WALKER & WALKER'S

ENGLISH LEGAL SYSTEM

Ninth Edition

RICHARD WARD

Professor of Public Law and Head of the Department of Law,
De Montfort University

AMANDA WRAGG

Senior Lecturer in Law, De Montfort University

OXFORD
UNIVERSITY PRESS

OXFORD

UNIVERSITY PRESS

Great Clarendon Street, Oxford OX2 6DP

Oxford University Press is a department of the University of Oxford.
It furthers the University's objective of excellence in research, scholarship,
and education by publishing worldwide in

Oxford New York

Auckland Cape Town Dar es Salaam Hong Kong Karachi
Kuala Lumpur Madrid Melbourne Mexico City Nairobi New Delhi
Shanghai Taipei Toronto

With offices in

Argentina Austria Brazil Chile Czech Republic France Greece
Guatemala Hungary Italy Japan South Korea Poland Portugal
Singapore Switzerland Thailand Turkey Ukraine Vietnam

Oxford is a registered trade mark of Oxford University Press
in the UK and in certain other countries

Published in the United States
by Oxford University Press Inc., New York

Eighth edition 1998

British Library Cataloguing in Publication Data

Data available

Library of Congress Cataloging in Publication Data

Data available

Typeset by RefineCatch Limited, Bungay, Suffolk
Printed in Great Britain
on acid-free paper by
Ashford Colour Press, Gosport, Hampshire

ISBN 0–40–695953–6   978–0–40–695953–9

1 3 5 7 9 10 8 6 4 2

WALKER & WALKER'S
ENGLISH LEGAL SYSTEM

PREFACE

The last seven years since the Eighth edition of this book have seen wholesale change and reform in virtually every aspect of the legal system. The aim of the book remains unchanged: to provide an accessible and relatively concise exposition of the main principles, rules, and issues. In writing this new edition we have sought, within the constraints of length, to reflect the areas and emphasis that we have found from our own experience to be important to the modern generation of students.

The aims of the book are one of the few things that have remained unchanged. The preparation of this edition has entailed wholesale rewriting, and a very large proportion of the book is to all intents and purposes new. By way of illustration, the chapters on the Human Rights Act 1998, on tribunals, on legal services, and on the civil process are almost entirely new, and the chapters on criminal justice and the courts are scarcely recognizable. We have sought to accommodate this vast morass of change whilst holding to the best qualities that this book has traditionally had.

In an area as wide and diverse as that covered by this book, input from a variety of individuals has helped us in developing our own understanding and perspectives. Needless to say we take responsibility for any errors or omissions. We would particularly like to thank our publishers for their ongoing support and seemingly inexhaustible patience.

On a more personal note, Richard Ward would like to thank Sarah for her unfailing support and greatly valued encouragement.

Amanda Wragg would like to thank Jang, and her parents Norma and Graham, for their love and seemingly endless patience.

We have stated the Law as we believe it to be as of 1 April 2005, but where possible we have sought at proof stage to reflect any later changes.

Richard Ward
Amanda Wragg

Leicester, April 2005

CONTENTS

Preface   v

Table of statutes   xxi

Table of statutory instruments   xxxvii

Table of EC legislation   xxxix

List of cases   xli

PART I SOURCES OF ENGLISH LAW

1 INTRODUCTORY ISSUES   3

  A   The historical context   3

      1   The role of the monarch   4

      2   The evolution of common law and equity   4

  B   The principal sources of law   5

      1   Legislation   5

      2   Common law   5

      3   Equity   6

      4   The European Union   6

      5   European Convention on Human Rights   7

      6   Other sources   7

  C   The distinction between civil and criminal matters   13

      1   The importance of the distinction   13

      2   Decision as to whether a matter is civil or criminal 15

  D   The administration of the English legal system   19

      1   The Lord Chancellor and the Department for Constitutional Affairs 19

      2   The Home Office   22

      3   The Law Officers   22

2 LEGISLATION   24

  A   Legislation and law reform   24

      1   Law reform   24

      2   Consolidation of enactments   26

      3   Codification   27

      4   Collection and disbursement of revenue   28

	5	Implementation of treaties	28
	6	Social legislation	28
B		Forms of legislation	29
	1	Acts of Parliament	29
	2	Delegated legislation	34
	3	Autonomic legislation	38
	4	Codes of Practice	39
C		The operation of statutes	41
	1	Geographical operation	41
	2	Temporal operation	42
D		The interpretation and construction of statutes	45
	1	The need for interpretation and construction	45
	2	Judicial approaches to interpretation	48
	3	Rules of interpretation and language	58
	4	Presumptions of substance	61
	5	Material aids to construction	66
	6	Interpretation of European Community legislation	76

3 CASE LAW, PRECEDENTS, AND LAW REPORTS 77

A		The relationship between law reports and the doctrine of precedent	77
B		The operation of the doctrine of precedent	78
	1	The doctrine of binding precedent	78
	2	The impact of the Human Rights Act 1998 on the doctrine of precedent	80
	3	The binding element in precedents	81
	4	Precedents which are not binding	85
	5	Reversing, overruling, and distinguishing	90
	6	The hierarchy of the courts	93
	7	Summary	103
C		Law reporting	103
	1	The Year Books	103
	2	The private reports	104
	3	The present system of law reporting	105

4 THE EUROPEAN COMMUNITY AND EUROPEAN UNION 110

A		Introduction	110
	1	The Single European Act and The Treaty on European Union	111
	2	The Treaty of Amsterdam	111
	3	The Treaty of Nice and the Charter of Fundamental Rights	113

	4	A Constitution for Europe?	113
B		The scope of European law	114
C		The institutions	117
	1	The Council	117
	2	The Commission	119
	3	The Parliament	119
	4	The Court of Justice	120
D		The sources of community law	121
	1	Legislation	121
	2	Case law	122
E		The relationship between community and national law	126
	1	The general approach of the Court of Justice	126
	2	Direct applicability and direct effect	127
F		Impact upon English courts	134
	1	The question of supremacy	134
	2	Interpretation	136
G		The European Court of Justice	138
	1	Composition and procedure	138
	2	Jurisdiction	139
	3	References for a preliminary ruling under Article 234	141

5 **THE HUMAN RIGHTS ACT 1998 AND THE EUROPEAN CONVENTION ON HUMAN RIGHTS** — 147

A		Introduction: the context	147
	1	The Convention and its history	147
	2	The status of the ECHR before the Human Rights Act 1998	149
	3	Bringing rights home	152
B		The Human Rights Act 1998	153
	1	The status of Convention rights and jurisprudence	153
	2	The impact on legislation	157
	3	Direct enforcement of Convention rights	163
C		Convention rights	170
	1	The nature of the rights protected	170
	2	Specific rights	173
D		The European Court of Human Rights	197
	1	The composition and procedure of the Court	198
	2	The admissibility of complaints	200

PART II THE ADMINISTRATION OF JUSTICE

6 THE ROYAL PREROGATIVE AND JUDICIAL REVIEW 205

  A   The royal prerogative 205

  B   Judicial review 206

      1   Historical origins of the powers of the High Court 206

      2   The scope of judicial review 207

      3   Limits to the judicial review jurisdiction 209

      4   Grounds for judicial review 214

      5   Procedure 217

7 THE COURTS 222

  A   Historical introduction 222

      1   The Curia Regis 222

      2   The Court of Exchequer 222

      3   The Court of Common Pleas 223

      4   The Court of King's Bench 223

      5   The Courts of Exchequer Chamber 223

      6   Assizes 224

      7   Justices of the peace 224

      8   The Star Chamber 225

      9   Court of Chancery 226

  B   The modern system of courts: an overview 227

      1   Classification of the courts 227

      2   The organization and administration of the courts 229

      3   The principle of open justice 231

      4   Contempt of court 236

  C   The European Court of Justice and European Court of Human Rights 241

  D   The House of Lords 241

      1   The House of Lords: constitution and procedure 241

      2   House of Lords: jurisdiction 242

      3   Reform: A Supreme Court for the United Kingdom 243

  E   The Court of Appeal 245

      1   Constitution 245

      2   Jurisdiction 246

  F   The High Court 249

      1   Constitution 249

		2	Jurisdiction	249
		3	The divisions	250
G			County courts	255
		1	Constitution	255
		2	Jurisdiction	255
H			The Crown Court	256
		1	Creation of the Crown Court	256
		2	Constitution	257
		3	Jurisdiction and procedure	258
I			Magistrates' Courts	259
		1	Constitution and organization	259
		2	Justices of the Peace	261
		3	Justices' clerks and justices' chief executives	262
		4	Jurisdiction	264
J			Coroners' Courts	266
		1	The office of coroner	266
		2	Jurisdiction	267
		3	The Review of Coroners' Services, 2003	268
K			Judicial Committee of the Privy Council	269
		1	Constitution	269
		2	Jurisdiction	270
L			Courts of particular jurisdiction	272
		1	Courts-martial	272
		2	Ecclesiastical courts	276

| 8 | TRIBUNALS AND INQUIRIES | 278 |

A			Tribunals: overview	278
		1	The characteristics of tribunals	278
		2	Composition	279
		3	Organization and control	281
B			Examples of tribunals	285
		1	Administrative tribunals	285
		2	Party and party tribunals	290
		3	Domestic tribunals	294
C			Control of tribunals by the courts	294
		1	Appeals from tribunals	294
		2	Supervisory control	295

	3	Challenging the decisions of 'private' disciplinary bodies	295
D		Inquiries	296
	1	Statutory inquiries	296
	2	Tribunals of inquiry	297

9 THE JUDICIARY — 300

A		The judicial hierarchy	300
B		The constitutional position of judges	303
	1	The changing political climate	304
	2	A new balance of powers?	312
C		Judicial appointments and security of tenure	313
	1	Appointments	313
	2	Tenure	319
	3	Training	321
	4	Judicial immunity	322
D		The judicial function	323

10 JURIES — 329

A		An historical growth of the jury system	329
B		The composition of the modern jury	330
	1	Qualifying for jury duty	330
	2	Selecting and summoning jurors	332
	3	Challenging the composition of the jury	332
C		The use of the jury trial at the present day	338
	1	Criminal cases	338
	2	Civil proceedings	340
	3	Jury secrecy	342
D		The merits of jury trial	344

11 LEGAL SERVICES — 347

A		The legal profession: the organizational framework	347
	1	The Courts and Legal Services Act 1990	348
	2	The Access to Justice Act 1999	348
B		The work of solicitors and barristers	349
	1	Solicitors	349
	2	Barristers	353
	3	The Director of Public Prosecutions and the Crown Prosecution Service	356
	4	The Law Officers	358

C	The education and training of lawyers		358
	1	Solicitors	358
	2	Barristers	359
D	The regulation of legal services		359
	1	The Law Society	359
	2	The Bar Council	361
	3	Review by the courts	361
	4	The Clementi Report: a review of the regulatory framework	362
E	Complaints against lawyers		364
	1	Solicitors	364
	2	Barristers	367
	3	The Legal Services Ombudsman	367
F	Civil liability		368
	1	Solicitors	368
	2	Barristers	369
G	The funding of legal services		371
	1	The remuneration of lawyers	371
	2	The cost of the law	373
	3	Legal Aid	374
	4	'Access to Justice': the new funding regime	375
	5	What has the new regime delivered? 'Access to Justice' or Justice Denied?	382

12 THE POLICE AND LAW ENFORCEMENT — 384

A	The law enforcement function		384
	1	The role of the individual	385
	2	The organization of the police	386
	3	Civilian officers: 'the extended police family'	390
B	Police accountability		391
	1	Rules of evidence	391
	2	Criminal proceedings	394
	3	Civil actions	395
	4	Judicial review	396
	5	Complaints against the police	396
C	Police powers		397
	1	General considerations	398
	2	Stop and search powers	401
	3	Surveillance	404

4	Arrest	405
5	Detention	409
6	Treatment of suspects	412
7	Access to legal advice	415
8	Interviews	417
9	Identification	420

PART III CIVIL PROCEDURE

13 THE CIVIL PROCESS — 425

A		Introduction	425
B		The Woolf analysis	426
	1	Delay and adversarial nature of civil litigation	426
	2	Expense	428
	3	Complexity	430
	4	Court of trial	430
	5	Recommendations	431
C		Administration of the civil justice system	432
	1	Rules of court	433
	2	The Overriding Objective	434
	3	The terminology	435
D		Settlement and alternative means of dispute resolution	436
	1	Introduction	436
	2	Arbitration	437
	3	Mediation and negotiation	441

14 PRE-TRIAL PROCESS — 446

A		Choice of court	446
B		Pre action protocols	448
C		Commencing a civil action	449
	1	The contents of the claim	450
	2	Parties to proceedings	451
	3	Representative and multi-party actions	452
	4	Issue and service of the claim	454
	5	Public or private law	455
	6	Counterclaims, contributions, and indemnities	455
D		Pre-commencement orders and procedures	456
	1	Disclosure and inspection of documents	456

2   Inspection, etc of property   457

3   The *Norwich Pharmacal* principle   458

4   Search orders   458

5   Freezing injunctions   460

15 CIVIL TRIALS   464

A   Introductory matters   464

1   The three-track approach   464

2   Small claims track   465

3   Fast track   466

4   Multi-track   466

B   Discontinuance and striking out   467

C   Settlement   469

D   Summary judgment   470

E   Part 36 payments and offers to settle   470

1   The principle   470

2   Effects of a payment into court or offer   471

F   Interim relief   472

1   Interlocutory injunction   472

2   Interim payment of damages   474

G   Statements of case   475

1   Background   475

H   Disclosure and inspection of documents   477

1   Relevant principles and background   477

2   Disclosure and inspection against other persons   480

3   Action for disclosure   480

I   Directions   481

J   Trial   481

1   Preparation of evidence   481

2   Procedure at the trial   484

16 COSTS   488

A   The power to award costs   488

1   The discretion   488

2   Orders against non parties   490

3   Costs order for misconduct and wasted costs orders   491

B   The assessment of costs   492
  1 The process   492
  2 The amount of costs   493
C   Costs and conditional fee agreements   495
D   Costs in multi party proceedings   497

17 APPEALS   498
A   Introduction   498
B   Rights of appeal   499
C   Procedure and powers on appeal   502
D   The approach to the determination of appeals   504
  1 Appeal on a point of law   504
  2 Appeal against a finding of fact   504
  3 Appeal against the exercise of a discretion   505
  4 Appeal against an award of damages   506

PART IV CRIMINAL PROCEEDINGS

18 CRIMINAL PROCEEDINGS AND THE CRIMINAL JUSTICE SYSTEM   511
A   Introduction   511
  1 The 'system'   511
  2 The aims of the criminal justice system   513
  3 Youth justice   514
  4 Victims of crime   516
B   The criminal process   518
  1 Adversarial nature   518
  2 The right to a fair trial   521
C   Case management   525

19 PRE-TRIAL PROCEDURE   527
A   The decision to commence proceedings   527
  1 Discretion and cautioning   527
  2 Conditional cautions for adult offenders   529
  3 Reprimands and warnings for juveniles   530
  4 Judicial scrutiny of the decision to prosecute or caution   531
  5 Police bail   532
  6 The decision to prosecute   533

B		Bringing the suspect before the court	540
	1	The old procedure	540
	2	The new procedure	542
C		Classification of offences	542
	1	Offences triable only on indictment	543
	2	Offences triable only summarily	543
	3	Offences triable either way	544
	4	Possible reform	545
D		Procedure for determining mode of trial	547
	1	The plea before venue process — adults	548
	2	Children and young persons	552
	3	Factors that influence mode of trial	553
E		Court bail	554
	1	Nature of bail	554
	2	Occasions for the grant of bail	556
	3	The right to bail	559
	4	Sureties	562
20		**TRIAL ON INDICTMENT**	**564**
A		Sending and transfer for trial	564
	1	Introduction	564
	2	The background	564
	3	Procedure	567
	4	Sending for trial	571
B		Delay and time-limits	572
C		Disclosure of evidence	574
	1	Introduction	574
	2	Prosecution disclosure	576
	3	Sensitive material	576
	4	Defence disclosure	579
	5	Further prosecution disclosure	582
	6	Expert evidence	583
D		The indictment	585
	1	Introduction	585
	2	Form and contents	586
	3	Joinder; separate trials	587
	4	Long trials: the number of counts and accused	589

		5	Non jury trial on indictment	590
		6	Duplicity	594
		7	Objecting to the indictment: amendment	594
	E	Pre-trial review		595
	F	Arraignment and pleas		597
		1	Attendance of the accused	597
		2	Arraignment	598
		3	Pleas	599
		4	Motion to quash the indictment	604
		5	Preliminary points of law	605
		6	Empanelling the jury: challenges	605
	G	Course of the trial		606
		1	Publicity	606
		2	Procedure at the hearing	607
		3	Witnesses	612
		4	The burden of proof and the right of silence	615
		5	Protection of the defendant	618
		6	Conclusion of the case	619
		7	Verdict	620
		8	Post verdict orders and sentence	621

21	SUMMARY PROCEDURE AND APPEALS			623
	A	Process		623
	B	Jurisdiction		625
	C	The course of the trial		625
		1	Time-limit	625
		2	Number of offences	627
		3	Pre-trial procedures	629
		4	Hearing	632
	D	Absences		635
		1	General effects of absence	635
		2	Pleading guilty by post	636
	E	Sentence		637
	F	Committals for sentence		639
	G	Youth justice		641
		1	Aims and provision of youth justice	641
		2	Court of trial	643

		3	The trial	644
		4	Youth offender contracts	646
		5	Imprisonment and community punishment	646
		6	Other orders	648
	H		Appeals following summary trial	648
		1	Appeal to the Crown Court	649
		2	Appeal by case stated to the Queen's Bench Division from magistrates' courts and the Crown Court	651
		3	Appeal to the House of Lords	654
	I		Judicial review	654
22	SENTENCES			656
	A		General principles	656
		1	The Halliday Report	656
		2	Principles of sentencing	658
		3	Consistency of sentencing and appropriate sentence	658
		4	The role of the Attorney-General	660
		5	Victims	661
	B		The sentencing process at the Crown Court	662
		1	Passing sentence	662
		2	Deferment of sentence	664
		3	Pre-sentence reports and other reports	664
		4	Pre-sentence drug testing	665
		5	Restraining orders	666
	C		The sentencing process in the magistrates' court	666
	D		Offence seriousness and sentencing thresholds	667
	E		Imprisonment	668
		1	Suspended sentence	668
		2	Length of custodial sentence	668
		3	Custody plus	670
		4	Intermittent custody	670
		5	Dangerous offenders	671
		6	Life sentences	673
		7	Young offenders	674
	F		Community sentences	675
	G		Fines	677
	H		Absolute and conditional discharges	677

I   Compensation and restitution   677

J   Miscellaneous orders   678

K   Restraining orders   679

23 APPEALS AND MISCARRIAGES OF JUSTICE   680

A   Introduction   680

   1   The development of the Court of Appeal (Criminal Division)   680

   2   The role of the Court of Appeal   681

B   The grounds of appeal   682

   1   Appeal against conviction   682

   2   Appeal against sentence   683

   3   Criminal Cases Review Commission   684

   4   Reference following acquittal   687

   5   Prosecution rights of appeal   688

C   Powers of the court   689

   1   Power to quash a conviction   689

   2   Power to substitute an alternative verdict   692

   3   Power to receive fresh evidence and to order a new trial   693

   4   *Venire de novo*   695

   5   Hospital orders   695

D   Appeals against sentence   695

E   Procedure   696

F   Appeal to the House of Lords   696

Selected reading   699

Index   709

TABLE OF STATUTES

Abortion Act 1967 . . . 31

Access to Justice Act 1999 . . . 247, 260, 267, 269,
    348, 357, 376
  Pt III . . . 348
  s 1(1) . . . 376
    (2)(a) . . . 376, 377
      (b) . . . 376, 380
    (3), (5) . . . 376
  s 3(1) . . . 376
  s 4(1) . . . 376, 377
    (2) . . . 377
    (4)(c) . . . 437
    (5) . . . 378
    (6) . . . 380
  s 6(1) . . . 377
  s 7 . . . 379
  s 8 . . . 378, 379
  s 12(1) . . . 376, 380
    (2) . . . 380
  s 13(2)(f) . . . 381
  s 14(2)(f) . . . 381
  s 16 . . . 381
  s 27 . . . 495
  s 28 . . . 373
  s 36 . . . 351
  s 37 . . . 351
  s 40 . . . 350
  s 42 . . . 435
  s 54(4) . . . 500
  s 55(1) . . . 247
  s 56 . . . 247
  s 57 . . . 247
    (12)(a) . . . 499
  s 59 . . . 502
  s 74 . . . 260
  s 75 . . . 259
  s 78 . . . 262, 264, 301
  s 83 . . . 260
  s 88 . . . 263
  s 90 . . . 263
  Sch 1, paras 14–15 . . . 376
  Sch 2 . . . 379
  Sch 13 . . . 263

Act of Settlement 1700 . . . 319

Acts of Parliament (Commencement) Act 1793
  . . . 42

Acts of Parliament Numbering and Citation Act
  1962 . . . 33

Administration of Estates Act 1925 . . . 51

Administration of Justice Act 1960 . . . 243
  s 1 . . . 654
  s 5 . . . 558

  s 13 . . . 240

Administration of Justice Act . . . 1968
  s 1(1)(a) . . . 241

Administration of Justice Act 1969 . . . 242, 475,
    499
  Pt II . . . 501
  s 12 . . . 243
  s 13 . . . 243

Administration of Justice Act 1970 . . . 253
  s 1 . . . 250
  s 3(1) . . . 252
  s 11 . . . 240

Administration of Justice Act . . . 1973
  s 9 . . . 321

Administration of Justice Act 1977 . . . 272

Administration of Justice Act . . . 1985
  Pt II . . . 350

Administration of Justice (Appeals) Act 1934 . . .
    242
  s 1 . . . 501

Administration of Justice (Miscellaneous
    Provisions) Act 1933 . . . 340

Administration of Justice (Miscellaneous
    Provisions) Act . . . 1938
  s 9 . . . 207

Adoption Act 1976 . . . 51

Agricultural Marketing Act 1958 . . . 211

Air Force Act 1955 . . . 44, 272, 560
  s 113 . . . 273
  s 133 . . . 273
  s 134 . . . 273

Anti-social Behaviour Act 2003 . . . 16

Anti-Terrorism, Crime and Security Act 2001 . . .
    162, 178
  s 23 . . . 161, 172
  s 90(1) . . . 412

Appellate Jurisdiction Act 1876 . . . 241, 242, 269
  s 6 . . . 314, 319

Appellate Jurisdiction Act 1947 . . . 241, 269

Arbitration Act 1950 . . . 437
  s 13A . . . 44
  s 21 . . . 439

Arbitration Act 1979 . . . 437

Arbitration Act 1996 . . . 437
  Pt I . . . 438
  s 1 . . . 438
  s 5(1) . . . 438
  s 9 . . . 438
  s 15(3) . . . 439

s 18 ... 439
s 24 ... 439
s 33 ... 440
  (1) ... 439
s 34(1) ... 439
s 36(1) ... 439
s 37(1) ... 439
s 41 ... 439
s 45 ... 440
s 46(3) ... 438
s 67 ... 440
s 68 ... 440
  (2) ... 440
s 69 ... 440
  (8) ... 441
s 85 ... 440
s 87 ... 438, 439
s 93 ... 441
Armed Forces Act 1981 ... 274
Armed Forces Act 1996 ... 150, 182, 272, 274
s 6 ... 272
Army Act 1955 ... 44, 272, 560
s 96 ... 273
s 113 ... 273
s 133 ... 273
s 134 ... 273
Asylum and Immigration (Treatment of
  Claimants etc) Act 2004 ... 286, 288, 289,
  310
s 26 ... 289
Bail Act 1976 ... 554, 557, 560
s 3 ... 555
  (2), (3), (6A) ... 555
s 4 ... 559
  (3) ... 559
s 5 ... 562
  (3), (4) ... 562
s 6(1) ... 555
  (3) ... 556
s 7 ... 640
  (3) ... 597
s 8(2) ... 562
s 9 ... 563
Sch 1 ... 559, 560, 561
  Pt I ... 560, 561
  para 1 ... 555
  para 2A ... 561
  para 9 ... 560
  Pt II ... 560
  para 1 ... 555
  para 9 ... 560
Sch 2 ... 558
Bail (Amendment) Act 1993 ... 558
Bankers Book Evidence Act 1879 ... 613
Betting Act ... 1853
s 1 ... 59
Betting, Gaming and Lotteries Act 1963 ... 75

Bill of Rights 1688 ... 44, 71
British Railways Board Act 1968 ... 29
Canada Act 1982 ... 67
Carriage by Air Act ... 1961
s 1(2) ... 70
Sch 1 ... 70
Chancel Repairs Act ... 1932
s 2(1) ... 196
Charitable Uses Act 1601 ... 44, 67
Child Abduction and Custody Act 1985 ... 254
Child Support Act 1991 ... 254
Children Act 1989 ... 25, 57, 158, 254, 255, 265,
  266, 378
s 25 ... 499
s 92 ... 254, 266
s 97 ... 232
Children and Young Persons Act ... 1933
s 37 ... 233
s 42 ... 645
s 43 ... 645
s 44 ... 514, 641, 645
s 45 ... 265
s 46 ... 644
s 47 ... 645
s 49 ... 265
s 53 ... 644, 674
  (2) ... 552
s 107 ... 265
Children and Young Persons Act 1969 ... 552
Church of England Assembly (Powers) Act 1919
  ... 276
Civil Evidence Act 1995 ... 25, 483
Civil Procedure Act 1997 ... 230, 253, 432
s 1 ... 35
  (3) ... 230, 432
s 6 ... 230, 432, 433
Clergy Discipline Measure ... 2003
s 2 ... 276
s 6(1), (2) ... 276
s 7 ... 276
s 22 ... 276
s 23 ... 276
s 30 ... 277
s 31 ... 277
Common Law Procedure Acts 1852 ... 6
Common Law Procedure Acts 1854 ... 6, 329,
  340
Commonwealth Immigrants Act ... 1962
Pt I ... 45
Companies Act 1985 ... 183
Companies Act 1989 ... 28
Consolidation of Enactments (Procedure) Act
  1949 ... 26
s 2 ... 26

Constitutional Reform Act 2005 . . . 3, 21, 182,
    229, 231, 244, 252, 281, 302, 309
  Pt 2 . . . 245, 250, 302
  Pt 3 . . . 3, 300
  s 2 . . . 21
  s 3 . . . 21, 317
    (5), (6) . . . 310
  s 5(1) . . . 22, 303, 310
  s 7(1) . . . 22, 303
    (2)(a) . . . 22, 303, 310
      (b), (c) . . . 22, 303
    (3), (4) . . . 303
  s 8 . . . 303
  s 9 . . . 254, 303
  s 12 . . . 303
  s 13 . . . 303
  s 16 . . . 269
  s 23 . . . 244
    (5), (6) . . . 244
  s 24 . . . 244, 303
  s 26 . . . 317
  s 27 . . . 316
  s 29 . . . 316
  s 38 . . . 244
  s 39 . . . 244
  s 40 . . . 244
    (4)(b) . . . 245
  s 42 . . . 244
  s 63 . . . 316
  s 65 . . . 316
  s 67–84 . . . 316
  s 85 . . . 281, 291
  s 88 . . . 316
  s 90 . . . 316
  s 108 . . . 320
  s 137 . . . 244
  s 138 . . . 270
  s 148(4) . . . 245
  Sch 1 . . . 303
  Sch 2 . . . 303
    Pt 1 . . . 22
  Sch 4 . . . 22
    para 115 . . . 250, 252
  Sch 8, Pt 1 . . . 316
  Sch 9 . . . 245
    Pt 2 . . . 271
  Sch 12 . . . 281
    Pt 1 . . . 316
  Sch 13 . . . 317
  Sch 14 . . . 291
  Sch 16 . . . 269, 270

Consumer Credit Act 1974 . . . 70, 195
  s 127(3) . . . 196
  s 188(1), (3) . . . 70
  Sch 2 . . . 70

Consumer Protection Act . . . 1987
  s 20 . . . 72

Contempt of Court Act 1981 . . . 149, 192, 345
  s 1 . . . 238
  s 2 . . . 238
  s 3(1) . . . 238
  s 4 . . . 235, 238, 596
    (2) . . . 235, 238, 606
  s 5 . . . 238
  s 6(c) . . . 238
  s 8 . . . 342, 343, 344, 590
    (1) . . . 238, 342
    (2)(a), (b) . . . 342
  s 9 . . . 239
  s 10 . . . 237
  s 11 . . . 235, 606
  s 12 . . . 228, 240
  s 14(1), (2), (4A) . . . 240
  Sch 1 . . . 238

Contracts (Rights of Third Parties) Act 1999 . . .
    25, 58

Coroners Act . . . 1988
  s 3 . . . 266
  s 8 . . . 267
    (2)(a) . . . 341
  s 16 . . . 267
  s 17A . . . 267
  s 30 . . . 267

County Courts Act 1846 . . . 255

County Courts Act 1984 . . . 255
  s 1 . . . 255, 320
  s 5 . . . 255
  s 6 . . . 255
  s 8 . . . 255
  s 38 . . . 472
  s 50 . . . 475
  s 66(3) . . . 341
  s 77 . . . 498

Court of Chancery Act 1841 (5 Vict, c 5) . . . 222

Court Probate Act 1857 . . . 271

Courts Act 1971 . . . 3, 245, 256, 257, 272
  s 8 . . . 259
  s 17(4) . . . 320
  s 24 . . . 258
  s 27 . . . 19
  s 28 . . . 19
  s 41 . . . 249
  s 43 . . . 4
  Sch 1 . . . 259

Courts Act 2003 . . . 19, 35, 230, 245, 254, 258,
    260, 264, 303, 662
  Pt 7 . . . 19
  s 1 . . . 19, 261, 303
    (1) . . . 230
  s 4 . . . 230, 261
  s 5 . . . 230, 261
  s 6 . . . 261, 264
  s 7 . . . 260
  s 8 . . . 260

s 10(2) . . . 260
s 11 . . . 320
s 12 . . . 262, 321
s 13 . . . 262, 321
s 15 . . . 261
s 19 . . . 261
s 22–26 . . . 262
s 22 . . . 320
s 26 . . . 262
s 27(1), (6) . . . 263
s 28(4), (5) . . . 263
s 29 . . . 264
s 31 . . . 323
s 32 . . . 323
s 63 . . . 623
  (1) . . . 300
s 66 . . . 265
s 69–74 . . . 525
s 69 . . . 35, 230
  (4) . . . 230
s 75–77 . . . 230
s 75–81 . . . 254, 266
s 75 . . . 35
  (5) . . . 230
Sch 1 . . . 261

Courts and Legal Services Act 1990 . . . 230, 256,
    313, 347, 348, 349, 350, 362, 431
s 1 . . . 256
s 8 . . . 507
  (5) . . . 361
s 15 . . . 77
s 17 . . . 348
  (3) . . . 348, 351
s 19 . . . 20
s 21 . . . 367
s 22 . . . 367
s 23–24 . . . 368
s 27 . . . 314, 348
  (9) . . . 352, 361
s 28 . . . 348, 349
s 29 . . . 350
s 31–33 . . . 348
s 31(1) . . . 354
  (2)(a) . . . 351
s 31A . . . 357
s 34–53 . . . 350
s 36 . . . 351
s 53 . . . 350
s 54 . . . 350
s 55 . . . 348, 350
s 58 . . . 372, 496
  (1) . . . 495
  (2)(a), (b) . . . 372
  (4)(b) . . . 372
s 58A . . . 372
s 58B . . . 373
s 61(1) . . . 355
s 66 . . . 348

s 71 . . . 262, 314
  (3) . . . 314
s 72 . . . 328
s 102 . . . 439
s 119 . . . 349
s 130 . . . 374
Sch 3 . . . 367
Sch 4 . . . 350, 352

Courts-Martial (Appeals) Act 1951 . . . 273
Courts-Martial (Appeals) Act 1968 . . . 273
s 39 . . . 273
Crime and Disorder Act 1998 . . . 265, 357, 516,
    521, 528, 529, 611, 629, 658, 671, 674
s 1 . . . 16
s 2 . . . 16
s 5–6 . . . 513
s 34 . . . 327, 552
s 36 . . . 273
s 37 . . . 513, 515, 642, 658
  (2) . . . 642
s 38 . . . 515, 642
s 40 . . . 573
  (5) . . . 574
s 41 . . . 19, 512, 573, 642, 643
s 42(5) . . . 515, 642
s 43–47 . . . 573
s 47 . . . 552, 629
s 48(2) . . . 629
s 49 . . . 263, 629
s 50A . . . 568
s 51–52 . . . 566, 567
s 51 . . . 569
  (2), (4), (6), (11) . . . 567
s 51A . . . 569
s 51B . . . 569, 571
  (8), (9) . . . 569
s 51C(3) . . . 569
s 51D(4) . . . 571
s 51E . . . 567
s 52A . . . 571
  (2), (7) . . . 571
s 54 . . . 562
  (2) . . . 555
s 56 . . . 559
s 57 . . . 557
s 65 . . . 523
  (1) . . . 530
s 66(1), (5) . . . 531
s 69_74 . . . 656
s 75 . . . 659
s 80 . . . 659
s 81 . . . 659
s 106 . . . 26
Sch 3 . . . 566, 567, 585
  para 1, 2, 5–6 . . . 568
Crime (Sentences) Act 1997 . . . 521, 659, 669,
    671
s 8–27 . . . 42

s 28 ... 178, 673
s 29 ... 673
Criminal Appeal Act 1907 ... 243, 248, 680, 692,
    493
    s 9(d), (e) ... 696
Criminal Appeal Act 1964 ... 681
    s 1 ... 681, 694
Criminal Appeal Act ... 1965
    s 14(4A) 687 ... 687
    s 15 ... 687
Criminal Appeal Act 1966 ... 243, 246, 248, 681
Criminal Appeal Act 1968 ... 246, 681, 696
    s 1 ... 682, 683
    s 2 ... 689, 690, 691
        (1) ... 689, 690
            (a) ... 691
            (c) ... 690
    s 3(1), (2) ... 692
    s 7–8 ... 694
    s 7 ... 681, 694
    s 8(2) ... 558
    s 17 ... 248, 684, 685, 686
        (1)(a) ... 684
    s 19 ... 558
    s 23 ... 693
        (1), (2) ... 693
    s 31 ... 558
        (3) ... 682
    s 36 ... 558
    s 37 ... 558
    s 45(2) ... 558
    s 50(1) ... 683
Criminal Appeal Act 1995 ... 681, 684, 685, 687,
    690, 693
    s 2 ... 686
    s 8(4), (5), (6) ... 685
    s 9 ... 248
    s 13 ... 686
        (2) ... 686
    s 19 ... 686
    s 21 ... 685
Criminal Attempts Act ... 1981
    s 4(2) ... 628
Criminal Damage Act ... 1971
    s 1 ... 544, 545
Criminal Evidence Act ... 1898
    s 1(3) ... 619
Criminal Evidence Act 1979 ... 24
Criminal Evidence Act ... 1999
    Pt II ... 232
    s 16 ... 233
    s 17 ... 233
    s 23 ... 233
    s 24 ... 233
    s 25 ... 233
        (3) ... 233

s 27 ... 233
s 28 ... 233
Criminal Injuries Compensation Act 1995 ...
    286, 287, 661, 662
Criminal Justice Act ... 1925
    s 41(1) ... 239
Criminal Justice Act 1948 ... 32, 242
    s 31(3) ... 329
Criminal Justice Act 1967 ... 374, 564, 570, 620
    s 11 ... 579, 581
    s 12 ... 574
    s 22 ... 558
Criminal Justice Act ... 1968
    s 23 ... 592, 614
    s 24 ... 614
Criminal Justice Act 1972 ... 330, 687
    s 36 ... 248
        (1) ... 678
Criminal Justice Act ... 1982
    s 37 ... 638
    s 48 ... 638
Criminal Justice Act 1987 ... 569, 581
    s 2 ... 384
    s 4 ... 565
        (2) ... 569
    s 6(2) ... 569
    s 7 ... 597
        (1) ... 595
    s 10 ... 581
    s 46 ... 569
Criminal Justice Act 1988 ... 43, 306, 660, 681,
    694
    Pt IV ... 246
    s 23–26 ... 633
    s 36 ... 248, 684
    s 40 ... 587
    s 46 ... 569
    s 51 ... 569
    s 75(6) ... 44
    s 108–117 ... 42
    s 118 ... 334
    s 119 ... 330
    s 154 ... 264
    s 159 ... 235, 606
    s 181 ... 264
    Sch 3 ... 684
    Sch 6 ... 42
    Sch 7 ... 42
Criminal Justice Act 1991 ... 521, 559, 569, 638,
    657, 667, 668, 669, 670
    s 3 ... 600, 629
    s 17 ... 638
    s 18–19 ... 638
    s 18 ... 638
    s 33(1)(a) ... 670
    s 34(2) ... 683

s 52 ... 613
s 53 ... 565
s 69 ... 637
s 70 ... 265
Sch 13 ... 552

Criminal Justice Act 1993 ... 521
s 65(1) ... 638

Criminal Justice Act ... 2001
s 53 ... 569

Criminal Justice Act 2003 ... 15, 179, 233, 248,
    258, 330, 331, 339, 357, 514, 521, 528, 529,
    533, 534, 540, 547, 548, 550, 557, 560, 573,
    581, 584, 605, 623, 630, 632, 633, 638, 656
Pt 9 ... 688
Pt 10 ... 43
Pt 12 ... 26, 178
s 4 ... 532
s 9 ... 413
s 13 ... 55
s 14 ... 561
s 15 ... 561
s 16 ... 556, 558
s 19 ... 561
s 22 ... 529
    (4) ... 529
s 23 ... 529
s 28–31 ... 542
s 28 ... 535
s 29(4) ... 624
s 32 ... 576
s 33 ... 582
    (3) ... 581
s 34 ... 582
s 35 ... 584
s 38 ... 581
s 40 ... 582
s 43–49 ... 259
s 43 ... 339, 590, 591, 592, 593
    (6), (7) ... 591
s 44 ... 333, 339, 591, 592
    (6) ... 592
s 46 ... 333, 338
s 48 ... 592
s 57–66 ... 605
s 58 ... 248, 688, 689
    (7) ... 689
s 62 ... 248
    (2) ... 689
s 75 ... 604
s 76(1) ... 248
s 84 ... 604
s 88–114 ... 588
s 98 ... 609, 619
s 100 ... 609
s 101 ... 593, 609, 619
s 114–131 ... 607
s 114 ... 614
s 115 ... 614

s 116 ... 592, 614
s 118 ... 66
    (2) ... 66
    (3) ... 66
s 119–120 ... 615
s 119 ... 608
s 126 ... 514
s 139 ... 615
s 142 ... 658
    (2) ... 658
s 143 ... 668
s 144 ... 600, 668
s 145 ... 668
s 147 ... 675
s 152 ... 667
s 154 ... 667
s 156(2) ... 665
s 161 ... 665
s 162 ... 665
s 167 ... 659
s 169 ... 659, 660
s 170 ... 554
    (5) ... 550
s 172(1) ... 660
s 177 ... 675
s 181 ... 670
s 183 ... 671
s 224(3) ... 671
s 225 ... 671
s 226 ... 672
s 227 ... 672
s 228 ... 672
s 237–268 ... 669
s 246 ... 669
s 247 ... 672
s 249 ... 672
s 269 ... 177, 673
s 278 ... 664
s 308 ... 542
s 315 ... 687
Sch 2 ... 357, 535, 664
Sch 3 ... 550, 553, 554, 564, 567, 630
    para 2 ... 519
    para 17 ... 568, 569, 571
    para 18 ... 567
    para 22 ... 549, 639
Sch 5 ... 604
    Pt 1 ... 248
Sch 8 ... 676
Sch 15 ... 671
Sch 21 ... 673
Sch 32 ... 568

Criminal Justice Act ... 2004
s 17 ... 558

Criminal Justice Administration Act 1956 ...
    257

Criminal Justice and Courts Services Act 2000
    ... 15, 656

s 2 . . . 512
s 69 . . . 661

Criminal Justice and Police Act 2001 . . . 419

Criminal Justice and Public Order Act 1994 . . .
    417, 521, 580
  s 1–18 . . . 656
  s 5 . . . 559
  s 26 . . . 560
  s 34–38 . . . 574, 632
  s 34 . . . 581, 619
  s 35 . . . 616
  s 36 . . . 581
  s 37 . . . 581, 619
  s 38 . . . 619
  s 40–42 . . . 665
  s 41 . . . 337
  s 44 . . . 566
  s 60 . . . 400, 403
  s 143 . . . 68
  s 149 . . . 19
  Sch 4 . . . 566
  Sch 9 . . . 569, 665

Criminal Law Act . . . 1967
  s 3 . . . 401
  s 6(1)(c) . . . 598
    (3) . . . 601

Criminal Law Act 1977 . . . 544, 545
  s Part III . . . 542, 543
  s 44 . . . 689
  s 56 . . . 267
  Sch 12 . . . 664

Criminal Procedure Act 1865 . . . 67
  s 3 . . . 608
  s 4 . . . 609
  s 6 . . . 609

Criminal Procedure and Investigations Act 1996
  . . . 521, 546, 548, 568, 578, 631
  Pt I . . . 575
  Pt II . . . 575
  Pt III . . . 596
  Pt IV . . . 596
  s 1 . . . 632
  s 3 . . . 576
    (1) . . . 576
    (6) . . . 577, 632
  s 5 . . . 580, 611
  s 6 . . . 632
  s 6A . . . 581
  s 6C . . . 582
  s 6D . . . 584, 632
  s 6E . . . 581
  s 7 . . . 582, 632
    (5) . . . 577
  s 8(5) . . . 577
  s 9(8) . . . 577
  s 11 . . . 584, 632
    (3) . . . 581

s 14 . . . 632
s 19 . . . 583
    (1) . . . 632
s 21A . . . 582
s 23 . . . 40
s 29(1), (2) . . . 596
s 31(4) . . . 597
s 40 . . . 596
s 47 . . . 568, 569
s 51–56 . . . 566
Sch 1 . . . 568
Sch 3 . . . 566
Sch 5 . . . 569

Criminal Procedure (Attendance of Witnesses)
    Act . . . 1965
  s 2 . . . 612
  s 3 . . . 239

Criminal Procedure (Insanity) Act 1964 . . . 598,
  661
  s 4 . . . 522, 598, 599
  s 4A . . . 18, 522, 598
  s 5 . . . 598, 599

Criminal Procedure (Insanity and Unfitness to
    Plead) Act 1991 . . . 598

Crown Proceedings Act 1947 . . . 65

Cyprus Act 1960 . . . 46

Dangerous Drugs Act . . . 1965
  s 5 . . . 627

Defamation Act . . . 1996
  s 12 . . . 507
  s 14 . . . 323

Deregulation and Contracting Out Act . . . 1994
  Pt 1 . . . 36

Disability Discrimination Act 1995 . . . 291

Domestic Proceedings and Magistrates Courts
    Act . . . 1978
  s 80 . . . 265

Domestic Violence, Crime and Victims Act 2004
  . . . 591, 592, 622, 661, 662
  s 5 . . . 594
    (2) . . . 594
  s 12 . . . 679
  s 14–16 . . . 678
  s 15 . . . 678
  s 16 . . . 678
  s 17 . . . 593
  s 22 . . . 598
  s 32(1) . . . 517
  s 45(2) . . . 661

Drug Trafficking Offences Act 1986 . . . 678

Drugs Act 1971 . . . 56

Ecclesiastical Jurisdiction Measure . . . 1963
  s 1 . . . 276, 277
    (3)(d) . . . 271
  s 3 . . . 277

s 5 . . . 277
s 6 . . . 276
s 7 . . . 277
s 8 . . . 271, 277
s 10 . . . 277
Employment Act 1989 . . . 28
Employment Protection Act . . . 1975
    s 87 . . . 292
Employment Protection (Consolidation) Act
    1978 . . . 26, 30, 136
Employment Rights Act 1996 . . . 26
    s 111 . . . 291
Employment Rights (Dispute Resolution) Act
    1998 . . . 291
    s 1 . . . 290
Employment Tribunals Act . . . 1996
    s 4 . . . 291
        (1)(b) . . . 292
        (3) . . . 291, 292
    s 6 . . . 292
    s 22 . . . 293
    s 28 . . . 293
    s 29 . . . 293
    s 36 . . . 292
    s 37 . . . 294, 295
Energy Act . . . 2004
    s 56 . . . 384
Equal Pay Act 1970 . . . 135, 137, 291
European Communities Act 1972 . . . 45, 120,
    127, 128, 134, 135
    s 2 . . . 30, 136
        (1) . . . 129, 134
        (2) . . . 36, 128, 129
        (4) . . . 55, 134, 157
    s 3 . . . 99
        (1) . . . 93
    Sch 2 . . . 36, 128
European Communities (Amendment) Act 1993
    . . . 111
European Communities (Amendment) Act 1998
    . . . 111
European Communities (Amendment) Act 1999
    . . . 119
European Communities (Amendment) Act 2002
    . . . 113
European Parliamentary Elections Act 1999 . . .
    32
European Parliamentary Elections Act 2002 . . .
    119
Evidence Act . . . 1851
    s 16 . . . 613
Explosives Act . . . 1875
    s 3(1) . . . 75
Explosive Substances Act . . . 1883
    s 4 . . . 75

Extradition Act . . . 1989
    s 9(2) . . . 16
    Sch 1, para 6(1) . . . 16
Family Law Act 1986 . . . 254
Family Law Act 1996 . . . 254, 265, 441
    s 29 . . . 441
Fatal Accidents Act 1976 . . . 476
Finance Act . . . 1960
    s 44 . . . 49
Firearms Act . . . 1968
    s 57(1) . . . 76
Fire Services Act 1947 . . . 34
Football (Offences) Act 1991 . . . 407
Foreign Compensation Act 1950 . . . 210
Foreign Compensation Act . . . 1969
    s 3 . . . 64
Gender Recognition Act 2004 . . . 58, 161, 185,
    194
Government of Ireland Act 1920 . . . 32
Government of Wales Act 1998 . . . 270, 271
Health and Safety at Work etc Act . . . 1974
    s 14 . . . 297
    s 16 . . . 41
    s 17(2) . . . 41
Health and Social Services and Social Security
    Adjudications Act 1983 . . . 286
Homicide Act . . . 1957
    s 2(2) . . . 616
Hostages Act 1982 . . . 28
Housing Act 1985 . . . 180
Housing (Homeless Persons) Act 1977 . . . 33
    Pt III . . . 33, 34
Human Fertilisation and Embryology Act 1990
    . . . 254
Human Rights Act 1998 . . . 7, 17, 18, 20, 30, 36,
    42, 45, 54, 55, 63, 65, 72, 76, 80, 95, 96, 99,
    102, 147, 149, 153, 211, 216, 232, 267, 269,
    305, 322, 324, 396, 397, 539
    s 1 . . . 37, 64, 73, 80, 153, 327
        (1) . . . 55
    s 2 . . . 86, 153
    s 3 . . . 43, 48, 55, 56, 57, 64, 157, 158, 159, 160,
        161, 162, 163, 192, 477, 618
        (1) . . . 55, 57, 80, 157
        (2) . . . 157, 159
            (b) . . . 57
    s 4 . . . 55, 159, 160, 161
        (5) . . . 55, 159
    s 5 . . . 159
    s 6 . . . 80, 157, 163, 164, 168, 327, 391
        (1) . . . 37, 163, 169, 192
        (2) . . . 38
        (3) . . . 165
            (b) . . . 163

s 7 . . . 168, 169
  (1) . . . 169
    (a) . . . 167, 168, 169
    (b) . . . 167, 169
  (3) . . . 168
  (5) . . . 168
  (6) . . . 169
s 8 . . . 169
  (2), (3), (4) . . . 169
s 9(1) . . . 168
  (3) . . . 169
  (5) . . . 169
s 10 . . . 37, 55, 159, 276
  (2) . . . 37
s 12 . . . 156, 157, 190, 474
  (3) . . . 474
s 13 . . . 157, 189
  (1) . . . 156
s 18 . . . 42
s 19 . . . 31, 73, 74, 162, 163
s 20 . . . 42
s 21(5) . . . 42
s 22(3) . . . 42
  (4) . . . 43, 169
Sch 1 . . . 31, 55, 153
Sch 2 . . . 160
  para 2(b) . . . 37, 38
Hunting Act 2004 . . . 32, 35
Immigration Act 1971 . . . 45
  Ss6 . . . 678
Immigration and Asylum Act 1999 . . . 57, 58,
  161, 183
Immunity Act . . . 1978
  s 3(1) . . . 89
Income and Corporation Taxes Act 1988 . . . 28
Income Tax Act . . . 1952
  s 25(3) . . . 49
Indemnity Act 1920 . . . 44
Indian Divorces (Validity) Act 1921 . . . 44
Indictment Act 1915 . . . 586, 594
  s 5(1) . . . 595
Industrial Relations Act 1971 . . . 40, 292
  s 113 . . . 291
Inquiries Act 2005 . . . 297
  s 17 . . . 298
  s 18 . . . 298
  s 19 . . . 298
  s 21 . . . 298
  s 40 . . . 298
Insolvency Act . . . 1986
  s 117 . . . 255
  s 373 . . . 255
Interception of Communications Act 1985 . . .
  151, 187, 404
Internationally Protected Persons Act 1978 . . .
  42
  s 1 . . . 42

Interpretation Act 1889 . . . 60
Interpretation Act 1978 . . . 60
  s 3 . . . 31
  s 5 . . . 60, 543
  s 6 . . . 60
  s 13 . . . 36
  s 15 . . . 45
  s 16(1) . . . 45
  Sch 1 . . . 60, 543
Judicial Committee Act 1833 . . . 269
  s 4 . . . 272
Judicial Pensions Act 1981 . . . 321
Judicial Pensions and Retirement Act . . . 1993
  s 26(1), (5), (7) . . . 321
  Sch 5 . . . 321
Juries Act . . . 1825
  s 29 . . . 334
Juries Act 1974 . . . 26, 330
  s 1 . . . 330
  s 2 . . . 605
  s 8 . . . 332
  s 9 . . . 331
  s 9A . . . 331
  s 9AA . . . 331
  s 10 . . . 337
  s 11 . . . 333
    (5)(a) . . . 333
  s 12(1)(a) . . . 334
    (2) . . . 334
    (4) . . . 335
    (6) . . . 337
  s 16 . . . 337, 621
    (1) . . . 337, 340, 621
  s 17 . . . 340
    (2) . . . 341
    (3), (4) . . . 620
  s 20 . . . 331
  Sch 1, Pts 1, 2 . . . 330
Justices of the Peace Act 1361 . . . 399
Justices of the Peace Act 1997 . . . 260
  s 5 . . . 19
  s 7 . . . 262, 321
  s 10 . . . 261
  s 10A–10E . . . 262
  s 10D . . . 262
  s 28 . . . 260
  s 41 . . . 263
  s 45 . . . 263
  s 51 . . . 323
  s 52 . . . 323
  s 64 . . . 261
Landlord and Tenant Act . . . 1954
  s 29(3) . . . 53
Landlord and Tenant Act 1988 . . . 25
Law Commissions Act 1965 . . . 25
  s 3(1) . . . 25, 44

Law Officers Act . . . 1997
  s 1 . . . 23, 358
Law of Property Act 1925 . . . 66
  s 40 . . . 97
  s 56 . . . 59
    (1) . . . 58
  s 205(1) . . . 59
Law of Property (Miscellaneous Provisions) Act
  1989 . . . 25
Law Reform (Limitation of Actions) Act 1954 . . .
  74, 75
Law Reform (Miscellaneous Provisions) Act 1970
  . . . 340
Law Terms Act 1830 (11 Geo 4 & Will 4, c 70) . . .
  224
Legal Aid Act 1960 . . . 374
Legal Aid Act 1964 . . . 374
Legal Aid Act 1974 . . . 374
Legal Aid Act 1979 . . . 374
Legal Aid Act 1988 . . . 375, 630
  Pt V . . . 375
  s 2 . . . 375
    (2), (3) . . . 375
  s 3 . . . 375
    (2) . . . 375
  s 6 . . . 375
  s 8(2) . . . 375
  Sch 2, Pt II, para 1 . . . 375
Legal Aid and Advice Act 1949 . . . 374
Legal Aid and Assistance Act 1949 . . . 374
Legal Aid and Assistance Act 1972 . . . 375
Limitation Act 1963 . . . 24, 41, 47
  s 7(3) . . . 84
  Pt I . . . 41
  s II . . . 41
  s III . . . 41
Limitation Act 1975 . . . 47
Limitation Act 1980 . . . 47, 65
  s s11 . . . 72
Local Government Act 1972 . . . 35, 272
  s 235(1) . . . 35
Local Government Finance Act 1992 . . . 228
  s 15 . . . 286
Magistrates' Courts Act 1957 . . . 636
Magistrates' Courts Act 1980 . . . 28, 570
  s 1 . . . 406, 624
    (2) . . . 541, 624
      (b) . . . 625
  s 2(1) . . . 625
    (6) . . . 624
  s 5A–5F . . . 568
  s 9(3) . . . 634
  s 10(3) . . . 634, 637
  s 11–16 . . . 635
  s 11(3), (4) . . . 637

s 12 . . . 542, 635, 636, 637
s 13(3) . . . 637
s 15 . . . 635
  (1) . . . 635
s 16 . . . 635
s 17–18 . . . 261
s 17 . . . 264, 544
s 17A . . . 549
  (9) . . . 549
s 18 . . . 261, 549
  (2), (3(. . . 551
s 19 . . . 553
  (2), (4) . . . 550
s 20 . . . 551
  (5), (6) . . . 551
  (7) . . . 261
s 20A(4) . . . 551
s 22 . . . 544
  (8) . . . 544
s 23(1), (3), (4) . . . 551
s 24 . . . 552, 643
  (1) . . . 552
  (2) . . . 553
s 24A–24D . . . 553
s 25 . . . 551
s 29 . . . 553, 644
s 30 . . . 557
s 31(1) . . . 637
s 34(3) . . . 638
s 39 . . . 638
s 40(1) . . . 638
s 41 . . . 556
s 63(3) . . . 254
s 66 . . . 266
s 67 . . . 266
s 69(2) . . . 266
s 82(5) . . . 637
s 97 . . . 633
s 98(7) . . . 634
s 101 . . . 13, 616, 617
s 102 . . . 633
s 108(1), (3) . . . 649
s 111 . . . 253, 688
  (1) . . . 651
  (2), (3), (4), (5), (6) . . . 652
s 113 . . . 557
s 117 . . . 541
s 120(3) . . . 562
s 121(1), (5) . . . 261
s 127 . . . 537
  (1), (2) . . . 625
s 128(1), (6) . . . 557
s 128A . . . 557
s 129(1) . . . 557
s 131(1) . . . 557
s 133 . . . 638
s 143 . . . 638
s 148 . . . 259
Sch 1 . . . 264, 544

Magistrates' Courts (Appeals from Binding Over Orders) Act 1956 . . . 650

Magistrates' Courts (Procedure) Act 1998 . . . 635, 637

Manchester General Improvement Act 1851 . . . 654

Marine Insurance Act 1906 . . . 27

Married Women (Maintenance in Case of Desertion) Act 1886 . . . 68

Matrimonial Causes Act 1857 . . . 271

Matrimonial Causes Act . . . 1973
   s 11 . . . 58, 158
   s 48(2) . . . 232

Matrimonial and Proceedings Act . . . 1984
   s 33 . . . 255

Medical Act . . . 1983
   s 1(3) . . . 294

Mental Capacity Act . . . 2005
   Pt 2 . . . 252

Mental Health Act 1983 . . . 14, 37, 63, 64, 161, 179, 252
   s 37 . . . 678
   s 65 . . . 286
   s 72(1) . . . 58
   s . . . 73
     (1) . . . 58

Merchant Shipping Act 1894 . . . 76

Merchant Shipping Act 1925 . . . 76

Merchant Shipping Act 1988 . . . 29, 135

Ministry of Defence Police Act . . . 1997
   s 2 . . . 384

Misuse of Drugs Act 1971 . . . 60, 183
   s 5 . . . 617
     (2), (3) . . . 561
   s 28 . . . 617

National Insurance Act 1911 . . . 286

Nationality, Immigration and Asylum Act 2002 . . . 58, 161
   Pt V . . . 288
   s 55 . . . 176
   s 81 . . . 289
   s 94 . . . 289
   s 101 . . . 289
   s 103A . . . 289, 311
   s 103B . . . 289
   Sch 4 . . . 289

Naval Discipline Act 1957 . . . 272, 560
   s 70 . . . 273
   s 129 . . . 273

Northern Ireland Act 1998 . . . 270, 271

Oaths Act . . . 1978
   s 1 . . . 333, 613
   s 5 . . . 333
     (2), (4) . . . 613

Obscene Publications Act 1959 . . . 31, 191
   s 4(1) . . . 60

Occupiers Liability Act 1957 . . . 65

Offences Against the Person Act . . . 1861
   s 20 . . . 547
   s 51 . . . 41
   s 57 . . . 50

Official Secrets Act . . . 1911
   s 1 . . . 543

Official Secrets Act 1920 . . . 407
   s 8(4) . . . 232

Official Secrets Act 1989 . . . 23
   Sch 1A . . . 407

Parliamentary Papers Act 1840 . . . 24

Parliament Act 1911 . . . 32, 35, 36, 67
   s 1 . . . 32
   s 2(1) . . . 32

Parliament Act 1949 . . . 32, 35, 36

Parliamentary Commissioner Act 1967 . . . 518

Patents Act 1977 . . . 251

Peace Act 1361 . . . 634

Perjury Act . . . 1911
   s 9 . . . 585

Planning (Listed Buildings and Conservation Areas) Act 1990 . . . 69
   s 1 . . . 69
   s 91 . . . 69

Police Act 1964 . . . 386
   s 41 . . . 387

Police Act 1976 . . . 396

Police Act 1996 . . . 386, 396
   s 3 . . . 386
   s 4 . . . 386
   s 5B . . . 386
   s 5C . . . 386
   s 6 . . . 386
   s 6A . . . 386, 387
     (2) . . . 388
   s 8 . . . 386, 387
     (3) . . . 388
   s 9B . . . 386
   s 11 . . . 386, 387
   s 13(3) . . . 386
   s 22 . . . 388
   s 24 . . . 387
   s 30 . . . 384
   s 36(1) . . . 387
   s 36A . . . 387
   s 37 . . . 387
   s 38 . . . 387
   s 39A . . . 387
   s 42(1) . . . 387
   s 49 . . . 297
   s 54 . . . 387
   s 88(1), (2), (4) . . . 395

s 89 . . . 395, 408
  (2) . . . 385
s 96 . . . 386
s 101 . . . 386
Sch 1 . . . 386
Sch 2 . . . 386
Sch 2A . . . 386

Police Act 1997 . . . 386
  s 1 . . . 388
  s 2 . . . 388
  s 48 . . . 388
  s 52(7) . . . 388
  s 91 . . . 404
  s 92 . . . 405
  s 93(1), (3), (4) . . . 404
  s 97 . . . 405
  Pt 1 . . . 384, 388
  Pt 2 . . . 384
  Pt 4 . . . 404

Police and Criminal Evidence Act 1984 . . . 15,
  17, 24, 27, 40, 357, 386, 396, 398, 412
  s 1 . . . 402, 403
    (1) . . . 402
    (6) . . . 402
    (7)(a), (b) . . . 402
    (8) . . . 402
    (8A) . . . 402
    (8B) . . . 402
    (9) . . . 402
  s 2 . . . 402
  s 3 . . . 16, 402
  s 18 . . . 409
  s 24 . . . 385, 406, 407, 408
    (1) . . . 407
    (5) . . . 408
  s 24A . . . 408
  s 25 . . . 407, 408
    (6) . . . 406
  s 26 . . . 406
  s 28 . . . 409
    (1), (3) . . . 408
  s 30 . . . 409, 532
    (10), (10A) . . . 409
  s 30A–30D . . . 532
  s 30A . . . 409
  s 32 . . . 409
    (2)(b) . . . 409
  s 34–36 . . . 532
  s 34 . . . 418
    (2A) . . . 418
  s 36 . . . 410, 418
  s 37 . . . 357, 410, 418, 535
  s 37A . . . 357
  s 37B . . . 357, 410, 519, 535
  s 37C . . . 357
  s 37C . . . 357
  s 38 . . . 410, 411
    (1) . . . 532

s 39 . . . 410
s 40 . . . 410, 411
s 41 . . . 411, 532
s 42(1) . . . 411
s 43 . . . 411
s 47 . . . 532
s 54 . . . 412
  (4) . . . 412
  (6A) . . . 412
  (9) . . . 413
s 54A . . . 412
s 55 . . . 389, 413
  (7) . . . 413
s 56 . . . 413
s 58 . . . 415, 416
  (8), (8A) . . . 415
s 60 . . . 387
s 60A . . . 40, 387, 401, 419
s 62(1) . . . 413
  (1A) . . . 413
  (10) . . . 414
s 63 . . . 414
s 65 . . . 413, 414
  (1) . . . 412
s 66 . . . 39, 387, 401
s 67(7) . . . 39
  (7A) . . . 39
  (11) . . . 40
s 69 . . . 50
s 76 . . . 69, 393, 419, 615, 618
  (2)(a) . . . 392
    (b) . . . 392, 393
  (8) . . . 69, 392
s 78 . . . 393, 394, 404, 417, 524, 607
s 79 . . . 611
s 80 . . . 611
  (3) . . . 612
s 81 . . . 583
s 82(3) . . . 392, 529
s 117 . . . 401
Sch 2 . . . 406
s Code A–F . . . 40, 401
  A . . . 400, 403, 404
  C . . . 410, 411, 412, 413, 414, 415, 416, 417,
    418, 419, 420
  D . . . 394, 420, 421
  E . . . 419
  F . . . 419

Police and Magistrates' Courts Act 1994 . . . 260,
  263

Police Reform Act 2002 . . . 16, 386, 387, 390
  s 6 . . . 387
  s 9 . . . 397
  s 10 . . . 397
  s 12 . . . 397
  s 17 . . . 397
  s 18 . . . 397
  s 20 . . . 397

s 38 . . . 384
  (2) . . . 390
  (6) . . . 390
s 39 . . . 391
  (4), (5) . . . 391
s 40–41 . . . 391
s 41(4) . . . 391
Sch 2, para 6 . . . 397
Sch 3, para 19 . . . 397
  para 15 . . . 397
  para 22 . . . 397
Sch 4 . . . 384
  Pts 1–4 . . . 390
Sch 5 . . . 391

Powers of Criminal Courts Act . . . 1973
s 21(1) . . . 650
s 42 . . . 641

Powers of Criminal Courts (Sentencing) Act 2000
  . . . 26, 557, 656, 667, 678
Pt III . . . 646
s 1 . . . 664
s 1A–1E . . . 664
s 2 . . . 664
s 3 . . . 549, 550, 639
s 3A . . . 550
s 4 . . . 639
s 12 . . . 648
s 16 . . . 646
s 17 . . . 646
s 21 . . . 646
s 60 . . . 648
s 7992) . . . 667
s 82A . . . 178
s 90 . . . 178, 646, 674
  (2) . . . 674
s 91 . . . 213, 643, 644
s 93 . . . 675
s 100–107 . . . 674
s 100 . . . 647
s 118 . . . 668
s 126 . . . 665
s 128 . . . 638
s 130 . . . 677
s 134 . . . 678
s 137 . . . 648
s 156 . . . 664

Prevention of Crime Act . . . 1953
s 1 . . . 616

Prevention of Terrorism Act 2005 . . . 17, 32, 162,
  308
s 1 . . . 179
s 4(7) . . . 17
s 9 . . . 17

Prevention of Terrorism (Temporary Provisions)
  Act 1984 . . . 172
s 14 . . . 178

Prison Act 1952 . . . 33, 151

Proceeds of Crime Act 2002 . . . 16
Prosecution of Offences Act 1985 . . . 572
s 1(3), (6) . . . 357
s 2 . . . 23, 356, 540
s 3 . . . 23
  (2) . . . 356
    (a), (b) . . . 533
s 6 . . . 533
s 7A . . . 357
s 10 . . . 535
s 19A . . . 362
s 22 . . . 573
  (3) . . . 573
s 23 . . . 536
s 28 . . . 585

Protection of Animals Act 1911 . . . 649
Protection from Harassment Act 1997 . . . 16
s 1 . . . 666
s 2 . . . 666
s 4 . . . 666
s 5 . . . 666, 679
s 7 . . . 666

Provisions of Oxford 1258 . . . 32
Public Interest Disclosure Act 1998 . . . 31
Public Order Act . . . 1936
s 5 . . . 627

Public Order Act 1986 . . . 23
s 5 . . . 191, 627
s 27 . . . 533

Quarter Sessions Act 1842 . . . 225
Race Relations Act 1968 . . . 64
Race Relations Act 1976 . . . 74, 291
s 57 . . . 255

Railways and Transport Safety Act . . . 2003
s 31 . . . 384

Regulation of Investigatory Powers Act 2000 . . .
  149, 151, 188, 404
Pt I . . . 405
Pt II . . . 405
s 5 . . . 405
s 6 . . . 405
s 17 . . . 405, 609
s 26(2), (3) . . . 405
s 28 . . . 405
s 29 . . . 405
s 32 . . . 405
s 65 . . . 286

Regulatory Reform Act 2001 . . . 36, 38
s 4(2) . . . 38

Rehabilitation of Offenders Act 1974 . . . 531
s 1 . . . 17

Rent Act 1977 . . . 56, 76, 80, 158, 185
s 141 . . . 255

Representation of the People Act 1983 . . . 228
s 3 . . . 19
s 120 . . . 253

Restriction of Offensive Weapons Act 1959 . . .
    47
Review of Justices Act 1872 . . . 653
Road Traffic Act 1930 . . . 41
Road Traffic Act 1988 . . . 26, 183
    s 5 . . . 46, 618
        (2) . . . 616
    s 7(6) . . . 628
    s 8 . . . 68
    s 16(2) . . . 189
    s 38(7) . . . 41
    s 163 . . . 402
    s 172 . . . 417, 523
Royal Assent Act 1967 . . . 32
Sale of Goods Act 1893 . . . 27
    s 22(1) . . . 11
School Standards and Framework Act . . . 1998
    s 95 . . . 286
Scotland Act 1998 . . . 30, 45, 270, 271
Serious Organised Crime and Police Act 2005 . . .
    390, 402
    Pt 1 . . . 384, 388
    Pt 2 . . . 385
    s 10 . . . 387
    s 65 . . . 385
    s 110 . . . 407
    s 117 . . . 413
    s 120–121 . . . 390, 410
    Sch 6, para 43 . . . 411, 415
    Sch 7, Pt 1 . . . 390
    Sch 8 . . . 390
Sex Discrimination Act 1975 . . . 137, 291
    s 6(4) . . . 136
    s 66 . . . 255
Sex Offenders Act . . . 1997
    Pt II . . . 41
    s 1(1)(b) . . . 18
Sexual Offences Act 1956 . . . 67
    s 14(1) . . . 62
Sexual Offences Act . . . 2003
    s 1 . . . 16
    s 9 . . . 185
    s 104 . . . 16
Sexual Offences (Amendment) Act . . . 1992
    s 1 . . . 234
    s 3 . . . 234
Sexual Offences (Amendment) Act 2000 . . . 32,
    185
Shops Act 1950 . . . 123
Short Titles Act . . . 1896
    s 2 . . . 33
Social Security Act . . . 1998
    s 4 . . . 286
    s 5 . . . 286
    s 7 . . . 286

s 13(2) . . . 287
s 14 . . . 287
s 15 . . . 287
Sch 1 . . . 286
Social Security Contributions and Benefits Act
    1992 . . . 26
    s 94 . . . 47
Solicitors Act 1957 . . . 61
Solicitors Act 1974 . . . 61, 352, 365
    s 1 . . . 358, 360
    s 2 . . . 358, 360
    s 3 . . . 358, 360
    s 20 . . . 61
    s 23 . . . 350
    s 31 . . . 360
    s 32 . . . 360
    s 35 . . . 360
    s 36 . . . 360
    s 37 . . . 360
    s 43 . . . 366
        (2) . . . 366
    s 46 . . . 294, 366
        (6) . . . 366
    s 47(1) . . . 366
        (2) . . . 366
        (2A) . . . 366
    s 49(1)(a) . . . 366
            (b) . . . 367
        (6) . . . 366
    s 50(2) . . . 361
    s 56 . . . 371
    s 57 . . . 371
    s 59 . . . 371
    s 64 . . . 371
    s 65(2) . . . 368
    s 70 . . . 371
    s 75 . . . 371
    s 87(1) . . . 371
    Sch 1 . . . 360
    Sch 2 . . . 360
Special Immigration Appeals Commission Act
    . . . 1997
    s 1 . . . 289
    s 2 . . . 289
Statute of Frauds 1677 . . . 44, 67
Statute of Gloucester 1278 . . . 32
Statute of Nisi Prius 11285 . . . 224
Statute of Uses 1535 . . . 67
Statute of Westminster I 1275 . . . 8
Statute of Westminster 1931 . . . 270
Statutory Instruments Act 1946 . . . 34
    s 3 . . . 35
    s 4 . . . 34
Street Offences Act . . . 1959
    s 2 . . . 232
Summary Jurisdiction Act 1857
    s 6 . . . 653

Supplies and Services (Transitional Powers) Act
   1945 . . . 36

Suppression of Terrorism Act . . . 1978
  s 4 . . . 42

Supreme Court Act 1981 . . . 245, 246, 251, 257
  s 1 . . . 257
  s 2 . . . 245
    (3) . . . 245, 300
  s 3(1) . . . 681
  s 5 . . . 250, 253
    (5) . . . 250
  s 7 . . . 250
    (2) . . . 250
  s 8 . . . 258
    (3) . . . 257
  s 9 . . . 246, 258, 301
    (4) . . . 650
  s 11(3), (8) . . . 319
  s 12 . . . 321
  s 15(2) . . . 246
  s 16 . . . 498
    (2) . . . 271
  s 17 . . . 508
  s 18(2) . . . 558
  s 20 . . . 252, 271
  s 28 . . . 229, 253, 654
    (2)(b) . . . 654
  s 28A . . . 253
  s 29(1) . . . 229
    (2) . . . 214
    (3) . . . 209, 213, 214, 257, 563
  s 30 . . . 207
  s 32(1) . . . 475
  s 32A . . . 487
  s 34 . . . 480
  s 35A . . . 89, 487
  s 37(1) . . . 472
  s 42 . . . 533
  s 45(1) . . . 257
  s 46 . . . 258
  s 47(2) . . . 663
  s 48 . . . 650
    (2)(a), (b) . . . 650
     (c) . . . 651
  s 49(3) . . . 468
  s 51 . . . 362, 490
    (6) . . . 491
  s 54(2–4) . . . 502
  s 54(2), (3)–(4A) . . . 246
  s 55(4) . . . 246
  s 59 . . . 100
  s 61 . . . 250, 251
  s 67 . . . 231
  s 68 . . . 253
  s 69 . . . 340
  s 71 . . . 249
    (1) . . . 251
  s 73(3) . . . 258

s 74(1) . . . 258
s 75 . . . 258, 259
s 78 . . . 258
s 81 . . . 557
s 128 . . . 371
s 151 . . . 301
Sch 1 . . . 250, 251, 254
Sch 2 . . . 253

Supreme Court of Judicature Acts . . . 1873
  s 34 . . . 251

Supreme Court of Judicature Acts 1873–75 . . . 4,
   6, 226, 227, 245, 249

Synodial Government Measure . . . 1969
  s 2(1) . . . 276

Taxation of Chargeable Gains Act 1992 . . . 26

Terrorism Act 2000 . . . 172, 183, 411, 533
  s 11 . . . 191, 618
    (2) . . . 191
  s 123 . . . 618
  s 41 . . . 178, 406
  s 44 . . . 400, 403
  s 45(1)(a), (b) . . . 403

Theft Act 1968 . . . 47, 545
  s 16 . . . 47
    (2)(a) . . . 47
  s 28(1) . . . 664

Theft Act 1978 . . . 47

Town and Country Planning Act 1990 . . . 296
  s 336 . . . 69

Trade Marks Act . . . 1994
  s 91 . . . 618
    (5) . . . 617

Trade Union and Labour Relations
   (Consolidation) Act 1992 . . . 40
  s 199 . . . 40
  s 207(2), (3) . . . 40

Transport Act . . . 1985
  s 117 . . . 286
  Sch 4 . . . 286

Transport Act . . . 2000
  s 219 . . . 35

Treason Act 1351 . . . 11

Treason Felony Act . . . 1848
  s 3 . . . 168, 191

Treasure Act 1996 . . . 267

Tribunal and Inquiries Act 1958 . . . 283

Tribunal and Inquiries Act 1992 . . . 283, 295
  s 1(1)(c) . . . 299
  s 2 . . . 283
  s 9 . . . 296
  s 11 . . . 295
  s 16(1) . . . 296

Tribunals of Inquiry (Evidence) Act 1921 . . . 298

War Crimes Act 1991 . . . 32, 42, 184
  Sch 1, para 4 . . . 569

War Damage Act 1965 . . . 24, 43, 90
 s 1(2) . . . 43
Water Industry Act 1991 . . . 26
Water Resources Act 1991 . . . 26
 s 210(1) . . . 35
 Sch 25 . . . 35
Weights and Measures Act 1985 . . . 30, 136
Welfare Reform and Pensions Act 199 . . . 254
Welsh Church Act 1914 . . . 32
Wildlife and Countryside Act 1981 . . . 65
Wills Act 1861 . . . 67
Youth Justice and Criminal Evidence Act . . .
     1999, 183, 517, 521, 613
 s 41 . . . 57, 158, 609
 s 45 . . . 234
 s 46 . . . 234
 s 47 . . . 518
 s 48 . . . 518
 s 49 . . . 518
 Sch 7 . . . 518
 Sch 8 . . . 518
Civil Procedure Rules 1998 (SI 1998/3132) . . .
     230, 426, 432, 464, 572, 623
 r 1(1) . . . 433
 r 1.2 . . . 434
 r 1.3 . . . 435
 r 3.1 . . . 434
 r 3.1(4) . . . 435
 r 3.3–3.9 . . . 468
 r 3.4 . . . 468
 r 3.9 . . . 468
 r 4(2)(e) . . . 436
 Part 8 . . . 465, 476
 Part 16 . . . 476
 r 16.2.3 . . . 476
 r 16.5.2 . . . 476
 PD 16 . . . 476
 r 17.1(2) . . . 476
 r 17.4(2) . . . 477
 Part 20 . . . 476
 r 22.1(6) . . . 476
 Part 23 . . . 473
 Part 24 . . . 470
 r 24.2 . . . 470
 Part 25 . . . 475
 r 26.2 . . . 256
 r 26.4(2) . . . 465
 r 26.6 . . . 465
 r 26.6(4) . . . 466
 r 26.6(5) . . . 466
 r 26.7(3) . . . 465
 r 26.8(1) . . . 465

 r 26.10 . . . 466
 r 28.2 . . . 466
 r 28.3 . . . 466
 r 28.5 . . . 466
 PD 29.4.13 . . . 466
 PD 29.5.3 . . . 466
 Part 30 . . . 249
 r 30.2 . . . 256
 r 31.6 . . . 479
 r 31.16 . . . 479
 r 31.22 . . . 478
 Part 36 . . . 470, 471, 472, 488
 r 36.5 . . . 470
 r 36.5(7) . . . 472
 r 36.20 . . . 472
 r36.20(2) . . . 471
 Part 38 . . . 468
 r 38.2 . . . 468
 r 38.4 . . . 468
 r 38.6 . . . 468, 488
 r 36.13(1) . . . 488
 Part 43 . . . 493
 r 43.4 . . . 492
 Part 44 . . . 493
 r 44.3 . . . 489
 r 44.3(1) . . . 488
 r 44.3(2) . . . 488
 r 44.3(6) . . . 489
 r 44.5(3) . . . 494
 44.14 . . . 491
 PD 44 . . . 492
 r 48.2 . . . 490
 r 48.6 . . . 497
 PD 48.53.4 . . . 491
 Part 49 . . . 252
 Part 52 . . . 247, 248, 498, 502
 r 52.3 . . . 499
 r 52.4 . . . 500
 r 52.9.1 . . . 500
 r 52.11 . . . 502, 504
 r 52.14.1 . . . 499
 PD 52 . . . 499, 500
 PD 52.7.7A . . . 500
 r 53.2 . . . 499
 r 53.2(3) . . . 499
 Part 54 . . . 206, 207, 217, 218, 219, 220, 253
 PD 54 . . . 206, 220, 221
 Part 58 . . . 252
 PD 58 . . . 252
Rules of the Supreme Court
 Ord 53 . . . 207, 217, 218, 253, 426
 Ord 59, r 11 . . . 508
 Ord 62, r 12(2) . . . 371
 Ord 114 . . . 653

TABLE OF STATUTORY INSTRUMENTS

Access to Justice Act 1999 (Destination of Appeals) Order 2000 (SI 2000/1071) . . . 247, 498
  Art 1(2)(c) . . . 499
    Art 4 . . . 247
    Art 5 . . . 247
Asylum and Immigration Tribunal (Procedure) Rules 2005 (SI 2005/230) . . . 289
Asylum (Designated Countries of Destination and Designated Safe Third Countries) Order 1996 (SI 1996/2671) . . . 37
Chartered Institute of Patent Agents Order 1999 (SI 1999/3137) . . . 350, 352
Children (Allocation of Proceedings) Order 1991 (SI 1991/1677) . . . 254, 255
  Art 3(1) . . . 266
  Sch 1 . . . 255
Civil Procedure (Amendment) Rules 2000 (SI 2000/221) . . . 247
Community Legal Service (Asylum and Immigration Appeals) Regulations 2005 (SI 2005/966) . . . 289
Community Legal Service (Financial) (Amendment) Regulations 2005 (SI 2005/1097) . . . 379
Community Legal Service (Financial) (Amendment No 2) Regulations 2005 (SI 2005/589) . . . 379
Community Legal Service (Financial) Regulations 2000 (SI 2000/516) . . . 379
Community Legal Service (Funding) (Amendment) Order 2005 (SI 2005/571) . . . 289
Conditional Fee Agreements Order 2000 (SI 2000/823) . . . 372
Conditional Fee Agreements Regulations 2000 (SI 2000/692) . . . 372, 496
Coroners (Amendment) Rules 1999 (SI 1999/3325) . . . 267
Coroners Rules 1984 (SI 1984/552) . . . 267
  r 22 . . . 267
County Courts Jurisdiction Order 1981 (SI 1981/1123) . . . 256
Crime and Disorder Act 1998 (Service of Prosecution Evidence) Regulations 2000 (SI 2000/3305) . . . 567, 574
Criminal Justice Act 2003 (Commencement No 1) Order 2003 (SI 2003/3282) . . . 514
Criminal Justice Act 2003 (Commencement No 1) Order 2004 (SI 2004/81) . . . 514
Criminal Procedure Rules 2005 (SI 2005/384) . . . 623, 635, 646
  r 3.2 . . . 631
  r 7.1 . . . 624
  r 7.3 . . . 627
    (3) . . . 627, 628
    (4) . . . 628
  Part 37 . . . 633
  r 37.1 . . . 634
  r 63 . . . 650
  r 64 . . . 653, 654
  r 68 . . . 653
Crown Court (Advance Notice of Expert Evidence) Rules 1987 (SI 1987/716) . . . 574, 583
Crown Court (Reference to the European Court) Rules 1972 (SI 1972) . . . 651
Disability Discrimination Act 1995 (Amendment) Regulations 2003 (SI 2003/1673) . . . 36, 123
Employment Appeal Tribunal (Amendment) Rules 2001 (SI 2001/1128) . . . 293
Employment Appeal Tribunal (Amendment) Rules 2004 (SI 2004/2526) . . . 293
Employment Appeal Tribunal Rules 1993 (SI 1993/2854) . . . 293
Employment Equality (Religion or Belief) Regulations 2003 (SI 2003/1660) . . . 36, 123, 291
Employment Equality (Sexual Orientation) Regulations 2003 (SI 2003/1661) . . . 36, 123, 291
Employment Tribunals (Constitution and Rules of Procedure) Order Regulations 2004 (SI 2004/1623) . . . 291
Employment Tribunals Extension of Jurisdiction (England and Wales) Order 1994 (SI 1994/1861) 292
  reg 4–9 . . . 291
  reg 9 . . . 291
Family Law Act 1996 (Part IV) (Allocation of Proceedings) Order 1997 (SI 1997/1896) 254
High Court and County Courts Jurisdiction Order 1991 (SI 1991/724) . . . 249, 256, 431
High Court and County Courts Jurisdiction (Amendment) Order 1999 (SI 1999/1014) . . . 249

Human Rights Act 1998 (Amendment No 2) Order 2001 (SI 2001/4032) . . . 161, 173, 178

Human Rights Act 1998 (Commencement No 2) Order 2000 (SI 2000/1851) . . . 42, 153

Indictment Rules 1971 (SI 1971/1253)
r 4(2) . . . 594
r 5(1) . . . 586
r 6 . . . 586
r 9 . . . 587, 588
r 10(1) . . . 585

Institute of Legal Executives Order 1998 (SI 1998/1077) . . . 352

Institute of Trade Mark Attorneys Order 2005 (SI 2005/240) . . . 352

Justices Clerks Rules 1999 (SI 1999/2784) . . . 541

Justices Clerks Rules 2005 (SI 2005/545) . . . 630

Judicial Committee (General Appellate Jurisdiction) Rules Order 1982 (SI 1982/1676)
Sch 2, para 16 . . . 270

Justices Clerks Rules 1999 (SI 1999/ 2784) . . . 630
r 2–3 . . . 541

Justices of the Peace (Commission Areas) (Amendment) Order 2001 (SI 2001/696)
Sch . . . 259

Justices' Clerks Rules 2005 (SI 2005/545) . . . 263

Legal Advice and Assistance Regulations 1989 (SI 1989/340) . . . 375

Legal Advice and Assistance (Scope) Regulations 1989 (SI 1989/550) . . . 375

Lord Justices Areas Order 2005 (SI 2005/554) . . . 260

Magistrates' Courts Rules 1981 (SI 1981/552) . . . 623
r 76(1) . . . 652

Maximum Number Judges Order 1994 (SI 1994/3217) . . . 241

Maximum Number Judges Order 2002 (SI 2002/2837) . . . 245

Mental Health Act 1983 (Remedial) Order 2001 (SI 2001/3712) . . . 37, 58, 64, 161, 179

Naval Discipline Act 1957 (Remedial) Order 2004 (SI 2004/66) . . . 272, 276

Police and Criminal Evidence Act 1984 (Codes of Practice) Order 2004 (SI 2004/1887) . . . 403

Police and Criminal Evidence Act 1984 (Visual Recording of Interviews) (Certain Police Areas) Order 2002 (SI 2002/1266) . . . 419

Police (Complaints and Misconduct) Regulations 2004 (SI 2004/643) . . . 391

Police (Conduct) Regulations 2004 (SI 2004/645) . . . 389

Police Regulations 2003 (SI 2003/527) . . . 389

Prison Rules 1964 (SI 1964/388) . . . 33
r 33(3) . . . 150

Prosecution of Offences (Custody Time Limits) Regulations 1987 (SI 1987/698) . . . 540

Race Relations Act (Amendment) Regulations 2003 (SI 2003/1626) . . . 36, 123

Regulation of Investigatory Powers (Directed Surveillance and Covert Human Intelligence Sources) Order 2003 (SI 2003/3171) . . . 405

Secretary of State for Constitutional Affairs Order 2003 (SI 2003/1887) . . . 21

Sex Discrimination Act 1975 (Amendment) Regulations 2003 (SI 2003/1657) . . . 36, 123

Social Security and Child Support (Decisions and Appeals) Regulations 1999 (SI 1999/991)
Sch 3 . . . 286

Solicitors (Non-Contentious Business) Remuneration Order 1994 (SI 1994/2616) . . . 371

Supreme Court Fees (Amendment) Order 1996 (SI 1996/3191) . . . 374
Art 3 . . . 374

Transfer of Functions (Miscellaneous) Order 2001 (SI 2000/3500) . . . 20

Youth Court (Constitution) Rules 1954 (SI 1954/1711) . . . 265

Youth Justice and Criminal Evidence Act 1999 (Commencement No 7) Order 2002 (SI 2002/1739) . . . 232

TABLE OF EC LEGISLATION

TREATIES

EC Treaty (Treaty of Rome 1957) . . . 110, 112, 121, 129
  Art 2 (ex 2) . . . 112, 123, 129
  Art 3–5 (ex 3, 3a, 3b) . . . 115
  Art 3 . . . 112
  Art 5 (ex 3b) . . . 116
  Art 6 . . . 124, 125
    (2) (ex Art F(2) . . . 112, 124
  Art 7 . . . 125
  Art 10 (ex 5) . . . 126
  Art 12 (ex 6) . . . 123
  Art 13 . . . 123
  Art 25 (ex 12) . . . 129
  Art 30 (ex 36) . . . 123
  Art 39 (ex 48) . . . 129
  Art 42 (ex 36) . . . 115
  Art 59 . . . 147
  Art 61–69 . . . 112, 142
  Art 81–83 (ex 85–87) . . . 119
  Art 90 (ex 95) . . . 129
  Art 94 (ex 100) . . . 112, 116, 117
  Art 133 (ex 113) . . . 116
  Art 137 (ex 189) . . . 119
  Art 138 (ex 118a) . . . 116, 117
  Art 141 (ex 119) . . . 115, 129, 134, 136, 137
  Art 174 (ex 130r) . . . 115
  Art 201 (ex 144) . . . 120
  Art 202 (ex 146) . . . 117
  Art 203 (ex 146) . . . 118
  Art 205 (ex 148) . . . 118
  Art 207 (ex 151) . . . 118
  Art 208 (ex 152) . . . 118
  Art 211 (ex 155) . . . 119
  Art 214 (ex 158) . . . 119
  Art 221 (ex 165) . . . 120, 138
  Art 222 (ex 166) . . . 138, 139
  Art 223 (ex 167) . . . 138
  Art 225 (ex 168a) . . . 120, 139
  Art 226 (ex 169) . . . 119, 140, 141
  Art 227 (ex 170) . . . 141
  Art 230 (ex 173) . . . 119, 122, 139
  Art 232 (ex 175) . . . 139
  Art 234 (ex 177) . . . 121, 131, 135, 139, 141, 142, 143, 144
    (1) . . . 142
  Art 235 (ex 178) . . . 141
  Art 236 (ex 178) . . . 141
  Art 249 (ex 189) . . . 121, 122, 129, 132
    (3) . . . 132
  Art 251 (ex 189b) . . . 120
  Art 288 (ex 215) . . . 141

Art 308 (ex 235) . . . 116
Protocol
  Art 4 . . . 119
EU Constitutional Treaty . . . 113
  Art I-2 . . . 114
  Art I-6 . . . 114
  Art I-7 . . . 113, 125
  Art I-9(2) . . . 125
  Art I-20(2) . . . 119
  Art I-22 . . . 117
  Art I-25 . . . 118
  Art I-26(6) . . . 119
  Art I-28 . . . 117
  Art I-29(1) . . . 139
    (2) . . . 138
  Art I-33 . . . 122
  Art I-34(1) . . . 120
  Protocol 2 . . . 114
  Protocol 3 . . . 138
EU Treaty (TEU) (Maastricht) 1992 . . . 7, 111, 121
Treaty of Amsterdam (1 May 1999) . . . 111, 112, 121, 123, 124, 142
  Protocol . . . 117
Treaty of Nice 2003 . . . 113, 119, 121, 139
  Protocol
    Art 3 . . . 118
Single European Act . . . 111, 121

DIRECTIVES

Employment Directive 2000/78/EC . . . 36, 123
Equal Treatment Directive 57/117 . . . 136
Equal Treatment Directive 76/207 . . . 123
Race Directive 2000/43/EC . . . 36, 123
Working Time Directive . . . 140

REGULATION

1612/68 . . . 123

CONVENTIONS

Convention for the Protection of Human Rights and Fundamental Freedoms, Rome, 4 November 1950 (European Convention on Human Rights (ECHR)) . . . 7, 28, 65, 112, 113, 124, 216, 616
  Art 2–12 . . . 37, 55, 73, 153

Art 2 . . . 155, 156, 172, 173, 174, 175, 176, 268, 269, 396
  (1) . . . 155
Art 3 . . . 148, 172, 175, 176, 414, 645
Art 4 . . . 148, 176
  (1) . . . 172
Art 5 . . . 37, 58, 64, 148, 161, 162, 166, 172, 173, 177, 178, 179, 400, 556, 559, 645
  (1) . . . 177
    (e), (f) . . . 179
  (2) . . . 409
  (4) . . . 154, 177, 178
  (5) . . . 169
Art 6 . . . 15, 17, 18, 20, 57, 125, 148, 150, 151, 155, 161, 166, 178, 180, 181, 182, 183, 196, 197, 210, 237, 240, 269, 272, 274, 275, 276, 281, 283, 315, 320, 335, 336, 343, 344, 373, 393, 405, 417, 418, 468, 477, 506, 514, 521, 522, 523, 524, 525, 537, 553, 570, 572, 578, 592, 609, 616, 617, 644, 645, 673
  (1) . . . 154, 180, 183, 232, 522
  (2) . . . 18, 181, 617
    (c) . . . 181
  (3) . . . 181, 523
Art 7 . . . 43, 148, 172, 183, 184
  (2) . . . 184
Art 8–11 . . . 171
Art 8 . . . 58, 148, 150, 151, 156, 161, 166, 167, 171, 175, 181, 184, 185, 186, 187, 188, 193, 194, 195, 325, 393, 394, 405, 523, 530, 556, 664
  (2) . . . 187
Art 9 . . . 148, 157, 175, 188, 189, 190
  (2) . . . 157, 188, 190
Art 10 . . . 124, 148, 150, 151, 156, 166, 169, 190, 191, 192, 193, 194, 237, 414, 478, 507
  (2) . . . 170, 190, 191, 193, 400
Art 11 . . . 148, 169, 193, 194
  (2) . . . 193, 400
Art 12 . . . 58, 148, 155, 161, 194
  (2), (3), (4) . . . 155
Art 13 . . . 148, 153, 155
Art 14 . . . 37, 73, 80, 153, 159, 162, 175, 179, 185, 192, 194, 195, 196
Art 18 . . . 153
Art 20 . . . 153, 199
Art 21 . . . 199
  (5) . . . 153
Art 22–29 . . . 198
Art 22 . . . 199
  (3) . . . 153
Art 23 . . . 199
Art 24–26 . . . 198
Art 24 . . . 198
Art 25–27 . . . 198
Art 26 . . . 200
Art 27 . . . 198, 199, 200
Art 28 . . . 199
Art 31–39 . . . 198
Art 34 . . . 167, 200, 201
Art 35–36 . . . 198
Art 35 . . . 198, 200, 201
Art 38–39 . . . 198
Art 38 . . . 199
Art 39 . . . 199
Art 41 . . . 169, 200
Art 43 . . . 200
Art 46 . . . 198, 200
Art 59 . . . 147, 198
Protocol 1 . . . 195
Art 1–3 . . . 37, 55, 73, 153
Art 1 . . . 64, 161, 195, 196, 197
Art 2 . . . 197
Art 3 . . . 197
Protocol 6 . . . 173
Art 1, 2 . . . 37, 55, 73, 153
Protocol 11 . . . 198
Protocol 13 . . . 173
Protocol 14 . . . 147, 198, 199, 200
Art 2 . . . 199
Art 6 . . . 200
Art 8 . . . 199
Art 12 . . . 198
Art 14 . . . 199
Art 16 . . . 200

LIST OF CASES

A (A Minor) (Costs), Re [1988] Fam Law 339, CA . . . 368

A (Children) (Conjoined Twins: Medical Treatment) (No 1), Re [2001] Fam 147; [2000] 4 All ER 961, CA . . . 175, 327

A v B plc [2002] EWCA Civ 337; [2003] QB 195; [2002] 2 All ER 545, CA . . . 167, 187, 328

A v France (1999) . . . 559

A v Secretary of State for the Home Department [2002] HRLR 45; [2002] EWCA Civ 1502; [2004] QB 335; [2003] 1 All ER 816, CA; [2004] UKHL 56; [2005] 2 WLR 87, HL . . . 12, 161, 172, 179, 242

A v United Kingdom (1999) 27 EHRR 611 . . . 176

ADT v United Kingdom (35765/97) (2001) 31 EHRR 33 . . . 186

AEI Rediffusion Music Ltd v Phonographic Performance Ltd (Costs) [1999] 1 WLR 1507; [1999] 2 All ER 299, CA . . . 489

AP v Switzerland (1998) 26 EHRR 541 . . . 522

ATB v Ministero per le Politiche Agricole (C402/98) [2000] ECR I-5501 . . . 123

A-G v De Keyser's Royal Hotel Ltd [1920] AC 508, HL . . . 12, 205

A-G v Hitchcock (1847) 1 Exch 91 . . . 609

Aaron v Shelton [2004] 3 All ER 561 . . . 490

Abidin Daver, The [1984] AC 398; [1984] 1 All ER 470, HL . . . 468

Abbassy v Commissioner of Police of the Metropolis [1990] 1 WLR 385; [1990] 1 All ER 193, CA . . . 408

Abbott v R [1977] AC 755; [1976] 3 All ER 140, PC . . . 270

Abdulaziz, Cabales and Balkandali v United Kingdom (A/94) (1985) 7 EHRR 471 . . . 185, 195

Accession of the Community to the European Human Rights Convention (Opinion 2/94), Re [1996] 2 CMLR 265 . . . 125

Adams v Naylor [1946] AC 543; [1946] 2 All ER 241, HL . . . 85

Adamson v United Kingdom (1999) App 42293/98 . . . 184

Adler v George [1964] 2 QB 7; [1964] 1 All ER 628 50

Adolf v Austria (A/49) (1982) 4 EHRR 313 . . . 522

Afrika v Cape plc [2003] 3 All ER 631 . . . 497

Ahmad v United Kingdom (8160/78) (1982) 4 EHRR 126 . . . 188, 189

Aiden Shipping Co Ltd v Interbulk Ltd (The Vimeira) (No 2) [1986] AC 965; [1986] 2 All ER 409, HL . . . 490

Air Canada v Secretary of State for Trade (No 2) [1983] 2 AC 394; [1983] 1 All ER 910, HL . . . 323, 577

Air India v Wiggins [1980] 2 All ER 593; [1980] 1 WLR 815, HL . . . 41

Airedale NHS Trust v Bland [1993] AC 789; [1993] 1 All ER 821, HL . . . 326

Aksoy v Turkey (1997) 23 EHRR 553 . . . 175, 200

Albert v Lavin [1982] AC 546; [1981] 3 All ER 878, HL . . . 385, 398, 399

Alcan Aluminium Raeren, SA Societe Franco-Belge des Laminoirs et Trefileries d'Anvers (Lamitref), and NV Werkhuizen Remy Claeys v Commission of the European Communities (C69/69) [1970] ECR 385 . . . 140

Alcatel Austria AG v Bundesministerium fur Wissenschaft und Verkehr (C81/98) [1999] ECR I-7671 . . . 132

Alderson v Booth [1969] 2 QB 216; [1969] 2 All ER 271 . . . 409

Alfons Lutticke GmbH v Hauptzollamt Sarrelouis (C57/65) [1966] ECR 293 . . . 129

Alfred F Beckett Ltd v Lyons [1967] Ch 449; [1967] 1 All ER 833, CA . . . 8

Ali v United Kingdom (1997) . . . 523

Allan v United Kingdom (2003) 36 EHRR 12 . . . 181

Allen v Emmerson [1944] KB 362; [1944] 1 All ER 344 . . . 60

Allen v Flood [1898] AC 1, HL . . . 241

Alliance & Leicester Building Society v Ghahremani (1992) 142 NLJR 313; (1992) The Times, 19 March . . . 362

Amand v Secretary of State for the Home Department [1943] AC 147; [1942] 2 All ER 381, HL . . . 16

Amber v Stacey [2001] 1 WLR 1225; [2001] 2 All ER 88, CA . . . 471

American Cyanamid Co v Ethicon Ltd [1975] AC 396; [1975] 1 All ER 504, HL . . . 156, 473, 474

American Cyanamid Co v Upjohn Co [1970] 3 All ER 785, HL . . . 501

Amministrazione delle Finanze dello Stato v
    Simmenthal SpA (No 2) (106/77) [1978] ECR
    629; [1978] 3 CMLR 263 . . . 45, 126

Ampthill Peerage, The [1977] AC 547; [1976] 2
    All ER 411, HL . . . 242

Anderson v Alnwick District Council [1993] 3 All
    ER 613; [1993] 1 WLR 1156 . . . 8

Anderson (Keith Anthony) v DPP [1978] AC 964;
    sub nom DPP v Anderson (Keith Anthony)
    [1978] 2 All ER 512 . . . 663

Anderson (Rupert) v R [1972] AC 100; [1971] 3
    All ER 768, PC . . . 689

Anderton v Ryan [1985] AC 560; [1985] 2 All ER
    355, HL . . . 95

Angelini v Sweden (1986) 51 D & R 41 . . . 188

Anisminic Ltd v Foreign Compensation
    Commission (No 2) [1969] 2 AC 147; [1969] 1
    All ER 208, HL . . . 64, 209, 212, 215, 311

Annandale and Hartfell Peerage Claim [1986] AC
    319; [1985] 3 All ER 577, HL . . . 242

Anon YB 6 Edw 2 (SS xiii), 43 . . . 103

Ansari v Puffin Investment Co Ltd [2002] EWCA
    234, CA . . . 502

Anton Piller KG v Manufacturing Processes Ltd
    [1976] Ch 55; [1976] 1 All ER 779, CA . . . 434

Antonio Munoz y Cia SA v Frumar Ltd (C253/00)
    [2003] Ch 328; [2003] All ER (EC) 56 . . . 129

Anufrijeva v Southwark LBC [2003] EWCA Civ
    1406; [2004] QB 1124; [2004] 1 All ER 833, CA
    . . . 169

Aoun v Bhari [2002] EWCA Civ 1141, CA . . .
    501

Arab Monetary Fund v Hashim (No 5) [1992] 2
    All ER 911 . . . 480

Aratra Potato Co Ltd v Taylor Joynson Garrett
    [1995] 4 All ER 695 . . . 373

Arbuthnot Latham Bank Ltd v Trafalgar Holdings
    Ltd [1998] 2 All ER 181; [1998] 1 WLR 1426,
    CA . . . 469

Arenson v Casson Beckman Rutley & Co [1977]
    AC 405; [1975] 3 All ER 901, HL . . . 83

Arrowsmith v United Kingdom (1978) 19 D & R
    5 . . . 188, 189

Arsenal v Reed [2003] EWCA Civ 865; [2003] 3
    All ER 865, CA . . . 146

Arthur J S Hall & Co v Simons and others [2002]
    1 AC 615; [2000] 3 All ER 673, HL . . . 82, 94,
    355, 370

Asher v Seaford Court Estates [1949] 2 KB 481;
    [1949] 2 All ER 155, CA . . . 48

Ashford v Thornton (1818) 1 B & Ald 405 . . . 6,
    10, 44

Ashworth Hospital Authority v MGN Ltd [2002]
    1 WLR 2033, HL . . . 481

Assam Railways and Trading Co Ltd v Inland
    Revenue Commissioners [1935] AC 445, HL
    . . . 71

Assicurazioni Generali SpA v Arab Insurance
    Group (BSC) [2002] EWCA Civ 1642; [2003] 1
    WLR 577, CA . . . 248, 504

Associated Provincial Picture Houses Ltd v
    Wednesbury Corporation [1948] 1 KB 223;
    [1947] 2 All ER 680, CA . . . 37, 215, 655

Astley v Younge (1759) 2 Burr 807 . . . 323

Aston Cantlow and Wilmcote with Billesley
    Parochial Church Council v Wallbank [2003]
    UKHL 37; [2004] 1 AC 546; [2003] 3 All ER
    1213, HL . . . 157, 164, 196, 209

Attorney-General v Associated Newspapers Ltd
    (1992) [1994] 2 AC 238; [1994] 1 All ER 556,
    HL . . . 342

Attorney-General v BBC [1981] AC 303; [1980] 3
    All ER 161, HL . . . 228, 240

Attorney General v BBC and Hat Trick
    Productions Ltd [1997] EMLR 76 . . . 239

Attorney General v Birmingham Post and Mail
    Ltd [1999] 1 WLR 361; [1998] 4 All ER 49 . . .
    239

Attorney-General v English (David) [1983] 1 AC
    116; [1982] 2 All ER 903, HL . . . 238

Attorney-General v Hislop and Pressdram [1991]
    1 QB 514; [1991] 1 All ER 911, CA . . . 236,
    238

Attorney-General v Leveller Magazine Ltd [1979]
    AC 440; [1979] 1 All ER 745, HL . . . 231, 235,
    237

Attorney-General v MGN Ltd [1997] 1 All ER 456
    . . . 239

Attorney General v Mulholland [1963] 2 QB 477;
    [1963] 1 All ER 767, CA . . . 239

Attorney-General v Punch [2002] UKHL 50;
    [2003] 1 AC 1046; [2003] 1 All ER 289, HL . . .
    192, 237, 238, 473

Attorney-General v Times Newspapers Ltd
    [1974] AC 273; [1973] 3 All ER 54, HL . . . 238

Attorney-General v Times Newspapers Ltd
    [1992] 1 AC 191; [1991] 2 All ER 398, HL . . .
    236, 238, 473

Attorney-General of Hong Kong v Lee Kwong-
    Kut [1993] AC 951; [1993] 3 All ER 939, PC
    . . . 56

Attorney-General v News Group Newspapers Ltd
    [1989] QB 110; [1988] 2 All ER 906 . . . 238

Attorney General of Ontario v Attorney General
    of Canada [1947] AC 127; [1947] 1 All ER 137,
    PC . . . 271

Attorney General of Northern Ireland v Gallagher
    (Patrick) [1963] AC 349; [1961] 3 All ER 299,
    HL . . . 687

Attorney-General of Northern Ireland's Reference (No 1 of 1975) [1977] AC 105; [1976] 2 All ER 937, HL . . . 401

Attorney General's Application, Re [1963] 1 QB 696; [1962] 3 All ER 326, CA . . . 236

Attorney General's Guidelines (Juries: Right to Stand By); *sub nom* Practice Note (Juries: Right to Stand By: Jury Checks) [1988] 3 All ER 1086 . . . 606

Attorney-General's Reference (No 1 of 1988), Re [1989] AC 971; [1989] 2 All ER 1, HL . . . 61

Attorney-General's Reference (No 1 of 1990), Re [1992] QB 630; [1992] 3 All ER 169, CA . . . 539

Attorney-General's Reference (No 1 of 2004), Re; R *v* Edwards [2004] All ER (D) 318 . . . 617, 618

Attorney-General's Reference (No 2 of 2001), Re [2004] 1 Cr App R 25 . . . 537

Attorney General's Reference (No 3 of 1979), Re (1979) 69 Cr App R 411, CA . . . 608

Attorney-General's Reference (No 3 of 1999), Re [2001] 2 AC 91; [2001] 2 WLR 56, HL . . . 188

Attorney-General's Reference (No 4 of 2002), Re [2004] UKHL 43; [2005] 1 All ER 237; [2004] 3 WLR 976, HL . . . 183, 191

Attorney-General's Reference (No 5 of 1989), Re; R *v* Hill-Trevor (Mark Charles) (1990) 90 Cr App R 358, CA . . . 660

Attorney-General's Reference (No 5 of 2002), Re [2004] UKHL 20; [2005] 1 AC 167; [2004] 4 All ER 901, HL . . . 405

Audergon *v* La Baguette Ltd [2002] EWCA Civ 10, CA . . . 502

Australian Consolidated Press Ltd *v* Uren (Thomas) [1969] 1 AC 590; [1967] 3 All ER 523, PC . . . 88

Avon CC *v* Hooper [1997] 1 All ER 53; [1997] 1 WLR 1605, CA . . . 72

Aydin *v* Turkey (1998) 25 EHRR 251 . . . 175

B *v* Chief Constable of Avon and Somerset [2001] 1 WLR 340; [2001] 1 All ER 562 . . . 14

B *v* United Kingdom (36337/97) [2001] 2 FLR 261; (2002) 34 EHRR 19 . . . 232

B *v* United Kingdom (2004) 39 EHRR 30 . . . 185

B (A Child) *v* DPP [2000] 2 AC 428; [2000] 1 All ER 833, HL . . . 62

B (A Child) (Adoption: Natural Parent), Re [2001] UKHL 70; [2002] 1 WLR 258; [2002] 1 All ER 641, HL . . . 188

Balabel *v* Air India [1988] Ch 317; [1988] 2 All ER 246, CA . . . 352

Bache *v* Essex County Council [2000] 2 All ER 847, CA . . . 292

Baker *v* R [1975] AC 774; [1975] 3 All ER 55, PC . . . 96

Balogh *v* St Albans Crown Court [1975] QB 73; [1974] 3 All ER 283, CA . . . 241

Barclays Bank Ltd *v* Cole (No 1) [1967] 2 QB 738; [1966] 3 All ER 948, CA . . . 74

Barclays Bank plc *v* Martin and Mortimer (2002) *The Times*, 19 August . . . 472

Barings plc (in liquidation) *v* Coopers & Lybrand (No 6) [2002] EWCA Civ 1163, CA . . . 501

Barras *v* Aberdeen Steam Trawling & Fishing Co Ltd [1933] AC 402, HL . . . 76

Barrington *v* Lee [1972] 1 QB 326; [1971] 3 All ER 1231, CA . . . 98

Barrister (Wasted Costs Order) (No 1 of 1991), Re [1993] QB 293; [1992] 3 All ER 429, CA . . . 362, 491

Barron *v* Lovell [199] CPLR 630 . . . 495

Becker *v* Finanzamt Munster-Innenstadt (C8/81) [1982] ECR 53; [1982] 1 CMLR 499 . . . 130

Beckles *v* United Kingdom (2003) 36 EHRR 13 . . . 183, 418

Begum (Runa) *v* Tower Hamlets [2003] UKHL 5; [200] 2 AC 430; [2003] 1 All ER 731, HL . . . 155, 180

Belasco *v* Hannant (1862) 3 B & S 13 . . . 67

Belgian Linguistic Case (No 2) (A/6) (1979–1980) 1 EHRR 252 . . . 197

Belgium *v* Spain (C388/95) [2000] E.C.R. I-3121 . . . 141

Bell Electric Ltd *v* Aweco Appliance Systems GmbH & Co [2002] EWCA Civ 501, CA . . . 501

Bellinger *v* Bellinger [2003] UKHL 21; [2003] 2 AC 467; [2003] 2 All ER 593, HL . . . 48, 58, 158, 161, 185, 194

Benedenoun *v* France (1994) 18 EHRR 54 . . . 522

Benham *v* United Kingdom (1996) 22 EHRR 293 . . . 17, 180, 181

Berrehab *v* Netherlands (A/138) (1989) 11 EHRR 322 . . . 185

Beswick *v* Beswick [1968] AC 58; [1967] 2 All ER 1197, HL . . . 58, 71

Beta Construction Ltd *v* Channel Four Television Co Ltd [1990] 1 WLR 1042; [1990] 2 All ER 1012, CA . . . 340

Bettison *v* Langton [2000] Ch 54; [1999] 2 All ER 367, CA (affirmed [2001] UKHL 24; [2002] 1 AC 27; [2001] 3 All ER 417, HL) . . . 12, 13

Bibby v Chief Constable of Essex (2000) 164 JP 297, CA . . . 399

Birkett v James [1978] AC 297; [1977] 2 All ER 801, HL . . . 468, 469

Black v Sumitomo [2002] 1 WLR 1562, CA . . . 479

Black Clawson International Ltd v Papierwerke Waldhof-Aschaffenburg AG [1975] AC 591; [1975] 1 All ER 810, HL . . . 74

Blackburn v Attorney General [1971] 2 All ER 1380; [1971] 1 WLR 1037, CA . . . 134, 208

Blyth v Blyth [1966] AC 643; [1966] 1 All ER 524, HL . . . 44

Boddington v British Transport Police [1999] 2 AC 143; [1998] 2 All ER 203, HL . . . 38, 219

Bonham's case (1609) 8 Co Rep 113 . . . 29

Bonsor v Musicians Union [1956] AC 104; [1955] 3 All ER 518, HL . . . 295

Booth v Britannia Hotels Ltd [2002] EWCA Civ 579, CA . . . 489

Bourgoin SA v Ministry of Agriculture, Fisheries and Food [1986] QB 716; [1985] 3 All ER 585, CA . . . 133

Bourne v Keane [1919] AC 815, HL . . . 92

Bourne (Inspector of Taxes) v Norwich Crematorium Ltd [1967] 2 All ER 576; [1967] 1 WLR 691 . . . 47

Boys v Chaplin [1968] 2 QB 1; [1968] 1 All ER 283, CA . . . 99

Brady v United Kingdom App (2001) 55151/100 . . . 173

Brannigan and McBride v United Kingdom (A/258-B) (1994) 17 EHRR 539 . . . 172, 178

Brasserie du Pecheur SA v Germany (C46/93); R v Secretary of State for Transport, ex parte Factortame Ltd (No 4) (C48/93) [1996] QB 404; [1996] All ER (EC) 301 . . . 133

Bratty (George) v Attorney General of Northern Ireland [1963] AC 386; [1961] 3 All ER 523, HL . . . 13

Bray (Inspector of Taxes) v Best [1989] 1 All ER 969; [1989] 1 WLR 167, HL . . . 105

Brennan v United Kingdom (39846/98) (2002) 34 EHRR 18 . . . 181

Brind v Secretary of State for the Home Department. See R v Secretary of State for the Home Department, ex parte Brind

British Railways Board v Herrington [1972] AC 877; [1972] 1 All ER 749, HL . . . 94

British Railways Board v Pickin [1973] QB 219; [1972] 3 All ER 923, CA (reversed [1974] AC 765; [1974] 1 All ER 609, HL) . . . 5, 29

Broekmeulen v Huisarts Registratie Commissie (C246/80) [1981] ECR 2311 . . . 142

Brogan v United Kingdom (A/145-B) (1989) 11 EHRR 117 . . . 172, 178

Broome v Cassell & Co Ltd (No 1) [1971] 2 QB 354; [1971] 2 All ER 187, CA . . . 88, 96

Brown v Bennett (Wasted Costs) (No 1) [2002] 2 All ER 273; . . . 1 WLR 713 . . . 76

Brown v Stott (Procurator Fiscal: Dunfermline) [2003] 1 AC 681; [2001] 2 All ER 97 . . . 183, 417, 271, 523, 617, 618

Brown v United Kingdom (1985) 8 EHRR 272 . . . 524

Brownsea Haven Properties v Poole Corporation [1958] Ch 574; [1958] 1 All ER 205, CA . . . 59, 60, 96

Buckley v United Kingdom (1997) 23 EHRR 101 . . . 186

Bugg v DPP [1993] QB 473; [1993] 2 All ER 815 . . . 220

Bulmer Ltd (H P) v J Bollinger SA (No 2) [1974] Ch 401; [1974] 2 All ER 1226, CA . . . 114, 142, 143, 144

Burmah Oil Co (Burma Trading) Ltd v Lord Advocate [1965] AC 75; [1964] 2 All ER 348, HL . . . 43, 90

Burns v Shuttlehurst Ltd [1999] 1 WLR 1449; [1999] 2 All ER 27, CA . . . 479

Bushell v Secretary of State for the Environment [1981] AC 75; [1980] 3 WLR 22, HL . . . 296

Bushell's Case (1670) Vaugh 135; 124 ER 1006 . . . 323, 329, 620

Button (Graham Cecil) v DPP [1966] AC 591; [1965] 3 All ER 587, HL . . . 11, 92

C (A Minor) (Interim Care Order: Residential Assessment), Re [1997] AC 489; [1996] 4 All ER 871, HL . . . 60

C (A Minor) v DPP [1994] 3 All ER 190, QBD (affirmed [1996] AC 1; [1995] 2 All ER 43, HL) . . . 326

CILFIT Srl v Ministro della Sanita (Minister of Health) (C283/81) [1982] ECR 3415; [1983] 1 CMLR 472 . . . 143

CR and SW v United Kingdom (1996) 21 EHRR 363 . . . 184

Callery v Gray (No 1) [2001] EWCA Civ 1117; [2001] 1 WLR 2112, CA; [2002] 3 All ER 652, HL . . . 496

Calpak SpA v Commission of the European Communities (C789–90/79) [1980] ECR 1949 . . . 140

Campbell v MGN Ltd [2004] ULHL 22; [2004] 2 AC 457; [2004] 2 All ER 995, HL . . . 187, 328

Campbell v United Kingdom (A/233A) (1993) 15 EHRR 137 . . . 187

Campbell and Cosans v United Kingdom (No 2) (A/48) (1982) 4 EHRR 293 . . . 197

Capital and Counties plc v Hampshire County Council [1997] QB 1004; [1997] 2 All ER 865, CA . . . 34

Cassell & Co Ltd v Broome (No 1) [1972] AC 1027; [1972] 1 All ER 801, HL . . . 79, 88, 96, 101, 506

Castorina v Chief Constable of Surrey [1988] NLJR 180 . . . 400

Cave v Robinson Jarvis & Rolf (A Firm) [2001] EWCA Civ 245; [2002] 1 WLR 581, CA . . . 99

Cayne v Global Natural Resources plc [1984] 1 All ER 225, CA . . . 474

Central Asbestos Co Ltd v Dodd [1973] AC 518; [1972] 2 All ER 1135, HL . . . 47, 84

Central Independent Television plc, Re [1991] 1 WLR 4; [1991] 1 All ER 347 . . . 235, 620

Central London Property Trust v High Trees House [1947] KB 130; [1956] 1 All ER 256n . . . 82, 324

Centrosteel Srl v Adipol GmbH (C456/98) [2000] ECR I-6007 . . . 132

Cha'are Shalom Ve Tsedek v France (2000) 9 BHRC 27 . . . 189

Chahal v United Kingdom (1997) 23 EHRR 413 . . . 176

Chandler (Terence Norman) v DPP [1964] AC 763; [1962] 3 All ER 142, HL . . . 68

Chapman v Honig [1963] 2 QB 502; [1963] 2 All ER 513, CA . . . 482

Chapman v United Kingdom (27238/95) (2001) 33 EHRR 18 . . . 186

Charter v Race Relations Board [1973] AC 868; [1973] 1 All ER 512, HL . . . 71

Chief Constable of Cleveland v McGrogan [2002] EWCA Civ 86; [2002] 1 FLR 707, CA . . . 398

Chief Constable of Norfolk v Clayton [1983] 2 AC 473; sub nom Clayton v Chief Constable of Norfolk [1983] 1 All ER 984, HL . . . 628

Chiron Corporation v Murex Diagnostics Ltd (No 8) [1995] All ER (EC) 88, CA . . . 142

City of London v Wood (1701) 12 Mod Rep 669 . . . 29

Christie v Leachinsky [1947] AC 573; [1947] 1 All ER 567, HL . . . 408

Clark v University of Lincolnshire and Humberside [2000] 3 All ER 752; [2000] 1 WLR 1988, CA . . . 99, 218

Clibbery v Allan [2002] EWCA Civ 45; [2002] 1 All ER 865, CA . . . 232

Cobbold v Greenwich LBC, unreported, 24 May 2001 . . . 477

Cocks v Thanet District Council [1983] 2 AC 286; [1982] 3 All ER 1135, HL . . . 218

Coggs v Bernard (1703) 2 Ld Raym 909 . . . 9, 10

Coles and Ravenshear Arbitration, Re [1907] 1 KB 1, CA . . . 433

Colley v Council for Licensed Conveyancers (Right of Appeal) [2001] 4 All ER 998, CA . . . 499

Collins v Wilcock [1984] 1 WLR 1172; [1984] 3 All ER 374 . . . 395, 527

Commission of the European Communities v France; sub nom Re Ban on British Bef Case (C1/00) [201] ECR I-9989; [2002] 1 CMLR 22 . . . 141

Commission v Italy (C39/72) [1973] ECR 101 . . . 129

Compagnie Financiere et Commerciale du Pacifique v Peruvian Guano Co (1882) LR 11 QBD 55

Court: . . . CA . . . 479

Compton, Re [1945] Ch 123; [1945] 1 All ER 198, CA . . . 91

Condron v United Kingdom (35718/97) (No 2) (2001) 31 EHRR 1; [2000] Crim LR 679 . . . 183, 418

Confédération Nationale des Producteurs de Fruits et Légumes v Council of the European Economic Community (C16/62) [1962] ECR 471 . . . 122

Connelly (Charles) v DPP [1964] AC 1254; (1964) 48 Cr App R 183, HL . . . 538, 602, 607

Consorzio del Prosciutto di Parma v Asda Food Stores Ltd [2001] UKHL 7; [2001] 1 CMLR 43, HL . . . 129

Conway v Rimmer [1968] AC 910; [1968] 2 WLR 998; [1968] 1 All ER 874, HL . . . 577

Cooper v United Kingdom (2004) 39 EHRR 8 . . . 155, 272, 275, 276

Corocraft Ltd v Pan American Airways Inc [1969] 1 QB 616; [1969] 1 All ER 82, CA . . . 70

Costa v Ente Nazionale per l'Energia Elettrica (ENEL) (C6/64) [1964] ECR 585; [1964] CMLR 425 . . . 126, 142

Costello-Roberts v United Kingdom (A/247-C) (1995) 19 EHRR 112 . . . 176

Council of Civil Service Unions v Minister for the Civil Service [1985] AC 374; [1984] 3 All ER 935, HL . . . 34, 37, 205, 208, 215, 216, 305

Courage Ltd v Crehan (C453/99) [2002] QB 507; [2001] All ER (EC) 886 . . . 134

Cowl (Frank) v Plymouth City Council [2001] EWCA Civ 1935; [2002] 1 WLR 803, CA . . . 219

Cowlishaw v Chalkley [1955] 1 WLR 101; [1955] 1 All ER 367n . . . 653

Cox v Army Council [1963] AC 48; [1962] 1 All ER 880, HL . . . 41

Crane v Director of Public Prosecutions [1921] 2 AC 299, HL . . . 587

Cream Holdings v Banerjee [2003] EWCA Civ 103; [2003] Ch 650; [2003] 2 All ER 318, CA; [2004] UKHL 44; [2004] 4 All ER 617; [2004] 3 WLR 918, HL . . . 156, 474

Crest Homes plc v Marks [1987] AC 829; [1987] 2 All ER 1074, HL . . . 478

Crook v Edmondson [1966] 2 QB 81; [1966] 1 All ER 833 . . . 67

Crowther v United Kingdom [2005] All ER (D) 06 (Feb) . . . 537

Culley v Harrison [1956] 2 QB 71; [1956] 2 All ER 254 . . . 59

Cuscani v United Kingdom (2003) 36 EHRR 2 . . . 181

Customs and Excise Commissioners v ApS Samex [1983] 1 All ER 1042 . . . 143, 145

Customs and Excise Commissioners v Savoy Hotel Ltd [1966] 2 All ER 299; [1966] 1 WLR 948 . . . 47

Cutler v Wandsworth Stadium Ltd [1949] AC 398; [1949] 1 All ER 544, HL . . . 33

Cutter v Eagle Star Insurance Co Ltd [1998] 4 All ER 417; [1998] 1 WLR 1647 . . . 47

Cyprus v Turkey (2002) 35 EHRR 30 . . . 200

D (An Infant), Re [1970] 1 All ER 1088 . . . 577

D v A & Co [1899] D 2136 . . . 362

D v United Kingdom (1997) 24 EHRR 423 . . . 176

D & C Builders Ltd v Rees [1966] 2 QB 617; [1965] 3 All ER 837, CA . . . 92

DPP v Ara [2001] EWHC Admin 493; [2002] 1 WLR 815 . . . 394

DPP v Boardman [1975] AC 421; sub nom Boardman v DPP [1974] 3 All ER 887, HL . . . 588

DPP v Bugg [1993] QB 473; [1993] 2 All ER 815 . . . 38

DPP v Channel Four Television Co Ltd [1993] 2 All ER 517 . . . 236

DPP v Corcoran (Terence) [1993] 1 All ER 912 . . . 627

DPP v Doot [1973] AC 807; [1973] 1 All ER 940, HL . . . 605

DPP v M [1997] 2 All ER 749 . . . 612

DPP v Manchester Crown Court and Huckfield [1993] 4 All ER 928, HL . . . 214

DPP v Johnson (David) [1995] 4 All ER 53; [1995] 1 WLR 728 . . . 46, 68

DPP v Jordan [1977] AC 699; [1976] 3 All ER 775, HL . . . 60

DPP v Hawkins [1988] 1 WLR 1166; [1988] 3 All ER 673 . . . 408

DPP v Humphrys (Bruce Edward) [1977] AC 1; [1976] 2 All ER 497, HL . . . 12, 538

DPP v Hutchinson [1990] 2 AC 783; [1990] 2 All ER 836 . . . 38

DPP v McKeown (Sharon) [1997] 1 All ER 737; [1997] 1 WLR 295, HL . . . 50

DPP v Merriman (John) [1971] 2 QB 310; [1971] 2 All ER 1424, CA (reversed [1973] AC 584; [1972] 3 All ER 42, HL) . . . 100

DPP v Ottewell [1970] AC 642; [1968] 3 All ER 153, HL . . . 61

DPP v P [1991] 2 AC 447; sub nom R v P (A Father) [1991] 3 All ER 337, HL . . . 587, 588

DPP v Schildkamp [1971] AC 1; [1969] 3 All ER 1640, HL . . . 68, 69

DPP v Shannon [1975] AC 717; sub nom R v Shannon (David Charles) [1974] 2 All ER 1009, HL . . . 689

DPP v Skinner [1990] RTR 254 . . . 413

DPP v Withers (Ian Douglas) [1975] AC 842; [1974] 3 All ER 984, HL . . . 326

D'Avigdor Goldsmid v Inland Revenue Commissioners [1953] AC 347; [1953] 1 All ER 403, HL . . . 61

Da Costa en Schaake NV v Nederlandse Belastingadministratie (C28–30/62) [1963] ECR 31; [1963] CMLR 224 . . . 144

Dalton v Angus (1881) 6 App Cas 740 . . . 10

Danchevsky v Danchevsky [1975] Fam 17; [1974] 3 All ER 934, CA . . . 240

Darnall v United Kingdom (A/272) (1994) 18 EHRR 205 . . . 182

Dauntley v Hyde (18410 6 Jur 133 . . . 368

Davies (Joy Rosalie) v Eli Lilly & Co (No 1) [1987] 1 WLR 428; [1987] 1 All ER 801, CA . . . 477, 497

Davis v Johnson [1978] 2 WLR 182; [1978] 1 All ER 841, CA (affirmed [1979] AC 264; [1978] 1 All ER 1132, HL) . . . 98, 99

Davis v Lisle [1936] 2 KB 434; [1936] 2 All ER 213 . . . 395

Davy v Spelthorne Borough Council [1984] AC 262; [1983] 3 All ER 278, HL . . . 218

De Coster v College des Bourgmestre et Echevins de Watermael Boitsfort (C17/00) [2001] I-9445 . . . 142

De Cubber v Belgium (Investigating Judge) (A/86) (1985) 7 EHRR 236 . . . 524

De Freitas v Permanent Secretary of Ministry of Agriculture, Fisheries, Lands and Housing [1999] 1 AC 69; [1998] 3 WLR 675, PC . . . 217

Defrenne v SABENA (C43/75) [1976] ECR 455; [1976] 2 CMLR 98 . . . 129

Demirel v Stadt Schwabisch Gmund (12/86) [1987] ECR 3719; [1989] 1 CMLR 421 . . . 124

Department of Health and Social Security v Ereira [1973] 3 All ER 421, CA . . . 469

Dillenkofer v Germany (C178/94) [1996] ECR I-4845 . . . 134

Director General of Fair Trading v Proprietary Association of Great Britain; sub nom Medicaments and Related Classes of Goods (No 2) [2001] 1 WLR 700; [2001] HRLR 17, CA 80, 182, 327, 335

Dixon v BBC [1979] QB 546; [1979] 2 All ER 112, CA . . . 89

Donald Campbell & Co Ltd v Pollack [1927] AC 732, HL . . . 488

Donoghue (or M'Alister) v Stevenson [1932] AC 562, HL . . . 85, 325

Doody v Secretary of State for the Home Department [1994] 1 AC 531; [1993] 3 All ER 92, HL . . . 282

Doorson v Netherlands (1996) 22 EHRR 330 . . . 234, 523

Doughty v Rolls Royce plc [1992] 1 CMLR 1045; [1992] ICR 538, CA . . . 131

Doughty v Turner Manufacturing Co [1964] 1 QB 518; [1964] 1 All ER 98, CA . . . 86

Douglas v Hello! Ltd (No 1) [2001] QB 967; [2001] 2 All ER 289, CA . . . 156, 167, 187, 328

Douglas v Hello! Ltd (No 6) [2003] EWHC 786 (Ch); [2003] 3 All ER 996 . . . 187

Doyle v Northumbria Probation Committee [1991] 4 All ER 294; [1991] 1 WLR 1340 . . . 6, 218

Dryden v Dryden [1973] Fam 217; [1973] 3 All ER 526 . . . 45

Dudgeon v United Kingdom (No 2) (A/45) (1982) 4 EHRR 149 . . . 170, 185, 195

Duke v Reliance Systems Ltd [1988] QB 108; [1987] 2 All ER 858, CA (affirmed [1988] AC 618; [1988] 1 All ER 626, HL) . . . 87, 137

Dulieu v White & Sons [1901] 2 KB 66985

Dun v Dun [1959] AC 272; [1959] 2 All ER 134, PC . . . 76

Dunbar (administrator of Dunbar, dec'd) v Plant [1998] Ch 412; [1997] 4 All ER 289, CA . . . 14

Duncan v Jones [1936] 1 KB 218; [1935] All ER Rep 710 . . . 399

Duport Steels v Sirs [1980] 1 All ER 529; [1980] 1 WLR 142, HL . . . 52, 54, 304, 324

Dunne v North Western Gas Board [1964] 2 QB 806; [1963] 3 All ER 916, CA . . . 84

Dunnett v Railtrack plc (Practice Note) [2002] EWCA Civ 302; [2002] 1 WLR 2434, CA . . . 435

Dunning v United Liverpool Hospital's Board of Governors [1973] 1 WLR 586; [1973] 2 All ER 454, CA . . . 479

Dyson Ltd v Registrar of Trademarks [2003] EWHC 1062 . . . 502

Dzodzi v Belgium (C297/88 and C197/89) [1990] ECR I-3763 . . . 144

ELH v United Kingdom (1997) App 32094/96 . . . 194

Ealing London Borough Council v Race Relations Board [1972] AC 342; [1972] 1 All ER 105, HL . . . 64

Earl of Oxford's case (1615) 1 Rep Ch 1 . . . 6

Earl Spencer v United Kingdom (1998) 25 EHRR CD 105 . . . 170, 187

Easterbrook v United Kingdom (2003) The Times, 18 June . . . 673

Eckle v Germany (A/51) (1983) 5 EHRR 1 . . . 537

Edwards v Jones [1947] KB 659; [1947] 1 All ER 830 . . . 628

Edwards v United Kingdom (A/247B) (1993) 15 EHRR 417 . . . 181

Edwards v United Kingdom (46477/99) (2002) 35 EHRR 19 . . . 175

Edwards and Lewis v United Kingdom App 396457/98 & 40451/98, 22 July 2003, (2003) The Times, 29 July . . . 520, 579, 592

Elderton v United Kingdom Totalisator Co Ltd (No 2) (1945) 61 TLR 529 (affirmed [1946] Ch 57; [1945] 2 All ER 624, CA) . . . 101

Ellen Street Estates v Minister of Health [1934] 1 KB 590, CA . . . 45

Ellenborough Park, Re [1956] Ch 131; [1955] 3 All ER 667, CA . . . 12

Ellerman Lines Ltd v Murray [1931] AC 126, HL . . . 69

Ellis v Deheer [1922] 2 KB 113, CA . . . 342

Emesa Sugar (Free Zone) NV v Aruba (C17/98) (No 1) [2000] ECR I-665 . . . 125, 139

Emmott v Minister for Social Welfare (C208/90) [1993] ICR 8 . . . 132

Engel v Netherlands (No 1) (A/22) (1979–1980) 1 EHRR 647 . . . 17, 180, 522

England v Cowley (1873) LR 8 Ex 126 . . . 92

Entick v Carrington (1795) 19 St Tr 1029 . . . 541

Equal Opportunities Commission v Secretary of

State for Employment [1995] 1 AC 1; [1994] 1
    All ER 910, HL . . . 30, 136

Ergi v Turkey (23818/94) (2001) 32 EHRR 18 . . .
    173

Esso Petroleum Co Ltd v Harper's Garage
    (Stourport) Ltd [1965] 3 WLR 469; [1965] 2
    All ER 933 . . . 102, 250

Estill v Cowling Swift & Kitchin [2000] Lloyd's
    Rep PN 378 . . . 370

European Commission v EC Council (81/72)
    [1973] ECR 575 . . . 123

Ewer v Ambrose (1825) 3 B & C 746 . . . 608

Ewing v Security Services [2003] EWCA Civ 581,
    CA . . . 278, 228

Ewing v United Kingdom (1986) 10 EHRR 141
    . . . 537

Excelsior Commercial & Industrial Holdings Ltd
    v Salisbury Hammer Asbden & Johnson,
    unreported, 12 June 2002 . . . 472, 494

Faccini Dori v Recreb Srl (C91/92) [1995] All ER
    (EC) 1; [1994] ECR I-3325 . . . 131, 132

Factortame v Secretary of State for the
    Environment, Transport and the Regions (No
    8) [2002] 3 WLR 104 . . . 472, 496

Factortame v Secretary of State for Transport. See
    R v Secretary of State for Transport, ex parte
    Factortame Ltd

Fairman v Perpetual Investment Building Society
    [1923] AC 74, HL . . . 84

Farrell v Alexander [1976] QB 345; [1976] 1 All
    ER 129, CA (reversed [1977] AC 59; [1976] 2
    All ER 721, HL) . . . 89

Fehily, Re (2002) CLW 26/9 . . . 574

Feldbrugge v Netherlands (A/99) (1986) 8 EHRR
    425 . . . 180

Fielden v Morley Corporation [1899] 1 Ch 1, CA
    . . . 67

Findlay v United Kingdom (1997) 24 EHRR 221
    . . . 150, 182, 274, 524, 537

Finucane v United Kingdom (2003) 37 EHRR 29
    . . . 174, 268

Firle Investments Ltd v Datapoint International
    Ltd [2001] EWCA Civ 1106, CA . . . 489

Firma Foto Frost v Hauptzollamt Lubeck-Ost
    (C314/85) [1987] ECR 4199; [1988] 3 CMLR
    57 . . . 121, 144

Fisher v Bell [1961] 1 QB 394; [1960] 3 All ER 731
    47

Fisher v Ruislip Northwood Urban District
    Council [1945] KB 584; [1945] 2 All ER 458,
    CA . . . 97

Fitzleet Estates Ltd v Cherry (Inspector of Taxes)

[1977] 3 All ER 996; [1977] 1 WLR 1345, HL
    . . . 95

Fitzpatrick v Sterling Housing Association Ltd
    [2001] 1 AC 27; [1999] 4 All ER 705, HL . . .
    48, 76, 80

Floor v Davis (Inspector of Taxes) [1980] AC 695;
    [1979] 2 All ER 677, HL . . . 60

Foakes v Beer (1883–84) LR 9 App Cas 605, HL
    . . . 92

Foenander v Bond Lewis & Co [2001] EWCA Civ
    759; [2002] 1 WLR 525; [2001] 2 All ER 1019,
    CA . . . 500

Foglia (Pasquale) v Novello (Mariella) (No 2)
    (C244/80) [1981] ECR 3045 . . . 144

Ford v GKR Construction Ltd [2000] 1 All ER
    802, CA . . . 433, 471, 472

Foster v British Gas plc (C188/89) [1991] 1 QB
    405; [1990] 3 All ER 89 . . . 131

Foster v British Gas plc [1991] 2 AC 306; [1991] 2
    All ER 705, HL . . . 131

Foster v Cranfield (1911) 46 L Jo 314 . . . 369

Foster v Diphwys Casson Slate Co (1887) LR 18
    QBD 428 . . . 59

Foster v Roussel Laboratories, unreported, 29
    January 1997 . . . 497

Fothergill v Monarch Airlines Ltd [1981] AC 251;
    [1980] 2 All ER 696, HL . . . 70, 72, 74

Foulkes v Chief Constable of Merseyside [1998] 3
    All ER 705; [1998] 2 FLR 789, CA . . . 399

Fox, Campbell and Hartley v United Kingdom
    (A/182) (1991) 13 EHRR 157 . . . 177, 400

France v UK (C141/78) [1979] ECR 2923 . . . 141

Francovich v Italy (C9/90) [1991] ECR I-5357;
    [1993] 2 CMLR 66 . . . 132

Franklin v Attorney General [1974] QB 185;
    [1973] 1 All ER 879 . . . 46

Froom v Butcher 1976] QB 286; [1975] 3 All ER
    520, CA . . . 102

Fullam v Newcastle Chronicle & Journal Ltd
    [1977] 3 All ER 32; [1977] 1 WLR 651, CA . . .
    482

G (Contempt: Committal), Re [2003] EWCA Civ
    489; [2003] 1 WLR 2051, CA . . . 240, 241

G v DPP [1997] 2 All ER 755 612

Gallie v Lee [1969] 2 Ch 17; [1969] 1 All ER 1062,
    CA (affirmed sub nom Saunders (Executrix of
    the Estate of Rose Maud Gallie) v Anglia
    Building Society (formerly Northampton
    Town and County Building Society) [1971] AC
    1004; [1970] 3 All ER 961, HL) . . . 79, 98

Garfield v Maddocks [1974] QB 7; [1973] 2 All
    ER 303 . . . 650

Garland v British Rail Engineering Ltd (No 2) [1983] 2 AC 751; [1982] 2 WLR 918, HL . . . 136

Garman v Plaice [1969] 1 WLR 19; [1969] 1 All ER 62 . . . 628

General of Berne Insurance Co Ltd v Jardine Reinsurance Management Ltd [1998] 2 All ER 301, CA . . . 493

Geveran Trading Co Ltd v Skjevesland [2002] EWCA Civ 1567; [2003] 1 WLR 912; [2003] 1 All ER 1, CA . . . 362

Ghaidan v Godin-Mendoza [2002] EWCA Civ 1533; [2003] Ch 380; [2002] 4 All ER 1162, CA ([2004] UKHL 30; [2004] 2 AC 557; [2004] 3 All ER 411, HL) 56, 57, 76, 80, 96, 99, 158, 160, 185, 195

Gilham v Browning [1998] 2 All ER 68, CA . . . 468

Gillingham v Gillingham [2001] EWCA Civ 906, CA . . . 502, 503

Gissing v Gissing [1971] AC 886; [1970] 2 All ER 780, HL . . . 97

Godwin v Swindon BC [2001] EWCA Civ 1478; [2002] 1 WLR 997; [2001] 4 All ER 641, CA . . . 435

Goode v Martin [2001] EWCA Civ 1899; [2002] 1 All ER 620, CA . . . 477

Goodwin v United Kingdom (2002) 35 EHRR 18 . . . 58, 158, 161, 185, 194

Goose v Wilson Sandford & Co (No 1) (1998) The Times, 19 February . . . 320

Gough v Chief Constable of Derbyshire [2002] EWCA Civ 351; [2002] QB 1213; [2002] 2 All ER 985, CA . . . 14

Gouriet v Union of Post Office Workers [1978] AC 435; [1977] 3 All ER 70, HL . . . 212

Gloucester (Bishop of) v Cunnington [1943] KB 101; [1943] 1 All ER 61, CA . . . 45

Grad (Franz) v Finanzamt Traunstein (C9/70) (C23/70) [1970] ECR 825; [1971] CMLR 1 . . . 130

Graff v Hauptzollamt Koln Rheinau (C351/92) [1994] ECR I-3361 . . . 123

Grant v Southwestern and County Properties Ltd [1975] Ch 185; [1974] 2 All ER 465 . . . 478

Greek case (1969) 12 YB ECHR 196 . . . 200

Green v United Kingdom 355 US 184 (1957); 2 Led 2nd 199 . . . 602

Gregory v United Kingdom (1998) 25 EHRR 577 . . . 336, 343

Grieves v United Kingdom (2004) 39 EHRR 2 . . . 272, 276

Griffin v South West Water Services Ltd [1995] IRLR 15 . . . 131

Griffith v Jenkins [1992] 2 AC 76; [1992] 1 All ER 65, HL . . . 653

Grobbelaar v News Group Newspapers Ltd [2001] EWCA Civ 33; [2001] 2 All ER 437, CA (reversed [2002] UKHL 40; [2002] 4 All ER 732; [2002] 1 WLR 3024, HL) . . . 341, 434, 505

Groos, In the Estate of [1904] P 269 . . . 67

Grovit v Doctor [1997] 2 All ER 417, HL . . . 469

Guerra v Italy (1998) 26 EHRR 357 . . . 186

Gundry v Sainsbury [1910] 1 KB 645, CA . . . 493

H and others (Minors) (Abduction: Acquiescence), Re [1998] AC 72; [1997] 2 All ER 225, HL . . . 70

H (A Healthcare Worker) v Associated Newspapers Ltd [2002] EWCA Civ 195, CA . . . 167, 187, 328

H v Ministry of Defence [1991] 2 QB 103; [1991] 2 All ER 834, CA . . . 341, 235

HM Advocate v McIntosh (Robert) (No 1) (Sentencing) [2001] UKPC D1; [2003] 1 AC 1099; [2001] 2 All ER 638, PC . . . 18

Hadmor Productions v Hamilton [1983] 1 AC 191; [1982] 2 WLR 322; [1982] 1 All ER 1042, HL . . . 506

Halford v Brookes (No 3) (1991) The Times 3 October . . . 14

Halford v United Kingdom (1997) 24 EHRR 523 . . . 149, 170, 188

Hall v Hall [1963] P 378; [1963] 2 All ER 140, CA . . . 254

Hall v Hall (1981) 3 FLR 379 . . . 97

Halloran v Delaney [2003] 1 WLR 28 . . . 496

Hamblin v Field (2000) The Times, 26 April, CA . . . 433

Hamilton v Al-Fayed (Costs) [2002] EWCA Civ 665, CA . . . 490

Hammond v DPP [2004] EWHC 69 (Admin); (2004) 168 JP 601 . . . 191

Hammond Suddards Solicitors v Agrichem International Holdings Ltd [2001] EWCA Civ 1915, CA . . . 501

Hamond v Howell (1677) 2 Mod Rep 218 . . . 322

Han (t/a Murdishaw Supper Bar) v Customs and Excise Commissioners [2001] 4 All ER 687, CA . . . 522

Handyside v United Kingdom (A/24) (1979–1980) 1 EHRR 737 . . . 170, 171, 190, 191

Hanlon v Law Society [1981] AC 124; [1980] 2 All ER 199, HL . . . 69

Hanning v Maitland (No 2) [1970] 1 QB 580; [1970] 1 All ER 812, CA . . . 98

Hanratty *v* Lord Butler of Saffron Walden (1971) 115 SJ 386, CA . . . 208

Hargreaves *v* Alderson [1964] 2 QB 159; [1962] 3 All ER 1019 . . . 628

Hargreaves *v* Bretherton [1959] 1 QB 45; [1958] 3 All ER 122 . . . 323

Harmony Shipping Co SA *v* Davis [1979] 1 WLR 1380; [1979] 3 All ER 177, CA . . . 482

Harold *v* Smith (1860) 17 ER 1229 . . . 493

Harper *v* National Coal Board (Intended Action) [1974] QB 614; [1974] 2 All ER 441, CA . . . 85

Harris *v* Bolt Burdon (2000) *The Times*, 8 December . . . 470

Harris *v* Tippett (1810) 2 Camp 637 . . . 609

Harris Simon & Co *v* Manchester City Council [1975] 1 WLR 100; [1975] 1 All ER 412 . . . 654

Harrow LBC *v* Shah [1999] 3 All ER 302; [2000] 1 WLR 83 . . . 62

Hasley *v* Milton Keynes General NHS Trust; Steel *v* Joy [2004] 4 All ER 920 . . . 489

Hatton *v* United Kingdom (2003) 37 EHRR 28 . . . 186

Hauschildt *v* Denmark (1990) 12 EHRR 416 . . . 524

Hedley Byrne & Co Ltd *v* Heller & Partners Ltd [1964] AC 465; [1963] 2 All ER 575, HL . . . 82, 83, 85, 368

Henn (Maurice Donald) *v* DPP [1981] AC 850; [1980] 2 All ER 166, HL . . . 145

Herczegfalvy *v* Austria (A/242B) (1993) 15 EHRR 437 . . . 14

Heydon's case (1584) 3 Co Rep 7a . . . 52

Hilal *v* United Kingdom (45276/99) (2001) 33 EHRR 2 . . . 176

Hill *v* Chief Constable of West Yorkshire [1989] AC 53; [1988] 2 All ER 238, HL . . . 396

Hilton *v* United Kingdom (1988) 57 D & R 108 . . . 200

Hirst *v* Secretary of State for the Home Department [2002] EWHC 602 (Admin); [2002] 1 WLR 2929 . . . 193

Hirst *v* United Kingdom (2004) 38 EHRR 40 . . . 193

Hoare *v* United Kingdom (1997) App 31211/96 . . . 181

Hobbs *v* CT Tinling & Co Ltd [1929] 2 KB 1, CA . . . 609

Hodgson *v* Lakeman [1943] KB 15 . . . 652

Hoffmann La Roche & Co AG *v* Secretary of State for Trade and Industry [1975] AC 295; [1974] 2 All ER 1128, HL . . . 38

Holden & Co *v* Crown Prosecution Service [1990] 2 QB 261; [1990] 1 All ER 368, CA . . . 361

Holgate-Mohammed *v* Duke [1984] AC 437; [1984] 1 All ER 1054, HL . . . 389, 406

Holiday in Italy, Re (Decision R (S) 4/74) [1975] 1 CMLR 184 . . . 143

Holy Monasteries *v* Greece (A/301-A) (1995) 20 EHRR 1 . . . 188

Home Office *v* Harman [1983] 1 AC 280; [1982] 1 All ER 532, HL . . . 478

Hope *v* Great Western Railway Co [1937] 2 KB 130; [1937] 1 All ER 625, CA . . . 340

Hornal *v* Neuberger Products [1957] 1 QB 247; [1956] 3 All ER 970, CA . . . 13

Houlden *v* Smith (1850) 14 QB 841 . . . 322

Huddersfield Police Authority *v* Watson [1947] KB 842; [1947] 2 All ER 193 . . . 101

Hughes *v* Holley (1986) 151 JP 233; (1986) 86 Cr App R 1230 . . . 399, 634

Hughes *v* Kingston upon Hull City Council [1999] QB 1193; [1999] 2 All ER 49 . . . 96, 101

Humphries *v* Connor (1864) 17 ICLR 1 . . . 399

Huntley *v* Attorney General of Jamaica [1995] 2 AC 1; [1995] 1 All ER 308, PC . . . 56

Hussain and Singh *v* United Kingdom (1996) 22 EHRR 1 . . . 177

ICI plc *v* Colmer (Inspector of Taxes) (C264/96) [1998] ECR I-4695 . . . 144

IM Properties plc *v* Cape & Dalgleish [1999] QB 297; [1998] 3 All ER 203, CA . . . 89

Ibrahim *v* R [1914] AC 599; [1914–15] All ER Rep 874, PC . . . 271

Inco Europe Ltd *v* First Choice Distribution [2000] 2 All ER 109; [2000] 1 WLR 586, HL . . . 53

Incorporated Council of Law Reporting for England and Wales *v* Attorney General [1971] Ch 626; [1971] 1 All ER 436 . . . (affirmed [1972] Ch 73; [1971] 3 All ER 1029, CA) . . . 67, 105

Industrial Properties (Barton Hill) Ltd *v* Associated Electrical Industries Ltd [1977] QB 580; [1977] 2 All ER 293, CA . . . 89

Ingleton *v* Dibble [1972] 1 QB 480; [1972] 1 All ER 275 . . . 385

Inland Revenue Commissioners *v* Hinchy [1960] AC 748; [1960] 1 All ER 505, HL . . . 49, 61

Inland Revenue Commissioners *v* National Federation of Self Employed and Small Businesses Ltd [1982] AC 617; [1981] 2 WLR 722, HL . . . 220

International Fruit Co NV *v* Commission of the

European Communities (C41–44/70) [1971] ECR 411 . . . 140

International Transport Roth GmbH v Secretary of State for the Home Department [2002] EWCA Civ 158; [2003] QB 728; [2002] 3 WLR 344; [2002] HRLR 31, CA . . . 57, 58, 161, 165, 183, 196, 217, 307, 308

Internationale Handelsgesellschaft mbH v Einfuhr- und Vorratsstelle fur Getreide und Futtermittel (11/70) [1970] ECR 1125; [1972] CMLR 255 . . . 123

Ireland v United Kingdom (A/25) (1979) 2 EHRR 25 . . . 175, 178, 200

Irish Creamery Milk Suppliers Association v Ireland (C36/80) [1981] ECR 735; [1981] 2 CMLR 455 . . . 145

Irving v Askew (1870) LR 5 QB 208 . . . 105

J H Rayner (Mincing Lane) Ltd v Department of Trade and Industry [1989] Ch 72; [1988] 3 All ER 257, CA (affirmed [1990] 2 AC 418; [1989] 3 All ER 523, HL) . . . 66

JS v Netherlands (1995) 20 EHRR CD 41 . . . 125

Jacobs v London County Council (No 2) [1950] AC 361; [1950] 1 All ER 737, HL . . . 84

James Buchanan & Co Ltd v Babco Forwarding & Shipping (UK) Ltd [1978] AC 141; [1977] 3 All ER 1048, HL . . . 69

Jégo-Quéré at Cie SA v Commission (Case T-1777/01) [2002] All ER (EC) 932; [2002] 2 CMLR 44 . . . 140

Jégo-Quéré at Cie SA v Commission (Case C-263/02) [2004] All ER (EC); [2005] 2 WLR 179 . . . 140

Jersey States, Re (1853) 9 Moo PCC 185 . . . 272

Jersild v Denmark (A/298) (1995) 19 EHRR 1 . . . 190

Johanna Oldendorff, The; E L Oldendorff & Co GmbH v Tradax Export SA [1974] AC 479; [1973] 3 All ER 148, HL . . . 95

John v MGN Ltd [1997] QB 586; [1996] 2 All E.R 35, CA . . . 341, 507

Johnson v Great Western Railway Co [1904] 2 KB 250, CA . . . 506

Johnson v Moreton [1980] AC 37; [1978] 3 All ER 37, HL . . . 242

Johnson v Phillips [1976] 1 WLR 65; [1975] 3 All ER 682 . . . 385

Johnson v United Kingdom (1999) 27 EHRR 296 . . . 179

Johnston v Chief Constable of the Royal Ulster Constabulary (C222/84) [1987] QB 129; [1986] 3 All ER 135 . . . 123, 128, 151

Jones v DPP [1962] AC 635; [1962] 1 All ER 569, HL . . . 697

Jones v Secretary of State for Social Services [1972] AC 944; [1972] 1 All ER 145, HL . . . 80, 91, 94, 324

Jordan v United Kinngdom (2003) 37 EHRR 2 . . . 174, 268, 269

Joscelyne v Nissen [1970] 2 QB 86; [1970] 1 All ER 1213, CA . . . 88

Joyce v DPP [1946] AC 347; [1946] 1 All ER 186, HL . . . 11, 42

K's Settlement Trusts, Re [1969] 2 Ch 1; [1969] 1 All ER 194 . . . 252

K and T v Finland (2003) 36 EHRR 18 . . . 185

Kammins Ballrooms Co Ltd v Zenith Investments (Torquay) Ltd (No 1) [1971] AC 850; [1970] 2 All ER 871, HL . . . 48, 53

Kampelmann v Landschaftsverband Westfalen-Lippe (C253/96) [1997] ECR I-6907 . . . 131

Karaduman v Turkey (1993) 74 D & R 14 . . . 189

Kaye v Robertson [1991] FSR 62 . . . 186

Keegan v Ireland (A/290) (1994) 18 EHRR 342 . . . 188

Keenan v United Kingdom (27229/95) (2001) 33 EHRR 38 . . . 148, 175, 176

Kelly v United Kingdom (1993) 74 D & R 139

Kembeare v K 4 Edw 2 (SS iv), 153 . . . 103

Kemp v Liebherr (Great Britain) Ltd [1987] 1 All ER 885; [1987] 1 WLR 607 . . . 625

Kenlin v Gardiner [1967] 2 QB 510; [1966] 3 All ER 931 . . . 395

Kennedy v Spratt [1972] AC 83; [1971] 1 All ER 805, HL . . . 242

Kerly, Son & Verden, Re [1901] 1 Ch 467, CA . . . 239

Khan v United Kingdom (35394/97) (2001) 31 EHRR 45 . . . 181, 188, 393

Khan (Sultan) v United Kingdom [2000] Crim LR 683 . . . 523

Khorasandjian v Bush [1993] QB 727; [1993] 3 WLR 476; [1993] 3 All ER 669, CA . . . 473

Kiam v MGN Ltd (No 2) (Costs) [2002] EWCA Civ 66; [2002] 2 All ER 242, CA . . . 495

Kingston-upon- Hull Dock Co v Browne (1831) 2 B & Ad 43 . . . 61

Kjeldsen, Busk Madsen & Pedersen v Denmark (A/23) (1979–1980) 1 EHRR 711 . . . 189

Kleinwort Benson Ltd v Lincoln City Council [1999] 2 AC 349; [1998] 4 All ER 513, HL . . . 79, 91

Knuller (Publishing, Printing and Promotions) Ltd v DPP [1973] AC 435; [1972] 2 All ER 898, HL . . . 95, 326

Kokkinakis v Greece (A/260-A) (1994) 17 EHRR 397 . . . 188

Korda *v* ITF Ltd (t/a International Tennis Federation) (1999) *The Independent*, 21 April . . . 295

Kremzow *v* Austria (C299/95) [1997] ECR I-2629 . . . 124

Kruhlak *v* Kruhlak (No 1) [1958] 2 QB 32; [1958] 1 All ER 154 . . . 52

Kruse *v* Johnson [1898] 2 QB 91; [1895–1899] All ER Rep 105 . . . 219

L (An Infant), Re [1968] P 119; [1968] 1 All ER 20, CA . . . 250

L *v* DPP [2002] 1 Cr App R 420 . . . 617

L'Office Cherifien des Phosphates Unitramp SA *v* Yamashita-Shinnihon Steamship Co Ltd (The Boucraa) [1994] 1 AC 486; 1994] 1 All ER 20, HL . . . 43, 44

Ladd *v* Marshall [1954] 3 All ER 745, CA . . . 502, 503

Laker Airways *v* Department of Trade [1977] 2 All ER 182, CA . . . 208

Langborger *v* Sweden (A/155) (1990) 12 EHRR 416 . . . 524

Langford *v* Law Society [2002] EWHC 2802 (Admin); [2003] 153 NLJR 176 . . . 367

Langley *v* North West Water Authority [1991] 3 All ER 610; [1991] 1 WLR 697, CA . . . 99, 361, 434

Laskey *v* United Kingdom (1997) 24 EHRR 39 . . . 186

Law *v* Jones [1974] Ch 112; [1973] 2 All ER 437, CA . . . 97

Law *v* National Greyhound Racing Club [1983] 1 WLR 1302; [1983] 3 All ER 300, CA . . . 294

Law Society *v* United Service Bureau Ltd [1934] 1 KB 343 . . . 61

Lawal *v* Northern Spirit Ltd [2003] UKHL 35; [2004] 1 All ER 187; [2003] ICR 856, HL . . . 182, 281, 293

Le Compte *v* Belgium (A/43) (1982) 4 EHRR 1 . . . 193

Lee *v* Leeds City Council [2002] EWCA Civ 6; [2002] 1 WLR 1488, CA . . . 188

Lee *v* Showmen's Guild of Great Britain [1952] 2 QB 329; [1952] 1 All ER 1175, CA . . . 58

Lehideux and Isorni *v* France (2000) 30 EHRR 665 . . . 190

Leigh *v* Michelin Tyre plc [2004] 2 All ER 173 . . . 492 . . .

Letang *v* Cooper [1965] 1 QB 232; [1964] 2 All ER 929, CA . . . 74

Letellier *v* France (A/207) (1992) 14 EHRR 83 . . . 559

Lewis *v* Chief Constable of South Wales [1991] 1 All ER 206, CA . . . 408

Lewis *v* Daily Telegraph Ltd [1964] AC 234; [1963] 2 All ER 975 . . . 507

Lilly ICOS Ltd *v* Pfizer Ltd (No 2) [2002] EWCA Civ 2; [2002] 1 All ER 842, CA . . . 478

Lincoln *v* Daniels [1962] 1 QB 237; [1961] 3 All ER 740, CA . . . 353

Lindley *v* Rutter [1981] QB 128; [1980] 3 WLR 660 . . . 389, 412

Linkletter *v* Walker 381 US 618 (1965) . . . 90

Linwood *v* Andrews and Moore (1888) 58 LT 612 . . . 362

Litster *v* Forth Dry Dock and Engineering Co Ltd [1990] 1 AC 546; [1989] 1 All ER 1134, HL . . . 137

Lloyd *v* Bow Street Magistrates' Court [2003] EWHC 2294 . . . 537

Lloyds Bank Ltd *v* Marcan [1973] 3 All ER 754; [1973] 1 WLR 1387, CA . . . 74

Locabail International Finance Ltd *v* Agroexport and Atlanta (UK) Ltd (The Sea Hawk) [1986] 1 WLR 657; [1986] 1 All ER 901, CA . . . 474

Locabail (UK) Ltd *v* Bayfield Properties Ltd (Leave to Appeal) [2000] 2 WLR 870 . . . 524

Lodwick *v* Saunders [1985] 1 WLR 382; [1985] 1 All ER 577 . . . 402

London Corporation *v* Cusack-Smith [1955] AC 337; [1955] 1 All ER 302, HL . . . 76

London Street Tramways Co Ltd *v* London County Council [1898] AC 375, HL . . . 93

Loose *v* Williamson [1978] 1 WLR 639; [1978] 3 All ER 89 . . . 480

Lopez Ostra *v* Spain (A/303-C) (1995) 20 EHRR 277 . . . 186

Lord Advocate *v* Dumbarton District Council [1990] 2 AC 580; [1990] 1 All ER 1, HL . . . 65

Lord Bishop of Natal (1864) 3 Moo PCCNS 115 . . . 205

Loveday *v* Renton (No 2) [1992] 3 All ER 184 . . . 372

Loveridge, Re [1902] 2 Ch 859, . . . 106

Lownds *v* Home Office [2002] EWCA Civ 365; [2002] 1 WLR 2450, CA . . . 493, 494

Luc Thiet Thuan *v* R [1997] AC 131; [1996] 2 All ER 1033, PC . . . 84, 86

Ludlow *v* Metropolitan Police Commissioner [1971] AC 29; [1970] 1 All ER 567, HL . . . 587

Lustig-Prean & Beckett *v* United Kingdom (2000) 29 EHRR 548 . . . 149, 185

Lyckeskog Case (C-99/00) [2002] ECR I-483; [2003] 1 WLR 9 . . . 142

M, Re; *sub nom* M *v* Home Office [1994] 1 AC 377; [1993] 3 All ER 537, HL . . . 240, 306

M (A Minor) (Care Order: Threshold Conditions), Re [1994] 2 AC 424; [1994] 3 All ER 298, HL . . . 48

M (Wardship: Freedom of Publication) [1990] 2 FLR 36 . . . 235

McC (a Minor) *v* Mullan [1985] AC 528; [1984] 3 All ER 908, HL . . . 322

McCann *v* United Kingdom (A/324) (1996) 21 EHRR 97 . . . 173

Macarthys Ltd *v* Smith [1979] 3 All ER 325; [1979] 1 WLR 1189, CA . . . 134, 136

McClaren *v* Home Office [1990] ICR 824, CA . . . 209

Macniven (Inspector of Taxes) *v* Westmoreland Investments Ltd [2001] UKHL 6; [2003] 1 AC 311; [2001] 1 All ER 865, HL . . . 54

McConnell *v* Chief Constable of Greater Manchester [1990] 1 WLR 364; [1990] 1 All ER 423, CA . . . 398, 399

Macdonald *v* Taree Holdings Ltd (2000), unreported . . . 493

McGonnell *v* United Kingdom (2000) 30 EHRR 289 . . . 20, 182

McGovern *v* Attorney General [1982] Ch 321; [1981] 3 All ER 493 . . . 67

McKerr's application for judicial review, Re [2004] UKHL 12; [2004] 1 WLR 807; [2004] 2 All ER 409, HL . . . 174

McKerry *v* Teesdale and Wear Valley Justices [2000] Crim LR 594 . . . 645

McLoughlin *v* O'Brian [1983] 1 AC 410; [1982] 2 All ER 298, HL . . . 5

Macmanaway, Re [1951] AC 161, PC . . . 272

McMichael *v* United Kingdom (A/308) [1995] 2 FCR 718; (1995) 20 EHRR 205 . . . 180

McMillan *v* Crouch [1972] 3 All ER 61; [1972] 1 WLR 1102, HL . . . 71

McMonagle *v* Westminster City Council [1990] 2 AC 716; [1990] 1 All ER 993, HL . . . 49

McPherson *v* Secretary of State for the Home Department [2001] EWCA Civ 1955; [2002] INLR 139, CA . . . 176

McPhilemy *v* Times Newspapers Ltd (Re-amendment: Justification) [1999] 3 All ER 775, CA . . . 476

Machent *v* Quinn [1970] 2 All ER 255 . . . 601

Madros Electric Supply Corp Ltd *v* Boarland (Inspector of Taxes) [1955] AC 667; [1955] 1 All ER 753, HL . . . 65

Magdalen College (1615) 11 Co Rep 66b . . . 104

Magor and St Mellons Rural DC *v* Newport Corporation [1950] 2 All ER 1226, CA; affirmed [1952] AC 189; [1951] 2 All ER 839, HL . . . 53

Maguire *v* Molin [2002] EWCA Civ 1083, CA . . . 477

Makanjuola *v* Commissioner of Police of the Metropolis [1992] 3 All ER 617, CA . . . 395, 577

Mallett *v* Restormel Borough Council [1978] 2 All ER 1057, CA . . . 245

Malone *v* Commissioner of Police of the Metropolis (No 2) [1979] Ch 344; [1979] 2 All ER 620 . . . 5, 80, 151, 325

Malone *v* United Kingdom (A/82) (1985) 7 EHRR 14 . . . 149, 151, 187

Mandla (Sewa Singh) *v* Dowell Lee [1983] QB 1; [1982] 3 All ER 1108, CA . . . 74

Mansell *v* R (1857) 8 E & B 54 . . . 337

Manuel *v* Attorney General [1983] Ch 77; [1982] 3 WLR 821, CA . . . 29

Marchiori *v* Environment Agency [2002] EWCA Civ 3; *The Independent*, 31 January 2002, CA . . . 210

Marcic *v* Thames Water Utilities Ltd [2003] UKHL 66; [2004] 2 AC 42; [2003] 1 All ER 135, HL . . . 186

Marckx *v* Belgium (A/31) (1979–1980) 2 EHRR 330 . . . 194

Mareva Compania Naviera SA *v* International Bulk Carriers SA (The Mareva) [1980] 1 All ER 213, CA . . . 434 . . .

Market-Overt case (1596) 5 Co Rep 83b . . . 11

Marks *v* Beyfus (1890) 25 QBD 494, CA . . . 577

Marleasing SA *v* La Comercial Internacional de Alimentacion SA (C106/89) [1990] ECR I-4135; [1992] 1 CMLR 305 . . . 132, 137, 138

Mars UK Ltd *v* Technology Ltd (No 2) [1999] TLR 501 . . . 489

Marsh *v* Joseph [1897] 1 Ch 213, CA . . . 361

Marshall *v* Southampton and South West Hampshire Area Health Authority (No 1) (C152/84) [1986] QB 401; [1986] 2 All ER 584 . . . 130, 137

Marshall *v* Southampton and South West Hampshire Area Health Authority (No 2) [1994] 1 AC 530; [1994] 1 All ER 736, HL . . . 130

Martins *v* Fowler [1926] AC 746, PC . . . 68

Matthews *v* Ministry of Defence [2002] EWCA Civ 773; [2002] 3 All ER 513; [2002] 1 WLR 2621; reversing [2002] EWHC 13; (2002] *The Times*, January 30, 2002 . . . 160

Matthews *v* United Kingdom (1999) 28 EHRR 361 . . . 125

Meco Pak AB Ltd v Electropaint Ltd [2001] EWCA Civ 1537, CA . . . 504

Mellacher v Austria (A/169) (1990) 12 EHRR 391 . . . 195

Melluish (Inspector of Taxes) v BMI (No 3) Ltd [1996] AC 454; [1995] 4 All ER 453, HL . . . 71

Mendoza v Ghaidan' [2003] 5 EHRLR 501 . . . 80

Mennitto v Italy (33804/96) (2002) 34 EHRR 48 . . . 180

Mepstead v DPP [1996] Crim LR 111 . . . 395

Mercer v Denne [1905] 2 Ch 538 . . . 8

Merkur Island Shipping Corporation v Laughton Shaw and Lewis (The Hoegh Anapa) [1983] 2 AC 570; [1983] 2 All ER 189; [1983] 1 All ER 334 . . . 27, 28

Metcalf v Wetherill (Wasted Costs Order) [2002] UKHL 27; [2003] 1 AC 120; [2002] 3 All ER 721, HL . . . 361, 491

Metropolitan Asylum District Managers v Hill (No 2) (1881) LR 6 App Cas 193, HL . . . 63

Metropolitan Police Commissioner v Wilson [1984] AC 242; sub nom R v Wilson (Clarence George) [1983] 3 All ER 448, HL . . . 601

Midland Bank Trust Co Ltd v Green (No 3) [1982] Ch 529; [1981] 3 All ER 744, CA . . . 80

Midland Bank Trust Co Ltd v Hett Stubbs & Kemp [1979] Ch 384; [1978] 3 All ER 571 . . . 368

Miliangos v George Frank (Textiles) Ltd (No 1) [1975] QB 487; [1975] 1 All ER 1076, CA (reversed [1976] AC 443; [1975] 3 All ER 801, HL) . . . 88, 91, 92, 96, 97, 98, 325

Miller v Ministry of Pensions [1947] 2 All ER 372 . . . 13

Mills v Colchester Corporation (1867) LR 2 CP 476 . . . 8

Minister of Social Security v Amalgamated Engineering Union [1967] 1 AC 725; [1967] 1 All ER 210, HL . . . 94

Mirehouse v Rennell (1833) 1 Cl & Fin 527 . . . 103

Modahl v British Athletic Federation Ltd (No 2) [2001] EWCA Civ 1447; [2002] 1 WLR 1192, CA . . . 295

Money v Leach (1765) 3 Burr 1742 . . . 541

More O'Ferrall Ltd v Harrow Urban DC [1947] KB 66; [1946] 2 All ER 489 . . . 653

Morelle v Wakeling [1955] 2 QB 379; [1955] 1 All ER 708, CA . . . 88

Morris v Crown Office [1970] 2 QB 114; [1970] 1 All ER 1079, CA . . . 239

Morris v United Kingdom (2002) 34 EHRR 52 . . . 155, 275

Moss v McLachlan (1984) 149 JP 167 . . . 399

Mount Murray Country Club Ltd v Macleod [2003] UKPC 53, (2003) The Times, 7 July . . . 296

Munroe v Crown Prosecution Service [1988] Crim LR 823 . . . 641

Munster v Lamb (1883) 11 QBD 588, CA . . . 323

Murphy v Brentwood DC [1991] 1 AC 398; [1990] 2 All ER 908, HL . . . 95

Murray v DPP [1999] 1 WLR 1 . . . 611

Murray v United Kingdom (A/300-A) (1995) 19 EHRR 193 . . . 177, 400

Murray v United Kingdom (Right to Silence) (1996) 22 EHRR 29 . . . 185, 418, 616

Nagle v Feilden [1966] 2 QB 633; [1966] 1 All ER 689, CA . . . 295

National Assistance Board (By JR Beattie) v Wilkinson [1952] 2 QB 648; [1952] 2 All ER 255 . . . 63

National Provincial Bank Ltd v Ainsworth [1965] AC 1175; [1965] 2 All ER 472, HL . . . 74

National Union of Teachers v Governing Body of St Mary's Church of England (Aided) Junior School [1997] 3 CMLR 630; [1997] IRLR 242, CA . . . 131

Nerva v United Kingdom, App No 42295/98, 11 July 2000 . . . 500

New Windsor Corporation v Mellor [1975] Ch 380; [1975] 3 All ER 44, CA . . . 8

Niemietz v Germany (A/251B) (1993) 16 EHRR 97 . . . 185

Noble v Kennoway (1780) 2 Doug KB 510 . . . 8

Nold (J) Kohlen und Baustoffgrosshandlung v Ruhrkohle AG (C4/73) [1977] ECR 491 . . . 124

Norris v Ireland (A/142) (1991) 13 EHRR 186 . . . 201

North Range Shipping Ltd v Seatrans Shipping Corporation [2002] 1 WLR 2397, CA . . . 500

Norwich Pharmacal Co v Customs and Excise Commissioners [1974] AC 133; [1973] 2 All ER 943, HL . . . 480

O'Donnell (Peter John) v Charly Holdings Inc (A Company Incorporated under the Laws of Burma), unreported, 14 March 2000 . . . 470

O'Hara v Chief Constable of the Royal Ulster Constabulary [1997] AC 286; [1997] 1 All ER 129, HL . . . 400

O'Hara v United Kingdom (37555/97) (2002) 34 EHRR 32 . . . 400

O'Loughlin v Chief Constable of Essex [1998] 1 WLR 374, CA . . . 401

O'Reilly v Mackman [1983] 2 AC 237; [1982] 3 All ER 1124, HL . . . 38, 217, 218

O'Rourke v Camden LBC [1998] AC 188; [1997] 3 All ER 23, HL . . . 33, 180

Oakley v Lyster [1931] 1 KB 148, CA . . . 92

Officier van Justitie v Kolpinghuis Nijmegen BV (C80/86) [1987] ECR 3969; [1989] 2 CMLR 18 . . . 122, 130

Ogden Industries Pty v Lucas (Heather Doreen) [1970] AC 113; [1969] 1 All ER 121, PC . . . 75

Oliver Ashworth (Holdings) Ltd v Ballard (Kent) Ltd [2000] Ch 12; [1999] 2 All ER 791, CA . . . 54

Olutu v Home Office [1997] 1 All ER 385; [1997] 1 WLR 328, CA 33

Olympic, The [1913] P 92, CA . . . 76

Open Door Counselling Ltd v Ireland (A/246) (1993) 15 EHRR 244 . . . 175

Orford v Rasmi Electronics [2002] EWCA Civ 1672, CA . . . 470

Oscroft v Benabo [1967] 2 All ER 548, CA . . . 504

Osman, Re (Practice Note) [1995] 1 WLR 1327; [1996] 1 Cr App R 126 . . . 337

Osman v United Kingdom (2000) 29 EHRR 245 . . . 174, 396

Otter v Norman [1989] AC 129; [1988] 2 All ER 897, HL . . . 47

Otto-Preminger Institute v Austria (A/295-A) (1995) 19 EHRR 34 . . . 192

Overseas Tankship (UK) Ltd v Morts Dock & Engineering Co (The Wagon Mound) (No 1) [1961] AC 388; [1961] 1 All ER 404, PC . . . 86

Ozturk v Germany (A/73) (1984) 6 EHRR 409 . . . 522

P, C and S v United Kingdom (2002) 35 EHRR 31 . . . 181

P, ex parte (1998) The Times, 31 March . . . 234

P Foster (Haulage) Ltd v Roberts [1978] 2 All ER 751 . . . 649

Padfield v Minister of Agriculture, Fisheries and Food [1968] AC 997; [1968] 1 All ER 694, HL . . . 211, 215

Pafitis v Greece (1999) 27 EHRR 566 . . . 125

Parfums Christian Dior SA v Evora BV (C337/95) [1997] ECR I-6013; [1998] 1 CMLR 737 . . . 144

Parker v British Airways Board [1982] QB 1004; [1982] 1 All ER 834, CA . . . 80

Partridge v Crittenden [1968] 2 All ER 421; [1968] 1 WLR 1204 . . . 47

Peach Grey & Co v Sommers [1995] 2 All ER 513; [1995] ICR 549 . . . 278, 228

Pearce v Ove Arup Partnership Ltd (Jurisdiction) [1999] 1 All ER 769, CA . . . 502

Peck v United Kingdom (2003) 36 EHRR 41 . . . . . . 167, 187, 328

Pepper (Inspector of Taxes) v Hart [1993] AC 593; [1993] 1 All ER 42, HL . . . 71, 72, 324

Percy v DPP [1995] 1 WLR 1382; [1995] 3 All ER 124 . . . 398

Percy v Hall [1997] QB 924; [1996] 4 All ER 523, CA . . . 38

Perry v Kendricks Transport Ltd [1956] 1 All ER 154; [1956] 1 WLR 85, CA . . . 84

Perry v United Kingdom (2004) 39 EHRR 3 . . . 188

Petrofina (Great Britain) Ltd v Martin [1965] Ch 1073; [1965] 2 All ER 176 . . . 102, 250

Petrotrade Inc v Texaco Ltd [2001] 4 All ER 853, CA . . . 470

Phillips v Brooks Ltd [1919] 2 KB 243 . . . 80

Phillips v United Kingdom (2001) . . . 537

Pickering v Liverpool Daily Post and Echo [1991] 2 AC 370; [1991] 1 All ER 622, HL . . . 278

Pickstone v Freemans plc [1987] 3 WLR 811; [1987] 3 All ER 756, CA (reversed [1989] AC 66; [1988] 2 All ER 803, HL) . . . 72, 137

Piddington v Bates [1961] 1 WLR 162; [1960] 3 All ER 660 . . . 399

Piersack v Belgium (A/53) (1983) 5 EHRR 69 . . . 524

Pillans v Van Mierop (1765) 3 Burr 1663 . . . 104

Pinnel's case (1602) 5 Co Rep 117a . . . 91

Piraiki-Patraiki Cotton Industry AE v Commission of the European Communities (11/82) [1985] ECR 207 . . . 140

Plaumann & Co v Commission of the European Communities (C25/62) [1963] ECR 95; [1964] CMLR 29 . . . 140

Plender v Hyams [2001] 2 All ER 179, CA . . . 500

Polemis and Furness Withy & Co Ltd, Re [1921] 3 KB 560, CA . . . 86

Polly Peck International plc v Nadir (Asil) (No 2) [1992] 4 All ER 769, CA . . . 463

Poplar Housing and Regeneration Community Association Ltd v Donoghue [2001] EWCA Civ 595; [2002] QB 48; [2001] 4 All ER 604, CA . . . 56, 158, 164, 186, 209

Port Line v Ben Line Steamers [1958] 2 QB 146; [1958] 1 All ER 787 . . . 85

Porter v Magill [2001] UKHL 67; [2002] 2 AC 357; [2002] 1 All ER 465, HL . . . 80, 182, 327, 335

Post Office v Estuary Radio Ltd [1968] 2 QB 740; [1967] 3 All ER 663, CA . . . 41

Powell v Kempton Park Racecourse Co Ltd [1899] AC 143, HL . . . 59

Practice Direction (Admin Ct: Establishment) [2000] 1 WLR 1654; [2000] 4 All ER 1071 . . . 253

Practice Direction (Amendment No 8) (Mandatory Life Sentences) [2005] 1 Cr App R 8 . . . 674

Practice Direction (Costs: Criminal Proceedings) [2004] 2 Cr App R 26 . . . 678

Practice Direction (Court of Appeal: Citation of Authorities) [2001] 2 All ER 510; [2001] 1 WLR 1001, CA . . . 77, 78, 87, 99, 105, 109

Practice Direction (Court of Appeal (Crim Div): Crime: Voluntary Bills) [1990] 1 WLR 1633; [1991] 1 All ER 288, CA . . . 570

Practice Direction (Criminal Proceedings: Consolidation) [2002] 3 All ER 904; [2002] 1 WLR 2870 . . . 337, 340, 553, 570

Practice Direction (Crown Court: Business) [2001] 1 WLR 1996; [2001] 4 All ER 635, CA . . . 258, 259

Practice Direction (Crown Court: Defendant's Evidence) [1995] 2 Cr App R 192 . . . 611

Practice Direction (Crown Court: Solicitors: Rights of Audience) [1988] 1 WLR 1427; [1988] 3 All ER 717 . . . 351

Practice Direction (Crown Court: Trial of Children and Young Persons) [2000] 2 All ER 285 . . . 553

Practice Direction (Jury Service: Excusal (Amendment)) (2005) *The Times*, 24 March . . . 337, 340

Practice Direction (QBD: Justices: Clerk to Court) [2000] 1 WLR 1886; [2000] 4 All ER 895 . . . 263

Practice Direction (Sup Ct: Form of Judgments, Paragraph Marking and Neutral Citation) [2001] 1 WLR 194; [2001] 1 All ER 193 . . . 107

Practice Direction (Sup Ct: Judgments: Neutral Citations) [2002] 1 All ER 351; [2002] 1 WLR 346 . . . 108

Practice Direction (Sup Ct: Solicitors: Rights of Audience) [1986] 1 WLR 545; [1986] 2 All ER 226 . . . 351

Practice Direction (Life Sentence for Murder) [2002] 4 All ER 1089 . . . 660

Practice Note [1987] 3 All ER 1064 . . . 572

Practice Note (CA: Reports: Citations) [1991] 1 All ER 352 . . . 105

Practice Note (Ch D: Motions: Agreed Adjournment) [1977] 2 All ER 540; *sub nom* Practice Direction [1977] 1 WLR 537 . . . 589

Practice Note (Commercial Court: Alternative Dispute Resolution) [1994] 1 All ER 34; [1994] 1 WLR 14 . . . 436

Practice Note (Juries: Right to Stand By: Jury Checks) [1988] 3 All ER 1086; (1989) 88 Cr App R 123 . . . 333

Practice Statement (Court of Appeal: Authorities) [1996] 3 All ER 382; [1996] 1 WLR 854, CA . . . 77

Practice Statement (Crime: Life Sentences) [2002] 1 WLR 1789 . . . 673

Practice Statement (House of Lords: Judicial Precedent) [1966] 3 All ER 77; [1966] 1 WLR 1234, HL . . . 93, 94, 95

Prais v Council of Ministers of the European Communities (130/75) [1976] ECR 1589 . . . 124, 151

Prasad v R [1981] 1 WLR 469; [1981] 1 All ER 319, PC . . . 271

Pratt v Attorney General of Jamaica [1994] 2 AC 1; [1993] 4 All ER 769, PC . . . 270

Pretty v United Kingdom (2002) 35 EHRR 1 . . . 175

Pride of Derby and Derbyshire Angling Association Ltd v British Celanese Ltd [1953] Ch 149; [1953] 1 All ER 179, CA . . . 68

Proclamations (1610) 12 Co Rep 74 . . . 104

Prohibitions del Roy (1607) 12 Co Rep 63 . . . 104, 205, 206

Prudential Assurance Co Ltd v London Residuary Body [1992] 2 AC 386; [1992] 3 All ER 504, HL . . . 92

Pubblico Ministero v Ratti (148/78) [1979] ECR 1629; [1980] 1 CMLR 96 . . . 130

Purdy v Cambran [1999] CPLR 843, CA . . . 433, 468

Pyx Granite Co Ltd v Ministry of Housing and Local Government [1960] AC 260; [1959] 3 All ER 1, HL . . . 64

Qualcast (Wolverhampton) Ltd v Haynes [1959] AC 743; [1959] 2 All ER 38, HL . . . 81, 82

Qualter, Hall & Co v Board of Trade [1962] Ch 273; [1961] 3 All ER 389, CA . . . 68

Qazi v Harrow LBC [2003] UKHL 43; [2004] 1 AC 983; [2003] 4 All ER 461, HL . . . 186

R (on the application of Abbasi) v Secretary of State for Foreign and Commonwealth Affairs [2002] EWCA Civ 442, CA . . . 208

R (on the application of Alconbury) v Secretary of State for the Environment, Transport and the Regions [2002] EWHC 13; [2001] HRLR 2 (reversed [2001] UKHL 23; [2003] 2 AC 295; [2001] 2 All ER 929, HL) . . . 58, 87, 160, 180

R (on the application of Amin) v Secretary of State for the Home Department [2003] UKHL

51; [2004] 1 AC 653; [2003] 4 All ER 1264, HL . . . 174, 269

R (on the application of Anderson) v Secretary of State for the Home Department [2001] EWCA Civ 1698; [2002] 2 WLR 1143, CA; [2002] UKHL 46; [2003] 1 AC 837; [2002] 4 All ER 1089, HL . . . 154, 178, 179, 673

R (on the application of Anufrijeva) v Secretary of State for the Home Department [2003] UKHL 36; [2004] 1 AC 604; [2003] 3 All ER 827, HL . . . 308

R (on the application of Beer (t/a Hammer Trout Farm)) v Hamshire Farmers Markets Ltd [2003] EWCA Civ 1056; [2004] 1 WLR 233, CA . . . 164

R (on the application of Begum) v Denbigh High School [2005] EWCA Civ 199; The Times, 4 March 2005, CA . . . 189

R (on the application of the Campaign for Nuclear Diarmament) v Prime Minister [2002] ALL ER (D) 245 . . . 210

R (on the application of Carson) v Secretary of State for Work and Pensions; R (on the application of Reynolds) v Secretary of State for Work and Pensions [2003] EWCA Civ 797; [2003] 3 All ER 577; [2003] HRLR 36, CA . . . 195, 196

R (on the application of D) v Secretary of State for the Home Department [2002] EWHC 2805 (Admin); [2003] 1 WLR 1315 . . . 179

R (on the application of Daly) v Secretary of State for the Home Department [2001] UKHL 26; [2001] 2 AC 532; [2001] 3 All ER 433, HL . . . 150, 165, 171, 187, 216

R (on the application of Davies) v HM Deputy Coroner for Birmingham [2003] EWCA Civ 1739; [2004] HRLR 13 . . . 174

R (on the application Director of Public Prosecutions) v Camberwell Youth Court [2005] 1 Cr App R 6 . . . 212, 570

R (on the application Director of Public Prosecutions) v Prestatyn Magistrates' Court [2002] LSG, 1 July 2002 . . . 544

R (on the application of Ebrahim) v Feltham Magistrates Court; Mouat v DPP; [2001] 1 All ER 381 . . . 539

R (on the application of Farrakhan) v Secretary of State for the Home Department [2002] EWCA Civ 606; [2002] QB 1391; [2002] 4 All ER 289, CA . . . 193

R (on the application of Giles) v Parole Board [2003] UKHL 42; [2004] 1 AC 1;[2003] 4 All ER 429, HL . . . 178

R (on the application of Gillan) v Commissioner of Police for the Metropolis [2004] EWCA Civ 1076; [2004] 3 WLR 114, CA . . . 177, 403

R (on the application of Grundy & Co Excavations Ltd) v Halton Division Magistrates' Court (2003) 167 JP 387 . . . 617

R (on the application of H) v Mental Health Review Tribunal for North and East London Region [2001] EWCA Civ 415; [2002] QB 1; [2001] 3 WLR 512, CA . . . 37, 58, 64, 161, 179

R (on the application of Heather) v Leonard Cheshire Foundation [2002] EWCA Civ 366; [2002] 2 All ER 936, CA . . . 164

R (on the application of Jackson) v A-G [2005] EWCA Civ 126; The Times 17 February 2005, CA . . . 29, 32, 35, 313

R (on the application of Khan) v Secretary of State for Health [2003] EWCA Civ 1129; [2003] 4 All ER 1239 . . . 269

R (on the application of Laporte) v Chief Constable of Gloucester [2004] EWHC 253 (Admin); [2004] 2 All ER 874 . . . (affirmed [2004] EWCA Civ 1639; [2005] 1 All ER 473, CA) . . . 177, 399, 400

R (on the application of Lichniak) v Secretary of State for the Home Department [2002] QB 296; [2001] 3 WLR 933, CA . . . 214

R (on the application of Limbuela) v Secretary of State for the Home Department [2004] EWHC 219 (Admin); (2004) The Times, 9 February, QBD; [2004] EWCA Civ 540; [2004] QB 1140; [2004] 3 WLR 561, CA . . . 307

R (on the application of M) v Dover Magistrates' Court [2003] EWCA Civ 237; [2003] QB 1238; [2003] 2 All ER 631, CA . . . 181

R (on the application of M) v Waltham Forest Magistrates Court and the DPP; R (on the application of W) v Thetford Youth Court and the DPP (2002) 166 JP 453 . . . 644

R (on the application of McCann) v Manchester Youth Court and others [2002] UKHL 39; [2003] 1 AC 787; [2002] 4 All ER 593, HL . . . 14, 15, 17, 181

R (on the application of N) v M [2002] EWCA Civ 1789; [2003] 1 WLR 562; [2003] 1 FLR 667, CA . . . 14

R (on the application of Pearson) v Secretary of State for the Home Department [2001] EWHC Admin 239; [2001] HRLR 39 . . . 197

R (on the application of Pretty) v DPP [2001] UKHL 61; [2002] 1 AC 800; [2002] 1 All ER 1, HL . . . 175, 327

R (on the application of ProLife Alliance) v BBC [2003] UKHL 23; [2004] 1 AC 185; [2003] 2 All ER 977, HL . . . 165, 166, 190, 191, 217, 307

R (on the application of Q) v Secretary of State for the Home Department [2003] EWHC 195 (Admin); (2003) The Times, 20 February,

QBD; [2003] EWCA Civ 364; [2004] QB 36; [2003] 2 All ER 905, CA . . . 176, 307

R (on the application of Robertson) v Wakefield Metropolitan DC [2001] EWHC Admin 915; [2002] QB 1052; [2002] 2 WLR 889 . . . 188

R (on the application of Rushbridger) v Attorney-General [2003] UKHL 38; [2004] 1 AC 357; [2003] 3 All ER 784, HL . . . 168, 191

R (on the application of S) v Chief Constable of South Yorkshire; R (on the application of Marper) v Chief Constable of South Yorkshire [2001] [2004] UKHL 39; [2004] 1 WLR 2196; [2004] 4 All ER 139, HL . . . 188

R (on the application of Saadi) v Secretary of State for the Home Department [2002] UKHL 41; [2002] 4 All ER 785; [2002] 1 WLR 3131, HL . . . 179, 180, 307

R (on the application of Samaroo) v Secretary of State for the Home Department [2001] EWCA Civ 1139; [2001] UKHRR 1150, CA . . . 172

R (on the application of Sivakumar) v Immigration Appeal Tribunal [2003] UKHL 14; [2003] 2 All ER 1097; [2003] 1 WLR 840, HL . . . 175

R (on the application of Telegraph Group plc) v Sherwood [2001] EWCA Crim 1075; [2001] 1 WLR 1983, CA . . . 183, 192, 235

R (on the application of U) v Metropolitan Police Commissioner [2002] 4 All ER 593 . . . 523

R (on the application of U) v Metropolitan Police Commissioner [2004] 1 All ER 419 . . . 523

R (on the application of Uttley) v Secretary of State for the Home Department [2004] UKHL 38; [2004] 1 WLR 2278; [2004] 4 All ER 1, HL . . . 184

R (on the application of W) v Lambeth LBC [2002] EWCA Civ 613; [2002] 2 All ER 901, CA . . . 88, 89

R. (on the application of Williamson) v Secretary of State for Education and Employment [2001] EWCA Civ 1926; [2003] QB 1300; [2003] 1 All ER 385, CA . . . 190, 197

R v A (Complainant's Sexual History) (No 2) [2001] UKHL 25; [2002] 1 AC 45; [2001] 3 All ER 1, HL . . . 56, 57, 157, 158, 159, 181, 307, 324

R v Absolam (Calvin Lloyd) (1989) 88 Cr App R 332, CA . . . 410, 417

R v Agar (Vincent Raymond) [1990] Crim LR 183, CA . . . 577

R v Ahluwalia [1992] 4 All ER 889; (1993) 96 Cr App R 133, CA . . . 84, 326, 693

R v Aitken (Peter Kenneth) (Practice Note) [1966] 1 WLR 1076; [1966] 2 All ER 453n, CA . . . 683

R v Alexander (Simon Christopher) [1974] 1 WLR 422; [1974] 1 All ER 539, CA . . . 620

R v Allen (1872) LR 1 CCR 367 . . . 50

R v Alladice (Colin Carlton) (1988) 87 Cr App R 380, CA . . . 393, 415, 580

R v Amersham Juvenile Court, ex parte Wilson [1981] 2 All ER 315 . . . 552

R v Andrews (Donald Joseph) [1987] AC 281; [1987] 2 WLR 413; [1987] 1 All ER 513, HL . . . 615

R v Andrews (Tracey) [1999] Crim LR 156, CA . . . 333

R v Armagh (1982) 76 Cr App R 190 . . . 328

R v Aspinall (Paul James) [1999] 2 Cr App R 115; (1999) 96(7) LG 35, CA . . . 40, 401

R v Assim (Ismet) [1966] 2 QB 249; [1966] 2 All ER 881, CA

R v Ayres (David Edward) (1984) 78 Cr App R 232, HL . . . 692

R v B [2003] 2 Cr App R 197, CA . . . 538

R v B [2003] EWCA Crim 319, CA . . . 692

R v Baines [1987] Crim LR 508, CA . . . 612

R v Barnet & Camden Rent Tribunal, ex parte Frey Investments Ltd [1972] 1 All ER 1185, CA . . . 215

R v Barry (Christopher) [1975] 1 WLR 1190; [1975] 2 All ER 760, CA . . . 620

R v Bates [1952] 2 All ER 842; [1953] 1 WLR 77 . . . 67, 68

R v Beck, ex parte Daily Telegraph plc [1993] 2 All ER 177, CA . . . 236

R v Beckford (Ian Anthony) [1996] 1 Cr App R 94, CA . . . 539

R v Bedfordshire County Council, ex parte Henlow [2001] EWHC Admin 179 . . . 219

R v Beedie (Thomas Sim) [1997] 2 Cr App R 167, CA . . . 603

R v Belmarsh Magistrates Court, ex parte Watts [1999] 2 Cr App R 188 . . . 539

R v Benjafield [2002] UKHL 2; [2003] 1 AC 1099; [2002] 1 All ER 815, HL . . . 18, 95, 181

R v Berry (John) (1978) 66 Cr App R 156, CA . . . 598

R v Berry (John Rodney Francis) (No 2) [1991] 1 WLR 125; [1991] 2 All ER 789, CA . . . 684

R v Berry (John Rodney Francis), unreported, 3 April 1992 684

R v Beycan [1990] Crim LR 185, CA . . . 416

R v Bezzina (Anthony) [1994] 3 All ER 964; [1994] 1 WLR 1057, CA . . . 62

R v Bibi (Bashir Begum) (1980) 71 Cr App R 360, CA . . . 659

R v Birmingham Justices, ex parte Wyatt (Joseph Michael) [1976] 1 WLR 260; [1975] 3 All ER 897 . . . 650

R v Blackburn (Raymond Francis) (1992) *The Times*, 1 December, CA . . . 417

R v Blandford (Harold Percy); R v Freestone (George Nightingale) [1955] 1 WLR 331; [1955] 1 All ER 681 . . . 541

R v Blandford Justices, ex parte G (An Infant) [1967] 1 QB 82; [1966] 1 All ER 1021 . . . 649

R v Blastland (Douglas) [1986] AC 41; [1985] 2 All ER 1095, HL . . . 607

R v Boal (Francis Steven) [1992] QB 591; [1992] 3 All ER 177, CA . . . 683, 692

R v Board of Visitors of the Maze Prison, ex parte Hone [1988] A.C 379; *sub nom* Hone v Board of Visitors of the Maze Prison [1988] 1 All ER 321, HL . . . 215, 282

R v Bone (Michael Edward) [1968] 1 WLR 983; [1968] 2 All ER 644, CA . . . 615

R v Bow Street Metropolitan Stipendiary Magistrate, ex parte Director of Public Prosecutions (1990) 91 Cr App R 283 . . . 539

R v Boyle (George Bainbridge) [1954] 2 QB 292; [1954] 2 All ER 721, CA . . . 598

R v Brentford Justices, ex parte Wong [1981] QB 445; [1981] 2 WLR 203; [1981] 1 All ER 884 . . . 626, 627

R v Broad (Mervyn) (1979) 68 Cr App R 281, CA . . . 599, 601

R v Bromley Magistrates Court, ex parte Smithy and Wilkins [1995] 4 All ER 146; (1995) 159 JP 251 . . . 631, 632

R v Brooks (Christopher) [1985] Crim LR 385, CA . . . 547

R v Brown [1995] 1 Cr App R 191 . . . 575

R v Brown (Winston) [1998] AC 367; [1997] 3 WLR 447; [1997] 3 All ER 769, HL . . . 524

R v Bryant (Horace Henry) and Dickson (Victor Richard) (1946) 31 Cr App R 146, CA . . . 575

R v Bryant (Philip Roy) [1979] QB 108; [1978] 2 All ER 689, CA . . . 619

R v Bullock (Peter John) [1964] 1 QB 481; [1963] 3 All ER 506, CA . . . 651

R v Burles (David John) [1970] 2 QB 191; [1970] 1 All ER 642, CA . . . 599

R v C (Barry) [2004] EWCA Crim 292; [2004] 1 WLR 2098; [2004] 3 All ER 1, CA . . . 184

R v Canale (Ramon Michael) [1990] 2 All ER 187, CA . . . 393, 394, 417

R v Cannan (John David) (1991) 92 Cr App R 16, CA . . . 588

R v Cannings [2004] 2 Cr App R 7 . . . 686

R v Canterbury and St Augustine Justices, ex parte Klisiak [1982] QB 398; [1981] 2 All ER 129 . . . 544

R v Canterbury and St Augustine Justices, ex parte Turner (1983) 147 JP 193 . . . 626

R v Carr-Briant [1943] KB 607; [1943] 2 All ER 156 . . . 13, 616

R v Caslin (Judy) [1961] 1 WLR 59; [1961] 1 All ER 246, CA . . . 692

R v Cavanagh (James Michael) [1972] 1 WLR 676; [1972] 2 All ER 704, CA . . . 608

R v Celaire and Poulton [2003] Crim LR 124 . . . 659

R v Central Criminal Court, ex parte Francis & Francis (A Firm) [1989] AC 346; [1988] 3 All ER 775, HL . . . 50

R v Central Criminal Court, ex parte Raymond [1986] 1 WLR 710; [1986] 2 All ER 379 . . . 214

R v Central Criminal Court and Nadir, ex parte Director of the Serious Fraud Office [1993] 1 WLR 949; [1993] 2 All ER 399 . . . 214

R v Central Criminal Court, ex parte Randle and Pottle (1991) 92 Cr App R 323 . . . 540

R v Central Criminal Court, ex parte Telegraph plc [1993] 1 WLR 980; [1993] 2 All ER 971, CA . . . 235

R v Chairman of Stephen Lawrence Inquiry, ex parte A (1988) *The Times*, 25 July . . . 297

R v Chan-Fook (Mike) [1994] 1 WLR 689; [1994] 2 All ER 552, CA . . . 326

R v Chard (Alan John) [1984] AC 279; [1983] 3 All ER 637, HL . . . 76

R v Charles (Derek Michael) [1976] 1 All ER 659; [1976] 1 WLR 248, CA (affirmed *sub nom* Commissioner of Police of the Metropolis v Charles (Derek Michael) [1977] AC 177; [1976] 3 All ER 112, HL) . . . 100

R v Chertsey Justices, ex parte Franks [1961] 2 QB 152; [1961] 1 All ER 825 . . . 626

R v Chief Constable of Avon and Somerset, ex parte Robinson [1989] 1 WLR 793; [1989] 2 All ER 15 . . . 390

R v Chief Constable of Devon and Cornwall, ex parte Central Electricity Generating Board [1982] QB 458; [1981] 3 All ER 826, CA . . . 389, 398

R v Chief Constable of Kent, ex parte L [1993] 1 All ER 756 . . . 212, 531

R v Chief Constable of Sussex, ex parte International Trader's Ferry Ltd [1998] QB 477; [1997] 2 All ER 65, CA . . . 115

R v Chief Constable of Warwickshire, ex parte Fitzpatrick [1998] 1 All ER 65 . . . 219

R v Chief Constable of the West Midlands, ex parte Wiley [1995] 1 AC 274; [1994] 3 All ER 420, HL . . . 578

R v Chief Immigration Officer, Heathrow Airport, ex parte Bibi (Salamat) [1976] 3 All ER 843; [1976] 1 WLR 979, CA . . . 65, 149, 150

R v Chief Rabbi of the United Hebrew Congregations of Great Britain and the Commonwealth, ex parte Wachmann [1992] 1 WLR 1036; [1993] 2 All ER 249 . . . 209

R v Chisnell [1992] Crim LR 507, CA . . . 608

R v Christou (George) [1997] AC 117; [1996] 2 WLR 620; [1996] 2 All ER 927, HL . . . 588

R v Clarke (Linda Vera) [1982] 1 WLR 1090; [1982] 3 All ER 232, CA . . . 328

R v Clerk to the Bradford Justices, ex parte Sykes [1999] Crim LR 748 . . . 541

R v Clowes (Peter) (No 1) [1992] 3 All ER 440 . . . 578

R v Cockley (Wayne Edward) [1984] Crim LR 429, CA . . . 610

R v Coe (Anthony William) [1968] 1 WLR 1950; [1969] 1 All ER 65, CA . . . 640

R v Cohen (1992) 142 NLJ 1267 . . . 589

R v Colchester Justices, ex parte North Essex Building Co [1977] 3 All ER 567 . . . 550

R v Colyer [1974] Crim LR 24 . . . 102

R v Comerford (Thomas Anthony) [1998] 1 WLR 191; [1998] 1 All ER 823, CA . . . 333

R v Commissioner of Police of the Metropolis, ex parte Blackburn (No 1) [1968] 2 QB 118; [1968] 1 All ER 763, CA . . . 211, 388

R v Commissioner of Police of the Metropolis, ex parte Blackburn (Albert Raymond) (No 3) [1973] QB 241; [1973] 1 All ER 324, CA . . . 211

R v Commissioner of Police of the Metropolis, ex parte P (1996) 8 Admin LR 6; 160 JP 369 . . . 212

R v Constanza (Gaetano) [1997] 2 Cr App R 492; [1997] Crim LR 576, CA . . . 326

R v Cooksley [2003] Crim LR 564 . . . 660

R v Cooper (Sean) and McMahon [1969] 1 QB 267; [1968] 3 WLR 1225; [1969] 1 All ER 32, CA . . . 686, 690

R v Cornwall County Council, ex parte Huntington [1992] 3 All ER 566 . . . (affirmed [1994] 1 All ER 694, CA) . . . 65, 210

R v Courtie (Thomas) [1984] AC 463; [1984] 1 All ER 740, HL . . . 594, 627, 628

R v Coventry City Council, ex parte Phoenix Aviation [1995] 3 All ER 37 . . . 115, 212, 215

R v Cowan (Donald) [1996] QB 373; [1995] 3 WLR 818; [1995] 4 All ER 939, CA . . . 611, 617

R v Coward (Anderson Ralph) (1980) 70 Cr App R 70, CA . . . 599

R v Cox (Rodney William) (1993) 96 Cr App R 464, CA . . . 417

R v Criminal Cases Review Commision, ex parte Pierson (1999) . . . 686

R v Criminal Injuries Compensation Board, ex parte Lain [1967] 2 QB 864; [1967] 2 All ER 770 . . . 208, 287, 662

R v Cripps, ex parte Muldoon [1984] QB 68; [1983] 3 All ER 72 . . . 228, 253

R v Cronin [1940] 1 All ER 618 . . . 695

R v Crook (Timothy) [1992] 2 All ER 687; (1991) 93 Cr App R 17, CA . . . 235

R v Croydon Justices, ex parte Dean [1993] QB 769; [1993] 3 All ER 129 . . . 539

R v Cruttenden (Roger Christian) [1991] 2 QB 66; [1991] 3 All ER 242, CA . . . 44

R v Cunningham (Brian Gregory) (1993) 14 Cr App R (S) 444, CA . . . 669

R v Cuthbertson (Brian George) [1981] AC 470; [1980] 2 All ER 401, HL . . . 60

R v D (Contempt of Court: Illegal Photography) [2004] EWCA Crim 1271; (2004) The Times, 13 May, CA . . . 239

R v DPP, ex parte Kebilene [2000] 2 AC 326; [1999] 4 All ER 801, HL . . . 55, 617

R v Da Silva (Michael Reginald) [1990] 1 WLR 31; [1990] 1 All ER 29, 608

R v Dabhade (Nitin Jayat) [1993] QB 329; [1992] 4 All ER 796, CA . . . 602

R v Danvers [1982] Crim LR 680 . . . 337

R v Davies (David) [1906] 1 KB 32 . . . 228, 240

R v Day [2003] EWCA Crim 1060, CA . . . 687

R v Delaney (Joseph Patrick) (1989) 88 Cr App R 338, CA . . . 393

R v Derby Magistrates Court, ex parte B [1996] AC 487; [1995] 4 All ER 526, HL . . . 352

R v Derby Crown Court, ex parte Brooks (1985) 80 Cr App R 164 . . . 538

R v Devizes Youth Court, ex parte M, unreported, 22 January 2000 . . . 644

R v Director of Public Prosecutions, ex parte Cooke (1992) 95 Cr App R 233 . . . 537

R v Director of the Serious Fraud Office, ex parte Smith [1993] AC 1; sub nom Smith v Director of the Serious Fraud Office [1992] 3 All ER 456, HL . . . 574

R v Disciplinary Committee of the Jockey Club, ex parte The Aga Khan [1993] 2 All ER 853; [1993] 1 WLR 909 . . . 209, 294

R v Denbigh Justices, ex parte Williams [1974] QB 759; [1974] 2 All ER 1052 . . . 231

R v Deputy Governor of Parkhurst Prison, ex parte Hague [1992] 1 AC 58; [1991] 3 All ER 733, HL . . . 33

R v Derbyshire County Council, ex parte Noble [1990] ICR 808; [1990] IRLR 332, CA . . . 220

R v Dickson (Robert) [1969] 1 WLR 405; [1969] 1 All ER 729, CA . . . 585

R v Dodd, unreported, 1971 . . . 693

R v Doheny (Alan James) [1997] 1 Cr App R 369, CA . . . 414

R v Doncaster Justices, ex parte Goulding [1993] 1 All ER 435 . . . 550

R v Dossi (Severo) (1918) 87 LJKB 1024 . . . 595

R v Dover Justices, ex parte Dover DC (1992) 156 JP 433 . . . 235

R v Drew [2003] UKHL 25; [2003] 4 All ER 557; [2003] 1 WLR 1213, HL . . . 176

R v Drummond [2002] All ER (D) 70 . . . 617

R v Dryden [1995] 4 All ER 987, CA . . . 84

R v Dudley Magistrates Court, ex parte Payne [1979] 1 WLR 891; [1979] 2 All ER 1089 . . . 637

R v Dunbar (Ronald Patrick) [1958] 1 QB 1; [1957] 2 All ER 737, CA . . .

R v Dundon [2004] EWCA Crim 621; (2004) The Times, 28 April . . . 276

R v Dunford (Nicholas James) (1990) 91 Cr App R 150, CA . . . 393

R v Durham Quarter Sessions, ex parte Virgo [1952] 2 QB 1; [1952] 1 All ER 466 . . . 649

R v E(T) [2004] 2 Cr App R 36 . . . 538

R v East Berkshire Area Health Authority, ex parte Walsh [1985] QB 152; [1984] 3 All ER 425, CA . . . 209, 218

R v El Faisal, 20 January 2003, unreported . . . 335

R v Ellis [2003] EWCA Crim 3556, CA . . . 687

R v Emmerson (Geoffrey) (1991) 92 Cr App R 284, CA . . . 392

R v Ensor (Maxie Angus Anderson) [1989] 1 WLR 497; [1989] 2 All ER 586, CA . . . 691

R v Epsom Justices, ex parte Gibbons [1984] QB 574; [1983] 3 All ER 523 . . . 628

R v Evans [1992] NLJR 1267 . . . 593

R v Evesham Justices, ex parte McDonagh and Berrows Newspapers Ltd [1988] QB 553; (1988) 87 Cr App R 28 . . . 233

R v Eyles (Charles Stanley) (1963) 47 Cr App R 260, CA . . . 683

R v Fairhead (Terry George) [1975] 2 All ER 737, CA . . . 664

R v Fisher (Charles) [1969] 1 All ER 100; [1969] 1 WLR 8, CA . . . 43

R v Football Association, ex parte Football League [1993] 2 All ER 833 . . . 295

R v Forbes (Anthony Leroy) [2001] 1 AC 473; [2001] 1 All ER 686, HL . . . 394, 421

R v Ford (Royston James) [1989] QB 868; [1989] 3 All ER 445, CA . . . 333, 335

R v Forde [1923] 2 KB 400; [1923] All ER Rep 479, CA . . . 683

R v Freeman (Brandford Augustus) [1970] 2 All ER 413; [1970] 1 WLR 788, CA . . . 76

R v Fulling (Ruth Susan) [1987] QB 426; 1987] 2 All ER 65, CA . . . 69, 392

R v Funderburk (Roy) [1990] 2 All ER 482, CA . . . 609

R v G [2002] EWCA 1992 . . . 523

R v Galbraith (George Charles) [1981] 2 All ER 1060, CA . . . 610

R v Galvin (Peter Anthony) [1987] QB 862; [1987] 2 All ER 851, CA . . . 67

R v General Council of the Bar, ex parte Percival [1991] 1 QB 212; [1990] 3 All ER 137 . . . 294, 531

R v Ghafour [2002] Crim LR 739 . . . 530

R v Gibson (Richard Norman) [1990] 2 QB 619; [1991] 1 All ER 439, CA . . . 326

R v Gilbert (1977) 66 Cr App R 237 . . . 579

R v Goldenberg (Meir) (1989) 88 Cr App R 285, CA . . . 393

R v Goldstein (Alexander Joseph) [1983] 1 All ER 434; [1983] 1 WLR 151, HL . . . 145

R v Goldstein (Harry Chaim) [2003] EWCA Crim 3450; [2004] 1 WLR 2878; [2004] 2 All ER 589, CA . . . 184

R v Goodson (Sean Eric) [1975] 1 WLR 549; [1975] 1 All ER 760, CA . . . 620

R v Gough (Robert) [1993] AC 646; [1993] 2 All ER 724, CA . . . 80, 335, 524

R v Gould (John Arthur Charles) [1968] 2 QB 65; [1968] 1 All ER 849, CA . . . 100, 683

R v Governor of Belmarsh Prison, ex parte Francis [1995] 3 All ER 634; [1995] 1 WLR 1121 . . . 15

R v Governor of Brixton Prison, ex parte Levin [1997] AC 741; [1997] 3 All ER 289, HL . . . 15, 16

R v Governor of Brixton Prison, ex parte Osman [1991] 1 WLR 281; [1992] 1 All ER 108 . . . 578

R v Governor of Brockhill Prison, ex parte Evans (No 1) [1997] QB 443; [1997] 1 All ER 439 . . . 656

R v Governor of Brockhill Prison, ex parte Evans (No 2) [2001] 2 AC 19; [2000] 4 All ER 15, HL ... 91

R v Grafton (John Peter) [1993] QB 101; [1992] 4 All ER 609, CA ... 599, 612

R v Grant (Ronald Morrison) [1951] 1 KB 500; [1951] 1 All ER 28, CA ... 640

R v Gray's Inn (1780) 1 Doug K353 ... 353

R v Greater London Council, ex parte Blackburn [1976] 1 WLR 550; [1976] 3 All ER 184, CA ... 220

R v Gregory [1993] Crim LR 623, CA ... 619

R v Guildford Crown Court, ex parte Siderfin [1990] 2 QB 683; [1989] 3 All ER 73 ... 331

R v H (Assault of Child: Reasonable Chastisement) [2001] EWCA Crim 1024; [2002] 1 Cr App R 7; [2001] 2 FLR 431, CA ... 176

R v HM Coroner for Greater Manchester, ex parte Tal [1985] QB 67; [1984] 3 All ER 240 ... 101

R v Inspectorate of Pollution, ex parte Greenpeace Ltd (No 2) [1994] 4 All ER 329 ... 220

R v H [2003] All ER (D) 403 (Feb) ... 539

R v H; R v C [2004] 2 Cr App R 10; (2004) The Times, 6 February ... 520

R v HM Treasury, ex parte British Telecommunications plc (C392/93) [1996] QB 615; [1996] All ER (EC) 411 ... 133

R v H (Fitness to Plead) [2003] UKHL 1; [2003] 1 All ER 497; [2003] 1 WLR 411 ... 18

R v Hackett [1986] Crim LR 462 ... 577

R v Haddy [1944] KB 442; [1944] 1 All ER 319, CA ... 689

R v Hallam (James Edward) [1957] 1 QB 569; [1957] 1 All ER 665, CA ... 61

R v Hallstrom, ex parte W (No 2) [1986] QB 1090; [1986] 2 All ER 306 ... 63

R v Hambery (Cyril) [1977] QB 924; [1977] 3 All ER 561, CA ... 621

R v Hanratty [2002] 2 Cr App R 30 ... 687

R v Harrison (1923) 17 Cr App R 156 ... 619

R v Harrow LBC, ex parte D [1990] Fam 133; [1990] 3 All ER 12, CA ... 211

R v Havering Justices, ex parte Gould (1993), unreported ... 212

R v Haynes (2002) CLW 25/6 ... 574

R v Hendon Justices, ex parte DPP [1994] QB 167; [1993] 1 All ER 411 ... 635

R v Hennessy (1979) 68 Cr App R 419 ... 577

R v Hereford Magistrates Court, ex parte Rowlands [1998] QB 110; [1997] 2 WLR 854 ... 213

R v Heyes (Percy) [1951] 1 KB 29; [1950] 2 All ER 587, CA ... 602

R v Highbury Corner Magistrates Court, ex parte McGinley (1986) 150 JP 257 ... 628

R v Hollington (David John) and Emmens (George Michael) (1986) 82 Cr App R 281, CA ... 600

R v Hopkins [2004] All ER (D) 356 (Feb) ... 538

R v Horseferry Road Magistrates Court, ex parte Bennett (No 1); sub nom Bennett v Horseferry Road Magistrates Court [1994] 1 AC 42; [1993] 3 All ER 138, HL ... 394, 539

R v Horseferry Road Justices, ex parte Independent Broadcasting Authority [1987] QB 54; [1986] 2 All ER 666 ... 62

R v Howe (Michael Anthony) [1986] QB 626; [1986] 1 All ER 833, CA (affirmed [1987] AC 417; [1987] 1 All ER 771, HL) ... 100

R v Howell (Errol) [1982] QB 416; [1981] 3 All ER 383, CA ... 398

R v Hughes (1879) 4 QBD 614 ... 541

R v Hughes (Patrick Darren) [1994] 1 WLR 876, CA ... 412

R v Hunt (Richard Selwyn) [1987] AC 352; [1987] 1 All ER 1, HL ... 616, 617

R v Inland Revenue Commissioners, ex parte Mead and Cook (No 2) [1993] 1 All ER 772 ... 212, 531

R v Inner London Crown Court, ex parte Benjamin (1987) 85 Cr App R 267 ... 214

R v Inner West London Coroner, ex parte Dallaglio [1994] 4 All ER 139, CA ... 268

R v Inspectorate of Pollution, ex parte Greenpeace Ltd (No 2) [1994] 4 All ER 329 ... 167

R v Insurance Ombudsman Bureau, ex parte Aegon Life Assurance Ltd [1994] COD 426 ... 209

R v Ireland (Robert Matthew) [1997] QB 114; [1997] 1 All ER 112, CA ... 326

R v Islington North Juvenile Court, ex parte Daley [1983] 1 AC 347; sub nom Daley, Re [1982] 2 All ER 974, HL ... 552, 643

R v Jackson (Clarence) [1974] QB 802; [1974] 1 All ER 640, CA ... 100

R v James (David John) [2002] EWCA Crim 1119, CA ... 182

R v Jefferies (William Charles James) [1969] 1 QB 120; [1968] 3 All ER 238, CA ... 652

R v Johnstone [2003] 3 All ER 884 ... 617, 618

R v K (Age of Consent: Reasonable Belief) [2001] 1 Cr App R 35; [2001] Crim LR 134, CA (reversed [2001] UKHL 41; [2002] 1 AC 462; [2001] 3 All ER 897, HL) ... 62

R v K (Trevor Douglas) (1993) 97 Cr App R 342 . . . 577

R v Kansal (Yash Pal) (No 2) [2001] UKHL 62; [2002] AC 69; [2002] 1 All ER 257, HL . . . 95, 169

R v Keane (Stephen John) (1994) 99 Cr App R 1, CA . . . 575

R v Kearley (Alan Robert) [1992] 2 AC 228; [1992] 2 All ER 345, HL . . . 607

R v Keenan (Graham) [1990] 2 QB 54; [1989] 3 All ER 598, CA . . . 294

R v Kennett Justices, ex parte Humphrey and Wyatt [1993] Crim LR 787 . . . 625

R v Khan (Sultan) [1997] AC 558; [1996] 3 All ER 289, HL . . . 404

R v Kidd (Philip Richard); R v Canavan (Darren Anthony) [1998] 1 WLR 604; [1998] 1 All ER 42, CA . . . 593

R v Kingston Crown Court, ex parte Bell (A Juvenile) (2000) 164 JPN 901 . . . 650

R v Kisko, unreported (1992) . . . 520

R v Knighton (William) (deceased) [2002] EWCA Crim 2227 . . . 687

R v Knightsbridge Crown Court, ex parte International Sporting Club (London) [1982] QB 304 . . . 211, 215

R v Kray (Ronald) [1970] 1 QB 125; [1969] 3 All ER 941, CA . . . 587

R v LPB (1990) 91 Cr App R 359 . . . 539

R v Lamb (Thomas) [1968] 1 WLR 1946; [1969] 1 All ER 45, CA . . . 585

R v Lambert (Steven) [2001] UKHL 37; [2002] 2 AC 545; [2001] 3 All ER 577, HL . . . 43, 56, 95, 169, 183, 307, 617

R v Lamont [1989] Crim LR 813, CA . . . 420

R v Lattimore (Colin George) (1976) 62 Cr App R 53; [1976] Crim LR 45, CA . . . 693

R v Leatham [1861–73] All ER Rep Ext 1646 . . . 391

R v Legal Aid Board, ex parte Bruce [1992] 1 WLR 694; [1992] 3 All ER 321, HL . . . 375

R v Legal Aid Board, ex parte Kaim Todner [1999] QB 966; [1998] 3 All ER 541, CA . . . 234

R v Leicester City Justices, ex parte Barrow [1991] 2 QB 260; [1991] 3 All ER 935, CA . . . 635

R v Leicester Crown Court, ex parte S (A Minor) [1993] 1 WLR 111; [1992] 2 All ER 659 . . . 234

R v Lewisham LBC, ex parte Shell UK Ltd [1988] 1 All ER 938 . . . 215

R v Liverpool City Magistrates Court, x parte DPP (1997) 161 JP 43 . . . 234

R v Liverpool Juvenile Court, ex parte R [1988] QB 1; 3 WLR 224; [1987] 2 All ER 668 . . . 633

R v Llandrindod Wells Justices, ex parte Gibson [1968] 1 WLR 598; [1968] 2 All ER 20 . . . 637

R v London County Quarter Sessions Chairman, ex parte Downes [1954] 1 QB 1; [1953] 2 All ER 750 . . . 602

R v Inner London Crown Court, ex parte Mentesh [2001] 1 Cr App R (S) 94 . . . 650

R v London Sessions Appeal Committee, ex parte Rogers [1951] 2 KB 74; [1951] 1 All ER 343 . . . 640

R v London Sessions Appeal Committee, ex parte Westminster Corporation [1951] 2 KB 508; [1951] 1 All ER 1032 . . . 652

R v Looseley (Grant Spencer); sub nom Attorney General's Reference (No 3 of 2000), Re [2001] UKHL 53; [2001] 4 All ER 897, HL . . . 181, 394

R v Lord Chancellor, ex parte Maxwell [1996] 4 All ER 751 . . . 215

R v Lord Chancellor, ex parte Witham [1998] QB 575; [1997] 2 All ER 779 . . . 207, 373, 425

R v Lord Chancellor's Department, ex parte Nangle [1992] 1 All ER 897 . . . 209

R v Lord President of the Privy Council, ex parte Page [1993] AC 682; [1993] 3 WLR 1112, HL 215

R v Lord Saville of Newdigate, ex parte A [1999] 4 All ER 860; [2000] 1 WLR 1855, CA . . . 183, 234

R v M; Kerr; H [2001] All ER (D) 67 . . . 522

R v McCann . . . 616

R v McGregor (John) [1968] 1 QB 371; [1967] 2 All ER 267, CA . . . 621

R v McHugh (David) (1977) 64 Cr App R 92, CA . . . 692

R v McIlkenny (Richard) [1992] 2 All ER 417, CA . . . 519, 520, 574, 680, 681, 694

R v McInerey and Keating [2003] Crim LR 209 . . . 659

R v McKendry, 6 March 2000, unreported, Aldershot Court-Martial Centre . . . 274

R v Mackerney and Pinfold [2003] EWCA Crim 3643 . . . 695

R v McKenna (William James) [1960] 1 QB 411; [1960] 1 All ER 326, CA . . . 620

R v McKenzie (David Stuart) (Practice Note) [1993] 1 WLR 453, CA . . . 610

R v Mclean (Alexander) [1911] 1 KB 332, CA . . . 663

R v Maguire (Anne Rita) [1992] QB 936; [1992] 2 All ER 433, CA . . . 520, 521, 583, 680, 690, 691

R v Maidstone Crown Court, ex parte Gill [1987] 1 All ER 129 . . . 214

R v Malvern Justices, ex parte Evans [1988] QB 540; [1988] 1 All ER 371 . . . 233, 235

R v Manchester Crown Court, ex parte Director of Public Prosecutions [1993] AC 9; *sub nom* Director of Public Prosecutions v Manchester Crown Court and Ashton [1993] 2 All ER 663, HL . . . 214

R v Manchester Crown Court, ex parte Williams and Simpson [1990] Crim LR 654; (1990) 154 JP 589 . . . 213, 570

R v Manchester Stipendiary Magistrate, ex parte Hill [1983] 1 AC 328; *sub nom* Hill v Anderton [1982] 2 All ER 963, HL . . . 541

R v Manley (Elizabeth) [1933] 1 KB 529, CA . . . 326

R v Mansfield Justices, ex parte Sharkey [1985] QB 613; [1985] 1 All ER 193 . . . 555

R v Marylebone Justices, ex parte Westminster LBC [1971] 1 WLR 567; [1971] 1 All ER 1025 . . . 640

R v Martin (Alan) [1998] AC 917; [1998] 1 All ER 193, HL . . . 272

R v Mason (Adrian Craig) [2002] EWCA Crim 385; [2002] 2 Cr App 38, CA . . . 393

R v Mason (Carl) [1988] 1 WLR 139; [1987] 3 All ER 481, CA . . . 393, 616

R v Mason (Vincent) [1981] QB 881; [1980] 3 All ER 777, CA . . . 334

R v Mattan (Mahmoud Hussein) (1998) *The Times,* 5 March . . . 687

R v Medical Appeal Tribunal, ex parte Gilmore [1957] 1 QB 574; [1957] 1 All ER 796, CA . . . 65

R v Medway (Andrew George) [1976] QB 779; [1976] 2 WLR 528; [1976] 1 All ER 527, CA . . . 696

R v Meek [1967] Crim LR 44; 110 SJ 867, CA . . . 610

R v Melville (Alan Brian) [1976] 1 WLR 181; [1976] 1 All ER 395, CA . . . 693

R v Melvin (Charles) and Eden (Clement) [1953] 1 QB 481; [1953] 1 All ER 294, CA . . . 692

R v Melvin and Dingle, unreported, 20 September 1993 . . . 575

R v Miah (Badrul) [1997] 2 Cr App R 12, CA . . . 342

R v Mildenhall Magistrates Court, ex parte Forest Heath DC (1997) 161 JP 401, CA . . . 652

R v Millberry, Morgan and Lackenby [2003] Crim LR 561 . . . 659

R v Miller (1993) 97 Cr App R 99, CA . . . 392

R v Mills (Gary) and Poole (Anthony Keith) [1998] 1 Cr App R 43; [2001] EWCA Crim 753; [2004] 1 Cr App R 7 . . . 687

R v Mills (Leslie Ernest) (1979) 68 Cr App R 154, CA . . . 686

R v Ministry of Agriculture, Fisheries and Food, ex parte Hamble (Offshore) Fisheries Ltd [1995] 2 All ER 714; [1995] 1 CMLR 533 . . . 123

R v Ministry of Agriculture, Fisheries and Food, ex parte Hedley Lomas (Ireland) Ltd (C5/94) [1996] All ER (EC) 493; [1996] ECR I-2553 . . . 133, 134

R v Ministry of Defence, ex parte Smith [1996] QB 517; [1996] 1 All ER 257, CA 210, 216

R v Mirza (Shabbir Ali) [2004] UKHL 2; [2004] 1 AC 1118; [2004] 1 All ER 925, HL . . . 342, 343, 344

R v Monopolies and Mergers Commission, ex parte Argyll Group plc [1986] 1 WLR 763; [1986] 2 All ER 257, CA . . . 220

R v Morpeth Ward Justices, ex parte Ward (1992) 95 Cr App R 215 . . . 211

R v Moss (Frank) (1990) 91 Cr App R 371, CA . . . 420

R v Mutford and Lothingland Justices, ex parte Harber [1971] 2 QB 291; [1971] 1 All ER 81 . . . 640

R v National Insurance Commissioners, ex parte Michael [1977] 2 All ER 420; [1977] 1 WLR 109, CA . . . 47

R v Neal (Frank) [1949] 2 KB 590; [1949] 2 All ER 438, CA . . . 620

R v Newcastle upon Tyne Justices, ex parte John Bryce (Contractors) Ltd [1976] 1 WLR 517; [1976] 2 All ER 611 . . . 626

R v Newland (Mark Anthony) [1988] QB 402; [1988] 2 All ER 891, CA . . . 586

R v Newsome (John Lee) [1970] 2 QB 711; [1970] 3 All ER 455, CA . . . 100

R v Newton (Robert John) (1983) 77 Cr App R 13, CA . . . 601, 662

R v Nicholson (James Kessack) (No 1) [1947] 2 All ER 535, CA . . . 663

R v Noble (Cyril Patrick Duncan) [1971] 3 All ER 361, CA . . . 696

R v Norfolk Justices, ex parte DPP [1950] 2 KB 558; *sub nom* R v South Greenhoe Justices, ex parte DPP [1950] 2 All ER 42 . . . 639

R v Northavon DC, ex parte Palmer (1995) 27 HLR 576, CA . . . 207

R v Northumberland Compensation Appeal Tribunal, ex parte Shaw [1952] 1 KB 338; [1952] 1 All ER 122, CA (affirmed [1951] 1 KB 711; [1951] 1 All ER 268) . . . 87, 101, 215

R v Norwich Crown Court, ex parte Belsham [1992] 1 WLR 54; [1992] 1 All ER 394 . . . 539

R v Novac (Andrew) (1977) 65 Cr App R 107, CA ... 589

R v O'Brian, unreported, 2000 ... 695

R v Oddy (Julian Farrar) [1974] 2 All ER 666, CA ... 677

R v Oldham Justices, ex parte Morrissey [1959] 1 WLR 58; [1958] 3 All ER 559 ... 637

R v Oliva (Joseph Francis) [1965] 1 WLR 1028; [1965] 3 All ER 116, CA ... 608

R v Oliver, Hartley and Baldwin [2003] Crim LR 127 ... 659

R v Oxford (Bullingdon) Justices, ex parte Bird [1948] 1 KB 100 ... 652

R v Oxford City Justices, ex parte Smith (1982) 75 Cr App R 200 ... 626 ...

R v Palmer (John) [2002] EWCA Crim 2202; [2003] 1 Cr App R (S) 12, CA ... 100

R v Panel on Take-overs and Mergers, ex parte Datafin plc [1987] QB 815; [1987] 1 All ER 564, CA ... 164, 209, 294

R v Pendleton (Donald) [2001] UKHL 66; [2002] 1 WLR 72; [2002] 1 All ER 524, HL ... 694

R v Peterborough Magistrates Court, ex parte Dowler [1997] QB 911; [1997] 2 WLR 843 ... 213

R v Pharmaceutical Society of Great Britain, ex parte Association of Pharmaceutical Importers [1987] 3 CMLR 951, CA ... 143, 145

R v Picher (1974) 60 Cr App R 1 ... 611

R v Pickford (John Andrew) [1995] 1 Cr App R 420, CA ... 692

R v Pigg (Stephen) [1983] 1 WLR 6; [1983] 1 All ER 56, HL ... 621

R v Plain (Martin John) [1967] 1 WLR 565; [1967] 1 All ER 614, CA ... 610

R v Plymouth Justices, ex parte Rogers [1982] QB 863; [1982] 2 All ER 175 ... 634

R v Pontypridd Juvenile Magistrates Court, ex parte B [1988] Crim LR 842 ... 625

R v Port Talbot BC, ex parte Jones [1988] 2 All ER 207 ... 215

R v Qureshi (Sajid) [2001] EWCA Crim 1807; [2002] 1 WLR 518; [2002] 1 Cr App R 33, CA ... 343

R v R [2003] Crim LR 898 ... 659, 660

R v R and R [2002] Crim LR 349 ... 529

R v R (Rape: Marital Exemption) [1992] 1 AC 599; [1991] 4 All ER 481, HL ... 90, 184, 326

R v Radley (Ronald George) (1974) 58 Cr App R 394, CA ... 595

R v Rankine (Elliston) [1986] 2 All ER 566, CA ... 577

R v Raymond (Stephen Patrick) [1981] QB 910; [1981] 2 All ER 246, CA ... 570

R v Reading Crown Court, ex parte Hutchinson [1988] QB 384; [1988] 1 All ER 333 ... 38, 219

R v Reading Crown Court, ex parte Malik [1981] QB 451; [1981] 1 All ER 249 ... 557

R v Redbridge Justices, ex parte Whitehouse (1991) 94 Cr App R 332 ... 548

R v Registrar General, ex parte Smith [1991] 2 QB 393; [1991] 2 All ER 88, CA ... 51

R v Richards (Randall) [1999] Crim LR 764, CA ... 233

R v Richardson (1977) 66 Cr App R 6 ... 609

R v Richardson (David Ernest) [1971] 2 QB 484; [1971] 2 WLR 889; [1971] 2 All ER 773, CA ... 608

R v Roberts (1984) 80 Cr App R 89 ... 519

R v Robertson (Eric John) [1968] 1 WLR 1767; [1968] 3 All ER 557, CA ... 598

R v Robinson (Wellesley Alphonso) (1969) 53 Cr App R 314, CA ... 601

R v Rowe (Ivor Clyde) [1955] 1 QB 573; [1955] 2 All ER 234, CA ... 652

R v Royle (Brian) [1971] 3 All ER 1359; [1971] 1 WLR 1764, CA ... 47

R v St Albans Crown Court, ex parte Cinnamond [1981] QB 480; [1981] 1 All ER 802 ... 655

R v St Albans Juvenile Court, ex parte Goodman [1981] 2 All ER 311 ... 552

R v Samuel (Cornelius Joseph) [1988] QB 615; [1988] 2 All ER 135, CA ... 393, 413, 415

R v Sang (Leonard Anthony) [1980] AC 402; [1979] 3 WLR 263; [1979] 2 All ER 1222, HL ... 524

R v Sanghera (Rashpal) [2001] 1 Cr App R 20; [2000] All ER (D) 1415, CA ... 40, 394

R. v Scothern [1961] Crim. LR 326, CA ... 695

R v Secretary of State for the Environment, ex parte National Association of Local Government Officers (1993) 5 Admin LR 785 ... 216

R v Secretary of State for the Environment, ex parte Ostler [1977] QB 122, CA ... 210

R v Secretary of State for the Environment, ex parte Rose Theatre Trust Co (No 2) [1990] 1 QB 504; [1990] 1 All ER 754 ... 220

R v Secretary of State for the Environment, Transport and the Regions, ex parte Spath Holme Ltd [2001] 2 AC 349; [2001] 1 All ER 195, HL ... 71, 72

R v Secretary of State for Foreign and Commonwealth Affairs, ex parte Lord

Rees-Mogg [1994] QB 552; [1994] 1 All ER 457 ... 111

R v Secretary of State for Foreign and Commonwealth Affairs, ex parte World Development Movement Ltd [1995] 1 WLR 386; [1995] 1 All ER 611 ... 167

R v Secretary of State for the Home Department, ex parte A [2002] EWCA Civ 1008; [2002] 3 CMLR 14 ... 144

R v Secretary of State for the Home Department, ex parte Bentley [1994] QB 349; [1993] 4 All ER 442 ... 208

R v Secretary of State for the Home Department, ex parte Brind 1990] 1 All ER 469, CA (affirmed [1991] 1 AC 696; [1991] 1 All ER 720; 1991] 2 WLR 588, HL) ... 150, 210, 215, 216, 324

R v Secretary of State for the Home Department, ex parte Bugdaycay [1987] A.. 514; [1987] 2 WLR 606, HL 216

R v Secretary of State for the Home Department, ex parte Cheblak [1991] 1 WLR 890; [1991] 2 All ER 319, CA ... 215

R v Secretary of State for the Home Department, ex parte Fire Brigades Union [1995] 2 AC 513; [1995] 2 All ER 244, HL ... 42, 210, 287, 304, 306

R v Secretary of State for the Home Department, ex parte Hickey (No 2) [1995] 1 WLR 734; [1995] 1 All ER 490 ... 687

R v Secretary of State for the Home Department, ex parte Hindley [2001] 1 AC 410; [2000] 2 All ER 385, HL ... 178

R v Secretary of State for the Home Department, ex parte Javed [2001] EWCA Civ 789; [2002] QB 129, CA ... 37, 176

R v Secretary of State for the Home Department, ex parte Khawaja [1984] AC 74; [1983] 1 All ER 765, HL ... 13, 94

R v Secretary of State for the Home Department, ex parte Ku (Kwai Chi) [1995] QB 364; [1995] 2 All ER 891, CA ... 81

R v Secretary of State for the Home Department, ex parte Leech (No 2) [1994] QB 198; [1993] 4 All ER 539, CA ... 150

R v Secretary of State for the Home Department, ex parte McQuillan [1995] 4 All ER 400 ... 216

R v Secretary of State for the Home Department and the Parole Board, ex parte Norney (1995) 7 Admin LR 861 ... 150

R v Secretary of State for the Home Department, ex parte Northumbria Police Authority [1989] QB 26; [1988] 1 All ER 556, CA ... 4, 387

R v Secretary of State for the Home Department,

ex parte Pierson [1998] AC 539; [1997] 3 All ER 577, HL ... 61, 312

R v Secretary of State for the Home Department, ex parte Saleem [2001] 1 WLR 443; [2000] 4 All ER 814, CA ... 37

R v Secretary of State for the Home Department, ex parte Simms [2000] 2 AC 115; [1999] 3 All ER 400, HL ... 30, 193

R v Secretary of State for the Home Department, ex parte Stafford [1999] 2 AC 38; [1998] 4 All ER 7, HL ... 154

R v Secretary of State for the Home Department, ex parte Swati [1986] 1 WLR 477; [1986] 1 All ER 717, CA ... 434

R v Secretary of State for the Home Department, ex parte Venables and Thompson [1998] AC 407; [1997] 3 All ER 97, HL ... 306, 673

R v Secretary of State for the Home Department, ex parte Wynne [1992] QB 406; [1992] 2 All ER 301, CA ... 29

R v Secretary of State for the Home Department, ex parte Zamir [1980] AC 930; [1980] 2 All ER 768, HL ... 94

R v Secretary of State for National Heritage, ex parte Continental Television BV [1993] 3 CMLR 387, CA ... 135

R v Secretary of State for Transport, ex parte Factortame Ltd (No 1) [1989] 2 CMLR 353, CA (reversed [1990] 2 AC 85; [1989] 2 All ER 692, HL) ... 30, 135, 145, 473

R v Secretary of State for Transport, ex parte Factortame Ltd (C213/89) [1990] ECR I-2433; [1990] 3 CMLR 1, ECJ ... 30, 120, 127, 133, 135, 145

R v Secretary of State for Transport, ex parte Factortame Ltd (No 2) [1991] 1 AC 603; [1991] 1 All ER 70, HL ... 29, 135

R v Secretary of State for Transport, ex parte Factortame Ltd (No 3) (C221/89) [1992] QB 680; [1991] 3 All ER 769 ... 29

R v Secretary of State for Transport, ex parte Factortame Ltd (No 4) (C48/93) [1996] QB 404; [1996] All ER (EC) 301 ... 29, 133

R v Secretary of State for Transport, ex parte Factortame Ltd (No 5) [2000] 1 AC 524; [1999] 4 All ER 906, HL ... 29

R v Seelig (Roger Hugh) [1992] 1 WLR 149; [1991] 4 All ER 429, CA ... 537

R v Sefton Metropolitan Borough Council, ex parte Help the Aged [1997] 4 All ER 532, CA ... 215

R v Seisdon Justices, ex parte Dougan [1982] 1 WLR 1479; [1983] 1 All ER 6 ... 635

R v Self (Graham) [1992] 1 WLR 657; [1992] 3 All ER 476, CA ... 407

R v Shayler (David Michael) [2002] UKHL 11; [2003] 1 AC 247; [2002] 2 All ER 477, HL . . . 192

R v Sheer Metalcraft Ltd [1954] 1 QB 586; 133 [1954] 1 All ER 542 . . . 35

R v Sheffield Crown Court, ex parte Brownlow [1980] QB 530; [1980] 2 All ER 444, CA . . . 213, 334

R v Sheffield Justices, ex parte Director of Public Prosecutions [1993] Crim LR 136 . . . 548

R v Shivpuri (Pyare) [1987] AC 1; [1986] 2 All ER 334, HL . . . 12, 95

R v Silcott, Braithwaite and Raghip (1991) The Times, 9 December, CA . . . 520

R v Simpson [2003] EWCA Crim 1499; [2004] QB 118; [2003] 3 All ER 531, CA . . . 100

R v Smith (Morgan James) [1999] QB 1079; [1998] 4 All ER 387, CA (affirmed [2001] 1 AC 146; [2000] 4 All ER 289, HL) . . . 86

R v Smith [2003] EWCA Crim 283; [2003] 1 WLR 2229, CA . . . 336

R v Smith (David Raymond) [1974] QB 354; [1974] 1 All ER 632, CA . . . 683

R v Snaresbrook Crown Court, ex parte Input Management Ltd (1999) 163 JP 533 . . . 650

R v Soanes (Dorothy Clara) [1948] 1 All ER 289, CA . . . 601

R v Socialist Worker Printers & Publishers Ltd, ex parte Attorney General [1975] QB 637; [1975] 1 All ER 142 . . . 234, 235, 237

R v Solicitor General, ex parte Taylor and Taylor [1996] 1 FCR 206 . . . 212

R v South Hackney Juvenile Court, ex parte RB and C (1983) 77 Cr App R. 294 . . . 550

R v South Worcestershire Magistrates, ex parte Lilley [1995] 4 All ER 186; (1995) 159 JP 598 . . . 631

R v Southampton Crown Court, ex parte K [2002] EWHC 1640 (Admin) . . . 644

R v Southampton Justices, ex parte Green [1976] QB 11; [1975] 2 All ER 1073, CA . . . 562

R v Southwark Crown Court, ex parte Customs and Excise Commissioners [1993] 1 WLR 764 . . . 214

R v Southwark Crown Court, ex parte Ward (Michael) [1996] Crim LR 123 . . . 214

R v Spear (John) and others; R v Saunby and others [2001] EWCA Crim 2; [2001] QB 804; [2001] 2 WLR 1692, CA (affirmed [2002] UKHL 31; [2003] 1 AC 734; [2002] 3 All ER 1074, HL) . . . 87, 155, 274, 275, 276

R v Spencer (Alan Widdison) [1987] AC 128; [1986] 2 All ER 928, HL . . . 337

R v Straw (Norma Margaret) [1995] 1 All ER 187, CA . . . 693

R v Sussex Justices, ex parte McCarthy [1924] 1 KB 256 . . . 231, 633

R v Taylor (Derek Roy), Roberts (David Eric) and Simons (Geoffrey) (1977) 64 Cr App R 182, CA . . . 659

R v Taylor (John William) [1950] 2 KB 368; [1950] 2 All ER 170, CA . . . 100

R v Taylor (Gary) [1995] Crim LR 253; (1994) The Times, 17 August, CA . . . 234

R v Taylor (Michelle Ann) and Taylor (Lisa Jane) (1994) 98 Cr App R 361, CA . . . 238

R v Thompson (1976) 64 Cr App R 96 . . . 613

R v Thompson (William) [1975] 1 WLR 1425; [1975] 2 All ER 1028, CA . . . 570

R v Thornton (Sara Elizabeth) (No 1) [1992] 1 All ER 306; (1993) 96 Cr App R 112, CA . . . 326

R v Tickner [1992] Crim LR 44, CA . . . 587

R v Tirado (Emilio) [1974] 59 Cr App R 80, CA . . . 595

R v Tottenham Justices, ex parte Joshi [1982] 1 WLR 631; [1982] 2 All ER 507 . . . 655

R v Tottenham Youth Court, ex parte Fawzy [1998] 1 All ER 365 . . . 553

R v Trew (Emmon Clement) [1996] 2 Cr App R 138, CA . . . 588

R v Trussler (Barry) [1988] Crim LR 446 . . . 392

R v Turnbull (Raymond) [1977] QB 224; [1976] 3 All ER 549, CA . . . 420

R v Turner (Bryan James) (1975) 61 Cr App R 67, CA . . . 328

R v Turner (Frank Richard) (No 1) [1970] 2 QB 321; [1970] 2 All ER 281, CA . . . 599

R v V [2004] All ER (D) 207 (Feb) . . . 540

R v Veneroso [2002] Crim LR 306 . . . 181, 394

R v Vickers (John Willson) [1957] 2 QB 664; [1957] 2 All ER 741, CA . . . 68

R v Vickers (Richard John) [1975] 1 WLR 811; [1975] 2 All ER 945, CA . . . 683

R v Visitors to the Inns of Court, ex parte Calder and Persaud [1994] QB 1; [1993] 2 All ER 876, CA . . . 328

R v Walsh (Gerald Frederick) (1990) 91 Cr App R 161; [1989] Crim LR 822, CA . . . 40, 401

R v Wandsworth LBC, ex parte Mansoor [1997] QB 953; [1996] 3 All ER 913, CA . . . 72

R v Ward (Judith Theresa) [1993] 2 All ER 577; [1993] 1 WLR 619, CA 578, 583, 584

R v Warwickshire County Council, ex parte Johnson [1993] AC 583; [1993] 1 All ER 299, HL . . . 72

R v Watford Justices, ex parte Outrim [1983] RTR 26 . . . 626

R v Wattam (1978) 68 Cr App R 293 . . . 558

R v Weekes (Alan John) (1982) 74 Cr App R 161, CA . . . 600

R v West (Rosemary Pauline) [1996] 2 Cr App R 374, CA . . . 588

R v West (Thomas William Edward) [1964] 1 QB 15; [1962] 2 All ER 624 . . . 547

R v West London Coroner, ex parte Gray [1988] QB 467; [1987] 2 All ER 129 . . . 14

R v West London Stipendiary Magistrate, ex parte Anderson (1985) 80 Cr App R 143 . . . 539

R v West London Metropolitan Stipendiary Magistrate, ex parte Klahn [1979] 1 WLR 933; [1979] 2 All ER 221 . . . 541

R v West Yorkshire Coroner, ex parte Smith (No 1) [1983] QB 335; [1982] 3 All ER 1098, CA . . . 267

R v Wheatley (Peter Richard) [1979] 1 All ER 954; [1979] 1 W.LR 144, CA . . . 75

R v Wicks (Peter Edward) [1998] AC 92; [1997] 2 All ER 801, HL . . . 219

R v Wilkins (Joseph Herbert) (1978) 66 Cr App R 49, CA . . . 601

R v Willesden Justices, ex parte Clemmings (1988) 87 Cr App R 280 . . . 626

R v Williams (Brian) (No 4) [1962] 1 WLR 1268; [1962] 3 All ER 639, CA . . . 663

R v Williams (Carl) [1982] 1 WLR 1398; [1982] 3 All ER 1092, CA . . . 683

R v Willis (Peter Charles) (1974) 60 Cr App R 146, CA . . . 659

R v Wilson [1991] Crim LR 838, CA . . . 619

R v Wimbledon Justices, ex parte Derwent [1953] 1 QB 380; [1953] 1 All ER 390 . . . 626

R v Wolverhampton Coroner, ex parte McCurbin (Desmond) [1990] 1 WLR 719; [1990] 2 All ER 759, CA . . . 14

R v Young (Eric Rutherford) [1964] 2 All ER 480, CA . . . 610

R v Young (Stephen Andrew) [1995] QB 324; [1995] 2 WLR 430, CA . . . 342, 343

Rampal v Rampal (No 2) [2001] EWCA Civ 989; [2002] Fam 85; [2001] 3 WLR 795, CA . . . 50

Randolph v Tuck [1962] 1 QB 175; [1961] 1 All ER 8 . . . 102

Rantzen v Mirror Group Newspapers (1986) Ltd [1994] QB 670; [1993] 4 All ER 975, CA . . . 507

Rasmussen v Denmark (A/87) (1985) 7 EHRR 371 . . . 171

Rastin v British Steel plc [1994] 1 WLR 732; [1994] 2 All ER 641, CA . . . 427

Raymond v Honey [1981] QB 874; [1981] 2 All ER 1084 . . . 236

Read v J Lyons & Co Ltd [1945] KB 216; [1945] 1 All ER 106, CA (affirmed [1947] AC 156; [1946] 2 All ER 471, HL) . . . 12, 84

Reed Executive plc v Business Information Ltd [2004] 4 All ER 943 . . . 489

Rees v United Kingdom (A/106) (1987) 9 EHRR 56 . . . 194

Reid v Commissioner of Police of the Metropolis [1973] QB 551; [1973] 2 All ER 97, CA . . . 11

Reid Hewitt & Co v Joseph [1918] AC 717, HL . . . 490

Remli v France (1996) 22 EHRR 253 . . . 343

Rice v Connolly [1966] 2 QB 414; [1966] 2 All ER 649 . . . 385, 404

Richards v R [1993] AC 217; [1992] 4 All ER 807, PC . . . 604

Rickards v Rickards [1990] Fam 194; [1989] 3 All ER 193, CA . . . 97

Riddick v Thames Board Mills [1977] QB 881; [1977] 3 All ER 677, CA . . . 478

Ridehalgh v Horsefield [1994] Ch 205; [1994] 3 All ER 848, CA . . . 491

Rippon (Highfield) Housing Confirmation Order 1938, Re [1939] 2 KB 838; [1939] 3 All ER 548, CA . . . 74

River Wear Commissioners v Adamson (1877) LR 2 App Cas 743 . . . 49

Robert Addie & Sons (Collieries) Ltd v Dumbreck [1929] AC 358, HL . . . 94

Roberts, Re [1967] 1 WLR 474 . . . 570

Roberts v Hopwood [1925] AC 578, HL . . . 215

Roberts Petroleum Ltd v Bernard Kenny Ltd (In Liquidation) [1983] 2 AC 192; [1983] 1 All ER 564, HL . . . 77, 109

Roe v Robert McGregor & Sons [1968] 2 All ER 636, CA . . . 502

Rondel v Worsley [1969] 1 AC 191; [1967] 3 All ER 993, HL . . . 82, 94, 369, 370

Rookes v Barnard (No 1) [1964] AC 1129; [1964] 1 All ER 367, HL . . . 12, 74, 87

Ross v Caunters [1980] Ch 297; [1979] 3 All ER 580 . . . 368

Ross v Costigan (1982) 41 ALR 319 . . . 296

Rost v Edwards [1990] 2 QB 460; [1990] 2 All ER 641 . . . 44

Royal Bank of Scotland plc v Etridge (No 1) [1997] 3 All ER 628, CA . . . 97

Royal Bank of Scotland plc v Etridge (No 2) [1998] 4 All ER 705, CA . . . 88, 97

Royal Brompton Hospital NHS Trust v

Hammond (No 7) [2001] EWCA Civ 206; 76 Con LR 148, CA . . . 476

Royal College of Nursing of the United Kingdom v Department of Health and Social Security [1981] AC 800; [1981] 1 All ER 545, HL . . . 52

Rowe and Davis v United Kingdom (2000) 30 EHRR 1 . . . 181

Roy v Kensington and Chelsea and Westminster Family Practitioner Committee [1992] 1 AC 624; [1992] 1 All ER 705, HL . . . 218

Royster v Cavey [1947] KB 204; [1946] 2 All ER 642, CA . . . 85

Rutili (Roland), Gennevilliers (France) v Ministry of the Interior of the France (C36/75) [1975] ECR 1219 . . . 151

Rylands v Fletcher (1868) LR 3 HL 330, HL 84

S (A Child) (Identification: Restrictions on Publication), Re [2004] UKHL 47; [2004] 3 WLR 1129; [2004] 4 All ER 683, HL . . . 234 . . . 234

S (Children) (Care Order: Implementation of Care Plan), Re; sub nom Re W and B (Children) (Care Plan) [2001] EWCA Civ 757; [2001] 2 FLR 582; [2001] HRLR 50, CA (reversed [2002] UKHL 10; [2002] 2 AC 291; [2002] 2 All ER 192, HL) . . . 57, 158

S (An Infant) v Manchester City Recorder [1971] AC 481; [1969] 3 All ER 1230, HL . . . 634, 640

SA Magnavision NV v General Optical Council (No 2) [1987] 2 CMLR 262 . . . 142

SCS Peterbroeck Van Campenhout & Cie v Belgium (C312/93) [1996] All ER (EC) 242 . . . 127

St Edmundsbury and Ipswich Diocesan Board of Finance v Clark (No 1) [1973] Ch 323; [1973] 2 All ER 1155 . . . 249

St John the Evangelist, Chopwel, Re [1995] Fam 254; [1996] 1 All ER 275 . . . 84

St Thomas, Pennywell, Re [1995] Fam 50; [1995] 4 All ER 167 . . . 84

Sagnata Investments Ltd v Norwich Corporation [1971] 2 QB 614; [1971] 2 All ER 1441, CA . . . 65, 75

Saif Ali v Sydney Mitchell & Co [1980] AC 198; [1978] 3 All ER 1033, HL . . . 369

Salamander AG v European Parliament & Council (T172 & T175/98) [2000] 2 CMLR 1099 . . . 122

Saliabaku v France (1988) 13 EHRR 379 . . . 617

Salomon v Customs and Excise Commissioners [1967] 2 QB 116; [1966] 3 WLR 1223, CA . . . 65

Sander v United Kingdom (2001) 31 EHRR 44 . . . 336, 343

Saltpetre (Case of) (1606) 12 Co Rep 12 . . . 208

Sampson v Croydon Crown Court [1987] 1 WLR 194; [1987] 1 All ER 609, HL . . . 213

Saunders v United Kingdom (1997) 23 EHRR 313; (1997) 2 BHRC 358 . . . 183, 618

Scanfuture UK Ltd v Secretary of State for Trade and Industry [2001] ICR 1096; [2001] IRLR 416 . . . 280, 281, 291, 320

Schenk v Switzerland (A/140) (1991) 13 EHRR 242 . . . 523

Schorsch Meier GmbH v Hennin [1975] QB 416; [1975] 1 All ER 152, CA . . . 88

Scott v Avery (1856) 5 HL Cas 811 . . . 438

Scott (Otherwise Morgan) v Scott [1913] AC 417; [1911–13] All ER Rep 1, HL . . . 231, 234, 606

Seaford, Re; sub nom Seaford v Seifert [1967] P 325; [1967] 2 All ER 458 . . . (reversed [1968] P 53; [1968] 1 All ER 482, CA) . . . 101

Secretary of State v M, unreported, 8 March 2004; affirmed [2002] EWCA Civ 1502; [2004] QB 335; [2003] 1 All ER 816 . . . 308

Secretary of State for Defence v Guardian Newspapers Ltd [1985] AC 339; [1984] 3 All ER 601, HL . . . 237

Secretary of State for Social Security v Tunnicliffe [1991] 2 All ER 712, CA . . . 43

Securum Finance Ltd v Ashton [2001] Ch 291; [2000] 3 WLR 1400, CA . . . 469

Selectmove, Re [1995] 1 WLR 474; [1995] 2 All ER 531, CA . . . 92

Senator Lines v 15 EU Member States, App 56672/00, 10 March 2004 . . . 125

Senator Lines GmbH v Commission of the European Communities (C364/99) [1999] ECR I-8733; [2000] 5 CMLR 600 . . . 125

Senior v Holdsworth, ex parte Independent Television News [1976] QB 23; [1975] 2 All ER 1009, CA . . . 478

Series 5 Software Ltd v Clarke [1996] 1 All ER 853 . . . 473

Services Ltd v Merent Psychometric Internationasl Ltd [2002] FSR 8 . . . 474

Shaaban bin Hussien v Chong Fook Kam [1970] AC 942; [1969] 3 All ER 1626, PC . . . 400

Shah v Karanjia [1993] 4 All ER 792 . . . 490

Shah (Nilish) v Barnet London Borough Council [1983] 2 AC 309; [1983] 1 All ER 226, HL . . . 52

Shah v Swallow [1984] 2 All E.R. 528; sub nom DPP v Shah [1984] 1 WLR 886, HL . . . 627

Shaker v Al-Bedrawi [2002] 4 All ER 835 . . . 502

Sharratt v London Central Bus Co Ltd (No 1); Hollins v Russell [2003] EWCA Civ 718; [2003] 1 WLR 2487; [2003] 4 All ER 590, CA; [2004] 3 All ER 325, HL . . . 372, 495, 496

Shaw v DPP [1962] AC 220; [1961] 2 All ER 446, HL . . . 326

Shaw v DPP and others [1993] 1 All ER 918 . . . 628

Shaw v Hamilton [1982] 1 WLR 1308; [1982] 2 All ER 718 . . . 650

Shaw v Vauxhall Motors Ltd [1974] 2 All ER 1185, CA . . . 479

Sheldrake v DPP [2005] 1 All ER 337 . . . 617, 618

Shenton v Tyler [1939] Ch 620; [1939 1 All ER 827, CA . . . 12

Shimizu (UK) Ltd v Westminster City Council [1997] 1 All ER 481; [1997] 1 WLR 168, HL . . . 69

Sibson v United Kingdom (A/258-A) (1994) 17 EHRR 193 . . . 193

Sidebotham, ex parte (1880) 14 Ch D 458, CA . . . 652

Sigsworth, Re [1935] Ch 89 . . . 51

Simms v Moore [1970] 2 QB 327; [1970] 3 All ER 1 . . . 633

Sinclair v Brougham [1914] AC 398; [1914–1915] All ER Rep 622, HL . . . 83

Singh v Secretary of State for the Home Department 2002 SLT 1058; (2004) The Times, 23 January . . . 281

Sirros v Moore [1975] QB 118; [1974] 3 All ER 776, CA . . . 322, 323

Six Clerks, ex parte the (1798) 3 Ves 589 . . . 226

Skone v Skone [1971] 2 All ER 582, HL . . . 503

Slater v May (1704) 2 Ld Raym 1071 . . . 104

Slim v Daily Telegraph [1968] 2 QB 157; [1968] 1 All ER 497, CA . . . 47

Smalley v Warwick Crown Court; sub nom Smalley, Re [1985] AC 622; [1985] 1 All ER 769, HL . . . 213, 214, 563

Smith v Benabo [1937] 1 KB 518; [1937] 1 All ER 523 . . . 45

Smith v Director of the Serious Fraud Office [1992] 3 All ER 456, HL . . . 384

Smith v Wilson (1832) 3 B & Ad 728 . . . 8

Smith, Grady & Beckett v United Kingdom (2000) 29 EHRR 493 . . . 149, 185, 194, 195

Smurthwaite v Gill [1994] 1 All ER 898; (1994) 98 Cr App R 437, CA . . . 394

Snell v Unity Finance Co [1964] 2 QB 203; [1963] 3 WLR 559; [1963] 3 All ER 50, CA . . . 504

Soering v United Kingdom (A/161) (1989) 11 EHRR 439 . . . 165, 170, 176

Sogbetun v Hackney London Borough Council [1998] ICR 1264; [1998] IRLR 676 . . . 292

Solicitor, Re [1966] 1 WLR 1604; [1966] 3 All ER 52 . . . 239, 362

Solicitor, ex parte Hales, Re [1907] 2 KB 539 . . . 362

Sorrell v Finch [1977] AC 728; [1976] 2 All ER 371, HL . . . 98

South Buckinghamshire DC v Porter; sub nom Wrexham CBC v Berry [2003] UKHL 26; [2003] 2 AC 558; [2003] 3 All ER 1, CA . . . 186

Spicer v Holt [1977] AC 987; [1976] 3 All ER 71, HL . . . 405, 654

Spicer v Warbey [1953] 1 All Er 284; [1953] 1 WLR 334 . . . 653

Spring Grove Services v Deane (1972) 116 SJ 844, CA . . . 469

Stafford v DPP [1974] AC 878; [1973] 3 All ER 762, HL . . . 690, 694

Stafford v United Kingdom (2002) 35 EHRR 32; (2002) 13 BHRC 360 . . . 154, 178, 179, 673

Starr v National Coal Board [1977] 1 All ER 243; [1977] 1 WLR 63, CA . . . 97

Starrs v Ruxton; sub nom Starrs v Procurator Fiscal 2000 JC 208; 2000 SLT 42 . . . 20, 182, 280, 320

Stedman v United States (1997) 89 D & R 104 . . . 189

Steel v United Kingdom (1999) 28 EHRR 603 . . . 17, 177, 180, 190, 194, 399

Steel and Morris v United Kingdom (2005) App 68416/01 . . . 181, 192

Steele Ford & Newton v Crown Prosecution Service (No 2) [1994] 1 AC 22; [1993] 2 All ER 769, HL . . . 490

Stephens v Cuckfield Rural District Council [1960] 2 QB 373; [1960] 2 All ER 716, CA . . . 68

Stevens v United Kingdom (1986) D & R 245 . . . 190

Stewart v United Kingdom (1985) 7 EHRR CD 453 . . . 173

Stirland v DPP [1944] AC 315; [1944] 2 All ER 13, HL . . . 689

Stoke-on-Trent City Council v B & Q plc (No 2) [1991] Ch 48; [1991] 4 All ER 221 . . . 123

Storer v British Gas plc [2000] 1 WLR 1237; [2000] 2 All ER 440, CA . . . 232

Stubbings v Webb [1993] AC 498; [1993] 1 All ER 322, HL . . . 72

Sullivan v Cooperative Insurance Society Ltd (1999) The Times, 19 May, CA . . . 494

Sunday Times v United Kingdom (No 1) (A/30) (1979–1980) 2 EHRR 245 . . . 149, 170, 192, 238

Sunworld Ltd v Hammersmith and Fulham LBC; R v Blackfriars Crown Court, ex parte Sunworld Ltd [2000] 2 All ER 837 . . . 652

Sussex Peerage Case (1844) 11 Cl & Fin 85 . . . 67

Sutcliffe v Pressdram Ltd [1991] 1 QB 153; [1990] 1 All ER 269, CA . . . 341

Swain v Hillman & Gay [2001] 1 All ER 91, CA . . . 470

Sweet v Parsley [1970] AC 132; [1969] 1 All ER 347, HL . . . 62

Swedish Engine Drivers Union v Sweden (A/20) (1979–80) 1 EHRR 617 . . . 193

Swinney v Chief Constable of Northumbria (No 1) [1997] QB 464; [1996] 3 All ER 449, CA . . . 396

Sydall v Castings [1967] 1 QB 302; [1966] 3 All ER 770, CA . . . 74

Symons v Rees (1876) 1 Ex D 416 . . . 105

Symphony Group plc v Hodgson [1994] QB 179; [1993] 4 All ER 143, CA . . . 490

T and V v United Kingdom [2000] 2 All ER 1024n; (2000) 30 EHRR 121 . . . 177, 181, 552, 553, 644, 645

TP and KM v United Kingdom (28945/95) (2002) 34 EHRR 2 . . . 185

Tai Hing Cotton Mill Ltd v Liu Chong Hing Bank Ltd (No 1) [1986] AC 80; [1985] 2 All ER 947, PC . . . 86

Taittinger SA v Allbev Ltd [1994] 4 All ER 75; [1993] 2 CMLR 741, CA . . . 124

Tamlin v Hannaford [1950] 1 KB 18; [1949] 2 All ER 327 . . . 65

Tanfern Ltd v Cameron-MacDonald [2000] 1 WLR 1311; [2000] 2 All ER 801, CA . . . 247, 498, 499, 500

Taylor v Chief Constable of Thames Valley [2004] EWCA Civ 858; [2004] 1 WLR 3155; [2004] 3 All ER 503, CA . . . 409

Taylor v United Kingdom (2003) 36 EHRR CD 104 . . . 184

Tehrani v Rostron [1972] 1 QB 182; [1971] 3 All ER 790, CA . . . 65

Teixeira de Castro v Portugal (1999) 28 EHRR 101 . . . 181

Telemarsicabruzzo SpA v Circostel (C320/90) [1993] ECR I-393 . . . 144

Thai Trading Co v Taylor [1998] 3 All ER 65, CA . . . 495

Thermawear Ltd v Linton (1995) The Times, 20 October, CA . . . 500

Thoburn v Sunderland City Council [2002] EWHC 195 (Admin); [2003] QB 151; [2002] 4 All ER 156 . . . 30, 45, 136, 312

Thornton v Kirklees MBC [1979] QB 626; [1979] 2 All ER 349, CA . . . 33

Three Rivers DC v Bank of England (No 2) [1996] 2 All ER 363 . . . 71, 72

Three Rivers DC v Bank of England (Disclosure) [2004] UKHL 48; [2004] 3 WLR 1274, HL . . . 352, 353

Thynne, Wilson and Gunnell v United Kingdom (A/190) (1991) 13 EHRR 666 . . . 177, 673

Tito v Waddell [1975] 1 WLR 1303; [1975] 3 All ER 997 . . . 249

Tiverton Estates Ltd v Wearwell Ltd [1975] Ch 146; [1974] 1 All ER 209, CA . . . 97

Todd v Adam [2002] EWCA Civ 509, CA . . . 504

Tolstoy Miloslavsky v United Kingdom (A/323) (1995) 20 EHRR 442 . . . 192, 341

Transocean Marine Paint Association v Commission of the European Communities (17/74) [1974] ECR 1063 . . . 123

Trendtex Trading Corporation v Central Bank of Nigeria [1977] QB 529; [1977] 1 All ER 881, CA . . . 89, 99

Trivedi v United Kingdom [1997] EHRLR 520; (1997) App 31700/96 . . . 181, 523

Trustees of the Dennis Rye Pension Fund v Sheffield City Council [1997] 4 All ER 747, CA . . . 219

Tucker v DPP [1992] 4 All ER 901 . . . 651

Tudor Grange Holdings Ltd v Citibank NA [1992] Ch 53; [1991] 4 All ER 1 . . . 68

Turton v Turton [1988] Ch 542; [1987] 2 All ER 641, CA . . . 97

Tyrer v United Kingdom (A/26) (1979–1980) 2 EHRR 1 . . . 176

U (A Child) (Serious Injury: Standard of Proof), Re [2004] EWCA Civ 567; [2004] 3 WLR 753, [2004] 3 FLR 263 . . . 14

UCB Corporate Services Ltd (formerly UCB Bank plc) v Halifax (SW) Ltd (Striking Out: Breach of Rules and Orders) (2000) 97(1) LSG 24, CA . . . 469

Ullah v Special Ajudicator [2004] UKHL 26; [2004] 2 AC 323; [2004] 3 All ER 785, HL . . . 190

Union de Pequeños Agricultores v Council (C-50/00) [2002] All ER (EC) 893; [2002] 3 CMLR 1 . . . 140

United Kingdom v Council of the European Union (C84/94) [1996] All ER (EC) 877 . . . 116, 140

United Railways of Havana and Regla
Warehouses Ltd, Re [1961] AC 1007; [1960] 2
All ER 332, HL . . . 88, 92

V v United Kingdom [2002] All ER 1024 . . . 673

Van der Mussele v Belgium (A/70) (1984) 6
EHRR 163 . . . 176

Van Duyn v Home Office (C41/74) [1975] Ch
358; [1975] 3 All ER 190 . . . 128, 129, 130

Van Gend en Loos v Nederlandse
Belastingadministratie (26/62) [1963] ECR 1;
[1963] CMLR 105 . . . 120, 126, 128, 129, 130

Van Marle and others v Netherlands (A/101)
(1986) 8 EHRR 483 . . . 195

Van Schijndel v Stichting Pensioenfonds voor
Fysiotherapeuten (C430/93 and C431/93)
[1996] All ER (EC) 259 . . . 127

Veater v G [1981] 1 WLR 567; [1981] 2 All ER 304
. 634

Venables and Thompson v News Group
Newspapers Ltd [2001] Fam 430; [2001] 1 All
ER 908 . . . 156, 167, 175, 187, 192, 434

Vereinigte Familiapress Zeitungsverlags- und
Vertriebs GmbH v Bauer Verlag (C368/95)
[1997] ECR I-3689; [1997] 3 CMLR 1329 . . .
124, 151

Vernon v Paddon [1973] 1 WLR 663; [1973] 3 All
ER 302 . . . 627

Verrechia (t/a Freightmaster Commercials) v
Commissioner of Police of the Metropolis
[2002] EWCA Civ 605, CA . . . 489

Vestey v Inland Revenue Commissioners [1980]
AC 1148; [1979] 3 All ER 976, HL . . . 95

Vetterlein v Hampshire County Council [2001]
EWHC Admin 560; [2002] Env LR 8 . . . 186

Vince v Chief Constable of Dorset [1993] 1 WLR
415; [1993] 2 All ER 321, CA . . . 410

Viscount De L'Isle v Times Newspapers [1987] 3
All ER 499; [1988] 1 WLR 49, CA . . . 340

Von Colson v Land Nordrhein-Westfahlen (C14/
83) [1984] ECR 1891; [1986] 2 CMLR 430 . . .
132, 137

W A Sherratt Ltd v John Bromley (Church
Stretton) Ltd [1985] QB 1038; [1985] 1 All ER
216, CA . . . 97

W B Anderson & Sons Ltd v Rhodes (Liverpool)
Ltd [1967] 2 All ER 850 . . . 82

Wagner-Miret v Fondo de Garantia Salarial
(C334/92) [1993] ECR I-6911 . . . 132

Wagon Mound, The (No 1). See Overseas
Tankship (UK) Ltd v Morts Dock &
Engineering Co

Wainwright v Home Office [2003] UKHL 53;
[2004] 2 AC 406; [2003] 4 All ER 969, HL . . .
167, 187, 325, 328

Waite v United Kingdom (2003) 36 EHRR 54 . . .
178

Wakefield v Duckworth & Co [1915] 1 KB 218
. . . 368

Wall v Radford [1991] 2 All ER 741 . . . 102

Walters v WH Smith & Son Ltd [1914] 1 KB 595;
[1911–13] All ER Rep 170 . . . 407 . . . 407

Wandsworth London Borough Council v Winder
(No 1) [1985] AC 461; [1984] 3 All ER 976, HL
. . . 218

Ward v Guinness Mahon & Co Ltd [1996] 4 All
ER 112, CA . . . 497

Ward v James (No 2) [1966] 1 QB 273; [1965] 1
All ER 563, CA . . . 340, 341, 345

Ware v Fox [1967] 1 WLR 379; [1967] 1 All ER
100 . . . 627

Warner v Sampson [1959] 1 QB 297; [1959] 1 All
ER 120, CA . . . 10

Warren v Warren [1997] QB 488; [1996] 4 All ER
664, CA . . . 323

Waugh v HB Clifford & Sons Ltd [1982] Ch 374;
[1982] 1 All ER 1095, CA . . . 369

Webb v EMO Air Cargo (UK) Ltd (C32/93)
[1992] 4 All ER 929; [1993] 1 CMLR 259, HL
. . . 137, 138

Webb v EMO Air Cargo (UK) Ltd (No 2) [1995]
1 WLR 1454; [1995] 4 All ER 577, HL . . . 138

Wells, Re (1840) 3 Moo PCC 216 . . . 272

Welsh Development Agency v Redpath Dorman
Long Ltd [1994] 1 WLR 1409; [1994] 4 All ER
10, CA . . . 99

Westdeutsche Landesbank Girozentrale v
Islington LBC [1996] AC 669; [1996] 2 All ER
961, HL . . . 83, 89

Westminster City Council v National Asylum
Support Services [2002] UKHL 38; [2002] 4
All ER 654; [2002] 1 WLR 2956, HL . . . 52, 73

Wheeler v Leicester City Council [1985] AC 1054;
[1985] 2 All ER 1106, HL . . . 215

Whiston v Whiston [1995] Fam 198; [1998] 1 All
ER 423, CA . . . 50

White v Jones [1993] 3 WLR 730; [1993] 3 All ER
481, CA . . . 369

Whitehead v Haines [1965] 1 QB 200; [1964] 2
All ER 530 . . . 653

Whitehouse (Albert), Re [1951] 1 KB 673; [1951]
1 All ER 353 . . . 640

Whitehouse v Jordan [1981] 1 All ER 267, HL . . .
505

Whitley v Stumbles [1930] AC 544, HL . . . 47

Wilkinson *v* Lord Chancellors Department [2003] EWCA Civ 95; [2003] 2 All ER 184; [2003] 1 WLR 1254, CA . . . 239

Williams *v* Cowell (t/a The Stables) (No 1) [2000] 1 WLR 187; [2000] ICR 85, CA . . . 181

Williams *v* Fawcett [1986] QB 604; [1985] 1 All ER 787, CA . . . 97

Williamson v Chief Constable of West Midlands [2003] EWCA Civ 337; [2004] 1 WLR 14, CA . . . 17, 177, 180, 399

Wilson *v* First County Trust Ltd (No 2) [2001] EWCA Civ 633; [2002] QB 74; [2001] 3 All ER 229, CA (reversed [2003] UKHL 40; [2004] 1 AC 816; [2003] 4 All ER 97, HL) . . . 43, 61, 72, 73, 160, 163, 195, 196

Wingrove *v* United Kingdom (1997) 24 EHRR 1 . . . 191

Wintle *v* Nye (No 2) [1959] 1 WLR 284; [1959] 1 All ER 552, HL

Wolstanton Ltd *v* Newcastle-under-Lyme Corporation [1940] AC 860; [1940] 3 All ER 101, HL . . . 9

Wood *v* Luscombe [1966] 1 QB 169; [1964] 3 All ER 972 . . . 102

Woolmington *v* DPP [1935] AC 462, HL . . . 13, 615

Worcester Works Finance *v* Cooden Engineering Co [1972] 1 QB 210; [1971] 3 All ER 708, CA . . . 86

Wraith *v* Sheffield Forgemasters Ltd [1998] 1 WLR 132; [1998] 1 All ER 82, CA . . . 494

Wright *v* Carter [1903] 1 Ch 27, CA . . . 352

Wynne *v* United Kingdom (A/294-A) (1995) 19 EHRR 333 . . . 178

X *v* Federal Republic of Germany (1981) 25 DR 240 . . . 500

X *v* United Kingdom (1974) 1 D & R 41 . . . 188, 189

X *v* United Kingdom (1993) 15 EHRR CD 113 . . . 183

X and Church of Scientology *v* Sweden (1978) 16 D & R 68 . . . 188, 190

X and Y *v* Netherlands (A/91) (1986) 8 EHRR 235 . . . 185

X, Y and Z *v* United Kingdom (1997) 24 EHRR 143 . . . 185

X Ltd *v* Morgan Grampian (Publishers) Ltd [1991] 1 AC 1; [1990] 2 All ER 1, HL . . . 237

Yagci and Sargan *v* Turkey (A/319) (1995) 20 EHRR 505 . . . 559

Yew Bon Tew alias Yong Boon Tiew *v* Kenderaan Bas Maria [1983] 1 AC 553; [1982] 3 All ER 833, PC . . . 43, 44

Yonge *v* Toynbee [1910] 1 KB 215, CA . . . 369

Young *v* Bristol Aeroplane Co Ltd [1944] KB 718; [1944] 2 All ER 293, CA (affirmed [1946] AC 163; [1946] 1 All ER 98, HL) . . . 87, 97, 98, 99, 100, 101

Young *v* United Kingdom (A/44) (1982) 4 EHRR 38 . . . 193

Younger *v* United Kingdom (2003) App 57420/00 . . . 175

Younghusband *v* Luftig [1949] 2 KB 354; [1949] 2 All ER 72 . . . 62, 101

Z *v* Finland (1998) 25 EHRR 371 . . . 171

Z *v* United Kingdom (2002) 34 EHRR 3 . . . 176

Zabala Erasun *v* Instituto Nacional de Empleo (C422–424/93) [1995] All ER (EC) 758 . . . 144

Zaera (Gimenez) *v* Instituto Nacional de la Seguridad Social (C126/86) [1987] ECR 3697 . . . 129

Zamora, The (No 1) [1916] 2 AC 77, PC . . . 39

Zockoll Group Ltd *v* Mercury Communications Ltd (No 1) [1998] FSR 354, CA . . . 474

PART I

SOURCES OF
ENGLISH LAW

1

INTRODUCTORY ISSUES

A THE HISTORICAL CONTEXT

The current legal system of England and Wales[1] has evolved over many centuries and it has changed considerably during this time. Modern problems and needs have led to widespread changes in the court system, the organization of the legal profession, and the procedures followed by the courts. New courts have been created,[2] and a whole body of administrative justice has developed, meaning that many disputes between the state and the individual are now resolved in tribunals and inquiries rather than in the courts themselves.[3] Indeed, increasing emphasis is placed on seeking to avoid formal legal proceedings altogether, with the trend towards greater use of arbitration and mediation procedures. Alongside this, old procedures have been developed and refined to meet modern needs.

Yet to concentrate exclusively upon modern developments would be to acquire an incomplete picture, for many institutions and procedures can only be understood in the light of an awareness of their historical background. Although the modern courts may be different from their predecessors, the court system is of ancient origins and many rules of procedure owe their existence to the nature of the institutions in which they first developed. For example, the fact that the modern criminal trial is still essentially oral in nature owes much to the old forms of trial for criminal offences, particularly trial by jury. Similarly, the current procedure of judicial review derives from powers exercised by the Crown since the twelfth century,[4] while modern principles of equity were developed in the old Court of Chancery. Moreover, the substantive rules of law are not immune from historical influence: the modern laws of contract and tort, for example, can best be understood in the light of their historical origins.[5]

---

[1] Scotland and Northern Ireland are separate jurisdictions with their own courts and laws. This book deals only with England and Wales.

[2] The Crown Court, for example, was created by the Courts Act 1971, and Part 3 of the Constitutional Reform Act 2005 provides for the creation of a new Supreme Court: see pp 20 and 243, *post*.

[3] See chapter 8.   [4] See chapter 6.

[5] See, for discussion: Maitland, *The Forms of Action at Common Law* (1948).

1 THE ROLE OF THE MONARCH

Historically, the sovereign was the fountain of justice in England, and the administration of justice was, and still is, one of the prerogative powers of the Crown.[6] In theory the Monarch continues to be the formal head of the legal system, and the Crown has a residual duty to ensure that justice is done[7] and that law and order is maintained.[8] The reality is that these functions are now exercised by or on behalf of ministers, and the role of the Monarch in the modern legal system is purely a nominal one. Historically however, the Monarch's role was more direct, and the development of the common law arose through the unifying influence of those administering justice on his behalf. Specifically, it was the assumption of control over the administration of justice by the Monarch's representatives which led to local courts and jurisdictions being replaced with a centralized system.[9] The new courts that evolved as a result of this process were the King's courts, administering justice under the inherent power of the Crown. Even though the vast majority of courts now have a statutory basis, these historical origins remain important.

The role of the Monarch in ensuring that justice is done was historically performed through the issue of writs, which were essentially royal commands. In addition to being the basis of the common law causes of action in contract and tort,[10] prerogative writs continue to form the basis for the most important remedies for controlling the misuse of executive power.[11]

2 THE EVOLUTION OF COMMON LAW AND EQUITY

Common law and equity are two of the main historical sources of English law, the third being legislation. The term 'common law' reflects the fact that the law administered by the King's courts became the common law of England and Wales, gradually supplanting the mass of local custom that previously existed. The King's legal functions were originally performed by the King's Council and by the justices who travelled the country on his behalf. The jurisdiction of the King's Council gave rise to the emergence of the old common law courts of Exchequer, Common Pleas, and King's Bench, which continued to operate until they were abolished by the Judicature Acts 1873–75.[12]

As the common law grew more rigid, principally through the writ system, those who felt that they had suffered injustice as a result would petition the King to exercise

---

[6] This is discussed further in chapter 6.

[7] Consider, for example, the prerogative of mercy, discussed at p 208, *post*.

[8] For a modern example, see *R v Secretary of State for the Home Department, ex parte Northumbria Police Authority* [1989] QB 26, [1988] 1 All ER 556.

[9] See, generally: Baker, *An Introduction to English Legal History* (4th edn, 2002). Certain local courts survived formally until 1973, when they were abolished by the Courts Act 1971, s 43.

[10] See: Milsom, *Historical Foundations of the Common Law* (2nd edn, 1981).

[11] See the discussion of judicial review in chapter 6.

[12] For the main courts prior to 1875, see pp 222–6, *post*.

his prerogative in their favour. These petitions were initially dealt with by the King in Council, but were later delegated to the King's chief minister, the Chancellor. Eventually the system became formalized, culminating in the development of rules of equity and the creation of the Court of Chancery. Equity then, evolved as a mechanism for remedying the deficiencies of the common law, and the Court of Chancery continued to be the principal forum for administering equity until its abolition in 1875.[13]

B THE PRINCIPAL SOURCES OF LAW

1 LEGISLATION

The emergence of Parliament as the dominant force within the United Kingdom constitution[14] led to the growth of legislation as a major source of law, transcending both common law and equity in its importance. Its role today is unquestioned. Common law and equity are nowadays concerned essentially with the application and development of existing principles, and whilst this does involve the making of law,[15] courts generally take the view that the development of entirely new principles should be left to Parliament.[16] Legislation can also change or abolish existing common law principles, and amend or repeal earlier statutes.

The nature, creation, and interpretation of legislation are the subject of detailed consideration in chapter 2 of this book.

2 COMMON LAW

Despite the significance of legislation in modern times, common law is still one of the most important sources of legal rules, and its application through the doctrine of judicial precedent is the subject of detailed consideration in chapter 3.

The basic principle underpinning the early development of the common law was that a right only existed if there was a procedure for enforcing it (*ubi remedium ibi ius*), and for this reason substantive law became inextricably bound up with procedure. The nature of the disputed right and the procedure through which it could be enforced determined which court dealt with the matter. Common law claims became highly technical, with the nature of the form of action often determining the content of the law and whether a particular claim could succeed. This rigid 'writ system' was

---

[13] Principles of equity are now administered and applied by all courts.

[14] Through the development of the doctrine of the legislative supremacy of Parliament. Under this, no court can question the validity of an Act of Parliament: see *British Railways Board* v *Pickin* [1974] AC 765, [1974] 1 All ER 609.

[15] See further, p 78, *post*.

[16] See *Malone* v *Metropolitan Police Commissioner (No 2)* [1979] Ch 344, [1979] 2 All ER 620, and p 325, *post*. See also *McLoughlin* v *O'Brian* [1983] 1 AC 410, [1982] 2 All ER 298.

effectively abolished by the Common Law Procedure Acts 1852 and 1854, resulting in the categorization of claims becoming far less important. The law now strives to concentrate upon substance rather than form. However, the dangers that rigid procedural distinctions can create have not totally disappeared. As recently as 1991, Henry J in *Doyle* v *Northumbria Probation Committees*[17] observed that the procedural requirements then involved in any challenge to a public body meant that:

[T]he forms of action abolished by the Common Law Procedure Act 1854 in the 19th Century appear to be in danger of returning to rule us from their graves.

The extent to which the modern law of judicial review has avoided this danger is considered in chapter 6.

In criminal matters the common law developed the forms of trial which, in nature if not in detail, still exist today. Ancient procedures such as trial by battle may have disappeared,[18] but trial on indictment involving trial by jury[19] is of ancient origin, and was undertaken in the old courts of Assize.[20] In addition, the criminal law was also enforced summarily through trial by justices of the peace without a jury. Though procedures are much changed, these forms of trial are distinctly recognizable to modern eyes.

3 EQUITY

Equity developed primarily to correct deficiencies in the common law, and this inevitably meant that the two systems were frequently in conflict. Although the conflict was ultimately resolved in favour of equity,[21] the existence of two systems of law and two sets of courts, each with their own procedures, remedies, and routes of appeal, continued to cause problems of jurisdiction. The Judicature Acts 1873–75 were intended to bring about fundamental reform, and their immediate effect was to create a unified system of courts and procedure. The Acts did not merge the substantive rules and it is still correct to talk about 'principles of equity' or 'equitable remedies', but the unification of the courts did lead to considerable fusion between the two sets of rules. Courts can now apply both rules of common law and equity, irrespective of their origins, and it is often unclear to which of the two historical systems a rule owes its parentage. The effect of equity upon substantive law is therefore beyond doubt, particularly in relation to matters affecting property and trusts, the law of contract, and important remedies like the injunction.

4 THE EUROPEAN UNION

While the traditional sources of English law continue to be important, two European sources have become increasingly significant. One of these is the European Union.

---

[17] [1991] 4 All ER 294, [1991] 1 WLR 1340.

[18] Trial by battle was not formally abolished until the decision in *Ashford* v *Thornton* (1818) 1 B & Ald 405 reminded Parliament that it still theoretically existed.

[19] See pp 329, 564, *post*.   [20] See p 256, *post*.   [21] *Earl of Oxford's case* (1615) 1 Rep Ch 1.

The Union was founded in 1992 upon the European Community,[22] a supra-national body with its own legal personality, institutions, and the capacity to make and enforce laws. The United Kingdom joined the European Community in 1972, and by virtue of the European Communities Act of the same year, Community laws were integrated into the English legal system. European Community law should therefore be regarded as a direct source of English law, and its importance is sufficient to warrant separate and more detailed treatment in chapter 4.

5 EUROPEAN CONVENTION ON HUMAN RIGHTS

The United Kingdom was one of the first signatories to the Convention for the Protection of Human Rights and Fundamental Freedoms in 1950.[23] This Convention, usually referred to as the European Convention on Human Rights (or ECHR), is a treaty of the Council of Europe, and unlike the law of the European Community it has never been incorporated directly into domestic law. While its principles have influenced the interpretation of statutes, the development of the common law, and decisions about the content of legislation, until recently its provisions could only be enforced by the European Court of Human Rights in Strasbourg. The position has now changed significantly as a result of the Human Rights Act 1998. This major piece of legislation obliges public authorities to act compatibly with Convention rights,[24] and in the event of a breach of those rights, it enables victims to seek a direct remedy in the domestic courts.[25] It also requires courts to interpret legislation in a manner compatible with Convention rights as far as it is possible to do so,[26] though it stops short of allowing the courts to disapply Acts of Parliament which cannot be interpreted in this way. Both the Human Rights Act and the Convention itself are the subject of more detailed discussion in chapter 5.

6 OTHER SOURCES

The following historical categories of law have now lost much of their original importance, and for this reason their content is not elaborated in detail in this book. They are not entirely without relevance however, and their wider contribution to the development of the common law does merit some consideration.

(a) Custom

Though custom is no longer an important source of law in its own right, much of the early common law developed through the application by the courts of existing English customs. Thus customs such as monogamy, parental rights, the right to use the

---

[22] Before the creation of the Union, this was known as the European Communities (plural), but the singular term 'Community' was adopted by the Maastricht Treaty in 1992.

[23] The Convention came into effect in 1953.

[24] Section 6.   [25] Section 7.   [26] Section 3; see p 157, post.

seashore for navigation and fishing,[27] and most of the early principles of criminal law,
have either become part of the common law or have been incorporated in statute.

The word 'custom' may also be used in a more specific sense, to describe conventional trade or business usage. This is really a misuse of the word however, since
trade usage is usually relevant only to imply terms into contracts, and whether such
terms can be implied in a particular case is a question of fact rather than law. Trade
customs need not be ancient[28] provided that they can be proved to be certain. However, they must not be illegal or unreasonable and they may always be expressly
excluded. Many trade customs were originally an elaborate method of granting
discounts to purchasers; hence the 'baker's dozen' and the fact that 1,000 rabbits
means 1,200 rabbits to rabbit-dealers.[29]

Another common use of the word 'custom' is to describe local custom; rules of law
which apply only in a definite locality. This type of custom *is* a separate source of law,
and it has two elementary and unvarying characteristics. First, it must be an exception
to the common law, and second, it must be confined in its application to a particular
locality or a class of persons within a locality, such as fishermen. Examples of the type
of local customary right still existing include rights of way, rights to indulge in sports
and pastimes on a village green,[30] and rights to dry fishing-nets on land within a
parish.[31]

Local customary rights only exist in law when recognized by judicial decision and
this means satisfying certain tests.[32] Firstly, the custom must have existed 'from time
whereof the memory of man runneth not to the contrary' (time immemorial) and
this has been fixed by statute at 1189.[33] In practice proof of existence in 1189 is rarely
available, and the courts are usually satisfied by evidence that the custom has existed
for a long time. It must have existed uninterrupted however, and any interruption of
the custom since 1189 defeats its existence. In addition, a custom can only exist by
common consent. This means that it must not have been exercised by the use of force,
nor secretly, nor under a revocable licence. Thus, where the right to fish depended
upon the grant of a licence by the owners of an oyster fishery, it was held that there
was no custom since enjoyment had never been as of right.[34] Other requirements are
that the custom is certain, that it is consistent with other local customs, and that any
duty imposed by the custom is obligatory. Finally, the most important test is that of
reasonableness. A custom that is repugnant to the common law cannot be reasonable,
and for this reason the House of Lords in one case rejected a custom which enabled a

---

[27] Though not for bathing or beachcombing; see *Alfred F Beckett Ltd v Lyons* [1967] Ch 449, [1967] 1 All
ER 833. For a modern example of reliance on customary fishing rights, see *Anderson v Alnwick District
Council* [1993] 3 All ER 613, [1993] 1 WLR 1156.

[28] See *Noble v Kennoway* (1780) 2 Doug KB 510 at 513, per Lord Mansfield.

[29] *Smith v Wilson* (1832) 3 B & Ad 728.

[30] *New Windsor Corporation v Mellor* [1975] Ch 380, [1975] 3 All ER 44.

[31] *Mercer v Denne* [1905] 2 Ch 538.

[32] These tests owe their origins to the work of Blackstone.   [33] Statute of Westminster I 1275.

[34] *Mills v Colchester Corporation* (1867) LR 2 CP 476; see also *Alfred F Beckett Ltd v Lyons* [1967] Ch 449,
[1967] 1 All ER 833.

lord to undermine his tenant's land without compensating him for the resulting damage.[35]

(b) Canon law

Canon law, which is the law of the Western or Catholic Church, has influenced the growth of English law in two ways. First, it was the basis of many concepts formulated in the law courts, and as such it is an original source of other, more modern sources. Examples include the nature of criminal law and its close association with moral fault, the use of imprisonment as a punishment for crime, and, of course, the nature of Christian marriage and family rights. Canon law also influenced the nature of equity, the strong moral content of which is attributable to the fact that the early Chancellors were clerics.

The second way in which canon law became a source of English law was by its application in the ecclesiastical courts. In this context it was a system of law wholly independent of the common law, and during the Middle Ages the ecclesiastical courts were completely outside the control of the King. Their jurisdiction remained separate from the common law except in the areas of probate and matrimonial jurisdiction, but since 1857 it has been confined to matters affecting members of the Church.[36]

(c) Roman law[37]

Roman law, the basis of most continental legal systems, is of surprisingly little importance as a source of English law. There was never a system of English courts applying solely Roman law and any influence that it did have was therefore indirect. The principal link between Roman law and common law is Bracton's treatise *De Legibus et Consuetudinibus Angliae*, written around 1250. Bracton was well versed in Roman law, and the civilian principles incorporated into his treatise owed much to the writings of the Roman jurist Justinian. Common law judges faced with a case of first impression have occasionally looked to Bracton for assistance, and in doing so have adopted Romanist principles. The leading example is the judgment of Holt CJ in *Coggs* v *Bernard*,[38] which classifies bailments according to Bracton's system.

(d) Textbooks

Unlike statutes and law reports, which are original literary sources of law, textbooks are merely a secondary source. Even the most highly regarded modern textbooks have little or no value as a source of law, since direct authority for a legal rule can almost always be found in a law report or Act of Parliament. However, in the infancy of law reporting textbooks were (and still are) the main source of authority for most common law rules. Indeed, during this period the line between a law report and a

---

[35] *Wolstanton Ltd and Duchy of Lancaster* v *Newcastle-under-Lyme Corporation* [1940] AC 860, [1940] 3 All ER 101.

[36] See p 276, *post.*   [37] See Lee, *Elements of Roman Law* (4th edn, 1986).

[38] (1703) 2 Ld Raym 909.

textbook opinion was often quite a narrow one, and Coke's *Institutes* (Inst) are generally accorded as much authority as his Reports. It will thus be apparent that there are two types of legal textbook. The first is the ancient textbook or 'book of authority', which is commonly used as an original source of common law. The second type is the modern textbook, which is not a source of law at all. The main functions of a modern textbook are to indicate where direct sources of law may be found and to provide an analysis of them. The dividing line between books of authority and modern textbooks is purely historical and depends on the availability of direct literary sources. Blackstone's *Commentaries on the Laws of England* is probably the watershed, in that although it is a book of authority, it was also the forerunner of the modern textbook.

Books of authority. Of the many works produced as legal textbooks only about a dozen are accepted as books of authority, and it is no accident that almost all the authors of these works were judges. The academic lawyer in the modern sense did not appear until Blackstone in the eighteenth century, and Blackstone himself was also a judge.

Glanvill's treatise *De Legibus et Consuetudinibus Angliae* (concerning the laws and customs of England) was written in Latin in about 1187. It deals mainly with the subject of land law and is the first major commentary on the common law in existence. It is still cited as a book of authority,[39] though not as frequently as the larger and more comprehensive treatise of Bracton. The latter treatise, dating from around 1250, was also written in Latin and entitled *De Legibus et Consuetudinibus Angliae*. It draws many Roman law analogies and virtually all the principles of Roman law which have found their way into English law have done so via Bracton. The development of the law of easements, for example, owes much to his exposition of Roman law.[40] Nevertheless, he was primarily a chronicler of common law and his treatise stands as the major academic work on this subject prior to Coke's *Institutes*.

Littleton's *Of Tenures* was published in the late fifteenth century, and it was the first comprehensive study of English land law. It appears that the work was intended for use as a textbook and it was in fact used for this purpose for centuries after its composition. It is also notable as being the first major legal work to be printed rather than written. It was described by Coke as 'the most perfect and absolute work that ever was written in any human science'. Coke himself was probably the greatest of the early textbook writers, and his four *Institutes of the Laws of England* are, alongside his law reports, his great contribution to academic literature. The first Institute was published in 1628 and is a treatise on Littleton's *Of Tenures*. The second is a summary of the principal medieval statutes. The third is concerned with criminal law, and the fourth deals with the jurisdiction of the courts. The reason for the exalted position of

---

[39] *Ashford* v *Thornton* (1818) 1 B & Ald 405; *Warner* v *Sampson* [1959] 1 QB 297, [1959] 1 All ER 120.

[40] *Dalton* v *Angus* (1881) 6 App Cas 740. See also *Coggs* v *Bernard* (1703) 2 Ld Raym 909, in which Holt CJ developed the law of bailments in accordance with Roman law concepts gleaned from Bracton.

the *Institutes* is Coke's mastery of the Year Books,[41] which has probably never been equalled. For this reason the Year Books are cited comparatively infrequently, while the Institutes have probably been cited to English courts more frequently than any other book of authority. In 1973, for example, the Court of Appeal in *Reid* v *Metropolitan Police Commissioner* looked to Coke for assistance in interpreting the words 'market overt' in section 22(1) of the Sale of Goods Act 1893:[42]

to solve this question we have to go back to the works of Sir Edward Coke. In 1596 there was an important case about market overt;[43] Coke reported it. He afterwards expounded the law of market overt in his Institutes.[44] I think we should follow the words of Sir Edward Coke rather than those of Sir William Blackstone.

The words that the Court of Appeal followed stated that 'the sale must not be in the night, but between the rising of the sun, and the going downe of the same'. The result was that a purchaser who bought goods an hour before sunrise at the New Caledonian Market was held not to have acquired a good title to them.

After Coke a large number of legal textbooks were produced. A few, such as those of Hawkins, Hale, and Foster are regarded as being particularly authoritative in the area of criminal law. In *Joyce* v *DPP*[45] for example, the House of Lords relied almost entirely on the work of Foster, Hale, Hawkins, East, and Coke, in deciding that a foreigner who enjoyed the protection of the Crown could be guilty of treason under the Treason Act 1351. More recently, in defining the common law offence of affray in the House of Lords, Lord Gardiner LC referred to Fitzherbert, Coke, Hale, Hawkins, and Blackstone.[46]

Blackstone's *Commentaries on the Laws of England*, published in 1765, deal with constitutional law, family law, the law of property, succession, contract, tort, criminal law, and civil and criminal procedure. It is, however, in the fields of tort and criminal law that Blackstone's authority is greatest. The *Commentaries* were probably the last work of authority to be written, and in the event of an inconsistency with earlier works, the older authorities are almost bound to prevail. This is well illustrated by the case of *Button* v *DPP*,[47] in which Blackstone's assertion that a common law affray could occur only in a public place[48] was rejected by the House of Lords as inconsistent with earlier statements of Hale and Hawkins.

Modern textbooks. The growth of law reporting since Blackstone's era has made it unnecessary to look at more recent textbooks as a direct source of common law rules. Nineteenth-century works such as Stephen's *Commentaries on the Laws of England* are sometimes consulted, but only as guides rather than sources.

There are nevertheless many standard textbooks which have considerable persuasive

---

[41] These are discussed further at p 103, *post*.
[42] [1973] QB 551 at 559, [1973] 2 All ER 97 at 99, per Lord Denning MR.
[43] *Market-Overt case* (1596) 5 Co Rep 83b.   [44] (1642) vol 2, pp 713–14.
[45] [1946] AC 347, [1946] 1 All ER 186.   [46] *Button* v *DPP* [1966] AC 591, [1965] 3 All ER 587.
[47] Ibid.   [48] 4 Comm 145.

authority. Virtually every branch of the law has its standard work and a judge will think twice before dismissing a statement of law appearing in such a work. However, in the event of a textbook being inconsistent with a principle contained in a precedent or a statute, the latter will always prevail. For example, in *Button v DPP*[49] the House of Lords drew attention to errors in *Archbold's Pleadings, Evidence & Practice in Criminal Cases* and *Russell on Crimes and Misdemeanours*; both standard works on the criminal law. Similarly, in *Shenton v Tyler*[50] the Master of the Rolls referred to a dozen textbooks on evidence before deciding that they were all mistaken as to the scope of marital privilege. These are exceptional occurrences however, and on the whole, the persuasive authority of a standard textbook is of considerable weight. There have been several cases in which a court has been willing to accept the view of a distinguished academic upon the law. Thus the Court of Appeal in *Re Ellenborough Park*[51] adopted the description of easements contained in Cheshire's *Modern Real Property*, while the House of Lords in *A-G v De Keyser's Royal Hotel Ltd*[52] expressly accepted Dicey's definition of the royal prerogative. To take this a step further, counsel for the respondents in *Rookes v Barnard*[53] suggested that the tort of intimidation had actually been created by Sir John Salmond in his work on the law of torts.

There used to be a rule of practice that a textbook could not be cited in court during the lifetime of its author, but this is no longer the case and several legal authors have had the satisfaction of seeing their opinions judicially endorsed during their lifetimes.[54] In *R v Shivpuri*, in which the House of Lords overruled one of its previous decisions in the face of considerable academic criticism, Lord Bridge (who had also been party to the earlier decision) ended his speech with the following tribute:[55]

I cannot conclude this opinion without disclosing that I have had the advantage, since the conclusion of the argument in this appeal, of reading an article by Professor Glanville Williams entitled 'The Lords and Impossible Attempts, or *Quis Custodet Ipsos Custodies?*' [1986] CLJ 33. The language in which he criticises the decision in *Anderton v Ryan* is not conspicuous for its moderation, but it would be foolish, on that account, not to recognise the force of the criticism and churlish not to acknowledge the assistance I have derived from it.

In a recent Court of Appeal decision concerned with grazing rights,[56] counsel cited at least fourteen different textbooks spanning a period of more than three centuries. As there had not been a single reliably reported case in which the particular issue had

---

[49] [1966] AC 591, [1965] 3 All ER 587.   [50] [1939] Ch 620, [1939] 1 All ER 827.
[51] [1956] Ch 131, [1955] 3 All ER 667.   [52] [1920] AC 508.
[53] [1964] AC 1129, [1964] 1 All ER 367.
[54] See, e.g., *Read v J Lyons & Co Ltd* [1945] KB 216, [1945] 1 All ER 106 (affirmed [1947] AC 156, [1946] 2 All ER 471); *DPP v Humphrys* [1977] AC 1, [1976] 2 All ER 497.
[55] [1987] AC 1 at 23, [1986] 2 All ER 334 at 345.
[56] *Bettison v Langton* [2000] Ch 54, [1999] 2 All ER 367 (affirmed [2001] UKHL 24, [2002] 1 AC 27, [2001] 3 All ER 417). See also *A v Secretary of State for the Home Department* [2004] UKHL 56, [2005] 2 WLR 87, in which Lord Walker relied heavily on academic literature in his discussion of the UK's anti-terror laws.

formed part of the ratio, Robert Walker LJ clearly found these works helpful. After reviewing the various authorities, he stated:[57]

In this case, [counsel for the plaintiffs] relies on textbook authority, not for an analysis of apparently conflicting decisions, but to make good a want of any clear decision. In those circumstances, and in such a technical area of the law of real property, textbooks may provide the court with valuable assistance.

He went on to conclude that:[58]

[T]he preponderance of authority—both in reported cases and in classic textbooks—appears to me . . . to support the [plaintiff's case]. In my judgment the cumulative effect of this authority, even if it is not strictly binding, is so powerful that it should be followed.

C THE DISTINCTION BETWEEN CIVIL AND CRIMINAL MATTERS

1 THE IMPORTANCE OF THE DISTINCTION

The law distinguishes between civil and criminal matters, and courts are sometimes classified into civil and criminal courts. This latter classification is useful for the purposes of exposition, but in reality it is not a valid one. Although certain courts do exercise a purely civil or criminal jurisdiction, most, including the House of Lords, Court of Appeal, High Court, Crown Court, and magistrates' courts, exercise jurisdiction in both civil and criminal matters.

This distinction between civil and criminal matters is important for several reasons. First, the terminology used is different. In civil proceedings a claimant (formerly called a plaintiff) sues a defendant or makes an application for a civil order, while in a criminal case a prosecutor prosecutes the accused.

Secondly, the burden and standard of proof differ. In a civil case the party asserting a particular matter bears the burden of proving it, usually to the civil standard of the balance of probabilities.[59] In contrast, the burden of proof in a criminal case normally rests with the prosecution,[60] and the standard is that of proof beyond reasonable doubt.[61] However, this statement disguises the fact that even in a civil case the standard

---

[57] [2000] Ch 54 at 64, [1999] 2 All ER 367 at 375.

[58] [2000] Ch 54 at 72, [1999] 2 All ER 367 at 382.

[59] The standard is not an absolute one: see *Hornal* v *Neuberger Products Ltd* [1957] 1 QB 247, [1956] 3 All ER 970; *R* v *Secretary of State for the Home Department, ex parte Khawaja* [1984] AC 74, [1983] 1 All ER 765.

[60] See *Woolmington* v *DPP* [1935] AC 462. For exceptions, see *Bratty* v *Attorney-General for Northern Ireland* [1963] AC 386, [1961] 3 All ER 523 (the defence of insanity); Magistrates' Courts Act 1980, s 101; and other specific statutory exceptions.

[61] For the meaning of this phrase, see *Miller* v *Minister of Pensions* [1947] 2 All ER 372, per Lord Denning. In a case where the burden of proof is on an accused the standard is the civil standard of the balance of probabilities: *R* v *Carr-Briant* [1943] KB 607, [1943] 2 All ER 156.

of proof may be high. In *R v Wolverhampton Coroner, ex parte McCurbin*,[62] an inquest (a civil inquiry into the cause of death by a coroners' court)[63] had to decide whether the death of an individual whilst being arrested amounted to an unlawful killing or death by misadventure. The Divisional Court upheld the coroner's view that the standard of proof needed to establish unlawful killing was the criminal standard, whilst that for establishing death by misadventure was the balance of probabilities. Findings of suicide in coroners' courts have also been held to require proof beyond reasonable doubt.[64] Similarly, in *Halford v Brookes*,[65] a civil case in which the defendant was effectively accused of murder, Rougier J observed:

No-one, whether in a criminal or a civil court, should be declared guilty of murder, certainly not such a terrible crime as this, unless the tribunal was sure that the evidence does not admit of any other sensible conclusion

More recently, in civil proceedings to obtain anti-social behaviour orders,[66] sex offender orders[67] and football banning orders,[68] it has been held that the standard of proof required for such purposes is indistinguishable from the criminal standard.

What is common to all of these situations is that they involve allegations of criminal or quasi-criminal conduct, even though they are challenged through civil proceedings.[69] It is this factor which is said to necessitate a more exacting standard of proof. Whether there are in fact two standards, or simply different levels of proof which vary according to what has to be determined, is a moot point. In *R (on the application of N) v M*[70] the Court of Appeal had to determine the standard to be applied when ordering that a person detained under the Mental Health Act 1983 could be treated without his consent. A European Court of Human Rights case[71] was cited, in which it had been said that proof of necessity must be 'convincingly shown', but the Court of Appeal maintained that this did not amount to using the criminal standard:[72]

[The defendant] submits that the test is, in effect, the same as the criminal standard of proof. We disagree. It seems to us that no useful purpose is served by importing the language of the

---

[62] [1990] 1 WLR 719, [1990] 2 All ER 759.　　　[63] See p 266, *post*.

[64] *R v West London Coroner, ex parte Gray* [1988] QB 467, [1987] 2 All ER 129. Cf. *Dunbar (administrator of Dunbar, dec'd) v Plant* [1998] Ch 412, [1997] 4 All ER 289, where in civil proceedings it was held that the standard of proof for establishing that a party had aided and abetted a suicide was the civil standard.

[65] (1991) *The Times* 3 October.

[66] *R (on the application of McCann) v Manchester Crown Court and others* [2002] UKHL 39, [2003] 1 AC 787, [2002] 4 All ER 593.

[67] *B v Chief Constable of Avon and Somerset* [2001] 1 All ER 562, [2001] 1 WLR 340.

[68] *Gough v Chief Constable of Derbyshire* [2002] EWCA Civ 351, [2002] QB 1213, [2002] 2 All ER 985.

[69] Different considerations apply where allegations of serious criminal conduct are made in the context of a care proceedings application. The welfare of the child is the paramount consideration in such a case, and the standard of proof is therefore the balance of probabilities: *Re U (A Child) (Serious Injury: Standard of Proof)* [2004] EWCA Civ 567, [2004] 3 WLR 753, [2004] 3 FLR 263.

[70] [2002] EWCA Civ 1789, [2003] 1 WLR 562, [2003] 1 FLR 667.

[71] *Herczegfalvy v Austria* (1993) EHRR 437.

[72] [2002] EWCA Civ 1789 at [18], [2003] 1 WLR 562 at [18], per Dyson LJ.

criminal law. The phrase 'convincingly shown' is easily understood. The standard is a high one. But it does not need elaboration or further explanation.

This case should, however, be compared with the recent decision in *R (on the application of McCann)* v *Manchester Crown Court,* which concerned the making of anti-social behaviour orders.[73] The House of Lords considered it impractical to leave individual magistrates to determine precisely what was required by a 'heightened civil standard' of proof: in the interests of pragmatism Lord Steyn concluded that the standard in all such cases should be the criminal one.[74]

The categorization of a matter as civil or criminal is not only relevant to the burden of proof; it also determines which rules of evidence apply to the case. The rules of evidence followed in civil proceedings often differ from those applicable in criminal cases. This was well illustrated in *R* v *Governor of Brixton Prison, ex parte Levin*[75] where the House of Lords held that because extradition proceedings were to be treated as criminal proceedings, they were subject to rules in the Police and Criminal Evidence Act 1984. Similarly, the finding in *R (on the application of McCann)* v *Manchester Crown Court*[76] that proceedings to obtain an anti-social behaviour order were civil in nature, meant that the court could accept hearsay evidence as to the conduct alleged. This would not have been the case if the same allegations had been made in criminal proceedings, though it should be noted that the Criminal Justice Act 2003 now provides for hearsay evidence to be more widely admissible in criminal cases.[77]

Finally, the fact that proceedings are criminal or are to be regarded as such, will affect the procedures to be followed and the standards that those procedures have to meet. Article 6 of the European Convention on Human Rights[78] specifies a number of minimum rights for the protection of those 'charged with a criminal offence'. It also requires such charges to be subject to a presumption of innocence. These rights have assumed added importance since the coming into force of the Human Rights Act 1998, as courts and public authorities are now obliged by domestic law to discharge their functions in a manner compatible with Convention rights.

2 DECISION AS TO WHETHER A MATTER IS CIVIL OR CRIMINAL

This decision is not always easy to make, and it cannot be made simply by asking whether the court that deals with the matter is a civil or a criminal court. An example of a case in which a court had to determine such a question is *ex parte Levin.*[79] The House of Lords had to decide whether extradition proceedings before a magistrates' court were civil or criminal in nature, since this was crucial to determining which rules of evidence applied. In an earlier case[80] a Divisional Court had apparently

---

[73] [2002] UKHL 39, [2003] 1 AC 787, [2002] 4 All ER 593.   [74] Ibid at [18].

[75] [1997] AC 741, [1997] 3 All ER 289.

[76] [2002] UKHL 39, [2003] 1 AC 787, [2002] 4 All ER 593.

[77] See Part 11 of the Act.   [78] See p 180, *post.*   [79] [1997] AC 741, [1997] 3 All ER 289.

[80] *R* v *Governor of Belmarsh Prison, ex parte Francis* [1995] 3 All ER 634, [1995] 1 WLR 1121.

concluded that such proceedings were not criminal, and the court noted counsel's argument that they were *sui generis* (i.e. a type of their own). Lord Hoffmann, giving the decision of the House, disagreed with this view, pointing to a contrary body of authority[81] and a statutory requirement to conduct extradition proceedings 'as near as may be' as if they were committal proceedings before magistrates.[82]

The difficulty facing the court in *Levin* is far from unique, and it is increasingly possible to identify areas where the boundary between criminal and civil proceedings has become blurred. For example, the same acts or omissions may give rise to both civil and criminal proceedings. Thus, while a motorist who causes damage, injury or loss of life may well be prosecuted for a motoring offence, that same motorist will almost certainly be liable in damages if sued by the aggrieved party. The relatives of a person who has been unlawfully killed, but in respect of whose death no prosecution has been brought, may sue in tort; ostensibly for compensation, but in reality to provide a forum in which the culpability of the defendant can be established. Similarly, if a rape victim sues his[83] or her assailant, the assailant is liable irrespective of whether he has been successfully prosecuted. Another example is contempt of court, which can be both civil and criminal in nature.[84]

The growing tendency for formal links to be made between civil and criminal procedures is perhaps of greater significance. The Protection from Harassment Act 1997 for example, makes it a criminal offence to pursue a course of conduct amounting to harassment of a person, or which causes a person to fear that violence will be used against him. However, section 3 creates a civil remedy in tort for a person who is (or may be) the victim of harassment. Similarly, a criminal court may make a restraining order when sentencing a person for an offence, or, under the Domestic Violence, Crime and Victims Act 2004, even after acquittal. While this is a civil order, a breach without reasonable excuse will constitute a criminal offence.

Other examples are to be found in the Crime and Disorder Act 1998[85] and the Sexual Offences Act 2003,[86] which permit magistrates' courts to make anti-social behaviour orders (ASBOs) and sexual offences prevention orders respectively. These are civil orders made in civil proceedings, yet non-compliance with such an order without lawful excuse amounts to a criminal offence triable before a magistrates' court. The Proceeds of Crime Act 2002 may also be considered. This establishes an Assets Recovery Agency with the power to instigate civil proceedings to recover property obtained by criminal conduct. It even allows any income generated by such conduct to be taxed. The exercise of these powers clearly involves proof of criminal activity, but as the proceedings are civil the standard is that of the balance of probabilities.

---

[81] *Amand* v *Secretary of State for Home Affairs* [1943] AC 147, [1942] 2 All ER 381, where Viscount Simon LC said that a matter may be 'criminal' even though a person is not charged with a breach of the criminal law.

[82] Extradition Act 1989, s 9(2) and Schedule 1, para 6(1).

[83] The offence of rape extends to male victims: Sexual Offences Act 2003, s 1.

[84] See p 236, *post*.

[85] Section 1, as amended by the Police Reform Act 2002 and the Anti-social Behaviour Act 2003.

[86] Section 104; this replaces the sex offender order provisions in the Crime and Disorder Act 1998, s 2.

The control order powers in the Prevention of Terrorism Act 2005 provide another interesting example. These powers may be used to impose unprecedented restrictions on individual liberties. Yet a court can confirm even the most serious orders if it is satisfied 'on the balance of probabilities' that the controlled person is or has been involved in terrorist-related activities.[87] Contravention of a control order 'without reasonable excuse' is a criminal offence punishable by imprisonment for up to five years.[88]

(a) The impact of the Human Rights Act 1998

As already noted, one consequence of the Human Rights Act 1998 is that courts and public authorities must now comply with the European Convention on Human Rights. Article 6 of this Convention concerns the right to a fair trial, and it contains a number of safeguards which apply specifically to those charged with criminal offences. Thus while the boundary between civil and criminal law is now becoming increasingly blurred, the ability to make the distinction is perhaps more important than ever.

The European Court of Human Rights has previously confirmed that the term 'criminal' has an autonomous meaning for these purposes. This means that while a State's classification of a matter as civil or criminal is undoubtedly important, it cannot be conclusive: the content of what is alleged and the nature of any penalty must also be taken into account.[89] It has previously been established that proceedings for non-payment of council tax are 'criminal' for the purposes of the Convention,[90] as are proceedings for binding over to keep the peace.[91] In contrast, the House of Lords recently used the Convention test to determine that anti-social behaviour orders (or ASBOs) are not criminal in nature.[92] Crucial to this decision was the finding that there was no 'penalty' involved in the making of such an order: the House observed that there appeared to be no case in which the European Court of Human Rights had classified proceedings as 'criminal' in the absence of a penalty. It also noted that an ASBO cannot be entered as a conviction on a defendant's record.[93] The decision has been criticised for attaching insufficient weight to the fact that in common with most criminal sanctions, the purpose of an ASBO is to prevent behaviour

---

[87] Section 4(7) of the 2005 Act; for further discussion, see p 179, *post*.

[88] Ibid, s 9; it is also punishable by a fine.

[89] *Engel* v *The Netherlands (No 1)* (1979–1980) 1 EHRR 647 at [678]–[679].

[90] *Benham* v *United Kingdom* (1996) 22 EHRR 293.

[91] See *Steel* v *United Kingdom* (1999) 28 EHRR 603. Cf. *Williamson* v *Chief Constable of West Midlands* [2003] EWCA Civ 337, [2004] 1 WLR 14, in which the Court of Appeal held that breach of the peace is not 'an offence' for the purposes of the Police and Criminal Evidence Act 1984. The court pointed out that since the term 'criminal offence' has an autonomous meaning within Convention jurisprudence, it is not essential for breach of the peace to be categorized as an offence in domestic law. On this view, what matters is not the classification of an act but whether any Convention rights are violated as a consequence of that classification.

[92] *R (on the application of McCann)* v *Manchester Crown Court and others* [2002] UKHL 39, [2003] 1 AC 787, [2002] 4 All ER 593.

[93] See the Rehabilitation of Offenders Act 1974, s 1.

detrimental to the public interest. Moreover, such orders arguably *do* have both a punitive and a deterrent element.[94] Nevertheless, the House of Lords has since applied a similar approach[95] to proceedings under section 4A of the Criminal Procedure (Insanity Act) 1964. A boy charged with indecent assault was declared incompetent to stand trial, and in the section 4A proceedings that followed, a second jury found that he had committed 'the act' in question. He was therefore required to register as a sex offender.[96] The House of Lords concluded that there was no incompatibility with Article 6 of the Convention, since the section 4A procedure did not involve the 'determination of a criminal charge' and therefore did not violate the presumption of innocence. Lord Bingham delivered the judgment for a unanimous House:[97]

Whether one views the matter through domestic or European spectacles, the answer is the same: the purpose and function of the s 4A procedure is not to decide whether the accused person has committed a criminal offence. The procedure can result in a final acquittal, but it cannot result in a conviction and it cannot result in punishment. Even an adverse finding may lead, as here, to an absolute discharge ... It is, indeed, difficult if not impossible to conceive of a criminal proceeding which cannot in any circumstances culminate in the imposition of any penalty, since it is the purpose of the criminal law to proscribe, and by punishing to deter, conduct regarded as sufficiently damaging to the interests of society to merit the imposition of penal sanctions.

The idea that the possibility of punishment is a distinguishing feature of a criminal act is consistent with conventional wisdom.[98] Nevertheless, being subjected to an ASBO or required to register as a sex offender must surely have adverse consequences, and it is safe to assume that such matters will continue to be hotly debated.

Finally, it was recently confirmed[99] that an application to confiscate the proceeds of criminal activity does not amount to a criminal charge and does not engage the protection of Article 6(2).[100] Thus, although confiscation proceedings are subject to a lesser standard of proof and impose a 'persuasive' burden on the person whose assets are disputed, they do not give rise to a breach of the Convention.[101]

---

[94] See Bakalis, 'Anti-Social Behaviour Orders—Criminal Penalties or Civil Injunctions' [2003] 62(3) CLJ 583.

[95] *R v H (Fitness to Plead)* [2003] UKHL 1, [2003] 1 All ER 497, [2003] 1 WLR 411. See also p 522, *post*.

[96] Under the Sex Offenders Act 1997, s 1(1)(b).

[97] *R v H (Fitness to Plead)* [2003] UKHL 1 at [18]–[19], [2003] 1 All ER 497 at [18]–[19], [2003] 1 WLR 411.

[98] See, for example, Glanville Williams, 'The Definition of Crime' (1955) 8 CLP 107.

[99] *R v Benjafield* [2002] UKHL 2, [2003] 1 AC 1099, [2002] 1 All ER 815. The application in question was made under s 4(3) of the Drug Trafficking Act 1994.

[100] The Privy Council had previously reached the same conclusion in *HM Advocate v McIntosh (Sentencing)* [2001] UKPC D1, [2003] 1 AC 1078, [2001] 2 All ER 638.

[101] The House of Lords also found that even if Article 6(2) had been engaged there would have been no breach. This was because, when interpreted in the light of the Human Rights Act, the burden on the defendant was a 'persuasive' rather than a legal one.

D THE ADMINISTRATION OF THE ENGLISH LEGAL SYSTEM

As outlined at the beginning of this chapter, the English legal system has developed in a piecemeal way over many centuries, with the result that no single institution has had overall responsibility for its administration. In contrast to many other states the UK does not have the equivalent of a Ministry of Justice, and responsibility for the administration of the system is instead shared between various government departments and a growing number of executive agencies and other bodies. For example, the police,[102] Crown Prosecution Service,[103] Prison Service,[104] Youth Justice Board[105] and Parole Board[106] all perform important functions with regard to the criminal justice system. In addition, Her Majesty's Courts Service provides administrative support for the major courts,[107] while the Legal Services Commission plays a central role in the funding of legal actions.[108] The work of each of these bodies is overseen, either directly or indirectly, by one of a small number of government departments, and the principal functions and responsibilities of these departments are set out in more detail below.

1 THE LORD CHANCELLOR AND THE DEPARTMENT FOR CONSTITUTIONAL AFFAIRS

For centuries, much of the responsibility for the administration of the legal system has rested with the office of Lord Chancellor. In modern times the holder of this office has exercised a wide range of functions, including those of Cabinet Minister, senior judge and 'speaker' of the House of Lords. Responsibility for overseeing the administration of the Supreme Court, county courts and magistrates' courts[109] has also fallen within his remit, along with the task of appointing Court Rule Committees and allowing or disallowing their rules.[110] Other functions have included making or advising on judicial appointments, appointing and providing training for justices of the peace, overseeing the funding of legal services, appointing a Legal Services Ombudsman, and

---

[102] See chapter 12.   [103] See p 356, *post.*

[104] This became an executive agency of the Home Office on 1 April 1993.

[105] Established under the Crime and Disorder Act 1998, s 41. Its principal functions are to monitor and set standards for the work of the youth justice system; see p 514, *post.*

[106] This is an executive non-departmental public body; Criminal Justice and Public Order Act 1994, s 149.

[107] Including magistrates' courts, but excluding the House of Lords and the future Supreme Court. Magistrates' courts were previously administered by independent Magistrates' Courts Committees: see p 260, *post.* The new agency was launched in March 2005 when the functions of these Committees were integrated into the existing Courts Service: see p 230, *post.*

[108] See chapter 11.

[109] Courts Act 2003, s 1 (replacing the duties previously set out in the Justices of the Peace Act 1997, s 5; and the Courts Act 1971, ss 27 and 28).

[110] For the most recent provisions, see Part 7 of the Courts Act 2003.

maintaining the National Archives[111] and Land Registry. To assist in performing these functions the Lord Chancellor has had his own government department, and has also been able to draw on the advice of the Lord Chancellor's Advisory Committee on Legal Education and Conduct (ACLEC).[112]

The ministerial dimension of the Lord Chancellor's work acquired a new significance when his Department was asked to oversee the implementation of the Human Rights Act 1998. This was followed in 2001 by the decision to transfer responsibility for constitutional affairs from the Home Office to the Lord Chancellor's Department.[113] These developments increasingly brought the Lord Chancellor into the political spotlight, and questions were raised about whether his role was compatible with the concept of an independent judiciary.[114] In *McGonnell* v *UK*[115] the European Court of Human Rights ruled that the right to a fair trial was breached when the Guernsey Royal Court Bailiff adjudicated in a planning case, having also been involved in making the applicable legislation. It was easy to see the parallels between the Bailiff's position and that of the Lord Chancellor.

On 13 June 2003 the Prime Minister announced plans to abolish the office of Lord Chancellor and transform his Department into a new Department for Constitutional Affairs. The proposal was part of a package of reforms designed to 'redraw the relationship between the Judiciary, the Government and Parliament.'[116] The idea was that the head of the new Department would inherit the Lord Chancellor's ministerial functions and hold the title of Secretary of State for Constitutional Affairs. The Lord Chancellor's judicial functions would be transferred to the Lord Chief Justice, and the mechanics of making judicial appointments would be handed to a new Judicial Appointments Commission. Plans to transfer the judicial functions of the House of Lords to a new Supreme Court were also part of the package.

Lord Falconer was immediately appointed as both Lord Chancellor and Secretary of State, with the intention being that he would hold both titles concurrently until the programme of reform was complete. He explained the rationale for the changes as follows:[117]

It can no longer be appropriate for a senior judge to sit in Cabinet or for a Government Minister to be our country's senior judge. I have myself made it clear that I shall not sit judicially, but it is now time to bring such anachronistic and questionable arrangements to an end.

Some of the Lord Chancellor's ministerial responsibilities were transferred to the

---

[111] Formerly the Public Record Office.

[112] Appointed pursuant to the Courts and Legal Services Act 1990, s 19.

[113] Transfer of Functions (Miscellaneous) Order 2001, SI 2001/3500.

[114] The right to a fair trial under Article 6, ECHR includes the right to have one's rights and obligations determined by 'an independent and impartial tribunal'.

[115] (2000) 30 EHRR 289; see also *Starrs* v *Ruxton* 2000 JC 208, 2000 SLT 42; p 320, *post.*

[116] Department for Constitutional Affairs, *Constitutional Reform: Reforming the Office of the Lord Chancellor* (2003) CP 13/03.

[117] Ibid, foreword.

Secretary of State within weeks,[118] and provisions to redistribute his remaining functions were included in the Constitutional Reform Bill. The Bill attracted formidable opposition when it was introduced in the House of Lords. The proposed Judicial Appointments Commission was relatively uncontroversial and a majority of the Lords were also prepared to accept the plans for a Supreme Court: what they could not accept however, was the idea of abolishing the historic office of Lord Chancellor.[119] By the time the Bill had its first reading in the House of Commons the government had been forced to make significant concessions. Instead of insisting that the office of Lord Chancellor should be abolished, it was now prepared to see the office continue in a modified form. This was a highly embarrassing climb-down but its practical significance should not be overstated. Although the title of Lord Chancellor has been retained, the effect of what is now the Constitutional Reform Act 2005 is that the holder of the officer ceases to have any judicial role. During the Commons stages of the Bill, the Courts Minister explained the government's position:[120]

Whether the post holder is called 'Secretary of State for Constitutional Affairs', 'Lord Chancellor', or has both titles, is not of great significance.

[. . .] what matters most is the substance of the post, the nature of the job, and whether it is reformed so that the post holder no longer has conflicting duties. If the role of the head of the judiciary can pass to the Lord Chief Justice, and with it many of the judicial functions that are incompatible with the political functions of a Cabinet Minister, the Office of Lord Chancellor can continue in that substantially reformed way.

Having gained acceptance of the idea that a senior Minister should not also be a judge, the government took the view that it was no longer essential for the Lord Chancellor to have a legal qualification and sit in the House of Lords.[121] Section 2 of the Act thus provides that the person appointed as Lord Chancellor must be 'qualified by experience': in deciding a person's suitability for the role his experience as a practitioner or academic is merely a factor to be 'taken into account'.[122] Experience gained as a Minister or MP in either House of Parliament may also be considered, along with any 'other experience that the Prime Minister considers relevant'. The person appointed has a duty to uphold the continued independence of the judiciary and to refrain from seeking to influence particular judicial decisions. He must also have regard to the need to *defend* judicial independence.[123]

The future of most of the functions hitherto exercised by the Lord Chancellor is set

---

[118] Secretary of State for Constitutional Affairs Order 2003, SI 2003/1887.

[119] Most of the concerns related to the possible impact on judicial independence: see at p 301, *post*.

[120] 430 HC Official Report (6th Series), coll 621–622, 31 January 2005, Christopher Leslie MP.

[121] This particular change was rejected by the Lords at the first time of asking, but it was eventually passed by a majority of just twelve.

[122] This provision is surely only enforceable at a political level—the idea of a court judicially reviewing the power to make Ministerial appointments is unthinkable: see p 210, *post*.

[123] Section 3.

out in detail in Schedule 4 of the Act.[124] Essentially, this provides that the Lord Chancellor will continue to be responsible for determining the geographical and jurisdictional boundaries of individual courts, and for ensuring an efficient and effective system to support them. At the same time, the Lord Chief Justice will assume the title of 'Presdident of the Courts of England Wales', and he will have the task of representing the judiciary's views to Parliament and the government.[125] The Lord Chief Justice will also be responsible for overseeing the deployment of individual judges, allocating work within the courts,[126] issuing Practice Directions,[127] and ensuring that appropriate structures are in place for the training and support of judges.[128]

2 THE HOME OFFICE

Even before the creation of the Department for Constitutional Affairs, the Lord Chancellor did not have exclusive responsibility for matters affecting the English legal system. The Home Secretary is responsible for criminal justice policies, and legislation in this area is developed, steered through Parliament, and implemented by the Home Office. The Home Secretary has responsibility for sentencing policy, the prison service, and the maintenance of police standards, and he also exercises those prerogative powers that concern the administration of justice and the maintenance of law and order. In addition, the Home Office conducts and sponsors research into the criminal justice system.

3 THE LAW OFFICERS

The Law Officers' Department is headed by the Attorney-General and the Solicitor-General, both of whom are Ministers and legal advisers to the Crown.

In addition to his political duties, which include advising government departments and answering questions in Parliament, the Attorney-General is responsible for appointing the Director of Public Prosecutions and for overseeing the work of the Serious Fraud Office and Treasury Solicitors Office. He represents the Crown in major international litigation, certain civil proceedings, and trials for treason and other offences with a constitutional element. Mention may also be made of 'relator' proceedings in which the Attorney-General appears on behalf of a section of the public; proceedings to restrain a public nuisance being one such example. In addition, the consent of the Attorney-General is required for the prosecution of certain categories

---

[124] The blueprint for this was the 'Concordat' agreed between the Lord Chancellor and the Lord Chief Justice in January 2004: DCA, *The Lord Chancellor's Judiciary-Related Functions: Proposals.*

[125] Sections 5(1), 7(1) and 7(2)(a). The fate of the Lord Chancellor's judicial functions is discussed further in chapter 9.

[126] Section 7(2)(c).   [127] Schedule 2, Part 1.   [128] Section 7(2)(b).

of offence,[129] and he is able to terminate prosecutions on indictment by the entry of a *nolle prosequi*.[130]

The Solicitor-General's role used to be to act as the Attorney-General's deputy, and to carry out those functions that had been delegated by the latter. This position has now changed, and the two Ministers are able to decide for themselves how to divide their various functions.[131]

The Director of Public Prosecutions is a barrister or solicitor of not less than ten years' standing, who is appointed by the Attorney-General[132] to head the Crown Prosecution Service (CPS). His duties under section 3 of the Prosecution of Offences Act 1985 include the following:

(a) taking over the conduct of all criminal proceedings instituted on behalf of a police force or immigration officer;

(b) instituting and conducting criminal proceedings where the importance or difficulty of the case makes it appropriate that the Director should institute the proceedings;

(c) taking over binding over proceedings brought by a police force;[133]

(d) giving advice to police forces on all matters relating to criminal offences; and

(e) appearing in certain appeals.

Thus the Director and the Crown Prosecution Service effectively control the prosecution process. They do not control the process of investigation—that is a matter for the police—but they may direct that certain enquiries be made. The work of the Law Officers and the CPS is considered in more detail in chapter 11.

---

[129] Including some offences under the Official Secrets Act 1989, the Public Order Act 1986, and the Anti-Terrorism, Crime and Security Act 2001.

[130] This is a prerogative power; see p 206, *post.*   [131] Law Officers Act 1997, s 1.

[132] Prosecution of Offences Act 1985, s 2.   [133] See p 399, *post.*

2

LEGISLATION

A LEGISLATION AND LAW REFORM

The broad function of all legislation is to create, alter, or revoke law to give effect to the intention of the legislative body. Subordinate legislation fulfils various specific functions, scarcely capable of classification. The functions of Acts of Parliament, by far the most important form of legislation, may be classified as follows.

1 LAW REFORM

Although all statutes are concerned with law revision in the broadest sense, relatively few are concerned with altering or revising substantive rules of law. When statutes are passed to revise existing legal rules, it is usually because these rules have become stale and incapable of adaptation. A statute may also be passed to alter the law following an unpopular decision of a court, and there are many examples of Acts passed with the apparent intention of overruling a House of Lords decision.[1] However, the process of law reform is often more haphazard and piecemeal, and sometimes the impetus for change comes from ad hoc committees, departmental working groups, or Royal Commissions. The Police and Criminal Evidence Act 1984 is one such example, having been enacted following the report of the Royal Commission on Criminal Procedure.[2] More recently, major changes to the civil justice system were implemented following the report of a committee chaired by Lord Woolf.[3] Reviews of the criminal justice and tribunal systems by other committees have prompted similar reforms.[4]

An example of what can happen if law reform is not carefully considered is provided by attempts to reform the system of committal proceedings in criminal cases. Committals for trial were 'abolished' in 1994, to be replaced by a new system of transfers for trial. However, the government soon recognized the force of objections

---

[1] Examples are: Parliamentary Papers Act 1840; Limitation Act 1963; War Damage Act 1965; Criminal Evidence Act 1979. The apparent intention of these Acts is to reverse House of Lords decisions immediately preceding them, though they do not expressly name the cases concerned.

[2] Cmnd 8092, 1981.

[3] Lord Woolf, *Final Report on Access to Justice* (1996): see Part 3 of this book for a detailed discussion.

[4] Lord Justice Auld, *Review of the Criminal Courts* (2001), discussed further in Part 4 of this book; Leggatt, *Tribunals for Users: One System, One Service* (2001), discussed in chapter 8.

put by those who would have to operate the new system, and the transfer for trial provisions were repealed in 1996 without ever having been introduced. Further changes were included in a 1998 Act, and in 2003 Parliament once again changed the procedures for allocating criminal cases and sending them to the Crown Court.[5]

(a) The Law Commission

A major addition to the machinery of law reform was made by the Law Commissions Act 1965, which established the Law Commissions.[6] Section 3(1) of the Act defines the duty of the Commissions thus:

[I]t shall be the duty of each of the Commissions to take and keep under review all the law with which they are respectively concerned with a view to its systematic development and reform, including in particular the codification of such law, the elimination of anomalies, the repeal of obsolete and unnecessary enactments, the reduction of the number of separate enactments and generally the simplification and modernisation of the law.

The creation of the Law Commissions was an important step forward in law reform. The Law Commission for England and Wales[7] has five full-time Commissioners and a full-time administrative staff, and it has produced a steady flow of reports, recommendations, and draft Bills, most of which have been implemented by Acts of Parliament.[8] By the time of its 37th Annual Report in 2003, the Law Commission had published 170 law reform reports.[9] Of these, around 120 had been implemented in full or in part, and of the thirty which were still outstanding, seventeen had been accepted by the government in principle.[10]

The mission of the Law Commission is to make the law simpler, fairer, and cheaper to use. Reform projects may be included in a programme of work submitted by the Commission to the Lord Chancellor, or they may be referred to the Commission by government departments. The Commission works through small teams, each of which is led by a Law Commissioner and usually comprises three government lawyers and three research assistants. Each team may have five or six projects. In some projects there may also be an academic consultant. The process involves the publication of a Consultation Paper, following research and analysis of case law, legislation, and academic and professional opinion. The consultation paper will describe the existing problems with the law, and suggest possible solutions and reform options. Following a consultation period a final report is published, and this may include a draft Bill. The Commission often gives assistance to government Ministers and departments, 'so as

---

[5] See p 548, post.

[6] Prior to 1965, the machinery for generating law reform consisted mainly of the Law Revision Committee and the Law Reform Committee, which considered, on their own initiative or at the invitation of the Lord Chancellor, branches of the law requiring change.

[7] There is a separate Commission for Scotland.

[8] See, for example, Landlord and Tenant Act 1988, Law of Property (Miscellaneous Provisions) Act 1989, Children Act 1989; Civil Evidence Act 1995; Contracts (Rights of Third Parties) Act 1999.

[9] Law Commission, *Annual Report 2002/03* (Law Com No 280), Appendix B, p 59.

[10] Ibid, Appendix C, p 61.

to ensure that best value is obtained from the effort and resources devoted to the project by the Commission and others'.[11]

Not all Law Commission reports and recommendations are implemented, although the statistics quoted above show that its record is extremely good. An example of a report that has *not* yet been implemented is the Law Commission's draft Criminal Law Bill.[12] This was intended to be a first step at criminal law codification, but it still awaits implementation and has been described as 'over technical, poor on exposition and a sore puzzle from beginning to end'.[13]

2 CONSOLIDATION OF ENACTMENTS

Where a branch of the law has evolved piecemeal, the existing law may effectively be re-enacted in a consolidating statute for the purpose of clarification. There are three sorts of consolidating Acts: (1) 'pure' consolidation (simple re-enactment); (2) consolidation under the Consolidation of Enactments (Procedure) Act 1949, which allows 'corrections and minor improvements';[14] and (3) consolidation with amendments recommended by the Law Commission. Many of the major consolidating Acts in recent years have fallen into the third category.[15]

Consolidation Acts are not subject to parliamentary debate, but there are special procedures designed to ensure that the Bill, when enacted, does not depart from the pre-existing statutory provisions which are to be consolidated. The type of consolidation effected appears from the long title of the Act in question.[16] Substantive changes in the law will often be made before the process of consolidation is undertaken. Thus, for example, section 106 of the Crime and Disorder Act 1998 has the side heading 'pre-consolidation amendments'.

Consolidation frequently proves to be a very temporary process. For example, the Powers of Criminal Courts (Sentencing) Act 2000 was enacted as a consolidating statute to repeal and replace the earlier sentencing powers of criminal courts. Yet it was amended in the same year by the Criminal Justice and Courts Act 2000, and has now been more extensively revised by Part 12 of the Criminal Justice Act 2003. Some

---

[11] Ibid.

[12] Law Commission, *Legislating the Criminal Code: Offences Against the Person and General Principles*, 1993 (Law Com No 218).

[13] Bennion (1994) 15 *Stat LR* 108; cf. Smith: 'The Law Commission's Criminal Law Bill—A Good Start for the Criminal Code' (1995) 16 Stat LR 105.

[14] These are defined by s 2 as amendments which have the effect of resolving ambiguities, removing doubts, bringing obsolete provisions into conformity with modern practice or removing unnecessary provisions or anomalies which are not of substantial importance, and amendments designed to facilitate improvement in the form or manner in which the law is stated. This category also covers any transitional provisions which may be necessary in consequence of such amendments.

[15] Examples are Water Industry Act 1991, Water Resources Act 1991, Social Security Contributions and Benefits Act 1992, Taxation of Chargeable Gains Act 1992.

[16] See, e.g., Employment Protection (Consolidation) Act 1978 (pure consolidation) (see, now, Employment Rights Act 1996); Road Traffic Act 1988 (Law Commission amendments); Juries Act 1974 (1949 Act 'corrections and improvements').

believe that the process of consolidation should be taken to the point of producing a consolidated statute book, in which the whole of our statute law would be arranged under titles and kept up to date by textual amendments. However, it is clear that this is not a reform that is likely to be implemented in the foreseeable future. In May 1973 the government set up the Renton Committee to review the form in which public Bills are drafted, 'with a view to achieving greater simplicity and clarity in statute law'. The Committee reported in 1975[17] and concluded that it would not be practicable to consolidate the whole statute book within a limited number of years, nor to do so on the principle of 'one Act, one subject'.

3 CODIFICATION

Codification differs from consolidation in that an Act may only be said to consolidate statute law, whereas it may codify both statute law *and* case law. The processes are similar in function however, in that the object is to simplify and clarify the existing law rather than to effect substantial alterations to it. Notable examples of major codifying statutes include the Sale of Goods Act 1893 (which was later consolidated in the Sale of Goods Act 1979) and the Marine Insurance Act 1906. Since then there has been very little codification, although one notable exception is the Police and Criminal Evidence Act 1984 (PACE). This statute radically altered and codified the pre-existing common law and statutory rules relating to police powers of search, entry to premises, the treatment and questioning of suspects, and the admissibility of confession evidence.

There is a pressing need for codification in many areas of the law, and this is largely due to the manner in which Parliament sometimes approaches the task of amending statutes. Rather than producing a comprehensive re-enactment which would enable the law on a topic to be set out in a single Act, piecemeal amendments have often been made, with one statute dealing with a large number of different topics and amending an equally large number of earlier statutes. Subsequently the amending provision may itself be repealed, so that in order to discover what the law is, it becomes necessary to pick one's way through a maze of separate statutory provisions. This situation, in the field of industrial relations legislation, led Sir John Donaldson MR to make the following observation:[18]

My plea is that Parliament, when legislating in respect of circumstances which directly affect the 'man or woman in the street' or the 'man or woman on the shop floor', should give as high a priority to clarity and simplicity of expression as to refinements of policy. Where possible, statutes, or complete parts of statutes, should not be amended but re-enacted in an amended form so that those concerned can read the rules in a single document. When formulating policy, ministers, of whatever political persuasion, should at all times be asking themselves and asking parliamentary counsel; 'Is this concept too refined to be capable of

---

17 *The Preparation of Legislation*, Cmnd 6053 (1975).
18 *Merkur Island Shipping Corporation* v *Laughton* [1983] 2 AC 570 at 594–5, [1982] 1 All ER 334 at 351.

expression in basic English?' Having to ask such questions would no doubt be frustrating for ministers and the legislature generally, but in my judgment this is part of the price which has to be paid if the rule of law is to be maintained.

Lord Diplock expressly adopted these remarks when the case reached the House of Lords.[19] Increasingly, Acts which significantly amend earlier legislation will substitute one or more sections, or sub-sections, for the pre-existing provision. One example of this is Schedule 1 to the Criminal Procedure and Investigations Act 1996, which introduced five new sections into the Magistrates' Courts Act 1980. This does not, of course, remove the need for a greater measure of codification.

4 COLLECTION AND DISBURSEMENT OF REVENUE

The annual Finance Act implementing the Budget proposals is concerned primarily with the collection of revenue by the Crown. Other Acts, notably the Income and Corporation Taxes Act 1988, fulfil the same function. Conversely, public expenditure is authorized by Parliament annually through Consolidated Fund Acts (which authorize payments out of the Consolidated Fund), and the Appropriation Act (which appropriates public expenditure to specific purposes).

5 IMPLEMENTATION OF TREATIES

The United Kingdom, by entering into treaties, undertakes to implement the laws that form the subject matter of those treaties. For example, the directives and decisions of the European Community usually require implementation by statute or statutory instrument,[20] and the UK may also be obliged to legislate in order to give effect to decisions on the European Convention on Human Rights.[21] Examples of domestic legislation intended to implement other treaties and conventions include the Taking of Hostages Act 1982, the Employment Act 1989, and the Companies Act 1989.

6 SOCIAL LEGISLATION

These Acts are varied in their scope and functions but may be classified together as social legislation. Such Acts are concerned with regulating the day-to-day running of the social system rather then with creating criminal offences or rights and duties between individuals, although there is an increasing tendency for Parliament to delegate the power to make regulations of this nature to subordinate bodies.[22]

---

[19] [1983] 2 AC 570 at 662, [1983] 2 All ER 189 at 198–9.
[20] See p 129, *post.*   [21] See p 149, *post.*   [22] See p 34, *post.*

B FORMS OF LEGISLATION[23]

Early legislation in England took several different forms, such as charters,[24] provisions, ordinances, and statutes. At the present day however, United Kingdom legislation may take one of three forms: Acts of Parliament, delegated legislation, and autonomic legislation.

1 ACTS OF PARLIAMENT

Subject to compliance with the overriding legislation of the European Community, Parliament is recognized as sovereign and as possessing unlimited legislative power. This has not always been so,[25] but in modern times it had not been seriously contended that the courts have any power to override the intention of the legislature until *British Railways Board* v *Pickin*.[26] In this case, an attempt was made to impugn the validity of the British Railways Act 1968, on the ground that the British Railway Board had fraudulently concealed certain matters from Parliament and had misled Parliament into an enactment which deprived the plaintiff of his land. If it was surprising that such a point should be pleaded, it was perhaps more surprising that the Court of Appeal should have held that it raised a triable issue.[27] The House of Lords, however, allowed the Board's appeal and restored the judge's order that the pleading be struck out as frivolous, vexatious, and an abuse of process. Accordingly, it is now clear that no court is entitled to go behind that which Parliament has enacted and that this rule is equally applicable to public and private Acts.[28]

However, where there is a potential conflict between a United Kingdom Act and legislation of the European Community, the courts have power to restrain enforcement of the former. This occurred in *R* v *Secretary of State for Transport, ex parte Factortame (No 2)*.[29] The applicants, who were companies controlled by Spanish nationals, sought to challenge the validity of the Merchant Shipping Act 1988 on the basis that it contravened the EC Treaty and deprived them of their Community law

---

[23] This chapter is confined to United Kingdom legislation. For EC legislation, see chapter 4, *post*.

[24] For an attempt to rely upon Magna Carta, see *R* v *Secretary of State for the Home Department, ex parte Wynne* [1992] QB 406, [1992] 2 All ER 301.

[25] See, e.g., dicta of Coke CJ in *Bonham*'s case (1609) 8 Co Rep 113 and of Holt CJ in *City of London* v *Wood* (1701) 12 Mod Rep 669.

[26] [1974] AC 765, [1974] 1 All ER 609.

[27] [1973] QB 219, [1972] 3 All ER 923. For another unsuccessful attempt to have a statute declared ultra vires, see *Manuel* v *A-G* [1983] Ch 77, [1982] 3 All ER 822.

[28] The Court of Appeal's decision in *R (on the application of Jackson)* v *A-G* [2005] EWCA Civ 126, *The Times* 17 February 2005, suggests that there may be a limited exception to this rule for legislation enacted using the Parliament Acts procedure: see p 35, *post*.

[29] [1991] 1 AC 603, [1991] 1 All ER 70. For the subsequent litigation see *R* v *Secretary of State for Transport, ex parte Factortame (No 3)* [1992] QB 680, [1991] 3 All ER 769; *R* v *Secretary of State for Transport, ex parte Factortame (No 4)* Case 48/93 [1996] QB 404, [1996] All ER (EC) 301; *R* v *Secretary of State for Transport, ex parte Factortame (No 5)* [2000] 1 AC 524, [1999] 4 All ER 906.

rights. Since determination of this issue by the European Court of Justice was likely to take some time, the applicants applied for an interim injunction to restrain the Secretary of State from enforcing the Act. The House of Lords initially decided that they had no power to make such an order,[30] but following a reference to the European Court of Justice[31] they granted the applicants the interim relief sought. The effect of this unprecedented decision was to 'disapply' Part II of the Merchant Shipping Act. The decision was taken a stage further in *Equal Opportunities Commission* v *Secretary of State for Employment*,[32] where the House of Lords held that it was entitled to judicially review legislation to ensure that it complied with European law. On the facts, provisions in the Employment Protection (Consolidation) Act 1978 were held to be contrary to European law, and a declaration to this effect was issued.

The impact of EC law on the legislative supremacy of Parliament was considered further in the recent case of *Thoburn* v *Sunderland City Council*.[33] The appellants had been convicted for selling produce in imperial measurements, contrary to delegated legislation implementing a European directive on the use of metric weights. The appeal by way of case stated centred on the claim that the Weights and Measures Act 1985 (which permitted the use of imperial weights) had, by implication, partially repealed section 2 of the European Communities Act 1972 (which authorizes the implementation of Community obligations by delegated legislation). The Divisional Court rejected this argument, and in doing so, Laws LJ sought to distinguish between 'constitutional statutes' such as the European Communities Act, and 'ordinary' Acts of Parliament:[34]

There are now classes or types of legislative provision which cannot be repealed by mere implication. These instances are given and can only be given, by our own courts, to which the scope and nature of Parliamentary sovereignty are ultimately confided.

He continued:[35]

In my opinion, a constitutional statute is one which (a) conditions the legal relationship between citizen and State in some general overarching manner, or (b) enlarges or diminishes the scope of what we would now regard as fundamental constitutional rights.

Other statutes said by Laws LJ to be immune from implied repeal include the Magna Carta, the Human Rights Act 1998, and the Scotland Act 1998.

In an earlier decision, Lord Hoffman had made similar observations about Parliament's ability to legislate contrary to fundamental human rights principles:[36]

The principle of legality means that Parliament must squarely confront what it is doing and accept the political cost. Fundamental rights cannot be overridden by general or ambiguous

---

[30] *R* v *Secretary of State for Transport, ex parte Factortame (No 1)* [1990] 2 AC 85, [1989] 2 All ER 692.
[31] Case C-213/89 [1990] ECR I-2433, [1990] 3 CMLR 1.
[32] [1995] 1 AC 1, [1994] 1 All ER 910.
[33] [2002] EWHC 195 (Admin), [2003] QB 151, [2002] 4 All ER 156.
[34] Ibid at [60].   [35] Ibid at [62].
[36] *R* v *Secretary of State for the Home Department, ex parte Simms* [2000] 2 AC 115 at 131, [1999] 3 All ER 400 at 412; see also Lord Steyn, 'Democracy through Law' [2002] EHRLR 723.

words . . . In the absence of express language or necessary implication to the contrary, the courts therefore presume that even the most general words were intended to be subject to the basic rights of the individual.

(a) Public and Private Acts

Most Acts of Parliament are what is known as 'Public General Acts',[37] and the impetus for the vast majority of these comes from the government. Some may be based on specific manifesto pledges but many originate within government departments. They are drafted by the Office of Parliamentary Counsel to the Treasury, in liaison with relevant Ministers. Occasionally, however, a Public General Act may begin life as a Private Members Bill. As the name indicates, such Bills are introduced by individual MPs rather than by Ministers acting on behalf of the government, and they rarely become law unless the government can be persuaded to lend its time and support. Examples of Private Members Bills which have been enacted with government support include the Obscene Publications Act 1959 (introduced by Roy Jenkins), the Abortion Act 1967 (David Steel), and the Public Interest Disclosure Act 1998 (Richard Shepherd).

Alongside Public General Acts there are also Private Acts, which are usually proposed by either local authorities (Local Acts) or large public companies and corporations (Personal Acts). Such Acts tend to affect only the interests of those who originally proposed them.

(b) The legislative process

Before a Bill is drafted the government may outline its intentions in a consultation paper, inviting feedback from interested parties on the range of options that is being considered. This consultation period will usually be followed by a White Paper setting out the government's revised proposals in detail. It is also becoming more common for Bills to be published in draft, providing an early opportunity for scrutiny and revision by the parliamentary Select Committees.

Once the government is satisfied with a Bill it will be introduced in Parliament. Money Bills and Bills dealing with politically contentious matters are usually presented to the House of Commons first, although less controversial Bills may begin life in the House of Lords. The title of the Bill will be read out in what is known as the first reading, and a date will be set for the second reading and the first opportunity for a full debate on the Bill's merits.[38] At the end of this debate, the Bill and any amendments that have been proposed will be put to the vote. It is unlikely that any government sponsored Bill will be defeated at this stage, although on 17 January 2004 the government's Higher Education Bill survived its second reading in the Commons by

[37] By virtue of the Interpretation Act 1978, s 3, every Act passed since 1850 is presumed to be a Public Act in the absence of a contrary provision.

[38] Section 19 of the Human Rights Act 1998 requires the Minister sponsoring a Bill to make a written statement before the Second Reading as to whether, in his view, its provisions are compatible with the rights specified in Schedule 1 of the 1998 Act: see p 162, *post.*

a margin of just five votes. Assuming that a Bill does get this far, it will be referred to a parliamentary Standing Committee for more detailed consideration. The Committee will then report back to the House in the report stage, before the Bill proceeds to the third reading and a final vote. If a simple majority of the House votes in favour of enacting the Bill it will be sent to the other House and the process will be repeated.[39] Only when it has received the approval of both Houses of Parliament can a Bill be presented for the Royal Assent and become an Act of Parliament.[40]

The Parliament Acts of 1911 and 1949 modify the principle that a Bill cannot be enacted without the approval of both the Commons and the Lords. Under the provisions of these Acts, the House of Lords no longer has the power of veto and can only delay Bills which have Commons support for a period of up to one year,[41] or in the case of money Bills, for up to one month.[42] If, at the end of this period the House of Lords rejects a Bill for a second time, the Commons can then invoke the Parliament Acts procedure and present the Bill for the Royal Assent. There is, however, no power enabling the House of Lords to legislate without the consent of the Commons. The Parliament Acts procedure has only been invoked on seven occasions, most recently to enact the Hunting Act 2004.[43] In most cases of disagreement between the two Houses a compromise has been reached, usually involving the House of Lords voting in favour of a Bill in return for the House of Commons accepting certain amendments. Indeed, in one of the most extraordinary episodes in British political history Parliament sat through the night to debate what became the Prevention of Terrorism Act 2005. The Bill 'ping-ponged' between the two Houses four times before a compromise was finally reached. The deadlock was only broken when the government reluctantly agreed to give Parliament the opportunity to make amendments to the Act at a later date.

Acts of Parliament are published in Queens' Printers' Copy form by Her Majesty's Stationery Office and they are also made available electronically on the HMSO web site.[44] The Stationery Office publishes these statutes in annual volumes and also publishes an annual Index to the Statutes in Force, for reference purposes.

(c) Citation

The mode of citation of statutes has undergone change. Early statutes were cited by the name of the place where Parliament met.[45] Subsequently statutes were cited by reference to their regnal year and chapter. Thus, for example, the Criminal Justice Act

---

[39] If any further amendments are proposed at this stage, the Bill must go back to the first House so that it can have the opportunity to vote on them.

[40] The usual procedure for this is set out in the Royal Assent Act 1967.

[41] Parliament Act 1911, s 2(1), as amended.   [42] Ibid, s 1.

[43] The Welsh Church Act 1914, the Government of Ireland Act 1920, the Parliament Act 1949, the War Crimes Act 1991, the European Parliamentary Elections Act 1999, and the Sexual Offences (Amendment) Act 2000 were also passed in this way. For a challenge to the validity of the 1949 Act and subsequent legislation, see *R (on the application of Jackson)* v *A-G* [2005] EWCA Civ 126, *The Times* 17 February 2005, and p 35, *post*.

[44] www.hmso.gov.uk.   [45] e.g. Statute of Gloucester 1278; Provisions of Oxford 1258.

1948 would be cited as 11 & 12 Geo 6, c 58 indicating that the Act was the fifty-eighth passed in the Parliamentary session extending over the eleventh and twelfth years of the reign of George VI. This exceedingly cumbersome method of citation was not abolished until 1962.[46] Although Acts still have chapter numbers (a legacy of the fiction that only one Act was passed in a parliamentary session), reference is now to the calendar year rather than to the regnal year. Acts are usually cited by reference to their short title, and this is permissible by section 2 of the Short Titles Act 1896.

(d) Enforcement of statutory duties

Due to the restrictive effect of the doctrine of judicial precedent, the creation of new rights and causes of action is virtually the prerogative of Parliament. Where a statute imposes a duty the question often arises whether a breach of that statutory duty is actionable in tort. The issue in such cases is whether the legislature intended to confer a cause of action on the claimant, not whether the claimant belongs to a class which the provision was intended to protect. It might be thought that where a statute created rules but provided no criminal penalty for their breach, the intention of Parliament must have been to create a right of civil action to a person who suffers as a result of the breach:

for, if it were not so, the statute would be but a pious aspiration.[47]

This is not, however, invariably the case. Thus in *R v Deputy Governor of Parkhurst Prison, ex parte Hague*[48] the House of Lords held that the Prison Rules 1964 (made under the Prison Act 1952) conferred no right to sue for damages upon a prisoner who had been restrained in a manner not permitted by those Rules. The prisoner's remedies were to complain to the governor or board of visitors. He might also challenge any administrative decision of the Secretary of State or the governor by judicial review proceedings.

The principles to be considered were discussed in *O'Rourke v Camden LBC*,[49] where the House of Lords considered whether the Housing (Homeless Persons) Act 1977 conferred private rights as well as public duties. Lord Hoffman explained the issue as follows:

There is no doubt that, like several other provisions in Pt III, [the 1977 Act] creates a duty which is enforceable by proceedings for judicial review. But whether it gives rise to a cause of action sounding damages depends upon whether the Act shows a legislative intention to create such a remedy . . . The indicator upon which [counsel] for Mr O'Rourke placed most reliance was the common sense proposition that a statute which appears intended for the protection of a limited class of people but provides no other remedy for breach should ordinarily be construed as intended to create a private right of action. . . . Camden, on the

---

[46] Acts of Parliament Numbering and Citation Act 1962 (10 & 11 Eliz 2, c 34).

[47] *Cutler v Wandsworth Stadium Ltd* [1949] AC 398 at 407, [1949] 1 All ER 544 at 548, per Lord Simonds.

[48] [1992] 1 AC 58, [1991] 3 All ER 733.

[49] [1998] AC 188, [1997] 3 All ER 23, overruling *Thornton v Kirklees MBC* [1979] QB 626, [1979] 2 All ER 349. The power to make delegated legislation may not necessarily include the power to create new enforceable rights: *Olutu v Home Office* [1997] 1 All ER 385, [1987] 1 WLR 328.

other hand, says that although Pt III does not expressly enact any remedy for breach, that does not mean that it would be toothless without an action for damages or an injunction in private law. It is enforceable in public law by individual homeless persons who have locus standi to bring proceedings for judicial review. Furthermore, there are certain contra-indications which make it unlikely that Parliament intended to create private law rights of action.

The first is that the Act is a scheme of social welfare, intended to confer benefits at the public expense on grounds of public policy. Public money is spent on housing the homeless not merely for the private benefit of people who find themselves homeless but on grounds of general public interest: because, for example, proper housing means that people will be less likely to suffer illness, turn to crime or require the attention of other social services. The expenditure interacts with expenditure on other public services such as education, the National Health Service and even the police. It is not simply a private matter between the claimant and the housing authority. Accordingly, the fact that Parliament has provided for the expenditure of public money on benefits in kind such as housing the homeless does not necessarily mean that it intended cash payments to be made by way of damages to persons who, in breach of the housing authority's statutory duty, have unfortunately not received the benefits which they should have done . . .

Ultimately the matter depends on the construction of each individual statute, but if the duty is of a general administrative or regulatory nature, a right in tort is unlikely to be implied.[50]

2 DELEGATED LEGISLATION

'Delegated legislation' is the term used to describe the vast body of rules, orders, regulations, and byelaws, created by subordinate bodies under powers delegated through Acts of Parliament. Parliament has neither the time nor the expertise to enact all the legislation needed in a modern, complex society, and the use of delegated legislation enables legal rules to be made and altered quickly without taking up valuable parliamentary time.[51]

Orders in Council are the highest form of delegated legislation.[52] They are nominally made by the Privy Council, though in most cases the Privy Council merely sanctions Orders that have in practice been made by the government. Orders in Council made pursuant to statutory powers are published in statutory instruments,[53]

---

[50] *Capital and Counties plc* v *Hampshire County Council and others* [1997] QB 1004, [1997] 2 All ER 865 (duty to ensure a water supply under Fire Services Act 1947 did not confer enforceable right).

[51] In 2002 for example, a total of 2,959 Statutory Instruments applicable to the UK were made, compared with just forty-four Public Acts of Parliament. Exceptionally, as many as 3,806 Statutory Instruments were made in 2001, but 597 of these related directly to the outbreak of Foot and Mouth disease in that year.

[52] Note that Orders in Council can also amount to primary legislation pursuant to the royal prerogative: *Council of Civil Service Unions* v *Minister for the Civil Service* [1985] AC 374, [1984] 3 All ER 935.

[53] See the Statutory Instruments Act 1946. Statutes conferring subordinate legislative powers frequently provide that the statutory instrument made thereunder shall be laid before Parliament. In this event a copy of the instrument must be so laid before it comes into operation: s 4. Some statutory instruments cannot take effect until expressly approved by resolution, while others take effect immediately subject to cancellation by negative resolution within forty 'sitting' days.

as are the various regulations, orders, directions, and rules made by Ministers of the Crown and other subordinate bodies.[54] Statutory instruments are published by Her Majesty's Stationery Office and are cited by calendar year and number: for example, SI 2003/1660. They also have a short title. Failure to publish does not affect the validity of a statutory instrument, but it may provide a defence to any prosecution brought in respect of it.[55]

Local authority byelaws are another form of delegated legislation.[56] Alongside numerous powers to make byelaws on specific matters, local authorities also have a general power under the Local Government Act 1972 to make byelaws 'for good rule and government and suppression of nuisances.'[57]

It has been argued[58] that statutes made using the Parliament Acts procedure are also a form of delegated legislation, and the Court of Appeal's decision in *R (on the application of Jackson)* v *A-G* lends support to this view.[59] When the Parliament Act 1911 removed the Lords' power to veto legislation, it replaced it with the power to delay Public Bills for up to two years. The 1911 Act was then itself used to pass the Parliament Act 1949, which reduced this delaying period to one year. The argument advanced in *Jackson* was that the 1911 Act had not created an alternative procedure for making Acts of Parliament, and that it was instead an enabling Act which delegated law-making powers to a body comprising the House of Commons and the Monarch. It followed that the 1949 Act was a subordinate instrument made pursuant to the 1911 Act, and to the extent that it sought to amend its own 'parent Act', it was ultra vires: a subordinate body could not give itself greater powers than those originally conferred by Parliament. The applicant therefore sought a declaration that both the 1949 Act and the Hunting Act 2004 (which was made under it) were invalid. The court refused to grant the declaration and rejected the argument that the 1911 Act could only be amended with the consent of the Lords. However, it indicated that the outcome might have been different if the 1949 Act had purported to make more than a 'relatively modest and straightforward amendment.'[60]

The result of the use of the 1911 Act was in form to produce an Act of Parliament as is contended by the Attorney General and [Counsel] but, as we have already pointed out, that Act will not be valid if it is outside the scope of the 1911 Act.

---

[54] Not all statutory instruments are made by Ministers. The Courts Act 2003, for example, empowers the Criminal Procedure Rule Committee to make rules of practice and procedure for the criminal courts (s 69), and gives equivalent powers to a new Family Procedure Rule Committee (s 75). See also the Civil Procedure Act 1997, s 1, for the powers of the Civil Procedure Rule Committee.

[55] Statutory Instruments Act 1946, s 3; *R v Sheer Metalcraft* [1954] 1 QB 586, [1954] 1 All ER 542.

[56] Certain other bodies are also empowered to make byelaws. For example, s 210(1) and Schedule 25 of the Water Resources Act 1991 empower the Environment Agency to make byelaws for purposes connected with the carrying out of its functions. See also the Transport Act 2000, s 219, which empowers the Strategic Rail Authority to make byelaws regulating the use of the railways.

[57] Section 235(1). Such byelaws only take effect when they are confirmed by the Secretary of State.

[58] Perhaps most famously by Wade: see *Constitutional Fundamentals* (1980) at p 27.

[59] [2005] EWCA Civ 126, *The Times* 17 February 2005.   [60] At [98], per Lord Woolf CJ.

[W]e do not, however, regard this as being an all or nothing situation. We do not believe that it will necessarily follow if we conclude that the 1949 Act is lawful legislation, that the 1911 Act can be used or amended, so as to produce results that will constitute a different constitutional settlement.[61]

Delegated legislation is not a new phenomenon and where it is concerned solely with implementing the detail of a general policy contained in an Act of Parliament, it is useful and unexceptionable.[62] However, it is increasingly common for delegated powers to be defined in extremely wide terms,[63] with the effect of conferring extensive legislative power upon government departments. One example of this is section 2(2) of the European Communities Act 1972, which confers a wide power on Ministers or Her Majesty in Council to make delegated legislation giving effect to Community obligations.[64] The potential scope of this power is vast. In 2003, for example, the government introduced a series of Regulations designed to give effect to two EC Directives on discrimination.[65] Entirely new grounds for challenging discrimination in employment were created,[66] and existing Acts of Parliament dealing with 'race', gender, and disability discrimination were substantially amended.[67] These reforms will have a significant impact on the entire field of anti-discrimination law; yet by relying on the enabling power in s 2(2) of the European Communities Act 1972, the government was able to bring about these changes without asking Parliament to enact further primary legislation.

There are numerous other examples of so-called 'Henry VIII clauses' which allow delegated legislation to amend Acts of Parliament. For instance, the Regulatory Reform Act 2001 empowers Ministers to amend or repeal primary legislation in order to reduce burdens on businesses and professions.[68] An even wider example can be found in the Human Rights Act 1998. Where a court has declared that a legislative

---

[61] Ibid, at [45]–[46].

[62] For example, many Acts of Parliament are brought into operation by Order in Council. An Act may be brought into force in this way, even though the power to make the Order derives from the Act itself; Interpretation Act 1978, s 13.

[63] Such powers tend to be very widely defined in time of war. See, for example, the extraordinarily wide powers conferred by the Supplies and Services (Transitional Powers) Act 1945 (now repealed).

[64] See p 128, *post*. The scope of s 2(2) is limited by Schedule 2, which excludes the power to make any provision imposing or increasing taxation, any retrospective provision or any criminal offence punishable with imprisonment for more than two years, or, on summary conviction with imprisonment for more than three months. Even with these limitations the power is far-reaching, and in 2003 138 statutory instruments affecting England and Wales were made pursuant to s 2(2) of this Act.

[65] EC Employment Directive (2000/78/EC); EC Race Directive (2000/43/EC).

[66] Employment Equality (Religion or Belief) Regulations 2003, SI 2003/1660; Employment Equality (Sexual Orientation) Regulations 2003, SI 2003/1661.

[67] Race Relations Act 1976 (Amendment) Regulations 2003, SI 2003/1626; Sex Discrimination Act 1975 (Amendment) Regulations 2003, SI 2003/1657; Disability Discrimination Act 1995 (Amendment) Regulations 2003, SI 2003/1673.

[68] This replaces and extends the power previously contained in Part 1 of the Deregulation and Contracting Out Act 1994.

provision is incompatible with a Convention right,[69] section 10 empowers a Minister to make such amendments to the legislation as he considers necessary to remove the incompatibility. In *R (on the application of H) v North and East London Regional Mental Health Tribunal* the Court of Appeal declared provisions of the Mental Health Act 1983 to be incompatible with the right to liberty under Article 5, ECHR.[70] The offending provisions were amended by the Mental Health Act 1983 (Remedial) Order 2001,[71] and because the Secretary of State considered that there were 'compelling reasons' for acting quickly he was able to make this Order without waiting for further parliamentary approval.[72]

(a) Scrutiny of delegated legislation

The vital feature that distinguishes Parliament from any other person or body with legislative powers is that only Parliament is sovereign. This means that delegated legislation is valid only if it is within the legislative powers conferred by Parliament (intra vires). Thus, while the courts have no power to declare Acts of Parliament invalid, delegated legislation *can* be declared invalid if it is ultra vires (outside the power). The scope of the courts' jurisdiction in such cases was considered in *R v Secretary of State for the Home Department, ex parte Javed*.[73] The case centred on an Order designating Pakistan as a country where there was 'no serious risk of persecution'.[74] The applicants were Pakistani asylum seekers who had been subjected to a fast-track procedure on the basis of this Order. The Court of Appeal confirmed that delegated legislation could be judicially reviewed on the grounds identified in the GCHQ case,[75] namely illegality, procedural impropriety, and *Wednesbury* unreasonableness.[76] The courts can also strike down subordinate legislation which is incompatible with the rights protected by the Human Rights Act,[77] unless the terms of the

---

[69] A 'Convention right' means any of the rights contained in Articles 2 to 12 and 14 of the ECHR, Articles 1 to 3 of the First Protocol and Articles 1 and 2 of the Sixth Protocol (Human Rights Act, s 1). Not all courts have the power to make such a declaration: see p 159, *post*.

[70] [2001] EWCA Civ 415, [2002] QB 1, [2002] 3 WLR 512. The provisions concerned the test to be applied when determining a restricted patient's entitlement to release from a secure hospital. The provision was held to be incompatible with Article 5 as the patient bore the burden of proving that his continued detention under the Act was no longer warranted.

[71] SI 2001/3712.   [72] Human Rights Act 1998, s 10(2); Schedule 2, para 2(b).

[73] [2001] EWCA Civ 789, [2002] QB 129.

[74] Asylum (Designated Countries of Destination and Designated Safe Third Countries) Order 1996, SI 1996/2671. The Order was purportedly made under powers conferred by the Asylum and Immigration Appeals Act 1993.

[75] *Council of Civil Service Unions v Minister for the Civil Services* [1985] AC 374, [1984] 3 All ER 935. See further, p 215, *post*.

[76] *Associated Provincial Picture Houses Ltd v Wednesbury Corpn.* [1948] 1 KB 223, [1947] 2 All ER 680. The Court of Appeal in *Javed* held that the 1996 Order was void for unreasonableness. Delegated legislation may also be declared ultra vires where it breaches a fundamental right, such as the right of access to a court— see *R v Secretary of State for the Home Department and others, ex parte Saleem* [2001] 1 WLR 443, [2000] 4 All ER 814.

[77] A Minister or other body exercising a power to make delegated legislation is subject to s 6(1) of the Act, which makes it unlawful for a public authority to act incompatibly with Convention rights.

enabling Act make the incompatibility inevitable.[78] However, unless and until declared ultra vires by a final judgment in the courts, a statutory instrument must be treated as part of the law and enforced accordingly.[79]

Although any challenge to delegated legislation is usually made in an application for judicial review,[80] it is also possible to raise the question of validity as a defence to a civil action[81] or a prosecution[82] in what is known as a 'collateral challenge'. However, the fact that part of delegated legislation is ultra vires does not necessarily invalidate the whole of that legislation. The valid part may be textually severable, meaning that the invalid part may be severed whilst the valid part remains intact and enforceable.[83] Alternatively, even where delegated legislation is not textually severable, it may nevertheless be upheld and enforced if it is *substantially* severable, so that what remains after severance is essentially unchanged in its legislative purpose, operation, and effect.[84]

Despite the possibility of judicial review, it must be remembered that the role of the court is limited to ensuring that the delegated legislation is authorized by the enabling Act. Where that Act has been drafted so as to confer very wide powers, the scope for judicial scrutiny of their exercise is necessarily limited. Such powers are always subject to control by Parliament, and the Joint Select Committee on Statutory Instruments is able to consider the technical aspects of individual instruments and draw them to the attention of Parliament. In addition, most, though not all statutory instruments must be laid before Parliament for a period of forty days before they can take effect, and some require an affirmative resolution of both Houses.[85] The sheer volume of delegated legislation that is now being made and the inability of the Joint Select Committee to review its merits does raise doubts about the effectiveness of parliamentary scrutiny. However, the ultimate form of parliamentary control is that without the authority of an Act of Parliament there would be no power to make delegated legislation.

3 AUTONOMIC LEGISLATION

This differs from delegated legislation in that an autonomous body has an independent power to legislate for its own members, and in some cases, for members of the

---

[78] s 6(2).

[79] Cf. *Hoffman-La Roche & Co AG v Secretary of State for Trade and Industry* [1975] AC 295 at 329, [1974] 2 All ER 1128; *Percy v Hall* [1997] QB 924, [1996] 4 All ER 523.

[80] See *O'Reilly v Mackman* [1983] 2 AC 237, [1982] 3 All ER 1124. See generally, Ch. 6.

[81] *R v Reading Crown Court, ex parte Hutchinson* [1988] QB 384, [1988] 1 All ER 333.

[82] *Boddington v British Transport Police* [1999] 2 AC 143, [1998] 2 All ER 203. The House of Lords confirmed in *Boddington* that a collateral challenge could be based on either substantive or procedural ultra vires. This overruled the earlier decision in *DPP v Bugg* [1993] QB 473, [1993] 2 All ER 815 to the effect that a collateral challenge could only be based on a claim of substantive ultra vires.

[83] 'A legislative instrument is textually severable if a clause, a sentence, a phrase or a single word may be disregarded, as exceeding the lawmaker's power, and what remains of the text is still grammatical and coherent.' (*DPP v Hutchinson* [1990] 2 AC 783 at 804, [1990] 2 All ER 836 at 839, per Lord Bridge.)

[84] Ibid.

[85] For example, deregulation orders made under the Regulatory Reform Act 2001 are subject to an affirmative resolution procedure; s 4(2). Cf. Human Rights Act 1998, Schedule 2, para 2(b).

general public. Though this power is usually conferred by Parliament, this is not always so. However, in all cases the power is sanctioned by Parliament. Examples of autonomous legislative bodies are public undertakings such as transport authorities, and bodies created by Royal charter, such as universities, whose byelaws may affect the public at large. The Church of England, the General Medical Council, The Law Society, trade unions, and even limited companies are autonomous in the sense that they have power to control their own internal structures and to legislate for their members. It is arguable that such legislation does not affect the public, but it does in a negative sense in that any individual who causes a breach of the regulations created by an autonomous body may commit a civil wrong.

In almost all cases autonomic legislation is confined in its extent by an Act of Parliament and is therefore subject to the doctrine of ultra vires. An important exception however, is the prerogative jurisdiction of the Privy Council. This jurisdiction is principally concerned with legislating by Order in Council for Crown Colonies. The power is subject to the ordinary rules of English law, though not to the doctrine of ultra vires.[86] It will thus be apparent that an Order in Council may be passed either under powers conferred by individual Acts or under a general prerogative power independent of statute. Both are subject to the power of the law to determine the existence and extent of the power to make the Order.[87]

4 CODES OF PRACTICE

Before leaving the topic of forms of legislation, it is necessary to refer to Codes of Practice, which are of increasing significance in certain legislative contexts. A number of Acts of Parliament specifically require or authorize the preparation of accompanying Codes of Practice, usually for the purpose of providing further guidance, instructions, or rules governing matters of practice and procedure. Whether such Codes are classifiable as 'legislation' is a moot point. In one sense they have the characteristic of delegated legislation in that the power to issue them is conferred by statute,[88] and presumably a Code of Practice could be declared ultra vires. Certain codes must be laid before Parliament before they can come into operation, and some are even subject to an affirmative resolution procedure.[89] On the other hand, the very nature of Codes of Practice means that they do not have the force of law. As discussed below however, this does not mean that they are without legal effect.

In the context of the enforcement of the criminal law several Codes are of particular importance. Section 66 of the Police and Criminal Evidence Act 1984 (PACE)

---

[86] *The Zamora* [1916] 2 AC 77.   [87] See p 208, *post*.

[88] Not all Codes of Practice are issued pursuant to statutory powers. Numerous voluntary codes exist in both the private and public sectors, but these do not raise the same legal issues as those backed by a statutory framework.

[89] Codes of Practice made under s 66 of the Police and Criminal Evidence Act 1984 (PACE) can only be brought into force by a statutory instrument which has been approved by both Houses of Parliament (s 67(7)). However, revisions to existing Codes are not subject to affirmative resolution (s 67(7A)).

authorizes the Home Secretary to make Codes of Practice dealing with the different stages of police investigations. Codes dealing with the exercise of stop and search powers (Code A), the execution of search powers (Code B), the treatment and questioning of suspects (Code C), the identification of suspects (Code D), and the tape-recording of police interviews (Code E) have been in operation for some time.[90] A new Code dealing with the visual recording of interviews has also been introduced (Code F).[91] The PACE Codes are important to both the practitioner and the police, and if there is a 'significant and substantial' breach of the Codes,[92] evidence obtained as a result of that breach may be excluded from consideration by the courts. The status of one of the PACE Codes was recently discussed by Lord Woolf CJ:[93]

The Code has statutory backing under the Police and Criminal Evidence Act 1984. However it remains a code and it does not have the status of subordinate legislation.

Another example is the Code of Practice on the preservation and disclosure of evidence, made under s 23 of the Criminal Procedure and Investigations Act 1996. This Code is intended to ensure that important material is made available to the prosecutor and disclosed to the defence if it may assist them.[94] It is very much intended to create a framework where miscarriages of justice become less likely.

In the context of the civil law, perhaps the most important example of a Code of Practice is that issued by the Advisory Conciliation and Arbitration Service (ACAS) under the Trade Union and Labour Relations (Consolidation) Act 1992. ACAS may issue Codes of Practice containing 'such practical guidance as the Service thinks fit for the purpose of promoting the improvement of industrial relations or for purposes connected with trade union learning representatives'.[95] Provision for codes of this type was first made by the Industrial Relations Act 1971 and the first such code, the Code of Practice on Disciplinary Practice and Procedures in Employment, has had a significant impact in the context of unfair dismissal.

(a) The status of Codes of Practice

As already indicated, although Codes of Practice cannot be directly enforced through the courts they are not without legal effect. For example, Codes issued under the Trade Union and Labour Relations (Consolidation) Act 1992 are specifically admissible in any proceedings before a court, industrial tribunal, or the Central Arbitration Committee.[96] Similarly, by section 67(11) of the Police and Criminal Evidence Act any

---

[90] Codes A–E. The latest version of these Codes came into effect on 1 August 2004. See p 401, *post*.

[91] Code F; issued under the authority of s 60A, PACE.

[92] *R v Walsh* (1990) 91 Cr App R 161, [1989] Crim LR 822; *R v Aspinall* [1999] 2 Cr App R 115, (1999) 96(7) LSG 35. See further, p 391, *post*.

[93] *R v Sanghera (Rashpal)* [2001] 1 Cr App R 20 at 6, [2000] All ER (D) 1415. The Court of Appeal upheld the trial judge's decision not to exclude evidence obtained in breach of Code B because there was no doubt as to its reliability.

[94] See p 575, *post*. For discussion of the Code of Practice, see Card and Ward, *Criminal Procedure and Investigations Act 1996* (1996), ch 3, and p 574, *post*.

[95] Section 199, as amended by the Employment Act 2002, s 43(1).   [96] Section 207(2), (3).

Code under the Act is admissible in evidence, and if appearing to be relevant to any question arising in the proceedings, 'it shall be taken into account in determining that question.'

Codes of Practice approved or issued by the Health and Safety Commission have even greater force, since a failure to comply with such a Code amounts to prima facie proof of a breach of the Act's provisions for the purposes of any criminal proceedings.[97] Reference may also be made to the Highway Code, first issued pursuant to the Road Traffic Act 1930. Failure to comply with its provisions is not an offence in itself, but it may be relied upon by any party in civil or criminal proceedings.[98]

C THE OPERATION OF STATUTES

In defining the scope of a statute it is necessary to advert both to its geographical area of operation and to the time during which it is operative.

1 GEOGRAPHICAL OPERATION

There is a presumption that an Act of Parliament is operative throughout the United Kingdom but not elsewhere unless a contrary intention appears in the Act itself.[99] The contrary intention may either limit or extend the geographical operation of the Act, and statutes frequently contain a section restricting their operation to exclude Scotland or Northern Ireland. The Limitation Act 1963 is a typical example. It was in three parts; Part I applying to England and Wales, Part II to Scotland, and Part III to Northern Ireland. Many other examples exist. A similar reduction in geographical operation occurs with Acts which are expressed to apply only to a limited locality. Such Acts are described as 'Local Acts'.

Conversely an Act may expressly or by necessary implication extend outside the United Kingdom, though there is a presumption against this.[100] For example, section 57 of the Offences Against the Person Act 1861 provides that the crime of bigamy is committed 'whether the second marriage shall have taken place in England or Ireland, or elsewhere.' Another example is Part II of the Sex Offenders Act 1997, which extends the jurisdiction of United Kingdom courts to allow trial in the UK of British citizens who commit certain sexual offences abroad. However, an Act with extraterritorial

---

[97] Health and Safety at Work Act 1974, ss 16 and 17(2).   [98] Road Traffic Act 1988, s 38(7).

[99] Since it lies within the prerogative power of the Crown to extend its sovereignty and jurisdiction across both land and sea, the words 'United Kingdom' incorporate such area of land or sea as may be formally declared by the Crown to be subject to its sovereignty and jurisdiction: see *Post Office* v *Estuary Radio Ltd* [1968] 2 QB 740, at 748, [1967] 3 All ER 663 at 680, per Diplock LJ.

[100] The presumption is particularly strong in criminal cases; see *Cox* v *Army Council* [1963] AC 48, [1962] 1 All ER 880; *Air-India* v *Wiggins* [1980] 2 All ER 593, [1980] 1 WLR 815.

operation will usually (but not always) apply only to British subjects or persons owing allegiance to the Crown.[101]

2 TEMPORAL OPERATION

(a) When a statute begins to be operative

Until 1793[102] a statute came into force on the first day of the parliamentary session in which it was passed. Consequently virtually all legislation was retrospective. The present law is that a statute comes into force on the day on which it receives the royal assent, unless some other date is specified in the Act itself. Increasingly, however, an Act may provide that it is to come into force on a 'day to be appointed' by statutory instrument, and different sections within an Act may be brought into force at different times. For example, most of the provisions of the Human Rights Act 1998 were brought into force in England and Wales approximately two years after the Act was passed, the commencement date having been effected by statutory instrument.[103] Certain provisions however, came into effect as soon as the Act received the royal assent.[104]

There are portions of Acts in existence which have never been brought into force,[105] and sometimes the decision not to implement is taken quite soon after the Act is passed. Thus, for example, sections 8 to 27 of the Crime (Sentences) Act 1997 introduced a new scheme for the early release of prisoners. Within months, and after a change of government, it was announced that the new scheme would not be implemented.[106]

Sometimes the failure to bring a statutory provision into force may give rise to problems, as was vividly demonstrated in *R v Secretary of State for the Home Department, ex parte Fire Brigades' Union.*[107] The Criminal Justice Act 1988 provided for a statutory compensation scheme for victims of violent crime, this being intended to replace the ex gratia Criminal Injuries Compensation Scheme established under the royal prerogative.[108] The statutory provisions were not brought into force and in 1994 the Home Secretary purported to introduce a new scheme pursuant to the royal

---

[101] *Joyce v DPP* [1946] AC 347, [1946] 1 All ER 186. Cf. the Internationally Protected Persons Act 1978, under which attacks upon the person or property of protected persons '(such as heads of state and their families) are offences justiciable in the United Kingdom, even though committed outside the United Kingdom by a person whether a citizen of the United Kingdom and Colonies or not' (s 1). See also the Suppression of Terrorism Act 1978, s 4 and the War Crimes Act 1991.

[102] Acts of Parliament (Commencement) Act 1793.

[103] For England and Wales—see s 22(3); Human Rights Act 1998 (Commencement No 2) Order, 2000 (SI 2000/1851).

[104] Sections 18 (appointment of judges to the European Court of Human Rights), 20 (the power to make supplementary orders) and 21(5) (abolition of the death penalty for certain military offences).

[105] *Current Law Statutes Annotated* incorporates a table of 'Legislation Not Yet in Force'. See also, *Is it in Force?*, which is published as an annual supplement to *Halsbury's Statutes of England.*

[106] See 299 HC Official Report (6th series) coll 342–350, 30 July 1997.

[107] [1995] 2 AC 513, [1995] 2 All ER 244; see p 210, *post.*

[108] Sections 108 to 117 and Schedules 6 and 7.

prerogative. The House of Lords held, by a majority, that the Home Secretary had acted unlawfully. Although he was not obliged to bring the statutory scheme into effect at any given time, he was under a duty to keep the matter under review. It was an abuse of prerogative power to exercise it in a manner inconsistent with bringing the statute into force. Lord Browne-Wilkinson observed that if the Home Secretary wanted to introduce a scheme inconsistent with that in the 1988 Act, he should have first asked Parliament to repeal the statutory provisions.

(b) Retrospective operation

As a general rule a statute only affects factual situations that arise during the period of its operation. There is a presumption against the statute being retroactive, although the courts have been keen to point out that it is in each case a question of ascertaining the intentions of Parliament. As Staughton LJ stated in *Secretary of State for Social Security* v *Tunnicliffe:*[109]

the true principle is that Parliament is presumed not to have intended to alter the law applicable to past events and transactions in a manner which is unfair to those concerned in them, unless a contrary intention appears. It is not simply a question of classifying an enactment as retrospective or non-retrospective. Rather it may well be a matter of degree— the greater the unfairness, the more it is expected that Parliament will make it clear if that is intended.

The presumption is particularly strong where a statute creates criminal penalties or would operate to deprive a person of a vested right in property.[110] In the case of the former, the presumption can only have been strengthened by section 3 of the Human Rights Act 1998, under which the courts must try to interpret legislation in a manner compatible with the prohibition on retrospective criminal offences in Article 7, ECHR.[111] Parliament is sovereign, however, and statutes are occasionally expressed to be retrospective even where this operates to deprive a person of a vested right in property. A modern illustration was the War Damage Act 1965, which operated to remove rights to compensation from the Crown, and which was expressed to apply to proceedings commenced before the Act came into force.[112] A more recent example is provided by the provisions in Part 10 of the Criminal Justice Act 2003. These

---

[109] [1991] 2 All ER 712 at 724, approved by the House of Lords in *L'Office Cherifien des Phosphates* v *Yamashita-Shinnihon Steamship Co Ltd* [1994] 1 AC 486, [1994] 1 All ER 20, and more recently in *Wilson* v *First County Trust (No 2)* [2003] UKHL 40, [2004] 1 AC 816, [2003] 4 All ER 97.

[110] *Yew Bon Tew* v *Kenderaan Bas Mara* [1983] 1 AC 553, [1982] 3 All ER 833. In *R* v *Fisher* [1969] 1 All ER 100, [1969] 1 WLR 8 the rule against retrospective operation operated *against* the accused, as he was convicted of an offence which had been abolished at some point between the commission of the offence and the date of his trial.

[111] See p 183, *post*. The Human Rights Act itself is presumed not to be retrospective, except to the extent that it can be relied upon in proceedings instigated by public authorities which concern events occurring before the Act came into force. See s 22(4); *R* v *Lambert* [2001] UKHL 37, [2002] 2 AC 545, [2001] 3 All ER 577.

[112] Section 1(2). The action affected was *Burmah Oil Co Ltd* v *Lord Advocate* [1965] AC 75, [1964] 2 All ER 348.

provisions bring about changes to the double jeopardy rule and are expressed to apply 'whether the acquittal was before or after the passing of this Act'.[113]

An Act of indemnity, the purpose of which is to validate or legalize that which was initially invalid or illegal, must by its nature be retroactive.[114] Similarly, a statute which alters rules of evidence or procedure is always retroactive in the absence of a contrary intention, since the rules of evidence and procedure that a court is bound to observe are those in existence at the time of the hearing.[115] On the other hand, sentencing provisions usually apply only in respect of offences committed after the provisions were introduced.

Even if the statutory provision does not take effect retrospectively, it may neverthe-less be held to entitle a court to have regard to what has occurred prior to its passage. Thus in *L'Office Cherifien des Phosphates* v *Yamashita-Shinnihon Steamship Co Ltd*,[116] the House of Lords held that an 'inordinate and inexcusable delay', which had occurred *before* section 13A of the Arbitration Act 1950 came into force, entitled an arbitrator to dismiss a claim.

(c) When a statute ceases to be operative

No statute becomes obsolete by the passing of time. Nevertheless there are many ancient statutes more honoured in the breach than in the observance. At one time the approach of the legislature was to do nothing until the need for repeal manifested itself. Thus, the plaintiff in a nineteenth century case was no doubt disturbed to discover that his opponent had a right to claim trial by battle,[117] and resort to such provisions as the preamble to the Charitable Uses Act 1601, the Statute of Frauds 1677, and the Bill of Rights 1688 is by no means uncommon.[118] The present position is that the Law Commissions are expressly required to review 'obsolete and unneces-sary enactments' with a view to repeal.[119] In consequence there are now regular Statute Law (Repeals) Acts, each of which repeals hundreds of obsolete enactments following recommendations of the Law Commissions.

There is an important exception to the rule that statutes do not become obsolete with the passing of time. Certain statutes are expressed to be operative only for a limited period, usually because they are experimental or transitional. The best known statutes of this type are the Army Act and the Air Force Act, and these are re-enacted periodically so as to avoid the prohibition on keeping a standing army in times of peace. Temporary statutes may acquire a new lease of life by the passing of an Expiring Laws Continuance Act, which is effected solely for the purpose of renewing statutes

---

[113] Section 75(6).

[114] Examples of Acts of indemnity are: Indemnity Act 1920; Indian Divorces (Validity) Act 1921.

[115] See *Blyth* v *Blyth* [1966] AC 643, [1966] 1 All ER 524; *R* v *Cruttenden* [1991] 2 QB 66, [1991] 3 All ER 242 (evidence); cf. *Yew Bon Tew* v *Kenderaan Bas Mara* [1983] 1 AC 553, [1982] 3 All ER 833 (limitation statute in Malaysia held not to revive statute-barred cause of action).

[116] [1994] 1 AC 486, [1994] 1 All ER 20.   [117] *Ashford* v *Thornton* (1818) 1 & Ald 405.

[118] See, e.g., *Rost* v *Edwards* [1990] 2 QB 460, [1990] 2 All ER 641.

[119] Law Commissions Act 1965, s 3(1).

which would otherwise expire. Thus Part I of the Commonwealth Immigrants Act 1962, an experimental measure expressed to last for only one year, was renewed annually until 1971 when the Immigration Act 1971 was passed to supersede it.

Unless it is expressed to be operative for a limited period, a statute ceases to have effect only when this is provided for by another statute, since only Parliament is competent to repeal (or authorize the repeal of) its own enactments.[120] Repeal of one statute does not have the effect of reviving any earlier legislative provision, statutory or otherwise, unless the contrary intention is expressed by Parliament.[121]

Repeal may be express or implied. In modern times almost all repeal is express and it is common for a schedule of repeals to be incorporated into the body of an Act. Implied repeal is possible however, and occurs where two statutory provisions are inconsistent with one another. In this situation the later provision impliedly repeals the earlier to the extent of the inconsistency.[122] The courts generally lean against implied repeal and will attempt to reconcile seemingly conflicting provisions wherever possible. Moreover, the recent decision of the Divisional Court in *Thoburn* v *Sunderland City Council and others* suggests that there is a certain class of legislation, labelled 'constitutional statutes', which can only be repealed expressly.[123] The European Communities Act 1972, the Human Rights Act 1998, and the Scotland Act 1998 are said to be examples of such legislation.[124] There is also a rule that a public Act does not impliedly repeal a private or local Act (*generalia specialibus non derogant*).[125]

D THE INTERPRETATION AND CONSTRUCTION OF STATUTES

1 THE NEED FOR INTERPRETATION AND CONSTRUCTION

Where the words of a statute are clear and unambiguous, persons affected by its provisions will regulate their conduct according to its terms and the need for judicial interpretation will not arise. However, if the meaning or extent of a statute is uncertain or ambiguous litigation is inevitable and the statute will fall to be interpreted. There is a technical distinction between interpretation and construction. 'Interpretation' is simply the process whereby a meaning is assigned to the words in a

---

[120] An enactment may be impliedly repealed by EC legislation: *Amministrazione delle Finanze dello Stato* v *Simmenthal SpA* [1978] ECR 629; see p 126 *post*. In addition, Parliament may confer power on a Minister to amend or repeal statutory provisions: see p 36, *ante*.

[121] Interpretation Act 1978, ss 15, 16(1).

[122] See, for example, *Smith* v *Benabo* [1937] 1 KB 518, [1937] 1 All ER 523; *Ellen Street Estates Ltd* v *Minister of Health* [1934] 1 KB 590; *Dryden* v *Dryden* [1973] Fam 217, [1973] 3 All ER 526.

[123] [2002] EWHC 195 (Admin) at [60], [2003] QB 151 at [60], [2002] 4 All ER 156, per Laws LJ.

[124] Ibid. See further, p 30, *ante*.

[125] See *Bishop of Gloucester* v *Cunnington* [1943] KB 101, [1943] 1 All ER 61.

statute. 'Construction', on the other hand, is the process whereby uncertainties or ambiguities are resolved. It follows that every statute that comes before a court is interpreted, whereas only uncertain or ambiguous provisions require construction. Judges do not usually distinguish the processes since litigation generally only arises where the wording of a statute is ambiguous or uncertain. Lawson J, however, did distinguish them in one case:[126]

Stage one is this; whether the meaning of the Cyprus Act 1960 in this respect is clear and unambiguous, and if so, what does it mean? At this stage I look at the words of the enactment as a whole, including the Schedule, and I use no further aids, no further extrinsic aids in order to reach a conclusion as to the clear and unambiguous meaning of the words . . . If I find that the answer on the first stage in my inquiry is that the meaning of the Act in this respect is ambiguous, then I have to go on to the second stage and consider two possible different meanings . . . Now if I get to this second stage, then in my judgment, and then only, am I entitled to look at extrinsic aids[127] such as the long title, the heading, the side notes, other legislation; then only am I entitled to resort to maxims of construction. . . .

(a) The words of the statute

The need for interpretation or construction may arise for a variety of reasons. One may be careless drafting, or the form and content of the Act having been the subject of hasty or ill thought-out amendments during the parliamentary process. However, many issues of construction arise simply because of the very uncertainty of words themselves. In the drink-driving case of *DPP* v *Johnson*,[128] for example, the Divisional Court had to consider the meaning of the word 'consume' in section 5 of the Road Traffic Act 1988. As Schiemann LJ put it:

It is not unusual to speak of a house being consumed by fire and it would not be strange to speak of a bottle of medical alcohol having been consumed by rubbing its contents into skin prior to administering an injection . . . One can also talk of consuming snuff by sniffing.

The meaning of a word depends on the context in which it is used. It was the context of section 5, together with the marginal note, that persuaded the court to reject the submission that 'consume' in section 5 meant 'consume by mouth', holding that a drink–drive offence could be committed even if the alcohol had, in part, been ingested by injection.

(b) Ambiguity

Ambiguity arises when words used in a statute are found to be capable of bearing two or more literal meanings. Language is an imprecise tool and even Parliamentary draftsmen, in using words intended to convey one meaning, occasionally contrive to give rise to an alternative meaning which neither they nor the legislature envisaged.

---

[126] *Franklin* v *A-G* [1974] QB 185 at 199, [1973] 1 All ER 879 at 886.

[127] The aids referred to by Lawson J are generally referred to as *intrinsic* (rather than extrinsic) aids since they appear in the text of the Queen's Printer's copy of the Act; see p 66, *post*.

[128] [1995] 4 All ER 53, [1995] 1 WLR 728.

Thus the Restriction of Offensive Weapons Act 1959 made it an offence to 'offer for sale' certain offensive weapons, including 'flick knives'. A shopkeeper who displayed weapons of this type in his window was held not to be guilty of an offence under the Act, because the exhibition of goods in a shop window does not constitute an offer.[129]

Where a statute concerns an intrinsically complex area of law, such as landlord and tenant or income tax, it seems to be virtually impossible to choose language which is entirely free from ambiguity. Nevertheless the judiciary has on occasion been less than sympathetic to the draftsman's plight. Thus in *R v Royle*[130] section 16 of the Theft Act 1968 was described as being so obscure as to have 'created a judicial nightmare', while in *Central Asbestos Co Ltd v Dodd*, Lord Reid said that the Limitation Act 1963 had 'a strong claim to the distinction of being the worst drafted Act on the statute book'.[131]

(c) Uncertainty

Uncertainty is far more common than ambiguity. Uncertainty occurs where the words of a statute are intended to apply to various factual situations and the courts are called upon to decide whether or not the set of facts before them were envisaged by the Act. For example, the words 'an accident arising out of and in the course of his employment' in the Workmen's Compensation Acts were the source of innumerable cases, not because they were in any way ambiguous but because their scope was adaptable to endless permutations of facts and was therefore uncertain.[132]

The use of general and ostensibly straightforward words, such as 'road',[133] 'premises',[134] and 'board'[135] has created problems of construction that the legislature could not have envisaged. More recently, the courts have had to resolve such conundrums as whether the cremation of humans is 'the subjection of goods or materials to any process',[136] whether an orange squeezed by hand is a 'manufactured beverage',[137] whether a partner in a long-term homosexual relationship is a member of the other

---

[129] *Fisher v Bell* [1961] 1 QB 394, [1960] 3 All ER 731. In reaching this decision, the Divisional Court relied heavily upon established common law principles of contract law: see also *Partridge v Crittenden* [1968] 2 All ER 421, [1968] 1 WLR 1204.

[130] [1971] 3 All ER 1359 at 1363, [1971] 1 WLR 1764 at 1767, per Edmund Davies LJ. The offending part of the section (s 16(2)(a)) was eventually repealed and replaced by the Theft Act 1978.

[131] [1973] AC 518 at 529, [1972] 2 All ER 1135 at 113; the Limitation Act 1975 (replacing that part of the 1963 Act) seemed to aim at similar distinction. The Acts concerned are now consolidated in the Limitation Act 1980.

[132] The words are still used in social security legislation (currently the Social Security Contributions and Benefits Act 1992, s 94) where they continue to cause trouble; see *R v National Insurance Commissioner, ex parte Michael* [1977] 2 All ER 420, [1977] 1 WLR 109.

[133] *Cutter v Eagle Star Insurance Co Ltd* [1998] 4 All ER 417, [1998] 1 WLR 1647.

[134] *Whitley v Stumbles* [1930] AC 544; *Maunsell v Olins* [1975] AC 373, [1975] 1 All ER 16.

[135] *Otter v Norman* [1989] AC 129, [1988] 2 All ER 897.

[136] *Bourne (Inspector of Taxes) v Norwich Crematorium Ltd* [1967] 2 All ER 576, [1967] 1 WLR 691.

[137] *Customs and Excise Commissioners v Savoy Hotel Ltd* [1966] 2 All ER 299, [1966] 1 WLR 948. For a delightfully sardonic exposition of the difficulty of ascertaining the 'right' meaning of words, see the judgment of Diplock LJ in *Slim v Daily Telegraph Ltd* [1968] 2 QB 157 at 171–2, [1968] 1 All ER 497 at 504.

partner's 'family',[138] and whether a male to female transsexual is a 'female'.[139] Lord Denning once expressed the difficulty as follows:[140]

It must be remembered that it is not within human powers to foresee the manifold sets of facts which may arise, and, even if it were, it is not possible to provide for them in terms free from all ambiguity.

2 JUDICIAL APPROACHES TO INTERPRETATION

The basic task of the judge is to ascertain the intention of Parliament. Nevertheless there are alternative approaches to this task. These approaches, which differ radically, are commonly known as the 'literal' approach and the 'purposive' approach. It is never possible to know in advance which approach any particular court will favour, and it may well be that a court will adopt the approach which best enables it to reach the conclusion considered just in all the circumstances. In *Re M (A Minor) (Care Order: Threshold Conditions)*[141] Lord Templeman spoke of: 'ascertaining and giving effect to the intention of Parliament by construing a statute in accordance with the spirit rather than the letter of the Act.'

Both of these approaches to interpretation are discussed below, though they must now be considered in the light of the obligation arising from section 3 of the Human Rights Act 1998.[142]

(a) The literal approach

The basic approach to statutory interpretation, as already stated, is to ascertain the intention of the legislature. The literal approach to this task is that this intention must be found in the ordinary and natural meaning of the language used in the statute. In other words, the focus is on the 'objective' meaning of the words, not on the subjective intention that might lie behind their use. While the approach may be defended as respecting the proper boundaries between the judicial and legislative functions,[143] it does have certain obvious shortcomings. Firstly, it relies on an assumption that the 'ordinary and natural meaning' of a word or phrase can always be ascertained. Yet as discussed previously, this is not always the case and the courts have often had considerable difficulty in interpreting seemingly straightforward words.[144] Secondly, if the words used in a provision are capable of *alternative* ordinary and natural meanings, the court still needs to find a mechanism for choosing between these alternatives.

---

[138] *Fitzpatrick* v *Sterling Housing Association Ltd* [2001] 1 AC 27, [1999] 4 All ER 705.

[139] *Bellinger* v *Bellinger* [2003] UKHL 21, [2003] 2 AC 467, [2003] 2 All ER 593.

[140] *Asher* v *Seaford Court Estates Ltd* [1949] 2 KB 481 at 499, [1949] 2 All ER 155 at 164.

[141] [1994] 2 AC 424, [1994] 3 All ER 298.

[142] The impact of the Human Rights Act on statutory interpretation is discussed at p 157, *post*. As to the interpretation of European Community legislation, see chapter 4, *post*.

[143] See, e.g., the judgment of Viscount Dilhorne in *Kammins Ballrooms Co Ltd* v *Zenith Investments (Torquay) Ltd* [1971] AC 850, [1970] 2 All ER 871.

[144] See p 47, *ante*.

Despite these shortcomings, the literal approach will, in most cases, produce a reasonable interpretation of the statute. Difficulty arises, however, where a literal interpretation produces either an improbable result or a manifest absurdity. Where the result is merely less plausible than that which Parliament might be assumed to have intended, a strict application of the literal approach means that this interpretation ought nevertheless to be given. Thus in *Inland Revenue Commissioners* v *Hinchy*[145] the House of Lords was called upon to construe section 25(3) of the Income Tax Act 1952, which provided that any person delivering an incorrect tax return should forfeit 'treble the tax which he ought to be charged under this Act'. Although Parliament presumably intended a penalty of treble the *unpaid* tax,[146] the House of Lords took a literal approach to the subsection, and held that the respondent was liable to pay treble the *whole* amount of tax payable by him for the year. *Fisher* v *Bell*, cited earlier,[147] is a further example of the application of the literal rule producing a result which appeared contrary to the intention of the legislature.

The golden rule. The strict application of the literal approach may be modified by the use of 'the golden rule'. This means that where the literal approach would produce a manifestly absurd outcome, judges may depart from the ordinary meaning of the word(s), in favour of an interpretation which avoids the absurdity. Lord Blackburn explained this approach as follows:[148]

[W]e are to take the whole statute and construe it all together, giving the words their ordinary signification, unless when so applied they produce an inconsistency or absurdity or inconvenience so great as to convince the Court that the intention could not have been to use them in their ordinary signification, and to justify the court in putting them in some other signification, which, though less proper, is one which the Court thinks the words will bear.

The use of the golden rule is well illustrated by the unanimous decision of the House of Lords in *McMonagle* v *Westminster City Council*.[149] The appellant was charged with using premises as a 'sex encounter establishment' without a licence. The statutory definition of these words was 'premises at which performances which are not unlawful are given, which wholly or mainly comprise the sexual stimulation of persons admitted to the premises.' The appellant's defence was that the prosecution had failed to prove that the performances were not unlawful, and that if they were, according to the plain words of the statute a licence was not required. The House of Lords rejected this interpretation as manifestly absurd. Lord Bridge explained his reasoning:[150]

---

[145] [1960] AC 748, [1960] 1 All ER 505.

[146] The law was in fact changed shortly after this decision by the Finance Act 1960, s 44.

[147] [1961] 1 QB 394, [1960] 3 All ER 731; see p 47, *ante*. The Law Commission report, *The Interpretation of Statutes*, 1969 (Law Com No 21) recommended a statutory provision to the effect that a construction which would promote the general legislative purpose underlying the provision in question 'is to be preferred to a construction which would not'.

[148] *River Wear Commissioners* v *Adamson* (1877) 2 App Cas 743 at 764–5.

[149] [1990] 2 AC 716, [1990] 1 All ER 993.

[150] [1990] 2 AC 716 at 727, [1990] 1 All ER 993 at 998.

I am satisfied that the main object of paragraph 3A(c) of Schedule 3 is to require any premises, not falling within the proviso, where live nude entertainment is provided to be licensed and that in order to avoid the substantial frustration of that object it is both necessary and legitimate that the words 'which are not unlawful' should be treated as surplusage and as having been introduced by incompetent draftsmanship for no other purpose than to emphasise that a licence confers no immunity from the ordinary criminal law.

Another example is provided by *Adler* v *George*.[151] In this case, a conviction for causing an obstruction '*in the vicinity of*' a prohibited place was upheld by the Divisional Court even though the incident had occurred *inside* the place in question. Similarly, in *R* v *Allen*[152] the court applied the golden rule to the statutory definition of bigamy in order to avoid a manifestly absurd outcome. Section 57 of the Offences Against the Person Act 1861 stated that, 'whosoever being married shall marry another person . . . shall be guilty of bigamy'. A literal interpretation of these words would have rendered it impossible to commit the offence, since any attempt to 'marry' whilst already being married to someone else would be ineffective. The court therefore interpreted the phrase 'shall marry' to mean 'shall go through a marriage ceremony'.[153]

The difficulty, of course, lies in drawing the line between a literal interpretation which appears to the court to produce a 'manifest absurdity', and one which merely appears to be improbable. For those who advocate a literal approach to statutory interpretation, the adoption of a different meaning in the former case may be accepted as a legitimate extension of this approach. To depart from the ordinary meaning of words in the latter case, however, might be seen as unacceptable judicial activism. Lord Bridge is amongst those to have warned against the judiciary substituting its own judgment for that of the legislature:[154]

It is one thing to abstain from giving to the language of a statute the full effect of its ordinary grammatical meaning in order to avoid some positively harmful or manifestly unjust consequence. This I would describe as a legitimate process of construction to avoid a positive absurdity. But it is quite another thing to read into a statute a meaning which the language used will not bear in order to remedy a supposed defect or shortcoming which, if not made good, will make the statutory machinery less effective than the court believes it ought to be in order to achieve its proper purpose.

A case which arguably stretches the limits of the golden rule is *DPP* v *McKeown*.[155] The House of Lords had to consider the meaning of section 69 of the Police and Criminal Evidence Act 1984, which allowed computer-generated documents to be admitted as evidence if the court was satisfied that any fault in the computer had not

---

[151] [1964] 2 QB 7, [1964] 1 All ER 628.   [152] (1872) LR 1 CCR 367.

[153] This reasoning should be compared with that applied in *Whiston* v *Whiston* [1995] Fam 198, [1998] 1 All ER 423, to prevent a bigamist from claiming financial relief under the Matrimonial Causes Act 1973. (Cf. *Rampal* v *Rampal (No 2)* [2001] EWCA Civ 989, [2002] Fam 85, [2001] 3 WLR 795.)

[154] *R* v *Central Criminal Court, ex parte Francis & Francis* [1989] AC 346 at 375, [1988] 3 All ER 775 at 783.

[155] [1997] 1 All ER 737, [1997] 1 WLR 295. The provision in question has now been repealed.

affected the production of the document or the accuracy of its contents. Because the computer's clock had been set inaccurately, the time stated on a document produced by the computer was wrong. On a literal interpretation, it was thus inadmissible: the contents were inaccurate. However, the House of Lords avoided this conclusion because it considered that Parliament could not have intended it—the inaccurate time shown on the document did not affect its reliability as proof of what was being disputed.

Finally, it should be noted that there is a residual category of cases in which a literal interpretation of a statute is rejected in order to avoid an outcome which would clearly be contrary to public policy. Thus in *Re Sigsworth*[156] the golden rule was applied to prevent a murderer from inheriting the estate of his victim, although he was, as her son, the 'sole issue' on a literal interpretation of the Administration of Estates Act 1925. In a later case, the Court of Appeal took a similar approach in rejecting the judicial review application of a double killer. The applicant had a psychotic illness which was known to involve extreme hatred of his adoptive parents. His application for a copy of his birth certificate was turned down by the Registrar General out of concern that he might use the information to find and harm his natural mother. Despite the fact that the ordinary words in the Adoption Act 1976 did not give the Registrar General any discretion to refuse the applicant's request, the Court of Appeal upheld his decision on the basis that Parliament could not have intended to facilitate the commission of a crime.[157]

(b) The purposive approach

The 'mischief rule', or rule in *Heydon's* case,[158] is a form of purposive interpretation with a relatively long history. It means that where a statute was passed to remedy a mischief the court will, if possible, adopt the interpretation of the statute which will have the effect of correcting that mischief. In *Heydon's* case itself, the rule was defined thus:

four things are to be discussed and considered; (1) what was the common law before the making of the Act; (2) what was the mischief and defect for which the common law did not provide; (3) what remedy the Parliament hath resolved and appointed to cure the disease of the commonwealth; and (4) the true reason of the remedy.

In order to ascertain the mischief which the statute was passed to correct, the judge may legitimately have regard to the preamble of the statute, the long title, headings, and extrinsic sources which may indicate the state of the law before the passing of the Act.[159]

The rule has often been used to resolve ambiguities in cases where the literal rule would produce an unsatisfactory outcome. For example, a 'single woman' for the

---

[156] [1935] Ch 89.
[157] *R v Registrar General, ex parte Smith* [1991] 2 QB 393, [1991] 2 All ER 88.
[158] (1584) 3 Co Rep 7a.
[159] For further discussion of the use of both internal and external aids, see pp 66–75, *post*.

purposes of affiliation proceedings was a woman with no husband to support her, not necessarily an unmarried woman—the Acts were passed to remedy the mischief of women having illegitimate children without the means of supporting them.[160] Similarly, medically-induced abortions brought about by nurses acting under the instruction of doctors constituted lawful 'termination by a registered medical practitioner', since the statute in question was intended to correct the mischief of legal uncertainty and to ensure that abortions were carried out safely.[161]

Unlike in Heydon's day, most modern legislation is not specifically concerned with rectifying mischief but with the fulfilment of some more general policy objective:

> Even for the lawyer, the expression [the mischief rule] is unsatisfactory. It tends to suggest that legislation is only designed to deal with an evil, and not to further a positive social approach.[162]

The 'mischief rule' has therefore given way to the slightly broader notion of 'purposive' interpretation. This emphasizes the need to construe the wording of a statute in its wider context, so as to give effect to its underlying purpose. One criticism that could be made of the wide application of this purposive approach is that it is inherently subjective. The judge who decides that a literal interpretation is contrary to the intention of the legislature is, *ipso facto*, ascertaining its intention from some source other than the statute, and this might be regarded as going beyond the judicial function. Moreover, the judge may expose himself to the criticism that he is giving effect to his own views of what the policy of Parliament *ought* to be.[163] The contrary view, however, is that a consideration of the context in which Parliament has used particular words can only enhance a judge's ability to ascertain their intended meaning:[164]

> The starting point is that language in all legal texts conveys meaning according to the circumstances in which it was used. It follows that the context must always be identified and considered before the process of construction or during it. It is therefore wrong to say that the court may only resort to evidence of the contextual scene when an ambiguity has arisen.

In *Shah v Barnet London Borough Council*,[165] the House of Lords offered *some* guidance as to when a purposive interpretation of a provision could be adopted in preference to its literal meaning. It concluded that this would only be legitimate where a clear expression of the legislative intention could be found in either the Act or permissible extrinsic sources.

---

[160] *Kruhlak v Kruhlak* [1958] 2 QB 32, [1958] 1 All ER 154.

[161] *Royal College of Nursing v Department of Health and Social Security* [1981] AC 800, [1981] 1 All ER 545.

[162] Law Commission, *The Interpretation of Statutes* (Law Com. No 21), 1969.

[163] See *Duport Steels Ltd v Sirs* [1980] 1 All ER 529, [1980] 1 WLR 142; *Shah v Barnet London Borough Council* [1983] 2 AC 309, [1983] 1 All ER 226.

[164] *Westminster City Council v National Asylum Support Service* [2002] UKHL 38 at [5], [2002] 4 All ER 654 at [5], [2002] 1 WLR 2956, per Lord Steyn.

[165] [1983] 2 AC 309, [1983] 1 All ER 226.

Supplying omissions. The legitimacy of going beyond a literal interpretation of a statute is often called into question when a court is faced with a factual situation for which the statute does not provide. Such a situation is termed a *casus omissus*, and it can only be remedied by attributing to Parliament an intention that it never had. This amounts to a legislative act on the part of the judiciary and is a function which the more conservative judges are slow to adopt. Denning LJ, in the Court of Appeal, expressed his personal view of the judicial function as follows:[166]

We sit here to find out the intention of Parliament and of Ministers and carry it out, and we do this better by filling in the gaps and making sense of the enactment than by opening it up to destructive analysis.

On appeal Lord Simonds condemned this approach, describing it as a 'naked usurpation of the legislative function under the thin disguise of interpretation'.[167] 'If a gap is disclosed,' Lord Simonds explained, 'the remedy lies in an amending Act.'

In *Kammins Ballrooms Co Ltd* v *Zenith Investments (Torquay) Ltd* a majority of the House of Lords were prepared to read words into section 29(3) of the Landlord and Tenant Act 1954. They held that they had the power to consider an application brought by a tenant less than two months after requesting a new tenancy, even though the provision stated that 'no application shall be entertained unless it is made *not less than* two nor more than four months' after such a request.[168] As Lord Diplock explained:[169]

[This conclusion] can be justified only upon the assumption that the draftsman of the Act omitted to state in any words used in the subsection an exception to the absolute prohibition to which Parliament must have intended it to be subject. A conclusion that an exception was intended by Parliament, and what that exception was can only be reached by using the purposive approach.

In *Inco Europe Ltd* v *First Choice Distribution* the House of Lords was unanimous in confirming that the courts do have the power to correct obvious drafting errors:[170]

Before interpreting a statute in this way the court must be abundantly sure of three matters: (1) the intended purpose of the statute or provision in question; (2) that by inadvertence the draftsman and Parliament failed to give effect to that purpose in the provision in question; and (3) the substance of the provision Parliament would have made, although not necessarily the precise words Parliament would have used, had the error in the Bill been noticed.

(c) The trend towards purposive interpretation

While the literal and purposive approaches to statutory interpretation may be alternative models, it would be wrong to treat them as mutually exclusive. Firstly, a literal

---

166 *Magor and St Mellons Rural District Council* v *Newport Corporation* [1950] 2 All ER 1226 at 1236.
167 [1952] AC 189 at 191, [1951] 2 All ER 839 at 841.
168 [1971] AC 850, [1970] 2 All ER 871 (emphasis added).
169 [1971] AC 850 at 880, [1970] 2 All ER 871 at 892.
170 [2000] 2 All ER 109 at 115, [2000] 1 WLR 586 at 592, per Lord Nicholls.

reading of a provision will not always be able to resolve an ambiguity, and secondly, even under a purposive approach the court's primary obligation is to interpret the words of the Act. As Lord Hoffman explained in one case:[171]

There is ultimately only one principle of construction, namely to ascertain what Parliament meant by using the language of the statute.

Moreover, since these are merely approaches rather than strict rules, judges can, and do, adopt whichever method of interpretation they consider appropriate, and it is common to find elements of both approaches influencing the same decision. Thus, as Laws LJ observed, 'the difference in purposive and literal construction is in truth one of degree only,'[172] and the cases do not always fall neatly into distinct categories.

For some judges, the choice of approach is a matter of principle, and it is inextricably linked with ideas about the role of the courts within the framework of the constitution and the separation of powers.[173]

[I]t cannot be too strongly emphasised that the British Constitution, though largely unwritten, is firmly based on the separation of powers. Parliament makes the laws, the judiciary interprets them. When Parliament legislates to remedy what the majority of its members at the time perceive to be a defect or lacuna in the existing law . . . the role of the judiciary is confined to ascertaining from the words that Parliament has approved as expressing its intention what that intention was, and giving effect to it. Where the meaning of statutory words is plain and unambiguous it is not for judges to invent fancied ambiguities as an excuse for failing to give effect to its plain meaning . . . Under our constitution it is Parliament's opinion on these matters that is paramount.

Increasingly however, many judges take the view that the approach to interpretation must be determined on an individual basis, taking into account all the circumstances of a case. It is clear that the willingness to look beyond a strict literal approach is growing, and the decision to permit limited use of *Hansard* as an extrinsic aid is evidence of this. It is equally beyond doubt that the particular approach adopted by the court will turn not only on the inclinations of the individual judge, but also upon the context in which the matter is being decided. As will be seen later, the courts are always anxious to adopt a purposive approach to statutes in order to give effect to international obligations, and in the context of EC law they are under a legal obligation to do so. In addition, the Human Rights Act 1998 obliges the courts to take a more creative approach to statutory interpretation in all cases which could impact on the protection of ECHR rights.

---

[171] *MacNiven* v *Westmoreland Investments* [2001] UKHL 6, [2003] 1 AC 311, [2001] 1 All ER 865.
[172] *Oliver Ashworth (Holdings) Ltd* v *Ballard (Kent) Ltd* [2000] Ch 12 at 34, [1999] 2 All ER 791 at 805.
[173] *Duport Steels* v *Sirs* [1980] 1 All ER 529 at 541, [1980] 1 WLR 142 at 157, per Lord Diplock.

(d) Statutory interpretation under The Human Rights Act 1998[174]

The Human Rights Act 1998 adds a new dimension to the task of statutory interpretation.[175] The long title describes it as 'an Act to give further effect to rights and freedoms guaranteed under the European Convention on Human Rights', and one of the principal mechanisms by which it seeks to do this is contained in section 3(1). This provides that:

So far as it is possible to do so, primary legislation and subordinate legislation must be read and given effect in a way which is compatible with the Convention rights.[176]

Section 3 applies to *all* legislation, whether enacted before or after the Human Rights Act,[177] and it significantly enhances the courts' powers of interpretation. However, it stops short of enabling them to disapply Acts of Parliament[178] and it does not affect the validity, continuing operation, or enforcement of any incompatible primary legislation. Nor does it affect the validity of incompatible subordinate legislation where primary legislation prevents removal of the incompatibility.[179] If a Convention compliant interpretation of an Act is not possible, a court[180] may issue a declaration of incompatibility but it must still give effect to the legislation as Parliament intended.[181] Thus, as Lord Steyn explained:[182]

It is crystal clear that the carefully and subtly drafted Human Rights Act 1998 preserves the principle of Parliamentary sovereignty. In a case of incompatibility which cannot be avoided by interpretation under section 3(1), the courts may not disapply the legislation. The court may merely issue a declaration of incompatibility which then gives rise to a power to take remedial action.

Section 3 is more than just a 'tool' which judges may consider in the event of an ambiguity, and its effect is not simply to add yet another approach to existing canons

---

[174] Much has been written about statutory interpretation under the Human Rights Act 1998. See for example, Clayton, 'The Limits of What's "Possible": Statutory Construction Under the Human Rights Act' [2002] *EHRLR* 559; Lord Lester, 'The Art of the Possible—Interpreting Statutes Under the Human Rights Act' [1998] *EHRLR* 665; Bennion 'What Interpretation is "Possible" Under s 3(1) of the Human Rights Act 1998' [2000] *Public Law* 77; Marshall, 'The Lynchpin of Parliamentary Intention: Lost, Stolen or Strained?' [2003] *Public Law* 236.

[175] The overall significance of this major piece of legislation is discussed in chapter 5.

[176] Section 1(1) provides that 'Convention rights' are those ECHR rights contained in Articles 2 to 12 and 14, Articles 1 to 3 of the First Protocol and Articles 1 and 2 of the Sixth Protocol. The text of these Articles is set out in Schedule 1 to the Act.

[177] Section 3(2).

[178] Cf. The European Communities Act 1972, s 2(4); discussed further in chapter 4, *post*.

[179] Section 3(2).

[180] For these purposes, the term 'court' means the House of Lords, the Judicial Committee of the Privy Council, the Courts-Martial Appeal Court, the Court of Appeal, the High Court, and the Scottish High Court of Justiciary (except when sitting as a trial court or Court of Session): s 4(5).

[181] Section 4. The effect of such a declaration is simply to bring the incompatibility to the attention of Parliament, and, where appropriate, to allow Ministers to take remedial action under s 10. Incompatible *subordinate* legislation may be declared invalid unless primary legislation prevents removal of the incompatibility. In the latter case a declaration of incompatibility may be issued.

[182] *R v DPP, ex parte Kebilene* [2000] 2 AC 326 at 333, [1999] 4 All ER 801 at 831.

of interpretation. Instead, it imposes an *obligation* on judges to seek a Convention compatible interpretation, regardless of whether the provision in question is ambiguous. Once it is established that Convention rights are engaged, courts are permitted to go far beyond previously accepted limits in seeking 'possible' meanings of words:[183]

[Section 3] will require a very different approach to interpretation from that to which the English courts are accustomed. Traditionally, the search has been for the true meaning: now it will be for a possible meaning that would prevent the making of a declaration of incompatibility.

On the other hand, section 3 need not be considered at all unless an 'ordinary' reading of the disputed legislation would give rise to a Convention breach:[184]

[U]nless the legislation would otherwise be in breach of the Convention section 3 can be ignored; so courts should always first ascertain whether, absent section 3, there would be any breach of the Convention . . .

Several cases decided since the Act came into force have considered the permissible boundaries of interpretation under section 3. In *Poplar Housing and Regeneration Community Association* v *Donoghue*, the Court of Appeal sought to distinguish between the tasks of legislation and interpretation:[185]

[I]f it is necessary in order to obtain compliance to radically alter the effect of the legislation this will be an indication that more than interpretation is involved.

It is clear that 'reading down' legislation to narrow the effect of a provision, and reading additional words *in*, are both legitimate techniques in Human Rights Act cases. Thus, in *R* v *Lambert*[186] the House of Lords read down a provision of the Misuse of Drugs Act 1971, so as to impose an evidential rather than a legal burden on the accused and thereby avoid a breach of the presumption of innocence. Similarly, in *Ghaidan* v *Godin-Mendoza*[187] the phrase 'as his or her wife or husband' was construed to mean '*as if they were* his or her wife or husband', in order to avoid a conclusion that the Rent Act 1977 discriminated against same-sex partners.

The leading case on section 3 is *R* v *A (No 2)*.[188] The defendant was prosecuted for rape and sought to rely on the defence of consent. He wanted to adduce evidence of the complainant's sexual history in support of this defence, but the use of such

---

[183] Lord Cooke, 582 HL Official Report (5th series) col 1272, 3 November 1997. (Even before the Human Rights Act, there is evidence that some judges were prepared to take a more teleological approach to the interpretation of human rights provisions. See, e.g., the Privy Council's experience of interpreting written constitutions and Bills of Rights from other jurisdictions: *Huntley* v *Attorney-General for Jamaica* [1995] 2 AC 1, [1995] 1 All ER 308; *Attorney-General of Hong-Kong* v *Lee Kwong-kut* [1993] AC 951, [1993] 3 All ER 939.)

[184] *Poplar Housing and Regeneration Community Association Ltd* v *Donoghue* [2001] EWCA Civ 595 at [75], [2002] QB 48 at [75], [2001] 4 All ER 604, per Lord Woolf CJ. This approach was endorsed by Lord Hope in *R* v *A (No 2)* [2001] UKHL 25 at [58], [2002] 1 AC 45 at [58], [2001] 3 All ER 1.

[185] [2001] EWCA Civ 595 at [76], [2002] QB 48 at [76], [2001] 4 All ER 604, per Lord Woolf CJ.

[186] [2001] UKHL 37, [2002] 2 AC 545, [2001] 3 All ER 577.

[187] [2004] UKHL 30, [2004] 2 AC 557, [2004] 3 All ER 411.

[188] [2001] UKHL 25, [2002] 1 AC 45, [2001] 3 All ER 1.

evidence appeared to be precluded by section 41 of the Youth Justice and Criminal Evidence Act 1999. Defence counsel contended that a refusal to admit the evidence would breach the right of the accused to a fair trial under Article 6 of the Convention: the issue for the court was whether it was 'possible' to interpret section 41 in a manner compatible with that right. The House of Lords held that it was, interpreting it as being subject to an implied discretion to permit evidence of sexual history in order to ensure a fair trial. Lord Steyn explained the effect of section 3 as follows:[189]

[T]he interpretive obligation under s 3 of the 1998 Act is a strong one. It applies even if there is no ambiguity in the language in the sense of the language being capable of two different meanings . . . Under ordinary methods of interpretation a court may depart from the language of the statute to avoid absurd consequences: s 3 goes much further. Undoubtedly, a court must always look for a contextual and purposive interpretation: s 3 is more radical in its effect. It is a general principle of the interpretation of legal instruments that the text is the primary source of interpretation: other sources are subordinate to it . . . Section 3 qualifies this general principle because it requires a court to find an interpretation compatible with Convention rights if it is possible to do so . . . In accordance with the will of Parliament as reflected in s 3 it will sometimes be necessary to adopt an interpretation, which linguistically may appear strained. The techniques to be used will not only involve the reading down of express language in a statute but also the implication of provisions.

Thus far, *R v A (No 2)* probably constitutes the 'high water mark' of judicial creativity under the Human Rights Act, and in subsequent decisions the courts have not always been willing to go quite this far. In *Re S (Children) (Care Order: Implementation of Care Plan)*[190] the Court of Appeal read words into the Children Act 1989 to give the courts increased discretionary powers concerning children taken into care. On appeal to the House of Lords however, this use of section 3 was rejected, and their Lordships cautioned against reading words into an Act to the point of making it unintelligible or unworkable:[191]

[Section] 3(2)(b) presupposes that not all provisions in primary legislation can be rendered convention compliant by the application of section 3(1) . . . For present purposes, it is sufficient to say that a meaning which departs substantially from a fundamental feature of an Act of Parliament is likely to have crossed the boundary between interpretation and amendment.

In *Ghaidan v Godin-Mendoza*[192] the House of Lords enthusiastically returned to the creative approach adopted in *R v A (No 2)*, and to date there have been only a handful

---

[189] Ibid at [40].   [190] [2001] EWCA Civ 757, [2002] 2 FLR 582, [2002] HRLR 50.

[191] [2002] UKHL 10 at [38]–[43], [2002] 2 AC 291 at [38]–[43], [2002] 2 All ER 192, per Lord Nicholls. See also *International Transport Roth GmbH v Secretary of State for the Home Department* [2002] EWCA Civ 158, [2003] QB 728, [2002] HRLR 31. In this case the Court of Appeal was unable to find a compatible interpretation of provisions in the Immigration and Asylum Act 1999 without crossing the boundaries of legitimate interpretation. A declaration of incompatibility was issued.

[192] [2004] UKHL 30, [2004] 2 AC 557, [2004] 3 All ER 411.

of cases which have resulted in a declaration of incompatibility.[193] In *R (on the application of H)* v *North and East London Regional Mental Health Tribunal,* the Court of Appeal declared sections 72(1) and 73(1) of the Mental Health Act 1983 to be incompatible with the right to liberty under Article 5.[194] The offending provisions were subsequently amended by the Mental Health Act 1983 (Remedial) Order 2001.[195] In another case, the Court of Appeal issued a declaration of incompatibility in relation to provisions of the Immigration and Asylum Act 1999. The provisions imposed a fixed penalty of £2,000 per entrant on hauliers responsible for bringing illegal entrants into the UK.[196] The legislative response to this decision was to amend the offending provisions by Act of Parliament.[197] A further example is provided by the House of Lords decision in *Bellinger* v *Bellinger.*[198] In this case, a provision stating that a marriage shall be void if 'the parties are not respectively male and female'[199] was held to be incompatible with the rights of the transsexual applicant under Articles 8 and 12. Parliament's response was to enact the Gender Recognition Act 2004.

3 RULES OF INTERPRETATION AND LANGUAGE

(a) The statute must be read as a whole

The meaning suggested by a word when used in isolation might be different from that suggested when used in conjunction with other words.[200] A statute must therefore be read as a whole, and every section must be interpreted in the light of other sections. The decision of the House of Lords in *Beswick* v *Beswick* provides an interesting illustration of this.[201] The case concerned the interpretation of section 56(1) of the Law of Property Act 1925, which states that 'a person may take an interest in land or other property . . . although he may not be named as a party to the conveyance or

---

[193] Of these, a number have been overturned on appeal. See, e.g., *R (on the Application of Alconbury)* v *Secretary of State for the Environment, Transport and the Regions* [2001] UKHL 23, [2003] 2 AC 295, [2001] 2 All ER 929, reversing [2002] HRLR 2; *Matthews* v *Ministry of Defence* [2002] EWCA Civ 773, [2002] 3 All ER 513, [2002] 1 WLR 2621, reversing [2002] EWHC 13.

[194] [2001] EWCA Civ 415, [2002] QB 1, [2002] 3 WLR 512. Section 73 of the Mental Health Act 1983 concerns the test to be applied when determining a restricted patient's entitlement to release from a secure hospital. The provision was held to be incompatible with Article 5 as the burden of proof rested on the patient to show that his continued detention under the Act was no longer warranted.

[195] SI 2001/3712.

[196] *International Transport Roth GmbH* v *Secretary of State for the Home Department* [2002] EWCA Civ 158, [2003] QB 728, [2002] HRLR 31.

[197] Nationality, Asylum and Immigration Act 2002.

[198] [2003] UKHL 21, [2003] 2 AC 467, [2003] 2 All ER 593. Their Lordships noted that the government had already indicated its acceptance of the decision in *Goodwin* v *UK* (2002) 35 EHRR 18, in which the European Court of Human Rights had concluded that UK law was in breach of the Convention.

[199] Matrimonial Causes Act 1973, s 11.

[200] See the observations on the words 'unfair competition' in *Lee* v *Showmen's Guild of Great Britain* [1952] 2 QB 329 at 338, [1952] 1 All ER 1175 at 1178.

[201] [1968] AC 58, [1967] 2 All ER 1197. Note that the law on privity of contract has now been substantially altered by the Contract (Rights of Third Parties) Act 1999.

other instrument'. The interpretation section of the same Act states that 'in this Act unless the context otherwise requires "property" includes any thing in action'.[202] It was argued that the combined effect of these provisions was to enable a stranger to a contract to enforce it, but the House of Lords rejected this argument. Their Lordships pointed out that section 56 is one of twenty-five sections in the Act grouped under the heading 'conveyances and other instruments', and in the context of the Act as a whole, it was held that the word 'property' must be interpreted to mean 'real property'.

Strictly speaking, the long title and the short title, being part of the enactment, must be consulted in interpreting any part of the Act. In practice, however, the courts will only refer to the long title to resolve an ambiguity and they do not regard the short title as an aid to interpretation at all. Headings, marginal notes, and punctuation are not part of the enactment, and their role as aids to interpretation is dealt with later.[203]

The general principle that a statute must be read as a whole has given rise to three specific presumptions concerning the use of language, each of which is known by a Latin title.

Noscitur a sociis. This translates as 'a thing is known by its associates', and in practical terms it means that where a provision contains a list of items, the meaning of each individual word in the list is coloured by the meaning of the others. In *Foster* v *Diphwys Casson Slate Co*[204] the court had to consider whether a statute prohibited the taking of explosives into a mine when carried in a cloth bag. The relevant statute stated that explosives could only be taken into a mine when carried in a 'case or canister'. Although in one sense a cloth bag might be thought of as a 'case', when interpreted in the context of the surrounding words it was held that the word only referred to containers of the same strength and solidity as a 'canister'.

Ejusdem generis. This rule means that general words which follow two or more particular words in an Act must be confined to a meaning of the same kind as the particular words. When the intention is to cover a wide range of similar circumstances, it is common drafting practice to use two or three particular examples, followed by a general expression such as 'or other place'. The effect of this is to extend the operation of the enactment to all circumstances within the same genus.

The operation of the rule can best be illustrated by two examples. Section 1 of the Betting Act 1853 prohibited the keeping of a 'house, office, room *or other place*' for the purposes of betting. In *Powell* v *Kempton Park Racecourse Co*[205] the issue was whether Tattersalls' ring at a racecourse was an 'other place' within the meaning of the Act. The House of Lords held that it was not, since the words 'house, office, room' created a genus of indoor places within which an outdoor place did not fall. *Brownsea*

---

[202] Section 205(1).   [203] See p 67, *post*.   [204] (1887) LR 18 QBD 428.
[205] [1899] AC 143; cf. *Culley* v *Harrison* [1956] 2 QB 71, [1956] 2 All ER 254.

Haven Properties Ltd v *Poole Corporation*[206] concerned a power to make traffic orders 'in all times of public processions, rejoicings, or illuminations, *and in any case when the streets are thronged or liable to be obstructed*'. It was held that this did not confer power to create a one-way traffic system for the six months of the summer holiday season.

It should be noted that there must be at least two specific words to create a genus. Thus where an Act referred to 'theatres and other places of amusement', it was held that a funfair was within the Act even though not ejusdem generis with the word 'theatres'.[207] Similarly, the ejusdem generis rule does not apply where the particular words in a statute are sufficiently different that they do not create a genus at all.[208]

Expressio unius est exclusio alterius. This translates as 'to express one thing is to exclude another'. It means simply that where a provision includes an item or list which is *not* followed by general words such as 'or other place', it is presumed that Parliament did not intend any unspecified items to be included. Thus, in *R* v *Cuthbertson*[209] a power to order forfeiture of property following a conviction for 'an offence under *this* Act' did not authorize forfeiture for *conspiracy* to commit an offence: the offence of conspiracy was not created by that Act.[210]

(b) Interpretation Act 1978

This Act, which consolidated and amended the Interpretation Act 1889, prescribes definitions of certain words and phrases which are commonly encountered in Acts of Parliament. Thus:

unless the contrary intention appears: (a) words importing the masculine gender include the feminine; (b) words importing the feminine gender include the masculine; (c) words in the singular include the plural and words in the plural include the singular.[211]

' "month" means calendar month'.[212]

However, these and other definitions are only presumptive and they yield to a contrary intention in the Act being interpreted. Thus, although the Interpretation Act defines the word 'person' to include a body corporate, a corporation carrying out

---

[206] [1958] Ch 574, [1958] 1 All ER 205; see also *DPP* v *Jordan* [1977] AC 699, [1976] 3 All ER 775. Section 4(1) of the Obscene Publications Act 1959 provides a public good defence in the case of articles considered to be 'in the interests of science, literature, art or learning, or of other objects of general concern'. The House of Lords held that when construed ejusdem generis with the preceding words, the phrase 'other objects of general concern', did not include the psychotherapeutic value of pornography to sexual deviants.

[207] *Allen* v *Emmerson* [1944] KB 362, [1944] 1 All ER 344.

[208] For an illustration of this, see *Re C (A Minor) (Interim Care Order: Residential Assessment)* [1997] AC 489, [1996] 4 All ER 871.

[209] [1981] AC 470, [1980] 2 All ER 401.

[210] The statute in question was the Misuse of Drugs Act 1971.

[211] Section 6. For an illustration of this rule, see *Floor* v *Davis* [1980] AC 695, [1979] 2 All ER 677.

[212] Section 5 and Schedule 1.

legal work was not held to be not guilty of acting as an unqualified 'person': the statute concerned could only apply to persons who could qualify as solicitors.[213]

4 PRESUMPTIONS OF SUBSTANCE

It is possible to express almost any rule of statutory interpretation in the form of a presumption. The rules against retrospective and extraterritorial operation are often expressed as presumptions, and the 'rules' concerning the interpretation of language can also be thought of as presumptions since their operation can be displaced by an express provision to the contrary. Nevertheless, although it is probably a mere matter of terminology, the following are always described as presumptions rather than rules.[214] Recent decisions indicate that these presumptions may simply be facets of the wider principle of legality:[215]

Parliament does not legislate in a vacuum. Parliament legislates for a European liberal democracy founded on the principles and traditions of the common law. And the courts may approach legislation on this initial assumption. But this assumption only has prima facie force. It can be displaced by a clear and specific provision to the contrary.

(a) Penal provisions are construed narrowly

Where a statute imposes criminal liability or tax obligations (which are treated as penal) and the statute is ambiguous or uncertain, it should be construed in favour of the individual.[216] Thus it has been held that the offence of 'knowingly possessing an explosive' requires knowledge on the part of the accused that the substance possessed is explosive, not merely that he possesses the substance.[217] One aspect of this general rule is the presumption against the imposition of liability without fault.

However, this rule of interpretation is not strong enough to displace the literal rule. Consequently, where a statute unambiguously creates a criminal offence or a tax the court is bound to give effect to it. The provision will be regarded as unambiguous if the court considers the intention of Parliament to be clear, notwithstanding that the words are capable of bearing more than one meaning.[218]

---

213 *Law Society* v *United Service Bureau Ltd* [1934] 1 KB 343. This lacuna was filled by the Solicitors Act 1957 (now Solicitors Act 1974, s 20).

214 For a useful discussion of several presumptions, see *Wilson* v *First County Trust (No 2)* [2003] UKHL 40 at [186]–[201], [2004] 1 AC 816 at [186]–[201], [2003] 4 All ER 97, per Lord Rodger.

215 *R* v *Secretary of State for the Home Department, ex parte Pierson* [1998] AC 539 at 587, [1997] 3 All ER 577 at 603, per Lord Steyn. In *Wilson* v *First County Trust (No 2)* [2003] UKHL 40 at [153], [2004] 1 AC 816 at [153], [2003] 4 All ER 97, Lord Scott described the presumption against giving retrospective effect to legislation as 'part of a broader presumption that Parliament does not intend a statute to have an unfair or unjust effect.'

216 *Kingston-upon-Hull Dock Co* v *Browne* (1831) 2 B & Ad 43; *D'Avigdor-Goldsmid* v *Inland Revenue Commissioners* [1953] AC 347, [1953] 1 All ER 403.

217 *R* v *Hallam* [1957] 1 QB 569, [1957] 1 All ER 665.

218 See, for examples, *DPP* v *Ottewell* [1970] AC 642, [1968] 3 All ER 153; *Attorney-General's Reference (No 1 of 1988)* [1989] AC 971, [1989] 2 All ER 1; *Inland Revenue Commissioners* v *Hinchy* [1960] AC 748, [1960] 1 All ER 505. See also, p 45, *ante*.

(b) Presumption against the imposition of criminal liability without fault

At common law mens rea is an element in all crimes,[219] and although the legislature can, and does, create strict liability offences, the intention so to do must be clear and unambiguous. In *Sweet v Parsley*[220] the House of Lords quashed a conviction for managing premises used for the smoking of cannabis, on the basis that the accused rented out the premises and did not know that her tenants were using drugs. Lord Reid explained the judicial approach as follows:[221]

our first duty is to consider the words of the Act; if they show a clear intention to create an absolute offence, that is an end of the matter. But such cases are very rare. Sometimes the words of the section which creates a particular offence make it clear that mens rea is required in one form or another. Such cases are quite frequent. But in a very large number of cases there is no clear indication either way. In such cases there has for centuries been a presumption that Parliament did not intend to make criminals of persons who were in no way blameworthy in what they did. That means that, whenever a section is silent as to mens rea, there is a presumption that, in order to give effect to the will of Parliament, we must read in words appropriate to require mens rea.

The more serious the alleged offence, the more difficult it will be to rebut the presumption of the need for mens rea. Thus, in *B v DPP*[222] the House of Lords allowed the appeal of a fifteen year old boy who had pleaded guilty to inciting a child under the age of fourteen to commit an act of gross indecency: the boy had honestly believed that the girl was over fourteen.[223] In contrast, where a statute is silent on the question of mens rea, a court *may* be prepared to treat an offence as one of strict liability if this would help to further some general social objective and if the offence is not 'truly criminal' in character.[224]

An analogous presumption is that Parliament does not intend to create new criminal offences. In *R v Horseferry Road Justices, ex parte Independent Broadcasting Authority*[225] the Queen's Bench Divisional Court held that, 'the inference that Parliament did not intend to create an offence in the absence of an express provision to that effect is, nowadays, almost irresistible.' This is of very limited application however,

---

[219] See *R v Tolson* (1889) LR 23 QBD 168; *Younghusband v Luftig* [1949] 2 KB 354, [1949] 2 All ER 72.
[220] [1970] AC 132, [1969] 1 All ER 347.   [221] [1970] AC 132 at 148, [1969] 1 All ER 347 at 349.
[222] [2000] 2 AC 428, 1 All ER 833.
[223] See also, *R v K (Age of Consent: Reasonable Belief)* [2001] UKHL 41, [2002] 1 AC 462, [2001] 3 All ER 897, where the same reasoning was applied to a charge of indecent assault under the Sexual Offences Act 1956, s 14(1). The fourteen year old alleged victim had in fact consented to the act and the defendant had a genuine belief that she was over the age of sixteen. The House of Lords reversed the Court of Appeal's finding and held that the prosecution was required to prove mens rea in respect of the girl's age. Interestingly, the Court of Appeal seems to have based its reasoning on an application of *expressio unius est exclusio alterius*: the Act expressly required mens rea in relation to other offences but was silent with regard to indecent assault: [2001] 1 Cr App R 35, [2001] Crim LR 134.
[224] See, for example, *R v Bezzina* [1994] 3 All ER 964, [1994] WLR 1057 (owning or handling a dog which is dangerously out of control in a public place); and *Harrow LBC v Shah* [1999] 3 All ER 302, [2000] 1 WLR 83 (selling a National Lottery ticket to a child under 16).
[225] [1987] QB 54 at 72, [1986] 2 All ER 666 at 674, per Lloyd LJ.

since when Parliament does intend to create a new criminal offence this is usually made clear by the fact that penalties for the offence are specified.

(c) Presumption against alteration of the law

Parliament, like the judiciary, is presumed to know the law. Consequently if an Act does not *expressly* alter the law it will be presumed that Parliament did not intend it to have that effect. In the words of Devlin J:[226]

a statute is not to be taken as effecting a fundamental alteration in the general law unless it uses words which point unmistakably to that conclusion.

It is important to remember, however, that Parliament can and does make fundamental alterations to the common law, and if such a change appears from a literal interpretation of the words used, the use of any presumption to the contrary is out of place.

The presumption against fundamental change also applies in relation to statute law. One aspect of this is the presumption that where a provision is re-enacted in a consolidating statute, a modest change in the wording does not necessarily introduce a fundamental change in meaning. Conversely the mere fact that a provision *is* re-enacted cannot be assumed to mean that Parliament is endorsing judicial interpretations of the earlier enactment. The court must interpret the enactment as it stands, though if the scales are equally balanced, the fact that Parliament has re-enacted a provision which has been the subject of judicial interpretation might tip the balance in favour of that interpretation.[227]

(d) Presumptions against deprivation of liberty and property

There is a well-established presumption that in the absence of express provision the courts will not construe a statute as depriving a person of any property right vested in him before the statute came into operation. For example, every person has a right to the use and enjoyment of his own land. The remedy for infringement of this right is an action in trespass or nuisance, depending on the character of the interference. Consequently where a statute authorizes the performance of an act which constitutes a nuisance to the claimant, the statute will not be construed as removing the claimant's right unless it is clearly intended to have that effect.[228] There is an even stronger presumption against the deprivation of a person's liberty. Thus, in a case concerning detention under the Mental Health Act 1983, it was said that:[229]

Parliament is presumed not to enact legislation which interferes with the liberty of a subject without making it clear that this was its intention.

Both presumptions must now be considered in the context of the Human Rights Act

---

[226] *National Assistance Board* v *Wilkinson* [1952] 2 QB 648 at 661, [1952] 2 All ER 255 at 260.
[227] See p 75, *post*.   [228] *Metropolitan Asylum District Managers* v *Hill* (1881) 6 App Cas 193.
[229] *R* v *Hallstrom, ex parte W* [1986] QB 1090 at 1104, [1986] 2 All ER 306, per McCullough J.

1998, which requires legislation to be interpreted as far as possible in a manner compatible with the rights to liberty and to peaceful enjoyment of possessions.[230] Even in the Human Rights Act era, however, liberty and proprietary rights may be taken away by express words. In *R (on the application of H)* v *North and East London Regional Mental Health Tribunal*[231] the Court of Appeal found it impossible to interpret provisions of the Mental Health Act 1983 in a manner compatible with the right to liberty. A declaration of incompatibility was issued, but this did not, of course, alter the validity of the legislation.[232]

(e) Presumption against ousting the jurisdiction of the courts

Individuals cannot, by contract, exclude the jurisdiction of the courts. Although Parliament may exclude an individual's recourse to the courts, the provision purporting so to do must be absolutely clear and unambiguous since the courts are extremely wary about permitting legislative or executive interference with their jurisdiction. The principle was stated by Viscount Simmons in *Pyx Granite Ltd* v *Ministry of Housing and Local Government*:[233]

[I]t is a principle not by any means to be whittled down that the subject's recourse to Her Majesty's courts for the determination of his rights is not to be excluded except by clear words.

So reluctant are the courts to see their jurisdiction ousted, that even seemingly clear words may not suffice. Thus in *Anisminic* v *Foreign Compensation Commission*,[234] a provision stating that any 'determination' of the Commission 'shall not be called into question in any court of law' did not prevent a court declaring that the Commission had made a fundamental error of law that deprived it of power to act. Because it had no power, no *valid* 'determination' was being called into question. Such legal sophistry can only be prevented by the clearest of words. An example of such words is the amended wording introduced following the *Anisminic* decision—section 3 of the Foreign Compensation Act 1969 prevents judicial review even of a 'purported determination'.

On the basis of this presumption, a provision stating that the decision of an inferior court, tribunal, or administrative body shall be 'final' will be held not to exclude the prerogative jurisdiction of the High Court to review the decision:

---

[230] Section 3: see p 55, *ante*. The rights to liberty (Article 5, ECHR) and the peaceful enjoyment of possessions (Article 1, Protocol 1, ECHR) are protected Convention rights under s 1.

[231] [2001] EWCA Civ 415, [2002] QB 1, [2001] 3 WLR 512.

[232] The offending provisions were subsequently amended by the Mental Health Act 1983 (Remedial) Order 2001, SI 2001/3712. See further, p 58 *ante* and p 75, *post*.

[233] [1960] AC 260 at 286, [1959] 3 All ER 1 at 6, cited with approval by Lord Donovan in *Ealing London Borough* v *Race Relations Board* [1972] AC 342 at 353, [1972] 1 All ER 105 at 108. The House of Lords held that the machinery established under the Race Relations Act 1968 for referring disputes to certain nominated county courts did not exclude the inherent jurisdiction of the High Court to make a declaration as to rights under the Act.

[234] [1969] 2 AC 147, [1969] 1 All ER 208. See also, p 209, *post*.

if a tribunal goes wrong in law and the error appears on the face of the record, the High Court will interfere by certiorari to quash the decision. It is not to be deterred by the enactment that the decision is 'final'. The decision may be final on the facts but it is not final on the law.[235]

In contrast, a statute permitting challenge within a limited period is likely to be effective in preventing any review after that period. In *R v Cornwall County Council, ex parte Huntington*[236] a Divisional Court held that the terms of the Wildlife and Countryside Act 1981, which excluded judicial challenge after a forty-two-day period, prevented the court from engaging in judicial review of an order made under the Act.

(f) Presumption that a statute does not bind the Crown

One of the few relics of the prerogative of the Crown is the rule that the Crown is not bound by a statute unless expressly named in it. The rule extends to the Crown and to its servants and agents, though not to nationalized industries.[237] The Crown Proceedings Act 1947 placed the Crown, with certain exceptions, in the same position as a private person in the law of torts. Consequently, statutes which affect common law rights and duties are usually expressed to bind the Crown. Examples are the Limitation Act 1980 and the Occupiers' Liability Act 1957. In practice the general trend of modern legislation is towards the removal of the Crown's privileges and immunities.[238]

(g) Presumption that Parliament does not intend to violate international law

There is a presumption that Parliament does not intend to legislate in a manner incompatible with international law. The courts generally take a purposive approach when interpreting statutes designed to give effect to treaty obligations, the presumption being that Parliament intends such legislation to achieve its objectives.[239] Similarly, where a provision is genuinely ambiguous the courts may take account of a treaty when choosing between two equally reasonable interpretations, regardless of whether the statute was enacted for the purpose of giving effect to that treaty.[240]

---

235 *Tehrani* v *Rostron* [1972] 1 QB 182 at 187, [1971] 3 All ER 790 at 793, per Lord Denning MR: see also *R v Medical Appeal Tribunal, ex parte Gilmore* [1957] 1 QB 574, [1957] 1 All ER 796, where the earlier authorities are reviewed; *Sagnata Investments Ltd* v *Norwich Corporation* [1971] 2 QB 614, [1971] 2 All ER 1441. See also p 310, *post*.

236 [1992] 3 All ER 566. The decision was upheld on appeal: see [1994] 1 All ER 694.

237 *Tamlin* v *Hannaford* [1950] 1 KB 18, [1949] 2 All ER 327; for an account of the history of this presumption and a recent illustration of its operation, see *Lord Advocate* v *Dumbarton District Council* [1990] 2 AC 580, [1990] 1 All ER 1.

238 See *Madros Electric Supply Corporation (in liquidation)* v *Boarland (Inspector of Taxes)* [1955] AC 667, [1955] 1 All ER 753.

239 *Salomon* v *Commissioners of Customs and Excise* [1967] 2 QB 116, [1966] 3 WLR 1223. The interpretation of legislation designed to give effect to obligations of EC law is discussed in chapter 4.

240 *R* v *Chief Immigration Officer, ex parte Salamat Bibi* [1976] 3 All ER 843, [1976] 1 WLR 979. It was held that where such an ambiguity arose, the courts had a discretion to take into account the UK's obligations under the European Convention on Human Rights. Since the introduction of the Human Rights Act 1998 however, courts have had a *statutory obligation* to seek an ECHR compatible interpretation of all legislation, whether it is ambiguous or not. See further, p 55, *ante*.

Of course, as with other presumptions, this is subject to the overriding principle that Parliament is legislatively supreme: clear and unambiguous words in the main body of an Act will take precedence over any inconsistent treaty obligations.[241]

International obligations cannot alter the clear meaning of statutes. They may, however, be permitted to make clear which of more than one reasonable meaning was intended by Parliament.

5 MATERIAL AIDS TO CONSTRUCTION

Alongside the various approaches and presumptions that are applied in the process of statutory interpretation, there are also several aids to construction which may be considered in the event of ambiguity. There are two classes of aids to construction; internal aids and external aids. The extent to which these are used varies from case to case, but those who advocate a strict literal approach to the task of interpretation would generally regard the use of *external* aids as illegitimate.

(a) Internal aids

An internal (or intrinsic) aid is an aid that is to be found within the Queen's Printer's copy of the statute itself. The principle that a statute must be read as a whole means that those parts of the statute which form part of the enactment should always be consulted as part of the general process of interpretation. Certain other parts of the statute such as punctuation, headings, and marginal notes may also be used in cases of ambiguity, even though they are not strictly part of the enactment.

'Notes' of the type found in section 118 of the Criminal Justice Act 2003 fall into a different category. The Act makes significant changes to the rules governing the admissibility of hearsay evidence in criminal cases and section 118 expressly preserves certain categories of evidence which were already admissible at common law. Thus section 118(2) preserves 'any rule of law under which in criminal proceedings evidence of a person's reputation is admissible for the purpose of proving his good or bad character'. This is qualified by a 'note', which states that the rule is 'preserved only so far as it allows the court to treat such evidence as proving the matter concerned.' Despite the label, this note is an integral part of the provision, and as such, it is likely to be crucial to its interpretation.[242]

Long title. The long title of an Act begins with the words 'an Act' and goes on to describe the general effect of the legislation. Thus the Law of Property Act 1925 has the long title; 'An Act to consolidate the enactments relating to Conveyancing and the Law of Property in England and Wales'. The long title is usually succinct rather than explanatory and it is unlikely to do more than identify the subject matter of the Act.

---

[241] *J. H. Rayner Ltd* v *Department of Trade and Industry* [1989] Ch 72 at 231, [1988] 3 All ER 257 at 342, per Ralph Gibson LJ (affirmed [1990] 2 AC 418, [1989] 3 All ER 523, HL).

[242] See also, s 118(3).

However, as it forms part of the enactment and may be debated or amended by Parliament, it is regarded as a legitimate aid to interpretation and construction.[243] It is though, a minor aid: there have been conspicuously few cases in which it has been consulted and it certainly cannot prevail over an express provision in the body of the Act. Thus an Act to 'amend the law with respect to wills of personal estate made by British subjects' (Wills Act 1861) was held to apply to the will of an alien.[244] The long title should not be confused with the preamble, although preambles are rare in modern statutes and judges occasionally use the terms interchangeably.[245]

Short title. This is the title by which Acts are commonly, and properly, cited. In theory the short title is a valid aid to both interpretation and construction, but there appears to be no reported case in which the short title has been used to determine a point of construction. The short title could certainly not be used to introduce ambiguity into the body of the Act: indeed, the short titles of certain Acts do not reflect their content accurately. The Criminal Procedure Act 1865, for example, applies to both civil and criminal proceedings.

Preamble. The preamble is that part of the statute which precedes the enacting words and sets out the reason for the statute being passed. In old cases great weight was attached to the preamble as an aid to construction.[246] Important Acts such as the Statute of Uses 1535, the Statute of Frauds 1677 and the Parliament Act 1911 have long and instructive preambles. Probably the best known preamble is that of the Charitable Uses Act 1601, which is still regarded as containing the criteria to be adopted when considering whether a particular object is a 'charitable' one.[247] Where a statute has a preamble, it traditionally begins with the word 'whereas'. Modern statutes, however, rarely contain a preamble and where one is included it is generally too brief to be of assistance.[248] Although the preamble is part of the enactment, like the long title, it cannot be introduced to create an ambiguity in the body of the Act.

Headings. A section or group of sections in an Act may be preceded by a heading. Such headings are not part of the enactment and for that reason logic would suggest their exclusion. In fact, however, headings are often consulted as an aid to construction where the enactment is uncertain or ambiguous.[249] The modern judicial tendency

---

[243] See *Fielding* v *Morley Corporation* [1899] 1 Ch 1 at 3, per Lindley MR. Before the nineteenth century the long title did not form part of the enactment and therefore could not be used in this way.

[244] *Re Groos* [1904] P 269; see also *R* v *Bates* [1952] 2 All ER 842, [1953] 1 WLR 77; *R* v *Galvin* [1987] QB 862, [1987] 2 All ER 851.

[245] e.g. Winn LJ in *Crook* v *Edmondson* [1966] 2 QB 81 at 89, [1966] 1 All ER 833 at 835. For an example of a statute with a preamble, see the Parliament Act 1911 or the Canada Act 1982.

[246] *Belasco* v *Hannant* (1862) 3 B & S 13; *Sussex Peerage Case* (1844) 11 Cl & Fin 85.

[247] See, e.g., *Incorporated Council of Law Reporting for England and Wales* v *A-G* [1971] Ch 626, [1971] 1 All ER 436; *McGovern* v *A-G* [1982] Ch 321, [1981] 3 All ER 493.

[248] Compare secondary legislation of the European Community, which invariably has a long preamble.

[249] For an instructive case see *Crook* v *Edmondson* [1966] 2 QB 81, [1966] 1 All ER 833, in which the words 'immoral purposes' were construed in the light of the group of sections of the Sexual Offences Act 1956 in which those words occurred.

appears to be to treat a heading as if it were a preamble.[250] In *DPP v Schildkamp*[251] Lord Upjohn was in favour of according greater weight to headings than were the other Law Lords. He observed:[252]

In my opinion, it is wrong to confine their role to the resolution of ambiguities in the body of the Act. When the court construing the Act is reading it through to understand it, it must read the cross-headings as well as the body of the Act and that will always be a useful pointer as to the intention of Parliament in enacting the immediately following sections.

Marginal notes. Marginal notes or 'clause titles' are not part of an Act and are inserted by the draftsman purely for facility of reference. Sometimes a marginal note bears no relation to the content of a section that has been considerably altered during the passage of the Bill.[253] More commonly, it may be misleading. For example, the marginal note to section 143 of the Criminal Justice and Public Order Act 1994 refers to 'male rape and buggery' despite the fact that the section relates to the latter, but not the former.

For this reason the old rule was that marginal notes were not regarded as a legitimate aid to construction, even in the event of ambiguity.[254] Nevertheless there have been cases in which the court has clearly adverted to the marginal note in construing a section.[255] Thus, as Upjohn LJ observed in one case:[256]

While the marginal note to a section cannot control the language used in the section, it is at least permissible to approach a consideration of its general purpose and the mischief at which it is aimed with the note in mind.

An example of a marginal note being used to resolve an ambiguity is *DPP v Johnson*,[257] where it was held that the note accompanying section 8 of the Road Traffic Act 1988 provided evidence that Parliament's intention was to reduce the number of people driving with alcohol in their bodies. The note referred to: 'driving or being in charge of a motor vehicle with alcohol consumption above the prescribed limit'. As a result, the court construed the word 'consuming' widely to embrace the ingestion of alcohol by any method, and held that it was not entitled to restrict consumption to the act of drinking. The appellant, who had had alcohol injected into his body as a constituent element of a pain-killing drug, was therefore guilty of an offence under section 8.

---

[250] *Martins v Fowler* [1926] AC 746; *Qualter, Hall & Co Ltd v Board of Trade* [1962] Ch 273, [1961] 3 All ER 389.

[251] [1971] AC 1, [1969] 3 All ER 1640.   [252] [1971] AC at 28, [1969] 3 All ER at 1656.

[253] Married Women (Maintenance in Case of Desertion) Act 1886, s 1(2).

[254] See *R v Bates* [1952] 2 All ER 842, [1953] 1 WLR 77; *Chandler v DPP* [1964] AC 763, [1962] 3 All ER 142.

[255] e.g. *Pride of Derby and Derbyshire Angling Association Ltd v British Celanese Ltd* [1953] Ch 149, [1953] 1 All ER 179; *R v Vickers* [1957] 2 QB 664, [1957] 2 All ER 741; *Tudor Grange Holdings Ltd v Citibank NA* [1992] Ch 53, [1991] 4 All ER 1.

[256] *Stephens v Cuckfield Rural District Council* [1960] 2 QB 373 at 383, [1960] 2 All ER 716 at 720.

[257] [1995] 4 All ER 53, [1995] 1 WLR 728.

Punctuation. Acts of Parliament were not punctuated before 1850, and as punctuation tends to be left to the draftsman and not scrutinized by Parliament there is some old authority for the proposition that punctuation cannot be taken into account as an aid to construction. Modern courts take a more realistic attitude however, and following the observations of Lord Reid in *DPP v Schildkamp*,[258] the House of Lords has held that punctuation can and should be taken into account by judges in interpreting statutes.[259]

Interpretation sections. Most modern statutes include at least one interpretation section indicating the meaning that Parliament intended to be given to particular words. The context in which a word is used is still important however, and where there is an inconsistency between the meaning given in an interpretation section and that suggested by the context in which the word is used, the latter prevails.

This is especially so when the interpretation section uses the word 'includes'. In this case it will be regarded as extending rather than restricting the normal meaning of the words in question. Thus, in *R v Fulling*[260] the court defined the term 'oppression' in section 76 of the Police and Criminal Evidence Act 1984 by reference to its ordinary, natural meaning, as stated in the *Oxford English Dictionary*. It did not even cite the content of section 76(8) of that statute, which provides that oppression 'includes' inhuman or degrading treatment, torture, violence, or the threat of violence.

Another example is *Shimizu (UK) Ltd v Westminster City Council*.[261] In that case the House of Lords had to consider the meaning of the term 'listed building' in the Planning (Listed Buildings and Conservation Areas) Act 1990. Section 336 of the Town and Country Planning Act 1990 defined a 'building' as including 'part of a building', unless the context otherwise requires. That definition was incorporated into the Listed Buildings Act by section 91 of the Act. Despite that, Lord Hope was able to conclude that the expression 'listed building' included *part* of a listed building for the purposes of section 1 of the Act, but did not do so in respect of virtually all other provisions of that Act.

Schedules. Acts of Parliament often contain one or more schedules. They are always placed at the end of the Act and are used (inter alia) for prescribing forms, furnishing illustrations, listing repeals effected by the Act, and setting out transitional provisions. They cannot be regarded as altering the ordinary meaning of words used in the Act, but it is probable that they can be considered in cases where a provision is otherwise uncertain or ambiguous.[262]

---

[258] [1971] AC 1 at 28, [1969] 3 All ER 1640 at 1654: see p 68, *ante.*

[259] *Hanlon* v *The Law Society* [1981] AC 124, [1980] 2 All ER 199; see also *Bodden* v *Commissioner of Police of the Metropolis* [1990] 2 QB 397, [1989] 3 All ER 833.

[260] [1987] QB 426, [1987] 2 All ER 65.   [261] [1997] 1 All ER 481, [1997] 1 WLR 716.

[262] In a case involving an Act passed to give effect to an international treaty, the House of Lords refused to look at a schedule containing the text of that treaty because it considered the words to be unambiguous: *Ellerman Lines Ltd* v *Murray* [1931] AC 126. The case has since been disapproved: *James Buchanan & Co Ltd* v *Babco Forwarding and Shipping* [1978] AC 141, [1977] 3 All ER 1048.

The Consumer Credit Act 1974 utilized a novel concept in parliamentary drafting
—the use of examples. Section 188(1) provides that 'Schedule 2 shall have effect for
illustrating the use of terminology employed in this Act'. The Schedule contains
twenty-four examples, each expressed in the form of a set of facts and an analysis of
the application of the new terminology to those facts. The examples are expressed not
to be exhaustive and section 188(3) provides that in the case of conflict between
Schedule 2 and any other provision of the Act, the latter shall prevail.

When an Act of Parliament is passed to implement an international treaty, the text
of that treaty will normally be included in a schedule to the Act. This may give rise to
difficulties in interpretation if the treaty is in a foreign language or is set out in more
than one language. A purposive approach will usually be adopted in such cases,[263] and
the court may consult extrinsic sources such as dictionaries, *travaux préparatoires*,
and the decisions of foreign courts. The words used in the treaty will be construed
so as to conform to the generally accepted meaning of the provision. As Lord
Browne-Wilkinson put it in *Re H and others (Minors) (Abduction: Acquiescence)*:[264]

An international convention, expressed in different languages and intended to apply to
a wide range of differing legal systems, cannot be construed differently in different
jurisdictions.

In *Fothergill* v *Monarch Airlines Ltd*[265] the House of Lords had to consider a provision
of the Warsaw Convention contained in Schedule 1 to the Carriage by Air Act 1961.
Reversing the decision of the Court of Appeal, it held that the loss of articles from a
suitcase constituted 'damage' to baggage. It reached this conclusion by taking a purposive approach, and by looking at extrinsic sources to ascertain that the word 'avarie'
(used in the French text) has a slightly wider meaning than the term 'damage' (used in
the English): it is also capable of meaning 'loss'.

(b) External aids

An external (or extrinsic) aid to construction is an aid which is not to be found in the
Queen's Printer's copy of the Act. The use of such aids is restricted and has always
been controversial: those who favour a literal approach would generally reject their
use on the basis that the courts should be concerned with what Parliament *actually*
said, not what it *intended* to say. Even for advocates of a more purposive approach, the
use of external aids is only legitimate to the extent that they can shed light on the
intentions of Parliament:

The task of the court is often said to be to ascertain the intention of Parliament expressed in
the language under consideration. This is correct and may be helpful, so long as it is

---

[263] In one case involving a statute designed to give effect to a treaty, the Court of Appeal adopted the text
of the treaty even though its meaning differed from the text used in the main body of the Act: *Corocraft Ltd* v
Pan American Airways Inc [1969] 1 QB 616, [1969] 1 All ER 82.

[264] [1998] AC 72, [1997] 2 All ER 225.

[265] [1981] AC 251, [1980] 2 All ER 696. Section 1(2) of the 1961 Act expressly provides that in the event of
inconsistency between the English and French texts, the latter is to prevail.

remembered that 'the intention of Parliament' is an objective concept, not subjective. The phrase is a shorthand reference to the intention which the court reasonably imputes to Parliament in respect of the language used. It is not the subjective intention of the Minister or other persons who promoted the legislation. Nor is it the subjective intention of the draftsman, or of individual members of . . . either House.[266]

Although the general rule in relation to external aids is one of exclusion,[267] there are some which are considered legitimate and these are set out below.

Reports of parliamentary debates. Since the function of the courts is to ascertain the intention of the legislature, it might be thought that they would readily refer to statements made in Parliament as to the intention of the member or party introducing the Bill. In fact, until recently the reports of debates on the Bill during its passage through Parliament were rigidly excluded.[268] However, in 1993 the House of Lords in *Pepper* v *Hart*[269] reconsidered the position, and held (Lord Mackay LC dissenting) that in certain circumstances a court should be entitled to refer to parliamentary materials. The objection that by so doing the courts would be calling proceedings in Parliament into question, contrary to the Bill of Rights 1688, was rejected. The pre-conditions for the exercise of the power were stated by Lord Browne-Wilkinson:

the exclusionary rule should be relaxed so as to permit reference to parliamentary materials where: (a) legislation is ambiguous or obscure, or leads to an absurdity; (b) the material relied upon consists of one or more statements by a Minister or other promoter of the Bill together if necessary with such other parliamentary material as is necessary to understand such statements, and their effect; (c) the statements relied upon are clear.

It should be noted that only statements made in respect of a Bill passing through Parliament can potentially be considered under *Pepper* v *Hart*. The rule does not permit the use of statements to indicate a Minister's understanding of the state of the law at the time;[270] nor does it permit the use of statements that are not concerned with the point at issue in the litigation.[271]

---

[266] *R* v *Secretary of State for the Environment, Transport and the Regions, ex parte Spath Holme Ltd* [2001] 2 AC 349 at 387, [2001] 1 All ER 195 at 206, per Lord Nicholls.

[267] The Law Commission Report, *The Interpretation of Statutes* (1969, Law Com No 21) recommended the admission of extrinsic material other than reports of parliamentary proceedings. Lord Simon more than once advocated reference to parliamentary proceedings and other preparatory material as an aid to judicial interpretation of statutes (cf. *McMillan* v *Crouch* [1972] 3 All ER 61 at 76, [1972] 1 WLR 1102 at 1119; *Charter* v *Race Relations Board* [1973] AC 868 at 900, [1973] 1 All ER 512 at 527) but his views on this topic attracted little support.

[268] *Assam Railways and Trading Co Ltd* v *Inland Revenue Commissioners* [1935] AC 445. In *Beswick* v *Beswick* [1968] AC 58 at 74, [1967] 2 All ER 1197 at 1202, reasons advanced for the rule were that it would add to the time and expense of preparing cases if counsel had to read all the debates in *Hansard*, and that reports of debates in select committees were not available to the public.

[269] [1993] AC 593, [1993] 1 All ER 42.

[270] *Hillsdown Holdings plc* v *Pensions Ombudsman* [1997] 1 All ER 862.

[271] *Pepper (Inspector of Taxes)* v *Hart* [1993] AC 593, [1993] 1 All ER 42; *Melluish (Inspector of Taxes)* v *BMI (No 3) Ltd* [1996] AC 454, [1995] 4 All ER 453; *Three Rivers District Council* v *Bank of England (No 2)* [1996] 2 All ER 363.

Lord Mackay's dissenting speech expressed concern that the costs of litigation would be immensely increased by the onerous task of researching the record of parliamentary proceedings in *Hansard*. The frequency with which the courts have been asked to apply *Pepper* v *Hart* appears to give some support to these concerns.[272] The House of Lords has recently endorsed the *Pepper* v *Hart* rule, but it has also expressed scepticism as to its value, cautioning that recourse to *Hansard* should be permitted only exceptionally.[273] On a related matter, it has held that it a court *is* entitled to have regard to ministerial statements and explanatory notes when seeking to determine whether legislation is compatible with the Human Rights Act 1998. However, their Lordships confirmed that extrinsic aids cannot be used in a manner which amounts to questioning proceedings in Parliament:[274]

The Human Rights Act 1998 requires the court to exercise a new role in respect of primary legislation. This new role is fundamentally different from interpreting and applying legislation. The courts are now required to evaluate the effect of primary legislation in terms of Convention rights and, where appropriate, make a formal declaration of incompatibility . . . Sometimes the court may need additional background information tending to show, for instance, the likely practical impact of the statutory measure and why the course adopted by the legislature is or is not appropriate . . . Beyond this use of Hansard as a source of background information, the content of parliamentary debates has no direct relevance . . . [I]t is a cardinal constitutional principle that the will of Parliament is expressed in the language used by it in its enactments. The proportionality of legislation is to be judged on that basis . . . The proportionality of a statutory measure is not to be judged by the quality of the reasons advanced in support of it in the course of parliamentary debate, or by the subjective state of mind of an individual Minister or other member.

The courts tend to take a more flexible approach to the use of *Hansard* and other external aids when interpreting legislation designed to implement international or European obligations.[275] In addition, it may be observed that most continental countries take a very positive view of extrinsic materials and encourage consultation of the parliamentary and political history of the statute. These materials are known as

---

[272] See, e.g., *R* v *Warwickshire County Council, ex parte Johnson* [1993] AC 583, [1993 1 All ER 299 (reference made to Minister's speech in debate on a proposed amendment to Consumer Protection Act 1987, s 20); *Stubbings* v *Webb* [1993] AC 498, [1993] 1 All ER 322 (reference made to the speech of the chairman of the Committee upon whose report s 11 of the Limitation Act 1980 was based); *Avon CC* v *Hooper* [1997] 1 All ER 532, [1997] 1 WLR 1605; *R* v *Wandsworth LBC, ex parte Mansoor* [1997] QB 953, [1996] 3 All ER 913; *Mirvahedy* v *Henley* [2001] EWCA Civ 1749, [2002] QB 769, [2002] 2 WLR 566 (reference to ministerial statements to ascertain the scope of s 2(2) of the Animals Act 1971.)

[273] *R* v *Secretary of State for the Environment, Transport and the Regions, ex parte Spath Holme Ltd* [2001] 2 AC 349, [2001] 1 All ER 195. By a majority of four to one, the House of Lords held that the *Pepper* v *Hart* conditions were not satisfied.

[274] *Wilson* v *First County Trust (No 2)* [2003] UKHL 40 at [61]–[67], [2004] 1 AC 816 at [61]–[67], [2003] 4 All ER, per Lord Nicholls. Their Lordships permitted the Speaker of the House of Commons and the Clerk of Parliaments to make submissions expressing their concern about any expansion in the use of *Hansard*.

[275] *Three Rivers District Council* v *Bank of England (No 2)* [1996] 2 All ER 363; *Pickstone* v *Freemans plc* [1989] AC 66, [1988] 2 All ER 803; *Fothergill* v *Monarch Airlines Ltd* [1981] AC 251, [1980] 2 All ER 696.

travaux préparatoires and are an invaluable aid to the task of discovering the intention of continental legislatures.

Explanatory notes. Since the 1998–99 session, an 'Explanatory Notes' document has been published with the majority of Bills presented to Parliament.[276] These notes set out the purposes and key provisions of the Bill in clear and simple terms, and they may be revised as and when the Bill is amended during the legislative process. They do not, however, form part of the enactment and they are not expressly approved by Parliament. Parliament has left it to the courts to determine what use, if any, can be made of Explanatory Notes when construing legislation, and their status was considered by Lord Steyn in *Westminster City Council* v *National Asylum Support Service.*[277] Despite having made some rather sceptical extra-judicial comments about the merits of allowing recourse to *Hansard,*[278] he was more enthusiastic about the use of Explanatory Notes:[279]

Insofar as the Explanatory Notes cast light on the objective setting or contextual scene of the statute, and the mischief at which it is aimed, such materials are . . . always admissible aids to construction. They may be admitted for what logical value they have . . . After all, the connection of Explanatory Notes with the shape of the proposed legislation is closer than pre-parliamentary aids which in principle are already treated as admissible.

It is recognized, however, that the distinction between legitimate and illegitimate uses of Explanatory Notes is a fine one:[280]

If exceptionally there is found in Explanatory Notes a clear assurance by the executive to Parliament about the meaning of a clause, or the circumstances in which a power will or will not be used, that assurance may in principle be admitted against the executive in proceedings in which the executive places a contrary contention before the court . . . What is impermissible is to treat the wishes and desires of the government about the scope of the statutory language as reflecting the will of Parliament. The aims of the government in respect of the meaning of clauses as revealed in Explanatory Notes cannot be attributed to Parliament. The object is to see what is the intention expressed by the words enacted.

Ministerial statements of compatibility. Section 19 of the Human Rights Act 1998 provides that before the Second Reading of a Bill, the Minister in charge of it must either: (a) make a statement that in his view the provisions of the Bill are compatible with Convention rights;[281] or (b) make a statement that although the Bill is *not*

---

[276] See Select Committee on Modernisation of HC, 2nd Report: Explanatory Material for Bills, 1997–1998, HC 389, at pp 1–2. Before 1998, the practice was for a Bill to be accompanied by an explanatory document prepared by the sponsoring department and indicating its broad provisions and likely financial impact.

[277] [2002] UKHL 38, [2002] 4 All ER 654, [2002] 1 WLR 2956.

[278] '*Pepper* v *Hart*: A Re-examination' (2001) 21 Oxford Journal of Legal Studies 59.

[279] [2002] UKHL 38 at [5], [2002] 4 All ER 654 at [5].

[280] Ibid, at [6]. See also *Wilson* v *First County Trust (No 2)* [2003] UKHL 40, [2004] 1 AC 816, [2003] 4 All ER 97.

[281] By section 1, 'Convention rights' are those ECHR rights contained in Articles 2 to 12 and 14, Articles 1 to 3 of the First Protocol and Articles 1 and 2 of the Sixth Protocol.

compatible, the government nevertheless wishes to proceed. This provision came into effect on 24 November 1998 and it is perhaps unsurprising that virtually all of the statements made under section 19 since that date have been to the effect that legislation is compatible. Section 19 statements do not include any explanation as to *why* the Minister thinks that an Act is compatible or not, and they do not take account of any amendments to the Bill made during the legislative process. For these reasons their probative value is limited, but when a court is considering whether it is possible to interpret an Act in a Convention compliant manner,[282] a section 19 statement may have some value as a general indication of Parliament's intention.

Dictionaries. Words in statutes are presumed to bear their ordinary and natural meaning, and it is legitimate to consult a dictionary to ascertain the meaning of words with no particular legal meaning. Thus in *Re Rippon (Highfield) Housing Confirmation Order 1938*[283] the court adopted the *Oxford English Dictionary* definition of the word 'park'. Nevertheless dictionaries bear only slight weight, and, in context, the dictionary meaning may not be the one which Parliament intended. In a Court of Appeal case concerning the interpretation of the word 'ethnic' in a 1976 Act,[284] Lord Denning MR rejected a 1972 dictionary definition of the term, in favour of one from 1934.[285] The House of Lords in the same case rejected both definitions and came to its own conclusions about the meaning of the word.[286] Words and phrases with a particular legal meaning are described as 'terms of art', and they do not necessarily bear the meaning which laymen would attribute to them.[287] In interpreting the foreign text of a convention, a court is entitled to consult foreign dictionaries, textbooks, and articles, and even to receive expert evidence.[288]

Reports of committees. Reports of the Law Commissions, Law Reform Committees, and similar bodies are legitimate aids to discovering the state of the pre-existing law and the mischief which a statute was passed to remedy.[289] Once again however, if the words of a statute are unambiguous, it is not legitimate to interpret them otherwise in order to accord with the recommendations of a Committee.[290] Thus in *Letang v Cooper*[291] the Court of Appeal held that the words 'negligence, nuisance or breach of duty' in the Law Reform (Limitation of Actions) Act 1954 were wide enough to embrace the tort of trespass to the person. This was despite the fact that the

---

[282] Section 3: see further, p 55, *ante*.   [283] [1939] 2 KB 838, [1939] 3 All ER 548.
[284] The Race Relations Act 1976.   [285] *Mandla* v *Dowell Lee* [1983] QB 1 at 12.
[286] [1983] 2 AC 548, [1983] 1 All ER 1062, HL.
[287] See *Sydall* v *Castings Ltd* [1967] 1 QB 302, [1966] 3 All ER 770 on the construction of the word 'descendants' as a term of art. See also *Barclays Bank Ltd* v *Cole* [1967] 2 QB 738, [1966] 3 All ER 948 on the meaning of the word 'fraud', and compare *Lloyds Bank Ltd* v *Marcan* [1973] 2 All ER 359, [1973] 1 WLR 339.
[288] *Fothergill* v *Monarch Airlines Ltd* [1981] AC 251, [1980] 2 All ER 696.
[289] See, e.g., *Rookes* v *Barnard* [1964] AC 1129, [1964] 1 All ER 367; *National Provincial Bank* v *Ainsworth* [1965] AC 1175, [1965] 2 All ER 472; *Black-Clawson International Ltd* v *Papierwerke Waldhof-Aschaffenburg AG* [1975] AC 591, [1975] 1 All ER 810.
[290] *Black-Clawson International Ltd* v *Papierwerke Waldhof-Aschaffenburg AG* (*ante*).
[291] [1965] 1 QB 232, [1964] 2 All ER 929.

Tucker Committee report,[292] which preceded the 1954 Act, expressed an intention to exclude this form of action from the shorter limitation period recommended in that report.

Other statutes. Where the words of one statute are ambiguous or uncertain, assistance as to their meaning may sometimes be gained from considering the way in which similar words have been used in statutes dealing with the same subject matter. Thus in *R v Wheatley*[293] the question before the Court of Appeal was whether a pipe bomb filled with a mixture of sodium chlorate and sugar was an 'explosive' substance within the meaning of section 4 of the Explosive Substances Act 1883. The defendant's expert evidence was to the effect that the materials would produce only a pyrotechnic effect, and not an explosive one. The judge directed the jury that this was no defence, having regard to the definition of 'explosive' in section 3(1) of the Explosives Act 1875, which included a substance used to produce a 'pyrotechnic effect'. It was held that this direction was correct, since the long title of the 1883 Act indicated that it was intended to amend the 1875 Act and both Acts dealt with the same subject matter. It followed that what was an explosive substance for the purposes of the 1883 Act was to be determined by applying the definition used in the 1875 Act.

(c) Judicial precedents

The application of judicial precedent to statutory interpretation has been explained as follows:[294]

It is quite clear that judicial statements as to the construction and intention of an Act must never be allowed to supplant or supersede its proper construction and courts must beware of falling into the error of treating the law to be that laid down by the judge in construing the Act rather than found in the Act itself. No doubt a decision on particular words binds inferior courts on the construction of those words on similar facts, but beyond that the observations of judges on the construction of statutes may be of the greatest help and guidance but are entitled to no more than respect and cannot absolve the court from its duty in exercising an independent judgment.

Thus where a superior court has interpreted the words of an Act, an inferior court is bound to adopt that interpretation if faced with the same words in the same Act. Similarly the Court of Appeal is bound to follow its own previous decision upon the interpretation of a statute to the same extent as it is bound to follow any of its other previous decisions. In addition, if an Act employs words or phrases that have been the subject of interpretation in an earlier statute dealing with the same subject matter it may be inferred that they are intended to bear the same meaning since Parliament is

---

292 Cmnd 7740. See also *Sagnata Investments v Norwich Corporation* [1971] 2 QB 614, [1971] 2 All ER 1441, in which the report of the Royal Commission on Betting, Lotteries and Gaming (Cmnd 8190, 1951) was used as an aid to the construction of the Betting, Gaming and Lotteries Act 1963.

293 [1979] 1 All ER 954, [1979] 1 WLR 144.

294 *Ogden Industries Pty Ltd v Lucas* [1970] AC 113 at 127, [1969] 1 All ER 121 at 126, per Lord Upjohn.

presumed to know the law.[295] For example, the House of Lords, in assigning a meaning to the word 'wreck' in the Merchant Shipping Act 1925, adopted the interpretation of that word which had been given in a case decided on the wording of the Merchant Shipping Act 1894.[296] This is, however, no more than a possible inference and it must not be supposed that by re-enacting a provision which has been the subject of judicial interpretation Parliament is necessarily giving statutory force to that interpretation. If it is a wrong interpretation, then provided it is not binding on the court in accordance with the doctrine of precedent, the court is perfectly free to disregard it.[297] Moreover, where the earlier decision is upon similar words in a statute that does not deal with the same subject matter, or where the words are used in a different context, that decision is of little, if any, value.[298] Finally, where the earlier case was decided before the Human Rights Act 1998 came into effect,[299] a court should not follow that decision if doing so would result in a finding that the legislation is in breach of Convention rights.[300]

6 INTERPRETATION OF EUROPEAN COMMUNITY LEGISLATION

The techniques of interpretation which English courts have developed over the centuries have been described above. As already noted, approaches to interpretation have influenced approaches to legislative drafting, and vice versa. Community legislation is drafted in a different mould. It is expressed in terms of broad principle, leaving the courts to supply the detail by giving effect, in particular cases, to the general intention of the body that enacted the instrument in question. Thus regulations, directives, and decisions of the Council and Commission have to state the reasons on which they have been based. They must also refer to any proposals or opinions that were required to be obtained pursuant to the Treaties. These reasons are normally set out in the preamble to the instrument in question. Accordingly, English judges are required to take a purposive approach to the interpretation of Community legislation, referring points of law to the Court of Justice when necessary or required. The 'literal' approach plays little or no part in this process.[301]

---

[295] Cf. *Maxwell on Interpretation of Statutes* (11th edn, 1962), p 303, cited with approval in *R v Freeman* [1970] 2 All ER 413, [1970] 1 WLR 788. In the *Freeman* case the Court of Appeal held that since there was no relevant distinction between the definition of 'firearm' in s 57(1) of the Firearms Act 1968 and the definitions in earlier Firearms Acts, Parliament must be taken to have adopted the interpretation of the earlier Acts when enacting the 1968 statute.

[296] *The Olympic* [1913] P 92; *Barras v Aberdeen Steam Trawling and Fishing Co Ltd* [1933] AC 402.

[297] See *Dun v Dun* [1959] AC 272, [1959] 2 All ER 134; *R v Chard* [1984] AC 279, [1983] 3 All ER 637 (in which the House of Lords expressly disapproved dicta to the contrary in *Barras v Aberdeen Steam Trawling and Fishing Co Ltd* (*ante*)).

[298] *London Corporation v Cusack-Smith* [1955] AC 337, [1955] 1 All ER 302; *Brown v Bennett (No 1)* [2002] 2 All ER 273, [2002] 1 WLR 713.

[299] 2 October 2000.

[300] See *Ghaidan v Godin-Mendoza* [2002] EWCA Civ 1533, [2003] Ch 380, [2002] 4 All ER 1162, in which the Court of Appeal declined to follow the House of Lords' interpretation of a provision in the Rent Act 1977 (*Fitzpatrick v Sterling Housing Association Ltd* [2001] 1 AC 27, [1999] 4 All ER 705). For a discussion of the impact of the Human Rights Act on the doctrine of judicial precedent, see chapter 3, *post*.

[301] The interpretation of Community law is discussed in more detail in chapter 4, *post*.

3

CASE LAW, PRECEDENTS, AND LAW REPORTS

A THE RELATIONSHIP BETWEEN LAW REPORTS AND THE DOCTRINE OF PRECEDENT

The operation of the doctrine of precedent is inextricably bound up with law reporting. Precedents are almost always contained in law reports and the modern doctrine of binding precedent did not develop until an integrated system of law reporting evolved in the nineteenth century. Nevertheless, until recently, any decision could be cited in court provided that it was vouched for by a barrister, solicitor, or other qualified person[1] who was present when the judgment was delivered, and decisions did not need to be reported in order to be relied upon in court. However, in the face of concern about the over-citation of cases, particularly those which are unreported, the judiciary is now seeking to limit the use of unreported decisions. In *Roberts Petroleum Ltd* v *Bernard Kenny* Lord Diplock caused considerable consternation among some sections of the profession by stating that:[2]

[T]he time has come when your Lordships should adopt the practice of declining to allow transcripts of unreported judgments of the Civil Division of the Court of Appeal to be cited on the hearing of appeals to this House unless leave is given to do so . . . such leave should only be granted on counsel's giving an assurance that the transcript contains a statement of some principle of law, relevant to an issue in the appeal to this House, that is binding on the Court of Appeal and of which the substance, as distinct from the mere choice, of phraseology, is not to be found in one of the generalised or specialised series of reports.

The Court of Appeal has since adopted much the same approach[3] and it recently issued a Practice Direction restricting the range of cases that can be cited in the civil courts.[4] The effect of this is that: (a) applications attended by one party only; (b) applications for permission to appeal; (c) decisions that an application is arguable; and (d) decisions of the county court,[5] cannot be cited unless there is a clear indication

---

[1] Courts and Legal Services Act 1990, s 115. See p 348, *post*.
[2] [1983] 2 AC 192 at 200–2, [1983] 1 All ER 564 at 566–8.
[3] *Practice Statement (Court of Appeal: Authorities)* [1996] 3 All ER 382, [1996] 1 WLR 854.
[4] *Practice Direction (Citation of Authorities)* [2001] 2 All ER 510, [2001] 1 WLR 1001.
[5] A county court decision may be cited if it deals with a point of law in respect of which no higher authority is available, or in order to illustrate the measure of damages in a personal injury case.

that the decision in question purports to establish a new principle or extend the present law.[6] The Practice Direction also discourages reliance on cases from foreign jurisdictions other than those of the European Court of Human Rights and European Court of Justice. Lord Woolf CJ explained the reasons for these changes:[7]

The current weight of available material causes problems both for advocates and for courts in properly limiting the nature and amount of material that is used in the preparation and argument of subsequent cases . . . Recent and continuing efforts to increase the efficiency, and thus reduce the cost, of litigation, whilst maintaining the interests of justice, will be threatened if courts are burdened with a weight of inappropriate and unnecessary authority.

It is important to distinguish a law report from a court record. A court record consists of the names of the parties, the pleadings, and the decision or order of the court. A law report contains most of these along with the judgment of the court setting out the reasoning upon which the decision was based. It is this reasoning which is important for the purposes of the doctrine of precedent, and court records are therefore of little value in this context.

One might suppose that because the doctrine of precedent is the cornerstone of the English legal system, the courts would have created a methodical system of producing law reports. In fact, however, this has never been done and law reporting has been left entirely to private enterprise. There is still an element of chance in the matter of whether or not a case is reported, although the growth of electronic legal databases such as LEXIS,[8] means that few cases decided by the superior courts[9] (other than the Crown Court) escape the scrutiny of researchers. In addition, certain key decisions of tribunals and rulings of trial judges in the Crown Court become known to practitioners and academics through specialist journals and encyclopaedias.

B THE OPERATION OF THE DOCTRINE OF PRECEDENT

1 THE DOCTRINE OF BINDING PRECEDENT

The traditional view of the function of an English judge has been that it is not to make law but to decide cases in accordance with existing legal rules. The doctrine of binding precedent (or *stare decisis*), whereby the judge is not merely referred to earlier decisions for guidance but is also bound to apply rules of law decided by those cases, was founded on this 'declaratory' view of the judicial process. However, few would now deny that judges have a powerful law-making function.

---

[6] Since the Practice Direction, if a decision falling into one of these categories does extend the law or establish a new principle it must include an express statement to this effect in the judgment.

[7] [2001] 2 All ER 510 at [1]–[2], [2001] 1 WLR 1001 at [1]–[2].   [8] See p 107, *post.*

[9] See chapter 7, *post.*

The theoretical position has been that judges do not make or change law: they discover and declare the law which is throughout the same. According to this theory, when an earlier decision is overruled the law is not changed: its true nature is disclosed, having existed in that form all along. This theoretical position is, as Lord Reid said in the article 'The Judge As Law Maker' (1972–1973) 12 J.S.P.T.L. (N.S.) 22, a fairy tale in which no-one any longer believes. In truth, judges make and change the law. The whole of the common law is judge-made and only by judicial change in the law is the common law kept relevant in a changing world.[10]

The operation of the doctrine depends upon the hierarchy of the courts. All courts stand in a definite relationship to one another. A court is bound by decisions of courts above itself in the hierarchy and, usually, by courts of equivalent standing. Given that the doctrine of precedent has binding force within this framework, the question naturally arises of how the law may develop if cases are always to be determined according to ageless principles. In practice there are several ways in which the doctrine retains its flexibility. These are dealt with in detail below, but two basic principles should be noted: first, that superior courts have power to overrule decisions of inferior courts and, in certain cases, to overrule their own earlier decisions; and second, that any rule of law may be changed by statute. Consequently every rule of law is subject to change, either by the judges themselves or by Parliament. Although legislation is the ultimate source of law, in the sense that Parliament has the constitutional authority to make or unmake any law, it should not in any way be regarded as a *superior* source of law. Although judges may be reluctant to make major changes which involve policy better settled by Parliament, judicial law-making has the advantage of being able to provide both flexibility and relative speed.

The advantages of the precedent system are said to be certainty, precision, and flexibility.[11] Legal certainty is achieved, at least in theory, because judges are bound to deal with like situations in a consistent way. Precision is achieved by the sheer volume of reported cases which provide specific solutions to innumerable factual situations. Finally, flexibility is achieved by the possibility of decisions being overruled or distinguished, thus allowing the law to adapt to new or previously unforeseen circumstances.

The obvious disadvantages of the system are its inherent rigidity, which may occasionally cause hardship, and the vast and ever-increasing bulk of reported cases to which the court must refer in order to determine what the law is. Indeed, it is this latter concern which has led the courts to take steps restricting the extent to which certain types of case can be cited as precedents.[12]

Finally, it is self-evident that there cannot be an infinite regression. Every rule of law

[10] *Kleinwort Benson v Lincoln City Council* [1999] 2 AC 349 at 358, [1998] 4 All ER 513 at 518, per Lord Browne-Wilkinson.

[11] See the observations of Russell LJ in *Gallie v Lee* [1969] 2 Ch 17 at 41, [1969] 1 All ER 1062 at 1076, and of Lord Hailsham in *Cassell & Co Ltd v Broome* [1972] AC 1027 at 1054, [1972] 1 All ER 801 at 809 ('in legal matters, some degree of certainty is at least as valuable a part of justice as perfection').

[12] See p 77, *ante*.

must have its origin, and if it was not created by statute then it must have been created by a court. Even in modern times cases arise for which there is no precedent, and the court's decision in such a case must inevitably be based on general principles. These cases are described as cases of first impression and they require the judge to make law rather than to simply apply it.[13] Although he will do this by reference to analogous principles, even legal principles must have their origin and the failure to properly account for this is an inherent weakness of the declaratory theory.[14]

2 THE IMPACT OF THE HUMAN RIGHTS ACT 1998 ON THE DOCTRINE OF PRECEDENT

Under the Human Rights Act 1998,[15] courts and tribunals are obliged to perform their functions in accordance with Convention rights,[16] and they must interpret legislation in a manner compatible with these rights so far as it is possible to do so.[17] Not only does this sanction the overruling of incompatible precedents by the appellate courts in the ordinary way, it also permits a 'year zero' approach to *stare decisis*,[18] because a court's obligations under the Act must prevail over any duty to obey the normal rules of precedent. This means that, for example, a pre-Human Rights Act decision of a higher court cannot stand in the way of a lower court coming to a different conclusion in order to give effect to Convention rights. Thus the Court of Appeal has already declined to follow a previous decision of the House of Lords, in order to avoid the conclusion that a provision of the Rent Act 1977 was in breach of Article 14 of the Convention.[19] Similarly, in *Director General of Fair Trading* v *Proprietary Association of Great Britain*[20] the same court made a 'modest adjustment' to the test for bias established by the House of Lords in *R* v *Gough*[21] in order to comply with the approach of the European Court of Human Rights. The modified approach adopted in this case has since been approved by the House of Lords in *Porter* v *Magill*.[22]

The Act also requires courts and tribunals determining matters involving Convention rights to take into account decisions of the European Court of Human Rights in

---

[13] e.g. *Philips* v *Brooks Ltd* [1919] 2 KB 243; *Malone* v *Metropolitan Police Commissioner (No 2)* [1979] Ch 344, [1979] 2 All ER 620; *Midland Bank Trust Co Ltd* v *Green (No 3)* [1982] Ch 529, [1981] 3 All ER 744; *Parker* v *British Airways Board* [1982] QB 1004, [1982] 1 All ER 834.

[14] See Lord Simon's observations on the declaratory theory of common law in *Jones* v *Secretary of State for Social Services* [1972] AC 944 at 1026, [1972] 1 All ER 145 at 198, quoted at p 324, *post*.

[15] The overall significance of this major piece of legislation is discussed in chapter 5, *post*.

[16] Section 6. Convention rights are defined in s 1.

[17] Section 3(1). The effect of the Act on statutory interpretation is discussed further in chapter 2, *ante*.

[18] See Mead, 'Swallowing the Camel, Straining at the Gnat: The Implications of *Mendoza* v *Ghaidan*' [2003] 5 EHRLR 501 at 509.

[19] *Ghaidan* v *Godin-Mendoza* [2002] EWCA Civ 1533, [2003] Ch 380, [2002] 4 All ER 1162 (affirmed: [2004] UKHL 30, [2004] 2 AC 557, [2004] 3 All ER 411). The House of Lords decision in question was *Fitzpatrick* v *Sterling Housing Association Ltd* [2001] 1 AC 27, [1999] 4 All ER 705.

[20] [2001] 1 WLR 700, [2001] HRLR 17; *sub nom Re Medicaments and Related Classes of Goods (No 2)*.

[21] [1993] AC 646, [1993] 2 All ER 724.

[22] [2001] UKHL 67, [2002] 2 AC 357, [2002] 1 All ER 465.

so far as they are relevant. The Act stops short of making these decisions binding on domestic courts, but they are regarded as highly persuasive.[23]

3 THE BINDING ELEMENT IN PRECEDENTS

(a) The ratio decidendi

Strictly speaking, it is a misstatement to say that a 'decision' is binding on anyone other than the parties to the case in question. Similarly, it is not technically correct to regard a 'decision' as having been overruled. It is not the decision which binds (or is overruled); it is the rule of law contained within the decision. This element of the decision is termed the *ratio decidendi*, and not every statement of law made by a judge in the case forms part of this *ratio*.

Every decision contains the following basic ingredients:

(1) findings of material facts, both direct and inferential;[24]

(2) statements of the principles of law applicable to the legal problems disclosed by the facts; and

(3) a judgment (or judgments) based on the combined effect of (1) and (2).

For the purposes of the parties themselves, (3) is the material element in the decision, for it is what ultimately determines their rights and liabilities in relation to the subject matter of the case. However, for the purpose of the doctrine of precedent, (2) is the vital element in the decision, and it is this which is termed the *ratio decidendi*. Thus the *ratio decidendi* may be defined as the statement of law applied to the legal problems raised by the facts, upon which the decision is based.

The two other elements in the decision are not precedents at all: the findings of fact are not binding on anyone, and the judgment is only binding on the parties to the case in question.[25] This means that even where the direct facts of a case appear to be identical to those before the court in an earlier decision, the judge or jury is not bound to draw the same inferences. *Qualcast (Wolverhampton) Ltd v Haynes*[26] is a good example of this point. In that case an employee sued his employers for negligence in failing to provide a safe system of work. At first instance the county court judge held himself bound to follow earlier cases in which employers who had acted in a similar manner had been held liable. The House of Lords held that this was not the correct

---

[23] The status of these decisions is discussed further at p 153, *post*.

[24] An inferential finding of fact is the inference which the judge (or jury) draws from the direct or perceptible facts. For example, negligence may be inferred from the direct facts of the speed of a vehicle, the length of skid marks, and the state of the road. Negligence is thus an inferential finding of fact. Similarly, unreasonable behaviour in matrimonial proceedings is an inference of fact which may be drawn from the direct facts of the respondent spouse's treatment of the other spouse.

[25] See *R v Secretary of State for the Home Department, ex parte Ku* [1995] QB 364, [1995] 2 All ER 891.

[26] [1959] AC 743, [1959] 2 All ER 38.

approach, since the cases relied upon by the judge were based upon inferences of fact which were not binding. Otherwise, as Lord Somervell observed:[27]

the precedent system will die from a surfeit of authorities.

Not every statement of law in a judgment is binding. Only those statements which are based upon the facts and upon which the decision is based are binding. Any other statement of law is, strictly speaking, superfluous and is described as an *obiter dictum* (something said 'by the way'). It should not, however, be concluded from this that *obiter dicta* are of little or no weight or importance.

(b) Obiter dicta

There are two types of *obiter dicta*. Firstly, a statement of law is regarded as *obiter* if it is based upon facts which either were not found to be material or were not found to exist at all. For example, the famous statement of equitable estoppel contained in the judgment of Denning J in *Central London Property Trust Ltd* v *High Trees House Ltd*[28] is clearly *obiter* since it applied to a set of facts which were not found to be present in the case. Similarly, in *Rondel* v *Worsley*[29] the House of Lords expressed opinions to the effect that a barrister might be held liable in tort when acting outside the province of litigation, and that a solicitor acting as an advocate might enjoy immunity from action. Since the case concerned only the liability of a barrister when acting as an advocate, these opinions were necessarily *obiter*.

Secondly, even where a statement of law *is* based on the facts as found, it will be regarded as *obiter* if it does not form the basis of the decision. A statement of law made in support of a dissenting judgment is an obvious example. Similarly, where a court makes statements of law leading to one conclusion but then comes to a contrary conclusion for a different reason, those statements are necessarily *obiter* since they do not support the decision. An example is provided by the seminal case of *Hedley Byrne & Co Ltd* v *Heller & Partners*.[30] The central proposition of law in that case was that the maker of a statement owes a duty of care, in certain circumstances, to persons whom he may expect to rely upon that statement. Strictly speaking however, this statement was *obiter*, as on the facts of the case it was found that the bank which had given the disputed advice was protected by a disclaimer of responsibility. That being so, the further statement as to what rule of law *would* have been applied but for the disclaimer cannot be regarded as essential to the decision. Nevertheless, *Hedley Byrne* illustrates that the strict rules for isolating the *ratio* of a case are sometimes of limited value, since the reasoning of the House of Lords undoubtedly represents the present state of the law:[31]

---

[27] [1959] AC 743 at 758, [1959] 2 All ER 38 at 43. In the tort of negligence, only the existence of a duty of care is a question of law; whether or not the defendant has broken this duty is a question of fact.

[28] [1947] KB 130, [1956] 1 All ER 256n.

[29] [1969] 1 AC 191, [1967] 3 All ER 993. The House of Lords has since overruled its decision in this case in *Arthur J S Hall* v *Simons and others* [2002] 1 AC 615, [2000] 3 All ER 673; see p 370, *post*.

[30] [1964] AC 465, [1963] 2 All ER 575.

[31] *W B Anderson and Sons Ltd* v *Rhodes* [1967] 2 All ER 850 at 857, per Cairns J.

When five members of the House of Lords have all said, after close examination of the authorities, that a certain type of tort exists, I think that a judge of first instance should proceed on the basis that it does exist without pausing to embark on an investigation whether what was said was necessary to the ultimate decision.

Hedley Byrne has since been expressly applied by the Court of Appeal and approved by the House of Lords.[32] It seems reasonable to conclude that where the House of Lords states a rule of law and expressly overrules earlier contrary decisions, that statement will be treated as binding even though not strictly essential to the decision.

(c) Ascertaining the ratio decidendi

Whilst in theory a clear definition can be proffered as to how to ascertain the *ratio decidendi* of a case, drawing a distinction between the *ratio* and *obiter dicta* in practice is often fraught with difficulty. First of all, a case may be argued on more than one ground. If the court is willing to decide the case on one ground it will usually refrain from expressing an opinion on any other point of law, but sometimes a court may feel compelled to deal with every point of law raised. Isolating the *ratio decidendi* in such a case may be extremely difficult. The problem is often particularly acute in the case of appellate decisions, since different members of the court may arrive at the same conclusion for different reasons. The starting point in this situation is that a reason adopted by a majority of the court is presumed to be *ratio*, whereas a reason adopted only by a minority is usually regarded as non-essential to the decision and therefore not binding. The position becomes complicated where no one reason is favoured by a majority, yet every case must be assumed to have a *ratio decidendi*. The answer seems to be that it depends upon which of the alternative reasons subsequent courts are prepared to accept as *rationes*. One classic example is the decision of the House of Lords in *Sinclair* v *Brougham*.[33] It was held in this case, that once the creditors of a society had been paid in full by agreement, the assets remaining were to be divided between depositors and members of the society in accordance with the proportion of new payments to the society. The reasons for this conclusion were far from clear, with one member of the court concurring with a judgment based on reasons which were at odds with his own.[34] The multiplicity of opinion and reasoning was sufficient to provoke Lord Browne-Wilkinson to observe in a later case that it was:[35]

a bewildering authority: no single *ratio* can be detected; all the reasoning is open to serious objection, it was only intended to deal with cases where there were no trade creditors in competition and the reasoning is incapable of application where there are such creditors.
In so far as the decision of the court in *Sinclair* v *Brougham* was discernible at all, it was overruled.

A further difficulty is that what may initially be considered to be *obiter dicta*, even

---

[32] *Arenson* v *Casson, Beckman, Rutley & Co* [1977] AC 405, [1975] 3 All ER 901.
[33] [1914] AC 398, [1914–1915] All ER Rep 622.   [34] Lord Dunedin.
[35] *Westdeutsche Handesbank Girozentrale* v *Islington LBC* [1996] AC 669 at 713, [1996] 2 All ER 961 at 996.

by the court itself, may subsequently be viewed differently. Thus, in *Luc Thiet Thuan* v *R*[36] the court considered that what may have been an *obiter dictum* in *R* v *Ahluwalia*[37] 'certainly ripened' into *ratio decidendi* in *R* v *Dryden*.[38]

It is certainly possible for a case to have two or more *rationes decidendi*. The case of *Fairman* v *Perpetual Investment Building Society*[39] is an example. The House of Lords in that case gave two reasons for its decision, both of which were accepted as binding by the House in *Jacobs* v *London County Council*.[40] On the other hand, in *Read* v *J Lyons & Co Ltd*.[41] the House of Lords advanced two reasons for its decision that the defendants were not liable under the rule in *Rylands* v *Fletcher*.[42] (1) that the rule did not apply in the absence of an escape of the dangerous substance from the defendant's occupation or control; and (2) that the rule did not apply unless the plaintiff had an interest in land affected by the escape. The second reason, which is principally contained in the speech of Lord Macmillan, was, in a later case,[43] treated by the Court of Appeal as *obiter*, on the basis that it was not essential to the decision. The position is further complicated by the fact that the Court of Appeal's statement on this point was itself *obiter*, because the plaintiff's action failed for another reason. The question of whether the second reason in *Read* v *J Lyons & Co Ltd* is *ratio* or *obiter* was therefore left unresolved.[44]

A variation of this problem can arise if a majority of the judges in a case favour a reason which does not actually support the court's decision. The reason cannot be a *ratio* because it does not support the decision, yet on the other hand it seems logically odd to conclude that the *ratio* can be found in the contrary reasoning of the minority. The occasions on which such a dilemma will arise are likely to be very rare, but the decision of the House of Lords in *Central Asbestos Co Ltd* v *Dodd*[45] was such an occasion. The question before the House turned on the construction of the ill-drafted provisions of section 7(3) of the Limitation Act 1963. Lords Reid and Morris took one view of the law, Lords Simon and Salmon a different view. The fifth member of the court, Lord Pearson, was in favour of deciding the appeal in the same way as Lords Reid and Morris, but his view on the point of law substantially supported that of Lords Simon and Salmon. It was not long before the Court of Appeal was called upon to decide the point of law which had arisen in *Dodd*'s case, and it concluded that since

---

[36] [1997] AC 131, [1996] 2 All ER 1033. See also, *St John the Evangelist, Chopwel* [1995] Fam 254, [1996] 1 All ER 275. In this case, the judge said that statements made in *Re St Thomas, Pennywell* [1995] Fam 50, [1995] 4 All ER 167, 'were not strictly necessary to that decision but now I adopt them as part of the *ratio decidendi* of the present case.'

[37] [1992] 4 All ER 889, (1993) 96 Cr App R 133.   [38] [1995] 4 All ER 987.

[39] [1923] AC 74.

[40] [1950] AC 361, [1950] 1 All ER 737. The case is particularly notable in that one of the two reasons given in *Fairman*'s case was clearly not essential to the decision.

[41] [1947] AC 156, [1946] 2 All ER 471.   [42] (1868) LR 3 HL 330.

[43] *Perry* v *Kendricks Transport Ltd* [1956] 1 All ER 154, [1956] 1 WLR 85.

[44] The Court of Appeal in *Dunne* v *North-Western Gas Board* [1964] 2 QB 806, [1963] 3 All ER 916, expressly left the point open.

[45] [1973] AC 518, [1972] 2 All ER 1135.

the case had no discernible *ratio* at all, it would go back to the law contained in the earlier cases.[46]

4 PRECEDENTS WHICH ARE NOT BINDING

(a) Persuasive authorities

Obiter dicta. Although *obiter dicta* lack binding authority, they may nevertheless have a strong persuasive influence. This is particularly so where the statement in question has come from a court of high authority and is a deliberate statement of law as opposed to a casual expression of opinion. Such a dictum will usually be followed in the absence of any binding authority to the contrary. In the case of *Adams v Naylor*[47] for example, the House of Lords disapproved the practice of government departments setting up a nominal defendant to avoid the Crown's immunity from actions in tort. Although this disapproval was *obiter*, the Court of Appeal in *Royster v Cavey*[48] adopted it and refused to sanction this long-standing practice. *Hedley Byrne & Co Ltd v Heller & Partners*[49] provides another example of *obiter dicta* which has subsequently had considerable influence, but perhaps the most striking example of all is the 'neighbour principle' propounded by Lord Atkin in *Donoghue (or M'Alister) v Stevenson*.[50] This statement of law has become the basis of the modern tort of negligence and has been cited and applied on occasions too numerous to mention, yet the statement was far wider than the case itself required and it was therefore strictly *obiter*.

Decisions of inferior courts. Decisions of courts lower in the hierarchy may have some persuasive authority for those courts above them. Court of Appeal decisions, for example, are generally regarded as having persuasive authority in the House of Lords.

Decisions of the Judicial Committee of the Privy Council. 'Decisions' of the Judicial Committee of the Privy Council are not strictly binding on any English court,[51] and in theory, even a first instance judge may legitimately decline to follow a Privy Council decision.[52] In practice, however, such decisions are of very great persuasive authority for the obvious reason that the Judicial Committee is in fact composed of those persons who usually sit in the House of Lords.

There had not been any suggestion that Privy Council authorities were of equivalent

---

[46] *Harper v National Coal Board* [1974] QB 614, [1974] 2 All ER 441.

[47] [1946] AC 543, [1946] 2 All ER 241.

[48] [1947] KB 204, [1946] 2 All ER 642. This decision precipitated the passing of the Crown Proceedings Act 1947, which enabled the Crown to be sued in tort.

[49] [1964] AC 465, [1963] 2 All ER 575; see p 82, *ante*.   [50] [1932] AC 562.

[51] Privy Council decisions on 'devolution questions' affecting Wales, Scotland and Northern Ireland *are* binding, even on the House of Lords: see p 271, *post*.

[52] Diplock J did so in *Port Line Ltd v Ben Line Steamers Ltd* [1958] 2 QB 146, [1958] 1 All ER 787; see also *Dulieu v White* [1901] 2 KB 669.

weight to House of Lords cases until the decision in *Doughty* v *Turner Manufacturing*.[53] In this case, the Court of Appeal expressed the view that its own decision in *Re Polemis*[54] was no longer good law in the light of the subsequent Privy Council decision in *The Wagon Mound*.[55] Similarly, when the Court of Appeal in *Worcester Works Finance Ltd* v *Cooden Engineering Co Ltd*.[56] was faced with a conflict of authority between one of its own previous decisions and a later decision of the Privy Council, it had no hesitation in preferring the latter. Since Privy Council decisions are merely persuasive, however, it cannot be assumed that they will always be followed, and in *R* v *Smith*[57] both the Court of Appeal and the House of Lords declined to follow an earlier decision of the Privy Council concerning the defence of provocation to murder.[58] For its own part, the Privy Council has stated that it will follow House of Lords decisions when deciding cases where the applicable law is English, on the basis that the House of Lords is the final judicial authority for the determination of English law.[59]

Decisions of the European Court of Human Rights. Section 2 of the Human Rights Act 1998 requires any court or tribunal determining a matter involving a Convention right, to take into account any judgment, decision, or advisory opinion of the European Court of Human Rights, along with certain decisions of the Commission and Committee of Ministers, in so far as they may be relevant. Decisions of the European Court of Human Rights and the other institutions are thus given the status of persuasive precedents, and it is left to individual courts and tribunals to decide whether they should be followed in any particular case. The suggestion that courts ought to be bound by the Strasbourg jurisprudence was rejected by the government during the passage of the Human Rights Bill through Parliament. The Lord Chancellor explained that to make the Strasbourg jurisprudence binding on domestic courts would be inconsistent with the spirit of the Convention itself:[60]

We must remember that Clause 2 requires the courts to take account of all the judgments of the European Court of Human Rights, regardless of whether they have been given in a case involving the United Kingdom . . . the United Kingdom is not bound in international law to follow that Court's judgments in cases to which the United Kingdom had not been a party, and it would be strange to require courts in the United Kingdom to be bound by such cases.

The precise effect of section 2 was subsequently considered by Lord Slynn in the leading

---

[53] [1964] 1 QB 518, [1964] 1 All ER 98.   [54] [1921] 3 KB 560.
[55] *Overseas Tankship (UK) Ltd* v *Morts Dock and Engineering Co Ltd* [1961] AC 388, [1961] 1 All ER 404.
[56] [1972] 1 QB 210, [1971] 3 All ER 708.
[57] *R* v *Smith* [1999] QB 1079, [1998] 4 All ER 387, CA; [2001] 1 AC 146, [2000] 4 All ER 289, HL.
[58] The decision in question was *Luc Thiet Thuan* v *R* [1997] AC 131, [1996] 2 All ER 1033.
[59] *Tai Hing Cotton Mill Ltd* v *Liu Chong Hing Bank Ltd* [1986] AC 80, [1985] 2 All ER 947.
[60] Lord Irvine of Lairg, 583 HL Official Report (5th series) col 511, 18 November 1997.

case of *R (on the Application of Alconbury) v Secretary of State for the Environment, Transport and the Regions:*[61]

In the absence of some special circumstances it seems to me that the court should follow any clear and constant jurisprudence of the European Court of Human Rights. If it does not do so there is at least a possibility that the case will go to that court which is likely in the ordinary case to follow its own constant jurisprudence.

Decisions from other jurisdictions. A third class of persuasive authorities consists of the decisions of Scottish, Irish, Commonwealth, and foreign courts. There is an increasing tendency on the part of English lawyers and judges to draw analogies from other legal systems, and decisions from other jurisdictions—particularly Scotland, Ireland, the USA, Australia, Canada, and New Zealand—are frequently cited. In an effort to reduce the sheer volume of cases being used in this way, the Court of Appeal recently felt compelled to take steps discouraging reliance on foreign cases except where they genuinely have something to add to existing domestic law.[62] At the same time however, the Lord Chief Justice acknowledged that 'cases decided in other jurisdictions can, if properly used, be a valuable source of law.'[63]

(b) Statements of law made per incuriam

The Court of Appeal in the leading case of *Young v Bristol Aeroplane Co Ltd*[64] established that it was entitled to depart from one of its previous decisions if satisfied that the decision in question was reached *per incuriam* (through lack of care). When a decision is described as having been made *per incuriam*, this usually, though not always, means that some relevant statutory provision or precedent which would have led the court to a different conclusion, was not brought to the court's attention.[65] Although the principle in *Young's* case was expressed to apply only to the Court of Appeal, it has since been applied in other courts. Thus in *R v Northumberland Compensation Appeal Tribunal, ex parte Shaw*[66] a Divisional Court of the King's Bench Division declined to follow a Court of Appeal decision on the ground that the latter had been reached *per incuriam*, a relevant House of Lords decision not having been cited to the Court of Appeal. However, when the Court of Appeal refused to follow a House of Lords decision on exemplary damages[67] which it considered to have been made *per*

---

[61] [2001] UKHL 23 at [26], [2003] 2 AC 295 at [26], [2001] 2 All ER 929. For an example of a case in which the Strasbourg jurisprudence was *not* followed, see *R v Spear and others; R v Saunby and others* [2002] UKHL 31, [2003] 1 AC 734, [2002] 3 All ER 1074, discussed at p 151, *post.*

[62] *Practice Direction (Citation of Authorities)* [2001] 2 All ER 510 at [9.1], [2001] 1 WLR 1001 at [9.1], per Lord Woolf CJ.

[63] Ibid.

[64] [1944] KB 718, [1944] 2 All ER 293 (affirmed [1946] AC 163, [1946] 1 All ER 98); see p 97, *post.*

[65] *Duke v Reliance Systems Ltd* [1988] QB 108, [1987] 2 All ER 858 (affirmed [1988] AC 618, [1988] 1 All ER 626).

[66] [1951] 1 KB 711, [1951] 1 All ER 268. See also *Hughes v Kingston upon Hull City Council* [1999] QB 1193, [1999] 2 All ER 49.

[67] *Rookes v Barnard* [1964] AC 1129, [1964] 1 All ER 367. This decision had already been subjected to devastating criticism in the courts of the Commonwealth and had been repudiated by the Privy Council; see

incuriam, it was roundly condemned by the House of Lords for having done so.[68] Lord Hailsham LC, in the course of the leading speech for the majority, asserted that:[69]

it is not open to the Court of Appeal to give gratuitous advice to judges of first instance to ignore decisions of the House of Lords in this way. The course taken would have put judges of first instance in an embarrassing position, as driving them to take sides in an unedifying dispute between the Court of Appeal and the House of Lords.

These words proved to be prophetic because in *Miliangos* v *George Frank (Textiles) Ltd*,[70] Bristow J found himself in the embarrassing position foreseen by Lord Hailsham. This was because the Court of Appeal in *Schorsch Meier GmbH* v *Hennin*[71] had held that the rule of law whereby money judgments could only be expressed in sterling had ceased to exist, notwithstanding clear House of Lords authority for the existence of the rule. Bristow J preferred to follow the House of Lords authority, but the Court of Appeal later stated that he was wrong to do so because *Schorsch Meier* was binding upon him. On appeal[72] the House of Lords decision in question[73] was overruled, although not on any of the grounds cited by the Court of Appeal.

The *per incuriam* principle is of limited application, and very few decisions have subsequently been regarded as having been reached in this way.[74] In *Morelle Ltd* v *Wakeling*[75] Sir Raymond Evershed MR reaffirmed that:

As a general rule the only cases in which decisions should be held to have been given *per incuriam* are those of decisions given in ignorance or forgetfulness of some inconsistent statutory provision or of some authority binding on the court concerned; so that in such cases some part of the decision or some step in the reasoning on which it is based is found, on that account, to be demonstrably wrong. This definition is not necessarily exhaustive, but cases not strictly within it which can properly be held to have been decided *per incuriam* must, in our judgment . . . be . . . of the rarest occurrence.

Thus the mere fact that a case was not fully or expertly argued,[76] or that it was argued on one side only (as *Schorsch Meier* was), does not entitle a court to disregard it as having been made *per incuriam*. Similarly, a case cannot be considered *per incuriam*

Australian Consolidated Press Ltd v *Uren* [1969] 1 AC 590, [1967] 3 All ER 523. No less devastating was the criticism of Lord Denning MR, culminating in the description of the doctrine laid down by Lord Devlin in *Rookes* v *Barnard* as 'hopelessly illogical and inconsistent': *Broome* v *Cassell & Co Ltd* [1971] 2 QB 354 at 381, [1971] 2 All ER 187 at 199.

[68] *Cassell & Co Ltd* v *Broome* [1972] AC 1027, [1972] 1 All ER 801.

[69] [1972] AC 1027 at 1054, [1972] 1 All ER 801 at 809.

[70] [1975] QB 487, [1975] 1 All ER 1076.   [71] [1975] QB 416, [1975] 1 All ER 152.

[72] [1976] AC 443, [1975] 3 All ER 801.

[73] *Re United Railways of the Havana and Ragla Warehouses Ltd* [1961] AC 1007, [1960] 2 All ER 332 (a decision to which Lord Denning himself had been a party).

[74] For two recent examples, see *Royal Bank of Scotland* v *Etridge (No 2)* [1998] 4 All ER 705 and *R (on the application of W)* v *Lambeth LBC* [2002] EWCA Civ 613, [2002] 2 All ER 901.

[75] [1955] 2 QB 379 at 406, [1955] 1 All ER 708 at 718; see also *Miliangos* v *George Frank (Textiles) Ltd* [1976] AC 443 at 477, [1975] 3 All ER 801 at 821, per Lord Simon.

[76] *Joscelyne* v *Nissen* [1970] 2 QB 86, [1970] 1 All ER 1213; *Morelle Ltd* v *Wakeling* [1955] 2 QB 379, [1955] 1 All ER 708.

solely because the court appeared to misunderstand the law or was not aware of the policy considerations behind a statute.[77] However, if it appears to a court that a previous interpretation of a statute was clearly wrong, then it would seem that the duty of the later court is to apply a correct interpretation.[78] Whether this is an example of the *per incuriam* doctrine or simply an illustration of a judge's general obligations concerning the interpretation of statutes is a moot point. In *IM Properties v Cape & Dalgleish*[79] the Court of Appeal was referred to an earlier House of Lords decision,[80] which it considered to be based on an incorrect interpretation of section 35A of the Supreme Court Act 1981. The Court of Appeal held that in these circumstances it had no option but to depart from the earlier decision, and it is clear that it regarded this as an application of the *per incuriam* doctrine:[81]

[U]nder these circumstances we are not bound by this aspect of the *Westdeutsche* decision and . . . we are entitled to determine this appeal upon what we consider is the correct construction of s 35A.

(c) Precedents embodying former rules of international law

The decision of the Court of Appeal in *Trendtex Trading Corporation Ltd v Central Bank of Nigeria*[82] indicates that there may be a further limited exception to the doctrine of binding precedent in respect of that part of English law which embodies current international law. The court in this case held that the defendant bank could not claim sovereign immunity from action because, inter alia, as a matter of international law the doctrine of state immunity was not applicable to ordinary commercial transactions. In reaching this decision the court declined to follow an earlier Court of Appeal decision which would otherwise have been considered binding, the majority holding that the rule of *stare decisis* could not stand in the way of a court giving effect to changes in international law. The point does not appear to have been judicially considered since this case, and the decision must therefore be taken as an accurate statement of the current law.

---

[77] *Farrell* v *Alexander* [1976] QB 345, [1976] 1 All ER 129 (decision reversed [1977] AC 59, [1976] 2 All ER 721); but see *Industrial Properties (Barton Hill) Ltd* v *Associated Electrical Industries Ltd* [1977] QB 580, [1977] 2 All ER 293. In the latter case, the Court of Appeal declared one of its previous decisions *per incuriam* where the court had misunderstood an earlier case because of deficiencies in the law report to which it had been referred. See also *Dixon* v *BBC* [1979] QB 546, [1979] 2 All ER 112 in which one *ratio* of an earlier case was treated as *per incuriam* on the ground that the statutory provision under construction had been considered in isolation rather than in context. See also, *R (on the application of W)* v *Lambeth LBC* [2002] EWCA Civ 613, [2002] 2 All ER 901.

[78] Ibid.   [79] [1999] QB 297, [1998] 3 All ER 203.

[80] *Westdeutsche Handesbank Girozentrale* v *Islington LBC* [1996] AC 669 at 713, [1996] 2 All ER 961 at 996.

[81] [1999] QB 297 at 308–9, [1998] 3 All ER 203 at 212, per Hobhouse LJ.

[82] [1977] QB 529, [1977] 1 All ER 881. The question at issue in the case has now been resolved by the State Immunity Act 1978, s 3(1).

5 REVERSING, OVERRULING, AND DISTINGUISHING

(a) Reversing

Reversing occurs when one of the parties to a case appeals against the decision of a lower court and the appellate court then reaches a different conclusion. The effect of this is literally to 'reverse' the lower court's decision in the case and to alter the outcome for the parties concerned. The process of reversing a decision must be carefully distinguished from that of 'overruling', since the latter does not change the outcome in the case that is overruled.

(b) Overruling

Overruling occurs when a court in one case makes a decision affecting the rule of law upon which the decision in a *different* case was based. This means that semantically, it is not correct to describe a decision as having been 'overruled' since it is only the rule of law contained in the decision which is affected, and not the decision itself.

A decision may be overruled either by statute or by a higher court. If overruled by a court, the earlier decision is deemed to have been based on a misunderstanding of the law, and on a strict application of the declaratory theory, the earlier rule is deemed never to have existed. On this view the common law is never changed; it is merely restated correctly. However, such a rationalization ignores the reality that judges do make law, and often change the law because of changing circumstances or attitudes. An example of such a decision is that of *R* v *R*,[83] in which the House of Lords held that the long-established rule that a husband cannot be criminally liable for raping his wife no longer formed part of English law.

Whatever the theoretical basis, all judicial overruling operates retrospectively, and this is one important respect in which it differs from most instances of overruling by statute.[84] Another difference between overruling by the courts and overruling by statute is that statutes do not expressly name the decisions that they overrule. Nevertheless it is not usually difficult to identify the cases which are overruled by a statute, particularly where the statute follows closely upon an unpopular decision of a superior court.[85]

The United States Supreme Court has the power to overrule decisions prospectively. This means that it may overrule an existing legal rule for the benefit of future decisions, yet still apply it to the particular case before it.[86] This power is said to be based on the common law, and though it has never been recognized in this country it has occasionally been the subject of judicial attention. In *Jones* v *Secretary of State*

---

[83] *R* v *R (Rape: Marital Exemption)* [1992] 1 AC 599, [1991] 4 All ER 481; see p 326, *post*.

[84] The War Damage Act 1965 is a rare example of an Act which was expressly stated to be retrospective, and which was passed with the apparent intention of overruling a House of Lords decision (*Burmah Oil Co Ltd* v *Lord Advocate* [1965] AC 75, [1964] 2 All ER 348). The presumption against the retrospective operation of statutes is discussed further in chapter 2.

[85] Ibid.   [86] *Linkletter* v *Walker* 381 US 618 (1965).

for Social Services,[87] Lord Simon suggested that the most satisfactory method of dealing with the case would have been to allow the appeal on the basis that it was covered by an existing House of Lords precedent, but to then overrule that precedent prospectively. In the event, however, he simply concurred with the majority of the House of Lords and decided to allow the appeal, observing that any extension of judicial power to include prospective overruling should preferably be left to Parliament:[88]

In the first place, informed professional opinion is probably to the effect that your Lordships have no power to overrule decisions with prospective effect only; such opinion is itself a source of law; and your Lordships, sitting judicially, are bound by any rule of law arising extra-judicially. Secondly, to proceed by Act of Parliament would obviate any suspicion of endeavouring to upset one-sidedly the constitutional balance between executive, legislature and judiciary. Thirdly, concomitant problems could receive consideration for example whether other courts supreme within their own jurisdictions should have similar powers as regards the rule of precedent; whether machinery could and should be devised to apprise the courts of the potential repercussions of any particular decision; and whether any court (including the appellate committee of your Lordships' House) should sit *in banc* when invited to review a previous decision.

The passage above illustrates clearly the reasons why it is preferable for major changes in the law to be made by Parliament, rather than by the judiciary. The House of Lords has revisited the question of whether it should have the power to prospectively over-rule in two recent cases,[89] but there appears to be no overwhelming support for change and the matter has been left open for future consideration.

A precedent does not lose its authority with the passing of time. Indeed the strength of a precedent arguably increases with age, and courts tend to be reluctant to overrule long-standing authorities unless they are clearly wrong. Apart from the desirability of attaining certainty, the main reason for the reluctance of judges to overrule old decisions is the fact that this might have the effect of disturbing existing financial arrangements, depriving persons of vested proprietary rights, or even imposing crim-inal liability retrospectively. Thus in *Re Compton*[90] the Court of Appeal was unwilling to overrule a long line of old authorities concerning charitable trusts, even though it considered these cases to be anomalous. Similarly although the rule in *Pinnel's case*[91] is plainly anomalous, even the House of Lords has refused to overrule it. Thus, in

87 [1972] AC 944, [1972] 1 All ER 145; see p 94, *post*.

88 [1972] AC 944 at 1026–7, [1972] 1 All ER 145 at 198; Lord Simon advanced similar suggestions in *Miliangos* v *George Frank (Textiles) Ltd* [1976] AC 443 at 490, [1975] 3 All ER 801 at 832.

89 *Kleinwort Benson Ltd* v *Lincoln City Council* [1999] 2 AC 349, [1998] 4 All ER 513; *R* v *Governor of Brockhill Prison, ex parte Evans (No 2)* [2001] 2 AC 19 at 26, [2000] 4 All ER 15 at 19. In the latter case, Lord Slynn stated that in his view, 'there may be situations in which it would be desirable, and in no way unjust, that the effect of judicial rulings should be prospective or limited to certain claimants.'

90 [1945] Ch 123, [1945] 1 All ER 198.   91 (1602) 5 Co Rep 117a.

Foakes v *Beer*[92] Lord Fitzgerald expressed doubt about the merits of the rule but felt that because of its longevity the House would not be justified in overruling it.[93]

On the other hand, the courts generally have little hesitation in overruling decisions which they consider to be clearly wrong. Thus, in *Bourne* v *Keane*[94] the House of Lords overruled a series of long-standing decisions on the law of trusts, even though this had the effect of disturbing many existing trusts and settlements. More recently in *Button* v *DPP*[95] the House of Lords held that the common law offence of affray could be committed in a private place, and thus overruled a line of authority to the effect that the offence could occur only in a public place. Similarly, in the leading case of *Miliangos* v *George Frank (Textiles) Ltd*[96] the House of Lords effectively overruled a decision which embodied one of the clearest and most firmly entrenched rules of English law, namely that judgment must be given in sterling.[97]

(c) Distinguishing

The process of 'distinguishing' is probably the major factor in enabling the doctrine of precedent to remain flexible and adaptable. Cases are distinguished on their facts. The *ratio decidendi* of a case is, by definition, based upon the material facts of that case and courts are only bound to apply precedents which share the same material facts. Consequently, if a court is willing to regard as material any fact which is not common to both the case before it and the precedent cited, the two cases can be distinguished. The law reports are full of strained distinctions where the court was evidently anxious not to follow an apparently binding precedent. In theory it is possible to distinguish virtually any precedent, since factual situations will almost never precisely duplicate themselves. Nevertheless there are practical limits beyond which the court will be unlikely to go. Cases which are indistinguishable are described as being 'on all fours' with one another.

To illustrate how fine a distinction may be drawn between ostensibly parallel factual situations, reference may be made to two cases concerning the tort of conversion. In *England* v *Cowley*[98] the defendant refused to allow the plaintiff to remove goods from his, the defendant's, premises. This was held not to be conversion since there was no absolute denial of title. This case was distinguished by the Court of Appeal in *Oakley* v *Lyster*,[99] in which the defendant refused to allow the plaintiff to remove material from

---

[92] (1883–84) LR 9 App Cas 605.

[93] Ibid at 630. The rule has, of course, been undermined by the doctrine of equitable estoppel; see *D & C Builders Ltd* v *Rees* [1966] 2 QB 617, [1965] 3 All ER 837. See also *Re Selectmove* [1995] 1 WLR 474, [1995] 2 All ER 531.

[94] [1919] AC 815. On the other hand, in *Prudential Assurance Co Ltd* v *London Residuary Body* [1992] 2 AC 386, [1992] 3 All ER 504, the House of Lords felt unable to overrule ancient authorities requiring the maximum duration of a term of years to be determinable at the outset. This conclusion was reached on the ground that overruling the earlier authorities might upset long-established titles, yet the House itself acknowledged that it led to a 'bizarre outcome' in the instant case.

[95] [1966] AC 591, [1965] 3 All ER 587.   [96] [1976] AC 443, [1975] 3 All ER 801.

[97] *Re United Railways of the Havana and Regla Warehouses Ltd* [1961] AC 1007, [1960] 2 All ER 332.

[98] (1873) LR 8 Exch 126.   [99] [1931] 1 KB 148.

his (the defendant's) land, and in addition asserted his own title to the material. This was held to be an act of conversion, the assertion of title apparently making the denial of title absolute.

6 THE HIERARCHY OF THE COURTS

It has already been noted that the doctrine of binding precedent rests upon the underlying principle that the courts form a hierarchy, with each court standing in a definite position in relation to every other court. The structure of this hierarchy must now be considered for the purposes of the doctrine of precedent.

(a) European Court of Justice[100]

In matters concerning: (1) the interpretation of the Treaties; (2) the validity and interpretation of acts of the Community institutions; and (3) the interpretation of the statutes of bodies established by an act of the Council, the Court of Justice of the European Communities is the supreme tribunal. Accordingly, its decisions in these areas of jurisdiction will be binding on all English courts. Indeed section 3(1) of the European Communities Act 1972 expressly provides that:

for the purpose of all legal proceedings any question as to the meaning or effect of any of the Treaties, or as to the validity, meaning or effect of any Community instrument, shall be treated as a question of law (and, if not referred to the European Court, be for determination as such in accordance with the principles laid down by and any relevant decision of the European Court or any court attached thereto).

The European Court of Justice does not observe a doctrine of binding precedent and does not regard itself as bound by its previous decisions. This does not, however, mean that its previous decisions have no influence upon it.

(b) House of Lords

The House of Lords stands at the summit of the English hierarchy of courts, and decisions of the House of Lords are binding upon all other courts trying civil or criminal cases.

Formerly the House of Lords regarded itself as strictly bound by its own earlier decisions, which were thus immutable except by legislation.[101] However in 1966 Lord Gardiner LC issued a Practice Statement to the effect that their Lordships would in future be willing to depart from their earlier decisions 'when it appears right to do so'.[102] They would, however, bear in mind the danger of disturbing financial arrangements and proprietary rights retrospectively and the especial need for certainty as to the criminal law. The Lord Chancellor made it clear, moreover, that this statement was not intended to apply elsewhere than in the House of Lords.

---

100 See chapter 4, *post.*
101 This principle was established in *London Tramways Co v London County Council* [1898] AC 375.
102 [1966] 3 All ER 77, [1966] 1 WLR 1234.

The practical consequences of this change in the law were, at first, slight. In the five years following Lord Gardiner's statement the House of Lords did not overrule any of its previous decisions. This reticence is aptly demonstrated by *Jones* v *Secretary of State for Social Services*.[103] In this case, a seven-member House declined to overrule one of its previous decisions[104] even though a majority of their Lordships were of opinion that the *ratio* of the earlier decision was wrong. Since there was no suggestion that the earlier authority could be distinguished it might appear that there was no alternative but to overrule it, and three members of the House were prepared to do this. Lord Simon, however, gave several reasons why he thought that it would be wrong to depart from the earlier case, even though he agreed that it had been wrongly decided. In particular, he emphasised that the power to depart from a previous decision 'is one to be most sparingly exercised', and he concluded that a variation of view on a matter of statutory construction would rarely provide a suitable occasion. The wait for a suitable occasion was not a long one, however, and in *British Railways Board* v *Herrington*[105] the House refused to follow a precedent which had stood for over forty years,[106] concerning the duty of care owed by an occupier of land to trespassers.

In *R* v *Secretary of State for the Home Department, ex parte Khawaja*[107] the House of Lords rejected a previous decision which had unduly restricted the power of the courts to review the detention and removal of suspected illegal immigrants.[108] Lord Scarman stated that the House must be satisfied of two things before it was entitled to take such a step:[109]

[T]he House must be satisfied not only that adherence to the precedent would involve the risk of injustice and obstruct the proper development of the law, but also that a judicial departure by the House from the precedent is the safe and appropriate way of remedying the injustice and developing the law. The possibility that legislation may be the better course is one which, though not mentioned in the [Practice] Statement, the House will not overlook.

Both conditions were clearly satisfied on the facts of the case because the liberty of the subject was at stake and the decision raised fundamental issues about the ability of the courts to review executive decisions.

A more recent example is provided by the case of *Arthur JS Hall & Co* v *Simons*,[110] in which the House of Lords departed from the precedent set in *Rondel* v *Worsley*[111] and removed the immunity of advocates from liability in tort. While their Lordships did not doubt that *Rondel* v *Worsley* had been correctly decided at the time, it was felt that the original justifications for the immunity no longer applied and that it was therefore in the interests of public policy for the immunity to be removed.[112]

---

[103] [1972] AC 944, [1972] 1 All ER 145.
[104] *Minister of Social Security* v *Amalgamated Engineering Union* [1967] 1 AC 725, [1967] 1 All ER 210.
[105] [1972] AC 877, [1972] 1 All ER 749.
[106] *Robert Addie & Sons (Collieries) Ltd* v *Dumbreck* [1929] AC 358.
[107] [1984] AC 74, [1983] 1 All ER 765.
[108] *R* v *Secretary of State for the Home Department, ex parte Zamir* [1980] AC 930, [1980] 2 All ER 768.
[109] [1984] AC 74 at 106, [1983] 1 All ER 765 at 778.   [110] [2002] 1 AC 615, [2000] 3 All ER 673.
[111] [1969] 1 AC 191, [1967] 3 All ER 993.   [112] This is discussed further in chapter 11, *post*.

Notwithstanding the especial need for certainty as to the criminal law, the House in *R* v *Shivpuri*[113] departed from its own previous decision in *Anderton* v *Ryan*[114] on the law of criminal attempts. *Anderton* had been decided less than a year earlier but had meanwhile been the subject of devastating academic criticism. Lord Bridge (who had also been a party to the earlier decision) gave the following reasons:[115]

Firstly, I am undeterred by the consideration that the decision in *Anderton* v *Ryan* was so recent. The 1966 Practice Statement is an effective abandonment of our pretention to infallibility. If a serious error embodied in a decision of this House had distorted the law, the sooner it is corrected the better. Secondly, I cannot see how, in the very nature of the case, anyone could have acted in reliance on the law as propounded in *Anderton* v *Ryan* in the belief that he was acting innocently and now find that, after all, he is to be held to have committed a criminal offence.

Despite these and other examples,[116] the House of Lords' power to depart from its previous decisions continues to be exercised sparingly. As Lord Reid observed in one case:[117]

our change of practice in no longer regarding previous decisions of this House as absolutely binding does not mean that whenever we think a previous decision was wrong we should reverse it. In the general interest of certainty in the law we must be sure that there is some very good reason before we so act.

As the recent decision in *R* v *Kansal*[118] confirms, the House will not overrule its own decisions lightly, and a belief that an earlier case was wrongly decided will not necessarily be a sufficient justification. In *Kansal*, the House declined to overrule a decision which it had reached only four months earlier,[119] despite a majority of the House agreeing that the earlier case had been wrongly decided. The unwillingness of their Lordships to invoke the Practice Statement on this occasion was largely due to the fact that the cases concerned the status of the Human Rights Act 1998 during the transitional period before it came into force. The decisions were therefore unlikely to have any long-term significance.

Apart from the possibility of the House of Lords being prepared to depart from its own earlier decisions there are now four other means by which a House of Lords decision may lose its authority. Firstly, and most obviously, it may be overruled by statute or as a result of a decision of the European Court of Justice. Secondly, the potential scope of a House of Lords decision may be lessened if it can be

---

113 [1987] AC 1, [1986] 2 All ER 334.   114 [1985] AC 560, [1985] 2 All ER 355.

115 [1987] AC 560 at 23, [1986] 2 All ER 355 at 345.

116 See *The Johanna Oldendorff* [1974] AC 479, [1973] 3 All ER 148; *Vestey* v *Inland Revenue Commissioners* [1980] AC 1148, [1979] 3 All ER 976; *Murphy* v *Brentwood District Council* [1991] 1 AC 398, [1990] 2 All ER 908.

117 *Knuller (Publishing, Printing and Promotions) Ltd* v *Director of Public Prosecutions* [1973] AC 435 at 455, [1972] 2 All ER 898 at 903; see also, *Fitzleet Estates Ltd* v *Cherry* [1977] 3 All ER 996, [1977] 1 WLR 1345.

118 *R* v *Kansal (No 2)* [2001] UKHL 62, [2002] AC 69, [2002] 1 All ER 257.

119 *R* v *Lambert* [2001] UKHL 37, [2002] 2 AC 545, [2001] 3 All ER 577. *Kansal* has since been applied in *R* v *Benjafield* [2002] UKHL 2, [2003] 1 AC 1099, [2002] 1 All ER 815.

distinguished. The process of distinguishing applies in the House of Lords as in other courts. Indeed, before the 1966 Practice Statement it was applied with more force in the House of Lords than elsewhere because there was no other judicial means of avoiding a precedent which the House felt to be wrong. Thirdly, the House of Lords may reject one of its own previous decisions if it was made *per incuriam*. This is, however, of limited application, since it would be virtually inconceivable in modern times for a case to progress through the House of Lords with a crucial authority being overlooked. Moreover, it is doubtful whether this option is open to other courts. As noted earlier, the Court of Appeal in *Broome v Cassell & Co Ltd*[120] regarded a House of Lords decision as being given *per incuriam* on the basis that two House of Lords authorities were not cited to the House. Not only did the House of Lords disapprove the Court of Appeal's application of the *per incuriam* doctrine, Lord Diplock stated clearly that the Court of Appeal had no power to treat a House of Lords' decision in this way:[121]

The Court of Appeal found themselves able to disregard the decision of this House in *Rookes v Barnard* by applying to it the label *per incuriam*. That label is relevant only to the right of an appellate court to decline to follow one of its own previous decisions, not to its right to disregard a decision of a higher appellate court or to the right of a judge of the High Court to disregard a decision of the Court of Appeal.

This dictum has been approved in subsequent cases[122] and it may therefore be assumed to be authoritative. Finally, the status of certain House of Lords decisions may be undermined by the application of the Human Rights Act 1998. As discussed earlier in this chapter, the Human Rights Act obliges courts to act consistently with the ECHR, and to interpret legislation in a Convention compatible way wherever it is possible to do so. Thus, a court may have no option but to depart from a precedent which would otherwise be binding upon it, in order to reach a decision which is consistent with its obligations under the Human Rights Act. This is so, even if the precedent concerned was established by the House of Lords.[123]

(c) Court of Appeal

Civil Division. Decisions of the Court of Appeal are binding on all inferior courts trying civil or criminal cases, including divisional courts.[124] The Court of Appeal itself is bound by decisions of the European Court, the House of Lords,[125] and by its own

---

[120] [1971] 2 QB 354, [1971] 2 All ER 187; see p 88, *ante*.

[121] *Cassell & Co Ltd v Broome* [1972] AC 1027 at 1131, [1972] 1 All ER 801 at 874.

[122] See *Baker v R* [1975] AC 774, [1975] 3 All ER 55; *Miliangos v George Frank (Textiles) Ltd* [1976] AC 443 at 479, [1975] 3 All ER 801 at 822–3, per Lord Simon. Cf. *Hughes v Kingston upon Hull City Council* [1999] QB 1193, [1999] 2 All ER 49, in which the Divisional Court of the Queen's Bench Division rejected a *per incuriam* decision of the Court of Appeal.

[123] See, e.g., the decision of the Court of Appeal in *Ghaidan v Godin-Mendoza* [2002] EWCA Civ 1533, [2003] Ch 380, [2002] 4 All ER 1162, discussed further at pp 56 and 80, *ante*.

[124] *Brownsea Haven Properties Ltd v Poole Corporation* [1958] Ch 574, [1958] 1 All ER 205.

[125] Subject to such decisions being compatible with EC law and with the Human Rights Act 1998; see p 99, *post*.

earlier decisions.[126] The latter principle was established in *Young* v *Bristol Aeroplane Co Ltd*.[127] In delivering the judgment in this case, Lord Greene MR cited three exceptional circumstances in which an earlier decision of the Court of Appeal would not be regarded as binding:

(1) Where there are two conflicting decisions, the court may choose which it will follow and the decision not followed will be deemed to have been overruled. Thus, in *Fisher* v *Ruislip-Northwood Urban District Council*[128] the court had to choose between conflicting lines of authorities concerning the liability of local authorities to motorists who collided with unlit air-raid shelters. Similarly, in *Tiverton Estates Ltd* v *Wearwell Ltd*[129] the Court of Appeal was able to avoid following its decision in the controversial case of *Law* v *Jones*[130] because it conflicted with earlier decisions of the court.

(2) The court is bound to refuse to follow a decision of its own, which, though not expressly overruled, cannot stand with a later House of Lords decision.[131]

(3) The court is not bound to follow a decision of its own if that decision was given *per incuriam*. Thus, in *Royal Bank of Scotland* v *Etridge (No 2)*[132] the court refused to follow its own decision in *Royal Bank of Scotland* v *Etridge (No 1)*[133] because it had not, in the earlier case, been referred to two previous decisions by which it ought to have been bound.

If a decision is described as having been given *per incuriam* this usually means that the court has overlooked a relevant statutory provision or a binding precedent,[134] but there is a residual category of other cases in which the principle may be invoked. Thus, in *Williams* v *Fawcett*[135] the Court of Appeal rejected a number of earlier authorities on the ground that there had been a 'manifest slip or error' affecting the liberty of the subject and it was unlikely that the House of Lords would have the opportunity to correct this error. The court applied the same test in *Rickards* v *Rickards*[136] and refused

---

[126] The Court of Appeal is also bound by the decisions of courts which exercised equivalent jurisdiction prior to 1875: the Court of Exchequer Chamber and the Chancery Court of Appeal; see *Re Stevens, ex parte M'George* (1882) 20 Ch D 697.

[127] [1944] KB 718, [1944] 2 All ER 293 (affirmed [1946] AC 163, [1946] 1 All ER 98).

[128] [1945] KB 584, [1945] 2 All ER 458.   [129] [1975] Ch 146, [1974] 1 All ER 209.

[130] [1974] Ch 112, [1973] 2 All ER 437. The effect of this decision was that it was unnecessary for a memorandum under s 40 of the Law of Property Act 1925 to acknowledge the existence of a contract. See also *Starr* v *National Coal Board* [1977] 1 All ER 243, [1977] 1 WLR 63; *WA Sherratt Ltd* v *John Bromley (Church Stretton) Ltd* [1985] QB 1038, [1985] 1 All ER 216.

[131] It is notable that this exception was not expressed to apply to cases in which a decision of the Court of Appeal is inconsistent with an *earlier* House of Lords decision. It may be that Lord Greene did not envisage that such a situation would ever arise, or, alternatively, he may have assumed that any such situation would be covered by the third of his exceptions. In *Turton* v *Turton* [1988] Ch 542, [1987] 2 All ER 641, the Court of Appeal disapproved its own decision in *Hall* v *Hall* (1981) 3 FLR 379, on the ground that it was inconsistent with the House of Lords case of *Gissing* v *Gissing* [1971] AC 886, [1970] 2 All ER 780. However, in *Miliangos* v *George Frank (Textiles) Ltd* [1976] AC 443 at 479, [1975] 3 All ER 801 at 823, Lord Simon indicated that the Court of Appeal should follow its own decision in such a case and give leave to appeal to the House of Lords.

[132] [1998] 4 All ER 705.   [133] [1997] 3 All ER 628.   [134] See p 87, *ante*.

[135] [1986] QB 604, [1985] 1 All ER 787.   [136] [1990] Fam 194, [1989] 3 All ER 193.

to follow an earlier decision involving a wrongful rejection of jurisdiction by the court in circumstances where there was no possibility of an appeal to the House of Lords.

While he was Master of the Rolls, Lord Denning engaged in a tireless but ultimately unsuccessful campaign to give the Court of Appeal the freedom to depart from its previous decisions at will. In *Gallie* v *Lee*[137] he made the following assertion:

We are, of course, bound by the decisions of the House [of Lords], but I do not think we are bound by prior decisions of our own, or at any rate, not absolutely bound. We are not fettered as it was once thought. It was a self-imposed limitation; and we who imposed it can also remove it. The House of Lords have done it. So why should not we do likewise?

This was, however, a minority opinion. Russell LJ saw the position of the House of Lords in quite a different light, saying of the Master of the Rolls:[138]

I think that in one respect he has sought to wield a broom labelled 'for the use of the House of Lords only'. I do not support the suggestion that this court is free to override its own decisions . . . the availability of the House of Lords to correct error in the Court of Appeal makes it in my view unnecessary for this court to depart from its existing discipline.

In *Barrington* v *Lee*,[139] a case concerned with liability in respect of an estate agent's default over a deposit, Lord Denning again made the bold statement that the Court of Appeal was not bound by a previous decision on similar facts. Again, however, he found himself in the minority: while Edmund Davies and Stephenson LJJ felt able to distinguish the earlier case and to concur with Lord Denning on the result of the appeal, they both reaffirmed the principles set out in *Young* v *Bristol Aeroplane*. Stephenson LJ's judgment epitomizes the traditional approach:[140]

what may be thought timorous subservience to judicial precedent is, in my judgment, preferable to the uncertainty which will be introduced into the law in fields not easy to delimit by the bolder work of demolition and restoration proposed by Lord Denning MR in this case. We must take care lest in struggling to straighten out the law we bend it until it breaks.

Faced with such opposition, Lord Denning was constrained to resile from the statements he had made in *Gallie* v *Lee* and *Barrington* v *Lee*, and in *Miliangos* v *George Frank (Textiles) Ltd*[141] he expressly applied the principles in *Young* v *Bristol Aeroplane Co Ltd*. Nevertheless in *Davis* v *Johnson*,[142] a controversial case dealing with the power of the courts to protect battered wives, Lord Denning led the full Court of Appeal in

---

[137] [1969] 2 Ch 17 at 37, [1969] 1 All ER 1062 at 1072 (affirmed *sub nom Saunders* v *Anglia Building Society* [1971] AC 1004, [1970] 3 All ER 961).

[138] [1969] 2 Ch 17 at 41, [1969] 1 All ER 1062 at 1082. The third member of the court, Salmon LJ, took a middle view and stated that any change in policy would require a pronouncement of the whole Court of Appeal. Nevertheless, in *Davis* v *Johnson* [1979] AC 264, [1978] 1 All ER 1132, Lord Salmon and other members of the House of Lords expressly reaffirmed *Young's* case.

[139] [1972] 1 QB 326 at 338, [1971] 3 All ER 1231 at 1238; see also *Hanning* v *Maitland (No 2)* [1970] 1 QB 580 at 587, [1970] 1 All ER 812 at 815.

[140] [1972] 1 QB 326 at 345, [1971] 3 All ER 1231 at 1245. The law was, eventually, clarified by the House of Lords in *Sorrell* v *Finch* [1977] AC 728, [1976] 2 All ER 371.

[141] [1975] QB 487, [1975] 1 All ER 1076.   [142] [1978] 2 WLR 182, [1978] 1 All ER 841.

yet another attack on *Young*. This attack was repulsed when the case reached the House of Lords,[143] and the rule in *Young* was, in Lord Diplock's words, 'expressly, unequivocally and unanimously' reaffirmed.

The general rule that the Court of Appeal is bound to follow its previous decisions is now well-settled, and in the light of the unequivocal House of Lords decision in *Davis* v *Johnson* it is difficult to envisage the Court making any further attempt to free itself from this position. This does not, however, preclude the possibility of adding to the list of recognized exceptions, and the Court of Appeal's willingness to depart from a previous decision in order to give effect to changes in international law may be regarded as one such example.[144] The Court of Appeal has also held that its is not bound by its previous decisions on applications for permission to appeal,[145] though an earlier finding that it was not obliged to follow previous interlocutory decisions made by only two judges[146] has now been rejected.[147]

Two further exceptions to the rule that the Court of Appeal is obliged to follow its previous decisions have arisen as a result of statutory intervention. Firstly, as already noted,[148] the Human Rights Act 1998 has important implications for the doctrine of precedent. Given that the Court of Appeal has already refused to follow an earlier House of Lords decision in order to give effect to Convention rights,[149] it seems certain that the Court will not hesitate to depart from its own previous decisions in similar circumstances. Secondly, when faced with a conflict between one of its own decisions (or a decision of the House of Lords) and a decision of the European Court of Justice, section 3 of the European Communities Act 1972 obliges the Court of Appeal to follow the latter.

It may be noted finally that a 'full court' of five or more judges of the Civil Division is sometimes convened to hear cases involving particularly important or difficult points of law. The full court has, however, no greater authority than the normal court and its decisions carry no more weight as precedents.[150]

Criminal Division. Decisions of the Criminal Division of the Court of Appeal are binding on all inferior courts, including the Divisional Court of the Queen's Bench

---

[143] [1979] AC 264, [1978] 1 All ER 1132.

[144] *Trendtex Trading Corporation Ltd* v *Central Bank of Nigeria* [1977] QB 529, [1977] 1 All ER 881; see p 89, *ante*.

[145] *Clark* v *University of Lincolnshire and Humberside* [2000] 3 All ER 752, [2000] 1 WLR 1988. This is, of course, consistent with the current rule of practice that decisions on applications for permission to appeal cannot normally be cited as precedents in the civil courts; *Practice Direction (Citation of Authorities)* [2001] 2 All ER 510, [2001] 1 WLR 1001.

[146] *Boys* v *Chaplin* [1968] 2 QB 1, [1968] 1 All ER 283; *Welsh Development Agency* v *Redpath Dorman Long* [1994] 1 WLR 1409, [1994] 4 All ER 10.

[147] *Cave* v *Robinson Jarvis and Rolfe* [2001] EWCA Civ 245, [2002] 1 WLR 581.

[148] See p 80, *ante*.

[149] *Ghaidan* v *Godin-Mendoza* [2002] EWCA Civ 1533, [2003] Ch 380, [2002] 4 All ER 1162, discussed further at pp 56 and 80, *ante*.

[150] *Young* v *Bristol Aeroplane Co Ltd* [1944] KB 718, [1944] 2 All ER 293. Likewise the authority of a two-judge court is no less than that of a three-judge court: *Langley* v *North West Water Authority* [1991] 3 All ER 610, [1991] 1 WLR 697.

Division. The Division regards itself as bound by decisions of its predecessor, the Court of Criminal Appeal, and also by decisions of the Civil Division of the Court of Appeal, subject to the exceptions contained in *Young* v *Bristol Aeroplane Co Ltd*. Thus in *DPP* v *Merriman*[151] the Criminal Division reluctantly allowed an appeal which was totally lacking in merit, because of the existence of a direct authority of the Court of Criminal Appeal in favour of the appellant. However, the court certified a point of law of general public importance and granted leave to appeal to the House of Lords. The appeal was subsequently allowed and the earlier authority was overruled.[152]

The Court of Criminal Appeal formulated the principle that it would not be bound by its own previous decisions where this would cause injustice to an appellant, the rationale being that the desire for justice transcends the desirability of certainty. In *R* v *Taylor*, Lord Goddard CJ explained the rule as follows:[153]

This court, however, has to deal with questions involving the liberty of the subject, and if it finds, on reconsideration, that, in the opinion of a full court assembled for that purpose, the law has been either misapplied or misunderstood in a decision which it has previously given, and that, on the strength of that decision, an accused person has been sentenced and imprisoned, it is the bounden duty of the court to reconsider the earlier decision with a view to seeing whether that person had been properly convicted. The exceptions which apply in civil cases ought not to be the only ones applied in such a case as the present.

This rule was adopted by the Criminal Division of the Court of Appeal in *R* v *Gould*.[154] A recent example of the application of the rule is the case of *R* v *Simpson*,[155] in which the Criminal Division declined to follow its previous decision in *R* v *Palmer* *(John)* because it considered that the law in the earlier case had been misunderstood and misapplied.[156]

In the past, decisions of the Court of Criminal Appeal were somewhat less reliable as precedents than the decisions of other appellate courts. This is accounted for by the fact that the court rarely reserved judgment, and that only one judgment was usually given and dissenting opinions were not recorded. Although section 59 of the Supreme Court Act 1981 expressly provides that separate judgments may be pronounced on a question of law, precedents of the Criminal Division of the Court of Appeal are still regarded with more circumspection than decisions of the Civil Division.

---

[151] [1971] 2 QB 310, [1971] 2 All ER 1424.   [152] [1973] AC 584, [1972] 3 All ER 42.

[153] [1950] 2 KB 368, [1950] 2 All ER 170. See also *DPP* v *Merriman* [1973] AC 584 at 605, [1972] 3 All ER 42 at 58, per Lord Diplock; *R* v *Howe* [1986] QB 626, [1986] 1 All ER 833 (affirmed [1987] AC 417, [1987] 1 All ER 771). Cf. *R* v *Charles* [1976] 1 All ER 659, [1976] 1 WLR 248 (affirmed *sub nom Metropolitan Police Commissioner* v *Charles* [1977] AC 177, [1976] 3 All ER 112).

[154] [1968] 2 QB 65, [1968] 1 All ER 849. The necessity for a 'full court' of five or more judges seems to have been tacitly abolished, though *R* v *Newsome* [1970] 2 QB 711, [1970] 3 All ER 455 suggests that a court of five has a greater power to depart from earlier decisions. On occasions when the need to choose between conflicting decisions arises, a full court is sometimes convened; see, e.g., *R* v *Jackson* [1974] QB 802, [1974] 1 All ER 640. See also, G Zellick, 'Precedent in the Court of Appeal, Criminal Division' [1974] Crim LR 222.

[155] [2003] EWCA Crim 1499, [2004] QB 118, [2003] 3 All ER 531.

[156] [2002] EWCA Crim 2202, [2003] 1 Cr App R (S) 12.

(d) High Court

Divisional courts. In civil matters, divisional courts are bound by decisions of the House of Lords and Court of Appeal. They are also bound by their own previous decisions to the same extent as the Court of Appeal, and this means that they are entitled to rely on the exceptions established in *Young* v *Bristol Aeroplane* and elsewhere.[157] Thus, when faced with a conflict between two of their previous decisions, divisional courts can choose which one to follow, and they need not follow previous decisions which are incompatible with EC law, the Human Rights Act 1998, or any decision of the Court of Appeal, House of Lords, or ECJ. Divisional courts can also depart from their own previous decisions if they are regarded as having been made *per incuriam*, and occasionally, they have even rejected Court of Appeal decisions on this basis.[158] Divisional court decisions in civil cases are binding on judges of the same division of the High Court sitting alone, and possibly on judges of other divisions.[159]

In criminal cases the position of the Divisional Court of the Queen's Bench Division is closely analogous to that of the Criminal Division of the Court of Appeal. Thus it is free to depart from its own decisions in the same circumstances as in that court.

Finally, when exercising its supervisory jurisdiction, a Divisional Court is in the same position as a High Court judge sitting alone, and it may depart from one of its own previous decisions if convinced that the decision is wrong. The above principles appear from the judgment of the Queen's Bench Divisional Court, delivered by Goff LJ in *R* v *Greater Manchester Coroner, ex parte Tal.*[160]

Judges at first instance. Decisions of High Court judges sitting alone at first instance are binding on inferior courts but not on other High Court judges. For this reason, principles of law contained only in first instance decisions should not be relied upon too heavily since they are not binding in any High Court action. Naturally, however, they are of persuasive authority and a High Court judge will hesitate before 'not following' the decision of one of his brethren, if only for reasons of comity. Nevertheless, where a first instance judge is clearly convinced that an earlier decision at first instance is wrong, he will be free to refuse to follow that decision.

There have been several direct clashes between judges deciding cases at first instance.

---

[157] See p 97, *ante*; *Huddersfield Police Authority* v *Watson* [1947] KB 842, [1947] 2 All ER 193.

[158] *R* v *Northumberland Compensation Tribunal, ex parte Shaw* [1952] 1 KB 338, [1952] 1 All ER 122; *Hughes* v *Kingston upon Hull City Council* [1999] QB 1193, [1999] 2 All ER 49. Cf. *Cassell & Co Ltd* v *Broome* [1972] AC 1027 at 1131, [1972] 1 All ER 801 at 874, in which Lord Diplock asserted that the *per incuriam* doctrine did not entitle either the Court of Appeal or the High Court to disregard any decision of a higher appellate court.

[159] *Re Seaford, Seaford* v *Seifert* [1967] P 325, [1967] 2 All ER 458 (reversed [1968] P 53, [1968] 1 All ER 482) in which a judge of the Probate, Divorce and Admiralty Division regarded himself as bound by a decision of the Divisional Court of the Queen's Bench Division. Cf. *Elderton* v *United Kingdom Totalisator Co Ltd* (1945) 61 TLR 529 (affirmed [1946] Ch 57, [1945] 2 All ER 624).

[160] [1985] QB 67, [1984] 3 All ER 240. A 'full' Divisional Court of five or more judges has no greater authority than a court of two or three: *Younghusband* v *Luftig* [1949] 2 KB 354, [1949] 2 All ER 72.

A notable modern example concerned the question of whether a failure to wear a seat belt in a motor vehicle should be treated as contributory negligence in the event of an accident in which injury is sustained. This question divided the judges of the Queen's Bench Division in some fourteen reported cases on the topic between 1970 and 1975, before the Court of Appeal finally resolved the conflict in *Froom* v *Butcher*.[161]

It is sometimes said that judges of the Chancery Division are less willing to depart from decisions of their brethren than are judges of other divisions. However, this is only true in the sense that there is often a greater risk in Chancery Division cases that a departure from an earlier case might have the effect of disturbing financial arrangements or depriving a person of a vested proprietary right.

High Court judges are bound by the decisions of divisional courts, the Court of Appeal, and the House of Lords. However, as with the appellate courts, the strict application of the *stare decisis* doctrine must be considered in the light of the High Court's statutory obligations to give effect to EC law and to decide cases in accordance with the requirements of the Human Rights Act 1998.[162]

(e) County courts, magistrates' courts, the Crown Court

Magistrates' courts and county courts are bound by the decisions of all superior courts, including first instance decisions of the High Court. Judges deciding cases in the Crown Court are also bound by these decisions, despite the bold assertion of one circuit judge that he was not bound by decisions of the Divisional Court.[163] The decisions of one inferior court do not bind other inferior courts, chiefly because they are unlikely to address any new legal principles and they are rarely reported. Decisions made by judges in the Crown Court *are* occasionally reported however, and they do have some persuasive authority for other inferior courts, especially when the Crown Court is presided over by a High Court judge.

(f) Tribunals

Lower tribunals do not set binding precedents for themselves or for any other court, and they are bound by the decisions of the appellate tribunals and superior courts. The Employment Appeal Tribunal and other appellate tribunals are bound by decisions of the Court of Appeal and House of Lords, but they do not generally regard themselves as being bound by their own decisions.

---

[161] [1976] QB 286, [1975] 3 All ER 520; all of the reported cases on the subject are reviewed in the judgment of Lord Denning, MR in this case. The Court of Appeal concluded that failure to wear a seat belt *did* amount to contributory negligence. For another illustration of clashes between judges at first instance, see *Esso Petroleum Co Ltd* v *Harper's Garage (Stourport) Ltd* [1965] 3 WLR 469, [1965] 2 All ER 933 and *Petrofina Ltd* v *Martin* [1965] Ch 1073, [1965] 2 All ER 176. See also *Wood* v *Luscombe* [1966] 1 QB 169, [1964] 3 All ER 972; *Wall* v *Radford* [1991] 2 All ER 741 and *Randolph* v *Tuck* [1962] 1 QB 175, [1961] 1 All ER 814.

[162] See pp 80 and 99, *ante*.

[163] *R* v *Colyer* [1974] Crim LR 24. The judge's refusal to follow a decision of the Divisional Court of the Queen's Bench Division must surely have been incorrect, given that decisions of the divisional courts are even binding upon themselves.

7 SUMMARY

In conclusion, it would be optimistic to state categorically that the doctrine of binding precedent achieves certainty while retaining flexibility. Its operation depends, as with the interpretation of statutes, on each judge or court's conception of the judicial function. The rules for determining the *ratio decidendi* of a case and the hierarchy of the courts are sufficiently well defined to achieve legal certainty. On the other hand, the *per incuriam* doctrine, the process of distinguishing, the capacity of superior courts to overrule decisions, and the absolute power of Parliament to change the law, all serve to keep the doctrine flexible. In the last analysis the doctrine of precedent is usually seen to operate fairly, though how far this is attributable to the inherent qualities of the doctrine and how far to the good sense of English judges is a matter of debate.

C LAW REPORTING

As stated at the beginning of this chapter, the doctrine of binding precedent became a part of English law only when the system of law reporting had become comprehensive. The doctrine of precedent, as such, is of far greater antiquity but it was only in the nineteenth century that precedents became binding rather than merely persuasive. If it were possible to mark the turning point, the decision in *Mirehouse* v *Rennell*[164] in 1833 would appear to herald the evolution of the modern system.

The history of law reporting can be roughly divided into three periods; the period of the Year Books extending approximately from 1272 to 1535; the period of the private named reporters extending from 1535 to 1865; and the modern, semi-official system of reporting which began in 1865.

1 THE YEAR BOOKS

The Year Books are the first available law reports. They were first compiled during the reign of Edward I and their exact purpose is uncertain. They were certainly not intended for use by the judges as precedents, and were probably just notes compiled by students and junior advocates for use, by advocates, as guides to pleading and procedure. However, there are indications that they may have been used by some judges as a direct source of precedent. Thus in 1310 Stanton J referred to a case decided at least ten years earlier,[165] while Bereford CJ in 1312 cited a decision some twenty-five years old.[166] By the fifteenth century there are many examples of Year Book cases in which the judge is reported as having relied upon a number of old authorities, and there is ample evidence that judges were conscious that their decisions were being

---

[164] (1833) 1 Cl & Fin 527.
[165] *Kembeare* v *K* YB 4 Edw 2 (SS iv), 153. Note the method of citation by regnal year.
[166] *Anon* YB 6 Edw 2 (SS xiii), 43.

recorded for use as precedents.[167] Compilation of printed Year Books ceased in about 1535.[168]

With the introduction of printing in the fifteenth century, many Year Book manuscripts were printed in the so-called 'Black Letter' editions. The most widely used modern versions of the Year Books are the Rolls Series (RS) and the Selden Society Series (SS), both of which date from the early twentieth century. They contain the original text of the Year Book manuscripts, which are in 'law French', a peculiar combination of Norman French, English, and Latin, together with an English translation.

2 THE PRIVATE REPORTS

As soon as the compilation of the Year Books ceased, private sets of reports began to be produced and published under the name of the law reporter. These reports proliferated in the period of 1535 to 1865 and the citation of precedents became progressively more common as the reports became more comprehensive.

The standard of reporting varied greatly. At one end of the scale were those whose reports contain what are still regarded as classic expositions of the common law, with Coke being the most notable example. Coke's Reports (Co Rep) are so well known as to be citable merely as 'reports' (Rep), and they contain comprehensive expositions of virtually every aspect of the common law. Published between 1600 and 1658, Coke's Reports contain many of the great constitutional cases of the seventeenth century, such as *Prohibitions del Roy*,[169] *Proclamations*,[170] and *Magdalen College*.[171] Alongside Coke, other highly regarded law reporters include Dyer (who was once Chief Justice of the Common Pleas), Saunders (a Chief Justice of the King's Bench), Plowden, and Burrow. Burrow's Reports of cases in the Court of King's Bench are widely regarded as the first set of law reports produced in the modern pattern, since they contain headnotes and the argument of counsel is carefully separated from the judgment.

It must not be thought that every one of the private law reporters was a Plowden or a Coke. At the other end of the scale were reporters such as Barnardiston, Atkyns, and Espinasse whose reports became virtually uncitable, so low were they held in judicial esteem.[172] Indeed, Lord Mansfield would not permit certain series of reports to be cited to him, while Holt CJ famously complained that 'these scrambling reports will make us appear to posterity for a parcel of blockheads'.[173]

The private reports are cited by the name of the reporter (usually abbreviated) and a volume and page number. The date of the report is not part of the reference but is usually inserted in ordinary round brackets. Thus the reference to the case of *Pillans* v *Van Mierop* (1765) 3 Burr 1664 indicates that the case can be found in the third volume of Burrow's Reports at page 1664. In practice most law libraries have the

---

[167] For examples see Allen, *Law in the Making* (7th edn), pp 190 *et seq.*

[168] Although manuscript Year Books continued to be produced into the seventeenth century.

[169] (1607) 12 Co Rep 63.   [170] (1610) 12 Co Rep 74.   [171] (1615) 11 Co Rep 66b.

[172] See Allen, *Law in the Making* (7th edn), pp 221 *et seq.*

[173] *Slater* v *May* (1704) 2 Ld Raym 1071.

reports of the private reporters in the reprinted edition known as 'the English Reports' (ER or Eng Rep).

3 THE PRESENT SYSTEM OF LAW REPORTING

(a) The Law Reports

In 1865 the system of private reporting gave way to current system. A Council was established to publish reports of superior court decisions as cheaply as possible, and it was, from its inception, under professional control. The Council was incorporated in 1870 as the Incorporated Council of Law Reporting for England and Wales.[174] It now produces the Law Reports, the Weekly Law Reports (WLR), the Industrial Cases Reports (ICR), and the Law Reports Statutes. The Law Reports are not an official publication but judges are given the opportunity to revise reports of their own judgments and they are the series of reports to which counsel should refer when citing a case which is reported in the Law Reports.[175] One advantage of these Reports over other series is that legal argument, as well as the judgments, is published. Where the court has adjourned to take time to consider its decision, judgment is said to be 'reserved'. This fact is indicated in the reports by the words *curia advisari vult, cur ad vult* or *cav*, and reserved judgments are generally accorded greater weight than *ex tempore* judgments.

Before 1875, cases published in the Law Reports were cited by reference to the court in which they were decided and a serial number dating from 1865, prefixed by the letters LR. The date was not part of the reference and was therefore inserted in ordinary round brackets. Thus *Irving* v *Askew* (1870) LR 5 QB 208 was reported in the fifth volume of Reports of cases in the Court of Queen's Bench, at page 208. Between 1875 and 1890 citation was by an abbreviation of the appropriate division of the High Court (Ch D; QBD; PD; CPD; Ex D[176]) or App Cas for an appeal case. The prefix LR was dropped but the date was still not part of the reference and the serial number dated from 1875. An example of citation during this period is *Symons* v *Rees* (1876) 1 Ex D 416.

In 1891 the date was made part of the reference in place of a serial number and the letter D (for Division) was dropped. The fact that the date is part of the reference is signified by its inclusion in square brackets. There is a separate volume of Reports for each division of the High Court (QB; Ch; Fam)[177] and a separate volume for House of

---

[174] The Council is a charity: *Incorporated Council of Law Reporting for England and Wales* v *A-G* [1972] Ch 73, [1971] 3 All ER 1029.

[175] *Practice Note (CA: Reports: Citations)* [1991] 1 All ER 352; *Practice Direction (Citation of Authorities)* [2001] 2 All ER 510, [2001] 1 WLR 1001. The House of Lords has stated that counsel may refer to a report in Tax Cases, rather than the Law Reports: *Bray* v *Best* [1989] 1 All ER 969, [1989] 1 WLR 167.

[176] The last two were abolished in 1880; see p 223, *post*.

[177] When the Family Division was named the Probate, Divorce and Admiralty Division, this volume of Reports was cited by the letter P.

Lords and Privy Council cases (AC).[178] Court of Appeal decisions are reported in the volume for the division of the High Court from which the appeal came. County court appeals and appeals to the Criminal Division of the Court of Appeal are usually reported in the volume for the Queen's Bench Division. There is thus nothing in the reference to distinguish a Court of Appeal decision from a decision at first instance.

(b) The Weekly Law Reports

The Weekly Law Reports have been published since 1953 and they include a report of every decision which will ultimately appear in the Law Reports proper.[179] The cases are reported in full, but legal argument is omitted because of the restriction on space. In addition, many cases are published in the Weekly Law Reports which are not subsequently included in the Law Reports. These cases make up Volume 1 whereas cases destined to reach the Law Reports can be found in Volumes 2 and 3.

As with the Law Reports, the year is part of the reference for cases published in the Weekly Law Reports, and it therefore appears in square brackets. There is, however, no attempt to classify cases by the court in which they were decided. All cases appear in 1 WLR, 2 WLR or 3 WLR irrespective of whether they are House of Lords or first instance decisions.

(c) Other series of reports

The All England Reports. Perhaps the most important of the commercially published reports are the All England Law Reports.[180] These are published by Butterworths on a weekly basis and are eventually collated in annual volumes. Their virtue lies principally in the speed with which they follow decisions and the fact that they include many cases which do not find their way into the Law Reports. The All England Law Reports are cited by the year in square brackets, followed a volume number,[181] the abbreviation All ER and a page number.

'Official' reports. Several series of reports are published under government authority, and unlike the Law Reports, Weekly Law Reports, and All England Reports, they concentrate on reporting cases in certain specialized areas. These series include Reports of Tax Cases, Reports, of Patent, Design and Trade Mark Cases, Immigration Appeal Reports, Industrial Tribunal Reports, and Value Added Tax Tribunal Reports.

---

[178] Before 1974 when a case reached the House of Lords, the Privy Council, or a Divisional Court on appeal, the appellant's name used to be cited first. Thus, for example, the case known in the Court of Appeal as *Lever Brothers Ltd* v *Bell* [1931] 1 KB 557 became *Bell* v *Lever Brothers Ltd* [1932] AC 161 in the House of Lords. This practice was altered in 1974, and petitions for leave to appeal and appeals to the House of Lords carry the same title that they had at first instance; [1974] 1 All ER 752, [1974] 1 WLR 305. In criminal cases this had the effect of terminating the practice whereby the Director of Public Prosecutions was substituted for *Rex* (or *Regina*).

[179] These replaced the 'Weekly Notes' (WN), which were published in the form of a current précis and were not strictly citeable as reports; see *Re Loveridge* [1902] 2 Ch 859 at 865, per Buckley J.

[180] The Law Journal Reports (LJ) and Law Times Reports (LT) have been incorporated in the All England Law Reports.

[181] There are usually three or four volumes published each year.

Specialist reports published commercially. There are many series of specialist reports published commercially. For example, the Criminal Appeal Reports (CAR or Cr App R), first published shortly after the creation of the Court of Criminal Appeal, are still produced and include a number of criminal cases not reported elsewhere. Similarly Lloyd's List Law Reports (Lloyd's Rep) contain a number of commercial cases not reported elsewhere while the Road Traffic Reports (RTR) contain, as the title would suggest, reports of road traffic cases. Other specialist series in general use are Local Government Reports (LGR), Building Law Reports (BLR), Simon's Tax Cases (STC), Property and Compensation Reports (PCR), Industrial Relations Law Reports (IRLR), Housing Law Reports (HLR), Fleet Street Patent Law Reports (FSR), and Human Rights Law Reports (HRLR).

European cases. European Community law decisions are to be found principally in the European Court Reports (ECR) published by the European Court of Justice, and the Common Market Law Reports (CMLR) which are an unofficial source. The main source of decisions of the European Court of Human Rights is the European Human Rights Reports series (EHRR).

Newspapers and periodicals. A number of legal periodicals such as the Solicitors Journal, Justice of the Peace, Estates Gazette, Criminal Law Review, New Law Journal, and Current Law include notes of cases to which reference may be made in the absence of a full report in a recognized series. In addition, *The Times, The Guardian,* and *The Independent* also publish reports of decided cases, and while these are inevitably brief, they may be cited in court in the absence of an alternative source.

(d) Electronic sources

Many of the different series of law reports are now available electronically, either on CD Rom or on the Internet, and the use of this technology allows lawyers to access an increasingly large volume of case law, often within a relatively short time of the decisions being made. An important example is the LEXIS database. This gives access to a vast range of cases, many of which are not reported elsewhere. LexisNexis can be accessed through the Butterworths web site,[182] which also gives online access to the All England Reports. Other online databases produced commercially include Westlaw and Lawtel. In addition, the decisions of several courts, including the House of Lords[183] and Privy Council,[184] can be accessed through official web sites,[185] as can cases decided by the European Court of Justice[186] and the European Court of Human Rights.[187]

(e) Neutral citation of judgments

With effect from 11 January 2001, the Lord Chief Justice issued a Practice Direction[188] establishing a new system of neutral citation for cases decided by the Administrative

---

[182] www.butterworths.com   [183] www.parliament.uk/judicial_work/judicial_work.cfm
[184] www.privy-council.org.uk   [185] See also: www.courtservice.gov.uk
[186] http:// europa.eu.int/eur-lex   [187] www.echr.coe.int
[188] *Practice Direction (Sup Ct: Form of Judgments)* [2001] 1 All ER 193, [2001] 1 WLR 194.

Court and Court of Appeal. Under this system an official number is assigned to each new decision, and when used in conjunction with the year and the abbreviation for the court issuing the decision, this gives each case a unique reference. In addition, judgments of the courts concerned are now issued with numbered paragraphs instead of page numbers. Thus, to adopt the example used in the Practice Direction, paragraph 30 of the tenth case decided by the Civil Division of the Court of Appeal in 2001 would be cited as [2001] EWCA Civ 10 at [30]. The Practice Direction further provides that when used in court, the neutral citation of a judgment should be given before the citation from the law report series. Lord Woolf CJ explained the reasons for this new system as follows:[189]

The main reason of these changes is to facilitate the publication of judgments on the World Wide Web and their subsequent use by the increasing numbers of those who have access to the Web. The changes should also assist those who use and wish to search judgments stored on electronic databases.

Although not covered by the Practice Direction, the House of Lords, the Privy Council, and even the Immigration Appeals Tribunal have adopted the same approach, and the system of neutral citation has now been extended to all divisions of the High Court.[190] The correct form of citation for these courts is illustrated in the examples below:

R v Lambert [2001] UKHL 37   (House of Lords)

A v B [2002] EWCA Civ 337   (Court of Appeal, Civil
                                                    Division)

R v Barker [2002] EWCA Crim 1508   (Court of Appeal, Criminal
                                                    Division)

Percy v DPP [2001] EWHC 1125 (Admin)   (Administrative Court)

Douglas v Hello [2003] EWHC 786 (QB)   (High Court, Queen's
                                                    Bench Division)

Re B [2002] EWHC 429 (Fam)   (High Court, Family
                                                    Division)[191]

B v Auckland District Law Society [2003] UKPC 38   (Privy Council)

S v Secretary of State for the Home Dept. [2003] UKIAT 3 (Immigration Appeals
                                                    Tribunal)

---

189 Ibid at [3].

190 *Practice Direction (Sup Ct: Judgments: Neutral Citations)* [2002] 1 All ER 351, [2002] 1 WLR 346.

191 Other categories of High Court decision use the following abbreviations in place of (Fam): Chancery Division (CH); Patent's Court (Pat); Commercial Court (Comm); Admiralty Court (Admlty); Technology and Construction Court (TCC).

(f) Weaknesses in the present system of reporting

The most obvious criticism that can be made of the present system of law reporting in England is that it remains informal and the selection of cases for reporting is entirely at the discretion of the law reporters. While there cannot be many important cases which escape the elaborate net of the law reporters, there are undoubtedly some; the Court of Appeal, for example, decides about 3,000 cases every year, of which only a small proportion are reported. This has been remedied to an extent by the proliferation of commercial series of law reports, and coupled with the availability of computerized databases such as LEXIS, this means that in one sense there is now hardly ever an 'unreported' case.

While this may have gone some way towards addressing the risk that important decisions may be overlooked, it has, paradoxically, led some to suggest that *too many* cases are now available to practitioners. The citation of unreported cases and cases which do not appear in the Law Reports has become increasingly common, and concern at the effect of this on the length and cost of litigation has led the courts to restrict the use of unreported decisions as precedents.[192]

It can also be argued that the system involves an unnecessary duplication of effort, since many cases are reported in full in at least four different series of reports, in addition to being noted in newspapers and numerous periodicals.

On the initiative of the then Lord Chancellor, a Committee was set up to report on the state of law reporting. Its report, published in 1940, was somewhat negative in character. It rejected the proposal to grant a monopoly to the Incorporated Council of Law Reporting, being content to state that the Law Reports should be cited in preference to any other series. The Committee also rejected a proposal that law reporters should be subject to a system of licensing. Most of the positive recommendations in the 1940 Report were contained in the minority report of Professor Goodhart, the main suggestion being that each court should produce an authenticated transcript which would be filed with the court records. Copies of these transcripts would be available for sale to law reporters and other interested persons, which would in effect make law reports 'official'. However, the majority of the Committee rejected this proposal as expensive and inconvenient, and the system of law reporting in England continues to operate on an unofficial and informal basis.

---

[192] *Roberts Petroleum Ltd* v *Bernard Kenny* [1983] 2 AC 192, [1983] 1 All ER 564; *Practice Direction (Citation of Authorities)* [2001] 2 All ER 510, [2001] 1 WLR 1001. See p 77, *ante.*

4

THE EUROPEAN COMMUNITY AND EUROPEAN UNION[1]

A INTRODUCTION

On 1 January 1973 the UK became a Member State of the European Communities. There were originally three communities: the European Coal and Steel Community (ECSC), the European Atomic Energy Community (Euratom), and the European Economic Community (EEC). The EEC, which was by far the most ambitious and significant of the three projects, was officially renamed 'the European Community' (EC) by the Treaty on European Union in 1992. The ECSC expired on 23 July 2002, leaving Euratom and the European Community as the two remaining elements of the European Communities.

Created in 1957 by the Treaty of Rome,[2] the European Community (or the EEC as it then was) initially comprised six members,[3] but has since expanded to its current composition of twenty-five Member States.[4] The Treaty reflected a post-war desire to achieve stability through European unity, and the aim set out in the Preamble was to create an 'ever closer union' amongst the peoples of Europe. This was to be achieved through common action in the economic field. The Community was to have its own institutions, along with laws that could regulate the powers and obligations of Member States in economic matters.

---

[1] See generally, Steiner and Woods, *Textbook on EC law* (8th edn, 2003); Hartley and Clayton, *The Foundations of European Community Law* (5th edn, 2003); Wyatt and Dashwood, *European Union Law* (4th edn, 2000); Craig and De Búrca, *EU Law: Text, Cases and Materials* (3rd edn, 2003); Fairhurst and Vincenzi, *Law of the European Community* (4th edn, 2003).

[2] This Treaty was significantly amended by the Treaty of Amsterdam (in force since 1 May 1999) and its provisions have consequently been re-organized and re-numbered. This chapter will adopt the new numbers when referring to the Treaty's provisions, with the old numbers following in brackets.

[3] Belgium, France, Germany, Italy, Luxembourg, and the Netherlands.

[4] Denmark, Ireland and the UK became members in 1973; Greece in 1981; Portugal and Spain in 1986; Finland, Austria and Sweden in 1995; and Cyprus, the Czech Republic, Estonia, Hungary, Latvia, Lithuania, Malta, Poland, the Slovak Republic, and Slovenia on 1 May 2004. Bulgaria and Romania are expected to join in 2007, and the number of Member States could eventually rise to thirty if negotiations with Croatia, Turkey, and Macedonia come to fruition.

1 THE SINGLE EUROPEAN ACT AND THE TREATY ON EUROPEAN UNION

The Community has now developed far beyond the original aims set by the Treaty of Rome. Not only has its membership increased, its role has expanded beyond the economic into social, financial, and political areas of competence. In 1987 the Single European Act was adopted,[5] and in addition to strengthening the institutional position of the European Parliament, it established the objective of making 'concrete progress towards European unity'. It sought to achieve this by amending the Treaty of Rome.

The process of amendment and reform was continued by the Treaty on European Union, which is more commonly referred to as the Maastricht Treaty. The UK ratified this Treaty in 1993 after considerable political controversy,[6] and it was given effect in law by the European Communities (Amendment) Act 1993. Not only did the Maastrich Treaty formally re-name the EEC as the 'European Community', it also radically amended the Treaty of Rome in order to achieve its aims. These aims are stated in the Preamble to be a continuation of the process of 'ever closer union', economic and monetary union, the development of a single currency,[7] common citizenship, common foreign and defence policies, and the enhancement of the demo-cratic functions of Community institutions.

The effects of the Maastricht Treaty were significant. Firstly, it extended the area of legal competence of the Community: it created a common citizenship, expanded existing rights of movement and voting, increased co-ordination of general economic policy, established a Central Bank, and increased the rights of workers. Secondly, the Treaty established a European Union (EU), founded on the existing Member States of the European Communities. The EC and its body of laws formed one of the three pillars of the European Union, the other two being concerned with (a) establishing a common foreign and security policy, and (b) achieving co-operation in justice and home affairs. These other two pillars did not form part of the EC framework, with the result that decisions made under them have thus far been made at a political level and have not been subject to the jurisdiction of the European Court of Justice. This position is now changing as a result of the Treaty of Amsterdam.

2 THE TREATY OF AMSTERDAM[8]

The next significant step in the development of the EC and EU was the signing of the Treaty of Amsterdam in 1997. The Treaty came into force on 1 May 1999 and

---

[5] Despite the name, this is a Treaty and should not be confused with an Act of the UK Parliament.

[6] For an unsuccessful challenge to the incorporation of the Treaty, see *R v Secretary of State for Foreign Affairs, ex parte Lord Rees-Mogg* [1994] QB 552, [1994] 1 All ER 457.

[7] The UK and Denmark reserved their positions on the later stages of economic and monetary union, as did Sweden when it joined the EU in 1995. The other twelve states replaced their national currencies with the Euro in 1999: their national currencies ceased to be legal tender three years later.

[8] Given effect in the UK by the European Communities (Amendment) Act 1998.

made substantive amendments to both the EC Treaty and the Treaty on European Union. It also made specific commitments to a number of important non-economic goals, including human rights, environmental protection, and equality. Another important objective was to simplify the existing treaties by removing obsolete provisions: an obvious consequence of this is that most of the provisions in the earlier treaties were renumbered.[9] The position of the European Parliament was also strengthened.[10]

Economic co-operation still lies at the heart of the 'closer Europe' objective, but this is now balanced against other important aims. Thus Article 2 of the amended EC Treaty states that in addition to 'establishing a common market and an economic and monetary union,' the Community shall also have the task of promoting:

[A] harmonious, balanced and sustainable development of economic activities, a high level of employment and of social protection, equality between men and women, sustainable and non-inflationary growth, a high degree of competitiveness and convergence of economic performance, a high level of protection and improvement of quality of life, and economic and social cohesion and solidarity among Member States.

An amended Article 3 identifies a wide range of activities permissible in order to achieve the Community's goals. These now include policies relating to education, health, consumer protection, tourism, civil protection, the environment, and 'the flowering of cultures', along with the original concerns of common agricultural policies, the elimination of trade barriers, and the free movement of workers, goods and services. In addition to the specific provisions of the Treaty, Article 94 (ex 100) provides for:

the approximation of such laws, regulations or administrative provisions of the Member States as directly affect the establishment or functioning of the common market.

From a legal perspective, one of the most important changes brought about by the Treaty of Amsterdam was the re-drawing of the boundaries between the EC and the EU. The Justice and Home Affairs pillar of the EU was re-titled 'Police and Judicial Co-operation in Criminal Matters', and a large part of it was brought within the framework of the EC pillar,[11] making it susceptible to the jurisdiction of the European Court of Justice. Another EU provision which was expressly made justiciable by the Treaty of Amsterdam is the new Article 6(2) (ex Art F(2)). This provides that:

The Union shall respect fundamental rights as guaranteed by the European Convention on Human Rights and Fundamental Freedoms . . . as general principles of Community law.

However, the second EU pillar—the Common Foreign and Security Policy—still lies beyond the jurisdiction of the Court of Justice.

---

[9] See n 2, *ante.*   [10] See p 120, *post.*   [11] See Articles 61–69, EC Treaty, as amended.

3 THE TREATY OF NICE AND THE CHARTER OF FUNDAMENTAL RIGHTS

The Treaty of Nice was signed by the Member States on 26 February 2001 but it did not come into force until 1 February 2003.[12] Unlike its predecessors this Treaty was primarily concerned with institutional reform, and it paved the way for the number of Member States to be increased from fifteen to twenty-five. In anticipation of the likelihood that achieving unanimity will become more difficult as the EU gets bigger, it also amended the existing treaties to allow more measures to be adopted by qualified majority.[13]

Another important document to be agreed when the European Council met in Nice was the Charter of Fundamental Rights of the European Union. The Charter sets out a number of economic and social rights of the kind that one might expect from an organization founded on an economic agenda. Thus it includes the right to education, the right to engage in work, the right not to be dismissed unjustifiably, and the right to collective bargaining. However, it also includes many of the civil and political rights found in most other international human rights agreements,[14] along with more novel ones such as the right to protection of family data. The civil and political rights correspond closely with those found in the ECHR,[15] and to avoid any inconsistency in interpretation the Charter states that:[16]

In so far as this Charter contains rights which correspond to rights guaranteed by the Convention for the Protection of Human Rights and Fundamental Freedoms, the meaning and scope of those rights shall be the same as those laid down by the said Convention. This provision shall not prevent Union law providing more extensive protection.

The Charter was signed on 15 December 2000, but at that time it was not expressed to be legally binding.

4 A CONSTITUTION FOR EUROPE

On 29 October 2004, almost three years after the idea was first accepted in principle, the Heads of State and Government formally signed the EU Constitutional Treaty. The intention was that this document should replace the four major treaties on which the Union is currently founded, and that the EU should be given a distinct legal personality.[17] If it is ever adopted, the Constitution will formally merge the EU with the EC and abolish its pillar structure. It will also incorporate the Charter of

---

[12] The Treaty had to be ratified by every Member State before it could take effect. The process was initially delayed when the Irish voted against ratification in a referendum in June 2001. The Irish government was eventually able to proceed with ratification following a second referendum in October 2002. The Treaty was given effect in the UK by the European Communities (Amendment) Act 2002.

[13] See p 147, *post.*

[14] For example, it includes provisions on equality, freedom of expression, and privacy.

[15] See chapter 5.   [16] Article 52(3).   [17] Article I-7.

Fundamental Rights into the main body of European Law. Article 1–2 of the Constitution sets out the Union's values:

The Union is founded on the values of respect for human dignity, freedom, democracy, equality, the rule of law and respect for human rights, including the rights of persons belonging to minorities. These values are common to the Member States in a society in which pluralism, non-discrimination, tolerance, justice, solidarity and equality between women and men prevail.

Another objective of the Constitution is to make the EU more democratic. Many of its provisions are concerned with institutional reform, and Article I-5 states that the Union shall respect the equality of Member States and their national identities. It makes it clear that essential state functions, such as law and order and national security, should remain the preserve of the Member States, but for the first time the primacy of Union law over national law is expressly acknowledged.[18] Protocol 1 of the Constitution is designed to give national Parliaments a greater role, by enabling them to consider draft EU legislation before it can take effect.[19] This is developed further in Protocol 2, under which the EU institutions will be forced to review any draft legislation which is deemed by at least a third of national Parliaments to infringe the principal of subsidiarity.[20]

The Constitution is perhaps the EU's most ambitious and controversial project to date, but at the time of writing it is increasingly uncertain whether it will ever get off the ground. Its future was thrown into doubt in the spring of 2005 when it was rejected by national referenda in both France and the Netherlands. Although several Member States have already completed the process of ratification, plans to hold referenda in the UK and a number of other states have been postponed indefinitely. Speaking in June 2005, the President of the European Commission acknowledged that the Constitution had been dealt a serious – and perhaps even fatal – blow:[21]

[It is difficult to see what a renegotiation would achieve, It is highly unlikely it would produce a radically different or better document. The Constitution is already the best possible compromise, It represents a delicate balance of competing views, which contains many improvements to the way in which the EU carries out its business. That is why there is no plan B.

B THE SCOPE OF EUROPEAN LAW

Far from being a separate system of law, European law is now a significant source of English law. In *Bulmer Ltd* v *J Bollinger SA*, Lord Denning MR stated:[22]

---

[18] Article I-6; see further, p 134, *post*.

[19] Protocol on the Role of National Parliaments in the European Union.

[20] 'Subsidiarity' means that decisions must be taken at a level which is as close as possible to the citizens of the Union.

[21] Jose Manuel Barroso, speaking at the National Forum on Europe, Dublin, 30 June 2005.

[22] [1974] Ch 401 at 418, [1974] 2 All ER at 1231; see p 144, *post*.

The first and fundamental point is that the treaty concerns only those matters which have a European element, that is to say matters which affect people or property in the countries of the Common Market besides ourselves. The treaty does not touch any of the matters which concern solely the mainland of England and the people in it. These are still governed by English law. They are not affected by the treaty. But when we come to matters with a European element, the treaty is like an incoming tide. It flows into the estuaries and up the rivers. It cannot be held back. In future, in transactions which cross the frontiers we must no longer speak or think of English law as something on its own. We must speak or think of Community law, of Community rights and obligations, and we must give effect to them.

This statement significantly underestimated the involvement of Community law beyond matters that 'cross frontiers', and today does not at all reflect the true legal position. Transactions which concern 'solely the mainland of England and the people in it' may nevertheless be affected by Community provisions. Some aspects of EC law concern obligations of an economic character, which are imposed on Member States rather than on individuals. Others, however, may create individually enforceable rights, even within litigation that appears on its face to have no European context. Article 141 (ex 119), for example, concerns equality of treatment between male and female employees, while Article 174 (ex 130r) provides for the regulation of environmental matters. Even where the implementation of Community obligations is achieved by domestic legislation, it is clear that the influence of European law is significant.

The impact of the EC across the whole range of English law is well demonstrated by the decision in *R v Coventry City Council, ex parte Phoenix Aviation*.[23] During a campaign against the export of live veal calves there were public disturbances at several UK ports. An airport and a ferry port refused to accept the trade because they each feared unlawful disruption, but the applicants sought an order of mandamus[24] compelling the respondents to accept it. A local authority also sought a declaration that it was entitled to ban the trade in veal calves. The Divisional Court made an order of mandamus and refused to grant the declaration. It held that in the absence of an emergency there was no statutory discretion to ban different types of trade. Further, it was an unlawful use of discretion to base decisions on the fact that trade would lead to unlawful disturbances and disruption. Although not deciding the point, the court doubted whether such a ban was lawful under Community Law.[25]

The scope of the Community's legal competence is subject only to the limits imposed by the EC Treaty, and many of its provisions are drafted in very wide terms. For example, legitimate areas of Community activity under Articles 3 to 5 (ex 3, 3a, and 3b) include the elimination of restrictions on the free movement of goods and services, a common commercial policy, the creation of an internal market, free movement of persons, common agricultural, fisheries and transport policies, competition policy, social and environmental policies, the strengthening of consumer

---

[23] [1995] 3 All ER 37. [24] Now known as a mandatory order; see p 207, *post*.

[25] Exceptions to the general principle of free movement of goods and services exist by virtue of Article 42 (ex 36). See *R v Chief Constable of Sussex, ex parte International Trader's Ferry Ltd* [1998] QB 477, [1997] 2 All ER 65.

protection, and measures in the spheres of energy, civil protection, and tourism. In addition, Article 94 (ex 100) empowers the Council to issue directives for the approximation of laws, regulations, or administrative provisions which directly affect the common market. The European Community may also enter into treaties and international agreements to fulfil the objectives set out in the Treaties,[26] and the terms of these Treaties sometimes leave scope for creative expansion. To add to this range of powers, Article 308 (ex 235) of the EC Treaty provides as follows:

If action by the Community should prove necessary to attain, in the course of the operation of the common market, one of the objectives of the Community and this Treaty has not provided the necessary powers, the Council shall, acting unanimously on a proposal from the Commission and after consulting the European Parliament, take the appropriate measures.

This has been a powerful tool in developing Community policy in areas such as environmental protection, which was not specifically within its competence when the Treaty was first drafted.[27]

Article 5 (ex 3b) outlines the Community's relationship with its Member States by reference to the principle of subsidiarity:

The Community shall act within the limits of the powers conferred upon it by this Treaty and of the objectives assigned to it therein.

In areas which do not fall within its exclusive competence, the Community shall take action, in accordance with the principle of subsidiarity, only if and in so far as the objectives of the proposed action cannot be sufficiently achieved by the Member States and can therefore, by reason of the scale or effects of the proposed action, be better achieved by the Community.

Any action by the Community shall not go beyond what is necessary to achieve the objectives of this Treaty.

The difficulty with Article 5 is that it does not define the circumstances in which action at Community level might be *necessary* to achieve Treaty objectives, and this leaves considerable room for disagreement. At one level, the wording is inconsistent with the principle that EC law is supreme, since this principle suggests that the Community should have the final word on *any* matter within its competence, regardless of whether this competence is 'exclusive' or not. Moreover, there is no agreed method for determining whether the Community's competence in a particular matter *is* exclusive.

Disputes are inevitable, and although the Court of Justice has been prepared to determine issues arising under Article 5, it is clear that it is keen to avoid being drawn into a more political role. In *UK v EU Council*[28] the UK challenged the Working Time Directive made under Article 138 (ex 118a) of the Treaty, arguing that it conflicted with the principle of subsidiarity. In the UK's view there was no evidence that the

---

[26] See Article 133 (ex 113).

[27] This Article can only be relied upon as the basis for legislative action not specifically authorised by other provisions: see *UK v EU Council* Case C-84/94, [1996] All ER (EC) 877.

[28] Ibid.

aims of the Directive could not instead be achieved by action at a domestic level. It also argued that the subject matter fell within the ambit of Article 94 (ex 100) rather than Article 138, which was significant because measures adopted under the former provision require unanimity: the UK believed that it should have had a power of veto. The Court of Justice rejected both arguments, stating that the Council had a wide discretion in making social policy changes, and that judicial review of that discretion would be limited to a consideration of whether there was a manifest error or misuse of power. It dealt with the specific subsidiarity point by stating that Health and Safety issues fell within the Council's competence, and that the Council had an obligation to adopt minimum standards.

The Member States sought to clarify the subsidiarity principle in a Protocol to the Treaty of Amsterdam.[29] This states that:

Subsidiarity is a dynamic concept and should be applied in the light of the objectives set out in the Treaty. It allows Community action within the limits of its powers to be expanded where circumstances so require, and conversely, to be restricted or discontinued where it is no longer required.

The Protocol also requires the memorandum accompanying new EC legislation to state how it complies with the principles of subsidiarity and proportionality.[30] In a further development, the European Constitution will, if it is ever implemented, allow national Parliaments to call for a review of any draft legislation which is thought to contravene the principle of subsidiarity.[31]

C THE INSTITUTIONS[32]

The EC and the EU operate through four main institutions, though these institutions have only a limited role with regard to foreign and security policy and certain other aspects of EU business. These institutions are the Council, the Commission, the Court of Justice, and the European Parliament.

1 THE COUNCIL

The Council of the European Union, formerly known as the Council of Ministers,[33] is the EC's main legislative and decision-making body. Article 202 (ex 146) of the EC

---

[29] The Protocol on the Application of the Principles of Subsidiarity and Proportionality.

[30] See p 123, *post*.   [31] See p 114, *ante*.

[32] See generally Craig and De Búrca, *EU Law: Text, Cases and Materials* (3rd edn, 2003) ch 2; Fairhurst and Vincenzi, *Law of the European Community* (4th edn, 2003) ch 3.

[33] It was re-named in 1993: Council Decision 93/592. It should not be confused with the European Council, which consists of the Heads of State and foreign ministers of the EU countries, together with the President and another member of the Commission. Articles I-22 and I-28 of the EU Constitution mean that the European Council will in future have both a President and a Minister for Foreign Affairs.

Treaty states that its task is to ensure that the Treaty's objectives are obtained, and that the general economic policies of the Member States are co-ordinated. It also empowers the Council to 'take decisions', which primarily means approving legislation proposed by the Commission.[34] The Council is also responsible for negotiating with non-EU states, approving the EU budget and making decisions under the Union's second and third pillars.[35]

The Council is composed of the ministers from each Member State,[36] with the precise composition at any given time being determined by the matter under discussion. For example, a Council meeting to discuss environmental issues would be attended by the environment Minister from each state and it would be referred to as 'the Environment Council'. For the purposes of continuity, a permanent committee of officials (COREPAR)[37] conducts much of the routine work of the Council, for later ratification. The Presidency of the Council is held by each State in turn for a period of six months. The main functions of the Presidency are to convene and chair meetings of the Council, and also to determine the agendas.

The Treaty requires decisions on matters such as immigration policy and taxation to be unanimous, but in most other matters the Council operates on the basis of qualified majority voting.[38] Each Member State is entitled to cast a certain number of votes, with the numbers being weighted to give the most votes to the most populous countries. Before the number of EU states rose from fifteen to twenty-five the UK, France, Germany, and Italy had ten votes each, whilst Luxembourg had just two. The total number of available votes was eighty-seven, and at least sixty-two of these had to be cast in favour of a measure in order for it to be accepted. Since November 2004 the rules have become more complicated. The UK, France, Germany, and Italy now have twenty-nine votes each, closely followed by Spain and Poland with twenty-seven. The least populous state, Malta, has just three. A qualified majority requires at least 72 per cent of the 321 available votes but it also requires the approval of a majority (or sometimes a two-thirds majority) of the Member States.[39] In addition, to alleviate the concerns of some of the largest states that they could be outvoted if all of the smaller countries acted together, a Member State can also ask for confirmation that the votes cast in favour represent at least 62 per cent of the EU's population. This means that if the UK, Germany, and France act together, they will be able to veto measures which have the support of the other twenty-two countries. If the European Constitution is ever accepted, its provisions will make further changes to the voting system with effect from November 2009.[40]

---

[34] Under Article 208 (ex 152) the Council may also initiate legislation by asking the Commission to examine a particular issue and submit its proposals.

[35] See p 111, *ante*.   [36] Article 203 (ex 146).   [37] Article 207 (ex 151).

[38] Article 205 (ex 148). In certain instances the Council can make decisions by a simple majority on the basis of one vote per State, but this is generally limited to decisions about procedural matters.

[39] See Article 3 of the Protocol on EU Enlargement, attached to the Treaty of Nice.

[40] See Article I-25, which provides that a 'blocking minority' must include at least *four* Member States.

If a Member State considers that a Community measure adopted by the Council is not valid, it may challenge that measure in the Court of Justice under Article 230 (ex 173).

2 THE COMMISSION

The powers of the Commission are set out in Article 211 (ex 155) of the EC Treaty and they principally concern the formulation of legislative proposals and the implementation and enforcement of measures adopted by the institutions. It can investigate potential breaches of Community law and may refer them to the European Court of Justice,[41] although frequently it is able to resolve such issues through political negotiations. The Commission can even impose its own sanctions where it finds breaches of the EC's competition laws, fining states and large companies which are found to have engaged in anti-competitive behaviour.[42] Finally, the Commission is also responsible for managing the EU budget, and acting together with the Council it is able to represent the EU at an international level.

The Commissioners hold office for a renewable term of five years,[43] with each one being responsible for a particular policy area. The size of the Commission was reduced from thirty to twenty-five in November 2004, which means that there is now one Commissioner per country.[44] The European Constitution envisages a further reduction in the size of the Commission from 2014 onwards.[45]

3 THE PARLIAMENT

Although originally comprising members nominated by Member States, the European Parliament has been directly elected since 1979.[46] Elections are held every five years, with June 2004 providing the first opportunity for citizens of the new Member States to elect representatives. The total number of MEPs now stands at 732, with the UK contributing seventy-eight (reduced from eighty-seven).[47] The European Constitution will eventually allow the number to rise to 750, with between six and ninety-six MEPs representing each state.[48] The Parliament holds plenary sessions in both Strasbourg and Brussels, although much of the preparatory work is done in committees. The General Secretariat and its departments are based in Luxembourg.

In the original Article 137 of the EC Treaty (now 189), the role of the Parliament

---

[41] Article 226 (ex 169).   [42] See Articles 81–83 (ex 85–87).   [43] Article 214 (ex 158).

[44] Article 4 of the Protocol on EU Enlargement.   [45] Article I-26(6).

[46] In 1999 a system of proportional representation was introduced in the UK for the election of MEPs; European Parliamentary Elections Act 1999 (replaced by the European Parliamentary Elections Act 2002).

[47] Germany currently contributes the most (ninety-nine) and Malta the least (five). The terms of the Treaty of Nice mean that the UK should now have only seventy-two MEPs, based on the assumption that Bulgaria and Romania will be joining the EU during the life of the 2004–2009 Parliament. However, transitional arrangements negotiated when the latest Treaties of Accession were signed have allowed the UK to retain seventy-eight seats until the 2009 elections.

[48] Article I-20(2).

was stated to be 'advisory and supervisory'. Its position has since been considerably strengthened and it now has much greater involvement in the legislative process It also has important roles in approving the Community budget and scrutinizing the other institutions. There are different legislative procedures for different areas of EC law, and many of them now require the approval or involvement of the Parliament. The most significant of these is the co-decision procedure established under Article 251 (ex 189b), which, although rather complicated, effectively gives the Parliament a power of veto in a wide range of matters. The range of measures made by this procedure will increase considerably if the European Constitution is ever adopted: so much so that it will be known in future as 'the ordinary legislative procedure'.[49] Despite this welcome development however, the European Parliament will still lack the power to legislate independently.

In addition to its legislative role, the Parliament can ask questions of the Commission and Council, and it can even censure the Commission and remove it on a motion passed by a two-thirds majority.[50] Though the power of censure was once regarded as a largely theoretical sanction, a significant milestone was reached in 1999 when the *threat* of a vote of no confidence forced the entire Commission to resign. This action followed a damning report into accusations of maladministration and fraud, in matters for which the Commission had overall responsibility. Had the Commission not resigned of its own accord, the Parliament would undoubtedly have forced it to do so by passing a motion of no confidence.[51]

4 THE COURT OF JUSTICE

The Court of Justice consists of one judge from each Member State, assisted by eight Advocates-General. It can sit either in chambers of three or five judges, in a Grand Chamber of eleven judges, or exceptionally, in plenary session.[52] It has a crucial role in enforcing Community obligations and in ensuring the uniform interpretation of European law throughout the Community.[53] Cases reach the Court either through direct actions or through references from national courts on points of Community law. Member States are obliged to apply its principles within their own jurisdictions, and the UK gives effect to this obligation by virtue of the European Communities Act 1972.

A Court of First Instance was created in 1988, to ease the problems of workload and delay which had bedevilled the Court of Justice.[54] The Court of First Instance deals with disputes between the Community and its servants, along with actions for judicial

---

[49] Article I-34(1).   [50] Article 201 (ex 144).

[51] See Craig, 'The Fall and Renewal of the Commission: Accountability, Contract and Administrative Organisation' (2000) 6 ELJ 98.

[52] Article 221 (ex 165), as amended by the Treaty of Nice.

[53] *Van Gend en Loos* v *Nederlandse Administratie de Belastingen* Case 26/62 [1963] ECR 1, [1963] CMLR 105; *R* v *Secretary of State for Transport, ex parte Factortame* Case C-213/89 [1990] ECR I-2433, [1990] 3 CMLR 1.

[54] Article 225 (ex 168a).

review brought by natural or other legal persons. Since the Treaty of Nice came into force on 1 February 2003, it has also been able to deal with some references from national courts under the Article 234 (ex 177) procedure. The work of both the Court of First Instance and the Court of Justice is considered in more detail later in this chapter.[55]

D THE SOURCES OF COMMUNITY LAW

1 LEGISLATION

The Treaties[56] are the primary source of European law, and they create a wide framework of powers, duties, and individual rights. Their provisions are framed in broad terms, requiring further legislative action and subsequent interpretation by the Court of Justice. By Article 249 (ex 189) the Community institutions are currently empowered to issue regulations, directives, decisions, recommendations, and opinions. These are the instruments through which the policies inherent in the Treaties are achieved. Regulations, directives, and decisions may be classed as 'secondary' or 'delegated' Community legislation, and their legality may be challenged in the Court of Justice. However, national courts have no power to declare Community measures invalid unless they have already been declared as such by the Court of Justice.[57] If the legality of a Community measure is raised as an issue in a domestic case, the national court may make a reference to the Court of Justice for a ruling on the matter. In some circumstances it will be under a duty to do so.[58]

The differences between the types of instrument set out in Article 249 (ex 189) are as follows:

A regulation shall have general application. It shall be binding in its entirety and directly applicable in all Member States.

A directive shall be binding, as to the result to be achieved, upon each Member State to which it is addressed, but shall leave to the national authorities the choice of form and methods.

A decision shall be binding in its entirety upon those to whom it is addressed.

Recommendations and opinions shall have no binding force.

There is thus a distinction between regulations and decisions on the one hand, and directives, recommendations, and opinions on the other. Only the former are

---

[55] See p 138, *post.*

[56] The most important of these are the Treaty of Rome (EC Treaty), the Single European Act, the Treaty on European Union (TEU or Maastricht Treaty), the Treaty of Amsterdam, and the Treaty of Nice. See also the European Constitution (discussed at p 113, *ante*) which was drafted with the aim of consolidating the existing Treaties into a single document.

[57] *Firma Foto-Frost* v *Hauptzollamt Lübeck-Ost* Case 314/85 [1987] ECR 4199, [1988] 3 CMLR 57.

[58] Article 234 (ex 177); see p 141, *post.*

immediately binding, although the doctrine of direct effects may confer a similar status on directives in practice. Where a measure does not attract immediate binding force the task of implementation is left to the Member States. It should also be noted that only regulations and decisions may be challenged directly by individuals under Article 230 (ex 173):[59]

Any natural or legal person may ... institute proceedings against a decision addressed to that person or against a decision which, although in the form of a regulation or decision addressed to another person, is of direct and individual concern to the former.

One of the aims of the new Constitution[60] is to simplify and rationalize the range of 'legal acts' that the institutions can adopt. If it is adopted, the system will create a clear distinction between 'legislative' and 'non-legislative' acts, and each of the current instruments will be renamed.[61] Thus, regulations will become 'European laws' and directives will become 'European framework laws': these will be the basic legislative instruments of the Union. There will also be four types of non-legislative instrument. Two of these will be non-binding, and they will still be called 'recommendations' and 'opinions'. The term 'decision' will continue to describe a binding non-legislative act, but whereas Article 249 assumed that all decisions would have a specific addressee, the new system will recognize that they may be of more general application. The other type of binding non-legislative instrument will be specifically concerned with implementing the Constitution and EU legislation. In a rather confusing move, the EU has decided that these instruments will be called 'regulations'.

2 CASE LAW

The other important source of Community law is the case law of the Court of Justice. The doctrine establishing the supremacy of Community law owes its origins to the court's creativity, as does the concept of direct effect. In addition, the Treaties are framed in broad terms and it is the duty of the court to interpret and apply Community law in ways that fulfil their underlying spirit and policy. Besides this interpretative role, the court has developed a number of general principles:

(a) *Legal certainty and legitimate expectations.* The principle of legal certainty applies in various ways: a measure may not be altered once it has been adopted and it will be presumed that provisions do not operate retropesctively. In *Officier van Justitie v Kolpinghuis Nijmegen BV*[62] the Dutch authorities sought to rely in criminal proceedings on a directive that had not been implemented. The Court of Justice held that

---

[59] Note that in applying this provision, the Court of Justice has regard to the substance rather than the form of the measure; see, e.g. *Confédération Nationale des Producteurs de Fruits et Légumes* v *Commission* Case 16/62 [1962] ECR 471; *Salamander AG v Parliament and Council* Cases T-172 and 175–77/98 [2000] 2 CMLR 1099.

[60] See p 113, *ante*.   [61] See Article I-33 of the Constitutional Treaty.

[62] Case 80/86 [1987] ECR 3969, [1989] 2 CMLR 18.

criminal liability could not be imposed in this way. The legitimate expectations[63] of individuals who are affected by Community measures will also be protected, though not to the point of fettering the Community's freedom of action.[64]

(b) Natural justice. Community bodies will be required to give reasons for their actions, and not to act arbitrarily.[65]

(c) Equality of treatment in comparable situations.[66] Until recently, EC legislation did not set out any general principle of equality, although there were specific provisions dealing with gender discrimination in employment and with the free movement of workers regardless of (EC) nationality.[67] A wider principle was established by the Court of Justice however, to the effect that comparable situations must be treated in the same way and different situations should be treated differently.[68] This principle has now been reinforced by the new Article 13 of the EC Treaty, which was inserted by the Treaty of Amsterdam. The Article does not in itself prohibit discrimination, but instead empowers the EC institutions to:

take appropriate action to combat discrimination based on sex, racial or ethnic origin, religion or belief, disability, age or sexual orientation.

The Article has already generated two major directives.[69]

(d) Proportionality. Obligations may not be imposed on an individual except to the extent necessary to achieve the purpose of the measure.[70] This concept applies not only in respect of Community measures, but also in determining the legality of the actions of Member States. Thus Hoffman J in *Stoke-on-Trent City Council* v *B & Q plc*[71] had to determine whether the restrictions on Sunday trading in the Shops Act 1950 were proportionate to those permitted by Article 30 (ex 36). The question was ultimately decided in the affirmative by the House of Lords. The concept of proportionality may apply equally to the remedy that the court is being asked to

---

[63] The phrase is borrowed from English law. See Usher: 'The Influence of National Concepts on Decisions of the European Court' [1976] 1 EL Rev 359. For an example, see *EC Commission* v *EC Council* Case 81/72 [1973] ECR 575.

[64] *ATB* v *Ministero per le Politiche Agricole* Case C-402/98 [2000] ECR I-5501. For an example of the domestic application of this principle in the European context, see *R* v *Ministry of Agriculture and Fisheries, ex parte Hamble Fisheries* [1995] 2 All ER 714, [1995] 1 CMLR 533.

[65] *Transocean Marine Paint Association* v *EC Commission* Case 17/74 [1974] ECR 1063.

[66] See generally: Bell, *Anti-Discrimination Law and the European Union* (2002).

[67] Articles 2 and 12 (ex 2 and 6) EC Treaty; Equal Treatment Directive 76/207; Regulation 1612/68.

[68] *Sabbatini* v *European Parliament* Case 20/71 [1972] ECR 345; *Graff* v *Hauptzollamt Köln-Rheinau* Case C-351/92 [1994] ECR-I-3361.

[69] EC Employment Directive 2000/78; EC Race Directive 2000/43. Statutory instruments to implement these measures in UK law have now been introduced: SI 2003/1626 (race), SI 2003/1657 (sex), SI 2003/1660 (religion or belief), SI 2003/1661 (sexual orientation), and SI 2003/1673 (disability).

[70] *Internationale Handelsgesellschaft GmbH* v *Einfuhr- und Vorratsstelle für Getreide* Case 11/70 [1970] ECR 1125, [1972] CMLR 255; *Johnston* v *Chief Constable of the RUC* Case 222/84 [1987] QB 129, [1986] 3 All ER 135.

[71] [1991] Ch 48, [1991] 4 All ER 221.

grant. In *Taittinger v Allbev*,[72] the court granted an injunction restraining the use of the expression 'Elderflower Champagne' on the basis that it infringed a Community directive. The Court of Appeal rejected a submission that the remedy was disproportionate to the infringement.

(e) Fundamental rights.[73] The original Treaties of the European Communities did not include any specific human rights provisions, but the protection of fundamental rights was nevertheless considered important. A Joint Declaration in 1977[74] stressed the role of the European Convention on Human Rights (ECHR), and in *Nold v Commission* the Court of Justice stated that:[75]

[F]undamental rights form an integral part of the general principles of law, the observance of which it ensures. In safeguarding these rights, the Court is bound to draw inspiration from constitutional traditions common to the Member States, and it cannot therefore uphold measures which are incompatible with fundamental rights recognised and protected by the Constitutions of those States. Similarly, international treaties for the protection of human rights on which the Member States have collaborated or of which they are signatories, can supply guidelines which should be followed within the framework of Community law.

In respect of national legislation which falls outside the scope of Community law, the Court does not have any general power to examine its compatibility with the ECHR.[76] However, the Court is increasingly prepared to take a generous approach to the question of whether Community law is engaged. Thus in the *Familiapress*[77] case the Court ruled that since a ban on the distribution of a magazine obstructed the free movement of goods, any justification for the ban would need to be compatible with the right to freedom of expression under Article 10 of the ECHR.

Following the lead of the Court of Justice, the Member States included a provision in the Treaty on European Union stating that the ECHR 'shall be respected by Member States'.[78] Though the provision was initially not justiciable, it was expressly brought within the Court's jurisdiction by the Treaty of Amsterdam. The wording was also strengthened, and the amended Article 6 now provides that:

(1) The Union is founded on the principles of liberty, democracy, respect for human rights and fundamental freedoms, and the rule of law, principles which are common to the Member States.

---

[72] [1994] 4 All ER 75, [1993] 2 CMLR 741.

[73] See Alston, Heenan and Bustelo, *The EU and Human Rights* (1999).

[74] Joint Declaration by the European Parliament, Council and Commission ([1977] OJ C103/1). See also *Prais v Council* Case C-130/75 [1976] ECR 1589.

[75] Case 4/73 [1974] ECR 491 at para 13; see Drzemczewski 'The Domestic Application of the European Human Rights Convention as European Community Law' (1981) 30 ICLQ 118.

[76] *Demirel v Stadt Schwabisch Gmund* Case 12/86 [1987] ECR 3719, [1989] 1 CMLR 421; *Kremzow v Austria* Case C-299/95 [1997] ECR I-2629.

[77] *Vereingte Familiapress Zeitungsverlags- und Vertriebs GmbH v Heinrich Bauer Verlag* Case C-368/95 [1997] ECR-I-3689, [1997] 3 CMLR 1329.

[78] Article 6 (ex F2).

(2) The Union shall respect fundamental rights, as guaranteed by the European Convention for the Protection of Human Rights and Fundamental Freedoms signed in Rome on 4 November 1950 and as they result from the constitutional traditions common to the Member States, as general principles of Community Law.

A new Article 7 allows the voting rights of Member States to be suspended in the event of a 'serious and persistent' breach of the Article 6 principles.

The suggestion that the EC might itself become a signatory to the ECHR has been mooted for some time,[79] and it now seems increasingly likely to happen. In 1994 the Court of Justice advised that the EU did not have any legal competence to accede to the Convention, and that a move in this direction would require an amendment to the Treaty.[80] Such an amendment has now been included in the European Constitution,[81] and the Council of Europe has agreed an amendment to the ECHR which paves the way for the EU's accession.[82] In any event, each Member State is a Convention signatory in its own right, and a number of EU Member States have been challenged under the Convention in relation to aspects of EC law and procedure.[83] A German company fined by the EU Commission for a breach of competition laws recently challenged *all* of the EU Member States before the Court of Human Rights. The essence of the claim was that by refusing to suspend the fine pending the outcome of a hearing, the Commission had violated the presumption of innocence and the right to a fair trial under Article 6 of the ECHR.[84] The Court of Human Rights declared the claim inadmissible because by this stage the EC's Court of First Instance had quashed the fines: the company was not a 'victim' of anything.[85] The rather more difficult question of whether the states *could* be collectively liable in this way was neatly side-stepped, but it is notable that the Strasbourg court did not rule out this possibility. From the other side, the European Court of Justice recently directed its own attentions to the compatibility of its institutions with Article 6, concluding that the involvement of the Attorney-General in cases before the court did not give rise to any breach of this provision.[86]

---

[79] Harmsen, 'National Responsibility for EC Acts under the ECHR: Recasting the Accession Debate' (2001) 7 EPL 625.

[80] *Re Accession of the Community to the European Human Rights Convention (Opinion 2/94)* [1996] 2 CMLR 265.

[81] Article I-9(2); see also Article I-7, which states that the EU shall have legal personality. See p 113, *ante*.

[82] An amendment to Article 59, ECHR, will be made by the new Protocol 14: see p 198, *post*.

[83] *Matthews* v *UK* (1999) 28 EHRR 361; *JS* v *Netherlands* (1995) 20 EHRR CD 41; *Pafitis* v *Greece* (1999) 27 EHRR 566; see Canor, 'Primus Inter Pares: Who is the Ultimate Guardian of Fundamental Rights in Europe?' (2000) 25(1) EL Rev 3.

[84] *Senator Lines* v *15 EU Member States*, App 56672/00, 10 March 2004; see also *Senator Lines GmbH* v *Commission* Case C-364/99 [1999] ECR I-8733, [2000] 5 CMLR 600.

[85] Whether there had been a breach initially was irrelevant, because until the company's case had been considered by the CFI its legal remedies had not been exhausted: see p 200, *post*.

[86] *Emesa Sugar* v *Aruba* Case C-17/98 [2000] ECR I-665. For more discussion on the role of the Advocates-General, see p 139, *post*.

Finally, on 15 December 2000 the Member States signed the Charter of Fundamental Rights of the European Union. Though the Charter was not initially expressed to be legally binding,[87] it forms an integral part of the proposed European Constitution.[88]

E THE RELATIONSHIP BETWEEN COMMUNITY AND NATIONAL LAW

1 THE GENERAL APPROACH OF THE COURT OF JUSTICE

In a series of important decisions the Court of Justice has developed the doctrine of supremacy of Community over national law. In *Van Gend en Loos* v *Nederlandse Administratie der Berlastingen*[89] the Court of Justice stated that Member States had:

[L]imited their sovereign rights, albeit within limited fields.

In *Costa* v *ENEL*[90] it stated that:

The transfer by the states from their domestic legal system to the Community legal system of the rights and obligations arising under the Treaty carries with it a permanent limitation of their sovereign rights, against which a subsequent unilateral act incompatible with the concept of the Community cannot prevail.

The supremacy of Community law means that national courts must enforce Community rights even if this involves overriding national legislation. In the *Simmenthal* case[91] the Court stated that:

Every national court must, in a case within its jurisdiction, apply Community law in its entirety and protect rights which the latter confers on individuals and must accordingly set aside any provision of national law which may conflict with it, whether prior or subsequent to the Community rule.

Thus, in any situation of conflict directly applicable Community law prevails. In addition, Member States are under a duty to take any action necessary to implement Community law. Article 10 (ex 5) states:

Member States shall take all appropriate measures, whether general or particular, to ensure fulfilment of the obligations arising out of this Treaty or resulting from actions taken by the institutions of the Community. They shall facilitate the achievement of the Community's

---

[87] See p 113, *ante*; for a discussion see Arnull, 'From Charter to Constitution and Beyond: Fundamental Rights in the New European Union' [2003] PL 774.

[88] See p 113, *ante*. The Charter provisions are set out in Part II of the Constitution.

[89] Case 26/62 [1963] ECR 1, [1963] CMLR 105.

[90] Case 6/64 [1964] ECR 585, [1964] CMLR 425.

[91] *Amministrazione delle Finanze dello Stato* v *Simmenthal* Case 106/77 [1978] ECR 629, [1978] 3 CMLR 263.

tasks. They shall abstain from any measure which could jeopardise the attainment of the objectives of this Treaty.

In *R v Secretary of State for Transport, ex parte Factortame*[92] the Court of Justice held that national courts must ensure the legal protection of rights derived from directly applicable Community law: i.e. those arising from the Treaty, Regulations, or rulings of the Court of Justice. Where rules of national law prevent this, they must be set aside. In cases where the Community and national authorities share jurisdiction, national courts must avoid reaching conclusions at variance with the Community institutions. They must also avoid the adoption of national procedural rules which render the exercise of Community rights virtually impossible or extremely difficult.[93]

2 DIRECT APPLICABILITY AND DIRECT EFFECT

(a) Identifying the concepts

Direct applicability. The Treaties, regulations, and some decisions of European law are said to be directly applicable. This means that they are automatically incorporated into domestic legal systems and come into force without the need for any further action on the part of Member States. Achieving direct applicability in the UK initially required an Act of Parliament: the UK is a dualist state and treaties do not become part of domestic law without specific legislation to implement them. Thus the European Communities Act 1972 was enacted, section 2(1) of which states that:

All such rights, powers, liabilities, obligations and restrictions from time to time created or arising by or under the Treaties, and all such remedies and procedures from time to time provided for by or under the Treaties, as in accordance with the Treaties are without further enactment to be given legal effect or used in the United Kingdom shall be recognised and available in law, and shall be enforced, allowed and followed accordingly; and the expression 'enforceable Community right'[94] and similar expressions shall be read as referring to one to which this subsection applies.

The wording of this provision is somewhat cumbersome and does not fully convey its immense significance: since it came into force all directly applicable European laws have automatically formed part of UK law, without any further legislation to incorporate them being needed.

Not all European laws are directly applicable: directives and most decisions usually require an act of implementation by the Member State before they can take effect. In

---

[92] Case C-213/89 [1990] ECR I-2433, [1990] 3 CMLR 1. For the *Factortame* litigation generally, see pp 133–5, *post.*

[93] *SCS Peterbroeck van Compeenhout and Cie v Belgium* Case 312/93 [1996] All ER (EC) 242. In deciding this, the basic principles of the domestic judicial system have to be taken into account: *Van Schijndel v Stichling Pensioenfonds* [1996] All ER (EC) 259.

[94] The European Union Bill A introduced in January 2005 B proposed to replace 'enforceable Community right' with 'enforceable Union right' C in the event of the EU Constitution being adopted.

the UK, the power to implement such provisions by statutory instrument is contained in section 2(2) of the 1972 Act. The scope of this section is limited by Schedule 2, which excludes the power to do any of the following:

(a) make any provision imposing or increasing taxation; or

(b) make any provision taking effect from a date earlier than that of the making of the instrument containing the provision; or

(c) confer any powers to legislate by means of orders, rules, regulations or other subordinate instrument, other than rules of procedure for any court or tribunal; or

(d) create any new criminal offence punishable with imprisonment for more than two years or punishable on summary conviction with a fine or imprisonment for more than three months.[95]

Even with these limitations the power is far-reaching: in 2003 alone, 138 statutory instruments affecting England and Wales were made pursuant to section 2(2).

Direct effect. In the context of European law, a provision is said to have 'direct effect' if it creates rights that an individual can rely upon in court. The courts have sometimes used the terms 'directly applicable' and 'direct effect' interchangeably,[96] but they are not, strictly speaking, synonymous.[97] Many directly applicable provisions can be described as having 'direct effect' because they are capable of creating rights enforceable by individuals. It does not necessarily follow however, that *all* directly applicable provisions will have such an effect. In order for a provision to have direct effect, certain criteria must be satisfied. These were set out in the important case of *Van Gend en Loos*:[98]

(a) it must not relate to inter-state relations alone;

(b) it must be clear and precise;

(c) no further action by the state for implementation must be necessary; and

(d) it must not be conditional at the time of enforcement.

Whether a particular provision fulfils these criteria is a question of interpretation, to be determined as a question of European law.

---

[95] Obligations in these areas can only be implemented by Act of Parliament or through some other enabling provision.

[96] See, e.g., *Johnston* v *Chief Constable of the RUC* Case 222/84 [1987] QB 129, [1986] 3 All ER 135; *Van Duyn* v *Home Office* Case 41/74 [1975] Ch 358, [1975] 3 All ER 190.

[97] See Winter, 'Direct Applicability and Direct Effects' (1972) 9 CML Rev 425; Ruffert, 'Rights and Remedies in European Community Law: A Comparative View' (1997) 34 CML Rev 307; Hilson and Downes, 'Making Sense of Rights: Community Rights in EC Law' (1999) 24 EL Rev 121.

[98] *Van Gend en Loos* v *Nederlandse Administratie der Belastingen* Case 26/62 [1963] ECR 1, [1963] CMLR 105.

(b) The Treaties

Treaty provisions are directly applicable and therefore require no further implementation. However, in order for a Treaty provision to have direct effect and give rise to individual rights, the *Van Gend en Loos* criteria must be satisfied.

A number of Articles of the Treaty of Rome have been held by the Court of Justice to be directly effective, and they must therefore be taken to create rights and obligations within English law. These include Article 25 (ex 12), which prohibits the introduction of new customs duties and was held in *Van Gend en Loos* to be enforceable at the instance of an individual. Other directly effective Treaty provisions include: Article 90 (ex 95), which prevents Member States from imposing discriminatory taxes on the products of other Member States;[99] Article 141 (ex 119), which states that men and women should receive equal pay for equal work;[100] and Article 39 (ex 48), which is concerned with the free movement of workers within the Community.[101]

These cases should be compared with the decision in *Zaera v Institutio Nacionale de la Seguriad Social*.[102] In this case the Court ruled that the commitment in Article 2 to 'raising the standard of living' was simply an aim of the Community and that it was insufficiently precise to confer any enforceable rights.

(c) Regulations[103]

Article 249 (ex 189) of the Treaty expressly provides that regulations are to be directly applicable and binding in their entirety. They automatically form part of UK law by virtue of section 2(1) of the European Communities Act 1972, and by their very nature they are likely to have the characteristics needed for direct effect.[104] In one recent case challenging the labelling of supermarket produce as 'Parma ham', it was said that the applicable regulation had been intended to establish rights over brand marks that could be relied upon in Member States: it was therefore directly effective.[105]

(d) Directives[106]

Unlike regulations, directives do not necessarily have immediate binding force. They are addressed to Member States but it is left to the individual national authority to implement them. In the UK this is normally done by an Order in Council or statutory instrument made pursuant to section 2(2) of the European Communities Act 1972. In principle then, although directives are binding on Member States as to the result to be achieved, they are not directly applicable. For this reason it was initially assumed that

---

[99] *Alfons Lütticke GmbH v Hauptzollamt Saarlouis* Case 57/65 [1966] ECR 293.

[100] *Defrenne v Sabena* Case 43/75 [1976] ECR 455, [1976] 2 CMLR 98.

[101] *Van Duyn v Home Office* Case 41/74 [1975] Ch 358, [1975] 3 All ER 190.

[102] Case 126/86 [1987] ECR 3697.

[103] To be renamed 'European laws' if the Constitution takes effect: see p 113, *ante*.

[104] *Commission v Italy* Case 39/72 [1973] ECR 101; *Antonio Muñoz v Frumar Ltd* Case C-253/00 [2003] Ch 328, [2003] All ER (EC) 56.

[105] *Consorzio del Prosciutto di Parma v Asda Stores Ltd* [2001] UKHL 7, [2001] CMLR 43.

[106] To be renamed 'European framework laws' if the Constitution takes effect: see p 113, *ante*.

they could not have any direct effect on individual rights, but in fact a rather more complicated position has developed through the case law of the Court of Justice.

In *Grad* v *Finanzampt Traunstein*[107] the Court of Justice ruled that a directive *could* create rights which would be enforceable by individuals if a state had failed to implement it by the due date. This approach was confirmed in *Van Duyn* v *Home Office*,[108] when the Court rejected the argument that a directive should be treated differently from a regulation. The purpose of this judicial creativity is to ensure that the fulfilment of Community objectives is not weakened by the failure of states to meet their obligations:[109]

[W]here the Community authorities have, by directive, imposed on Member States the obligation to pursue a particular course of conduct, the useful effect of such an act would be weakened if individuals were prevented from relying on it before their national courts and if the latter were prevented from taking it into consideration as an element of Community law.

There are, however, various limitations to the doctrine. Firstly, the conditions for direct effect must be fulfilled, and this means that the directive must be precise and unconditional as set out in *Van Gend en Loos*.[110] In addition, the deadline for implementation must have expired. In *Publico Ministero* v *Ratti*[111] the Court of Justice held that whilst one directive could have direct effect and prevent the Italian authorities from relying on domestic laws relating to solvents, another could *not* have this effect because the date for implementation had not yet passed.

Even where these conditions are met, directives can only have 'vertical' direct effect: in other words, they can only be enforced against the state.[112] They do not have 'horizontal' direct effect and therefore cannot be enforced against private individuals. This was confirmed in *Marshall* v *Southampton and South West Hampshire Area Health Authority*, in which it was stated that:[113]

[T]he binding nature of a directive, which constitutes the basis for the possibility of relying on the directive before a national court, exists only in relation to 'each Member State to which it is addressed.' It follows that a directive may not of itself impose obligations on an individual and that a provision of a directive may not be relied upon as such against such a person.

Marshall itself concerned a challenge to an employer's policy of operating different retirement ages for men and women. Female employees were normally required to

---

[107] Case 9/70 [1970] ECR 825, [1971] CMLR 1.

[108] Case 41/74 [1975] Ch 358, [1975] 3 All ER 190.

[109] [1975] Ch 358 at 376–7, [1975] 3 All ER 190 at 205.

[110] See p 000, *ante*; *Becker* v *Finanzamt Münster-Innenstadt* Case 8/81 [1982] ECR 53, [1982] 1 CMLR 499.

[111] Case 148/78 [1979] ECR 1629, [1980] 1 CMLR 96.

[112] Note that the doctrine does not operate the other way round and a state cannot enforce an unimplemented directive against an individual; see *Officier van Justitie* v *Kolpinghuis* Case 80/86 [1987] ECR 3969, [1989] 2 CMLR 18.

[113] Case 152/84 [1986] QB 401 at 422, [1986] 2 All ER 584, at 600. For the subsequent litigation, see *Marshall* v *Southampton and South West Hampshire Area Health Authority (No 2)* [1994] 1 AC 530, [1994] 1 All ER 736.

retire at the age of sixty, whereas their male colleagues were able to continue working until they reached sixty-five. This policy potentially violated the Equal Treatment Directive,[114] and since Miss Marshall's employer happened to be a state body, it was held that she was entitled to rely upon the directive as having direct effect. Yet if Miss Marshall had been employed by a private company she would have had no remedy.

The meaning of 'the state' for these purposes was considered in *Foster* v *British Gas*,[115] which, like *Marshall*, was a case concerning discriminatory retirement ages. On a reference under Article 234 (ex 177), the Court of Justice ruled that the Equal Treatment Directive could be relied upon against a body if it provided a public service under the control of the state and exercised special powers for that purpose. In applying this guidance to the facts of the case, the House of Lords held[116] that British Gas (at a time when it was a public corporation) was provided by statute with the duty of performing a public service. It had a monopoly power and it was also under the control of the state, since the state could dictate its policies and reclaim revenue. The directive was therefore directly effective.

Though not definitive, *Foster* is the leading case in this area and it is the starting point for any consideration of whether a body is 'an emanation of the state'. On the basis of the *Foster* test, the governing body of a voluntary-aided school in receipt of state funding has been held to be an emanation of the state,[117] as has a privatized water company.[118] On the other hand, in *Doughty* v *Rolls-Royce*[119] it was held that Rolls Royce was *not* a state body, even though the Crown owned 100 per cent of the company's shares at the time. More recently, the approach of the Court of Justice in *Kampelmann*[120] seems to suggest that the criteria set out in *Foster* are alternative rather than cumulative, and that a body may be regarded as an emanation of the state as long as *some* of these criteria can be satisfied.

This distinction between vertical and horizontal direct effects cause difficulties, not only in determining when a body is under the control of the state, but also in applying the rules evenly. For example, it has already been noted that rights in employment law may depend upon whether the employer is within the public or private sector. In insisting that directives can have only vertical direct effect the courts are attempting to maintain a distinction between regulations and directives, but the fact that cases can hinge on seemingly incidental matters, such as the identity of a claimant's employer, has led to considerable criticism.[121] In the light of other rulings of the Court of Justice

---

[114] Directive 76/207.   [115] Case C-188/89 [1991] 1 QB 405, [1990] 3 All ER 897.

[116] [1991] 2 AC 306, [1991] 2 All ER 705.

[117] *National Union of Teachers* v *Governing Body of St Mary's Church of England (Aided) Junior School* [1995] 3 CMLR 630, [1997] IRLR 242.

[118] *Griffin* v *South-West Water Services Ltd.* [1995] IRLR 15.

[119] [1992] 1 CMLR 1045, [1992] ICR 538

[120] *Kampelmann* v *Landschaftsverband Westfalen-Lippe* Cases C 253–258/96 [1997] ECR I-6907 at para 46.

[121] See, e.g. Lenz A-G *in Faccini Dori* v *Recrab Srl* Case C-91/92 [1994] ECR I-3325, [1995] All ER (EC) 1; Craig and De Búrca, *EU Law: Text, Cases and Materials* (3rd edn, 2003) at pp 207–8; Arnull, 'The Direct Effect of Directives: Grasping the Nettle' (1986) 35 ICLQ 939.

however, the distinction is less important than it may at first appear to be. This is because directives can also have what are called 'indirect effects'.

Indirect effects. In *von Colson* v *Land Nordrhein-Westfalen*[122] the Court of Justice stated:

[I]n applying the national law and in particular the provisions of a national law specifically introduced in order to implement [a directive], national courts are required to interpret their national laws in the light of the wording and the purpose of the directive in order to achieve the result referred to in the third paragraph of Article 189.

This approach was strengthened by the decision in *Marleasing SA* v *La Commercial International de Alimentatión SA*:[123]

[I]n applying national law, whether the provisions concerned pre-date or post-date the directive, the national court asked to interpret national law is bound to do so in every way possible in the light of the text and the aims of the directive to achieve the results envisaged by it and thus comply with Article 189(3) of the Treaty.

The Court of Justice has since endorsed this strong interpretive obligation in a number of other cases,[124] and as far as possible, national courts must now interpret all legislation in a manner consistent with the provisions of directives. In adopting this approach the Court of Justice has undoubtedly reduced the significance of the direct effects doctrine,[125] but it should be remembered that the obligation described in *Marleasing* is merely one of interpretation. Its application depends upon whether a compatible interpretation of national law is 'possible', and the Court of Justice has generally left it to the domestic courts to answer this question.[126]

Damages. In some circumstances the failure of a Member State to implement a directive may give rise in Community law to an action for damages. In *Francovich* v *Italian Republic*[127] the Court of Justice ruled that an individual could claim for financial loss resulting from the non-implementation of a directive. In order for an action for damages to succeed, it was held that three conditions must be satisfied:

(1) The directive must be intended to confer individual rights;

(2) It must be possible to identify the content of those rights on the basis of the provisions of the directive; and

---

[122] Case 14/83 [1984] ECR 1891, [1986] 2 CMLR 430; note that Article 189 was re-numbered as Article 249 by the Treaty of Amsterdam.

[123] Case C-106/89 [1990] ECR I-4135, [1992] 1 CMLR 305; ibid.

[124] See *Centrosteel* v *Adipol* Case C-456/98 [2000] ECR I-6007.

[125] See Craig, 'Directives: Direct Effect, Indirect Effect and the Construction of National Legislation' (1997) 22 EL Rev 519; Prechal, 'Does Direct Effect Still Matter?' (2000) 37 CML Rev 1047.

[126] *Wagner-Miret* v *Fondo de Garantia Salarial* Case C-334/92 [1993] ECR I-6911; *Faccini Dori* v *Recrab Srl* Case C-91/92 [1994] ECR I-3325, [1995] All ER (EC) 1; *Alcatel Austria* v *Bundesministerium für Wissenschaft und Verkehr* Case C-81/98 [1999] ECR I-7671. For the approach of the English courts, see p 136, *post*.

[127] Case C-6, 9/90 [1991] ECR I-5357, [1993] 2 CMLR 66. Note that in *Emmott* v *Minister for Social Welfare* Case C-208/90 [1993] ICR 8 the Court of Justice ruled that where a State fails to implement a directive properly the individual may sue the state in reliance on that directive (if directly effective) until proper implementation occurs.

(3) There must be a causal link between the breach of the state's obligation and the damage suffered.

English law was slow to accept the right to seek damages in such cases,[128] but the decision in *R v Secretary of State for Transport, ex parte Factortame*[129] made it clear that domestic courts have a duty to confer effective protection for Community rights. The position was put beyond doubt by the decisions in *Brasserie du Pêcheur SA v Germany* and *R v Secretary of State for Transport ex parte Factortame (No 4)*.[130] In the first of these two companion cases, it was alleged that a German law relating to the purity of beer contravened European law, whilst in the second, the breach of Community law had already been established.[131] The Court of Justice confirmed the approach in *Francovich* and ruled that even where the infringement of Community law had resulted from the legislation of a national Parliament, liability for damages could still arise. The general principle to emerge from these cases is that if a state is responsible for a breach of Community obligations—even if those obligations derive from a measure which does not have direct effect—the state may be liable in damages for any losses that result. In determining whether the breach of Community law is sufficient to warrant compensation, the decisive test is whether the state manifestly and gravely disregarded the limits of its discretion. Factors to be considered by the court include: (a) the clarity and precision of the rule breached; (b) the measure of discretion left to the authorities; (c) whether the infringement and the damage caused was intentional; (d) whether any error of law was excusable; and (e) whether the position taken by a Community institution may have contributed to the omission. Following the clear statement of principle outlined by the Court of Justice, the House of Lords in *Factortame (No 5)* entered judgment[132] for the plaintiff, thus accepting its duty to provide a remedy for breach of Community obligations.

In the subsequent case of *R v HM Treasury, ex parte British Telecommunications plc*[133] the Court of Justice confirmed the approach set out in *Factortame*, stating that in order for a Member State to be liable in damages:

[T]he rule of law infringed must be intended to confer rights on individuals; the breach must be sufficiently serious; and there must be a direct causal link between the breach of the obligation resting on the state and the damage sustained by the injured parties.

On the facts of the case, which concerned the incorrect implementation of a directive, the Court of Justice held that the breach was not sufficiently serious to give rise to damages: the UK had acted in good faith and the wording of the directive was imprecise. By contrast, in *R v Ministry of Agriculture, Fisheries & Food, ex parte Hedley*

---

128 *Bourgoin SA v Ministry of Agriculture Fisheries & Food* [1986] QB 716, [1985] 3 All ER 585.
129 Case C-213/89 [1990] ECR I-2433, [1990] 3 CMLR 1.
130 Cases C-46/93 and 48/93 [1996] QB 404, [1996] All ER (EC) 301.   131 See p 135, *post.*
132 [2000] 1 AC 524, [1999] 4 All ER 906.
133 Case C-392/93 [1996] QB 615 at 655, [1996] All ER (EC) 411 at para 39.

Lomas[134] the breach was blatant. The UK had refused to grant a licence for the export of sheep for slaughter in Spain, without any legal justification for so doing. The fact that the UK believed that the Spanish abattoir was operating in breach of Community law was irrelevant.

More recently, the Court of Justice has held that a breach of a directly effective Treaty Article, which concerns anti-competitive agreements, could potentially give rise to an action for compensation to cover damage caused by a non-state party.[135] The full implications of this decision are still, as yet, uncertain.

(e) Decisions

Decisions may be made by the Council and Commission as a formal method of enunciating policies or initiating actions. They are binding upon those to whom they are addressed, and like directives, they are capable of having direct effect.

F IMPACT UPON ENGLISH COURTS

1 THE QUESTION OF SUPREMACY

The insistence of Community law that it shall prevail over conflicting national law presents distinct challenges to the UK's constitutional orthodoxy. It was this potential conflict that led to the unsuccessful attempt in *Blackburn* v *AG*[136] to challenge the UK's accession to the Treaty of Rome and the passage of the 1972 Act. The Court of Appeal ruled that the treaty-making power of the Crown was beyond challenge, though it also confirmed that Parliament retained the theoretical power to legislate in any way that it saw fit: if it chose to do so it could repeal the 1972 Act.

Implementation of the Treaty in English law was achieved by the passage of section 2(1) of the Act. In addition, section 2(4) states that:

[A]ny enactment passed or to be passed, other than one contained in this part of this Act, shall be construed and have effect subject to the foregoing provisions of this section.

Directly applicable Community obligations therefore take precedence over conflicting national provisions. By these means Parliament has ensured that most conflicts between English law and European law are resolved in favour of the latter. The constitutional challenge can be avoided by relying on the will of Parliament itself. In *Macarthys Ltd* v *Smith*[137] the majority of the court held that the individual rights arising under what was then Article 119 (now 141) should prevail over the clear and

---

[134] Case C-5/94 [1996] ECR I-2553, [1996] All ER (EC) 493; see also *Dillenkofer* v *Germany* Cases C178–9/94 and 188–90/94 [1996] ECR I-4845.

[135] *Courage* v *Crehan* Case C-453/99 [2002] QB 507, [2001] All ER (EC) 886. The provision in question was Article 81 (ex 85) of the EC Treaty.

[136] [1971] 2 All ER 1380, [1971] 1 WLR 1037.   [137] [1979] 3 All ER 325, [1979] 1 WLR 1189.

unambiguous words of the Equal Pay Act 1970. By contrast Lord Denning used the Article as an aid to construction, concluding that the terms of the 1970 Act were capable of bearing a meaning that would allow compliance with Community obligations. Alternatively he considered that if Parliament had intended to derogate from its obligations under the Treaty, it would (and could) do so by express words: in the absence of such words, an intention to comply with Treaty obligations would be presumed.

The authority conferred by the 1972 Act has enabled courts both to quash executive actions and to declare delegated legislation invalid. More fundamentally, the courts have now accepted that it may require them to declare the provisions of a subsequent Act of Parliament to be inoperative. This occurred in *Factortame v Secretary of State for Transport (No 2)*.[138] The applicants, who were companies controlled by Spanish nationals, sought to challenge the validity of the Merchant Shipping Act 1988 on the basis that it contravened the EC Treaty and deprived them of their Community law rights. The Divisional Court had made a reference to the Court of Justice under Article 234 (ex 177), but since determination of the issues was likely to take some time, the applicants applied for an interim injunction to restrain the Secretary of State from enforcing the Act. The House of Lords initially decided that they had no power to make such an order,[139] but following a further reference to the Court of Justice[140] they granted an interim injunction to suspend the operation of the Merchant Shipping Act 1988. Lord Bridge stated:[141]

Whatever limitation of its sovereignty Parliament accepted when it enacted the European Communities Act 1972 was entirely voluntary. Under the terms of the 1972 Act it has always been clear that it was the duty of a United Kingdom court, when delivering final judgment, to override any rule of national law found to be in conflict with any directly enforceable rule of Community law. Similarly, when decisions of the Court of Justice have exposed areas of United Kingdom statute law which failed to implement Council directives Parliament has always legally accepted the obligation to make appropriate and prompt amendments. Thus there is nothing in any way novel in according supremacy to rules of Community law in those areas to which they apply, and to insist that, in the protection of rights under Community law, national courts must not be inhibited by rules of national law from granting interim relief in appropriate cases is no more than a logical recognition of that supremacy.

Whether such an injunction will be granted depends upon the merits of the particular case, and it is certainly not automatic. A significant factor will be the likelihood of the Court of Justice giving a ruling which favours one party or the other. If a trial judge considers that this likelihood is evenly balanced, he is entitled to decide that the applicant's interest in having the Act of Parliament struck down is outweighed by the public interest in enforcing it.[142]

---

[138] [1991] 1 AC 603, [1991] 1 All ER 70.   [139] [1990] 2 AC 85, [1989] 2 All ER 692.

[140] Case C-213/89 [1990] ECR I-2433, [1990] 3 CMLR 1.

[141] [1991] 1 AC 603 at 659, [1991] 1 All ER 70 at 107.

[142] Ibid; see also *R v Secretary of State for the National Heritage, ex parte Continental Television BV* [1993] 3 CMLR 387.

The impact of EC law on the legislative supremacy of Parliament was revisited in the recent case of *Thoburn* v *Sunderland City Council and others*.[143] The appellants had been prosecuted for selling produce in imperial measurements, contrary to delegated legislation implementing a directive on the use of metric weights. The appeal by way of case stated centred on the claim that the Weights and Measures Act 1985 (which permitted the use of imperial weights) had, by implication, partially repealed section 2 of the European Communities Act 1972. The Divisional Court rejected this argument, and in doing so, Laws LJ stated expressly what many had assumed for some time:[144]

There are now classes or types of legislative provision which cannot be repealed by mere implication. These instances are given and can only be given, by our own courts, to which the scope and nature of Parliamentary sovereignty are ultimately confided.

In the view of Laws LJ, the European Communities Act forms part of this special class of legislative provisions, which he collectively termed 'constitutional statutes', and it is therefore immune from implied repeal.[145] Although not a decision of the House of Lords, *Thoburn* is the strongest indication yet that as far as the national courts are concerned, the supreme status of European law is still dependent on the authority of the 1972 Act. However, unless and until Parliament chooses to expressly repeal that Act, it seems that any conflict between domestic and European law will be resolved in favour of the latter.

The supremacy of Community law has thus been achieved, and in appropriate cases the courts will be prepared to disapply Acts of Parliament in order to give it proper effect. In an action for judicial review, a court may also consider a declaration to the effect that the UK is in breach of its Community obligations.[146]

2 INTERPRETATION

In most of the cases to come before the domestic courts, judges have been able to avoid confronting the issue of supremacy. The approach of Lord Denning in *Macarthys Ltd* v *Smith* was to use European law as an aid to construction, and it is this interpretative approach that has generally found favour with English judges. In *Garland* v *British Rail Engineering*, Lord Diplock stated:[147]

[I]n the instant case the words of section 6(4) of the Sex Discrimination Act 1975 that fall to be construed, 'provision in relation to retirement', without any undue straining of the ordinary meaning of the language used, are capable of bearing either the narrow meaning accepted by the Employment Appeal Tribunal or the wider meaning preferred by the Court

---

[143] [2002] EWHC 195 (Admin), [2003] QB 151, [2002] 4 All ER 156.   [144] Ibid. at [60].
[145] See p 30, *ante*.
[146] *Equal Opportunities Commission* v *Secretary of State for Employment* [1995] 1 AC 1, [1994] 1 All ER 910. On the facts, provisions in the Employment Protection (Consolidation) Act 1978 were declared to be contrary to the Equal Pay Directive (57/117) and Article 141 (ex 119) of the Treaty.
[147] [1983] 2 AC 751 at 771. Article 119 was re-numbered as Article 141 by the Treaty of Amsterdam.

of Appeal but acknowledged by that court to be largely a matter of first impression. Had the attention of the court been drawn to Article 119 of the EEC Treaty and the judgment of the European Court of Justice in *Defrenne* v *Sabena* I have no doubt that, consistently with statements made by Lord Denning MR in previous cases, they would have construed section 6(4) so as not to make it inconsistent with article 119.

The same approach was adopted in *Pickstone* v *Freeman's plc*,[148] where the House of Lords considered that an amendment to the Equal Pay Act 1970, which was intended to give effect to the ruling of the Court of Justice in *Marshall*,[149] was capable of being so construed. Although on a literal reading the amendment did not achieve its object- ive, the House of Lords felt able to read words into the legislation to give effect to the clear intention of Parliament. This purposive approach can be contrasted with that of the Court of Appeal in the same case: the Court of Appeal had found the words of the 1970 Act to be clear and unambiguous, but it nevertheless held that the obligations of Community law prevailed over them.[150] In *Litster* v *Forth Dry Dock and Engineering Co Ltd*[151] regulations were made to give effect to a directive. The claimant could not rely on the directive itself because the defendant company was not an organ of the state and there was thus no direct effect. In a clear application of the *von Colson* principle, the House of Lords nevertheless accepted that it had a duty to interpret the regulation in a manner consistent with the directive.

In both *Pickstone* and *Litster*, the courts were concerned with the interpretation of laws which had been made or amended to give effect to European law. This was not the case in *Duke* v *GEC Reliance* however,[152] and the House of Lords refused to distort the meaning of a statute to give effect to a Community provision which was not directly effective. The House held that in such circumstances it was required by English law to give the words of the statute their ordinary and natural meaning, and that the *von Colson* ruling[153] was not applicable because the court had no discretion as to the approach to interpretation. The reasoning in this case is unconvincing, and in *Marleasing*[154] the Court of Justice confirmed that the duty to interpret national law in the light of European law is not confined to measures passed with the intention of implementing European provisions.

The House of Lords returned to this issue in *Webb* v *EMO Air Cargo (UK) Ltd*. The claimant in this case had been hired to cover for another employee who was on maternity leave, but she was dismissed when she too became pregnant. Her situation did not appear to fall within the scope of the Sex Discrimination Act 1975, but she argued that it *was* covered by the Equal Treatment Directive and that the 1975 Act should be interpreted in the light of the latter instrument. The House of Lords

---

[148] [1989] AC 66, [1988] 2 All ER 803.
[149] Case 152/84 [1986] QB 401, [1986] 2 All ER 584. See p 130, *ante*.
[150] [1987] 3 WLR 811, [1987] 3 All ER 756.   [151] [1990] 1 AC 546, [1989] 1 All ER 1134.
[152] [1988] AC 618, [1988] 1 All ER 626.
[153] Case 14/83 [1984] ECR 1891, [1986] 2 CMLR 430; see p 132, *ante*.
[154] Case C-106/89 [1990] ECR I-4135, [1992] 1 CMLR 305; see p 132, *ante*. For criticism of the *Duke* decision, see Foster, 'The Effect of the European Communities Act 1972, s 2(4)' (1988) 51 MLR 775.

accepted the principle expressed in *Marleasing*, but emphasized that the obligation to interpret statutes in a manner compatible with European law applied only to the extent that a compatible interpretation was 'possible':[155]

It is for a United Kingdom court to construe domestic legislation in any field covered by a Community directive so as to accord with the interpretation of the directive as laid down by the European Court, *if that can be done without distorting the meaning of the domestic legislation.* [emphasis added]

The House of Lords initially took the view that a compatible interpretation was *not* possible in this case. However, following a reference to the Court of Justice,[156] it accepted that the provision could be interpreted so as to comply with the directive without distorting the meaning of the Act.[157]

G THE EUROPEAN COURT OF JUSTICE

1 COMPOSITION AND PROCEDURE

The Court of Justice comprises one judge for each Member State, assisted by eight Advocates-General.[158] Both the judges and the Advocates-General are appointed for a renewable period of six years, and appointments are staggered so that a proportion of the court is replaced or re-appointed every three years. Article 223 of the EC Treaty (ex 167) provides that members of the Court shall:

be chosen from persons whose independence is beyond doubt and who possess the qualifications required for appointment to the highest judicial offices in their respective countries or who are jurisconsults of recognised competence.

Article 223 further stipulates that the judges must nominate one of their number as President of the Court. The President holds this position for a renewable term of three years, and is responsible for directing the judicial business of the Court and for overseeing its administration. The Court also appoints its own registrar and lays down rules governing his service.

The Court may sit either in chambers of three or five judges, in a Grand Chamber of eleven judges, or exceptionally, in plenary session.[159] Its organization and

---

[155] [1992] 4 All ER 929 at 939, [1993] 1 CMLR 259 at 270, per Lord Keith of Kinkel.

[156] Case C-32/93 [1994] QB 718, [1994] 4 All ER 115.

[157] *Webb* v *EMO Air Cargo (UK) Ltd (No 2)* [1995] 1 WLR 1454, [1996] 4 All ER 577.

[158] Articles 221 and 222 of the EC Treaty (ex 165 and 166). The nationality of the judges is not specified at present but it is assumed that each state will be represented. Article I-29(2) of the European Constitution will, if adopted, make this explicit, by providing that 'the Court of Justice shall consist of one judge from each Member State'. Protocol 3 of the Constitution sets out a new Statute of the Court of Justice.

[159] Article 221 (ex 165), as amended by the Treaty of Nice. The number of judges in a Grand Chamber will increase to thirteen if the European Constitution is implemented.

procedures are set out in the Statute of the Court (annexed to the EC Treaty by the Treaty of Nice) and in the Rules of Procedure adopted by the court itself.

(a) Advocates-General

The role of Advocate-General has no direct parallel within the English legal system. Comparisons with counsel acting as *amicus curiae* are inexact, because despite the name, an Advocate-General does not act on anyone's behalf. Instead his role is to present independent, reasoned conclusions on cases submitted to the Court, in order to assist the Court in performing its duties.[160] The opinion of the Advocate-General is not binding but it is clearly of persuasive value. It will be reported with the judgment of the Court and may therefore be important in assisting in the development of legal doctrine.

(b) The Court of First Instance

The Court of First Instance was created in 1988 in an attempt to ease the workload of the Court of Justice.[161] It deals mainly with disputes between the Community and its servants and with actions for judicial review brought under Article 230 (ex 173). Since the Treaty of Nice came into force in February 2003, it has also been able to deal with some references from national courts under the Article 234 (ex 177) procedure. The jurisdiction of the Court of First Instance will be further expanded under the European Constitution, and it will in future be known as 'the General Court'.[162]

The Court has one judge for each Member State but there are no separate Advocates-General. In most other respects, the structure of the Court is very similar to that of the Court of Justice: judges are appointed for six years, they nominate a President who holds office for three years, and they normally sit in chambers of three or five. There is a right of appeal to the Court of Justice on a point of law.

2 JURISDICTION

The main jurisdiction of the Court of Justice is as follows:

(a) Judicial review of the actions of the Community institutions. Under Article 230 (ex 173) the Court can review the legality of an act of the Council or the Commission. Under Article 232 (ex 175) failures to act can also be challenged.

Member States, the Council and the Commission have the status of privileged applicants, and may bring an action under these provisions on the grounds of lack of competence, infringement of an essential procedural requirement, infringement of

---

[160] Article 222 (ex 166). The compatibility of the Advocate-General's role with the right to a fair trial was recently considered in *Emesa Sugar v Aruba* Case C-17/98 [2000] ECR I-665; see p 125, *ante*.

[161] Article 225 (ex 168a); see Brown, 'The First Five Years of the Court of First Instance and Appeals to the Court of Justice' (1995) 32(3) CML Rev 743.

[162] Article I-29(1).

Community law, or misuse of power.[163] An individual or 'non-privileged applicant' can only challenge (a) decisions addressed to him, and (b) decisions or regulations which are of direct and individual concern. The requirement for standing has been restrictively interpreted, and matters cannot be of direct concern to an individual if there is a discretion as to their implementation.[164] Where no real discretion exists, or where implementation is automatic, then the 'direct concern' test is satisfied.[165] The established approach is typified by the decision in *Plaumann & Co v EEC Commission*:[166]

Persons other than those to whom a decision is addressed may only claim to be individually concerned if that decision affects them by reason of certain attributes which are peculiar to them or by reason of circumstances in which they are differentiated from all other persons and by virtue of these factors distinguishes them individually just as in the case of the person addressed.

Thus, even though the applicants were German importers of clementines, they did not have standing to challenge a decision on the import duties on clementines, since any person could potentially be a clementine importer. Despite the restrictive effect of this ruling, it has been followed in numerous subsequent cases.[167] In the recent case of *Jégo-Quéré at Cie SA v Commission* the Court of First Instance adopted a more relaxed approach, citing the importance of providing an effective remedy for those whose rights and freedoms are affected by Community law:[168]

[I]n order to ensure effective judicial protection for individuals, a natural or legal person is to be regarded as individually concerned by a Community measure of general application that concerns him directly if the measure in question affects his legal position, in a manner which is both definite and immediate, by restricting his rights or by imposing obligations on him. The number and position of other persons who are likewise affected by the measure, or who may be so, are of no relevance in that regard.

The Court of Justice later overturned the decision,[169] and confirmed the *Plaumann* approach as correct.

(b) Direct actions against Member States. A Member State may be challenged directly in the Court of Justice for a failure to fulfil its Community obligations. Actions against Member States may be brought either by the Commission[170] or by other Member

---

[163] See, e.g. the UK's unsuccessful challenge to the Working Time Directive in *UK v EU Council* Case C-84/94, [1996] All ER (EC) 877.

[164] *Alcan v EC Commission* Case 69/69 [1970] ECR 385.

[165] *International Fruit Co v NV Commission* Case 41–44/70 [1971] ECR 411.

[166] Case 25/62 [1963] ECR 95, [1964] CMLR 29.

[167] See, e.g. *Calpak SpA v EC Commission* Cases 789–90/79 [1980] ECR 1949; *Piraiki-Patraiki v Commission* Case 11/82, [1985] ECR 207. The approach to standing in these cases can be compared with that of the domestic courts on applications for judicial review; see p 220, *post.*

[168] Case T-177/01 [2002] All ER (EC) 932 at [51], [2002] 2 CMLR 44.

[169] Case C-263/02 [2004] All ER (EC), [2005] 2 WLR 179; see also *Unión de Pequeños Agricultores v Council* Case C-50/00 [2002] All ER (EC) 893, [2002] 3 CMLR 1.

[170] Article 226 (ex 169).

States.[171] Proceedings by the latter are extremely rare,[172] although the *threat* of a challenge from a Member State can sometimes lead the Commission to take action under Article 226 (ex 169). In 1999 for example, France refused to allow the importation of UK beef even though the Community had decided to lift the worldwide ban which had been imposed in response to a health scare. The UK notified the Commission of its intention to bring an action against France, and the Commission responded by successfully challenging the ban itself under Article 226.[173]

(c) Cases concerning the liability in damages of the Community and its servants. Under Articles 235 and 288 (ex 178 and 215), the Court of Justice has jurisdiction over disputes concerning damage caused by the Community institutions and their servants in the performance of their duties. The Court of First Instance can also hear disputes between the Community and its servants.[174]

(d) Appeals from the Court of First Instance

(e) References from national courts requesting a preliminary ruling. This is a major source of work for the Court, and has important consequences for the courts of Member States. The jurisdiction is governed by Article 234 (ex 177) of the EC Treaty and is considered in more detail in the sections below.

3 REFERENCES FOR A PRELIMINARY RULING UNDER ARTICLE 234[175]

Article 234 (ex 177) creates a power, and in some circumstances imposes a duty, to refer questions concerning the interpretation of European law to the Court of Justice. It plays a key role in ensuring that the treaties and other instruments are applied consistently throughout the Community. Article 234 states:

(1) The Court of Justice shall have jurisdiction to give preliminary rulings concerning:

    (a) the interpretation of this Treaty;

    (b) the validity and interpretation of acts of the institutions of the Community and of the European Central Bank;

    (c) the interpretation of the statutes of bodies established by an act of the Council, where those statutes so provide.

(2) Where such a question is raised before any court or tribunal of a Member State, that court or tribunal may, if it considers that a decision on the question is necessary to enable it to give judgment, request the Court of Justice to give a ruling thereon.

(3) Where any such question is raised in a case pending before a court or tribunal of a

---

[171] Article 227 (ex 170).

[172] See *France* v *UK* Case 141/78 [1979] ECR 2923; *Belgium* v *Spain* Case C-388/95 [2000] ECR I-3121.

[173] *Commission* v *France*; sub nom *Re Ban on British Beef* Case C-1/00 [2001] ECR I-9989, [2002] 1 CMLR 22.

[174] Article 236 (ex 178).

[175] See generally Craig and De Búrca, *EU Law: Text, Cases and Materials* (3rd edn, 2003), ch 11; Arnull, 'The Use and Abuse of Article 177, EEC' (1989) 52(5) MLR 622.

Member State, against whose decisions there is no judicial remedy under national law, that court or tribunal shall bring the matter before the Court of Justice.

The Court of Justice also has a limited jurisdiction to give preliminary rulings on aspects of the EU's 'third pillar'.[176] The provisions in question concern matters such as visas, asylum, and immigration. However, a reference may only be made by courts and tribunals against whose decisions there is no judicial remedy in national law: unlike with Article 234, there is no discretion for other courts to seek a ruling. Certain measures adopted under the rest of the third pillar (now titled 'Police and Judicial co-operation in Criminal Matters') may also be the subject of a preliminary ruling, but only for Member States which have accepted the court's jurisdiction in such matters. The UK is not one of these states.

(a) The power to refer

This power to refer matters under Article 234 is conferred upon courts and tribunals. It is for the Court of Justice to decide whether a body constitutes a 'court or tribunal', and the term has been held to include state bodies exercising judicial or quasi-judicial functions.[177]

(b) When is a reference mandatory?

If the interpretation of European law is raised as an issue in a case, the domestic court or tribunal involved in that case must decide whether to refer the matter to the Court of Justice. If the domestic court is one 'against whose decisions there is no judicial remedy', a reference to the Court of Justice will be mandatory. Thus if a matter falling within the scope of Article 234(1) is raised in a case before the House of Lords, that matter *must* be referred to the Court of Justice since there is no possibility of a further appeal. A reference is not only mandatory for courts whose decisions can *never* be challenged:[178] what matters is whether an appeal is possible in the particular case in question. On this basis, it could be suggested that the Court of Appeal would often be obliged to make a reference, since an appeal from a decision of this court is only possible with leave and leave may not be granted. However, if leave is not granted by the Court of Appeal it may still be requested from the House of Lords, and this means that the Court of Appeal usually has a discretion as to whether to seek a ruling:[179]

[176] Articles 61–69, EC Treaty; incorporated by the Treaty of Amsterdam in 1999—see p 111, *ante*.

[177] *Broekmeulen v Huisarts Registratie Commissie* Case 246/80 [1981] ECR 2311; *De Coster v Collège des Bourgmestre et Échevins de Watermael-Boitsfort* Case C-17/00 [2001] ECR I-9445.

[178] Cf. Lord Denning in *HP Bulmer Ltd v J Bollinger SA* [1974] Ch 401, [1974] 2 All ER 1226, who suggested that only the House of Lords could be under an obligation to make a reference.

[179] *Chiron Corporation v Murex Diagnostics* [1995] All ER (EC) 88 at 93, per Balcombe LJ. See also *Costa v ENEL* Case 6/64 [1964] ECR 585, [1964] CMLR 425; *Lyckeskog* Case C-99/00 [2002] ECR I-4839, [2003] 1 WLR 9. The position is arguably different in the case of a Divisional Court which refuses to certify a point of law on appeal from a decision of a magistrates' court, since this extinguishes any possibility of taking the case further; see *SA Magnavision MN v General Optical Council (No 2)* [1987] 2 CMLR 262.

Except . . . where the Court of Appeal is the court of last resort, the Court of Appeal is not *obliged* to make a reference to the ECJ . . . If the Court of Appeal does not make a reference to the ECJ, and gives its final judgment on the appeal, then the House of Lords becomes the court of last resort.

It should also be noted that the concept of a judicial remedy under Article 234 is wide enough to encompass the possibility of judicial review. Since inferior courts and tribunals are under the supervisory jurisdiction of the High Court it would appear that such bodies will never be caught by the mandatory reference requirement, even if no right of appeal exists.[180]

(c) When is a decision on a point of European law 'necessary'?

Unless a decision on a point of European law is 'necessary' for the determination of a case, there is neither a duty nor a discretion to make a reference to the Court of Justice: necessity is a pre-condition to the use of the preliminary ruling procedure. In *HP Bulmer Ltd v J Bollinger SA*, Lord Denning stressed that a decision on a matter is not 'necessary' if substantially the same point has already been decided by the Court of Justice or if the point is 'reasonably free from doubt'.[181] In the *CILFIT Case*[182] the Court of Justice stated that there is no need to refer a question if the answer to it 'can in no way affect the outcome of the case.' Other English courts have interpreted the phrase as meaning 'reasonably necessary' or 'substantially determinative' of the litigation.[183]

The doctrine of acte clair. Lord Denning's suggestion that a matter need not be referred if it is already reasonably free from doubt, mirrors the European law doctrine of *acte clair*. In *CILFIT* the Court of Justice stated:[184]

[T]he correct application of Community law may be so obvious as to leave no scope for any reasonable doubt as to the manner in which the question raised is to be resolved. Before it comes to the conclusion that such is the case, the national court or tribunal must be convinced that the matter was equally obvious to the courts of the other Member States and to the Court of Justice.

The Court also stated that in determining whether a point is *acte clair*, regard should be had to the fact that Community law is drafted in different languages and may not always translate easily. In addition, it emphasized that Community concepts may bear different meanings from similar concepts in domestic law, and that such points need to be considered in the context of Community law as a whole. In *R v Pharmaceutical Society of Great Britain, ex parte the Association of Pharmaceutical Importers*[185] Kerr LJ

---

180 See *Re a Holiday in Italy* [1975] 1 CMLR 184.
181 [1974] Ch 401, [1974] 2 All ER 1226. He also suggested that the point of law must be conclusive of the case, but this goes too far and is inconsistent with the approach of the Court of Justice.
182 *CILFIT Srl v Ministro della Sanita* Case 283/81 [1982] ECR 3415, [1983] 1 CMLR 472.
183 *Customs and Excise Commissioners v Aps Samex* [1983] 1 All ER 1042.
184 Case 283/81 [1982] ECR 3415 at para 16, [1983] 1 CMLR 472.
185 [1987] 3 CMLR 951. See also the judgment of Bingham J in *Customs and Excise Commissioners v ApS Samex* [1983] 1 All ER 1042.

observed that an English court should 'hesitate long' before concluding that a point of European law was so obvious as to leave no room for reasonable doubt. Note also that since a national court has no power to declare actions of the Community invalid, a reference under Article 234 may sometimes be necessary even where the point of law is clear.[186]

The existence of a 'precedent'. Though the Court of Justice does not operate a rigid doctrine of precedent,[187] it does tend to follow its previous decisions in the interests of legal certainty. A national court may therefore consider it unnecessary to refer a point which has been answered by the Court of Justice in a previous case,[188] though much will depend on the national court's view of whether the earlier decision was correct. In *Da Costa*,[189] the Court of Justice suggested that an obligation to make a reference will not arise where a 'precedent' exists, though there will still be a discretion to ask for a preliminary ruling.

(d) The discretion to refer

The discretion to refer is ultimately that of the national court or tribunal, and its decision will not be reviewable by the Court of Justice unless the reference is spurious or an abuse of process:[190]

A request for a preliminary ruling from a national court may be rejected only if it is manifest that the interpretation of Community law sought by that court bears no relation to the true facts or the subject matter of the main proceedings.
The Court of Justice will not, however, deliver advisory opinions or opinions on hypothetical questions.[191]

It will be for the national court to formulate the question to be answered, and it should also define the factual and legislative context. In one case,[192] the Court of Justice held that it could not rule on the questions posed by the national court as it had not been provided with sufficient information. In *Bulmer v Bollinger*[193] Lord Denning set out some guidelines for the exercise of the discretion by English courts. These guidelines are not binding however: indeed, as a matter of Community law, the decision to make a reference must rest with the court or tribunal concerned. Nevertheless, the following factors were considered by Lord Denning to be relevant:

---

[186] *Firma Foto-Frost v Hauptzollamt Lubeck-Ost* Case 314/85 [1987] ECR 4199, [1988] 3 CMLR 57.

[187] See chapter 3.

[188] *R v Secretary of State for the Home Department, ex parte A* [2002] EWCA Civ 1008, [2002] 3 CMLR 14; *Parfums Christian Dior v Evora BV* Case C-337/95, ECR I-6013, [1998] 1 CMLR 737.

[189] *Da Costa v Nederlandse Belastringadministratie* Cases 28–30/62 [1963] ECR 31, [1962] CMLR 224.

[190] *ICI Chemical Industries v Colmer (HM Inspector of Taxes)* Case C-264/96 [1998] ECR I-4695; *Dzodzi v Belgium* Cases C-297/88 and C-197/89 [1990] ECR I-3763; *Foglia v Novello (No 2)* Case 244/80 [1981] ECR 3045.

[191] *Zabala Erasu v Instituto National de Empleo* Cases C-422–424/93 [1995] All ER (EC) 758.

[192] *Telemarsicabruzzo SpA v Circostel and others* Cases C-320–322/90 [1993] ECR I-393.

[193] [1974] Ch 401, [1974] 2 All ER 1226.

(i) the time needed to obtain a ruling;

(ii) the importance of not overloading the European Court with references;

(iii) the difficulty and importance of the point;

(iv) the expense involved; and

(v) the wishes of the parties.

He also stated that the facts should be established first; an 'injunction of obvious merit'.[194] The importance of deciding the facts first is that they provide the legal context for the point at issue, and indeed may determine whether or not a reference is in fact necessary. However, as the Court of Justice stated in *Irish Creamery Milk Suppliers Association* v *Ireland*,[195] the national court has responsibility for giving judgment in the case and it is therefore in the best position to judge when a reference is required. There is nothing to prevent a reference being made at an interlocutory stage, and important issues were raised and resolved in this way in the *Factortame* litigation.[196] In each case however, it is a matter for the discretion of the trial court. In *Henn and Darby* v *DPP*[197] Lord Diplock indicated that a reference in a criminal case should be dealt with if necessary *after* the trial, at the appellate stage. By contrast, in *R* v *Goldstein* it was said that in a criminal case the best time to deal with such a matter would be on a motion to quash the indictment.[198] It would seem that the real issue in all cases is whether the interests of justice provide a compelling reason for going ahead with the trial, pending determination of the reference.

In deciding whether to make a reference, the workload of the Court of Justice appears not to be a relevant factor, despite the dicta of Lord Denning: the problems of the Court of Justice should not be resolved through the mechanism of restricting references. By contrast, expense *is* an important factor to consider. In *R* v *Pharmaceutical Society of Great Britain, ex parte Association of Pharmaceutical Importers*[199] Kerr LJ expected the case to reach the House of Lords, at which point a reference would become mandatory. He considered that an immediate reference would therefore save considerable time and costs. As Hodgson J observed in the *Factortame* case, if a reference is going to be made, 'the sooner it is done the better.'[200]

The wishes of the parties will be a relevant but not decisive factor. The concept of 'reference by consent' should not creep into the practice of the English courts, for it is the court's judgment as to the need for a reference that is important. However, where only one party wishes a reference there is no inevitability: it will usually be the case that a reference will assist one party only. A reference may be appropriate even against the wishes of both parties. The court may also take into account the fact that the

---

[194] *Customs and Excise Commissioners* v *ApS Samex* [1983] 1 All ER 1042 at 1055, per Bingham J.

[195] Case 36/80 [1981] ECR 735, [1981] 2 CMLR 455.

[196] *R* v *Secretary of State for Transport, ex parte Factortame* Case C-213/89 [1990] ECR I-2433, [1990] 3 CMLR 1.

[197] [1981] AC 850, [1980] 2 All ER 166.   [198] [1983] 1 All ER 434, [1983] 1 WLR 151.

[199] [1987] 3 CMLR 951.

[200] *R* v *Secretary of State for Transport, ex parte Factortame (No 1)* [1989] 2 CMLR 353 at 380.

matter is one upon which the European Commission has strong views. Once a decision to make a reference is taken however, the domestic court is not at liberty to disregard the outcome, and it must apply the ruling of the Court of Justice to the facts before it.[201]

[201] See *Arsenal* v *Reed* [2003] EWCA Civ 696, [2003] 3 All ER 865, which raises some interesting questions about the extent to which courts should follow any views expressed by the Court of Justice about the application of the law to the facts.

5

THE HUMAN RIGHTS ACT 1998 AND THE EUROPEAN CONVENTION ON HUMAN RIGHTS

A INTRODUCTION: THE CONTEXT

1 THE CONVENTION AND ITS HISTORY[1]

The UK is a signatory to the Convention for the Protection of Human Rights and Fundamental Freedoms, usually referred to as the European Convention on Human Rights or ECHR. It is an instrument of the Council of Europe, which, like the European Communities,[2] is an intergovernmental body formed in the aftermath of the Second World War. Since it was established in 1949 the membership of the Council of Europe has steadily increased from ten to forty-six states,[3] and it includes all of the current Member States of the EC. In recent years there has been talk of the EC itself acceding to the Convention,[4] but it is important to remember that the Council of Europe and the EC are separate bodies with their own separate treaties and institutions. Whereas the EC was initially established as a vehicle for greater economic co-operation, human rights were at the centre of the Council of Europe's agenda from the outset. The ECHR was the Council's first major project and is undoubtedly its single most important achievement. The UK played a significant role in the drafting process and was one of the first countries to sign the Convention in November 1950. It entered into force in the UK on 3 September 1953.

---

[1] For a comprehensive account, see Simpson, *Human Rights and the End of Empire: Britain and the Genesis of the European Convention* (2001).

[2] See chapter 4.

[3] Albania, Andorra, Armenia, Austria, Azerbaijan, Belgium, Bosnia and Herzegovina, Bulgaria, Croatia, Cyprus, the Czech Republic, Denmark, Estonia, Finland, France, Georgia, Germany, Greece, Hungary, Iceland, Ireland, Italy, Latvia, Liechtenstein, Lithuania, Luxembourg, Malta, Moldova, Monaco, the Netherlands, Norway, Poland, Portugal, Romania, Russia, San Marino, Serbia and Montenegro, Slovenia, the Slovak Republic, Spain, Sweden, Switzerland, Turkey, the former Yugoslav Republic of Macedonia, the Ukraine, and the UK.

[4] See p 125, *ante*. When brought into effect, Protocol 14 will amend Article 59 of the Convention so as to make this possible: Protocol 14 is discussed further in Part 'D' of this chapter.

The emphasis of the Convention is on protecting basic 'human rights', along with what might be termed civil and political rights,[5] and its text is closely modelled on the UN's Universal Declaration on Human Rights, 1948. The key rights are the right to life (Article 2), freedom from torture (Article 3), freedom from slavery (Article 4), the right to liberty and security of the person (Article 5), the right to a fair trial (Article 6), the right not to be subject to retrospective criminal liability or penalties (Article 7), respect for private and family life (Article 8), freedom of thought, conscience, and religion (Article 9), freedom of expression (Article 10), freedom of assembly and association (Article 11), and the right to marry and found a family (Article 12). These rights are considered in more detail later in this chapter.[6] One other provision should be noted: Article 13 guarantees the availability of a remedy at national level to enforce the substance of Convention rights in whatever form they are secured in domestic law.

[T]he remedy required by Article 13 must be 'effective' in practice as well as in law. In particular its exercise must not be unjustifiably hindered by the acts or omissions of the . . . respondent State.[7]

The list of Convention rights has been enhanced over the years by a number of additional protocols. Though acceptance of the Convention is now a pre-requisite for Council of Europe membership, most of the protocols are optional,[8] and this has enabled the Convention to address issues which probably would not have been brought within its framework at all if unanimity had been required. To date, fourteen protocols have been added to the Convention. Some of these have been concerned solely with institutional reform, but others have added new substantive rights. Protocol 1 includes the right to peaceful enjoyment of possessions, to education, and to free elections, while Protocol 6 is concerned with the abolition of the death penalty in peace time. Both of these Protocols have been signed and ratified by the UK, as has Protocol 13, which strengthens Protocol 6 by banning the use of the death penalty in *any* circumstances. However, the UK has thus far not accepted Protocol 4, (which prohibits the imprisonment of debtors, the expulsion of nationals, and the collective expulsion of aliens), Protocol 7, (which, inter alia, guarantees equality between spouses and the right not to be tried more than once for the same offence), or Protocol 12 (which prohibits discrimination on a wide range of grounds).

What distinguishes the ECHR from most other international human rights treaties is not the catalogue of rights that it protects, but its machinery for enforcement. It established both a Commission and a Court of Human Rights, which together were given the task of ensuring that the Convention was observed. The Commission was

---

[5] The European Social Charter (1961) addresses economic, social and cultural rights, but is not backed up by the same mechanisms for enforcement; see Gomien, Harris and Zwaak, *Law and Practice of the European Convention on Human Rights and the European Social Charter* (1996).

[6] See p 173, *post*.   [7] *Keenan* v *UK* (2001) 33 EHRR 38 at para 122.

[8] Acceptance of Protocol 6 is now mandatory: see p 173, *post*.

abolished in 1998, but the Court, based in Strasbourg, has gone from strength to strength. It received over 40,000 individual complaints in 2004 alone.[9]

2 THE STATUS OF THE ECHR BEFORE THE HUMAN RIGHTS ACT 1998[10]

Unlike the European Communities, the Council of Europe did not set out to establish a superior legal order, and the ECHR does not oblige Member States to directly incorporate its provisions into their national legal systems. The UK's constitutional arrangements mean that international treaties are not binding in domestic law unless accompanied by an Act of Parliament,[11] and it was not until the implementation of the Human Rights Act 1998[12] that it was possible for Convention rights to form the basis of a domestic legal challenge. Even before the Act, however, decisions of the Court of Human Rights provided the impetus for several pieces of legislation and Convention rights were occasionally taken into account by the national courts. In addition, the Convention was able to have a subtle and indirect influence through the decisions of the European Court of Justice.

(a) The impact of findings of the European Court of Human Rights

Since the UK accepted the jurisdiction of the European Court of Human Rights and the right of individuals to petition that court,[13] it has been found to be in breach of Convention rights on numerous occasions. States are obliged to give effect to any decision of the Court in cases to which they are parties, and several Acts of Parliament have been enacted in response to adverse findings in Strasbourg. For example, the Contempt of Court Act 1981 followed the decision in *Sunday Times* v *UK*[14] that the common law approach to contempt was incompatible with freedom of expression. Similarly, the finding in *Malone* v *UK*[15] that there was insufficient legal regulation of telephone tapping led to the enactment of the Interception of Communications Act 1985. Decisions in Strasbourg have also triggered changes in the procedures for dealing with life prisoners[16] and the abandonment of the policy preventing homosexuals from serving in the military.[17] Occasionally, the mere *likelihood* of an adverse finding has been enough to bring about legislative reform. Thus in anticipation that aspects of

[9] European Court of Human Rights, *Survey of Activities, 2004*. The majority of applications are declared inadmissible or otherwise resolved: 718 judgments were delivered in 2004, twenty-three of which concerned the UK. See p 200, *post*.

[10] See Beloff and Mountfield, 'Unconventional Behaviour? Judicial uses of the European Convention in England and Wales' [1996] EHRLR 467.

[11] *R* v *Chief Immigration Officer, Heathrow Airport, ex parte Bibi (Salamat)* [1976] 3 All ER 843, [1976] 1 WLR 979.

[12] See p 153, *post*.   [13] On 14 January 1966.

[14] (1979–1980) 2 EHRR 245; see p 192, *post*.

[15] (1985) 7 EHRR 14. The 1985 Act was replaced by the Regulation of Investigatory Powers Act 2000 following further criticism in *Halford* v *UK* (1997) 24 EHRR 523.

[16] See p 177, *post*.

[17] *Smith and Grady* v *UK* (2000) 29 EHRR 493; *Lustig-Prean and Beckett* v *UK* (2000) 29 EHRR 548.

the court-martial system would be found to breach the fair trial provisions in Article 6, the government introduced the Armed Forces Act 1996. This Act made a number of changes to the courts-martial system, though it did not, of course, prevent the Strasbourg court from finding a breach of Article 6 in the case in question.[18]

(b) An indirect influence on the domestic courts

There is a presumption that Parliament does not intend to legislate in a manner incompatible with international law,[19] and where a statutory provision is genuinely ambiguous it is legitimate to take account of an international treaty when choosing between two equally reasonable interpretations. Thus even before the passage of the Human Rights Act, the ECHR could be taken into account as an aid to statutory interpretation. The position was discussed in *R* v *Chief Immigration Officer of Heathrow Airport, ex parte Bibi (Salamat)*. Immigration officials had refused to give the applicant leave to enter the UK to join a man that she said was her husband, and this was alleged to constitute an interference with the right to respect for family life under Article 8 of the Convention. In the course of his judgment, Lord Denning stated that:[20]

The position as I understand it is that if there is any ambiguity in our statutes, or uncertainty in our law, then these courts can look to the Convention as an aid to clear up the ambiguity and uncertainty ... but I would dispute altogether that the Convention is part of our law. Treaties and declarations do not become part of our law until they are made law by Parliament.

The issue was also considered by the House of Lords in *R* v *Secretary of State for Home Affairs, ex parte Brind*.[21] The Home Secretary had made a directive prohibiting the broadcasting of statements by representatives of proscribed organizations, and the applicant argued that this contravened the right to freedom of expression under Article 10. In dismissing the applications, the House recognized that the Convention *could* be used for the resolution of a legislative ambiguity. However, it held that it did not require an administrative body such as the Home Office to exercise its discretion within the terms of the Convention. To conclude otherwise would amount to incorporation of the Convention by the judiciary, and this would be a usurpation of the legislative function.

The courts were more willing to use the Convention when interpreting statutes enacted to give effect to decisions of the Court of Human Rights,[22] or when considering the scope of the common law. In most cases however, its effect (if any) was limited to reinforcing a conclusion which would have been reached in any event. For example, in *R* v *Secretary of State for the Home Department, ex parte Leech (No 2)*,[23] rule 33(3) of

---

[18] *Findlay* v *UK* (1997) 24 EHRR 221; see p 274, *post*.   [19] See p 65, *ante*.

[20] [1976] 3 All ER 843 at 847, [1976] 1 WLR 979 at 984.

[21] [1991] 1 AC 696, [1991] 1 All ER 720.

[22] *R* v *Secretary of State for the Home Department, ex parte Norney* (1995) 7 Admin LR 861.

[23] [1994] QB 198, [1993] 4 All ER 539; cf. the Human Rights Act case of *R (on the application of Daly)* v *Secretary of State for the Home Department* [2001] UKHL 26, [2001] 2 AC 532, [2001] 3 All ER 433; discussed at pp 165 and 187, *post*.

the Prison Rules was found to be ultra vires the Prison Act 1952 because it created an unrestricted right for a governor to read prisoners' correspondence. It thus interfered with the right to seek legal advice and to have unimpeded access to the courts. The court based its conclusion on the idea that access to the courts is a 'constitutional right', but it also noted that its approach was consistent with Article 8 of the Convention.

More often, the Convention had no decisive effect on domestic cases at all, and on a number of occasions the courts made it clear that they felt unable to use it to develop the common law. Thus in *Malone v Metropolitan Police Commissioner (No 2)*[24] Sir Robert Megarry considered the legality of the police interception of telephone calls. Even though not bound by any authority, and despite considering that the practice could breach Article 8 of the Convention,[25] he declined to develop the law in a way that would ensure compliance, suggesting that any reform in this area would be best left to Parliament.[26]

(c) An influence through the EC / EU

Though the EC itself has not acceded to the Convention,[27] its individual Member States are all signatories and the European Court of Justice has frequently asserted that Convention rights form part of its legal order. The rights guaranteed by the Convention have now been given express recognition in Article 6 of the Treaty on European Union, and where national legislation falls within the scope of Community law, the Court of Justice will examine its compatibility with the ECHR.[28] In the *Familiapress*[29] case, for example, the Court ruled that any justification for a ban on the distribution of a magazine would need to be compatible with the right to freedom of expression under Article 10, ECHR. This led some to conclude that a measure of indirect incorporation was being achieved through the influence of EC law:[30]

There is no case in which the European Court [of Justice] has upheld the validity of actions which conflicted with the European Convention on Human Rights. It seems therefore, that in those areas affected by the EEC Treaties, the ECHR is already indirectly incorporated into English domestic law. The principles of the Convention form an integral part of EEC law and English domestic law is subject to EEC law. United Kingdom legislation must comply with directly applicable legislation, which itself falls to be construed so as to give effect to the European Convention on Human Rights.

---

24 [1979] Ch 344, [1979] 2 All ER 620.

25 In that it failed to be prescribed by law. The Strasbourg court later agreed with this assessment: *Malone* v *UK* (1985) 7 EHRR 14. Parliament responded by enacting the Interception of Communications Act 1985, which was later replaced by the more extensive Regulation of Investigatory Powers Act 2000.

26 [1979] Ch 344 at 380, [1979] 2 All ER 620 at 649.

27 The possibility of its accession is now being considered: see p 125 and p 147, n 4 *ante*.

28 *Johnston* v *Chief Constable of the RUC* Case C-222/84 [1987] QB 129, [1986] 3 All ER 135, *Prais* v *Council* Case C-130/75 [1976] ECR 1589; *Rutili* v *Minister of the Interior* Case C-36/75, [1975] ECR 1219.

29 *Vereingte Familiapress Zeitungsverlags und Vertriebs GmbH* v *Heinrich Bauer Verlag* Case C-368/95 [1997] ECR-I-3689, [1997] 3 CMLR 1329.

30 Browne-Wilkinson, 'The Infiltration of a Bill of Rights' [1992] PL 397 at p 401. See also Grief, 'The Domestic Impact of the European Convention on Human Rights as Mediated through Community Law' [1991] PL 555; Beyleveld, 'The Concept of a Human Right and Incorporation of the ECHR' [1995] PL 577.

3 BRINGING RIGHTS HOME

Despite the influence of the Convention on aspects of domestic law, its impact prior to 1998 was inevitably limited by the fact that it was merely an international treaty and could not be directly enforced in the national courts. This meant that a 'victim' of a Convention breach had to either depend on the processes of interpretation described above, or take the case through the long, slow procedures of the Court of Human Rights. Moreover, the fact that the government might choose to bring the law into line with the rulings of the court did not provide an automatic remedy for those who were aggrieved. Calls to incorporate the ECHR into national law had been made for decades,[31] but it was not until 1998 that the UK finally enacted legislation to give it domestic effect. The argument that the UK had an exemplary human rights record and that incorporation was therefore unnecessary, did not stand up to scrutiny: by the time of the Human Rights Bill the UK had lost more cases in Strasbourg than any other state except Italy.[32] The government's White Paper explained the rationale for incorporation as follows:[33]

The rights, originally developed with major help from the United Kingdom Government, are no longer seen as British rights. And enforcing them takes too long and costs too much. It takes on average five years to get an action into the European Court of Human Rights once all domestic remedies have been exhausted; and it costs an average of £30,000. Bringing these rights home will mean that the British people will be able to argue for their rights in the British courts – without this inordinate delay and cost. It will also mean that the rights will be brought much more fully into the jurisprudence of the courts throughout the United Kingdom, and their interpretation will thus be far more subtly and powerfully woven into our law. And there will be another distinct benefit. British judges will be able to make a distinct contribution to the development of the jurisprudence of human rights in Europe.

The following analysis is divided into three main areas. The first concerns the content and structure of the Human Rights Act itself, while the second focuses on the interpretation of specific Convention rights. The final part of the chapter will examine the role of the European Court of Human Rights.

---

[31] A detailed discussion of the campaign is beyond the scope of this work, but see Zander, *A Bill of Rights* (4th edn, 1996); Bingham, 'The European Convention on Human Rights: Time to Incorporate' [1993] LQR 390; Lester, 'The Mouse that Roared: The Human Rights Bill 1995' [1995] PL 198; Klug and Wadham, 'The "Democratic" Entrenchment of a Bill of Rights: Liberty's Proposals' [1993] PL 579; Gardner, *Aspects of Incorporation of the European Convention on Human Rights* (1993).

[32] Lord Irvine (Lord Chancellor), 582 HL Official Report (5th series) col 1227, 3 Nov 1997.

[33] *Rights Brought Home: The Human Rights Bill*, Cm 3782, at para 1.14. See also, Jack Straw MP and Paul Boateng MP, 'Bringing Rights Home: Labour's Plans to Incorporate the European Convention on Human Rights into UK Law' [1997] 1 EHRLR 71.

B THE HUMAN RIGHTS ACT 1998

The Human Rights Act 1998, which came fully into force on 2 October 2000,[34] is described in its long title as 'an Act to give further effect to rights and freedoms guaranteed under the European Convention on Human Rights'. The UK's constitutional framework means that the Act is not 'entrenched' in the same manner as the human rights documents adopted by many other states, but it is presumed that any attempt to repeal or amend its provisions would require the clearest possible words.[35]

The scheme of the Act is complex: it obliges public authorities to perform their functions in a manner compatible with Convention rights, and it gives the Convention and its jurisprudence a significant influence over the interpretation of domestic law. However, it stops short of allowing the courts to 'disapply' or invalidate incompatible Acts of Parliament, and in this crucial respect it does not give the Convention primacy over domestic law.[36]

1 THE STATUS OF CONVENTION RIGHTS[37] AND JURISPRUDENCE

(a) Section 1: The rights protected

Section 1 provides that the 'Convention rights' given effect shall be those contained in Articles 2 to 12 and 14 of the Convention, in Articles 1 to 3 of the First Protocol, and in Articles 1 and 2 of the Sixth Protocol. These rights are reproduced in Schedule 1 of the Act. The 'missing' right, Article 13, is the right to a remedy for an infringement of the Convention. The government took the view that the very existence of the Human Rights Act was sufficient to give effect to Article 13, and that to expressly incorporate it would involve unnecessary duplication.[38]

(b) Section 2: The Strasbourg case law[39]

Section 2 requires any court or tribunal determining a matter involving a Convention right, to take into account any judgment, decision, or advisory opinion of the European Court of Human Rights, along with certain decisions of the Commission and Committee of Ministers, *in so far as they may be relevant*. It is clear from this wording that the national courts are not bound by Strasbourg decisions, and they thus have the status of persuasive precedents. The fact that Parliament chose not to *oblige* the courts to follow the Strasbourg case law is entirely consistent with the Convention itself, as

---

[34] For England and Wales—s 22(3); SI 2000/1851. Sections 18, 20 and 21(5) came into force on the date of Royal Assent.

[35] *Thoburn v Sunderland City Council and others* [2002] EWHC 195 (Admin), [2003] QB 151, [2002] 4 All ER 156. The Act was described in this case as a 'constitutional statute'.

[36] Cf. the status given to EC law by the European Communities Act 1972: see chapter 4 for a discussion.

[37] The content of these rights is considered in greater depth at p 170, *post*.

[38] Jack Straw MP (Home Secretary), 312 HC Official Report (6th series) col 975, 20 May 1998.

[39] See also p 86, *ante*.

states are afforded a generous margin of appreciation in the application of its provisions. Moreover, domestic courts will frequently be required to determine cases under the Human Rights Act where the only relevant case law concerns other jurisdictions: it would be illogical to prevent the English courts from coming to their own conclusions in such cases.

The domestic courts have made it clear that in the absence of exceptional circumstances they are unlikely to depart from any 'clear and constant jurisprudence of the European Court of Human Rights'.[40] This means that so far, most judges have adhered fairly closely to the Strasbourg case law. For example, despite considering that mandatory and discretionary life sentences raised similar issues, the Court of Appeal in *R (on the application of Anderson) v Secretary of State for the Home Department*[41] followed the Strasbourg line and ruled that mandatory sentences were not subject to the same requirements as those which were discretionary. Their Lordships were clearly influenced by the knowledge that another case on the same point was already pending before the Court of Human Rights, and as Simon Brown LJ explained:[42]

In the end there are two factors which have persuaded me to regard the Strasbourg case law as for the present determinative. First, that whatever advantage we might enjoy through our domestic knowledge and experience of the mandatory life sentence regime could perhaps be thought balanced (or even conceivably outweighed) by the Court of Human Rights' deeper appreciation of the true ambit and reach of Articles 5(4) and 6(1) of the Convention . . .

The second factor which weighs with me is that of comity. True, this court is not bound by Court of Human Rights judgments, any more than that court is bound by them. Where, however, as here, the Court of Human Rights itself is proposing to re-examine a particular line of cases, it would seem somewhat presumptuous for us, in effect, to pre-empt its decision. For my part, I shall be surprised if the present regime for implementing mandatory life sentences survives the Court of Human Rights' re-examination of the issue in Stafford. The final decision, however, I am persuaded should be theirs.

As predicted, when the Strasbourg court did have the opportunity to revisit the issue in *Stafford v UK*,[43] it departed from its previous jurisprudence and agreed that the regime for implementing mandatory life sentences did infringe the Convention. Consequently, when the House of Lords heard the appeal in *Anderson*[44] it felt able to declare that the Home Secretary's power to determine the tariff for mandatory life prisoners was incompatible with the Convention. What is particularly notable is that in reaching its conclusions in *Stafford*, the Court of Human Rights drew heavily on the opinions expressed by the domestic courts in both *Stafford*[45] and *Anderson*, including those of Simon Brown LJ. Thus, although the Court of Appeal thought it appropriate to leave the final decision to Strasbourg, it was able to influence that decision through its own jurisprudence.

---

[40] *R (on the Application of Alconbury) v Secretary of State for the Environment, Transport and the Regions*: [2001] UKHL 23 at [26], [2003] 2 AC 295 at [26], [2001] 2 All ER 929.
[41] [2001] EWCA Civ 1698, [2002] 2 WLR 1143.   [42] Ibid at [65]–[66].
[43] (2002) 35 EHRR 32.   [44] [2002] UKHL 46, [2003] 1 AC 837, [2002] 4 All ER 1089.
[45] *R v Secretary of State for the Home Department, ex parte Stafford* [1999] 2 AC 38, [1998] 4 All ER 7, HL.

In other cases, the national courts have felt less constrained by the Strasbourg case law. For example, in dismissing a claim that the courts-martial system was incompatible with Article 6, Lord Steyn politely suggested that a recent Strasbourg case[46] on the point had been wrongly decided:[47]

It goes without saying that any judgment of the European Court commands great respect, and section 2(1) of the Human Rights Act 1998 requires the House to take any such judgment into account, as it routinely does. There were, however, a large number of points in issue in *Morris*, and it seems clear that on this particular aspect the European Court did not receive all the help which was needed to form a conclusion.

Similar comments were made by Lords Bingham and Rodger. At the next available opportunity,[48] a unanimous Grand Chamber of the Strasbourg court took account of these judgments and again departed from its previous case law, declaring itself satisfied that there was, after all, no incompatibility with the Convention. As these cases demonstrate, the obligation to *consider*, rather than to *follow* Strasbourg decisions, means that there is at least the potential for the national courts to develop a human rights jurisprudence of their own. Moreover, the flexibility in section 2 means that 'domestic courts are perfectly entitled to accord *greater* rights than those guaranteed by the Convention';[49] though it is still too early to tell whether they will in fact do so.

(c) Sections 12 and 13: The special status of freedom of religion and freedom of expression

Section 12 applies when a court is considering whether to grant relief which could affect the right to freedom of expression. Section 12(2) provides that relief should not be granted against a party who is neither present nor represented unless the court is satisfied that all reasonable attempts to notify him have been made, or that there are compelling reasons for not notifying him. Section 12(3) adds that the publication of disputed material should not be restrained before trial unless the applicant is 'likely to establish that publication should not be allowed.' Finally, section 12(4) requires the court to have particular regard to the importance of freedom of expression. It states that when considering granting relief in relation to material which is 'journalistic, literary or artistic', it must take into account (a) the extent to which the material is (or is about to become) available to the public; (b) whether publication would be in the public interest; and (c) any relevant privacy code.

Section 12 was included in the Act in response to strong lobbying from sections of the media who were concerned that incorporation might be the catalyst for new rights of privacy. In fact however, the provision has not been interpreted to give freedom of

---

[46] *Morris* v *UK* (2002) 34 EHRR 52.

[47] *R* v *Spear and others; R* v *Saunby and others* [2002] UKHL 31 at [12], [2003] 1 AC 734 at [12], [2002] 3 All ER 1074.

[48] *Cooper* v *UK* (2004) 39 EHRR 8.

[49] *Begum (Runa)* v *Tower Hamlets* [2003] UKHL 5 at [69], [2003] 2 AC 430 at [69], [2003] 1 All ER 731, per Lord Hoffman.

expression priority over other rights. In *Douglas v Hello! Ltd (No 1)*, for example, Sedley LJ stated that:[50]

That Convention right, when one turns to it, is qualified in favour of the reputation and rights of others and the protection of information received in confidence. In other words, you cannot have particular regard to Article 10 without having equally particular regard at the very least to Article 8.

The irony here is that not only was section 12 assumed to make Article 10 directly applicable between private parties, it was also assumed that it indirectly did the same for the right to respect for private life in Article 8. This approach led one commentator to observe that section 12 was proving to be 'largely irrelevant' in practice.[51]

In a recent breach of confidence case the Court of Appeal confirmed that section 12 does not require freedom of expression to take priority over other Convention rights: it simply means that any attempt to restrict free speech must be clearly justified:[52]

It is one thing to say . . . that the media's right to freedom of expression, particularly in the field of political discussion 'is of a higher order' than 'the right of an individual to his good reputation'; it is, however, another thing to rank it higher than competing rights.

This point was not challenged when the case went to the House of Lords, but it was held that section 12 nevertheless required a new approach to the granting of pre-trial injunctions.[53] Lord Nicholls concluded that in the light of section 12 it would not necessarily be sufficient for the party seeking an injunction to establish 'a real prospect of succeeding'[54] at trial. Instead, he stated that the courts should be 'exceedingly slow to make interim restraint orders where the applicant has not satisfied the court that he will *probably* ("more likely than not") succeed at the trial.'[55]

The other Convention right given a special status under the Human Rights Act is freedom of religion. Section 13(1) provides that if the determination of an issue under the Act could affect the exercise by a religious organization or its members of the right to freedom of thought, conscience, and religion, a court must have particular regard to the importance of that right.[56] This provision was included in response to lobbying from church leaders, who were concerned that they may find themselves compelled to conduct gay marriages or to employ those whose lifestyles or beliefs were

---

[50] [2001] QB 967 at 1003, [2001] 2 All ER 289 at 322.

[51] Amos, 'Can We Speak Freely Now? Freedom of Expression under the Human Rights Act' [2002] 6 EHRLR 750 at 755.

[52] *Cream Holdings v Banerjee* [2003] EWCA Civ 103 at [54], [2003] Ch 650 at [54], [2003] 2 All ER 318, per Simon Brown LJ. See also *Venables and Thompson v News Group Newspapers* [2001] Fam 430, [2001] 1 All ER 908, in which the Article 10 right had to give way to the Article 2 rights of individuals whose lives could be endangered if details of their whereabouts were published.

[53] [2004] UKHL 44, [2004] 4 All ER 617, [2004] 3 WLR 918.

[54] This is the test established in *American Cyanamid Co v Ethicon Ltd* [1975] AC 396, [1975] 1 All ER 504.

[55] [2004] UKHL 44 at [22], [2004] 4 All ER 617 at [22] (emphasis added). Their Lordships overturned the Court of Appeal's decision on the facts and discharged the injunction that had been granted.

[56] For a discussion, see Cumper, 'The Protection of Religious Rights under s 13 of the Human Rights Act' [2000] PL 254.

incompatible with their doctrines.[57] In fact, the churches probably overestimated the extent to which they would be affected by the Act. The guarantees under Article 9 are already sufficient to ensure that a Minister of religion could not be compelled to perform a marriage ceremony against his conscience, and most of the functions of a church would not be caught by section 6 in any event.[58] Moreover, the interpretation given to section 12 makes it unlikely that section 13 will allow freedom of religion to trump other Convention rights, and having 'particular regard' to the right will mean paying equal regard to the grounds upon which religious freedom can be restricted in Article 9(2).

2 THE IMPACT ON LEGISLATION

(a) Section 3: The interpretative obligation

One of the principal mechanisms by which the Act seeks to give effect to Convention rights is set out in section 3(1). This provides that:

So far as it is possible to do so, primary legislation and subordinate legislation must be read and given effect in a way which is compatible with the Convention rights.

This interpretive obligation applies to *all* legislation, whether enacted before or after the Human Rights Act,[59] and it permits the courts to go far beyond previously accepted limits in seeking 'possible' meanings of words. Once it is established that a provision engages a Convention right, the court must then consider whether it appears on its face to be compatible with that right. Most Convention rights are not absolute and the interference with the right may be a legitimate one: if this is the case the court need do nothing except give effect to the provision in the ordinary way. If, however, the provision appears to be inconsistent with the Convention, section 3 obliges the court to seek a different interpretation.

It is important to note that section 3 does not authorize the courts to disapply Acts of Parliament,[60] and it does not affect the validity, continuing operation, or enforcement of any incompatible primary legislation.[61] Nevertheless, it is clear that the interpretive obligation under section 3 is a strong one. In the leading case of *R v A (No 2)*, Lord Steyn explained that:[62]

It applies even if there is no ambiguity in the language in the sense of the language being

---

[57] A House of Lords amendment which would have allowed Article 9 to prevail over other Convention rights was removed in the Commons: what is now s 13 was inserted in its place.

[58] See *Aston-Cantlow and Wilcote with Billesley Parochial Church Council v Wallbank* [2003] UKHL 37 at [63], [2004] 1 AC 546 at [63], [2003] 3 All ER 1213. Lord Hope confirmed that a church council was not a 'core' public authority for the purposes of the Human Rights Act: see p 164, *post*.

[59] Section 3(2). The impact of the Act on statutory interpretation is discussed further at p 55, *ante*.

[60] Cf. The European Communities Act 1972, s 2(4); discussed further in chapter 4, *ante*.

[61] Nor does it affect the validity of incompatible subordinate legislation where primary legislation prevents removal of the incompatibility: s 3(2).

[62] [2001] UKHL 25 at [40], [2002] 1 AC 45 at [40], [2001] 3 All ER 1.

capable of two different meanings . . . In accordance with the will of Parliament as reflected in s 3 it will sometimes be necessary to adopt an interpretation, which linguistically may appear strained. The techniques to be used will not only involve the reading down of express language in a statute but also the implication of provisions.

The implications of this approach are potentially dramatic. In *R v A* itself, the disputed provision[63] had been specifically enacted to prevent defendants in sex offence cases from adducing evidence of a complainant's sexual history. Yet in reliance on section 3, the House of Lords interpreted the provision as being subject to an implied discretion to *allow* such evidence in the interests of a defendant's right to a fair trial. Section 3 does have its limits however, and in other cases the courts have cautioned against reading words into an Act to the point of making it unworkable:[64]

[I]f it is necessary in order to obtain compliance to radically alter the effect of the legislation this will be an indication that more than interpretation is involved.

In *Re S (Children) (Care Order: Implementation of Care Plan)*[65] the Court of Appeal read words into the Children Act 1989 to create new discretionary powers for the courts to supervise local authority care orders. On appeal, however, the House of Lords rejected this use of section 3 on the basis that it would have undermined a fundamental feature of the 1989 Act: namely, that 'the courts are not empowered to intervene in the way local authorities discharge their parental responsibilities under final care orders.'[66] Their Lordships also noted that the Court of Appeal had failed to identify any specific provision of the Children Act that was capable of being interpreted in the manner suggested.[67] Similarly, in *Bellinger v Bellinger*[68] the House of Lords held that section 11 of the Matrimonial Causes Act 1973 could not be interpreted so as to allow a male to female transsexual to marry a man. Such an interpretation would have represented a major change in the law and would have had far-reaching ramifications which were best left to Parliament to determine.[69]

It has been argued that *Re S* and *Bellinger v Bellinger* are evidence of a shift away from the 'high water mark' of *R v A* towards a more restrictive approach,[70] but the recent decision in *Ghaidan v Godin-Mendoza*[71] suggests that this is not the case. By a majority of 4:1, the House of Lords construed provisions in the Rent Act 1977 so as to

---

[63] Youth Justice and Criminal Evidence Act 1999, s 41.

[64] *Poplar Housing and Regeneration Community Association Ltd* v *Donoghue* [2001] EWCA Civ 595 at [76], [2002] QB 48 at [76], [2001] 4 All ER 604, per Lord Woolf CJ.

[65] [2001] EWCA Civ 757, [2002] 2 FLR 582, [2001] HRLR 50: *sub nom Re W and B (Children) (Care Plan)*.

[66] [2002] UKHL 10 at [42], [2002] 2 AC 291 at [42], [2002] 2 All ER 192, per Lord Nicholls.

[67] Ibid, at [43].

[68] [2003] UKHL 21, [2003] 2 AC 467, [2003] 2 All ER 593.

[69] At the time of this decision the House of Lords was aware that legislation to remedy the defect was already imminent: the government had accepted that UK law was in breach of the Convention following the decision of the Court of Human Rights in *Goodwin* v *UK* (2002) 35 EHRR 18.

[70] Nicol, 'Statutory Interpretation and Human Rights After *Anderson*' [2004] PL 274. Cf. Kavanagh, 'Statutory Interpretation and Human Rights After *Anderson*: A More Contextual Approach' [2004] PL 537.

[71] [2004] UKHL 30, [2004] 2 AC 557, [2004] 3 All ER 411.

confer the tenancy rights of spouses on same-sex partners, thus avoiding the conclusion that the Act was incompatible with the non-discrimination requirements in Article 14. Lord Nicholls confirmed that section 3 required a radical approach:[72]

Section 3 enables language to be interpreted restrictively or expansively. But section 3 goes further than this. It is also apt to require a court to read in words which change the meaning of the enacted legislation, so as to make it Convention-compliant. In other words, the intention of Parliament in enacting section 3 was that, to an extent bounded only by what is 'possible', a court can modify the meaning, and hence the effect, of primary and secondary legislation.

Lord Nicholls acknowledged that there would inevitably be some cases in which a Convention-compliant interpretation was not possible, and both *Re S* and *Bellinger* v *Bellinger* were said to be examples of such cases:[73]

Parliament . . . cannot have intended that in the discharge of this extended interpretative function the courts should adopt a meaning inconsistent with a fundamental feature of legislation. That would be to cross the constitutional boundary section 3 seeks to demarcate and preserve.

Nevertheless, the majority of the House felt that the Rent Act could be given a Convention-compliant interpretation without crossing this constitutional boundary, and all five Law Lords endorsed the decision in the earlier case of *R* v *A (No 2)*. It is clear then that the interpretative obligation decreed by section 3 is of an 'unusual and far-reaching character'.[74]

(b) Sections 4, 5 and 10—Declarations of incompatibility and remedial orders

If a court[75] concludes that a compatible interpretation of a provision is not possible, it may issue a declaration of incompatibility under section 4 of the Act. The effect of a declaration is to bring the matter to the attention of the government so that a change in the law can be considered. It does not affect the validity, continuing operation, or enforcement of the statute, and the court must give effect to the incompatible provision as Parliament intended.[76] Nevertheless, where a court is contemplating such a step, the Crown is entitled to be given notice and the relevant Minister or his nominee is entitled to be joined as a party to the proceedings.[77]

Where a declaration of incompatibility has been made, or where the Strasbourg court has made an equivalent finding, section 10 empowers a Minister to make such

---

[72] Ibid, at [32].   [73] Ibid, at [33].   [74] Ibid, at [30], per Lord Nicholls.

[75] For these purposes, the term 'court' covers the House of Lords, the Judicial Committee of the Privy Council, the Courts-Martial Appeal Court, the Court of Appeal, the High Court, and the Scottish High Court of Justiciary (except when sitting as a trial court or Court of Session): s 4(5). Even the lower courts are bound by s 3 and may occasionally need to decide that a compatible interpretation of legislation is impossible. However, as they have no power to make formal declarations of incompatibility, such decisions cannot trigger the power to make a remedial order under s 10.

[76] Incompatible *subordinate* legislation may be declared invalid unless primary legislation prevents removal of the incompatibility: s 3(2). In the latter case a declaration of incompatibility may be issued.

[77] Section 5.

amendments to the legislation as he considers necessary to remove the incompatibility. It is important to note that this is a power, not an obligation, and it only arises where the Minister considers that there are 'compelling reasons' for proceeding under this section. The requirement for compelling reasons was inserted during the committee stage in the House of Lords, as many MPs were concerned to limit this potentially far-reaching power.[78] Ironically however, it has been argued that the amendment may be to the detriment of human rights protection:[79]

The consequence of this unfortunate amendment could be that a breach of human rights may go uncorrected for want of parliamentary time or because it relates to an unpopular group or a controversial cause. But it is precisely this domination of majority over minority interests which human rights law is designed to prevent. The amendment therefore had the unfortunate effect of weakening the structure of the Act.

So far, relatively few declarations have been made, and some have been overturned on appeal.[80] What this tells us about the level of human rights protection has been the subject of considerable debate, and much has been written about the extent to which deference plays a part in the courts' decisions.[81] A detailed examination of these issues is beyond the scope of this work, but it is worth remembering that a declaration of incompatibility does not oblige Parliament or the government to take remedial action. If there is a reluctance to use section 4 because of a concern that elected bodies should have the final word on policy matters, it is therefore unwarranted. On the other hand, the desire to avoid declarations is not always due to excessive deference. From a human rights perspective, a declaration of incompatibility may be the least desirable outcome: it will not affect the validity of the legislation and there is no guarantee of remedial action. Even if remedial action is taken it will not assist those involved in the original case. A compatible interpretation under section 3 is potentially far more powerful because it means *giving effect* to the provision in a Convention-compliant way. During the debates on the Human Rights Bill, the government made its own preference in these situations clear:[82]

---

[78] Remedial orders are normally subject to affirmative resolution but this may be avoided if the Minister certifies that a more urgent response is necessary. In the latter case, the remedial order will expire after 120 days unless it has been approved by an affirmative resolution of both Houses: Schedule 2.

[79] Wadham and Mountfield, *Blackstone's Guide to the Human Rights Act 1998* (2nd edn, 1999) at p 49.

[80] See, e.g., *R (on the Application of Alconbury) v Secretary of State for the Environment, Transport and the Regions* [2001] UKHL 23, [2003] 2 AC 295, [2001] 2 All ER 929, reversing [2001] HRLR 2; *Matthews v Ministry of Defence* [2002] EWCA Civ 773, [2002] 3 All ER 513, [2002] 1 WLR 2621, reversing [2002] EWHC 13, (2002) *The Times*, January 30; *Wilson v First County Trust (No 2)*; sub nom *Wilson v Secretary of State for Trade and Industry* [2003] UKHL 40, [2004] 1 AC 816, [2003] 4 All ER 97, reversing [2001] EWCA Civ 633, [2002] QB 74, [2001] 3 All ER 229.

[81] See p 165, *post*.

[82] Jack Straw MP (Home Secretary), 313 HC Official Report (6th series) coll 421–2, 3 June 1998. In *Ghaidan v Godin-Mendoza* [2004] UKHL 30 at [39], [2004] 2 AC 557 at [39], [2004] 3 All ER 411 Lord Steyn observed that in the first three and a half years of the Human Rights Act there had been at least as many declarations of incompatibility as there had been uses of section 3. On the basis of these statistics he suggested that the law may have taken 'a wrong turning'.

[W]e want the courts to strive to find an interpretation of legislation that is consistent with Convention rights, so far as the plain words of the legislation allow, and only in the last resort to conclude that the legislation is simply incompatible with them.

Nevertheless, the very existence of section 4 means that Parliament must have envisaged that a compatible interpretation would not always be 'possible'. The danger in placing so much emphasis on section 3 is that the courts may interpret Convention rights quite narrowly, in order to make a finding of compatibility easier. More generally, there is concern that some judges may be too ready to accept that an interference with a right is justifiable, thus avoiding the need to fully engage with either section.

In respect of the few declarations that have not been successfully challenged, the government has generally been prepared to take remedial action, and it has tended to opt for the mechanism of primary legislation. Thus, provisions of the Immigration and Asylum Act 1999 which were found to be incompatible with the Convention[83] were amended by the Nationality, Immigration and Asylum Act 2002, while laws which breached the Convention rights of transsexuals[84] were amended by the Gender Recognition Act 2004. In contrast, section 10 was used following the Court of Appeal's finding that provisions of the Mental Health Act 1983 were incompatible with the right to liberty under Article 5.[85] The Secretary of State was satisfied in this case that there were compelling reasons for acting quickly, and the offending provisions were amended by the Mental Health Act 1983 (Remedial) Order 2001.[86]

The government was presented with perhaps its most difficult Human Rights Act challenge to date by the decision of the House of Lords in *A* v *Secretary of State for the Home Department*.[87] The case was brought by a number of foreign nationals who had been detained without trial for almost three years under powers in the Anti-Terrorism, Crime and Security Act 2001.[88] The purpose of these powers was to enable the government to deal with those foreign nationals who were suspected of involvement in terrorism, but who could not be put on trial and who could not be deported for humanitarian reasons. The government had sought to pre-empt any legal challenge to these powers by derogating from the Article 5 right to liberty and security of the person.[89] However, by a majority of 8:1 their Lordships held that by singling out non-nationals for detention, the Act was interfering with the right to liberty in a

---

[83] *International Transport Roth GmbH* v *Secretary of State for the Home Department* [2002] EWCA Civ 158, [2003] QB 728, [2002] HRLR 31. The provisions imposed a fixed penalty on hauliers responsible for bringing illegal entrants into the UK and were found to be incompatible with Article 6 and with Article 1 of the First Protocol.

[84] The inability of transsexuals to marry in accordance with their 'new' gender was found to be incompatible with Articles 8 and 12 in both *Goodwin* v *UK* (2002) 35 EHRR 18 and *Bellinger* v *Bellinger* [2003] UKHL 21, [2003] 2 AC 467, [2003] 2 All ER 593.

[85] *R (on the application of H)* v *North and East London Regional Mental Health Review Tribunal* [2001] EWCA Civ 415, [2002] QB 1, [2001] 3 WLR 512. The provisions had effectively required a restricted patient seeking release from a secure hospital to prove that his continued detention was no longer warranted.

[86] SI 2001/3712.   [87] [2004] UKHL 56, [2005] 2 WLR 87.   [88] Section 23.

[89] The concept of derogation is discussed at p 172, *post*. The derogation in question was registered by the Secretariat General on 18 December 2001; SI 2001/ 4032.

discriminatory manner and was therefore in breach of both Article 5 *and* Article 14. The Court of Appeal had taken the view that the difference in treatment was justifiable because foreign nationals, unlike British nationals, had no right to remain in the UK.[90] In the House of Lords' view, however, the logic of this argument was flawed. Once it was accepted that the threat of terrorism was not confined to non-nationals, the different legal status of such persons could not provide an objective basis for the difference in treatment. A declaration of incompatibility was therefore granted, and the Order dealing with the derogation from Article 5 was quashed. The government did not release the detainees immediately but it did agree to seek alternative ways of dealing with them. Within three months the internment powers in the 2001 Act had been replaced with a system of 'control orders'. These control orders may involve restricting the movement or communications of suspected terrorists, but crucially they can be used in respect of both nationals and non-nationals.[91] The Home Office has also agreed to seek assurances about human rights from other states, so that more suspected foreign terrorists can be deported.[92]

(c) Section 19: Ministerial statements of compatibility[93]

The courts may be aided in their efforts under section 3 by ministerial statements made under section 19 of the Act. This provides that before the Second Reading of a Bill, the Minister in charge of it must either: (a) make a statement that in his view its provisions are compatible with Convention rights; or (b) make a statement that although it is *not* compatible, the government nevertheless wishes to proceed. The purpose of section 19 is presumably to aid the legislative process and to enable incompatible Bills to be subjected to heightened scrutiny. However, governments will inevitably be reluctant to declare that they are advocating Bills which infringe human rights. Indeed, virtually all of the statements made under section 19 have been to the effect that legislation is compatible,[94] and as the section does not require a Minister to explain *how* he arrived at his conclusion, the probative value of these statements is greatly limited. For this reason, they risk being seen as little more than labels of approval, which give no real indication as to the true human rights implications of the Bills concerned. Much will depend in practice on the willingness of MPs to engage with human rights issues, and to subject ministerial statements to proper scrutiny. The Joint Committee on Human Rights has an important role to play here:[95]

The Joint Committee . . . is able to monitor the operation of section 19 of the HRA speedily

---

[90] [2002] EWCA Civ 1502, [2004] QB 335, [2003] 1 All ER 816.

[91] Prevention of Terrorism Act 2005.

[92] Charles Clarke MP (Home Secretary), 430 HC Official Report (6th series) col 307, 26 January 2005.

[93] See also, p 73, *ante*.

[94] The knowledge that provisions of the Anti-Terrorism, Crime and Security Bill would almost certainly *not* be compatible led the government to announce a derogation from Article 5: see the discussion of *A v Secretary of State for the Home Department* [2004] UKHL 56, [2005] 2 WLR 87, above.

[95] Lester, 'Parliamentary Scrutiny Under the Human Rights Act 1998' [2002] 4 EHRLR 432, at 437.

and effectively, and reports to each House of Parliament its views as to the compatibility or lack of compatibility of legislative proposals.

The knowledge that a statement of compatibility must be made might also serve to concentrate the Minister's mind during the preparatory stages of a Bill. In addition, section 19 statements may be considered by the courts,[96] and it has been said that they will 'inevitably be a strong spur to the courts to find the means of construing statutes compatibly with the Convention.'[97] They are not, of course, binding, and a ministerial statement of compatibility does not prevent a court from making a declaration of *in*compatibility in the future. Nevertheless, the ministerial statement may give tacit encouragement to the judiciary to maximize the interpretive obligation under section 3. After all, if a Minister considers a Bill to be compatible, and Parliament enacts it on that basis, it might be suggested that Parliament must intend a compatible interpretation to be found.

3 DIRECT ENFORCEMENT OF CONVENTION RIGHTS

(a) Section 6: The duty of public authorities to act compatibly with the ECHR

Section 6(1) of the Act makes it unlawful for a public authority to act in a way which is incompatible with a Convention right. However, the authority will have a defence if it can be shown that:

(a) as the result of one or more provisions of primary legislation, the authority could not have acted differently; or

(b) in the case of one or more provisions of, or made under, primary legislation which cannot be read or given effect in a way which is compatible with the Convention rights, the authority was acting so as to give effect to or enforce those provisions.

The Act takes a functional approach to the meaning of 'public authority', and this means that even seemingly 'private' bodies may be subject to the Act if certain of their functions are public in nature.[98] A person or body may fall into one of three categories for these purposes: (1) 'standard' public authorities, which must act compatibly with the Convention at all times; (2) 'hybrid' or 'quasi-public' bodies, which are only caught by the Act when performing their public functions; and (3) private bodies, which are not subject to the duty under section 6(1) at all. The first category includes bodies such as government departments, the police, and local authorities, which are all self-evidently public in nature and present relatively few difficulties. The precise scope of the second category is rather more complex, and predictably the courts have

---

[96] *Wilson v First County Trust (No 2)*; *sub nom Wilson v Secretary of State for Trade and Industry* [2003] UKHL 40 at [61]-[67], [2004] 1 AC 816 at [61]-[67], [2003] 4 All ER 97, per Lord Nicholls.

[97] Lord Irvine of Lairg, 'The Development of Human Rights in Britain under an Incorporated Convention on Human Rights' [1998] PL 221.

[98] Section 6(3)(b)

drawn upon principles which were already established in the field of judicial review.[99] In one of its early Human Rights Act decisions, the Court of Appeal held that a registered social landlord was subject to section 6 in respect of its relationship with its tenants. The fact that the landlord performed functions which a public authority would otherwise have to carry out was relevant but not conclusive, and Lord Woolf CJ suggested that a private body providing such services would not always be performing a 'public function':[100]

What can make an act, which would otherwise be private, public, is a feature or a combination of features which impose a public character or stamp on the act. Statutory authority for what is done can at least help to mark the act as being public; so can the extent of control over the function exercised by another body which is a public authority. The more closely the acts that could be of a private nature are enmeshed in the activities of a public body, the more likely they are to be public. However, the fact that the acts are supervised by a public regulatory body does not necessarily indicate that they are of a public nature.

It was considered relevant that the housing association had been specifically created to take over a large proportion of residential council property.[101] It was also in receipt of state funding, had various statutory duties and was supervised by a statutory body. The Court of Appeal later distinguished this case when ruling that a care home run by a charitable foundation was *not* performing public functions.[102] This was the case even though a substantial proportion of the home's residents were funded by the local authority. More recently, the House of Lords held that a parochial church council was not performing public functions when exercising a statutory power to compel a landowner to repair a church chancel:[103]

It may be said that, as the church is a historic building which is open to the public, it is in the public interest that these repairs should be carried out. It is also true that the liability to repair the chancel rests on persons who need not be members of the church . . . But none of these factors leads to the conclusion that the PCC's act in seeking to enforce the lay rector's liability on behalf of the parishioners is a public rather than a private act. The nature of the act is to be found in the nature of the obligation which the PCC is seeking to enforce. It is seeking to enforce a civil debt. The function which it is performing has nothing to do with the responsibilities which are owed to the public by the State.

---

[99] See, e.g., *R v Panel on Takeovers and Mergers, ex parte Datafin* [1987] QB 815, [1987] 1 All ER 564. For a critique of the courts' approach to section 6, see Oliver, 'Functions of a Public Nature under the Human Rights Act' [2004] PL 329.

[100] *Poplar Housing and Regeneration Community Association Ltd v Donoghue* [2001] EWCA Civ 595 at [65], [2002] QB 48 at [65], [2001] 4 All ER 604.

[101] See also *R (on the application of Beer (t/a Hammer Trout Farm)) v Hampshire Farmers Markets Ltd* [2003] EWCA Civ 1056, [2004] 1 WLR 233: a company created by a local authority to manage a farmers' market was deemed to be exercising public functions when licensing stall-holders.

[102] *R (on the application of Heather) v Leonard Cheshire Foundation* [2002] EWCA Civ 366, [2002] 2 All ER 936.

[103] *Aston-Cantlow and Wilcote with Billesley Parochial Church Council v Wallbank* [2003] UKHL 37 at [64], [2004] 1 AC 546 at [64], [2003] 3 All ER 1213, per Lord Hope: see p 196, *post*.

Finally, section 6(3) of the Act makes it clear that neither House of Parliament constitutes a public authority for these purposes. Persons exercising functions in connection with proceedings in Parliament are also excluded. However, courts and tribunals are expressly *included* within the definition, and thus have an obligation to perform their functions in a manner compatible with Convention rights.

(b) Judicial deference and proportionality

In determining whether public authorities have acted in breach of Convention rights, the courts are required to assess the legitimacy of any interference with those rights and to measure the extent of the interference against the yardstick of proportionality. This concept is discussed further at p 170, but in essence it means that a balance must be struck between the general interests of the community and the rights of the individual,[104] and that any restriction on a right must be limited to the extent necessary to achieve a legitimate aim. The House of Lords confirmed at an early stage that the actions of public authorities in Human Rights Act cases must be measured against this principle of proportionality:[105]

First, the doctrine of proportionality may require the reviewing court to assess the balance which the decision maker has struck, not merely whether it is within the range of rational or reasonable decisions. Secondly, the proportionality test may go further than the traditional grounds of review inasmuch as it may require attention to be directed to the relative weight accorded to interests and considerations. Thirdly ... the intensity of the review ... is guaranteed by the twin requirements that the limitation of the right was necessary in a democratic society, in the sense of meeting a pressing social need, and the question whether the interference was really proportionate to the legitimate aim being pursued.

These principles require a different level of scrutiny to that traditionally applied in judicial review cases, and the debate about how much judicial deference should be paid to the executive in human rights cases is ongoing.[106] In a recent House of Lords' decision Lord Walker endorsed an earlier attempt by Laws LJ to establish some general principles:[107]

(1) greater deference is to be paid to an Act of Parliament than to a decision of the executive or subordinate measure;

---

[104] *Soering* v *UK* (1989) 11 EHRR 439.

[105] *R (on the application of Daly)* v *Secretary of State for the Home Department* [2001] UKHL 26 at [27], [2001] 2 AC 532 at [27], [2001] 3 All ER 433, per Lord Steyn. A blanket policy authorizing searches of a prisoner's cell and requiring his correspondence with his lawyer to be examined in his absence was *not* a proportionate response to the legitimate objective of maintaining prison discipline. (Judicial review is discussed further in chapter 6.)

[106] See Klug, 'Judicial Deference Under the Human Rights Act 1998' [2003] 2 EHRLR 125; Clayton, 'Judicial Deference and "Democratic Dialogue": the Legitimacy of Judicial Intervention under the Human Rights Act 1998' [2004] PL 33; Jowell, 'Judicial Deference: Servility, Civility or Institutional Incapacity?' [2003] PL 592; Edwards, 'Judicial Deference under the Human Rights Act' (2002) 65 MLR 859. See also, p 306, *post.*

[107] *R (on the application of ProLife Alliance)* v *BBC* [2003] UKHL 23 at [136], [2004] 1 AC 185 at [136], [2003] 2 All ER 977 (applying the judgment of Laws LJ in *International Transport Roth GmbH* v *Secretary of State for the Home Department* [2002] EWCA Civ 158, [2003] QB 728, [2002] HRLR 31).

(2) there is more scope for deference where the Convention itself requires a balance to be struck, much less so where the right is stated in terms which are unqualified;

(3) greater deference will be due to the democratic powers where the subject-matter in hand is peculiarly within their constitutional responsibility, and less when it lies more particularly within the constitutional responsibility of the courts;

(4) greater or less deference will be due according to whether the subject matter lies more readily within the actual or potential expertise of the democratic powers or the courts.

It is certainly the case that the courts have taken a more 'interventionist' stance under the 'due process' rights in Articles 5 and 6, which might be regarding as falling within their particular sphere of expertise. On the other hand, they have tended to concede a wider margin of discretion to Parliament and the executive under Articles such as 8 and 10, which require individual rights to be balanced against the public interest and which leave more scope for restrictions on policy grounds.[108] For this reason, Lord Hoffman has taken exception to the word 'deference' being used at all:[109]

I do not think that its overtones of servility, or perhaps gracious concession, are appropriate to describe what is happening . . . The principle that the independence of the courts is necessary for a proper decision of disputed legal rights or claims of violation of human rights is a legal principle. It is reflected in Article 6 of the Convention. On the other hand, the principle that majority approval is necessary for a proper decision on policy or allocation of resources is also a legal principle. Likewise, when a court decides that a decision is within the proper competence of the legislature or executive, it is not showing deference. It is deciding the law.

(c) Horizontal effect

In keeping with the scheme of the Convention, the Act does not oblige private bodies and individuals to act compatibly with Convention rights, and it does not expressly require the courts to give effect to the Convention in developing the common law. However, given that the courts are clearly under a general duty to perform their functions in accordance with the Convention, there was much academic speculation from the outset about whether the Human Rights Act would have 'indirect horizontal effect'.[110] In other words, would the courts be obliged to give effect to the Convention in developing the common law, and would this mean that Convention rights could be directly enforced against private individuals?

---

[108] The judicial application of individual Convention rights is discussed in Part 'C' of this chapter.

[109] *R (on the application of ProLife Alliance) v BBC* [2003] UKHL 23 at [75]–[76], [2004] 1 AC 185 at [75]–[76], [2003] 2 All ER 977.

[110] Buxton, 'The Human Rights Act and Private Law' (2000) 116 LQR 48; Hunt, 'The "Horizontal Effect" of the Human Rights Act' [1998] PL 424; Phillipson, 'The Human Rights Act: "Horizontal Effect" and the Common Law: A Bang or a Whimper?' (1999) 62(2) MLR 825; Wade, 'Horizons of Horizontality' (2000) 116 LQR 217.

It soon became apparent that Convention rights and principles would have an influence on judicial reasoning in common law cases. For example:[111]

If there is an intrusion in a situation in which a person can reasonably expect his privacy to be respected then that intrusion will be capable of giving rise to liability in an action for breach of confidence unless the intrusion can be justified.

Thus far, however, the courts have stopped short of recognizing any new common law torts, preferring instead to take the Convention into account when applying established torts such as breach of confidence and nuisance. Thus in *Wainwright v Home Office* the House of Lords held that a new tort of privacy could only be recognized by Parliament, but that the courts could develop existing torts and remedies in order to satisfy Article 8.[112]

(d) Section 7: Challenging public authorities under the Act

Where a person claims that a public authority has acted (or is proposing to act) in breach of Convention rights, proceedings may be brought against that authority under section 7(1)(a) of the Act. However, such proceedings can only be brought by a person who is able to show that he is (or would be) 'a victim of the unlawful act'. This is consistent with the criteria for bringing a Strasbourg application under Article 34 of the Convention, but it is rather stricter than the 'sufficient interest' test applied in conventional judicial review cases.[113] Public interest groups with a particular interest and expertise in an area may have standing to bring a judicial review action on conventional grounds, but they will not be considered 'victims' under the Human Rights Act unless they are actually affected by a Convention breach. The government considered that the Strasbourg approach would help to prevent the courts from becoming clogged up with test cases, and it rejected the suggestion that the 'victim' test could lead to injustice:[114]

If there is an unlawful action or if unlawful action is threatened, then there will be victims or potential victims who will complain and who will in practice be supported by interest groups. If there are no victims, the issue is probably academic and the courts should not be troubled.

In addition to being able to bring a direct action under section 7(1)(a), section 7(1)(b) allows a victim (or potential victim) of a Convention breach to raise the issue

---

[111] *A v B; H v Associated Newspapers* [2002] EWCA Civ 337 at [11], [2003] QB 195 at [11], [2002] 2 All ER 545, per Lord Woolf CJ. See also *Douglas v Hello! Ltd (No 1)* [2001] QB 967, [2001] 2 All ER 289; *Venables and Thompson v News Group Newspapers* [2001] Fam 430, [2001] 1 All ER 908.

[112] [2003] UKHL 53, [2004] 2 AC 406, [2003] 4 All ER 969. Cf. *Peck v UK* (2003) 36 EHRR 41, which revealed significant deficiencies in the ability of domestic law to safeguard the right to respect for private life: see p 187, *post*.

[113] See, e.g., *R v Inspectorate of Pollution, ex parte Greenpeace (No 2)* [1994] 4 All ER 329; *R v Secretary of State for Foreign and Commonwealth Affairs, ex parte World Development Movement* [1995] 1 WLR 386, [1995] 1 All ER 611. See also Marriott and Nicol, 'The Human Rights Act, Representative Standing and the Victim Culture' [1998] EHRLR 730.

[114] Lord Irvine (Lord Chancellor), 583 HL Official Report (5th series) col 832, 24 Nov 1997.

in proceedings which have been commenced on some other basis. Thus, a Convention issue may be raised by a party to a civil action involving a public authority, by a defendant in a criminal case, or by an applicant in a judicial review action based on other grounds. However, a 'judicial act' of a court or tribunal may only be challenged in judicial review proceedings or during the course of an appeal.[115] In addition, section 7(3) states that:

If the proceedings are brought on an application for judicial review, the applicant is to be taken to have a sufficient interest in relation to the unlawful act only if he is, or would be, a victim of that act.

This provision is designed to prevent public interest groups from circumventing the victim requirement by raising Convention issues in judicial review proceedings brought on other grounds. Nevertheless, a court conducting a judicial review of statutory powers will be obliged to seek a Convention-friendly interpretation of those powers, even if the applicant is not a 'victim'.[116] It would also appear that if a court accepts a judicial review application from a public interest group, it will be obliged to act compatibly with the Convention when conducting that review, in order to fulfil its own obligations under section 6.

The time limit for bringing an action under section 7 creates a further anomaly. Actions for judicial review must normally be brought within three months,[117] whereas section 7(5) specifies a one-year time limit for actions brought under section 7(1)(a).[118] In this respect, an applicant whose complaint is based solely on a breach of Convention rights appears to be in a better position than an applicant seeking review on both Convention and non-Convention grounds. In addition, it has been persuasively argued that claims under section 7(1)(a) need not necessarily be brought by way of judicial review at all, and that they could instead take the form of an action for breach of statutory duty.[119] The comments of the Under-Secretary of State for the Home Department during the committee stage of the Bill seem to support this view:[120]

Clause 7(1)(a) creates a cause of action, and the Bill would be open to criticism if it did not clearly state what limitation period was to apply to proceedings under that paragraph. As I

---

[115] Section 9(1).

[116] See, e.g., R (on the application of Rusbridger) v Attorney-General [2003] UKHL 38, [2004] 1 AC 357, [2003] 3 All ER 784. The House of Lords confirmed that the editor of the Guardian did not need to be a 'victim' in order to seek a declaration that s 3 of the Treason Felony Act 1848 was incompatible with the Convention. However, the action failed because the provision had not actually been applied and the issue was purely hypothetical: see p 191, post.

[117] See p 217, post.

[118] The courts have a discretion to allow a longer period if it is considered equitable.

[119] See, e.g. Fenwick, Civil Liberties and Human Rights (3rd edn, 2002) at p 168; Clayton and Tomlinson, Human Rights Law (2000) at p 1498.

[120] Mike O'Brien MP, 314 HC Official Report (6th series) coll 1095 and 1099, 24 June 1998. Mr O'Brien took the view that the standard three-month time limit would normally be appropriate if judicial review proceedings were used.

have said, we believe that the right balance is provided by a 12-month period, with the power to extend it for the benefit of the complainant. Suggestions for a two or three-year period fail to take account of the existing three-month period for judicial review, to which *many* claims under clause 7(1)(a) will be *similar*. [emphasis added]

Finally, section 7(6) confirms that Convention issues may be raised in proceedings brought by or at the instigation of a public authority, or in any appeal against the decision of a court or tribunal. Most of the Act's provisions did not come into force until 2 October 2000, and a section 7 claim may only be brought against a public authority in respect of acts occurring on or after this date. However, section 22(4) states that where proceedings are instigated or brought by a public authority, a breach of the Convention may be challenged under section 7(1)(b) whenever the act in question took place. In other words, a demonstrator arrested for a public order offence in September 2000 would have been entitled to raise issues based on Articles 10 or 11 in the course of his defence. In *R v Lambert*[121] however, the House of Lords gave a restrictive interpretation to this provision and held that where a person had actually been tried and convicted before the commencement of the Act, pre-commencement breaches of the Convention could not be raised in a subsequent appeal. Within months a differently constituted House suggested that *Lambert* had been wrongly decided, but it was nevertheless unwilling to overrule the decision.[122]

(e) Section 8: Remedies

Where a court or tribunal has found that a public authority has acted unlawfully under section 6(1), it may grant 'such relief or remedy, or make such order within its powers as it considers just and appropriate'.[123] An award of damages can only be made by a court which already has the power to award damages in civil proceedings,[124] and only where the court is satisfied that an award is necessary to afford 'just satisfaction'.[125] In exercising the power to award damages a court must take into account the principles applied by the European Court of Human Rights under Article 41 of the Convention.[126] Section 9(3) states that courts and tribunals cannot be liable in damages for judicial acts done in good faith unless there has been a breach of Article 5(5). Where there has been such a breach the award must be made against the Crown and the 'appropriate person'[127] must be joined to the proceedings.

---

[121] [2001] UKHL 37, [2002] 2 AC 545, [2001] 3 All ER 577.

[122] *R v Kansal (No 2)* [2001] UKHL 62, [2002] AC 69, [2002] 1 All ER 257.

[123] Section 8(1). For a discussion of when an award of damages might be 'just and appropriate', see *Anufrijeva v Southwark LBC* [2003] EWCA Civ 1406, [2004] QB 1124, [2004] 1 All ER 833. See also Hartshorne, 'The Human Rights Act 1998 and Damages for Non-Pecuniary Loss' [2004] EHRLR 660.

[124] Section 8(2).   [125] Section 8(3).   [126] Section 8(4).

[127] The 'appropriate person' is defined by s 9(5) to mean 'the Minister responsible for the court concerned, or a person or government department nominated by him'.

C CONVENTION RIGHTS[128]

1 THE NATURE OF THE RIGHTS PROTECTED

The Convention only imposes obligations on states and it is not possible to bring an action against a private individual at Strasbourg level. However, where an individual interferes with a Convention right the state may be liable if it has failed to take appropriate steps to protect that right or if it has failed to provide an adequate remedy. In *Earl Spencer* v *UK*[129] for example, the European Court of Human Rights was prepared to consider a claim based on alleged breaches of privacy by several newspapers, because the applicant had made an arguable case that UK law did not protect individual rights of privacy.

Most Convention rights are not absolute. Although the rights to freedom from torture and slavery are unqualified and non-derogable,[130] the other rights are subject to certain limitations, and in determining the permissible extent of these limitations the doctrines of proportionality and the margin of appreciation are both important.[131]

(a) Proportionality[132]

Inherent in the Convention is the principle that a fair balance must be struck between the general interests of the community and the individual's fundamental rights.[133] Where limitations on specific rights are permitted, they are usually expressed to be subject to a requirement of necessity, and this is given effect in the court's jurisprudence by the application of the principle of proportionality. For example, Article 10(2) states that any limitation on the right to freedom of expression must go no further than is 'necessary in a democratic society'. In other words, the restriction must conform to a 'pressing social need' and the interference must be proportionate to the legitimate aim pursued.[134]

This principle applies equally to the other qualified rights in the Convention. Thus in *Dudgeon* v *UK*,[135] laws criminalizing homosexual acts between consenting adult

---

[128] See Harris, O'Boyle and Warbrick, *Law of the European Convention on Human Rights* (1995); Janis, Kay and Bradley, *European Human Rights Law: Text and Materials* (2nd edn, 2000); Van Dijk and Van Hoof, *The Theory and Practice of the European Convention on Human Rights* (3rd edn, 1998); Mowbray, *Cases and Materials on the European Convention on Human Rights* (2000); Ovey and White (eds), *Jacobs and White: European Convention on Human Rights* (3rd edn, 2002); Gomien, Harris and Zwaak, *Law and Practice of the European Convention on Human Rights and the European Social Charter* (1996).

[129] (1998) 25 EHRR CD 105. The claim was ultimately unsuccessful because the applicants failed to demonstrate the inadequacy of domestic law. See also, *Halford* v *UK* (1997) 24 EHRR 523.

[130] See below.   [131] For the application of these principles in EC law, see p 123, *ante*.

[132] See Fordham and de la Mere, 'Identifying the Principles of Proportionality', in Jowell and Cooper (eds), *Understanding Human Rights Principles* (2001) at 27; Blake, 'Importing Proportionality: Clarification or Confusion?' [2002] 1 EHRLR 19.

[133] *Soering* v *UK* (1989) 11 EHRR 439.

[134] See *Sunday Times* v *UK* (1979–1980) 2 EHRR 245; *Handyside* v *UK* (1979) 1 EHRR 737.

[135] (1982) 4 EHRR 149.

males were contrary to the right to respect for private life under Article 8 because the impact of the laws failed the test of proportionality. This was so, notwithstanding the fact that the state was pursuing the 'legitimate aim' of protecting vulnerable young members of society. The House of Lords has confirmed that the actions of public authorities in Human Rights Act cases must be measured against the principle of proportionality, and that this involves a different level of scrutiny to that traditionally applied in judicial review cases.[136]

(b) The margin of appreciation

The 'margin of appreciation' describes the degree of deference shown to States in areas where there is room for discretion in the interpretation of Convention provisions. It arises most often in the context of the 'personal freedom' provisions in Articles 8 to 11,[137] since these are subject to a wide range of possible exceptions and there is room for disagreement about their scope. The principle was clearly articulated in the *Handyside* case:[138]

By reason of their direct and continuous contact with the vital forces of their countries, State authorities are in principle in a better position than the international judge to give an opinion on the exact content of these requirements as well as on the 'necessity' of a 'restriction' or 'penalty' intended to meet them.

The existence or non-existence of common ground between the states is an important factor in determining the extent of any national margin,[139] but opinion is divided as to whether the doctrine is really an appropriate response to European diversity and national sovereignty. In a partly dissenting judgment in *Z* v *Finland*, De Meyer J stated that:[140]

[W]here human rights are concerned, there is no room for a margin of appreciation which would enable the states to decide what is acceptable and what is not. On that subject the boundary not to be overstepped must be as clear and precise as possible. It is for the Court, not each state individually to decide that issue.

When deciding Human Rights Act cases, domestic courts are not required to apply Convention rights to a diverse group of states, and the margin of appreciation doctrine therefore has no application.[141] However, the role of the courts in reviewing the

---

[136] *R (on the application of Daly)* v *Secretary of State for the Home Department* [2001] UKHL 26, [2001] 2 AC 532, [2001] 3 All ER 433: see the quote from this decision at p 165, *ante*.

[137] See Yourrow, *The Margin of Appreciation Doctrine in the Dynamics of European Human Rights Jurisprudence* (1996).

[138] *Handyside* v *UK* (1979) 1 EHRR 737 at para 48.

[139] *Rasmussen* v *Denmark* (1984) 7 EHRR 371.

[140] (1997) 25 EHRR 371 at 415. Jones suggests that the doctrine 'can only . . . devalue Convention rights and freedoms at the expense of the limitations': 'The Devaluation of Human Rights Under the European Convention' [1995] PL 430, at 449. Cf. Schokkenbroek, 'The Basis, Nature and Application of the Margin of Appreciation Doctrine in the Case-Law of the European Court of Human Rights' (1998) 19(1) HRLJ 30.

[141] Singh et al, 'Is there a Role for the "Margin of Appreciation" in National Law after the Human Rights Act?' [1999] 1 EHRLR 15.

actions of public authorities is essentially supervisory, and although the standard of scrutiny under the Human Rights Act is a heightened one, decision-makers are still afforded a measure of discretion. This is particularly relevant in cases which hinge on whether a restriction on a Convention right is 'necessary',[142] though any restriction is, of course, subject to a requirement of proportionality.

(c) Derogation

Most Convention rights are subject to the possibility of derogation in times of war or other public emergency.[143] The UK entered a derogation in respect of Article 5 following the decision[144] that provisions of the Prevention of Terrorism (Temporary Provisions) Act 1984 were in breach of the Convention. At the time the UK deemed the situation in Northern Ireland to constitute an 'emergency threatening the life of the nation', and the European Court of Human Rights was not prepared to disagree with this assessment.[145] The provisions were eventually replaced by more stringent measures in the Terrorism Act 2000 and the derogation was withdrawn in February 2001. However, in December of the same year, the UK once again derogated from Article 5 in respect of the newly enacted power[146] to detain suspected foreign terrorists without trial. The public emergency this time was said to stem from the heightened threat of terrorism in the wake of September 11th and the presence of suspected international terrorists in the UK.[147] When this derogation was challenged, a majority of the House of Lords accepted the government's assertion that the UK was facing a public emergency, but in doing so they demonstrated far less deference than that generally exhibited by the Court of Human Rights:[148]

The courts' power to rule on the validity of the derogation is another of the safeguards [contained in the Human Rights Act 1998] . . . It would be meaningless if we could only rubber-stamp what the Home Secretary and Parliament have done. But any sensible court, like any sensible person, recognises the limits of its expertise. Assessing the strength of a general threat to the life of the nation is, or should be, within the expertise of the Government and its advisers. They may, as recent events have shown, not always get it right. But courts too do not always get things right. It would be very surprising if the courts were better able to make that sort of judgment than the Government. Protecting the life of the nation is one of the first tasks of a Government in a world of nation states. That does not mean that

---

[142] See e.g. *R (on the application of Samaroo)* v *Secretary of State for the Home Department* [2001] EWCA Civ 1139 [2001] UKHRR 1150.

[143] No derogation from Articles 3, 4(1) and 7 is possible. The right to life in Article 2 is only derogable in respect of 'deaths resulting from lawful acts of war'.

[144] *Brogan* v *UK* (1989) 11 EHRR 117.

[145] *Brannigan and McBride* v *UK* (1994) 17 EHRR 539.

[146] Anti-Terrorism, Crime and Security Act 2001, s 23. The power was limited to circumstances in which the suspect could not be deported because of the risk that he or she would face persecution or torture.

[147] Declaration registered by the Secretariat General on 18 December 2001.

[148] *A* v *Secretary of State for the Home Department* [2004] UKHL 56 at [226], [2005] 2 WLR 87 at [226], per Baroness Hale. Lord Hoffman dissented on this point, concluding at [96] that 'terrorist violence, serious as it is, does not threaten our institutions of government or our existence as a civil community'. Judicial deference under the Human Rights Act generally is discussed at p 165, *ante*.

the courts could never intervene. Unwarranted declarations of emergency are a familiar tool of tyranny. If a Government were to declare a public emergency where patently there was no such thing, it would be the duty of the court to say so. But we are here considering the immediate aftermath of the unforgettable events of 11 September 2001 . . .

The House of Lords concluded that the government had not demonstrated the necessity of singling out foreign nationals for detention in circumstances where some British nationals posed an equally serious threat. The derogation was thus held to be incompatible with the Convention, and the government's Derogation Order[149] was quashed.

2 SPECIFIC RIGHTS

(a) Article 2: The right to life

This states that 'everyone's right to life shall be protected by law' and that 'no-one shall be deprived of his life intentionally save in the execution of a sentence of a court following his conviction of a crime for which this penalty is provided by law'. This form of words originally allowed states to retain the use of capital punishment, but the possibility of imposing the death penalty in peace time has effectively been removed by Protocol 6. Acceptance of this Protocol is now mandatory,[150] and as of 1 February 2005, only Russia and Monaco had still to ratify it. Thirty states, including the UK, had also ratified the more extensive provisions in Protocol 13, which ban the use of the death penalty in *any* circumstances.

The remaining limitations on the right to life permit the use of force where this is necessary to defend a person from unlawful violence, to effect a lawful arrest, to prevent the escape of a lawfully detained person, or to quell a riot or insurrection. In *McCann* v *UK*[151] the SAS shot and killed three members of the Provisional IRA who were suspected of planning a terrorist attack in Gibraltar. Although the court accepted that force had been used in pursuit of a legitimate aim, it found a violation of the Convention because it was not persuaded that the use of lethal force had been absolutely necessary.[152] Where a state is mounting a legitimate security operation, a breach of Article 2 will be established if the state does not take all reasonable precautions to avoid or minimise loss of life.[153] However, no violation was found in *Stewart* v *UK*[154]

---

[149] Human Rights Act (Amendment No 2) Order 2001, SI 2001/ 4032. Further derogations from Article 5 are contemplated by the Prevention of Terrorism Act 2005, which replaced the internment powers with a system of control orders: see p 179, *post*.

[150] Parliamentary Assembly, Resolution 1044 (1994).

[151] (1996) 21 EHRR 97. See also *Kelly* v *UK* (1993) 74 D & R 139 (the use of fatal force against a joyrider attempting to evade an army checkpoint).

[152] Cf. *Brady* v *UK* (2001) App 55151/00: the police shooting of an unarmed robbery suspect did not give rise to an admissible Article 2 claim because the officer had genuinely and reasonably believed that the suspect was reaching for a gun.

[153] *Ergi* v *Turkey* (2001) 32 EHRR 18.   [154] (1985) 7 EHRR CD 453.

when a thirteen year-old boy was killed by plastic baton rounds fired into a crowd during a riot.

Article 2 imposes a procedural obligation to investigate deaths caused by state action or while the deceased was in the state's care. In *Jordan* v *UK*[155] the Court of Human Rights ruled that the holding of an inquest does not discharge this obligation, because an inquest is not a forum for determining the identity or culpability of those responsible for causing death. This decision triggered the government's Review of Coroner Services,[156] along with several domestic cases. In *R (on the application of Amin)* v *Secretary of State for the Home Department*[157] an inquest was held to be an inadequate forum to investigate the death of a prisoner at the hands of his racist cellmate. An inquest into the death of a prisoner who was suffering from heroin withdrawal was also unsatisfactory, because the jury was not invited to consider a verdict of systemic neglect.[158] Similarly, a breach of Article 2 was established in *Finucane* v *UK*, because allegations that RUC officers had colluded in the murder of a solicitor were not properly investigated.[159] However, the House of Lords has held that a failure to investigate a death under Article 2 can only be challenged at domestic level where the death in question occurred after the Human Rights Act came into force.[160]

In *Osman* v *UK*[161] the Court of Human Rights confirmed that Article 2 may impose a positive duty on states to protect life. The case challenged the failure of the police to arrest a teacher who was known to have formed an obsessive attachment to a former pupil. The teacher subsequently shot and killed the boy's father but the court found no breach of Article 2 on the facts, stating that:[162]

[W]here there is an allegation that the authorities have violated their positive obligation to protect the right to life . . . it must be established . . . that the authorities knew or ought to have known at the time of the existence of a real and immediate risk to the life of an identified individual or individuals . . . and that they failed to take measures within the scope of their powers which, judged reasonably, might have been expected to avoid that risk.

This dictum was instrumental in persuading the High Court to grant injunctions to the killers of James Bulger upon their release from prison. The court accepted that the applicants would face a real threat of revenge attacks if their whereabouts and new identities were revealed, and it granted permanent injunctions to prevent the media

---

[155] (2003) 37 EHRR 2 (an unarmed member of the Provisional IRA shot by RUC officers): see Ní Aoláin, 'Truth Telling, Accountability and the Right to Life in Northern Ireland' [2002] 5 EHRLR 572.

[156] See p 268, *post*.

[157] [2003] UKHL 51, [2004] 1 AC 653, [2003] 4 ALL ER 1264. See also *R on the application of Khan)* v *Secretary of State for Health* [2003] EWCA Civ 1129, [2004] 1 WLR 971, [2003] 4 All ER 1239 (Article 2 breached because of a failure to provide funds enabling Mr Khan to be legally represented at his daughter's inquest). These decisions prompted an amendment to the exceptional funding provisions in the Access to Justice Act 1999.

[158] *R (on the application of Davies)* v *HM Deputy Coroner for Birmingham* [2003] EWCA Civ 1739, [2004] HRLR 13: a finding of accidental death had been reached.

[159] (2003) 37 EHRR 29.

[160] *Re McKerr's application for judicial review* [2004] UKHL 12, [2004] 1 WLR 807, [2004] 2 All ER 409.

[161] (2000) 29 EHRR 245.   [162] Ibid at para 116.

from publishing this information.[163] The House of Lords has also emphasized that the right to life must underpin any determination of asylum applications.[164] In general however, it seems that a failure to *protect* life will only breach Article 2 if the authorities knew or should have known of an imminent and specific threat. In *Younger* v *UK*[165] a failure to prevent a suicide in police custody did not violate the right to life because the police had no prior knowledge that the deceased was a suicide risk. In contrast, a failure to protect a mentally ill prisoner from being kicked to death by his cellmate did give rise to a breach of Article 2.[166]

Finally, the European Court of Human Rights[167] has confirmed the decision in *R (on the application of Pretty)* v *DPP*[168] that Article 2 does not guarantee the right to *end* life. The applicant was suffering from motor neurone disease and was said to have only months left to live. She wanted to end her own life so as to avoid further suffering and loss of dignity, but she was physically unable to commit suicide alone and the DPP refused to undertake not to prosecute her husband if he assisted. Both the House of Lords and the Strasbourg court stressed that Article 2 was concerned with the *protection* of life, and that it did not confer any right to die. However, Article 2 does not prevent a state from permitting the carrying out of lawful abortions;[169] nor does it prevent surgery to separate conjoined twins which will inevitably result in the death of one of them, but which is necessary to preserve the life of the other.[170]

(b) Article 3: The prohibition of torture and inhuman or degrading treatment

Article 3 is concerned with different levels of ill treatment. 'Degrading treatment' is treatment which grossly humiliates a person beyond the level of humiliation inherent in any punishment, or which drives him to act against his own will or conscience. 'Inhuman treatment' involves the causing of physical or mental suffering. 'Torture' is an aggravated form of deliberate inhuman treatment, which causes 'very serious and cruel suffering'.[171] Article 3 has been used on several occasions to provide a standard against which the treatment of suspects and prisoners can be judged. In *Ireland* v *UK* the use of certain interrogation techniques on suspected terrorists was found to constitute degrading treatment.[172] Article 3 was also breached in *Keenan* v

---

[163] *Venables and Thompson* v *News Group Newspapers* [2001] Fam 430, [2001] 1 All ER 908.

[164] *R (on the application of Sivakumar)* v *Home Secretary* [2003] UKHL 14, [2003] 2 All ER 1097, [2003] 1 WLR 840.

[165] (2003) App 57420/00.   [166] *Edwards* v *UK* (2002) 35 EHRR 19.

[167] *Pretty* v *UK* (2002) 35 EHRR 1. Claims under Articles 3, 8, 9, and 14 were also rejected. Mrs Pretty died from her illness twelve days after this decision. For an extended analysis see Morris, 'Assisted Suicide Under the European Convention on Human Rights: a Critique' [2003] 1 EHRLR 65.

[168] [2001] UKHL 61, [2002] 1 AC 800, [2002] 1 All ER 1.

[169] *Open Door Counselling* v *Ireland* (1993) 15 EHRR 244.

[170] *Re A (Children) (Conjoined Twins: Surgical Separation)* [2001] Fam 147, [2000] 4 All ER 961.

[171] *Ireland* v *UK* (1979) 2 EHRR 25.

[172] Ibid. Detainees were forced to wear hoods, to stand against a wall in an uncomfortable position, to go without food, drink and sleep for long periods, and to endure loud and continuous noise. In some cases the treatment of prisoners has been sufficiently cruel and severe to constitute torture: see *Aydin* v *Turkey* (1998) 25 EHRR 251 (the rape of a detainee by an official); *Aksoy* v *Turkey* (1997) 23 EHRR 553 (being stripped naked, hung by the arms, beaten and subjected to electric shocks).

UK,[173] when the authorities failed to provide adequate medical care to a mentally ill prisoner who eventually committed suicide. By contrast, the House of Lords[174] found no breach of this Article when a mentally ill defendant was sentenced to life imprisonment following his conviction for a second serious offence.

The positive obligations imposed by Article 3 have been addressed in several immigration and asylum cases. Thus, in *Chahal* v *UK* it was held that to deport a Sikh separatist leader to India, in the face of a real risk that he would be ill-treated, would amount to a violation of Article 3.[175] Similarly, in *R (on the application of Q)* v *Secretary of State for the Home Department*, it was held that certain procedural safeguards must be met before late asylum seekers could lawfully be deprived of state support.[176] Article 3 was also the basis of a successful challenge to the designation of Pakistan as a safe third country.[177]

The Article has also been used in more novel ways. In has been held, for example, that it may be breached by extraditing a man to a country where he could face the death penalty,[178] or by deporting an AIDS sufferer to a country with inadequate medical facilities.[179] The Article has even been considered in the context of a failure to protect an applicant from domestic violence,[180] and in relation to the use of corporal punishment in schools[181] and homes.[182]

(c) Article 4: Prohibition of slavery and forced labour

Very few cases have arisen under Article 4 and none of them have been successful. The most significant case thus far is *Van der Mussele* v *Belgium*,[183] in which a lawyer challenged his obligation to provide free legal services to clients who could not afford to pay for them. His claim failed because he knew when he chose to become a barrister that he would be expected to do some pro bono work.

There may be scope for using Article 4 in the context of human trafficking,[184] since those who are helped to gain clandestine entry into other states often find themselves coerced or forced into economically exploitative situations. Article 4 would arguably be engaged if it could be established that a state had failed to protect individuals from

---

[173] (2001) 33 EHRR 38 (the family's claim under Article 2 was unsuccessful).

[174] *R* v *Drew* [2003] UKHL 25, [2003] 4 All ER 557, [2003] 1 WLR 1213.

[175] (1996) 23 EHRR 413. See also *Hilal* v *UK* (2001) 33 EHRR 2; *McPherson* v *Secretary of State for the Home Department* [2001] EWCA Civ 1955, [2002] INLR 139.

[176] [2003] EWCA Civ 364, [2004] QB 36, [2003] 2 All ER 905. Support had been denied to six applicants under s 55 of the Nationality, Immigration and Asylum Act 2002, on the grounds that their asylum claims had not been made as soon as reasonably practicable after arrival in the UK.

[177] *R* v *Secretary of State for the Home Department, ex parte Javed* [2001] EWCA Civ 789, [2002] QB 129.

[178] *Soering* v *UK* (1989) 11 EHRR 439.   [179] *D* v *UK* (1997) 24 EHRR 423.

[180] *Z* v *UK* (2002) 34 EHRR 3 (failure to remove children from a home environment in which they were known to be neglected and abused).

[181] *Tyrer* v *UK* (1979–1980) 2 EHRR 1; *Costello-Roberts* v *UK* (1995) 19 EHRR 112.

[182] *A* v *UK* (1999) 27 EHRR 611; *R* v *H (Reasonable Chastisement)* [2001] EWCA Crim 1024, [2001] 2 FLR 431, [2002] 1 Cr App R 7.

[183] (1984) 6 EHRR 163.

[184] See Drew, 'Human Trafficking: A Modern Form of Slavery?' [2002] 4 EHRLR 481.

a specific, known risk of exploitation. As yet however, the potential for using Article 4 in this way is untested.

(d) Article 5: The right to liberty and security of the person

Article 5 provides that no-one shall be deprived of his liberty save in accordance with a procedure prescribed by law and for one of the purposes specified in Article 5(1). These purposes include: (a) detention after conviction; (b) arrest or detention for failing to comply with a court order or legal obligation; and (c) arrest or detention for the purpose of bringing a person before a competent legal authority on reasonable suspicion of having committed an offence. With regard to the latter, the requirement for 'reasonable suspicion' is an essential safeguard against arbitrary detention. An 'honest belief' that an offence has been committed will not suffice,[185] and this raises doubts about the legitimacy of those police powers that do not depend upon a reasonable suspicion.[186] The power to arrest for breach of the peace has also been challenged, but the Strasbourg court has found it to be compatible with Article 5— even though breach of the peace is not 'an offence' in domestic law.[187]

Article 5 lists a number of procedural safeguards for the benefit of those lawfully detained: an arrested person must be informed promptly of the reasons for his detention in a language which he understands, and he must be brought promptly before a judge. A detainee is also entitled to trial within a reasonable time, or to release pending trial, and he must have the right to challenge his detention. These requirements have had a significant impact on the procedures for making decisions about life prisoners in England and Wales. In *Thynne, Wilson and Gunnell v UK*[188] the Court of Human Rights ruled that those serving discretionary life sentences were entitled to periodic reviews to determine whether their continued detention could be justified. A similar conclusion was reached in respect of juveniles detained at Her Majesty's Pleasure.[189] The Home Secretary's involvement in setting the 'tariff' in such cases was also contrary to Article 5(4), because it meant that the period of detention was not controlled by a court.[190] Following these decisions, new arrangements were put in

---

[185] *Fox, Campbell and Hartley v UK* (1991) 13 EHRR 157; cf. *Murray v UK* (1995) 19 EHRR 193 (mere suspicion sufficient in circumstances where officers could demonstrate an objective basis).

[186] Mead, 'The Likely Effect of the Human Rights Act on Everyday Policing Decisions in England and Wales' (2000) 5(1) J Civ Lib 5; Fenwick, *Civil Liberties and Human Rights* (3rd edn, 2002) at pp 775–7. Both authors also suggest that stop and search powers may lack a legitimate Article 5 purpose, although in *R (on the application of Gillan) v Commissioner of Police for the Metropolis* [2004] EWCA Civ 1067, [2004] 3 WLR 114, the Court of Appeal concluded that a *brief* detainment under stop and search powers would not amount to a deprivation of liberty at all.

[187] *Steel v UK* (1999) 28 EHRR 603; see *Williamson v Chief Constable of West Midlands* [2003] EWCA Civ 337, [2004] 1 WLR 14. Any detention beyond the period necessary to prevent an imminent breach of the peace or to bring a person before magistrates will be unlawful: *R (on the application of Laporte) v Chief Constable of Gloucester* [2004] EWHC 253 (Admin), [2004] 2 All ER 874 (affirmed on appeal, though without express reliance on Article 5: [2004] EWCA Civ 1639, [2005] 1 All ER 473).

[188] (1991) 13 EHRR 666.   [189] *Hussain and Singh v UK* (1996) 22 EHRR 1.

[190] *T and V v UK* (2000) 30 EHRR 121. The 'tariff' is the minimum prison term that must be served before a person can be considered for parole. This element of the sentence is intended to satisfy the demands of retribution and deterrence. It is now known as the 'minimum term': see the Criminal Justice Act 2003, s 269.

place for determining and reviewing the detention of discretionary life prisoners and those detained at Her Majesty's Pleasure.[191]

Mandatory life sentences were thought to raise different issues because the Strasbourg court had previously found that they were not indeterminate and did not need to be periodically reviewed.[192] However, in *Stafford* v *UK*[193] the Court concluded that there was no material difference between discretionary and mandatory life prisoners. In both cases the setting of the tariff was a sentencing exercise, and Articles 5 and 6 required that it should be performed by a court. Mr Stafford had in fact been released on life licence, but the Home Secretary had revoked the licence following his conviction for fraud. This also violated Article 5, because the original life sentence could not authorize a further period of detention for an unrelated, non-violent offence.[194] Shortly after this decision, the House of Lords concluded that it was impossible to interpret the mandatory life sentence powers in a manner compatible with Article 6 without doing 'judicial vandalism' to the legislation.[195] It therefore issued a declaration of incompatibility. Provisions to bring the arrangements for mandatory life prisoners into line with these judgments were included in Part 12 of the Criminal Justice Act 2003.[196]

Article 5 issues have also been raised in relation to the detention of suspected terrorists. In *Brogan* v *UK*[197] laws allowing suspected terrorists to be detained for up to seven days without being brought before a judicial authority were found to breach Article 5. Instead of amending the offending legislation the government derogated from Article 5,[198] and the derogation remained in force until February 2001. The withdrawal of the derogation followed the decision to replace the existing anti-terror laws with the Terrorism Act 2000. Section 41 of this Act continues to permit detention without charge for up to seven days, but judicial authority must now be obtained where the period of detention exceeds forty-eight hours.

The UK entered a further derogation from Article 5 following the enactment of the Anti-Terrorism, Crime and Security Act 2001.[199] This Act provided that where

---

[191] Crime (Sentences) Act 1997, s 28; Powers of Criminal Courts (Sentencing) Act 2000, ss 82A, 90.

[192] *Wynne* v *UK* (1995) 19 EHRR 333; see also *R* v *Secretary of State for the Home Department, ex parte Hindley* [2001] 1 AC 410, [2000] 2 All ER 385.

[193] (2002) 35 EHRR 32.

[194] See also *Waite* v *UK* (2003) 36 EHRR 54 (revocation of licence following conviction for further offences); *R (on the application of Giles)* v *Parole Board* [2003] UKHL 42, [2004] 1 AC 1, [2003] 4 All ER 429 (no breach of Article 5(4) in respect of judicial powers to impose an extended determinate sentence on public safety grounds).

[195] *R (on the application of Anderson)* v *Secretary of State for the Home Department* [2002] UKHL 46 at [30], [2003] 1 AC 837 at [30], [2002] 4 All ER 1089, per Lord Bingham. The provision was the Crime (Sentences) Act 1997, s 29. See Amos, 'R v Secretary of State for the Home Department, ex parte Anderson: Ending the Home Secretary's Sentencing Role' (2004) 67(1) MLR 108; see also p 154, *ante*.

[196] See p 673, *post*

[197] (1989) 11 EHRR 117; Prevention of Terrorism (Temporary Provisions) Act 1984, s 14.

[198] The derogation was unsuccessfully challenged in *Brannigan and McBride* v *UK* (1994) 17 EHRR 539; see p 000, *ante*. See also *Ireland* v *UK* (1979) 2 EHRR 25.

[199] Declaration registered by the Secretariat General on 18 December 2001; SI 2001/ 4032.

a foreign national was suspected of terrorism but could not be deported on humanitarian grounds, the Secretary of State could certify that he was believed to present a threat to national security. The suspect could then be detained indefinitely, without trial. The government sought to pre-empt any legal challenge to this provision by derogating from Article 5 immediately, but in *A v Secretary of State for the Home Department*[200] the House of Lords nevertheless made a declaration of incompatibility. It held that by singling out non-nationals for detention the Act was interfering with the right to liberty in a discriminatory manner, and that it was therefore in breach of Articles 5 *and* 14. The government's response was the Prevention of Terrorism Act 2005, which replaces the interment powers with a system of control orders. This Act avoids the element of discrimination inherent in the earlier legislation, by providing that the new powers may be exercised against any person suspected on reasonable grounds of involvement in terrorism-related activity. Nevertheless, the range of controls permitted by the Act will have serious consequences for the liberties of those affected. The list of possible obligations contemplated by section 1 is long and non-exhaustive. It includes, inter alia: (a) prohibitions or restrictions on being in particular places or areas at specified times; (b) restrictions on movement to, from and within the United Kingdom; (c) restrictions regarding residence; (d) restrictions relating to work or business; and (e) restrictions on associating or communicating with others. It is clear then that the anti-terror laws will continue to interfere with the right to liberty as set out in Article 5, and on this basis the 2005 Act allows for further derogations to be made.

Article 5(1)(e) expressly permits the lawful detention of persons of unsound mind, but the state must demonstrate an objective and reliable basis for the detention, and it must be subject to periodic review.[201] In a 2001 case[202] the Court of Appeal declared provisions of the Mental Health Act 1983 to be incompatible with Article 5, because the patient bore the burden of proving that his continued detention was no longer necessary. The Act was subsequently amended by remedial order.[203] Following the decisions in *Stafford* and *Anderson*, a further declaration of incompatibility was made in *R (on the application of D) v Secretary of State for the Home Department*,[204] because the Act failed to provide an adequate right of review to restricted patients serving prison sentences. Consequently, further amendments to the Act were made by the Criminal Justice Act 2003.[205]

Article 5(1)(f) also permits the detention of persons pending deportation or extradition, and for the purpose of preventing unauthorized entry into the country. In *R (on the application of Saadi) v Secretary of State for the Home Department* the policy of

---

[200] *A v Secretary of State for the Home Department* [2004] UKHL 56, [2005] 2 WLR 87. For more detailed discussion, see pp 161 and 308, *ante*.

[201] *Johnson v UK* (1997) 27 EHRR 296.

[202] *R (on the application of H) v North and East London Regional Mental Health Review Tribunal* [2001] EWCA Civ 415, [2002] QB 1, [2001] 3 WLR 512.

[203] Mental Health Act 1983 (Remedial) Order 2001, SI 2001/3712.

[204] [2002] EWHC 2805 (Admin), [2003] 1 WLR 1315.   [205] See ss 294 and 295.

detaining asylum seekers at 'reception centres' was challenged, on the basis that it affects those whose applications have yet to be determined, and in respect of whom no decision to deport has been taken.[206] However, the House of Lords held that as asylum applicants were only detained where there was a reasonable belief that they might abscond, the policy was a lawful and proportionate means of controlling entry.

(e) Article 6: The right to a fair trial

Article 6(1) concerns the right to a fair trial, the main elements of which are: (a) a fair and public hearing; (b) an independent and impartial tribunal; (c) a trial within a reasonable period of time; (d) a public judgment; and (e) a reasoned decision. It applies to all proceedings which involve a criminal charge or the determination of civil rights and obligations. A broad view is taken of what constitutes 'civil rights and obligations', and it is not confined to matters regarded as 'civil' for other purposes. Administrative decisions affecting 'personal, economic and individual' rights are also covered,[207] and this means that decisions relating to social security,[208] planning,[209] care proceedings,[210] and welfare payments[211] have all been held to engage Article 6(1). Conventional wisdom suggests that the extent of any discretion in conferring a benefit is crucial to the question of whether a 'right' exists,[212] but the Convention juris-prudence is not entirely consistent.[213] The English courts have indicated a willingness to go further than Strasbourg in extending due process obligations to a range of 'public law' matters. However, they have also expressed concern that administrative decisions should not be subjected to an unreasonable level of review. In one recent case[214] a decision that a homeless person had unreasonably been refused accommodation was *assumed* to engage Article 6(1), but the point was left open for future consideration.

The term 'criminal' also has an autonomous meaning for Article 6 purposes: the content of what is alleged and the nature of any penalty must be taken into account.[215] Proceedings for non-payment of council tax[216] and for binding over to keep the peace[217] are both considered to be 'criminal'. However, proceedings relating

---

[206] [2002] UKHL 41, [2002] 4 All ER 785, [2002] 1 WLR 3131.

[207] *Feldbrugge* v *Netherlands* (1986) 8 EHRR 425 at para. 37.   [208] Ibid.

[209] *R (on the Application of Alconbury)* v *Secretary of State for the Environment, Transport and the Regions* [2001] UKHL 23, [2003] 2 AC 295, [2001] 2 All ER 929.

[210] *McMichael* v *UK* (1995) 20 EHRR 205.   [211] *Mennitto* v *Italy* (2002) 34 EHRR 48.

[212] Cf. *O'Rourke* v *Camden LBC* [1998] AC 188, [1997] 3 All ER 23, where the existence of a discretion was a key factor in persuading the House of Lords that provisions of the Housing Act 1985 could not be subject to a private law action for damages; see p 33, *ante*.

[213] It is difficult to see, for example, why social security decisions are protected by Article 6(1), but not taxation decisions.

[214] *Begum (Runa)* v *Tower Hamlets* [2003] UKHL 5, [2003] 2 AC 430, [2003] 1 All ER 731. See Loveland, 'Does Homelessness Decision-Making Engage Article 6(1) of the ECHR?' [2003] 2 EHRLR 176; Craig, 'The Human Rights Act, Article 6 and Procedural Rights' [2003] PL 753.

[215] *Engel* v *The Netherlands (No 1)* (1979–1980) 1 EHRR 647.

[216] *Benham* v *UK* (1996) 22 EHRR 293.

[217] *Steel* v *UK* (1999) 28 EHRR 603. Cf. *Williamson* v *Chief Constable of West Midlands* [2003] EWCA Civ 337, [2004] 1 WLR 14. The civil/criminal distinction is discussed at p 13, *ante*.

to anti-social behaviour orders,[218] the forfeiture of goods seized by customs and excise,[219] and the confiscation of the proceeds of criminal activity,[220] are not. Additional safeguards for the benefit of those charged with a criminal offence are set out in Article 6(2) and 6(3). These include the presumption of innocence, the right to be promptly informed of the nature of any charges, the right to adequate time and legal assistance in preparing a defence, and the right to call and examine witnesses.

Article 6 provides an important yardstick against which to measure any aspect of the trial process, and it has generated far more case law than any other Convention right. The idea that there should be equality of arms between the parties to an action is an important theme. Amongst other things, it entails an obligation to ensure the disclosure of relevant evidence,[221] the ability to challenge that evidence,[222] and the ability to participate effectively in the proceedings. The latter requirement may be breached where a child is tried in an adult court[223] or where language difficulties prevent a party to an action from fully understanding the proceedings.[224] Article 6 may also be breached by the operation of certain evidential rules,[225] or by the admission of unfairly or covertly obtained evidence.[226] The right of unimpeded access to legal advice is also fundamental,[227] and the availability of legal aid is an important factor here. The requirement for legal aid to be available is more explicit where criminal charges are involved,[228] but the Court of Human Rights recently found a breach of Article 6(1) when legal aid was denied to the defendants in a complex libel action.[229] The 'McLibel Two' were sued for libel after distributing leaflets containing allegations about the fast-food giant, McDonalds. Legal aid is generally unavailable in

---

[218] *R (on the application of McCann)* v *Manchester Crown Court and others* [2002] UKHL 39, [2003] 1 AC 787, [2002] 4 All ER 593.

[219] *R (on the application of Mudie)* v *Dover Magistrates' Court* [2003] EWCA Civ 237, [2003] QB 1238, [2003] 2 All ER 631.

[220] *R* v *Benjafield* [2002] UKHL 2, [2003] 1 AC 1099, [2002] 1 All ER 815.

[221] *Edwards* v *UK* (1992) 15 EHRR 417; *Rowe and Davis* v *UK* (2000) 30 EHRR 1.

[222] *R* v *A (No 2)* [2001] UKHL 25, [2002] 1 AC 45, [2001] 3 All ER 1.

[223] *T and V* v *UK* (2000) 30 EHRR 121.

[224] *Cuscani* v *UK* (2003) 36 EHRR 2. Cf. *Williams* v *Cowell (t/a The Stables)* [2000] 1 WLR 187, [2000] ICR 85 (the refusal of the EAT to conduct its proceedings in Welsh did not prevent the applicant from having a fair trial because he was perfectly able to understand and speak English.)

[225] *Trivedi* v *UK* (1997) App 31700/96 (exceptions to the hearsay rule); *Hoare* v *UK* (1997) App 31211/96 (the availability of expert evidence): both applications were found to be inadmissible on the facts.

[226] *R* v *Looseley; sub nom Attorney-General's Reference (No 3 of 2000)* [2001] UKHL 53, [2001] 4 All ER 897 (entrapment); *Teixeira de Castro* v *Portugal* (1999) 28 EHRR 101 (entrapment); *Khan* v *UK* (2001) 31 EHRR 45 (use of a covert listening device breached Article 8 but not Article 6); *Allan* v *UK* (2003) 36 EHRR 12 (placing an informant in a cell to obtain a confession infringed the privilege against self-incrimination); *R* v *Veneroso* [2002] Crim LR 306 (drugs found while officers were illegally on the defendant's premises were inadmissible on the basis of Article 8, though the judge indicated that the outcome might have been different if semtex had been found.).

[227] *Brennan* v *UK* (2002) 34 EHRR 18 (Article 6 breached by the presence of a police officer at a meeting between the defendant and his solicitor); *P, C and S* v *UK* (2002) 35 EHRR 31 (refusal to adjourn proceedings to free a child for adoption in order to allow the mother to obtain legal advice).

[228] See Article 6(2)(c); *Benham* v *UK* (1996) 22 EHRR 293.

[229] *Steel and Morris* v *UK* (2005) App 68416/01.

defamation cases, and although the defendants received some help from volunteer lawyers, they represented themselves throughout the trial. The trial itself lasted for two and a half years, and became the longest running action in English legal history. The Court held that whether legal aid was necessary for a fair civil trial had to be determined on a case by case basis. In this case the complexity of the issues, the potential severity of the consequences,[230] and the capacity of the applicants to defend themselves effectively against the lawyers and resources of McDonalds, had all contributed to an unacceptable inequality of arms.

Several cases have examined the requirement for an 'independent and impartial tribunal', and decisions on this aspect of Article 6 have had a considerable influence on the English legal system. The principle that decisions should be free from bias is well established in English law, but when the Human Rights Act came into force the Court of Appeal held that a 'modest adjustment' to the existing test was needed.[231] Article 6 was also instrumental in bringing about reforms to the procedures for dealing with life prisoners,[232] and the Armed Forces Act 1996 pre-empted a finding that the courts-martial system lacked sufficient guarantees of independence.[233] In addition, following the decision in *Lawal* v *Northern Spirit*,[234] barristers will no longer be used as part-time EAT judges. However, it is the decision in *McGonnell* v *UK*[235] that may prove to be the most significant. The facts of the case were that the Guernsey Royal Court Bailiff had adjudicated in a planning case, having also been involved in making the applicable legislation. The Court concluded that this amounted to a breach of Article 6, and although the decision was not concerned with wider constitutional issues, it had clear implications for both the Appellate Committee of the House of Lords and the office of Lord Chancellor. It is partly because of this decision that the government was persuaded of the need to reform both institutions, and its proposals for doing so form the basis of the Constitutional Reform Act 2005.[236]

The question of whether a trial has taken place within a 'reasonable time' can only be resolved by reference to both the circumstances of the case and the complexity of the issues. In one case, a nine year delay in resolving a tribunal action was held to constitute a breach of Article 6,[237] but in *R* v *James (David John)*, a five year delay in dealing with a complicated fraud case was not considered unreasonable.[238] The principle that justice should be seen to be done is also highly valued, but it is subject to the

---

[230] The defendants had been ordered to pay damages totalling £76,000, although McDonalds had not sought to enforce the award.

[231] *Director General of Fair Trading* v *Proprietary Association of Great Britain; sub nom Re Medicaments and Related Classes of Goods (No 2)* [2001] 1 WLR 700, [2001] HRLR 17. The modification was subsequently approved by the House of Lords in *Porter* v *Magill* [2001] UKHL 67, [2002] 2 AC 357, [2002] 1 All ER 465.

[232] See p 177, *ante*.

[233] The Strasbourg court made such a ruling in *Findlay* v *UK* (1997) 24 EHRR 221: see p 274, *post*.

[234] [2003] UKHL 35, [2004] 1 All ER 187, [2003] ICR 856: see p 239, *post*.

[235] (2000) 30 EHRR 289. See also *Starrs* v *Ruxton; sub nom Starrs* v *Procurator Fiscal* 2000 JC 208, 2000 SLT 42; p 320, *post*.

[236] These reforms are considered in more detail in chapters 1, 7, and 9.

[237] *Darnall* v *UK* (1994) 18 EHRR 205.   [238] [2002] EWCA Crim 1119.

proviso that publicity may be restricted where the interests of justice demand it. Private hearings may be necessary in order to protect the identity of vulnerable witnesses,[239] and fairness may also require the imposition of reporting restrictions pending the outcome of proceedings. In *R (on the application of the Telegraph Group plc) v Sherwood*[240] the decision to delay the reporting of one trial until a second, related trial had been concluded, was held to be a justifiable and proportionate response to a substantial risk of prejudice.

The right to be presumed innocent of a criminal charge is expressly protected under Article 6(2), and in several Human Rights Act cases[241] the courts have modified the interpretation of burden of proof provisions. Freedom from self-incrimination and the related idea of the right to silence are not specifically mentioned, but both principles have been held to be covered by the fair trial concept in Article 6(1). In *Saunders v UK* the Court of Human Rights considered the effect of provisions of the Companies Act 1985, under which Mr Saunders was compelled to answer questions put to him during a fraud investigation.[242] The use made of these answers at Mr Saunders' trial, and the fact that they had been obtained under compulsion, was held to infringe Article 6. The right to silence is not absolute however, and allowing a court to draw adverse inferences from a defendant's silence will not automatically involve a breach of the Convention. Thus, restrictions on the right to silence in *Murray v UK*[243] did not violate Article 6 because the weight of evidence meant that the drawing of inferences had not been unfair. Moreover, the case was tried by a single judge who was required to give a reasoned decision. The risk of unfairness is considered to be greater where a defendant is tried by jury: Article 6 may be breached if the judge does not ensure that appropriate weight is given to any explanation offered by the accused.[244]

(f) Article 7: The right not to be subject to retrospective criminal liability or penalties

Article 7 prohibits the imposition of criminal liability for an act which was not an offence when it was carried out. Legislation imposing retrospective criminal liability

---

[239] See *X v UK* (1993) 15 EHRR CD 113 (witnesses gave evidence in open court, but they did so from behind a screen and could not even be seen by the defendant). See also *R v Lord Saville of Newdigate, ex parte A* [1999] 4 All ER 860, [2000] 1 WLR 1855, discussed at p 234, n 75, *post*.

[240] [2001] EWCA Crim 1075, [2001] 1 WLR 1983.

[241] *R v Lambert* [2001] UKHL 37, [2002] 2 AC 545, [2001] 3 All ER 577 (provisions of the Misuse of Drugs Act 1971 read down so as to impose an evidential rather than a legal burden); *Attorney-General's Reference (No 4 of 2002)* [2004] UKHL 43, [2005] 1 All ER 237, [2004] 3 WLR 976 (provisions of the Terrorism Act 2000 read down so as to impose an evidential rather than a legal burden); *International Transport Roth GmbH v Secretary of State for the Home Department* [2002] EWCA Civ 158, [2003] QB 728, [2002] HRLR 31 (a compatible interpretation of provisions in the Immigration and Asylum Act 1999 could not be found and a declaration of incompatibility was issued).

[242] (1997) 23 EHRR 313. The Companies Act was later amended by the Youth Justice and Criminal Evidence Act 1999. Cf. *Brown v Stott* [2003] 1 AC 681, [2001] 2 All ER 97 (requirement to answer a potentially incriminating question under the Road Traffic Act 1988 did not infringe the Convention).

[243] (1996) 22 EHRR 29.

[244] *Condron v UK* (2001) 31 EHRR 1; *Beckles v UK* (2003) 36 EHRR 13.

is virtually unknown in modern times,[245] but issues may arise where offences are given a different interpretation to that which might have been expected. Article 7 may also be infringed if an offence is not sufficiently precise to enable an individual to regulate his conduct. In practice however, it will be rare for this type of challenge to succeed. In *CR and SW* v *UK* for example, the applicants claimed that the removal of the marital rape exemption in *R* v *R*[246] amounted to the creation of a retrospective offence, contrary to Article 7. Yet the Strasbourg court held that the applicants should have foreseen that their conduct would be considered criminal, and that there was there-fore no breach of the Convention.[247] In another case, a defendant argued unsuccess-fully that the offence of public nuisance was too vague to satisfy the need for legal certainty.[248] He had been convicted of the offence after causing an anthrax scare when a package of salt that he had sent to a friend leaked out at a postal sorting office. The Court of Appeal held that he could have foreseen that his conduct was capable of amounting to a public nuisance, and that there was therefore no breach of Article 7.

Article 7 also forbids the imposition of a heavier criminal penalty than that in force at the time of the offence. Most of the cases that arise in this context hinge on whether a particular requirement constitutes a penalty, and the purpose of the requirement is usually crucial to this determination. Compelling a person to register as a sex offender has been held not to constitute a penalty—even though non-compliance is a criminal offence—because the purpose of the requirement is not to punish.[249]

In *R (on the application of Uttley)* v *Secretary of State for the Home Department*, the defendant was sentenced to twelve years imprisonment more than a decade after committing a series of sex offences. He argued that his release on licence after eight years amounted to a breach of Article 7, on the grounds that if he had been given the same sentence at the time of his offences, he would have been released after the same number of years but *without* licence. His argument was rejected by the House of Lords on the basis that Article 7 was only concerned with the maximum 'applicable' sentence, and not with the sentence that a particular offender was likely to receive.[250]

(g) Article 8: The right to respect for a person's private and family life, his home and correspondence

Article 8 may be subject to limitations which are in accordance with law and which are necessary in a democratic society in the interests of national security, public safety or

---

[245] See p 43, *ante*. The War Crimes Act 1991 is a notable exception but it is the type of legislation envisaged by Article 7(2). This allows the retrospective criminalisation of acts which would have been recognised as criminal at the time under general principles of international law.

[246] *R* v *R (Rape: Marital Exemption)* [1992] 1 AC 599, [1991] 4 All ER 481: see p 326, *ante*.

[247] (1996) 21 EHRR 363. The Court of Appeal reached the same conclusion on similar facts in *R* v *C (Barry)* [2004] EWCA Crim 292, [2004] 1 WLR 2098, [2004] 3 All ER 1.

[248] *R* v *Goldstein (Harry Chaim)* [2003] EWCA Crim 3450, [2004] 1 WLR 2878, [2004] 2 All ER 589.

[249] *Adamson* v *UK* (1999) App 42293/98.

[250] [2004] UKHL 38, [2004] 1 WLR 2278, [2004] 4 All ER 1. See also *Taylor* v *UK* (2003) 36 EHRR CD 104 (a boy who committed a crime at the age of fourteen was punished as a young offender because he was fifteen when sentenced—Article 7 held not to be engaged).

the economic well-being of the country, for the prevention of disorder or crime, for the protection of health or morals, or for the protection of the rights and freedoms of others. Although the Article covers four key areas—private life, family life, home, and correspondence—it is often unnecessary to distinguish clearly between them, and they can be 'read together as guaranteeing collectively more than the sum of their parts.'[251] For example, the right to respect for private life includes the right to develop personal relationships with others,[252] and relationships which do not establish a conventional 'family' may nevertheless fall within the scope of Article 8. Moreover, where national laws confer particular rights or benefits on family members, there may be a breach of Article 8 if the state's interpretation of what constitutes a family is too narrow. Thus, in *X, Y and X, Y and Z* v *UK*[253] the relationship between a woman, a female to male transsexual and a child that the woman had conceived through artificial insemination, was held to constitute a family. Similarly, in *Ghaidan* v *Godin-Mendoza*[254] the House of Lords upheld a ruling that the Rent Act 1977 should be interpreted to confer the rights of a 'spouse' on the surviving gay partner of a protected statutory tenant.

The ability to maintain family ties is of fundamental importance, and any denial of parental rights of access to a child will be subject to strict scrutiny.[255] Indeed, the failure of the authorities to involve a parent in otherwise justified decisions about the care and custody of a child may amount to a breach of Article 8.[256] Article 8 may also be violated by immigration and deportation decisions which have a disproportionate impact on the ability to maintain family relationships.[257] However, states are not obliged to respect the choice of married couples as to their country of residence.[258]

Article 8 entails respect for personal identity and sexual preferences, and it has been used alongside Article 14 in several cases concerning discrimination against homosexuals and transsexuals. The decision in *Smith and Grady* v *UK*[259] forced the Ministry of Defence to abandon its ban on gays in the military, and recent decisions in both the UK and Strasbourg provided the impetus for a new law conferring legal rights on transsexuals.[260] The Strasbourg court also found breaches of Articles 8 and 14 in a case concerning the UK's discriminatory age of consent laws, though the offending laws were amended before the case was even decided.[261] Article 8 was successfully

---

[251] Ovey and White (eds), *Jacobs and White: European Convention on Human Rights* (3rd edn, 2002) at p 218.

[252] *Niemietz* v *Germany* (1993) 16 EHRR 97; *X and Y* v *Netherlands* (1986) 8 EHRR 235.

[253] (1997) 24 EHRR 143.   [254] [2004] UKHL 30, [2004] 2 AC 557, [2004] 3 All ER 411.

[255] *K and T* v *Finland* (2003) 36 EHRR 18.   [256] *TP and KM* v *UK* (2002) 34 EHRR 2.

[257] *Berrehab* v *Netherlands* (1989) 11 EHRR 322 (refusal of residence permit to a Moroccan national living in the Netherlands who maintained regular contact with his ex-wife and their child).

[258] *Abdulaziz, Cabales and Balkandali* v *UK* (1985) 7 EHRR 471.

[259] (2000) 29 EHRR 493; *Lustig-Prean and Beckett* v *UK* (2000) 29 EHRR 548.

[260] The Gender Recognition Act 2004, introduced following *Goodwin* v *UK* (2002) 35 EHRR 18 and *Bellinger* v *Bellinger* [2003] UKHL 21, [2003] 2 AC 467, [2003] 2 All ER 593.

[261] *B* v *UK* (2004) 39 EHRR 30. The age of consent for male homosexuals was 18; it was 16 for heterosexuals. The age of consent was equalized at sixteen by the Sexual Offences (Amendment) Act 2000. The relevant law is now contained in s 9 of the Sexual Offences Act 2003, which states that 'it shall be an offence to have sex with a child under the age of 16'. See also *Dudgeon* v *UK* (1982) 4 EHRR 149, discussed at p 170, *ante*.

relied upon by a gay man prosecuted for gross indecency after he had videotaped consensual sex acts for his own private use.[262] However, the decision to prosecute a group of men who recorded themselves engaging in acts of sado-masochism did not involve a similar breach.[263] The Court accepted that the interference in the latter case was in the interests of public health.

The effectiveness of Article 8 in protecting environmental and housing rights has been rather more measured.[264] In *Hatton* v *UK*,[265] for example, the Grand Chamber[266] overturned a finding that night flights from Heathrow Airport breached the Article 8 rights of local residents. In another case the House of Lords rejected a nuisance action brought by a householder whose property was flooded by water from the sewers.[267] In the latter case the defendant's activities were subject to scrutiny by an independent regulator, and the statutory regime was held to strike an appropriate balance between the rights of those such as the claimant and those who depended on the defendant for sewerage services. Nevertheless, it is clear that severe pollution affecting home and family life *is* capable of being addressed under Article 8,[268] and in certain circum-stances the state may have a positive obligation to provide information about serious environmental hazards.[269] Planning decisions concerning the occupation of land by the Roma community will also raise Article 8 issues, but thus far the courts have tended to find any interference with the right to a home to be legitimate.[270] An even more restrictive approach was taken in a recent housing case,[271] in which a joint tenant had given notice to quit on a property still occupied by her former husband. The husband wanted to continue living in the property but a majority of the House of Lords held that the public authority landlord had an unqualified right to recover possession and that it was unnecessary to establish a justification under Article 8(2).[272]

Article 8 has, of course, been applied in cases involving more 'conventional' privacy claims, and in an important line of domestic jurisprudence the national courts have considered whether the Human Rights Act requires them to develop a common law tort of privacy. It is clear that no such tort existed before the Act,[273] though it was possible to bring some privacy claims within the scope of existing torts such as breach

---

[262] *ADT* v *UK* (2001) 31 EHRR 33.   [263] *Laskey* v *UK* (1997) 24 EHRR 39.

[264] See Sands, 'Human Rights, the Environment and the Lopez Ostra Case' [1996] 29 EHRLR 597; Cook, 'Environmental Rights as Human Rights' [2002] 2 EHRLR 196.

[265] (2003) 37 EHRR 28.   [266] See p 200, *post*.

[267] *Marcic* v *Thames Water Utilities* [2003] UKHL 66, [2004] 2 AC 42, [2003] 1 All ER 135.

[268] *Lopez Ostra* v *Spain* (1995) 20 EHRR 277; *Vetterlein* v *Hampshire County Council* [2001] EWHC 560 (Admin), [2002] Env LR 8.

[269] *Guerra* v *Italy* (1998) 26 EHRR 357.

[270] *Buckley* v *UK* (1997) 23 EHRR 101; *Chapman* v *UK* (2001) 33 EHRR 18; *South Buckinghamshire DC* v *Porter (No 1)*; *sub nom Wrexham CBC* v *Berry* [2003] UKHL 26, [2003] 2 AC 558, [2003] 3 All ER 1.

[271] *Qazi* v *Harrow LBC* [2003] UKHL 43, [2004] 1 AC 983, [2003] 4 All ER 461.

[272] In a strong dissenting opinion Lord Steyn suggested that any European challenge to this decision was likely to prove successful; ibid at [27]. See also *Poplar Housing and Regeneration Community Association Ltd* v *Donoghue* [2001] EWCA Civ 595, [2002] QB 48, [2001] 4 All ER 604.

[273] *Kaye* v *Robertson* [1991] FSR 62.

of confidence, nuisance and trespass. In the first post-Human Rights Act 'privacy' case to come before the national courts, Sedley LJ famously asserted that:[274]

[W]e have reached a point where it can be said with confidence that the law recognises and will appropriately protect a right of personal privacy.

However, in subsequent decisions the courts have stopped short of recognising the existence of a new tort. In the first such case to reach the House of Lords it was held that the creation of new torts was a matter for Parliament, and that Article 8 could instead be given effect by developing established torts and remedies.[275] The Strasbourg court has rarely had to consider claims involving media intrusions, and it rejected Earl Spencer's claim that the government had failed to protect him from such interference because it was not convinced that he lacked a remedy in domestic law.[276] Recently however, it found a breach of Article 8 when CCTV footage recorded shortly after the applicant's suicide attempt was broadcast on television.[277] The case highlighted significant weaknesses in the ability of domestic law to safeguard individual privacy, and further developments in this field now seem inevitable. The only question is whether Parliament will finally grasp the nettle before the judiciary's hand is forced:[278]

The recent judgment in *Peck v United Kingdom* in the ECtHR, given on January 28 2003, shows that in circumstances where the law of confidence did not operate, our domestic law has already been held to be inadequate. That inadequacy will have to be made good and if Parliament does not step in then the courts will be obliged to. Further development by the courts may merely be awaiting the first post-Human Rights Act case where neither the law of confidence nor any other domestic law protects an individual who deserves protection.

Police and prison searches and the use of covert surveillance techniques will obviously give rise to privacy issues, but they will generally be justifiable on one of the grounds set out in Article 8(2). However, in order to avoid a breach of the Convention such actions must be in accordance with a lawful procedure and must satisfy the requirements of proportionality. Breaches of Article 8 have been established in several cases concerning the interception of prisoners' correspondence, on the basis that the authorities' objectives could have been achieved by less restrictive means.[279] In *Malone v UK*[280] the finding that police telephone tapping was not properly regulated led to the enactment of the Interception of Communications Act 1985, and further criticism in

---

[274] *Douglas v Hello! Ltd (No 1)* [2001] QB 967 at 997, [2001] 2 All ER 289 at 316.

[275] *Wainwright v Home Office* [2003] UKHL 53, [2004] 2 AC 406, [2003] 4 All ER 969. See also, *Venables and Thompson v News Group Newspapers* [2001] Fam 430, [2001] 1 All ER 908; *A v B*; *H v Associated Newspapers* [2002] EWCA Civ 337, [2003] QB 195, [2002] 2 All ER 545; *Campbell v MGN* [2004] UKHL 22, [2004] 2 AC 457, [2004] 2 All ER 995.

[276] *Earl Spencer v UK* (1998) 25 EHRR CD 105.   [277] *Peck v UK* (2003) 36 EHRR 41.

[278] *Douglas v Hello! Ltd (No 6)* [2003] EWHC 786 (Ch) at [229], [2003] 3 All ER 996 at [229], per Lindsay J. See Singh and Strachan, 'Privacy Postponed' [2003] EHRLR Special Issue 12.

[279] *R (on the application of Daly) v Secretary of State for the Home Department* [2001] UKHL 26, [2001] 2 AC 532, [2001] 3 All ER 433; *Campbell v UK* (1993) 15 EHRR 137.

[280] (1985) 7 EHRR 14.

Halford v *UK* prompted a more comprehensive piece of legislation.[281] More recently, a breach of the Convention was established when covertly obtained footage of a defendant was used in a video identification parade, following his refusal to take part in a police line-up.[282]

Article 8 rights have also been considered in the context of adoption decisions,[283] the condition of local authority housing,[284] the sale of electoral registers,[285] and the police retention of DNA samples and fingerprints.[286]

(h) Article 9: The right to freedom of thought, conscience, and religion

This right includes the freedom to change religion or belief, and the freedom to manifest one's religion or belief in worship, teaching, practice, and observance. The bare right to freedom of thought, conscience, and religion is absolute, but the right to *manifest* a religion or belief is qualified by Article 9(2). This permits the right to be restricted on the grounds of public safety, public order, the protection of health or morals, and the protection of the rights and freedoms of others. To comply with Article 9(2), any such restriction must be prescribed by law and must be 'necessary in a democratic society'.

The term 'religion or belief' has been interpreted widely to extend beyond purely theistic beliefs and beliefs with a metaphysical element:[287]

[Article 9] is, in its religious dimension, one of the most vital elements that go to make up the identity of believers and of their conception of life, but it is also a precious asset for atheists, agnostics, sceptics and the unconcerned.

Alongside major world faiths such as Islam[288] and Christianity,[289] pacifism,[290] the Church of Scientology,[291] atheism,[292] and Buddhism[293] have all been assumed to constitute protected beliefs. Thus far however, most Article 9 cases have been unsuccessful: the Court or former Commission has generally found either that there has been no interference with a protected 'manifestation', or that any interference was justified.

'Manifestations' covered by Article 9 include worship,[294] proselytism,[295] observing

---

[281] (1997) 24 EHRR 523; Regulation of Investigatory Powers Act 2000. See also *Khan* v *UK* (2001) 31 EHRR 45.

[282] *Perry* v *UK* (2004) 39 EHRR 3.

[283] *Re B (A Minor) (Adoption: Natural Parent)* [2001] UKHL 70, [2002] 1 All ER 641, [2002] 1 WLR 258; *Keegan* v *Ireland* (1994) 18 EHRR 342.

[284] *Lee* v *Leeds City Council* [2002] EWCA Civ 6, [2002] 1 WLR 1488.

[285] *R (on the application of Robertson)* v *Wakefield Metropolitan DC* [2001] EWHC 915 (Admin), [2002] QB 1052, [2002] 2 WLR 889.

[286] *Attorney-General's Reference (No 3 of 1999)* [2001] 2 AC 91, [2001] 2 WLR 56; *R (on the application of S)* v *Chief Constable of South Yorkshire; R (on the application of Marper)* v *Chief Constable of South Yorkshire* [2004] UKHL 39, [2004] 1 WLR 2196, [2004] 4 All ER 139.

[287] *Kokkinakis* v *Greece* (1994) 17 EHRR 397 at para. 31.   [288] *Ahmad* v *UK* (1982) 4 EHRR 126.

[289] *Kokkinakis* v *Greece* (1994) 17 EHRR 397.   [290] *Arrowsmith* v *UK* (1978) 19 D&R 5.

[291] *X and Church of Scientology* v *Sweden* (1978) 16 D&R 68.

[292] *Angelini* v *Sweden* (1986) 51 D&R 41.   [293] *X* v *UK* (1974) 1 D&R 41.

[294] *Holy Monasteries* v *Greece* (1995) 20 EHRR 1.   [295] *Kokkinakis* v *Greece* (1994) 17 EHRR 397.

dietary restrictions,[296] and religious education.[297] In *Arrowsmith* v *UK*[298] however, the distribution of leaflets urging troops not to serve in Northern Ireland was held not to be a manifestation of pacifism because the leaflets were not actually an expression of the applicant's pacifist views. In addition, although there is a positive obligation for states to ensure the peaceful enjoyment of religious freedom, there is no requirement to guarantee equality between religions or to prohibit religious discrimination.[299] It seems that religious discrimination will only violate Article 9 where there is an element of compulsion. Thus, where an individual has voluntarily put himself in a position where his religious freedom is restricted, the Strasbourg institutions have generally found either that there has been no interference with Convention rights, or that the interference is justified. In *X* v *UK*,[300] for example, the Commission agreed with the UK government that a law requiring Sikh motorcyclists to wear crash helmets was a 'necessary' restriction on religious freedom. However, the government subsequently changed its mind and turban-wearing Sikhs are now exempt from the law in question.[301] In another case[302] the Commission rejected the claim of a Muslim teacher who was dismissed for missing forty-five minutes of classes each week in order to attend the mosque. The Commission concluded that the teacher had accepted restrictions on his religious freedom when taking up his post.[303] This decision can be contrasted with the approach of the Court of Appeal in a recent Human Rights Act case.[304] A fourteen year old Muslim girl claimed that she had been excluded from the defendant school for refusing to comply with its uniform policy on religious grounds. Her position could not be compared with that of an employee because pre-sixteen education is not a contractual choice: she was required by law to go to school. The school's policy allowed girls to wear a form of dress—the shalwar kameeze—which was acceptable to the vast majority of its Muslim students. However, the applicant believed that she was obliged by her religion to wear a more loose fitting garment—the jilbab. The Court found that there had been a restriction on her freedom to manifest her religious beliefs, and that the school had failed to justify this restriction. It was no answer to say that the school's policy was compatible with the beliefs of most Muslim students, because the applicant's beliefs were different and the school could not pick and choose which religious beliefs to accommodate.

Despite the symbolic importance attached to freedom of religion in section 13 of

---

[296] *Cha'are Shalom Ve Tsedek* v *France* (2000) 9 BHRC 27.

[297] *Kjeldsen, Busk Madsen and Pedersen* v *Denmark* (1979–1980) 1 EHRR 711.

[298] (1978) 19 D&R 5.

[299] This will change when Protocol 12 comes into force, but only for states which have ratified it.

[300] (1978) 14 D&R 234.   [301] Road Traffic Act 1988, s 16(2).

[302] *Ahmad* v *UK* (1982) 4 EHRR 126; see also *Stedman* v *UK* (1997) 89 D&R 104.

[303] See also *Karaduman* v *Turkey* (1993) 74 D&R 14, in which the complaint of a Muslim woman who was refused permission to wear a headscarf for a photograph on a university identity card was rejected on similar grounds. These cases may be criticised for ignoring the discriminatory impact of the restrictions: the 'choice' in both cases need not have been made by a non-Muslim.

[304] *R (on the application of Begum)* v *Denbigh High School* [2005] EWCA Civ 199, *The Times* 4 March 2005.

the Human Rights Act,[305] relatively few cases under the Act have involved Article 9. One example is *Ullah* v *Special Adjudicator*, in which it was held that a refusal to grant asylum to a person fleeing religious persecution could theoretically amount to a breach of Article 9.[306] In another case[307] it was held that a belief that physical chastisement was essential to a Christian upbringing did not require such chastisement to be administered by teachers. The banning of corporal punishment in schools did not, therefore, infringe the religious freedom of parents. However, it is noteworthy that a majority of the court accepted that the belief itself could fall within the scope of Article 9.

(i) Article 10: The right to freedom of expression

Article 10 covers the right to hold opinions and to receive and impart information and ideas. The right may be restricted in the interests of national security, territorial integrity or public safety, for the prevention of disorder or crime, for the protection of health, morals or the rights and freedoms of others, in order to prevent the disclosure of confidential information, or in order to maintain the authority and impartiality of the judiciary.[308] Freedom of expression lies at the heart of the Convention system, and its importance is expressly recognized by section 12 of the Human Rights Act.[309] Protected forms of expression can include words, pictures, dress, and even conduct,[310] though some types of expression are more highly valued than others. Commercial speech, for example, does not attract the same level of protection as political speech.[311] In addition, Article 17 states that the Convention does not confer any right to engage in activities aimed at the destruction of protected rights and freedoms, and this may provide a basis for denying protection to speech inciting racial or religious hatred.[312] In any event, laws aimed at restricting hate speech will generally fall within the exceptions permitted under Article 10(2), subject to the principle of proportionality.

The fact that certain ideas are controversial or may 'offend, shock or disturb',[313] is not a sufficient justification for preventing their expression. Yet the House of Lords recently held that the BBC acted lawfully in refusing to broadcast an election video containing graphic images of aborted foetuses.[314] It accepted that the video constituted a form of protected speech but found the BBC's decision to be consistent with Article 10(2) and with its statutory duty not to screen items which offend against

---

[305] See p 156, *ante*.

[306] [2004] UKHL 26, [2004] 2 AC 323, [2004] 3 All ER 785. It was thought, however, that a refugee entitled to succeed under Article 9 would in any event be entitled to asylum on the ground of a well-founded fear of persecution.

[307] *R (on the application of Williamson)* v *Secretary of State for Education and Employment* [2002] EWCA Civ 1926, [2003] QB 1300, [2003] 1 All ER 385.

[308] Article 9(2).   [309] See p 155, *ante*.

[310] *Stevens* v *UK* (1986) D&R 245; *Steel* v *UK* (1999) 28 EHRR 603.

[311] *X and the Church of Scientology* v *Sweden* (1978) 16 D&R 68.

[312] *Lehideux and Isorni* v *France* (2000) 30 EHRR 665.

[313] *Handyside* v *UK* (1979) 1 EHRR 737 at 48; see also *Jersild* v *Denmark* (1995) 19 EHRR 1.

[314] *R (on the application of ProLife Alliance)* v *BBC* [2003] UKHL 23, [2004] 1 AC 185, [2003] 2 All ER 977.

good taste and decency. Lord Walker explained that although material likely to cause 'a significant degree of revulsion' could potentially be justified by its purpose, the BBC had considerable experience in determining accepted standards of taste and decency and its decision was within the limits of its discretion.[315] The degree of deference shown to the BBC in this case has been criticized,[316] and in a strong dissenting judgment Lord Scott concluded that the restriction was not 'necessary':[317]

A broadcasters' mind-set that rejects a party election television programme dealing with an issue of undeniable public importance such as abortion, on the ground that large numbers of the voting public would find the programme 'offensive' denigrates the voting public, treats them like children who need to be protected from the unpleasant realities of life, seriously undervalues their political maturity and can only promote . . . voter-apathy.

In another recent case a man was convicted of a public order offence[318] after preaching in a city centre whilst displaying a sign with the words 'Stop Immorality. Stop Homosexuality. Stop Lesbianism.' The Administrative Court held that although the man had been motivated by sincerely held religious beliefs and had intended to preach rather than to cause offence, his conviction was compatible with Article 10.[319]

Freedom of expression is limited in numerous ways by domestic law, but most of the restrictions seem to fall within the legitimate exceptions permitted under Article 10(2). Thus in *Handyside v UK*[320] a prosecution under the Obscene Publications Act 1959 was held to be a legitimate and proportionate means of protecting public morals: the court was prepared to grant a wide margin of appreciation in the absence of a uniform conception of morality. In another case,[321] the refusal to give a film certificate to an allegedly blasphemous video was found to be a legitimate way of protecting the rights and freedoms of others. Recently the House of Lords suggested that section 11 of the Terrorism Act 2000, which makes it an offence to profess membership of a proscribed organization, is consistent with Article 10 because it does not prohibit the holding of particular views and is a proportionate response to concerns about terrorism.[322] In another case the House was asked to issue a declaration as to whether a treason provision was compatible with the right to freedom of expression.[323] It declined to grant the relief sought because the applicants had already published a series of articles advocating the peaceful overthrow of the monarchy

---

[315] Ibid, at [122].

[316] MacDonald, 'R (on the application of ProLife Alliance) v British Broadcasting Corporation' [2003] 6 EHRLR 651; Barendt, 'Free Speech and Abortion' [2003] PL 580.

[317] [2003] UKHL 23 at [99], [2004] 1 AC 185 at [99], [2003] 2 All ER 977.

[318] The offence of causing harassment, alarm, or distress: Public Order Act 1986, s 5.

[319] *Hammond v DPP* [2004] EWHC 69 (Admin), (2004) 168 JP 601. (It was also held to be compatible with Article 9.)

[320] (1979) 1 EHRR 737. [321] *Wingrove v UK* (1997) 24 EHRR 1.

[322] *Attorney-General's Reference (No 4 of 2002)* [2004] UKHL 43, [2005] 1 All ER 237, [2004] 3 WLR 976. However, their Lordships concluded that the defence under s 11(2) must be read down so as to impose an evidential rather than a legal burden on the defendant: see p 56, *ante*.

[323] *R (on the application of Rusbridger)* v *Attorney-General* [2003] UKHL 38, [2004] 1 AC 357, [2003] 3 All ER 784; Treason Felony Act 1848, s 3.

and no-one had attempted to prosecute them. Their freedom of expression had therefore not been inhibited and the question before the court was purely hypothetical. Nevertheless, Lord Scott did not refrain from expressing his opinion on the matter:[324]

It is plain as a pike staff to the respondents and everyone else that no-one who advocates the peaceful abolition of the monarchy . . . is at any risk of prosecution. Whatever may be the correct construction of s 3, taken by itself, it is clear beyond any peradventure first, that the section would now be 'read down' as required by s 3 of the Human Rights Act 1998 so that the advocacy contemplated by the respondents could not constitute a criminal offence, and second, that no Attorney-General or Director of Public Prosecutions would or could authorise a prosecution for such advocacy without becoming a laughing stock. To do so would plainly be an unlawful act under s 6(1) of the 1998 Act.

The Strasbourg court has criticized the UK's blasphemy laws on the basis that they only apply to the Anglican faith and thus discriminate between religions, but it has also ruled that restrictions on blasphemous speech are not inherently incompatible with Article 10.[325] Should an appropriate set of facts arise in a Human Rights Act case, the courts would have to apply the law of blasphemy in a non-discriminatory manner to avoid a breach of Article 14. However, given that blasphemy is a common law doctrine it has been suggested that it would be open to the courts to abolish it altogether.[326]

Reporting restrictions pending the outcome of legal proceedings are also permissible under the Convention, in the interests of protecting the rights and freedoms of others and maintaining the impartiality of the judiciary. However, any restrictions must be prescribed by law and proportionate to their objectives, and criticism that the common law contempt jurisdiction was too uncertain in scope[327] led to the enactment of the Contempt of Court Act 1981.[328] It has also been held that the law of defamation is compatible with freedom of expression, as long as the level of damages awarded in successful cases is not so high as to have a chilling effect on the essence of the right.[329]

Article 10 cases decided under the Human Rights Act include the related cases of *R v Shayler*[330] and *Attorney-General v Punch*.[331] In the first case a former MI5 officer was prosecuted under the Official Secrets Act 1989 for disclosing information obtained during the course of his employment. In a ruling on a preliminary matter the House

---

[324] Ibid at [23].   [325] *Otto-Preminger Institut* v *Austria* (1995) 19 EHRR 34.

[326] Fenwick, *Civil Liberties and Human Rights* (3rd edn, 2002) at p 321.

[327] *Sunday Times* v *UK* (1979–1980) 2 EHRR 245.

[328] A line of Human Rights Act cases is already developing concerning the circumstances in which reporting restrictions and injunctions should be imposed: see *Venables and Thompson* v *News Group Newspapers* [2001] Fam 430, [2001] 1 All ER 908. In *R (on the application of the Telegraph Group plc)* v *Sherwood* [2001] EWCA Crim 1075, [2001] 1 WLR 1983, the Court of Appeal suggested that the pre-Human Rights Act approach was already broadly compatible with the Convention.

[329] *Tolstoy Miloslavsky* v *UK* (1995) 20 EHRR 442. In *Steel and Morris* v *UK* (2005) App 68416/01, it was held that Article 10 could also be infringed if the defendant in a defamation case had no access to legal aid and faced a significant inequality of arms: see p 181, *ante*.

[330] [2002] UKHL 11, [2003] 1 AC 247, [2002] 2 All ER 477.

[331] [2002] UKHL 50, [2003] 1 AC 1046, [2003] 1 All ER 289.

of Lords held that the restrictions on free speech fell within Article 10(2) because they were a legitimate and proportionate response to the interests of national security. Moreover, the House did not consider it necessary to read a public interest defence into the Act in order to render it compatible. In the second case a magazine published an article by David Shayler while proceedings against him were still ongoing. Injunctions had already been obtained to prevent Mr Shayler from publishing such information, and it was held that the publishers could be liable for contempt of court. The fact that they did not believe the material to be harmful to the national interest did not amount to a defence: the purpose of the injunction was to preserve the confidentiality of the information until its status had been determined, and the terms of the order were proportionate to this objective.

Article 10 was also considered in *R (on the application of Farrakhan) v Secretary of State for the Home Department.*[332] In this case the Home Office had refused to allow a controversial political figure to enter the UK on the basis that his radical views might inflame religious tensions and lead to disorder. The Court accepted that Article 10 was engaged, even though Mr Farrakhan remained outside the territorial jurisdiction of the Convention. However, it held that the decision to refuse entry had been legitimate. In other cases consideration has been given to the right of prisoners to speak to the media on matters of public interest,[333] and freedom of expression has also played a significant role in the domestic jurisprudence on Article 8.[334]

(j) Article 11: Freedom of peaceful assembly and of association with others

Limitations on this right are permitted if prescribed by law and necessary in a democratic society in the interests of national security or public safety, for the prevention of disorder or crime, for the protection of health or morals, or for the protection of the rights and freedoms of others.[335] The Article expressly protects the right to 'form and join a trade union for the protection of one's interests', and it has been held that this imposes a positive duty on states to create conditions in which the exercise of this right is possible.[336] Article 11 has also been held to protect the right *not* to join a union, although it may be that this right is only breached if the individual is opposed to union membership for reasons of conscience and principle.[337] Professional associations are generally not considered to be trade unions for these purposes, and requiring members of a particular profession to join a relevant association is not contrary to Article 11.[338]

---

[332] [2002] EWCA Civ 606, [2002] QB 1391, [2002] 4 All ER 289.

[333] *Hirst v Secretary of State for the Home Department* [2002] EWHC 602 (Admin), [2002] 1 WLR 2929; *Hirst v UK* (2004) 38 EHRR 40. See also the pre-Human Rights Act case of *R v Secretary of State for the Home Department, ex parte Simms* [2000] 2 AC 115, [1999] 3 All ER 400.

[334] See p 184, *ante.*   [335] Article 11(2).

[336] *Swedish Engine Drivers Union v Sweden* (1979–1980) 1 EHRR 617.

[337] *Young v UK* (1982) 4 EHRR 38; cf. *Sibson v UK* (1994) 17 EHRR 193 (no breach in respect of a worker who simply wanted to change from one union to another and who had been offered redeployment).

[338] *Le Compte v Belgium* (1982) 4 EHRR 1.

Alongside the specific protection given to union rights, Article 11 has been used alongside Article 10 in the context of the right to peaceful protest. The Strasbourg court has criticized the power to bind over to keep the peace as being too vague and imprecise to constitute a limitation 'prescribed by law'.[339] However, the power to *arrest* for breach of the peace is accepted to be a legitimate and proportionate restriction on Convention rights.[340]

(k) Article 12: The right to marry and found a family

This Article provides that 'men and women of marriageable age have the right to marry and to found a family, according to the national laws governing the exercise of this right.' On its face the wording appears to restrict the right to marry to couples of the opposite sex, and it also gives states considerable scope to regulate the exercise of the right as they see fit. Recently however, the Court of Human Rights has departed from its previous jurisprudence[341] and ruled that the refusal to recognize the change in gender of a post-operative transsexual, and the negative impact of this decision on the right to marry, was a violation of Articles 8 and 12.[342] In the view of the Court, evidence of changing attitudes towards gender and marriage meant that there was less scope for affording states a wide margin of appreciation.

In *R (on the application of Mellor)* v *Secretary of State for the Home Department*[343] it was held that the refusal to provide a prisoner with facilities for artificial insemination did not breach the right to found a family. It has also been established that Article 12 does not entitle a prisoner to receive conjugal visits.[344]

(l) Article 14: The right not to be discriminated against with regard to other Convention rights

The substantive rights set out in the Convention must, by virtue of Article 14, be respected and protected in a non-discriminatory way:

The enjoyment of the rights and freedoms set forth in this Convention shall be secured without discrimination on any grounds such as sex, race, colour, language, religion, political or other opinion, national or social origin, association with a national minority, property, birth or other status.

The list of prohibited grounds of discrimination is broad and non-exhaustive, and the reference to 'other status' has enabled additional grounds such as sexual orientation[345] and illegitimacy[346] to be brought within its ambit. However, Article 14 does not create

---

[339] *Steel* v *United Kingdom* (1999) 28 EHRR 603.

[340] For criticism, see Fenwick, 'The Right to Protest, the Human Rights Act and the Margin of Appreciation' (1999) 62 MLR 491.

[341] See, e.g. *Rees* v *UK* (1986) 9 EHRR 56

[342] *Goodwin* v *UK* (2002) 35 EHRR 18; applied in *Bellinger* v *Bellinger* [2003] UKHL 21, [2003] 2 AC 467, [2003] 2 All ER 593. The Gender Recognition Act 2004 was introduced in response to these decisions.

[343] [2001] EWCA Civ 472, [2002] QB 13, [2001] 3 WLR 533.

[344] *ELH* v *UK* (1997) App 32094/96.   [345] *Smith and Grady* v *UK* (2000) 29 EHRR 493.

[346] *Marckx* v *Belgium* (1979–1980) 2 EHRR 330.

a free-standing right, and a breach of the non-discrimination principle can only be established in conjunction with another Convention right. An applicant merely needs to demonstrate that an act or omission 'falls within the ambit of' a substantive right, in order to raise a discrimination issue. This means that even where the Convention does not *require* a state to take positive steps to protect or enhance a particular freedom, if it *chooses* to do so in respect of *some* groups, Article 14 may demand that the benefit is extended to all. For example, *Abdulaziz, Cabales and Balkandali* v *UK*[347] concerned an immigration rule governing when spouses who were non-nationals would be granted indefinite leave to remain in the UK, and which treated men and women differently. There was no breach of Article 8 but the rule fell 'within the ambit' of the right to family life, and as it discriminated on gender grounds it was held that there had been a breach of Article 14. Other laws and policies challenged success-fully under Article 14 include the criminalisation of homosexual acts in Northern Ireland,[348] the denial of rights to same-sex partners which would be afforded to other unmarried couples,[349] and the ban on gays in the military.[350]

Protocol 1. Protocol 1 of the Convention is concerned with three distinct rights: the right to peaceful enjoyment of possessions, the right to education, and the right to participate in free and fair elections.

The right to peaceful enjoyment of possessions is set out in Article 1 of the First Protocol. It may be restricted 'in the public interest' and subject to the conditions provided for by domestic and international law. In addition, the right does not 'in any way impair the right of a State to enforce such laws as it deems necessary to control the use of property in accordance with the general interest or to secure the payment of taxes or other contributions or penalties.' The term 'possessions' has been interpreted quite widely:[351] it may even include entitlements to pensions and social security benefits under a contributions-based system in which the applicant's 'share' can be quantified.[352] On the other hand, the right is subject to a wide range of exceptions, and states are afforded considerable discretion in deciding when a restriction is in the public interest. For example, in *Wilson* v *First County Trust (No 2)* a provision of the Consumer Credit Act 1974, which could render a credit agreement unenforceable if

---

[347] (1985) 7 EHRR 471.

[348] *Dudgeon* v *UK* (1982) 4 EHRR 149 (a breach of Articles 8 and 14 because of the disproportionate impact on the applicant's private life).

[349] See, e.g. *Ghaidan* v *Godin-Mendoza* [2004] UKHL 30, [2004] 2 AC 557, [2004] 3 All ER 411.

[350] *Smith and Grady* v *UK* (2000) 29 EHRR 493.

[351] For example, it is capable of including licences, patents, planning permission, leasehold interests, and even goodwill in a business: see *Van Marle and others* v *Netherlands* (1986) 8 EHRR 483; *Mellacher* v *Austria* (1990) 12 EHRR 391.

[352] In *R (on the application of Carson)* v *Secretary of State for Work and Pensions; R (on the application of Reynolds)* v *Secretary of State for Work and Pensions* [2003] EWCA Civ 797, [2003] 3 All ER 577, [2003] HRLR 36, it was held that jobseeker's allowance fell within Article 1 of the First Protocol as it was contribution based, but that income support did not.

the amount of credit was calculated incorrectly, was held to be a proportionate mechanism for achieving the legitimate objective of consumer protection:[353]

[Section] 127(3) may be drastic, even harsh, in its adverse consequences for a lender. He loses all his rights under the agreement, including his rights to any security which has been lodged. Conversely, the borrower acquires what can only be described as a windfall. He keeps his money and recovers his security. These consequences apply just as much where the lender was acting in good faith throughout and the error was due to a mistaken reading of the complex statutory requirements as in cases of deliberate non-compliance . . .

[Nevertheless] it must be open to Parliament to decide that, severe though this sanction may be, it is an appropriate way of protecting consumers as a matter of social policy.

Claims under Article 1 of the Protocol are unlikely to succeed unless there is a clear lack of proportionality or a defective procedure. As a consequence, such claims are often made in conjunction with a claim under Article 6 or 14 of the Convention. For example, differentials in pensions and benefit payments corresponding with differences in age or country of residence were recently challenged under Article 1 of the Protocol and Article 14 of the Convention. The differences in treatment were found to be justifiable however, and the challenge failed on both grounds.[354] The right to peaceful enjoyment of possessions was also considered in *Aston Cantlow* v *Wallbank*.[355] The defendant owned the freehold over a plot of rectorial land, and the Parish Council had sought to invoke section 2(1) of the Chancel Repairs Act 1932, under which the owners of such land could be obliged to repair the chancel of the parish church. The defendants claimed that this was a breach of both Article 14 of the Convention and Article 1 of the First Protocol: they argued that requiring them to pay for the repairs was an arbitrary deprivation of property which discriminated against them as owners of the land. The defendants ultimately lost their case because the House of Lords found that the Parish Council was not a public authority and was not performing a public function.[356] However, it also held that there would have been no interference with Convention rights in any event, because the defendant had acquired her property with full knowledge of the accompanying repair obligation. *International Transport Roth*[357] is an example of a challenged based on a procedural defect. The case centred on a penalty regime under which hauliers could be fined £2,000 for every clandestine immigrant brought into the country by their vehicles. The challenge was partially

---

[353] [2003] UKHL 40 at [72]–[77], [2004] 1 AC 816 at [72]–[77], [2003] 4 All ER 97, per Lord Nicholls. Their Lordships considered that, in any event, there were no property rights at stake because the effect of the Act meant that the credit company had never possessed any right to enforce the payments. On the facts the issue did not directly arise because the agreement had been made before the Human Rights Act came into force and the Act did not have retrospective effect: see p 169, *ante*.

[354] *R (on the application of Carson)* v *Secretary of State for Work and Pensions; R (on the application of Reynolds)* v *Secretary of State for Work and Pensions* [2003] EWCA Civ 797, [2003] 3 All ER 577, [2003] HRLR 36.

[355] *Aston-Cantlow and Wilcote with Billesley Parochial Church Council* v *Wallbank* [2003] UKHL 37, [2004] 1 AC 546, [2003] 3 All ER 1213.

[356] See p 164, *ante*.

[357] *International Transport Roth GmbH* v *Secretary of State for the Home Department* [2002] EWCA Civ 158, [2003] QB 728, [2002] HRLR 31.

based on Article 6 because hauliers were required to prove that they had an effective scheme for preventing such incidents, and this amounted to a reversal of the burden of proof. However, there was also an issue under Article 1, Protocol 1, because officials were empowered to detain vehicles in order to ensure payment. The regime was found to be in breach of both provisions and a declaration of incompatibility was issued

Article 2 of the Protocol states that 'no person shall be denied the right to education', and it imposes a specific obligation on states to 'respect the right of persons to ensure such education and teaching in conformity with their own religious and philosophical convictions'. Upon signing the Protocol, the UK entered a specific reservation in respect of this Article, which provides that it is accepted 'only so far as it is compatible with the provision of efficient instruction and training and the avoidance of unreasonable public expenditure.' The wording of the first part of the Article is deliberately restrictive, referring to the negative right not to be denied education, rather than a positive right to receive it. The effect of this is that it is primarily concerned with ensuring that existing educational facilities are available on an equal basis: it does not, for example, include any positive right to have children educated in a particular language.[358] In *Campbell v UK*[359] the use of corporal punishment in a school was successfully challenged under Article 2 of the First Protocol, on the basis that it contravened the parental right of the applicant to have her child educated in accordance with her religious and philosophical beliefs. This can be contrasted with the decision in *R (on the application of Williamson) v Secretary of State for Education and Employment*,[360] in which a ban on the use of physical chastisement in schools was held *not* to conflict with the contrary belief—i.e. the belief that corporal punishment was an integral part of a Christian upbringing.

Finally, Article 3 of the Protocol obliges states to hold 'free elections at reasonable intervals by secret ballot, under conditions which will ensure the free expression of the opinion of the people.' The Article does not expressly create any individual rights, but the right to participate in elections is implied. In 2001, this Article was used in an unsuccessful challenge to section 3 of the Representation of the People Act 1983, which disqualifies prisoners from voting during their time in custody.[361]

D THE EUROPEAN COURT OF HUMAN RIGHTS

With its highly legalistic character and its several decades of interpretive jurisprudence, the European Convention on Human Rights has engendered the most sophisticated jurisprudence of any of the international judicial instruments promulgated to protect human

---

[358] *Belgian Linguistics Case (No 2)* (1979–1980) 1 EHRR 252.   [359] (1982) 4 EHRR 293.

[360] [2002] EWCA Civ 1926, [2003] QB 1300, [2003] 1 All ER 385.

[361] *R (on the application of Pearson) v Secretary of State for the Home Department* [2001] EWHC 239 (Admin) [2001] HRLR 39. For a critique of this decision, see Lardy, 'Prisoner Disenfranchisement: Constitutional Rights and Wrongs' [2002] PL 524.

rights . . . in many respects, the theory and practice of the European Convention on Human Rights parallel the theory and practice of the United States Supreme Court more closely that any domestic system operating in Europe. The key to understanding the Convention lies in the case-law of the European Commission and Court, whose role it is to interpret the Convention, unlike the role of British and most Commonwealth judges, whose role it is to apply the law as passed by the legislature.[362]

In its original form, the ECHR established both a Commission and a Court of Human Rights. The Commission's role was to examine applications under the Convention and to reject at an early stage those which were manifestly unfounded or otherwise inadmissible. Admissible claims were then subject to the Commission's attempts to negotiate a 'friendly settlement'. Only if a settlement could not be reached would the matter finally be referred to the Court, but not before the Commission had examined the case and prepared a written opinion as to the merits. In the 1990s the Committee of Ministers[363] decided to streamline the complaints procedure in order to cope with the growing number of applications that were being received each year. The reforms were set out in Protocol 11 and came into effect on 1 November 1998. After a brief transitional period to allow the resolution of cases that were already in the system, the Commission was abolished and a re-vamped, full-time Court now deals with all stages of a complaint.

Further reforms are due to be implemented under Protocol 14. This was opened for signature on 12 May 2004, but requires ratification by all forty-six member states before it can take effect. The Committee of Ministers aims to secure its entry into force by 2006.[364] Whereas Protocol 11 brought about wholesale changes to the Strasbourg system, the reforms introduced by Protocol 14 will be rather more modest. The aim is to ease the pressure on the Court by allowing clearly inadmissible claims to be filtered out by a single judge at a preliminary stage.[365] The Protocol will also introduce an additional admissibility criterion for individual applications.[366] Several Convention Articles will be amended or renumbered as a result of these changes,[367] though none of the provisions dealing with substantive rights will be affected. (References in this chapter are to the old Article numbers: the new numbers are given in brackets where applicable.)

1 THE COMPOSITION AND PROCEDURE OF THE COURT

The number of judges of the Court is equal to the number of parties to the Convention, though judges are appointed to sit in an individual capacity and there are no

---

[362] Gomien, Harris and Zwaak (1996) at p 19; see n 5 *ante*.

[363] The Council of Europe's political and executive body.

[364] For a discussion, see Beernaert, 'Protocol 14 and New Strasbourg Procedures: Towards Greater Efficiency? And at What Price?' [2004] EHRLR 544.

[365] See the new Article 27.   [366] Article 35, as amended; Protocol 14, Article 12.

[367] Article 24 will be deleted, the old Articles 25–27 will become Articles 24–26, and a new Article 27 will be inserted. Articles 22–29, 31–32, 35–36, 38–39, 46, and 59 will be amended.

requirements as to nationality.[368] Like their counterparts in the European Court of Justice,[369] judges are currently appointed for a renewable period of six years, but under the reforms introduced by Protocol 14 they will serve for a single nine-year term.[370] Judges are elected by the Parliamentary Assembly from a list of candidates supplied by each Member State,[371] and the Court is divided into four sections. Rule 25(2) of the Rules of Procedure provides that 'the composition of the sections shall be geographically and gender balanced and shall reflect the different legal systems among the Contracting Parties.' The sections are headed by two Vice-Presidents and two Presidents of Section. The holders of these positions are elected by the judges from amongst their ranks, as is the Court's President.[372]

Applications to the Court may be made in any language used by the Member States, though once a case reaches the merits stage proceedings must normally be conducted in English or French.[373] Each application is assigned to a section, and a rapporteur decides whether to refer the case directly to a Chamber of seven judges, or whether to allocate it to a three-member committee for a preliminary examination.[374] Committees perform a filtering role similar to that performed by the former Commission and may strike out inadmissible claims without a hearing.[375] Under the new system it will also be possible for claims that are clearly inadmissible or without merit to be struck out by a single judge.[376]

Applications not struck out at a preliminary stage are currently referred to a Chamber for a full determination. This will continue to be the case for most applications brought under the new system, but the committees will also have the power to decide both the admissibility *and* the merits of repetitive claims. Thus, 'if the underlying question in [a] case . . . is already the subject of well-established case law', it will be possible for a committee of three judges to deal with all aspects of it in a single judgment, instead of admissible claims automatically being referred to a Chamber.[377] Where a decision is made by a Chamber, its membership will include the section President or Vice-President and the judge elected in respect of the Member State concerned. During this stage it may be possible for the parties to negotiate a friendly settlement with the assistance of the Court's Registrar,[378] but if the case cannot be resolved the Chamber will deliver its judgment. Within three months of the judgment, any party may request that the case be referred to the Grand Chamber on the grounds that it raises a serious issue of interpretation or some other serious issue of general

---

[368] Articles 20 and 21, ECHR. The judge currently occupying Liechtenstein's seat in the court is Swiss.

[369] See p 138, *ante.*   [370] Article 23, as amended; Protocol 14, Article 2.

[371] Article 22, as amended.   [372] Rule 8, Rules of Procedure.   [373] Rule 34.

[374] Rule 49. Under rule 48, all inter-state applications must be referred to a Chamber.

[375] Article 28, as amended.

[376] New Article 27 (which has no equivalent in the old Convention structure). Where a single judge is used, he or she cannot be the judge elected in respect of the state with which the case is concerned.

[377] Article 28; Protocol 14, Article 8.

[378] Article 38. (The relevant provisions are moved to Article 39 by Protocol 14, Article 14, and the changes introduced allow the Court to facilitate a friendly settlement at *any* stage in proceedings.)

importance.[379] The Grand Chamber consists of seventeen judges, including the President, Vice-Presidents, and section Presidents, and is constituted for a period of three years.[380] Exceptionally, where a case raises sufficiently important issues, the Chamber may decline to deliver a judgment and may instead refer the case directly to the Grand Chamber for a ruling.[381]

By Article 41, if a violation of the Convention is established the Court can afford 'just satisfaction' to the injured party. This may involve an order for a state to pay compensation and recompense for costs. Final judgments of the Court are binding on the member states concerned, and the Committee of Ministers is responsible for overseeing their execution and for ensuring that any remedial action is taken. Failure to comply with a judgment might lead to a state being suspended from the Council of Europe, or, under Protocol 14, to the Committee of Ministers bringing proceedings in the Court for persistent infringement.[382]

2 THE ADMISSIBILITY OF COMPLAINTS

Complaints may be brought either by other Convention states or by individual victims of a Convention breach.[383] Inter-state applications are rare, but this is perhaps inevitable given the likely diplomatic consequences of bringing such an action. Most inter-state cases have been brought by countries directly connected to the 'victims' of the complaints,[384] but the *Greek Case* is a notable exception.[385] Several countries pursued this case when the 'regime of the colonels' seized power in Greece in a military coup. Specific complaints included the use of torture, the use of courts-martial to sentence political prisoners, the prohibition of political activity, censorship of the press, and suspension of the rule of law. In total, violations of ten different Convention rights were established, forcing Greece to withdraw from the Council of Europe. It did not return until democracy was restored in 1974.

The vast majority of complaints lodged with the Court are from individual applicants. The basic admissibility criteria are set out in Article 35 of the Convention. This stipulates that the applicant must have already exhausted all effective remedies in his own country, and that he must have lodged his complaint within six months of a final decision by a national court or tribunal.[386] These criteria are applied fairly rigidly, though a journalist who was refused a job following a secret vetting process was able to make a later application because the alleged breach was not discovered until nine years later.[387] An additional admissibility criterion is introduced by Protocol 14. This

---

[379] Article 43.   [380] Article 27 (new Article 26), as amended; Protocol 14, Article 6.

[381] Article 30.   [382] Article 46, as amended; Protocol 14, Article 16.

[383] Recognition of the right of individual petition has been compulsory on Convention states since 1998: Article 34. The UK accepted this right on 14 January 1966.

[384] *Ireland* v *UK* (1979) 2 EHRR 25; see p 178, *ante*. See also *Cyprus* v *Turkey* (2002) 35 EHRR 30.

[385] (1969) 12 YB ECHR 196.

[386] Article 35, as amended. There is no obligation to have recourse to remedies which are inadequate or ineffective: *Aksoy* v *Turkey* (1997) 23 EHRR 553.

[387] *Hilton* v *UK* (1988) 57 D&R 108.

empowers the Court to declare an individual application inadmissible if the applicant 'has not suffered a significant disadvantage'. However, the case should still be examined on its merits if respect for human rights requires it.[388] The complainant must also be a victim or potential victim of a Convention breach,[389] and a 'victim' for these purposes is a person directly affected by a violation of a right, or who runs the risk of being directly affected in the future. In *Norris* v *Ireland*,[390] for example, a gay man who risked prosecution under a law criminalizing homosexual acts was considered to be a 'victim' for the purposes of Article 34.

[388] Article 35, as amended; Protocol 14, Article 12.   [389] Article 34.
[390] (1991) 13 EHRR 186.

PART II

THE
ADMINISTRATION OF
JUSTICE

6

THE ROYAL PREROGATIVE
AND JUDICIAL REVIEW

A THE ROYAL PREROGATIVE

Historically the sovereign is the fountain of justice in England. For this reason the administration of justice is, strictly speaking, a prerogative of the Crown. This prerogative has, however, been substantially whittled away. Thus it was decided by Coke CJ in the case of *Prohibitions del Roy*[1] that the King (James I) could not, in his own person, judge any case. The Crown no longer has a general power to create new courts by prerogative, and while it can, theoretically, create courts to administer only the common law,[2] there would be no money to finance them in the absence of statutory authority. With the drastic curtailment of the immunity of the Crown in respect of civil proceedings (other than in a personal capacity) the position of the Crown is effectively formal. The remaining powers and privileges, though nominally vested in the Crown, are in reality those of its Ministers.[3]

Dicey defined the prerogative as follows:

The prerogative is the name for the remaining portion of the Crown's original authority, and is therefore, as already pointed out, the name for the residue of discretionary power left at any moment in the hands of the Crown, whether such power be in fact exercised by the King himself or by his Ministers.[4]

Most of the remaining vestiges of prerogative control over the administration of justice are formal rather than substantive. The superior courts are termed the 'Queen's Courts' and the judges of those courts styled 'Her Majesty's Judges'. Criminal proceedings, on indictment, are pursued in the name of the Queen and all criminal proceedings are conducted on behalf of the Crown. These so-called prerogatives are, however, illusory. There is no power in the Crown to intervene in civil proceedings and any private individual may usually commence criminal proceedings.

---

[1] (1607) 12 Co Rep 63.

[2] *Re Lord Bishop of Natal* (1864) 3 Moo PCCNS 115. The Criminal Injuries Compensation Board was an example of a tribunal created by prerogative act; see p 287, *post*.

[3] In accordance with constitutional principle, exercisable by and on the advice of Ministers.

[4] *Introduction to the Study of the Law of the Constitution* (8th edn, 1915), p 421, cited with approval in *A-G v De Keyser's Royal Hotel Ltd* [1920] AC 508. See also: *Council of Civil Service Unions v Minister for the Civil Service (the GCHQ case)* [1985] AC 374; [1984] 3 All ER 935.

The parts of the royal prerogative which have continuing influence on the administration of justice are few. Among them may be included the power of the Attorney-General to stop a prosecution on indictment by entering a *nolle prosequi*, the power to pardon a convicted person and the prerogative of mercy under which the Crown may, through the Home Secretary, suspend, commute, or remit any sentence.[5] The process of judicial review, though, provides an important mechanism for judicial scrutiny and control over parts of the administration of justice, and governed by the rules and procedures set out in para 54 of the Civil Procedure Rules.[6]

B JUDICIAL REVIEW

1 HISTORICAL ORIGINS OF THE POWERS OF THE HIGH COURT

Historically, the superior common law courts controlled the conduct of inferior courts of record, in the name of the King and under the royal prerogative.[7] The existence of the prerogative itself was a matter claimed to be within the province of the common law courts. In the *Case of Proclamations*[8] the court stated that 'the King hath no prerogative, but which the law of the land allows him.' The errors of these courts, whether errors as to jurisdiction or errors of law within jurisdiction, were again controlled through the use of the prerogative. This supervisory function was achieved through use of the prerogative writs. These were as follows:

(1) *prohibition*: inferior courts or administrative bodies could be prohibited from acting in excess of jurisdiction or unlawfully;

(2) *mandamus*: an inferior court could be ordered to exercise jurisdiction where it was declining to do so or an official ordered to perform a function which the law required of him;

(3) *certiorari*: the record of an inferior court could be examined by the King's Bench and the proceedings quashed on the ground of error of law, excess of jurisdiction, or abuse of process;

(4) *habeas corpus*: requiring a person holding another in custody to justify the confinement to the court;

(5) *quo warranto*: enabling a party to challenge the jurisdiction of a court or person in public office purporting to exercise jurisdiction over him. Exercised by means of a writ ordering the sheriff to summon the claimant to show by what authority (quo warranto) he asserted jurisdiction.

---

[5] See p 208, *post.*
[6] Supplement by *Practice Direction (PD 54)*
[7] See p 223, *post.*
[8] (1610) 12 Co Rep 74.

Of the above, *quo warranto* fell into disuse long before its abolition in 1938.[9] The various forms of the writ of habeas corpus still exist and are still frequently used, often as a means of testing the validity of detention effected for the purpose of extradition. The remaining three writs were abolished in 1938 but were replaced by orders of prohibition, mandamus, and certiorari. These in turn were renamed by the Civil Procedure Rules as *Prohibition Orders*, *Mandatory Orders*, and *Quashing Orders* respectively. Together with injunctions and declarations they form the armoury of the Administrative Court,[10] which performs the supervisory functions inherent in the term 'judicial review'.[11] An application for any of the orders named above, or for an injunction or declaration, must be made by way of application for judicial review. Damages may be awarded, perhaps where there is found to be a breach of contract or a tort committed by a public authority,[12] but in fact they are rarely awarded in judicial review proceedings, and are more appropriate remedies in private law actions.

2 THE SCOPE OF JUDICIAL REVIEW

This has widened greatly in recent years. Despite occasional judicial confusions, it was always clear that judicial review lay against any inferior court or tribunal, and against any body exercising statutory functions affecting the rights of individuals. A striking recent example of this principle is provided by the case of *R v Lord Chancellor, ex parte Witham*.[13] The applicant in this case challenged the validity of regulations which purported to repeal provisions contained in an earlier order. The earlier order had exempted litigants in receipt of certain state benefits from the obligation to pay court fees. The applicant was on income support and wished to bring proceedings for defamation, but without the exemption he would not have had the financial means to do so. The Divisional Court[14] upheld his challenge to the regulations, holding that access to the courts was a constitutional right at common law and could not be abrogated without the clear authority of an Act of Parliament. There was no such authority of an Act of Parliament. There was no such authority in this instance and the regulations were therefore ultra vires.

The scope of judicial review has developed to allow challenges to the actions of bodies affecting the legitimate expectations of individuals[15] Doubt remained, however, about the reviewability of actions taken by or on behalf of the Crown under the royal prerogative. The traditional position was that though the court was entitled to

---

9 By Administration of Justice (Miscellaneous Provisions) Act 1938, s 9, which provided that the remedy would, in effect, be replaced by injunction; see now Supreme Court Act 1981, s 30.

10 Part of the Queen's Bench Division: see p 252, *post*.

11 Under Part 54 CPR, and, formerly, under RSC Ord 53.

12 See, e.g., *R v Northavon DC, ex parte Palmer* (1995) 27 HLR 576.

13 [1998] QB 575, [1997] 2 All ER 779.

14 The court responsible for dealing with applications for judicial review prior to the creation formally of the Administrative Court.

15 See Lord Diplock in the GCHQ case, *ante*, n 4. The legitimate expectation can be either as to the receipt of a benefit, or of being treated procedurally in a particular way.

rule as to the existence or extent of prerogative power, it was not entitled to review the exercise of such power.[16] Thus an attempt in *Hanratty* v *Lord Butler*[17] to challenge the exercise the prerogative power of mercy inevitably failed. After a period of judicial re-evaluation,[18] the matter was effectively put beyond doubt by the House of Lords in *Council of Civil Service Unions* v *Minister for the Civil Service*.[19] The litigation arose out of an instruction by the Minister to the effect that the conditions of employment of staff at Government Communications Headquarters (GCHQ) would be revised so as to prohibit membership of any trade union (other than an approved departmental staff association). This instruction was issued pursuant to power conferred upon the Minister by an Order in Council made under the royal prerogative.[20] The appellants applied for judicial review of the Minister's instruction. It was contended (inter alia) on behalf of the Minister that the instruction was not open to review by the courts because it came from a use of the prerogative. In the event, adjudication on this contention became unnecessary because the House of Lords held that the evidence disclosed the Minister's instruction to have been justified on the ground of national security. This being so, any observations by their Lordships upon the contention raised were necessarily obiter. However, the majority proceeded on the basis that the key question was not the source of the power, but rather whether it was of a nature suitable for judicial adjudication (i.e. justiciable).

In the GCHQ case, Lord Roskill identified certain prerogative powers as of a type not suitable for judicial determination. These included the making of treaties, the defence of the realm, the prerogative of mercy, the grant of honours, the dissolution of Parliament, and the appointment of Ministers. What is fundamental though, is the nature of the issue to be determined by the court.[21] Lord Roskill's list is not absolute, as shown by a successful challenge being made to the exercise of the prerogative of mercy in *R* v *Secretary of State for Home Affairs, ex parte Bentley*.[22] In that case, a Divisional Court held that the courts have jurisdiction to review the exercise of the royal prerogative of mercy by the Home Secretary. The Home Secretary, in consider-ing whether or not to grant a posthumous free pardon to B, a person hanged in 1952 for murder, had failed to have regard to the fact that such a pardon might be used in a variety of circumstances and take different forms. It might constitute a full pardon, or, as might have been appropriate in this case, a conditional pardon substituting a lesser sentence for that in fact imposed. The Secretary of State thus had made an error

---

[16] *Case of Saltpetre* (1606) 12 Co Rep 12; *Blackburn* v *A-G* [1971] 2 All ER 1380; [1971] 1 WLR 1037.

[17] (1971) 115 Sol Jo 386.

[18] See *R* v *Criminal Injuries Compensation Board, ex parte Lain* [1967] 2 QB 864 (though this was not a case of the direct exercise of prerogative power); *Laker Airways Ltd* v *Department of Trade* [1977] 2 All ER182, per Lord Denning.

[19] See n 4, *ante*.

[20] This is primary legislation, to be distinguished from the use of Orders in Council as delegated legislation.

[21] *R (On the application of Abbasi)* v *Secretary of State for Foreign and Commonwealth Affairs* [2002] EWCA Civ 598.

[22] [1994] QB 349, [1993] 4 All ER 442.

of law by failing to have regard to all relevant considerations, and therefore his refusal was unlawful. In so deciding the court was applying the reasoning of the House of Lords in the GCHQ case. Even the exercise of the prerogative of mercy could be judicially reviewed if the grounds of challenge did not involve the court in deciding policy questions. Thus, whilst the policy to be adopted for the granting of pardons was not justiciable, the present decision was, because the Secretary of State had failed to recognize the extent of his powers.

The trend set by the GCHQ case has continued. Recent case law shows that it is now the nature of the function that matters, and which determines whether judicial review is available. In R v Panel on Take-overs and Mergers, ex parte Datafin[23] the court ruled that the absence of a statutory or prerogative power was not decisive: judicial review would lie in respect of any body performing a public law function.[24] In this case, the Take-Over Panel was acting 'governmentally' in engaging in regulatory functions which would otherwise be performed by a statutory body on behalf of the state.[25] The application of the Datafin principle is far from easy. In R v Disciplinary Committee of the Jockey Club, ex parte Aga Khan[26] the Court of Appeal decided that the Jockey Club was not a public body for the purposes of judicial review, despite its important regulatory function in respect of the sport of horseracing. The key features in reaching this decision were the lack of integration into a scheme of public regulation, the fact that the Jockey Club was not a 'surrogate organ of government', the fact that its powers derived from consent, and the fact that effective private law remedies existed.

3 LIMITS TO THE JUDICIAL REVIEW JURISDICTION

Statute may attempt to prohibit judicial review by the use of a so-called 'ouster clause'. If the words of such a clause are clear then the courts will be bound by them. One example is section 29(3) of the Supreme Court Act 1981 discussed below, which prevents judicial review of matters relating to trial on indictment. However, the courts generally seek, where possible, to construe ouster clauses restrictively. One such example was Anisminic Ltd v Foreign Compensation Commission, which concerned a

---

[23] [1987] QB 815, [1987] 1 All ER 564.

[24] Which is not created simply by the body concerned being a public body: see R v East Berkshire Area Health Authority, ex parte Walsh [1985] QB 152; [1984] 3 All ER 425. For the relevant principles, see McClaren v Home Office [1990] ICR 824; R v Lord Chancellor's Department, ex parte Nangle [1992] 1 All ER 897. Significant overlaps also exist with the cases dealing with the question of 'public body' for the purposes of the Human Rights Act 1998, s 6. See, p 163, ante, and, in particular, Poplar HRCA v Donoghue [2001] 4 All ER 604; Aston Cantlow and Wilmcote with Billesley Parochial Church Council v Wallbank [2001] 3 All ER 393.

[25] The effect of the Datafin decision appears weakened by subsequent cases; See R v Chief Rabbi of the United Hebrew Congregations of Great Britain, ex parte Wachmann [1992] 1 WLR 1036. In R v Insurance Ombudsman Bureau and the Insurance Ombudsman, ex parte Aegon Life Assurance Ltd [1994] COD 426, the court held that if the exercise of the power was consensual or contractual then it was not a public law matter, despite being woven into a system of governmental control.

[26] [1993] 2 All ER 853.   [27] [1969 2 AC 147.

section in the Foreign Compensation Act 1950. The section[27] purported to prevent judicial review of any 'determination' of the Commission but the House of Lords ruled that it could not prevent judicial review of a matter which the Commission had no power to deal with in the way it had. The Commission had, on the particular facts, had made an error of law which deprived it of jurisdiction.[28] Clearly, courts are reluctant to be deprived of their power to engage in scrutiny of the legal basis of any decision or action, but their ability to sidestep an ouster clause will depend on its extent and nature. A partial ouster clause is more likely to be upheld.[29] Such provisions must also be viewed in the light of the wider context of the European Convention: the interference with the liberty or rights of an individual without some opportunity for either review or appeal may raise important issues under Article 6 of the Convention.[30]

One key limit on judicial review is the nature of the question to be decided by the court.[31] For example, many (though not all) of the prerogative powers involving the administration of justice may be beyond judicial review, because of their unsuitability for judicial determination. However, Simon Brown LJ observed[32] that 'only the rarest cases will today be ruled strictly beyond the court's purview'. The role of the courts is clear: to examine matters of legality, not matters that infringe upon the proper role of the Executive or Parliament. On judicial review the courts are concerned with legality, not the merits of the case.[33] That gives the court the right to review the legal basis on which any action is taken. A good example is *R v Secretary of State for the Home Department, ex parte Fire Brigades Union*,[34] where an attempt to replace a scheme governing payments to the victims of crime with an extra-statutory scheme under the Royal Prerogative was held unlawful. The statutory scheme had been passed by Parliament, but never introduced. Even though the Minister had the right to decide whether, if at all, to bring the statutory scheme into force, he was not entitled in law to use royal prerogative powers to frustrate the will of Parliament. He should have sought to have the statutory provisions changed, by repeal or amendment, through statute. In short, he was misusing his powers and acting unlawfully.

Whilst it is easy to draw this distinction in theory, the reality is rather different. When judicially reviewing the exercise of a statutory discretion the court will seek to establish, or impute, the intention of Parliament. At first sight that might appear to be a simple question of statutory construction and interpretation, but, as already noted,[35] the principles that govern construction and interpretation are sufficiently broad to

---

[28] For these purposes we may equate the word 'jurisdiction' with 'power'.

[29] *R v Secretary of State for the Environment, ex parte Ostler* [1977] QB 122; *R v Cornwall County Council, ex parte Huntington* [1992] 3 All ER 526.

[30] See p 180, *ante*.

[31] See Lord Roskill in GCHQ case, *ante*. See also *R (on the application of the Campaign for Nuclear Disarmament v Prime Minister* [2002] All ER (D) 245; *Marchiori v Environment Agency* [2002] EWCA Civ 3, *The Independent*, 31 January 2002.

[32] In *R v Ministry of Defence, ex parte Smith* [1996] QB 517, [1996] 1 All ER 257.

[33] *R v Secretary of State for the Home Department, ex parte Brind* [1991] 1 AC 696.

[34] [1995] 2 All ER 244   [35] See pp 48–58, *ante*.

give the court real choices. Thus in *Padfield v Agriculture, Fisheries and Food*[36] the House of Lords concluded that Parliament could not have intended a seemingly unlimited discretion under the Agricultural Marketing Act 1958 to be used in the way that it had. Further, the methodology and case law of the European Convention means that, by virtue of the Human Rights Act 1998, the courts are required to have regard to questions of policy and proportionality.[37] The scope of judicial review has therefore widened, raising important issues concerning the proper role of the judiciary.

Judicial review should be carefully contrasted with appeals. Appeals are concerned with the question of the merits of a decision or action, either on matters of fact or law. By contrast, judicial review is concerned with questions of legality. In the context of the administration of justice, there is obviously an overlap. Superior courts have the power to make errors of law, and the correct way of correcting them is by an appeal on a point of law.[38] By contrast, errors of law of inferior courts and tribunals may be corrected by judicial review if they are apparent on the face of the record.[39] Even then, however, if a matter of fact may be in issue the better approach may be to bring an appeal by way of case stated on a point of law.[40]

Sometimes judicial review may be available, but only to a limited extent. In *R v Harrow LBC, ex parte D*,[41] for example, it was said that a local authority's decision to place a name on its child abuse register would rarely be a matter for review. The court indicated that judicial review would only be appropriate if the decision in question could be shown to be wholly unreasonable or to raise an important point of principle. Presumably, a slightly wider approach to reflect the need to protect the Convention rights of the child or parents might now be called for. Another area where judicial review may be limited relates to policing and prosecution. The courts have held that the actions of the police may be reviewed, but that the scope of that review is restricted. An example of this is judicial review of the prosecution process. In *R v Commissioner of Police for the Metropolis, ex parte Blackburn*[42] the applicant sought an order of mandamus to compel the Commissioner of Police to reverse a policy statement which appeared to limit the enforcement of the gaming laws. The Court of Appeal held that mandamus might be appropriate if there was a complete failure to perform a duty imposed by law, but it declined to make an order in the particular case before the court because the Commissioner had in fact reversed his policy. In a subsequent case involving the obscene publications laws,[43] the court stressed that the discretion was that of the Commissioner, and that the court could only intervene

---

[36] [1968 AC 997

[37] See p 165, *ante*. For proportionality as a ground of challenge, see p 216, *post*.

[38] As to which see chapter 17 and chapter 23, *post*.

[39] *R v Crown Court at Knightsbridge, ex parte International Sporting Club (London) Ltd* [1982] QB 304

[40] *R v Morpeth Ward JJ, ex parte Ward* (1992) 95 Cr App R 215. For appeals by way of case stated, see p 651, *post*.

[41] [1990] Fam 133, [1990] 3 All ER 12.   [42] [1968] 2 QB 118, [1968] 1 All ER 763.

[43] *R v Commissioner of Police for the Metropolis, ex parte Blackburn (No 3)* [1973] QB 241, [1973] 1 All ER 324.

where there was what amounted to an abdication of function. By contrast it will be much easier to justify judicial intervention if the decisions of the police affect the ability of an individual to exercise legally protected rights. Such a case was *R v Coventry City Council, ex parte Phoenix Aviation*[44] where the actions of the police in failing to prevent the obstruction by demonstrators of the applicants' rights, under EU law, to export live animals were judicially reviewable. The application succeeded on the facts.

One area which has evolved in tune with modern approaches to judicial review is that in respect of decisions to institute proceedings. The decisions of the Law Officers appear generally to be beyond challenge. In *Gouriet v Union of Post Office Workers*[45] the power to enforce the criminal law through applications for injunctive relief was held to be for the Attorney-General alone. More recently, in *R v Solicitor-General, ex parte Taylor and Taylor*,[46] a Divisional Court decided that the decision whether to bring proceedings for contempt of court was not justiciable. However, in the context of judicial review of the decision to prosecute the courts are more willing to intervene. A distinction has, in the past, been drawn between decisions involving juveniles and those involving adults. In *R v Chief Constable of Kent, ex parte L*[47] the court stated that, where a policy exists in respect of cautioning juveniles, the decision to commence or discontinue criminal proceedings was subject to judicial review, but only where it could be shown that the decision was made regardless of, or contrary to, that policy.[48] This was applied by another Divisional Court in *R v Commissioner of Police for the Metropolis, ex parte P*,[49] where the cautioning of a juvenile improperly, and in contravention of the Code for Crown Prosecutors, was judicially reviewable. The courts have also been prepared to consider judicial review of decisions to prosecute an adult. The challenge in *R v Inland Revenue Commissioners ex parte Mead*[50] failed on the facts, because the prosecuting authority (the Inland Revenue) had considered the matter fairly, and appropriately, and had taken all relevant matters into account.

Moving to judicial review of the actions of the courts themselves, it is an effective means for the control of the inferior courts, ensuring a means of challenge where failures to comply with jurisdictional requirements, or with principles of fair procedure, have occurred. Judicial review also provides a remedy where no right of appeal against a decision exists.[51] A good example was seen in *R (Director of Public Prosecutions) v Camberwell Youth Court*.[52] In that case, the DPP was concerned about the decisions by youth courts in a series of cases to retain jurisdiction to sentence certain young offenders rather than to commit them to the Crown Court for

---

[44] [1995] 3 All ER 37.   [45] [1978] AC 435, [1977] 3 All ER 70.   [46] [1996] 1 FCR 206.
[47] [1993] 1 All ER 756.   [48] See *R v Havering Justices, ex parte Gould* (1993), unreported.
[49] (1996) 5 Admin LR 6, 160 JP 369.   [50] [1993] 1 All ER 772.
[51] Judicial review can only be prevented by the clearest of words: *Anisminic Ltd v Foreign Compensation Commission* [1969] 2 AC 147, [1969] 1 All ER 208.
[52] [2005] 1 Cr App R 6.

sentence.[53] To achieve the desired result voluntary bills of indictment were preferred,[54] a procedure against which there was no appeal.[55] On an application for judicial review, the court deprecated that practice, holding that if the DPP considered the decision of the youth court wrong the correct way of proceeding was by means of an application for judicial review to quash the decision of the inferior court.

However, where a right of appeal does exist, leave to apply for judicial review may be declined unless the complaint raised is one of procedural impropriety, unfairness, or bias, leaving the applicant to deal with other matters by way of appeal.[56] Similarly with the actions of other forms of judicial adjudication, such as tribunals or public inquiries.

Judicial review does not generally lie against superior courts. The Crown Court is a superior court of record, but despite this, it is amenable to judicial review when dealing with an appeal from a magistrates' court. This is because it is then exercising the jurisdiction of that court, an inferior court. Its actions are also subject to review in other cases, subject to the important limitation in section 29(3) of the Supreme Court Act 1981, which concerns judicial review 'in matters relating to trial on indictment'. The reason for this provision is historical: the Crown Court took over the appellate jurisdiction of the old courts of Quarter Sessions, which were inferior courts and thus subject to judicial review. However, the application of section 29(3) has proved less than easy. In *R v Crown Court at Sheffield, ex parte Brownlow*[57] Lord Denning sought to interpret the subsection as preventing judicial review of any matter arising 'in the course of trial on indictment'. This extremely narrow construction was not adopted by the majority of the court, which concluded that section 29(3) prevented judicial review where a decision arose out of, or incidentally to, the jurisdiction to try cases on indictment. On this view, a decision by the trial judge as to information concerning the jury panel was held to be caught by section 29(3) and thus was not judicially reviewable.

The approach taken by the majority has not been followed in subsequent cases. In *Smalley v Crown Court at Warwick*[58] the House of Lords considered a decision to forfeit a recognizance entered into by a witness to be judicially reviewable. Lord Bridge stressed the need to proceed on a case-by-case basis. He set out a working test: the limitation in section 29(3) applied to 'any decision affecting the conduct of a trial on indictment'. However, it has since been stressed that this is a guideline, and was not an attempt to re-write the words of the subsection.[59] In addition, the real difficulty is in applying the guidance given by Lord Bridge. Decisions to allow counts of an indictment effectively to remain untried, and applications to quash an indictment,

---

[53] Under Powers of Criminal Courts (Sentencing) Act 2000, s 91. See, further, p 639, *post.*

[54] See p 570, *post.*

[55] *R v Manchester Crown Court, ex parte Williams and Simpson* [1990] Crim LR 654.

[56] *R v Hereford Magistrates' Court, ex parte Rowlands* [1998] QB 110; cf. *R v Peterborough Magistrates' Court, ex parte Dowler* [1997] QB 911.

[57] 1980] QB 530, [1980] 2 All ER 444.   [58] [1985] AC 622, [1985] 1 All ER 769.

[59] Per Lord Bridge in *Sampson v Crown Court at Croydon* [1987] 1 All ER 609, [1987] 1 WLR 194.

are instances which have been held to be subject to the restrictions upon judicial review.[60] So too are matters relating to sentence.[61]

The problem was extensively considered by the House of Lords in two cases. The first was *R v Manchester Crown Court, ex parte Director of Public Prosecutions*[62] where the court held that an order of the Crown Court made upon an application to stay the proceedings for abuse of process was an order affecting the conduct of the trial, and therefore fell within section 29(2). The second was *Director of Public Prosecutions v Crown Court at Manchester and Huckfield*,[63] where a decision by a circuit judge to quash an indictment for lack of jurisdiction was held to be a matter 'relating to trial on indictment' and thus not judicially reviewable. One test is whether the decision sought to be reviewed arises in the issue between the Crown and the defendant formulated by the indictment, including issues relating to costs. If it does, then judicial review might well lead to delay in the trial, and therefore is probably caught by the restrictions imposed by section 29(3).

The House of Lords stressed that this test might not always be appropriate. In particular, the question was left open as to whether judicial review was available in respect of the procedures to be followed in cases of serious fraud.[64] However, the test formulated by the court would have the effect of permitting judicial review where an order was made affecting a person other than the defendant,[65] or where the court was acting under a different jurisdiction.[66]

4 GROUNDS FOR JUDICIAL REVIEW

As already noted, judicial review is not a form of appeal. The High Court should not substitute its own decision for that of the court, tribunal, or body below on the ground that it appears to be wrong, and it is generally at pains to avoid doing so. The circumstances in which the court will interfere are want or excess of jurisdiction or failure to comply with the rules of natural justice and procedural fairness. These standards of procedural fairness vary from case to case but generally include the right of each party to state his case, the prohibition on a person being judge in his own cause, the right to be informed of the reasons for a decision and, in some cases, the

---

[60] See *R v Central Criminal Court, ex parte Raymond* [1986] 2 All ER 379, [1986] 1 WLR 710.; *R v Southwark Crown Court, ex parte Ward* [1996] Crim LR 123

[61] *R (On application of Lichniak) Secretary of State for the Home Department* [2002] QB 296.

[62] [1994] AC 9; *sub nom Director of Public Prosecutions v Crown Court at Manchester and Ashton* [1993] 2 All ER 663.

[63] [1993] 4 All ER 928.

[64] In *R v Central Criminal Court, ex parte Serious Fraud Office* [1993] 2 All ER 399, [1993] 1 WLR 949 such proceedings were held not to be caught by the restriction in s 29(3). See also *R v Crown Court at Southwark* [1993] 1 WLR 764. For procedures relating to serious fraud cases see p 589, *post.*

[65] See *Smalley v Crown Court at Warwick*, n 58 *ante* (forfeiture of recognizance of third party); *R v Crown Court at Maidstone, ex parte Gill* [1987] 1 All ER 129 (forfeiture of property of third party).

[66] See, e.g. *R v Crown Court at Inner London, ex parte Benjamin* (1986) 85 Cr App R 267 (binding over of acquitted person).

right to legal representation before a tribunal.[67] In respect of inferior courts or tribunals, the court can intervene by way of judicial review if there is an error of law on the face of the record,[68] although this principle is of little practical importance given the wide interpretation the courts have given to the concept of excess of power or jurisdiction for non judicial bodies.[69]

In addition, in the case of an administrative person or body the court will intervene when a discretion has been misused. This could have occurred because relevant matters have not been taken into account,[70] or regard paid to irrelevancies, or because the discretion has been fettered improperly[71] or otherwise used contrary to the principles of the enabling power. These are often known as 'the *Wednesbury* principles'.[72] These matters are couched in legal terms but often bring the courts to a position where care has to be taken not to cross the boundaries between legitimate executive judgment and proper judicial intervention. Finally, if the body reaches a decision that no sensible authority could reach it may be held to be invalid on the grounds of '*Wednesbury* unreasonableness', now usually referred to as 'irrationality'.[73]

These grounds of judicial review were described by Lord Diplock in *Council of Civil Service Unions* v *Minister for the Civil Service*[74] as (1) 'illegality'; (2) 'irrationality' (i.e. *Wednesbury* unreasonableness); and (3) 'procedural impropriety'. Whilst these terms have become widely accepted and used, it is important to recognize that they amount to no more than convenient labels,[75] and do not amount to the creation of new grounds of challenge. The meaning and scope of 'irrationality' has been the subject of doubt, and has been described, graphically, as applying in respect of decisions which are so unreasonable as to 'jump off the page at you'.[76] It is a controversial ground that raises constitutional issues and issues about the proper role of the

---

[67] See *R* v *Board of Visitors of HM Prison, The Maze, ex parte Hone* [1988] AC 379, *sub nom Hone* v *Maze Prison Board of Prison Visitors* [1988] 1 All ER 321; *R* v *Secretary of State for the Home Department, ex parte Cheblak* [1991] 2 All ER 319, [1991] 1 WLR 890.

[68] *R* v *Northumberland Compensation Appeal Tribunal, ex parte Shaw* [1952] 1 KB 338, [1952] 1 All ER 122. This used to be confined to the record itself and excluded jurisdiction to correct errors in the reasons leading to the record but it is now held to extend to errors in reasons given in support of the recorded decision: *R* v *Crown Court at Knightsbridge, ex parte International Sporting Club (London) Ltd* [1982] QB 304, [1981] 3 All ER 417.

[69] See *Anisminic Ltd* v *Foreign Compensation Commission*, p 209, *ante*, and Lord Browne-Wilkinson in *R* v *Lord President of the Privy Council, ex parte Page* [1993] AC 682.

[70] See, e.g. *R* v *Port Talbot BC, ex parte Jones* [1998] 2 All ER 207; *R* v *Barnet & Camden Rent Tribunal* [1972] 1 All ER 1185; *Roberts* v *Hopwood* [1925] AC 578

[71] See, e.g. *Wheeler* v *Leicester City Council* [1985] 2 All ER 1106; *R* v *Lewisham LBC, ex parte Shell UK Ltd* [1988] 1 All ER 938; *R* v *Coventry City Council, ex parte Phoenix Aviation* [1995] 3 All ER 37.

[72] *Associated Provincial Picture Houses Ltd* v *Wednesbury Corporation* [1948] 1 KB 223, [1947] 2 All ER 680. For examples see, e.g., *Padfield* v *Minister of Agriculture, Fisheries and Food* [1968] AC 997, [1968] 1 All ER 694; *Wheeler* v *Leicester City Council* [1985] AC 1054, [1985] 2 All ER 1106; *R* v *Sefton Metropolitan Borough Council, ex parte Help the Aged* [1997] 4 All ER 532.

[73] For discussion, see *R* v *Secretary of State for the Home Department, ex parte Brind* [1991] 1 AC 696, [1990] 1 All ER 469, CA, [1991] 1 AC 696, [1991] 1 All ER 720, HL.

[74] See p 208, *ante*.   [75] Per Lord Donaldson in *ex parte Brind, ante*.

[76] *R* v *Lord Chancellor, ex parte Maxwell* [1996] 4 All ER 751.

judiciary, because, in effect, it requires the reviewing court to take a view as to the merits, or lack of merits of the decision under review. Lord Lowry in *R v Secretary of State for the Home Department, ex parte Brind*[77] summed up the issues well when he said:

> ... what we are accustomed to call Wednesbury unreasonableness is a branch of the abuse, or misuse, of power: the court's duty is not to interfere withy a discretion which Parliament has entrusted to a statutory body or an individual but to maintain a check on excesses in the exercise of discretion. That is why it is not enough if a judge feels able to say ... 'I think that is unreasonable: that is not what I would have done.' It also explains the emphatic language which judges have used in order to drive home the message and the necessity ... for the act to be 'so unreasonable that no reasonable [body] would have done it.' In that strong and necessary emphasis lies the danger. A less emotive but, subject to one qualification, reliable test is to ask: 'Could a decision-maker acting reasonably have reached that decision?' The qualification is that the supervising court must bear in mind that it is not sitting on appeal, but satisfying itself whether the decision-maker has acted within the bounds of his discretion. ...

These issues become even more acute in the context of Convention rights and the Human Rights Act 1998. Lord Templeman in *Brind* and Simon Brown LJ in *R v Ministry of Defence, ex parte Smith*[78] each appeared to suggest that the decision of a public authority was challengeable more readily on grounds of irrationality if it involved the fundamental rights of the individual. This was somewhat controversial, and was not firmly settled by authority.[79] Lord Diplock in the GCHQ case[80] canvassed 'proportionality' as a possible fourth ground of challenge. This was rejected in *Brind* v *Secretary of State for the Home Department*[81]—the House of Lords concluded that no such ground existed as a general ground of challenge by judicial review, but rather that it formed part of the process by which allegations of breach of the *Wednesbury* principles, or of *Wednesbury* unreasonableness, would be judged. In any event, such a ground is more likely to be relevant to the review of administrative actions or discretions than to the judicial actions of inferior courts.

There is now no doubt that the Human Rights Act 1998 widens the role and approach of the court on judicial review, particularly because the passage of the Human Rights Act 1998 takes the courts, in human rights cases, into questions of proportionality. In *R (Daly) v Secretary of State for the Home Department*[82] the challenge on judicial review was as to the legality of a policy relating to the searching of prison cells and the impact of that policy on prisoners' rights to private and confidential

---

[77] [1991] 1 AC 696.

[78] [1996] QB 517, [1996] 1 All ER 527. See, to similar effect, Lord Bridge in *R v Secretary of State for the Home Department, ex parte Bugdaycay* [1987] AC 514 at 531; *R v Ministry of Defence, ex parte Smith* [1996] QB 517.

[79] See, e.g. *R v Secretary of State for the Environment, ex parte National Association of Local Government Officers* (1993) 5 Admin LR 785, per Neill LJ; cf. *R v Secretary of State for Home Department, ex parte McQuillan* [1995] 4 All ER 440.

[80] See p 208, *ante*.   [81] [1991] 1 All ER 720 [1991] 2 WLR 588.   [82] [2001] 2 AC 532.

communication with their lawyers. In allowing the appeal, the House of Lords confirmed that the doctrine of proportionality under the Convention may require the court to consider the appropriateness of the balance struck by the decision-maker, and that it overlapped with the traditional grounds of challenge. The question was whether the measures designed to meet the legislative objective were proportionate to the needs of that objective, and whether they went no further than necessary.[83] This approach was confirmed as correct in R (Pro-Life Alliance) v BBC[84] where the balancing function with this wider role led to the upholding of a limitation on a party political broadcast, and thus a justifiable limitation on the right of freedom of expression. It was for the court to review the decision with intensity appropriate to the circumstances of the case. The latitude, or deference, that the court will, or should, give to the decision-maker will depend on the subject matter, and whether it lies more readily within the actual or potential expertise of the decision-maker or the court.[85]

5 PROCEDURE

An application for any one of the prerogative orders, or for a declaration that a public law decision is unlawful, must be made by way of application for judicial review. A Pre-Action Protocol[86] requires (except in emergency cases) an applicant to send a letter before claim, seeking to establish whether litigation can be avoided, and setting out details of the decision or matter to be challenged. A defendant should normally respond within fourteen days, and indicate which matters are contested and which conceded. It should also supply certain other information or copies of relevant documents requested.

Judicial review is is the normal, though not exclusive, means of challenge where questions of public law arise. Matters relating to the administration of justice are likely to be public law matters.

Where in reality an action raises issues of public law, the normal procedure for determination of those questions is by an application for judicial review under Part 54 CPR. Historically, a failure to use the correct procedure could have been potentially fatal to the success of the application. The Order 53 RSC procedure that existed prior to 1977 had defects that often meant that proceeding by way of writ in the Queen's Bench Division was more attractive. Certain procedures such as discovery[87] and cross-examination of those who swore affidavits were not available on judicial review; nor was it open to a court dealing with such an application to make an award for damages, or issue a declaration. These, and other, defects were remedied in 1977 when a revised Order 53 came into effect. As a result, in 1981 the House of Lords in O'Reilly

---

[83] Citing with approval the formulation in de Freitas v Permanent Secretary of Ministry of Agriculture, Fisheries, Lands and Housing [1999] 1 AC 69. See, further p 170, ante.

[84] [2003] 2 All ER 977.

[85] See the formulation, and summary, of Laws LJ in International Transport Roth Gmbh v Secretary of State for the Home Department [2002] 3 WLR 344. See also, p 165; ante.

[86] As to which, see, generally, p 448, post.   [87] See p 477, post.

v *Mackman*[88] indicated firmly that the Order 53 procedure was to be the usual method of challenging public law actions or decisions. Lord Diplock stressed the advantages of the limited time for challenge under Order 53, and the safeguard that the filter of requiring leave to apply creates. To seek to avoid these safeguards by proceeding by writ would amount in most cases to an abuse of process, although Lord Diplock accepted that there were exceptions to this general rule.

This distinction between public and private law matters, and the procedures to be followed, has caused the courts considerable difficulty.[89] The position was somewhat clarified, if not entirely so, by the House of Lords in *Roy* v *Kensington and Chelsea and Westminster Family Practitioners Committee*.[90] In that case the plaintiff, a doctor, commenced an action by writ in which he sought to obtain payments that he alleged were due to him, and which he claimed were being withheld by the defendant committee. The doctor's terms and conditions of employment were governed by regulation made pursuant to statute, and the committee sought to have the plaintiff's action struck out, arguing that it raised public law matters which should be decided on an application for judicial review under Order 53.[91] This application initially succeeded, but was rejected both by the Court of Appeal and by the House of Lords. The plaintiff was seeking to recover money allegedly owed to him. This raised private law rights, which could be enforced by private law action even if they involved challenge to a public law decision. In his speech, Lord Lowry identified two approaches. The first, the 'narrow' approach was that taken by the court in *O'Reilly* v *Mackman*: that the Order 53 procedure ought generally to be followed if there was a public law issue. The second, the 'broad' approach, was favoured by him: that the Order 53 procedure was only obligatory if no private law issue was involved. He preferred the broad approach to the narrow, although did not formally decide the matter, concluding that on either basis the case of *Roy* fell within the exception to the general rule in *O'Reilly*.

Such an approach is consistent with a series of cases where a claim for money from a party was held to be a private law matter, even if the defence involved an assertion that the claim was invalid because it was made pursuant to an ultra vires action.[92] The mere fact that one party to an action is a public body does not turn the matter into a public law matter.[93] The position was put on a much more sensible and pragmatic footing in 2000 with the decision of the Court of Appeal in *Clark* v *University of Lincolnshire and Humberside*.[94] In this case an action for judicial review of a decision of the respondent university was struck out because judicial review was an inappropriate

---

[88] [1983] 2 AC 237, [1982] 3 All ER 1124; see also *Cocks* v *Thanet District Council* [1983] 2 AC 286, [1982] 3 All ER 1135.

[89] See the cri de coeur of Henry J in *Doyle* v *Northumbria Probation Committee* [1991] 4 All ER 294, [1991] 1 WLR 340. For discussion of the issues, see Lord Woolf, 'Public Law—Private Law: Why the Divide? A Personal View' [1986] 2 PL 220.

[90] [1992] 1 AC 624; [1992] 1 All ER 705.   [91] Now CPR, Part 54.

[92] See in particular: *Wandsworth London Borough Council* v *Winder* [1985] AC 461, [1984] 3 All ER 976; *Davy* v *Spelthorne Borough Council* [1984] AC 262, [1983] 3 All ER 278.

[93] *R* v *East Berkshire AHA, ex parte Walsh* [1985] QB 152, [1984] 3 All ER 425.

[94] [2000] 3 All ER 752.

process for dealing with what were essentially matters of academic judgment. Nonetheless the court allowed a statement of claim to be amended alleging breach of contract. Lord Woolf observed:

Where a student has . . . a claim in contract, the court will not strike out a claim which could more properly be made under [Part 54] solely on the basis of the procedure that has been adopted. It may however do so if it comes to the conclusion that in all the circumstances, including the delay in instituting the proceedings, there has been an abuse of the process of the court under the CPR.

Whatever the technical and analytical difficulties, the courts are looking to the practicalities. In *Trustees of the Dennis Rye Pensions Fund v Sheffield City Council*[95] the Court of Appeal stated that a court should look at the practical consequences and not merely at the technical distinctions between public and private rights and bodies. In the case before the court it was obvious that the issues, which related to claim for payment for work done, could be dealt with more conveniently in a private law action than in an application for judicial review. More recently, in *R v Bedfordshire CC, ex parte Henlow Grange Health Farm Ltd*[96] the court dismissed an application for judicial review in respect of a planning resolution that was ineffective because the decision had been 'called in' (i.e. taken over) by the Secretary of State. What the applicant was seeking was effectively an advisory declaration to influence the decision of the Secretary of State, and that was an abuse of process of the Part 54 jurisdiction. The court also took into account the fact that the planning legislation provided a comprehensive scheme for the decision-making in terms of planning applications. The courts have also, unsurprisingly given the trend towards encouraging settlement rather than litigation,[97] concluded that judicial review should not be permitted (except for good reasons) if a significant part of the issues could be resolved outside the litigation process.[98]

Further, the authorities show that it is open to a party to proceedings to raise the invalidity of a public law action as a defence to criminal proceedings. The extent to which this is permissible has, until recently, been unclear. The right to use the invalidity of the by-law as a defence to criminal proceedings was accepted in the nineteenth century,[99] and confirmed in *R v Reading Crown Court, ex parte Hutchinson*.[100] More recently in *Boddington v British Transport Police*[101] the House of Lords put beyond doubt the fact that a defendant in criminal proceedings is entitled to challenge the validity of subordinate legislation (or an administrative decision made pursuant to subordinate legislation) where the prosecution is based on the assumption that

---

95 [1997] 4 All ER 747. See also *R v Chief Constable of Warwickshire, ex parte Fitzpatrick* [1998] 1 All ER 65 (complainant should not challenge search warrant by judicial review, which was unsuitable for a fact-finding exercise, but should rely on his private rights).

96 [2001] EWCA Admin 179.   97 See p 436, *post*.

98 *Frank Cowl and others v Plymouth CC* [2001] EWCA Civ 1935.

99 See, e.g. *Kruse v Johnson* [1898] 2 QB 91, [1895–1899] All ER Rep 105.

100 [1988] QB 384, [1988] 1 All ER 333.

101 [1998] 2 All ER 203. See also *R v Wicks* [1998] AC 92, [1997] 2 All ER 801.

the subordinate legislation is valid. The only exception to this is where there is a clear Parliamentary intention to the contrary. The ability to challenge as part of one's defence (i.e. collateral challenge) does not depend on the grounds of challenge, nor on whether those grounds are of a substantive or procedural nature. The House over-ruled authority which appeared to suggest the contrary.[102]

The procedure under Part 54 is supplemented by the requirements of a Practice Direction (PD 54). The applicant must apply promptly and in any event within three months from the date when the grounds of the application first arise, unless the court considers that there is good reason for extending this period. The application is by originating motion, to the Administrative Court. The applicant requires permission (formerly known as leave) to apply for judicial review, a matter which is dealt with without a hearing. The judge can in fact require a hearing if he wishes. If the application for permission is refused the applicant may renew it by applying, in criminal cases to the Administrative Court or, in any other case, to a single judge sitting in open court (or, if the court so directs, to the Administrative Court).

Applications for interlocutory orders, such as discovery, interrogatories, and cross-examination of witnesses, may be made to a judge or master. However, it should be borne in mind that:

in the ordinary way judicial review is designed to deal with matters which can be resolved without resorting to these procedures.'[103]

On the hearing of the application for judicial review the court will hear any party served with the motion or summons and any other person who appears to be a proper person to be heard. An applicant must have sufficient interest (formerly known as locus standi). This principle is designed to prevent the court being troubled by 'mere busybodies'.[104] On the other hand, standing is not confined to persons who have a legal or financial interest.[105] Whether standing exists ultimately turns on the nature of the statutory provision and the nature of the person or organization claiming a sufficient interest. In *R v HM Inspectorate of Pollution and Ministry of Agriculture Fisheries and Food, ex parte Greenpeace (No 2)*,[106] the environmental organization Greenpeace was held to have standing to challenge the actions of the respondents in varying an authorization to discharge radioactive waste. The organization was a large organization with internationally recognized expertise in environmental matters.

The court has the power to make prohibition, mandatory and quashing orders, and to grant injunctions and declarations. It can also award damages if an applicant could have recovered damages by bringing an action rather than an application for judicial review. In addition the court has power to grant interim relief, such as interlocutory

---

[102] *Bugg* v *DPP* [1993] QB 473, [1993] 2 All ER 815.

[103] *R* v *Derbyshire County Council, ex parte Noble* [1990] 1 CR 808, [1990] IRLR 332, per Woolf LJ.

[104] See *R* v *Greater London Council, ex parte Blackburn* [1976] 3 All ER 184, [1976] 1 WLR 550; *R* v *Monopolies and Mergers Commission, ex parte Argyll Group* [1986] 2 All ER 257, [1986] 1 WLR 763.

[105] *Inland Revenue Commissioners* v *National Federation of Self Employed and Small Businesses* [1982] AC 617; *R* v *Secretary of State for the Environment, ex parte Rose Theatre Trust* [1990] 1 All ER 754, [1990] 1 QB 5.

[106] [1994] 4 All ER 329. Cf. Rose Theatre Trust case, *ante*.

injunctions. Where the relief sought is a declaration, an injunction, or damages the court may, in certain circumstances, order the proceedings to continue as if they had been commenced by writ. As already observed, the essential feature of judicial review is that it applies to public law rather than private law matters. Thus it is not appropriate where the applicant's complaint is of a purely private nature, such as, for example, where he has been wrongfully dismissed by his employer, even where that employer is a public authority. Conversely, if the applicant wishes to challenge a public law decision he must proceed by way of application for judicial review and he cannot avoid the procedural requirements of Part 54 (notably the need for permission and the prescribed time-limit) by bringing an ordinary action seeking a declaration or an injunction.

7

THE COURTS

A HISTORICAL INTRODUCTION

Any examination of the modern legal system would be incomplete without an awareness of its historical background. As noted in chapter 1 the monarch had a pivotal role in the development of the early courts, and the exercise of regal power through the King's Council or Curia Regis is therefore a useful starting point for this analysis.

1 THE CURIA REGIS

In medieval times the King's Council exercised legislative, executive, and judicial functions, and it is therefore the predecessor of both Parliament and the courts. Over a period of time the courts began to assume an independent jurisdiction, and the three main common law courts—the Court of Exchequer, the Court of Common Pleas, and the Court of King's Bench—split off from the Council. Their judges exercised jurisdiction over civil disputes and major criminal cases in London and on assize, and the King's justices assumed jurisdiction over other criminal offences. The residual jurisdiction of the King persisted however, and it was not until the seventeenth century that the Council finally discontinued its judicial function.

2 THE COURT OF EXCHEQUER

This was the first of the three main common law courts to split off from the Curia Regis. Originally its jurisdiction was confined to disputes between subjects and the Crown concerning revenue, but it later acquired jurisdiction over disputes between subjects, such as writs of debt and covenant.[1] It also appears to have exercised an equity jurisdiction in its early days. When the Court of Exchequer was finally abolished in 1875, its common law jurisdiction was transferred to the newly formed High Court. Its equity jurisdiction had already been transferred by statute to the Chancery in 1841.[2]

---

[1] These were the earliest personal actions recognized by the common law. Debt was an action for a fixed sum of money in return for consideration already given. Covenant lay for breach of any obligation entered into under seal. For more detailed discussion, see the 6th edition of this work, pp 22–29.

[2] 5 Vict, c 5.

3 THE COURT OF COMMON PLEAS

While the King was determining civil disputes in Council, suitors were obliged to follow the court wherever it travelled. Because of the inconvenience this caused it became the practice for some judges to remain permanently in Westminster Hall to try Common Pleas.[3] These judges were senior advocates who were highly paid and had an exclusive right of audience in the court. The court had jurisdiction over disputes between subjects where the King's interest was not involved, and it therefore tried all real actions, the personal actions of debt, convenant, and *detinue*, and trespass actions where the title to land was involved. When the court was abolished in 1875, its jurisdiction was transferred to the High Court.

4 THE COURT OF KING'S BENCH

This was the last of the three central courts to break away from the Council, and through its close association with the King it acquired jurisdiction to issue the prerogative writs of *mandamus, prohibition*, and *certiorari*,[4] and thus to restrain abuses of power by inferior courts and public officials. It also had the power to issue the writ of *habeas corpus*, which was later of great constitutional importance in curbing the personal exercise of prerogative powers by the King. The court was presided over by the Chief Justice of England, and it had both original and appellate functions. The court's judges had criminal jurisdiction in courts of assize but its original jurisdiction was exercised principally in civil matters, covering most actions in tort (nearly all of which are offshoots of trespass), and contract. It also used various procedural means to filch jurisdiction over writs of debt and other cases from the Court of Common Pleas, to the point where the very existence of the latter court was threatened. The King's Bench had appellate jurisdiction in both civil and criminal cases, though the right of appeal was based on an error in procedure in the court below.[5]

5 THE COURTS OF EXCHEQUER CHAMBER

At different times there have been no less than four courts bearing the title 'Exchequer Chamber':

(1) The oldest was established in 1357 and consisted of the Chancellor and the Treasurer, assisted by judges of the common law courts. Its jurisdiction was solely as a court of error from the Exchequer.

(2) Even before 1357 there was a practice of judges reserving difficult points of

---

[3] As opposed to Pleas of the Crown, which were based upon breaches of the King's peace and usually involved a fine or forfeiture.

[4] Now called mandatory orders, prohibiting orders, and quashing orders. This 'judicial review' jurisdiction is still exercised by the Queen's Bench Division of the High Court: see chapter 6.

[5] 31 Edw 3, St 1, c 12.

law for consideration by a bench of judges drawn from different courts. The meetings were relatively informal and initially the opinions delivered were purely persuasive, but by the fifteenth century its judgments were regarded as binding.[6] The court was known as the Court of Exchequer Chamber because that was where it usually sat, and many of the leading common law cases were decided in this court. It continued to determine civil cases until the seventeenth century, and decided criminal matters until the nineteenth century.

(3) A third Court of Exchequer Chamber was created by statute in 1585[7] as a court of error from the King's Bench. Thus there were at this time three courts of error: the Court of Exchequer Chamber (1357) from the Court of Exchequer, the King's Bench from the Common Pleas, and the Court of Exchequer Chamber (1585) from the King's Bench. In addition, the House of Lords could hear errors directly from the King's Bench. This complex hierarchy prevailed until the creation of the last Court of Exchequer Chamber in 1830.

(4) The court created in 1830[8] was the court of error from all three common law courts, and any appeal from this court lay to the House of Lords. It existed until 1875 when its jurisdiction was transferred to the Court of Appeal.

6 ASSIZES

Even in the Middle Ages it was impossible to hold all criminal trials in London, and Norman and Plantagenet monarchs adopted the system of sending out royal justices to hold 'assizes' (or sittings) of the royal courts. The jurisdiction of these courts was at first purely criminal but was later extended to civil matters. Assize judges held office under royal commission, and while most were judges of the common law courts they could also be serjeants-at-law or even prominent laymen. The system was organized on the basis of circuits, with each circuit consisting of a group of counties visited three or four times a year. In addition, the *Statute of Nisi Prius* 1285 extended the system to certain civil actions triable by jury. It was further extended in the fourteenth and fifteenth centuries to cover all types of civil action, though initially only the issues of fact in civil cases could be tried *nisi prius*; the pleading still took place in Westminster.[9]

7 JUSTICES OF THE PEACE

Justices of the peace[10] originate from a royal proclamation of 1195, which created the knights of the peace to assist the sheriff in enforcing the law. Initially the office was

---

[6] In 1483 the Chief Justice of the Common Pleas followed a decision of the Exchequer Chamber even though he thought it wrong (Y1 Ric 3, Michs, no 2).

[7] 31 Eliz 1, c 1.   [8] 11 Geo 4 & 1 Will 4, c 70.

[9] The assize system survived until 1 January 1972, when the Courts Act 1971 came into operation.

[10] The term dates from about 1327: Plucknett, *A Concise History of the Common Law* (5th edn, 1956), p 168.

administrative in nature, but it assumed a judicial function in the fourteenth century because of the declining criminal jurisdiction of the local courts and the inability of the assizes to deal with the growing number of offenders. By 1330, the holders of the office had become so powerful that they were given statutory power to punish the sheriff if he abused his powers of granting bail to prisoners.

Statutes of Labourers were passed from 1351 in an attempt to regulate wages, and the enforcement of these statutes was placed in the hands of 'justices of labourers'. In 1361 these justices were included in the same commissions as the keepers of the peace, and it is from this date that the office of 'justice of the peace' in its modern sense originates. The criminal jurisdiction of the new justices was at first exercised solely in the quarter sessions which they were compelled by statute[11] to hold, but in 1496[12] they were given jurisdiction to try offences out of sessions. This summary jurisdiction was exercised without a jury by what is now termed a 'magistrates' court.'[13] In 1590 justices in quarter sessions were given jurisdiction over all criminal offences, including capital felonies, and it was not until the Quarter Sessions Act 1842 that their jurisdiction was limited to exclude treason, murder, and felonies punishable with life imprisonment.

The administrative functions of justices of the peace declined as their criminal jurisdiction grew, and most of these functions are now in the hands of local authorities. However, certain important functions remain; notably the power to issue warrants of arrest and summonses. The task of conducting preliminary investigations into indictable offences was conferred on justices of the peace in 1554.[14]

8 THE STAR CHAMBER

The Star Chamber derived its jurisdiction from the King in the same way as the common law courts, but because it retained its links with the King in Council it actually administered the royal prerogative rather than the common law. Opinions differ as to the origins of the court, but it seems to have originated from sittings of the Council in a chamber in Westminster known as the Star Chamber, possibly on account of its interior decor. It consisted of members of the Council, the Chancellor, Treasurer and Privy Seal and common law judges, and it had jurisdiction over a range of civil matters outside the common law. It is, however, the Star Chamber's criminal jurisdiction which is of the greatest interest, since it recognized and tried many new offences, including riot, unlawful assembly, conspiracy, criminal libel, perjury, and forgery.

Procedure differed radically from that in the common law courts. Criminal proceedings were commenced by the Attorney-General and the defendant was examined in an inquisitorial procedure, sometimes under torture. Evidence was frequently given by affidavit, thus denying the accused any opportunity to cross-examine witnesses,

---

[11] 36 Edw 3, st 1, c 12.   [12] 11 Hen 7, c 3.   [13] See p 259, *post*.
[14] 1 & 2 P & M, c 13 and 2 & 3 P & M, c 10.

and guilt or innocence was determined by members of the court rather than by a jury. Despite this, even Coke, that most noted champion of the common law, described the court as 'the most honourable Court (our Parliament excepted) that is in the Christian world.'[15] Eventually the court came to be seen as a symbol of prerogative power, and one of the first legislative acts of the Long Parliament was the abolition of the Star Chamber in 1641.

9 COURT OF CHANCERY

The development of principles of equity to supplement the common law has already been noted.[16] The Court of Chancery was the principal court of equity, and its most important jurisdiction was the recognition and enforcement of equitable principles. The office of Chancellor and the principles of equity are, historically, inexorably linked, and the nature and effectiveness of the court depended upon the characteristics of the particular Chancellor. The court was brought into disrepute in the seventeenth century by the sale of offices in the court,[17] and the scale of the corruption was so great that on the 'bursting' of the South Sea Bubble in 1725 (an eighteenth-century speculative venture) a deficiency of £100,000 in court funds was discovered.

A further defect in the court was its organization. It had an excess of court officials who attempted to extend their duties so as to increase their revenue, and this naturally made litigation extremely slow and expensive. The excess of court officers was equalled only by the paucity of judges. At first the Chancellor himself was the only judge, but by the sixteenth century he was accustomed to delegate his judicial functions to the Masters in Chancery. This did little to speed up the conduct of litigation however, since the parties had a right to apply to the Chancellor for a rehearing. During Lord Eldon's time in office (1807–1827) there are records of judgments being reserved for months and even years, and in 1813 he approved the appointment of a Vice-Chancellor. The Court of Chancery was eventually abolished by the Judicature Acts 1873–1875, and most of its jurisdiction was transferred to the Chancery Division of the High Court.

In addition to its equitable jurisdiction, the court acquired jurisdiction over other miscellaneous matters. For example, the Crown had protective custody of all infants within the realm, and this jurisdiction, comprising such matters as the power to appoint guardians, was assigned to the Court of Chancery.[18] A similar concept existed in relation to persons of unsound mind, and this jurisdiction continues to be exercised by the Court of Protection.[19]

---

[15] 4 Inst, p 65.   [16] See p 6, *ante.*
[17] The office of Master of the Rolls was apparently worth £6,000 in the eighteenth century. See *ex parte the Six Clerks* (1798) 3 Ves 589.
[18] It is now exercised by the Family Division of the High Court: see p 253, *post.*
[19] See p 252, *post.*

B THE MODERN SYSTEM OF COURTS: AN OVERVIEW

The impact of the Judicature Acts 1873–1875 in sweeping away many of the old courts has already been noted, and the modern system is very different from that which preceded it. The superior courts in England and Wales continue to derive their jurisdiction from the Crown, but they are now heavily regulated by statute and some courts and tribunals owe their origins entirely to statutory intervention.

1 CLASSIFICATION OF THE COURTS

Courts can be classified in various ways. It is, for example, possible to classify them on the basis of the types of cases that they hear, or according to whether their jurisdiction is original or appellate. These divisions are not entirely satisfactory however, since courts often do not fall neatly into one particular category and the divisions have little formal significance. Nevertheless, they do have some value for the purposes of exposition, and the principal divisions are therefore set out below.

(a) Civil and criminal courts

The most obvious division is between civil and criminal courts, but this classification is problematic because most English courts—including the House of Lords, Court of Appeal, High Court, Crown Court, and magistrates' courts—exercise jurisdiction in both civil and criminal matters.

(b) Courts of original jurisdiction and appellate courts

An alternative method of classification is to distinguish between appellate courts and courts of original jurisdiction. Again however, it is not possible to place all courts into one category or the other. While courts such as the Court of Appeal exercise a purely appellate jurisdiction, and those such as magistrates' courts have no appellate role, many other courts have both original and appellate functions. Indeed, the Queens Bench Divisional Court is neither a court of first instance nor a court of appeal; it is primarily a court of review. In addition, although the Court of Justice of the European Communities (the European Court of Justice) is not technically a court of appeal, its decisions are binding on all domestic courts.

(c) Courts and tribunals

Strictly speaking, the term 'tribunal' is an umbrella term capable of encompassing not only the bodies that generally use this name, but also those that are usually labelled 'courts'. It also has a narrower meaning however, and when used in this sense it refers only to those tribunals which cannot be described as courts.

Whether a particular tribunal can properly be called a 'court' is sometimes a matter of dispute. The description becomes important in the context of contempt of court,[20] since as the name suggests, this offence can only be committed in relation to a 'court'. In *A-G v BBC*[21] the House of Lords held that a local valuation court[22] was not a 'court' for the purposes of the contempt jurisdiction, since its functions were essentially administrative and it was not established to exercise the judicial power of the state. By contrast, employment tribunals *have* been held to constitute 'courts' for these purposes.[23]

Whether a particular tribunal can be called 'a court' or not appears to be of no other practical significance: it is not central to the question of whether it is subject to the High Court's supervisory jurisdiction, and it does not determine whether it is under a duty to act judicially.[24]

(d) Courts of record

Historically, the distinction between courts of record and other courts depended upon whether the court maintained records of its proceedings and preserved them in the Public Record Office. The central characteristic of a court of record now is that it has the power to punish for contempt. However, it should be noted that magistrates' courts, which are not courts of record, have a statutory power to punish contempts committed in the face of the court.[25] In addition, the High Court has a common law jurisdiction to punish contempts committed before courts which are not courts of record.[26]

(e) Superior and inferior courts

Traditionally, the most significant division has been between superior and inferior courts.[27] The jurisdiction of superior courts is limited neither by geography nor by the value of the cases that they can hear. The House of Lords, Court of Appeal, High Court, Crown Court, Privy Council, and Employment Appeal Tribunal are all superior courts. The most important of the inferior courts are the county courts and magistrates' courts. One of the distinctive features of inferior courts is that they are amenable to the supervisory jurisdiction of the High Court.[28] However, the Crown Court is also subject to this jurisdiction in the exercise of its appellate functions, even

---

[20] See p 85, *post.*   [21] [1981] AC 303, [1980] 3 All ER 161.

[22] These courts were replaced by valuation tribunals: Local Government Finance Act 1992.

[23] *Peach Grey & Co v Sommers* [1995] 2 All ER 513, [1995] ICR 549; applied in *Ewing v Security Services* [2003] EWCA Civ 581.

[24] See chapter 8.   [25] Contempt of Court Act 1981, s 12: see p 239, *post.*

[26] *R v Davies* [1906] 1 KB 32.

[27] Whether a court is an inferior or a superior court can usually be ascertained by reference to its historical origins or, where applicable, to the terms of the statute creating it. If this does not settle the matter it is necessary to look at the nature and powers of the court to see whether they are analogous to those of a superior or an inferior court. See, e.g., *R v Cripps, ex parte Muldoon* [1984] QB 68, [1983] 3 All ER 72, in which the Queen's Bench Divisional Court held an election court (under the Representation of the People Act) to be an inferior court.

[28] See chapter 6.

though it is a superior court.[29] The distinction is also important in relation to contempt of court, as the superior courts are able to inflict more stringent penalties than those available to the inferior courts.[30]

2 THE ORGANIZATION AND ADMINISTRATION OF THE COURTS

Leaving aside the work of tribunals,[31] the principal courts exercising jurisdiction in England and Wales are the Court of Appeal, the High Court, the Crown Court, the House of Lords, county courts, and magistrates' courts. The first three courts in this list collectively comprise the Supreme Court of England and Wales.[32] The constitution and jurisdiction of each of these courts is considered in detail later in this chapter, but their roles can be summarized as follows:

(1) First instance jurisdiction over civil matters is primarily shared between the county courts and the High Court. The Crown Court and magistrates' courts also have a limited civil jurisdiction.

(2) Jurisdiction over criminal cases at first instance is divided between magistrates' courts and the Crown Court.

(3) The Crown Court and High Court exercise certain appellate functions alongside their original jurisdiction.

(4) The Court of Appeal hears appeals from the decisions of courts lower down in the hierarchy, though not from the decisions of magistrates' courts.

(5) Except in matters of European law,[33] the House of Lords is the final court of appeal for England and Wales, Scotland, and Northern Ireland. However, in 2003 the government announced plans to transfer the judicial functions of the House of Lords to a new Supreme Court: the Constitutional Reform Act 2005 will give effect to these changes.[34]

As outlined in chapter 1, the English legal system has evolved in a piecemeal way over many centuries, and responsibility for its administration is now divided between three government departments and numerous other bodies.[35] The rules governing the procedure and jurisdiction of the courts are contained in a multitude of statutes, practice directions, court rules, and other statutory instruments, all of which seem to be subject to constant revision and amendment. The distribution of business between the courts has been revised many times, and the legal system has been the focus of

---

[29] The Crown Court is only open to the supervisory jurisdiction of the Divisional Court where jurisdiction is expressly granted by the Supreme Court Act 1981, ss 28 and 29(1). Matters relating to 'trial on indictment' are not within that jurisdiction.

[30] See p 240, *post*.　　[31] See chapter 8.

[32] They will be renamed 'the Senior Courts of England and Wales' when the Judicial Committee of the House of Lords is replaced by a new Supreme Court: see p 243, *post*.

[33] The jurisdiction and functions of the European Court of Justice and European Court of Human Rights are discussed in chapters 4 and 5 respectively. Note that the ECJ is not technically a court of appeal.

[34] See p 243, *post*.　　[35] See p 19, *ante*.

numerous reports and recommendations. In 1996 for example, the Woolf Report on *Access to Justice* led to a major restructuring of the civil justice system, less than a decade after fundamental changes were brought about by the Courts and Legal Services Act 1990.[36] Lord Justice Auld's review of the criminal justice system produced similarly far-reaching recommendations,[37] and although the government rejected his proposal to replace the Crown Court and magistrates' courts with a unified criminal court, a number of his other recommendations were given effect by the Courts Act 2003. In 1998 the Civil Justice Council was established, with a remit of keeping the civil justice system under review and considering new ways of making it accessible, fair and efficient.[38] Following recommendations in the Auld Report[39] the government created a Criminal Justice Council with equivalent functions. A Criminal Justice Board with responsibility for direction and strategy at a national level was also established.

The absence of a truly national framework applicable to all courts has been criticized, and the focus of many of the recent reforms has been on achieving greater harmonization and efficiency. The Auld Report had much to say on this subject, describing the criminal justice system as 'structurally inefficient, ineffective and wasteful.'[40] Prior to the Woolf reforms the county courts and the High Court were subject to different procedural rules, despite the fact that their jurisdiction is largely concurrent. The Civil Procedure Act 1997 changed this by establishing a Civil Procedure Rule Committee with the authority to make Rules for the High Court, the county courts, and the Civil Division of the Court of Appeal.[41] The Courts Act 2003 has introduced a similar approach for the criminal justice system: instead of being subject to three different sets of rules, all criminal cases are now governed by new Criminal Procedure Rules regardless of which court they are heard in.[42] A Family Procedure Rule Committee has similar powers to make rules governing family proceedings.[43] All rule committees are subject to an overriding duty to ensure that the system is 'accessible, fair and efficient', and that any rules made are both 'simple and simply expressed.'[44]

Under section 1(1) of the Courts Act 2003 the Lord Chancellor has a duty to ensure that there is an efficient and effective system to support the business of the Supreme Court, county courts, and magistrates' courts. The Act also provides for England and Wales to be divided into separate local justice areas, with each area having its own Courts Board. Courts Boards are responsible for scrutinizing and reviewing the administration of the courts and for making recommendations to the Lord Chancellor.[45] The principal aim of the Courts Act is to provide a framework for

---

[36] Most of Woolf's recommendations were adopted in the Access to Justice Act 1999 and the Civil Procedure Rules 1998, SI 1998/3132: see p 426, *post*.

[37] *Review of the Criminal Courts of England and Wales* (2001); see p 521, *post*.

[38] Civil Procedure Act 1997, s 6.   [39] See chapter 8 of the Report.

[40] At para 14.   [41] Civil Procedure Rules 1998, SI 1998/3132, or 'CPR'.

[42] 2003 Act, s 69; Criminal Procedure Rules 2005, SI 2005/384.   [43] 2003 Act, ss 75–77.

[44] Ibid, ss 69(4); 75(5); Civil Procedure Act 1997, s 1(3), as amended.   [45] Sections 4 and 5.

a unified court structure, and to this end the Lord Chancellor has transferred administrative responsibility for all but one of the major courts to a single executive agency. The new agency is to be known as 'Her Majesty's Court Service' and it was formally launched on 1 April 2005. It administers all of the courts that were previously managed by the Courts Service—that is, the Crown Court, High Court, Court of Appeal, and county courts—and it has also assumed responsibility for managing the network of magistrates' courts.[46] This leaves the House of Lords (or its replacement) as the only major court not covered by the new agency. However, it is considered appropriate for the latter court to be administered separately because of its unique position as an appellate court for all parts of the United Kingdom. The new arrangements will allow for greater sharing of resources, making it easier, for example, to use the same facilities as a venue for magistrates' and county court business, as well as for sittings of the Crown Court. It also opens up the possibility of creating specialist centres where magistrates, county courts, and High Court judges can exercise their family jurisdiction under one roof.

Despite the wholesale changes of recent years, it seems inevitable that there will be further reforms in the near future. Indeed, while the House of Commons was still debating legislation that will lead to the creation of a new Supreme Court,[47] the Department for Constitutional Affairs was already looking at the possibility of combining the existing civil courts.[48]

3 THE PRINCIPLE OF OPEN JUSTICE[49]

'Open justice' is a key principle of the English legal system, and amongst other things it requires that the courts should sit in public. In the words of Lord Hewart CJ in *R v Sussex Justices, ex parte McCarthy*:[50]

a long line of cases shows that it is not merely of some importance but is of fundamental importance that justice should not only be done, but should manifestly and undoubtedly be seen to be done.

The principle, and the circumstances which may justify departure from it, were set out by the House of Lords in *Scott v Scott*[51] and later explained by Lord Diplock in *A-G v Leveller Magazine Ltd*:[52]

As a general rule the English system of administering justice does require that it be done in public: *Scott v Scott*. If the way the courts behave cannot be hidden from the public ear and

---

[46] These were previously managed by forty-two separate Magistrates' Courts Committees: see p 260, *post*.

[47] Constitutional Reform Act 2005: see p 243, *post*.

[48] DCA, *A Single Civil Court? The Scope for Unifying the Civil Jurisdictions of the High Court, the County Courts and the Family Proceedings Courts* (2005) CP 06/05.

[49] For a detailed analysis, see Jaconelli, *Open Justice: A Critique of the Public Trial* (2002).

[50] [1924] 1 KB 256 at 259; see also *R v Denbigh Justices, ex parte Williams* [1974] QB 759, [1974] 2 All ER 1052; Supreme Court Act 1981, s 67.

[51] [1913] AC 417.   [52] [1979] AC 440, [1979] 1 All ER 745.

eye this provides a safeguard against judicial arbitrariness or idiosyncrasy and maintains the public confidence in the administration of justice.

More recently the principle was endorsed by Butler-Sloss P, quoting from the work of Jeremy Bentham:[53]

Publicity is the very soul of justice. It is the keenest spur to exertion and the surest of all guards against improbity. It keeps the judge himself while trying under trial.

From this it follows that if at all possible, proceedings should be held in open court and fair and accurate reports of those proceedings should be permissible. In *Storer* v *British Gas*[54] the Court of Appeal quashed the decision of an industrial tribunal because the hearing had taken place in an office which was kept locked and marked 'Private'. On the other hand, certain restrictions on the principle of open justice may be permitted where this is necessary to protect the administration of justice, or where Parliament has created a specific exception.

Article 6(1) of the European Convention on Human Rights is also relevant in this context, and has assumed added importance since the coming into force of the Human Rights Act 1998.[55]

Article 6(1)

In the determination of his civil rights and obligations or of any criminal charge against him, everyone is entitled to a fair and public hearing . . . Judgment shall be pronounced publicly but the press and public may be excluded from all or part of the trial in the interests of morals, public order or national security in a democratic society, where the interests of juveniles or the protection of the private life of the parties so require, or to the extent strictly necessary in the opinion of the court in special circumstances where publicity would prejudice the interests of justice.

(a) A hearing in open court

Parliament has granted a power to sit in camera in various types of proceedings. These include proceedings covered by the Children Act 1989,[56] applications relating to a caution for soliciting,[57] cases involving evidence of sexual capacity in suits for the annulment of marriage,[58] and proceedings under the Official Secrets Acts.[59] In addition, provisions designed to assist vulnerable witnesses in criminal proceedings are contained in the Youth Justice and Criminal Evidence Act 1999.[60] Part II of this Act enables courts to take 'special measures' to assist certain categories of witnesses

---

[53] *Clibbery* v *Allan* [2002] EWCA Civ 45 at [16], [2002] Fam 261 at [16], [2002] 1 All ER 865.

[54] [2000] 2 All ER 440, [2000] 1 WLR 1237.

[55] See chapter 5. For an illustration of the correct approach to this issue under Article 6(1), see *B* v *UK* [2001] 2 FLR 261, (2002) 34 EHRR 19. It was found in this case that a county court hearing to determine the residence of a child did not breach the Convention, even though it was held in private.

[56] Section 97.   [57] Street Offences Act 1959, s 2.

[58] Matrimonial Causes Act 1973, s 48(2).   [59] Official Secrets Act 1920, s 8(4).

[60] Most of the relevant provisions have been in force since 24 July 2002; see Youth Justice and Criminal Evidence Act 1999 (Commencement No 7) Order 2002, SI 2002/1739.

(though not defendants) who might have difficulty giving evidence or who might be reluctant to do so. These categories include those under the age of seventeen, alleged victims of sex offences, those suffering from a mental or physical impairment likely to affect the quality of evidence given, and those whose evidence is likely to be impaired by fear or distress.[61] One of the special measures available to the courts is the power to allow a vulnerable witness to give evidence in camera,[62] subject to section 25(3) which states that one representative of the press must be allowed to stay. Other special measures include the possibility of screening the witness from the accused,[63] or allowing the witness to give evidence via a pre-recorded video or live video link.[64]

In addition to these specific provisions, the courts also have a general jurisdiction to sit in camera where the presence of the public would render the administration of justice impracticable. This was confirmed in R v Richards[65] when a judge decided to clear the court so that a witness to a murder could give evidence. The witness had refused to testify under any other circumstances, and in denying an application for leave to appeal, the Court of Appeal observed that courts have an inherent jurisdiction to do what is necessary for the proper administration of justice.

The courts are not, however, permitted to restrict open justice for any other reason, and there is no jurisdiction to hear a case in private purely for the convenience of the parties. Thus in R v Evesham Justices, ex parte McDonagh[66] it was held that a court could not prohibit publication of the defendant's address to save him from being harassed by his ex-wife. This case may be compared with that of R v Malvern Justices, ex parte Evans,[67] in which magistrates sat in camera to hear a mitigation plea in respect of a driving offence. The mental health of the defendant was such that if the court had not sat in camera, the defendant would have been inhibited in making her plea. An appeal against the making of the order was dismissed, but the Divisional Court observed that it would rarely be appropriate to make such an order, and they doubted whether it had in fact been appropriate in this particular case.

(b) Withholding particular information or evidence from the public

The second aspect of open justice is the principle that all evidence should be communicated publicly. However, just as there are limitations on the principle that

---

[61] Sections 16 and 17.

[62] Section 25. This applies only to evidence given in relation to a sex offence, or where there are grounds for believing that the witness has been or may be intimidated. See also s 37 of the Children and Young Persons Act 1933. For an analysis of the 1999 Act, see Birch, 'A Better Deal for Vulnerable Witnesses?' [2000] Crim LR 223. The Home Office has produced its own guidelines on the new provisions: *Achieving Best Evidence in Criminal Proceedings: Guidance for Vulnerable and Intimidated Witnesses, including Children.*

[63] Section 23.

[64] Section 24, 27, and 28. Note however, that the use of both live and pre-recorded video evidence will be possible in a wider range of circumstances under the Criminal Justice Act 2003.

[65] [1999] Crim LR 764.   [66] [1988] QB 553, (1988) 87 Cr App R 28.

[67] [1988] QB 540, [1988] 1 All ER 371.

proceedings should be conducted in public, there are also circumstances which may justify a court restricting publicity of evidence. To give a common example, a court will usually permit a victim of blackmail to be identified during proceedings by a title such as 'Mr X', and to communicate his name and address to the court by writing it down.[68] There are also statutory provisions for preserving the anonymity of young witnesses,[69] complainants in sex offence cases,[70] and other vulnerable parties.[71] Exceptionally, the identity of witnesses may be protected even from other parties to the proceedings. The obvious situation in which this may occur is where an informant has a genuine fear of reprisals if he gives evidence in a criminal case. Withholding relevant information from a defendant is an extreme step however, and it would usually be assumed to compromise his right to a fair trial.[72]

The parties to proceedings will not normally be granted anonymity. The position was discussed by the Court of Appeal in *R v Legal Aid Board, ex parte Kaim Todner*,[73] where a firm of solicitors sought anonymity in judicial review proceedings against the Legal Aid Board. In rejecting any special rule relating to the legal profession, Lord Woolf MR stressed that any exception to the general rule in *Scott v Scott* could only be justified if this was necessary in the interests of justice. This was a matter for the court and could not be determined by any agreement of the parties in the case. As had been noted in *ex parte P*,[74] 'when both sides agreed that information should be kept from the public that was when the court had to be the most vigilant.' Public scrutiny was necessary in order to deter inappropriate behaviour by the courts, and to maintain confidence in the administration of justice. In addition, members of the public could not come forward with relevant evidence if they were unaware of its relevance to proceedings. In deciding whether to protect the anonymity of a party to an action, it was not unreasonable for a court to assume that a party who initiated proceedings had accepted the normal consequences of that action. On the other hand, a witness with no interest in the proceedings would have a stronger claim if he or she would be prejudiced by publicity, though even this would not attract automatic anonymity.[75]

---

[68] *R v Socialist Worker Printer and Publishers Ltd, ex parte A-G* [1975] QB 637, [1975] 1 All ER 142.

[69] Youth Justice and Criminal Evidence Act 1999, s 45; see also the Children and Young Persons Act 1933, s 39. For the relevant principles, see *R v Leicester Crown Court, ex parte S* [1992] 2 All ER 659, [1993] 1 WLR 111; *Re S (A Child) (Identification: Restrictions on Publication)* [2004] UKHL 47, [2004] 3 WLR 1129, [2004] 4 All ER 683.

[70] Sexual Offences (Amendment) Act 1992, s 1 (as amended). Once an allegation of an offence has been made, it is an offence to publish information likely to lead members of the public to identify the complainant unless the judge has lifted these restrictions under s 3.

[71] Youth Justice and Criminal Evidence Act 1999, s 46.

[72] The relevant principles are discussed in *R v Taylor (Gary)* (1994) Times, 17 August, [1995] Crim LR 253; *R v Liverpool City Magistrates' Court, ex parte DPP* (1997) 161 JP 43. For the ECHR dimension, see also *Doorson v Netherlands* (1996) 22 EHRR 330.

[73] [1999] QB 966, [1998] 3 All ER 541.   [74] (1998) Times, 31 March.

[75] An exceptional case in which there were sound reasons for preserving the anonymity of witnesses is *R v Lord Saville of Newdigate, ex parte A* [1999] 4 All ER 860, [2000] 1 WLR 1855. The Court of Appeal agreed with the Divisional Court that it had been unreasonable to deny anonymity to 17 members of the armed

This area of law was also considered in *A-G* v *Leveller Magazine*.[76] The House of Lords accepted that a court was entitled to sit in private or to withhold the name of a witness if this was in the interests of the administration of justice. On the facts however, the judge had not made a clear order restricting publication, and the identity of the witness could be readily ascertained from evidence which was freely reportable. The defendant's conviction for contempt of court was therefore quashed.[77] Any such order will now be made pursuant to section 11 of the Contempt of Court Act 1981 unless restrictions are permissible at common law.[78] It is possible to appeal against the making of such an order,[79] and an order should only be made where the administration of justice justifies the restriction. Personal embarrassment is not a sufficient reason.[80]

(c) The reporting of proceedings in court

A final principle of open justice is that reports of judicial proceedings should not be prevented or discouraged, as long as they are fair, contemporaneous, and accurate. The publication of such reports is expressly permitted by section 4 of the Contempt of Court Act 1981, but the law recognizes that there are circumstances where a departure from the general rule may be justified. Section 11 for example, confers a power to prevent the reporting of details which have not been disclosed in open court. In addition, section 4(2) of the Act empowers a court to *postpone* reporting where this is necessary in the interests of justice. If, however, those interests can be satisfied in less restrictive ways, the section 4(2) power should not be used. This was the approach before the Human Rights Act came into effect,[81] and the decision in *R (on the application of the Telegraph Group plc)* v *Sherwood* suggests that it is still correct.[82] The Court of Appeal in this case identified three key principles. Firstly, a judge has no discretion to restrict publication unless there is a substantial risk of prejudice to particular legal

---

forces who were due to give evidence to the Bloody Sunday Inquiry. Though not strictly concerned with a trial, this decision indicates the principles to be applied when considering a restriction on open justice. On the facts, it was found that revealing the identity of the witnesses was not vital to the fairness of the inquiry, and in any event, the clear risk that the lives of the witnesses could be threatened if their identities were made public outweighed any other considerations.

[76] [1979] AC 440, [1979] 1 All ER 745.

[77] For a discussion of contempt of court, see below at p 236.

[78] See *R* v *Socialist Worker Printer and Publishers Ltd, ex parte A-G* [1975] QB 637, [1975] 1 All ER 142; *Re M (Wardship: Freedom of Publication)* [1990] 2 FLR 36.

[79] Criminal Justice Act 1988, s 159; *R* v *Crook* [1992] 2 All ER 687, (1991) 93 Cr App R 17.

[80] See, e.g. *R* v *Malvern Justices, ex parte Evans* [1988] QB 540, [1988] 1 All ER 371; *R* v *Dover JJ, ex parte Dover DC* (1992) 156 JP 433 (publicity embarrassing to a restaurant); *H* v *Ministry of Defence* [1991] 2 QB 103, [1991] 2 All ER 834 (publication of embarrassing medical evidence restrained).

[81] In *Re Central Independent Television* [1991] 1 All ER 347, [1991] 1 WLR 4 an order prohibiting radio or television reporting whilst a jury was staying overnight at a hotel was held to be excessive. See also, *Ex parte Telegraph plc* [1993] 2 All ER 971, [1993] 1 WLR 980.

[82] [2001] EWCA Crim 1075, [2001] 1 WLR 1983. For a discussion of the effect of reporting restrictions on the Convention right to freedom of expression, see Cram, 'Reporting Restrictions in Criminal Proceedings and Article 10 of the ECHR' [1998] EHRLR 742.

proceedings. Secondly, where such a risk exists, an order should not be made unless the judge is satisfied that it is the least restrictive means of avoiding that risk. Finally, any risk of prejudice must be balanced against the public interest in the proceedings being reported. On the facts of the case a decision to delay the reporting of one trial until a second, related trial had been concluded, was held to be a justifiable and proportionate response to a substantial risk of prejudice.[83] The rules governing the reporting of legal proceedings are considered in more detail below, in the context of the law of contempt.

Given the high-technology age in which we now live, some would question whether allowing printed reports of legal proceedings is still sufficient to ensure that justice is done in public. The government is now considering whether there is a case for allowing the television cameras to have access to the courts, and it published a consultation paper on 'broadcasting the courts' at the end of 2004.[84] Allowing the televising of trials would be a big step however, and it seems likely that if the government does decide to move in this direction it will proceed with extreme caution.

4 CONTEMPT OF COURT[85]

Judges have an inherent jurisdiction to punish conduct calculated to prejudice or interfere with the process of the law. Such conduct is termed a contempt of court and may be either criminal or civil in nature.

(a) Criminal contempt

Criminal contempt is an offence at common law and comprises conduct which interferes with the administration of justice or which creates a substantial risk that the course of justice will be prejudiced.[86] Thus, it is a criminal contempt to interfere with a juror or witness,[87] or to prevent or unlawfully deter a party from pursuing a legal action.[88] A journalist who refuses to disclose his source of information when required to do so by a court may also be liable for contempt.[89] However, a court may only

---

[83] Cf. the earlier decision in *R v Beck, ex parte Daily Telegraph plc* [1993] 2 All ER 177, in which reporting restrictions were refused in similar circumstances. The court in the recent case felt able to distinguish *Beck* on the facts however, and did not doubt that it was correctly decided.

[84] Department for Constitutional Affairs, *Broadcasting Courts* (2005) CP 28/04.

[85] See generally: Miller, *Contempt of Court* (3rd edn, 2000); Borrie and Lowe, *The Law of Contempt* (3rd edn, 1996).

[86] *A-G v Times Newspapers Ltd* [1992] 1 AC 191, [1991] 2 All ER 398.

[87] *Re Attorney-General's Application* [1963] 1 QB 696, [1962] 3 All ER 326.

[88] *Raymond v Honey* [1981] QB 874, [1981] 2 All ER 1084 (prisoner unlawfully prevented from making an application to the High Court); *A-G v Hislop and Pressdram* [1991] 1 QB 514, [1991] 1 All ER 911 (defendant in a libel case published further articles to deter the claimant from pursing the action).

[89] In *DPP v Channel 4 Television Co Ltd* [1993] 2 All ER 517, fines totalling £75,000 were imposed on the defendant for failure to comply with an order to produce documents.

require disclosure if satisfied that this is necessary in the interests of justice, national security, or the prevention of crime or disorder.[90]

It is also a contempt to publish the name of a party or witness where publication is prohibited by statute or is contrary to a court order.[91] In *Attorney-General v Punch*[92] the publishers and editor of a magazine were convicted of contempt after publishing an article by the former MI5 officer, David Shayler. Mr Shayler was being prosecuted for disclosing intelligence obtained while working for the security services, and he was the subject of an injunction preventing him from making further disclosures while his case was still pending. The injunction did not apply to the defendants directly, but on appeal to the House of Lords it was held that their publication nevertheless amounted to a contempt of court:[93]

The primary effect of such an injunction is to regulate the conduct of the person against whom it is made. But it also has an indirect effect upon the conduct of third parties. In general, it is a contempt of court for anyone, whether party to the proceedings or not, deliberately to interfere with the due administration of justice. One species of such interference . . . is the deliberate publication of information which the court has ordered someone else to keep confidential. Publication interferes with the administration of justice because it destroys the subject-matter of the proceedings. Once the information has been published, the court can no longer do justice between the parties by enforcing the obligation of confidentiality.

Their Lordships acknowledged that the injunction had implications for the right to freedom of expression, and that Article 10 of the ECHR was therefore engaged. Nevertheless, they emphasized that the Article 10 right could be lawfully restricted on a number of grounds, and held that the injunction in this case had been proportionate to the legitimate objective of protecting national security.[94] The defendants' motive was not important and the fact that they did not believe the material to be harmful to national security was irrelevant: what mattered was that their conduct was intentional.

It has . . . to be shown that there was an intention . . . to interfere with or impede the administration of justice. This is an essential ingredient, and it has to be established to the criminal standard of proof. But the intent need not be stated expressly or admitted by the defendant. As is the case where the question of intention, or mens rea, arises in criminal

---

[90] Contempt of Court Act 1981, s 10; *Secretary of State for Defence v Guardian Newspapers Ltd* [1985] AC 339, [1984] 3 All ER 601; *X Ltd v Morgan-Grampian (Publishers) Ltd* [1991] 1 AC 1, [1990] 2 All ER 1. Cf. *Goodwin v UK* (1996) 22 EHRR 123. See also, the discussion of Article 10, ECHR, at p 192, *ante*.

[91] *R v Socialist Worker Printers and Publishers Ltd, ex parte A-G* [1975] QB 637, [1975] 1 All ER 142; There must, however, be a clear direction and not merely a request: *A-G v Leveller Magazine Ltd* [1979] AC 440, [1979] 1 All ER 745.

[92] [2002] UKHL 50, [2003] 1 AC 1046, [2003] 1 All ER 289.   [93] Ibid at [66], per Lord Hoffman.

[94] Other legitimate grounds for restricting freedom of expression include maintaining judicial independence and protecting the rights and freedoms of others. The right must also be balanced against the right to a fair trial under Article 6.

cases, it can be inferred from all the circumstances including the foreseeability of the consequences of the defendant's conduct.[95]

In addition to the common law rule, contempt of court may also be committed under certain statutory provisions. For example, it is a contempt to obtain, disclose or solicit any particulars of statements made, opinions expressed, arguments advanced, or votes cast by members of a jury in the course of their deliberations.[96] There is also a strict liability rule covering publications that are seriously prejudicial to a fair trial.

Strict liability contempt. The strict liability rule is set out in sections 1 and 2 of the Contempt of Court Act 1981, and it covers the publication of material which creates a substantial risk of impeding or prejudicing 'active'[97] legal proceedings. In assessing whether a risk of prejudice is substantial, it is relevant to take into account the lapse of time between the publication and the date of any trial, and the likelihood of the material being encountered by potential jurors.[98] A publication creating such a risk will amount to a contempt of court, regardless of whether there was any intention to interfere with the course of justice.[99] However, publications *intended* to prejudice the course of justice can still be dealt with at common law,[100] as can material published when proceedings are imminent but not active.[101]

There are three statutory defences to the strict liability rule: (a) innocent publication or distribution;[102] (b) fair and accurate reports of legal proceedings held in public, which are published contemporaneously and in good faith;[103] and (c) discussion of public affairs or other matters of general public interest, where the risk of prejudice to particular legal proceedings is incidental.[104] An illustration of the defence of incidental discussion is provided by the case of *Attorney-General* v *English*,[105] in which the House of Lords decided that an article discussing the merits of mercy killing did not amount to contempt, even though at the time of publication a doctor was on trial accused of the mercy killing of a disabled child.

---

[95] [2002] UKHL 50 at [87], [2003] 1 AC 1046 at [87], [2003] 1 All ER 289, per Lord Hope. See also, *A-G* v *News Group Newspapers plc* [1989] QB 110, [1988] 2 All ER 906.

[96] Contempt of Court Act 1981, s 8(1). Proposals to relax this rule to allow legitimate jury research are discussed at p 344, *post.*

[97] In criminal cases proceedings will be active from the time of an arrest, the issue of an arrest warrant, or the issue of a summons. In civil proceedings the relevant date will usually be the date of setting down for trial: ibid, Schedule 1. See also, *A-G* v *Hislop and Pressdram* [1991] 1 QB 514, [1991] 1 All ER 911.

[98] In *R* v *Taylor and Taylor* (1994) 98 Cr App R 361 it was held that the prejudicial impact of an article could be heightened by the use of photographs.

[99] The position was previously governed by common law, which made it an offence to publish material prejudging the issues to be determined in pending litigation: *A-G* v *Times Newspapers* [1974] AC 273, [1973] 3 All ER 54. The 1981 Act was passed following the ruling of the European Court of Human Rights in *Sunday Times* v *UK* (1979–1980) 2 EHRR 245, which found that the common law rule was too vague and imprecise and went further than was necessary in a democratic society.

[100] Contempt of Court Act 1981, s 6(c); *A-G* v *Punch* [2002] UKHL 50, [2003] 1 AC 1046, [2003] 1 All ER 289.

[101] *A-G* v *Times Newspapers* [1992] 1 AC 191, [1991] 2 All ER 398.   [102] 1981 Act, s 3(1).

[103] Ibid, s 4. Note that the court may order publication to be postponed under s 4(2): see p 235, *ante.*

[104] Ibid, s 5.   [105] [1983] 1 AC 116, [1982] 2 All ER 903.

Where a publication is sufficiently prejudicial to justify the quashing of a conviction or a stay of proceedings, a finding of contempt will usually be possible. However, the case of *Attorney-General* v *MGN*[106] illustrates some of the difficulties that may arise. Criminal proceedings against the partner of a well-known actress were abandoned when highly prejudicial reports appeared in five tabloid newspapers. The court found that there was a risk of prejudice stemming from the cumulative effect of these reports, but that when considered separately, none of them were sufficiently prejudicial to satisfy the test for contempt. Conversely, a finding of contempt may be made in circumstances where a stay of proceedings is unnecessary, as in *Attorney-General* v *BBC and Hat Trick Productions.*[107] The case concerned satirical remarks about Robert Maxwell's sons, which were broadcast six months before the brothers stood trial on serious fraud charges. The judge in the fraud case refused to order a stay of proceedings, on the basis that the six-month gap and the likely length and complexity of the trial would concentrate the juror's minds on the evidence presented in court. Nevertheless, the broadcaster and producers of the programme were convicted of strict liability contempt.

Contempt in the face of the court. If judicial proceedings are actually disrupted, or a contempt is committed in the vicinity of the courtroom, this will constitute contempt in the face of the court. This offence may be committed by, for example, distributing leaflets and shouting during proceedings,[108] using a tape-recorder in court without leave,[109] taking a photograph or making an unauthorized sketch in court,[110] or refusing to give evidence when summoned as a witness.[111] In one case a man was sentenced to six months imprisonment after attacking his wife and her solicitor during a child custody hearing.[112] In addition, disobeying a witness summons is punishable as a contempt in the same way as if it had been committed in the face of the court.[113]

(b) Civil contempt

Civil contempt will occur where a party fails to comply with a court order. For example, a civil contempt may be committed by a failure to comply with an injunction, or by the failure of a solicitor to comply with an undertaking.[114] Mere failure to

---

[106] [1997] 1 All ER 456.

[107] [1997] EMLR 76. See also *A-G* v *Birmingham Post and Mail Ltd* [1998] 4 All ER 49, [1999] 1 WLR 361, where it was suggested that strict liability contempt requires a lesser degree of prejudice than would be needed to stay proceedings or quash a conviction.

[108] *Morris* v *Crown Office* [1970] 2 QB 114, [1970] 1 All ER 1079.

[109] Contempt of Court Act 1981, s 9.

[110] Criminal Justice Act 1925, s 41(1), as amended; *R* v *D (Contempt of Court: Illegal Photography)* [2004] EWCA Crim 1271, (2004) *The Times*, 13 May—the defendant in this case was given an immediate twelve months custodial sentence for using his mobile phone to take photographs during proceedings.

[111] *A-G* v *Mulholland* [1963] 2 QB 477, [1963] 1 All ER 767.

[112] *Wilkinson* v *Lord Chancellor's Department* [2003] EWCA Civ 95, [2003] 2 All ER 184, [2003] 1 WLR 1254.

[113] Criminal Procedure (Attendance of Witnesses) Act 1965, s 3, as amended.

[114] *Re Kerly* [1901] 1 Ch 467; *Re A Solicitor* [1966] 3 All ER 52, [1966] 1 WLR 1604.

pay a judgment debt is not contempt, although wilful refusal to do so is.[115] In addition, if an alternative method of securing compliance with a court order is available, the Court of Appeal has stated that this method should be adopted rather than sending the contemnor to prison.[116]

The House of Lords made an important decision on civil contempt in *M v Home Office*.[117] M was seeking leave to apply for judicial review of the Home Secretary's decision to refuse his asylum application. At the end of the hearing the judge made it clear that he wished M to remain in the country until his application had been determined, and he understood the Home Secretary to have given an undertaking not to deport him. M was nevertheless flown out of the country, and the judge made an order obliging the Home Secretary to return him to the jurisdiction. When the Minister failed to comply, he was found to be in contempt of court.

(c) Jurisdiction to punish contempt

The jurisdiction to punish for contempt is inherent in superior courts of record. Such courts may commit for contempt and can punish contempt in the face of the court by an immediate fine and a prison term of up to two years.[118] Although a county court is an inferior court, it is treated as a superior court for these purposes.[119] Most other contempts relating to inferior courts are dealt with by the Queen's Bench Division,[120] although inferior courts of record can punish contempt in the face of the court by an immediate fine and a prison term not exceeding one month.[121] In addition, although not courts of record, magistrates' courts have equivalent powers to punish the wilful interruption of magistrates' proceedings and other forms of misbehaviour in court.[122] Until 1960 there was no right of appeal against punishment for criminal contempt, but this position was altered by section 13 of the Administration of Justice Act 1960. Appeal lies to the Court of Appeal, Divisional Court or House of Lords, as the case may be.

Contempt may be punished by a summary procedure far removed from the ordinary processes of the law: no precise charges are put, the accused may have no opportunity to consult a lawyer, and the judge making the decision may have been the person insulted. Article 6 of the ECHR establishes certain safeguards for a person charged with a criminal offence, including the presumption of innocence, the right to be informed of the nature of any charges, the right to adequate time and legal

---

[115] Debtors Act 1869, as amended by the Administration of Justice Act 1970, s 11.

[116] *Danchevsky v Danchevsky* [1975] Fam 17, [1974] 3 All ER 934; *Re G (Contempt: Committal)* [2003] EWCA Civ 489, [2003] 1 WLR 2051.

[117] *Re M* [1994] 1 AC 377; *sub nom M v Home Office* [1993] 3 All ER 537.

[118] Contempt of Court Act 1981, s 14(1).   [119] Ibid, s 14(4A).

[120] *R v Davies* [1906] 1 KB 32. Note that this jurisdiction is limited to 'courts' properly so-called, and it may therefore be important to ascertain whether a particular tribunal is a court: *A-G v BBC* [1981] AC 303, [1980] 3 All ER 161: see p 228, *ante*.

[121] 1981 Act, s 14(1), (2).

[122] Ibid, s 12. Magistrates can also punish the making of insults against justices, witnesses, solicitors, barristers, and officers of the court.

assistance in preparing a defence, and the right to be dealt with by an independent and impartial tribunal. Doubts have been raised about the compatibility of the summary procedure with these requirements, and the Court of Appeal has indicated that it should not be used in the absence of a clear contempt that cannot wait to be dealt with:[123]

Nearly all contempt proceedings require to be adjourned to a separate hearing, in many cases to a different judge, with the rest of the case continuing if possible. An adjournment will usually be necessary if the first judge has already heard evidence from the party alleged to be in contempt which he would not be obliged to give, for risk of self-incrimination, if he were faced with an allegation of contempt.

C THE EUROPEAN COURT OF JUSTICE AND EUROPEAN COURT OF HUMAN RIGHTS

These courts play an increasingly important role in the English legal system, and their functions and powers are considered in detail in chapters 4 and 5.

D THE HOUSE OF LORDS

1 THE HOUSE OF LORDS: CONSTITUTION AND PROCEDURE

Parliament is the oldest common law court, and its judicial functions have been exercised by the House of Lords since the fifteenth century. In theory, an appeal to the House of Lords is an appeal to the whole House, and until the nineteenth century this was literally true in that any member of the House could and did vote in judicial sessions. Even those peers who were lawyers were rarely the most senior and well-respected judges of their day, and puisne judges were frequently invited to advise their Lordships on the law.[124] The convention against lay peers participating in judicial sittings of the House was not firmly established until the Appellate Jurisdiction Act 1876 provided for the creation of salaried life peers to hear appeals. The new life peers were called Lords of Appeal in Ordinary ('Law Lords'), and their number was subsequently fixed at between seven and twelve.[125]

---

[123] *Re G (Contempt: Committal)* [2003] EWCA Civ 489 at [21], [2003] 1 WLR 2051 at [21], per Butler Sloss P. See also, *Balogh v St Albans Crown Court* [1975] QB 73, [1974] 3 All ER 283.

[124] The last case in which this appears to have happened was *Allen v Flood* [1898] AC 1.

[125] Appellate Jurisdiction Act 1947; Administration of Justice Act 1968, s 1(1)(a); Maximum Number of Judges Order 1994, SI 1994/3217. By custom, one or two Law Lords have always been from Scotland and one from Northern Ireland: these members have usually sat in appeals from the Court of Session and the Court of Appeal of Northern Ireland.

The 1876 Act provided that appeals should be heard by at least three members from the following list: (a) the Lord Chancellor; (b) the Lords of Appeal in Ordinary; and (c) certain other peers 'who hold or have held high judicial office'. In practice, most appeals are heard by a committee of at least five Lords of Appeal (or occasionally seven),[126] and they are generally argued in a committee room at the Palace of Westminster and not in the Chamber of the House itself. Each Law Lord is entitled to deliver a separate opinion, with the decision of the majority prevailing. In the unusual case of *Kennedy v Spratt*[127] Lord Upjohn, who was one of the five Law Lords to have heard the appeal, died before the judgment was delivered. This resulted in the vote being equally split and the appeal was therefore dismissed.[128]

2 HOUSE OF LORDS: JURISDICTION

(a) Original jurisdiction

In modern times the House of Lords has had very little original jurisdiction. The right of a peer to be 'tried by his peers'[129] was abolished by the Criminal Justice Act 1948, and while the House theoretically retains the jurisdiction to conduct impeachment proceedings, this has not been exercised since the impeachments of Warren Hastings and Viscount Melville in 1795 and 1805 respectively. Both the House of Lords and the House of Commons have jurisdiction over breaches of privilege, including contempt of the House, and either House may imprison the offender. Beyond this, the original jurisdiction of the House of Lords is limited to hearing disputed peerage claims through the Committee of Privileges.[130]

(b) Appellate jurisdiction

Civil cases. The House of Lords hears appeals in civil cases from the Court of Appeal, but only with leave of either the Court of Appeal or the Appeals Committee of the House itself.[131] Most cases to reach the House of Lords have involved points of law of public importance, though this is not a pre-requisite in civil cases.[132]

The Administration of Justice Act 1969 introduced a 'leap-frog' procedure, allowing

---

[126] The appeal in *A v Secretary of State for the Home Department* [2004] UKHL 56, [2005] 2 WLR 87 was of such significance that it was heard by nine Law Lords: see p 161, *ante*.

[127] [1972] AC 83, [1971] 1 All ER 805.

[128] Ibid. As it happens, the opinion written by Lord Upjohn before his death indicated that he was in favour of dismissing the appeal. Had his opinion indicated that he was in favour of allowing the appeal, an anomalous situation would have arisen whereby his death would have deprived the appellant of success. It is uncertain how their Lordships would have responded to this situation.

[129] This is thought to originate from the Magna Carta.

[130] For examples, see the *Ampthill Peerage* case [1977] AC 547, [1976] 2 All ER 411, and the *Annandale and Hartfell Peerage Claim* [1986] AC 319, [1985] 3 All ER 577.

[131] Administration of Justice (Appeals) Act 1934. The House also hears appeals from the equivalent civil courts of Scotland (Court of Session) and Northern Ireland (Court of Appeal).

[132] In *Johnson v Moreton* [1980] AC 37 at 53, [1978] 3 All ER 37 at 44, Lord Hailsham suggested that nine out of ten House of Lords cases concerned the construction of Acts of Parliament.

appeals to bypass the Court of Appeal and go directly from the trial court to the House of Lords. A leapfrog appeal is only possible if two conditions are satisfied:[133]

(1) The trial judge must grant a certificate (with the consent of all parties) that the case involves a point of law of general public importance. The point of law must either relate wholly or mainly to the construction of an enactment, or it must be one in respect of which the judge would be bound by a previous decision of the Court of Appeal or House of Lords; and

(2) The House of Lords must grant leave.

Criminal cases. The House of Lords' jurisdiction in criminal cases is of comparatively modern origin, and it was not until the Court of Criminal Appeal was created in 1907[134] that there was any general right to appeal to the Lords in a criminal case. The right of appeal from the Queen's Bench Divisional Court was created by the Administration of Justice Act 1960, and appeal also lies from the High Court, the Courts-Martial Appeal Court, and the Court of Appeal of Northern Ireland.[135] There is no right of appeal to the House of Lords from Scotland's highest criminal court, the High Court of Justiciary.

3 REFORM: A SUPREME COURT FOR THE UNITED KINGDOM

On 12 June 2003 the government unexpectedly announced that it planned to transfer the jurisdiction of the House of Lords' Appellate Committee to a new Supreme Court. This was to be part of a package of measures aimed at modernizing the constitution and ensuring a more formal separation of powers. Other parts of the package included reforming the office of Lord Chancellor,[136] the creation of a government department with administrative responsibility for most major courts,[137] and the creation of an independent Judicial Appointments Commission.[138] A consultation paper explained that the idea behind the proposed new court was to formally separate the judiciary from Parliament and the executive. 'Transparency of independence' was cited as the key issue:[139]

The considerable growth of judicial review in recent years has inevitably brought the judges more into the political eye. It is essential that our systems do all that they can to minimise

---

[133] Sections 12 and 13.

[134] Criminal Appeal Act 1907. The jurisdiction of this court was transferred to the Criminal Division of the Court of Appeal by the Criminal Appeal Act 1966.

[135] The conditions required for an appeal are discussed at p 682, *post*.

[136] Department for Constitutional Affairs, *Constitutional Reform: Reforming the Office of the Lord Chancellor* (2003) CP 13/03. The original proposal was for abolition; see p 20, *ante*.

[137] The Department for Constitutional Affairs (DCA); ibid.

[138] DCA, *Constitutional Reform: A New Way of Appointing Judges* (2003) CP 10/03; see p 314, *post*.

[139] DCA, *Constitutional Reform: A Supreme Court for the United Kingdom* (2003) CP 11/03, at para 1.2. The proposed reforms were considered sufficiently fundamental for at least one journal to devote an entire edition to the issue: (2004) 24 Legal Studies.

the danger that judges' decisions could be perceived to be politically motivated. The Human Rights Act 1998, itself the product of a changing climate of opinion, has made people more sensitive to the issues and more aware of the anomaly of the position whereby the highest court of appeal is situated within one of the chambers of Parliament.

In its published response to the consultation paper,[140] the Judges' Council broadly accepted the proposals, whilst making it clear that not all of its members were convinced of the need for change. The main area of disagreement concerned the proposal to remove the senior judges from the legislature entirely:[141]

While the House of Lords remains wholly, or mainly, an appointed (rather than elected) body there is a strong case for the Lord Chief Justice of England and Wales, the Lord President of the Court of Session, the Lord Chief Justice of Northern Ireland and the President of the Supreme Court being members. It would not be sensible to exclude from a House of Lords those best placed to contribute to debates on the justice system and the judiciary. All other members of the Supreme Court, should cease to exercise any rights they may have to speak or vote in the House while they serve as judges.

The final blueprint for the new Court was included in the Constitutional Reform Act 2005. The Act reflects most of the preferences expressed by the Judges' Council as to the Court's membership, size, composition, and jurisdiction.[142] Crucially however, the recommendation that some senior judges should continue to sit in the House of Lords has not been adopted. Section 23 provides that 'there is to be a Supreme Court of the United Kingdom', and that it shall consist of twelve judges.[143] The Court will be properly constituted when an uneven number of not less than three judges is sitting, more than half of whom must be permanent members.[144] The current Lords of Appeal will become the first members of the new Court, and at this point they will cease to be entitled to sit in Parliament.[145] They will be called 'Justices of the Supreme Court',[146] and the Court's two most senior members will hold the offices of President and Deputy President.[147] The President will be able to supplement the Court's permanent membership by asking other senior judges to sit on a temporary basis. Former Law Lords and Supreme Court Justices will also be eligible to sit.[148]

The Supreme Court will not be able to strike down legislation as unconstitutional or contrary to the ECHR, and its jurisdiction will be broadly the same as that currently exercised by the House of Lords.[149] It will, however, inherit jurisdiction over

---

[140] Judges' Council Response to the Consultation Papers on Constitutional Reform (available online at www.dca.gov.uk/judicial/pdfs/jcresp.pdf). The Law Lords' response is discussed at p 315, *post*.

[141] Ibid, at para 17.

[142] Some of the Council's recommendations were *not* adopted. For example, the Act does not include provisions making the Lord Chief Justice, Master of the Rolls, Lord President of the Court of Session, and Lord Chief Justice of Northern Ireland *ex officio* members of the new court; nor does it prevent leapfrog appeals from the High Court in criminal cases.

[143] This number may be varied by Order in Council, subject to an affirmative resolution procedure.

[144] Section 42.   [145] Sections 24 and 137.   [146] Section 23(6).

[147] Sections 23(5) and 24.   [148] Sections 38 and 39.   [149] Section 40.

devolution matters from the Privy Council.[150] As it will hear appeals from all parts of the UK it will remain legally separate from the existing courts of England and Wales.

Although the Constitutional Reform Act was passed in 2005, the provisions establishing the Supreme Court will not be brought into force until it can be properly housed.[151] The government's preferred venue for the new Court is Middlesex Guildhall, but the planned refurbishments to this building are unlikely to be complete before the end of 2008.

E THE COURT OF APPEAL

The English superior courts were completely reorganized by the Supreme Court of Judicature Acts 1873–1875. The Acts created the Supreme Court of Judicature[152] and transferred to it the jurisdiction of the existing superior courts: the appellate jurisdiction was transferred to the Court of Appeal and the original jurisdiction was transferred to the High Court. The Crown Court was added to the list by the Courts Act 1971. The Supreme Court of Judicature now consists of three courts: the Court of Appeal, the High Court, and the Crown Court. The relevant law is consolidated in the Supreme Court Act 1981.

1 CONSTITUTION

The Court of Appeal is split into Civil and Criminal Divisions, and is composed of a number of *ex officio* judges along with the Lords Justices of Appeal.[153] The *ex officio* judges comprise the Lord Chief Justice, the Master of the Rolls, the President of the Family Division of the High Court, the Vice-Chancellor,[154] former Lord Chancellors,[155] and the Lords of Appeal in Ordinary.[156] Of these, only the Master of the Rolls

---

[150] Section 40(4)(b); Schedule 9. The Privy Council's jurisdiction is discussed at p 269, *post.*

[151] Section 148(4).

[152] Renamed 'the Supreme Court of England and Wales' by the Supreme Court Act 1981. It will become 'the Senior Courts of England and Wales' when the new Supreme Court is established: see above.

[153] Supreme Court Act 1981, s 2. Section 2(3) was amended by the Courts Act 2003 to permit the use of the title 'Lady Justice of Appeal' where appropriate. The maximum number of ordinary Court of Appeal judges is thirty-seven: Maximum Number of Judges Order, SI 2002/2837.

[154] The Constitutional Reform Act 2005 provides for the Vice-Chancellor to be re-titled 'Chancellor of the High Court'. It also provides for the appointment of a President of the Queen's Bench Division: the holders of both offices will be *ex officio* Court of Appeal judges.

[155] When Lord Falconer was appointed to this position in June 2003 he made it clear that he did not intend to sit in a judicial capacity. The effect of Part 2 of the Constitutional Reform Act 2005 is that future Lord Chancellors will not have any judicial functions: see further, pp 20 and 301.

[156] The Court has sometimes been composed of three Law Lords: see *Mallett* v *Restormel Borough Council* [1978] 2 All ER 1057. The Lords of Appeal will become 'Justices of the Supreme Court' when the new Court is established.

(in civil cases) and the Lord Chief Justice (in criminal cases) usually sit, and they are in fact the Presidents of the Civil and Criminal Divisions respectively. In addition to the regular judges of the Court, any High Court judge or circuit judge may be required to sit.[157] Former High Court and Court of Appeal judges may also be asked to sit, but they cannot be compelled to do so.

The Civil Division may be duly constituted with only one judge present, but most cases are heard by three judges sitting together.[158] At least two judges must be present to hear appeals against sentence,[159] and three or more judges are required for any of the following:[160]

(a) an appeal against conviction;

(b) an appeal against a verdict of not guilty by reason of insanity;

(c) an appeal against a finding of unfitness to plead;

(d) an application for leave to appeal to the House of Lords;

(e) a refusal of leave to appeal against conviction (or against any of the verdicts and findings referred to above), unless the application has already been refused by a single judge; or

(f) a review of a sentencing decision which has been referred by the Attorney-General under Part IV of the Criminal Justice Act 1988.

In addition, a single judge of the Criminal Division has jurisdiction under the Criminal Appeal Act 1968 to hear certain types of application; notably for leave to appeal.[161] Either division may occasionally convene a 'full court' of five or more members to hear appeals involving novel or difficult points of law. However, such a court has no wider powers than the normal court.

2 JURISDICTION

The Court of Appeal has consisted of a Civil and a Criminal Division since 1 October 1966, which is when the Criminal Appeal Act 1966 came into operation.

(a) Civil Division

The Civil Division exercises:

(a) all jurisdiction conferred on it by the Supreme Court Act 1981 or any other Act; and

(b) all jurisdiction exercisable by it prior to the commencement of the 1981 Act.[162]

---

[157] Supreme Court Act 1981, s 9: note that circuit judges can only sit in the Criminal Division.

[158] Ibid, s 54(2), as amended. The Master of the Rolls may give directions about the minimum number of judges needed for (a) any description of proceedings, or (b) any particular proceedings; s 54(3)–(4A).

[159] Ibid, s 55(4).   [160] Ibid; there must be an odd number. For details, see p 696, *post.*

[161] Section 31, as amended.   [162] Supreme Court Act 1981, s 15(2).

Its jurisdiction is entirely civil and entirely appellate. Until recently, appeals in civil cases from both the county court and the High Court were generally heard by the Court of Appeal, but in 1997 a review carried out by Sir Jeffrey Bowman concluded that the Civil Division's workload was unnecessarily high.[163] Two of the Review's most important recommendations were that:

(a) any appeal against the first instance decision of a civil court should normally require leave;[164] and

(b) more appeals should be dealt with at a lower level, the guiding principle being simply that the judge or court hearing an appeal should have a superior jurisdiction to the first instance decision maker.

The main aim of these proposals was to reduce the workload of the Civil Division and to improve the speed and overall efficiency of the appeals process.

Reform under the Access to Justice Act 1999. The Bowman recommendations were broadly implemented by the Access to Justice Act 1999 and the Civil Procedure Rules, Part 52.[165] Under section 56 of the Act the Lord Chancellor is empowered to make more detailed rules for the allocation of civil appeals by way of statutory instrument.[166] Appeals against many county court decisions are now dealt with by High Court judges, whilst the Court of Appeal continues to hear appeals against final decisions in multi-track[167] and specialist proceedings cases.[168] In addition, there is a discretion to allow any civil appeal which would normally be heard by a lower court to be dealt with instead by the Court of Appeal.[169]

Any second appeal against the decision of a county court or High Court judge will also lie to the Court of Appeal, but second appeals can only be granted exceptionally and the Court of Appeal must be satisfied that either:

(a) the appeal would raise an important point of principle or practice; or

(b) there is some other compelling reason for hearing it.[170]

Finally, the Civil Division has jurisdiction to hear appeals on points of law from the

---

[163] *Report to the Lord Chancellor by the Review of the Court of Appeal* (Lord Chancellor's Department, 1997); see also Jacob J, 'Bowman Review of the Court of Appeal' (1998) 61(3) MLR 390. Similar recommendations were made in Woolf's *Final Report on Access to Justice* (1996).

[164] The Review recommended that an appeal should still be as of right in cases where the liberty of the subject was at stake, and in certain cases involving children.

[165] SI 2000/221; in force since 2 May 2000. For a discussion of the key changes, see *Tanfern Ltd v Cameron-MacDonald* [2000] 2 All ER 801, [2000] 1 WLR 1311.

[166] An Order pursuant to this provision has been made: see the Access to Justice Act 1999 (Destination of Appeals) Order 2000, SI 2000/1071.

[167] Ibid, Article 4. Multi-track cases are discussed at p 466, *post*.

[168] Ibid. Specialist proceedings are those involving the Patents Court or Technology and Construction Court, commercial proceedings, admiralty matters, and proceedings under the Companies Acts.

[169] 1999 Act, s 57. This discretion may be exercised by either the Master of the Rolls or a court involved in the case.

[170] Ibid, s 55(1); SI 2000/1071, Article 5.

Competition Commission, the Employment Appeal Tribunal, the Lands Tribunal, and various other tribunals.

The appeal itself normally takes the form of a limited review unless the court considers that it would be in the interests of justice to hold a rehearing, or exceptionally, to order a new trial.[171] The appeals system applicable to civil cases is discussed further in chapter 18 of this book.

(b) Criminal Division

The Criminal Division of the Court of Appeal was established by the Criminal Appeal Act 1966 as the successor to the Court of Criminal Appeal.[172] Its jurisdiction is entirely criminal and entirely appellate. Its principal function is to hear appeals against conviction and sentence from persons convicted in the Crown Court. It can also consider sentencing decisions referred by the Attorney-General on the grounds that they are unduly lenient.[173] In addition, where a trial on indictment has ended in a conviction, a finding of not guilty by reason of insanity, or a finding that a person did the act in question but is under a disability, the case can be referred by the Criminal Cases Review Commission for determination as an appeal.[174]

Where a trial on indictment has ended in acquittal, the Attorney-General has the power to refer points of law arising from the case to the Court of Appeal.[175] However, the purpose of such a reference is simply to clarify the law for future cases, and the Court of Appeal's opinion on the matter does not affect the outcome for the defendant. Indeed, before the Criminal Justice Act 2003, a jury's decision to acquit a defendant was final and could not be challenged by the prosecution. However, the 2003 Act gives prosecutors new powers to appeal against the outcome of a trial on indictment. As of 4 April, they can ask the Court of Appeal to quash an acquittal and order a re-trial, where a person has been tried for a qualifying offence and certain conditions are met.[176] They can also appeal against a judge's decision to terminate a prosecution or to make an evidentiary ruling which significantly weakens their case.[177] A more detailed discussion of the criminal appeals system is set out in chapter 24 of this book.

---

[171] Civil Procedure Rules, Part 52. The difference between a review and a re-hearing is considered in *Assicurazoni Generali Spa* v *Arab Insurance Group* [2002] EWCA Civ 1642, [2003] 1 WLR 577.

[172] Established by the Criminal Appeal Act 1907, to supersede the Court for Crown Cases Reserved.

[173] Criminal Justice Act 1988, s 36; see p 684, *post*.

[174] Criminal Appeal Act 1995, s 9: see p 684, *post*. This power was formerly exercisable by the Home Secretary: Criminal Appeal Act 1968, s 17.

[175] Criminal Justice Act 1972, s 36; see p 687, *post*.

[176] 2003 Act, s 76(1): see p 688, *post*. 'Qualifying offences' are listed in Schedule 5, part 1. For a more detailed analysis see Ward and Davies, *Criminal Justice Act 2003: A Practitioners' Guide* (2004).

[177] Sections 58 and 62.

F THE HIGH COURT

1 CONSTITUTION

The High Court was established by the Supreme Court of Judicature Acts 1873–75 and to it was transferred the jurisdiction of several existing superior courts. These included the three superior common law courts of first instance, the Court of Chancery, and the Courts of Admiralty, Probate, and Divorce and Matrimonial Causes.[178] The constitution and jurisdiction of the High Court are now governed by the Supreme Court Act 1981. The court sits primarily in London, but by virtue of section 71 of the Act sittings may be conducted at any place in England or Wales.[179] The centres at which sittings are actually held are determined in accordance with the Lord Chancellor's directions, and ad hoc directions may be given to enable the Court to sit at a particular location. Thus, in a case concerning a disputed right of way in Iken, a small village in Suffolk,[180] the Lord Chancellor authorised the Court to sit at Iken so that the evidence of an elderly witness could be taken.

2 JURISDICTION

The jurisdiction of the High Court is both civil and criminal. In civil actions its jurisdiction is virtually unlimited and it is broadly concurrent with that of the county courts. However, there is a minimum financial limit for the value of claims that can be commenced in the High Court, and subject to any statutory exceptions this is currently £50,000 for personal injury actions, and £15,000 for other cases.[181] For claims exceeding these limits proceedings can be commenced in either court, and there are provisions for transferring appropriate cases from one court to the other.[182] Following the Woolf reforms, the allocation of cases between the High Court and the county courts now depends not only on the sums involved but also on whether they are designated as 'small claims', 'fast track', or 'multi track' cases.[183] These reforms are the subject of more detailed analysis in chapter 15, but for present purposes it is sufficient to note that the majority of the High Court's workload now consists of multi-track cases, and most civil actions continue to be determined at county court level.

In addition to its original jurisdiction in civil cases, the High Court also has both appellate and supervisory functions. The historic role of the courts in supervising the

---

[178] The jurisdiction of the Chancery Courts of the Counties Palatine of Lancaster and Durham was *not* transferred, but these courts were merged with the High Court under s 41 of the Courts Act 1971.

[179] Evidence may be taken outside the jurisdiction. In *Tito v Waddell* [1975] 3 All ER 997, [1975] 1 WLR 1303 the judge visited two Pacific islands in order to view land at the centre of a legal dispute.

[180] *St Edmundsbury and Ipswich Diocesan Board of Finance v Clark* [1973] Ch 323, [1973] 2 All ER 1155.

[181] High Court and County Courts Jurisdiction Order 1991, SI 1991/724; High Court and County Courts Jurisdiction (Amendment) Order 1999, SI 1999/1014.

[182] CPR, Part 30.   [183] See p 464, *post*.

actions of inferior bodies and tribunals has already been noted,[184] and this role is now performed mainly by a Divisional Court of the Queen's Bench Division. All three divisions of the High Court also have an appellate role, and this has increased since the restructuring of the civil appeals system in 1999.[185]

3 THE DIVISIONS

The High Court initially consisted of five divisions, but these were reduced in 1880 to the three that currently exist:[186] the Chancery Division, the Queen's Bench Division, and the Family Division.[187] Each division handles a different type of subject matter, though it is important to note that the divisions are of equal competence and they are not separate courts. Indeed, the inherent jurisdiction of the High Court judge may be exercised by a judge of any division,[188] and the fact that a matter falls within a particular division's class of business does not necessarily mean that that the matter must be allocated accordingly.[189] Moreover, in certain cases the jurisdiction of the divisions overlaps, and this means that claimants sometimes have a choice about where to commence their actions. Many actions for professional negligence for example, can be commenced in either the Queen's Bench Division or the Chancery Division.[190] Nevertheless, the overall effect of the relevant statutes and rules of procedure is to confer a distinct jurisdiction upon each division,[191] and suggestions that the divisions should be merged have thus far been rejected.[192]

(a) Chancery Division

The business of the Chancery Division is carried out by the Vice-Chancellor and seventeen puisne judges.[193] Before 1972, sittings of the Chancery Division were held only in the Royal Courts of Justice in London, and Chancery judges did not go on

---

[184] See p 223, *ante*.   [185] See p 498, *post*.

[186] See now, the Supreme Court Act 1981, s 5. Section 7 of the Act provides that the number of divisions may be increased or reduced on the recommendation of the senior judges specified in s 7(2).

[187] The Family Division was originally called the Probate, Divorce and Admiralty Division, but was renamed by the Administration of Justice Act 1970, s 1. Its Admiralty jurisdiction was re-assigned to the Queen's Bench Division and contentious probate business was assigned to the Chancery Division.

[188] Supreme Court Act 1981, s 5(5): see *Re L* [1968] P 119, [1968] 1 All ER 20.   [189] Ibid.

[190] The contract disputes in *Petrofina (Great Britain) Ltd v Martin* [1965] Ch 1073, [1965] 2 All ER 176 and *Esso Petroleum Co Ltd v Harper's Garage (Stourport) Ltd* [1965] 3 WLR 469, [1965] 2 All ER 933 may also be considered in this context. The two cases concerned very similar issues, yet the former was tried in the Chancery Division and the latter in the Queen's Bench Division.

[191] For the distribution of business between the divisions, see Supreme Court Act 1981, s 61 and Schedule 1.

[192] See, e.g. Woolf, *Final Report on Access to Justice* (1996), at p 261.

[193] *Judicial Statistics 2003*, p 99. The Lord Chancellor has historically been head of the Division but modern Lord Chancellors have rarely sat at first instance. When Lord Falconer was appointed in 2003 he announced that he did not intend to sit at all, and Part 2 of the Constitutional Reform Act 2005 is designed to formally strip the Lord Chancellor of all judicial functions: see pp 20 and 301. The Act also provides for the office of Vice-Chancellor to be replaced with that of 'Chancellor of the High Court'; Schedule 4, para 115.

assize. The Supreme Court Act 1981 authorizes sittings of the High Court to be held anywhere in England and Wales,[194] but most Chancery business is still heard in London.[195]

Jurisdiction. Section 34 of the Supreme Court of Judicature Act 1873 gave the Chancery Division jurisdiction over matters which were previously heard in the Court of Chancery. The distribution of High Court business is now governed by section 61 and Schedule 1 of the Supreme Court Act 1981, and under these provisions the Chancery Division is assigned jurisdiction over all causes and matters concerning:

(a) the sale, exchange or partition of land, or the raising of charges on land;

(b) the redemption or foreclosure of mortgages;

(c) the execution of trusts;

(d) the administration of estates of deceased persons;

(e) bankruptcy;

(f) the dissolution of partnerships or the taking of partnership or other accounts;

(g) the rectification, setting aside or cancellation of deeds or other instruments in writing;

(h) probate business, other than non-contentious or common form business;

(i) patents, trade marks, registered designs or copyright;

(j) the appointment of a guardian of a minor's estate, and

(k) matters relating company law.

Various other statutes and rules of procedure give the Chancery Division jurisdiction over revenue matters, town and country planning, and landlord and tenant disputes.

The appellate jurisdiction of the Chancery Division has always been limited, and has primarily related to taxation, insolvency and land registration. As stated previously however, reforms since 1999 mean that many more appeals from county court decisions can now be determined at High Court level. The implications of these changes are discussed further in chapter 17, but their overall effect is to extend the appellate jurisdiction of all three divisions of the High Court to cover a broader spectrum of cases.

Patents Court. The Patents Court is part of the Chancery Division and is one of a number of 'specialist courts' within the High Court. It was established by the Patents Act 1977 and hears patent actions at first instance and on appeal from the Comptroller-General of Patents, Designs and Trademarks.

---

[194] Section 71(1).

[195] Cases are also heard in Birmingham, Bristol, Cardiff, Leeds, Liverpool, Manchester, Newcastle-upon-Tyne, and Preston.

Court of Protection. When sitting as the Court of Protection, judges of the Chancery Division hear applications concerning the property[196] and affairs of persons of unsound mind within the meaning of the Mental Health Act 1983. At the time of writing, the 1983 Act also governs the constitution and jurisdiction of the court However, Part 2 of the Mental Capacity Act 2005 will give the court an enhanced jurisdiction and make it a superior court of record in its own right.

(b) Queen's Bench Division

At the time of writing, the Queen's Bench Division has seventy-two puisne judges[197] and is headed by the Lord Chief Justice. However, the Constitutional Reform Act 2005 provides for the creation of a new post of President of the Queen's Bench Division,[198] which will *not* be held by the Lord Chief Justice. The Division has both a civil and a criminal jurisdiction, and performs original, appellate, and supervisory functions.

Civil jurisdiction. The most important aspect of this Division's business is its first instance jurisdiction over civil matters, and most of its workload consists of actions in contract and tort. Its role in the civil appeals system has always been very limited, though High Court judges of all divisions were given a greater appellate jurisdiction when the system was restructured in 1999.[199] In addition, a Divisional Court of the Queen's Bench Division, consisting of two or more judges, has a limited civil jurisdiction to hear appeals by way of case stated from the Crown Court and magistrates' courts.[200]

Commercial Court. This court has jurisdiction over commercial matters, and like the Patents Court, it is a specialist court operating within a division of the High Court. It was officially designated as a court by the Administration of Justice Act 1970,[201] though a 'commercial list' of cases has been maintained since 1895. The Court has its own rules of procedure[202] and is served by nominated puisne judges with particular expertise in this area of law.

Admiralty Court. This is also a specialist court, and it has jurisdiction over matters assigned to the Queen's Bench Division by section 20 of the Supreme Court Act 1981. Its business includes actions to enforce claims for damages arising out of collisions between ships, claims to the possession or ownership of ships, claims for loss of or damage to goods carried in a ship, towage claims, and other specified proceedings. When trying admiralty actions the judge often sits with lay assessors.

Technology and Construction Court. Since 1998 this specialist court has been responsible for dealing with disputes involving construction, engineering, surveying, and similar matters, along with certain cases concerning information technology, the sale

---

[196] The power is exercisable in the High Court if the sum involved is small: *Re K's Settlement Trusts* [1969] 2 Ch 1, [1969] 1 All ER 194.

[197] *Judicial Statistics 2003*, p 99.   [198] Schedule 4, para 115.   [199] See p 498, *post.*

[200] Appeals from magistrates' courts in family cases lie to the Family Division.

[201] Section 3(1).   [202] See CPR, parts 49 and 58, and the accompanying *Practice Direction 58.*

of goods, trespass, and nuisance.[203] However, a dispute will only warrant allocation to this court if it involves technically complex questions of fact.

As a final point, it should be noted that judges of the Queen's Bench Division also exercise many other functions. Not only do they handle most of the business of the Criminal Division of the Court of Appeal, they also sit in the Courts-Martial Appeal Court and determine disputed parliamentary elections when sitting as an election court.[204] In addition, the 'first-tier' jurisdiction of the Crown Court is exercised principally by judges from this Division.[205]

Criminal jurisdiction. The criminal jurisdiction of the High Court is exercised exclusively by the Queen's Bench Division and is entirely appellate. It comprises appeals by way of 'case stated'[206] from magistrates' courts, and also from the Crown Court when acting in its capacity as an appellate court. These appeals are heard by a Queen's Bench Divisional Court consisting of at least two but often three judges.

Supervisory jurisdiction. The supervisory jurisdiction of the Queen's Bench Division is also exercised by a Divisional Court. It includes the power to make mandatory orders, prohibition orders, and quashing orders,[207] which compel inferior courts and tribunals to exercise their powers properly and within the scope of their authority (intra vires). It also includes the power to issue the prerogative writ of habeas corpus. The Division's supervisory jurisdiction is exercised through the procedure known as 'judicial review', which is currently governed by Part 54 of the Civil Procedure Rules.[208] These cases used to be dealt with as part of the Crown Office list, but the group of increasingly specialized judges who determine judicial review matters is now known as 'the Administrative Court'.[209]

(c) Family Division

The Family Division[210] consists of the President and eighteen nominated puisne judges,[211] who are assisted in their work by a number of district judges. Its jurisdiction

---

[203] Supreme Court Act 1981, s 68 and Schedule 2, as amended by the Civil Procedure Act 1997. The matters dealt with by the court were formally known as 'Official Referee's Business'.

[204] Representation of the People Act 1983, s 120. This is not actually part of the Queen's Bench Division: indeed, it is an inferior court and is therefore subject to judicial review (*R v Cripps, ex parte Muldoon* [1984] QB 68, [1984] 3 All ER 72).

[205] See p 258, *post.*

[206] Magistrates' Courts Act 1980, s 111; Supreme Court Act 1981, ss 28 and 28A. For details of the procedure, see p 651, *post.*

[207] Formerly known as orders of mandamus, prohibition, and certiorari.

[208] This replaces RSC, Ord 53: for more detail, see chapter 6.

[209] *Practice Direction (Administrative Court: Establishment)* [2000] 4 All ER 1071, [2000] 1 WLR 1654.

[210] Prior to the Administration of Justice Act 1970, it was known as the Probate, Divorce and Admiralty Division. Sir Alan Herbert described the jurisdiction as 'wills, wives and wrecks': of these, 'wills' have gone to the Chancery Division, and 'wrecks' (other than the wrecks of marriages) to the Queen's Bench Division.

[211] Supreme Court Act 1981, s 5; *Judicial Statistics 2003*, p 99.

is set out in the Supreme Court Act 1981, and is both original and appellate. The following functions are assigned to it by Schedule 1 of the Act:

(a) all High Court matrimonial causes and matters (whether at first instance or on appeal);

(b) all causes and matters (whether at first instance or on appeal) relating to:
   (i) legitimacy;
   (ii) the exercise of the inherent jurisdiction of the High Court with respect to minors, the maintenance of minors and any proceedings under the Children Act 1989, except proceedings solely for the appointment of a guardian of a minor's estate;
   (iii) adoption;
   (iv) non-contentious or common-form probate business;

(c) applications for consent to the marriage of a minor;

(d) proceedings on appeal from an order or decision made under section 63(3) of the Magistrates' Courts Act 1980 to enforce an order of a magistrates' court made in matrimonial proceedings or with respect to the guardianship of a minor;

(e) certain proceedings under the Family Law Act 1986;

(f) proceedings under the Children Act 1989;

(g) proceedings under various other statutory provisions.[212]

The effect of these provisions is to give the Division exclusive High Court jurisdiction over matrimonial disputes and children, thus avoiding the conflicts which used to arise between the Family and Chancery Divisions before 1970.[213]

For proceedings arising under the Children Act 1989, magistrates' courts, county courts, and the Family Division each have jurisdiction.[214] The distribution of work between the three courts is governed by an order made by the Lord Chancellor,[215] which also provides for the transfer of cases between the three courts. In addition, the Courts Act 2003 establishes a Family Procedure Rule Committee with the power to make Family Procedure Rules governing practice and procedure across all three courts.[216] The Constitutional Reform Act 2005 also provides for the creation of a new post of Head of Family Justice, which will be held *ex officio* by the President of the Family Division.[217]

The appellate business of the Family Division consists largely of appeals from family courts concerning matrimonial causes and children.

---

[212] Family Law Acts 1986 and 1996; Child Abduction and Custody Act 1985; Human Fertilisation and Embryology Act 1990; Welfare Reform and Pensions Act 1999; Child Support Act 1991.

[213] See, e.g. *Hall v Hall* [1963] P 378, [1963] 2 All ER 140.   [214] Children Act 1989, s 92.

[215] Children (Allocation of Proceedings) Order 1991, SI 1991/1677, as amended. See also, the Family Law Act 1996 (Part IV) (Allocation of Proceedings) Order 1997, SI 1997/1896.

[216] Sections 75–81.   [217] Section 9.

G COUNTY COURTS

1 CONSTITUTION

The county courts were established by the County Courts Act 1846 to meet the need for a system to deal with small claims. There are currently 218 county courts in England and Wales, each serving a particular district. Every county court district is assigned at least one circuit judge and one district judge, and deputy district judges may also be appointed.[218] In theory, even High Court and Court of Appeal judges may be asked to sit,[219] but it would be extremely rare to find such a senior judge being used in this capacity.

2 JURISDICTION

The jurisdiction of the county courts is entirely civil, and in terms of subject matter it is broadly concurrent with the civil jurisdiction of the High Court. Thus the County Courts Act 1984 gives them jurisdiction over cases involving tort, contract, land, equity, family law, probate, and even admiralty, whilst other statutes confer jurisdiction in matters such as discrimination, divorce, landlord and tenant, and insolvency.[220] However, as county courts owe their origins entirely to statute they only have jurisdiction in matters specifically assigned to them by legislation. They do not, for example, have any inherent jurisdiction to conduct judicial review proceedings; nor can they grant the associated prerogative remedies.[221]

Not all county courts deal with the full range of cases eligible for determination at this level: almost a quarter do not have jurisdiction to hear divorce petitions, and over a third do not deal with insolvency matters. In addition, some county courts have been designated as specialist centres for dealing with particular types of action. For example, whilst all county courts have jurisdiction to hear proceedings under the Children Act 1989, a number have been designated as specialist 'family hearing centres' to which difficult cases may be transferred.[222] One county court in London even specializes in patent cases. There is also a Bulk Centre at Northampton County Court, which processes computer-generated debt recovery claims from major claimants such as public utilities and mail order companies. The same court also processes a large volume of claims for unpaid car parking charges.

There are two further limitations on the county courts' jurisdiction, the first of which is geographical. Unlike the High Court, which is a single court with the

---

[218] County Courts Act 1984, ss 1, 5, 6, and 8.   [219] Ibid, s 5.

[220] See, e.g. Race Relations Act 1976, s 57; Sex Discrimination Act 1975, s 66; Matrimonial and Family Proceedings Act 1984, s 33; Rent Act 1977, s 141; Insolvency Act 1986, ss 117 and 373.

[221] See chapter 6.

[222] Children (Allocation of Proceedings) Order 1991, SI 1991/1677, as amended. The designated centres are listed in Schedule 1 of the Order.

jurisdiction to sit anywhere in England and Wales, each county court is a separate entity serving a particular district. Although most claims can be commenced in any county court, a defended action to recover a sum of money will normally be transferred to the defendant's home district. Other claims may also be transferred at the court's discretion.[223]

The second limitation is a financial one. County courts were created primarily to handle minor civil actions such as the recovery of small debts, and until 1991 their jurisdiction in tort and contract was limited to claims involving £5,000 or less. Reforms under the Courts and Legal Services Act 1990 led to this upper ceiling being removed,[224] and the emphasis shifted to setting *minimum* financial limits for cases commenced in the High Court. Cases involving less than £25,000 generally had to be commenced at county court level. Further reforms since 1999 mean that the allocation of cases between the two courts now depends not only on the financial value of the claim, but also on whether it is designated as a 'small claims', 'fast track', or 'multi track' case.[225] The allocation and management of civil cases is discussed further in chapters 14 and 15, but in essence, 'small claims' (involving less than £5,000) continue to be dealt with by the county courts, and other actions involving less than £15,000 (or £50,000 for personal injuries) must also begin life at this level. Most claims for higher amounts can be commenced in either court, and the decision about where a case is ultimately determined depends not only on the sums involved, but also on the importance and complexity of the issues. County courts now have unlimited jurisdiction in tort, contract, and land cases, but financial limits are still in place for certain other types of action. For example, in equity matters and contentious probate cases, the upper limit is currently £30,000.[226]

Finally, it should be noted that although the jurisdiction of the county courts is largely original, circuit judges do have jurisdiction to hear appeals from the decisions of district judges.[227]

H THE CROWN COURT

1 CREATION OF THE CROWN COURT

The Crown Court was created by the Courts Act 1971 and came into operation on 1 January 1972. Before this date trials on indictment took place at quarter sessions or assizes. Both quarter sessions and assizes had local jurisdiction and were generally confined to dealing with offences that had been committed locally.

---

[223] CPR, rr 30.2 and 26.2.
[224] Section 1; High Court and County Courts Jurisdiction Order 1991, SI 1991/724.
[225] See p 464, *post*.
[226] This is the effect of the County Courts Jurisdiction Order 1981, SI 1981/1123.
[227] See p 498, *post*.

The assize courts were grouped into circuits and did not sit continuously: judges were sent out on circuit by royal commission and sat at each assize town for the duration of the assize. Their jurisdiction was equivalent to that of the High Court and at least two Queen's Bench Division judges were usually named in the commissions. County court judges and Queen's Counsel were also included, and even the Master of the Rolls and Lords Justices of Appeal could theoretically be asked to sit. The assize courts generally dealt with the most serious criminal offences, though they also handled a certain amount of civil work. Less serious offences tried on indictment were dealt with at quarter sessions. These were held four times a year at almost 150 different courts, and like the assizes they dealt with both civil and criminal cases. Quarter sessions also had jurisdiction to hear appeals from the decisions of magistrates' courts, and to sentence persons committed for sentencing following summary conviction. The whole of this jurisdiction was subsequently transferred to the Crown Court.

Before leaving the pre-1972 system, three other courts should also be mentioned. The Central Criminal Court—popularly known as the 'Old Bailey'—was the assize court with jurisdiction over indictable offences committed in Greater London and on the high seas. In addition, the Criminal Justice Administration Act 1956 established Crown Courts in Liverpool and Manchester. These courts exercised a criminal jurisdiction equivalent to that of the assizes and quarter sessions in their respective areas.

This plethora of courts with workloads determined largely by historical factors led to the establishment of a Royal Commission chaired by Lord Beeching. The Commission's recommendations[228] formed the basis for the system introduced by the Courts Act 1971. The Act abolished all courts of assize and quarter sessions, including the Crown Courts of Liverpool and Manchester and the Central Criminal Court in London.[229] It replaced them with a single court, to be known as the Crown Court, which is part of the Supreme Court of England and Wales[230] and a superior court of record.[231] Its constitution and jurisdiction are now governed by the Supreme Court Act 1981.

2 CONSTITUTION

As already indicated, the essential feature of the Crown Court is that it has a national jurisdiction. There are not various Crown Courts throughout the country: there is

[228] See *Report of the Royal Commission on Assizes and Quarter Sessions*, Cmnd 4153, 1969.

[229] The latter has been retained in name however, as s 8(3) of the Supreme Court Act 1981 provides for the Crown Court to be known as the Central Criminal Court when sitting in London. The same section preserves the right of the Lord Mayor and Aldermen of the City to sit as judges with any High Court judge, circuit judge, recorder or district judge (magistrates' courts). The reasons for this are unclear, but a seat in the Old Bailey is still traditionally left vacant for the Lord Mayor.

[230] See p 245, n 152 *ante*.

[231] Supreme Court Act 1981, ss 1, 45(1). When exercising its appellate jurisdiction the Crown Court is subject to the High Court's supervisory jurisdiction as if it were an inferior court: s 29(3) (see p 228, *ante*). It is not, however, subject to this jurisdiction in matters relating to trial on indictment.

just one Crown Court, sittings of which may be held anywhere, at any time.[232] There are currently seventy-eight Crown Court centres in England and Wales, and for administrative purposes they are grouped into six circuits. Each centre falls into one of three categories:

(1) 'First tier' centres—these deal with the full range of Crown Court business and also provide a venue for High Court judges to handle some of their civil work;

(2) 'Second tier' centres—these deal with the full range of the Crown Court's criminal work; and

(3) 'Third-tier' centres—High Court judges do not usually visit third-tier centres, which means that the workload of these venues is generally confined to less serious criminal cases.

The Supreme Court Act 1981 provides that the Crown Court's jurisdiction may be exercised by High Court judges, circuit judges, recorders, and, under an amendment inserted by the Courts Act 2003, by district judges from magistrates' courts.[233] Deputy circuit judges may also be appointed.[234] The most serious or difficult cases are usually reserved for High Court judges, who in practice are almost invariably drawn from the Queen's Bench Division.[235] In addition to the regular judges of the Court, any judge of the Court of Appeal and any former Court of Appeal or puisne judge may also be asked to sit, though they cannot be compelled to do so.[236] Crown Court judges normally sit alone, but when hearing appeals from magistrates' courts they must sit with between two and four justices of the peace.[237] A judge may also sit with justices of the peace when hearing a case on indictment, unless the case has been listed for a plea of not guilty.[238] Where justices do sit they must play a full part in all decisions, and in the event of disagreement the decision of the majority prevails.[239]

3 JURISDICTION AND PROCEDURE

The Crown Court has exclusive jurisdiction over all trials on indictment, including proceedings on indictment for offences within the jurisdiction of the Admiralty in England.[240] Before the Criminal Justice Act 2003, all trials on indictment were tried by a judge sitting with a jury, but the new Act will make it possible for cases where there is a real risk of jury tampering to be tried by a judge sitting alone. A similar power

---

[232] Ibid, s 78.

[233] Section 8; at the time of writing the amendment had yet to be brought into force.

[234] Courts Act 1971, s 24.   [235] As to the distribution of business, see p 571, post.

[236] Supreme Court Act 1981, s 9.   [237] Ibid, ss 8 and 74(1).

[238] Ibid, s 75; Practice Direction (Crown Court: Business) [2001] 4 All ER 635 at 638, [2001] 1 WLR 1996 at 2000.

[239] If the court is evenly split, the regular judge has the casting vote: s 73(3).

[240] Supreme Court Act 1981, s 46.

has been introduced in relation to complex fraud cases—a highly controversial change.[241] The jurisdiction formerly exercised by the quarter sessions is also vested in the Crown Court.[242] This includes hearing appeals against summary conviction from the magistrates' courts,[243] sentencing those committed for sentence following summary conviction,[244] and exercising a limited civil jurisdiction in relation to licensing appeals.

The Lord Chief Justice is empowered by section 75 of the Supreme Court Act to give directions for the distribution of Crown Court business. The current directions[245] establish four different classes of offence. Class 1 offences are the most serious, and must be tried by a High Court judge. Class 2 offences must be tried by a High Court judge unless a particular case is released by or on the authority of a presiding judge.[246] Most other offences triable only on indictment fall into Class 3, and may be listed for trial by a High Court judge, circuit judge, or recorder. Class 4 comprises the few remaining indictable offences and all offences triable either way. These offences will normally be tried by a circuit judge or recorder.[247]

I MAGISTRATES' COURTS

A magistrates' court is defined by section 148 of the Magistrates' Courts Act 1980, as 'any justice or justices of the peace[248] acting under any enactment or by virtue of his or their commission or under the common law'. Magistrates currently sit in over 1,500 courtrooms throughout England and Wales.[249]

1 CONSTITUTION AND ORGANIZATION

Before April 2005, each area of England and Wales had a separate commission of the peace,[250] and each commission area was divided into petty session areas.[251]

---

[241] Criminal Justice Act 2003, ss 43–49: see pp 339 and 591, *post*.

[242] Courts Act 1971, s 8, Schedule 1; though note that certain administrative functions were transferred to local authorities.

[243] See p 649, *post*.   [244] See p 639, *post*.

[245] *Practice Direction (Crown Court: Business)* [2001] 4 All ER 635 at 638, [2001] 1 WLR 1996 at 1999. The directions permit presiding judges to reserve particular cases for trial by a High Court judge. For further details of the classification of offences, see p 571, *post*.

[246] A presiding judge is a High Court judge with special responsibility for a particular circuit.

[247] Class 4 offences cannot be listed for trial by a High Court judge without the consent of that judge or the presiding judge.

[248] For the historical role of justices of the peace, see p 224, *ante*.

[249] *Magistrates' Courts Business Returns, Annual Report 2002–2003*, p 4.

[250] In December 2003 there were forty-seven such areas in England and a further five in Wales: Justices of the Peace (Commission Areas) (Amendment) Order 2001, SI 2001/696, Schedule.

[251] Commission areas were formerly divided into both petty session areas and petty divisional areas, but these became a single category under s 75 of the Access to Justice Act 1999.

Magistrates' Court Committees (MCCs)[252] were responsible for the 'efficient and effective administration' of the courts in each commission area, and magistrates were appointed on a local basis to exercise a local jurisdiction. All of this has now changed as a result of the Courts Act 2003, which is the latest in a long line of reforms to affect the magistrates' courts.

Executive responsibility for magistrates' courts was transferred from the Home Office to the Lord Chancellor's Department in 1992, and in 1993 the Magistrates' Court Service Inspectorate was established. This was followed by the Police and Magistrates' Courts Act 1994, which reduced the size of the MCCs and attempted to give them a more clearly defined management role. It also empowered the Lord Chancellor to reduce the number of commission areas in order to improve efficiency. Prior to the 1994 Act, it had been suggested that the local committees should be abolished and replaced with a national executive agency,[253] but this proposal was widely opposed by magistrates and the government did not pursue it.

The Justices of the Peace Act 1997 was primarily a consolidating Act, but the process of reform continued under the Access to Justice Act 1999. A unified Greater London Magistrates' Courts Authority replaced the twenty-two MCCs in London,[254] and the Lord Chancellor was given greater powers to alter commission areas.[255] In the Explanatory Notes accompanying the Act, the government set out the need to develop a 'coherent geographical structure' for the criminal justice system, by moving towards common boundaries for the various agencies involved.[256] This meant that not only should MCCs be able to reorganize the petty session areas within their commission boundaries, but also that there should be greater alignment between the commission boundaries, police force areas, and Crown Prosecution areas.

(a) Reform under the Courts Act 2003

In his review of criminal justice,[257] Lord Justice Auld made the radical recommendation that the Crown Court and magistrates' courts should be replaced with a single Criminal Court. The government rejected this particular proposal but accepted that the criminal courts should be more closely aligned. This provided the impetus for the White Paper *Justice for All*, and for the subsequent Courts Act 2003. The Act repeals the Justices of the Peace Act 1997, though many of its provisions are re-enacted.

The Courts Act establishes a single commission of the peace for England and Wales,[258] and gives magistrates a national jurisdiction. It also provides for magistrates to be assigned to local justice areas,[259] which means in practice that they will continue

---

[252] Consisting of justices of the peace and other members co-opted by the committee or appointed by the Lord Chancellor: Justices of the Peace Act 1997, s 28.

[253] See the Home Office study, *Magistrates' Courts: Report of a Scrutiny* (HMSO, 1989).

[254] Access to Justice Act 1999, s 83 (amending the 1997 Act).

[255] Ibid, s 74 (amending the 1997 Act).   [256] At paras 248–250.

[257] *Review of the Criminal Courts of England and Wales* (2001).   [258] Section 7.

[259] Sections 8 and 10(2). At the time of writing these areas are identical to the former petty session areas: Local Justice Areas Order 2005, SI 2005/554.

to sit locally. The MCCs and the Greater London Magistrates' Courts Authority have been abolished,[260] and the Lord Chancellor is now under a general duty to ensure that there is an efficient and effective system to support the Supreme Court, county courts, and magistrates' courts.[261] Magistrates' courts, like most other major courts, are now administered by Her Majesty's Courts Service, which is an executive agency of the Department for Constitutional Affairs.[262] An element of local accountability has been retained through the creation of Local Courts Boards, which are established and appointed by the Lord Chancellor.[263] The membership of these Boards must include at least one judge, at least two local representatives, at least two other persons with 'appropriate knowledge or experience', and two or more justices of the peace.[264] They are concerned not only with magistrates' courts but also with the Crown Court and county courts in their areas,[265] and they are responsible for scrutinizing the management of the courts and making recommendations where appropriate.

2 JUSTICES OF THE PEACE

The vast majority of justices of the peace are lay magistrates, who are appointed by the Lord Chancellor on the advice of Local Advisory Committees. They are unqualified and unpaid, but they are required to attend training courses[266] and may claim allowances for travel, subsistence, and loss of earnings.[267] They are expected to be available for at least twenty-six half-days each year, and normally sit in pairs or groups of three.[268] A single lay justice has a limited jurisdiction and cannot order a person to pay more than one pound or impose imprisonment for more than fourteen days.[269] However, a single justice can hear proceedings to determine the allocation of cases that are triable either way, and can also transfer cases to the Crown Court for trial on indictment.[270] Under amendments made by the Criminal Justice Act 2003,[271] a single justice may also accept a guilty plea in a case which is to be dealt with summarily.

Appointments to the lay magistracy are intended to reflect all sections of the community, but there is persistent criticism that the majority of justices tend to be white, middle class, Conservative, and old.[272] In fact, recent research by Morgan and Russell[273] suggests that around 4 per cent of lay magistrates are black or Asian, with a further 1 per cent coming from other ethnic minority backgrounds. At a national level, this

---

[260] 2003 Act, s 6.　　[261] Ibid, s 1.

[262] This was launched on 1 April 2005: see p 231, *ante*.

[263] 2003 Act, s 4; Schedule 1.　　[264] Ibid, Schedule 1.

[265] Ibid, s 5.　　[266] Ibid, s 19 (replacing the Justices of the Peace Act 1997, s 64).

[267] Ibid, s 15 (replacing s 10 of the 1997 Act).　　[268] Magistrates' Courts Act 1980, s 121(1).

[269] Ibid, s 121(5).　　[270] Ibid, ss 17–18 (as amended).

[271] Ibid, ss 18 and 20(7) (as amended).

[272] See Darbyshire, 'For The New Lord Chancellor: Some Causes for Concern About Magistrates' [1997] Crim LR 861, at 862–6.

[273] *The Judiciary in the Magistrates' Courts* (2000), chapter 2. This study was jointly commissioned by the Home Office and the Lord Chancellor's Department.

means that the magistracy is 'approaching ethnic representativeness',[274] but in cities with large ethnic minority populations the bench is still disproportionately white. The same study shows that around 94 per cent of lay justices are aged between forty and seventy, and that they are 'disproportionately middle class, and almost certainly financially well-off, compared to the population at large'.[275] For example, 69 per cent of lay magistrates in the survey described their current or former occupation as 'professional or managerial', while only 3 per cent described themselves as skilled manual workers. Given that lay magistrates are unpaid, it should come as no surprise that those who are retired or in well-paid employment are more likely to volunteer their services, and Morgan and Russell conclude that achieving greater diversity would inevitably be costly:[276]

A more socially representative magistracy could almost certainly be recruited, but:

- the members would be unlikely to be so willing or able to sit as often as many lay magistrates do today
- we believe that more socially representative recruits would be more likely to claim loss of earnings and expenses.

Which is to say that a more socially representative lay magistracy would be a more expensive one.

Upon reaching the age of seventy, lay magistrates join the supplemental list and can no longer serve as justices of the peace.[277]

In April 2004 there were 28,705 lay justices in England and Wales, but the magistracy is also served by 106 District Judges (Magistrates' Courts) and around 150 Deputy District Judges (Magistrates' Courts).[278] These judges used to be called stipendiary magistrates, but they were renamed by section 78 of the Access to Justice Act 1999. The same provision also merged the metropolitan and provincial benches.[279] Unlike lay magistrates, District Judges (Magistrates' Courts) are legally qualified and serve on a full-time, professional basis. They have all the powers of two lay justices and therefore sit alone.[280]

3 JUSTICES' CLERKS AND JUSTICES' CHIEF EXECUTIVES

Justices' clerks are responsible for advising magistrates on matters of law. They are appointed by the Lord Chancellor and must have either: (a) a five-year magistrates' court qualification;[281] (b) five years' experience as an assistant to a justices' clerk and a

---

[274] Ibid, at p 14.   [275] Ibid, at p 16.   [276] Ibid, at p 108.

[277] Courts Act 2003, ss 12 and 13 (replacing Justices of the Peace Act 1997, s 7). A younger magistrate may have his name added to this list at his own request or on the grounds of incapacity.

[278] *Magistrates' Courts Business Returns, Annual Report 2002–2003*, p 4; *Judicial Statistics 2003*, tab 9.5.

[279] The functions and terms of appointment of District Judges (Magistrates' Courts) are set out in the Courts Act 2003, ss 22–26 (replacing sections 10A–10E of the 1997 Act).

[280] Ibid, s 26 (replacing section 10D of the 1997 Act).

[281] Within the meaning of the Courts and Legal Services Act 1990, s 71.

qualification as a solicitor or barrister; or (c) previous experience as a justices' clerk. The functions of a justices' clerk include:[282]

[G]iving advice to any or all of the justices of the peace to whom he is clerk about matters of law (including procedure and practice) on questions arising in connection with the discharge of their functions, including questions arising when the clerk is not personally attending on them.

Most justices' clerks cover more than one court and it is impossible for them to personally advise every courtroom for which they are responsible. As a result, many of their functions are delegated to justices' clerks' assistants or 'court clerks', not all of whom are professionally qualified. Concerns have been raised in the past[283] about the number of lay magistrates being advised by unqualified clerks, and more stringent professional requirements have now been introduced. Since January 1999, all newly appointed court clerks must be qualified solicitors or barristers, and those in post before this date have until 2010 to reach the same standard.[284]

The primary function of a clerk is to provide legal advice, and he has a duty to offer such advice whenever he considers it appropriate, regardless of whether it has been specifically requested.[285] However, care must be taken to ensure that he does not appear to interfere with the magisterial function. This means that a clerk should not play any part in helping magistrates to make findings of fact, and that any legal advice given should normally be stated in open court.[286] In addition to his advisory functions, a justices' clerk may also perform many of the pre-trial functions otherwise carried out by a single judge. These include setting the date and time of a trial, giving directions for the conduct of the trial, and making an order for public funding to assist defendants in criminal cases.[287]

In the past justices' clerks were responsible for the general administration of magistrates' courts, in addition to their role as legal advisers. Concerns about this mixing of administrative and legal functions were partly addressed by the Police and Magistrates' Courts Act 1994, which created the new position of justices' chief executive. Many of the clerks' administrative functions were transferred to the holders of this new office,[288] leaving the clerks free to concentrate on their advisory and judicial roles. Each MCC was required to appoint its own chief executive, and his role was to ensure the efficient and effective administration of magistrates' courts in the area. The chief executive was responsible for allocating work between clerks,[289] but the Act expressly

---

[282] Courts Act 2003, s 28(4). This largely re-enacts s 45 of the Justices of the Peace Act 1997.

[283] See, e.g. Derbyshire, 'For the New Lord Chancellor: Some Causes for Concern about Magistrates' [1997] Crim LR 861 at 872.

[284] Section 27(1) of the Courts Act 2003 makes it possible for a clerk without professional qualifications to remain in post for the time being. However, s 27(6) confers a power to remove this exception at a future date.

[285] Courts Act 2003, s 28(5); replacing s 45 of the 1997 Act.

[286] *Practice Direction (QBD: Justices: Clerk to Court)* [2000] 4 All ER 895, [2000] 1 WLR 1886.

[287] Crime and Disorder Act 1998, s 49; Justices' Clerks Rules 2005, SI 2005/545, Schedule.

[288] Many of those that remained were transferred by the Access to Justice Act 1999: s 90; Schedule 13.

[289] Justices of the Peace Act 1997, s 41 (since amended by s 88 of the 1999 Act).

provided that clerks should not be subject to his direction when performing their legal functions.[290] The emphasis on separating administrative and legal functions has been continued by the Courts Act 2003, and like its predecessors the Act includes an express guarantee of the clerks' independence.[291] However, now that Her Majesty's Courts Service has taken over the management of magistrates' courts,[292] the office of justices' chief executive has been abolished.[293]

4 JURISDICTION

It is common to suppose that the jurisdiction of magistrates' courts is entirely criminal, but they also have a wide and varied civil jurisdiction. In both civil and criminal cases however, this jurisdiction is limited to relatively minor matters when compared with the cases heard by the High Court, county courts, and Crown Court. Before examining the jurisdiction of the magistrates' courts more closely, it should be noted that when justices of the peace exercise such important functions as the granting of bail and the issuing of summonses and warrants, they are not strictly acting as 'magistrates' courts'.

(a) Criminal jurisdiction

The criminal jurisdiction of magistrates' courts principally concerns summary offences, which are offences triable without a jury. All summary offences are created by statute, and all are of a fairly minor character. Indeed, most summary convictions are for road traffic offences, and so numerous are the convictions for speeding and unauthorized parking, that offenders are able to plead guilty by post.[294] Almost two million persons each year are found guilty of summary offences in England and Wales.

Before the Criminal Justice Act 2003, the maximum penalty that could be imposed for a summary offence was six months' imprisonment and a fine limited in amount.[295] However, the 2003 Act enables the Secretary of State to set a maximum penalty of up to fifty-one weeks imprisonment for a range of summary offences,[296] and it increases the sentencing powers of magistrates accordingly.[297] The Act also establishes the new 'custody plus' sentence, which (when eventually introduced) will replace all short prison sentences (except for intermittent custody) with a short period of imprisonment followed by a period of supervision in the community.[298]

In addition to their jurisdiction over summary offences, magistrates' courts also have jurisdiction over offences 'triable either way',[299] though this is subject to a

---

[290] Section 78; see now Courts Act 2003, s 29. Proposals to transfer justices' clerks to a system of fixed-term contracts and performance related pay only added to concerns about judicial independence, and were dropped from the 1994 Bill at an early stage.

[291] 2003 Act, s 29.   [292] See p 261, *ante*.   [293] 2003 Act, s 6.

[294] See p 636, *post*   [295] See p 637, *post*.   [296] Section 281(2).

[297] Section 154.   [298] Section 181.

[299] See Magistrates' Courts Act 1980, s 17; Schedule 1. For details of the procedure for determining the mode of trial of such offences, see p 547, *post*.

defendant's right to insist on trial by jury. Where a defendant is convicted of an either-way offence, a magistrates' court may impose penalties similar to those which may be imposed following conviction for a summary offence.

(b) Youth courts and youth justice

Youth courts are magistrates' courts exercising jurisdiction over offences committed by children and young persons.[300] Until 1991 they were known as juvenile courts.[301] A youth court consists of up to three justices selected from a specially trained juvenile panel, and must normally include at least one man and one woman.[302] The chair of the court remains constant, although other members serve by rotation. A youth court may also consist of a District Judge (Magistrates' Courts), sitting alone.[303]

Youth courts aim to treat juvenile suspects differently from adult defendants, and the procedures adopted are deliberately less formal. The only persons admitted to the court are the court officers, witnesses, bona fide members of the press, the parties and their representatives, and other persons authorized by the court to be present. In addition, the media is normally prohibited from publishing or broadcasting the identity of any child or young person involved in the proceedings,[304] though the court may lift these reporting restrictions if it is in the public interest to do so. The terms 'conviction' and 'sentence' are avoided, and the terms 'finding of guilt' and 'order made upon a finding of guilt' are used instead.

The Crime and Disorder Act 1998 established in statutory form that the basic aim of the youth justice system is to prevent offending. It also contains provisions relating to youth justice services, a new Youth Justice Board, and youth offending teams. All of these are considered further in chapter 18.

(c) Civil jurisdiction

This aspect of the magistrates' courts' jurisdiction is extremely varied. It includes the recovery of certain civil debts such as income tax, national insurance contributions, council tax, and electricity, gas, and water charges. It also includes the licensing of pubs, clubs, and gambling establishments. However, the most important aspect of the magistrates' courts' civil workload is their jurisdiction over family law matters. This is exercised principally under the Family Law Act 1996 and Children Act 1989, in what are known as 'family proceedings courts'.

(d) Family proceedings courts

These courts were created by section 80 of the Domestic Proceedings and Magistrates' Courts Act 1978, and were then known as domestic courts. They were renamed

---

[300] For these purposes a 'child' is a person under fourteen years, and a 'young person' is someone aged fourteen-seventeen: Children and Young Persons Act 1933, s 107.

[301] Criminal Justice Act 1991, s 70.

[302] Children and Young Persons Act 1933, s 45 (as amended); Youth Court (Constitution) Rules 1954, SI 1954/1711 (as amended), r.12.

[303] 1933 Act, s 45 (as amended); Courts Act 2003, s 66.   [304] 1933 Act, s 49 (as amended).

'family proceedings courts' by the Children Act 1989.[305] They normally consist of two or three justices drawn from a specially trained panel, and as far as practicable they should include a man and a woman.[306] Nominated District Judges (Magistrates' Courts) may sit alongside one or two lay justices, though it is possible for a judge to deal with family proceedings matters when sitting alone.[307] The only persons who may be present during proceedings are officers of the court, the parties, their legal representatives, witnesses, newspaper representatives, and any other persons permitted by the court.[308]

Family proceedings courts have jurisdiction to deal with maintenance applications and to make various orders in respect of children, domestic violence, and the occupation of the family home. They also have a public law jurisdiction to deal with care proceedings brought by local authorities under the Children Act 1989. In fact, their jurisdiction under the Children Act is largely concurrent with that of county courts and the Family Division of the High Court, except that public law actions can only be commenced in a family proceedings court.[309] In view of their overlapping jurisdictions, the Courts Act 2003 established a new Family Procedure Rule Committee with the power to make procedural rules governing all three courts.[310]

J CORONERS' COURTS

1 THE OFFICE OF CORONER

This ancient office dates from the twelfth century, when it principally concerned the custody of revenue accruing to the King from fines and forfeiture. In addition, the coroner occasionally exercised the jurisdiction of the sheriff and enquired into treasure trove and unexplained deaths. Some of these functions have since been removed, and the primary role of the modern coroner is to hold inquests into unexplained deaths. The appointment and jurisdiction of coroners is now governed by statute.[311] They may be barristers, solicitors, or registered medical practitioners of not less than five years' standing, and they may be removed from office for misbehaviour or inability to discharge their duties.[312]

---

[305] Section 92.   [306] Magistrates' Courts Act 1980, ss 66 and 67 (as amended).
[307] Ibid.   [308] Ibid, s 69(2).
[309] Children (Allocation of Proceedings) Order 1991, SI 1991/1677, Article 3(1). Such cases may be transferred to the county court or to the Family Division if they are sufficiently complex or serious, or where there would otherwise be an unacceptable delay.
[310] Sections 75–81.   [311] Coroners Act 1988 (a consolidation Act).   [312] Ibid, s 3.

2 JURISDICTION

The coroner's jurisdiction is principally concerned with inquests into the deaths of persons 'whose bodies are lying within his district'.[313] The jurisdiction arises where there is reasonable cause to suspect that a person has died a violent or unnatural death, or has died suddenly from an unknown cause. Deaths in prison or police custody, and deaths occurring as a result of injury caused by a police officer in the purported execution of his duty, also fall within the coroner's jurisdiction.[314] The holding of an inquest in such cases is mandatory. In *R v West Yorkshire Coroner, ex parte Smith*[315] the Court of Appeal held that the phrase 'lying within his jurisdiction' (which was the form of words used prior to the passing of the Coroners Act 1988) applied to a body brought into the district from abroad. This would appear to remain the position.

To hold an inquest the coroner may, and in some cases must, summon a jury of between seven and eleven members.[316] Witnesses attend and give evidence and the coroner has the power to compel their attendance if necessary. The procedure is inquisitorial however, and although interested persons may be represented and may ask questions, it is the coroner who conducts the proceedings and no speeches are made to the jury. The jury's verdict need not be unanimous provided that there are not more than two dissentients. Detailed matters of procedure are governed by the Coroners Rules 1984.[317]

Prior to the passing of the Criminal Law Act 1977 the jury might return a verdict of murder, manslaughter, or infanticide by a named person, and the coroner could then commit that person for trial. This was abolished by section 56 of the 1977 Act and a coroner's inquisition cannot now charge a person with any offence. Moreover, although coroners have the power to compel the attendance of witnesses, a witness cannot be obliged to answer questions 'tending to incriminate himself.'[318] These limitations have given rise to a number of cases under the ECHR and the Human Rights Act 1998,[319] and were among the issues considered by the Review of Coroner Services (discussed below).

Where criminal proceedings are in hand, any inquest relating to the same issues should be adjourned.[320] The coroner has a discretion to resume the inquest on conclusion of the criminal proceedings, but if he does so, any findings as to the cause of death must not be inconsistent with the outcome of the criminal case.[321] A coroner must also adjourn an inquest if he is informed that the circumstances surrounding a death are to be the subject of a public inquiry, unless there is an 'exceptional reason' for not doing so.[322]

---

[313] Ibid, s 8. Coroners also retain their historical jurisdiction to hold inquests in relation to treasure (s 30: see the Treasure Act 1996), but the recent Review of Coroners' Services recommended that this should be removed: see n 324, *post*.

[314] 1988 Act, s 8.   [315] [1983] QB 335, [1982] 3 All ER 1098.   [316] 1988 Act, s 8.

[317] SI 1984/552, as supplemented by the Coroners (Amendment) Rules 1999, SI 1999/3325.

[318] SI 1984/552, r 22.   [319] See pp 183 and 616 for further discussion of the issues.

[320] 1988 Act, s 16; the decision ultimately rests with the DPP.   [321] Ibid, s 16.

[322] Ibid, s 17A, as inserted by the Access to Justice Act 1999.

There is no appeal from an inquest, but the proceedings are subject to judicial review and may be challenged if, for example, there is evidence of bias.[323]

3 THE REVIEW OF CORONERS' SERVICES, 2003[324]

In July 2001 the government announced that it was setting up a Review of Coroners' Services, to be chaired by Tom Luce. The Review was completed in April 2003 and it highlighted a number of 'critical defects' in the system. The fact that coroners operate 'in isolation from the mainstreams of medicine and justice administration' was identified as a particular weakness,[325] as was the fact that most coroners are part-time.[326] The Review also criticized the absence of a national structure for leadership and administration,[327] along with the lack of 'a clear and reliable process for clarifying the relationship between the inquest and other formal processes for investigating death.'[328] The reforms recommended by the Review would essentially remodel the coroners' service along the lines of the other major courts:[329]

The death investigation service—the coroner service—should become a service of predominantly full-time legally qualified professionals, appointed, trained and supported to modern judicial and public service standards.

Specific recommendations included:

(1) Making the Lord Chancellor responsible for appointing and supporting the coroners' service, in the same way as for other courts;

(2) Requiring coroners to be full-time and to be legally (rather than legally *or medically*) qualified;

(3) Appointing a 'Statutory Medical Assessor' (a doctor) to assist each coroner;

(4) Establishing a standing Rules Committee to formulate procedural rules for the conduct of inquests;

(5) Creating a statutory Coronial Council to oversee the work of the service; and

(6) Restructuring the service in England and Wales to create a single jurisdiction headed by a Chief Coroner.[330] The jurisdiction would be split into around sixty districts, based on the existing police areas.

Another issue for the Review group was how to respond to the decision in *Jordan* v *UK*.[331] Article 2 of the ECHR implies a duty on the state to investigate deaths occurring

---

[323] For an example, see *R* v *Inner West London Coroner, ex parte Dallaglio* [1994] 4 All ER 139.

[324] *Death Certification and Investigation in England, Wales and Northern Ireland: The Report of a Fundamental Review,* Cm 5831, 2003.

[325] Ibid, at para 2.4.e.

[326] The Review found that only twenty-three of the 123 coroners in England and Wales were full-time.

[327] Para 2.4.j.   [328] Para 2.4.k.   [329] Para 3.2.

[330] A second jurisdiction would cover Northern Ireland.

[331] (2003) 37 EHRR 2; see also *Finucane* v *UK* (2003) 37 EHRR 29.

as a result of state action or while the deceased was in state custody. In *Jordan*, the European Court of Human Rights found that the holding of an inquest does not discharge this duty, because it is not a forum for determining the identity and culpability of those responsible for causing death. This decision has since been applied in a number of domestic cases under the Human Rights Act 1998.[332] The matter is further complicated by Article 6. For example, although the ability to compel witnesses to attend an inquest is necessitated by Article 2, the right to a fair trial under Article 6 would seem to require that a witness is not obliged to give evidence which could incriminate him.

The Review recommended that the rule preventing a witness from being compelled to answer incriminating questions should be removed. It proposed instead that there should be a limited immunity, preventing incriminating testimony given by a witness from being used against him in criminal or disciplinary (but not civil) proceedings.[333] More generally, it concluded that the scope of an inquest should be limited only by the proviso that its findings 'do not determine civil or criminal liability',[334] and that the inquest should be the 'default process' for handling the vast majority of Article 2 cases.[335]

At the time of writing, the government has yet to respond in detail to these recommendations, but it has accepted that legislative reform is needed and is awaiting the outcome of further research.[336]

K JUDICIAL COMMITTEE OF THE PRIVY COUNCIL

1 CONSTITUTION

Prior to the Judicial Committee Act 1833, the jurisdiction of the Privy Council was exercised principally by laymen. The 1833 Act[337] created the Judicial Committee, which at the time of writing consists of the Lord President of the Council, the Lord Chancellor, ex-Lord Presidents, the Lords of Appeal in Ordinary, and certain other

---

[332] See *R (on the application of Amin)* v *Secretary of State for the Home Department* [2003] UKHL 51, [2004] 1 AC 653, [2003] 4 All ER 1264 (inquest into the death of a prisoner who had been murdered by his cellmate did not satisfy Article 2). See also *R (on the application of Khan)* v *Secretary of State for Health* [2003] EWCA Civ 1129, [2003] 4 All ER 1239 (Article 2 breached because Mr Khan was unable to obtain legal aid enabling him to be legally represented at his daughter's inquest). These decisions prompted an amendment to the exceptional funding provisions in the Access to Justice Act 1999. Further examples are discussed at p 174, *ante*.

[333] Para 9.38.   [334] Para 21.33.   [335] Para 10.61.

[336] In November 2003 the Home Office asked Tom Luce to link his findings to an inquiry into the failure of various institutions to prevent a GP from murdering his patients: see *The Shipman Inquiry's Third Report: Death Certification and the Investigation of Deaths by Coroners*.

[337] As amended by the Judicial Committee Act 1844, the Appellate Jurisdiction Acts 1876–1947 and other Acts. Further amendments will be made by Schedule 16 of the Constitutional Reform Act 2005.

members who have held high judicial office. From time to time membership has also been extended to persons who have held high judicial office in Commonwealth countries, though such persons may not sit when the Committee is determining 'devolution issues' under the Scotland Act 1998, the Government of Wales Act 1998, and the Northern Ireland Act 1998.

The Lord Chancellor and the Lords of Appeal in Ordinary are the members of the Committee who usually sit. Decisions of the Privy Council therefore enjoy great authority, though they are not strictly binding on English courts.[338] The transfer of the House of Lords' judicial functions to a new Supreme Court will necessarily affect the Privy Council's composition: when this happens, it is intended that the Justices of the Supreme Court should take the positions currently occupied by the Lords of Appeal in Ordinary.[339]

Appeals are heard at the bar of the Privy Council before not less than three—and usually five—members of the Committee.[340] The procedure is similar to that currently followed by the House of Lords.

2 JURISDICTION

Although all English courts derive their jurisdiction directly or indirectly from the sovereign, the Judicial Committee of the Privy Council is slightly different, in that its jurisdiction is that of the sovereign in Council. Consequently the Privy Council does not pass judgment: it merely tenders advice to the sovereign, which is then implemented by Order in Council. Only one opinion is usually read and until recently dissents were not even recorded.[341] However, it is now provided by Order in Council that dissenting opinions may be delivered in open court.[342]

The main aspects of the Privy Council's jurisdiction are as follows:[343]

(a) *Appeals from courts outside the United Kingdom.* Since the sovereign is the fountain of justice for all her Dominions, the Privy Council has jurisdiction to hear appeals from the Isle of Man, the Channel Islands, independent Commonwealth countries, and British Colonies and Protectorates. However, since the Statute of Westminster 1931, many Commonwealth States have legislated to

---

[338] See p 85, *ante*. The Privy Council's decisions on devolution issues are, of course, binding in respect of Wales, Scotland and Northern Ireland.

[339] This will be the effect of the Constitutional Reform Act 2005, s 138; Schedule 16.

[340] A greater number has been known: see, e.g. *Pratt v A-G for Jamaica* [1994] 2 AC 1, [1993] 4 All ER 769, where a committee of seven judges declared gross delays in carrying out death sentences in Jamaica to amount to inhuman and degrading treatment.

[341] Cf. the Criminal Division of the Court of Appeal, which also delivers only one judgment but for different reasons.

[342] Judicial Committee (General Appellate Jurisdiction) Rules Order 1982, SI 1982/1676, Schedule 2, para 16. For a particularly vigorous dissent, see *Abbot v R* [1977] AC 755, [1976] 3 All ER 140.

[343] Until recently the Privy Council had jurisdiction to hear appeals from tribunals governing healthcare professionals, but this jurisdiction has been transferred to the High Court, Queen's Bench Division.

exclude appeal to the Privy Council.[344] Thus the Privy Council held in 1947 that Canada could validly legislate to make the decisions of its own Supreme Court final and exclusive.[345] Leave to appeal in criminal matters is only given in exceptional cases, and mere misdirection will not suffice: there must be some clear departure from the 'requirements of justice', or something which 'deprives the accused of the substance of fair trial and the protection of the law.'[346]

(b) *Admiralty jurisdiction.* Prior to 1875, appeal lay from the High Court of Admiralty to the Privy Council. Since the Judicature Acts most appeals from the High Court now lie to the Court of Appeal, but the Privy Council has retained its jurisdiction to hear appeals from the High Court when sitting as a 'prize court'.[347] A prize court is a court convened to determine issues concerning the ownership of ships and cargo, and the validity of their capture by enemy warships.

(c) *Appeals from ecclesiastical courts.* The jurisdiction of the ecclesiastical courts was drastically curtailed in 1857,[348] and is now confined to matters affecting the clergy and church buildings. Appeals from the highest ecclesiastical courts lie to the Privy Council.[349] Although archbishops and bishops are not members of the Privy Council, an archbishop (or the Bishop of London) and four other bishops are summoned to sit in an advisory capacity whenever the Council is hearing ecclesiastical appeals.

(d) *Devolution questions.* The Privy Council currently has jurisdiction over devolution questions arising under the Scotland Act 1998, the Government of Wales Act 1998, and the Northern Ireland Act 1998. Matters relating to the functions of the devolved legislative and executive bodies may be referred directly to the Judicial Committee of the Privy Council, or they may reach it through the appeals process.[350] This jurisdiction was conferred on the Privy Council to avoid the House of Lords having to determine disputes in which it had an interest as part of the UK Parliament. This will cease to be an issue when the House of Lords' judicial functions are transferred to an independent Supreme Court, and the new court will therefore take over jurisdiction in devolution cases.[351]

---

[344] Territories which have ended or ceased to recognize the Privy Council's jurisdiction include: Aden, Australia, Botswana, Burma, Canada, Cyprus, Ghana, Guyana, Hong Kong, India, Kenya, Malaysia, Malta, Nigeria, Pakistan, Sierra Leone, Singapore, Sri Lanka, Tanzania, and Uganda.

[345] *A-G for Ontario* v *A-G for Canada* [1947] AC 127, [1947] 1 All ER 137.

[346] *Ibrahim* v *R* [1914] AC 599 at 614–615, per Lord Sumner: see also *Prasad* v *R* [1981] 1 All ER 319, [1981] 1 WLR 469.

[347] Supreme Court Act 1981, s 16(2). By s 20, the High Court's jurisdiction to sit as a prize court is exercised by the Admiralty Court (part of the Queen's Bench Division); see p 252, *ante.*

[348] Court of Probate Act 1857; Matrimonial Causes Act 1857.

[349] Ecclesiastical Jurisdiction Measure 1963, s 1(3)(d); s 8.

[350] For an example, see *Brown* v *Stott* [2003] 1 AC 681, [2001] 2 ALL ER 97.

[351] Constitutional Reform Act 2005, Schedule 9, part 2; see p 244, *ante.*

(e) *Special references.* In addition to its appellate jurisdiction, the Privy Council is sometimes required to advise on matters of law at the request of the sovereign.[352] In the past it has advised on such diverse matters as the powers of colonial judges,[353] legislation in Jersey,[354] and the eligibility of a person to sit and vote in the House of Commons.[355]

L COURTS OF PARTICULAR JURISDICTION[356]

Certain courts do not fit within the general hierarchy because they are concerned with matters outside the scope of the ordinary civil and criminal law. The authority of these specialist courts is usually limited to certain members of society who have impliedly agreed to submit to their jurisdiction, though in some instances it extends to all members of the community.

1 COURTS-MARTIAL[357]

Courts-martial exercise jurisdiction over members of the armed forces, and over their dependants if an alleged offence is committed overseas. Their constitution, jurisdiction, and procedures are governed by various statutes, including the Army and Air Force Acts 1955, the Naval Discipline Act 1957, and the Armed Forces Act 1996. They cannot generally exercise jurisdiction over civilians, except where Her Majesty's forces are in armed occupation of hostile territory and a state of martial law has been declared. In addition, civilians who are employed by the forces and are on active service outside the United Kingdom may be tried in 'standing civilian courts'.[358]

Air Force and military courts-martial are similar in constitution and procedure.[359] The accused may be arrested by a superior officer for any offence against military law.

---

[352] Judicial Committee Act 1833, s 4.   [353] *Re Wells* (1840) 3 Moo PCC 216.

[354] *Re Jersey States* (1853) 9 Moo PCC 185.   [355] *Re Macmanaway* [1951] AC 161.

[356] Prior to 1977 there were many courts of local jurisdiction, but the judicial functions of most of them were abolished by the Courts Act 1971, the Local Government Act 1972 and the Administration of Justice Act 1977. The few that remain are listed in the Law Commission report, *Jurisdiction of Certain Ancient Courts* (Law Com No 72).

[357] See generally, Lyon, 'After Findlay—A Consideration of Some Aspects of the Military Justice System' [1998] Crim LR 109.

[358] Armed Forces Act 1976, s 6. This power was challenged in *R v Martin* [1998] AC 917, [1998] 1 All ER 193.

[359] They are described in detail in the European Court of Human Rights' judgment in *Cooper* v *UK* (2004) 39 EHRR 8. Naval courts-martial follow similar procedures, but there are slight differences in their composition. These differences proved to be crucial in the recent case of *Grieves v UK* (2004) 39 EHRR 2. In *Cooper* the court accepted that the army and Air Force courts-martial were 'independent and impartial' tribunals for the purposes of Article 6, ECHR. In *Grieves* however, the court concluded that the naval system fell short of the required standard because it had no permanent President and Judge Advocates were appointed by a serving naval officer. The government has now introduced delegated legislation to address the issues raised: Naval Discipline Act 1957 (Remedial) Order 2004, SI 2004/66. See further, p 276, *post*.

If the offence is merely a 'summary' one he will be tried by superior officers, but in other cases he has a choice as to whether to be tried summarily or by court-martial. Serious offences are always tried at courts-martial, except that murder, manslaughter, treason, and rape committed within the United Kingdom must be tried in the ordinary criminal courts. In all other cases, the jurisdiction of civilian and military courts is concurrent. However, a person who has already been convicted or acquitted by a civilian court cannot subsequently be tried by court-martial, and vice versa.[360]

A court-martial consists of a Permanent President of Courts-Martial (PPCM), a Judge Advocate from the Judge Advocate General's department[361] and at least two other officers. The Judge Advocate's role is to advise on questions of law and to give rulings and directions on matters of practice and procedure. The President and the other officers are the sole arbiters of fact. The trial itself takes place in open court and is in many ways similar to a trial in the ordinary criminal courts. It is subject to similar rules of evidence and procedure, and the accused is sent for trial on a charge sheet which may be compared with an indictment. The prosecution case is conducted by an Army or Air Force officer, either personally or through a civilian counsel, and the accused may appear in person or be represented by counsel, solicitor, or a defending officer. There is no jury however, and at the conclusion of the evidence the Judge Advocate summarizes the legal and factual issues before leaving the court to arrive at its decision. A majority decision is acceptable.[362] All guilty verdicts and sentences are subject to confirmation by a Reviewing Authority.[363] This body has the power to reduce sentences, quash convictions, and order retrials, but it cannot increase a sentence or interfere with an acquittal. Any person convicted by court-martial has a right to appeal against both conviction and sentence to the Courts-Martial Appeal Court.

(a) Courts-Martial Appeal Court

The Courts-Martial Appeal Court was established by the Courts-Martial (Appeals) Act 1951,[364] and in terms of composition and procedure it closely resembles the Criminal Division of the Court of Appeal. It comprises the *ex officio* and ordinary members of the Court of Appeal, nominated[365] judges of the Queen's Bench Division, certain Scottish and Irish judges, and other persons of legal experience who may be appointed to sit. Appeals are heard by at least three judges, though only one judgment is delivered. Any subsequent appeal lies to the House of Lords and can only be made with leave.[366]

---

[360] Army Act 1955, ss 133, 134; Air Force Act 1955, ss 133, 134; Naval Discipline Act 1975, s 129.

[361] The corresponding department in the Navy is the Judge Advocate of the Fleet's department.

[362] See, e.g. Army Act 1955, s 96. Before the possibility of such a penalty was finally removed by the Crime and Disorder Act 1998 (s 36), any decision to impose the death sentence had to be unanimous.

[363] Army Act 1955, s 113; Air Force Act 1955, s 113; Naval Discipline Act 1957, s 70.

[364] It is now governed by the Courts-Martial (Appeals) Act 1968. Before 1951 there was no right of appeal against conviction.

[365] By the Lord Chief Justice.   [366] See p 696, *post*; Courts-Martial (Appeals) Act 1968, s 39.

(b) Issues of fairness

In *Findlay* v *UK* the court-martial procedure was found to be incompatible with the fair trial provisions in Article 6, ECHR, because there were insufficient safeguards to guarantee impartiality.[367] At the time, several aspects of the courts-martial procedure were under the control of a 'Convening Officer'. This Officer had the task of selecting the President and other members of the court, and this usually meant selecting officers who were inferior in rank and perhaps even under his direct command. The Convening Officer was also responsible for procuring the attendance of witnesses, deciding which charges should be brought against the accused, and sending an abstract of the evidence to the prosecution. All of this gave the impression of a tribunal lacking in impartiality.

The Armed Forces Act 1996, which came into force on 1 April 1997, anticipated the decision in *Findlay* and introduced changes designed to safeguard the independence of the system. It abolished the Convening Officer role and distributed his former functions between the prosecuting authority and the Commanding Officer, in liaison with the court-martial administration officer and the Reviewing Authority. However, despite these reforms, the court-martial procedure has been the subject of further Article 6 challenges. In *R* v *McKendry*, the Judge Advocate advised that the office of Permanent President of Courts-Martial (PPCM) was incompatible with the idea of an independent tribunal. He noted that PPCMs are appointed for a limited number of years and do not have any formal security of tenure. He also voiced concern that PPCMs could, as military officers, be subject to periodic review by their superiors:[368]

Those particular concerns are sufficient in my view for me to rule that in the particular circumstances of the system as it now stands, the appointments of permanent presidents do not give rise to an impartial and independent tribunal.

Following *McKendry* the use of PPCMs was suspended. However, in *R* v *Spear* the Courts-Martial Appeal Court held that the involvement of PPCMs in a number of earlier hearings had not violated Article 6:[369]

There is as we understand it no jurisprudence to show that the 'guarantees' referred to in Findlay's case . . . must as a matter of law be formal . . . We consider that in the context of our domestic jurisdiction, a useful but by no means exclusive approach to the objective requirements of Article 6 may be to invoke the common law's reasonable man. Would the reasonable man, *apprised of all the relevant facts about the particular case and the general practice*, conclude that there existed any real doubt as to the court's impartiality or independence?

In each of the appeals before the court, the PPCM had been in his last posting before retirement and was therefore unlikely to have been influenced by the prospect of

---

[367] (1997) 24 EHRR 221. Procedures at the time were governed by the Armed Forces Act 1981.

[368] *R* v *McKendry* (unreported) 6 March 2000, Aldershot Court-Martial Centre.

[369] *R* v *Spear and others* [2001] EWCA Crim 2 at [35], [2001] QB 804 at 819, [2001] 2 WLR 1692, per Laws LJ.

promotion or preferment. The court noted that PPCMs effectively operated outside the military chain of command, that (in the army at least) they were no longer subject to periodic reviews, and that despite the absence of any written guarantees of tenure, no PPCM had ever actually been removed from his position. On this basis, the Courts-Martial Appeal Court was satisfied that each appellant had been tried by an independent and impartial tribunal.

Spear was given leave to appeal to the House of Lords. Before the appeal could be heard however, the European Court of Human Rights in *Morris* v *UK*[370] decided that despite the improvements made since *Findlay*, the courts-martial system still fell short of what was required by Article 6. The Court noted that the roles of the PPCM and the Judge Advocate were important safeguards of independence, but it considered that they were not sufficient to exclude the risk of outside pressure being brought to bear on the other members. In particular, it expressed concern that (a) these other members received no legal training; (b) there were no statutory or other bars to prevent them from being subjected to external influence; and (c) they remained subject to army discipline and reporting.

Morris was not followed when *R* v *Spear* reached the House of Lords,[371] their Lordships having taken the view that the Strasbourg court had not had sufficient information upon which to base its decision. It was noted that although the ordinary courts-martial members were still subject to army discipline and reporting, their 'judicial' decisions were not evaluated or discussed as part of the reporting process: indeed, officers were prohibited from discussing their deliberations with anyone who was not a member of the court. It was also noted that any attempt to influence a court-martial would probably constitute the offence of attempting to pervert the course of justice. Lord Bingham concluded that:[372]

In my opinion the rules governing the role of junior officers as members of courts-martial are in practice such as effectively to protect the accused against the risk that they might be subject to 'external army influence', as I feel sure the European Court would have appreciated had the position been more fully explained.

Lord Rodger concurred, pointing out that:[373]

Article 6 does not require that the members of the tribunal should not share the values of the military community to which they belong, any more than it requires that the judge or members of the jury in a civil court should be divorced from the values of the wider community.

In *Cooper* v *UK*[374] a unanimous Grand Chamber of the Strasbourg court took account of these judgments and departed from its previous case law, declaring itself satisfied that there was, after all, no incompatibility with the Convention. However, the courts

---

[370] (2002) 34 EHRR 52.
[371] *R* v *Spear and others; R* v *Saunby and others* [2002] UKHL 31, [2003] 1 AC 734, [2002] 3 All ER 1074. For the status of European Court of Human Rights decisions as precedents, see pp 86 and 153, *ante*.
[372] Ibid at [12]; see also p 155, *ante*.   [373] Ibid at [57].   [374] (2004) 39 EHRR 8.

in both *Cooper* and *Spear* suggested that the role of the Reviewing Authorities was anomalous, and while they found no unfairness in the proceedings on the facts, they expressed concern that PPCMs in the RAF were still subject to review by their superior officers. In addition, in *Grieves* v *UK*[375] the Royal Navy's courts-martial were found to be incompatible with Article 6, due to the lack of a permanent President and the fact that Judge Advocates were appointed by (and answerable to) a serving naval officer. The government responded quickly to this decision, and made a Remedial Order providing that naval Judge Advocates will in future be appointed by the Judge Advocate of the Fleet; a civilian.[376] The Courts-Martial Appeal Court recently quashed the conviction of a defendant found guilty under the old system, and indicated that other appeals brought on the same grounds were also likely to succeed.[377]

2 ECCLESIASTICAL COURTS

These courts have a history as old as the common law itself. Although they have been subject to control by the sovereign since the reign of Henry VIII, and their jurisdiction over laymen has been abolished, there remains a hierarchy of courts within the Church of England. In addition, the General Synod of the Church of England has statutory powers[378] to pass Measures concerning any matter affecting the Church of England, and even concerning Acts of Parliament. These Measures have statutory force upon receiving the Royal Assent.

Each diocese has a consistory court with jurisdiction over matters such as parochial libraries, the restoration of churches, and acts relating to land within the diocese.[379] Until now these courts have also had jurisdiction over disciplinary matters, but a Measure passed in 2003 provides for the creation of separate Disciplinary Tribunals for each diocese. These Tribunals have jurisdiction over priests and deacons, and can determine allegations of neglect of duty, conduct unbecoming a clerk in Holy Orders, and other forms of misconduct.[380] The Vicar-General's Court for each province continues to have jurisdiction over allegations of misconduct involving bishops.[381] Appeals from the above courts lie to the Arches Court of Canterbury or the Chancery

---

[375]　(2004) 39 EHRR 2.

[376]　Naval Discipline Act 1957 (Remedial) Order 2004, SI 2004/66. The Order was made under section 10 of the Human Rights Act 1998: see p 159, *ante.*

[377]　*R* v *Dundon* [2004] EWCA Crim 621, (2004) *The Times,* 28 April.

[378]　Under the Church of England Assembly (Powers) Act 1919, as amended by the Synodial Government Measure 1969, s 2(1).

[379]　Ecclesiastical Jurisdiction Measure 1963, ss 1 and 6.

[380]　Clergy Discipline Measure 2003, ss 2, 6(1), 7 and 22. It is clear from this Measure that the Church of England is not immune from the mood of reform that has swept through the legal system in recent years. Its effect will be to transform the ecclesiastical courts into something more recognisable as a judicial system. Amongst other things, it provides for the appointment of a President of Tribunals, the creation of a Disciplinary Commission with an advisory role, and the formulation of a Code of Practice. It also ensures that members of ecclesiastical courts enjoy greater security of tenure and cannot be removed from office without due process.

[381]　Ibid, ss 6(2), 7 and 23.

Court of York: both of these are presided over by officers who must either be barristers of ten years' standing, or persons who have held high judicial office.[382] Any further appeal lies to the Privy Council.[383]

The Court of Ecclesiastical Causes Reserved has jurisdiction over all members of the clergy in matters of 'doctrine, ritual or ceremonial'. This court is composed of five judges appointed by Her Majesty, and must include two persons who have held high judicial office.[384] Any appeal lies to a Commission of Review, which is currently composed of three Lords of Appeal in Ordinary and two Lords Spiritual.[385]

The ecclesiastical courts can impose a range of penalties, including removal from office. Such a penalty may be imposed when a clergyman is sentenced to imprisonment, or has a decree of divorce or order of separation pronounced against him on one of certain specified grounds.[386]

---

[382] Ecclesiastical Jurisdiction Measure 1963, ss 1, 3, and 7.   [383] Ibid, s 8.
[384] Ibid, ss 5 and 10. The others must be bishops.   [385] Ibid, s 7.
[386] Clergy Discipline Measure 2003, ss 30 and 31.

8

TRIBUNALS AND INQUIRIES

A TRIBUNALS: OVERVIEW

In 2001 Sir Andrew Leggatt reported that there were over seventy administrative tribunals operating in England and Wales,[1] in addition to a number of domestic tribunals and other regulatory bodies. The overwhelming majority of these were created during the twentieth century to provide cheap and informal mechanisms for resolving particular types of dispute. Most, though not all, adjudicate on matters involving the citizen and the state. Over the past half a century the Welfare State has grown rapidly, and virtually every aspect of life—from the economy and industry, to housing and the environment—is increasingly subject to governmental intervention and regulation. The potential for disputes between the citizen and the state has increased phenomenally, and this has been matched by an increase in the jurisdiction and workload of the tribunals. As far back as 1979, tribunals were dealing with almost six times as many cases as the courts.[2] They now handle around a million cases each year:[3]

That number of cases alone makes their work of great importance to our society, since more of us bring a case before a tribunal than go to any other part of the justice system. Their collective impact is immense.

1 THE CHARACTERISTICS OF TRIBUNALS

The distinction between tribunals and courts is not a technical one. Both courts and tribunals have been described as 'machinery for adjudication',[4] and both have a duty to act judicially. Although the offence of contempt of court[5] can only be committed in relation to a court, some tribunals have been held to be 'courts' for these purposes,[6]

---

[1] *Tribunals for Users: One System, One Service—Report of the Review of Tribunals* (2001), overview, para 2.
[2] Royal Commission on Legal Services, Cmnd 7648, 1979.
[3] *Tribunals for Users* (2001) at para 1.1.   [4] Royal Commission on Legal Services, para 40.
[5] See p 236, *ante*.
[6] *Peach Grey & Co v Sommers* [1995] 2 All ER 513, [1995] ICR 549 (employment tribunals); applied in *Ewing v Security Services* [2003] EWCA Civ 581. *Pickering v Liverpool Daily Post and Echo Newspapers plc* [1991] 2 AC 370 [1991] 1 All ER 622 (Mental Health Review Tribunals).

and the Employment Appeal Tribunal is actually a superior court of record. The choice of terminology therefore has no formal significance, and in a general sense, *any* type of court or judicial body can be called a 'tribunal'. In the context of the English legal system however, the term is usually reserved for bodies which have more specialized areas of jurisdiction than the ordinary courts, and which often comprise both lawyers and expert lay members.

When compared to courts, tribunals are said to be relatively informal, accessible, quick, and inexpensive, but in fact there is enormous variation in the extent to which different tribunals possess these characteristics. Much depends on the nature of the matter being determined. Thus, industrial tribunals are rather more formal than social security appeals tribunals, and the Lands Tribunal exhibits a degree of formality similar to that of the ordinary courts. There are also differences in the types of decisions that individual tribunals are required to make. Some tribunals deal with appeals against the decisions of government departments and public officials,[7] and some even hear appeals against the decisions of other tribunals.[8] Others have original jurisdiction to determine matters such as the discharge of patients in compulsory detention.[9] In addition, a small number of tribunals—notably employment tribunals and rent assessment panels—have jurisdiction to hear disputes between private citizens.

Although the jurisdiction of most tribunals concerns 'administrative' disputes, it would be a mistake to assume that these disputes are any less important than those coming before the courts. Some tribunals adjudicate on matters affecting fundamental rights, such as asylum decisions, claims of unlawful discrimination, and applications to be discharged from compulsory detention. Others, such as the Lands Tribunal, sometimes deal with claims involving very large sums of money. However, with the exception of the EAT,[10] tribunals are generally regarded as inferior to the ordinary courts, and they are subject to the supervisory jurisdiction of the High Court. In some cases they are also subject to the appellate jurisdiction of the High Court or Court of Appeal.[11]

2 COMPOSITION

The composition of most tribunals differs from that of the average court, and usually includes both legally qualified persons and lay people with relevant expertise. For example, an employment tribunal typically comprises a legally qualified chairman and two 'wing members'. One wing member will be a layman with experience of representing employers' interests; the other will have experience of representing the

---

[7] Social Security Appeals Tribunals, School Admission Appeal Panels and the Immigration Adjudicators are just a few examples.

[8] See, e.g., the Immigration Appeal Tribunal, discussed at p 288, *post.*

[9] Mental Health Review Tribunals.   [10] Employment Appeal Tribunal: see p 292, *post.*

[11] This is discussed further in part 'C' of this chapter.

rights of workers. Similarly, experts in the fields of medicine, disability and finance sit alongside lawyers in social security appeals tribunals.

The lay members who serve on tribunals are generally drawn from panels of experts appointed by government Ministers. As tribunals frequently have to adjudicate upon decisions made by those same Ministers, concerns have been raised about the extent to which panel members are genuinely independent. The arrangements for appointing the lay members of employment tribunals were the subject of a Human Rights Act challenge in *Scanfuture Ltd v Secretary of State for Trade and Industry*.[12] Before 1999 lay members were appointed by the Secretary of State on a short-term basis and they had no real security of tenure. The renewal of their contracts was entirely at the Secretary of State's discretion, and their remuneration was determined by the same Minister. The Employment Appeal Tribunal ruled that 'a fair-minded and informed observer' would justifiably fear that members appointed like this were not independent and impartial. For a tribunal including such members to determine a case involving the Minister was therefore incompatible with the right to a fair trial under Article 6 of the ECHR:[13]

[H]ow would [an] observer react? He would see the DTA, a party to the proceedings, to have had a large role in the appointment of two of the three Members of the Employment Tribunal (all three having an equal voice), having a substantial role in the fixing of their lengths of appointment, in their possible re-appointment, in their possible removal, and in their remuneration. He would no doubt be comforted to some extent upon reflecting that, whatever the full theoretical range of the Secretary of State's powers, in practice the observer would not have come across any instance of any unwarranted or improper pressure upon any lay member, [but] . . .

In our judgment the fair-minded and informed observer in 1999 would have harboured an objectively justifiable fear that the Employment Tribunal as it was in April-June 1999 lacked both impartiality and independence within the meaning of that expression in Article 6.

The government had anticipated such a challenge,[14] and the arrangements for appointing the lay members of employment and other tribunals had already been reformed by the time that *Scanfuture* was decided. Thus, although the wing members of employment tribunals continue to be appointed by the Secretary of State, they are now appointed for a three-year term which is automatically renewable. The Secretary of State still has the power to remove members from their posts, but only one on of five specified grounds[15] and not without judicial involvement. The EAT concluded that there is now 'no need or reason, if ever there was, for any lay member to think that . . . it would help him acquire a renewal of his office by his leaning in favour of

---

[12] [2001] ICR 1096, [2001] IRLR 416.

[13] Ibid, at [33]–[36], per Lindsay J. Article 6 is discussed further at p 180, *ante*.

[14] It was clear from the decision in *Starrs v Ruxton* 2000 JC 208, 2000 SLT 42 that the terms upon which many part-time judges and tribunal members held office would have to be reviewed: see; p 320, *post*.

[15] These grounds are: (a) misbehaviour; (b) incapacity; (c) failure as to training; (d) failure to satisfy the sitting requirements; and (e) sustained failure to observe reasonably expected standards.

the Secretary of State in any hearing.'[16] Thus, in the opinion of the EAT, the new arrangements for appointing lay tribunal members are compatible with Article 6.

A similar issue arose in *Singh v Secretary of State for the Home Department*[17] in the context of a part-time immigration adjudicator. The adjudicator had been appointed for an initial term of one year, and although it was 'normal' for such appointments to be renewed on expiry, his conditions of service made it clear that renewal could not be guaranteed. They also stated that the Lord Chancellor reserved the right to terminate his appointment 'without cause' at one month's notice. The Scottish Court of Session held that these arrangements did not provide security of tenure and were therefore incompatible with both Article 6 and the existing common law test for bias. Again however, the court noted that a modified appointments system had been in place in the immigration tribunals since 2000, and it would appear that the new system does provide the necessary safeguards.[18]

Sir Andrew Leggatt's recent review of tribunals[19] raised similar concerns about independence, and it recommended that tribunal members should be appointed in the same way as members of the judiciary. Provisions to give effect to this recommendation were included in the Constitutional Reform Act 2005. In future, judges, magistrates, and most tribunal members will be selected by a Judicial Appointments Commission:[20] the Lord Chancellor's role in approving or recommending the Commission's selections will be largely a formality.

3 ORGANIZATION AND CONTROL

There is a danger that tribunals might be viewed as part of the process of government rather than as part of a legal system providing an independent means of review. Extensive powers of adjudication have been granted to tribunals which are not demonstrably independent of government departments, and for almost a century concerns have been growing[21] about executive encroachment into the legislative and judicial areas. Some of these concerns were addressed by the Donoughmore Committee in 1932.[22] This recommended that:

(a) the supervisory jurisdiction of the High Court over tribunals should be maintained;

(b) tribunals should be compelled by the High Court to observe natural justice;

---

[16] *Scanfuture v Secretary of State for Trade and Industry* [2001] ICR 1096 at [41], [2001] IRLR 416 at [41], per Lindsay J.

[17] 2002 SLT 1058, (2004) *The Times* 23 January, Inner House.

[18] The composition of the Employment Appeal Tribunal was the subject of a different type of Article 6 challenge in *Lawal v Northern Spirit* [2003] UKHL 35, [2004] 1 All ER 187, [2003] ICR 856: see p 293, *post*.

[19] *Tribunals for Users* (2001) at para 2.32.

[20] See, in particular, s 85 and Schedule 12 of the 2005 Act. See also, p 314, *post*.

[21] See, e.g., Lord Hewart CJ's reference to 'administrative lawlessness' in *The New Despotism* (1929).

[22] Report of the Committee on Ministers' Powers, Cm 4060, 1932.

(c) the reports of statutory inquiries should be published; and

(d) there should be the possibility of an appeal from tribunals on a question of law.

These recommendations were generally given effect,[23] but concerns about independence persisted. Then, in 1957, the Franks Committee carried out a major review of administrative tribunals and inquiries.[24]

(a) The Franks Committee

The Franks Committee Report described tribunals as follows:[25]

[They] are not ordinary courts, but neither are they appendages of Government Departments . . . tribunals should properly be regarded as machinery provided by Parliament for adjudication rather than as part of the machinery of administration. The essential point is that in all these cases Parliament has deliberately provided for a decision outside and independent of the Department concerned . . . and the intention of Parliament to provide for the independence of tribunals is clear and unmistakable.

The Report highlighted the need for tribunals to have the three key characteristics of openness, impartiality, and fairness. These are in fact the key principles underpinning the judicial system in England and Wales, and a court in an application for judicial review would consider them to be the basic standards of procedural fairness.[26] The Franks Report described these characteristics as follows:[27]

Openness appears to us to require the publicity of proceedings and knowledge of the essential reasoning underlying the decisions; fairness to require the adoption of a clear procedure which enables parties to know their rights, to present their case fully and to know the case which they have to meet; and impartiality to require the freedom of tribunals from the influence, real or apparent, of departments concerned with the subject matter of their decisions.

The Report also noted that tribunals have certain advantages over courts: cheapness, accessibility, informality, expert knowledge of their own areas of operation, and an ability to deal with cases relatively quickly. The volume of work however, is now very substantial, and this militates against the speedy disposal of applications. By 1999, employment tribunals alone were dealing with in excess of 83,000 cases each year.[28]

(b) The Council on Tribunals

One of the key recommendations of the Franks Report was the creation of a permanent statutory body to supervise and review the working of tribunals within its remit.

---

[23] The courts' supervisory jurisdiction over tribunals is discussed at p 295, *post*.

[24] Report of the Committee on Administrative Tribunals and Enquiries, Cmnd 218, 1957.

[25] Ibid, at para 2.45.

[26] See, e.g., *Doody v Secretary of State for Home Affairs* [1994] 1 AC 531, [1993] 3 All ER 92; *R v Board of Visitors of HM Prison, The Maze, ex parte Hone* [1988] AC 379, [1988] 1 All ER 321. See further, p 295, *post*.

[27] Paragraph 42 of the Report.

[28] *Tribunals for Users* (2001), chapter on Employment Tribunals at para 3.

This recommendation was given effect by the creation of the Council on Tribunals.[29] The Council consists of between ten and fifteen members appointed by the Lord Chancellor.[30] Those tribunals subject to its scrutiny are listed in the First Schedule to the Tribunal and Inquiries Act 1992. They include employment tribunals, the Lands Tribunal, Mental Health Review Tribunals, and the General and Special Commissioners of Income Tax. The Council does not have any role in respect of inquiries set up by the government to investigate issues of public concern, but inquiries that form part of a statutory administrative procedure do fall within its remit.

The Council's role is advisory and consultative, and it has no independent executive authority. Its primary function is to keep the workings of tribunals under review and to report on them from time to time. Its work also includes giving advice on the appointment and training of tribunal members and on the rules under which they operate. In 1991 it published a set of model tribunal rules and it also produces various Annual Reports. Its influence is limited however, and one commentator[31] suggested that its reports did 'little more than recite facts and make the occasional grumble.' Clearly, there are limits to the effectiveness of what is essentially an advisory watchdog.

(c) The Leggatt Review of Tribunals: One System, One Service

In 2000, Sir Andrew Leggatt was asked to chair the first major review of tribunals since the Franks Report. His objective was to recommend a system that would be 'coherent, professional, cost-effective and user-friendly',[32] and which would also be compatible with the requirements for independence under Article 6 of the ECHR.[33] He reviewed the work of more than different tribunals and concluded that they could not really be described as a 'system' at all:[34]

[T]he present collection of tribunals has grown up in an almost entirely haphazard way. Individual tribunals were set up, and usually administered by departments, as they developed new statutory schemes and procedures. The result is a collection of tribunals, mostly administered by departments, with wide variations of practice and approach, and almost no coherence. The current arrangements seem to us to have been developed to meet the needs and conveniences of the departments and other bodies which run tribunals, rather than the needs of the user.

Leggatt expressed concern that most tribunals were still administered by the departments whose policies they had a duty to consider:[35]

The very fact that a department is responsible for the policy and the legislation, under which cases are brought in the tribunal it sponsors, leads users to suppose that the tribunal is part of the same enterprise as its sponsoring department.

---

29 Tribunals and Inquiries Act 1958: this was superseded by the Tribunals and Inquiries Act 1992.

30 1992 Act, s 2. Its members are disqualified from membership of the House of Commons.

31 Lomas, 'The Twenty-Fifth Annual Report of the Council on Tribunals—An Opportunity Sadly Missed' (1985) 48 MLR 694.

32 *Tribunals for Users: One System, One Service—Report of the Review of Tribunals* (2001), overview, para 1.

33 See pp 182 and 280, *ante.*   34 *Tribunals for Users*, para 1.3.

35 Ibid, overview, para 11.

He concluded that greater independence and efficiency could be achieved by establishing a common administrative service with responsibility for *all* tribunals. A more coherent system could be developed by grouping the existing tribunals into nine divisions, with each division relating to a particular subject area. Thus, there should be divisions dealing with education, finance, health and social services, immigration, land and valuation, social security and pensions, transport, regulatory matters, and employment.[36] Each division should have a corresponding appellate or 'second-tier' tribunal, and there should be a right to appeal against first-tier decisions but only on a point of law. Any further appeal should lie to the Court of Appeal.[37] Leggatt also recommended a number of reforms designed to make tribunals more 'understandable, unthreatening and useful to users'.[38] These included training chairmen to provide better assistance to those presenting their own cases, improving tribunal procedures, making relevant information more accessible, and ensuring that voluntary and other advice groups were properly funded.

(d) The government's response: Transforming Public Services

The Leggatt Review made a total of 361 separate recommendations and received a fairly cautious welcome from the government. A consultation paper published in August 2001 said that the government had an open-mind but wanted to consult more widely.[39] The responses to the consultation revealed very strong support for reform, and in July 2004 the Department for Constitutional Affairs published a White Paper setting out its own vision for the future. This vision was described as 'different from, but compatible with' that of Leggatt:[40]

We accept Sir Andrew Leggatt's key recommendation that tribunals provided by central government should be brought together into a unified system within what is now the Department for Constitutional Affairs. We believe that this will be more effective and efficient, and will firmly embed the principle of independence. But we see this new body as much more than a federation of existing tribunals. This is a new organisation and a new type of organisation. It will have two central pillars: administrative justice appeals, and employment cases. Its task, together with a transformed Council on Tribunals, will not be just to process cases according to law. Its mission will be to help to prevent and resolve disputes, using any appropriate method and working with its partners in and out of government, and to help to improve administrative justice and justice in the workplace, so that the need for disputes is reduced.

Plans to bring tribunals together into a single service are already underway. The new Tribunals Service will be accountable to the Department for Constitutional Affairs and will be formally launched in April 2006. It will initially be based on those tribunals for which the DCA is already responsible, but others—including the

---

[36] Ibid, para 9.   [37] Ibid, para 14.   [38] Ibid, para 6.

[39] Lord Chancellors Department, *Tribunals for Users: Consultation Paper about the Report of the Review of Tribunals by Sir Andrew Leggatt* (2001).

[40] *Transforming Public Services: Complaints, Redress and Tribunals*, at para 1.14.

Appeals Service, employment tribunals, and EAT—will be transferred to the Service before 2008.

Leggatt's proposed nine-division structure has been rejected as unnecessary, but there will be separate 'employment' and 'administrative justice' pillars.[41] The general thrust of Leggatt's recommendations for appeals has been accepted, and the White Paper proposes to create a new Administrative Appeals Tribunal. This will hear appeals on points of law from all but a handful of first-tier tribunals, and will bring together the jurisdictions of the existing appellate tribunals.[42] The only exception will be the EAT, which will remain a separate entity and will constitute the second tier of the employment pillar. An appeal from a second-tier tribunal will only be possible where a novel or difficult point of law is raised, and it will lie not to the High Court but to the Court of Appeal.[43] In addition, the government suggests that with an enhanced system of appellate tribunals and an increased role for the Court of Appeal, there will be no scope for the High Court to retain its supervisory jurisdiction. A person who is refused leave to appeal will, however, be able to seek a statutory review of this decision on paper by a judge of the Court of Appeal.[44] This is probably the White Paper's most controversial proposal. Other specific plans include:

- Imposing a statutory duty on the new organisation to work with administrative bodies to improve the quality of original decision-making;
- Renaming the legally qualified members of tribunals 'Tribunal Judge' and 'Tribunal Appellate Judge';
- Creating the post of Senior President of Tribunals;
- Creating a statutory tribunals rule committee; and
- Establishing a new and enhanced role for the Council on Tribunals, which will in time evolve into an Administrative Justice Council.

B EXAMPLES OF TRIBUNALS

1 ADMINISTRATIVE TRIBUNALS

Administrative tribunals are generally concerned with the resolution of disputes between the citizen and the state. Most tribunals fall into this category, and the range is extensive and diverse. Examples include the Criminal Injuries Compensation Appeals

---

[41] Ibid, para 6.38.

[42] Ibid, para 717. The DCA appears to envisage something similar to the divisional structure of the High Court, with appeals tribunal members having a common jurisdiction but being assigned to hear particular types of case according to their expertise.

[43] Ibid, para 7.27.   [44] Ibid, para 7.28.

Panel,[45] the General Commissioners of Income Tax,[46] the Asylum and Immigration Tribunal,[47] the Investigatory Powers Tribunal,[48] Mental Health Review Tribunals,[49] School Admission Appeals Panels,[50] the Traffic Tribunal,[51] Valuation Tribunals,[52] and the Appeals Service. Three of these are considered in more detail below.

(a) The Appeals Service

In 1998 the social security appeals tribunals[53] were combined with the disability appeals tribunals, medical appeal tribunals, vaccine damage tribunals, and child support appeal tribunals to form a unified system with a single jurisdiction.[54] This system, known as the Appeals Service, handles around 270,000 cases each year.[55] Its workload consists mainly of appeals against decisions concerning entitlement to welfare benefits and other payments.

The Service has two distinct components: a judicial wing and an administrative wing. Its judicial wing has a President,[56] seven Regional Chairmen, sixty District Chairmen and over 2,000 other full-time and part-time panel members.[57] Around 750 of its members are legally qualified: the rest are appointed for their expertise in the fields of medicine, finance, and dealing with the needs of the disabled.[58] The President's role is primarily managerial and administrative. He has a statutory obligation to provide panel members with training, and he produces an annual report on the standard of the Secretary of State's decision-making in cases reaching appeal.[59] The administrative wing of the Service is an executive agency of the Department of Work and Pensions and is headed by a Chief Executive.

Certain cases can only be determined by a lawyer sitting with one or two other panel members, but many can be heard by a lawyer sitting alone.[60] The conduct of hearings is deliberately informal, and panel members are expected to be pro-active in eliciting the facts and applying the relevant law. This is extremely important because most applicants are not represented at the hearing[61] and many do not even

---

[45] Criminal Injuries Compensation Act 1995: see p 287, *post*.

[46] This is the oldest tribunal still in existence and dates from 1798.

[47] A new tribunal created by the Asylum and Immigration (Treatment of Claimants etc.) Act 2004: see p 288, *post*.

[48] Regulation of Investigatory Powers Act 2000, s 65.   [49] Mental Health Act 1983, s 65.

[50] School Standards and Framework Act 1998, s 95.   [51] Transport Act 1985, s 117; Schedule 4.

[52] Local Government Finance Act 1992, s 15.

[53] These tribunals were themselves borne out of a merger, in that they were created by combining supplementary benefits tribunals and National Insurance tribunals: Health and Social Services and Social Security Adjudications Act 1983. The origins of the system can be traced back to the Court of Referees, created by the National Insurance Act 1911.

[54] Social Security Act 1998, s 4.   [55] *The Appeals Service Annual Report 2002–2003*, at p 5.

[56] 1998 Act, s 5. The President must be a lawyer of ten years standing.

[57] *Annual Report 2002–2003*, at p 4.

[58] Social Security and Child Support (Decisions and Appeals) Regulations 1999, SI 1999/991, Schedule 3.

[59] Schedule 1 of the 1998 Act.   [60] Ibid, s 7.

[61] Public funding is not available for representation in Appeals Service cases. The proportion of applicants who are legally represented is therefore very small.

attend.[62] An appeal to a Social Security or Child Support Commissioner on a point of law is possible, but only with the leave of the tribunal or its chairman.[63] Any further appeal from the decision of a Commissioner normally lies to the Court of Appeal.[64]

In certain respects the Appeals Service was the model for the unified tribunals service proposed by Leggatt. Replacing five separate jurisdictions with one has enabled the adoption of common procedures, and allowed greater flexibility in the deployment of resources: tribunal members appointed to the single jurisdiction can now be allocated to any type of case for which they have suitable expertise.[65] Although Leggatt did not suggest that all tribunals should be unified in this way, he did recommend that there should be greater harmonization of procedures. He also thought that it should be possible for suitably qualified members to sit in more than one tribunal. On the other hand, Leggatt was concerned that the Appeals Service's administrative wing remained an executive agency of a government department:[66]

So close a relationship with a sponsoring department facilitates links between the tribunal and decision-makers and policy makers. But it also brings with it a perception that the tribunal is not independent.

Some of these concerns should be addressed when administrative responsibility for the system is transferred to the new Tribunals Service.[67]

(b) The Criminal Injuries Compensation Appeals Panel

In 1964 the government used prerogative powers[68] to create a scheme for compensating the victims of violent crime. Claims were administered by the Criminal Injuries Compensation Board and were assessed on the same basis as common law damages.

The scheme was placed on a statutory footing in 1995[69] and the Board was replaced by the Criminal Injuries Compensation Authority.[70] Awards are now calculated by reference to a tariff, which sets minimum and maximum amounts for each type of injury. A claimant who is dissatisfied with the decision of a claims officer can apply in writing to have it reviewed by someone in a more senior position. If the review is unsuccessful the claimant then has ninety days in which to appeal to the Criminal Injuries Compensation Appeals Panel.

---

62 See Wikeley, Ogus, and Barendt, *The Law of Social Security* (5th edn, 2002). The success rate for unrepresented applicants is quite low.

63 1998 Act, s 14. If a person considering an application for leave to appeal is satisfied that the decision is wrong in law, he has the power to set it aside and refer it for re-determination to the same or a differently constituted tribunal: s 13(2).

64 Ibid, s 15.   65 *Review of Tribunals* (2001), chapter on the Appeals Service, at para 16.

66 Ibid, at para 8.   67 See p 284, *ante.*

68 See *R v Criminal Injuries Compensation Board, ex parte Lain* [1967] 2 QB 864, [1967] 2 All ER 770; for a discussion of the royal prerogative, see chapter 6.

69 Criminal Injuries Compensation Act 1995. Provisions to establish a statutory regime were included in the Criminal Justice Act 1988 but were never actually implemented: see *R v Secretary of State for the Home Department, ex parte Fire Brigades Union* [1995] 2 AC 513, [1995] 2 All ER 244. The scheme created under the 1995 Act has since been revised and the current version dates from 2001.

70 The Board was abolished on 1 April 2000.

The Panel has a chairman and approximately 145 other members, around half of whom are legally qualified. Appeals are usually heard by either two or three members, though larger tribunals are sometimes convened to enable recently appointed members to gain experience.[71] At the hearing the appellant must prove his case on a balance of probabilities. He may choose to have a legal advisor or other representative present, and he may call, examine and cross-examine witnesses. The procedure is informal and adjudicators are not bound by strict rules of evidence. The Leggatt Report found that around 60 per cent of claimants were represented at appeal hearings, although it praised the supportive and constructive way in which unrepresented appellants were dealt with.[72] There is no right of appeal against the Panel's decisions but they are subject to the possibility of judicial review.[73]

The Panel is currently funded jointly by the Home Office and the Scotland Office, but administrative responsibility will be transferred to the Department for Constitutional Affairs when the Tribunals Service is launched in 2006.[74]

(c) The Asylum and Immigration Tribunal

Launched in April 2005, this tribunal has jurisdiction to hear appeals against Home Office decisions in matters relating to immigration and asylum.[75] Its predecessor, the Immigration Appellate Authorities (IAA) comprised two separate bodies: the Immigration Adjudicators and the Immigration Appeal Tribunal (IAT). The Adjudicators handled appeals from decisions made by entry clearance officials, immigration officers, and the Home Secretary, whilst the IAT had jurisdiction to hear second-tier appeals from decisions of the Adjudicators. Before 2002, appeals to the IAT could be based on grounds of both fact and law. This made it almost inevitable that an unsuccessful appeal to the Adjudicators would be the subject of a further challenge in the IAT. In his Review of Tribunals, Leggatt concluded that these arrangements had a negative effect on the perceived authority of the Adjudicators and contributed to a 'culture of challenge'. He also suggested that the expert contribution of non-lawyers was made too late in the process: all Immigration Adjudicators were legally qualified and usually sat alone, but appeals to the IAT were heard by a legally qualified chairman sitting with one or two lay members. Leggatt recommended that lay members and lawyers should sit together at the Adjudicator stage to determine both the facts and the law: any further appeal to the IAT should only be possible on a point of law and should therefore be determined by a lawyer sitting alone.[76] His recommendations were given partial effect by the Nationality, Immigration and Asylum Act 2002,

---

[71] See *Tribunals for Users* (2001), chapter on the Criminal Injuries Compensation Appeals Panel, at para 10. The Review concluded that panels of four or more members were intimidating for claimants and that they should therefore be avoided.

[72] Ibid, at paras 4 and 9.   [73] See pp 294–5, *post*.   [74] See p 284, *ante*.

[75] The key provisions are contained in Part V of the Nationality, Immigration and Asylum Act 2002 (as amended by the Asylum and Immigration (Treatment of Claimants etc.) Act 2004).

[76] *Tribunals for Users* (2001), Part III, recommendations 298–301.

which restricted the jurisdiction of the IAT to appeals based on points of law.[77] The involvement of lay members remained unchanged however, with the rather odd result that they were only able to contribute to the appeals process at a stage where purely legal issues were being determined. Just two years after these reforms were introduced the entire system was radically overhauled by the Asylum and Immigration (Treatment of Claimants etc.) Act 2004. The system of second-tier appeals was ended, and both the Adjudicators and the IAT were replaced with a single-tier Asylum and Immigration Tribunal.[78]

As with the previous system, the new Tribunal has no jurisdiction in respect of decisions taken on national security grounds,[79] and it cannot review asylum claims certified by the Home Secretary as being manifestly unfounded or as having originated in a country which is presumed safe.[80] The government had originally intended that the Tribunal's decisions should not be subject to judicial review, but its proposed ouster clause was withdrawn from the Asylum Bill in the face of considerable opposition.[81] The compromise eventually reached means that the Tribunal's decisions may be judicially reviewed on the grounds of an error of law, but any challenge must be made within five days of the original decision and only written submissions will be examined.[82] Where a Tribunal decision has already been reconsidered, any further challenge on a point of law lies to the Court of Appeal and can only be made with leave.[83]

The Tribunal itself comprises both lawyers and persons with suitable non-legal experience, and the Lord Chancellor is required to appoint a President and at least one Deputy President. It is for the President to determine how many members should hear particular cases or classes of case, having regard to their complexity and other circumstances.[84] It should be remembered that immigration and asylum cases are often complex and have potentially serious consequences for the individuals concerned. In addition, the hearings themselves are usually quite formal and few appellants are fluent in English. This means that most asylum applicants will require the assistance of both an interpreter and a representative in order to have a realistic prospect of success. Representation in asylum and immigration cases has been covered by the Community Legal Service scheme since January 2000, and this will continue to be the case for appeals heard by the new Tribunal.[85] However, where a decision of the

---

[77] 2002 Act, s 101 (now repealed).   [78] Ibid, s 81; as substituted by the 2004 Act, s 26.

[79] On this point see the powers and jurisdiction of the Special Immigration Appeals Commission, as conferred by the Special Immigration Appeals Commission Act 1997, ss 1 and 2.

[80] 2002 Act, s 94 (as amended). The 2004 Act extends the powers of the Secretary of State in this regard, allowing him to certify that all or part of a country is presumed safe for particular classes of person.

[81] See the discussion of clause 11 at p 310, *post*.

[82] 2002 Act, s 103A (inserted by the 2004 Act). Those applying from abroad must do so within twenty-eight days.

[83] Ibid, s 103B

[84] Detailed rules regarding the Tribunal are set out in a new Schedule 4 to the 2002 Act, and in the Asylum and Immigration Tribunal (Procedure) Rules 2005, SI 2005/230

[85] Community Legal Service (Funding) (Amendment) Order 2005, SI 2005/571.

Tribunal is itself being challenged the availability of legal aid will depend on the merits of the applicant's case, and no payment can be awarded until *after* the review or reconsideration is complete.[86]

2 PARTY AND PARTY TRIBUNALS

Although most tribunals are primarily concerned with public law disputes involving the citizen and the state, 'party and party tribunals' have jurisdiction to hear disputes between individuals. Employment tribunals are by far the most important example,[87] and with the exception of a small number of cases involving the Secretary of State for Trade and Industry, their workload consists mainly of disputes between employers and employees.

One of the issues addressed by Leggatt was whether party and party tribunals should be linked more closely with the courts, but on balance he concluded that this would not be in the interests of the user:[88]

There are arguments for ... keeping party and party [tribunals] separate from those dealing with administrative law. They are the parts of the tribunal system closest in essential function to the ordinary courts. The need for a fundamentally adversarial approach to cases has produced similarities in procedure. There is therefore an argument for party and party tribunals either to be merged with the ordinary courts, or to remain a separate body of tribunals but in a closer relationship with the courts ... [P]arty and party tribunals are falling behind the modern courts in terms of speed, active case management, the effective conduct of hearings, and even informality. A closer relationship might promote modernisation and further the development of the new civil procedures ...

Against these arguments should be set the distinctive benefits for the user in having cases decided by tribunals: the opportunities if procedures and hearings are simple and informal enough for users reasonably to expect to handle cases themselves, if properly supported; and better decisions if they are taken jointly by lawyers and experts ... This has led us to conclude that the features which are common to citizen and state tribunals and party and party tribunals are much more important than those which divide them. Both should therefore form part of the Tribunals System.

(a) Employment tribunals

First established in 1964, and until 1998 known as industrial tribunals,[89] employment tribunals now have jurisdiction to hear more than eighty different types of complaint. Their jurisdiction includes most claims in damages for breach of an employment

---

[86] Community Legal Service (Asylum and Immigration Appeals) Regulations 2005, SI 2005/966. For strong criticism of the new funding arrangements, see Select Committee on Constitutional Affairs, *5th Report: Legal Aid—Asylum Appeals* (House of Commons Papers, Session 2004–05, 276).

[87] Rent assessment panels and the Lands Tribunal also have some 'party and party' jurisdiction.

[88] *Tribunals for Users* (2001), paras 3.18–3.19.

[89] They were renamed by the Employment Rights (Dispute Resolution) Act 1998, s 1.

contract,[90] along with claims relating to unfair dismissal,[91] unlawful discrimination,[92] and equal pay.[93] They are currently administered by the Employment Tribunals Service, which is an agency of the Department of Trade and Industry. By 2008 the government intends to transfer responsibility for this agency to the Department for Constitutional Affairs, where it will then be integrated with the enlarged Tribunals Service.

In common with many other tribunals, employment tribunals comprise both lawyers and expert lay members. The lawyers must be barristers or solicitors of seven years standing, and the lay members must be persons with knowledge and experience of industrial relations. The lay members are divided into two panels: one comprising those with experience of representing workers; the other consisting of persons experienced in representing employers' interests. Until now the members of both panels have been appointed by the Secretary of State for Trade and Industry, prompting concerns that they are not sufficiently independent of the Minister whose policies they often have to consider.[94] These concerns are now being addressed however, and in future all those who sit on employment tribunals will be selected by an independent Judicial Appointments Commission.[95] In the meantime, lay members' conditions of service have been modified to ensure that they have greater security of tenure.[96]

The system is headed by a President of Employment Tribunals,[97] who must be a lawyer of seven years standing. His functions include determining the number and location of tribunals, selecting chairmen and lay members for hearings, and sitting as a chairman himself.[98] Section 4 of the Employment Tribunals Act 1996[99] states that cases should normally be heard by a legally qualified chairman sitting with two lay members. Regulations[100] further stipulate that one lay member should be drawn from each of the two panels, so that both sides of the industry are represented. Decisions are made by majority, and the chairman may therefore be outvoted if the lay members agree with each other as to the appropriate conclusion. Certain types of case can be determined by a chairman sitting alone,[101] including breach of contract cases and cases concerning the minimum wage. In addition, the parties may consent to *any* case being heard by a

---

[90] Employment Tribunals Extension of Jurisdiction Order 1994, SI 1994/1623. Employment Tribunals do not have jurisdiction over claims relating to personal injuries and certain other matters, and cannot make awards exceeding £25,000. The Lord Chancellor was given the power to confer the breach of contract jurisdiction in 1971 (Industrial Relations Act 1971, s 113), but did not exercise it until 1994.

[91] Employment Rights Act 1996, s 111.

[92] Sex Discrimination Act 1975, Race Relations Act 1976, Disability Discrimination Act 1995, Employment Equality (Religion or Belief) Regulations 2003, SI 2003/1660; Employment Equality (Sexual Orientation) Regulations 2003, SI 2003/1661.

[93] Equal Pay Act 1970.   [94] See p 280, *ante*.

[95] Constitutional Reform Act 2005, s 85; Schedule 14. See further, p 314, *post*.

[96] See p 280, *ante*; *Scanfuture* v *Secretary of State for Trade and Industry* [2001] ICR 1096, [2001] IRLR 416.

[97] For England and Wales. A President of the Scottish Employment Tribunals is also appointed.

[98] Employment Tribunals (Constitution and Rules of Procedure) Regulations 2004, SI 2004/1861, regs 4–9.

[99] This was originally called the Industrial Tribunals Act but was renamed by the Employment Rights (Dispute Resolution) Act 1998.

[100] SI 2004/1861, reg 9.   [101] These are set out in s 4(3) of the 1996 Act.

chairman sitting alone or with one lay member,[102] though the tribunal can override their wishes if a three-member panel is considered more suitable.[103]

Hearings are conducted in much the same way as in the ordinary civil courts, with rules of evidence generally, though not always, being adhered to.[104] An applicant may appear in person or be represented by counsel, a solicitor, a representative of a trade union or employers' association, or any other person whom he desires to represent him.[105] Many parties do appear in person, but there is concern that it is becoming increasingly difficult for unrepresented parties to contest cases successfully; particularly where aspects of European or anti-discrimination law are involved.[106] Public funding is not currently available for legal representation at employment tribunals, and an obvious way of assisting users would be to lift this restriction. Such a move would be extremely costly however,[107] and Leggatt suggested that it would be better to concentrate on improving the informality and accessibility of the system.[108] On the other hand, the nature of employment law is such that the Employment Tribunal Taskforce has doubted whether a less formal and complex system can really be achieved.[109]

Appeals against the decisions of employment tribunals lie to the Employment Appeal Tribunal (EAT) on a point of law. The proportion of cases which are the subject of an appeal to the EAT is very low—around 4 per cent[110]—and this is probably due in part to the number of parties who contest employment cases without the benefit of professional advice.

(b) The Employment Appeal Tribunal

The Employment Appeal Tribunal (EAT) was established in 1976[111] to hear appeals against the decisions of employment tribunals. It is a superior court of record and has all the characteristics of a court.[112] It comprises a number of judges nominated from the High Court and the Court of Appeal, at least one judge from Scotland's Court of

---

[102] Ibid, s 4(1)(b); s 4(3).

[103] *Sogbetun* v *London Borough of Hackney* [1998] IRLR 676, [1998] ICR 1264.

[104] See the 2004 Regulations: SI 2004/1861. See also, MacMillan, 'Employment Tribunals: Philosophies and Practicalities' (1999) 28(1) ILJ 4.

[105] Employment Tribunals Act 1996, s 6. The right to be represented by a person of one's choosing is unqualified and cannot be restricted by the tribunal: *Bache* v *Essex County Council* [2000] 2 All ER 847.

[106] For a recent study of the experiences of tribunal users, see Adler and Gulland, *Tribunal Users' Experiences, Perceptions and Expectations: A Literature Review* (2003). Earlier research by Genn and Genn suggested that the benefits of representation for the tribunal user were significant: 'The Effectiveness of Representation at Tribunals' (1989, Lord Chancellor's Department).

[107] In 2000/01, employment tribunals received 130,408 applications: *Report of the Employment Tribunal Taskforce* (2002), at para 1.9.

[108] *Tribunals for Users* (2001), chapter on Employment Tribunals, at para 11.

[109] *Report of the Employment Tribunal Taskforce* (2002), at para 8.25.   [110] Ibid, para 8.47

[111] Employment Protection Act 1975, s 87. Its predecessor, the National Industrial Relations Court, was established under the Industrial Relations Act 1971 and abolished after only three years.

[112] It can only punish for contempt with the consent of one of its judicial members: Employment Tribunals Act 1996, s 36.

Session, and such other lay members as may be appointed.[113] One of the judges is appointed President. The lay members are persons with special knowledge or experience of industrial relations, and they hold the highest judicial office available to a person without legal qualifications. The EAT is duly constituted when sitting with a judge and either two or four of the lay members.[114] As with employment tribunals, the lay members must be drawn in equal numbers from panels representing both sides of industry.

Senior barristers have sometimes been used as part-time EAT judges, but this practice was called into question when a barrister appeared as an advocate before lay members with whom he had sat in a judicial capacity. The claimant complained that this situation gave rise to a real possibility of bias, and the EAT agreed that his appeal should be heard by a differently constituted tribunal. The issue of principle was eventually referred to the House of Lords,[115] which held that for a judge to appear as an advocate under these circumstances would be contrary to both the common law and the ECHR right to a fair trial:[116]

Would . . . an observer consider that it was reasonably possible that the wing member[s] may be subconsciously biased? The observer is likely to approach the matter on the basis that the lay members look to the judge for guidance on the law, and can be expected to develop a fairly close relationship of trust and confidence with the judge.[117]

Their Lordships noted that the chairmen of employment tribunals were not permitted to appear as advocates before other tribunals in the same region, and they recommended that the EAT should adopt the same policy. Following this decision, it was announced that the practice of allowing barristers to sit as part-time EAT judges would be phased out.

The EAT's rules of procedure[118] aim at informality: no-one appears robed, there is no bench or witness box, and parties and their advisers sit at tables and address the court seated. In most other respects however, EAT hearings are very similar to those found in the ordinary courts. A party may appear in person or he may be represented by counsel, a solicitor, a representative of a trade union or employers' association, or any other person whom he desires to represent him.[119] Although employment tribunals are not covered by the Community Legal Service scheme, eligible persons can apply for public funding for representation at EAT hearings. Any decision of the EAT on a question of fact is final, and as a superior court of record, its decisions are not

---

113 Employment Tribunals Act 1996, s 22.

114 Ibid, s 28. With the consent of the parties cases may be heard by a judge and either one or three other members.

115 *Lawal* v *Northern Spirit* [2003] UKHL 35, [2004] 1 All ER 187, [2003] ICR 856.

116 European Convention on Human Rights, Article 6: see pp 182 and 280, *ante*.

117 [2003] UKHL 35 at [21], [2004] 1 All ER 187 at [21], per Lord Steyn.

118 Employment Appeal Tribunal Rules 1993, SI 1993/2854; Employment Appeal Tribunal (Amendment) Rules 2001, SI 2001/1128; Employment Appeal Tribunal (Amendment) Rules 2004, SI 2004/2526; *Practice Direction (EAT: Appeal Procedure)* [2005] IRLR 94.

119 Employment Tribunals Act 1996, s 29.

subject to the High Court's supervisory jurisdiction.[120] Any appeal on a point of law lies to the Court of Appeal.[121]

The EAT is currently administered by the Employment Tribunals Service, making it the only appellate tribunal which is not the responsibility of the Department for Constitutional Affairs. This anomaly will be corrected when the EAT and employment tribunals are integrated into the new Tribunals Service.[122]

3 DOMESTIC TRIBUNALS

A number of private and professional associations have set up their own bodies for resolving disputes between their members and enforcing internal discipline. As these bodies are concerned with matters of private rather than public importance, they are often referred to as 'domestic tribunals'. Their jurisdiction is based primarily on contract: by becoming a member of the association or professional body concerned, a person contracts to accept the jurisdiction of its governing tribunal. Nevertheless, in several cases these tribunals exist on a statutory basis with a right of appeal to the courts. Examples of domestic tribunals constituted under statute are the Solicitors Disciplinary Tribunal[123] and the Investigation Committee of the General Medical Council.[124] Examples of tribunals created by private bodies themselves include the Disciplinary Tribunal of the Bar[125] and the Football Association's Disciplinary Committee. The decisions of a non-statutory tribunal cannot be the subject of an appeal to the ordinary courts and they will not be amenable to judicial review unless the tribunal concerned is a public body performing public functions.[126] It may, however, be possible to mount a legal challenge using some other means: this is considered in more detail below.

C CONTROL OF TRIBUNALS BY THE COURTS

1 APPEALS FROM TRIBUNALS[127]

There is no right to appeal against the decision of a tribunal at common law, but in some cases a right to appeal on a point of law is provided by statute. The Tribunals

---

[120] See p 253, *ante*   [121] 1996 Act, s 37.

[122] See p 284, *ante*. The transfer is due to be completed by 2008.

[123] Solicitors Act 1974, s 46: see p 366, *post*.   [124] Medical Act 1983, s 1(3), as amended.

[125] See p 367, *post*.

[126] *Law* v *National Greyhound Racing Club* [1983] 3 All ER 300, [1983] 1 WLR 1302; *R* v *Disciplinary Committee of the Jockey Club, ex parte the Aga Khan* [1993] 2 All ER 853, [1993] 1 WLR 909. The relevant test was established in *R* v *Panel on Take-overs and Mergers, ex parte Datafin plc* [1987] QB 815, [1987] 1 All ER 564. In *R* v *General Council of the Bar, ex parte Percival* [1991] 1 QB 212, [1990] 3 All ER 317 a decision of the Bar Council's Professional Conduct Committee was held to be judicially reviewable. See p 207, *ante*.

[127] For an outline of the government's most recent proposals, see p 285, *ante*.

and Inquiries Act 1992 establishes a statutory right to appeal to the High Court[128] against the decisions of a number of tribunals, and the EAT is a rare example of a tribunal from which an appeal to the Court of Appeal is possible.[129]

2 SUPERVISORY CONTROL

Administrative and 'party and party' tribunals are public bodies performing public functions, and they are amenable to the High Court's supervisory jurisdiction in the same way as the inferior courts. This common law jurisdiction provides a basis for challenging decisions which have been made ultra vires or which are contrary to principles of natural justice. It is usually exercised by issuing one of the prerogative orders[130] in an application for judicial review,[131] though these remedies are not available in respect of bodies whose functions are essentially private in nature.

3 CHALLENGING THE DECISIONS OF 'PRIVATE' DISCIPLINARY BODIES

Few domestic tribunals have public functions, and most derive their authority from a contractual relationship with those under their supervision. The decisions of these private bodies cannot be the subject of a prerogative order[132] but the courts still have jurisdiction to determine whether they have been made fairly and in accordance with natural justice. The High Court has shown an increased willingness to intervene in the affairs of bodies which can deprive individuals of their livelihoods, and an aggrieved party may be able to challenge a decision by seeking a declaration or injunction.[133] Thus, in *Korda* v *International Tennis Federation*[134] the court granted a declaration as to the correct interpretation of the Federation's rules. The defendant's Disciplinary Committee had sanctioned the claimant for a breach of its anti-doping policy, but a dispute arose concerning the circumstances in which the defendant could refer the matter to the Court of Arbitration in Sport. On this occasion the issue was resolved in the defendant's favour: the Court of Appeal found that the rules allowed the Federation to appeal against the decision on the grounds that it was too lenient.

In the absence of an express contractual relationship, the courts may be prepared to find the existence of an *implied* contract between the parties and then to make a ruling as to its terms. In *Modhal* v *British Athletic Foundation Ltd (No 2)*[135] the claimant

---

[128] Section 11. These appeals are heard by a Divisional Court of the Queen's Bench Division.

[129] Employment Tribunals Act 1996, s 37.

[130] Mandatory orders, prohibiting orders and quashing orders.   [131] See chapter 6.

[132] In *R v Football Association Ltd, ex parte Football League Ltd* [1993] 2 All ER 833 it was held that the FA was not susceptible to judicial review because it was a private body which derived its authority from a contractual relationship with its members. See n 126, *ante*.

[133] In *Nagle* v *Feilden* [1966] 2 QB 633, [1966] 1 All ER 689 the Court of Appeal held that a person had an arguable right not to be arbitrarily excluded from his chosen profession by a governing body. See also: *Bonsor* v *Musicians Union* [1956] AC 104, [1955] 3 All ER 518.

[134] (1999) *The Independent,* April 21.   [135] [2001] EWCA Civ 1447, [2002] 1 WLR 1192.

failed a dope test and was banned from competing in events recognised by her sport's governing body. She successfully challenged the ban by using the defendant's own appeals process, but then commenced a civil action for damages. On appeal from the Queen's Bench Division, the Court of Appeal held that the claimant had an implied contract with the defendant, which derived from her participation in the defendant's events and her submission to its disciplinary rules and procedures. The Court of Appeal found that the defendant had not failed in its contractual obligation to provide a fair disciplinary process, and the action was therefore unsuccessful. Nevertheless, this decision demonstrates that that there is at least a theoretical possibility of a civil remedy being awarded in such circumstances.

D INQUIRIES

Inquiries are established for the purpose of investigating specific issues and their role is one of fact-finding rather than adjudication. They are not generally required to adhere to strict rules of evidence[136] and the courts are slow to interfere with their decisions in the absence of a clear breach of natural justice:[137]

In determining what is relevant to [an] inquiry, regard must be had to its investigatory character. Where broad terms of reference are given to it, as in this case, the [inquiry] is not determining issues between parties but conducting a thorough investigation into the subject matter. It may have to follow leads. It is not bound by rules of evidence. There is no set order in which evidence must be adduced ... If [the inquiry] bona fide seeks to establish a relevant connection between certain facts and the subject matter of the inquiry, it should not be regarded as outside its term of reference by doing so ...

[A] court ... should be very slow to restrain [an inquiry] from pursuing a particular line of questioning and should not do so unless it is satisfied ... [that it] is going off on a frolic of its own.

1 STATUTORY INQUIRIES

Some statutes require a Minister or public authority to hold an inquiry before a particular type of decision can be taken. These 'statutory inquiries' are covered by the Tribunals and Inquiries Act 1992 and may be the subject of procedural rules made pursuant to section 9 of that Act. Inquiries held at a Minister's discretion will also be subject to the Act if they are designated as statutory inquiries by the Lord Chancellor.[138] Statutory inquiries are an integral part of town and country planning, compulsory purchase, and highways development schemes.[139] They are conducted by

---

[136] See *Bushell* v *Secretary of State for the Environment* [1981] AC 75, [1980] 3 WLR 22.

[137] *Ross* v *Costigan* (1982) 41 ALR 319 at 334–5, per Ellicott J; cited with approval by Lord Walker in *Mount Murray Country Club Ltd* v *MacLeod* [2003] UKPC 53 at [28], *The Times*, 7 July.

[138] Section 16(1).   [139] See, e.g. the Town and Country Planning Act 1990.

inspectors and are usually triggered when objections are lodged against the decisions of public authorities.

The conduct of a statutory inquiry will be governed by the statute under which it is held, though the inspector will often be left with considerable discretion. Any rights of appeal will also be governed by the particular statutory scheme and will usually be restricted to points of law. An aggrieved party may, however, have recourse to judicial review.[140]

2 TRIBUNALS OF INQUIRY

Some inquiries are instigated by Ministers for the purposes of investigating specific events or issues of public concern. A recent consultation paper described the rationale for such inquiries as follows:[141]

There has been a long standing practice in the UK of setting up formal and open inquiries, where necessary, to look into matters that have caused public concern. Ministers are not under any statutory duty to set up such inquiries, but have found them to be a useful method of dealing with matters that have warranted formal, independent investigation.

Inquiries of this nature can fall into one of three categories:

(a) Inquiries instigated by Ministers acting under specific statutory provisions

An example of a provision conferring the power to order such an inquiry is section 49 of the Police Act 1996. This has enabled Home Secretaries to instigate local inquiries into matters connected with the policing of an area.[142] Sir William MacPherson's inquiry into the racially motivated killing of Stephen Lawrence is a striking example of an inquiry ordered under this provision.[143] The police had investigated certain individuals in relation to the killing, but the Crown Prosecution Service had declined to prosecute because of a lack of evidence. A private prosecution brought by the victim's family was thrown out by the judge for the same reason. The scope of the inquiry was limited to an examination of alleged failings in the police investigation. Attempts to question those suspected of the killing in order to establish their guilt were successfully challenged in the Divisional Court, and it was made clear that the inquiry was not a proper forum for conducting a murder trial.[144]

The Inquiry into the Southall Rail Accident in 1997 is another example of an inquiry set up under subject-specific legislation. The statutory basis for this inquiry was section 14 of the Health and Safety at Work etc. Act 1974.

---

[140] See chapter 6.

[141] Department for Constitutional Affairs, *Effective Inquiries* (2004) CP 12/04 at p 7.

[142] Such inquiries will in future fall within the scope of the Inquiries Act 2005, which repeals section 49: for a discussion, see p 298, *post*.

[143] *Inquiry into the Death of Stephen Lawrence*, 1997–1998.

[144] *R v Chairman of Stephen Lawrence Inquiry, ex parte A* (1988) *The Times*, 25 July.

(b) Inquiries established under the Inquiries Act 2005

The Inquiries Act 2005 provides a framework under which a Minister can establish an inquiry into events that have caused public concern. The procedures adopted by such an inquiry are for the chairman to determine, but the Act confers specific powers to compel the production of documents, to summon witnesses, and to receive evidence on oath.[145] Inquiries that are subject to the Act must generally sit in public and the proceedings may be broadcast or recorded at the chairman's discretion.[146] However, the chairman also has a discretion to restrict publicity if he considers this to be conducive to the inquiry or in the wider public interest.[147]

The predecessor to the 2005 Act—the Tribunals of Inquiry (Evidence) Act 1921—was rarely used,[148] and its procedures were usually reserved for inquires into allegations of misconduct on the part of public authorities. The second Bloody Sunday Inquiry is a notable example: at the time of writing, this inquiry had been ongoing for seven years and its eventual cost was expected to reach £155 million.[149] In 1966 the Royal Commission on Tribunals of Inquiry[150] made a number of recommendations regarding inquiries under the 1921 Act. In particular, it recommended that any person affected by allegations against him should have the right to be legally represented and to cross-examine witnesses, and that any testimony given by such a person should not be admissible as evidence in subsequent criminal or civil proceedings.[151] It also recommended that the facts should be presented to the inquiry panel by independent counsel. To date none of these recommendations have been adopted, and the extent to which cross-examination and legal representation are permitted is still a matter for individual inquiry chairmen.[152]

(c) Non-statutory inquiries

Some inquiries are established on a non-statutory basis, which means that they lack any formal powers of investigation and can only be effective to the extent that those involved are willing to co-operate. Inquiries that could have national security implications or cause political embarrassment are often conducted in this way. They are usually chaired by senior judges and may sit in private, though their findings are generally made public. A good example of a non-statutory inquiry was the inquiry into the export of arms to Iraq in breach of international embargoes.[153] It was established

---

[145] Sections 17 and 21.   [146] Section 18.   [147] Section 19.

[148] See Winetrobe, 'Inquiries After Scott: the Return of the Tribunal of Inquiry' [1997] PL 18.

[149] Department for Constitutional Affairs, *Effective Inquiries* (2004) CP 12/04, Annex B. The inquiry was commenced in 1998. For the first inquiry, see *Inquiry into Disorders in Northern Ireland ('Bloody Sunday')* Cmd 556, which reported in 1972.

[150] Cmnd 3121. The Commission was chaired by Lord Justice Salmon.

[151] Similar recommendations have been made with regard to testimony given in coroners' courts: see p 269 *ante*.

[152] For an argument that there is already a presumption in favour of allowing legal representation, see Willmott, 'A Presumption of Legal Representation at Judicial Inquiries' (2003) 12(2) Nott LJ 34. Note also that s 40 of the new Act allows chairmen to award payments of 'reasonable amounts' to witnesses, including awards in respect of legal representation.

[153] *Inquiry into the Export of Defence Equipment and Dual-Use Goods to Iraq*, 1996.

when several prosecutions collapsed amid allegations that ministers had turned a blind eye to the illegal trade and that the businessmen involved had spied for the security services. The inquiry was chaired by Sir Richard Scott and took four years to complete. Its five-volume report criticized both ministers and officials, and generated a considerable amount of academic literature.[154]

The Hutton Inquiry into the circumstances surrounding the death of Dr David Kelly was also conducted on a non-statutory basis.[155] The government had published an intelligence dossier on Iraq shortly before the second Gulf War, and a journalist made a number of highly critical statements about the dossier in an item broadcast on BBC radio. Dr Kelly was a government scientist and he later admitted to officials in the Defence Department that he had been the journalist's 'anonymous' source. He then found himself at the centre of a very public row between the BBC and the government, and he apparently took his own life after his identity was revealed by the media. Lord Hutton's inquiry was highly critical of both the BBC and its journalist, but the government's handling of the incident was largely vindicated. This prompted concerns that the credibility of public inquiries was being undermined, with some suggesting that Lord Hutton had interpreted his terms of reference too narrowly and failed to address the real issues. In the aftermath of the Hutton Report the government established a further inquiry into the intelligence upon which it based its controversial dossier and its subsequent decision to go to war with Iraq. The inquiry was conducted by Privy Councillors under the chairmanship of Lord Butler and it reported in July 2004.[156]

A common criticism of non-statutory inquiries is that although their main function is to investigate concerns about government action, they can only be instigated by ministers. Moreover, it is for the Minister instigating an inquiry to appoint its chair and determine its terms of reference. As a matter of law however, there is nothing to prevent a member of the public from setting up his own inquiry and finding someone to chair it: the real issue is whether anyone outside the government would be able to fund one and to persuade the relevant people to participate.

The Council on Tribunals does not have any duty to keep tribunals of inquiry under review, but it is nevertheless empowered to report to the government on any procedural matters that it considers to be of special importance.[157] Following recommendations made by the Scott Report, the Council provided ministers with written guidelines for the conduct of inquiries into matters of public concern. These guidelines were published in 1996.[158]

---

[154] See, for example, Blom-Cooper, 'Witnesses and the Scott Inquiry' [1994] PL 1; Howe, 'Procedure at the Scott Inquiry' [1996] PL 445; Leigh and Lustgarten, 'Five Volumes in Search of Accountability: the Scott Report' (1996) 59(5) MLR 695; Scott, 'Procedures at Inquiries: the Duty to be Fair' (1995) 111 LQR 596.

[155] It reported in January 2004: see Blom-Cooper and Munro, 'The Hutton Inquiry' [2004] PL 472.

[156] *Review of Intelligence on Weapons of Mass Destruction* (HC Paper 898 (2004)).

[157] Tribunals and Inquiries Act 1992, s 1(1)(c).

[158] Advice to the Lord Chancellor on the Procedural Issues Arising in the Conduct of Public Inquiries set up by Ministers (1996). The role of the Council on Tribunals is discussed at p 282, *ante.*

9

THE JUDICIARY[1]

A THE JUDICIAL HIERARCHY

The twelve Lords of Appeal in Ordinary—the 'Law Lords'—perform the judicial functions of both the House of Lords[2] and the Privy Council,[3] and are currently the most senior judges in the United Kingdom. The Constitutional Reform Act 2005 provides for the creation of a new Supreme Court,[4] which means that the both the Appellate Committee of the House of Lords and the title 'Lord of Appeal' are due to be abolished. Under the Act the current Law Lords will automatically become the first Justices of the new court, but they will also lose their entitlement to sit and vote in Parliament.[5]

Next in order of seniority are the thirty-seven Lords (and Lady) Justices of Appeal.[6] Along with a number of *ex officio* members they are the permanent Court of Appeal judges, and they also sit in the Courts-Martial Appeal Court and Employment Appeal Tribunal. They can even be asked to hear High Court, Crown Court, and county court cases, but it would be unlikely in practice to find such a senior judge sitting below High Court level.[7]

Next in line are the 107 full-time High Court judges or 'puisne judges'. All puisne judges have jurisdiction to sit anywhere in the High Court, although in practice each judge is assigned to a particular division.[8] Puisne judges also hear the most serious types of Crown Court case,[9] and frequently sit alongside Lords Justices in the Court of

---

[1] See generally: Pannick, *Judges* (1987); Griffith, *The Politics of the Judiciary* (5th edn, 1997); Malleson, *The New Judiciary: The Effects of Expansion and Activism* (1999); Stevens, *The English Judges: Their Role in the Changing Constitution* (2002).

[2] See p 241 *ante.*   [3] See p 269 *ante.*

[4] See Part 3 of the Constitutional Reform Act 2005, and the discussion at p 243, *ante.*

[5] Ibid, ss 24 and 137.

[6] See p 245, *ante.* The title 'Lady Justice' has been officially recognized since January 2004: Supreme Court Act 1981, s 2(3), as amended by the Courts Act 2003, s 63(1). The Court of Appeal's first female judge was originally referred to by the masculine title.

[7] In 2003, Lords Justices of Appeal collectively sat 200 days in the High Court, accounting for just over 1 per cent of all High Court sitting days. They did not sit in the Crown Court or county courts at all during this period: *Judicial Statistics 2003*, table 9.2.

[8] See p 250, *ante.*   [9] See p 258, *ante.*

Appeal—usually in the Criminal Division. Deputy High Court judges are also appointed, and they exercise the same jurisdiction as their full-time counterparts.

Circuit judges carry out the majority of Crown Court work,[10] and in 2003 they accounted for just over 73 per cent of all sitting days in this court. However, they are also responsible for around a quarter of sitting days in the county courts, and a similar proportion of High Court work. They can even sit in the Criminal Division of the Court of Appeal if called upon, and actually did so in approximately 10 per cent of the Division's cases in 2003.[11] Circuit judges are assisted in both their criminal and civil work by deputy circuit judges and recorders, although these judges do not have jurisdiction to sit in the Court of Appeal.

District judges and deputy district judges are responsible for most county court business,[12] in addition to hearing a small number of cases in the High Court. Finally, there are the District Judges (Magistrates' Courts) and their deputies.[13] These judges were formerly known as stipendiary magistrates, and as the name indicates, they have jurisdiction to sit as justices of the peace in magistrates' courts.[14]

(a) Specific judicial offices

The Lord Chancellor. Historically, the highest judicial office in the United Kingdom has been that of Lord Chancellor, and the holder of this office has been the most senior member of the Appellate Committee of the House of Lords. He has also been an *ex officio* member of the Court of Appeal, head of the High Court's Chancery Division, 'speaker' of the House of Lords, and a Cabinet Minister. He has therefore been a member of the judicial, legislative, *and* executive branches of the state, giving him a unique position within the constitution. His executive role means that he has never had the security of tenure enjoyed by other judges, and to this day he can be replaced at the whim of the Prime Minister in the same way as any other member of government.[15]

In June 2003, the government announced plans to abolish the office of Lord Chancellor in order to achieve a more formal separation of powers.[16] The intention was to transfer the Lord Chancellor's ministerial functions to the new office of Secretary of State for Constitutional Affairs, leaving his judicial functions to be performed by the Lord Chief Justice. Lord Falconer was given the task of implementing the changes, and he was simultaneously appointed as both Lord Chancellor and Secretary of State. There was, however, widespread criticism that the government had not consulted senior judges before making the announcement, and many felt that it

---

[10] Ibid. Section 151 of the Supreme Court Act 1981 provides that unless the context requires otherwise, a reference to a judge of the Supreme Court shall not include a reference to a judge of the Crown Court.

[11] Supreme Court Act 1981, s 9; *Judicial Statistics 2003*, table 9.3.   [12] See p 255, *ante.*

[13] See p 262, *ante.*

[14] They were renamed by the Access to Justice Act 1999, s 78: see p 262, *ante.*

[15] In June 2003 for example, Lord Falconer was appointed Lord Chancellor when it became clear that his predecessor, Lord Irvine, did not support the government's plans for constitutional reform.

[16] For other aspects of the reform package, see p 243, *ante.*

had underestimated the implications of its decision.[17] The Lord Chief Justice was among those to express his concerns:[18]

[T]he announcement of 12 June . . . clearly indicated an extraordinary lack of appreciation of the significance of what was being proposed. This was followed . . . without consultation, by the transfer of the Court Service from the Lord Chancellor to the Secretary of State for Constitutional Affairs. This last action could well have been due to oversight but it demonstrates there is a lack of appreciation of the significance of the independence of the judiciary in the corridors of government.

Several weeks *after* announcing its intentions, the government did publish a consultation paper.[19] The Lord Chief Justice was ultimately persuaded of the need for reform, and on behalf of the judiciary he negotiated a lengthy Concordat with the Secretary of State.[20] This document was intended as a blueprint for the future relationship between the courts and the government, and the subsequent Constitutional Reform Bill broadly reflected its contents. The Lord Chief Justice later said that if the Concordat was accepted in its entirety it would be 'a highly satisfactory outcome',[21] but not everyone was convinced that change was necessary. Many in the House of Lords felt that abolishing the Lord Chancellor's office would *damage* judicial independence rather than enhance it, and these sentiments were echoed by the Judges' Council:[22]

The office has played a critical role in binding together the three arms of the State: the legislature, the executive and the judiciary. The office is a key pillar of the constitution. If it had not been for the office of Lord Chancellor, it is doubtful whether this country would have managed without a formal written constitution. The Lord Chancellor's wide range of responsibilities, including those of a Cabinet Minister with major responsibilities for the administration of justice, has resulted in him being a cohesive force. As Head of the Judiciary he has been able to represent the judiciary at the highest level within government . . . [he] has been the constitutional link between The Queen and the judiciary.

In the end the Judges' Council did not oppose the proposals, but many in the House of Lords did. By the time the Bill reached the House of Commons it had already been significantly amended: instead of abolishing the office of Lord Chancellor, Part 2 of what is now the Constitutional Reform Act 2005 provides for it to continue in a modified form. The Lord Chancellor will not, in future, have any judicial functions, but his role as a Member of Parliament and Cabinet Minister will continue.[23] He will

---

[17] See Stevens, 'Reform in Haste and Repent at Leisure: Iolanthe, the Lord High Executioner and *Brave New World*' (2004) 24 LS 1.

[18] Lord Woolf, 'The Rule of Law and a Change in the Constitution' (2004) 63(2) CLJ 317, at p 323.

[19] Department for Constitutional Affairs, *Constitutional Reform: Reforming the Office of the Lord Chancellor* (2003) CP 13/03.

[20] DCA, *The Lord Chancellor's Judiciary-Related Functions: Proposals* (2004). The document is widely referred to as 'the Concordat'.

[21] 'The Rule of Law and a Change in the Constitution' (2004) 63(2) CLJ 317 at p 325.

[22] Judges' Council Response to the Consultation Papers on Constitutional Reform, at para 21. The Response is available online at www.dca.gov.uk/judicial/pdfs/jcresp.pdf

[23] If anything this role is likely to be expanded, as the Act paves the way for Lord Chancellors to be appointed from the House of Commons instead of the Lords.

still be responsible for overseeing the administration of most major courts,[24] and for appointing Court Rule Committees,[25] allowing or disallowing Court Rules,[26] making and advising on judicial appointments,[27] and overseeing the funding of legal services.[28] He will not, however, be eligible to sit in any court.

The Lord Chief Justice and other senior posts. The Lord Chief Justice is President of the Criminal Division of the Court of Appeal and head of the Queen's Bench Division of the High Court. Following the decision to end the judicial role of the Lord Chancellor he is also the country's most senior judge, and the Constitutional Reform Act gives him the additional title of President of the Courts of England and Wales.[29] This office entitles him to sit in any of the ordinary courts in the jurisdiction,[30] and it carries with it a number of responsibilities. These include overseeing the arrangements for judicial education,[31] supervising the deployment of judges and allocating work within the courts,[32] issuing Practice Directions (with the concurrence of the Lord Chancellor),[33] and representing the judiciary's views to Parliament and the government.[34] Once the new arrangements have been fully implemented, it is envisaged that someone other than the Lord Chief Justice will hold the new post of President of the Queen's Bench Division.

The other Heads of Division are the Master of the Rolls (who heads the Civil Division of the Court of Appeal), the Vice-Chancellor (whose *de facto* status as head of the High Court's Chancery Division is formalised by the 2005 Act[35]), and the President of the Family Division of the High Court.

Two other senior posts are those of Head and Deputy Head of Civil Justice. These positions were created by the Courts Act 2003[36] and may be held by the Vice-Chancellor, the Master of the Rolls, or any of the Lords Justices of Appeal. In addition, the Constitutional Reform Act provides for the creation of a further six senior posts. These are: Head and Deputy Head of Criminal Justice, Head and Deputy Head of Family Justice, and President and Deputy President of the Supreme Court.[37]

B THE CONSTITUTIONAL POSITION OF JUDGES

There is much debate about whether judges are 'servants' of the Crown. One view is that they *are* servants, as they are technically appointed by the Queen and are paid out

---

[24] With the exception of the Appellate Committee of the House of Lords: Courts Act 2003, s 1.
[25] See p 230, *ante*.   [26] Constitutional Reform Act 2005, s 12; Schedule 1.
[27] See p 313, *post*.
[28] See p 371, *post*. Some of the Lord Chancellor's other functions are considered at p 19, *ante*.
[29] 2005 Act, s 7(1).   [30] Ibid, s 7(3); (4).   [31] Ibid, s 7(2)(b).
[32] Ibid, s 7(2)(c).   [33] Ibid, s 13; Schedule 2.   [34] Ibid, ss 5(1); 7(2)(a).
[35] Ibid, Schedule 4, para 115. The Vice-Chancellor will in future be called 'Chancellor of the High Court'.
[36] Section 62.
[37] 2005 Act, ss 8, 9, and 24. The Lord Chief Justice (or a person appointed by him) will be *ex officio* Head of Criminal Justice, and the President of the Family Division will be *ex officio* Head of Family Justice.

of the Consolidated Fund. There is no doubt, however, that judges cannot be controlled in the exercise of their office by either Parliament or the executive, and judicial
independence is a fundamental principle of English law. This independence is essential if the courts are to perform their constitutional role of reviewing executive action.
The idea is closely linked to the doctrine of the separation of powers, which for many
judges is a cornerstone of the constitution:[38]

It is a feature of the peculiarly British conception of the separation of powers that Parliament, the executive and the courts have each their distinct and largely exclusive domain.
Parliament has a legally unchallengeable right to make whatever laws it thinks right. The
executive carries on the administration of the country in accordance with the powers
conferred on it by law. The courts interpret the laws, and see that they are obeyed.

It is clear, however, that the separation of powers within the UK is incomplete,[39] and
the *balance* of powers between the legislature, executive, and judiciary is unequal. The
legislative supremacy of Parliament was described by Wade as 'the ultimate political
fact' upon which the system hangs,[40] and the traditional view is that this supremacy is
unrestricted.[41] The UK does not have a written constitution with a superior status to
ordinary laws, and as 'the weakest and least dangerous department of government'[42]
the judiciary has no authority to strike down legislation as unconstitutional or
invalid.[43] Yet within this framework there is room for genuine debate about the limits
of judicial authority, and about the proper relationship between the courts and the
other 'departments of government'.

1 THE CHANGING POLITICAL CLIMATE

Since the 1940s most governments have enjoyed large majorities in the House of
Commons, and this has enabled them to control the legislative agenda. The post-war
era was characterized by political consensus, but the two main parties became more
polarized and ideological during the 1970s, and the political climate since then has
been distinctly adversarial. Successive governments have used their large majorities to
steer controversial laws through Parliament, prompting Lord Hailsham's famous
warning that the UK was becoming an 'elective dictatorship'.[44] Disputes with a

---

[38] *R* v *Secretary of State for the Home Department, ex parte Fire Brigades' Union* [1995] 2 AC 513 at 567,
[1995] 2 All ER 244 at 267, per Lord Mustill. See also, *Duport Steels* v *Sirs* [1980] 1 All ER 529 at 541, [1980] 1
WLR 142 at 157, per Lord Diplock.

[39] Given that the UK does not have a written constitution and that it draws its Ministers from the
legislature, several academics have questioned whether there is a separation of powers at all: see, e.g. Hood
Phillips, 'A Constitutional Myth: Separation of Powers' (1977) 93 LQR 11.

[40] Wade, 'The Basis of Legal Sovereignty' [1955] CLJ 172 at p 188.

[41] This view of parliamentary supremacy is closely associated with the work of Dicey: see *Introduction to
the Study of the Law of the Constitution* (10th edn, 1959).

[42] See Lord Steyn: 'The Weakest and Least Dangerous Department of Government' [1997] PL 84.

[43] But see the discussion at p 312, *post*.

[44] In 1976: see Lewis, *Lord Hailsham: A Life* (1997) at p 136. Lord Hailsham ceased to voice such concerns
when he was made Lord Chancellor a few years later.

political dimension have frequently come before the courts, and the courts have responded by developing more sophisticated principles of review. Since the 1980s, some Law Lords have felt compelled to break the convention against speaking in legislative debates,[45] and the rules preventing judges from commenting on matters of public interest have been abandoned.[46] These developments, along with the involvement of judges in several high-profile inquiries,[47] have created the impression that the judiciary is being drawn into the political arena.

(a) Judicial inquiries

Governments often appoint senior judges to head inquiries into matters of public interest. A government with a difficult or sensitive issue to address may rely on the 'borrowed authority'[48] of a judge to conduct an independent review, and to use his forensic ability to examine witnesses and sift evidence. Inevitably however, the outcome of an inquiry rarely pleases everyone, and judges cannot be expected to produce non-political solutions to political problems. The Denning Report into the Profumo scandal,[49] the Scott Inquiry into the sale of arms to Iraq,[50] and the Hutton Inquiry into the death of Dr David Kelly,[51] are just three examples of inquiries that have generated intense controversy,[52] and which have arguably had a negative impact on the appearance of judicial impartiality.

(b) Judicial review and judicial activism

Judicial review[53] is the principal mechanism for holding the executive accountable to the law, and it is therefore central to the constitutional role of the courts. Over the last twenty years the courts have developed more sophisticated principles of review, and in GCHQ[54] and other cases they have extended the application of these principles to new situations. The courts' powers of review have been further enhanced by the Human Rights Act 1998, and judicial review has thus assumed considerable importance in recent years. This partly explains why the last two decades have witnessed an unprecedented level of conflict between the judiciary and the government. Ministers have increasingly found themselves on the receiving end of adverse judicial comment, and owing to the nature of their responsibilities—and perhaps the personalities

---

[45] See: Stevens, *The English Judges: Their Role in the Changing Constitution* (2002) at pp 93–4.

[46] The so-called 'Kilmuir rules' (named after a former Lord Chancellor) were abandoned in 1989.

[47] See p 297, *ante*.

[48] See Griffith, *The Politics of the Judiciary* (4th Edn, 1991), at pp 52–5; Drewery, 'Judicial Inquiries and Public Reassurance' [1996] PL 368.

[49] Cmnd 2152, 1963.

[50] *Inquiry into the Export of Defence Equipment and Dual-Use Goods to Iraq*, 1996.

[51] This reported in January 2004: see p 299, *ante*.

[52] The Inquiries Act 2005 is aimed at making their procedures more efficient and effective: see Department for Constitutional Affairs, *Effective Inquiries: A Consultation Paper* (2004) CP 12/04.

[53] See chapter 6.

[54] *Council of Civil Service Unions* v *Minister for the Civil Service* [1985] AC 374, [1984] 3 All ER 935. In this case it was held that the use of prerogative powers was potentially amenable to judicial review.

involved—Home Secretaries have been particularly susceptible. For example, when Kenneth Baker authorized the deportation of an asylum seeker and ignored a judge's order to return him to the jurisdiction, he became the first Minister in British legal history to be held liable for contempt of court.[55] In the Court of Appeal, Nolan LJ reminded him that:[56]

[T]he proper constitutional relationship of the executive with the courts is that the courts will respect all acts of the executive within its lawful province, and that the executive will respect all decisions of the courts as to what its lawful province is.

Another Home Secretary, Michael Howard, was defeated in the House of Lords when he purported to use prerogative powers to establish a Criminal Injuries Compensation scheme instead of implementing the scheme provided for by statute.[57] His attempts to extend the minimum prison term served by the killers of James Bulger were also thwarted by the courts.[58] On each occasion the courts asserted the importance of the separation of powers, but critics accused them of interfering in matters of policy. This was not, however, an argument accepted by Lord Steyn. Writing extra-judicially, he stated that:[59]

[T]he principle of the separation of powers is an essential constitutional safeguard of judicial independence, and the integrity of the administration of justice. It exists not to eliminate friction between the judiciary and the executive. It exists not to promote efficiency. It exists for one reason only: to prevent the rise of arbitrary executive power.

Lord Steyn was not the only judge to express his views outside the courtroom. Home Office policies on crime and sentencing were publicly criticized by the Lord Chief Justice,[60] and Laws LJ wrote various articles about the constitution and the role of the courts within it.[61] Some judges even added their voices to campaigns for a written constitution and the incorporation of the European Convention on Human Rights.[62]

The Convention was eventually given domestic effect by the Human Rights Act 1998, which requires the courts to balance individual rights against competing public

---

[55] *Re M; sub nom M v Home Office* [1994] 1 AC 377, [1993] 3 All ER 537, HL: see p 240, *ante*.

[56] [1992] QB 270 at 314–15, [1992] 4 All ER 97 at 146.

[57] *R v Secretary of State for Home Affairs, ex parte Fire Brigades Union* [1995] 2 AC 513, [1995] 2 All ER 244. The statute in question was the Criminal Justice Act 1988. Several Law Lords had spoken out against the scheme in Parliament, which effectively meant that they could not sit when this case reached the House of Lords.

[58] *R v Secretary of State for the Home Department, ex parte Venables and Thompson* [1998] AC 407, [1997] 3 All ER 97.

[59] 'The Weakest and Least Dangerous Department of Government' [1997] PL 84, at p 87.

[60] See Stevens, *The English Judges: Their Role in the Changing Constitution* (2002), at pp 50–2.

[61] See, e.g. 'Law and Democracy' [1995] PL 80; 'The Constitution: Morals and Rights' [1996] *PL* 622.

[62] See, e.g. Bingham, 'The European Convention on Human Rights: Time to Incorporate' [1993] LQR 390; Scarman, *Why Britain Needs a Written Constitution* (1992). Many academics and politicians were opposed to such developments, on the basis that they would require the courts to make political judgments: see Griffiths, 'The Political Constitution' (1979) 42 MLR 1; Lyell, 'Whither Strasbourg? Why Britain Should Think Long and Hard Before Incorporating the European Convention on Human Rights' [1997] EHRLR 132.

interest claims.[63] It also requires them to engage in creative statutory interpretation, and, wherever possible, to give effect to legislation in a manner that is compatible with Convention rights. Decisions under the Act therefore require a greater level of scrutiny than that previously adopted in judicial review cases, and this has created further opportunities for clashes with the government.

The question of how much judicial 'deference' is appropriate in human rights cases is still unresolved, but it is clear that less deference will be shown where the courts regard the subject matter of a case as falling within their own sphere of expertise.[64] Once again, this has led to conflict between the judiciary and the Home Office. A series of cases, both domestically and in Strasbourg, have effectively wrestled control of sentencing decisions from the Home Secretary.[65] The courts have also modified the interpretation of various statutes, so as to protect the right to a fair trial and to the presumption of innocence.[66] However, it is in the field of asylum and immigration that some of the most significant clashes have occurred. The government's policies in this area have been challenged in several recent cases, and at least one Home Secretary has responded by publicly attacking the courts' decisions. Thus, when Collins J held that six asylum seekers had been unlawfully denied state support,[67] the then Home Secretary, David Blunkett, complained that:[68]

Frankly, I am personally fed up with having to deal with a situation where Parliament debates issues and the judges then overturn them. I don't want any mixed messages going out so I am making it absolutely clear that we don't accept what Justice Collins has said.

The same judge had previously ruled that detaining asylum seekers at 'reception centres' was unlawful.[69] This decision was later overturned on appeal,[70] but not before the Secretary of State had complained that his policies were being thwarted by unaccountable judges.[71] Mr Blunkett was further infuriated when the Special Immigration Appeals Commission—again chaired by Collins J—declared that the

---

[63] For a discussion, see p 165, *ante*.

[64] *R (on the application of Prolife Alliance) v BBC* [2003] UKHL 23 at [136], [2004] 1 AC 185 at [136], [2003] 2 All ER 977, per Lord Walker; *International Transport Roth GmbH v Secretary of State for the Home Department* [2002] EWCA Civ 158, [2003] QB 728, [2002] HRLR 31, per Laws LJ. For further discussion, see p 165, *ante*.

[65] See p 177, *ante*. See also: Amos, 'R v Secretary of State for the Home Department, ex parte Anderson: Ending the Home Secretary's Sentencing Role' (2004) 67(1) MLR 108.

[66] See, e.g. *R v A (No 2)* [2001] UKHL 25, [2002] 1 AC 45, [2001] 3 All ER 1; *R v Lambert* [2001] UKHL 37, [2002] 2 AC 545, [2001] 3 All ER 577.

[67] *R (on the application of Q) v Secretary of State for the Home Department* [2003] EWHC 195 (Admin), *The Times*, 20 February. See also, *R (on the application of Limbuela) v Secretary of State for the Home Department* [2004] EWHC 219 (Admin), *The Times*, 9 February, QBD; [2004] EWCA Civ 540, [2004] QB 1140, [2004] 3 WLR 561, CA.

[68] These comments were made in a radio interview and reported by *The Independent*, 20 February 2003: see also Bradley, 'Judicial Independence Under Attack' [2003] PL 397. Justice Collins' decision was upheld by the Court of Appeal on slightly modified grounds: [2003] EWCA Civ 364, [2004] QB 36, [2003] 2 All ER 905.

[69] *R (on the application of Saadi) v Secretary of State for the Home Department* [2001] EWHC 670 (Admin).

[70] [2002] UKHL 41, [2002] 4 All ER 785, [2002] 1 WLR 3131.

[71] Stevens, *The English Judges: Their Role in the Changing Constitution* (2002) at pp 130–1.

detention without trial of suspected foreign terrorists was incompatible with the Human Rights Act.[72] In a landmark decision the Commission's ruling was endorsed by the House of Lords,[73] forcing the government into a major rethink of its anti-terror laws. The internment provisions were subsequently replaced with a new system of control orders,[74] and all of those detained were eventually released. Other decisions of note include the ruling that an asylum seeker's benefits could not be withdrawn without notification,[75] and the declaration that penalties applied to hauliers who assisted illegal immigrants were incompatible with Convention rights.[76]

The issues raised by these and other cases have continued to divide lawyers and politicians. Many feel that the courts have been seeking to uphold the rule of law, and they view the government's reaction to certain decisions as an affront to judicial independence. Indeed, when Lord Irvine was Lord Chancellor, he issued a tacit reminder to his own Cabinet colleagues about the need to respect judicial authority:[77]

In a democracy under the rule of law, it is not mature to cheer the judges when a win is secured and boo them when a loss is suffered . . .

[The Human Rights Act] was drafted sensitively to the balance of forces within our substantially unwritten constitution. And that means the government can accept adverse court decisions, not as defeats, but as steps on the road to better governance . . .

In giving greater responsibility to our judges, we are merely confirming that ours is a society governed by the rule of law . . . We ask our judges to decide many difficult cases. Some are between private citizens. Some are criminal appeals. Others are against ministers; and of these, some are lost and some are won. That is neither avoidable nor unconstitutional. It is simply proof that 'be you ever so high, the law is above you'.

Others however, would argue that the courts have at times undermined the will of Parliament, and that concerns about judicial independence are misplaced:[78]

Once appointed, judges of the English High Court and above can be removed only on an address by both Houses of Parliament, which means that they are virtually irremovable. So, against whom does the judiciary need protection? Against the government? Yet, there has

---

[72] *A v Secretary of State for the Home Department* [2002] HRLR 45. Collins J later ordered the release of one detainee, having described evidence presented by the Home Office as 'inaccurate' and 'clearly misleading': *Secretary of State v M*, unreported, 8 March 2004; affirmed [2002] EWCA Civ 1502, [2004] QB 335, [2003] 1 All ER 816.

[73] [2004] UKHL 56, [2005] 2 WLR 87. The significance of this case was such that it was heard by nine of the twelve Law Lords. Coincidentally, Mr Blunkett resigned as Home Secretary the day before their Lordships delivered their opinions, and it was left to his successor to plan the government's response.

[74] Prevention of Terrorism Act 2005: the background to this legislation is discussed further at pp 161 and 178, *ante*.

[75] *R (on the application of Anufrijeva) v Secretary of State for the Home Department* [2003] UKHL 36, [2004] 1 AC 604, [2003] 3 All ER 827.

[76] *International Transport Roth GmbH v Secretary of State for the Home Department* [2002] EWCA Civ 158, [2003] QB 728, [2002] HRLR 31.

[77] 'The Impact of the Human Rights Act: Parliament, the Courts and the Executive' [2003] PL 307, at pp 323–4.

[78] Arnheim, 'The Rule of Law or the Rule of Lawyers?' (2004) 154 NLJ 776.

never been a time when government decisions have been struck down with greater abandon than now, and even Acts of Parliament have been savaged by the courts . . .

The real loser is democracy. In a parliamentary democracy like the UK, legislation is intended to give expression to the will of the people. If it fails to do so, the people can turn the government out at the next election. But for unelected judges to make up the law as they go along is contrary not only to the doctrine of the separation of powers, but is also a usurpation of the role of Parliament.

Whichever view is taken, the relationship between the government and the judiciary has undoubtedly been tested over the last two decades, and it is said that Ministers have even considered amending the Human Rights Act so as to curb the courts' power. Yet it is not only the courtroom that clashes have occurred: the enactment of a number of recent statutes has also proved contentious, and two of these are discussed below.

(c) The Constitutional Reform Act 2005

The original aims of the Constitutional Reform Bill have been considered in detail elsewhere in this book, but they can be broadly summarized as follows:

(a) to abolish the post of Lord Chancellor and transfer his judicial responsibilities to the Lord Chief Justice, leaving his ministerial functions to the Secretary of State for Constitutional Affairs;

(b) to replace the Appellate Committee of the House of Lords with an independent Supreme Court, so that the most senior judges cease to occupy seats in Parliament; and

(c) to establish an independent Judicial Appointments Commission.

On its face, the Bill was intended to achieve a more formal separation of powers, and a judiciary that is more transparently independent of government. One might therefore have expected it to be well received by most judges, but in fact, initial reactions ranged from the mildly sceptical to the deeply suspicious. The government's failure to consult judges before announcing its decision didn't help matters, and the Lord Chief Justice could barely conceal his anger that the reforms were thought to be 'capable of being achieved by a press release.'[79] The biggest cause for concern was the proposed abolition of the Lord Chancellor's office.[80] The Judges' Council expressed serious reservations about this proposal, pointing out that the new Secretary of State would be a political figure, who would not be constrained by 'judicial responsibilities and constitutional conventions'.[81] The Law Lords agreed that the Lord Chancellor's role had been a safeguard of judicial independence, and that 'the constitution would be gravely

---

[79] Lord Woolf, 'The Rule of Law and a Change in the Constitution' (2004) 63(2) CLJ 317, at p 320.

[80] See p 20, *ante*.

[81] Response to the Consultation Papers on Constitutional Reform; available at www.dca.gov.uk/judicial/pdfs/jcresp.pdf.

weakened if that safeguard were removed and not replaced.'[82] The judiciary's main concern was whether a Secretary of State, who might not necessarily be a lawyer, could properly defend judicial interests within government. Their unease was exacerbated by the fact that certain politicians appeared not to respect their authority,[83] and they had previously opposed plans to transfer the Court Service to the Home Office for similar reasons:[84]

It was disturbing that—at that time—it was not appreciated within government that it was inappropriate for the department that most frequently had to defend proceedings for judicial review in the courts and that had to lead responsibility for criminal justice policy to be in charge of what should be seen as an impartial Court Service.

Judges were more ambivalent about the plans for a Supreme Court, but six of the twelve Law Lords publicly opposed the proposals, and eight were in agreement that if the reforms *did* go ahead, at least some of the Court's members should continue to sit in the House of Lords.[85] Lord Hobhouse, for example, argued that the Lord Chief Justice and other senior figures should retain their parliamentary seats so that they could continue to speak on behalf of the judiciary.[86] By the time that the Bill was presented to Parliament, many of the judges' preferences had been accommodated, and the Concordat[87] negotiated by the Lord Chief Justice had helped to allay some of their concerns.

The proposed abolition of the Lord Chancellor's office also faced opposition from within Parliament, and the government was 'persuaded' to accept that the office should continue in a modified form. The Constitutional Reform Act 2005 thus removes the Lord Chancellor's judicial functions[88] whilst reminding him of the need to defend judicial independence.[89] It also removes the requirement for him to be either a lawyer or a peer,[90] which means that he will, in effect, be a Secretary of State in all but name. The suggestion that certain judges should retain their parliamentary seats was also rejected by the government, and the Act leaves it to the Lord Chief Justice to ensure that their interests are represented by other means.[91]

(d) The 'mother of all ouster clauses'

While the debate about constitutional reform was still ongoing, a second government Bill was generating further controversy. The main purpose of what is now the Asylum and Immigration (Treatment of Claimants) Act 2004 was to create a new, single-tier

---

[82] The Law Lords' Response to the Government's Consultation Paper on Constitutional Reform: A Supreme Court for the United Kingdom, CP 11/03 July 2003, at para 5.

[83] See the discussion at p 307, *ante*.

[84] Lord Woolf, 'The Rule of Law and a Change in the Constitution' (2004) 63(2) CLJ 317 at p 323.

[85] The Law Lords' Response (*ante*, n 82), at paras 2 and 21.   [86] Ibid, at para F.2.

[87] See p 302, *ante*.

[88] Most of these are transferred to the Lord Chief Justice by Schedules 2 and 4.

[89] Section 3(6); s 3(5) prohibits *all* Ministers from seeking to influence judicial decisions.

[90] Section 2: see p 21, *ante*.   [91] Sections 5(1) and 7(2)(a).

tribunal to deal with appeals in immigration and asylum cases.[92] In what was described as the 'mother of all ouster clauses',[93] clause 11 of the Bill purported to exclude the tribunal's decisions from any possibility of judicial review. Previous attempts to oust the jurisdiction of the courts have been interpreted narrowly: it has generally been assumed that Parliament would not have intended to prevent the review of a decision made without its authority.[94] Clause 11 however, was clearly drafted with the intention of making it 'judge-proof'.[95] If enacted, it would have expressly precluded the courts from considering claims based on: (i) lack of jurisdiction; (ii) irregularity; (iii) error of law; (vi) breach of natural justice; or (v) any other matter. Senior judges publicly condemned the clause, and the Lord Chief Justice was particularly scathing:[96]

The provision has to be read to appreciate the lengths to which the government has gone to try and exclude the possibility of intervention by the courts. Extensive consultation took place with myself and other members of the judiciary before the Bill was introduced . . . our advice was that a clause of the nature now included in the Bill was fundamentally in conflict with the rule of law and should not be contemplated by any government if it had respect for the rule of law.

We advised that the clause was unlikely to be effective and identified why. The result was that clause 11 was extended to close the loopholes we had identified, instead of being abandoned as we had argued . . . we pointed out that the danger of the proposed ouster clause was that it could bring the judiciary, the executive and the legislature into conflict. Apparently this was of little concern . . .

I am not over-dramatising the position if I indicate that, if this clause were to become law, it would be so inconsistent with the spirit of mutual respect between the different arms of government that it could be the catalyst for a campaign for a written constitution . . . The response of the government and the House of Lords to the chorus of criticism of clause 11 will produce the answer to the question of whether our freedoms can be left in their hands under an unwritten constitution.

In the end, the level of opposition to the clause forced the government to withdraw it,[97] and the compromise reached means that the Tribunal's decisions can be reviewed on the grounds of an error of law.[98] It remains to be seen, however, whether a constitutional crisis was avoided or merely postponed.

---

[92] See p 288, *ante.*   [93] See Jowell, 'Heading for a Constitutional Crisis' (2004) 154 NLJ 401.

[94] *Anisminic* v *Foreign Compensation Commission* [1969] 2 AC 147, [1969] 1 All ER 208: see p 64, *ante.*

[95] Jowell, 'Heading for a Constitutional Crisis' (2004) 154 NLJ 401.

[96] Lord Woolf, 'The Rule of Law and a Change in the Constitution' (2004) 63(2) CLJ 317, at pp 328–9.

[97] Lord Falconer, 659 HL Official Report (5th series) col 51, 15 March 2004. For a discussion, see Le Sueur, 'Three Strikes and it's out? The UK Government's Strategy to Oust Judicial Review from Immigration and Asylum Decision-Making' [2004] PL 225.

[98] Nationality, Immigration and Asylum Act 2002, s 103A: discussed at p 289, *ante.*

2 A NEW BALANCE OF POWERS?

Lord Woolf is one of a small but growing number of judges to assert a more powerful role for the courts. Before he was appointed as Lord Chief Justice, he said that if Parliament was to do the unthinkable and attempt to abolish judicial review, he would:[99]

[C]onsider there were advantages in making it clear that ultimately there are even limits on the supremacy of Parliament which it is the courts' inalienable responsibility to identify and uphold.

Similar comments have been made by Laws LJ:[100]

[T]hose who exercise democratic political power must have limits set to what they may do: limits which they are not allowed to overstep . . . the doctrine of Parliamentary sovereignty cannot be vouched by Parliamentary legislation; a higher order law confers it and must limit it.

Lord Justice Sedley has presented an alternative view, based on:[101]

[A] bi-polar sovereignty of the Crown in Parliament and the Crown in the courts, to each of which the crown's ministers are answerable—politically to Parliament, legally to the courts.

Not only are these judges asserting their own role within the constitution, they are also re-examining what is required by the rule of law.[102] Lord Steyn's judgment in *Pierson*, for example, suggests that in addition to requiring some lawful authority for government action, the rule of law might also be capable of tempering Parliament's supremacy:[103]

Unless there is the clearest provision to the contrary, Parliament must be presumed not to legislate contrary to the rule of law. And the rule of law enforces minimum standards of fairness.

By arguing that Parliament must be *presumed* to legislate in accordance with the rule of law, Lord Steyn avoids making a direct challenge to Parliament's authority. Lord Justice Laws adopted a similar approach in *Thoburn* v *Sunderland City Council*, when he asserted that there are 'constitutional statutes' which can only be repealed by express words.[104] Lord Woolf's approach is more direct however, and he suggests that

---

[99] Woolf, 'Droit Public—English Style' [1995] PL 57 at p 69.

[100] Laws, 'Law and Democracy' [1995] PL 80.

[101] Sedley, 'Human Rights: A Twenty-First Century Agenda' [1995] PL 386.

[102] In a work of this nature it is not possible to give a detailed account of the issues, but see: Allan, 'The Limits of Parliamentary Sovereignty' [1985] PL 614; Allan, 'The Conceptual Foundations of Judicial Review: Conceptual Conundrum or Interpretative Inquiry?' (2002) 61(1) CLJ 87; Craig, 'Public Law, Political Theory and Legal Theory' [2000] PL 211.

[103] *R* v *Secretary of State for the Home Department, ex parte Pierson* [1998] AC 539 at 575, [1997] 3 All ER 577 at 607. The rule of law is explicitly recognized as a 'constitutional principle' by s 1 of the Constitutional Reform Act 2005: the Act does not, however, attempt to define it.

[104] [2002] EWHC 195 (Admin) at [60], [2003] QB 151 at [60], [2002] 4 All ER 156. For a discussion, see p 30, *ante*.

the rule of law may impose modest but substantive limits on Parliament's ability to legislate.[105] The ideas expressed by these judges may seem radical, but they are a reminder of Hart's idea that supremacy is 'a rule of recognition',[106] and that its existence depends on Parliament's authority being accepted as legitimate. In other words, if Parliament purports to legislate in an arbitrary or unjust manner, its authority to do so may be called into question.

These views are by no means universally—or even generally—accepted,[107] and outside the field of European law[108] no judge in modern times has attempted to disapply an Act of Parliament. Moreover, even if it could be agreed that there *should* be limits on legislative power, many would dispute whether an unelected and unaccountable judiciary should have the authority to police those limits. Nevertheless, there are signs that the UK is 'inching towards becoming a constitutional state',[109]and if this trend continues it is likely to lead to a more influential—and perhaps more equal—role for the judges.

C JUDICIAL APPOINTMENTS AND SECURITY OF TENURE

1 APPOINTMENTS

(a) The present system

The Lords of Appeal in Ordinary and the Lords Justices of Appeal are currently appointed by the Queen on the advice of the Prime Minister, as are the Heads of Division for both the High Court and the Court of Appeal. High Court judges, circuit judges, recorders, and district judges (magistrates' courts) are appointed by the Queen on the advice of the Lord Chancellor, while district judges and lay magistrates are appointed by the Lord Chancellor directly.

Until recently, only experienced barristers were eligible for most judicial appointments, and solicitors could only be appointed at the level of recorder or district judge. However, the Courts and Legal Services Act 1990 removed these barriers by linking

---

[105] See the above extracts. Woolf has described the legislative intent approach as 'a harmless fairytale': see 'Droit Public—English Style' [1995] PL 57. See also *R (on the application of Jackson) v A–G* [2005] EWCA Civ 126, *The Times* 17 February 2005, which suggests that there may be modest limits on the use that can be made of the Parliament Acts procedure (discussed at p 32, *ante*).

[106] *The Concept of Law* (1961).

[107] See, e.g. Lord Irvine of Lairg, 'Judges and Decision Makers: the Theory and Practice of Wednesbury Review' [1996] PL 59.

[108] See pp 29 and 135, *ante*.

[109] Steyn, 'Democracy Through Law' [2002] EHRLR 723 at p 734. Stevens agrees that 'it is becoming slowly more accurate to describe Britain as a constitutional democracy rather than a parliamentary democracy': *The English Judges: Their Role in the Changing Constitution* (2002) at p 148.

the criteria for appointment to its new provisions on rights of audience.[110] Thus, Lords of Appeal in Ordinary must now have held high judicial office for two years or have a Supreme Court qualification,[111] while Lords Justices of Appeal must have a ten-year High Court qualification or experience as a High Court judge.[112] High Court judges require a ten-year High Court qualification or experience as a circuit judge, and circuit judges must have a ten-year Crown Court or county court qualification.[113] This means that it is now possible for a solicitor to be appointed directly to the High Court bench.

The Department for Constitutional Affairs has a Legal and Judicial Services Group, which assists the Lord Chancellor in making judicial appointments. Its staff conduct interviews, gather information about potential candidates, and administer the selection procedure according to the Lord Chancellor's guidelines. In addition to possessing the required legal knowledge and experience, the guidelines state that judicial candidates must satisfy a number of other criteria. These include having a high level of intellectual ability, being of sound judgement, having good communication and listening skills, being fair and impartial, and being mature, courteous, and of sound temperament.[114]

Appointments at the level of circuit judge and below are advertised nationally, and potential candidates are short-listed by a panel comprising a judge, an independent non-lawyer, and an official from the Department for Constitutional Affairs. Since 1998, High Court vacancies have also been advertised, though the Lord Chancellor reserves the right to make appointments at this level by personal invitation. All appointments at appellate level continue to be made by invitation only. In 2003 an independent audit of High Court appointments concluded that the 'dual route' system was unfair to both applicants and nominees, and it recommended that all future appointments should be made by application.[115]

(b) Reform: a new way of appointing judges

The independence of the judiciary is of fundamental importance, and many feel strongly that the power to appoint judges should not be in the government's hands. The judiciary is a predominantly male, white, middle-class, and middle-aged institution, and some argue that it has an inherent tendency to support 'conventional, settled and established interests'.[116] Yet English judges are said to rank highly on any

---

[110] See ss 27 and 71.

[111] Appellate Jurisdiction Act 1876, s 6, as amended by the Courts and Legal Services Act 1990. Section 71(3) of the 1990 Act defines a Supreme Court qualification to mean a right of audience for all Supreme Court proceedings (see p 348, post). In practice the Law Lords are generally appointed from the ranks of the Court of Appeal, although exceptionally a first instance judge may be appointed.

[112] This means having a right of audience for all High Court proceedings: ibid. See p 348, post.

[113] Within the meaning of the 1990 Act, s 71(3).

[114] Judicial Appointments in England and Wales (2003), ch 1.

[115] Her Majesty's Commissioners for Judicial Appointments, Report of the Commissioners' Review of the High Court 2003 Competition (2004) at para E.4.8.

[116] Griffith, The Politics of the Judiciary (5th edn, 1997), at p 20.

international scale of objectivity,[117] and few would seriously contend that they are subject to direct political interference. Indeed, the last two decades have been a period of 'unprecedented antagonism between judiciary and government'.[118] Nevertheless, the right to a fair trial before an 'independent and impartial tribunal'[119] requires judges to not only *be* independent, but to be demonstrably so. Now that this right has been given statutory effect by the Human Rights Act, concerns about the appointments system have gained momentum.

In 1999 Sir Leonard Peach carried out an independent scrutiny of the system, and on the basis of his recommendations the government established a Commission for Judicial Appointments.[120] However, the Commission's role is merely advisory and supervisory: it audits the selection process and can consider individual complaints, but beyond this its powers are limited and it has no direct role in making appointments. In 2003 it carried out an audit of appointments to the High Court bench, and it concluded that fundamental changes were needed:[121]

Our review of the 2003 High Court appointment competition has left us convinced that radical change is needed, to bring the system into line with best practice in other fields. We would be concerned to see any further High Court Judge selection processes take place on the basis of the present system, which we have found to be seriously lacking in transparency and accountability.

By the time that the audit was completed, the government had already published a consultation paper setting out is plans for a more powerful commission:[122]

In a modern democratic society it is no longer acceptable for judicial appointments to be entirely in the hands of a Government Minister. For example the judiciary is often involved in adjudicating on the lawfulness of actions of the Executive. And so the appointments system must be, and must be seen to be, independent of Government. It must be transparent. It must be accountable. And it must inspire public confidence.

More than half of those who responded to the consultation felt that the Commission should be able to make actual appointments, and a further 13 per cent (including the Bar Council, Law Society and Judges' Council) said that it should at least be able to make appointments to the lower ranks.[123] The government had emphasized the need

---

[117] Stevens, *The English Judges: Their Role in the Changing Constitution* (2002) at p 82.

[118] Lord Irvine of Lairg, 'The Impact of the Human Rights Act: Parliament, the Courts and the Executive' [2003] PL 307, at p 323. Although Lord Irvine wrote these words as Lord Chancellor and was referring to the period before the Labour government took office, the antagonism between the courts and the executive has actually increased subsequently. For a discussion, see p 307, *ante*.

[119] Article 6, ECHR: see p 180, *ante*.

[120] *Appointment Processes of Judges and Queen's Counsel in England and Wales.* The Commission was established in 2001. For a discussion, see The Law Society, *Broadening the Bench* (2000), ch 5.

[121] *Review of the High Court 2003 Competition* (supra, n 115) at para E.10.2.

[122] DCA, *Constitutional Reform: A New Way of Appointing Judges* (2003) CP 10/03, foreword.

[123] DCA, *Constitutional Reform: A New Way of Appointing Judges—Summary of Responses to the Consultation*, January 2004. See also: Malleson, 'Creating a Judicial Appointments Commission: Which Model Works Best?' [2004] PL 102; The Law Society, *Broadening the Bench* (2000).

for accountability, and its preference was for a 'recommending commission' which would leave the final decision to the Minister. However, it was persuaded that the Minister's discretion should be kept to a minimum, and this is reflected in the provisions that were eventually included in the Constitutional Reform Act 2005.

The Act provides that the Commission itself should comprise six lay members, five judges, a solicitor, a barrister, a tribunal member, and one lay justice. One of the lay members must be appointed as chairman.[124] The procedures for selecting the different categories of Commissioner are rather complicated, but they require the Lord Chancellor to consult with the Judges' Council, the Bar Council, the Law Society, and other bodies.[125] Nigel Wicks was announced as the Commission's first chairman in April 2005.

For appointments to the High Court bench and lower judicial ranks, the Act requires the Commission to determine its own selection procedure and to recommend a single candidate to the Minister.[126] The Lord Chancellor has the power to reject the initial selection and to ask the Commission to reconsider or put forward an alternative. However, if he does reject the Commission's preferred candidate, he must then appoint either (a) the next candidate selected, or (b) the Commission's original choice.[127] If at the first stage the Lord Chancellor merely asks the Commission to *reconsider* its selection, he will be entitled to reject the candidate put forward at the second stage (who may or may not be the same person), but he must then appoint the next selection. Though the rules are again complicated, they mean in essence that the Commission will never be required to put forward more than two or three selections for each post, and that the Lord Chancellor will only ever have one right of rejection. The Act sets out similar arrangements for the appointment of the Lord Chief Justice, Heads of Division, and Lords Justices of Appeal, but the Commission is required to convene a special selection panel before making any recommendation. The precise membership of this panel is determined by the nature of the appointment.[128] At all levels the Commission must make its selections on the basis of merit and good character,[129] and must take into account any guidelines issued by the Lord Chancellor.[130]

When a vacancy arises in the Supreme Court,[131] the Lord Chancellor will be required to convene a panel comprising the President of the Supreme Court, the Deputy President, and a member of each of the appointments bodies for England and Wales, Scotland, and Northern Ireland.[132] That panel will in turn be required to consult senior judges and the relevant Minister for each of the UK jurisdictions.[133] The Lord Chancellor will again have only one right of rejection,[134] and the actual

---

[124] See Schedule 12, part 1. This composition is more varied than that originally envisaged by the government: its consultation paper had proposed (at paras 118–121) that there should be five lay members, five judges, and five lawyers.

[125] Ibid.   [126] Section 88.   [127] Section 90.   [128] Sections 67–84.

[129] Section 63.   [130] Section 65.   [131] See p 243, *ante.*   [132] Schedule 8, part 1.

[133] Section 27: for England and Wales the Lord Chancellor is the relevant Minister.

[134] Section 29.

appointment of these judges will be formally made by the Prime Minister:[135] the Lord Chancellor's role will be to notify him of the selection.

As outlined previously, section 3 of the 2005 Act means that all Ministers will have a duty to uphold judicial independence, and to refrain from attempting to improperly influence judicial decisions. It further provides that the Lord Chancellor must have regard to the need to *defend* judicial independence, and must ensure that judges have the support necessary to enable them to perform their functions. The Act also provides for the appointment of a Judicial Appointments and Conduct Ombudsman, with the power to investigate complaints about appointments and disciplinary matters.[136]

It should be noted, however, that not everyone is convinced of the need to limit political involvement in the appointments process. Writing in 2002, more than a year before the government's proposals were announced, Robert Stevens argued that:[137]

Judges choosing judges is the antithesis of democracy. In all major common law countries em;the US, Canada, Australia and South Africa—the executive chooses the judiciary, although sometimes with advice from a Judicial Appointments Commission. To hand over the appointment of judges to a commission might well ensure bland appointments. The courts do have important political powers and responsibilities . . . the choice of judges is too important to be left to a quango . . . At the very least, if there is to be a Constitutional or Supreme Court, its judges must be chosen by elected officials and subject to examination by a democratic body.

(c) Diversity in the judiciary

Members of the judiciary continue to be drawn from a fairly narrow section of society. The first female Law Lord was appointed in January 2004, but there were only two Lady Justices in the Court of Appeal at this time, and less than 7 per cent of High Court judges were women. Women were slightly better represented in the lower ranks, accounting for 11 per cent of circuit judges and almost 40 per cent of district judges,[138] but the figures for ethnic minorities were less encouraging. Ethnic minorities comprised just 3 per cent of district judges and 1.5 per cent of circuit judges, and not a single black or Asian judge was appointed above the level of the circuit bench.[139] For obvious reasons, the composition of the judiciary has always mirrored that of the Bar, and although the number of female and ethnic minority barristers is increasing, it will be some time before this is reflected in the senior judicial ranks. Changes in the law in 1990 enabled solicitors to be considered for more judicial posts,[140] and in 2002 the Lord Chancellor removed the minimum age requirements that had previously limited the field of potential applicants. Over time, these developments are likely to aid the government's efforts to recruit a more diverse judiciary, but the rate of change

---

[135] Section 26.   [136] Section 62; Schedule 13.

[137] Stevens, *The English Judges: Their Role in the Changing Constitution* (2002) at p 144.

[138] DCA, *Statistics: Women in the Judiciary* (2004)

[139] DCA, *Statistics: Ethnic Minorities in the Judiciary* (2004)   [140] See p 313, *ante.*

will also be influenced by the willingness of suitable candidates to put themselves forward. The latest DCA guidelines suggest that the Lord Chancellor is himself frustrated at the slow rate of progress:[141]

Appointments must and will be made on merit irrespective of ethnic origin, gender, marital status, political affiliation, sexual orientation, religion or disability. These are not mere words. They are firm principles . . . I want every vacancy on the Bench to be filled by the best person available, but I can only appoint the judiciary from among those who are ready and willing to do the job. I would like all eligible practitioners to have the confidence to apply.

The implication here is that suitably qualified female and ethnic minority lawyers may be less inclined than their white, male counterparts to apply for judicial office. This perception is borne out by at least some empirical research. Writing in 1991 for example, Hughes suggested that opening up the system to greater competition made it *less* likely that female judges would be appointed, because a sizeable proportion of women lawyers would not put themselves forward without direct encouragement.[142] Similarly, while the Judges' Council is broadly in favour of the new Appointments Commission, it insists that there should still be a place for headhunting:[143]

The very best candidates frequently do not actively seek appointment. In practice, many judges take an appointment only when encouraged to do so out of a sense of duty.

On the other hand, it would be naïve to rely on such headhunting to remedy centuries of inequality and under-representation. Writing extra-judicially, Lady Justice Hale (as she then was) recently observed that, 'women have been entering the [legal] profession in significant numbers for a long time . . . But [there are] . . . systemic obstacles to making sufficient progress to be regarded as a serious candidate.'[144] The long hours culture, the fact that women's lifestyles may make it more difficult to devote time to 'networking', and the fact that High Court judges are still regularly appointed from a handful of elite chambers, are all cited as examples of such obstacles. A number of academics have argued that the overwhelmingly white, male culture of the judiciary has a real impact on both the development of the law, and the treatment of those who appear before the courts.[145] For Hale however, the issue is even more fundamental:[146]

---

[141] *Judicial Appointments in England and Wales* (2003), at p 1.

[142] *The Circuit Bench: A Women's Place* (1991). Cf. Malleson and Banda, *Factors Affecting the Decision to Apply for Silk and Judicial Office* (2000) Lord Chancellor's Department Research Series 02/00; Holland and Spencer, *Without Prejudice? Sex Equality at the Bar and in the Judiciary* (1992).

[143] Judges' Council Response to the Consultation Papers on Constitutional Reform, at para 76: see www.dca.gov.uk/judicial/pdfs/jcresp.pdf. Cf. the conclusions of Her Majesty's Commissioners for Judicial Appointments: see p 314, n 115 *ante*.

[144] Hale, 'Equality and the Judiciary: Why We Should Want More Women Judges' [2001] PL 489 at 492. See also, The Law Society, *Broadening the Bench* (2000).

[145] See, e.g.: Kennedy, *Eve Was Framed: Women and British Justice* (1992); Temkin, *Rape and the Legal Process* (1987); Genn, *Paths to Justice* (1997) at p 229; Smart (ed), *Law, Crime and Sexuality: Essays in Feminism* (1995).

[146] [2001] PL 489 at 502.

Judges . . . are set in authority over others and can sometimes wield enormous power over individuals and businesses. In a democratic society, in which we are all equal citizens, it is wrong in principle for that authority to be wielded by such a very unrepresentative section of the population.

It could also be argued that the pool of potential applicants is unduly restricted by statute, because eligibility for appointment is still linked to rights of audience.[147] Although the Lord Chancellor has made it clear that he no longer regards advocacy experience as essential,[148] few solicitors hold the qualifications needed for appointment to the High Court Bench,[149] and academic lawyers without a practitioner qualification are excluded from judicial office altogether. The government hopes that the new Judicial Appointments Commission will be able to find new and more inclusive ways of recruiting and selecting candidates:[150]

[T]he current judiciary is overwhelmingly white, male, and from a narrow social and educational background. To an extent, this reflects the pool of qualified candidates from which judicial appointments are made: intake to the legal professions has, until recently, been dominated by precisely these social groups.

Of course the fundamental principle in appointing judges is and must remain selection on merit. However the Government is committed to opening up the system of appointments, to attract suitably qualified candidates both from a wider range of social backgrounds and from a wider range of legal practice. To do so, and, to create a system which commands the confidence of professionals and the public, and is seen as affording equal opportunities to all suitably qualified applicants, will require fresh approaches and a major re-engineering of the processes for appointment.

2 TENURE

(a) Removal and discipline

Before Stuart times judges could be removed at the will of the King, but this position was altered by the Act of Settlement 1700. The Act provided that as long as they conducted themselves properly, judges of the superior courts could only be removed on an address by both Houses of Parliament,[151] and this rule still applies to judges of the High Court, Court of Appeal, and House of Lords.[152] No English judge has ever been removed under this procedure, although an Irish judge was removed in 1830 when he was discovered to have misappropriated court funds. Judges of the lower ranks can be removed by the Lord Chancellor without parliamentary approval, but

---

[147] See p 313, *ante.*   [148] *Judicial Appointments in England and Wales* (2003), ch 1.

[149] See p 351, *post.*

[150] DCA, *Constitutional Reform: A New Way of Appointing Judges* (2003), CP 10/03, foreword.

[151] The Lord Chancellor has always been an exception: see p 301, *ante.*

[152] Supreme Court Act 1981, s 11(3) (High Court and Court of Appeal); Appellate Jurisdiction Act 1876, s 6 (House of Lords). Special provisions allow the Lord Chancellor to remove a judge who is disabled by permanent infirmity and who does not have the capacity to resign: see the 1981 Act, s 11(8).

this can only be done on the grounds of incapacity or misbehaviour.[153] Judges of all ranks thus enjoy considerable security of tenure.

Serious judicial misconduct is almost unheard of in modern times. In 1983 a circuit judge was removed from office after being convicted of various smuggling offences, but this is an extreme example. On the rare occasions when judges have been disciplined, this has usually taken the form of a reprimand for a lesser 'offence' such as incompetence, neglect, unacceptable delay, or unacceptable personal behaviour.[154] Some judges have responded to allegations of such behaviour by offering their resignation, and others have been asked to do so. Thus, a High Court judge resigned in 1998 after being castigated by the Court of Appeal for taking twenty months to deliver a judgment:[155]

Conduct like this weakens public confidence in the whole judicial process. Left unchecked, it would be ultimately subversive of the rule of law. Delays on this scale cannot and will not be tolerated.

(b) Starrs v Ruxton and the problem of fixed-term appointments

Unlike other judges, recorders are appointed on a part-time basis and for a specific term of office. Before 2000 the standard length of appointment was three years, and at the end of this period the Lord Chancellor had a discretion as to whether a contract should be renewed. These arrangements were called into question by the decision of the Scottish High Court of Justiciary in Starrs v Ruxton.[156] The court ruled that the use of temporary judges infringed Article 6 of the ECHR, because a judge without security of tenure could not be considered 'independent'. The case was concerned with the use of temporary sheriffs in Scotland, but it had obvious implications for the appointment of recorders and the Lord Chancellor was quick to respond. The terms upon which part-time judges hold office were reviewed, and all are now appointed for a minimum period of five years. They can only be removed on the grounds of misbehaviour, incapacity, failure to comply with sitting requirements, failure to comply with training requirements, or sustained failure to observe reasonably expected standards. In the absence of one of these grounds, contracts will normally be renewed automatically at the end of each five-year term. However, exceptions may be made if there is a need to reduce numbers for operational reasons, or to make way for the

---

[153] Courts Act 1971, s 17(4) (circuit judges); County Courts Act 1984, s 11 (district judges); Courts Act 2003, s 22 (district judges (magistrates' courts)). Lay justices have not previously enjoyed the same security of tenure as their professional counterparts, but this position was rectified by s 11 of the Courts Act 2003.

[154] The *Judicial Appointments Annual Report 2002–2003* records that two formal reprimands were issued during the relevant period, although the Lord Chancellor received a total of 370 complaints relating to the personal conduct of judges: para 12.2. In future, the Lord Chief Justice will have greater powers in this area: Constitutional Reform Act 2005, s 108.

[155] *Goose v Wilson Sandford & Co* (1998), *The Times*, February 19, per Peter Gibson LJ. The judge, Mr Justice Harman, had regularly featured at the top of a legal journal's 'Worst Judge' poll: see 'Controlling the Judges' (1998) 148 NLJ 234.

[156] 2000 JC 208, 2000 SLT 42, *sub nom Starrs v Procurator Fiscal*. See also: *Scanfuture v Secretary of State for Trade and Industry* [2001] ICR 1096, [2001] IRLR 416, discussed at p 280, *ante*.

recruitment of new appointees.[157] The Lord Chancellor also took the opportunity to abolish the separate office of 'assistant recorder', and those who already held this title were re-appointed as recorders.

(c) Retirement

The standard retirement age for judges is seventy,[158] although a judge who has completed twenty years of service can retire with full pension rights at the age of sixty-five.[159] In addition, a judge of the circuit bench or lower ranks may be asked to stay on until he reaches seventy-five,[160] and any retired judge below this age may sit on an ad hoc basis.[161] Lay magistrates also 'retire' at seventy, which is when their names are added to the supplemental list and they cease to be able to perform judicial functions.[162] They are, however, unsalaried, and unlike their professional counterparts they do not receive a pension.

(d) Salaries

Judicial salaries are determined by the Lord Chancellor with the consent of the Minister for the Civil Service (the Prime Minister). They are paid from the Consolidated Fund[163] and are not subject to a vote in Parliament. They are deliberately set at a high level so as to provide a further safeguard of independence, the idea being that a well-paid judge will not be vulnerable to bribery and corruption. In fact however, the high earning capacity of the most successful practitioners means that accepting a judicial appointment will often involve a reduction in income. As of April 2003, district judges in both the magistrates' and the civil courts received a salary of £88,546, while High Court judges received £147,198 and the Lord Chief Justice got £200,236.[164] By contrast, the most successful barristers can earn over £500,000 per annum, although the income of the *average* barrister is much less than this.[165]

3 TRAINING

It was once assumed that those appointed to the Bench already had sufficient training and experience to enable them to perform judicial functions. It is now accepted that this is not inevitably the case, and in 1979 the Judicial Studies Board was established to provide training for both new and experienced judges. The Board is run by judges themselves, and through training courses and refresher courses it seeks to create an

---

157 The new rules are explained in the *Judicial Appointments Annual Report 2002–2003*.

158 Judicial Pensions and Retirement Act 1993, s 26(1); Schedule 5.

159 Judicial Pensions Act 1981. The twenty-year rule means that even if a judge continues until the age of seventy, he will be ineligible to receive a full pension unless he was called to the bench by the age of fifty.

160 Judicial Pensions and Retirement Act 1993, s 26(5).   161 Ibid, s 26(7).

162 Courts Act 2003, ss 12 and 13 (replacing the Justices of the Peace Act 1997, s 7).

163 Supreme Court Act 1981, s 12; Administration of Justice Act 1973, s 9.

164 *Judicial Appointments Annual Report 2002–2003*, at para 12.4.

165 *Chambers Guide to the Legal Profession 2001–2002*, at p 1247.

awareness of best practice and to equip judges to deal with common problems.[166] It also runs courses covering developments in procedure, substantive law, evidence, and sentencing, and in 1998 it began a major training programme to educate judges about the Human Rights Act. Judges are also exposed to related disciplines such as penology, and all judges now receive equal treatment training.

4 JUDICIAL IMMUNITY

The doctrine of judicial immunity is an offshoot of the principle of independence. Historically, the degree of immunity recognized has varied with the status of the judge, and the old cases distinguish between judges of superior and inferior courts. Superior court judges were immune from liability even if acting maliciously, while judges of the inferior courts enjoyed immunity only while acting within their jurisdiction. Thus, a Recorder who unlawfully imprisoned a jury for ignoring his direction to convict was held immune from suit,[167] while an unfortunate county court judge was held liable in damages for making an innocent mistake of law.[168]

In the modern case of *Sirros* v *Moore* the Court of Appeal rejected the idea that the degree of immunity should depend upon the status of the court. The claimant was a foreign national who unsuccessfully appealed to the Crown Court against a recommendation that he should be deported. The circuit judge who rejected his appeal was under the mistaken impression that the claimant was in custody, and at the end of the hearing he ordered a police officer to arrest and detain him. The detention was clearly unlawful, and the claimant brought an action for false imprisonment against both the judge and the police officer. However, the Court of Appeal held that the judge was immune from liability, despite the fact that he was a judge of an inferior court. The police officer was also held to be immune on the basis that he was following the judge's orders. Lord Denning MR even suggested that the principle of immunity should extend to justices of the peace:[169]

Every judge of the courts of this land from the highest to the lowest should be protected to the same degree, and liable to the same degree. If the reason underlying this immunity is to ensure 'that they may be free in thought and independent in judgment', it applies to every judge, whatever his rank. Each should be protected from liability to damages when he is acting judicially. Each should be able to do his work in complete independence and free from fear. He should not have to turn the pages of his books with trembling fingers, asking himself; 'If I do this, shall I be liable in damages?' So long as he does his work in the honest belief that it is within his jurisdiction, then he is not liable to an action.

In the later case of *McC* v *Mullan*,[170] the House of Lords questioned the assertion that inferior and superior courts are now subject to the same rules. It also confirmed that

---

[166] For a more detailed discussion, see Partington, 'Training the Judiciary in England and Wales' (1994) 13 CJQ 319; Malleson, *The New Judiciary: The Effects of Expansion and Activism* (1999), ch 5.

[167] *Hamond* v *Howell* (1677) 2 Mod Rep 218.   [168] *Houlden* v *Smith* (1850) 14 QB 841.

[169] [1975] QB 118 at 136, [1974] 3 All ER 776 at 785.   [170] [1985] AC 528, [1984] 3 All ER 908.

justices of the peace could be sued if they acted outside their jurisdiction. Nevertheless, *Sirros* v *Moore* remains good law, and justices of the peace now have statutory
immunity for acts done in good faith and in the purported execution of their duty.[171]
In addition, a judge cannot be compelled to give evidence of matters relating to the
performance of his judicial functions, although he is a competent witness to such
matters and may testify if he is willing to do so.[172]

The immunity that attaches to judicial proceedings is not personal to the judge.
No civil action lies in respect of words spoken in the course of proceedings by parties,[173] witnesses,[174] or advocates;[175] nor can an action be brought in respect of the
verdict of a jury.[176] In addition, media reports of judicial proceedings are absolutely
privileged in the law of defamation. They must, however, be fair, accurate and
contemporaneous.[177]

D THE JUDICIAL FUNCTION

Most of the judges' work is 'judicial', in the sense that they have to adjudicate upon
disputes. This means that they must deduce the facts from the evidence presented in
court, and apply the law to the facts so that they can give the 'right decision'. Appellate
courts have repeatedly pointed out that the judicial function goes no further than this,
and that a court has no duty to seek out some 'independent truth'. Thus:[178]

If [a] decision has been in accordance with the available evidence and with the law, justice
will have been fairly done.

Having found the facts, a judge must apply the existing legal rules to those facts. This
function has two elements: (a) the interpretation and construction of statutes; and
(b) the application of precedent.

(a) Statutes

Where a case concerns a rule of statute law, the judge's task is to ascertain the intention of the legislature. Different approaches to this task have already been identified,[179] but the traditional view is that judges must interpret statutes in accordance

---

[171] Justices of the Peace Act 1997, ss 51 and 52: in due course these provisions will be superseded by the
Courts Act 2003, ss 31 and 32.

[172] *Warren* v *Warren* [1997] QB 488, [1996] 4 All ER 664.

[173] *Astley* v *Younge* (1759) 2 Burr 807.

[174] *Hargreaves* v *Bretherton* [1959] 1 QB 45, [1958] 3 All ER 122.

[175] *Munster* v *Lamb* (1883) 11 QBD 588.   [176] *Bushell's Case* (1670) Vaugh 135.

[177] Defamation Act 1996, s 14.

[178] *Air Canada* v *Secretary of State for Trade (No 2)* [1983] 2 AC 394 at 438, [1983] 1 All ER 910 at 919, per
Lord Wilberforce.

[179] See p 48, *ante.*

with the literal meaning of the words used.[180] However, strict adherence to this rule is not always possible: the law being considered may be uncertain or ambiguous, and the Act may not provide for the circumstances in question. Judges must create new law in such cases, and this obviously raises questions about the limits of the judicial function. Most would accept that the role of the courts is to decide questions of law, and not to impinge upon the right of the executive to make and apply policy.[181] Yet deciding where this line should be drawn is not easy, particularly in the context of the Human Rights Act and in judicial review cases. In judicial review[182] for example, the courts are often required to determine whether executive bodies have acted within their statutory authority, and this means that they must engage in an interpretative function. Yet where the exercise of discretionary powers is concerned, Parliament's intention may be elusive.[183] Moreover, under section 3 of the Human Rights Act this intention may have to give way to an interpretation that is compatible with Convention rights.[184] The nature of these rights means that the courts may also have to take a view as to the proportionality of any action or provision interfering with them, and this inevitably requires a measure of policy evaluation.[185]

(b) Common law

Traditional views are also changing in relation to the development of common law principles. In *Jones* v *Secretary of State for Social Services* Lord Simon stated:[186]

In this country it was long considered that judges were not makers of law but merely its discoverers and expounders. The theory was that every case was governed by a relevant rule of law, existing somewhere and discoverable somehow, provided sufficient learning and intellectual rigour were brought to bear. . . . [T]he theory, however unreal, had its value in limiting the sphere of law-making by the judiciary (inevitably at some disadvantage in assessing the potential repercussions of any decision, and increasingly so in a complex modern industrial society), and thus also in emphasising that central feature of our constitution, the sovereignty of Parliament. But the true, even if limited, nature of judicial law-making has been more widely acknowledged of recent years.

Judges do sometimes establish new legal principles, and a good example of this is the judgment of Denning J in *Central London Property Trust Ltd* v *High Trees House Ltd*,[187] which effectively created the doctrine of equitable estoppel. Similarly, the 'neighbour

---

[180] See, for example, the words of Lord Diplock in *Duport Steels Ltd* v *Sirs* [1980] 1 All ER 529 at 541, [1980] 1 WLR 142, at 157: quoted at p 54, *ante.*

[181] See *R* v *Secretary of State for Home Affairs, ex parte Brind* [1991] 1 AC 696, [1991] 1 All ER 720.

[182] See p 207, *ante.*

[183] In some cases this intention may be ascertained from the records of parliamentary debates: see *Pepper* v *Hart* [1993] AC 593, [1993] 1 All ER 42.

[184] See e.g. *R* v *A (No 2)* [2001] UKHL 25 at [40], [2002] 1 AC 45 at [40], [2001] 3 All ER 1: discussed at p 56, *ante.*

[185] See the discussion at p 165, *ante.*

[186] [1972] AC 944 at 1026, [1972] 1 All ER 145 at 198. See also p 78, *ante.*

[187] [1947] KB 130, [1956] 1 All ER 256n.

principle' propounded by Lord Atkin in *Donoghue (or M'Alister) v Stevenson*[188] is widely acknowledged as the basis of the modern law of negligence. Indeed, it is fair to say that some judges deem the creation of new law to be part of the judicial function, but others believe that any far-reaching change should be left to Parliament. The latter approach is exemplified by the vigorous dissenting speech of Lord Simon in *Miliangos v George Frank (Textiles) Ltd*:[189]

I am sure that an expert committee, including or taking evidence from departmental officials, would apprehend a great number of not immediately apparent repercussions of the decision which my noble and learned friends propose to take. Such a committee might conclude that the repercussions make the decision unacceptable. Or they might suggest some means of mitigating any adverse effect. Or they might advise that the repercussions were on balance acceptable. But at least the crucial decision would be taken in the light of all the consequences involved.

By contrast . . . judicial advance should be gradual. I am not trained to see the distant scene; 'one step enough for me' should be the motto on the wall opposite the judge's desk. It is, I concede, a less spectacular method of progression than somersaults and cartwheels; but it is the one best suited to the capacity and resources of a judge.

Lord Simon was a lone dissenting voice in this case, and the House of Lords effected a radical reform of the law by holding that English courts have the power to give judgments expressed in foreign currency. However, on other occasions judges have exercised restraint on the basis that the resolution of a problem is best left to Parliament. In *Malone* v *Metropolitan Police Commissioner (No 2)* for example, Sir Robert Megarry considered that the practice of telephone tapping 'cried out' for legislation, but he declined to develop common law rules to fill the vacuum:[190]

I am not unduly troubled by the absence of English authority: there has to be a first time for everything, and if the principles of English law, and not least analogies from the existing rules, together with the requirements of justice and common sense, pointed firmly to such a right existing, then I think the court should not be deterred from recognising the right. On the other hand, it is no function of the courts to legislate in a new field. The extension of the existing laws and principles is one thing, the creation of an altogether new right is another.

Twenty-five years later, the House of Lords held that although the Human Rights Act had given greater recognition to the right to respect for private life,[191] this did not entitle the courts to create a new tort:[192]

For the reasons so cogently explained by Sir Robert Megarry in *Malone* v *Metropolitan Police Comissioner*, this is an area which requires a detailed approach which can be achieved only by legislation rather than the broad brush of common law principle.

The earliest criminal offences were, of course, judge-made, but since the nineteenth

---

[188] [1932] AC 562.   [189] [1976] AC 443 at 481–2, [1975] 3 All ER 801 at 824–5.
[190] [1979] Ch 344 at 372, [1979] 2 All ER 620 at 642.   [191] Article 8, ECHR.
[192] *Wainwright v Home Office* [2003] UKHL 53 at [33], [2004] 2 AC 406 at [33], [2003] 4 All ER 969, per Lord Hoffman.

century it has been accepted that judges have no power to create new criminal offences.[193] Nevertheless, they have occasionally sought to enforce public morality by declaring that the common law recognizes certain conduct to be criminal. Thus in *R* v *Manley*[194] the defendant falsely alleged that she had been attacked and robbed, and this put the police to considerable trouble and expense. She was convicted of the offence of public mischief, and despite counsel's protestations that no such offence was known to the law, her conviction was upheld on appeal. The decision of the House of Lords in *Shaw* v *DPP*[195] is equally striking. An agreement to publish the 'Ladies Directory', which advertised the names, addresses, and photographs of prostitutes, was held to constitute the offence of conspiracy to corrupt public morals. The following observation from the speech of Viscount Simonds has been widely quoted:[196]

In the sphere of criminal law I entertain no doubt that there remains in the courts of law a residual power to enforce the supreme and fundamental purpose of the law, to conserve not only the safety and order but also the moral welfare of the State.

In *Knuller* v *DPP*[197] a similar publication aimed at the homosexual market was held to give rise to the same offence, and a majority of the House of Lords suggested that an offence of outraging public decency also existed. In the light of these authorities, the principle that judges have no power to create new offences would appear to be illusory. However, in *DPP* v *Withers*[198] the House of Lords explained that conspiracy to effect a public mischief is not an offence in itself, and that conduct such as that in *R* v *Manley* (above) is criminal only because it amounts to some other established offence.

The approach to such matters is not always consistent, and judicial activism sometimes comes to the fore. Thus, in *R* v *R.* the House of Lords concluded that the rule that a husband could not be criminally liable for raping his wife was no longer part of English law.[199] Other examples of judicial creativity include the recognition of psychological harm as a form of assault,[200] the development of the law of provocation in the context of domestic violence,[201] and the decision that medical treatment may be lawfully withdrawn from a patient in a permanent vegetative state.[202] By contrast, in *C* v *DPP*[203] the House of Lords declined to abolish the *doli incapax* rule. The rule created

---

[193] This was virtually the only point upon which all five members of the House of Lords were agreed in *Knuller (Publishing, Printing and Promotions) Ltd* v *DPP* [1973] AC 435, [1972] 2 All ER 898. Lord Diplock's speech contains a useful account of the historical background: see [1973] AC 435 at 474, [1972] 2 All ER 898 at 918.

[194] [1933] 1 KB 529.   [195] [1962] AC 220, [1961] 2 All ER 446.

[196] [1962] AC 220 at 267–268, [1961] 2 All ER 446 at 452.

[197] [1973] AC 435, [1972] 2 All ER 898. See also *R* v *Gibson* [1990] 2 QB 619, [1991] 1 All ER 439.

[198] [1975] AC 842, [1974] 3 All ER 984.   [199] [1992] 1 AC 599, [1991] 4 All ER 481.

[200] *R* v *Chan-Fook* [1994] 2 All ER 552, [1994] 1 WLR 689; *R* v *Ireland* [1997] QB 114, [1997] 1 All ER 112; *R* v *Constanza* [1997] 2 Cr App R 492, [1997] Crim LR 576.

[201] *R* v *Thornton* [1992] 1 All ER 306, (1993) 96 Cr App R 112; *R* v *Ahluwalia* [1992] 4 All ER 889, (1993) 96 Cr App R 133.

[202] *Airedale NHS Trust* v *Bland* [1993] AC 789, [1993] 1 All ER 821.

[203] [1996] AC 1, [1995] 2 All ER 43.

a rebuttable presumption that a child under the age of fourteen could not possess criminal intent, and at first instance Laws J had said:[204]

[T]his presumption at the present time is a serious disservice to our law. It means that a child over ten who commits an act of obvious dishonesty, or even grave violence, is to be acquitted unless the prosecution specifically prove . . . that he understands the obliquity of what he is doing . . .

In the House of Lords, Lord Lowery set out five general principles:

(1) If the solution is doubtful the judges should beware of imposing their own remedy; (2) caution should prevail if Parliament has rejected opportunities of clearing up a known difficulty or has legislated while leaving the difficulty untouched; (3) disputed matters of social policy are less suitable areas for judicial intervention than purely legal problems; (4) fundamental legal doctrines should not lightly be set aside; (5) judges should not make a change unless they can achieve finality and certainty.

The application of these principles led him conclude that the presumption should not be abandoned. It has, however, now been abolished by statute.[205]

Where a case gives rise to a potential Human Rights Act issue, different considerations apply. As discussed previously, the Act does not oblige private bodies to act compatibly with the Convention, and it does not expressly require the courts to give effect to the Convention at common law. It does, however, oblige them to perform their functions in a manner consistent with Convention rights,[206] and since this is a statutory obligation it must prevail over any duty to obey established common law principles. A court may even conclude that it has no option but to depart from a precedent that would otherwise be binding, as when the Court of Appeal made a modest adjustment to the House of Lords' test for bias.[207] The open-textured language of Convention rights also leaves considerable room for interpretation, and on occasions judges have had to determine matters that involve as many moral choices as they do legal ones. In *R (on the application of Pretty) v DPP*[208] for example, the House of Lords found itself grappling with the difficult question of whether the right to life also gave a terminally ill woman the right to die. Similarly, in *Re A*[209] a court had to consider whether the same right could prevent surgery to separate conjoined twins, in circumstances where this would inevitably result in the death of one of them.

Convention rights have undoubtedly had an influence on judicial reasoning, but as indicated above, the courts have thus far stopped short of asserting the authority to create new common law torts. They have, however, sought to give effect to Convention

---

[204] [1994] 3 All ER 190 at 196–7.   [205] Crime and Disorder Act 1998, s 34.

[206] Section 6. Convention rights are defined in s 1 of the Act: see pp 170–97, *ante*.

[207] *Director General of Fair Trading v Proprietary Association of Great Britain (No 2)* [2001] 1 WLR 700, *sub nom Re Medicaments and Related Classes of Goods (No 2)* [2001] HRLR 17. The approach was subsequently approved by the House of Lords in *Porter v Magill* [2001] UKHL 67, [2002] 2 AC 357, [2002] 1 All ER 465.

[208] [2001] UKHL 61, [2002] 1 AC 800, [2002] 1 All ER 1: see p 175, *ante*.

[209] *Re A (Children) (Conjoined Twins: Surgical Separation)* [2001] Fam 147, [2000] 4 All ER 961.

rights—notably the right to respect for private life—by developing established torts such as breach of confidence.[210]

Finally, it should be noted that judges occasionally go beyond the function of dispute resolution by issuing guidelines for future cases. Thus the rates of interest to be awarded on damages in personal injury actions,[211] and the principles to be applied in determining applications for interlocutory injunctions,[212] have both been the subject of House of Lords guidelines. Similarly, the Criminal Division of the Court of Appeal has established a practice of issuing sentencing guidelines to assist Crown Court judges.[213]

(c) Administrative functions

In addition to resolving disputes, judges also exercise certain administrative functions. This is particularly true of justices of the peace, whose functions include licensing and the issuing of summonses and warrants. Chancery Division Judges sitting as a Court of Protection administer the affairs of persons of unsound mind,[214] and in their capacity as 'visitors' of the Inns of Court, High Court judges hear appeals from the Senate of the Inns of Court and the Bar.[215] Courts also deal with various types of non-contentious business, such as the administration of trusts, the winding-up of companies, adoption, and legitimacy. In addition, judges issue Practice Directions, act as presiding judges[216] and Heads of Division, and sit on the various Court Rule Committees which make Rules for court practice and procedure.[217]

---

[210] See, e.g. *A v B; H v Associated Newspapers*, [2002] EWCA Civ 337, [2003] QB 195, [2002] 2 All ER 545; *Douglas v Hello! Ltd (No 1)* [2001] QB 967, [2001] 2 All ER 289; *Campbell v Mirror Group Newspapers* [2004] UKHL 22, [2004] 2 AC 457, [2004] 2 All ER 995. These and other cases are discussed at pp 166 and 186, *ante*. Cf. *Wainwright v Home Office* [2003] UKHL 53, [2004] 2 AC 406, [2003] 4 All ER 969. Note also that in *Peck v UK* (2003) 36 EHRR 41, the European Court of Human Rights highlighted significant deficiencies in the ability of domestic law to protect privacy.

[211] See p 487, *post*.   [212] See p 472, *post*.

[213] This practice seems to have originated in *R v Turner* (1975) 61 Cr App R 67 in relation to sentences for robbery and has since been followed in many other sentencing areas. See, e.g., *R v Clarke (Linda)* [1982] 3 All ER 232, [1982] 1 WLR 1090 (partially suspended sentences); and *R v Armagh* (1982) 76 Cr App R 190 (drugs offences). See now, pp 659–60, *post*.

[214] The future of this court is discussed at p 252, *ante*.

[215] For this general jurisdiction, see *R v Visitors to the Inns of Court, ex parte Calder and Persaud* [1994] QB 1, [1993] 2 All ER 876.

[216] Courts and Legal Services Act 1990, s 72.   [217] See pp 230 and 303, *ante*.

10

JURIES

A HISTORICAL GROWTH OF THE JURY SYSTEM

The jury system has always been seen as one of the cornerstones of common law procedure, though there is evidence that some forms of jury trial existed in England even before the Norman Conquest. The trial of criminals by jury evolved in the thirteenth century to replace trial by ordeal, and by the middle of the fourteenth century the separate roles of the petty jury and grand jury were established.

The grand jury was not a 'trial jury' in the modern sense. Its original function was to present persons for trial at the start of assizes or quarter sessions,[1] but when the system of preliminary investigation by magistrates developed, its role was reduced to a mere formality. The grand jury was finally abolished by the Criminal Justice Act 1948.[2]

The twelve member petty jury was the equivalent of the modern trial jury, though in its early stages jurors were summoned for their local knowledge and acted as witnesses rather than judges of fact. The petty jury's function changed gradually as the practice of examining independent witnesses grew and by the fifteenth century it had assumed its modern role as arbiter of fact. A landmark decision in 1670[3] established that jurors should decide cases according to their consciences and that they could not be punished for returning a verdict contrary to the evidence or the judge's direction.

In civil cases there was only ever one type of jury: the trial jury of twelve members. This had its origins in the Assize of Clarendon, 1166, and by 1304 it was established that all trespass actions in common law courts had to be tried with a jury. As with criminal juries, jurors in civil trials originally acted as witnesses, but a similar transition from witnesses to judges of fact took place. The steady decline of the jury in civil cases began with the Common Law Procedure Act 1854, which allowed common law actions to be tried without a jury if both parties agreed. The use of juries in civil cases is now extremely limited.[4]

---

[1] See p 224, *ante.*

[2] Section 31(3). Grand juries are still used in some United States jurisdictions.

[3] *Bushell's case* (1670) Vaugh 135.   [4] See p 340, *post.*

B THE COMPOSITION OF THE MODERN JURY

1 QUALIFYING FOR JURY DUTY

Eligibility for jury service used to depend upon the existence of a property qualification, and juries were criticized for being 'predominantly male, middle-aged,
middle-minded and middle-class'.[5] Following the recommendations of the Morris
Committee[6] the property qualification was abolished and the present system of selecting jurors from the electoral register was introduced.[7] The law was consolidated in the
Juries Act 1974 and was most recently amended by the Criminal Justice Act 2003.
Section 1 of the 1974 Act now provides that[8] a person will be qualified to serve as a
juror and liable to attend for jury service when summoned, if:

(a) he is registered as a parliamentary or local government elector and is not less
than eighteen nor more than seventy[9] years of age;

(b) he has been ordinarily resident in the United Kingdom, the Channel Islands or
the Isle of Man for any period of at least five years since attaining the age of
thirteen;

(c) he is not a mentally disordered person; and

(d) he is not disqualified for jury service.

Thus, assuming that the residential and age qualifications are met, anyone listed on
the electoral register may be required to serve as a juror unless he is *ineligible* by
reason of mental disorder[10] or *disqualified* under Schedule 1, Part 2.[11]

The government considers jury service to be 'one of the most important civic duties
that anyone can be asked to perform'.[12] Those eligible have a legal obligation to attend
if summoned unless they can satisfy the 'appropriate officer'[13] that there is a good

---

[5] Devlin, *Trial By Jury* (1956), at p 20.

[6] *Report of the Departmental Committee on Jury Service*, 1965, Cmnd 2627.

[7] Criminal Justice Act 1972. For the effect of these reforms on the composition of juries, see Baldwin and
McConville, *Jury Trials* (1979) at p 94.

[8] As amended by the 2003 Act: with effect from 5 April 2004.

[9] The upper age limit was raised from sixty-five by the Criminal Justice Act 1988, s 119.

[10] This is defined in Schedule 1, Part 1 of the 1974 Act (as amended).

[11] There are three basic categories of disqualification. (1) A person who has been given an extended
sentence, or who has been sentenced to a term of imprisonment or detention of five years or more, or to
imprisonment or detention for public protection, is effectively disqualified from jury service for life. (2) A
person who has served a period of imprisonment, youth custody or detention or who has been the subject of
one of the community or rehabilitation orders listed in paragraph 7 of the Schedule is disqualified for ten
years after completion of the sentence. (3) A person who is on bail in criminal proceedings is also disqualified.

[12] Department for Constitutional Affairs, *Jury Summoning Guidance* (consultation paper; 2003), *foreword*.

[13] In practice, this task now falls to the Jury Central Summoning Bureau: see p 332, *post*.

reason to excuse or defer them.[14] In a recent Home Office study of 50,000 people summoned for jury duty,[15] 38 per cent of those in the sample were excused and nearly 17 per cent were granted a deferral.[16] The most common grounds for excusal were child-care responsibilities, illness, and work commitments. Recent guidelines[17] state that excusals should only be granted to those who can show good reason for not serving at any time within the following twelve months. Religious objections[18] or being out of the country are cited as examples of good reasons for excusal, but deferral is considered more appropriate for those with holiday plans or work commitments.

Before 5 April 2004, Members of Parliament, medical professionals and members of the armed forces were entitled to be excused from jury service as of right, the rationale being that such persons would generally have more pressing duties to perform elsewhere. Those aged over sixty-five and those belonging to religious societies with beliefs incompatible with jury service[19] could also insist on being excused. In addition, ministers of religion, members of the legal profession, and certain other persons involved in the administration of justice were *ineligible* to serve as jurors by reason of their occupation. The Morris Committee had suggested these occupational exclusions because of concerns that a clergyman or someone with professional knowledge of the justice system might exercise undue influence in a jury room. There was also an argument that someone working in the legal system might find it difficult to follow a judge's directions if this meant putting aside his own legal 'knowledge'.

In his *Review of the Criminal Courts* Lord Justice Auld concluded that despite the reforms of previous decades, juries still lacked diversity and were not sufficiently representative of the communities from which they were drawn. With a view to widening participation, he recommended that 'no-one should be automatically ineligible or excusable from jury service simply because he or she is a member of a certain profession or holds a particular office or job'.[20] This recommendation was given effect by the Criminal Justice Act 2003. The government dismissed concerns that the presence of lawyers in the jury room might be problematic:[21]

In England and Wales, a large number of people with extensive knowledge of the criminal justice system—legal academics, law students and civil servants working in criminal justice em;currently do jury service. There is no evidence to suggest that the involvement of any of

---

[14] Juries Act 1974, ss 9 and 9A. Failure to attend is a criminal offence punishable by a fine (s 20), although 'offenders' are rarely pursued: see Darbyshire, Maughan and Stewart, *What can the English Legal System Learn from Jury Research Published up to 2001?—Findings for the Criminal Courts Review* (2001) at p 6.

[15] Airs and Shaw, *Jury Excusal and Deferral*, Home Office Research Findings No 102 (1999), at p 1.

[16] A further 13 per cent were ineligible, disqualified or excused as of right, and 15 per cent had their summonses returned as 'undelivered' or simply did not attend.

[17] Issued in April 2004 under the new section 9AA of the Juries Act 1974: Department for Constitutional Affairs, *Guidance for Summoning Officers when considering deferral and excusal applications*.

[18] In *R v Crown Court at Guildford, ex parte Siderfin* [1990] 2 QB 683, [1989] 3 All ER 73 it was held that excusal on religious grounds should only be granted where the religious belief would stand in the way of proper performance of the jury function.

[19] Ibid.   [20] *Review of the Criminal Courts of England and Wales* (2001) at para 5.14.

[21] DCA, *Jury Summoning Guidance*, (consultation paper; 2003) at p 9.

these groups in jury service has been a problem. More generally, the diluting effect of the process of random selection, and the group dynamic of the jury, serve to protect the integrity of the deliberative process.

Those who would previously have been ineligible or excused as of right because of their occupations are now subject to the same regime as everyone else: if they wish to be excused from jury service they must persuade the summoning officer that they have a good reason. Even judges may now be called upon to serve as jurors and the Lord Chief Justice recently wrote to all judges offering advice on what to do if summoned.[22] The only persons automatically entitled to be excused are those who have served (or attended to serve) on a jury within the previous two years.[23] The Department for Constitutional Affairs estimates that a person's chances of doing jury service during his lifetime are roughly one in six.[24]

2 SELECTING AND SUMMONING JURORS

Before 2000, jurors were selected locally by the summoning officers for each court centre, but a Central Summoning Bureau has now been established at Blackfriars Crown Court. The Bureau operates on a national basis and randomly selects names from the electoral register by computer, taking into account the number of prospective jurors needed for each area. It is then responsible for issuing summonses and for dealing with applications for excusal or deferral. Under the old system, many local summoning officers developed their own methods for selecting names from the electoral lists, and the approach to dealing with excusals and deferrals differed from area to area. The move to a centralised system has gone some way towards improving the randomness and consistency of the selection process, and it should also enable automatic checks to be made to ensure that those disqualified by their criminal convictions do not serve. It does not, however, address the more fundamental criticism that thousands of otherwise eligible people do not qualify for jury service at all because their names do not appear on the electoral register.[25]

3 CHALLENGING THE COMPOSITION OF THE JURY

Once the summonses have been issued, the court officer prepares a 'panel' of prospective jurors and the parties have the right to inspect a list of their names and addresses. The names of those on the list are then put on cards and placed in a box. At the

---

[22] The text of the letter can be accessed through the Department for Constitutional Affairs website: www.dca.gov.uk.

[23] Juries Act 1974, s 8. Lord Justice Auld's *Review of the Criminal Courts* (2001) recommended that this time-scale should be extended (at para 5.224).

[24] *Jury Summoning Guidance* (consultation paper; 2003) at p 6.

[25] Recent research suggests that around 8 per cent of those eligible to vote (and up to 24 per cent of eligible black people) do not actually register: Airs and Shaw, *Jury Excusal and Deferral*, Home Office Research Findings No 102 (1999), at p 2.

beginning of a trial, cards are drawn from the box by a ballot in open court[26] and those named on the cards are sworn in as jurors.[27] It is at this point that the parties may exercise their limited rights to challenge those selected.[28] However, as the parties are given no information about the panel except for a list of names and addresses,[29] they will generally have very little to go on. Characteristics such as gender and race are not legitimate grounds for a challenge,[30] and the parties are not permitted to question jurors to ascertain whether any other grounds exist. In exceptional cases a judge may agree to the use of a questionnaire to determine whether jurors have been influenced by pre-trial publicity,[31] but exposure to pre-trial publicity in itself is not a sufficient basis for a challenge.

The effect of this is that unless a potential juror happens to be personally known to the defendant or one of the witnesses, it is unlikely in practice that the defence will have any basis for a challenge. The prosecution however, may have a slight advantage over the defence because of the controversial practice known as 'jury vetting'.

(a) Jury vetting

This practice came to light in 1978 when it was discovered that the prosecution in an official secrets trial had 'vetted' the names on the jury panel in order to identify those who might be 'disloyal'. The Attorney-General responded to the criticism that followed by publishing his guidelines on the use of the practice. The current guidelines date from 1988[32] and permit two types of checks. The first involves checking the names of potential jurors against police records to ensure that disqualified persons are excluded from the panel.[33] The second type of vetting is more controversial and involves making 'authorised checks' against the records of Special Branch and the security services. Authorized checks can only be made in national security and terrorism cases, and they require the personal consent of the Attorney-General. The aim is to identify potential jurors with extreme political views, on the basis that such persons

---

[26] Juries Act 1974, s 11. A jury should only be used once except where a second trial commences within twenty-four hours of the jury being constituted: s 11(5)(a). However, individual jurors may be returned to the pool at the conclusion of a trial and may try other cases if their names are drawn in subsequent ballots. The usual period of jury service is two weeks.

[27] For the manner of taking an oath for these purposes, see the Oaths Act 1978, ss 1 and 5.

[28] For a discussion, see Buxton, 'Challenging and Discharging Jurors—Part 1' [1990] Crim LR 225.

[29] It is legitimate to withhold the names of jurors from a court if there is a real risk of the jury being 'nobbled'. However, the parties still have the right to challenge for cause and are entitled to insist on inspecting the list of names on the panel: R v Comerford [1998] 1 All ER 823, [1998] 1 WLR 191. Note however, that under sections 44 and 46 of the Criminal Justice Act 2003, a jury trial may be dispensed with altogether if there is a 'real and present' danger of jury tampering which cannot be avoided by other measures. The defendant in such a case may be tried by a judge sitting alone.

[30] R v Ford [1989] QB 868, [1989] 3 All ER 445.

[31] In R v Andrews (Tracey) [1999] Crim LR 156 the Court of Appeal confirmed that this was a possibility, but it upheld the decision of the trial judge to refuse a questionnaire in Miss Andrews' case.

[32] Practice Note (Juries: Right to Stand by: Jury Checks) [1988] 3 All ER 1086, (1989) 88 Cr App R 123.

[33] The creation of the Central Summoning Bureau makes it possible for such checks to be made before jurors are even summoned and it is a criminal offence for a person who knows that he is disqualified from jury service to sit.

might find it impossible to assess a case fairly, and might exert improper pressure on other jurors or reveal evidence heard *in camera*. If the checks reveal information about a juror which is of concern to the Director of Public Prosecutions, the prosecutor in the case may then seek to exclude that person by asking him or her to 'stand-by' for the Crown.

The legitimacy of jury vetting was challenged in *R v Sheffield Crown Court, ex parte Brownlow*, in which Lord Denning MR expressed the view that:[34]

> To my mind it is unconstitutional for the police authorities to engage in jury vetting. So long as a person is eligible for jury service, and is not disqualified, I cannot think it right that, behind his back, the police should go through his record so as to enable him to be asked to 'stand by for the Crown' or to be challenged for the defence. If this sort of thing is to be allowed, what comes of a man's right of privacy?

These comments were merely obiter however, and although jury vetting is not specifically sanctioned by the Juries Act it has been held that the practice is not unlawful.[35]

(b) Standing by for the Crown

The prosecution has always had the right to request that a juror 'stand by for the Crown'. This means, in effect, that he will be moved to the back of the queue of potential jurors and will not be called upon for the trial unless and until the entire panel is exhausted. In this way the prosecution is able to prevent the juror from serving, without showing cause, as long as there are enough members of the panel left to form a jury. The most obvious situation in which this form of challenge may be used is in connection with jury vetting. The Attorney-General's guidelines[36] make it clear that jurors should only be stood by in exceptional cases. They also state that where jury vetting has revealed information which strongly suggests that someone on the panel may be biased against the defendant, the prosecution has a duty to make defence counsel aware of the risk.

The right of stand by is controversial because it is not open to the defence. Defence counsel used to have the right to exclude up to three jurors without showing cause in what was known as a peremptory challenge. However, this was abolished by the Criminal Justice Act 1988[37] and the only form of challenge now open to the defence is the right to challenge for cause.

(c) Challenging for cause

Both parties have the right to challenge any or all of the jurors for cause,[38] and this means establishing a good reason why the juror(s) in question should not be involved in the particular case. If prima facie grounds for a challenge can be shown, the issue will be tried by the judge.[39] The fact that a juror is ineligible or disqualified from jury

---

[34] [1980] QB 530 at 542, [1980] 2 All ER 444 at 453.
[35] *R v Mason* [1981] QB 881, [1980] 3 All ER 777.
[36] *Practice Note (Juries: Right to Stand by: Jury Checks)* [1988] 3 All ER 1086, (1989) 88 Cr App R 123.
[37] Section 118.   [38] Juries Act 1974, s 12(1)(a); Juries Act 1825, s 29.   [39] Ibid, s 12(2).

service would clearly be grounds for a challenge,[40] but a juror may also be challenged on the ground of bias.

Bias. Before the implementation of the Human Rights Act 1998, the leading case on the meaning of bias was *R* v *Gough*.[41] The appellant in the case had been indicted on a single count that he had conspired with his brother to commit robbery. His brother's name and address had been disclosed in open court during the trial, and a photograph of both men had been shown to the jury. One of the jurors was a next-door neighbour of the brother but she did not realize this until he started shouting in court after the appellant was convicted. Gough appealed on the ground that a reasonable and fair-minded person would have had a reasonable suspicion that a fair trial was not possible under these circumstances. The appeal was dismissed however, and the House of Lords held that no such danger arose on the facts of the case.

When the Human Rights Act came into force the Court of Appeal[42] made a 'modest adjustment' to the *Gough* test in order to satisfy the requirement that cases should be determined by an 'independent and impartial tribunal'.[43] The modified approach makes the objective nature of the test more explicit and asks whether a 'fair-minded and informed observer' would conclude that there was 'a real possibility of bias'.[44]

The issue of race. The principle of random selection lies at the heart of the jury system and jurors are not generally selected on the basis of gender or ethnic origin. In his 2001 review, Lord Justice Auld recommended that in racially sensitive cases there should be a modified selection procedure to ensure that up to three ethnic minority jurors were chosen.[45] However, the government rejected this proposal on the basis that it was potentially divisive, and there is still no lawful mechanism for interfering with the composition of a jury in order to achieve a racial balance.[46]

In England and Wales there is virtually no mechanism to ensure that juror bias may be removed. Certainly there remains challenge for cause but the defence are given no facts about jurors upon which to base a challenge. Thus, short of a juror having a swastika tattoo in full view of the court, challenge for cause is practically redundant.[47]

---

[40] Ibid, s 12(4). If a person serves on a jury and is subsequently discovered to have been disqualified or unfit to serve, this will not constitute grounds for reversing the jury's verdict unless an objection was raised at the time: s 18(1).

[41] [1993] AC 646, [1993] 2 All ER 724.

[42] *Director General of Fair Trading* v *Proprietary Association of Great Britain; sub nom Re Medicaments and Related Classes of Goods (No 2)* [2001] 1 WLR 700, [2001] HRLR 17.

[43] Article 6, ECHR.

[44] The modified test has since been approved by the House of Lords in *Porter* v *Magill* [2001] UKHL 67, [2002] 2 AC 357, [2002] 1 All ER 465.

[45] *Review of the Criminal Courts of England and Wales* (2001) at para 5.59.

[46] *R* v *Ford* [1989] QB 868, [1989] 3 All ER 445. In the unreported case of *R* v *El Faisal* (20 Jan 2003), a judge excluded Hindu and Jewish jurors from the trial of a Muslim cleric accused of soliciting the murder of Hindus and Jews. This was, however, a truly exceptional case: see Tausz and Ormerod [2003] Crim LR 633.

[47] Darbyshire Maughan and Stewart, *What can the English Legal System Learn from Jury Research Published up to 2001?—Findings for the Criminal Courts Review* (2001) at p 18. The authors supported Auld's recommendation that special selection procedures should be used in racially sensitive cases.

The European Court of Human Rights has held that this position is not inherently incompatible with the right to a fair trial. Indeed, in *Gregory* v *UK*[48] the Strasbourg court held that a black defendant had received a fair trial even though the judge had refused to excuse a member of the jury following complaints of racial bias from another juror. The judge had reminded the jury of the importance of deciding the case according to the evidence, and this was held to be sufficient to satisfy Article 6. The Court of Appeal recently took a similar approach[49] in the case of a black defendant convicted of GBH by an all-white jury. The offence had been committed during a violent incident involving the defendant and a group of white men, but the Court of Appeal confirmed that the judge had no discretion to discharge jurors for the purposes of altering the jury's composition. Although the defendant framed his appeal in terms of the right to a fair trial, the court held that fairness was ensured by the principle of random selection.

The present system rests on the assumption that a randomly selected jury with twelve white members is not necessarily incapable of fairly trying a black defendant. Indeed, research done for the Commission for Racial Equality suggests that black defendants are marginally more likely to be acquitted by a jury than white ones.[50] Although racism undoubtedly exists,[51] since other forms of prejudice also exist, it is questionable whether 'race' should be singled out for special treatment. On this point, Auld argued that:[52]

[W]hite juries are, or are perceived to be, less fair to black than to white people. It is [the] quality of visible difference and the prejudice that it may engender that singles out race for different treatment from other special interest groups.

Auld's proposal for a modified selection procedure was confined to 'racially sensitive' cases: he did not think that a special procedure should be used simply because a defendant happened to be black. Yet there is surely a 'visible difference' between a white jury and a black defendant in a robbery case, just as there would be if the black defendant was accused of racially motivated violence. Moreover, the absence of a visible difference between the defendant and the jury would not guarantee a bias-free decision in other sensitive cases. It would not, for example, assist a gay man tried before a homophobic jury if the fact of his homosexuality was relevant to the case and revealed during the evidence. Similarly, a religious leader prosecuted for inciting violence towards 'non-believers' would not be able to conceal the fact of his religious difference from members of the jury.[53] Of course, judges already have a discretion to

---

[48] (1998) 25 EHRR 577. This decision was distinguished in the later case of *Sander* v *UK* (2001) 31 EHRR 44: see p 343, *post*.

[49] *R* v *Smith* [2003] EWCA Crim 283, [2003] 1 WLR 2229.

[50] Bridges, Choongh and McConville, *Ethnic-Minority Defendants and the Right to Elect Jury Trial* (2000). It is at least possible that black defendants are more likely than whites to be taken to trial on comparatively weak evidence. See also: Enright, 'Multi-racial Juries' (1991) 41 NLJ 992.

[51] In 1995, the victims of nearly 400,000 crimes considered the offences to have been racially motivated: Auld, *Review of the Criminal Courts of England and Wales* (2001), at para 5.56.

[52] Ibid, at para 5.59.   [53] See n 46, *ante*.

discharge any juror who is incapable of properly performing his functions,[54] and an alternative to Auld's proposal might be to allow questionnaires to be used in appropriate cases for the purpose of uncovering possible bias.[55] Such an approach would, however, mark a significant inroad into the principle of random selection.

(d) Challenging the array

At common law it is possible for either party to challenge the entire jury on the ground that the person responsible for summoning the jurors is biased or has acted improperly.[56] This is known as a challenge to the array. Such challenges are now extremely rare, although there was an unsuccessful attempt to challenge an all-white jury on this basis in *R* v *Danvers*.[57]

(e) The judge's discretion to discharge

Where there are doubts about the capacity of a person to act effectively as a juror because of language difficulties[58] or a physical disability,[59] the 1974 Act empowers a judge to discharge that person from jury service. Judges also have a residual discretion to prevent a person from serving in any other circumstances where it is proper to do so.[60] A judge may, for example, discharge a person who is manifestly unsuited for jury service because of illiteracy, or who might otherwise be the subject of a challenge for cause. It is implicit in section 16 of the Juries Act that a juror may also be discharged once a trial is underway. This may be necessary, for example, if he is taken ill or if it becomes apparent during the course of the trial that he may be biased. A judge may also discharge a juror who experiences professional or personal difficulties during the trial, and a recent practice direction asks judges to be sensitive to the inconvenience that jury service may cause. However, it suggests that where a juror in a longer trial encounters a temporary difficulty such as a child-care problem or an urgent public service commitment, the judge may be able to avoid discharging the juror by allowing a short adjournment instead.[61]

In some circumstances, a failure to discharge a juror may constitute grounds for a subsequent appeal against conviction,[62] and as long as the number of jurors does not fall below nine it is possible for the trial to continue.[63] Exceptionally, the judge may

---

[54] See above.　　　[55] See p 333, *ante*.

[56] This common law power is expressly preserved by s 12(6) of the Juries Act 1974.

[57] [1982] Crim LR 680.　　　[58] Section 10.

[59] Section 9B, as inserted by the Criminal Justice and Public Order Act 1994, s 41. In *Re Osman* [1995] 1 WLR 1327, [1996] 1 Cr App R 126, a profoundly deaf person was discharged on the basis that he could only have understood the case with the assistance of an interpreter: as a non-juror, the interpreter could not have been allowed into the jury room. The Lord Chancellor subsequently indicated that he could see no objection to deaf people serving as jurors: Auld, *Review of the Criminal Courts* (2001), at para 5.56.

[60] *Mansell* v *R* (1857) 8 E & B 54; see Buxton, 'Challenging and Discharging Jurors—1' [1990] Crim LR 225.

[61] *Practice Direction (Jury Service: Excusal (Amendment))* (2005) *The Times*, 24 March (amending *Practice Direction (Criminal Proceedings: Consolidation)* [2002] 1 WLR 2870).

[62] *R* v *Spencer* [1987] AC 128, [1986] 2 All ER 928.　　　[63] 1974 Act, s 16(1).

discharge the entire jury if it appears that jury tampering has taken place,[64] or that the jury may be unable to reach a fair verdict because of adverse media reporting.[65]

C THE USE OF THE JURY TRIAL AT THE PRESENT DAY

Before the present century the jury system was widely pronounced to be one of the chief safeguards against the abuse of prerogative and judicial power. The right to trial by jury was thought to be essential and inviolable, and Blackstone saw the jury in criminal cases as a barrier between the liberties of the people and the prerogative of the Crown.[66] Lord Camden, reflecting the mood of the age, observed:

Trial by jury is indeed the foundation of our free constitution; take that away, and the whole fabric will soon moulder into dust.[67]

By the middle of the nineteenth century the idea that the jury trial was sacrosanct was disappearing, and the jury began to decline as a factor in both civil and criminal cases. The rapid growth in the volume of civil cases and the even more rapid growth of summary jurisdiction in criminal cases contributed to this decline, but there was also an increasing awareness that juries were both fallible and unpredictable. Yet although the use of the jury trial has steadily diminished, the debate about its merits continues, and the jury trial is still regarded by many as the hallmark of the English criminal justice system.

1 CRIMINAL CASES

In criminal cases the loss of faith in the jury system has been less marked than in civil cases. Trial by jury is still the standard mode of trial for indictable offences, and where a defendant aged eighteen or over[68] is prosecuted for an either way offence, he or she normally has the right to insist on trial by jury. Nevertheless, the percentage of criminal cases actually tried by jury is surprisingly low. The vast majority of offences committed are triable only summarily, and not all defendants who have the right to insist on trial by jury actually do so:[69] In 2001, some 1.84 million defendants were

---

[64] Criminal Justice Act 2003, s 46. The judge must then decide whether to continue the proceedings without a jury (see p 339), or whether to terminate the trial.

[65] In 2001 the judge in the trial of four footballers prosecuted for attacking an Asian student ruled that there was no evidence of a racial motive for the assault. The jury was later discharged when a national newspaper ran a story alleging that the attack *was* racially motivated. Three of the footballers were eventually tried before a second jury but two were cleared of all charges. One was convicted of affray.

[66] 3 Comm 379.

[67] See Jackson, *The Machinery of Justice in England* (1989, 8th edn), pp 391 *et seq*.

[68] There are special provisions for children and young persons; see p 552, *post*.

[69] The procedure for the allocation of offences is discussed further at p 547, *post*.

tried summarily, compared with only 78,000 in the Crown Court.[70] Many of those whose cases are disposed of in the Crown Court plead guilty, and the proportion of defendants whose fate is actually determined by a jury is only around 1 per cent. Thus, although the jury trial still has great symbolic importance in the context of serious offences, in the overall scheme of things it actually plays a fairly minor role.

The right to trial by jury for either way offences has been under review for a number of years. Critics have pointed out that jury trials cost considerably more than the summary alternative, and that most defendants who opt for trial by jury eventually plead guilty.[71] However, attempts to remove or diminish the right have always met with stiff opposition.[72] The Auld Report[73] recommended that the final decision about mode of trial should rest with the court and not the defendant, but the changes eventually introduced by the Criminal Justice Act 2003 did not go this far. Instead, a variety of procedural changes have been introduced to encourage more defendants to elect summary trial, together with increased sentencing powers for magistrates courts.

The Roskill Report in 1986 recommended that serious fraud cases should not be tried by jury at all, but should instead be tried by a judge sitting with two lay assessors. This was also advocated by the Auld Review.[74] The 2003 Act, when in force, will permit trial without jury in either of the following types of case:[75]

(a) cases in which there is a real and present danger of jury tampering;[76] and

(b) complex fraud cases in which the trial judge (with the approval of the Lord Chief Justice or his deputy) is satisfied that it is in the interests of justice to hear the case without a jury.[77]

The government undertook not to bring these provisions into effect for the time being. However, the issue resurfaced in March 2005 following the collapse of the 'Jubilee Line Extension' case. The trial of six defendants on allegations of fraud had lasted for 272 days and had been thwarted by excessive delays and problems with the jury. By the time the trial was abandoned, one juror had already been discharged after becoming pregnant and another had been discharged on the grounds of financial hardship. A third juror had requested a discharge on medical grounds, and the health of one of the defendants was also deteriorating. The trial was discontinued at the prosecution's request, and an inquiry ordered by the Attorney-General. On exactly the same day the Lord Chief Justice issued a Protocol for the Control and

---

[70] *Criminal Statistics 2001*, at p 18.

[71] See, e.g., the *Report of the Royal Commission on Criminal Justice*, Cm 2263, 1993; *The Review of Delay in the Criminal Justice System ('the Narey Report')* (1997).

[72] The Criminal Justice (Mode of Trial) Bill 1999 and the Criminal Justice (Mode of Trial) Bill (No 2) 2000, would both have removed the defendant's right to insist on jury trial for an either way offence. Both Bills were defeated in the House of Lords.

[73] *Review of the Criminal Courts of England and Wales* (2001) at para 5.166.   [74] (2001) at para 5.192.

[75] A clause which would have allowed a defendant charged with an indictable offence to request trial by judge alone was dropped from the Bill, following considerable opposition.

[76] Section 44.   [77] Section 43.

Management of Heavy Fraud and other Complex Cases. It provides that serious fraud and other complex trials should not normally be permitted to last longer than three months, although it acknowledges that a small number of exceptional cases may take longer than this. A practice direction issued at the same time reminds judges that they may occasionally need to use their discretion to adjourn a trial or discharge members of a jury. Where the length of a trial is expected to be particularly long, it is said to be good practice for the judge to enquire at the outset whether members of the jury panel foresee any difficulties with this.[78]

Majority verdicts. The standard size of a jury in a criminal case is twelve, but if this figure is reduced because a juror dies or is discharged, it will still be validly constituted as long as the number does not fall below nine.[79] Where a jury has eleven or twelve members, a majority verdict can be accepted if at least ten jurors agree; if a jury has ten members, a majority of nine is acceptable.[80] The verdict of a nine-member jury must be unanimous. The possibility of a majority verdict reduces the likelihood of a jury's decision being affected by bias or tampering, because a single juror will not normally be able to force a re-trial. Before a majority verdict can be accepted however, the jury must have deliberated for a minimum of two hours and the foreman of the jury must state in open court how many jurors agreed with it.[81]

2 CIVIL PROCEEDINGS

It is in civil cases that the decline of the jury has been most marked. Until 1854 most civil actions in the common law courts were tried by jury, but the Common Law Procedure Act 1854 allowed cases to be tried by judge alone if both parties consented. The real turning point was the Administration of Justice (Miscellaneous Provisions) Act 1933, which limited the right to claim trial by jury in a civil action to cases of libel, slander, malicious prosecution, false imprisonment, seduction, breach of promise of marriage, and fraud.[82] So far as the Queen's Bench Division is concerned, the right to a jury trial in these cases is now governed by section 69 of the Supreme Court Act 1981. A jury may only be refused in such a case if the court considers that the trial will involve a scientific or local investigation or a prolonged examination of documents.[83] For all other types of case the grant of a jury is at the discretion of the court. This discretion was once absolute,[84] but in the leading case of *Ward* v *James*[85] the full Court of Appeal established that it had to be exercised judicially. It also stated that unless

---

[78] *Practice Direction (Jury Service: Excusal (Amendment))* (2005) *The Times*, 24 March (amending *Practice Direction (Criminal Proceedings: Consolidation)* [2002] 1 WLR 2870).

[79] Juries Act 1974, s 16(1).   [80] Ibid, s 17.   [81] Ibid, s 17.

[82] Actions for seduction and breach of promise of marriage were abolished by the Law Reform (Miscellaneous Provisions) Act 1970.

[83] *Beta Construction* v *Channel Four Television* [1990] 2 All ER 1012, [1990] 1 WLR 1042; *Viscount De L'Isle* v *Times Newspapers* [1987] 3 All ER 499, [1988] 1 WLR 49.

[84] *Hope* v *Great Western Rly Co* [1937] 2 KB 130, [1937] 1 All ER 625.

[85] [1966] 1 QB 273, [1965] 1 All ER 563.

there were special circumstances, trials in personal injury cases should be by judge alone. The court noted the unpredictability of damages awards in jury cases, and suggested that juries tended to make disproportionate awards because they often assumed that the substantive defendant was a deep-pocketed insurance company.

Immediately before *Ward v James*, approximately 2 per cent of trials in the Queen's Bench Division took place before a jury. The figure is now minimal. In *H v Ministry of Defence*[86] the court was able to identify only one personal injury case since *Ward v James* in which trial by jury had been ordered, and if the Law Commission's recommendations are implemented, the use of the jury in personal injury cases will disappear entirely.[87] Consequently, in little more than a century, jury trial in civil cases has been virtually superseded by trial by judge alone, the one notable exception being trials for defamation. Jury trials in the county courts are even less common, though it is still possible for a county court to try a case before an eight-person jury,[88] and this occasionally happens in civil actions involving the police. Juries of between seven and eleven persons are also used in coroners' cases.[89]

Coroners' cases aside, the role of juries in civil actions remains controversial, and the extremely large awards of damages made by juries in some defamation cases have attracted considerable criticism. The European Court of Human Rights has suggested that such awards could unlawfully restrict freedom of expression, contrary to Article 10 of the ECHR.[90] In *John v Mirror Group Newspapers*, libel damages awarded to the singer Elton John were reduced from £625,000 to £125,000 on appeal, leading the Master of the Rolls to observe that:[91]

It is in our view offensive to public opinion . . . that a defamation plaintiff should recover damages for injury to reputation greater, perhaps by a significant factor, than if the same plaintiff had been rendered a helpless cripple.

In *Grobbelaar v News Group Newspapers*,[92] the House of Lords famously awarded damages of just £1 to a goalkeeper who sued for defamation when match-fixing allegations were published in a national newspaper. Their Lordships clearly took the view that the claimant was the author of his own misfortunes, and they also ordered him to pay his own costs. However, they refused to interfere with the jury's finding of liability on the facts, reversing the Court of Appeal's decision in this respect.

---

[86] [1991] 2 QB 103, [1991] 2 All ER 834.

[87] *Damages for Personal Injury: Non Pecuniary Loss* (HC Working Paper (1995) no 140), p 125. For an argument that there should still be a role for jury trials in personal injury cases, see Morris, 'Jury Trials in Personal Injury Claims—is there a Place for them?' [2002] 3 Journal of Personal Injury Law 310.

[88] County Courts Act 1984, s 66(3). A majority verdict of seven to one is acceptable in such a case: Juries Act 1974, s 17(2).

[89] See Coroners Act 1988, s 8(2)(a), and p 267, *ante*.

[90] *Tolstoy Miloslavksy v UK* (1995) 20 EHRR 442.

[91] [1997] QB 586 at 614, [1996] 2 All ER 35 at 54, per Sir Thomas Bingham MR. See also the comments of Lord Donaldson MR in *Sutcliffe v Pressdram Ltd* [1991] 1 QB 153, [1990] 1 All ER 269. Such cases are discussed further at p 506, *post*.

[92] [2002] UKHL 40, [2002] 4 All ER 732, [2002] 1 WLR 3024.

3 JURY SECRECY

A key principle of the jury system is that what takes place in the jury room must not be disclosed, and the secrecy of jurors' deliberations is protected by both common law and statute. Section 8(1) of the Contempt of Court Act 1981 makes it an offence to obtain, disclose, or solicit any particulars of statements made, opinions expressed, arguments advanced, or votes cast by members of a jury in the course of their deliberations. There are only two exceptions to this rule: (a) disclosures for the purpose of enabling the jury to arrive at and deliver its verdict;[93] and (b) disclosures made where an offence is alleged to have been committed in relation to the jury.[94] In *R v Miah*[95] section 8 was held to apply to 'anything said by one juror to another about the case from the moment the jury is empanelled, at least provided what is said is not overheard by anyone else who is not a juror.' Breach of this rule amounts to contempt of court, even if the breach is indirect. In *Attorney-General v Associated Newspapers*[96] a conviction for publishing the views of the jurors in a long and abortive fraud case was upheld, even though the appellants had obtained the information from a researcher and not directly from the jurors.

At common law, the rule is that 'the court will not investigate, or receive evidence about, anything said in the course of the jury's deliberations while they are considering their verdict in their retiring room.'[97] Evidence of the jury's behaviour *outside* the jury room can be admitted however, and in *R v Young (Stephen)*[98] the Court of Appeal quashed a murder conviction after hearing that the jury had attempted to contact the deceased using a oujia board in a hotel room. The rationale for maintaining the secrecy of jury deliberations was explained by Atkin LJ:[99]

[O]n the one hand it is in order to secure the finality of decisions arrived at by the jury, and on the other to protect the jurymen themselves and prevent their being exposed to pressure to explain the reasons which actuated them in arriving at their verdict.

It is also assumed that jurors are more likely to express their views honestly and frankly if they feel confident that their deliberations will remain confidential. On the other hand, the law operates with such rigidity that there is a serious risk of miscarriages of justice going undiscovered and unchallenged.

The scope of both the common law and statutory prohibitions was recently considered by the House of Lords in *R v Mirza (Shabbir Ali)*.[100] The defendant was a Pakistani man charged with six counts of indecent assault. As English was not his first language he was assisted in court by an interpreter, but the jury sent two separate

---

[93] Section 8(2)(a). It is lawful, for example, for notes to be passed between the judge and jury for this purpose.

[94] Section 8(2)(b).   [95] [1997] 2 Cr App R 12 at 18, per Kennedy LJ.

[96] [1994] 2 AC 238, [1994] 1 All ER 556.

[97] *R v Mirza (Shabbir Ali)* [2004] UKHL 2 at [95], [2004] 1 AC 1118 at [95], [2004] 1 All ER 925, per Lord Hope.

[98] [1995] QB 324, [1995] 2 WLR 430.   [99] *Ellis v Deheer* [1922] 2 KB 113 at 121.

[100] [2004] UKHL 2, [2004] 1 AC 1118, [2004] 1 All ER 925.

notes to the judge, indicating that they found the use of the interpreter suspicious. The judge directed the jury that they should draw no adverse inference from the use of the interpreter, but a letter written by a juror six days after the defendant's conviction indicated that they had ignored these instructions and were possibly influenced by racial prejudice. The Court of Appeal dismissed the defendant's appeal against conviction. The issue for the House of Lords was whether a court was prevented, either at common law or under the 1981 Act, from considering evidence of jury deliberations indicating a breach of Article 6. In a partial departure from the previous case law,[101] their Lordships held that section 8 of the 1981 Act was addressed to third parties and did not prevent a court from investigating allegations of injustice. A court had a responsibility to ensure that the defendant received a fair trial and it could not be in contempt of itself. However, a majority of their Lordships also upheld the common law rule against receiving evidence of jury deliberations. Exceptions to this rule could only be made where it was alleged that the jury had been affected by 'extraneous influences' or had declined to deliberate at all.[102]

The Article 6 dimension. The majority in *Mirza* clearly felt that the existing approach to jury secrecy was not incompatible with the right to a fair trial, but in a strong dissenting judgment, Lord Steyn argued that:[103]

[T]here is a positive duty on judges, when things have gone seriously wrong in the criminal justice system, to do everything possible to put it right. In the world of today, enlightened public opinion would accept nothing less. It would be contrary to the spirit of these developments to say that in one area, namely the deliberations of the jury, injustice can be tolerated as the price for protecting the jury system.

In *Gregory* v *UK*,[104] the European Court of Human Rights accepted the rules governing the secrecy of jury deliberations as a crucial and legitimate feature of English trial law. Thus, a judge who refused to investigate a juror's allegations that another member of the jury had made racist remarks, and who dealt with the matter by reminding the jury to decide the case according to the evidence, was held to have satisfied Article 6. By contrast, a breach of Article 6 was established on similar facts in *Sander* v *UK*.[105] The judge in this case had responded to the original allegation of racism by asking

---

[101] In *R* v *Young (Stephen)* [1995] QB 324, [1995] 2 WLR 430 the Court of Appeal held that it was prevented by section 8 from hearing evidence concerning improper conduct in the jury room: see p 342, *ante*. See also *R* v *Qureshi* [2001] EWCA Crim 1807, [2002] 1 WLR 518, [2002] 1 Cr App R 33, in which a juror made allegations of racial bias three days after the verdict. Leave to appeal was refused on the basis that the jury's verdict had been accepted by the trial judge and section 8 of the 1981 Act prevented any investigation into its deliberations.

[102] The 2005 consultation on jury research asks whether clarification of this area of law is needed, though it makes it clear that the government's own preference is to leave such matters to the courts: *Jury Research and Impropriety* CP 04/05, discussed at p 344, *post*.

[103] [2004] UKHL 2 at [4], [2004] 1 AC 1118 at [4], [2004] 1 All ER 925.

[104] (1998) 25 EHRR 577 at 594.

[105] (2001) 31 EHRR 44. See also, *Remli* v *France* (1996) 22 EHRR 253 (breach of Article 6 established when a court failed to investigate allegations of juror bias which came to light after the verdict); Zander, 'The Complaining Juror' (2000) 150 NLJ 723.

the jurors to search their consciences, and after receiving a note from the entire jury refuting the allegations, he had declined to do anything further. The distinction between these cases is a fine one, but it would appear that as long as a judge takes reasonable steps to address allegations made during the course of a trial, the court's duty under Article 6 will have been satisfied.

On a related matter, Darbyshire and others have questioned whether the failure of the jury system to provide a defendant with a reasoned verdict is itself a breach of Article 6:[106]

It is hard to see, in an era when every tribunal and magistrates' court provides a reasoned decision, how the secrecy of jury trials can survive.

Darbyshire concludes that juries should be required to respond to a series of written questions formulated by counsel and the judge, arguing that this would ensure compliance with Article 6 and would also help to reduce the scope for 'perverse verdicts'. The recommendation was endorsed by Lord Justice Auld in his Review of the Criminal Courts.[107] In his dissenting opinion in *Mirza*, Lord Steyn suggested that a jury is a judicial tribunal in its own right, and that its obligation to comply with the requirements of Article 6 is independent of any obligation on the judge.[108] This was not, however, a view endorsed by the majority.

Jury research. Section 8 of the 1981 Act has been criticized for severely restricting the scope for conducting research into the jury system, and in 1993 the Royal Commission on Criminal Justice proposed an amendment which would make legitimate jury research possible. In 2005 the Department for Constitutional Affairs revealed that such an amendment was finally being considered. The proposal outlined in its consultation paper would allow the Secretary of State to authorise specific research projects. Such research would be subject to strict conditions agreed in consultation with the Lord Chief Justice and would also be governed by a Code of Conduct. Unauthorized research into jury deliberations would remain unlawful.[109]

D THE MERITS OF JURY TRIAL

Jury trial has been the subject of significant criticism in recent years, with the most contentious issue being what some regard as an unacceptably high acquittal rate in

---

[106] Darbyshire, Maughan and Stewart, *What can the English Legal System Learn from Jury Research Published up to 2001?—Findings for the Criminal Courts Review* (2001) at p 39. See also, Pritchard, 'A Reform for Jury Trial?' (1998) 148 NLJ 45.

[107] (2001) at para 11.41.

[108] [2004] UKHL 2 at [6], [2004] 1 AC 1118 at [6], [2004] 1 All ER 925.

[109] *Jury Research and Impropriety* (2005) CP 04/05.

criminal cases.[110] Statistically, jury trials do result in proportionately more acquittals than magistrates' cases,[111] but the proportion of defendants acquitted by juries on all counts is still quite low.[112] In addition, it is difficult to make direct comparisons because the statistics are calculated differently and are influenced by different factors. For example, much of the business of magistrates' courts consists of strict liability offences where the scope for contesting guilt is reduced and the stakes are lower. The proportion of defendants pleading guilty in summary cases is therefore much higher than for cases in the Crown Court. Similarly, the acquittal rate for either way cases in the Crown Court may be at least partly explained by the fact that those who have a comparatively weak defence are less likely to elect trial by jury because of the risk of receiving a stiffer sentence if convicted.

The reality is that too little is known about how juries work, and as stated previously, research into how juries reach their verdicts is currently prohibited by the Contempt of Court Act 1981. In an attempt to work around this restriction some research has been carried out using 'shadow juries', where a panel of 'shadow' jurors is asked to follow a real case.[113] Some anecdotal and personal accounts of real jurors have also been published, and in 2001 a group of academics carried out a comprehensive review of jury research published in the UK and elsewhere.

The merits of the jury system are sometimes stated in terms of the deficiencies of alternative modes of trial. Although the summary process in the magistrates' courts is relatively quick and cheap, it is by no means beyond criticism, and it is often thought that jury trial favours an accused. Other advocates of jury trial rely upon its constitutional importance, and on the safeguards that it is said to provide for defendants.[114] In *Ward v James*, Lord Denning MR explained the role of the modern jury as follows:[115]

Let it not be supposed that this court is in any way opposed to trial by jury. It has been the bulwark of our liberties too long for any of us to seek to alter it. Whenever a man is on trial for serious crime, or when in a civil case a man's honour or integrity is at stake, or when one or other party must be deliberately lying, then trial by jury has no equal.

It was put more graphically by Lord Devlin, who described jury trial as 'the lamp that shows that freedom lives'.[116] Not all commentators are convinced by this romanticism, pointing out that this 'bulwark of our liberties' did not prevent any of the famous

---

[110] See, e.g. Darbyshire, 'For the New Lord Chancellor: Some Causes for Concern about Magistrates' [1997] Crim LR 861.

[111] In 2002 just over 30 per cent of contested cases in the magistrates' courts were dismissed. In the same year, 65 per cent of those pleading not guilty in the Crown Court were either acquitted by the jury or had the case discharged by the judge—*Criminal Statistics 2002*, at p16.

[112] In 2001, 8.6 per cent of cases committed for trial in the Crown Court resulted in the defendant being acquitted by a jury on all counts. A further 17.3 per cent were acquitted by or on the direction of the judge and 14.8 per cent were convicted on some or all counts after pleading not guilty. The majority of defendants —56.3 per cent—pleaded guilty: *Judicial Statistics 2001*, at pp 68–9.

[113] See McCabe and Purves *The Shadow Jury at Work* (1974).

[114] On this argument, see: Cornish, *The Jury* (1970).

[115] [1966] 1 QB 273 at 295, [1965] 1 All ER 563 at 571.   [116] Devlin, *Trial By Jury* (1956).

miscarriages of justice exposed in the 1990s.[117] Critics have also pointed to the potentially random factors that may affect a jury's deliberations. The fact that juries are laymen who are not required to explain their decisions leaves greater scope for them to be influenced by factors which have nothing to do with the law or the evidence. Thus, they may occasionally reach perverse verdicts because they have acted on the basis of prejudice and stereotypes or because they have failed to properly understand the legal and evidential issues. Juries may also return verdicts motivated by conscience, and there are many well-known examples of cases in which juries are thought to have acquitted defendants on moral rather than legal grounds. In 1985 for example, a jury found Clive Ponting not guilty of committing official secrets offences, despite clear evidence that he had in fact done what he was accused of. Similarly, in 2000, a multiple sclerosis sufferer was acquitted on charges of possessing cannabis after the jury was told that the defendant used the drug to relieve the symptoms of the disease. For some, the ability of a jury to deliver a moral verdict in such cases is one of the system's great strengths, but for others, these perverse acquittals are an affront to the rule of law.

Academic opinion on the jury system may be divided, but it seems that jurors themselves are strongly in favour of it. A recent Home Office survey, based on interviews with those summoned for jury service in six courts, found that:[118]

[T]he majority of respondents had a more positive view of the jury trial system after completing their service than they did before. Furthermore, virtually all jurors interviewed considered jury trials to be an important part of the criminal justice system.

---

[117] See Darbyshire, 'The Lamp that Shows that Freedom Lives: is it Worth the Candle?' [1991] Crim LR 740. Ironically, the primacy of jury trial has also been used as a justification for judicial non-interference with verdicts in alleged miscarriage of justice cases: see p 681, *post*.

[118] Matthews, Hancock and Briggs: *Jurors' Perceptions, Understanding, Confidence and Satisfaction in the Jury System: A Study in Six Courts* (2004) Home Office Research Study 227, at p 1.

11

LEGAL SERVICES

A THE LEGAL PROFESSION: THE ORGANIZATIONAL FRAMEWORK

A distinctive feature of the English legal system is the division of the legal profession into two separate branches: solicitors and barristers. Such a division is unknown outside Britain and the Commonwealth, and elsewhere all practitioners are simply described as 'lawyers'. The division dates back to around 1340, which is when professional advocacy first evolved:[1] attorneys, who were the forerunners of solicitors, were responsible for carrying out the preparatory stages of an action, but only serjeants and barristers had rights of audience in the common law courts. This basic distinction still exists at a formal level, but the differences between the two professions are rapidly diminishing in practice. Thus, while barristers are still thought of primarily as advocates, most spend a lot of time engaged in 'paper-work' such as the drafting of pleadings, opinions, and divorce petitions. Employed barristers can even conduct litigation.[2] Similarly, while solicitors are still responsible for the preparatory stages of litigation, they also deal with a range of non-litigious matters such as conveyancing and the drafting of wills, and all solicitors have rights in audience in at least some courts and tribunals.[3]

In 1976 a Royal Commission was set up to inquire into the provision of legal services. Its report was published in 1979 and it suggested that the legal profession was performing its functions well.[4] The Report was broadly supportive of the status quo and did not advocate fusing the two branches of the profession.[5] It did, however, prompt further debate and discussion. Over the next ten years the government published White Papers on civil justice,[6] legal services,[7] the legal profession,[8] conveyancing services,[9] and contingency fees.[10] Eventually, in 1990, the Courts and Legal Services Act was passed.

---

[1] For details see Baker, *An Introduction to English Legal History* (4th edn, 2002).
[2] See p 355, *post.*   [3] See p 350, *post.*
[4] Report of the Royal Commission on Legal Services (Cmnd 7648, 1979)—'The Benson Report'.
[5] Ibid, paras 17.45–17.46.   [6] Report of the Review Body on Civil Justice, Cm 394, 1988.
[7] Legal Services: A Framework for the Future, Cm 740, 1989.
[8] The Workload and Organisation of the Legal Profession, Cm 570, 1989.
[9] Conveyancing by Authorised Practitioners, Cm 572, 1989.   [10] *Contingency Fees*, Cm 571, 1989.

1 THE COURTS AND LEGAL SERVICES ACT 1990

The 1990 Act is based on a distinct philosophy, as set out in section 17(1):

The general objective of this Part is the development of legal services in England and Wales (and in particular the development of advocacy, litigation, conveyancing and probate services) by making provision of new or better ways of providing such services, and a wider choice of persons providing them, while maintaining the proper and efficient administration of justice.

In addition to preserving the existing rights of audience of solicitors and barristers,[11] section 17(3) of the Act established the 'general principle' that rights of audience should be linked to the following criteria:

(i) possession of appropriate qualifications;

(ii) membership of a professional body with effective and enforceable rules of conduct;

(iii) the existence of satisfactory arrangements for ensuring that legal services are not withheld on objectionable grounds; and

(iv) the existence of appropriate rules of conduct.

The Act provided a framework for solicitors to break the monopoly that barristers had enjoyed over advocacy work in the higher courts,[12] and it opened up the possibility that rights of audience might be extended to members of other professions.[13] The rules governing the provision of litigation[14] and probate[15] services were also relaxed, and section 66 of the Act removed the legal obstacles preventing solicitors from forming partnerships with non-solicitors.[16] The Act thus laid the foundations for significant changes to the way in which legal services were provided. It also provided for the appointment of a Legal Services Ombudsman[17] with the power to review complaints handling by the professional regulatory bodies.[18]

2 THE ACCESS TO JUSTICE ACT 1999

The Access to Justice Act 1999 made important changes to the funding of legal services: it established two separate schemes to replace what used to be known as 'Legal Aid', and it relaxed some of the rules governing the remuneration of lawyers through private funds.[19] Part III of the Act continued the theme of the Courts and Legal

---

[11] Sections 31 to 33.   [12] See p 350, *post*.

[13] Section 27: for more detailed discussion of rights of audience, see p 350, *post*.

[14] Section 28: see p 349, *post*.

[15] Section 55, which was not implemented until 2004: see p 350, *post*. Due to a lack of demand, provisions which would have further relaxed the rules governing conveyancing services have not been implemented at all: see p 350, *post*.

[16] There had been no such legal obstacles relating to barristers, though both solicitors and barristers have been prevented from entering into multi-disciplinary partnerships by their own professional rules.

[17] See p 367, *post*.   [18] See p 364, *post*.   [19] Sections 27–28: see p 373, *post*.

Services Act, by establishing the general principle that all lawyers with appropriate qualifications should be able to exercise full rights of audience in all proceedings. It also simplified the procedure for approving any further changes to rights of audience and rights to conduct litigation,[20] in addition to conferring additional powers on the Legal Services Ombudsman.[21]

B THE WORK OF SOLICITORS AND BARRISTERS

1 SOLICITORS

For most people seeking legal services or advice, a solicitor will be their first point of contact. In addition to conducting the preparatory stages of litigation, solicitors as a profession provide a wide range of other services. These include conveyancing work, the drafting of wills, the supervision of trusts and settlements, the administration of estates, the provision of advice on matters such as welfare law, immigration, and divorce, and the provision of advice and assistance to persons in custody. In addition, all solicitors enjoy at least some rights of audience before the courts,[22] and advocacy is an increasingly important part of the work of many solicitors. There is thus consider-able variety in the types of work that different solicitors do, and there is a growing trend towards specialisation. For example, while many high-street firms offer a gen-eral range of services, others—particularly sole practitioners—elect to specialize in certain areas such as conveyancing or personal injury work. At the other end of the scale, many solicitors now work in very large firms which deal only with corporate and commercial law, whilst others provide legal services as employees of local governments or Law Centres.[23]

(a) The right to conduct litigation

The right to conduct litigation is defined in the Courts and Legal Services Act 1990 as the right:[24]

(a) to issue proceedings before any court; and

(b) to perform any ancillary functions in relation to proceedings (such as entering appearances to actions).

Section 28 of the Act established the principle that any person should be entitled to conduct litigation where the right to do so has been conferred by an appropriate body. At the time, the only body authorized to confer the right was the Law Society, and the Act thus had the effect of preserving the monopoly that solicitors had enjoyed in this

---

[20] See pp 350–1, *post.*   [21] See p 367, *post.*   [22] See p 350, *post.*

[23] For a survey of recent trends, see the Law Society's *Annual Statistical Report, 2003.*

[24] Section 119 (as amended).

area. In 1999 the Bar Council and the Institute of Legal Executives were added to the list of 'authorised bodies' capable of granting litigation rights to their members.[25] However, the Bar Council has so far declined to grant such rights to barristers in independent practice.[26] The Act also established a process by which other organizations could apply to the Lord Chancellor for recognition as authorized bodies.[27] At the time of writing, two organizations had made successful use of this system: the Chartered Institute of Patent Agents and the Institute of Trade Mark Attorneys.[28]

(b) Other monopolies: conveyancing and probate

The monopoly of solicitors over conveyancing work was formally ended by the Administration of Justice Act 1985. Part II of this Act introduced a system of licensed conveyancers and established the Council for Licensed Conveyancers to regulate and oversee the new profession. Provisions in the Courts and Legal Services Act 1990[29] were designed to further liberalize the market and to create a new supervisory body, the Authorised Conveyancing Practitioners Board. The implementation of these provisions was postponed indefinitely due to a lack of demand, but following the publication of the Clementi Report in 2004[30] it seems that reform may once again be on the agenda.[31]

Solicitors have also had a virtual monopoly over the right to perform probate work,[32] but the government is now looking at ways of opening up this market to competition. Section 55 of the 1990 Act provides that any organization which has been 'approved' by the Lord Chancellor may authorize suitably qualified persons to provide probate services for reward. This provision was brought into force in December 2004, and the government envisages that the Council for Licensed Conveyancers will be one of the first bodies to seek approved status.[33] Banks, building societies, and insurance companies will also be able to offer probate services when section 54 of the 1990 Act is implemented.[34]

(c) Rights of audience

Solicitors may be slowly losing their monopolies over litigation, conveyancing, and probate work, but they are also making in-roads into an area that has historically been

[25] Access to Justice Act 1999, s 40.

[26] Such rights *have* been granted to employed barristers: see p 355, *post.*

[27] Courts and Legal Services Act 1990, s 29; Schedule 4 (as amended).

[28] Chartered Institute of Patent Agents Order 1999, SI 1999/3137; Institute of Trade Mark Attorneys Order 2005/240.

[29] Sections 34–53

[30] Final Report of the Review of the Regulatory Framework for Legal Services in England and Wales: see p 362, post

[31] As indicated by the Lord Chancellor at the Legal Services Reform Conference, 21 March 2005.

[32] At the time of writing, only solicitors, barristers and public notaries may undertake probate work for reward: Solicitors Act 1974, s 23.

[33] See also: Courts and Legal Services Act 1990, s 53.

[34] Department for Constitutional Affairs, Competition and Regulation in the Legal Services Market—A Report following the Consultation 'In the Public Interest?' (2003) at para 41.

the preserve of barristers: that of advocacy. Prior to the Courts and Legal Services Act 1990, solicitors had only limited rights of audience: they could appear on behalf of clients in magistrates' courts, county courts, and most tribunals, but barristers had exclusive rights of audience in most Crown Court and High Court cases and in all cases coming before the Court of Appeal and House of Lords.[35] The 1990 Act established the general principle that rights of audience should be determined on the basis of: (a) qualifications; and (b) membership of a properly regulated profession.[36] The Act did not affect the rights of audience acquired by solicitors and barristers on joining their respective professions, but it did authorize the Law Society and the Bar Council to confer rights of audience on their members. The Law Society's criteria for granting higher court rights of audience to solicitors were approved in 1994.[37]

The Bar Council had argued that their monopoly over higher court advocacy was necessary for the maintenance of high standards and for the preservation of a strong and effective Bar.[38] They had also noted that solicitors had no equivalent of the 'cab-rank' rule,[39] meaning that they had greater freedom than barristers in choosing which cases to accept. The Law Society had responded by pointing out that solicitors were already doing advocacy work in the lower courts, and that the cab-rank rule was often ineffective in practice.[40] In the end the new system appeared to satisfy no-one. As Humphries observed in 1998:[41]

The levels of competence, experience and training required to achieve the qualification have been kept so high that today only 624 out of more than 70,000 solicitors have the right to appear in the higher courts.

The Access to Justice Act 1999 simplified matters by providing that all solicitors who have complied with the Law Society's training requirements should have a full right of audience before every court.[42] By 2004 it was reported that around 2,000 solicitors had obtained higher court advocacy rights.[43]

The principle set out in section 36 applies equally to barristers, and the restrictions on rights of audience which had once been imposed on employed barristers have now been lifted for most purposes.[44] Note also that the Institute of Legal Executives, the Chartered Institute of Patent Agents, and the Institute of Trade Mark Attorneys have

---

[35] These limitations were derived from the practices of the courts themselves. See, e.g. *Practice Direction (Supreme Court: Solicitors: Rights of Audience)* [1986] 2 All ER 226, [1986] 1 WLR 545; *Practice Direction (Crown Court: Solicitors: Rights of Audience)* [1988] 3 All ER 717, [1988] 1 WLR 1427.

[36] Section 17(3): see p 348, *ante.*

[37] These rules required the approval of the Lord Chancellor, the Master of the Rolls, the Lord Chief Justice, and the Vice-Chancellor before they could take effect.

[38] Bar Council, *The Quality of Justice—The Bar's Response* (1989) at pp 128–146.

[39] See p 355, *post.*

[40] See *Striking the Balance: The Final Response of the Council of the Law Society on the Green Papers* (1989).

[41] 'Preparing for the New Order in Court', *The Lawyer*, 21 July 1998 at p 14.

[42] Section 36, which substitutes section 31(2)(a) of the Courts and Legal Services Act 1990.

[43] Final Report of the Review of the Regulatory Framework for Legal Services in England and Wales (2004) at para 6.

[44] Access to Justice Act 1999, s 37: see p 356, *post.*

been designated as 'authorised bodies' by the Lord Chancellor.[45] This means that they are able to confer limited rights of audience on their members.[46]

(d) The relationship between solicitor and client

A solicitor's authority derives from the retainer given to him by his client, the effect of which is to create a contractual relationship. The precise scope of this relationship will depend on the terms of the retainer, but a solicitor will generally acquire the authority to act as an agent on his client's behalf,[47] and he will be entitled to remuneration on completion of the work agreed. The relationship is not governed solely by the law of contract however, and it is circumscribed by a variety of statutory rules.[48]

The solicitor–client relationship is also a fiduciary one, which means that a solicitor has an obligation derived from equity to act in good faith in all dealings with his client. In particular, a solicitor who enters into a transaction with his client must ensure: (a) that he has made a full and honest disclosure of all facts within his knowledge; (b) that the financial terms are fair to the client; and (c) that the transaction was not procured by undue influence. A failure to do any of these things may result in the transaction being set aside.[49] A presumption of undue influence will also arise if a client gives his solicitor an inter vivos gift: in *Wright* v *Carter* it was held that this presumption could only be rebutted by evidence that the gift had been made or affirmed after the fiduciary relationship had ended.[50] The presumption of undue influence does not apply to gifts made by will, but where a solicitor prepares a will under which he receives a large benefit a court will require affirmative proof that the testator knew and fully approved of its contents.[51]

Another feature of this fiduciary relationship is the confidential nature of solicitor–client communications. This gives rise to two types of privilege: privilege in the tort of defamation and privilege from disclosure in evidence. This latter privilege, legal professional privilege, is regarded as fundamental.[52] Communications between solicitor and client are privileged provided they were made in confidence and for the purposes of obtaining or giving legal advice about the client's rights, liabilities, obligations, or remedies. In the important case of *Three Rivers District Council* v *Bank of England (Disclosure)*[53] Lord Scott endorsed the view expressed by Taylor LJ in an earlier case:[54]

[L]egal advice is not confined to telling the client the law; it must include advice as to what should prudently and sensibly be done in the relevant legal context.

---

[45] Courts and Legal Services Act 1990, s 27(9); Schedule 4.

[46] Institute of Legal Executives Order 1998, SI 1998/1077; Chartered Institute of Patent Agents Order 1999, SI 1999/3137; Institute of Trade Mark Attorneys Order 2005/240.

[47] See p 368, *post*.   [48] See generally, the Solicitors Act 1974, and p 360, *post*.

[49] *Wright* v *Carter* [1903] 1 Ch 27 at 60, per Stirling LJ.

[50] Ibid: evidence that the client had received independent advice from another solicitor did not suffice.

[51] *Wintle* v *Nye* [1959] 1 All ER 552, [1959] 1 WLR 284.

[52] See *R* v *Derby Magistrates' Court, ex parte B* [1996] AC 487, [1995] 4 All ER 526; *Three Rivers District Council* v *Bank of England (Disclosure)* [2004] UKHL 48, [2004] 3 WLR 1274.

[53] [2004] UKHL 48 at [38], [2004] 3 WLR 1274 at [38].

[54] *Balabel* v *Air India* [1988] Ch 317 at 330, [1988] 2 All ER 246 at 254.

The *Three Rivers* case itself concerned advice given to the Bank of England about its submissions to a public inquiry. Despite being largely presentational, the advice was held to be covered by legal professional privilege: the fact that the Bank may have been the subject of criticism by the inquiry gave the advice a legal context. On the other hand, their Lordships made it clear that not all communications between lawyer and client would necessarily be protected in this way. It was observed, for example, that advice relating to investments, finance, and other business matters would often lack a legal context.[55] This decision also confirms that legal professional privilege is absolute, and that once established it can only be waived by the client or overridden by statute.[56] Note finally that privilege also attaches to communications made in connection with current or contemplated litigation, and that in this context it may extend to cover communications with third parties.

2 BARRISTERS

(a) Inns of Court

A person may only practice as a barrister in England if he has been 'called to the Bar' of one of the four Inns of Court: Lincoln's Inn, the Inner Temple, the Middle Temple, and Gray's Inn. These Inns are as old as the profession itself and appear to have originated as living quarters for apprentices-at-law. Their jurisdiction derives from the judiciary and is subject to judicial control.[57]

A person seeking to qualify as a barrister must join one of the four Inns before he can begin the vocational stage of his legal training.[58] He must also keep a number of terms,[59] which means attending some of the dinners, educational days, and residential weekends that are organized by each Inn. The benchers of an Inn, who are judges or senior members of the Bar, have absolute control over the admission of students and the call of barristers. In principle the benchers also have jurisdiction over disciplinary matters, though for most purposes this jurisdiction is in practice delegated to the disciplinary tribunals appointed by the Inns Council. Any appeal against a decision of the benchers lies to the 'Visitors' of the Inns of Court—a domestic tribunal comprising the judges of the High Court.

(b) Practice at the bar

Most barristers work in independent practice in sets of chambers, which are associations of barristers sharing common facilities and administrative support. The work of each barrister is organized and arranged by the barrister's clerk, who also plays a

---

[55] [2004] UKHL 48 at [38], [2004] 3 WLR 1274 at [38], per Lord Scott.   [56] Ibid at [25].

[57] *R v Gray's Inn* (1780) 1 Doug K353, per Lord Mansfield; *Lincoln v Daniels* [1962] 1 QB 237 at 250, [1961] 3 All ER 740 at 745, per Sellers J.

[58] The various stages of a barrister's training are discussed further at p 359, *post.*

[59] The current requirement is that a student should complete twelve 'qualifying units': a dinner counts as one unit, an educational day counts as two, and a residential weekend counts as three.

key role in re-allocating cases when a barrister is unable to appear because of other commitments. The role of the barrister is primarily that of an advocate, and barristers are deemed to have been granted rights of audience before every court in relation to all proceedings.[60] They also deal with matters such as the giving of advice and the drafting of legal documents, though self-employed barristers are currently prevented by Bar Council rules from conducting litigation.[61] The practice of wearing robes continues despite some debate as to its utility,[62] and counsel cannot generally be 'heard' in court unless they are dressed in the appropriate wig, gown, and bands. They do not, however, wear robes when appearing before courts which are themselves unrobed, magistrates' courts being one example.

Barristers are divided into junior counsel and Queen's Counsel (QCs). The latter are known as 'silks' because they wear silk gowns as opposed to the stuff gowns worn by juniors. Appointments to the office of Queen's Counsel are made by the Crown on the advice of the Lord Chancellor, and are based on ability and experience. Silks are instructed in the most difficult, complex, or important of cases and are able to command much higher fees than their junior counterparts. At one time they were subject to rules preventing them from doing drafting work or giving written opinions on evidence, and they were not permitted to appear in court without a junior. Such formal restrictions no longer exist, though a QC is not obliged to accept instructions to act without a junior if he feels that it would not be in the interests of his client to do so. The established practice has been for appointments to the office of Queen's Counsel to be made annually, but in 2003 the process was suspended pending the outcome of a consultation exercise.[63] Changes were made to the selection process as a result of this consultation,[64] and the annual round of appointments resumed in 2005. Although the consultation revealed *some* support for the idea that a two-tier system works against the public interest, the overall conclusion was that the title of QC serves as a useful 'kitemark' or indication of quality.[65]

(c) The relationship between barrister and client

Whereas the relationship between solicitor and client is to some extent regulated by statute, a barrister's obligations towards his client are largely governed by self-imposed standards.[66] The common law rule which historically prevented self-employed

---

[60] Courts and Legal Services Act 1990, s 31(1).

[61] Code of Conduct of the Bar of England and Wales (8th edn, 2004) para 401: see also pp 349, and 356.

[62] A recent survey commissioned by the Lord Chancellor's Department found strong support for the reform of court dress from both court users and members of the public. There was no consensus as to what form any change might take, though only 34 per cent of advocates favoured the retention of wigs: ORC International, *Public Perceptions of Working Court Dress in England and Wales* (2002). See also: Lord Chancellor's Department, *Consultation on Court Working Dress in England and Wales* (2003) CP 05/03. At the time of writing it remains unclear whether the practice will survive.

[63] Department for Constitutional Affairs, *The Future of Queen's Counsel* (2003) CP 08/03.

[64] QC's are now selected by a panel comprising solicitors, barristers, laymen, and a judge, with the Lord Chancellor having no direct input into the decision.

[65] See Lord Falconer (Lord Chancellor), 661 HL Official Report (5th series) col WS54, 26 May 2004.

[66] See Code of Conduct of the Bar of England and Wales (8th edn, 2004).

barristers from entering into contracts for the provision of their services was abolished in 1990.[67] However, it was not until 2001 that the Bar Council relaxed its own rules and allowed barristers to accept instructions from solicitors on contractual terms.[68] Further changes in 2004 mean that barristers can now accept instructions directly from lay clients, though they are prohibited from doing so in certain types of case.[69] Barristers may advertise their services by any means permitted by law, though the Bar Council's Code of Conduct[70] prohibits them from publicising their success rates or making direct comparisons with their competitors.

A barrister has an obligation to preserve the confidences of his client, and he is deemed to have the authority to conduct proceedings on his client's behalf. The scope of this authority is subject to the ordinary principles of agency,[71] and it includes the authority to compromise proceedings and to make admissions on the client's behalf in civil proceedings. Note should also be taken of the 'cab-rank' principle. In theory this obliges barristers to accept any brief in an area in which they practice, provided that they are available and are offered a proper fee. A busy barrister can easily be committed elsewhere however, and the extent to which the cab-rank principle operates in practice is questionable.[72] Indeed, in 1973 some twenty-four QCs declined to accept briefs on behalf of the IRA Old Bailey bombers.[73] This is undoubtedly an extreme example and it is impossible to know the reasons given by those who were unable to accept the brief. Nevertheless, it seems unlikely that barristers are regularly forced to undertake work which they would not otherwise have accepted,[74] and in any event the cab-rank rule does not apply to work undertaken on the basis of a contract or conditional fee agreement.[75] In addition, barristers are required by the Bar's Code of Conduct to refuse to accept instructions which might cause 'professional embarrassment' or create a conflict of interests.

(d) Employed barristers

Although most barristers are self-employed and working in independent practice, a sizeable minority supply legal services as salaried employees. Some are employed by solicitors' firms, but barristers are also employed in other sectors such as government and commerce. Employed barristers may not supply legal services for reward except in the course of their employment, and in most cases this means that they may only supply legal services to their own employers. However, a barrister in the employment

---

[67] Courts and Legal Services Act 1990, s 61(1).

[68] See Annexe G2 of the Code of Conduct: 'The Contractual Terms of Work on Which Barristers Offer their Services to Solicitors'.

[69] See Annexe F2 of the Code of Conduct: 'The Public Access Rules'.   [70] At para 710.

[71] See p 368, post.

[72] See the survey covered by Walson, 'Advocacy for the Unpopular' (1998) 162 JP 499.

[73] Robertson, *The Justice Game* (1998) at p 379.

[74] See the observations of Lord Steyn in *Arthur JS Hall & Co* v *Simons* [2002] 1 AC 615 at 678, [2000] 3 All ER 673 at 759.

[75] Barristers have also voted to abandon the rule in certain public-funded cases: see p 382, post.

of a solicitor, authorized litigator, legal advice centre, or the Legal Services Commission may also provide legal services for his employer's clients.[76]

All employed barristers are permitted by the Bar's Code of Conduct to conduct litigation,[77] provided that they comply with the relevant rules and have completed the necessary training.[78] In addition to performing the other functions normally undertaken by barristers, an employed barrister may also interview witnesses, take statements, and handle his employers' funds. However, a barrister who has never practised in chambers may only exercise full rights of audience if he practises (or has practised) from the office of an experienced advocate for a period of at least three years.[79]

3 THE DIRECTOR OF PUBLIC PROSECUTIONS AND THE CROWN PROSECUTION SERVICE

Before 1985 there was no national system for the prosecution of offences, and arrangements varied considerably from one police area to the next. Some forces relied on local authority solicitors or solicitors in private practice, but many had their own prosecuting solicitors departments. The role of the Director of Public Prosecutions was supervisory and advisory, and he assumed responsibility for the prosecution of serious offences such as murder. The Royal Commission on Criminal Procedure[80] concluded that an independent system of public prosecutions was essential, and it recommended that once a police force had decided to prosecute, the conduct of that prosecution should be entrusted to a separate authority.[81] The Commission recommended that this new authority should be locally based,[82] but the government opted to create a national prosecution service under the control of the DPP. The government's decision was given effect by the Prosecution of Offences Act 1985, which established the Crown Prosecution Service (CPS).

Section 2 of the Act provides that the DPP must be a barrister or solicitor of not less than ten years' standing, and that he must be appointed by the Attorney-General. His duties are set out in section 3(2) of that Act, and they include the following:

(a) to take over the conduct of all criminal proceedings instituted on behalf of a police force;

(b) to institute and conduct criminal proceedings where the importance or difficulty of the case makes it appropriate that he should do so;

(c) to take over binding over proceedings brought by a police force;

(d) to give advice to police forces on all matters relating to criminal offences; and

---

[76] Code of Conduct of the Bar of England and Wales, Part V. Employed barristers are not prohibited from supplying legal services to the public free of charge.

[77] At para 504: cf. the position of self-employed barristers, at p 354, ante.

[78] Code of Conduct, Annexe I: Employed Barristers (Conduct of Litigation) Rules.

[79] He must also have completed a pupillage: see p 359, post. A person who has not completed a pupillage may be employed as a barrister without rights of audience if he was called to the Bar before 2002.

[80] Cm 8092, 1981.   [81] Ibid, at para 7.3.   [82] Ibid, at para 7.22.

(e) to appear in certain appeals.

Any member of the Crown Prosecution Service who is a barrister or solicitor may be designated by the DPP as a Crown Prosecutor.[83] Crown Prosecutors have all the powers of the DPP to institute and conduct proceedings, though they are subject to the direction of the DPP in the exercise of these powers.[84] Crown Prosecutors have the same rights of audience as solicitors, and since 2000 they have been able to appear before the higher courts if qualified to do so.[85] The DPP may also confer limited rights of audience on CPS employees who are not Crown Prosecutors.[86]

The CPS itself is a national organization with offices in regional centres. Its role is to prosecute offences and it does not control the process of investigation. Since it was established however, the context within which it operates has changed significantly: levels of serious crime have risen and a series of high profile cases have raised concerns about its effectiveness. The Glidewell Report,[87] which reported in May 1998, concluded that the structure of the CPS should be reorganized so as to achieve greater devolution of responsibility. It proposed that each Area should be headed by a Chief Crown Prosecutor and supported by an Area Business Manager, with the CPS National Headquarters having responsibility for resourcing and monitoring. The Report suggested that each CPS 'Area' should be regarded as equivalent to a large legal firm specializing in criminal prosecution, and that it should enjoy a large degree of autonomy in carrying out its professional functions. These aims were broadly accepted by the government, and the CPS was the subject of major structural changes in 1999. In particular, the boundaries of CPS Areas have been realigned to correspond with police areas,[88] and CPS staff are increasingly being located in or close to police stations.

Coupled with this structural review, Glidewell also considered the operational performance of the CPS. Statistics showed that more than half of all acquittals in the Crown Court resulted from an order or direction of the judge, and this was viewed with some concern. The Report also noted the suspicion that charges were sometimes dropped or downgraded in circumstances where such action was inappropriate, although it found no firm evidence that this actually occurred.[89] Glidewell took the view that where a case had been reviewed by the CPS it ought to be strong enough to put to a jury, and it recommended that the preparation of case files in future should be the responsibility of the CPS rather than the police. The idea that the CPS should become involved in the decision making at an earlier stage was given effect by the Criminal Justice Act 2003. Schedule 2 of the Act amends the Police and Criminal Evidence Act 1984,[90] with the result that the CPS now has much greater involvement in deciding whether a charge should be laid, and what the nature of any charge should be.[91]

---

[83] 1985 Act, s 1(3).   [84] Ibid, s 1(6).
[85] Courts and Legal Services Act 1990, s 31A (as inserted by the Access to Justice Act 1999).
[86] Prosecution of Offences Act 1985, s 7A (as inserted by then Crime and Disorder Act 1998).
[87] Review of the Crown Prosecution Service (Cm 3960, 1998).   [88] See p 386, post.
[89] The power to discontinue proceedings is discussed at p 536, post.
[90] By amending s 37 and inserting new ss 37A, 37B, 37C and 37D.
[91] These reforms are discussed in greater detail at p 534, post.

4 THE LAW OFFICERS

The 'law officers' are the Attorney-General and the Solicitor-General. They are legal advisers to the Crown and *ex officio* members of the Bar Council, though they may not engage in private practice during their time in office. They are assisted by practising barristers known as Treasury Counsel.

Apart from his political duties, which include advising government departments and answering questions in Parliament, the Attorney-General represents the Crown in certain civil proceedings and in trials for treason and other offences with a political or constitutional element. He also exercises the prerogative power of staying prosecutions on indictment by the entry of a *nolle prosequi*, and certain criminal proceedings can only be commenced with his authority.

The Solicitor-General's position is basically that of the Attorney-General's deputy, and he may exercise any power vested by statute in the Attorney-General (unless the statute in question provides otherwise).[92]

C THE EDUCATION AND TRAINING OF LAWYERS

1 SOLICITORS

Section 2 of the Solicitors Act 1974 provides that the Law Society may, with the concurrence of the Lord Chancellor, the Lord Chief Justice, and the Master of the Rolls, make regulations governing the education and training of solicitors. No person may be admitted as a solicitor without a certificate stating that he has complied with these training regulations and that the Society is satisfied as to his character and suitability.[93]

The current training regulations date from 1990 and they divide the training process into three distinct stages: the academic stage, the vocational stage, and continuing professional development. For many would-be solicitors the academic stage of training is satisfied by graduating with a qualifying law degree.[94] Graduates with a non-qualifying degree can meet the Law Society's requirements by completing a one-year[95] Common Professional Examination course (CPE) or by obtaining a Graduate Diploma in Law (GDL). The only way for non-graduates to complete the academic stage is to follow the ILEX route, which involves working in a legal office and passing the exams needed to qualify as a Member or Fellow of the Institute of Legal Executives. A Legal Executive who wishes to qualify as a solicitor can then undertake further

---

[92] Law Officers Act 1997, s 1.   [93] Solicitors Act 1974, ss 1; 3.

[94] One which covers 'The Foundations of Legal Knowledge': Public Law, EU Law, Criminal Law, the Law of Obligations, Property Law, and Equity and the Law of Trusts. See the Joint Statement on Qualifying Law Degrees issued by the Law Society and the Bar Council (effective 1 September 2001).

[95] Or a longer period for part-time or distance-learning students.

training and go on to sit the CPE. The ILEX route is described by the Law Society as 'lengthy, demanding and academically challenging',[96] and in practice the overwhelming majority of solicitors enter the profession as graduates. Having completed the academic stage of training, a student can then commence the vocational stage, which means passing a practical-orientated Legal Practice Course and entering into a training contract.[97] The third stage of a solicitor's training—continuing professional development—is undertaken once a solicitor is actually qualified, but it is nevertheless compulsory.

2 BARRISTERS

The Bar Council has its own Education and Training Department which makes recommendations on the requirements for entry to the profession. Its terms of reference are to formulate, oversee, and implement policy with regard to all aspects of the academic, vocational, and post-qualification stages of a barrister's training. As far as the academic stage is concerned, the requirements are essentially the same as for a would-be solicitor: they can be satisfied by obtaining either a qualifying law degree[98] or a non-qualifying degree followed by a CPE certificate or Graduate Diploma in Law. There is no equivalent for barristers of the ILEX route. The vocational stage of training comprises the one-year[99] Bar Vocational Course (BVC), which a student cannot commence until he or she has joined one of the Inns of Court.[100] This is followed by a twelve-month pupillage in chambers, the first half of which is spent shadowing a pupil supervisor. Pupils may accept instructions during the last six months of a pupillage, though not without the permission of their supervisors. It is only after each of these requirements has been fulfilled that a person can be called to the Bar and practise as a barrister. Like solicitors, barristers must also undertake continuing professional development activities on a regular basis.[101]

A THE REGULATION OF LEGAL SERVICES

1 THE LAW SOCIETY

The Law Society is the professional regulatory body governing the work of solicitors. It received its first Royal Charter in 1831 and was originally called 'The Society of Attorneys, Solicitors, Proctors and others not being Barristers, practising in the Courts of Law and Equity of the United Kingdom'. Its name was officially changed to 'the

---

[96] See the Law Society publication, 'Ways to Qualify as a Solicitor'.
[97] ILEX Fellows are exempt from the requirement to enter a training contract.
[98] See n 94, *ante*.   [99] If full-time: two-years if part time.   [100] See p 353, *ante*.
[101] This is a fairly recent innovation: CPD was not a requirement of all barristers until January 2005.

Law Society' by the Supplemental Charter of 1903. It has a President, a Vice-President and a Deputy Vice-President, and it is governed by a Council of between 100 and 105 members. At present the Council has 105 members, comprising sixty-one solicitors representing regional constituencies, thirty-nine other solicitors, and five lay members.

The Law Society has important regulatory powers affecting all solicitors, and these are currently derived from the Solicitors Act 1974.[102] By section 2 of this Act the Society may, with the concurrence of the Lord Chancellor, the Lord Chief Justice, and the Master of the Rolls, make 'training regulations' governing the education and training of persons seeking admission to practise as solicitors. It may also make training regulations applicable to those already in practice. No person may be admitted as a solicitor without a certificate from the Law Society stating that he has complied with its training regulations and that the Society is satisfied as to his character and suitability.[103] In addition to holding a current certificate, a solicitor wishing to practice is also required to have his name on the Law Society's Roll of Solicitors.[104]

Alongside its role in regulating entry to the profession, the Law Society has a number of other important functions. For example, section 32 of the 1974 Act requires the Council to make rules governing the handling by solicitors of clients' money, and section 31 empowers it to make rules regulating professional practice, conduct, and discipline. The Law Society also looks after the welfare of solicitors generally and attempts to maintain good relations with other bodies and with the public. To this end the Council examines the activities of unqualified persons doing the work of solicitors, and in appropriate cases it institutes proceedings. It also performs educative and public relations activities.

The Society protects the interests of the public by the maintenance of a compensation fund.[105] Grants may be made from this fund to any person who suffers hardship through the failure of a solicitor to account for money due in connection with his practice. The result is that members of the public are indemnified against losses which might be suffered as a result of a solicitor's default in handling their moneys. The Law Society then assumes, through the doctrine of subrogation, the rights and remedies of the person to whom the grant was made. By way of further protection of the public, the Society has power to take over and reorganize the practice of any solicitor who cannot safely be relied upon to continue the handling of his clients' affairs.[106] In addition, solicitors are required by rules made under section 37 of the

---

[102] The constitution and general purposes of the Law Society are still governed by its Royal Charter of 1845, which refers to its role in 'promoting professional improvement and facilitating the acquisition of legal knowledge'.

[103] Solicitors Act 1974, ss 1; 3.   [104] Ibid, s 1.

[105] Ibid, s 36 and Schedule 2. The fund is made up of special annual contributions payable by solicitors on application for practising certificates.

[106] Ibid, s 35; Schedule 1. The Society can intervene on the grounds of dishonesty, undue delay on the part of the personal representatives of a deceased solicitor, failure to comply with professional rules, bankruptcy, imprisonment, removal from or striking off the roll, suspension from practice, and incapacity or abandonment of practice by a sole practitioner.

Solicitors Act to secure professional indemnity insurance from one of the 'Qualifying Insurers' approved by the Society.[107] Without valid indemnity insurance solicitors are not permitted to practise.

2 THE BAR COUNCIL

The General Council of the Bar (usually referred to as the Bar Council) was founded in 1894, though it was reconstituted by the Bar and the Senate of the Inns of Court in 1987. Its membership of 115 barristers includes representatives of the Inns and Specialist Bar Associations, along with ex officio members such as the Attorney-General, Solicitor-General, and the Director of Public Prosecutions.

Like the Law Society, the Bar Council is both a representative and a regulatory body, and it has a wide range of functions. Its regulatory powers do not derive from statute but it is deemed to be an 'authorised body' for the purposes conferring rights of audience and rights to conduct litigation.[108] Other functions include compiling and implementing the Bar's Code of Conduct, maintaining and enhancing professional standards, and representing the interests of the profession to the government and other bodies. It also determines the Bar's policies on education and training and is thus able to regulate entry to the profession.

3 REVIEW BY THE COURTS

Solicitors are officers of the Supreme Court,[109] and judges of this court have an inherent jurisdiction to suspend a solicitor for misconduct or to strike his name from the Roll of Solicitors. In their capacity as officers of the court, solicitors may be ordered to meet any costs incurred as a result of improper, unreasonable, or negligent conduct,[110] and they may also be liable for any losses which are the natural and probable consequence of such conduct.[111] Barristers are not officers of the Supreme Court and have historically not been subject to this jurisdiction,[112] but since 1990 the major civil and criminal courts have had a statutory jurisdiction to order *any* legal

---

[107] Before 2000, all solicitors had been required to contribute to the Society's Solicitors' Insurance Fund.

[108] Courts and Legal Services Act 1990, ss 27(9); 8(5).

[109] To be renamed 'the Senior Courts of England and Wales' when a new 'Supreme Court' is established to replace the Appellate Committee of the House of Lords: see p 243, *ante*.

[110] This jurisdiction is preserved by the Solicitors Act 1974, s 50(2). See, e.g. *Holden & Co* v *Crown Prosecution Service* [1990] 2 QB 261, [1990] 1 All ER 368 (inherent jurisdiction to order defence solicitor to pay prosecution costs following a serious dereliction of duty); *Langley* v *North West Water Authority* [1991] 3 All ER 610, [1991] 1 WLR 697 (solicitor personally liable for costs resulting from failure to comply with county court Practice Direction).

[111] *Marsh* v *Joseph* [1897] 1 Ch 213.

[112] In *Metcalf* v *Wetherill (Wasted Costs Order)* [2002] UKHL 27, [2003] 1 AC 120, [2002] 3 All ER 721 the House of Lords suggested, obiter, that the inherent jurisdiction could be applied to any legal representative. However, it also accepted that the jurisdiction had largely been superseded by statute.

representative to pay the whole or part of any wasted costs.[113] The courts also have an inherent jurisdiction to prevent abuse of their procedures, and in exercising this jurisdiction they could refuse to hear an advocate or restrain his participation in a particular trial. In practice however, a court will only take such a drastic step in the most exceptional of cases.[114]

In addition to the above, a solicitor may incur liability as an officer of the court by giving an undertaking to the court,[115] or by giving an undertaking to an individual when acting in his capacity as a solicitor.[116] Such an undertaking will be enforced by the court summarily, not as a contractual obligation but in order to secure the proper conduct of its officers. Finally, both solicitors and barristers may be liable for contempt of court for acts done in a professional capacity.[117]

4 THE CLEMENTI REPORT: A REVIEW OF THE REGULATORY FRAMEWORK

In 2003 the Department for Constitutional Affairs announced a major review of the regulation of legal services.[118] The review was chaired by Sir David Clementi and had two main terms of reference: (a) 'to consider what regulatory framework would best promote competition, innovation and the public and consumer interest in an efficient, effective and independent legal sector'; and (b) 'to recommend a framework which will be independent in representing the public and consumer interest, comprehensive, accountable, consistent, flexible, transparent, and no more restrictive or burdensome than is clearly justified'. The final report of the review was published in December 2004.[119]

The Report made a number of significant recommendations which, if implemented, could have a profound effect on the legal landscape. Clementi's concerns fell into three main categories: (a) concerns about the complexity and ineffectiveness of the existing regulatory framework; (b) concerns about the current approach of the professions to the handling of complaints; and (c) concerns about the restrictive nature of current business practices. With regard to the first of these concerns, he recommended the creation of a new Legal Services Board with responsibility for overseeing

---

[113] Supreme Court Act 1981, s 51 (civil courts) as amended by the Courts and Legal Services Act 1990; Prosecution of Offences Act 1985, s 19A (criminal courts) as inserted by the 1990 Act. The principles to be applied were considered by the Court of Appeal in *Re A Barrister (Wasted Costs Order (No 1 of 1991))* [1993] QB 293, [1992] 3 All ER 429 and are discussed at p 491, *post*.

[114] *Geveran Trading Co v Skjevesland* [2002] EWCA Civ 1567, [2003] 1 WLR 912, [2003] 1 All ER 1.

[115] *D v A & Co* [1899] D 2136.

[116] *Re A Solicitor, ex parte Hales* [1907] 2 KB 539; *Re A Solicitor* [1966] 3 All ER 52, [1966] 1 WLR 1604

[117] *Linwood v Andrews and Moore* (1888) 58 LT 612; *Alliance and Leicester Building Society v Ghahremani* [1992] NLJR 313, (1992) Times 19 March; *Daw v Eley* (1868) LR 7 Eq 49.

[118] Competition and Regulation in the Legal Services Market—A Report following the Consultation 'In the Public Interest?' (2003).

[119] Final Report of the Review of the Regulatory Framework for Legal Services in England and Wales (2004).

the regulation of all legal service providers.[120] In addition to exercising regulatory powers in respect of the Law Society and Bar Council, the new body would also oversee the Institute of Legal Executives, the Council for Licensed Conveyancers, the Chartered Institute of Patent Agents, the Institute of Trade Mark Attorney, and the Office of the Immigration Services Commissioner. The existing professional bodies would still have front-line responsibility for regulating their own members, but the Legal Services Board would be able to intervene if standards were not being maintained. The Board would also assume a number of powers currently exercised by the Lord Chancellor, including the power to authorize bodies to confer rights of audience and the right to conduct litigation. In addition, Clementi recommended that all front-line regulatory bodies should be required to 'separate out' their regulatory and representative functions.[121]

On this issue of complaints, the Report proposed the creation of an Office for Legal Complaints, which would be a single, independent body responsible for handling all consumer complaints. Matters of professional conduct and discipline however, would continue to be dealt with by the existing professional bodies.[122] Finally, Clementi considered a range of options for opening up the legal services market to alternative business structures. His key recommendation here was that steps should be taken to enable lawyers from different professional backgrounds to work together to provide legal services to the public. This could be achieved by lifting the restrictions preventing solicitors from entering into partnerships with those from other disciplines, and by the Bar Council changing its own rules to permit barristers to enter into partnerships with others. Such changes would mean, for example, that solicitors and barristers would be able to join together to create 'Legal Disciplinary Practices', in which non-lawyers performing a managerial or administrative role might also be partners. Clementi recognized however, that if lawyers and non-lawyers were to be able to enter into partnerships, special safeguards would be needed to ensure the maintenance of ethical standards.[123]

The Clementi Report was 'warmly welcomed' by the government, and its recommendations were broadly accepted. Even before it was published, the Lord Chancellor had made it clear that he was keen to explore new way of delivering legal services:[124]

I want us to adopt the Heineken approach and find legal services which reach parts of the community that no other services have reached . . .

I want to see a market where everyone, except those with limited means who get free access, can get access to legal services at affordable cost in a modern setting. Shopping centres are the most obvious example of this, where clusters of problems such as employment, housing, debt and family problems can be dealt with together. And this leads to the use of employed solicitors by other businesses . . . for the legal profession to thrive and

---

[120] Ibid, at paras B70–B71.
[121] Including the Law Society and the Bar Council: ibid, at para B39. [122] Ibid, paras C88–C89.
[123] Ibid, at paras F11 and F25.
[124] The quote is taken from a speech to the Law Society's Annual Conference, 26 September 2003.

survive we must continue to be competitive in the legal market of today and we must not be frightened of innovation and change.

Shortly before this book was completed, the Lord Chancellor announced that he would be publishing a White Paper to take forward Clementi's proposals, with legislation to follow in 2005/2006.[125] The reaction of the professions to this news was mixed. The proposal for a new complaints body received a particularly frosty reception from the Bar Council, which pointed out that its existing complaints system already had a good track record and did not need to be fixed. It also voiced concerns about the possible effect on standards and legal ethics if lawyers were to be allowed to join 'Legal Disciplinary Practices', and it stated that it would continue to oppose the idea of barristers being able to form partnerships with other barristers.[126] For its part, the Law Society was rather more enthusiastic. It had already begun to move towards the separation of regulatory and representative functions envisaged by Clementi, and the prospect of solicitors being able to form alternative business structures was particularly welcomed.[127]

E COMPLAINTS AGAINST LAWYERS

Broadly speaking, complaints about lawyers fall into one of three main categories: (1) complaints involving allegations of professional misconduct; (2) complaints about inadequate professional service; and (3) complaints that a lawyer has acted with negligence. Both branches of the profession have their own internal mechanisms for dealing with complaints about misconduct and inadequate service, but a client who alleges that a lawyer has acted with negligence must generally look to the civil courts for a remedy.

1 SOLICITORS

(a) Complaint handling by the Law Society

In 1996 the Law Society replaced its existing Solicitor's Complaints Bureau with a new Office for the Supervision of Solicitors (OSS). The OSS handled complaints about the quality of service provided by solicitors in addition to dealing with allegations of professional misconduct. It was also responsible for overseeing the Solicitors' Compensation Fund. Like its predecessor, the OSS was much criticized for its inefficiency and its perceived lack of independence: despite its semi-autonomous status and the inclusion of a number of lay members, it was directly funded by the Law Society and

---

[125] Lord Falconer, 671 HL Official Report (5th series) col WS3, 21 March 2005.
[126] 'Clementi Must not be used to Compromise the Independence of Lawyers'—press release from the Chairman of the Bar Council, 15th December 2004.
[127] 'The Future of Legal Services'—press release from the President of the Law Society, 22 March 2005.

its membership included several solicitors who sat on the Law Society's Council. The OSS was widely criticized during its short history,[128] and in 2004 the Legal Services Ombudsman reported that the quality of its complaints handling was satisfactory in only 53.3 per cent of cases.[129] Three months before the Ombudsman's report was published, the OSS was replaced by two new bodies: the Consumer Complaints System and the Compliance Directorate.

Complaints that a solicitor has provided an 'inadequate professional service'—e.g. by involving the client in unreasonable delays or failing to keep him informed—are handled by the Consumer Complaints Service (CCS). The CCS also offers a free service for checking that solicitors' bills are fair and reasonable, though this is only offered in respect of work that has not involved court proceedings. The emphasis of the CCS is on conciliation, but in appropriate cases it can reduce a solicitor's Bill or order a solicitor to pay compensation of up to £5,000. Where some form of professional misconduct is alleged, such as a breach of lawyer-client confidentiality or the mishandling of client funds, the complaint is referred to the Society's Compliance Directorate. No compensation can be awarded in respect of such an allegation unless there is also an element of 'inadequate professional service'.[130] However, the Law Society can take disciplinary action against the solicitor concerned, place conditions on his practising certificate, or intervene in the solicitor's practice. Serious or persistent cases of professional misconduct will be referred to the Solicitors Disciplinary Tribunal.[131] The Law Society also has an Independent Commissioner with responsibility for overseeing its handling of complaints. The Commissioner has no involvement in dealing with individual complaints but he produces an annual report on the Law Society's performance and has the power to make recommendations. His office is funded by the Law Society and has no statutory basis: his independence derives from the fact that he is appointed by the Master of the Rolls and is not a lawyer.

In dividing responsibility for complaints handling between the CSS and its Compliance Directorate, the Law Society was responding to the Independent Commissioner's recommendation that it should separate its regulatory function from its handling of 'consumer redress'.[132] However, its efforts failed to impress the Legal Services Ombudsman:[133]

Regardless of the precise motives or details of this latest reorganisation, there is no doubt that it represents a high profile change to the Law Society's complaints-handling operations. I was therefore extremely disappointed that the Law Society took such a radical step without

---

[128] See, e.g. Moorhead, Sherr and Rogers, 'Willing Blindness? OSS Complaints Handling Procedures (2000); DCA, Complaints and Regulation in the Legal Services Market: A Scoping Study' (2003).

[129] *In Whose Interest?*—Annual Report of the Legal Services Ombudsman for England and Wales, 2003/ 2004 at p 13. The role of the Legal Services Ombudsman is discussed further at p 367, *post.*

[130] The Solicitors Act 1974 itself makes a distinction between 'conduct' and 'service' issues.

[131] See p 366, *post.*

[132] See Sir Stephen Lander, Independent Commissioner to the Law Society, *Redress or Rules? Whither the Consumer Redress Scheme?* (2003).

[133] *Ante*, n 129, at p 51.

any consultation or communication with either my Office . . . or, as far as I am aware, with any other external stakeholders. This hardly represents the actions of a model regulator prepared to engage openly and transparently with its stakeholders.

The Ombudsman also pointed that 'the most obvious single contribution to improving client satisfaction . . . would of course be to remove the causes that give rise to complaints in the first place'.[134]

Before the Law Society will consider a complaint about inadequate professional service, it will normally insist that a client has first made use of a solicitor's own 'in-house' complaints procedure. Rule 15 of the Solicitors Practice Rules requires all solicitors to have a complaints-handling procedure in place, and a breach of this rule may itself be a disciplinary matter. Both the Legal Services Ombudsman and the Independent Commissioner have indicated that the Law Society has not done enough to enforce this rule in the past, and the Society is now taking steps to address this.[135]

(b) The Solicitors Disciplinary Tribunal

Allegations of serious professional misconduct are dealt with by the Solicitors Disciplinary Tribunal. The Tribunal consists of 'solicitor members', who must be practising solicitors of not less than ten years' standing, and 'lay members', who are neither solicitors nor barristers.[136] It is independent of The Law Society and like other judicial tribunals it may receive evidence on oath and compel the attendance of witnesses. It is properly constituted when at least three members are present, the majority of whom must be solicitor members. There must also be at least one lay member present.[137]

Most of the Tribunal's caseload consists of referrals from the Law Society, though it can also hear applications from solicitors, judges, and members of the public. In addition to dealing with a variety of disciplinary matters it can hear any application to strike a solicitor's name from the Roll, or to re-instate a solicitor who has previously been struck-off or suspended.[138] It can also hear applications concerning the conduct of solicitors' employees.[139] The Tribunal can dispose of an application involving a solicitor by making any such order as it thinks fit:[140] in particular, an adverse finding may result in a solicitor being struck off, suspended, reprimanded, fined, or prevented from carrying out work funded by the Legal Services Commission.[141] In the case of an application concerning a solicitor's employee the Tribunal may make an order preventing that person from being employed or remunerated by a solicitor without the Law Society's written permission.[142] Any appeal against a refusal to revoke such an order lies to the Master of the Rolls, and his decision is final.[143] The Master of the Rolls

---

[134] Ibid, at p 52.

[135] See *In Whose Interest?*—Annual Report of the Legal Services Ombudsman for England and Wales, 2003/2004 at p 53; Annual Report of the Independent Commissioner to the Law Society 2003, Annex III, recommendation 3. See also Moorhead, 'Self-Regulation and the Market for Legal Services'—paper published by the Cardiff Centre for Ethics, Law and Society (Cardiff University, 2004).

[136] Solicitors Act 1974, s 46.   [137] Ibid, s 46(6).   [138] Ibid, s 47(1).

[139] Ibid, s 43.   [140] Ibid, s 47(2).   [141] Ibid, ss 47(2); 47(2A).

[142] Ibid, s 43(2).   [143] Ibid, ss 49(1)(a); 49(6).

also hears appeals against decisions relating to the reinstatement of a solicitor who has been struck off or suspended.[144] Appeals in all other cases lie to the High Court, and from there (with leave) to the Court of Appeal.[145]

2 BARRISTERS

Although barristers have always been subject to the disciplinary jurisdiction of the Inns of Court, the Bar Council did not have a system for dealing with complaints from lay clients until the appointment of a Complaints Commissioner in 1997. The Commissioner is an independent non-lawyer and his function is to examine all complaints received by the Bar Council and to filter out those that are clearly without justification. Complaints which appear to have merit are referred by the Commissioner to the Council's Professional Conduct and Complaints Committee (PCCC). If the PCCC agrees that the complaint may be justified it will refer the matter to another body for a final determination. Complaints which only raise issues of inadequate professional service are referred to an Adjudication Panel comprising the Commissioner, a layman, and two barristers: if a complaint is upheld the barrister may be ordered to repay his fees or to pay compensation of up to £5,000. Where a complaint is based wholly or partly on an allegation of professional misconduct[146] the PCCC has three options: (1) to refer the matter to an informal hearing; (2) to refer it to a summary procedure panel; or (3) to refer it to a disciplinary tribunal comprising a judge, two barristers and two laymen. Disciplinary tribunals deal with the most serious cases and can disbar or suspend a barrister if appropriate. A barrister can appeal against the decision of a tribunal or summary procedure panel to the Visitors of the Inns of Court (the High Court Judges).

3 THE LEGAL SERVICES OMBUDSMAN

The Ombudsman is an independent non-lawyer appointed for a renewable term of three years.[147] Her role is to investigate allegations made by persons who are dissatisfied at the handling of their complaints by the professional bodies. The focus of any investigation will be on the handling of the complaint itself, and the Ombudsman's role is not to review the actions of the lawyer who was originally the subject of that complaint.[148] Depending on the outcome of her investigations, the Ombudsman has the power to require that a complaint is reconsidered and/or that compensation is paid by the professional body or the lawyer concerned. She may also make

[144] Ibid.

[145] Ibid, s 49(1)(b). See, e.g. *Langford* v *Law Society* [2002] EWHC 2802 (Admin); [2003] 153 NLJR 176.

[146] The Code of Conduct of the Bar of England and Wales states that any failure to comply with the Code shall amount to professional misconduct (8th edn, 2004; para 901). It would be unusual however, for very minor breaches to be dealt with as misconduct in practice.

[147] Courts and Legal Services Act 1990, s 21; Schedule 3.

[148] The Ombudsman's functions are set out in detail in section 22 of the 1990 Act.

recommendations of a more general nature.[149] In 2003/04 the Ombudsman's Office completed 1,731 investigations and ordered compensation payments totalling £199,840.[150]

F CIVIL LIABILITY

1 SOLICITORS

(a) Liability to the client

A solicitor's authority derives from the retainer given to him by his client, the effect of which is to create a contractual relationship between the two parties. This relationship is subject to the ordinary law of contract and in particular to that part of contract law concerning agency.[151] Consequently the solicitor has a right to be indemnified by his client for acts done within the scope of his authority, and he is entitled to be put in funds for disbursements. If he is engaged to conduct contentious business he may also require payment of a reasonable sum on account of costs.[152] Beyond this however, the general rule is that a solicitor undertakes to complete the transaction for which he was retained, and he is not entitled to remuneration until the transaction is completed. In addition to his liability in contract, a solicitor who fails to act with due skill and care may also incur liability in tort. In *Midland Bank Trust Co Ltd* v *Hett, Stubbs and Kemp*[153] it was held that the relationship between solicitor and client was a 'special relationship' of the kind envisaged in *Hedley Byrne* v *Heller*.[154] A solicitor could thus be liable in tort for negligent advice given in the context of such a relationship. A solicitor may also be liable to his client if incompetent counsel is instructed,[155] or if counsel is not given adequate instructions upon which to act.[156]

(b) Liability to third parties

Where a solicitor contracts on behalf of a client with the knowledge of the other party, the transaction will be subject to the ordinary law of agency: contractual liability to the third party will be assumed by the client rather than the solicitor.[157] This principle applies equally to contracts made by the solicitor with the *ostensible* authority of his client: if the solicitor's actual authority to act is disputed, his liability will be to the

---

[149] Ibid, ss 23–24.
[150] *In Whose Interest?*—Annual Report of the Legal Services Ombudsman, 2003/2004 at p 13.
[151] See the discussion of liability to third parties, above.   [152] Solicitors Act 1974, s 65(2).
[153] [1979] Ch 384, [1978] 3 All ER 571. See also *Ross* v *Caunters* [1980] Ch 297, [1979] 3 All ER 580.
[154] [1964] AC 465, [1963] 2 All ER 575.   [155] *Re A (A Minor)* [1988] Fam Law 339.
[156] *Dauntley* v *Hyde* (1841) 6 Jur 133.
[157] *Wakefield* v *Duckworth & Co* [1915] 1 KB 218 (solicitor not liable for failure to pay a photographer).

client rather than the third party.[158] A solicitor will, however, be contractually liable to a third party if he fails to disclose that he is acting on someone else's behalf.[159] He will also incur liability to a third party if he purports to act with the authority of a client but no such authority exists.[160]

A solicitor may be liable in tort for any tortious act to which he has been a party, whether or not he was acting with the authority of a client. For example, a solicitor who fraudulently induces a third party to buy an estate with a defective title commits the tort of deceit. In some circumstances a solicitor may even be liable to a third party for economic loss caused by his negligence. This occurred in *White* v *Jones*,[161] where a solicitor's negligence in failing to draft a new will deprived the intended beneficiaries of an inheritance.

2 BARRISTERS

(a) Liability to the client

As noted previously, barristers were historically prevented from entering into contractual relationships with clients, but this rule has now changed.[162] Since 2004 it has been possible for barristers who comply with certain criteria to undertake 'public access' work, which means that they may accept instructions directly from lay clients. The relationship between barrister and client in such a case will normally be contractual, and the barrister may thus be liable in contract for any failure to perform.

Barristers were historically assumed to be immune from liability in negligence, and in *Rondel* v *Worsley*[163] the House of Lords accepted that this immunity could be justified. Various public policy arguments were cited: it was pointed out, for example, that barristers have an overriding duty to the court which could potentially conflict with a client's wishes, and the fact that barristers are not free to pick and choose their clients was also noted. A particular concern was that disgruntled clients might attempt to sue their barristers as a way of reopening cases that had already been lost. Some of their Lordships also thought that barristers might be inhibited in carrying out their duties if they had to operate under the threat of being sued. Although their Lordships differed in the emphasis that they placed on each of these grounds, they were agreed that barristers should continue to enjoy immunity in respect of their conduct at trial.

In the subsequent case of *Saif Ali* v *Sydney Mitchell & Co*[164] the House of Lords was once again called upon to consider the scope of barristers' immunity, but this time in relation to work done in chambers in the course of litigation. The effect of this

---

[158] A solicitor has ostensible authority to do any act which is within the scope of his retainer, and thus may bind his client to compromise of an action whether or not he has the client's actual authority so to do: *Waugh* v *HB Clifford and Sons Ltd* [1982] Ch 374, [1982] 1 All ER 1095.

[159] *Foster* v *Cranfield* (1911) 46 L Jo 314.   [160] *Yonge* v *Toynbee* [1910] 1 KB 215.

[161] [1993] 3 All ER 481, [1993] 3 WLR 730.   [162] See p 354, *ante.*

[163] [1969] 1 AC 191, [1967] 3 All ER 993.   [164] [1980] AC 198, [1978] 3 All ER 1033.

decision was to limit the immunity to matters of pre-trial work which were intimately connected with the conduct of the case in court. Since the barrister's advice and pleadings in the instant case had prevented the claimant's dispute from coming to court at all, it was not within the sphere of a barrister's immunity. Finally, in *Arthur JS Hall & Co v Simons*[165] the House of Lords departed from *Rondel v Worsley*[166] and abolished the controversial immunity altogether. Though their Lordships accepted that some of the justifications for it had merit, they concluded that none of them were sufficient to outweigh the interests of the client in having a remedy for the negligence of his advocate. They pointed out that doctors have no such immunity despite being bound by an ethical code, and they also stressed that a barrister would never be deemed negligent for acting in accordance with his duty to court. Concerns that barristers acting in criminal cases might be particularly at risk from unmeritorious claims persuaded a minority of the House that the immunity should only be lifted in respect of civil litigation. The majority however, shared Lord Hoffman's view that 'it would ordinarily be an abuse of process for a civil court to be asked to decide that a subsisting conviction was wrong',[167] and as Lord Millett pointed out:[168]

[To retain the immunity for criminal cases] would mean that a party would have a remedy if the incompetence of his counsel deprived him of compensation for (say) breach of contract or unfair dismissal, but not if it led to his imprisonment for a crime he did not commit and the consequent and uncompensated loss of his job.

The majority thus concluded that the immunity should be removed across the board.

(b) Liability to third parties.

In principle, barristers are in the same position as solicitors with regard to their potential liability to third parties. In one case for example, a barrister who gave negligent advice about the setting up of a trust was successfully sued in tort by its trustees.[169] In practice however, the nature of the barrister's role means that third party liability is much less likely to be an issue. One specific point to note is that the standard terms on which a barrister would normally accept a brief from a solicitor do not give rise to any contractual liability. There is, however, nothing to stop barristers from accepting a retainer on contractual terms.[170]

---

[165] [2002] 1 AC 615, [2000] 3 All ER 673.   [166] [1969] 1 AC 191, [1967] 3 All ER 993.
[167] [2002] 1 AC 615 at 706, [2000] 3 All ER 673 at 785.
[168] [2002] 1 AC 615 at 752, [2000] 3 All ER 673 at 829.
[169] *Estill v Cowling* [2000] Lloyd's Rep PN 378.
[170] Code of Conduct of the Bar of England and Wales, Annexe G2: The Contractual Terms of Work on which Barristers Offer their Services to Solicitors, 2001.

G THE FUNDING OF LEGAL SERVICES

1 THE REMUNERATION OF LAWYERS

The remuneration of solicitors is subject to a variety of statutory and other rules, the application of which depends upon whether the work done by the solicitor is contentious or non-contentious. 'Contentious business' is defined in section 87(1) of the Solicitors Act 1974 as:

Business done, whether as solicitor or advocate, in or for the purpose of proceedings begun before a court or before an arbitrator appointed under the Arbitration Act 1950, not being business which falls within the definition of non-contentious or common form probate business in the Supreme Court Act 1981, s 128.

The essence of the test is whether proceedings have begun: if they have, then all business relating to those proceedings is contentious. Section 59 of the Solicitors Act authorizes solicitors to enter into agreements with their clients to regulate remuneration in contentious business. In the absence of such an agreement a solicitor may submit either a Bill containing detailed items or one charging a gross sum.[171] The client is entitled to apply to the High Court for a detailed assessment (formerly known as 'taxation') of his bill.[172] If the application is granted the Bill will be assessed on an 'indemnity' basis,[173] which means that all costs which have been reasonably incurred and are reasonable in amount will be allowed.[174] Different rules apply where a Bill is to be paid from Legal Services Commission funds.

   Work done in respect of a dispute which is settled before proceedings are commenced is regarded as 'non-contentious business'. This term also covers a wide range of other matters, such as conveyancing and the drafting of wills and settlements. Save in certain exceptional cases under specific enactments,[175] remuneration for non-contentious business is regulated by an order made under section 56 of the 1974 Act. The basis of remuneration under the current order[176] is that the solicitor's costs must be fair and reasonable, having regard to all the circumstances of the case. Particular regard must be had to the complexity of the matter, the skill, specialized knowledge and responsibility involved, the number of documents, the time involved, the value of any property or amount of any sum involved, whether any land was registered, and the importance of the matter to the client.[177] As with contentious business the parties are at liberty to make their own agreement as to costs,[178] but any such agreement may still be subject to review by the courts.

   Barristers are not covered by the same regulatory regime as solicitors, and they may be remunerated on any basis agreed by the parties as long as it is permitted by law.

---

[171] Solicitors Act 1974, s 64.   [172] Ibid, s 70.   [173] See p 493, *post*.
[174] RSC, Ord 62, r 12(2).   [175] Preserved by s 75 of the 1974 Act.
[176] Solicitors' (Non-Contentious Business) Remuneration Order 1994, SI 1994/2616.
[177] Ibid, Article 3.   [178] 1974 Act, s 57.

This principle is, however, subject to the detailed rules regulating the cost of work funded by the Legal services Commission. In addition, counsel's fees may come under scrutiny when costs fall to be considered at the end of a trial and a barrister will not be permitted to charge for work which he has not been instructed to do.[179]

(a) Conditional fee agreements

Conditional fee arrangements are becoming an increasingly important way of funding legal services. A conditional fee agreement is defined by section 58(2)(a) of the Courts and Legal Services Act 1990 as:

[A]n agreement with a person providing advocacy or litigation services which provides for his fees and expenses, or any part of them, to be payable only in specified circumstances.

In other words, a lawyer who enters into a conditional fee agreement will only be paid for his services in certain circumstances. The vast majority of such agreements are entered into on what is described as a 'no win, no fee' basis, which means that the solicitor does not receive a fee from his client if he loses the case, but is paid a 'success fee' if he wins. A success fee is an amount which increases the standard fee by a given percentage.[180] Conditional fee agreements were once thought to be contrary to public policy, but the Courts and Legal Services Act 1990 legitimized their use in certain classes of case. These classes are designated by Order and were originally fairly limited, but current legislation permits the use of conditional fees in the vast majority of cases. The only remaining statutory exceptions are: (a) criminal cases; and (b) specified family proceedings cases.[181] For a conditional fee agreement to be enforceable it must be in writing and its effects must have been made clear to the client. In particular, the agreement must specify the circumstances in which the client may be liable to pay the legal representative's costs, and it must also state what percentage increase (if any) is attributable to a success fee.[182] The maximum percentage increase permitted by the regulations is currently 100 per cent of the normal fee.[183] The existence of a conditional fee agreement places most of the financial risks of litigation with the lawyer, and it is on this basis that an increase in the standard fee is said to be justified. Even with such an arrangement in place however, there will still be some element of risk for the client: the unsuccessful litigant may not have to pay his own lawyer but he will generally be liable to pay the other side's costs. He may also be liable for court fees, the cost of obtaining expert reports, and so on. The current regulations require the lawyer to explain this risk to the client and to advise him as to how this risk might be offset. The result is that most litigants who enter into these arrangements are protected by

---

[179] *Loveday* v *Renton (No 2)* [1992] 3 All ER 184.
[180] Courts and Legal Services Act 1990, ss 58(2)(b); 58(4)b.   [181] Ibid, s 58A.
[182] Ibid, s 58; Conditional Fee Agreement Regulations 2000, SI 2000/692. See also the decision in *Sharratt* v *London Central Bus Co Ltd (No 1)*; *Hollins* v *Russell* [2003] EWCA Civ 718, [2003] 1 WLR 2487, [2003] 4 All ER 590, in which the Court of Appeal held that a conditional fee arrangement will normally be enforceable as long as the general purpose of the statutory rules designed for the client's protection has been complied with.
[183] Conditional Fee Agreements Order 2000, SI 2000/823.

some form of insurance policy covering any potential liability for costs. In principle, both the lawyer's success fee and the cost of after-the-event insurance are recoverable from the losing party to an action. Ultimately however, this is a matter for the court's discretion.[184]

Note finally that conditional fee agreements must be carefully distinguished from other types of contingency agreement, such as those common in the United States which involve the lawyer receiving a percentage of any damages awarded. This type of arrangement has historically been unenforceable in England and Wales on public policy grounds.[185] The argument is that a contingency arrangement would give a lawyer an incentive to try to win at all costs and might therefore encourage unscrupulous conduct. In fact, the same argument could be made in respect of conditional fee agreements, and the Middleton Report recommended that the case for contingency fees should be reconsidered.[186]

(b) Litigation funding agreements

'Litigation funding agreements' are a variation on conditional fee agreements. They are made not with lawyers but with third party funders such as insurance companies, the idea being that these funders agree to bears the financial risk of litigation, in return for which they can claim a success fee if their clients win. This type of arrangement is provided for in principle by section 28 of the Access to Justice Act 1999, which will insert a new section 58B into the Courts and Legal Services Act 1990. At the time of writing however, this provision has yet to be implemented.

2 THE COST OF THE LAW

Access to legal advice is a fundamental right under the European Convention on Human Rights, and this right has now been given direct effect in English law.[187] Without access to advice an individual may remain unaware of his legal rights and obligations, and he may be unable to make effective use of the courts. Yet the cost of exercising this 'right' is high: the Woolf Report[188] found the average cost of litigation in medical negligence cases to be £38,252, while in personal injury cases it was £20,413. The majority of defendants in criminal cases will be in receipt of public funding, but the cost of such cases may still be considerable. The fees charged by lawyers are often high, and in recent years the Lord Chancellor has 'named and shamed' barristers considered to earn excessive amounts from doing publicly funded work.[189] The cost of justice is not solely a matter of lawyers' fees however: court fees

---

[184] See p 488, *post* for more detail on the recovery of costs.
[185] *Aratra Potato Co Ltd* v *Taylor Jaynson Garrett (A Firm)* [1995] 4 All ER 695.
[186] Review of Civil Justice and Legal Aid: A Report to the Lord Chancellor (1997), at para 5.50.
[187] Article 6: given effect by the Human Rights Act 1998 and discussed at p 180, *ante*.
[188] Access to Justice: Interim Report, Annex III, pp 251–6.
[189] See 'Fat Cats': the Facts behind 'those Figures', *Counsel*, June 1998 at 12. See also p 383, *post*.

and other expenses may also be significant, and achieving access to justice in this climate is a real challenge for the government.

One of the aims of recent civil justice reforms has been to reduce cost with a view to improving access to justice.[190] In addition, many lawyers have sought to address some of these difficulties by not charging for work done on behalf of financially strapped clients. In the past it was common for solicitors to tender initial advice free of charge, and the Bar's Free Representation and Pro Bono schemes have provided free legal services to many deserving clients. The work done by bodies such as Law Centres and Citizens' Advice Bureaux is also important, and legal expenses insurance is becoming increasingly significant as an alternative source of funding. However, its is the legal aid and advice scheme that has, since the Second World War, been the most important mechanism for ensuring affordable access to justice. Pressure on resources has inevitably increased as actions have become more complex and legal costs have risen, and these pressures have forced successive governments to keep the operation of the system under review. In 1991, the expenditure on legal aid was some £682 million. By 1997, this figure had increased to £1,477 million,[191] and by 2004 the total expenditure on publicly funded legal services was almost £2 billion.[192]

One government response to these pressures has been to try and recoup money by raising court fees. In 1996 it also sought to repeal certain rules which had exempted persons in receipt of state benefits from paying such fees.[193] However, in *R v Lord Chancellor, ex parte Witham*[194] its authority to take such action was successfully challenged. Witham was in receipt of income support and wished to bring proceedings for defamation, but since legal aid was unavailable and he was apparently no longer entitled to an exemption, he did not have the financial means to issue proceedings. Laws J upheld his claim that the change in the rules was ultra vires, stressing that access to the courts was a constitutional right at common law, and that it could not be abrogated without the clear and specific authority of an Act of Parliament. The Lord Chancellor had claimed that such authority was provided by section 130 of the Courts and Legal Services Act 1990, but Laws J disagreed and found the regulations in question to be invalid.

3 LEGAL AID

A civil legal aid scheme was introduced in the aftermath of the Second World War as part of the new Welfare State.[195] It was not fully implemented and its impact was limited, but the system expanded in subsequent decades as further legislation was enacted.[196] Criminal legal aid came later,[197] followed by the introduction of the duty

---

[190] See pp 375–83, *post.*   [191] See Middleton Report, p 288, *post.*
[192] Legal Services Commission, *Annual Report 2003–04*, preface.
[193] Supreme Court Fees (Amendment) Order 1996, Article 3, SI 1996/3191.
[194] [1998] QB 575, [1997] 2 All ER 779.   [195] Legal Aid and Advice Act 1949.
[196] See the Legal Advice and Assistance Act 1972 and the Legal Aid Acts of 1960, 1964, 1974, and 1979.
[197] Criminal Justice Act 1967.

solicitor scheme.[198] Eventually, the Legal Aid Act 1988 established a more comprehensive scheme covering both civil and criminal matters.[199] Section 3 of the Act created a Legal Aid Board to administer the new system and ensure the availability of advice, assistance, and representation.[200] The Board was responsible for managing the scheme in its application to civil matters, and also for maintaining a legal aid fund.[201] It could contract with law centres, Citizens Advice Bureaux, and other information agencies, in addition to entering into franchise arrangements with individual firms of solicitors.

The Act incorporated the 'Green Form' scheme, which was originally established under the Legal Advice and Assistance Act 1972. It was applicable to both civil and criminal matters and was designed to secure the availability of legal advice and information to those who would otherwise be unable to afford it. It covered oral or written advice given by a legal representative[202] in relation to any question of English law,[203] and a person who met the criteria for eligibility could obtain assistance equivalent to two hours' worth of work. 'Assistance by way of representation' was also available.[204] In principle, this could cover any steps taken on behalf a person in the institution or conduct of proceedings before a court, tribunal, or statutory inquiry, whether by representing him in those proceedings or otherwise. However, the precise application of the scheme was subject to more detailed rules,[205] and not all proceedings were actually covered. The scheme did not, for example, cover representation in defamation cases.[206]

The framework governing legal aid in criminal cases was set out in Part V of the Act, and as under the previous system the scheme was administered by the courts.[207] In principle, where legal aid was granted it could cover representation by a solicitor and counsel, in addition to the provision of advice. In magistrates' courts however, the cost of representation by counsel would only be covered where a case concerned an unusually grave or difficult indictable offence. In both civil and criminal cases, an assisted person could be ordered by the court to pay such contribution as appeared reasonable, having regard to his commitments and resources. Such means-testing did not apply to the duty solicitor scheme however,[208] which continued to fund the provision of free legal advice in police stations and magistrates' courts.

4 'ACCESS TO JUSTICE': THE NEW FUNDING REGIME

The Middleton Committee, which reported in 1997,[209] identified a number of weaknesses in the Legal Aid scheme. In particular, it raised serious concerns about the

---

[198] See p 381, *post*.
[199] See Legal Aid in England and Wales—A New Framework (Cmnd 118, 1987).
[200] 1988 Act, s 3(2). For the meaning 'advice', 'assistance', and 'representation' see s 2.
[201] Ibid, s 6.   [202] *R v Legal Aid Board, ex parte Bruce* [1992] 1 All ER 133, [1991] 1 WLR 1231.
[203] 1988 Act, s 2(2).   [204] Ibid, ss 2(3); 8(2).
[205] Legal Advice and Assistance (Scope) Regulations 1989, SI 1989/550, reg 9.
[206] 1988 Act, Schedule 2, Part II, para 1.   [207] See p 197, *ante*.
[208] Legal Advice and Assistance (Scope) Regulations 1989, SI 1989/340.
[209] Review of Civil Justice and Legal Aid: A Report to the Lord Chancellor (1997).

rapid growth in the cost of the scheme and its inability to target resources on priority areas. The Committee reported that expenditure on Legal Aid had risen from £682 million in 1991 to £1,477 million in 1997, an increase of some 115 per cent.[210] Some 90 per cent of that expenditure was said to have gone on lawyers' fees. In civil legal aid, expenditure since 1993 had increased by 43 per cent, yet the number of people assisted had gone down by 9 per cent. On the basis of such evidence, the Committee concluded that significant reforms were needed. It proposed that the Legal Aid Board should use its purchasing power to contract for legal services in a pro-active way, setting requirements of quality, access, and value for money. Only contracted suppliers should be able to do legal aid work, and consideration should be given to the possibility of the Board employing its own lawyers to provide legal services. Users of the system should be required to contribute as much as they could afford to the costs of their case, and everyone should be required to pay something. The Middleton Report was followed by publication of the government's own plans for the reform of Legal Aid.[211] These plans were part of a package of measures which would result in significant changes to the entire civil justice system.[212] In the government's view it was important to reduce the cost of civil justice for all users, so as to ensure greater accessibility and better value for money for both the taxpayer and the individual litigant. The government's proposals drew heavily on the Middleton Report and were given effect by the Access to Justice Act 1999.

(a) The Legal Services Commission

Section 1(1) of the Access to Justice Act 1999 established a new Legal Services Commission (LSC) to replace the Legal Aid Board. The Commission is required by the Act to 'establish, maintain and develop' two separate services: (a) the Community Legal Service;[213] and (b) the Criminal Defence Service.[214] It consists of between seven and twelve members,[215] who are appointed for their knowledge and experience in matters such as the provision of legal services, the work of the courts, consumer affairs, social conditions, and management.[216] The Commission has a wide range of powers and responsibilities and it may do anything which it considers necessary or appropriate for the discharge of its functions.[217] It is required to publish an annual plan setting out how it intends to fund its services for the forthcoming year, and at the end of that year it must also publish a report on its performance. Both documents must be submitted to the Lord Chancellor and laid before Parliament.[218]

The aim of the LSC is not only to improve the public's access to advice, but to ensure that the advice available is of good quality. It has therefore introduced a range of Quality Marks to recognize high standards in the delivery of different types of service. Three different standards of Quality Mark are available: (a) information;

---

[210] Ibid, at para 3.3.   [211] *Modernising Justice* (White Paper), December 1998.
[212] See the discussion at p 432, *post*.   [213] 1999 Act, ss 1(2)(a); 4(1). See p 377, *post*.
[214] Ibid, ss 1(2)(b); 12(1). See p 380, *post*.   [215] Ibid, s 1(3).   [216] Ibid, s 1(5).
[217] Ibid, s 3(1).   [218] Ibid, Schedule 1, paras 14–15.

(b) general help; and (c) specialist help. Within these categories there are specific Quality Marks for things such as mediation and telephone advice, and there is also a Quality Mark for the Bar. The 'specialist help' standard is aimed at legal professionals and other specialized agencies, and without this Quality Mark it is not possible to obtain LSC funding. It will be apparent from this that the other Quality Mark standards enable the LSC to accredit a range of services which it does not actually fund.

Contracts. Under the old Legal Aid system the vast majority of funding was provided on a case-by-case basis. Any lawyer could undertake legal aid work and there were no restrictions on the amount that he could do. A new scheme was introduced in 1994 whereby practitioners could apply for a Legal Aid franchise in one or more areas of law. Those operating under a franchise had to comply with strict quality and auditing requirements, in return for which they were able to undertake legal aid work on more favourable terms and without seeking prior approval for each case. At this stage the scheme was voluntary, and those who were unwilling (or unable) to obtain a franchise could still do legal aid work on the same terms as before. Since the launch of the Legal Services Commission however, things have changed significantly.

The position now is that publicly funded legal services can only be provided by those who hold LSC contracts. The terms of these contracts restrict the categories of law in which LSC-funded services can be offered, and they also limit the volume of cases that a provider can undertake. In this way, the LSC is able to exercise much greater control over expenditure than its predecessor: by regulating the types of contract awarded it can concentrate its funds on the areas in which they are most needed, and by auditing contracted suppliers it can ensure that proper standards are being maintained. In the government's view, this approach is the key to ensuring a high quality of service for the client and better value for money for the taxpayer.

(b) The Community Legal Service

The Community Legal Service (CLS) was established under section 1(2)(a) of the 1999 Act and is the responsibility of the Legal Services Commission. Its statutory purpose is to promote the availability of a range of services, and to secure access to those services so as to effectively meet individual needs.[219] The services specifically falling within its remit concern: (a) the provision of information about the law and the legal system; (b) the provision of help and advice about the application of the law to particular circumstances; (c) the provision of help in preventing, settling or otherwise resolving disputes about legal rights and duties; (d) the provision of help in enforcing decisions about the resolution of such disputes; and (e) the provision of help in relation to legal proceedings not relating to disputes.[220] The Commission must decide how to prioritize the allocation of its resources, but it must do so within the framework of directions laid down by the Lord Chancellor.[221] Priorities identified

---

[219] Ibid, s 4(1).   [220] Ibid, s 4(2).

[221] Ibid, s 6(1); Community Legal Service Fund Funding Priorities (2000).

thus far include proceedings under the Children Act 1989 and other proceedings concerning child welfare, civil proceedings where the client is at real risk of loss of life or liberty, domestic violence proceedings, and proceedings which allege serious breaches of human rights on the part of public authorities. The Commission is required to maintain a separate fund to support the provision of such services in accordance with the terms of the Act,[222] and in this sense the Community Legal Service can be seen as a replacement for civil legal aid.

What work is covered by community legal service contracts?. The Funding Code issued under section 8 of the 1999 Act lists seven levels of service that may be provided by contracted suppliers:

(1) Legal help (this covers the provision of advice as to the application of the law and assistance in resolving disputes—in essence it replaces the old Green Form scheme);[223]

(2) Help at court (help and advocacy for a client in relation to a particular hearing but falling short of formal legal representation);

(3) Approved family help (legal help and some types of representation in family disputes);

(4) Legal representation (including litigation and advocacy services and related preparatory work);

(5) Support funding (assistance with representation in cases which are otherwise privately funded);

(6) Family mediation

(7) Such other services as may be authorized by the Lord Chancellor.

Precisely which services are available is determined by the nature of the client's case and the terms of the provider's contract with the LSC. Work done under a Community Legal Service contract may be 'controlled' or 'licensed'. Controlled work is work for which the contract provides full authorization, and for which the supplier does not need to seek approval before accepting each new case. It encompasses all 'legal help' and 'help at court', in addition to covering 'legal representation' before certain tribunals.[224] All other work done under a general contract is known as 'licensed work', and it must be authorized on a case-by-case basis. In 2003/2004, 93 per cent of all solicitors holding General Civil Contracts had been allocated a quota of controlled work.[225] The LSC's total expenditure on controlled work was £383.3m.[226] In the same year the LSC spent £514.1m funding licensed work, the majority of which involved legal representation.[227]

---

[222] Ibid, s 4(5).   [223] See p 375, *ante*, for a brief explanation of the Green Form scheme.
[224] Mental Health Review Tribunals and the Asylum and Immigration Tribunal: Funding Code, para A3.
[225] Legal Services Commission, *Annual Report 2003–04*, p 21.
[226] Ibid, p 79.   [227] Ibid, p 78.

Work which falls outside the general contract altogether may be authorized separately under an 'individual case contract', and there are special arrangements for remunerating work done in 'high cost' cases. As with the Legal Aid scheme however, there are certain types of work for which Community Legal Service funding is not available at all. These exclusions are listed in Schedule 2 of the 1999 Act, and they comprise: (a) most claims in negligence (except those relating to clinical negligence); (b) conveyancing; (c) boundary disputes; (d) the making of wills; (e) matters of trust law; (f) defamation or malicious falsehood; (g) matters of company or partnership law (i) other business matters; and (j) asylum decisions. Many areas of work *are* covered by CLS funding, including (a) family; (b) housing; (c) debt; (d) immigration; (e) employment; (f) contract and consumer law; (g) welfare law; (h) community care; (i) clinical negligence; (j) education; (k) mental health; (l) public law; and (m) actions against the police. However, funding for advocacy is only available in relation to certain courts and certain types of proceedings,[228] with the result that representation before most tribunals is not covered by the scheme.

Eligibility for Community Legal Service assistance. An individual must satisfy both a merits test and a means test in order to obtain services from the CLS. The merits test derives from section 8 of the Access to Justice Act and from the Funding Code issued under it. Factors to be considered include: (a) the potential benefit to the client of providing the service in question and the likely cost to the CLS of funding it; (b) the availability and suitability of other sources of funding, such as conditional fee agreements; (c) the prospects of any legal action being successful; (d) the principle that mediation is often better than litigation in family cases; and (e) the public interest. 'High cost' cases and cases in areas such as clinical negligence and judicial review are subject to additional considerations.[229]

The rules governing financial eligibility are set out in regulations made under section 7 of the 1999 Act. The current regulations date from 2000,[230] though they have recently undergone considerable revision.[231] Different types of service used to be subject to different eligibility limits, but standard limits have now been introduced. Those with very low incomes and little capital will be entitled to full CLS assistance,[232] while those who are slightly better-off will be required to pay a contribution towards certain services.[233] The financial limits are reviewed each year and are increased by Statutory Instrument. More people qualify for assistance under the current regime

---

[228] Access to Justice Act 1999, Schedule 2.   [229] See generally, parts 6 to 13 of the Funding Code.

[230] Community Legal Service (Financial) Regulations 2000, SI 2000/516.

[231] Community Legal Service Financial (Amendment) Regulations 2005, SI 2005/589; Community Legal Service (Financial) (Amendment No 2) Regulations 2005, SI 2005/1097.

[232] Capital is not taken into account if the client is a pensioner or if the capital is the subject matter of the dispute. Those on Income Support and certain other benefits automatically qualify for full assistance.

[233] Services for which no contribution is required include: the provision of general information about the law and legal services; the provision of Legal Help or Help at Court; and Legal Representation in some cases involving children or asylum and immigration disputes—SI 2000/516, Article 3 (as amended).

than were covered by the Legal Aid system,[234] but the means test is still set at quite a low level—so much so that the Director of the Legal Aid Practitioner's Group has suggested that 'only loan sharks would loan money to someone who is poor enough to qualify for legal aid.'[235]

Not-for-profit organizations and Community Legal Service Partnerships. It should not be assumed that the CLS is only about the work done by solicitors' firms. Bodies like Shelter and the Citizens' Advice Bureaux can hold General Civil Contracts and receive LSC funding in much the same way as the private sector. In fact the LSC is increasingly looking to the not-for-profit sector as the number of solicitors doing publicly funded work declines, and in 2003/2004 it funded almost a million caseworker hours.[236] Another important feature of the new system is that it requires the LSC to work with other bodies and organizations to find ways of improving access to justice.[237] To this end it has brought solicitors together with law centres, Citizens Advice Bureaux, and local authority advice agencies to establish over 200 Community Legal Service Partnerships. A key function of these Partnerships is to identify areas of 'unmet legal need' and to find ways of addressing them at a local level.[238]

(b) The Criminal Defence Service

The other service managed by the LSC is the Criminal Defence Service (CDS). This was established under section 1(2)(b) of the Access to Justice Act and its role is to secure advice, assistance, and representation to persons involved in criminal investigations or proceedings.[239] All solicitors providing services for the CDS[240] must hold a General Criminal Contract and a Specialist Quality Mark. In this respect the CDS operates in a similar way to the Community Legal Service, although work done on behalf of the CDS is not subject to strict quotas.[241] As of March 2004, 2,669 solicitors' firms were operating under General Criminal Contracts.[242] Three basic levels of service may be provided: (1) advice and assistance; (2) advocacy assistance; and (c) representation. All services funded by the CDS are subject to some form of merits test, though many of them are not means-tested. With regard to initial advice and assistance, the merits test will automatically be satisfied if a suspect or defendant has a statutory right to legal advice,[243] but the provision of any additional assistance must be justified on a case-by-case basis.

---

[234] Controversial proposals to treat the equity in a person's home as 'capital' for these purposes were recently abandoned: see LSC, *A New Focus for Civil Legal Aid—Consultation Outcomes* (2005).

[235] Miller, 'Getting the Focus Right for Civil Legal Aid' (2004) NLJ 1673.

[236] Legal Services Commission, *Annual Report 2003–04*, p 78.   [237] 1999 Act, s 4(6).

[238] The Director of JUSTICE has concluded that not-for-profit bodies have benefited considerably from the creation of the CLS: Smith, *Paper for Legal Services Authority Conference on the Future of Community Legal Services: Law for those in Disadvantage* (4 October 2002) at para 44.

[239] 1999 Act, s 12(1). For these purposes the term 'criminal proceedings' includes proceedings relating to sentencing, appeals, extradition, binding over, and contempt of court: s 12(2).

[240] With the exception of those employed by the Public Defender Service: see p 381, *post*.

[241] Cf. the concept of 'controlled work' under CLS contracts, discussed at p 378, *ante*.

[242] Legal Services Commission, *Annual Report 2003–04*, p 6.   [243] See p 415, *post*.

One of the most important functions of the CDS is to provide duty solicitor schemes in police stations and magistrates' courts. These schemes cover the provision of 'advice and assistance' to persons who are held in police custody or who are appearing before magistrates in certain types of proceedings.[244] Their services are provided free of charge on a non-means-tested basis, and for the most part they are supplied by solicitors working in private practice. Recent changes to the General Criminal Contract mean that advice to those detained in connection with less serious offences will normally be provided by telephone only. Face-to-face assistance will be available if a police interview or identification procedure is to take place, or where the client is a young or vulnerable person, requires the assistance of an interpreter, or has complained of serious mistreatment. It may also be offered if the duty solicitor is already present at the police station.

Court duty solicitors may provide 'advocacy assistance' in connection with bail applications and binding-over proceedings, and *any* CDS-contracted solicitor may provide advocacy assistance in relation to ASBOs and certain other court orders, or in cases where a person risks imprisonment for non-payment of fines. Representation is subject to a merits test and will only be funded where a representation order has been made by a court or the LSC. It is not means-tested at the point of access but the Crown Court has the power to make a Recovery of Defence Costs Order at the conclusion of a case. The government has proposed changes which, if enacted, will reintroduce means testing in magistrates' courts and require convicted defendants to repay their defence costs if they can afford to do so.[245]

The Public Defender Service. In addition to delivering services through contracted lawyers in private practice, the CDS is also able to provide legal services through lawyers in its own employment.[246] A Public Defender Service has been launched, which now has offices in Birmingham, Cheltenham, Chester, Darlington, Liverpool, Middlesbrough, Pontypridd, and Swansea. Public Defenders participate in local duty solicitor schemes, and provide other CDS services—including representation—directly to their own clients. In 2003/2004 they handled 4,291 cases.[247] Public Defenders are an established feature of the legal system in the US and other jurisdictions, but they are a radical new development for England and Wales. There are concerns about the extent to which Public Defenders can be genuinely independent, though the Code of Practice established under section 16 of the Act aims to address some of these concerns.

---

[244] Including bail applications and applications relating to anti-social behaviour and sex-offender orders.
[245] The Criminal Defence Service Bill, which was announced on 17 May 2005.
[246] 1999 Act, s 13(2)(f) (advice and assistance); s 14(2)(f) (representation).
[247] Legal Services Commission, *Annual Report 2003–04*, p 6.

5 WHAT HAS THE NEW REGIME DELIVERED? 'ACCESS TO JUSTICE' OR JUSTICE DENIED?

The task faced by the LSC is undoubtedly a difficult one. The cost of funding legal services has been rising for many years, placing an increasing strain on public finances. Delivering access to justice in this climate was never going to be easy, and defenders of the new system would argue that the LSC has made a number of improvements. Changes to the means-test have enabled more people to benefit from LSC services than were covered by the old Legal Aid system, and the idea of concentrating funds on early dispute resolution has much to commend it in principle. The increase in funding for not-for-profit organizations has been welcomed, as has the greater emphasis on quality and accountability. There have also been many completely new initiatives, such as the development of Community Legal Service Direct,[248] the introduction of Housing Possession Duty Court Schemes,[249] and the launch of the Public Defender Service.

Critics however, would argue that in spite of the LSC's efforts to target funds where they are most needed, access to justice has actually diminished since its launch. The contract system has limited the number of suppliers who are able to provide publicly funded services, and those who do hold contracts are subject to considerable regulatory and administrative burdens. The professional bodies continue to complain that public funded work is poorly remunerated, and all of these factors are having a negative effect on the number of providers willing to work in this sector. A recent survey by Citizens' Advice found that 68 per cent of their bureaux experienced difficulties in finding Community Legal Service lawyers to do immigration work, with 60 per cent facing similar problems in the field of housing law.[250] Some 39 per cent of bureaux said that they were operating in 'an advice desert',[251] and the overall conclusion of the report was that publicly funded legal services were declining in all parts of the country[252]

In an effort to tackle rising costs and to make its budget go further, the LSC has introduced a mandatory system of fixed fees covering all types of controlled[253] civil work except immigration. It argues that by rewarding service providers for 'outputs' rather than for the actual time spent on each case, the new system will be more cost efficient and will ensure that payments to suppliers reflect market conditions.[254] It remains to be seen whether the profession will see things this way: when graduated fixed fees were introduced for family and criminal work, barristers took the view that they were being denied 'proper remuneration' and they voted to abandon the cab rule for cases which were subject to this system.

---

[248] Formerly called 'Just Ask!', this web site provides the public with information about how to get advice, and it also includes a national directory of service providers: www.clsdirect.org.uk.

[249] Which make housing advisers available in courts; cf. the duty solicitor scheme: see p 381, *ante*.

[250] *Geography of Advice* (2004) at para 2.15.   [251] Ibid, at para 2.14.

[252] Ibid, at para 5.1.   [253] See p 378, *ante*.

[254] Legal Services Commission, *Tailored Fixed Fee Scheme Consultation Paper: Civil (Non-Immigration) Controlled Work* (2004). The system became mandatory on 1 April 2005.

Recent statistics suggest that not all lawyers engaged in public funded work are impoverished. In 2003/2004, one barrister reportedly earned £800,000 in fees for work done for the Criminal Defence Service, while another barrister was paid £606,000 by the Community Legal Service over the same period. These figures add weight to a point made by the Lord Chancellor in a speech to the Law Society in 2003:[255]

I know lawyers complain about remuneration rates but may I point out that over the last ten years the average cost per family case in civil representation has gone up by 91 per cent. Inflation in the same period was 30 per cent. I do *not* argue that this is all to the benefit of lawyers. But it does show that arguments about rates are not as straightforward as they first appear.

It is likely that lawyers and politicians will continue to disagree about the fees paid for public funded work, but there is a growing consensus about the need to correct the imbalance between the civil and criminal budgets. Although overall spending on public funded work has continued to rise since the Legal Services Commission was launched, expenditure on civil work is actually declining. Unlike the Legal Aid Board the LSC is required to work to a particular budget, and since criminal work is not subject to quotas and continues to be demand-led, funding for the Community Legal Service has inevitably been squeezed. The Lord Chancellor is now promising to address this, and though he has rejected calls for the CLS budget to be ring-fenced, measures in the new Criminal Defence Bill[256] are designed to bring spending on criminal defence work under control. As far as the civil side is concerned, one of the most important developments on the agenda for the Community Legal Service is the introduction of salaried lawyers performing an equivalent role to Public Defenders. A pilot of such a scheme is likely to be introduced in the near future.[257]

---

[255] Law Society Annual Conference, London (26 September 2003).

[256] Announced in the Queen's Speech, May 2005: a previous Bill failed due to lack of parliamentary time.

[257] DCA, *Final Report of the Independent Review of the Community Legal Service* (2004).

12

THE POLICE AND LAW ENFORCEMENT[1]

A THE LAW ENFORCEMENT FUNCTION

Law enforcement functions in England and Wales are performed primarily, but not exclusively, by the jurisdiction's forty-three local police forces. These forces are served by over 140,000 full-time police officers, each one of whom exercises the legal powers and privileges of a 'constable'.[2] These salaried officers are assisted by around 10,000 'special constables', who serve on a part-time, unpaid basis. Since 2002, a number of civilian officers have also been designated, though their 'powers and privileges' are less extensive.[3]

In addition to local police forces, several other organizations perform law enforcement functions. The Ministry of Defence Police, the British Transport Police, and the Civil Nuclear Constabulary are examples of specialist police forces, and their officers hold the office of constable within their jurisdictions.[4] Other bodies operating at a national level include the National Criminal Intelligence Agency and the National Crime Squad,[5] which in 2006 will be combined to form a powerful new 'Serious Organised Crime Agency'.[6] The role of other agencies should also be considered. The Director of the Serious Fraud Office has wide ranging powers to assist in the investigation of complex or serious fraud offences.[7] Bodies such as the Inland Revenue and the Health and Safety Executive also have important investigative roles. It is, however, the police who perform the bulk of investigatory and law enforcement work.

---

[1] The literature on the police is extensive. See, e.g. the Report of the Royal Commission on Criminal Procedure, and the research studies listed in Annex D (Cmnd 8092, 1981); Lustgarten, *The Governance of the Police* (1986); Reiner, *The Politics of the Police* (3rd edn, 2000); English and Card, *Butterworth's Police Law* (8th edn, 2003); Newburn (ed), *Handbook of Policing* (2003); Newburn and Reiner, 'From PC Dixon to Dixon plc: Policing and Policing Powers since 1954' [2004] Crim LR 601.

[2] Police Act 1996, s 30.   [3] Police Reform Act 2002, s 38; Schedule 4. See p 390, *post*.

[4] Ministry of Defence Police Act 1997, s 2; Railways and Transport Safety Act 2003, s 31; Energy Act 2004, s 56.

[5] See Parts 1 and 2 of the Police Act 1997.

[6] Serious Organised Crime and Police Act 2005, part 1: see p 388, *post*. Parts of the Immigration Service and Her Majesty's Customs and Excise will also become part of the new Agency.

[7] Criminal Justice Act 1987, s 2; see *Smith v Director of Serious Fraud Office* [1992] 3 All ER 456.

1 THE ROLE OF THE INDIVIDUAL

All individuals have a duty to preserve the peace, though this is a duty of 'imperfect obligation' and there is generally no sanction for its breach. In *Albert* v *Lavin*[8] Lord Diplock stated:

every citizen in whose presence a breach of the peace is being, or reasonably appears to be about to be, committed has the right to take reasonable steps to make the person who is breaking or threatening to break the peace refrain from doing so; and those reasonable steps in appropriate cases will include detaining him against his will. At common law this is not only the right of every citizen, it is also his duty, although, except in the case of a citizen who is a constable, it is a duty of imperfect obligation.

Citizens also have powers of arrest in respect of offences which are being (or have been) committed:[9] it is these powers that are used by so-called 'store detectives'.

Beyond this however, a citizen has no general duty to assist the police. The law proceeds on the basis that individuals have a 'right to silence',[10] and a person is generally under no obligation to answer police questions or to co-operate with any investigation.[11] There is, however, a duty not to mislead or hinder an investigation: intentional, positive acts which make it more difficult for an officer to do his job may constitute the offence of wilfully obstructing a constable in the execution of his duty.[12] In *Rice* v *Connolly* Lord Parker CJ stated that whilst it was not unlawful to refuse to answer police questions, deliberately giving a false story undoubtedly *could* constitute an offence.[13] In *Ingleton* v *Dibble* a motorist who was about to be breathalysed grabbed a whisky bottle from another man and took a swig from it. His intention was clearly to make it impossible to ascertain whether he had been intoxicated whilst driving, and it was held that his actions amounted to a wilful obstruction of an officer in the execution of his duty.[14] In another case a motorist was convicted of the same offence after ignoring a constable's order to reverse the wrong way down a one way street to allow an ambulance to pass.[15]

Note finally, that in certain circumstances the Serious Fraud Office has the power to compel persons to answer questions or disclose relevant documents and information. In due course, Part 2 of the Serious Organised Crime and Police Act 2005 will make similar powers available to police officers. The use of these powers will be confined to the investigation of specific serious offences, and the consent of the Attorney-General or Director of Revenue and Customs Prosecutions will be required.[16]

---

8 [1982] AC 546 at 565, [1981] 3 All ER 878 at 880.

9 Police and Criminal Evidence Act 1984, s 24: see p 406, *post*.   10 Though see p 417, *post*.

11 *Rice* v *Connolly* [1966] 2 QB 414, [1966] 2 All ER 649.

12 Police Act 1996, s 89(2): see p 395, *post*.

13 [1966] 2 QB 414 at 420, [1966] 2 All ER 649 at 652.

14 [1972] 1 QB 480, [1972] 1 All ER 275.

15 *Johnson* v *Phillips* [1976] 1 WLR 65, [1975] 3 All ER 682.

16 It will not normally be possible to use statements made under such compulsion as evidence in any criminal proceedings against their maker: 2005 Act, s 65.

2 THE ORGANIZATION OF THE POLICE

The structures and organization of the police were radically changed by the Police Act 1964, the Police and Criminal Evidence Act 1984, and the Police and Magistrates' Courts Act 1994. The relevant provisions were consolidated by the Police Act 1996, and further changes have since been made by the Police Act 1997 and the Police Reform Act 2002. Policing is, for the most part, organized on a local basis, and each of the forty-three police areas[17] in England and Wales has its own police authority.[18] Most police authorities outside London have seventeen members, comprising members of local authorities, justices of the peace, and certain other persons nominated by the Home Secretary.[19] The Metropolitan Police Authority has twenty-three members, but is otherwise similarly constituted.[20] Slightly different arrangements exist for the City of London area, where the Common Council of the City of London performs the functions of a police authority.[21]

There is no direct democratic element in the management of policing, though democratic input is achieved indirectly through the representatives of local authorities. In addition, section 96 of the Police Act 1996 states that:

(1) Arrangements shall be made for each police area for obtaining —

    (a) the views of people in that area about matters concerning the policing of the area, and

    (b) their co-operation with the police in preventing crime in that area.

The primary duty of a police authority is 'to secure the maintenance of an efficient and effective police force for its area'.[22] To this end, the authority is required to appoint a Chief Constable[23] and to produce an annual policing plan with its proposed arrangements for policing the area.[24] In conjunction with the force's chief police officer, it must also produce a three-year strategy plan setting out its medium and long-term objectives.[25] In addition, although the appointment of individual police officers is a matter for the Chief Constable,[26] it is for the police authority to decide how many officers are needed for its area. Despite this apparent local autonomy, there are numerous mechanisms for ensuring the accountability of local police forces to central government, and the last two decades have seen an increasing trend towards centralization.

---

[17] See Schedule 1 of the Police Act 1996 for a list of police areas outside London.
[18] Police Act 1996, ss 3; 5B.   [19] Ibid, s 4; Schedule 2.   [20] Ibid, s 5C; Schedule 2A.
[21] Ibid, s 101.   [22] Ibid, s 6.
[23] Ibid, s 11: any appointment requires the Home Secretary's approval. The Metropolitan Police Authority is subject to different arrangements: both the Authority and the Mayor of London have the power to recommend a person for appointment as the Metropolitan Police Commissioner, but the actual appointment is made by the Monarch on the advice of the Home Secretary: 1996 Act, s 9B.
[24] Ibid, s 8.   [25] Ibid, s 6A.   [26] Ibid, s 13(3).

(a) Police authorities and central government

A Police Authority cannot appoint, remove, or suspend a Chief Constable without the approval of the Home Secretary,[27] and the Home Secretary can require a Chief Constable to retire in the interests of efficiency.[28] The Home Secretary can also direct that a police force be given assistance or reinforced in the interests of justice, safety, or public order, and he can do this with or without the agreement of the Police Authority.[29] Indeed, the Home Secretary has a wide range of powers that can be used to 'promote the efficiency and effectiveness of the police',[30] and it is to him that police authorities must send their local and strategic reports.[31] The Inspectorate of Constabulary also reports to the Secretary of State,[32] and an adverse report regarding a force may result in the police authority being required to submit an 'action plan' of proposed remedial measures.[33] It may also lead to the withholding of all or part of the central government grant made to each police authority.[34] The threat to withhold funds is a powerful one, and it can be used as a lever to secure change in the way a force is run.[35] For his part, the Secretary of State is required to produce a National Policing Plan at the beginning of each financial year, setting out his 'strategic policing priorities' and his proposals for addressing them.[36] He may also set objectives and performance targets for the policing of local police areas,[37] and he can issue Codes of Practice[38] and make regulations for the use of equipment.[39]

In addition to these statutory powers, the royal prerogative allows the Home Secretary to take all reasonably necessary steps to ensure the preservation of the Queen's peace.[40] In *R v Secretary of State for the Home Department, ex parte Northumbria Police Authority*[41] the Court of Appeal considered the scope of section 41 of the Police Act 1964. At the time, this was the provision authorizing the Home Secretary to provide and maintain services for promoting the efficiency of the police. The Court held that the Home Secretary was entitled under this provision to supply riot control equipment from central stores, without the approval of the police authority. It also held that even if section 41 could not be construed in this way, the Home Secretary's actions would have been lawful under the prerogative.

It would be wrong to view police authorities as acting always in isolation. Chief Constables can seek mutual aid from other forces,[42] and regional organizations have been created, both formally and informally. An example of the former is the national

---

27 Ibid, s 11: see also, n 23 above.   28 Ibid, s 42(1).   29 Ibid, s 24.

30 Ibid, s 36(1).   31 Ibid, ss 6A; 8.   32 Ibid, s 54.

33 Ibid, s 41A.   34 Ibid, s 46.

35 In 1992 for example, an adverse report from the Inspectorate of Constabulary led to significant changes in the running of the Derbyshire Police Force

36 1996 Act, s 36A (inserted by the Police Reform Act 2002).   37 Ibid, ss 37; 38.

38 See, e.g. Police and Criminal Evidence Act 1984, ss 60, 60A, and 66 (codes for the exercise of police powers and duties); Police Act 1996, s 39A (codes for chief police officers); Serious Organised Crime and Police Act 2005, s 10 (codes for the Serious Organised Crime Agency).

39 Police Reform Act 2002, s 6.

40 For a discussion of prerogative powers generally, see chapter 6, *ante*.

41 [1989] QB 26, [1988] 1 All ER 556.   42 Police Act 1996, s 24.

DNA database, which is managed by the Home Office Forensic Science Service on behalf of the Association of Chief Police Officers. The creation of the National Reporting Centre during the miners' strike in the mid-1980s provides an example of a rather less formal organization.[43] Another important national body is the National Criminal Intelligence Service (NCIS). This was originally created in 1992 but was given a statutory basis by Part I of the Police Act 1997. It is accountable to its own Service Authority and its primary function is to provide support and criminal intelligence to police forces and other law enforcement agencies.[44] The 1997 Act also created the National Crime Squad.[45] This brought the pre-existing Regional Crime Squads together in a single organization, and was effectively given the status of a police force in its own right. Its Director-General has the status and rank of a Chief Constable,[46] and its role is to tackle major crimes which cross force boundaries and which can better be handled at a national level. Part 1 of the Serious Organised Crime and Police Act 2005 makes provision for these bodies to be combined to form a new Serious Organised Crime Agency. The Agency will also replace parts of the Immigration Service and Her Majesty's Customs and Excise, and it is expected to begin operating in 2006. Billed as 'an FBI for the UK', its remit will extend throughout the UK and its focus will be on tackling drugs trafficking, money laundering, and other serious offences. The Agency will also have a number of new investigative powers at its disposal.[47]

(b) Police authorities and Chief Constables

A Chief Constable is required to produce drafts of policing and strategic plans for the Police Authority to finalise,[48] and he must also submit a general report to the Authority at the end of each financial year.[49] Beyond this, the Police Authority's rights are limited, and it has sometimes been said that a Chief Constable cannot be challenged on operational matters. In reality the position is not so straightforward, but the law does recognize that the Chief Constable has a wide discretion to determine strategy and other matters. The scope for judicially reviewing a Chief Constable's decisions is thus extremely limited, and neither the deployment of police resources nor individual policing decisions are normally matters for the courts. In *R v Commissioner of Police for the Metropolis, ex parte Blackburn* the Court of Appeal considered the legality of a policy by which the Commissioner had directed his officers to enforce the Gaming Acts only in certain circumstances. Lord Denning MR stated:[50]

[It is the duty of the Commissioner], as it is of every Chief Constable, to enforce the law of the land. He must take steps so to post his men that crimes may be detected; and that honest

---

[43] See generally, Freeman, 'Law and Order in 1984' [1984] CLP 175.
[44] Police Act 1997, ss 1, 2.   [45] Ibid, s 48.   [46] Ibid, s 52(7).
[47] In addition to Part 1 of the Act, see: *One Step Ahead: A 21st Century Strategy to Defeat Organised Crime* (Cm 6167, 2004). See also, p 385, *ante*.
[48] Police Act 1996, ss 6A(2); 8(3).   [49] Ibid, s 22.
[50] [1968] 2 QB 118 at 136, [1968] 1 All ER 763 at 769.

citizens may go about their affairs in peace. He must decide whether or not suspected persons are to be prosecuted . . . but in all these things he is not the servant of anyone, save of the law itself. No Minister of the Crown can tell him that he must, or must not . . . prosecute this man or that one. Nor can any police authority tell him so. The responsibility for law enforcement lies on him. He is answerable to the law and to the law alone [but] there are many fields in which [a chief police officer has] a discretion with which the law will not interfere. For instance, it is [for him] to decide in any particular case whether enquiries should be pursued, or whether an arrest should be made . . . It must be for him to decide on the disposition of his force and the concentration of his resources on any particular crime or area. No court can or should give him direction on such a matter

The court added that it *could* intervene if what was at issue was effectively an abdication of duty, but the matter was not put to the test because the policy statement had already been withdrawn. In another case the House of Lords accepted that police discretion could be the subject of judicial review, but it stressed that as long it was used for a legitimate purpose, the courts would not interfere with the exercise of that discretion.[51] Although these cases do not deal directly with the relationship between the Chief Constable and his police authority, they clearly illustrate the extent of a Chief Constable's discretion and the level of autonomy that he has.

(c) Chief Constables and individual officers

Constables are office holders under the Crown, though they are not Crown servants or employees of the Chief Constable. As stated previously, all police officers derive their powers from their status as constables, though certain powers can only be exercised by officers holding a particular rank. An intimate search of a suspect, for example, can only be authorized by an officer at least the rank of inspector.[52]

The reality of modern policing is that each force has its own policies and command structure, and all officers are subject to rules governing their employment, personal conduct, and discipline.[53] However, when exercising the powers of a constable an officer is legally responsible for his own actions, and he cannot be directed to exercise them in a particular way. In *Lindley* v *Rutter*[54] it was held that a police officer had acted unlawfully in removing an item of underwear from a drunken, arrested woman. The officer had wrongly regarded a standing instruction as depriving her of any discretion as to whether such garments should be removed. Although there was a common law power which could have provided the authority for the officer's conduct, she had not considered whether the conditions for exercising this power were satisfied: her actions were therefore unlawful. This does not mean that it will always be

---

[51] *Holgate-Mohammed* v *Duke* [1984] AC 437, [1984] 1 All ER 1054; cf. *R* v *Chief Constable of Devon & Cornwall, ex parte Central Electricity Generating Board* [1982] QB 458, [1981] 3 All ER 826. See also, Ch. 6, *ante*.

[52] Police and Criminal Evidence Act 1984, s 55.

[53] Police Regulations 2003, SI 2003/527; Police (Conduct) Regulations 2004, SI 2004/645.

[54] [1981] QB 128, [1980] 3 WLR 660.

improper to rely on a policy or standing instruction; what matters is whether there has been a genuine exercise of discretion.[55]

3 CIVILIAN OFFICERS: 'THE EXTENDED POLICE FAMILY'[56]

The Police Reform Act 2002 allows Chief Constables to confer limited law enforce-ment powers on civilians employed by police authorities. The idea is that if civilians are able to perform basic public order and support functions, constables can be given more time to focus on their core policing role. Section 38(2) of the Act provides that a civilian employee may be designated as one or more of the following: (a) a com-munity support officer, (b) an investigating officer, (c) a detention officer, or (d) an escort officer. Community support officers have specific powers to deal with low-level disorder and anti-social behaviour problems. Thus, where a community support officer has reason to believe that a person has committed a relevant offence or has been acting in an anti-social manner, he may require that person to give his name and address. If the person fails to comply with this requirement, or if the officer has reasonable grounds to suspect that he has been given false information, the officer may detain that person for up to thirty minutes until a constable arrives. Community support officers also have the power to issue some fixed penalty notices.[57] Investigat-ing officers on the other hand, are essentially civilian 'scene of crime' officers: they have the power to apply for and execute search warrants, and once a suspect has been lawfully arrested they can exercise many of the search and seizure powers available to constables.[58] Detention officers perform various functions with regard to persons in police custody, and they have powers to search, photograph, and fingerprint suspects.[59] Finally, escort officers, as the name indicates, are primarily involved in transporting detainees to and from police stations.[60]

The Serious Organised Crime and Police Act 2005 will further extend the police family by allowing civilian employees to be designated as 'staff custody officers'.[61] It will also extend the range of powers that can be conferred on community support officers: in future, such officers may be given powers to direct traffic, to assist at the scene of serious accidents, and to deal with begging and offences relating to the sale of alcohol. They will also have limited search and seizure powers.[62]

Some police powers can be conferred on civilians who are *not* employed by police authorities. Thus, where a police force has contracted a private company to provide

---

[55] See, e.g. *R* v *Chief Constable of Avon and Somerset Constabulary, ex parte Robinson* [1989] 2 All ER 15, [1989] 1 WLR 793.

[56] See *Policing in the New Century: A Blueprint for Reform* (Cm 5326, 2001); Morris, 'Extending the Police Family: Issues and Anomalies' [1992] PL 670; Ormerod and Roberts, 'The Police Reform Act 2002—Increasing Centralisation, Maintaining Confidence and Contracting out Crime' [2003] Crim LR 141; Jason-Lloyd, *Quasi-Policing* (2003).

[57] Ibid, s 38(6); Schedule 4, part 1.   [58] Ibid, s 38(6); Schedule 4, part 2.

[59] Ibid, s 38(6); Schedule 4, part 3.   [60] Ibid, s 38(6); Schedule 4, part 4.

[61] 2005 Act, ss 120–121; Schedule 8. See p 409, *post.*

[62] Ibid, Schedule 7, part 1. Schedule 8 adds to the range of powers exercisable by other civilian officers.

some of its escort and detention services, the Chief Constable can designate employees of that company as escort or detention officers.[63] The Act also enables Chief Constables to establish schemes whereby other non-police employees, such as security guards and traffic wardens, may be accredited to perform community safety functions. Accredited persons cannot exercise the full range of powers available to community support officers, but they can, for example, issue fixed penalty notices for littering and dog-fouling, and in some circumstances they can also require a person to provide his name and address.[64] Before any powers under the Act can be conferred on a non-police employee, the Chief Constable must be satisfied that he is a suitable person to exercise those powers, and that he is capable and adequately trained.[65] He must also be satisfied that the person's employer is a 'fit and proper person' to supervise him for these purposes.[66]

Private sector employees designated as detention or escort officers are subject to the police complaints regime, as are civilian officers employed by police authorities.[67] There is also little doubt that all those who exercise police powers, including those accredited under community safety schemes, will be liable under the Human Rights Act 1998 if they infringe Convention rights.[68] Nevertheless, the idea of extending police powers to persons who are not trained as constables remains controversial, particularly where those persons are not employed by the police authority and are not directly subject to police control. Paradoxically, some critics have also suggested that the new powers do not go far enough. As Jason-Lloyd has noted:[69]

[I]t is wrong to give civilians *limited* police powers when they are likely to face *unlimited* situations on the streets. The present structure of their powers is restricted to certain incidents, but this will not prevent other incidents from occurring within the same scenario where they have not been given specific powers to deal with them.

B POLICE ACCOUNTABILITY

The accountability of Chief Constables to police authorities and the Home Secretary has already been discussed, but police accountability is also achieved through a variety of other mechanisms.

1 RULES OF EVIDENCE

In general, English courts adhere to the principle that it is no part of their task to punish the police by excluding evidence. In *R v Leatham*,[70] Crompton J observed that:

---

[63] 2002 Act, s 39.   [64] Ibid, ss 40–41; Schedule 5.   [65] Ibid, ss 39(4); 41(4).
[66] Ibid, ss 39(5), 41(4).   [67] Police (Complaints and Misconduct) Regulations 2004, SI 2004/643.
[68] See the discussion of section 6 of this Act at p 163, *ante*.
[69] 'Police Reform—A Better Way?' (2003) 167 JP 805.   [70] [1861–73] All ER Rep Ext 1646.

It matters not how you get it; if you steal it even, it would be admissible.

However, in criminal cases the rules of admissibility may have the effect of excluding improperly obtained evidence. Confession evidence, for example, is only admissible if the prosecution can show beyond reasonable doubt that it was not obtained (a) by oppression of the person who made it;[71] or (b) in consequence of anything said or done which was likely to render it unreliable.[72] 'Oppression' is defined in section 76(8) of PACE to include 'torture, inhuman or degrading treatment, and the use or threat of violence (whether or not amounting to torture)'. Beyond this, the term carries its ordinary, natural meaning, and in R v *Fulling* the Court of Appeal adopted a definition from the Oxford English Dictionary:[73]

the exercise of authority or power in a burdensome, harsh or wrongful manner; unjust or cruel treatment of subjects, inferiors, etc.; the imposition of unreasonable or unjust burdens.

Deliberate or gross police misconduct, whether involving physical mistreatment or other forms of bullying, may constitute oppression. In making this assessment the court must take into account the individual characteristics of the suspect. In R v *Miller* the Court of Appeal had no doubt that the confession of the defendant, who was 'on the borderline of mental handicap', had been obtained by oppression:[74]

We are bound to say that on hearing [the interview tape], each member of this Court was horrified. Miller was bullied and hectored. The officers . . . were not questioning him so much as shouting at him what they wanted him to say. Short of physical violence, it is hard to conceive of a more hostile and intimidating approach by officers to a suspect. It is impossible to convey on the printed page the pace, force and menace of the officer's delivery . . .

Miller had denied being involved in any offence over 300 times before finally 'confessing' to murder. The finding that his confession had been obtained by oppression led the Court of Appeal to quash his conviction, along with the convictions of his co-accused. It is rare however, for a court to find that a confession has been obtained by oppression. Where police misconduct does result in confession evidence being excluded, it is usually on the grounds of unreliability. Thus, in R v *Trussler* a drug addict's confession was excluded because he had been denied access to a solicitor and had been interviewed after eighteen hours in custody without a rest period.[75] In another case, it was held that confession evidence should have been excluded from the defendant's trial because his interview had not been properly recorded. Although this

---

[71] PACE, s 76(2)(a). The term 'confession' is defined in s 82(3) to mean a statement wholly or partly adverse to the person who made it

[72] Ibid, s 76(2)(b).

[73] [1987] QB 426 at 432, [1987] 2 All ER 65 at 69, per Lord Lane CJ. On the facts, telling the defendant that her lover had been having an affair was held not to constitute oppression.

[74] (1993) 97 Cr App R 99 at 103, per Lord Taylor CJ. Cf. R v *Emmerson* (1991) 92 Cr App R 284: an officer raising his voice and using bad language did not amount to oppression.

[75] [1988] Crim LR 446.

could not have *caused* him to make unreliable admissions,[76] it had deprived the court of cogent evidence as to what had happened during the interview, and this made it impossible to be sure that section 76(2)(b) had not been breached. The officers had also offered improper inducements to persuade the defendant to admit his guilt, and this was a further reason for excluding the evidence. By contrast, section 76 did not provide a basis for excluding the confession of a heroin addict who claimed that he would have said anything to get bail and get access to drugs: the suspect had not been offered any inducements to confess and his admissions were not made 'in consequence of anything said or done'.[77]

Section 78 of PACE is another important provision and is potentially far wider in scope than section 76. It gives the court a discretion to exclude evidence on which the prosecution proposes to rely, where to admit it would create unfairness to the proceedings. It applies to both confession and non-confession evidence and *may* provide a basis for excluding evidence which has been obtained in breach of PACE and the Codes of Practice. In *R v Samuel* for example, the Court of Appeal quashed the conviction of a man who 'confessed' after being denied access to a lawyer. The Court noted that section 78 requires a judge to take account of how disputed evidence has been obtained, and in this case the police had acted in breach of a 'fundamental' right.[78] Improperly obtained evidence will not always be excluded however, and the courts have often asserted that their exclusionary powers should not be used as a way of disciplining the police. Thus in *R v Alladice* it was not 'unfair' to admit a confession made in breach of the right to legal advice, because the defendant conceded that he had understood his rights and coped well with police interviews.[79] In *R v Mason*, evidence obtained by placing a covert listening device in the defendants' cells was also held to have been properly admitted.[80] The lack of regulation of such surveillance meant that Article 8 of the ECHR had undoubtedly been breached, but the defendants had not been oppressed or tricked into making their admissions and the use of the evidence did not render the proceedings unfair. This approach reflects that adopted in *Khan v UK*, where the use of a similar device in a suspect's house was found to breach the right to respect for private life, but not the right to a fair trial under Article 6.[81]

It has been argued that despite statements to the contrary, judges often adopt a disciplinary approach in practice. In one case a suspect 'confessed' after he and his solicitor were falsely told that his fingerprints had been found on incriminating evidence. In quashing his conviction the Court of Appeal stated that its decision was not about police discipline; yet it was undoubtedly influenced by the fact that the police had acted in bad faith and had deliberately set out to deceive.[82] In *R v Canale* it

---

[76] *R v Delaney* (1989) 88 Cr App R 338.   [77] *R v Goldenberg* (1989) 88 Cr App R 285.

[78] *R v Samuel* [1988] QB 615, [1988] 2 All ER 135.

[79] (1988) 87 Cr App R 380; see also, *R v Dunford* (1990) 91 Cr App R 150.

[80] *R v Mason (Adrian Craig)* [2002] EWCA Crim 385, [2002] 2 Cr App R 38.

[81] (2001) 31 EHRR 45. *See* generally, p. 180, *ante*.

[82] *R v Mason (Carl)* [1987] 3 All ER 481, [1988] 1 WLR 139; see Birch, 'The Pace Hots Up: Confessions and Confusions Under The 1984 Act' [1989] Crim LR 95 at 107.

was held that confession evidence should have been excluded because of 'flagrant . . . deliberate and cynical' breaches of the recording requirements in PACE;[83] yet in *R v Sanghera (Rashpal)* the defendant's trial was held to have been fair despite the admission of evidence obtained during an improper search.[84] In the latter case the Court of Appeal noted that the police had acted in a bona fide manner, and that at the time of the search they had believed the defendant to be a victim rather than a suspect. They also noted that the defendant had not objected to the search at the time. As this last case demonstrates, judges are generally reluctant to exclude 'real' evidence on the grounds of impropriety, because there is often little doubt about its reliability. With confession evidence on the other hand, the issues of propriety and reliability cannot always be so easily separated. It should be remembered of course, that section 78 is concerned with 'fairness to the *proceedings*', rather than simply with fairness to the accused: the court in *Sanghera* clearly felt that a greater injustice might be done if the evidence was excluded from the jury.[85] Similarly, evidence that a witness in *R v Forbes* had made an 'unequivocal' identification of the accused was held to have been fairly admitted. This was despite the fact that the police had breached Code of Practice D by failing to hold a formal identification parade.[86]

Finally, police misconduct may provide the basis for an application to dismiss a prosecution on the grounds of an abuse of process.[87] The defendant in *DPP v Ara* had made an admission in the absence of a lawyer, and had subsequently made numerous unsuccessful requests to obtain a copy of the interview tape. His solicitor stated that without the tape he was unable to advise his client whether to accept a police caution, and the defendant was eventually charged with an offence of assault occasioning actual bodily harm. At a hearing before magistrates it was decided that it would be an abuse of process to proceed with the prosecution.[88] In general, it will also be an abuse of process to proceed with a case where police entrapment has caused a suspect to commit a crime which would not otherwise have occurred.[89]

2 CRIMINAL PROCEEDINGS

Quite apart from its possible effect on the prosecution of a suspect, police misconduct can sometimes amount to a criminal offence in itself. A number of highly-publicized

---

[83] *R v Canale* [1990] 2 All ER 187; see also, *R v Keenan* [1990] 2 QB 54, [1989] 3 All ER 598.

[84] [2001] 1 Cr App R 20, [2000] All ER (D) 1415.

[85] Cf. *R v Veneroso* [2002] Crim LR 306: drugs found while officers were illegally on the defendant's premises were held to be inadmissible on the basis of Article 8 of the ECHR. The judge did indicate however, that the outcome might have been different if semtex had been found.

[86] [2001] 1 AC 473, [2001] 1 All ER 686.

[87] *R v Horseferry Road Magistrates' Court, ex parte Bennett; sub nom Bennett v Horseferry Road Magistrates' Court* [1994] AC 42, [1993] 1 All ER 138.

[88] [2001] EWHC 493 (Admin), [2002] 1 WLR 815. The magistrates were held to have acted lawfully.

[89] *R v Looseley; sub nom Attorney-General's Reference (No 3 of 2000)* [2001] UKHL 53, [2001] 4 All ER 897. Cf. *Smurthwaite v Gill* [1994] 1 All ER 898, (1994) 98 Cr App R 437: no grounds for a stay of proceedings or the exclusion of evidence where officers had merely provided a suspect with the opportunity to offend.

miscarriages of justice have involved allegations of police misconduct,[90] and in some cases officers have been prosecuted for perjury or conspiracy to pervert the course of justice. More often, the legality of police conduct has been tested in prosecutions brought under section 89 of the Police Act 1996. This section makes it an offence to assault, or to resist or wilfully obstruct, a constable acting in the execution of his duty. The expression 'execution of duty' has a technical meaning for these purposes: an officer who infringes the rights of an individual in the absence of some legal authority will have acted outside the execution of his duty. The effect of such action is that any prosecution under section 89 must fail. Thus, a police officer who is trespassing and who is ejected from the premises using reasonable force will not succeed in a prosecution under section 89.[91] Similarly, a person who is being unlawfully restrained will not be committing a section 89 offence if he uses physical force to secure his release.[92] The key to each of these situations is the concept of unlawful interference with individual rights. If there is no interference with individual rights, or if there is some authority in law for the interference, the constable remains within the execution of duty.

3 CIVIL ACTIONS

Police misconduct may give rise to a civil action for assault, trespass, or false imprisonment. The legality of police detention may also be tested by applying for a writ of *habeas corpus*.

A Chief Constable is liable for any unlawful conduct of an officer acting in the performance of police functions.[93] Police authorities have a duty to indemnify Chief Constables in such cases, and at their discretion they may also indemnify *any* member of the police force against whom unlawful conduct is alleged.[94] What is within 'the performance of police functions' was considered in *Makanjuola* v *Commissioner of Police for the Metropolis*,[95] where an off-duty officer committed a serious sexual assault after using his warrant card to gain entry to premises. The Chief Constable was held not liable in damages for the assault, because it was not a fraudulent performance of what the constable had the authority to do honestly. Exemplary damages were awarded against the constable. The fact remains though, that the effectiveness of the civil law remedy may depend upon the liability of the Chief Constable, since an individual officer may be of modest means and not worth suing.

Unless a police authority is itself in breach of a statutory or common law obligation, it will not be directly liable for the actions of its officers. Moreover, it owes no general duty of care to members of the public in respect of the investigation and

---

[90] Some of these are discussed in Walker and Starmer, *Miscarriages of Justice: A Review of Justice in Error* (1999).

[91] *Davis* v *Lisle* [1936] 2 KB 434, [1936] 2 All ER 213.

[92] *Kenlin* v *Gardiner* [1967] 2 QB 510, [1966] 3 All ER 931; *Collins* v *Wilcock* [1984] 3 All ER 374, [1984] 1 WLR 1172. Cf. *Mepstead* v *DPP* [1996] Crim LR 111: a constable who took a person by the arm to calm him and to emphasize what was being said was acting within the execution of his duty.

[93] Police Act 1996, s 88(1).   [94] Ibid, s 88(2), (4).   [95] [1992] 3 All ER 617.

prevention of crime.[96] A duty of care may be established however, if a special relationship with a particular member of the public can be identified. In *Swinney* v *Chief Constable of the Northumbria Police* it was said to be arguable that a special relationship had arisen between the police and a police informant.[97] In addition, police officers and police authorities have a duty under the Human Rights Act 1998 to act compatibly with Convention rights. At least some of these rights may be breached by a failure to respond to a 'real and immediate risk' to an identified individual.[98]

4 JUDICIAL REVIEW

It has already been seen that police discretion is judicially reviewable,[99] but the restricted role of the courts in judicial review means that this is not always a satisfactory way of challenging police actions.

5 COMPLAINTS AGAINST THE POLICE

The police complaints system provides a non-legal mechanism for dealing with allegations of police misconduct. Pressure for such a system led to the creation of the Police Complaints Board in 1976,[100] but this body was widely regarded as unsatisfactory because the investigation of complaints was handled by the police themselves. As Lord Scarman observed in his Report into the Disturbances at Brixton:[101]

The evidence has convinced me that there is a widespread and dangerous lack of public confidence in the existing system for handling complaints against the police: unless there is a strengthening of the independent 'non-police' element, public confidence will continue to be lacking.

In an attempt to address some of this criticism, the Police and Criminal Evidence Act 1984 established a new regime under the supervision of the Police Complaints Authority.[102] Although the creation of this new, independent body was generally welcomed, critics pointed out that its role was largely supervisory, and that there was still no independent mechanism by which complaints could actually be investigated. As the Macpherson Inquiry noted in 1999:[103]

[The] investigation of police officers by their own or another Police Service is widely regarded as unjust, and does not inspire public confidence.

---

[96] *Hill* v *Chief Constable of West Yorkshire* [1989] AC 53, [1988] 2 All ER 238.

[97] [1997] QB 464, [1996] 3 All ER 449: the police were accused of allowing the informant's identity to fall into the public domain.

[98] *Osman* v *UK* (2000) 29 EHRR 245. This case concerned the failure of the police to prevent the death of a man who was murdered by his son's teacher. The teacher was known to have formed an obsessive attachment to the son, and the Court of Human Rights confirmed that Article 2 may impose a positive duty to protect life. It did not, however, find a breach of Article 2 on the facts.

[99] See p 389, *ante*.   [100] Police Act 1976.   [101] 1981, HMSO.

[102] The system was subsequently governed by provisions in the Police Act 1996.

[103] *Report of the Stephen Lawrence Inquiry* (Cm 4262-I, 1999) at ch 47, para 58.

(a) The Independent Police Complaints Commission (IPCC)

In response to criticism in the Macpherson Report and elsewhere, the Police Complaints Authority was recently replaced by the Independent Police Complaints Commission.[104] The IPCC was formally launched in April 2004, and it handles complaints about both officers and civilians who serve with the police. It is also required to record incidents involving criminal conduct on the part of such persons, in addition to recording behaviour justifying disciplinary proceedings.[105] Alongside those who have experienced or witnessed alleged misconduct, any other person who has been adversely affected by it has the right to complain to the Commission.[106] The Commission itself has a Chairman, two Deputy Chairmen, and fifteen regional Commissioners.[107] It has the power to conduct its own investigations into allegations of serious misconduct,[108] and to this end it can temporarily second officers from any police force in the UK.[109] Chief Police Officers have a duty to co-operate with any IPCC investigation, and they must ensure that the Commission is provided with access to police premises and relevant evidence.[110] Most complaints continue to be investigated locally by individual police forces, but the IPCC has the power to supervise or manage investigations where appropriate.[111] In determining how an incident should be dealt with, the IPCC must take into account both the seriousness of the case and the public interest.[112] A report must be submitted to the Commission at the end of any investigation that it has supervised, managed, or conducted, and a copy of this report must also be sent to the relevant police force.[113] The complainant has a right to be informed about the progress and outcome of the investigation,[114] and if evidence of criminal activity or misconduct is found, criminal or disciplinary proceedings will normally follow.

C POLICE POWERS

Authority to act in a particular way is conferred on the police by a wide range of authority, both common law and statutory. The detail of such powers is beyond the scope of this book, but a discussion of the general framework is set out below. A crucial issue is the whether the system achieves the right balance between protecting the public on the one hand, and maintaining safeguards for individuals on the other. The need to secure this balance has been highlighted by several miscarriage of justice cases, and it has assumed particular importance since the rights to liberty and to a fair trial were given explicit recognition by the Human Rights Act 1998.[115]

---

[104] Police Reform Act 2002, s 9.   [105] Ibid, s 10.
[106] Ibid, s 12. A complaint may also be made by a representative acting on behalf of such a person.
[107] The minimum requirement is for a Chairman and ten Commissioners: Ibid, s 9(2)
[108] Ibid, Schedule 3, para 19.   [109] Ibid, Schedule 2, para 6.   [110] Ibid, ss 17; 18.
[111] Schedule 3, para 15.   [112] Ibid.   [113] Ibid, Schedule 3, para 22.
[114] Section 20.   [115] For a discussion of these rights, see pp 177–83, *ante*.

Historically, police powers were piecemeal and ill-defined, creating problems for both the police and suspects. The Royal Commission on Criminal Procedure, which reported in 1981,[116] carried out a major review of the investigative powers of the police, and the questioning and treatment of suspects. The Report provided the basis for the Police and Criminal Evidence Act 1984 (PACE), though not all of its recommendations were accepted in their entirety.

1 GENERAL CONSIDERATIONS

Before looking at the legal framework in more detail, certain matters merit further discussion: (a) the common law concept of breach of the peace; (b) the concepts of 'reasonable suspicion' and 'reasonable belief'; (c) the use of force in the exercise of police powers; and (d) the role of the Codes of Practice.

(a) Breaches of the peace

At common law, a police officer is entitled to take any action necessary to prevent an imminent breach of the peace or to restrain a breach of the peace that is actually occurring.[117] Where a breach of the peace has already happened and there is a likelihood of reoccurrence, it would appear that an officer may also take *reasonable* steps to prevent such reoccurrence. In *Chief Constable of Cleveland* v *McGrogan*[118] it was held that the police had not acted unlawfully in detaining a man for almost twenty-four hours, because there was a real apprehension that if released sooner he would have committed a further breach of the peace within a short time.

Definitions of what constitutes a breach of the peace have varied. In *R* v *Chief Constable of Devon & Cornwall, ex parte Central Electricity Generating Board*, Lord Denning stated:[119]

There is a breach of the peace whenever a person who is lawfully carrying out his work is unlawfully and physically prevented by another from doing it.

This definition has been doubted however, on the basis that it is too wide.[120] It is now generally accepted that the correct approach is that identified in *R* v *Howell*:[121]

We cannot accept that there can be a breach of the peace unless there has been an act done or threatened to be done which either actually harms a person, or in his presence his property, or is likely to cause such harm, or which puts somebody in fear of such harm being done.

---

[116] Cmnd 8092, 1981.

[117] *Albert* v *Lavin* [1982] AC 546, [1981] 3 All ER 878. The power extends to acts occurring on private property: *McConnell* v *Chief Constable of the Greater Manchester Police* [1990] 1 All ER 423, [1990] 1 WLR 364.

[118] [2002] EWCA Civ 86, [2002] 1 FLR 707.

[119] [1982] QB 458 at 471, [1981] 3 All ER 826 at 832.

[120] See *Percy* v *DPP* [1995] 1 WLR 1382, [1995] 3 All ER 124.

[121] [1982] QB 416 at 426, [1981] 3 All ER 383 at 389, per Watkins LJ.

Once the likelihood of an imminent breach of the peace is established, a police officer has the power to take reasonable steps to prevent it from happening or continuing. This may involve restraining and temporarily detaining an individual,[122] removing an item from his possession,[123] or entering on to private property.[124] It may also mean requiring an individual not to travel along a certain route,[125] or requiring him to carry on his activities elsewhere or in a different way.[126] In addition, where a breach of the peace is reasonably apprehended, a person may be arrested and taken before a magistrates' court, where he may then be bound over to be of good behaviour and to keep the peace.[127] This 'binding over' power has been criticized by the European Court of Human Rights for its uncertainty,[128] and the Law Commission has recommended its abolition.[129] However, a recent Home Office consultation paper argued that 'it would be better to resolve the underlying issues of certainty and fairness,' rather than to remove the power altogether.[130] It also recommended that the sanction for non-compliance should be a fine rather than imprisonment.[131]

It will be apparent that alongside the extensive body of police powers conferred by Acts of Parliament, the police also have a wide measure of discretionary power that is still governed by the common law. It will be equally apparent that the use of this power can impinge upon conduct which in itself is perfectly lawful. In the Irish case of *Humphries* v *Connor* for example, an officer was held to have acted lawfully when he removed a political emblem from the lapel of a woman who was attracting a hostile crowd.[132] More recently however, the courts have emphasized that where a person is not acting unlawfully and is not himself 'threatening' to breach the peace, the power of arrest should only be used exceptionally.[133]

The use of the breach of the peace power may also contravene the Human Rights Act if it interferes with a Convention right in a manner that is not proportionate to a legitimate purpose. For example, detention for longer than is necessary to prevent an imminent breach of the peace or to bring a person before magistrates could amount

---

[122] *Albert* v *Lavin* [1982] AC 546, [1981] 3 All ER 878.

[123] *Humphries* v *Connor* (1864) 17 ICLR 1.

[124] *McConnell* v *Chief Constable of the Greater Manchester Police* [1990] 1 All ER 423, [1990] 1 WLR 364.

[125] *Moss* v *McLachlan* (1984) 149 JP 167; *R (on the application of Laporte)* v *Chief Constable of Gloucester* [2004] EWCA Civ 1639, [2005] 1 All ER 473. Note that there must be some proximity in terms of time and place to the apprehended breach of the peace.

[126] *Duncan* v *Jones* [1936] 1 KB 218, [1935] All ER Rep 710; *Piddington* v *Bates* [1960] 3 All ER 660, [1961] 1 WLR 162.

[127] For powers in relation to binding over, see the Justices of the Peace Act 1361, discussed in *Hughes* v *Holley* (1986) 151 JP 233. For a review of the law, see Law Commission Working Paper 103.

[128] See *Steel* v *UK* (1999) 28 EHRR 603. The Court also ruled that binding over proceedings must be regarded as 'criminal proceedings' for the purposes of the Convention. Note however, that the Court of Appeal has subsequently confirmed that breach of the peace itself is not a crime: *Williamson* v *Chief Constable of West Midlands* [2003] EWCA Civ 337, [2004] 1 WLR 14. See further, p 177, *ante*.

[129] *Binding Over*, Law Commission Report No 222 (1994).

[130] Home Office, *Bind Overs: A Power for the 21st Century* (2003) consultation paper, at para 9.4.

[131] Ibid, at para 7.10.7.   [132] (1864) 17 ICLR 1: the emblem in question was an orange lily.

[133] *Foulkes* v *Chief Constable for Merseyside* [1998] 3 All ER 705, [1998] 2 FLR 789; *Bibby* v *Chief Constable of Essex* (2000) 164 JP 297.

to an unlawful interference with the right to liberty.[134] Moreover, if through such detention a person is prevented from participating in a demonstration, there may also be an interference with the rights to freedom of expression and freedom of assembly. Whether the detention is unlawful in this respect will depend on whether it can be justified under Articles 10(2) and 11(2) of the ECHR.[135]

(b) Reasonable suspicion and reasonable belief

Most police powers depend for their rightful exercise on the officer having a particular state of mind at the relevant time. The usual requirement is for a 'reasonable suspicion' of certain facts,[136] and this provides an essential safeguard against the arbitrary use of power. In *Shaaban Bin Hussien* v *Chong Fook Kam*[137] Lord Devlin observed that 'suspicion in its ordinary meaning is a state of conjecture or surmise where proof is lacking: "I suspect but cannot prove" '. More recently, in *Castorina* v *Chief Constable of Surrey*[138] the Court of Appeal stated that an honest belief was not a necessary precondition. By contrast, an arrest which is based *solely* on an honest belief that an offence has been committed may not satisfy the requirements of Article 5 of the ECHR.[139]

Whether or not a reasonable suspicion exists is a matter to be determined objectively by the court. In order to be reasonable a suspicion must be based on evidence, but this need not be evidence that would be acceptable in a court of law. A suspicion may also be reasonable if based on information from an informant or a fellow officer: it need not be based entirely on the officer's own observations.[140] However, in the context of stop and search powers, PACE Code of Practice A makes it clear that a suspicion will not be reasonable if it is based on personal factors alone:[141]

[R]easonable suspicion cannot be based on generalisations or stereotypical images of certain groups or categories of people as more likely to be involved in criminal activity.

The Code also states that:[142]

[R]easonable suspicion should normally be linked to accurate and current intelligence or information, such as information describing an article being carried, a suspected offender, or a person who has been seen carrying a type of article known to have been stolen . . .

---

[134] *R (on the application of Laporte)* v *Chief Constable of Gloucester* [2004] EWHC 253 (Admin), [2004] 2 All ER 874 (affirmed on appeal, though without express discussion of this right: [2004] EWCA Civ 1639, [2005] 1 All ER 473).

[135] Ibid. See pp 190–4, *ante*, for a discussion of these rights.

[136] For examples of exceptions, see the powers conferred by the Criminal Justice and Public Order Act 1994, s 60 and the Terrorism Act 2000, s 44; discussed at p 403, *post*.

[137] [1970] AC 942 at 948, [1969] 3 All ER 1626 at 1630.   [138] [1988] NLJR 180.

[139] *Fox, Campbell and Hartley* v *UK* (1991) 13 EHRR 157; cf. *Murray* v *UK* (1995) 19 EHRR 193 (mere suspicion sufficient in circumstances where officers could demonstrate an objective basis). For further discussion of Article 5, see p 177, *ante*.

[140] *O'Hara* v *Chief Constable of the Royal Ulster Constabulary* [1997] AC 286, [1997] 1 All ER 129; *O'Hara* v *UK* (2002) 34 EHRR 32.

[141] At para 2.4.   [142] Ibid, at para 2.2; see further, p 403, *post*.

(c) Force

The law allows reasonable force to be used, where necessary, in the exercise of police powers. Section 3 of the Criminal Law Act 1967 provides that a person may use such force as is reasonable in the circumstances, to: (a) prevent crime; or (b) effect or assist in the lawful arrest of an offender, suspected offender, or person unlawfully at large. In addition, section 117 of the Police and Criminal Evidence Act 1984 provides that any power under the Act may be exercised using no more force than is reasonably necessary. Both provisions permit the use of force against property as well as persons. For example, an officer seeking to execute a lawful power of arrest may use reasonable force to gain entry on to premises, as long as he can demonstrate the necessity of his actions.[143]

Where police officers have used force in the past, they have generally been armed only with a truncheon. Nowadays, a growing number of police officers also have access to firearms. The test for the lawful use of force is unchanged however, and in all cases the issue is whether the degree of force used was necessary and reasonable in the circumstances.[144]

(d) Codes of Practice

Section 66 of PACE authorises the Home Secretary to make Codes of Practice dealing with the different stages of police investigations. Codes dealing with the exercise of stop and search powers (Code A), the execution of search powers (Code B), the treatment and questioning of suspects (Code C), the identification of suspects (Code D), the tape-recording of police interviews (Code E), and the visual recording of interviews (Code F) have all been introduced.[145]

The PACE Codes are important to both the practitioner and the police, and as noted above, if there is a 'significant and substantial' breach of the Codes, evidence obtained as a result of that breach *may* be excluded from consideration by the courts.[146] A breach of the Codes can also form the basis for disciplinary action against the officer.

2 STOP AND SEARCH POWERS

Stop and search powers are amongst the most controversial of police powers. On the one hand, they authorize action which some would argue to be necessary for the prevention and detection of crime. On the other, they provide the potential for misuse and for the harassment of minority groups. Before 1984 there existed a wide range of

---

[143] *O'Loughlin* v *Chief Constable of Essex* [1998] 1 WLR 374: on the facts of the case the use of force was *not* lawful, as the officer had not first made it clear that he wanted to enter to make an arrest.

[144] See *A-G's Reference Northern Ireland (No 1 of 1975)* [1977] AC 105 [1976] 2 All ER 937.

[145] Code F was issued under the authority of s 60A of PACE. The latest version of all six Codes came into effect on 1 August 2004: see also, p 39, *ante.*

[146] See p 391, *ante.* See also, *R* v *Walsh* (1990) 91 Cr App R 161, [1989] Crim LR 822; *R* v *Aspinall* [1999] 2 Cr App R 115, (1999) 96(7) LSG 35. See further, p 414, *post.*

stop and search powers, which were exercisable on different criteria, in different circumstances and by different people. The Royal Commission on Criminal Procedure concluded that these powers were too vague and that they were not always focused on true policing needs. It expressed concern that they could potentially be abused and applied on the basis of stereotypes, and it recommended that many of them should be rationalised or repealed.[147]

Following the Royal Commission's recommendations, general powers of stop and search were included in the Police and Criminal Evidence Act 1984. Section 1 provides that any person or vehicle may be detained and searched by a constable if he has reasonable grounds to suspect that he will find stolen or prohibited articles.[148] An offensive weapon constitutes a 'prohibited article' for these purposes, and this term covers any article made or adapted for causing injury to a person, or any article intended to cause injury by the person who is carrying it with him.[149] The other articles prohibited by section 1 are articles made, adapted, or intended for use in connection with burglary, theft, taking a motor vehicle without authority, obtaining property by deception, or destroying or damaging property.[150] Articles with a blade or point may also be the subject of a stop and search, even if they do not constitute offensive weapons.[151] It will be appreciated that the range of articles potentially within these definitions is very large.

The power to stop and search is exercisable in any place to which the public have access,[152] and any stolen or prohibited article found may be seized.[153] There is no specific power to seize any other item discovered, but an officer can make an arrest if he finds anything that he reasonably believes to be evidence of a crime.[154] Care must be taken to ensure that the stop and search powers are not abused, and the requirement for reasonable suspicion is thus an important safeguard. The constable must also give certain information to the detained person before he is searched. Specifically, the officer must give his name, the name of the police station to which he is attached, the object of the search, and his grounds for proposing to make it. If he is not in uniform, he must also provide documentary evidence that he is, in fact, a police officer.[155] A further safeguard is the requirement for the officer to make a written record of the search, either at the time or as soon as practicable afterwards.[156] The person searched is entitled to a copy of this record if he requests one within twelve months.

Not all stop and search powers are so precisely circumscribed. Where a senior

---

[147] Cmnd 8092, 1981, at p 1011.

[148] Section 163 of the Road Traffic Act 1988 provides uniformed constables with a general power to require a person driving a vehicle on a road to stop. It does not in itself authorise the detention or search of the vehicle, though in some circumstances the power to detain may be implied by the courts: see *Lodwick* v *Sanders* [1985] 1 All ER 577, [1985] 1 WLR 382.

[149] Sections 1(7)(a) and 1(9).   [150] Sections 1(7)(b) and 1(8), as amended.

[151] Section 1(8A). The Serious Organised Crime and Police Act 2005 creates a stop and search power in respect of prohibited fireworks: it inserts a new s 1(8B) of PACE to this effect.

[152] Section 1(1).   [153] Section 1(6).   [154] Powers of arrest are discussed at p 405, *post*.

[155] Section 2.   [156] Section 3.

officer anticipates violence in a particular locality, he can authorize what amounts to a random power of stop and search for a period not exceeding twenty-four hours.[157] Under such an authorization, a constable may stop and search any person or vehicle for offensive weapons or dangerous instruments. The officer does not need to reasonably suspect the person of being in possession of such an article, and thus for a limited period there is a power to stop and search that is effectively unchallengeable. An even more extensive power may be authorized under section 44 of the Terrorism Act 2000. This power can only be authorized by an officer of at least the rank of assistant chief constable, and only where it is considered expedient for the prevention of acts of terrorism. Once such an authorization is in place, any person or vehicle in the locality may be searched for articles that could be used in connection with terrorism.[158] Section 45(1)(b) expressly states that the power may be exercised 'whether or not the constable has grounds for suspecting the presence of articles of that kind.'[159] The authorization can last for up to twenty-eight days and may be renewed at the end of this period.

The exercise of stop and search powers is subject to more detailed guidance in PACE Code of Practice A.[160] The Code states that where a person is searched under section 1 of PACE, he or she cannot be required to remove any clothing in public other than an outer coat, jacket, or gloves. A person searched under the terrorism powers may also be required to remove headgear or footwear. The Code makes it clear that for searches which require a 'reasonable suspicion', that suspicion cannot be based on personal factors alone unless there is reliable supporting intelligence or information. It expressly states that 'a person's race, age, appearance, or the fact that the person is known to have a previous conviction, cannot be used alone or in combination with each other as the reason for searching that person'. Despite this, studies have repeatedly shown that that Black and Asian people are disproportionately more likely to be stopped and searched than those from other ethnic groups.[161] Moreover, research carried out by one police force showed that a reduction in the use of stop and search had had little effect on levels of crime in the area: the force's detection rate had actually increased during the same period.[162] Throughout the UK the proportion of searches that result in an arrest is consistently low, and Lustgarten

---

[157] Criminal Justice and Public Order Act 1994, s 60.   [158] Section 45(1)(a).

[159] Doubts have been raised about the extent to which stop and search powers which do not depend on a reasonable suspicion are compatible with Article 5, ECHR. However, in *R (on the application of Gillan) v Commissioner of Police for the Metropolis* [2004] EWCA Civ 1067, [2004] 3 WLR 114 it was held that a *brief* detainment under stop and search powers would not be subject to Article 5 as it would not involve a deprivation of liberty: see p 177, *ante*.

[160] The latest version of the Code came into force on 1 August 2004: Police and Criminal Evidence Act 1984 (Codes of Practice) Order 2004, SI 2004/1887.

[161] *Report of the Stephen Lawrence Inquiry*, Cm 4262-I, 1999 at para. 45.8; Miller, Bland and Quinton, *The Impact of Stops and Searches on Crime and the Community*, Police Research Series Paper No 130 (2000), ch 4; Home Office, *Statistics on Race and the Criminal Justice System*, 2000, ch 3.

[162] Lustgarten, 'The Future of Stop and Search' [2002] Crim LR 603, at p 614.

has concluded that 'it is hard to see how a suspicion which misfires so often and so consistently can be credibly described as "reasonable" '.[163]

PACE does not affect the capacity of an officer to speak to or question a person in the normal course of his duties, as long as there is no attempt to detain and no element of compulsion.[164] Frequently, routine questioning will provide the reasonable suspicion needed to justify detention for the purposes of a search. However, the converse is equally true: the Act allows reasonable suspicion to be eliminated by questioning, and in these circumstances there is no obligation to search. A written record of the encounter should still be made however, and police officers and staff are also required to record any incident where a person in a public place is asked to account for himself.[165]

3 SURVEILLANCE

The police sometimes need to use surreptitious means of investigation, and this may involve the use of technical devices such as eavesdropping equipment. Police telephone tapping has been regulated by statute since 1986,[166] but until 1997 there was no statutory regime covering the use of other forms of surveillance. In *R v Khan (Sultan)*[167] the House of Lords had to consider the legality of police action in attaching a listening device to a man's home. The police had thereby obtained incriminating evidence against the appellant, who was a visitor to that home. The appellant argued, unsuccessfully, that that evidence should have been excluded from his trial by virtue of section 78 of PACE. The House of Lords dismissed his appeal against conviction on the basis that the police had not acted unlawfully, but Lord Nolan described the lack of statutory regulation as 'astonishing'. Covert surveillance interfering with property or wireless telegraphy is now regulated by Part IV of the Police Act 1997. Section 93(1) provides that an 'authorising officer'[168] may authorize 'the taking of such action as he may specify', if he believes that:

(a) the action is necessary for the purpose of preventing or detecting serious crime;[169] and

(b) the taking of the action is proportionate to what it seeks to achieve.

Authorizations relating to property used mainly as a dwelling, hotel bedroom or office premises must be approved by a Commissioner appointed under section 91 of the

---

[163] Ibid, at p 615.

[164] For the general principles, see *Rice v Connolly* [1966] 2 QB 414, [1966] 2 All ER 649 (refusal to answer police questions not a wilful obstruction of a constable acting in the execution of duty).

[165] See Code of Practice A, paras 4.7 and 4.11. The latter requirement came into effect in April 2005.

[166] Interception of Communications Act 1985; since repealed and replaced by the more extensive provisions in the Police Act 1997 and the Regulation of Investigatory Powers Act 2000.

[167] [1997] AC 558, [1996] 3 All ER 289.

[168] A Chief Constable or one of the other high ranking officials listed in s 93(3).

[169] 'Serious crime' is defined for these purposes by s 93(4).

Act. Authorizations which are likely to result in the acquisition of legal, journalistic, or confidential personal information also require approval.[170] Where covert surveillance has been carried out pursuant to an authorization under the Act, section 92 confers immunity from criminal or civil proceedings.

Other forms of covert surveillance are subject to the provisions of the Regulation of Investigatory Powers Act 2000. Surveillance involving interference with postal or communications systems is governed by Part 1 of the Act. Under section 5, the Secretary of State may issue a warrant for the interception of communications if he believes that it is necessary for national security, for the prevention and detection of crime, or for safeguarding the economic well-being of the UK. A warrant can only be requested by one of the high-ranking officers listed in section 6, and section 17 prevents intercept material from being disclosed or adduced in connection with legal proceedings. The effect of the latter provision is that such surveillance can be used for intelligence purposes but is inadmissible as evidence at any trial. In this respect it can be argued that the Act fails to satisfy the ECHR with regard to both the fair trial requirements in Article 6 and the privacy provisions in Article 8.[171] However, in January 2005 the government ruled out the possibility of a change in the law, stating that it would present 'serious risks' for the ability of the interception agencies to fight serious crime and terrorism.[172]

Part II of the 2000 Act regulates the use of covert human intelligence. Intrusive surveillance—that which involves physical intrusion on to residential premises or into a private vehicle—can only be authorized by the Secretary of State or a 'senior authorising officer'. The person making the authorization must be satisfied that such intrusion is necessary for national security, for the prevention and detection of crime, or for safeguarding the economic well-being of the UK.[173] Non-intrusive surveillance can be authorized on a much wider range of grounds, and authorization can be granted can by a police superintendent or by certain other senior officials designated by the Secretary of State.[174] Rules for the conduct of covert operations involving human intelligence sources are set out in section 29 of the Act.

4 ARREST

Arrest is a matter of fact rather than a legal concept, though it does have legal consequences. As Viscount Dilhorne put it in *Spicer v Holt*:[175]

---

[170] Section 97.

[171] See Ormerod and McKay, 'Telephone Intercepts and their Admissibility' [2004] Crim LR 15. Section 17 has been interpreted as allowing a limited enquiry where it is alleged that communications within a private system have been intercepted with the consent of the owner: *Attorney-General's Reference (No 5 of 2002)* [2004] UKHL 20, [2005] 1 AC 167, [2004] 4 All ER 901.

[172] Charles Clarke MP (Home Secretary), 430 HC Official Report (6th series), col 18WS, 26 January 2005.

[173] Sections 26(3) and 32.

[174] Sections 26(2) and 28; Regulation of Investigatory Powers (Directed Surveillance and Covert Human Intelligence Sources) Order 2003, SI 2003/3171.

[175] [1977] AC 987, [1976] 3 All ER 71.

'Arrest' is an ordinary English word [and] whether or not a person has been arrested depends not upon the legality of his arrest but on whether he has been deprived of his liberty to go where he pleases.

The essence of arrest is therefore the deprivation of liberty. The concept was explained further by Lord Diplock in *Holgate-Mohammed* v *Duke*:[176]

First it shall be noted that arrest is a continuing act: it starts with the arrester taking a person into his custody (by action or words restraining him from moving elsewhere beyond the arrester's control) and it continues until the person so restrained is either released from custody, or, having been brought before a magistrate, is remanded in custody by the magistrate's judicial act.

In that case an officer arrested a person on reasonable suspicion of burglary because he wanted to continue questioning the suspect at the police station. Given that the power to arrest existed, its use to facilitate further questioning was a legitimate use of police discretion. Thus, whilst a person cannot simply be 'detained' by an officer so that he can be questioned, there is nothing to prevent the officer from exercising a lawful power of arrest in order to achieve this objective.

In order for an arrest to be lawful, the arresting officer must be able to point to a specific power of arrest, and he must comply with any necessary procedural requirements.

(a) Powers of arrest

An arrest may be lawfully made with or without a warrant. In respect of the former, the Magistrates' Courts Act 1980 confers a power on magistrates to issue a warrant of arrest.[177] In relation to arrest without warrant, the Police and Criminal Evidence Act 1984 made radical changes. Section 26 repealed all statutory powers authorizing arrest without a warrant, with the exception of twenty-one specific powers which were expressly preserved by Schedule 2.[178] The Act also preserved the common law power to arrest for breach of the peace.[179]

Section 24 confers general powers of arrest in respect of past, present, and future offences. In some situations these powers are available to both police officers and members of the public. Thus, any person can arrest an individual who has already committed an offence, or who is suspected on reasonable grounds of having done so. Any person can also arrest an individual who is (or is reasonably suspected to be) *in the act of* committing an offence. As might be expected, the powers available to a police officer are more extensive: in addition to the above, a constable can arrest any person who is (or is reasonably suspected to be) *about to* commit an offence. He can also make an arrest if he reasonably suspects that an arrestable offence has been

---

[176] [1984] AC 437, [1984] 1 All ER 1054.   [177] Section 1.

[178] Other statutory arrest powers have since been created: s 41 of the Terrorism Act 2000 for example, empowers a constable to arrest a person 'whom he reasonably suspects to be a terrorist.'

[179] This is the effect of PACE, s 25(6).

committed and that a particular individual was responsible. It is therefore possible for him to make a lawful arrest in circumstances where it turns out that no crime has actually occurred. The powers of the private citizen are rather more limited. In *R v Self*[180] for example, the defendant was charged with assault to escape lawful arrest. The arrest had been made by a citizen assisting a store detective, but the defendant was able to show that he had not in fact stolen the goods in question. Since no offence had been committed by anyone, the arrest was unlawful and the defendant was not guilty of the assault. As this case suggests, it is unwise for a citizen to make an arrest if he is not absolutely sure of his facts.

In its present form, the power of arrest conferred by section 24 can only be exercised in respect of 'arrestable offences'. This term is defined by section 24(1) to cover:

(a) offences for which the sentence is fixed by law (murder, with its mandatory life sentence, being the most obvious example);

(b) offences for which a person aged twenty-one years or over could receive a maximum sentence of at least five years imprisonment; and

(c) certain other specified offences.[181]

An arrest for a 'non-arrestable' offence can only be made without a warrant where it appears to a constable that it would be impractical to issue a summons because one of the 'general arrest conditions' is satisfied. These conditions are set out in section 25 and cover circumstances where:

(a) the name of the person is unknown to the constable and cannot readily be ascertained;

(b) there are reasonable grounds for doubting whether a name furnished is the person's real name;

(c) the person has failed to furnish a satisfactory address for service of a summons, or the constable reasonably doubts whether an address furnished is a satisfactory address for service;

(d) the constable has reasonable grounds for believing that an arrest is necessary to prevent the relevant person causing injury to himself or another; suffering physical injury; causing loss or damage to property; committing an offence against public decency; or causing an unlawful obstruction of the highway; or

(e) the constable has reasonable grounds for believing that an arrest is necessary to protect a child or other vulnerable person.

Under changes introduced by the Serious Organised Crime and Police Act 2005,[182] the

---

180 [1992] 3 All ER 476, [1992] 1 WLR 657. This decision confirms the pre-PACE position, as set out in *Walters v WH Smith & Son Ltd* [1914] 1 KB 595, [1911–13] All ER Rep 170.

181 Including offences under the Football (Offences) Act 1991 and the Official Secrets Acts of 1920 and 1989: Schedule 1A.

182 2005 Act, s 110.

section 24 powers are to be extended to cover all offences. The concept of a 'non-arrestable' offence will thus be abolished. The amended section 24 will provide that *any* arrest made without a warrant must be believed, on reasonable grounds, to be necessary for one of the reasons listed in section 24(5). The first four of these reasons will largely replicate the general arrest conditions currently found in section 25. The other lawful reasons for making an arrest will be to allow 'the prompt investigation of an offence', or to 'prevent the prosecution of an offence from being hindered by the disappearance of the person concerned'. The circumstances in which a citizen's arrest can be made will be narrowed. A new section 24A will mean that a person other than a constable may only make an arrest for an indictable offence, and only where it is not reasonably practicable for a constable to make it instead. In addition, the person making the arrest must have reasonable grounds for believing that his actions are necessary to prevent injury, to prevent loss or damage to property, or to prevent the suspect from making off.

(b) Mechanics of arrest

Even where a power of arrest exists, an arrest will only be lawful if the person arrested is told (a) that he is under arrest,[183] and (b) on what grounds he has been arrested. This information must be given at the time of the arrest or as soon as practicable afterwards.[184] Thus if a suspect manages to escape before a constable is able to explain the grounds for his arrest, the arrest will nevertheless be lawful. Once the suspect is re-captured and the situation is under control, any further delay in explaining the grounds will render the arrest invalid, but only from that moment onwards.[185] Similarly, where an arrest is initially unlawful because of a failure to comply with these requirements, it will become lawful subsequently once the reasons for the arrest are given. In *Lewis and another v Chief Constable of the South Wales Constabulary*[186] the Court of Appeal identified arrest as a continuing act: the plaintiffs' action for damages failed because they had only been unlawfully detained for a short period.

The statement of reasons does not have to specify a particular crime, or give a technical definition of the offence charged. What is needed is sufficient information to enable the arrested person to know the substance of why his liberty is being interfered with. In *Abbassy v Commissioner of Police*[187] the plaintiff was told that he was being arrested for 'unlawful possession' of a vehicle. He had been asked four times about ownership of the vehicle, but had responded in a rude and abusive fashion. Police inquiries later showed that he was in fact authorized to drive the vehicle. The plaintiff was charged with wilfully obstructing a constable in the execution of his duty, contrary to what is now section 89 of the Police Act 1996. The charges were later dropped and the plaintiff sought damages for unlawful arrest and false imprisonment. However,

---

[183] Section 28(1).   [184] Section 28(3).
[185] *DPP* v *Hawkins* [1988] 3 All ER 673, [1988] 1 WLR 1166.   [186] [1991] 1 All ER 206.
[187] [1990] 1 All ER 193, [1990] 1 WLR 385. The decision confirms that the approach outlined in the pre-PACE case of *Christie* v *Leachinsky* [1947] AC 573, [1947] 1 All ER 567 is still correct.

the court ruled that it had been made clear to him that the arrest was for unlawful possession of the vehicle. The fact that the officer had not specifically mentioned the vehicle in his statement of reasons was irrelevant. The judge had therefore misdirected the jury on a matter of law, and a re-trial was ordered. The claimant in *Taylor v Chief Constable of Thames Valley Police*[188] was a ten year old child who was arrested 'on suspicion of violent disorder': he had been throwing stones whilst participating in a demonstration. The child brought an action for false imprisonment and trespass to the person, alleging that he had not been given sufficient information for the arrest to be lawful. The Court of Appeal held that in order for an arrest to comply with section 28 of PACE and Article 5(2) of the ECHR,[189] a person had to be informed of the basis for the arrest in non-technical language that he could understand. The information given to the claimant in this case had been sufficient for these purposes, and the trial judge had been wrong to direct that a reference to throwing stones was needed.

An arrest also has certain physical requirements: it comprises compulsion and submission to that compulsion. There must either be a touching symbolic of seizure of the body, or alternatively, words of compulsion to which there is submission.[190]

(c) The consequences of arrest

By sections 30 and 30A, an arrested person must be taken to a police station or released on bail as soon as practicable after the arrest. However, these steps may be delayed if it is necessary to the investigation for the arrestee to be present elsewhere.[191] By section 32, an arrested person may be searched if the constable has reasonable grounds to believe that (a) he may present a danger to himself or others, (b) he may have concealed on him an article that may assist him in escaping from lawful custody, or (c) he may have concealed on him an article which is evidence relating to an offence.

Section 32(2)(b) confers the power to enter and search the premises where the suspect was arrested, or where he was immediately prior to his arrest. Section 18 confers a similar power in respect of premises occupied or controlled by the arrested person. Under the former provision the officer can only search for evidence of the offence for which the arrest was made. Under section 18 however, the officer may also search for evidence of 'connected' or 'similar' offences. The exercise of both powers is dependent on a lawful arrest having been made.

5 DETENTION

The custody officer performs a key role in relation to the detention, treatment, and questioning of suspects. Each designated police station must have at least one custody

---

[188] [2004] EWCA Civ 858, [2004] 1 WLR 3155, [2004] 3 All ER 503.

[189] See p 177, *ante* for a discussion of Article 5(2).

[190] *Alderson v Booth* [1969] 2 QB 216, [1969] 2 All ER 271.

[191] Section 30(10); (10A). Note that in some cases the Criminal Justice Act 2003 may in future permit a constable to release an arrested person on 'street bail'.

officer,[192] and it is to a 'designated station' that an arrested person should normally be taken. Until now, section 36 of PACE has required the person appointed to this role to be a police officer with at least the rank of sergeant. However, amendments made by the Serious Organised Crime and Police Act 2005[193] pave the way for civilian 'staff custody officers' to be appointed. The main functions of a custody officer are set out in sections 36, 38, 39, and 40 of PACE. They broadly encompass a duty to ensure that the treatment of all detained persons is in accordance with the requirements of the Act, and that the record-keeping required by the Act actually occurs. If these requirements are not complied with, the detention of the suspect is likely to become unlawful. The custody officer also has an important role in ensuring compliance with PACE Code of Practice C, which provides more detailed guidance for the detention, treatment, and questioning of those in police custody.

In order to protect the interests of the suspect, PACE envisages a separation of functions between the custody officer and those investigating the offence. Whether this concept is sustainable in practice is a moot point. Quite apart from the loyalties and pressures that membership of the same force might create, the custody officer may find it difficult on occasion to cure a natural desire to assist the investigation himself.[194]

In determining the legality of a suspect's detention and his treatment whilst in custody, a number of points must be considered:

(a) A person who attends a police station voluntarily is free to leave at any time, unless and until he is arrested.[195]

(b) A custody record must be kept, detailing all actions taken in respect of the arrested person. The custody officer is responsible for the accuracy and completeness of this record, and the timing of each entry must be noted. A solicitor or appropriate adult representing the detainee must be permitted to consult the record at any time.[196]

(c) If an investigating officer concludes that there is sufficient evidence to provide a realistic prospect of conviction, he must refer the case to the custody officer. It is for the custody officer to determine whether the suspect should be charged or released, and whether or not police bail should be granted. In certain cases he may seek guidance from the Crown Prosecution Service.[197]

(d) Within six hours of a suspect's detention being authorized, there must be a review to determine whether that detention continues to be necessary. Further

---

[192] *Vince v Chief Constable of the Dorset Police* [1993] 2 All ER 321, [1993] 1 WLR 415.
[193] Sections 120, 121.   [194] See, e.g. *R v Absolam* (1988) 88 Cr App R 332.
[195] PACE, s 29.
[196] Code C, para 2. There are references throughout PACE to the various matters that must be recorded.
[197] PACE, ss 37 and 37B; Code C, paras 16.1–16.2.

reviews should be conducted at intervals of nine hours or less for as long as the detainee remains in police custody[198]

(e) There are strict limits on how long an arrested person can be detained before being either charged or released. The basic rule is that detention shall not last longer than twenty-four hours from the time of arrest, or time of arrival at the police station, whichever is earlier.[199] This twenty-four hour period may be extended by a further twelve hours (i.e. thirty-six hours in total) by an officer of at least the rank of superintendent.[200] The officer must have reasonable grounds to believe that: (a) detention is necessary to secure or preserve evidence relating to the offence for which the arrest was made, or to obtain such evidence by questioning; (b) that the offence is a serious arrestable offence;[201] and (c) that the offence is being investigated diligently and expeditiously.

If the police wish to detain a person beyond thirty-six hours, a warrant of further detention must be obtained from a magistrates' court. The period of further detention granted by such a warrant cannot exceed thirty-six hours, though at the end of this period the police can apply to extend the warrant for a further thirty-six hours.[202] Four days (or ninety-six hours) is therefore the maximum permitted period of detention without charge.[203] The grounds for issuing or extending a warrant of further detention are the same as those for authorizing an initial extension of detention by a senior officer.

(f) Once a person has been charged with an offence, the custody officer must order his release unless one of the conditions in section 38 applies. These conditions are that:

(i) the person's name or address cannot be ascertained, or is reasonably believed to be false;

(ii) it is reasonably believed that the person will fail to appear in court to answer bail;

(iii) in the case of a person arrested for an imprisonable offence, it is reasonably believed that detention is necessary to prevent him from committing a further offence;

(iv) detention is necessary to enable a urine or non-intimate sample to be taken for the purposes of a drugs test;

(v) it is reasonably believed that detention is necessary for the protection of, or to prevent physical injury to, any other person or property;

---

[198] PACE, s 40; Code C, para 15. This review should be carried out by the custody officer if the arrested person has already been charged; otherwise, the review officer must be an officer of at least the rank of inspector who has not been directly involved in the investigation.

[199] PACE, s 41.   [200] Ibid, s 42(1).

[201] Once the concept of an 'arrestable offence' has been abolished, the power to extend the detention of a suspect will apply only to indictable offences: Serious Organised Crime and Police Act 2005, Schedule 6, para 43. See also, p 407, ante.

[202] PACE, s 43.   [203] This period is longer for those detained under the Terrorism Act 2000.

(vi) detention is necessary to prevent the arrestee from interfering with the administration of justice or with police investigations of that or other offences; or

(vii) detention is necessary for his own protection.

6 TREATMENT OF SUSPECTS

The Police and Criminal Evidence Act 1984 includes provisions designed to give proper protection to a suspect in the police station. The objective is to ensure not only that suspects are treated in accordance with minimum standards, but also that admissions and other evidence are obtained in such a way that they can safely be relied upon in court. The courts also regard the right of silence as important, and amongst other things, Code of Practice C seeks to prevent improperly induced self-incrimination.

(a) Search

Section 54 of PACE requires the custody officer to ascertain everything that a detained person has with him when he is brought to the police station. He has the power to cause the person to be searched for this purpose, although such a search is not obligatory. Much will depend upon how long a suspect is being detained, whether he is to be placed in the cells, and so on. In addition, a search may be carried out at any time whilst the person is in custody to ascertain whether he is in possession of an item that could be seized under section 54(4).[204] Articles covered by this provision are those which the custody officer believes might be used to: (a) cause physical injury; (b) damage property; (c) interfere with evidence; or (d) assist an escape. The same provision allows the custody officer to seize items in the detainee's possession if he has reasonable grounds for believing them to be evidence of an offence.[205] If necessary, a detained person can also be searched or examined by officers for the purposes of identification.[206] However, the extent of any search must be strictly limited to what is necessary in the circumstances. A detainee should not be strip searched, for example, unless the officer reasonably believes that he might have concealed an article which he would not be allowed to keep.[207]

Intimate searches—those which involve the physical examination of a person's body orifices other than the mouth[208]—are governed by different rules. An intimate search can only be authorized by an officer of at least the rank of inspector, and only where there are reasonable grounds to believe that the detainee may have concealed a

---

[204] Section 54(6A.)

[205] Cf. the pre-PACE position as stated in *Lindley* v *Rutter* [1981] QB 128, [1980] 3 WLR 660.

[206] PACE, s 54A, as amended by the Anti-Terrorism, Crime and Security Act 2001, s 90(1). Such a search can only be authorised by an officer of at least the rank of inspector.

[207] Code C, Annex A, para B.10.

[208] PACE, s 65(1). This definition was amended to make it easier for the police to deal with suspects who concealed drugs in their mouths. In *R* v *Hughes* [1994] 1 WLR 876 the holding of a suspect's nose and jaw, causing the extrusion of articles in the mouth, was held to be a search, but not an intimate search.

Class A drug or an item which he might use to injure himself or others.[209] Intimate searches should normally be carried out by a registered nurse or medical practitioner. Any search conducted by a police officer or civilian detention officer, whether intimate or otherwise, must be performed by an officer of the same gender as the detainee.[210]

(b) Information about rights

The arrested person must be informed of the right to have someone notified of his arrest. Section 56 provides that a person held in custody is entitled, at his request, to have a friend, relative, or other person notified of his whereabouts as soon as practicable. If the person named by the detainee is unobtainable he may nominate two others, and the police may extend the right further if they wish. The right is an important one, to be denied only in limited circumstances where to grant it would interfere with the investigation. Even if grounds for denying contact with an individual exist, they are unlikely to apply to making contact with a solicitor.[211] The arrested person also has the right to consult the Codes of Practice.[212]

(c) The taking of fingerprints and other samples

When PACE was first enacted, section 61 provided that a detainee who had not been charged could only have his fingerprints taken on the authority of a senior officer, and only then in certain circumstances. The provision has since been amended however,[213] and any person who has been arrested or charged in respect of a recordable offence may now have his fingerprints taken, either by conventional or electronic means.

An 'intimate sample' is defined by section 65 of PACE to mean: (a) a sample of blood, semen or any other tissue fluid, urine, or pubic hair; (b) a dental impression; or (c) a swab taken from a person's genitals or from a body orifice other than the mouth. Before an intimate sample can be taken, an officer must have both the written consent of the detainee and the authorization of a senior officer.[214] Such authorization should only be granted where the officer has reasonable grounds for (a) suspecting the detainee of involvement in a recordable offence, and (b) believing that the sample will tend to prove or disprove his involvement. An intimate sample may also be taken from a person who is not in police custody, but who has provided at least two non-intimate samples during the course of an investigation which have proved insufficient for the purpose of analysis.[215] Where a detainee refuses, without good cause, to consent to the taking of an intimate sample, adverse inferences may be drawn from this fact in any

---

[209] Ibid, s 55.   [210] Ibid, ss 54(9) and 55(7).

[211] *R v Samuel* [1988] QB 615, [1988] 2 All ER 135.

[212] Code C, para 3.1; *DPP v Skinner* [1990] RTR 254.

[213] Criminal Justice Act 2003, s 9. More recent amendments will, once implemented, allow fingerprints to be taken at a place *away* from the police station where an officer has doubts about the identity of a suspect: Serious Organised Crime and Police Act 2005, s 117.

[214] PACE, s 62(1).   [215] Ibid, s 62(1A).

subsequent criminal proceedings.[216] By creating a legal framework for such samples to be taken, PACE paved the way for the introduction of a national DNA database in 1995. By March 1998 this database contained the DNA profiles or more than 255,000 suspects and convicted persons, along with 30,000 profiles developed from material found at crime scenes.[217]

Hair samples (other than pubic hair), samples taken from the nails, and swabs taken from body parts not covered by section 65, constitute 'non-intimate samples' for the purposes of the Act. Section 63 provides that where a person has been arrested for a recordable offence, a non-intimate sample may be taken without his consent and without the need for authorization from a senior officer. There is also a power to take a non-intimate sample from a person held in police custody on the authority of a court, although in this case the authorization of a senior officer *is* required. As indicated above, samples taken from the mouth are no longer to be regarded as intimate samples, and they may therefore be taken without consent.

(d) Conditions of detention

Minimum standards for the conditions of police detention are set out in Parts 8 and 9 of Code of Practice C. They provide that cells should be adequately heated, cleaned and ventilated, that clean bedding should be supplied, and that access to toilet and washing facilities should be granted. They also stipulate that a replacement must be supplied for any item of clothing taken away for investigation, and that adequate meals must be provided. Brief outdoor exercise should be permitted where practicable, and suspects should be visited at least once an hour (or once every half an hour if a suspect is intoxicated). The custody officer must call for medical treatment if a suspect appears to be suffering from an illness, injury, or mental disorder, or is otherwise in need of clinical attention.

A serious failure to maintain adequate standards could amount to a breach of Article 3 of the ECHR, which prohibits torture and 'inhuman or degrading treatment'.[218] In an extreme case such a failure could also constitute a breach of Article 10 of the Bill of Rights, which prohibits 'cruel and unusual punishments'.

(e) Vulnerable suspects

Special rules apply to vulnerable persons. If the custody officer cannot establish effective communication with a detainee who appears to be deaf, or if there are doubts about the detainee's ability to hear, speak, or understand English, the officer must call for the assistance of an interpreter.[219]

If the person arrested is a juvenile, the 'appropriate adult' must be told of the arrest as soon as possible, and he must be asked to come to the police station.[220] Where the

---

[216] Ibid, s 62(10).

[217] See Redmayne, 'The DNA Database: Civil Liberty and Evidentiary Issues' [1998] Crim LR 437. The use of DNA evidence in court was considered in *R v Doheny and Adams* [1997] 1 Cr App R 369.

[218] See p 175, *ante*.   [219] Code C, para 13.10.

[220] Code C, para 3.15. For the meaning of 'appropriate adult', see para 1.7.

appropriate adult is not the person normally responsible for the juvenile's welfare, the latter party must also be informed of the situation.[221] Similar rules apply to those who are mentally disordered or otherwise mentally vulnerable.

7 ACCESS TO LEGAL ADVICE

In R v Samuel[222] the right of access to legal advice was described as 'fundamental'. The key provision is section 58 of PACE, which states that a person who is in police detention 'shall be entitled, if he so requests, to consult a solicitor privately at any time'. Access to a solicitor can only be delayed in respect of a person arrested for a serious offence,[223] and such a delay can only be authorized by an officer of at least the rank of superintendent. Before authorizing a delay, an officer must reasonably believe that the exercise of the right will do one of the following: (a) lead to interference with or harm to evidence connected with a serious offence;[224] (b) lead to interference with or physical injury to other persons; (c) lead to the alerting of other persons suspected of having committed such an offence; (d) hinder the recovery of any property obtained as a result of such an offence; or (e) hinder the recovery of the value of any property obtained by criminal conduct.[225] In the case of a person arrested under the terrorism provisions, the scope for restricting access to legal advice is greater.

These powers of delay have been construed very narrowly by the courts. In R v Samuel[226] the accused was denied access to a solicitor because the police feared that the solicitor might unwittingly alert other suspects. The court stated that any decision to deny access to legal advice had to be justified by the facts of the case. In this case the police had failed to demonstrate a reasonable belief that the solicitor in question might jeopardize their investigation: even if he had presented such a risk, the appropriate response would have been to ask the suspect to nominate an alternative, or to call the duty solicitor instead. The court also made it clear that legal advice cannot be delayed on the grounds that a solicitor might advise silence or make the investigation harder.[227]

More detailed rules are set out in Part 6 of Code of Practice C. This states that a suspect under arrest at a police station must be informed clearly of his right to consult privately with a solicitor, free of charge, at any time during his period in custody. Posters with this information must be displayed prominently in the charging area of each police station, and at certain stages in the process the suspect must be reminded of the right. There is no obligation on the police to request a solicitor on their own initiative, though if a solicitor attends at the request of the suspect's family, the

---

[221] Code C, para 3.13.   [222] [1988] QB 615, [1988] 2 All ER 135.

[223] At the time of writing, the Act refers specifically to a 'serious arrestable offence': these words will be replaced by the term 'indictable offence' when amendments made by the Serious Organised Crime and Police Act 2005 are implemented (2005 Act, Schedule 6, para 43).

[224] Ibid.   [225] PACE, ss 58(8); (8A)   [226] [1988] QB 615, [1988] 2 All ER 135.

[227] Ibid. See also R v Alladice (1988) 87 Cr App R 380.

suspect has the right to see him. The police must not take any action to discourage the exercise of the right, and they must not misrepresent the position.[228]

Once it has been requested, the police must generally wait until legal advice has been tendered before proceeding with an interview. The advice may be given over the telephone or in person, and may come either from a solicitor or from an 'accredited or probationary representative'.[229] Such a representative may be refused access if an officer of at least the rank of inspector considers that his presence would hinder the investigation:[230] the officer may take into account whether the representative's identity has been properly established, and whether he has a criminal record or is otherwise an unsuitable character. Restricting the presence of a solicitor is a far more serious step, but a solicitor may be asked to leave an interview if his conduct is preventing the police from being able to properly put questions to the suspect.[231]

The impact of the right under section 58 has been much debated. It seems likely that the mere presence of a lawyer at the police station will reduce the incidence of procedural irregularities, but research suggests that the quality of legal advice received by those in custody is variable.[232] Moreover, whilst the proportion of detainees obtaining legal advice has undoubtedly increased since PACE was introduced, the figure is still quite low. Research by Bucke and Brown found that legal advice was requested by around 40 per cent of detainees in 1997,[233] with most of the other 60 per cent taking the view that they simply did not need a lawyer.[234] The precise reasons for this low uptake are unclear but it seems that a variety of ploys, whether inadvertent or intentional, can dissuade suspects from taking advantage of their rights. For example, many of the detainees in Bucke and Browne's study said that they would wait until later before deciding whether they needed a lawyer: the authors suggest that custody officers may have encouraged this by emphasizing that suspects could change their minds about seeking legal advice at any time.[235] Similarly, Phillips and Brown found that some of the suspects in their study had declined legal advice after being told that they probably would not be charged.[236]

The effectiveness of the right to legal advice also depends on the availability of suitably qualified legal advisers, and the duty solicitor scheme has an important role here. The scheme is provided through the Criminal Defence Service and funded by the Legal Services Commission.[237] A detainee may seek advice from a duty solicitor at

---

[228] See *R v Beycan* [1990] Crim LR 185.   [229] See Code C, para 6.12.

[230] Ibid, para 6.12A.   [231] Code C, paras 6.9–6.11.

[232] McConville and Bridges, *Custodial Advice and the Right to Silence* (1993) RCCJ Research Study No 16. See also the Legal Services Commission's Evaluation of the Public Defender Service, which was conducted by Bridges and Sherr: http://www.legalservices.gov.uk/criminal/pds/evaluation.asp.

[233] *In Police Custody: Police Powers and Suspects' Rights under the Revised PACE Codes of Practice* (1997) HORS 174, at p 19.

[234] Ibid, at p 22.   [235] Ibid.

[236] *Entry into the Criminal Justice System: A Survey of Police Arrests and their Outcomes* (1998) HORS 185, at p 159.

[237] See p 381, *ante.*

any time, and the operation of a rota system amongst local practitioners means that, in theory, someone should always be available.

A denial of the right to legal advice is generally taken very seriously by the courts, and any confession made whilst the police are in breach of their obligations is likely to be excluded from evidence under section 78 of PACE.[238] The importance of the right to legal advice is also recognized by Article 6 of the ECHR.[239]

8 INTERVIEWS

One of the most serious problems identified in recent years is the possibility that confessions made by suspects may not always be reliable. The 1984 Act and Code of Practice C provide a detailed framework for the conduct and recording of interviews, the importance of which was explained by Lord Lane CJ in *R v Canale*:[240]

The object is two-fold: not merely to ensure that the suspect's remarks are accurately recorded and that he has an opportunity when he goes through the contemporaneous record afterwards of checking each answer and initialling each answer, but likewise it is a protection for the police, to ensure, so far as possible, that it cannot be suggested that they induced the suspect to confess by improper approaches or improper promises. If the contemporaneous note is not made then each of those two laudable objects is apt to be stultified.

Initially, there was a danger that the police might seek to circumvent the rules governing interviews by questioning suspects before they were brought to the police station. Amendments to Code C mean that the term 'interview' now covers any questioning of a person regarding his involvement or suspected involvement in a criminal offence or offences.[241] It does not, however, cover routine questioning in the ordinary course of an officer's duties.[242]

(a) The right of silence

The notion of 'the right of silence' is closely linked to the idea of freedom from self-incrimination. A suspect has the right not to be required to self-incriminate, which means that he cannot generally be compelled to answer questions put to him by a police officer[243] or to testify at any subsequent trial. Before 1994, a jury could not be invited to draw any adverse inference from the fact that a defendant had elected to remain silent during police questioning. This has now changed however, following the enactment of the Criminal Justice and Public Order Act 1994. If a person who is being questioned under caution fails to mention a fact later relied on in his defence, section

---

[238] See p 393, *ante.*   [239] See p 181, *ante.*   [240] [1990] 2 All ER 187 at 190.

[241] For an interpretation of this, see *R v Cox* (1992) 96 Cr App R 464.

[242] Distinguishing between interviews and other forms of questioning is not always easy in practice: see *R v Absolam* (1988) 88 Cr App R 332; *R v Blackburn and Wade* (1992) Times, 1 December.

[243] There are some limited exceptions to this rule. Section 172 of the Road Traffic Act 1988, for example, imposes a duty to give information about the driver of a vehicle in certain circumstances: see *Brown v Stott* [2003] 1 AC 681, [2001] 2 All ER 97.

34 of the Act provides that a court or jury may draw such inferences from this failure as appear proper. Similar inferences may be drawn from the failure of a suspect to account for certain matters during questioning,[244] or from the failure of a defendant to testify in his own defence at trial.[245]

Though the right to silence is not expressly mentioned in the European Convention on Human Rights, the watering down of this right does have implications for Article 6 and the right to a fair trial. In *Murray* v *UK* the Court held that the right to silence was not essential to a fair trial: indeed, there was no breach of Article 6 on the facts of this case because the weight of evidence against the accused meant that the drawing of inferences was not unfair.[246] On the other hand, a judge must ensure that appropriate weight is given to any explanation offered by the defendant, and Article 6 would clearly be breached if a defendant was convicted solely on the basis of his silence.[247] Where a suspect has remained silent on the advice of his lawyer, the effect of this advice must be taken into account. However, the fact that a suspect has acted on legal advice will not *necessarily* preclude the court from drawing adverse inferences. Conversely, the risk of inferences being drawn from silence means that any delay in granting access to lawyer will be regarded as a particularly serious matter.[248] Indeed, section 34(2A) of PACE provides that if a suspect is questioned before he has had the opportunity to consult a lawyer, no adverse inferences may be drawn from any failure to answer police questions.

(b) Cautions

A caution must be administered before a suspect is questioned with a view to obtaining evidence which may be given in court. A caution must also be administered on arrest. The standard wording of this caution was modified in 1994 to reflect changes in the right to silence. It now states:[249]

You do not have to say anything. But it may harm your defence if you do not mention when questioned something which you later rely on in court. Anything you do say may be given in evidence.

(c) The conduct of interviews

Interviews must take place at a police station, unless delay would lead to: (a) interference with or harm to evidence connected with an offence; (b) interference with or harm to other people; (c) serious loss of, or damage to, property; (d) the alerting of other persons suspected of committing an offence; or (e) hindrance to the recovery of property obtained in consequence of the commission of an offence.[250]

---

[244] Sections 36 (failure to account for objects, substances or marks) and 37 (failure to account for presence at a particular place).

[245] Section 35.   [246] (1996) 22 EHRR 29.

[247] *Condron* v *UK* (2001) 31 EHRR 1; *Beckles* v *UK* (2003) 36 EHRR 13.

[248] Ibid; *Murray* v *UK* (1996) 22 EHRR 29.   [249] Code C, para 10.5.

[250] Code C, para 11.1.

Code C requires that the suspect should be reminded of his right to free legal advice before any interview is conducted. It also contains specific requirements about breaks from questioning, maximum periods of questioning, and the provision of proper food and refreshments as appropriate.

Section 76 of PACE provides that a confession obtained by oppression or in circumstances likely to lead to unreliability must be excluded from evidence at any trial.[251]

(d) Records of interviews

Code C requires the police to keep an accurate record of all interviews with suspects, including details of the time, date, location, breaks, and the names of all persons present.[252] Any interview conducted at a police station with a person suspected of an indictable offence must now be tape-recorded in accordance with Code of Practice E.[253] The recording must be carried out openly and two copies must be made. The master copy must be sealed in the suspect's presence,[254] and if the suspect is to be charged or prosecuted, he must be supplied with his own copy as soon as practicable after the conclusion of the interview. Where a suspect objects to being tape-recorded his objections must be recorded on the tape, but the interviewer may then turn off the tape and record the interview in writing.[255]

Where an interview is recorded in writing, the record must be made contemporaneously with the interview or as soon as possible afterwards.[256] The suspect should be shown the record for the purposes of verification, and he should be given the opportunity to sign it as correct.[257] If he declines to do so, this must itself be recorded, along with any unsolicited comments made.[258]

The visual recording of interviews is a more recent innovation, which was given a statutory basis in 2001.[259] Visual recording is not currently mandatory[260] but where it is carried out it must comply with Code of Practice F.

(e) Vulnerable suspects

There is a recognition that certain groups require additional safeguards, and specific rules exist for the protection of juveniles and those who are mentally disordered or otherwise mentally vulnerable. Such persons should not be interviewed or asked to sign an interview record in the absence of an appropriate adult[261] unless the criteria governing urgent interviews are satisfied. Specifically, the police must wait for an

---

[251] See p 392, *ante.* [252] Code C, para 11.7.

[253] A separate Code of Practice governs the recording of interviews with persons detained under the terrorism provisions.

[254] Code E, para 2.2. [255] Ibid, para 4.8. [256] Code C, para 11.8.

[257] Ibid, para 11.11. [258] Ibid, paras 11.13–11.14.

[259] PACE, s 60A, as amended by the Criminal Justice and Police Act 2001.

[260] A pilot study was conducted between 2002 and 2003, which made visual recording compulsory in certain police areas: Police and Criminal Evidence Act 1984 (Visual Recording of Interviews) (Certain Police Areas) Order 2002, SI 2002/ 1266.

[261] Code C, para 11.15. See p 414, *ante,* for the meaning of 'appropriate adult'.

appropriate adult unless an officer of at least the rank of superintendent considers that a delay would do one of the following: (a) lead to interference with or harm to evidence connected with an offence; (b) lead to interference with or physical harm to persons or property; (c) lead to the alerting of other persons suspected of having committed an offence; or (d) hinder the recovery of any property obtained as a result of an offence.[262] The officer must also be satisfied that the person's physical or mental state will not be significantly harmed by the interview.[263]

Those suffering temporary disability due to drink, drugs, or illness should not normally be interviewed until they are fit, though the courts are generally willing to leave this judgment to the police.[264]

9 IDENTIFICATION

Following a series of wrongful convictions, the Devlin Committee was established to investigate how the law dealt with identification evidence. The Committee recommended[265] that in all but the most exceptional cases, juries should be directed not to convict on the basis of eye-witness testimony unless it was supported by substantial other evidence. No legislation followed, but the Court of Appeal in *R v Turnbull* laid down certain guidelines.[266] The guidelines suggest that identification evidence can be split into good and poor quality identification. If, for example, the identification was made in good conditions of light and weather, with ample opportunity to observe, the matter can safely be left to the jury. On the other hand, if the identification is of poor quality, the case should be withdrawn from the jury unless it is supported and confirmed by other evidence. In all cases that depend wholly or substantially on identification evidence, the judge should direct the jury to proceed with special caution. In addition, there is no difference for these purposes between recognition evidence and evidence involving the identification of a stranger: although it might be assumed that the former would be more reliable, the witness in each case is using his particular knowledge of a person to identify him, and the *Turnbull* guidelines therefore apply.

To minimize the risks associated with identification evidence, Code of Practice D sets out specific rules as to how suspects are to be identified. Failure to comply with this Code is likely to result in the evidence being excluded from any trial. If the identity of a suspect is not known, a witness may be shown photographs or taken to a particular locality to observe possible candidates, but certain safeguards must be met.[267] Once the identity of the suspect is known, a video identification, group identification or identification parade may be organized. One of these procedures *must* be

---

[262] Ibid, para 11.1.   [263] Ibid, para 11.18.

[264] *R v Lamont* [1989] Crim LR 813; *R v Moss* (1990) 91 Cr App R 371.

[265] *Report to the Secretary of State for the Home Department of the Departmental Committee on Evidence of Identification in Criminal Cases* (1976, HC 338).

[266] [1977] QB 224, [1976] 3 All ER 549. Note that the guidelines appear to apply only to the identification of humans, and not to the identification of vehicles and other objects.

[267] Code D, paras 3.2–3.3.

offered if a suspect disputes an identification, except where such a procedure would not be practicable or would serve no useful purpose in proving or disproving his involvement in the offence.[268] Such a procedure may also be organized if the officer in charge of the investigation considers that it would be useful. The preferred method of identification in either case is video identification. Paragraph 3.14 of the Code states that a suspect should be offered video identification unless one of the other procedures would be a more suitable and practicable alternative. In all cases a suspect must be reminded of his entitlement to free legal advice, and his consent to the procedure must be sought. In the absence of consent the police may use covert or other means of identification, and the suspect's refusal to participate may be given in evidence at any subsequent trial.[269]

---

[268] In *R v Forbes* [2001] 1 AC 473, [2001] 1 All ER 686 an earlier version of the Code was interpreted to mean that an identification procedure had to be held in all cases, even where the suspect was already well known to the witness. The wording adopted since 2002 ensures that parades need not be held in cases where they would serve no useful purpose.

[269] Code D, para 3.17.

PART III

CIVIL PROCEDURE

13

THE CIVIL PROCESS

A INTRODUCTION

Access to justice is a fundamental right. It has even been described as a constitutional right, insofar as such rights exist.[1] For society to operate effectively, there must be means whereby disputes between individuals, and between the state and individuals, can be resolved. The civil justice process provides those means, but must be accessible to those who need such access. Procedural, financial, or other restrictions defeat the whole purpose of the civil justice process, as does unnecessary delay or length.

Civil litigation has, for the most part,[2] traditionally been regarded as adversarial in nature.[3] Within a framework of substantive and procedural law established by the state for the resolution of civil disputes, the main responsibility for the initiation and conduct of proceedings has traditionally rested with the parties to each individual case, with the person bringing the action (the claimant)[4] setting the pace at which the litigation proceeds. The parties to the litigation controlled the commencement of the action, the setting of the legal agenda within which the case was to be decided,[5] the progress of the case, the question of interim relief whilst the case was in progress, the settlement or otherwise of the case, and the acquisition and adducing of evidence. The role of the judge was to adjudicate on issues selected by the parties when they choose to present them to the court. That approach is not intended to have survived the reforms of the 1990's and early 2000's, which followed two landmark reports by Lord Woolf. The Woolf Interim Report and the Woolf Final Report[6] were the foundations on which reform of the civil justice system was built, culminating in

---

[1] See Laws J in *R v Lord Chancellor, ex parte Witham* [1998] QB 575, [1997] 2 All ER 779. The significance of the constitutional right is that it should only be abrogated by the clear words of an Act of Parliament. For the detail of this case, see p 30, *ante*.

[2] Proceedings involving children might be regarded as an exception.

[3] Access to Justice: Interim Report to the Lord Chancellor on the Civil Justice System in England and Wales, June 1995 ('the Woolf Interim Report'), at para 3. See also the Final Report (the 'Woolf Final Report', 1996)

[4] Formerly known as the '*plaintiff*'. For changes in nomenclature, see p 435, *post*.

[5] The 'pleadings'.

[6] *Access to Justice: Final Report.* For general comment and reference, see Zuckerman and Cranston *Reform of Civil Procedure: Essays on Access to Justice* (1995); Zander *The Government's Plans on Civil Justice* (1998) 61 MLR 383; Zander 'Forwards or Backwards for the New Lord Chancellor' (1997) 16 CJQ 208. Note that not all comment was dismissive of the pre-existing process: see, e.g. Conrad Dehn QC Reform of Civil Justice: Essays on 'Access to Justice' (1995) at pp 149–61.

the new Civil Procedure Rules (CPR).[7] The success of the Woolf Reforms of course remains to be fully evaluated but have been endorsed by subsequent reports.[8]

The civil justice process has long been criticized for its cost, delay, and complexity.[9] Since the mid-nineteenth century there have been some sixty or so reports on aspects of procedure, including the Civil Justice Review.[10] In 1993 (the year before Lord Woolf's review was commissioned) that civil justice process was condemned by a report published by the Bar Council and Law Society,[11] and was described as 'fragmented and confusing' by the Middleton Report[12] in 1997. The Woolf Interim Report identified a key reason for this as being the absence of effective judicial control. Without this, the adversarial process was likely to encourage an adversarial culture and to degenerate into an environment in which the litigation process was too often seen as a battlefield where no rules apply. In this environment, questions of expense, delay, compromise, and fairness might have only low priority. The consequence was that expense is often excessive, disproportionate, and unpredictable; and delay is frequently unreasonable.[13]

B THE WOOLF ANALYSIS

The fact that the Woolf Interim and Final Reports identified fundamental shortcomings in the civil justice process has already been noted above. At the heart of the problems were the adversarial approach of litigation, the expense and complexity of litigation, and the delays with which it was surrounded, although mot all such criticisms applied to all proceedings. We have already noted the existence of specialist courts or jurisdictions.[14] For example, the Commercial Court developed specialist procedures and protocols to facilitate the handling of cases within its remit. So, too, with judicial review, where[15] the procedures and processes under Order 53 of the old Rules of the Supreme Court provided speedy (if not necessarily inexpensive) means for the challenge of actions and decisions of public bodies. The question of choice of court also was an important factor contributing to delay, inefficiency, and cost.

1 DELAY AND ADVERSARIAL NATURE OF CIVIL LITIGATION

As already noted, the conduct of civil litigation has, historically, been in the hands of the parties, operating within a framework of rules of court, creating the potential for

---

[7] See p 431, *post.*   [8] See pp 427 and 432, *post.*   [9] Woolf Interim Report, *op cit*, para 8.

[10] Report of the Review Body on Civil Justice, Cm 394, 1988, HMSO.

[11] *Civil Justice on Trial: The Case for Change*, 1993.

[12] Review of Civil Justice and Legal Aid: Report to the Lord Chancellor by Sir Peter Middleton GCB ('the Middleton Report'), Lord Chancellors' Dept, September 1997, at para 1.7.

[13] Woolf Interim Report, *op cit*, para 4.   [14] See p 252 *et seq ante.*

[15] See chapter 6, *ante.*

delay. In *Rastin* v *British Steel plc*,[16] Sir Thomas Bingham pointed out that 'delay has long been recognised as the enemy of justice'. An adversarial process encourages an adversarial culture, and this worked well where all parties were keen to see the case progress, were appropriately represented, and the court had little need to intervene.[17] But the adversarial system in civil litigation has not always in the past delivered that. In one analysis, extra-judicially, Sir Gavin Lightman[18] identified a number of 'disturbing features for those who are more interested in the achievement of justice than playing the game'.[19] These included the fact that success depends very much on the events at court itself, which in turn turns on the investment made by the respective parties in the litigation—'money talks loud and clear', and the judge has limited opportunity to redress the balance. The quality of advice varies enormously, from (to quote the metaphor used) 'fine wine' to 'unfit to drink'. The judge has to achieve fairness on the material put before him. Above all, Lightman concluded that the system is expensive and time-consuming: 'you must purchase your "champions" for the tournament, and champions do not come cheap'. This disenchantment with the adversarial system was heightened by the plethora of judicial pronouncements on matters of substantive law. The Woolf reforms were viewed as advances, but substantial litigation remains 'extravagantly expensive and unpredictable . . .'.

Clearly, whatever the pros and cons of the system, the rules governing preparation for trial often highlighted these problems. The Woolf Interim Report observed that the whole process could be much like a battleground, with the parties waging 'war' often devoid of judicial intervention or control.[20] In 1994, High Court cases on average took 163 weeks in London and 189 weeks elsewhere to progress from commencement of the action to trial. The great majority of this time was between commencement and setting down: 123 weeks in London and 148 weeks elsewhere. The equivalent county court figures were around eighty weeks overall from commencement to trial, with typically around sixty weeks elapsing. In the majority of cases the delay arose from a failure to progress the case efficiently, wasting time on peripheral issues, or from procedural skirmishing to wear down an opponent or to excuse failure to get on with the case.[21] Woolf considered that this approach was too often condoned by the courts, paradoxically for fear of disadvantaging the litigant. Excessive discovery,[22] the use of experts in heavy demand, and the exertion of partisan pressure on experts also each contributed to delay.

Delay, Woolf concluded, was of more benefit to the lawyers than to the parties.[23] It

---

[16] [1994] 2 All ER 641, [1994] 1 WLR 732.

[17] See Andrews, *English Civil Procedure* (2003) at paras 2.22–2.23.

[18] High Court judge, in Edward Bramley Memorial Lecture: see (2003) 22 CJQ 235.

[19] His comments were focused on the criminal justice system but may be thought, by some, to have some value in the context of the criminal justice system. For the adversarial system, see p 518, *post*.

[20] *Interim Report op cit*, paras 29 *et seq*.

[21] For condemnation of the culture, see Lightman, 'Civil litigation in the 21st Century' (1998) 17 CJQ 383.

[22] The process whereby documents in hands of one party are made available to other parties in the litigation, and now known as disclosure.

[23] Interim Report, Ch 3, para 31.

allowed litigators to carry excessive caseloads in which the 'minimum possible action occurs over the maximum possible timescale'. The process of case settlement was addressed at a very late stage, not facilitating speed but, by contrast, creating extra costs. Rules of court were flouted on a vast scale. The timetables they contained were generally ignored and their other requirements complied with when convenient to the interests of one of the parties and not otherwise. Woolf considered that the powers of the courts had fallen behind the more sophisticated and aggressive tactics of some litigators. Orders for costs which resulted[24] were of little value, applied after the damage was done. The delay in being able to obtain effective intervention by the court encouraged rule-breaking and discouraged the party who would be prejudiced from applying for preventive measures. The main procedural tools for conducting litigation efficiently had become subverted from their proper purpose. Pleadings often failed to state the facts as the rules require, leading to a fundamental deficiency, namely the failure to establish the issues in the case at a reasonably early stage, and from which many problems resulted.[25] New procedures had become bogged down in technicalities or excesses, especially in respect to expert evidence and discovery.

The Report also focused on equally fundamental issues that result. He wrote:[26]

Delay is an additional source of distress to parties who have already suffered damage. It postpones the compensation or other remedy to which they may be entitled. It interferes with the normal existence of both individuals and businesses. In personal injury cases, it can exacerbate or prolong the original injury. It can lead to the collapse of relationships and businesses. It makes it more difficult to establish the facts because memories fade and witnesses cannot be traced. It postpones settlement but may lead parties to settle for inadequate compensation because they are worn down by delay or cannot afford to continue.

Many of his recommendations address directly issues of delay.

2 EXPENSE

Delay and expense are, of course, inextricably linked. If litigation is unaffordable then there is a denial of justice.[27] This problem has not, historically, been fully addressed by the civil legal aid system, which has often catered for the needs of those on the lowest income levels, leaving a range of middle-income earners unable to seek redress in the courts and thus with unmet legal needs. This is a situation addressed by the growth of conditional fee agreements following the gradual phasing-out of civil legal aid.[28] Disproportionality was also a problem: a claim which can only be pursued, or defended, at disproportionate cost is one that cannot in reality be brought or defended easily. Woolf noted that the costs in some cases, particularly smaller value cases, were often in excess of the value of what was in dispute. Research undertaken for the Woolf Inquiry showed that in half of the cases examined by the research team, the costs for one party to litigation equalled or exceeded the value of the claim

---

[24] See p 488, post.   [25] Interim Report, para 9.   [26] Interim Report, para 30.
[27] Ibid, Ch 3, para 13.   [28] See p 375, *ante*.

disproportionately.[29] It considered that disproportionate costs permeated many aspects of the civil justice process. In part, this flowed from the cost of legal services, and the level of fees charged by lawyers. It also stemmed from the fact that solicitors generally charge by an hourly rate, thus compounding the effect of cumbersome rules, procedures, or structures that allow the parties to dictate the pace of litigation, and issues to be determined. The question of the awards of costs was also relevant.[30] As noted earlier, if no effective rules apply, priority is not always given to the taking of steps to settle the litigation, or to progress it quicker, and therefore more cheaply. Woolf concluded[31] that the expense of litigation is one of the most fundamental problems confronting the civil justice system. He quoted Sir Thomas Bingham, the Master of the Rolls, as describing it as 'a cancer eating at the heart of the administration of justice'. The problem of cost is fuelled by the combative environment in which litigation is conducted.

Excessive cost deters people from making or defending claims. A number of businesses told the Woolf Inquiry that it is often cheaper to pay up, irrespective of the merits, than to defend an action.[32] This is particularly true at the lower end of the scale of litigation. For individual litigants the unaffordable cost of litigation constitutes a denial of access to justice. This problem of disproportionate cost is most acute in smaller cases where the costs of litigation, for one side alone, frequently equal or exceed the value of what is at issue. The result is often that it was impossible for ordinary people to take or defend smaller cases unless they are legally aided, have insurance backing, or believe they can be certain of winning their case and their costs. Like the Middleton Report was to do, Woolf also focused on the overall costs to the state, with inexorable rises in the costs of legal aid. This has now of course been reversed by the expedient of removing state funding for many classes of litigation. For individual legally-aided litigants, the high cost of litigation impacted through the increased contributions which they had to pay throughout the duration of the case and the statutory charge on any compensation they recover. The Report concluded that this approach to litigation which then applied usually resulted in total uncertainty for the parties as to what litigation will require, and consequently increased the amount of expenditure in which they may be involved and the timescale of that involvement. This arose from a number of factors:

(a) the rule that costs normally follow the event and the inevitable uncertainty as to the outcome of litigation;

(b) the procedures when management of the case is primarily a matter for the parties and that either side could influence not only its own costs but also its opponent's;

(c) the requirement of the adversarial system that every aspect of a case be fully investigated. This encouraged excessive work and cost on issues which were often recognized from an early stage as peripheral;

---

[29] Ibid, para 19, citing research of Professor Hazel Genn.   [30] See p 375, *post*.
[31] Interim Report, *op cit*, Ch 1.   [32] Ibid, para 13.

(d) the charging system, on a daily or hourly basis, which meant that the more that is done on a case, the more lawyers were paid;

(e) the lack of continuity in the handling of cases, resulting in the additional work necessary to refresh memories.

3 COMPLEXITY

Alongside delay and expense is complexity—what one writer has described as 'the unholy trinity of consequences which flow once a lawyer gets hold of a dispute'.[33] Woolf concluded that unnecessary complexity was caused by the then state of the rules of court, the multiplicity of procedures and jurisdictions, the multiplicity of methods of commencing actions, and the multiplicity of Practice Directions. None of the above was helped by 'obscure and uncertain' substantive law.[34] All these factors created additional problems where, whether for financial or other reasons, there was a growth in the number of unrepresented parties.

4 COURT OF TRIAL

Allied to all of the above are issues relating to the structure of the various courts of trial.[35] The question of which court tries an action was at the forefront of the various factors which contribute to current problems about delay, inefficiency, and cost. The jurisdictions of the county court and High Court were separate, but overlapping, with each having similar, but different, regimes of procedure and rules, adding to the complexity and other related problems.

Historically, determination of civil claims has been undertaken by the High Court and the county courts. In some matters, the jurisdiction of the High Court was exclusive, in others concurrent with the county court, in the sense that an action could be commenced in either. The jurisdiction of the county court in respect of which the Queens Bench Division has jurisdiction had been limited by the financial value of the claim. Prior to 1991, in contract or tort actions, the value of the claim had to be no greater than £5,000. In equity and property matters the figure was £30,000. If the amount of the claim exceeded the jurisdiction of the county court then the matter had to be dealt with by the High Court, subject to statutory powers of transfer between the two courts. Proceedings in the county court were potentially cheaper, but the procedures followed in the county court were not always either speedy or effective. It was hardly surprising, therefore, that the Review Body on Civil Justice[36] found that much of the work tried at High Court level was not of sufficient importance, complexity, and substance to justify the time and expense involved in High Court

---

[33] Andrews, *English Civil Procedure* (2003), at para 2.6. The author was reflecting on what was identified as a possibly cynical response of a layman.

[34] Interim Report Ch 3, para 44.   [35] As to which, see p 249, *et seq.*

[36] See Civil Justice Review, *op cit*, n 10, *ante.*

proceedings. It identified the types of cases that did in fact justify proceedings at High Court level. These included:

(a) public law matters, which should be dealt with by way of judicial review;[37]

(b) those matters dealt with in specialist jurisdictions, especially the Commercial Court;[38]

(c) ordinary cases, which were important, complex, or which involved a substantial claim. The Review recommended changes to the jurisdiction of the county court, and improved mechanisms for transfer between the two jurisdictions.

As a result of this Review, the Courts and Legal Services Act 1990 altered the whole basis of distribution of work between High Court and county court, although did not adopt in their entirety the recommendations of the Review Body. In 1991 the Lord Chancellor made the High Court and County Court Jurisdiction Order,[39] which adjusted fundamentally the distribution of work between the two courts. By virtue of this order, there was no longer to be any limit to the jurisdiction of the county court in contract or tort. The general principle was that a claimant should be free to choose whichever court is preferred, although in deciding where in fact to commence an action a claimant will usually have regard to the court by which such an action will ultimately be tried. The general principle of freedom of choice expressed above was subject to one important qualification: any action of a value less than £50,000 and involving a claim of damages for personal injuries, had to be commenced in the county court. There was also a presumption that a non-personal injuries claim of the value between £25,000 and £50,000 would be started in the county court.

Woolf recognized the value of such changes, but saw the need to go much further, as part of his philosophy that some of the problems identified above stemmed from in the then inability of the court itself to manage the progress and conduct of the case. As noted later,[40] this has led to changes where the jurisdiction of the court is to be determined through a multi-track approach whereby the court of trial, and the procedure followed, will be determined by the nature of the claim, including its financial value.

5 RECOMMENDATIONS

Woolf did not consider the situation analysed above to be inevitable. The Woolf Report analysed the whole civil process, particularly case management, and the procedures adopted both prior to, and at, trial. In his recommendations he sought to increase the speed proceedings should achieve, to simplify both the language and the process itself, to ensure greater accessibility, to promote settlement and out-of-court resolution of disputes, and to make litigation more efficient and cost effective. In particular, his approach envisaged that pre-trial process and procedure should be managed and overseen by the court, to ensure that proceedings are conducted at the appropriate speed.

---

[37] See p 206, *ante.*   [38] See p 252, *ante.*   [39] SI 1991/724.   [40] See p 466, *post.*

Amongst the detailed recommendations were:

(a) an expanded small claims jurisdiction;

(b) a new fast track for straightforward cases not exceeding £10,000 to be a strictly limited procedure designed to take cases to trial within a short but reasonable timescale;

(c) a new multi-track, for cases above £10,000, spanning both High Court and county court cases, and providing appropriate and proportionate case management. Individual hands-on case management was concentrated on those cases which require significant attention and which most benefit from it. Other cases in the multi-track would proceed on standard or individually tailored timetables, according to standard or individual directions;

(d) within the multi-track there would be effective case management, through case management conferences and pre-trial review;

(e) the most complex and important cases were to be heard only by High Court judges and not by deputies. Other cases would be managed and heard by the appropriate level of judge and able to move flexibly within the system to ensure this.

The implementation and effect of the Woolf recommendations are noted at the appropriate part of our discussion about the new system.

The Woolf recommendations were broadly endorsed by the Middleton Report,[41] and accepted generally by the government. To facilitate these fundamental changes, the government took through Parliament what is now the Civil Procedure Act 1997. That Act paved the way for detailed changes. It does so by, in section 1, providing for a new set of procedural rules (the Civil Procedure Rules) which will apply to Court of Appeal, High Court, and county court proceedings. The power to make new rules is to be exercised with a view to securing that the civil justice system is accessible, fair, and efficient.[42] Civil Procedure Rules are made by a Civil Procedure Rule Committee. In addition, a Civil Justice Council is established by section 6 of the 1997 Act.

C ADMINISTRATION OF THE CIVIL JUSTICE SYSTEM

The growing impetus for change was also driven by the need to achieve efficiency and cost-effectiveness. As the Middleton Report put it:[43]

The civil justice system as a whole is not managed coherently, nor do its individual parts seem to be managed with efficiency much in mind. There is indeed a view that efficiency might be incompatible with justice: that it is always desirable and necessary to take infinite

---

[41] See p 426, *ante.*   [42] 1997 Act, s 1(3).   [43] See p 426, *ante.*

pains in order to achieve the best possible result in each case. Desirable though this may seem as a principle, it inevitably comes up against the limitation of available resources . . . I have therefore concentrated on efficiency. I take that to mean getting more out of a given level of resources, or the same amount at lower cost.

Responsibility for administration of civil justice now lies with the Lord Chancellor and the Department of Constitutional Affairs.[44] The Woolf Report[45] recommended the establishment of a Civil Justice Council as a body with on-going responsibility for overseeing and co-ordinating the proposals for reform contained in that Report. Such a Council was established in 1998. Its primary task is to advise the Lord Chancellor on how the civil justice system can be improved. Section 6 of the Civil Procedure Act imposes a duty on the Council to keep the civil justice system under review, to consider how to make the civil justice system more accessible fair and efficient, to advise the Lord Chancellor and the judiciary on the development of the civil justice system, and to refer proposals for change to the Lord Chancellor and the Civil Procedure Rule Committee.

The Council comprised representatives from the judiciary, the legal profession, civil servants with knowledge of the administration of justice, persons with experience and knowledge of consumer affairs, individuals with knowledge and experience of the lay advice sector, and those able to represent the interests of particular kinds of litigants (for example, companies or business).[46]

1 RULES OF COURT

Civil litigation is conducted by the parties in accordance with rules of court. Prior to the implementation of the Woolf recommendations separate rules existed in respect of the county court (County Court Rules) and the Supreme Court (the Rules of the Supreme Court). The Civil Procedure Rules (CPR) replace both, and amount to a new procedural code.[47] They are intended to be free-standing, applied individually to the facts of the case, and certainly not limited by pre-CPR case law.[48] That does not mean that the development of principles in pre-CPR case law should be ignored, still less that the appeal courts should not continue to develop principles as to how the rules should be used.[49]

The rules do not directly affect rules of substantive law.[50] Nor do the rules prevent the courts within their own jurisdiction, from innovating where the rules are silent on

---

[44] Formerly with the Lord Chancellor's Department. For issues relating to this, see p 19, *ante*.

[45] *Op cit*, para 19.

[46] For general information about the Council, see http://www.civiljusticecouncil.gov.uk.

[47] CPR 1(1).   [48] *Hamblin* v *Field The Times*, 26 April 2000; *Purdy* v *Cambran* [1999] CPLR 843.

[49] See, e.g. *Ford* v *GKR Construction* [2000] 1 All ER 802.

[50] The comments of Henn Collins MR in *Re Coles and Ravenshear* [1907] 1 KB 1, at 4, to the effect that 'the relation of the rules of practice to the work of justice is intended to be that of handmaiden rather than mistress' remains true in concept, but must be viewed in accordance with the *Overriding Objective*, as to which see p 434.

a point,[51] or deprive the courts of any inherent jurisdiction. In *Grobbelaar* v *News Group Newspapers*[52] Lord Bingham described this as follows:

... the inherent jurisdiction of the court may be defined as the reserve or fund of powers, a residual source of powers, which the court may draw upon as necessary whenever it is just and equitable to do so, and in particular to ensure the observance of the due process of law to prevent improper vexation or oppression, to do justice between the parties and to secure a fair trial between them.

The power of a judge to refuse to hear persons who have no right of audience before the court, or counsel who are improperly dressed, or to sit in camera, or to abort a trial and start a new one where a procedural irregularity has occurred, or to adjourn the proceedings are all inherent powers. The important development of *Mareva* injunctions[53] and *Anton Piller* orders[54] (under the old regime) derived from the inherent jurisdiction of the court, and there is no reason to doubt that such judicial creativity can continue under the new regime. Likewise, the court has always had inherent power to regulate its own procedure. In *Langley* v *North West Water Authority*[55] the Court of Appeal held that a Liverpool solicitor was bound to comply with a Code of Practice issued by the Liverpool County Court. This amounted to a local Practice Direction which the court was entitled to issue under its inherent jurisdiction, except to the extent that it was concurrent with statute law or rules of court. There is probably no reason why action consistent with the CPR, and in particular the *Overriding Objective*, cannot continue.

2 THE OVERRIDING OBJECTIVE

The CPR commence with the statement of an *Overriding Objective* to which any court must seek to give effect when exercising any power given by the rules, or when it interprets any rule (CPR 1.2). At the start this code defines what dealing with cases 'justly' means. It includes, so far as practicable:

(a) ensuring that the parties are on an equal footing;

(b) saving expense;

(c) dealing with the case in ways that are proportionate —

---

[51] See Andrews, *English Civil Procedure* (2003), at para 1.10 citing as an example *Venables* v *News Group Newspapers Ltd* [2001] 1 All ER 908: perpetual injunction to restrain publication of details of T and V being revealed. T and V had been convicted of the notorious murder of James Bulger, a crime attracting outrage and vigilantism.

[52] [2002] 4 All ER 732, citing Jacob 'The Inherent Jurisdiction of the Court' (1970) CLP 23.

[53] *Mareva Compania Naviera SA* v *International Bulkcarriers SA* [1980] 1 All ER 213. These are known as Freezing Injunctions: see p 460, *post*.

[54] *Anton Pillar KG* v *Manufacturing Processes Ltd* [1976] Ch 55, [1976] 1 All ER 779. These are now known as Search Orders: see p 458, *post*.

[55] [1997] 2 FLR 841. See also Sir John Donaldson in *R* v *Secretary of State for the Home Department, ex parte Swati* [1986] 1 All ER 717, [1986] 1 WLR 477. See, now CPR, 3.1.

(i) to the amount of money involved;

(ii) to the importance of the case;

(iii) to the complexity of the issues;

(iv) to the financial position of each party

(d) ensuring that it is dealt with fairly and expeditiously;

(e) allotting it to an appropriate share of of the court's resources, whilst taking into account the need to allocate resources to other cases.

It is the duty of all parties, and their lawyers, to comply with this objective.[56] It may on occasion guide how a court actually decides a case, or how it deals with questions of costs. One key example of this is the debate that has been on-going as to whether a court has the right to compel unwilling parties to engage in Alternative Dispute Resolution (ADR) and whether a failure to do so could, and should, be penalized by a refusal to award costs that otherwise the party would expect to receive.[57]

The CPR contain the relevant rules. They also contain *Practice Directions*, which amount to guides to the interpretation of the rules themselves[58] and also pre-action protocols, with which a court will expect a party to comply. A failure to do so may be reflected by a court in the grant, or refusal, of a discretionary remedy or procedure, or may be reflected in any orders for costs: CPR 3.1(4)).

3 THE TERMINOLOGY

As part of the process of seeking to simplify and demystify civil litigation recommended by Woolf, the CPR change many of the names, terms, and expressions formerly used, and to be found in the pre-CPR case law and texts. Whether the changes achieve their objective, or are simply change for change's sake, is a matter of taste and opinion. Where necessary these are dealt with at the appropriate part of the text, but the following should be noted at the outset:

- Plaintiff—now **claimant**

- Guardian ad litem—now **litigation friend**

- Writ—now **claim form**

- Leave—now **permission**

- Pleadings—now **statement of case**

- Interlocutory relief—now **interim remedies**

- Ex parte—now **without notice**

---

[56] CPR, 1.3; Access to Justice Act 1969, s 42.

[57] For discussion of this important issue, see p 436, *post*, and see, e.g., *Dunnett v Railtrack (Practice Note)* [2002] 1 WLR 2434. For the rules relating to costs, see p 488, *post*.

[58] *Godwin v Swindon BC* [2001] EWCA Civ 1478 per May LJ.

D SETTLEMENT AND ALTERNATIVE MEANS OF DISPUTE RESOLUTION

1 INTRODUCTION

Increasingly, those with disputes have sought alternative means of dispute resolution. As noted above, litigation, particularly in the High Court, is both time-consuming and expensive, and suffers the disadvantage of, generally, being conducted in public. Arbitration has long been seen as an accepted alternative to court procedures, particularly in the sphere of commerce and business, and involves a binding resolution of a dispute by an arbitrator. The principle of arbitration was adopted in respect of small claims in the county court, evolving into the small-claims track introduced as part of the Woolf reforms.[59] In addition, there has begun a tendency to look for other, more informal forms of mechanism for the resolution of disputes, generally known as Alternative Dispute Resolution (ADR).

Unlike arbitration, the characteristics of such mechanisms are, often, those of conciliation, mediation, and negotiation, and which by their nature will not generally involve the imposition of the verdict or conclusion. Such means of avoiding full-scale litigation are particularly helpful to parties to disputes in the commercial or business sectors. As long ago as 1994,[60] the Commercial Court encouraged alternative dispute resolution, particularly where the costs of litigation were likely to be wholly disproportionate to the amount at stake, and cost-effective.[61] Woolf envisaged a 'landscape of civil litigation . . . fundamentally different from what it is now', starting with the premise that litigation should be avoided where possible, but, if it occurred, less adversarial and more cooperative. He urged the use of ADR in the civil justice process, a fact reflected in the provisions of the CPR. 'Active case management' is one of the key principles introduced by the CPR, and that includes a court's 'encouraging parties to use an alternative dispute resolution procedure if it considers that appropriate, and facilitating the use of such a procedure.'[62] ADR is a 'method of resolving disputes otherwise than through the use of such a procedure.'[63] Pre-action protocols[64] emphasize the exchange of information at an early stage and promotion of negotiations leading to settlement. Parties are required to follow a 'reasonable procedure' intended to avoid litigation, and the parties must state whether they are willing to enter into ADR.[65] The effect of decisions elsewhere in the civil justice system also

---

[59] See p 465, *post*.

[60] *Practice Note (Commercial Court Alternative Dispute Resolution)* [1994] 1 All ER 34, 1 WLR 14.

[61] See, generally, Partington, 'Alternative Dispute Resolution: Recent Developments, Future Challenges' (2004) 23 CJQ 99; Genn, 'Court-Based Initiative for Non Family Civil Disputes: The Commercial Court and the Court of Appeal', Research Report for LCD, 2002.

[62] CPR 4 (2)(e).   [63] Glossary, CPR.   [64] See p 448, *post*.

[65] *Practice Direction for Pre Action Protocols*, para 4.2. Some specific pre-action protocols specifically require such consideration: e.g. clinical negligence protocol.

should not be overlooked. Section 4(4)(c) of the Access to Justice Act 1999 requires persons carrying out functions under the Community Legal Service[66] to do so with a view to achieving 'the swift and fair resolution of disputes without unnecessary or unduly protracted proceedings in court'. There are thus financial incentives, which may be increased with potential changes to the Community Legal Services approach to legal aid.[67] As things currently exist, however, the legal aid scheme does not always encourage litigation to be seen as a last resort, because of the higher rates lawyers are paid for representation as opposed to Legal Help (which provides support for early resolution of disputes), and because most legal aid remuneration is paid on hourly rates (with therefore greater rewards for more adversarial processes).[68]

Distinctions must be made between the different forms of process mentioned above. Arbitration is an alternative form of dispute adjudication, with the result usually binding on both sides. Mediation, conciliation, and negotiation are, in effect, means of assisted dispute settlement:[69] no settlement can be imposed and the onus is on the parties to come to an agreement. The nature of the process may vary: it can be a process 'designed to facilitate agreement'[70] or can be evaluative by encouraging settlement through evaluation of the parties' rights and case. Different mediators adopt different styles and approaches.[71] And the mediation may not be wholly voluntary: distinctions can be drawn between ADR which forms an alternative to the commencement of proceedings in the first place, and court-ordered ADR once proceedings are under way.[72]

We now turn to discuss these different strands.

2 ARBITRATION

Arbitration is one, long-standing alternative form of dispute resolution used by parties to contracts, particularly contracts involving the construction industry, and favoured as a form of dispute resolution by parties to international commercial contracts. The law hitherto has been governed by statutory provision, principally the Arbitration Acts of 1950 and 1979, as explained and developed by common law. In 1996 a new Arbitration Act was passed, which repealed earlier legislation, and which was designed to provide a statutory statement of the relevant statutory and common law principles,

---

[66] As to which, see p 377, *ante*.

[67] See Consultation Paper. '*A New Focus for Civil Legal Aid—encouraging early resolution, discouraging unnecessary litigation*,' DCA, 2004.

[68] *Consultation Paper, op cit*, n 67, at p 8.

[69] *Alternative Dispute Resolution: A Discussion Paper*, LCD November 1999, at 2.4.

[70] See also Department of Constitutional Affairs Public Service Agreement 3 which aims to reduce the proportion of disputes resolved by resort to the courts.

[71] See the analysis by Prince in *Court-based mediation: a preliminary analysis of the small claims mediation scheme at Exeter Crown Court*, Research Report for the Civil Justice Council, March 2004, at p 12.

[72] For court-ordered ADR and its implications, see p 443, *post*.

in clear and comprehensible language, complying where appropriate with international rules and principles governing arbitration.[73]

Section 1 of that Act states the general principles governing arbitration:

(a) the object of arbitration is to obtain the fair resolution of disputes by an impartial tribunal without unnecessary delay or expense;

(b) the parties should be free to agree how their disputes are resolved, subject only to such safeguards as are necessary in the public interest;

(c) in matters governed by Part I of the Act (which governs arbitration under an arbitration agreement) the court should not intervene except as the Act provides. The Act applies where the 'seat' of the arbitration is in England and Wales, in other words, that England and Wales is the jurisdiction designated by the parties to the arbitration agreement, or by or in accordance with that agreement.

The jurisdiction of arbitrators usually arises out of contract, though there are numerous statutory provisions which provide for the reference of disputes to arbitration. An agreement to refer disputes to arbitration is a contract and, as such, is subject to the ordinary law of contract. Such an agreement must be in writing if the provisions of the 1996 Act are to apply.[74] Any provision purporting to oust the jurisdiction of the courts is not effective to do so,[75] though there is no objection to a clause which makes reference to arbitration a condition precedent to a right of action. The effect of such a clause, traditionally known as a *Scott v Avery*[76] clause, is that if a party does institute proceedings without referring the dispute to arbitration, the clause may be pleaded as a defence in those proceedings and the other party may, after acknowledging service of the writ but before taking any other step in the proceedings, apply to the court for an order staying the proceedings.[77] The court must grant a stay unless satisfied that the arbitration agreement is null and void, inoperative, or incapable of being performed. Unlike the position at common law (which sometimes applies) the poverty or insolvency of such a claimant is not a ground for refusing a stay.[78]

(a) Procedure

Procedure on arbitrations is governed (except, in relation to statutory references, where the statute in question otherwise provides) by the Arbitration Act 1996. The issues arising must (in the absence of contrary agreement) be decided according to the rules of law considered by the court to be applicable decided in accordance with the principles of conflict of laws.[79] The arbitrator must act fairly and impartially as

---

[73] See Report of the Department of Trade and Industry Departmental Advisory Committee on International Commercial Arbitration, 1985 (the Mustill Report). That Committee prepared the draft Bill in 1995.
[74] 1996 Act, s 5(1).   [75] Ibid, s 87.   [76] (1856) 5 HL Cas 811.
[77] Arbitration Act 1996, s 9.
[78] Cf. *Fakes v Taylor Woodrow Construction Ltd* [1973] QB 436, [1973] 1 All ER 670. The 1996 Act, s 9, does not include the limited grounds accepted as just reason for a stay in this case.
[79] 1996 Act, s 46(3).

between the parties, giving each party a reasonable opportunity of putting his case, and for dealing with his opponents' case, and must adopt procedures suitable to the circumstances of the particular case, avoiding unnecessary delay and expense.[80] The arbitrator must decide all procedural and evidential matters, subject to the right of the parties to agree any matter. The arbitrator may thus decide when and where proceedings are to be held, in what language, what documents should be produced and disclosed, what questions should be put to and answered by the parties, whether to apply strict rules of evidence, the extent to which there should be oral or written submissions, and whether the tribunal should take the initiative in ascertaining the facts and the law.[81] In other words, the arbitrator has complete discretion to depart from traditional procedures, and to act inquisitorially. Arbitrators may appoint experts, legal advisers, or assessors to advise them.[82] Parties to arbitration are entitled to legal representation unless they agree otherwise.[83] Since 1990,[84] an arbitrator had no power to dismiss an arbitration for want of prosecution. Section 41 of the 1996 Act entitles an arbitrator to dismiss a claim where:

(a) there has been inordinate and inexcusable delay on the part of the claimant in pursuing the claim; and

(b) the delay
  (i) will give rise to a substantial risk that it is not possible to have a fair resolution of the issues in that claim; or
  (ii) has caused, or is likely to cause or have caused, serious prejudice to the respondent.

In the absence of specific provision reference to arbitration connotes reference to a single arbitrator.[85] Where specific provision is made for the appointment of two arbitrators there is a requirement to appoint an additional person as chairman. Under section 18 of the 1996 Act the High Court has various powers to appoint arbitrators and umpires in default of appointment by the parties, the Act specifying in detail the various powers that arise so that disputes are resolved without recourse to the court. The High Court also has power to revoke the authority of an arbitrator or umpire on the ground of delay, bias, or improper conduct[86] and has inherent jurisdiction to stay arbitration proceedings by injunction. There used to be provision whereby an arbitrator might, and, if directed by the court, had to, state in the form of a 'special case' for the opinion of the High Court, either his award or any question of law arising in the reference.[87] The power to apply for a special case was sometimes exercised by a party to delay unduly the resolution of the dispute and to add needlessly to costs. This was altered in 1979, the current provision being found in section 87 of the 1996 Act. This provides that the parties may enter into an 'exclusion agreement', but only if they do so after the arbitration has commenced. There will then be no power in the High

---

[80] Ibid, s 33(1).   [81] Ibid, s 34(1).   [82] Ibid, s 37(1).   [83] Ibid, s 36(1).
[84] Introduced by the Courts and Legal Services Act 1990, s 102.   [85] 1996 Act, s 15(3).
[86] Ibid, s 24.   [87] Arbitration Act 1950, s 21.

Court to consider a question of law arising in the course of the arbitration; nor will there be any right of appeal. Therefore (subject to the limited power of the High Court to set aside or remit an award for misconduct the arbitrator's decision will be final. Exclusion agreements entered into before the arbitration is commenced are effective only in a limited class of cases and in particular, are invalid in the case of a 'domestic arbitration agreement', that is, basically, an agreement which does not provide for arbitration outside the United Kingdom and is not one to which no United Kingdom national or resident is a party.[88] The decision of the arbitrator is in the form of an 'award', dealing with all the issues on which reference was made. The award may contain provision for the payment of money, costs, or an order of specific performance (except of a contract relating to land).[89] As between the parties the award binds the parties in relation to the issues decided, thus extinguishing any cause of action in relation thereto.

(b) Intervention by the court

An arbitration award may, with leave of the High Court, be enforced in the same way as a judgment or order of that court and, where leave is granted, judgment may be entered in the terms of the award. In addition action may be brought on the award as a contractual debt.

The court's powers over arbitration proceedings were altered and extended by the 1979 Act and are now contained in section 69 of the 1996 Act. The court may hear an application challenging the award if there has been an error by the arbitrator as to a matter relating to substantive jurisdiction, or where there has been a serious irregularity.[90] A right of appeal on any question of law arising out of an award made on an arbitration agreement exists (unless excluded by a valid 'exclusion agreement' (*ante*)) but only by consent of all parties or with leave of the court; the court may not grant leave unless it considers that the determination of the question of law could affect substantially the rights of the parties, that the question was one the arbitrator was asked to determine, that on the basis of the findings of fact the decision is obviously wrong or one of general public importance and the arbitrator's decision is open to serious doubt, and, finally that it is just and proper in all the circumstances for the court to determine the question. It may attach conditions to the grant of leave (for example the provision of security for the amount claimed). In addition to the right of appeal, there is jurisdiction in the High Court (save where there is a valid exclusion agreement) to determine any question of law arising in the course of the reference,[91]

---

[88] 1996 Act, s 85.   [89] Ibid, s 67.

[90] Ibid, s 68. The term 'serious irregularity' is broadly defined by s 68(2) and includes one or more of the following matters which the court considers has caused or will cause substantial injustice to the applicant: failure to comply with general duties under s 33, exceeding its powers, failure to conduct proceedings in accordance with agreed procedures, uncertainty or ambiguity about its award, the award being obtained by fraud, or irregularity in the conduct of the proceedings.

[91] Ibid, s 45.

but only with the consent of the arbitrator or of all the parties. There is an appeal from the High Court to the Court of Appeal, from decisions under Act, but only

(a) with leave of the High Court; and

(b) if the High Court certifies that the question of law is one of general public importance or one which for some other special reason should be considered by the Court of Appeal.[92]

Where an arbitrator has misconducted himself or the proceedings the court may remove him and may set aside the award, or may remit it for reconsideration. The parties may nominate any person they wish to act as arbitrator. Members of the Bar are not infrequently appointed. In addition, by section 93 of the Arbitration Act 1996 a judge of the Commercial Court may, if in all the circumstances he thinks fit, accept appointment as sole arbitrator or as umpire where the dispute appears to him to be of a commercial character and provided the Lord Chief Justice has informed him that, having regard to the state of business in the High Court, he can be made available to do so. Similar powers exist in respect of official referees. Where a judge has acted as arbitrator or umpire under this section appeal lies by case stated to the Court of Appeal.

3 MEDIATION AND NEGOTIATION

(a) Family matters

Conciliation and mediation plays a significant role in divorce proceedings. The trend generally is towards less court intervention in matrimonial matters. Divorce itself is basically a paper exercise, and the majority of financial matters, and matters relating to children are dealt with by consent. The 1990's saw a general trend towards encouraging, and requiring, mediation in the context of families. The Family Law Act 1996 encourages and requires mediation to occur. The same philosophy applies in the context of cases involving children, and a range of projects aimed to complement the judicial process through alternative dispute resolution in child care cases, by identifying and exploring the issues to be determined and exploring options on which the parties could agree. Pilot projects have been run in child care cases involving public law issues: these include a joint Alternative Dispute Resolution Project run by National Family Mediation and the Tavistock Centre, funded by the Department of Health, aiming to provide mediation as an alternative to the court process in child protection, fostering, adoption, or contact cases where there is a dispute between parents, carers, and local authority social workers.[93] National Family Mediation has also developed policies involving mediation in domestic violence cases. Since section 29 of the Family Law Act 1996 was introduced, the Legal Services Commission will require divorcing or separating couples who are eligible for legal aid and who are in dispute on matters

---

[92] Ibid, s 69(8).
[93] See Walsh, 'Working in the Family Justice System' [1997] Fam Law at 109–10.

relating to children, to attend an interview with a mediator as a pre-condition to the consideration of an application for legal aid. Mediation services are available at a growing number of major centres.

In the future it is intended to accelerate this process by changes to legal aid funding. The Community Legal Service proposes to restructure Legal Help, General Family Help, and Help with Mediation,[94] with a single level of service called Family Help, intended to cover all non-adversarial family dispute resolution, coupled with a further reduction in funding for representation in contested proceedings.[95] This is likely to be piloted and rolled out through the Family Advice and Information Service during 2006. The philosophy of diverting from the courts was well summarized as follows:[96]

[Research] has highlighted parents' awareness of the negative impact of conflict and sub-optimal contact arrangements on their children and their desire to find a better way of sorting these issues out . . . most do not want to resort to the courts. They are led or feel pressed there. Courts are not possibly the best equipped to deal with the emotional and practical problems being brought before them. The process can be (and is) criticised for being too backward-looking and focused on fact-finding: it is adversarial and may actually increase and prolong conflict . . . Courts certainly have a place in this—for those cases where safety is an issue or where no amount of help will reduce the conflict—but we estimate that there might be up to 60 per cent of the current court caseload that need not and should not really be there.

(b) Contractual and regulatory disputes

Some contracts specify a form of dispute resolution which, at any rate initially, requires disputes to be arbitrated or decided by an arbitrator or complaint resolution procedure. Examples of this are many, and include not only standard building agreements, but also more consumer-orientated matters such as some disputes between holidaymaker and travel company. Such agreements do not necessarily oust the jurisdiction of the courts. In addition, a range of dispute resolution mechanisms may exist, and are on the increase.[97] The Confederation of British Industry has established the Centre for Effective Dispute Resolution (CEDR). The City Disputes Panel was created to deal with disputes in the banking and finance sector.

In the public sector, the government has sought to increase the use of ADR as an alternative to litigation. The Environment Council offers an ADR service for public interest and environmental disputes. The NHS has been involved in pilot mediation projects. The Housing Ombudsman refers disputes in relation to public sector housing. The Planning Inspectorate has a pilot project in the context of planning appeals.

---

[94] As to which see p 442, *ante*.

[95] Parental disputes about arrangements for their children amount to some 28 per cent of civil legal aid budget.

[96] *Community Legal Service Consultation Paper op cit*, at p 18.

[97] See Nesic, 'Mediation—On the Rise in the United Kingdom?' to be found at http://www. adr.civiljusticecouncil.gov.uk/updocs.

Indeed, Woolf in his Final Report[98] identified the fact that applicants for judicial review should be encouraged to settle their disputes without recourse to the courts, through grievance procedures and ombudsman remedies which are increasingly available. Such complaints mechanisms exist increasingly in the sphere of public law, for example the National Health Service complaints procedure or the independent Housing Ombudsman noted above.[99]

All these mechanisms may have consequences for the availability of judicial remedies. For example, section 26 of the Children Act 1989 provided for a mechanism for dealing with complaints. In R v Birmingham City Council, ex parte A,[100] the applicant sought judicial review of the actions of the local authority in failing to provide suitable accommodation for a severely disturbed child. The application failed, the court holding that the appropriate response was to utilize the statutory complaints mechanism, not to seek judicial review. Again, and more recently, in Frank Cowell v Plymouth City Council[101] Lord Woolf himself criticized the abuse of judicial review in a case involving the re-housing of elderly residents of a care home, describing the process as 'over judicialised'.

(c) Court based schemes and court- led ADR requirements

It will be clear from the above that some courts have played a role in the development of ADR. Since 1993 the Commercial Court has been identifying cases regarded as appropriate for ADR. In some cases judges have suggested ADR. In others an order has been made requiring the parties to attempt ADR, a position that needs now to be reviewed in the light of the decision in Halsey v Milton Keynes General NHS Trust.[102] It stops short of compulsion. It was described as follows in Halsey:

It is the strongest form of encouragement. It requires the parties to exchange lists of neutral individuals who are available to conduct 'ADR procedures', to endeavour in good faith to agree a neutral individual or panel and to 'take such reasonable steps they may be advised to resolve their disputes by ADR procedures before the neutral individual or panel so chosen . . .' The order also provides that if the case is not settled 'the parties shall inform the court what steps towards ADR have been taken and (without prejudice to matters of privilege) why such steps have failed.

If following an ADR order there has been a failure to settle the parties must explain what steps were taken towards ADR, and why they failed. By 2000 the number of such orders had reached sixty-eight in a six-month period.[103] Typically, ADR occurred in about 50 per cent of cases where such an order was made, with a success rate for settlement in those cases of about 52 per cent. The research showed that ADR had some impact in reducing the proportion of cases going to trial, even if the ADR itself had proved unsuccessful. It identified the fact that orders can have a positive effect in

---

[98] At p 251.   [99] See Nichol, 'Available Dispute Resolution' Legal Action, Dec 1997, p 6.
[100] [1991] 3 All ER 610, [1991] 1 WLR 697.   [101] The Times 8 January 2002.
[102] See p 444, post.
[103] See Genn, Court-Based Initiatives for Non-Family Civil Disputes. Research Report for LCD, 2002.

opening up communication between the parties and avoiding the fear of one side showing weakness in being the first to suggest settlement.

Many other court-based initiatives can be identified. They include schemes at the Patents Court and the Central London County Court, a scheme in Exeter,[104] and in several other centres.

Given the growth in interest and activity in ADR since the early 1990's, and now the positive obligation to seek to avoid litigation contained in the CPR, key questions remain as to whether the parties can be forced to engage in mediation. Of course, the parties to a contract may have stipulated that a negotiated settlement or mediation is the first step, before litigation may be considered. An agreement to negotiate has been held not to be enforceable, because of the lack of sufficient certainty as to what is means,[105] but, by contrast, the House of Lords in *Channel Tunnel Group Ltd v Balfour Beatty Construction Ltd*[106] held that a court has a discretionary power to stay proceedings[107] if there is a dispute mediation clause equivalent to an agreement to arbitrate. Although the matter may not be completely clear,[108] a prior agreement is likely, if it is sufficiently clear and certain, to be binding.[109]

That conclusion is probably inevitable given the attitude of the courts since the introduction of the CPR and its requirement to consider ADR. A contrary conclusion would fly in the face of public policy.[110] Under the CPR parties may seek a stay to attempt ADR[111] and a failure to engage in ADR following a court's direction may be reflected in any costs order sought or made. In *Dunnet v Railtrack plc*[112] a defendant's application for costs was refused because of a failure to mediate. If parties 'turned down out of hand the chance of alternative dispute resolution when suggested by the court . . . they may have to face uncomfortable costs consequences . . .'.[113] Another court considered that the right question to ask was: is there on an objective viewpoint any real chance of mediation succeeding?[114] On the particular facts the court did not think so, and therefore did not deprive the claimant of his costs.

The authorities generally have proved inconsistent.[115] For that reason the guidance given in two cases in the Court of Appeal, *Halsey v Milton Keynes General NHS Trust* and *Steel v Joy*[116] is to be welcomed. In neither case was a party deprived of costs because of a failure to mediate. In *Halsey*, a clinical medical case, the defendant believed that it had a very strong case, that mediation costs would be disproportionately high,

---

[104] See Interim Research Report by Prince: *Court-Based Mediation—A Preliminary Analysis of Small Claims Mediation Scheme at Exeter County Court*, Civil Justice Council, March 2004.

[105] *Walford v Miles* [1992] 1 All ER 453.

[106] [1993] AC 334. See also *Scott UK Ltd v F E Barber Ltd* [1997] 3 All ER 540.

[107] As to which, see p 467, *post*.

[108] See *Halifax Financial Services Ltd v Intuitive Systems Ltd* [1999] 1 All ER (Comm) 303.

[109] The key question may be the mandatory nature of the procedure agreed: see *Cable & Wireless v IBM*.

[110] *Cable & Wireless v IBM* per Colman J.　　　[111] CPR, 26.4(1).　　　[112] [2002] CP Rep 35.

[113] *Dunnet v Railtrack plc*, Supra, per Brooke LJ.

[114] See *Hurst v Leeming* [2002] C P Rep 59; cf. *Leicester Circuits v Coates* [2003] EWCA 333.

[115] *Neal v Jones; Societe Internationale de Telecommunications Aéronautiques v Wyatt* [2002] EWHC 2401.

[116] (2004) EWCA (Civ) 576.

and the claimant's requests in pre-action correspondence was highly tactical. In *Steel*, a personal injury case, the claim involved a point of law which it was reasonable to wish to be resolved by the court. The case was probably intrinsically unsuitable for mediation.

The court gave general guidance. It does not have power to order reluctant litigants to mediate. To do so would violate art. 6 of the Convention, because it would be an unacceptable obstruction to right of access to the courts. The court can encourage, not compel. All those involved in litigation should routinely consider whether the dispute is suitable for ADR. If a party refuses to mediate, the court can displace the normal costs rule and order that party to pay the costs despite winning at trial. This should occur only if that party has acted unreasonably in refusing ADR. The burden of showing that lies with the unsuccessful party. If the case *is* mediated the parties are entitled to adopt whatever position they want, and the court is not, later, entitled to ask why that position was in fact adopted. This thus preserves the confidentiality of mediation. Above all, although most cases are suitable for ADR there is not a presumption in favour mediation. In deciding what cases suitable, regard should be had to the nature of the case, its merits, the extent to which other settlement methods have been attempted, whether the costs of mediation are disproportionately high and whether delay in arranging mediation would be prejudicial.

None of the above prevents a court from a court imposing an order requiring the parties to consider the suitability of mediate. Refusal will still carry the risk of deprivation of costs.

14

PRE-TRIAL PROCESS[1]

A CHOICE OF COURT

The Woolf Civil Justice Reforms[2] made fundamental changes to the commencement of actions. As already noted,[3] jurisdiction in civil matters has historically been divided between the county court and High Court.[4] The latter has had almost unlimited jurisdiction, unless statute has given jurisdiction exclusively to a county court The jurisdiction of the county court has been limited historically by value, or by the nature of the subject matter. For example, the county court has not had (and does not have) jurisdiction to deal with claims in libel or slander.[5]

Within that structure, the choice of where to commence the action turned on what was the appropriate court of trial. If the matter was within the exclusive jurisdiction of either the High Court, or of the county court, it was in that court that the action should have been commenced, usually by writ (in the case of the High Court) or summons (in the case of the county court). If the matters fell to be regarded as a small claim, the county court was the appropriate forum for the case. If judicial review[6] was sought an application had to be made to the Administrative Court (formerly, the Queens' Bench Divisional Court). Increasingly, though, the High Court and county court have had concurrent jurisdiction in respect of most matters. The county court can now deal with any matters that are founded on contract or tort whatever the financial value or complexity, jurisdiction over claims in equity and contentious probate where the value involved does not exceed £30,000[7] and unlimited jurisdiction to hear cases for the recovery of land.[8] The county court has now many of the same powers in respect of procedure and remedies as does the High Court. Yet, despite the concurrence of many aspects of jurisdiction the intention has been to keep the High Court for only the most valuable, complex, or important cases. Section 1 of the Courts and Legal Services Act 1990 empowers the Lord Chancellor to make provision for the allocation of business. Article 7 of the High Court and County Court

---

[1] See, generally, Zuckerman, *Civil Procedure* (2003); Andrews, *English Civil Procedure* (2002); Loughlin and Gerlis, *Civil Procedure* (2004).

[2] See p 426, *ante.*   [3] See p 255, *ante.*   [4] See p 249, *ante.*

[5] County Court Act 1984, s 15(2).   [6] See p 206, *ante.*

[7] County Courts Act 1984, ss 23, 32; County Courts Jurisdiction Order 1981, SI 1981/123.

[8] 1984 Act, s 21.

Jurisdiction Order 1991[9] creates a presumption that cases of a value less than £25,000 must be tried in the county court: a claim of less than £15,000 *cannot* be commenced in the High Court. The presumption is that a claim of a value of £50,000 or more *will* be eligible for High Court trial. The position will be otherwise if the application of certain criteria shows that a different court of trial is in fact appropriate. These criteria also apply in deciding in which court cases falling between these two financial figures should be tried, with one proviso. Cases involving personal injury claims of an estimated amount less than £50,000 must be commenced in the county court (except in the case of clinical medical negligence claims) The criteria mentioned above are set out in art. 7(5) of the order, which deals primarily with the transfer of cases between the two jurisdictions.[10] However, they are equally relevant to the question of initial choice of jurisdiction. The factors identified are as follows:

(i) the financial substance of the action, including that of any counter-claim;

(ii) whether the action is otherwise important, for example by raising issues of general public importance, or where the case will amount to a test case;

(iii) the complexity of the facts, legal issues, remedies, or procedures involved. Complex cases are more suitable for High Court trial;

(iv) whether transfer of the case will lead to more speedy trial, although this alone should not be a determining factor.

To facilitate the greater use of the county court jurisdiction, section 38 of the County Courts Act 1984 gave to the county court, generally speaking, the power to make any order which could be made by the High Court if the proceedings were in that court. That power is subject to any limitation imposed by regulations, and examples of such matters are freezing orders[11] or search orders.[12] In substantial cases where such orders may be crucial to the obtaining of information or prevention of dissipation of assets, these restrictions may conclusively influence the choice of High Court rather than county court jurisdiction. Some cases, such as professional negligence, claims under the Fatal Accidents Act 1976, claims of fraud or of undue influence, malicious prosecution, and false imprisonment, claims against the police, and contentious probate may be particularly suitable for High Court trial.[13] All concerned are bound by the Civil Procedure Rules. A claim should be started in the High Court only if by reason of its financial value and the amount in dispute and/or the complexity of the facts, legal issues, or procedures involved, and/or the public importance of the matters involved the claimant believes the claim should be dealt with by a High Court judge.[14] If a case does not fall within these criteria, nor is required to be tried in the High Court by statute or falls within a specialist jurisdiction (such as the Administrative

---

[9] SI 1991/724. [10] See CPR, 30.3(1), 30.3(2). [11] See p 460 *post.*
[12] See p 458, *post.* [13] Practice Direction 29, para 2.6.
[14] Practice Direction 7, para 2.4.

Court)[15] it will be transferred to the county court.[16] In a case where the choice of court was known to be wrong, and intended to intimidate the opponent, or to run up costs, a court might strike out the case.[17] This should not happen where there has been a bona fide error or misjudgment, because this would not only be contrary to the spirit of the 'overriding objective'[18] but possibly a breach of the fair trial provisions of art. 6 of the European Convention which encompasses the right of access to the court. A further sanction may be a reduction in the costs allowed at the conclusion of the case.[19]

The total effect of these changes is that the vast majority of actions, some 90 per cent, commence in the county court. The High Court is the forum for the more specialist and difficult cases.[20] The general powers to transfer between the two levels of court must be exercised having regard to the matters identified in the Civil Procedure Rules. These include:[21]

(a) the financial value of the claim, or the amount in dispute;

(b) the convenience or fairness of hearings being held in another court;

(c) the availability of a judge specializing in the type of claims in question;

(d) the complexity of facts, legal issues, remedies, or procedures;

(e) the public ignorance of the claim; the facilities available at the court where the claim is being dealt with, in particular with regard to the disabilities of a party or witness;

(f) whether any possibility of the making of a declaration of incompatibility.[22]

The court may have regard to matters as diverse as the convenience of the defendant[23] and the suitability of the court.

B PRE ACTION PROTOCOLS

We have already seen that Pre Action Protocols supplement the Civil Procedure Rules.[24] Their purpose was well explained by Brooke LJ in *Carlson v Townsend*[25] as 'guides to good litigation and pre-litigation practice, drafted by those who know the difference between good and bad practice ...'. There is not one general protocol: a government Consultation Paper that mooted that possibility[26] came in the end to the

---

[15] For judicial review, see p 206, *ante*.

[16] Count Court Act 1984, s 40; Practice Direction 29, para 2.6. Similar powers exist to transfer cases from the county court to the High Court if the latter is the more appropriate venue.

[17] *Restrick* v *Crickmore* [1994] 2 All ER 112.   [18] As to which, see p 434, *ante*.

[19] Supreme Court Act 1981, s 51(8), (9). For costs, see p 488, *post*.

[20] See Report of the Review Body on Civil Justice, Cm 394, 1988, HMSO.   [21] CPR, 30.3(2).

[22] As to which, see p 159, *ante*.   [23] *Pepin* v *Taylor* [2002] EWCA Civ 1522.

[24] See p 433, *ante*.   [25] [2001] 3 All ER 663.

[26] *Consultation Paper: General Pre-Action Protocol*, 2002, www.dca.gov.uk/consult/preactionresp.htm

conclusion that it was better to proceed by way of Practice Direction setting out a general framework within which parties in dispute should act prior to the commencement of formal action.[27] The essential elements are that the claimant should set out details of the matter in question, copies of essential documents relied on, and a response within a stated period (a period of one month is identified as a standard). Such a pre-action letter should indicate whether Alternative Dispute Resolution (ADR)[28] is sought. It should also give details of any conditional fee agreement.[29] A response should then follow from the defendant, with an acknowledgement within twenty-one days. This will set out (if that be the case) why the claim is not accepted, again with relevant detail. Clearly the objective is to avoid litigation if that is possible, and the Protocol envisages negotiation to try to avoid litigation prior to the actual commencement of proceedings.[30]

Specific pre-action protocols have been developed for particular kinds of litigation. These include Protocols in respect of personal injury cases, clinical disputes, construction and engineering disputes, defamation cases, professional negligence cases, and judicial review. The detail of them is beyond the scope of this book,[31] but the common features of clear statements designed to identify what matters are in dispute, what matters are claimed, and the extent to which the parties disagree are all evident. What is also important is their impact on the courts. They are intended to assist the process of negotiation and settlement before costly proceedings are begun. The main sanction for their disregard lies in the area of costs.[32] The Civil Procedure Rules seek to encourage pre-action settlement, and, as noted below,[33] Part 36 of CPR sets out a procedure where one party can offer to settle by making an offer or payment. If this is not accepted, and the ultimate judgment or award of the court at trial is not as generous as that offered under the Part 36 procedure, the party who refused the Part 36 offer may be penalized in costs for the expense of a trial unnecessarily incurred. The effect of this may be to increase the chances of settlement and the avoidance of litigation, but it may, perhaps, also 'front-load' some costs, bringing forward some costs from the litigation to the pre-litigation stage.[34]

C COMMENCING A CIVIL ACTION

Prior to the introduction of the Woolf Reforms a complex range of methods of commencement of civil action existed. A county court action was, generally, commenced by summons. An action in the Queen's Bench Division was in most cases commenced by writ of summons, generally referred to as a writ. The last writ was

---

[27] Practice Direction Protocols para 4.1.
[28] See p 443, *ante.*   [29] See p 49 and p 372, *ante.*   [30] Protocol, *op cit*, para 4.7.
[31] For a convenient summary, see Loughlin and Gerlis, *Civil Procedure*, 2nd edn (2004), at pp 87–97.
[32] See, e.g., *Ford* v *GKR Construction Ltd* [2000] 1 All ER 802.   [33] See p 470, *post.*
[34] See *Andrews op cit*, para 1.17.

issued on 24 April 1999.[35] Alternative methods of commencement also existed, of which the most important was the originating summons. This was an appropriate method of proceeding in the High Court where the parties' dispute was such that it could be determined without evidence on matters of fact. Woolf recommended that one form should be used for every civil dispute.[36] This in fact has not been completely achieved, but the basis of all procedure is, now, that the *main* way of commencing a civil action, whether in the High Court or county court, is by the issue of a claim form (Part 7 procedure).[37] But not all proceedings are begun by a claim. As noted above, it was possible to commence an action by way of originating summons. This procedure was used, for example, where the matter involved the question of the construction of a statute, or document, or where an application was made to the High Court other than one in pending proceedings and where no other procedure was specified, such as for discovery of documents before commencement of an action.[38] An equivalent pro-. cedure was introduced by Part 8 of the Civil Procedure Rules (Part 8 procedure). This is a process used where a decision is sought from the court on a question unlikely to involve a substantial dispute of fact. This could, again, involve the construction of a statute, contract, deed, or will. Part 8 may also be used in other circumstances speci-fied in the CPR, such as the agreement by the court of a settlement agreed on behalf of a child.[39] The choice is not that of the parties alone: the court may overturn the decision of the claimant,[40] if the Part 7 procedure is thought more appropriate because of the way it identifies complex issues to be determined.

1 THE CONTENTS OF THE CLAIM

A Part 7 claim identifies the claimant and defendant, although, exceptionally, it may be valid despite a failure to name the defendant provided it identifies those included in the action with sufficient particularity. One example was seen in *Bloomsbury Pub-lishing Group Ltd* v *News Group Newspapers Ltd*,[41] where the question in issue centred on whether the defendants had been adequately identified. Copies of the well-known Harry Potter children's' novels had been taken from the printers, pre-publication, by unauthorized persons. The court, in upholding the validity of an order against 'the person (or persons) who have offered [the books] for sale', observed that the overriding objective of the Civil Procedure Rules[42] was inconsistent with any rule that preferred form to substance.

The claim instructs the defendant to satisfy the claim, or, alternatively, acknowledge service and state whether the claim will be contested. Without this, the claimant may obtain judgment in default without giving further notice to the defendant. The claim will contain a concise statement of its nature, a description of the remedy sought

---

[35] Andrews, *op cit*, para 10.2.   [36] Woolf Final Report, *op cit*, Ch 2, para 3, Ch 12, para 1.
[37] CPR 7.2.
[38] Under Supreme Court Act 1981, s 33(2). For the equivalent post-Woolf procedure, see p 477, *post*.
[39] CPR Practice Direction 8A, 1.4.   [40] CPR, 8.1(3).   [41] [2003] 3 All ER 736.
[42] See p 433, *ante*.

although, when it comes to trial the court may grant such remedy to which the defendant is entitled.[43] The claim will state the amount of any money claimed, or contain a statement of value, which then allows the court to allocate the case to the correct court and track.[44] Importantly, a party who has entered into a conditional fee agreement and who will wish to recover a success fee[45] or an after-the-event insurance premium, must file details of those arrangements so that the defendant is aware of the possible financial effects should he lose.

A Part 8 claim will set out the nature of the issue or question the claimant wishes the court to resolve, the remedies sought, and the basis on which such remedies might be granted. The evidence supporting the claim, in the form of written statements or affidavits (sworn statements) must accompany the claim. The defence respond in kind. There is, though, no power to strike out an application in default of such a response.[46]

2 PARTIES TO PROCEEDINGS

A single claim form may start several claims that can conveniently be disposed of in the same proceedings.[47] This may amount to several claims against a single defendant, or may involve multiple defendants. An action may be representative in nature: where more than one person has the same interest, an action may be conducted by or against the same interest as representative of any other persons who have that same interest.[48] Thus, where several persons have the same interest, whether as claimants or defendants, one or more persons may be authorized to appear on behalf of all persons so interested. However a representative action is only appropriate where all the persons to be represented have a common grievance and will all benefit from the relief claimed if claimants[49] or are jointly liable if defendants.[50] Thus where the liability of defendants is several, for example in conspiracy[51] or defamation, they cannot be represented and must be sued in their own names. Nevertheless an action for negligence has been allowed to proceed against representatives of the members of a club on the ground that they were joint occupiers of the club premises.[52] A judgment against representative defendants is binding on them all.

---

[43] CPR, 16.2(5).   [44] CPR, 16.3.   [45] See p 495, *post*.   [46] CPR, 8.1(5).

[47] CPR, 7.3.   [48] CPR, 19.6.

[49] *Smith v Cardiff Corporation* [1954] 1 QB 210, [1953] 2 All ER 1373, distinguished in *John v Rees* [1970 Ch 345, [1969] 2 All ER 274.

[50] *Mercantile Marine Service Association v Toms* [1916] 2 KB 243.

[51] *Hardie & Lane v Chilton* [1928] KB 663.

[52] *Campbell v Thompson* [1953] QB 445, [1953] 1 All ER 831; see also *Wallersteiner v Moir (No 2)* [1975] QB 373, [1975] 1 All ER 849, where a minority shareholders' action was likened to a representative action on behalf of the company and it was stated by the Court of Appeal that the shareholder, after issuing proceedings, should in effect apply to the court for an order sanctioning the proceedings, the effect of which would be to give the shareholder a right to have the company pay his costs.

3 REPRESENTATIVE AND MULTI-PARTY ACTIONS

Representative actions have been somewhat circumvented by group actions whereby several actions out of a large number of potential claims are litigated to establish liability and the principles for the award of damages. The types of situations suitable for multi-party actions were summarized in 1997[53] as follows:

(a) Major one off disaster claims (such as the ferry disaster at Zeebrugge and Kings Cross tube station fire disaster) where causation is generally common to all the cases and may not be in dispute and where the class of those affected is clearly defined from the outset. In many cases the number of individuals in the class will be high.

(b) Product liability claims (especially those involving pharmaceutical products such as Opren and benzodiazepine) where liability may be difficult to determine and common issues may be difficult to identify. Such claims are frequently complicated by a multiplicity of defendants who all manufactured similar products as well as by a multiplicity of claimants. In a case involving the drug Opren there were some 1,500 claimants against a drug company, which were litigated on the basis of a 'master' statement of claim, and with certain 'lead cases' to determine different aspects of the overall issue

(c) Multiple claims relating to industrial diseases deriving from the same cause, such as asbestosis claims, industrial deafness, and vibration white finger claims.

(d) Environmental cases deriving not only from specific incidents but also from damage occurring over a period of time, such as seepage from an industrial plant, or a nuclear installation, or prolonged use of chemicals in particular circumstances. These types of claim may involve both personal injury and property damage as well as, in some cases, loss of amenity.

(e) Claims relating to use or consumption of defective goods or services causing damage to property, or personal injury and/or financial loss. Examples are claims by tenants of a block of flats or an estate for a landlord's failure to repair; shareholders against a company or its auditors for disseminating misleading information; residents of a neighbourhood against a public authority's decision to build a road or to permit development in their area; a group of package holiday customers against a tour operator; a group of customers who have bought defective goods; or for professional negligence claims. Often, but by no means always, the claims may be individually small, but together quite substantial.

Development of group actions in the UK has centred on a variety of types of case. There are cases involving 'mass disasters' involving large numbers of individual

---

[53] *Multi-Party Actions: Consultation Paper from Civil Justice Working Group*, Lord Chancellor's Department, 1997.

claims. Instead of having to try separately a whole series of cases arising out of the same 'disaster' it was more efficient for the courts to try the common questions as one action. As a result, the evolution of multi-party actions has largely occurred because of 'an innovative approach by the courts and practitioners to procedure rules, in particular those relating to lead actions, or test cases, and the joining of parties to the action.' Their development was well summarized by Longmore LJ in *Afrika and others* v *Cape Plc; X, Y and Z and others* v *Schering Healthcare Ltd; Sayers and others* v *Merck & Smithkline Beecham plc.*[54]

Multi-party actions are a comparatively novel feature of English litigation and the courts have attempted over recent years to fashion new types of order to enable viable actions to be brought in situations where a single individual would find it prohibitively expensive to bring proceedings on his or her own. The present appeals arise in three separate multi-party actions: the first is what is known as the MMR/MR litigation in which claims are made for injuries allegedly suffered by children as a result of the administration of vaccine against measles, mumps and rubella (or just measles rubella); the second action is the oral contraception litigation in which claimants seek damages for injuries sustained by the taking of oral contraceptives; the third action is brought by workers in South Africa against the English holding company of the South Africa subsidiary, which employed them, for injuries suffered as a result of exposure to asbestos. Typically defendants are drug manufacturers, health trusts on whose behalf drugs are prescribed, or other large corporations some of whom (or whose insurers) have deep pockets. Claimants are typically individuals who could not contemplate financing litigation themselves, and obtain assistance for that purpose from the Legal Services Commission or, perhaps, under a Conditional Fee Agreements . . . These actions are difficult, as well as expensive, to run and impose great burdens on the practitioners who conduct them and the judges who try them. They can, however, be a service to many who suffer severe injuries and it is the policy of the courts to facilitate such actions in appropriate cases and adapt traditional procedures accordingly . . .

The impact of the actions of the Legal Services Commission contracting representation in this type of case has already been noted.[55]

The Woolf Report identified objectives that any new system for multi-party actions should aim to achieve. Firstly, it should provide access to justice where large numbers of people have been affected by another's conduct, but individual loss is so small that it makes an individual action economically unviable. Secondly, it should provide expeditious, effective, and proportionate methods of resolving cases, where individual damages are large enough to justify individual action but where the number of claimants and the nature of the issues involved mean that the cases cannot be managed satisfactorily in accordance with normal procedure. Thirdly, the rules should achieve a balance between the normal rights of claimants and defendants, to pursue and defend cases individually, and the interests of a group of parties to litigate the action as a whole in an effective manner. Rules of court will seek to achieve these objectives.

Part 19 of the Civil Procedure Rules makes provision for Group Litigation pursuant

---

[54] [2001] EWCA Civ 2017. [55] See p 376, *ante.*

to a Group Litigation Order. Solicitors representing claimants in such a potential case are encouraged to form a Solicitor's Group, and to appoint one of their number as the lead in seeking a Group Litigation Order.[56] An application is made to the court. When made, such an order provides for the registration of all the claims in being, and identify the court which is to manage the case under the case management approach envisaged by Woolf. This will set a timetable, give directions, and generally manage the case through its often difficult and long processes. The judge will identify the lead solicitor, provide for a cut-off date for joining the group, and identify test claims. A judgment given relating to a Group Litigation Order issue is binding on the parties to all other claims on the group register at the time the judgment or order is made, unless the court orders otherwise.[57] An individual adversely affected may, however, seek permission to appeal.

4 ISSUE AND SERVICE OF THE CLAIM

Once issued the claim is normally valid for four months beginning with the date of issue.[58] However it may on application be renewed for a further period not exceeding twelve months if the court is satisfied that it has not been possible to serve it during that period. Such an application is made without giving notice to the other party. An extension will only be granted where the application for extension has been made promptly, and only if the court has been unable to serve the claim form, or the claimant has taken all reasonable steps to serve it, but has been unable to do so.[59] There are provisions in the rules which provide for a series of dates for 'deemed service'. For example, where service is by first class post, service is deemed to have been effected on the second day[60] after the claim form was posted. These dates are applied rigidly. In *Godwin* v *Swindon BC*[61] the court recognized this as a total fiction. Service was deemed to have occurred on Monday 11 September 2000, it having been posted on Thursday 7 September 2000, and thus out-of-time, even though the letter was in fact received on Friday 8 September, which was within time. This extraordinary result can be justified only on the basis of simplicity and certainty, and raises some issues about whether the individual's right of access to the courts is being limited in an unreasonable and disproportionate way, possibly infringing the fair trial provisions of art. 6 of the European Convention.[62]

The claim is served on the defendant by the court unless the claimant informs the court that he wishes to serve the claim himself, or unless there is a rule, order, or practice direction releasing the court from this obligation.[63] The Civil Procedure Rules

---

[56] Practice Direction 19B.
[57] CPR, 19.12(1)(a).   [58] CPR, 7.5(2).   [59] CPR, 7.6(3).
[60] This includes *all* days, and not simply working days: *Anderton* v *Clwydd CC (No 2)* [1992] 1 WLR 374.
[61] [2002] 1 WLR 997.
[62] See *Andrews op cit*, at para 10.48. See also *Sealy* v *Consignia plc* [2002] 3 All ER 801; *Vinos* v *Marks and Spencer plc* [2001] 3 All ER 784; *Naglegan* v *Royal Free Hospital NHS Trust* [2002] 1 WLR 1043.
[63] CPR, 6.3, 6.13.

specify the mode of service.[64] This may be by whatever means are agreed, by personal service, by leaving the claim at an address provided by the defendant for that purpose, leaving the claim at the usual or last-known address of an individual, or through a document exchange system. However, service by post is permitted and is the normal method of service by the court.[65] Electronic service by e-mail or fax is also envisaged in some circumstances where it has been indicated in writing by an individual that this will be accepted.

The court also has the power to order service by some other means, a process known as 'substituted service'. This might take, for example, the form of service by registered or recorded delivery post to the defendant's last known address, service on the defendant's solicitor or agent, or service by advertisement in the press. It also has the power to dispense totally with service,[66] but this power should not be used to validate late service.[67]

5 PUBLIC OR PRIVATE LAW

A second preliminary factor of importance which must be considered is whether the proposed action involves questions of public law. Where in reality an action raises issues of public law, the normal procedure for determination of those questions is by an application for judicial review under Part 54 of the Civil Procedure Rules.[68] A failure to use the Part 54 procedure, with its time limits and the requirement to obtain permission, may result subsequently in an application by the defendant to have the action struck out as an abuse of process of the court. The courts have developed a much more liberal approach to these matters, as was seen earlier.[69]

6 COUNTERCLAIMS, CONTRIBUTIONS, AND INDEMNITIES

Although counterclaims, contributions, and indemnities logically are issues and procedures that arise once the proceedings have been commenced, it is convenient to deal with them here. We have noted the Part 7 and Part 8 procedures for the commencement of actions. Where a party wishes to advance a new claim within existing procedures, Part 20 applies. It permits the making of a counterclaim (i.e. a claim that the claimant, or the claimant and others, is himself liable to the defendant). Thus if the supplier of goods is suing for the unpaid price, a counterclaim might claim damages of defective goods. But a counterclaim can be against a third party, although the permission of the court will be needed to bring in as a further defendant a third party.[70] Thus a purchaser who is defending an action brought by the retailer of a motor vehicle might wish to bring into the action the manufacturer of the car if he defendant wishes to allege gross design or construction faults. A counterclaim can be

---

[64] See, generally, CPR, 6.8–6.9.   [65] Practice Direction 6, para 8.1.   [66] CPR 6.9.
[67] *Godwin* v *Swindon BC* [2001] 4 All ER 641, disapproving *Infantino* v *Maclean* [2001] 4 All ER 641.
[68] Formerly Ord 53 RSC.   [69] See Ch, 6, *ante*.   [70] CPR, 20.5.

served as of right against the claimant at the same time as the service of the defence, but otherwise permission is required.

A contribution may be sought from someone who is liable to pay part of any damages awarded. Thus a driver potentially liable in damages for injuries caused to a pedestrian may seek a contribution from another driver considered to be partly at fault and responsible for the accident giving rise to the claim. By contrast a defendant may see an indemnity, usually from an insurance company. Part 20 provides for the procedure to be followed in such cases. This involves the service of a notice setting out the nature and grounds of the claim for a contribution of indemnity. Permission of the court is not required.

D PRE-COMMENCEMENT ORDERS AND PROCEDURES

Questions concerning disclosure and inspection of documents and the inspection, preservation, and the like of property are dealt with during the course of proceedings, usually after the statements of case and defence, and these matters are dealt with below in that context.[71] However statutory provisions enable parties to obtain orders of this type prior to the commencement of proceedings. There are two distinct procedures of this type, set out below. There are also common law powers.

1 DISCLOSURE AND INSPECTION OF DOCUMENTS

A potential litigant often will not know whether a cause of action exists, or a cause of action with realistic prospects of success exists, without knowing the contents of documents held by the potential defendant. For example, the strength of a potential claim in medical negligence against a hosipital trust may turn on the contents of medical records held by the hospital. In 1991 a power was introduced by section 33(2) of the Supreme Court Act 1981, which provided that a person who appears to the High Court to be likely to be a party to subsequent proceedings in respect of a claim of personal injuries or death could apply for pre-trial discovery of documents in the possession, custody, or power of a person. The Woolf Report recommended the extension of this power to all categories of case.[72] This was achieved in the Civil Procedure Rules.

For an order to be made, the following conditions must be satisfied:[73]

(a) The person against whom the order is sought must be a likely party to the proceedings; it is not enough that that person is a potential witness.

---

[71] See p 477, post.   [72] Woolf Final Report, *op cit*, p 127.   [73] See, generally, CPR, 31.

(b) The document or documents sought would be disclosable under the standard rules of disclosure if the action was in progress[74]

(c) Pre-action disclosure is desirable in order to dispose fairly of the anticipated proceedings, or to assist the dispute to be resolved without proceedings, or to save costs.

That party may be ordered to disclose whether those documents are in his custody, possession, and power and, if so, to produce them to the applicant, unless they are protected from disclosure by the doctrine of privilege. It is immaterial that the likelihood of the claim being made is dependent upon the outcome of the disclosure; the words 'likely' in the rules is to be construed as meaning 'may or may well be made' if, on disclosure, the documents in question indicate that the applicant has a good cause of action.[75] On the other hand a 'thin and fragile case' in *Snowstar Shipping Co Ltd* v *Graig Shipping Co*[76] was the context when a too-widely drawn application was refused.

If the relevant evidence is not in the possession of a person who is likely to be a party, rule 34 applies. If the pre-conditions are satisfied the court can order disclosure of documents in the possession of a person or body who is not a party or not likely to be so. The preconditions are that the documents must be likely to support the case of the applicant or adversely affect one of the parties to it.

2 INSPECTION, ETC OF PROPERTY

Section 33(1) of the Supreme Court Act 1981 empowers the High Court, in some circumstances, to make an order providing for the inspection, photographing, preservation, custody, or detention of property (including land or chattels) which appears to the court to be property which may become the subject matter of subsequent proceedings in the court, or as to which any question may arise in such proceedings, or for the taking of samples of any such property and the carrying out of any experiment on or with any such property. This is not limited to articles in the possession of a party, a position which may be contrasted with that that exists after commencement of proceedings. The relationship between the power of inspection and that of disclosure was examined in *Huddleston* v *Control Risks Information Services Ltd.*[77] The court drew a distinction between a party wishing to examine 'the medium' (i.e. the document itself) as opposed to being concerned with 'the message' (i.e. with the contents of the document). Section 33(1), inspection, applied to the former, section 33(2), discovery, to the latter. Since in this case the claimant's concern was for the contents, which were believed to be defamatory, what was being sought was discovery, for which the relevant conditions, described above, did not apply. The power of inspection could not be used to circumvent these criteria.

---

[74] See p 477, *post*.

[75] This was the position under pre-existing law: see *Dunning* v *United Liverpool Hospital's Board of Governors* [1973] 2 All ER 454, [1973] 1 WLR 586. See, now *Swain* v *Hillman* [2001] 1 All ER 91; *Three Rivers DC and others* v *HM Treasury and Governor and & Co of the Bank of England* [2002] EWCA Civ 1182.

[76] [2003] EWHC 1367.   [77] [1987] 2 All ER 1035, [1987] 1 WLR 701.

3 THE *NORWICH PHARMACAL* PRINCIPLE

In addition to the powers described above, a court may in some circumstances order disclosure against a third party who has information. If it does so it is doing so as part of its inherent jurisdiction. Whilst this will often be during litigation, it may be appropriate to obtain such disclosure prior to action, in order to discover whether a basis of action exists, and against whom. The principle, which was first stated by the court in *Norwich Pharmacal Co* v *Commissioners of Customs and Excise* does not permit disclosure in all circumstances: it is only where the third party is in some way involved in the wrongdoing alleged that the court will order disclosure against that third party.[78] However, the rule has been extended to cases where a third party has information necessary for locating and recovering missing funds,[79] and to a case where the defendant (which ran a discussion board on an internet site), knew the identity of an individual posting allegedly defamatory material in respect of the claimant. [80]

4 SEARCH ORDERS

The High Court developed what was known as an *Anton Piller* order, named after the case in which the Court of Appeal first sanctioned the making of such an order.[81] This allowed a court to order a defendant to permit a claimant to enter the defendant's premises in order to inspect, remove, or make copies of documents belonging to the claimant or relating to the claimant's property. The procedure and power is now governed by section 7 of the Civil Procedure Act 1997. An order may be obtained without notice, but will only be made where the claimant shows that there is a grave danger of property being smuggled away or vital evidence destroyed; it is usually applicable to infringement of copyright cases, passing off, or breaches of confidence, or cases of that sort.[82]

A search order may, at first sight, appear to be in the nature of a search warrant issued to a private individual, but in fact it is not; it confers upon the claimant no right to enter the defendant's premises, but rather imposes a duty on a defendant to permit the claimant to enter his premises. Failure on the part of the defendant to comply will, however, be a contempt of court. The use of the power has become extremely popular with claimants and their advisers. By its very nature it may enable a claimant to strike gold in relation to wrongful acts, such as misuse of confidential information or infringement of copyright, which but for the order the claimant might

---

[78] *Harrington* v *North London Polytechnic* [1984] 3 All ER 666 [1984] 1 WLR 1293. In *Ricci* v *Chow* [1987] 3 All ER 534, [1987] 1 WLR the Court of Appeal decided that disclosure of the identity of the publisher and printer of an alleged defamatory article would not be ordered against the defendant, a person involved in no way in the publication, but who knew the publisher's name.

[79] *Arab Monetary Fund* v *Hashim (No 5)* [1992] 2 All ER 911; *Bankers Trust* v *Shapira* [1980] 3 All ER 353.

[80] *Totalise plc* v *Motley Fool Ltd* [2001] EWCA Civ 1897.

[81] *Anton Pillar KG* v *Manufacturing Processes Ltd* [1976] Ch 55.

[82] See, e.g., *ex parte Island Records Ltd* [1978] Ch 122, [1978] 3 All ER 824.

possibly never have been in a position to prove (defendants in these matters frequently being less than frank as to voluntary disclosure); all that the claimant risks is having to pay his opponent's costs of the application and damages if any are caused.

There are three pre-conditions for the making of a search order. First, there must be a strong prima facie case. Secondly, the damage or potential damage to the applicant must be very serious. Thirdly, there must be clear evidence that the defendants have in their possession incriminating documents or things, and there must be evidence of a real possibility that the defendant may destroy such material before any application on notice can be heard.

In order to minimize speculative and oppressive applications the courts have formulated several procedural safeguards. Thus the claimant's solicitor should attend when the order is executed; if permission to enter premises is refused no force should be used; the defendant should have the opportunity to contact his solicitor, and should be advised of his right to obtain legal advice.[83] The requirement to allow entry does not in fact operate immediately, despite the use of the word 'forthwith' in an order, but operates only after there has been a reasonable period of time to obtain legal advice. The applicant must make full disclosure to the court of all matters relevant to his application and if material facts are omitted the order will be discharged. The nature of the search order is exceptional, and creates potential for abuse. In *Universal Thermosensors Ltd* v *Hibben*[84] Sir Donald Nicholls V-C identified certain key points, that are now reflected in Practice Direction 25:

(1) An order normally contain a term that, before compliance, the defendant may obtain legal advice, if this is done forthwith. If such a term is to be of use, generally such order should be executed only on working days in office hours, when a solicitor can be expected to be available.

(2) If an order is to be executed on private premises and a woman may be at the house alone, the solicitor serving the order must be, or be accompanied by, a woman.

(3) The order should expressly provide that, unless seriously impracticable, a detailed list of the items being removed should be prepared at the time of removal, with the defendant being given the opportunity to check that list.

(4) Orders sometimes contain a restraining order restraining those on whom they are served from informing others of the existence of the order for a limited period, subject to an exception in respect of communication with a lawyer to gain legal advice. The length of time governed by the restraining order should not be an excessively long period. In the instant case, one week was too long.

(5) An order should not be executed at business premises without a responsible officer or representative being present.

(6) Consideration should be given as to how a competitor of the business subject

---

[83] Practice Direction 25.   [84] [1992] 3 All ER 257, [1992] 1 WLR 840.

to the order can be prevented from having unlimited access to the documents of that business.

(7) An order should, where possible, be served by a solicitor other than a member of the firm of solicitors acting for the claimant. That solicitor should also have experience of the search order procedure. The defendant against whom an *ex parte* order has been made may apply to have the order set aside (as can any litigant against whom an *ex parte* order is made); he may even refuse compliance with the order and apply urgently to have it set aside but he does so at his peril since if his application fails he will be in contempt of court and liable to severe penalties if he has in the interim breached the order, for example by destroying records.

It was held by the House of Lords in *Rank Film Distributors Ltd* v *Video Information Centre*[85] that defendants could resist the making of an order on the ground of privilege against self-incrimination.[86] This was a serious inroad into the scope of what were then known as *Anton Piller* orders since, in the nature of things, persons against whom such orders are made are frequently engaged in fraudulent activity. To remedy this, section 72 of the Supreme Court Act 1981 withdrew the privilege in relation to High Court proceedings for infringement of rights pertaining to any intellectual property or for passing-off, including proceedings brought to prevent any apprehended such infringement or passing-off and proceedings brought to obtain disclosure of information relating thereto. Other exceptions to the privilege also exist.

The extent to which such orders can be resisted on the grounds of the privilege against self-incrimination was considered by the House of Lords in *AT & T Istel Ltd* v *Tully*.[87] The House was of the opinion that the privilege, which itself in a civil case was an 'archaic and unjustifiable survival from the past', only protected the defendant if compliance with the order would provide evidence against him in a criminal trial. If the defendant could be protected against being exposed to the reasonable risk of the information to be disclosed being used in a criminal prosecution by other means, then the courts were entitled to rely on those other means. In that case the Crown Prosecution Service had agreed not to seek to use in criminal proceedings the documents disclosed.

5 FREEZING INJUNCTIONS

(a) Jurisdiction

It will be appreciated that the prospective claimant in an action for debt or damages faces two distinct obstacles. The first is to obtain a judgment (or settlement) in his favour; the second is to enforce that judgment. It is of little consolation to most litigants to succeed in the action and yet be unable to enforce the judgment. Regrettably, where

---

[85] [1982] AC 380, [1981] 2 All ER 76.   [86] As for this, see p 615, *post.*
[87] [1993] AC 45, [1992] 3 All ER 523.

a defendant is uninsured against his liability this is a situation which often arises. Where the defendant is simply insolvent this is a misfortune that the claimant must bear. However the courts can and will intervene to prevent a defendant from avoiding his liability to the claimant by disposing of his assets, and in particular removing them outside the jurisdiction of the English courts. The jurisdiction to issue an injunction to restrain a defendant from removing assets was developed in the *Mareva*[88] case, are now to be found in the Civil Procedure Rules, and which reflect principles developed by case law.[89] The purpose of the injunction is to prevent the defendant from evading justice by disposing of assets. The claimant must show a good arguable case in relation to the substantive claim.[90] The defendant must have assets, whether inside or outside the jurisdiction. There must also be proved a real risk that, if the court does not grant an order, the defendant will take the opportunity to dissipate those assets or otherwise put them beyond the reach of the court. The standard is a high one: it will be insufficient to show that the defendant is short of money.[91]

The words 'dealing with' encompass disposing of, selling or charging assets. Until recently it had been thought that one important restriction on the court's power to grant a freezing injunction lay in the fact that the injunction is ancillary to a cause of action; it is not a cause of action in itself. Thus, if a claimant's claim is not justiciable in the English courts he cannot obtain an injunction. For example, if the defendant is domiciled in a country to which section 25 of the Civil Jurisdiction and Judgments Act 1982 does not apply, leave to serve a writ outside the jurisdiction will be required. If this was not granted, there would be no basis for a successful application for a freezing injunction. This view was supported by the Court of Appeal in *The Veracruz I*[92] where it was stressed that the powers of the High Court to grant an injunction derived from section 37 of the Supreme Court Act 1981, and were to grant an injunction in all cases where it was just and convenient to do so. The right to obtain an interlocutory injunction was not a cause of action in itself. However, this conclusion is called into doubt by the decision of the House of Lords in *Channel Tunnel Group Ltd* v *Balfour Beatty Construction Ltd.*[93] In that case Lord Mustill indicated that the fact that proceedings in an English court could be the subject of a stay did not prevent the court from granting interlocutory relief. Lord Browne-Wilkinson doubted whether the authority on which this restriction was based remained good law.

(b) Procedure

An applicant for a freezing injunction is well advised to act quickly. To this end the customary practice is to apply without notice in the first instance, sometimes even before issuing a claim (in which case the claimant will be required to undertake to issue a claim within a specified period or 'forthwith') whereupon an order will be made to take effect until the return date on the claim which the claimant will have

[88] *Mareva Compania SA* v *International Bulkcarriers SA* [1975] 2 Lloyds Rep 509.   [89] CPR, 25.1.
[90] *Derby* v *Weldon* [1990] Ch 48.   [91] *Midas Merchant Bank plc* v *Bello* [2002] EWCA Civ 274.
[92] [1992] Lloyds Rep 353.   [93] [1993] AC 334, [1993] 1 All ER 664.

issued or undertaken to issue. The claimant must swear an affidavit in support of his application. In *Third Chandris Shipping Corporation* v *Unimarine SA*[94] the Court of Appeal stated guidelines that judges should follow on such applications:

(i)   the claimant should make full and frank disclosure of all matters in his knowledge which are material for the judge to know;

(ii)   the claimant should give particulars of this claim and the amount thereof and of the defendant's case against it;

(iii)   the claimant should give some grounds for believing that the defendant has assets within the jurisdiction;

(iv)   the claimant should give some grounds (not merely that the defendant is abroad) for believing that there is a risk of the assets of the defendant being removed before the judgment is satisfied;

(v)   the claimant should give an undertaking in damages, in a suitable case to be supported by a bond or security.

The court has power to order disclosure of documents or to administer interrogatories as to the amount, whereabouts or other details of the defendant's assets, with a view to securing the efficacy of the injunction. Copies of the injunction will generally be served upon the defendant's bank or other body having custody of his assets, so as to fix such body with knowledge of the injunction (since such body would itself be guilty of contempt of court if it assisted the defendant to act in breach of the injunction, knowing that it is probable that the asset is being disposed of in breach of the injunction). The receipt by a bank of such notice overrides its customer's instructions, e.g. to honour cheques.

(c) Principles upon which the court acts

By section 37(1) of the Supreme Court Act 1981 the High Court may grant an injunction 'in all cases in which it appears to the court to be just and convenient to do so'. However, although not subject to statutory fetters, the courts have developed principles on the basis of which to grant or refuse injunctions. The general principles affecting the discretion whether to grant or refuse an interlocutory injunction are those laid down by the House of Lords in *American Cyanamid Co* v *Ethicon Ltd*[95] and will be considered in due course. However there are additional principles which particularly apply to *Mareva* applications. As a first step the claimant must satisfy the court (i) that he has at least a good arguable case; and (ii) that the refusal of an injunction would involve a real risk that a judgment or award in the claimant's favour would remain unsatisfied because of the defendant's removal of assets from the jurisdiction or dissipation of assets within the jurisdiction. An injunction will not be granted merely for the purpose of providing a claimant with security for a claim, even where it appears likely to succeed and even where the granting of the injunction will

---

94 [1979] QB 645.   95 See p 473, *post.*

not cause hardship to the defendant. An injunction will not be granted so as to give the claimant priority over other creditors, nor to prevent the defendant from paying his debts as they fall due or carrying on his legitimate business. It is also common for the injunction to be expressed so as to exclude periodical payments of reasonable amounts to provide for the living or other expenses of the defendant, including amounts to be paid to his legal advisers to contest the litigation.

(d) Position of third parties

It has been noted that service of a copy of the injunction upon a third party, such as a bank, operates in effect to freeze the account. This has led to problems and the courts are vigilant to ensure that banks and other third parties do not suffer in consequence of the grant of a freezing injunction. Thus, a bank is entitled to a variation of the injunction to enable it to set off against any funds which it holds any right that it has in respect of facilities granted to the client, for example bank charges, interest, or the balance on another account. Similarly an injunction will not be granted, or will be discharged, where the effect would be to interfere substantially with the business of a third party. In *Polly Peck International plc v Nadir (No 2)*[96] the court indicated that a freezing injunction ought not to be granted against a bank, except where that bank was likely to act so as to avoid judgment. Where a bank or third party is compelled to enter the proceedings in order to obtain an order, or discharge of an order, the claimant will ordinarily be required to pay its cost on an indemnity basis.

[96] [1992] 4 All ER 769.

15

CIVIL TRIALS

A INTRODUCTORY MATTERS

In previous chapters we have examined the nature of the new landscape for civil litigation, introduced following the Woolf Report,[1] and the process that applies in respect of avoiding disputes and in commencing them if that is inevitable. With the Woolf Reforms in place it is neither possible, or appropriate, to discuss the civil pre-trial and trial procedure simply, for the complexity of the Civil Procedure Rules, and their applicability in many different ways to different types of action, prevents this within the scope of a general text on the English legal system. This chapter concentrates on key principles, issues, and processes.

1 THE THREE-TRACK APPROACH

The Woolf Report proposed[2] that cases be allocated to one of three tracks—the *Small Claims* track, the *Fast* Track, and the *Multi-Track,* except where the procedural judge believed that particular characteristics of the individual case made it appropriate for it to be allocated to a different track: This approach reflects the general thrust of the Woolf Report, and of the civil justice reforms, in trying to ensure that the processes undertaken, the requirements made of the parties, that the mode of trial reflect the nature and complexity of what has to be decided and that procedural requirements (and costs)[3] are proportionate to the dispute with which the law has to deal. In part the pre-existing structures did that by defining specific jurisdictions for the county court and High Court, with powers of transfer between the two. The new procedures under the Civil Procedure Rules address these issues in the context of a common form of commencement of civil process, by reference to criteria that are likely to be good indicators as to the level appropriate to the dispute.

Allocation to the appropriate track is done by a district judge or master, following the completion of an allocation questionnaire. Parties completing an allocation

---

[1] See generally Ch 13 at p 426, *ante.*

[2] See *Access to Justice: Judicial Case Management: The Fast track and Multi Track, A Working Paper,* July 1997; See also Middleton Report, op cit, at paras 2.24–2.27.

[3] It will later be noted that costs recovery in the small claims and fast tracks are limited: see p 465, *post.*

questionnaire can request a stay to pursue settlement, or the court can impose a stay of its own initiative,[4] reflecting the philosophy that where cases can be resolved without course to a hearing they should be. Decisions about the allocation of some matters are automatic: Part 8 proceedings (the old originating summons procedure)[5] go automatically to the multi-track. So too with proceedings destined for one of specialist lists—the Commercial Court and the Technology and Construction Court, which provide specialist adjudication in their respective areas.[6] The scope of each track is defined by the Rules,[7] but there is no inevitability about that allocation. However, the process in many instances will be almost automatic. The court has to consider the appropriateness of the relevant track, and, in deciding that, must have regard to the following:[8]

(a) the financial value of the claim;

(b) the nature of the remedy sought;

(c) the complexity of facts, law; or evidence;

(d) the number of parties;

(e) the value of any counterclaim, and its complexity;

(f) the likely amount of oral evidence;

(g) the importance of the claim to those who are not parties;

(h) the views expressed by the parties;

(i) the circumstances of the parties.

Special rules apply in respect of multiple claims: they will normally be allocated to the track appropriate to that of highest value, but the parties may agree otherwise.[9]

2 SMALL CLAIMS TRACK

This is the small claims jurisdiction of the county court, and designed to provide a procedurally simple and inexpensive means of disposing of small claims. It is the track to which cases with a financial value of £5,000 or less will normally be allocated, including personal injury claims within that where the element of compensation sought for pain and suffering is less than £1,000. Its jurisdiction extends to tenant claims against landlords in relation to defective premises where the cost of repairs does not exceed £1,000. It also has power to deal with cases where counterclaims exceed £5,000.

The procedure adopted in this track is simplified. No interim relief is available except interim injunctions; disclosure is limited; expert evidence may not be called without the leave of the court. When notified of a hearing date parties are required to exchange all documents on which each intends to rely. Costs are not generally recoverable.[10]

---

[4] CPR, 26.4(2).   [5] See p 450, *ante.*   [6] See p 252, *ante.*   [7] CPR, 26.6.
[8] CPR, 26.8(1).   [9] CPR, 26.7(3).   [10] See p 488, *post.*

3 FAST TRACK

This normally apply to all claims above £5,000, but less than £15,000,[11] and claims under that limit that are excluded from the small claims jurisdiction (for example personal injuries claims where in excess of £1,000 is sought for pain and suffering). The trial must be likely to last no more than one day, and will generally be in the county court. The amount of expert evidence that may be called is limited to one, or in some cases two, expert per party.[12] The rules provide for directions about the appointment of a joint expert or for experts to try and agree matters.

When a case is allocated to the fast track directions relating to disclosure, service of witness statements, expert evidence, and as to date of trial will be given. A timetable will be set with the aim of ensuring trial within thirty weeks. A directions hearing will not generally be held.[13] A pre trial process will occur to ensure that the timetable imposed and directions made have been complied with,[14] to ensure that parties give notice of any applications that are to be made to the court and to ensure that an estimate of likely costs is given to the court.

If it becomes evident that the case is no longer suitable for the fast-track procedure because it is of a greater value than anticipated or for any other reason, the court may (though does not have to) reallocate to the multi track.[15]

4 MULTI-TRACK

The multi-track will normally apply to all defended claims valued at more than the fast track limit, all clinical negligence claims, all claims in categories in respect of High Court jurisdiction, e.g. judicial review, test cases, cases where there is a right to a jury trial, or cases where fraud is alleged against a party. Effective case management, which is inherent in the civil justice reforms,[16] is obviously crucial at the highest level, dealing with a wide variety of the most difficult or complex cases, but the extent to which the court needs to get involved beyond the issuing of standard directions will depend on the nature, complexity, and value of the matter. Directions without a hearing may be given at the allocation stage. The court can require further information from the parties beyond the statement of case, and may give directions relating to disclosure, case management timetables, and expert evidence. A case management conference may be necessary in an appropriate case, and must be held if the court proposes to appoint a joint expert or assessor.[17] At such a conference the court will consider a range of matters, including whether the issues are clear, whether amendments to the claim are needed, what disclosure of documents is necessary, what expert evidence is required, what evidence should be obtained and disclosed, and how matters of law and fact should be tried.[18] Necessary directions will be given all

---

[11] CPR, 26.6(4).   [12] CPR, 26.6(5).   [13] CPR, 28.2, 28.3.   [14] CPR, 28.5.
[15] CPR, 26.10.   [16] See p 427, *ante*.   [17] Practice Direction 29, para 4.13.
[18] Practice Direction 29, para 5.3.

designed to secure the achievement of minimizing delay and cost and ensuring compliance with the overriding objective. In due course (which may in cases of real complexity be after a very long process) a pre-trial checklist is completed, and in some cases a pre-trial review occurs, shortly before trial.

The above snapshot of the different forms of procedure anticipated in the different tracks serves only to demonstrate the key principle: that processes should be appropriate and proportionate to the matter being litigated, within the overall principle of active case management. As noted earlier, effective case-management aims to achieve early settlement where that is possible, the diversion of cases to alternative methods for the resolution of disputes, the encouragement of a spirit of co-operation between the parties, the identification of the issues, and progressing a case to trial as quickly and cheaply as possible.

Only the most complex and important cases are heard by High Court judges. Other cases will be managed and heard by the appropriate level of judge and the system permits cases to move flexibly within it to ensure this. As noted earlier, most claims will fall within the jurisdiction of the County Court. The case management role is managed by procedural judges who will generally be Masters or district judges working in teams with High Court and Circuit judges. For the heavier cases, requiring full 'hands-on' judicial control, the procedural judge may be a High Court or Circuit judge. The procedural judge will:

(a) conduct the initial scrutiny of all cases to allocate them to the appropriate management track;

(b) conduct the case management conference unless it is more appropriate for the trial judge to do so;

(c) generally monitor the progress of the case and investigate if parties are failing to comply with timetables or directions; and

(d) draw the existence of Alternative Dispute Resolution (ADR) to parties' attention where this is appropriate or desirable.

The trial judge will normally conduct the pre-trial review.

The salient features of the 'fast-track' will be a set timetable of twenty–thirty weeks, with a fixed date or 'warned week' set at the outset for trial; limited discovery, short trials (not exceeding one half day); no oral evidence from experts; and limited evidence from non-experts, and a firm timetable for all actions.

B DISCONTINUANCE AND STRIKING OUT

A party may wish to discontinue an action. The parties and their solicitors, at every stage of the proceedings, will generally be attempting to resolve their dispute without the expense of a trial. In fact very few actions come to trial. If the claimant is satisfied that his cause of action was misconceived or has ceased to exist he may at any time consent to judgment being entered against him with costs. The result will be to determine finally the issues he has raised in his claim. However the claimant is better advised simply to discontinue his action since this course will not prevent him from suing again at a more convenient time. This can be done, usually as of right, under Part 38 of the Civil Procedure Rules. However, the permission of the court will be needed to discontinue a claim, or any part of a claim, in respect of which the court has issued an interim injunction, given an undertaking to the court, or has received an interim payment.[19] If the claimant serves notice of discontinuance the defendant has the power to apply, within twenty-eight days, to have that set aside.[20] The court will then have to decide whether the defendant has suffered any injustice as a result of the discontinuance. This power to strike out a notice of discontinuance will be exercised rarely, and then in cases where it effectively amounts to an abuse of process of the court. Such was the case in *Gilham v Browning*[21] where the counterclaim that was being discontinued was raised only to circumvent an evidential restriction in that case. A party who discontinues is usually going to be liable in costs.[22]

A court also has the power to strike out a statement of case.[23] This it may do if the case discloses no reasonable grounds to bring or defend the claim, that the statement of claim amounts to an abuse of the court's process, or there have been failures to comply with a rule, practice direction, or court order. This provision is in addition to the power preserved by section 49(3) of the Supreme Court Act 1981, to stay proceedings as part of its inherent jurisdiction, which may perhaps be exercised where there are concurrent proceedings in another country.[24]

The question of striking out for delay or 'want of prosecution' is a key one especially because one of the objectives of the Civil Justice reforms was to remove unnecessary delay from civil proceedings, to secure justice within a reasonable time. Questions of default and delay can under the Civil Procedure Rules be dealt with by sanctions,[25] from which the parties can seek relief, a power to be exercised in the light of the matters identified in rule 3.9 as those to which the court should have regard. The decision appears to be that which the court considers just in all the circumstances,[26] but in a way which respects the overriding objective[27] but which also respects the fair trial provisions of art. 6 of the European Convention.[28] One way of achieving compliance is through a peremptory ('or unless') order of the court; in such cases the action is liable to be dismissed on account of the conduct of the party in failing to comply with the court's peremptory order; But the power to strike out a case for delay is an extreme one. Prior to the Civil Procedure Rules, the traditional position of the courts was not generally to use the striking out power in cases of delay. In

---

[19] CPR, 38.2.   [20] CPR, 38.4.   [21] [1998] 2 All ER 68.
[22] CPR, 38.6. For costs, see p 488, *post.*   [23] CPR, 3.4.
[24] *The Abadin Daver* [1984] AC 398, [1984] 1 All ER 470.   [25] See CPR 3.3–3.9.
[26] *Purdy v Cambran* [1999] CPLR 843.   [27] See p 434, *ante.*
[28] Zuckerman, *Civil Procedure, op cit,* para 10.97.

Birkett v *James*[29] the House of Lords held that in cases in which the limitation period had not expired (so that if the action were dismissed the plaintiff could simply issue a fresh writ), the court would not, save in rare and exceptional cases, dismiss an action for want of prosecution, unless some factors other than mere delay have prejudiced the defendant. As stated above, such cases are likely to be very rare. Such a position grew increasingly under challenge,[30] In *Arbuthnot Latham Bank Ltd* v *Trafalgar Holdings Ltd*[31] Lord Woolf MR observed:

In *Birkett* v James the consequences to other litigants and to the courts of inordinate delay was not a consideration which was in issue. From now on it is going to be a consideration of increasing significance. Litigants and their legal advisers must recognise that any delay which occurs from now on will be assessed not only from the point of view of the prejudice caused to the particular litigants whose case it is, but also in relation to the effect it can have on other litigants who are wishing to have their cases heard and the prejudice which is caused to the due administration of justice. . . .

There has thus been a 'change of culture'.[32] The fact that there may be another way of penalizing the delay is not inevitably decisive against a striking out for delay, although, arguably, is a matter that the court has to bear in mind.[33]

C SETTLEMENT

The importance of settling any claim without it reaching the stage of a hearing has already been noted.[34] The overriding objective and the pre-action protocols, and indeed the case management arrangements put in place by the CPR, all lay emphasis at attempting to resolve disputes outside the courtroom. It is usually also in the interests of the parties (or their insurance companies) who are likely to be in constant communication to effect a settlement of the action. This they may do with complete candour since letters which pass between them are privileged from production and any offer or admission of liability made therein is said to be made 'without prejudice'. The nature of a settlement is that it is a contract whereby the parties abandon their previous rights and obligations in return for the creation of new rights and obligations.

The parties may effect a settlement without the consent of the court by giving

---

[29] [1978] AC 297; [1977] 2 All ER 801. For exceptions at common law, see, e.g., *Spring Grove Services Ltd* v *Deane* (19720 116 Sol Jo 844, which case was exceptional in that the defence depended essentially on the evidence of two witnesses who were no longer available to the defendant when the second action was brought; cf. *Department of Health and Social Security* v *Ereira* [1973] 3 All ER 421. The matter is one for the discretion of the court: *Arbuthnot Latham Bank Ltd* v *Trafalgar Holdings Ltd* [1998] 2 All ER 181 [1998] 1 WLR 1426.

[30] See, e.g., *Grovit* v *Doctor* [1997] 2 All ER 417.   [31] [1998] 2 All ER 181.

[32] Per Chadwick LJ in *Securum Finance Lyd* v *Ashton* [2001] Ch 291 at 310.

[33] *UCB Corporate Services Ltd (formerly UCB Bank plc)* v *Halifax SW Ltd* [2000] LS Gaz R 24.

[34] See p 436, *ante*.

notice of withdrawal before trial. Where an order of the court is required, which will usually be the case when the action is settled during the trial, the required terms will be drawn up and indorsed on counsels' briefs, or, more usually, the parties will submit to judgment on agreed terms. The settlement of any action on behalf of an infant or patient must be approved by the court.

D SUMMARY JUDGMENT

A party to proceedings may have little or no prospect of successfully succeeding in his claim or defence. Part 24 of the Civil Procedure Rules permits summary judgment to be given, either on the application of the claimant or of the defendant, or on the court's own initiative. The court has to be satisfied that there is no real prospect of success on the claim or issue, or no real prospect of successfully defending the claim or issue, and, in either situation, there is no other compelling reason why the claim or issue should be disposed of at a trial.[35]

The power is an important one in the context of active case management.[36] A judge should, in an appropriate case consider of his own initiative the merits of a case, and if it has no prospects of success it should not be allowed to continue.[37] The power should, though, be exercised with caution in the context of a litigant in person.[38]

E PART 36 PAYMENTS AND OFFERS TO SETTLE

1 THE PRINCIPLE

In any action for debt or damages the defendant may, at any time, pay money into court in satisfaction of any or all of the claims being pursued in the action by the claimant. Prior to the Civil Procedure Rules these were known as 'payments into court', but now are known as Part 36 payments. Part 36 also deals with offers to settle.[39]

Part 36 has been described as 'one of the cornerstones of procedure made by the CPR'.[40] This statement serves only to emphasize the key principle, noted throughout, that the promotion of settlement is one of the key aims, which the conduct of litigation should seek to promote, facilitate, and encourage.[41] We have already noted[42] that

---

[35] CPR, r 24.2.

[36] See *Harris* v *Bolt Burdon* (2000) *The Times* 8 December; *Swain* v *Hillman & Gay* [2001] 1 All ER 91.

[37] *Peter John O'Donnell and others* v *Charly Holdings Inc (A Company Incorporated under the Laws of Burma) and another.* Unreported 14 March 2000.

[38] *Orford* v *Rasmi Electronics* and others [2002] EWCA Civ 1672.

[39] Formerly known as *Calderbank* offers. See, now, CPR, 36.5.

[40] *Petrotrade Inc* v *Texaco Ltd* [2001] 4 All ER 853.

[41] Woolf, *Final Report*, op cit, Ch 10, para 2.   [42] See p 449, *ante*.

Part 36 provides for pre-action offers to settle. An offer to settle can be made at any time before proceedings are commenced. Whilst this might seem self-evident, its recognition in Part 36 and in the Pre-Action Protocols is significant: if a party to proceedings unreasonably fails to accept a pre-action Part 36 offer, that is a matter to which the courts can have regard on questions of cost.[43]

A party may make a Part 36 payment into court at any stage in the proceedings, or may make an offer to settle, although if the claim is one for money the appropriate action is a payment under Part 36 rather than an offer. Offers to settle are appropriate in respect of proceedings where non-pecuniary relief is being sought (for example, an injunction). This was made clear in *Amber v Stacey*[44] where the defendant had made an offer of settlement in the sum of £4,000, followed, later, by a payment into court. When the judge eventually made a judgment for a sum less than that paid into court he made a costs order in favour of the defendant as from the date of offer of settlement.[45] This was held to be wrong in principle, the court varying the costs order made.

To make a payment into court the defendant deposits his payment with the Courts Fund, and serves a written notice to this effect on the claimant and on every co-defendant. Where the claimant has included in his claim two or more claims the defendant may either: (1) make a separate payment in respect of each, or (2) make one payment in respect of any or all of those claims. The latter course is usually disadvantageous to the claimant, since he must either continue with all of his claims or accept the payment and abandon them all. Accordingly where the payment in of a lump sum in respect of several causes of action embarrasses the claimant, he may apply to the court for an order that the defendant apportion his payment in respect of the several causes of action. However, the defendant will not be required to sever his payment in unless the causes of action are substantially different. Alternatively, the issue may be in respect of a claim that involves both pecuniary and non-pecuniary elements. In such circumstances a payment into court applies only to the pecuniary element: the non pecuniary element must be dealt with by an offer to settle.

2 EFFECTS OF A PAYMENT INTO COURT OR OFFER

Unless the court considers it unjust to do so, the court will order the claimant to pay any costs incurred by the defendant after the latest date on which the payment or offer could have been accepted without needing the permission of the court.[46]

A Part 36 offer or payment will have been made by notice being given to the claimant and other parties. The notice will state various details prescribed by the Rule and Practice Directions It can be given at any time, but if that is given less than twenty-one days before trial the payment or offer can only be accepted if the parties

---

[43] *Ford v GKR Construction* [2000] 1 All ER 802. For costs generally, see p 488, *post*.
[44] [2001] 1 WLR 1225.   [45] For the costs implications, see p 472, *post*.
[46] CPR, 36.20(2).

agree liability for costs or the court gives permission.[47] Thus within twenty-one days of the trial the court permission or agreement of the parties is a key pre-requisite. The court has discretion in the matter which is not simply confined to the application of the costs sanction envisaged by Part 36. In *Barclays Bank plc Martin and Mortimer*[48] the court stressed that it had to consider whether unfairness to the defendant, potentially caused by a change in the circumstances of the litigation, would arise if the claimant was allowed, late, to accept a Part 36 payment.

If an offer is wrongly rejected the issue of costs arise. Costs will be given to a claimant who, having failed to accept a payment or offer to settle, fails to 'beat' the payment (i.e. obtain more by way of monetary sum) or fails to obtain more advantageous terms of judgment than those contained in the offer to settle.[49] Those costs will usually, but not inevitably be on the standard basis.[50] On occasion, if the conduct of the claimant was wholly unjustified, costs might be on an indemnity basis,[51] although such cases are likely to be rare. This costs sanction is not, though, automatic. Whether the defendant gets his costs after a failure by the claimant to beat the payment-in is a matter of judicial discretion.[52] That discretion should, though, normally be exercised in accordance with the general principle that, in this situation, a defendant should receive his costs. Thus in *Factortame Ltd v Secretary of State for the Environment, Transport and the Regions*[53] the defendant was entitled to his costs after the rejection of a Part 36 offer, even though the defendant had not provided accurate figures as to matters which would have affected the levels of compensation. It was, in each, case a matter for the discretion of the trial judge.

F INTERIM RELIEF

1 INTERLOCUTORY INJUNCTION

An injunction is 'a court order prohibiting a person from doing something or requiring a person to do something.'[54] The power of the High Court to issue injunctions is, of course, inherited from the jurisdiction in equity,[55] but now extends to both High Court and county court by virtue of statutory provisions. In addition to the court's inherent power to grant an injunction by way of final remedy, section 37(1) of the Supreme Court Act 1981[56] empowers the court to grant an injunction by an interlocutory order 'in all cases in which it appears to the court to be just or convenient so to

---

[47] CPR, 36.5(7).   [48] (2002) *The Times*, 19 August.   [49] CPR, 36.20.

[50] See p 493, *post*.

[51] *Excelsior Commercial & Industrial Holdings Ltd v Salisbury Hammer Asbden & Johnson* unreported 12 June 2002. For the indemnity principle, see p 493, *post*.

[52] See *Ford v GR Construction* [2000] 1 All ER 802.

[53] [2002] 3 WLR 104. For other aspects of the Factortame litigation, see p 29, *ante*.

[54] Glossary to CPR.   [55] See p 6, *ante*.   [56] See County Courts Act 1984, s 38.

do.'[57] It may be noted that the injunction need not be directed at achieving the same relief as that which is sought by way of final relief in the proceedings. Their purpose was well explained by Lord Oliver in *Attorney–General* v *Times Newspapers*[58]

interlocutory injunctions are designed to ensure the effective administration of justice, so that the rights which it is the duty of the courts to protect can fairly be determined and effectively protected and enforced by the courts.

Procedures for obtaining such interim relief are governed by the Civil Procedure Rules, Part 23 and reflect the key principles for the grant of an interim injunction explained in the leading case of *American Cyanamid Co* v *Ethicon Ltd*.[59] Lord Diplock stated that the approach referred to above was incorrect and, in a speech with which the remainder of their Lordships agreed, laid down the following principles:

(1) The claimant must first satisfy the court 'that the claim is not frivolous or vexatious; in other words that there is a serious question to be tried'.

(2) The court should then go on to consider the 'balance of convenience'.

(3) As to that, the court should first consider whether, if the claimant were to succeed at the trial in establishing his right to a permanent injunction, he would be adequately compensated by an award of damages for the loss he would have sustained by refusal of an interlocutory injunction.

(4) If damages would not provide an adequate remedy (for example because the defendant may be impecunious) the court should consider whether the defendant would be adequately compensated by the claimant's undertaking as to damages (*infra*) in the event of an interlocutory injunction being granted but a permanent injunction being refused at the trial.

(5) Where other matters are equal, it is a 'counsel of prudence to take such measures as are calculated to preserve the status quo'.

(6) Finally, 'if the extent of the uncompensatable disadvantage to each party would not differ widely, it may not be improper to take into account in tipping the balance the relative strength of each party's case as revealed by the affidavit evidence.' By this is meant that the court should consider whether the strength of the case of one party is disproportionate to the other.[60]

Lord Diplock made it clear that there may be special factors which operate in 'individual cases' in addition to the principles enumerated above. Nevertheless it is clear that the courts should not embark on anything resembling a trial of the action.

The Court of Appeal initially showed little enthusiasm for these principles. In

---

[57] The position of the Crown was discussed in *Factortame* v *Secretary of State for Transport* [1990] 2 AC 85, [1989] 2 All ER 692.

[58] [1992] 1 AC 191, see also *Attorney-General* v *Punch Ltd* [2002] UKHL 50.

[59] 1975] AC 396, [1975] 1 All ER 504.

[60] See *Series 5 Software Ltd* v *Clarke* [1996] 1 All ER 853. A court should not grant interim relief where a new cause of action is relied on: see *Khorasandjian* v *Bush* [1993] QB 727.

Cayne v *Global Natural Resources plc*[61] the Court of Appeal pointed out that where the grant or refusal of an interlocutory injunction will have the practical effect of putting an end to the action the task of the court is to do its best to avoid injustice, and to balance the risk of doing an injustice to either party. In such cases the *American Cyanamid* guidelines cannot apply and unless the claimant can show an overwhelming case he will not be granted an injunction the effect of which would be tantamount to shutting the defendant out from contesting the action. May LJ justified this departure by observing:

> I think that one must be very careful to apply the relevant passages from Lord Diplock's familiar speech in the *Cyanamid* case not as rules but only as guidelines, which is what I am certain Lord Diplock intended them to be.

Special issues arise in the context of publications, and attempts to restrain them by interim injunction. That arises because of the special emphasis that has to be given by a court to the right of freedom of expression, pursuant to section 12 of the Human Rights Act 1998.[62] In *Cream Holdings Ltd* v *Banerjee*[63] the Court of Appeal held that, in such a case, it was insufficient that there was a serious issue to be tried. Section 12(3) required the courts to look at the merits, putting the *American Cyanamid* test on one side.

Application for an interim injunction must be made to a judge. In cases of extreme urgency application can be made without leave on affidavit, in which event an injunction will be granted for a very short period until an application by summons or motion can be brought before the court.

As an alternative to injunction the court will usually accept an undertaking from the defendant (which has precisely the same effect). In addition, as a condition of being granted an interim injunction the claimant is customarily required to give his undertaking as to damages, that is an undertaking to indemnify the defendant in respect of any damages which the latter sustains by reason of the injunction in the event of the action failing. For this reason it is generally improvident for a claimant to apply for an interlocutory injunction unless he has a strong case in circumstances in which the interim will cause the defendant heavy expense, for example by delaying building works.

2 INTERIM PAYMENT OF DAMAGES

One long-standing criticism of civil procedure in the English courts was that wholly innocent parties, such as injured passengers in road accidents, had to wait for long periods for their damages while disputes between other parties, such as the car drivers

---

[61] [1984] 1 All ER at 237. The *Cyanamid* principles do not apply to mandatory injunctions: *Locabail International Finance Ltd* v *Agroexport* [1986] 1 All ER 901, [1986] 1 WLR 657. The factors to be taken into account in the context of mandatory injunctions were set out in *Zockell Group Ltd* v *Mercury Communications Ltd* [1998] FSR 354. See also *Services Ltd* v *Merent Psychometric International Ltd* [2002] FSR 8.

[62] As to which, see p 155, *ante*.   [63] [2003] EWCA Civ 103.

(in fact, their insurers) were being resolved. The Report of the Committee on Personal Injuries Litigation[64] recommended that in such litigation, courts should have power to make interim payments and effect was given to this recommendation by the Administration of Justice Act 1969. This was replaced by section 32(1) of the Supreme Court Act 1981[65] which authorizes rules of court enabling the High Court:

in such circumstances as may be prescribed to make an order requiring a party to the proceedings to make an interim payment of such amount as may be specified in the order, with provision for the payment to be made to such other party to the proceedings as may be so specified or, if the order so provides, by paying it into court.

The power is regulated in deal by rule 25 of the Civil Procedure Rules. An interim payment may only be made if the defendant admits liability in whole or in part, or judgment that damages be assessed has already been obtained, or the court is satisfied that if the matter went to trial the claimant would receive a sum of money substantial in nature. Additional criteria apply in personal injury cases.

G STATEMENTS OF CASE

1 BACKGROUND

Statements of case replace the old pre-Woolf system of pleadings. These were written statements served by each party on his opponent, containing the allegations of fact on which the party pleadings relied. They were supposed to serve various purposes. Principally they enabled each party to determine exactly which facts are alleged against him. This could save a party from preparing evidence to meet allegations which are not being made against him. Also it enabled parties to establish their 'common ground', that is to say facts on which they are in agreement, thus saving the expense of proving these matters at the trial. Secondly, the action was decided upon the pleadings. Thus the parties and their successors could, by reference to the pleadings, determine in the future exactly what the case decided, so that they may not have to, and indeed may not be allowed to, fight the same issues again. Similarly reference to the pleadings in an action might disclose the *ratio decidendi* of the case for the purpose of the doctrine of precedent, since any fact not pleaded would not usually be regarded as a fact upon which a judgment is based.

Whether pleadings always in fact fulfilled these objectives is a matter of doubt. The Woolf Report[66] considered the use of pleadings by plaintiffs often had the effect not of clarifying the issues, but of merely adding to the adversarial conflict responsible for delay. The system caused extra and unnecessary cost, complications; and delays. The

---

[64] Cmnd 3691 of 1968 (the Pearson Committee).
[66] *Op cit*, paras 153–164.

[65] See also County Court Act 1984, s 50.

Report recommended that pleadings should have to spell out the facts relied on so that the parties can identify and define the matters in issue. Their content needed to be verified by the parties, so enabling the court to determine the range and scale of material required to progress the case and the necessary extent of disclosure, witness statements, and the use of experts. In short, this important part of the process should be such as to enable the court adequately to make decisions as to how a case should be managed, in accordance with the overriding objective.[67]

The old 'pleadings' are replaced by the new 'statements of case', a term defined widely to include a claim form,[68] particulars of claim, a defence, a Part 20 claim,[69] a reply to a defence, and any other information supplied either voluntarily or under a court order.[70] They should be characterized by conciseness, and by their capacity to clarify rather an obscure the issues,[71] but obviously have to be sufficiently clear and detailed to achieve that.[72]

The new regime for civil procedure from the outset seeks to achieve these aims. The information disclosed pre-action,[73] the contexts of the claim form[74] and duties to exchange documents and information[75] all form part and parcel of this process. Specific types of claim require specific types of information to be supplied. A few examples suffice. A claim under a contract requires a copy of the documents relied on to be attached to, or served with, the particulars of claim.[76] A Fatal Accidents Act 1976 claim should identify details of the dependant. In a personal injury claim, which relies on medical evidence, a report from a medical practitioner about the injuries sustained should be attached with the particulars of claim or otherwise served. A defendant who wishes to resist the claim will need to serve details of his defence. This will address every allegation made in the particulars of claim, with admissions or non-admissions (as appropriate). These admissions will identify facts which are agreed or not in dispute, as well as the response on the issues of liability. The basis and detail of any denials or non admissions must be set out.[77] A claimant is entitled to serve a reply to a defence, but is not obliged to do so.

All statements of case must be accompanied by a statement of truth, a statement that the party putting it forward believes it to be true.[78] A party must also supply relevant details of any conditional funding agreements.[79]

Statements of case may be amended by consent or with permission.[80] Amendments made by agreement will be formally dealt with by means of a consent order, but otherwise the permission of the court will be required. The court has a discretion in the matter, to be exercised in accordance with the overriding objective.[81] Amendments

---

[67] See p 434, ante.   [68] See p 450, ante.   [69] See p 455, ante.
[70] CPR, 2.3 Part 16. The Part 16 procedure does not apply to Part 8 proceedings (as to which see p 000, ante.
[71] McPhilemy v Times Newspapers Ltd [1999] 3 All ER 775, per Lord Woolf MR.
[72] The Royal Brompton Hospital NHS Trust v Hammond and others (2001) 76 Con LR 148.
[73] See p 456, ante.   [74] See p 450, ante.   [75] See p 449, ante, and p 456, post.
[76] Practice Direction 16.   [77] CPR, 16.5.2.   [78] CPR, 22.1(6).
[79] See p 372, ante, and p 495, post.   [80] CPR, 17.1(2).   [81] See p 434, ante.

which allow the court to adjudicate on the real issues in the case will generally be allowed, provided they are not inconsistent with facts which have already been asserted as part of the statement of case.[82] But prejudice might arise if the statement of case is amended in a way that affects the track in which the case is dealt with, or the defendant's response to the case. One example is *Maguire* v *Molin*[83] where the amendment sought and refused was to increase the value claimed from £15,000 (the maximum for the fast-track) to £80,000. Amendments which introduce effectively new claims after the expiration of any limitation period will not generally be permitted, for otherwise the limitation periods themselves would be circumvented.[84] However, questions of the operation of the Human Rights Act 1998[85] arose in *Goode* v *Martin*[86] where, although the court recognized a limitation period as potentially compatible with Article 6 of the Convention, the court used section 3 of the 1998 Act to interpret the requirement so as to allow a new claim beyond the limitation period where it was based on facts which were already in issue.

H DISCLOSURE AND INSPECTION OF DOCUMENTS

1 RELEVANT PRINCIPLES AND BACKGROUND

Disclosure (formerly known as discovery) is the procedure whereby a party discloses, to the court or to any other party, the relevant documents in the action that he has, or has had, in his possession, custody, or power. Documentary evidence plays an important part in nearly all civil cases. Its purpose was explained by Sir John Donaldson as follows:[87]

In plain language litigation is conducted 'cards face up on the table'. Some people from other lands regard this as incomprehensible. 'Why' they ask 'should I be expected to provide my opponent with the means of defeating me?' The answer, of course, is that litigation is not a war or even a game. It is designed to do real justice between opposing parties and, if the court does not have all the relevant information, it cannot achieve this object.

In an action for breach of contract, for example, the transactions between the parties may be contained entirely in letters which have passed between them. One party's letters may not be intelligible unless read in conjunction with letters in the possession of the other party. Similarly, in an industrial injuries action, the employers are likely to have internal accident reports, machine maintenance records, records of complaints, and the like which it is very much in the claimant's interests to see, while, on the other hand, the claimant may have documents relating to his medical condition, or to his

---

[82] *Cobbold* v *Greenwich LBC* Unreported 24 May, 2001.　　[83] [2002] EWCA Civ 1083.
[84] CPR, 17.4(2).　　　[85] See p 153, *ante*.　　[86] [2001] EWCA Civ 1899.
[87] *Davies* v *Eli Lilly & Co* [1987] 1 All ER 801, [1987] 1 WLR 428.

earnings since the accident or state benefits which he has received, all of which may be highly relevant to the quantification of his claim by the defendants.

Accordingly a party will want to have his opponent disclose which documents the latter has, or has had, in his possession (disclosure), and, secondly, to inspect and take copies of those documents in his opponent's possession (inspection).[88] Sometimes a party may have documents which are relevant to the litigation, and therefore disclosable, but which he wishes to safeguard against circulation either to third parties, or occasionally to the claimant himself for extraneous reasons. As to this point, the traditional position has been that on disclosure each party impliedly undertakes not to use the documents which are disclosed for any ulterior or improper purpose. The use of such documents in breach of that implied undertaking has been held to a contempt of court. Thus in *Home Office v Harman*[89] a solicitor who passed documents to a journalist to assist in the preparation of an article was held to be in contempt, even though the documents had been read in open court. Nor can a party generally rely upon such documents in other proceedings. Thus where a claimant in proceedings against his employers obtained discovery of a memorandum about him which contained an alleged libel, the court held that he could not found a libel action on that publication since that would be an abuse of the process of the court.[90] In *Crest Homes plc v Marks*[91] the court indicated that it would release a party from that undertaking if the applicant could demonstrate 'cogent and persuasive reasons' for such a release, and that the release did not cause injustice. If there is a real risk of the claimant using documents for an improper collateral purpose, the court could restrict inspection, for example to a party's legal advisers.

The position is now governed by the Civil Procedure Rules.[92] A party to whom a document is disclosed may use it only for the purposes of the proceedings and not for any other purpose, except where the document has been read to or by the court, or referred to at a public hearing, the court gives permission, or those who disclosed and received agree. Despite these exceptions the court nonetheless has discretion to restrict or prohibit the use of a document. The presumption will be that a document produced in open court will be disclosable.[93] If as in the *Lilly Icos* case the document was of only peripheral importance in the hearing and the contained highly sensitive commercial information there might be a case for restricting disclosure.

---

[88] 'Inspection' is not limited to ocular inspection but includes examination by any of the senses. Thus, a tape-recording is a document, inspection of which would be effected by playing the same upon a tape-recorder to the inspecting party: *Grant v Southwestern and County Properties Ltd* [1975] Ch 185, [1974] 2 All ER 465; similar considerations apply to untransmitted television film: *Senior v Holdsworth, ex parte Independent Television News Ltd* [1976] QB 23, [1975] 2 All ER 1009.

[89] [1983] 1 AC 280, [1982] 1 All ER 532. This finding was held to be in breach of the European Convention of Human Rights, Article 10 by the Court of Human Rights in *Harman v United Kingdom*, in that it infringed the right of freedom of expression and the right to impart and receive information under Article 10.

[90] *Riddick v Thames Board Mills Ltd* [1977] QB 881, [1977] 3 All ER 677.

[91] [1987] AC 829, [1987] 2 All ER 1074.   [92] CPR, 31.22.

[93] *Lilly Icos Ltd v Pfizer Ltd* [2002] EWCA Civ 2.

The pre-existing system of discovery was roundly condemned by the Woolf Report. One overseas judge observed:

If there was a hell to which disputatious, uncivil, vituperative lawyers go, let it be one in which the damned are eternally locked in discovery disputes with other lawyers of equally repugnant attributes.

Whatever the element of overstatement, reform was another key objective of the civil justice reforms. The pre-existing law allowed discovery not only of relevant documents, but of others which might lead to the production of relevant documents.[94] It should be borne in mind that the greater the level of disclosure the greater burden is imposed on parties to identify and produce information. This can potentially add to the length of time litigation takes, and its cost. It is for this reason that the Woolf Report recommended that disclosure should be controlled by the court as part of its case-management function, it being regulated with regard to the size of the case, the cost of disclosure, and the likely cost. For the future it is envisaged that disclosure on the scale that it used to happen will rarely take place.

The rules[95] now define 'standard disclosure' as involving documents on which the party will rely, documents which adversely affect his own case, which adversely affect another parties' case, or which support that case. In addition documents which are required to be disclosed by any Practice Direction must be disclosed. An on-going duty to disclose exists. The rules governing disclosure apply to fast-track and multi-track litigation, but not claims in the small claims track.

Obligations to disclose can arise pre-action. The Court of Appeal in *Black* v *Sumitomo*[96] considered pre-action disclosure to be important, particularly where the claim had not been fully established enabling a potential claimant to decide whether a claim might succeed and on what basis. This was particularly the case in personal injury and medical negligence cases. It was also a necessary pre-requite in some case in order to obtain funding, to establish what the likelihood of success is in a case potentially the subject of a conditional fee agreement. On the other hand the court must discourage 'fishing expeditions'. Pre trial protocols govern what should, ideally, be disclosed voluntary. But the CPR make provision for an order requiring pre-trial disclosure.[97] This was discussed in chapter 14.[98]

---

[94] See *Compagnie Financire* v *Peruvian Guano Co* (1882) 11 QBD 55. Interesting parallels exist with the development of disclosure in criminal cases.

[95] CPR, 31.6.

[96] [2002] 1 WLR 1562. The court reviewed earlier caselaw including *Dunning* v *United Liverpool Hospitals Board of Governors* [1973] 1 WLR 586; *Shaw* v *Vauxhall Motors Ltd* [1974] 2 All ER 1185; *Burns* v *Shuttlehurst* [1999] 1 WLR 1449.

[97] CPR, 31.16.   [98] See p 456, *ante*.

2 DISCLOSURE AND INSPECTION AGAINST OTHER PERSONS

We have already noted the procedure whereby orders for disclosure and inspection of documents against proposed parties may be made before the commencement of proceedings. Under section 34 of the Supreme Court Act 1981 there is, in addition, power, in actions for damages for death or personal injuries, to order a person who is not a party to the proceedings and who appears to be likely to have or have had in his possession, custody, or power any documents which are relevant to an issue arising out of the action to disclose whether these documents are in his possession, custody, or power and to produce those which he has to the applicant. This power is exercisable only after the commencement of proceedings, the application being by summons (which must be served on the person against whom the order is sought and on all parties to the action) supported by affidavit and now applies to all proceedings.

3 ACTION FOR DISCLOSURE

Save for the limited exception, in personal injuries actions, discussed above, there is, as a rule, no procedure for obtaining discovery against persons who are not parties to an action. They can, of course, be compelled to attend the trial and to produce, at that stage, documents in their possession (by means of court order) but there is a rule, sometimes known as the 'mere witness' rule, whereby discovery cannot be obtained against a person against whom no relief is sought but who might be a witness in an action. It follows that if a party wishes to inspect documents in the possession of a person against whom he has no cause of action, he cannot sue that person simply for the purpose of obtaining evidence, by way of disclosure of documents, for use against the party against whom there is a cause of action. This rule appears to have little in the way of logic to commend it but it is, nevertheless, too firmly entrenched to be altered save by way of legislation.

However, it has already been seen that a limited exception to the rule was formulated by the House of Lords in the case of *Norwich Pharmacal Co* v *Customs and Excise Commissioners.*[99] The facts of the case were unusual. The appellants, who were the owners of a patent covering a chemical compound, learned from information published by the respondents that a number of consignments of the compound had been imported between 1960 and 1970, none of which had been licensed by the appellants. The appellants therefore knew that others were infringing their patent but did not know their identity. The respondents refused to disclose the identity of the importers whereupon the appellants brought an action against the respondents seeking an order for discovery of documents relating to the importations. The House of Lords granted such an order; the reasoning behind the decision was expressed by Lord Reid, as follows:

[99] 1974] AC 133, [1973] 2 All ER 943, applied in *Loose* v *Williamson* [1978] 3 All ER 89, [1978] 1 WLR 639, [1974] AC, at 175, [1973] 2 All ER, at 948; see also, on the *Norwich Pharmacal* principle, *Arab Monetary Fund* v *Hashim (No 5)* [1992] 2 All ER 911.

if through no fault of his own a person gets mixed up in the tortious acts of others so as to facilitate their wrong-doing he may incur no personal liability but he comes under a duty to assist the person who has been wronged by giving him full information and disclosing the identity of the wrongdoers.

In *Ashworth Hospital Authority* v *MGN Ltd*[100] Lord Woolf stressed that the court should start from the proposition that a non-party should not be subjected to the civil process and made to disclose information. He should at least be 'involved', however innocently, in another person's wrongdoing.

I DIRECTIONS

It will be evident from the above that the case-management role of the court throughout the case will give the courts the opportunity to make directions relating to the whole management, conduct, and progress of the case. Amongst those, already identified are matters of disclosure, evidence, expert evidence, place, time, and mode of trial. Unlike the pre-Woolf system there is not simply one time when these matters will be considered. They are on-going issues. The involvement of the court will in part depend on the nature and complexity of the matters in issue, and the track the case is on.

J TRIAL

1 PREPARATION OF EVIDENCE

At an early stage of the action the papers will usually have been sent to counsel or solicitor (as appropriate).[101] Counsel will normally settle the statement of case but, in any event, will advise appropriately through the progress of the case through its various stages. Cases are won and lost in their preparation. Counsel will therefore wish to consider which applications should be made, whether the statement of case requires amendment, and similar matters. The first consideration upon preparing an action for trial is on whom the burden of proof rests. The general rule is that where any allegation of fact is in issue the party who alleges that fact must prove it. The statement of case will disclose where the general burden lies. If an allegation in the statement of case is admitted (expressly or impliedly) it need not be proved at all. If it is denied then the burden rests on the claimant. If it the defendant denies liability because of other facts, the burden of proving them lies on him. Throughout the

---

[100] [2002] 1 WLR 2033.   [101] For rights of audience, see p 350, *ante.*

standard of proof is the balance of probabilities (the 51 per cent rule), although it must be noted that this is a variable and not absolute standard.[102] However, the burden may shift during the action by the effect of presumptions. If a presumption is raised in favour of a party, the effect is to shift the burden of disproving the matter presumed to his opponent.

Having decided which matters he must prove, counsel will decide how he proposes to prove them. The two principal methods of proof are by witnesses and by documents.

(a) Witnesses

Counsel or solicitor will name the witnesses whom he requires. There is no property in a witness, so that there is no objection to interviewing or calling any witness even if he has been served with a witness summons by an opponent.[103] It is, of course, wrong to call a witness whose testimony is unlikely to support one's case, since a party cannot cross-examine a witness he has called, unless the court gives leave to treat the witness as hostile. Also, to intimidate or otherwise tamper with a witness amounts to a contempt of court.[104] Usually a witness will be prepared to attend voluntarily if he is tendered a reasonable fee. Where he will not, his attendance may be compelled by order. A witness who fails to comply may be committed for contempt of court.

(b) Evidence

Facts to be proved in a civil case are proved by the testimony of a witness in person and in open court. To that basic rule there are exceptions. Facts can be proved by formal admissions. A party need produce no proof of any matter admitted in his favour. Admissions may also be made in answer to interrogatories. A useful means of compelling an opponent to admit a fact is to serve him with a 'notice to admit facts', calling upon him to admit the facts listed in the notice. If he will not admit these facts and they are proved at the trial, unless the court otherwise orders, he will bear the costs of proof. This is, of course, a powerful weapon but it must not be abused. A party should not be asked to admit the facts in issue or any inference of fact, such as negligence. He should only, in practice, be asked to admit facts of a formal nature or facts which can easily be proved against him if he does not admit them. If admissions are made which clearly establish one party's liability the other party may, without waiting for a trial, apply for judgment based on those admissions.[105] Similar to such a notice is a 'notice to admit documents', calling upon the party served to admit the authenticity of the documents listed, though not the truth of their contents. The effect of failure to admit is, again, that the party who was served with the notice has to pay

---

[102] See p 000, ante.

[103] 3 See observations of Lord Denning MR in *Fullam* v *Newcastle Chronicle and Journal Ltd* [1977] 3 All ER 32, [1977] 1 WLR 651; see also *Harmony Shipping Co SA* v *Davis* [1979] 3 All ER 177, [1979] 1 WLR 1380.

[104] *Chapman* v *Honig* [1963] 2 QB 502, [1963] 2 All ER 513.

[105] For summary judgment see p 470, ante.

the costs of proving the documents at the trial, unless the court otherwise orders, which may involve an extra witness, such as a handwriting expert.

Wide powers are conferred on the judge by the Civil Procedure Rules as to the means of proof. Thus he may order evidence to be given at the trial by affidavit or in any other specified manner. For example, he may order the date on which an important event occurred to be proved by production of a newspaper containing a report of the event. In addition he may restrict the number of medical or other expert witnesses who may be called at the trial. Finally, it should be noted that a court may direct that a written statement be treated as the evidence in chief of the witness.

(c) Documents

Documentary evidence, especially in contract cases, frequently forms the basis of a party's case. Where he is in possession of the documents himself, he is in no difficulty. However the documents which are needed by a party may be in the possession of an opponent or of a third party. That problem may be overcome through the revised rules relating to disclosure, which should identify relevant documents in the hands of opponents or third parties.[106] If they are in the possession of a third party, the proper course is to serve him with an order requiring the witness to attend and produce the relevant documents.

(d) Notices under the Civil Evidence Act 1995

Where it is desired to put in evidence at the trial statements admissible under the provisions of the Civil Evidence Act 1995, the party desiring to do so must within twenty-one days after setting down serve on every other party a notice containing prescribed particulars of (if the statement is oral) the time, place, and circumstances in which the statement was made, the persons by whom and to whom it was made and the substance of the statement or, if material, the words used. In the case of written statements admissible by virtue of the Act, the notice must annex a copy of the document in question as well as contain certain prescribed particulars relating to the circumstances of its compilation. If the party giving the notice alleges that the maker cannot be called as a witness at the trial because he is dead, beyond the seas, unfit by reason of his bodily or mental condition to attend as a witness, cannot be found, or cannot reasonably be expected to have any recollection of matters relevant to the accuracy of his statement, the notice must contain a statement to this effect otherwise a party served with a notice may within twenty-one days serve a counter-notice requiring the maker of any statement to be called as a witness by the party who served the original notice, in which event if that person is not called as a witness, his statement is not admissible under the 1995 Act.

When the evidence for each side has been prepared the parties must await trial. Neither party need serve any notice of the date of trial on his opponent. Accordingly (unless the case has been given a fixed date) all parties must watch carefully the lists.

---

[106] See p 472, *ante*.

The Week's List is published on Mondays and contains the cases expected to be tried in that week. Each day there is published a Daily Cause List containing the actions to be heard that day and a Warned List consisting of actions likely to be tried in the near future. Thus neither side has any excuse if his case is not ready when the action comes on for trial. If one party fails to appeal, the trial may proceed in his absence. However, if application is made within seven days, a judgment obtained in the absence of a party may be set aside, generally on condition that he pay the costs thrown away. Although adjournment is possible, last minute postponements are looked upon with disfavour by the judge in charge of the list and may result in the offending firm of solicitors being penalized personally with the extra costs incurred.

2 PROCEDURE AT THE TRIAL

Jury trials are now rare in civil proceedings,[107] so a trial is almost certainly by judge and judge alone. It must also be borne in mind that procedures in respect of the small claims track will be very informal and very different from procedures in a complex multi-track case. The following gives some indication of the procedure followed in a High Court or contested county court action in the multi-track, or, to some extent, fast-track.

(a) Right to begin

If damages are unliquidated or the burden of proving any single issue on the pleadings rests on the claimant, then the claimant begins. Thus the only case where the defendant has the right to begin is a case in which the claimant claims only liquidated damages and the defendant has not traversed any allegation in the statement of claim. The right to begin and the right to the last word are advantages which are probably exaggerated, especially in the absence of a jury.

(b) Case for the claimant

Counsel for the claimant opens his case stating the facts on which the claimant relies The court will already have a large amount of information in the case 'bundle' containing skeleton arguments, statement of case, relevant documents, and other appropriate documents. It will be assumed that these have been read and thus the style and content of the advocacy will be very different from that in jury trial. The advocate should not rely upon any fact which he is not permitted to prove, which means, of course, that he cannot allege any fact not pleaded, although he may, even at this late stage, be allowed to amend the statement of case. The claimant's witnesses are then called and sworn. They are examined and may be cross-examined and re-examined. In the course of cross-examining the claimant's witnesses, counsel for the defendant must 'put his case' which includes making clear which part of the claimant's case is challenged and what positive allegations are being made in relation to the

---

[107] See p 338, *ante*.

evidence of the claimant's witnesses, so that they may have the opportunity of dealing with those allegations. This is important to the efficient conduct of trials because if counsel for the claimant calls a witness whose evidence is not challenged on a particular point, then he is entitled to assume that the point is not in issue and he will not call any other witnesses to deal with it. If the defence lead evidence as to matters which should have been put but were not put to the claimant's witnesses, judicial rebuke is virtually inevitable and, unless counsel was responsible for the oversight (in which event he will, in the interests of his client, immediately accept responsibility for it), the judge is likely to infer, and find, that the evidence in question is a recent invention. His documents, including answers to interrogatories which he wishes to put in, are then put in evidence. Finally counsel argues the propositions of law upon which he relies, citing to the court all relevant authorities on the point whether they support his own case or that of his opponent. If they tend to support his opponent's case, he must attempt to distinguish them from the present case on their facts. He cannot, however, ignore them, since this would infringe his duty to the court.

(c) Case for the defence

At the close of the claimant's case the defendant has the following courses open to him:

(1) he may submit 'no case to answer'. This is a submission that the claimant has failed to make out a prima facie case, or to establish the elements of a recognized cause of action. The submission is rare in a civil action since the objection will usually have been taken long before the trial. If it is made, the judge, before deciding, may require the defendant to 'stand on his submission', which means that he can call no evidence if his submission fails. Counsel for the claimant has a right to reply to the submission. If it succeeds, judgment is entered for the defendant. If it fails and the defendant has been put to his election, judgment is entered for the claimant.

(2) He may state that he intends to call no evidence, oral or documentary. Counsel for the claimant will then address the court followed by defence counsel who thus obtains the right to the last word.

(3) In most cases the defence will be a mixture of law and fact and the defendant will want to put in some evidence. In this event defence counsel may make an opening speech outlining his defence. His witnesses give their evidence in the same way as those of the claimant followed by the defendant's documents and legal submissions. The claimant may be permitted to adduce evidence in rebuttal where the defence case has raised matters which could not reasonably have been foreseen. Defence counsel then makes a closing speech, following which counsel for the claimant has a right to make a closing speech in reply. Where a party in his closing speech raises any fresh point of law, the other party is entitled to reply but only in relation to that point.

(d) Verdict and judgment

At the conclusion of all the evidence and the legal argument for both sides the judge sums up (in the rare case where there is a jury) or gives judgment, or reserves his judgment if there is not. He must direct the jury (if there is one) as to the issues in the case, stating on whom the burden of proving the individual issues rests, and outlining the evidence in support of those issues. He must also direct upon the standard of proof required from the party on whom the burden rests. He will direct on the law applicable to the issues of fact, for example, whether the words are capable of bearing the defamatory meaning alleged or whether the defendant owes the claimant a duty of care in negligence. He must leave the actual issues of fact and the assessment of damages to the jury, but, now, following a series of cases involving disproportionate damages awards, may give them guidance as to the appropriate level of damages that may be awarded. A modern tendency is for the judge to pose a series of questions to the jury calling for their decision on the facts and, if they find for the claimant on any issue, the amount of damages. Where the claimant has sought an equitable remedy as an alternative or in addition to damages, the grant of this remedy is in the discretion of the judge.

It remains for judgment to be entered in accordance with the verdict. A judgment crystallizes the rights of the parties in respect of the subject matter of the action. Thus they are estopped from litigating the same issues of fact again. Even if fresh damage becomes apparent the claimant cannot sue because his right is extinguished. Counsel for the unsuccessful party may apply for a stay of execution pending an appeal. This may be granted on terms. After judgment on the issues of liability and damages the judge may make orders as to interest and costs.

Historically damages have always been expressed in English currency. This has caused hardship in cases in which sterling has been devalued, so a party who bargained for payment in foreign currency has been awarded damages in sterling, the rate of exchange being calculated at the date upon which his entitlement to payment arose (the 'breach-date' rule). Accordingly in 1975 the House of Lords changed this rule. Since 1975 the English courts have shown an increasing willingness to give judgment in foreign currency. At first limited to contract actions where the sum was due under the contract in a foreign currency and the proper law of the contract was the law of that country in whose currency the obligation was expressed, the power is now exercised in cases where the claimant's loss would be most truly expressed in a foreign currency, in which case judgment will be given in that currency, and in tort actions, where damages may be awarded in a currency which the claimant has used to make good the loss which he has suffered. Nevertheless a judgment can only be enforced in terms of sterling. Accordingly if enforcement becomes necessary the judgment will be converted into its sterling equivalent at the date when leave is given to enforce the judgment.

Finally, there is, save in personal injuries actions, no procedure for successive awards of damages in the same action. Damages have to be assessed once and for all at the trial. This may cause hardship to either side, since subsequent events may demonstrate the hypotheses upon which the award of damages were based to be false with the result that the damages were too high or too low. This is particularly so in personal injury actions where, for example, an award of damages for loss of future earnings capacity must necessarily be highly speculative. To remedy this situation section 32A of the Supreme Court Act contains provision for 'provisional damages' in personal injury actions.

Section 35A of the Supreme Court Act 1981 empowers the court to award simple (but not compound) interest on debts or damages 'at such rate as the court thinks fit or as rules of court may provide'. In commercial cases the usual rate is 1 per cent above United Kingdom clearing banks' base rates over the relevant period. Different rules exist in respect of personal injury actions, where on most awards, the court must grant interest:

(1) the claimant is awarded interest on general damages for pain, suffering and loss of amenities from the date of service of the writ to the date of trial at a conventional rate of 2 per cent per annum;

(2) the claimant is awarded interest on special damages from the date of the accident to the date of trial at half the rates which during that period were payable on money in court placed on special account;

(3) no interest is awarded on future loss of earnings or other prospective financial losses.

16

COSTS

A THE POWER TO AWARD COSTS

In his Report, Lord Woolf identified the question of costs as one of the key problems that the civil justice system had to address.[1] Much of his Report was addressing how litigation could be made more efficient, less cumbersome, and thus cheaper and more affordable. At the same time the move to Conditional Fee Agreements[2] has created new funding opportunities in respect of many types of litigation, but raises important issues about costs.[3]

The basic rule is that costs are within the discretion of the court. In most cases the judge will order one side to pay all or a proportion of the costs of his opponent. At common law a successful litigant had a right to costs but this right has been virtually removed by legislation so that at the present day the award of costs is discretionary. A court has discretion as to whether costs are payable by one party, the amount to be paid, and when they are to be paid.[4] It is not, of course, an absolute discretion and it is a wrong exercise of the discretion to deprive a party of his costs if he has been completely successful and guilty of no misconduct.[5] Unless there are special factors present, a successful party may expect his costs from an unsuccessful opponent. This is the basic rule that costs normally follow the event, on an indemnity basis.[6] Further, there are some circumstances where a party is generally entitled to costs unless the court orders otherwise. A defendant is prima facie entitled to costs if the claim is struck out for non payment of fees, or the claim is discontinued.[7] A claimant is likewise entitles to costs where he accepts a Part 36 offer or payment.[8]

1 THE DISCRETION

When deciding how this discretion is to be used, the court will have regard to the conduct of the parties. It will need to have regard to the overriding objective[9] and the extent, for example, to which Pre Action Protocols have been followed, with appropri-

---

[1] See Interim Report, *op cit* Ch 25, para 1.   [2] See p 372, *ante*.   [3] See p 495, *post*.
[4] CPR, 44.3(1).
[5] *Donald Campbell & Co Ltd v Pollack* [1927] AC 732, per Viscount Cave at 811–12.
[6] CPR, 44.3(2); see p 493, *post*.   [7] CPR, r 38.6.   [8] CPR, 36.13(1).
[9] See p 434, *ante*.

ate disclosure, or the extent to which the parties have engaged in ADR.[10] CPR, 44.3 provides that the relevant conduct includes:

(a) pre-action conduct;[11]

(b) whether it was reasonable for a party to consider, raise, or contest a particular allegation or issue;

(c) the manner in which a case has been pursued or defended, or how a particular issue or issues has been produced;

(d) whether a claimant has exaggerated his claim.[12]

The issues will turn on the particular facts of the case. But, in the context of ADR,[13] the court in *Halsey* v *Milton Keynes General NHS Trust, Steel* v *Joy*[14] observed:

In deciding whether to deprive a successful party of some or all of his costs on the grounds that he has refused to agree to ADR, it must be borne in mind that such an order is an exception to the general rule that costs should follow the event. In our view the burden is on the successful party to show why there should be a departure from that general rule. The fundamental principle is that such departure is not justified unless it is shown (the burden being on the successful party) that the successful party acted unreasonably in refusing to agree to ADR.

The rules envisage that costs may be awarded, or not awarded, in respect of specific issues within the litigation. Lord Woolf in *AEI Rediffusion Music Ltd* v *Phonographic Performance Ltd*[15] observed:

It is now clear that too robust an application of the 'follow the event' principle encourages litigants to increase the costs of litigation, since it discourages from being selective as to the points they take. If you recover all your costs as long as you win, you are encouraged to leave no stone unturned in your effort to do so.

CPR, 44.3(6) provides that a party may be ordered to pay a proportion of other party's costs, a stated amount, costs from or to a certain date, costs incurred before the proceedings were begun, costs in respect of particular steps, costs relating to distinct parts of the proceedings, or interest on costs. Where the court considers that only parts of the costs should be recoverable, it is good practice where possible to express that in percentage terms (e.g. 60 per cent of the total) rather than on specific issues, in order to avoid difficulties in calculation and apportionment.[16] However, such an order

---

[10] See p 445, *ante*.

[11] For an example see *Dunnett* v *Railtrack* [2002] EWCA Civ 302, *Reed Executive plc* v *Business Information Ltd* [2004] 4 All ER 943, where it could not be established without reference in inadmissible evidence whether ADR was justified (though the court concluded on other evidence that it was not).

[12] See, e.g., *Booth* v *Brittania Hotels Ltd* [2002] EWCA 579.   [13] As to which, see p 443, *ante*.

[14] [2004] 4 All ER 920.   [15] [1999] 1 WLR 1507.

[16] *Verrechia* v *Commissioner of Police for the Metropolis* [2002] EWCA Civ 605; see also *AEI Rediffusion* v *Phonographic Performance Ltd* [1999] 2 All ER 299; *Firle Investments Ltd* v *Datapoint International Ltd* [2001] EWCA Civ 1106; *Mars UK Ltd* v *Technology Ltd (No 2)* [1999] TLR 501.

should be made where possible by the trial judge who has knowledge of the conduct of the case.[17]

There has been a considerable volume of litigation as to what is 'the event' in an action.[18] In a simple action involving one claimant, one defendant, and a single issue, no difficulty arises; the event is judgment on that issue. However, where there are several parties or several issues the situation is more complex, and the court will have deal with costs where appropriate on an issue basis. In the context of multi party actions special provisions apply.[19]

2 ORDERS AGAINST NON PARTIES

As already noted costs are completely within the discretion of the court. In *Aiden Shipping Co Ltd* v *Interbulk Ltd*[20] the House of Lords stressed that section 51 of the Supreme Court Act 1981 permitted the ordering of costs against non-parties, and that:

Courts of first instance are . . . well capable of exercising their discretion under the statute in accordance with reason and justice.

It should, however, be noted that this was a case where a close relationship existed between the third party (who was in fact a party to a related action) and the parties to the cause in respect of which the costs were awarded.[21] Guidance as to how the power to award costs in such cases should be used was given by the Court of Appeal in *Symphony Group plc* v *Hodgson*:[22] it was established that it was exceptional for a non-party to be ordered to pay such costs, particularly if the party had a cause of action against the non-party. Fair procedures should be followed to ensure that the non-party had the opportunity to make representations, and to ensure that cross-examination of a non-party is not simply being directed to the issue as to whether the court should make a costs order against that non-party. These procedures are now contained in CPR r 48.2.

A good example of the limits of the power was seen in *Hamilton* v *Al Fayed*[23] where the well-known defendant, who had proved successful in a libel action, was unable to recover his costs from the claimant, who was declared bankrupt. The defendant then sought a section 51 order against the group of individuals who had funded the claimant in the litigation. In rejecting the application for a section 51 costs order, the court confirmed that a general principle protects a person who funds litigation from being made the subject of a section 51 order, a principle which extends to any person whose reasons for funding are either familial, out of natural affection, but also where the contribution was motivated to see that a genuine dispute was not lost by default.

---

[17] *Aaron* v *Shelton* [2004] 3 All ER 561.   [18] *Reid, Hewitt & Co* v *Joseph* [1918] AC 717.
[19] See p 497, *post*.   [20] [1986] AC 965, [1986] 2 All ER 409.
[21] See [1986] 2 All ER 416; *Steele, Ford and Newton* v *Crown Prosecution Service* [1994] 1 AC 22, [1993] 2 All ER 769; *Shah* v *Karanjia* [1993] 4 All ER 792.
[22] [1994] QB 179, [1993] 4 All ER 143.   [23] [2002] EWCA Civ 665.

The right of the defendant to recover his costs had to give way to the public interest in access to the courts.

3 COSTS ORDER FOR MISCONDUCT AND WASTED COSTS ORDERS

The court may disallow all or any part of costs being claimed, or order a party of his legal representative personally to pay the costs incurred by the other party, if the party or the legal representative is at fault because of failure to comply with a rule, practice direction, or court order, or if he has behaved unreasonably or improperly before or during the proceedings.[24] This can include an attempt to inhibit the court from furthering the overriding objective,[25] and is additional to the power to make a wasted costs direction, discussed below.

Section 51(6) of the Supreme Court Act 1981 (as substituted) permits the court to make a 'wasted costs' order against a legal or other representative. It permits the court to disallow costs incurred, or to make an order requiring personal payment, as a result of improper, unreasonable, or negligent acts or omissions by such representatives, or in respect of costs which, in the light of such an act or omission, it would be unreasonable to expect the party on whose behalf they were incurred to pay.

This provision was the subject of judicial scrutiny and comment in *Re a Barrister (Wasted Costs Order) (No 1 of 1991)*.[26] The court identified a three-stage test, now reflected in a Practice Direction.[27]

(a) Had the legal representative of whom complaint was made acted improperly, unreasonably, or negligently?

(b) If so, did such conduct cause the applicant to incur unnecessary costs?

(c) If so, was it in all the circumstances just to order the legal representative to compensate the applicant for the whole or part of the relevant costs?

However, in *Ridehalgh v Horsefield*[28] the court stressed that care should be taken not to create a new and costly form of satellite litigation, a point reinforced by the House of Lords in *Metcalfe v Wetherill*,[29] where it was stressed that the discretion to make a wasted costs order should be reserved for those cases where the unjustifiable conduct can be demonstrated without recourse to disproportionate procedures. It is 'the last resort'.

'Improper conduct' is conduct which would justify disciplinary action; 'unreasonable', means not permitting of reasonable explanation. Sometimes, of course, the legal representative may not be in a position to give a full explanation as to why a particular course of action was undertaken, or not undertaken, because of the doctrine of legal professional privilege. The court should in these circumstances be slow to invoke the wasted costs jurisdiction.[30]

---

[24] CPR, 44.14.   [25] See p 434, *ante*.   [26] [1993] QB 293, [1992] 3 All ER 429.
[27] PD 48, para 53.4.   [28] [1994] Ch 205, [1994] 3 All ER 848.   [29] [2002] UKHL 27.
[30] See *Ridehalgh v Horsefield* [1994] 3 All ER 848; *Metcalfe v Wetherill*, n 23 above.

'Negligent' bears the meaning of a failure to act with the competence to be reasonably expected of ordinary members of the profession. It is not improper to pursue a hopeless case, unless that amounts to an abuse of process. Nor is any distinction to be drawn between legally aided and self-financing litigants. A wasted costs order may well be justified where an advocate's conduct of court proceedings is quite plainly unjustifiable. Above all, such applications should not be used as a means of intimidation, and should normally be dealt with at the conclusion of the trial.

Having considered the question of which side must pay costs, the judge must decide what is to be the basis on which the costs are to be assessed, in order to determine how much of an opponent's costs the loser will have to pay.

B THE ASSESSMENT OF COSTS

1 THE PROCESS

'Assessment of costs' is the new term for what was traditionally known as 'taxation of costs', and is the process by which the amount due under a costs order is determined. It takes one of two forms: 'summary assessment' and 'detailed assessment'. Summary assessment is the assessment by the court at the end of the hearing of the costs due, without consideration of the detailed components of the amount claimed. At certain stages during proceedings a party must serve a costs estimate on other parties. These costs estimates identify the potential costs liability of other parties and will be used to inform the court as to the appropriate costs order to make on summary assessment. However, an inadequate costs estimate will not inevitably mean that that the party claiming costs fails to recover what he ultimately claims.[31] Detailed assessment by contrast involves the detailed scrutiny of a party's costs by a costs officer.[32]

A summary assessment will, unless there is good reason to do otherwise, occur[33] in respect of:

(a) the whole claim for costs following a fast-track trial;[34]

(b) any hearing which has lasted no longer than one day;

(c) some hearings in the Court of Appeal.

The objective is to try and reduce the amount of time, effort, and cost involved in determining issues relating to costs where it is possible to do so. The summary assessment of cost, will consider the costs estimates and a statement of costs which will set out the number of hours claimed, the hourly charging rate of the lawyers involved in handling the case, the level of fee earner (i.e. his seniority and experience) disbursements, and costs for attending the hearing. A failure to supply such a statement

---

[31] *Leigh* v *Michelin Tyre plc* [2004] 2 All ER 173.
[32] CPR, 43.4.   [33] Practice Direction 44.   [34] As to which, see p 466, *ante.*

may not totally deprive a party of costs under summary assessment, but may affect the nature and content of the costs order made.[35] A detailed assessment involves a detailed consideration of a Bill of costs following the commencement of assessment proceedings after the conclusion of the trial, and within three months of that trial. After a variety of procedural steps, the detailed assessment hearing will occur (unless the parties reach agreement and appropriate orders are made) and a final costs certificate issued.

2 THE AMOUNT OF COSTS

At the outset, one must distinguish between costs between a solicitor and his own client, which amount to a contract debt, and costs between the parties with which, here, we are concerned. Regarding costs between a solicitor and his own client, each party must pay his own solicitor's costs,[36] although the advent of conditional fee agreements creates an important, and relatively new, context. The effect is that costs will be permitted on an indemnity basis.[37] This means that 'all costs shall be allowed except in so far as they are unreasonable in amount or have been unreasonably incurred.' All costs incurred with the express or implied approval of the client are deemed to be reasonable. This may be significantly more than the amounts recoverable under a costs order, which perhaps may amount only to 75–80 per cent of the total costs calculated on an indemnity basis.[38] Of course, if there is a conditional fee agreement the problem becomes theoretical, because the funding arrangements are designed to secure that the litigant is not liable to pay costs.

In respect of costs between parties under a costs order, these will be assessed on either the 'standard basis' or the 'indemnity basis', but within the established principle that no party is liable to pay more than the expense and costs incurred by the party claiming costs.[39] Standard costs provide for the recovery of expenditure and costs which have been reasonably incurred.[40] By contrast indemnity costs are more generous, allowing the recovery of all costs not unreasonably incurred. The benefit of the doubt is given to the party who is entitled to costs, and the doctrine of proportionality does not apply.[41] There are, though, some cases where the costs that can be recovered are limited. Small claims[42] costs are restricted to court fees, travelling expenses, and loss of earnings through attendance at court, limitations that are self-evidently necessary if the purpose of a small claims jurisdiction free from large potential costs is to be realized. In fast track proceedings,[43] the costs that may be recovered for advocacy at court are limited depending on the amount of the claim.

---

[35] *Macdonald* v *Taree Holdings Ltd* (2000), Unreported.   [36] See p 352, *ante*.
[37] See p 494, *post*.   [38] See Andrews, *English Civil Procedure, op cit*, para 36.22.
[39] Confusingly called 'the indemnity principle'. See *Harold* v *Smith* (1860) 17 ER 1229; *Gundry* v *Sainsbury* [1910] 1 KB 645; *General of Berne Insurance Co* v *Jardine Reinsurance Management Ltd* [1998] 2 All ER 301.
[40] See CPR, r 43, 44.   [41] *Lownds* v *Home Office* [2002] 1 WLR 2450.
[42] See p 351, *ante*.   [43] See p 352, *ante*.

(a) Standard costs

Costs on the standard basis is the normal basis of calculation for party and party costs. It requires costs not only to have been incurred necessarily, but also proportionality.[44] The facts of *Lownds* v *Home Office* illustrate the issue, with costs of approximately £17,000 being incurred in respect of a claim compromised at £3,000 damages. Although the appeal failed for transitional reasons in respect of the introduction of the Civil Procedure Rules, the case demonstrates vividly the fact that what is appropriate depends on the whole context of the case. In guidance given in its judgment, the court stated that the question of costs must be assessed (in the context of the claimant's costs) in terms of the proportionality of the expenditure to the likely amounts at stake and recoverable. By contrast the proportionality of the defendant's expenditure will be in relation to the amount claimed, for the defendant is entitled to take the claim at face value.

But even if the total costs may be proportionate, that of itself will not suffice. The court will look at each item on the statement of costs and determine whether it was reasonably incurred, and of a reasonable amount. On the other hand, if the total bill was disproportionate, the court would allow items which were necessary (as opposed to reasonable) to incur, to the extent that the amount of such items was reasonable.

The Civil Procedure Rules[45] identify the factors to be taken into account in deciding whether expenditure is reasonably or unreasonably incurred:

(a) the conduct of all the parties, including pre-commencement conduct, and the efforts made to resolve the dispute before and during proceedings;

(b) the amount or value of the money or property involved;

(c) the importance of the matter to all the parties;

(d) the particular complexity of the matter or the difficulty or novelty of the questions raised;

(e) the skill, effort, specialized knowledge, and responsibility involved;

(f) the time spent on the case;

(g) the place where and the circumstances in which work or any part of it was done. In particular it may be unreasonable to employ more expensive London lawyers if it was unnecessary to do so.[46]

(b) Indemnity costs

As noted above, these provide a more generous measure of cost recovery. The courts have a wide discretion as to whether, and in what circumstances, to award costs on an indemnity basis.[47] Despite the fact that the courts have sometimes held that

---

[44] *Lownds* v *Home Office, ante* n 35.   [45] CPR, 44.5(3).

[46] *Sullivan* v *Co-Operative Insurance company Ltd, The Times* 19 May 1999; *Wraith* v *Sheffield Forgemasters Ltd* [1998] 1 WLR 132.

[47] *Excelsior Commercial & Industrial Holdings Ltd* v *Salisbury Hammere Aspden & Johnson* 12 June 2002, unreported.

indemnity costs ought only to be awarded if a party has been engaged in culpable misconduct in the conduct of the litigation,[48] there is no need for moral misconduct or lack of probity. Any conduct might be considered by a judge to justify an indemnity costs order, and it was not for the appeal court to limit that discretion. Arguing a case devoid of merit might be one example, or clear breaches of the Civil Procedure Rules another.[49]

Indemnity costs are also awarded in certain other situations apart from the court's discretion: these include costs awarded in favour of a trustee or personal representative of an estate, where the parties have entered into an agreement regarding the payment of 'all costs', or a claimant has made an offer to settle the case under the Civil Procedure Rules, Part 36, and it was reasonable for the defendant to have accepted that offer.

C COSTS AND CONDITIONAL FEE AGREEMENTS

We have already noted the development of conditional fee agreements as a means of securing funding for litigation and access to justice.[50] These agreements have largely superseded legal aid as a means of funding most types of litigation, were authorized by the Courts and Legal Services Act 1990 (as amended in 1999 by the Access to Justice Act 1999), and allow litigation to be entered into by a claimant on a somewhat inaccurately so-called 'no win, no fee basis'. They achieve this by providing for the client's fees and expenses to be payable only in certain specified circumstances.[51] The agreement specifies a 'success fee' which is chargeable if the case is won, and which provides an uplift to the costs that would normally be charged. The costs and the success fee will be, in principle, recoverable from the losing party (subject to the court's discretion already discussed). There is, though, the prospect of lack of success. For that reason, the claimant will also incur the cost of pre-action insurance to cover costs should the claim fail and costs be awarded against the claimant. It is also possible to purchase insurance (After the Event legal expenses insurance) to cover potential liability for the claimant's own costs. To prove liability for such matters the claimant will have to produce a copy of the agreement, with non relevant confidential detail obscured or deleted.[52]

The reasons for this development are well-documented, and reflect the modern movement away from state-funded civil litigation through the legal aid scheme. They

---

[48] *See Kiam v MGN Ltd (No 2)* [2002] 2 All ER 242.   [49] *Barron v Lovell* [1999] CPLR 630.

[50] See p 372, *ante.*

[51] 1990 Act, s 58(1) (as substituted by Access to Justice Act 1999, s 27) For a good summary of the legislative history, and the development of a principle discussed in *Thai Trading Co (A Firm) v Taylor* [1998] 3 All ER 65, see *Sharratt v London Central Bus Co Ltd (The Accident Group Test Cases)* [2003] 4 All ER 590 (CA), [2004] 3 All ER 325.

[52] *Sharratt v London Central Bus Co Ltd, ante*, n 46.

also potentially widen access to justice.[53] But they also clearly have a significant impact on questions of costs between parties because of the potential liability of a losing defendant for the success fee and the insurance premium. That is one cogent reason for the requirement that details of any Conditional Fee Agreement funding arrangement be given at the commencement of proceedings by the claimant to the defendant.[54]

The principles to be applied in determining costs due in such circumstances have been worked-through in a series of cases. One basic issue is the enforceability of the agreement, which must comply with section 58 of the 1990 Act and the Conditional Fee Agreements Regulations of 2000.[55] Insurers have been increasingly concerned to challenge agreements where breach of the regulations and statutory requirements could be shown. The point was eventually disposed of in *Sharratt v London Central Bus Co Ltd (The Accident Group Test Cases)*,[56] where the court held that only where departure from the requirements had a material adverse effect on either the protection afforded to the client or upon the proper administration of justice would a conditional fee agreement be unenforceable. If the client would have no cause for complaint then the costs basis inherent in the agreement would apply.

Another issue is the level of success fee recoverable from the losing party. This can be reduced if it is disproportionate and, in determining that, regard must be had to the risk that the fee would not be payable, to the legal representative's liability for disbursements, and the availability of other forms of funding.[57] These are not easy issues: the Court of Appeal in *Callery v Gray (No 1)*[58] pointed to a reasonable success fee in a road traffic personal injury claim being no more than 20 per cent, bearing in mind that 99 per cent of such cases succeed. The facts of that case demonstrate the problem. The agreed success fee in the agreement was 60 per cent. An after the event insurance policy cost £367. The amount of compensation agreed by way of settlement was approximately £1,500. The costs judge reduced the success fee to 40 per cent, a figure, as noted above, reduced to 20 per cent on appeal. Yet in *Halloran v Delaney*[59] it was said that the appropriate success fee in such cases would normally use a figure of 5 per cent as a starting point, unless persuaded otherwise by the particular circumstances of the case, a conclusion supported by the House of Lords in *Callery v Gray*[60] in the context of modest and straightforward cases of this type. It also recognized the need, perhaps, for different success fee uplifts for different costs or different parts of the litigation.

There remains the question of the insurance fee. In deciding whether the recovery of such costs is permissible, the court will have regard to the availability of any pre-existing insurance cover, level and extent of the cover provided, whether any part of the premium was debateable in the event of early settlement, and any commission

---

[53] See, e.g., Lord Phillips MR in *R (Factortame Ltd) v Secretary of State for the Environment, Transport and the Regions (No 8)* [2002] 3 WLR 104.

[54] See p 372, *ante*.   [55] SI 2000/692.   [56] [2003] 4 All ER 590.

[57] Practice Direction (44) 11.8.   [58] [2001] 1 WLR 2112.   [59] [2003] 1 WLR 28.

[60] [2002] 3 All ER 652.

received by the claimant or his agents.[61] The stage at which it is appropriate to take out the insurance over will be a matter for the court to decide on an individual basis.

D COSTS IN MULTI PARTY PROCEEDINGS

The use of multi party actions to determine complex issues has already been discussed.[62] They can, though, raise difficult issues. The Woolf Report observed:[63]

If the treatment of costs is not examined from the outset, the result is either subsidiary litigation or protracted problems when the matter comes to [assessment]. My general proposals for information on costs to be made available at every stage when the managing judge is involved are all the more important in relation to multi-patty actions, where many claimants will be legally aided and have no direct control over costs and where costs can escalate dramatically. At every stage of the [multi-party situation] the judge should consider, with the help of the parties, the potential impact on costs of the directions that are contemplated and whether they are justified in relation to what is at issue. Parties and their legal representatives, as in other cases on the multi-track, should provide information on cost already incurred and be prepared to estimate the cost of proposed further work. . . .

Rule 48.6A of the Civil Procedure Rules provides for costs where a Group Litigation Order has been made. This provides for cost sharing orders in respect of common costs, which are divided equally, an approach that was developed further by the court in *Davies* v *Eli Lilly*, applied in *Ward* v *Guinness Mahon plc*[64] Procedures have also been developed to allow quarterly calculation of costs, relevant to those parties who discontinue their own claim or who settle.[65]

---

[61] Practice Direction (44), para 11.100.
[62] See p 452, *ante*. [63] Final Report, *op cit*, at Ch 17, para 57.
[64] [1996] 4 All ER 112. See *Afrika and others* v *Cape plc, and other related case* [2003] 3 All ER 631.
[65] *Foster* v *Roussel Laboratories* Unreported 29 January 1997.

17

APPEALS

A INTRODUCTION

The modern appellate process in civil cases has, like all other aspects of civil procedure, undergone significant change.[1] Prior to the implementation of the Woolf interim and final reports[2] the process was governed by the Supreme Court Act 1981. Now, Part 52 of the Civil Procedure Rules governs appeals both from the High Court and from the county court as well as in respect of certain other specialist appeals. These include jurisdiction to hear appeals from the Employment Appeal Tribunal,[3] the Lands Tribunal,[4] and various other statutory tribunals.[5]

Prior to the civil justice reforms, the Court of Appeal (Civil Division) was the fulcrum of the civil appellate system, with it dealing with all matters arising from the High Court. The Court of Appeal had jurisdiction to hear appeals from any judgment or order of the High Court, except where appeal went direct to the House of Lords under what was known as the 'leapfrog' procedure.[6] Likewise appeals from the county courts generally, but not always,[7] went to the Court of Appeal.[8]

The new structure creates a hierarchy, with appeals normally going to the next level. Which court will deal with which appeals is dealt with by the Access to Justice (Destination of Appeals) Order 2000.[9] Thus an appeal from the decision of a county court district judge will normally go to a circuit judge.[10] All appeals from a county court judge are normally dealt with by a High Court judge. Decisions of the High Court Master or District Judge[11] will, again, normally lie to a High Court judge. As before, decisions of High Court judges lie to the Court of Appeal. The purpose is clear: to ensure that the ever-increasing burden on the Court of Appeal prior to the Woolf reforms[12] was addressed by ensuring that only cases that need to be dealt with

---

[1] See the remarks of Brooke LJ in *Tanfern v Cameron-McDonald* [2000] 2 All ER 801.

[2] As to which, see p 426, *ante*.   [3] See p 292, *ante*.   [4] See Ch. 9, *ante*.

[5] See Ch. 9, *ante*.

[6] Supreme Court Act 1981, s 16. For appeal to the House of Lords, see p 000, *post*.

[7] Appeals from orders in bankruptcy matters lay in the first instance to a Divisional Court of the Chancery Division, and then with leave to the Court of Appeal.

[8] County Courts Act 1984, s 77.   [9] SI 2000/1071.   [10] See p 301, *ante*.

[11] See p 501, *ante*.

[12] See *Review of the Court of Appeal (Civil Division)* (the Bowman Report) to be found at www.dca.gov.uk/civil/. For commentary see Jacob at (1998) 61 MLR 390.

by the full Court of Appeal should be. However, such an approach might sometimes exclude from Court of Appeal consideration important points of law or practice. Accordingly, a 'leapfrog' procedure permits some cases to be transferred directly to the Court of Appeal. This is where an appeal would otherwise lie to a Circuit Judge or High Court judge, but the appeal raises important points of principle or practice, or there is some other compelling reason.[13] The Master of the Rolls also has the power to require a direct first appeal to the Court of Appeal.[14] And despite this hierarchy one important further exception exists: a 'final decision' can proceed to the Court of Appeal. A 'final decision' is one which would finally determine the entire proceedings.[15] This might include points of law, or evidence, such as limitation periods, but does not include the striking out the proceedings or a statement of case.[16]

Appeals from the Court of Appeal in limited circumstances lies to the House of Lords.[17] As noted above, there may, exceptionally, be an appeal directly from the High Court to the House of Lords.[18]

B RIGHTS OF APPEAL

Until the implementation of the civil justice reforms many rights of appeal existed as of right, with permission ('leave') to appeal needed only in a minority of cases.[19] The changed procedures now generally require 'permission'[20] to appeal to be granted.[21] That is not the case if a statutory scheme of appeal exists, because the scheme of appeal permits appeal as of right,[22] nor does it apply in certain situations where the liberty of the individual is at stake. The cases that fall within this category include orders committing an individual to prison, secure accommodation orders made under section 25 of the Children Act 1989, or cases where an application for an order of habeas corpus is refused.[23]

A party wishing to appeal must make an oral application to the court whose decision he seeks to appeal.[24] That is made to the relevant appeal court, or, if that application is refused, an application for permission can be made to the relevant appeal court provided the procedures that have been prescribed are followed.[25] These

---

[13] CPR, 52.14(1).　　　[14] Access to Justice Act 1999, s 57(1)(a).

[15] Destination of Appeals Order. *Op cit*, art. 1(2)(c).

[16] *Tanfern* v *Cameron-McDonald* [2000] 1 WLR 1315.　　　[17] See p 501, *post*.

[18] Administration of Justice Act 1969. See, further, p 000, *post*.

[19] The more important cases included: appeals from Divisional Courts of the High Court; appeals from consent orders or orders solely as to costs; from interim orders or judgments; from decisions of a county court judge where the value of the claim in contract, tort or certain other monetary claims did not exceed £5,000 (£15,000 in equity or probate); from a commercial judge on an arbitration appeal.

[20] For the change in terminology made by CPR, see p 000, *ante*.　　　[21] CPR, 52.3.

[22] *Colley* v *Council for Licensed Conveyancers* [2001] 4 All ER 998.

[23] As to which, see p 206, *ante*.　　　[24] CPR, 53.2(3).

[25] See CPR, 53.2; Practice Direction 52.

require an appeal notice and an 'appeal bundle' to be prepared. Unless statute provides otherwise, the time period for the lodging of the appeal notice is fourteen days. Leave to extend the time for the filing of an appeal notice may be granted by the court whose decision or order is being appealed, or by the appeal court provided the relevant procedure is complied with.[26] The question of extension is one for the court, not for the parties, a position reflecting the obligation of the courts under the Civil Procedure Rules to manage effectively the progress of cases. The decision not to grant an extension is itself a matter that is appealable.[27]

The appeal bundle will include copies of the appeal notice, a skeleton legal argument,[28] a copy of the order being appealed, a copy of the reasons for the decision, any written statements in support of the application,[29] and any other documents reasonably considered to be necessary to enable the appeal court to reach its decision. If there are relevant documents which are not available, for example the judgment giving written reasons for the decision, an explanation must be given. The record of the judgment or ruling being appealed is crucial if the appeal court is to be able to take an informed view of the appeal.[30] More limited documentation is needed if the appeal is one arising from a decision in the small claims track.[31]

The appeal court has various powers in respect of an appeal notice. It may, of course, grant permission. The criteria the court will apply will be to ask whether the appeal would have a real prospect of success, or whether there is some other compelling reason why the appeal should be heard.[32] Where there has already been an appeal, the criteria are even more strict: the case must raise an important issue of principle, or there must be other compelling reasons why a further appeal should be permitted. This is designed to facilitate the speedier resolution of disputes by making second appeals a rarity.[33]

Permission is unlikely to be granted in respect of case management decisions. In *Thermawear Ltd v Linton*[34] Lord Bingham MR stressed that procedural initiatives would be futile if every decision or initiative could be appealed

No right to appeal lies against a refusal of permission to appeal,[35] nor, apparently, are reasons for the refusal of permission needed to be given.[36] Alternatively it may:[37]

(a) strike out the whole or part of an appeal notice;

(b) set aside permission to appeal either in whole or in part

(c) impose conditions, or vary conditions, upon which an appeal may be brought.

---

[26] See CPR, 52.4.   [27] *Foenander v Bond Lewis & Co* [2001] EWCA Civ 759.

[28] Not required from a litigant in person: Practice Direction 52, para 7.7A.   [29] See p 502, *post*.

[30] *Plender v Hyams* [2001] 2 All ER 179.

[31] See Practice Direction 52. For the small claims track see p 465, *ante*.   [32] CPR, 52.3(6).

[33] *Tanfer Ltd v Cameron-McDonald* [2000] 1 WLR 1311.

[34] *The Times* 20 October 1995.   [35] Access to Justice Act 1999, s 54(4).

[36] *North Range Shipping Ltd v Seatrans Shipping Corporation* [2002] 1 WLR 2397; *X v Federal Republic of Germany* (1981) 25 DR 240; *Nerva v United Kingdom* App No 42295/98, 11 July 2000.

[37] CPR, 52.9(1).

A notice will be struck out only rarely, and usually if the court has been misled or the point at issue is clearly dealt with by statutory provision which had been overlooked.[38] Conditions should only be imposed where there is a 'compelling reason' to do so.[39] These might include security for costs, as in *Aoun v Bahri*, where such a requirement in respect of the costs of the lower court proceedings was held unreasonable. Other examples are an order to pay a judgment debt,[40] or the payment of money into court.[41] The discretion of the court is not in any way limited, subject to questions of reasonableness.

Appeal lies from the civil division of the Court of Appeal to the House of Lords only with permission of the Court of Appeal or of the House of Lords.[42] There is no requirement that the appeal be based on a point of law, though almost always appeal to the House of Lords is based upon a point of law rather than on an issue of fact or an award of damages. Although permission is the only prerequisite for appealing, no appeal lies from the decision of the Court of Appeal where any statute expresses the decision of the Court of Appeal to be final. As noted earlier, the Administration of Justice Act 1969, Part II provided for a 'leapfrog' appeal direct from the High Court to the House of Lords subject to the grant of a certificate by the trial judge and of leave by the House of Lords in any case in which appeal lies to the Court of Appeal (with or without permission). The criteria which apply as pre-conditions to the grant of such a certificate were stated by the House of Lords in the first 'leapfrog' case under the 1969 Act procedure, *American Cyanamid v Upjohn Co.*[43] These are—(1) the consent of all parties must be given, and (2) the case must involve a point of law of general public importance either relating to the construction of an enactment or is a point on which the judge was bound by precedent.

For the purpose of European Community law the House of Lords is clearly 'a court or tribunal of a Member State, against whose decision there is no judicial remedy under national law', so that where a question arises concerning:

(a) the interpretation of the Treaty;

(b) the validity and interpretation of acts of the institutions of the Community; or

(c) the interpretation of the statutes of bodies established by an Act of the Council, where those statutes so provide,

the House of Lords is bound to refer that question to the European Court for a preliminary ruling (unless, of course, the High Court or Court of Appeal has already referred the question in the same case) and, having obtained the ruling, is bound to follow it.[44]

---

[38] *Nathan* v *Smilovich* [2002] EWCA Civ 759; *Barings Bank plc (in liquidation)* v *Coopers & Lybrand* EWCA Civ 1155.

[39] Per *Brooke LJ* in *Aoun* v *Bahri* EWCA Civ 1141.

[40] *Hammond Suddards Solicitors* v *Agrichem International Holdings Ltd* [2001] EWCA Civ 1915.

[41] *Bell Electric Ltd* v *Aweco Appliance Systems GmbH & Co* [2002] EWCA Civ 501.

[42] Administration Of Justice (Appeals) Act 1934, s 1.   [43] [1970] 3 All ER 785.

[44] See p 141, *ante*.

C PROCEDURE AND POWERS ON APPEAL

The purpose of an appeal is to review the decision of the lower court, and not, generally, a rehearing of the original argument. In *Audergon* v *La Baguette Ltd*[45] the Court of Appeal held that it was undesirable to formulate criteria to be applied when deciding whether to rehear the case, but the Court must have good reason for ordering such a re-hearing. In that case the judge hearing the appeal did not have such a good reason, because the Master who had conducted the original matter had considered all the relevant evidence. But good reason might exist if the judge had given inadequate, or no, reasons, because then the process of review would be impossible.[46]

Appeals in the Court of Appeal have traditionally been heard by two or three judges of the Court, the court may now consist of a single judge.[47] The Court hears full legal argument from both sides and may substitute its own judgment for that of the court below. Even though it is not a complete rehearing, In addition, the appellant is normally confined to the points of law which he raised in the court below. He may in certain circumstances, discussed below, be allowed to take new points on appeal but he cannot, except with leave of the Court of Appeal, rely on any grounds of appeal or apply for any relief not specified in his notice of appeal.[48]

The Court of Appeal has all the powers, authority, and jurisdiction of the court or tribunal from which the appeal was brought in any matter before it. An appeal court will not generally admit evidence not before the lower court, but does have the power to admit new evidence.[49] This discretion must be exercised in accordance with the overriding objective,[50] in the light of all the circumstances of the case. The Civil Procedure Rules state[51] that appeal courts will not receive oral evidence or evidence that was not before the lower courts, unless it orders otherwise.

The Court has power to examine trial witnesses though it rarely does so, being content in most cases to rely upon the judge's note or a transcript of the official shorthand note. It has power to receive further evidence orally, by affidavit or by deposition taken before an examiner but, where there was a trial or hearing on the merits, but, as noted above, the Court will not admit further evidence (other than evidence as to matters which have occurred since the trial) except on special grounds. In *Ladd* v *Marshall*,[52] Denning LJ prescribed the following three conditions for the reception of fresh evidence in the Court of Appeal:

---

[45] [2002] EWCA Civ 10.

[46] *Ansari* v *Puffin Investment Co Ltd* [2002] EWCA 234; cf. *Dyson Ltd* v *Registrar of Trademarks* [2003] EWCHC 1062.

[47] Supreme Court Act 1981, s 54(2)–(4), substituted by Access to Justice Act 1999, s 59.

[48] CPR, 52.　　　[49] CPR, 52.11.

[50] *Gillingham* v *Gillingham* [2001] EWCA Civ 906. *Hamilton* v *Al-Fayed* (2002), EWCA Civ, 605. For the overriding objective, see p 434, *ante*. For discussion of *Ladd* v *Marshall*, see *Pearce* v *Ove Harup Partnership* [1999] 1 All ER 769; *Shaker* v *Al-Bedrawi* [2002] 4 All ER 835.

[51] CPR, 52.11.

[52] [1954] 3 All ER 745, applied in *Roe* v *Robert McGregor & Sons Ltd* [1968] 2 All ER 636.

first, it must be shown that the evidence could not have been obtained with reasonable diligence for use at the trial; secondly, the evidence must be such that, if given, it would probably have an important influence on the result of the case, though it need not be decisive; thirdly, the evidence must be such as is presumably to be believed, or, in other words, it must be apparently credible though it need not be incontrovertible.

This statement was approved by the House of Lords in *Skone* v *Skone*[53] where the evidence consisted of a bundle of love letters written by the co-respondent in a divorce suit to the wife which tended to prove adultery between them. The trial judge had dismissed the husband's petition and accepted the co-respondent's evidence to the effect that adultery had not taken place. It was argued that these letters (which were in the possession of the wife) could have been obtained by seeking discovery of documents from the wife. The House of Lords rejected this argument on the basis that the husband had no reason to suspect the existence of such letters, that the letters, if genuine, falsified the judge's finding to such an extent that it would be unjust to leave matters where they were and, furthermore, that there was a strong prima facie case of deception of the court. It must be emphasized that these rigorous conditions need not be satisfied in respect of evidence of matters occurring after the trial. Evidence will be admitted of matters occurring after the trial where the basis on which the trial judge gave his decision has been clearly falsified by subsequent events.

Of course, such authorities pre-date the civil justice reforms, and the approach to the old case law is that it is often no longer relevant or appropriate.[54] But In *Gillingham* v *Gillingham*[55] the principles in *Ladd* v *Marshall* were considered to remain good law, not as rules but, rather, as indicators of matters which should be taken into account. In *Gillingham* the evidence was forgotten correspondence, which had not been disclosed by the other party. Although, with reasonable diligence it might have been discovered, the matter could not fairly or satisfactorily resolved without it, and it was therefore right to allow the appeal and order a new trial.

On appeal the Court has full power to make any order which should have been made in the court below and to substitute its own order as to liability, quantum, or costs for that of the court below. In addition the Court of Appeal is not confined to the points raised in the notice of appeal or respondent's notice. It may, though it rarely does, take any point of law or fact so far as is necessary to ensure the determination on the merits of the real question in issue between the parties. Should the Court of Appeal wish to decide an issue of fact which has not been raised in the statement of case, an extremely infrequent contingency, it may allow the grounds of appeal to be amended.

---

53 [1971] 2 All ER 582. 54 See p 433, *ante*. 55 See n 50, *ante*.

D THE APPROACH TO THE DETERMINATION OF APPEALS

1 APPEAL ON A POINT OF LAW

Most appeals are based on a point of law. It has already been stated that, notwithstanding the general power to take a point not raised therein, the Court usually confines itself to the points raised in the notice of appeal or respondent's notice. Furthermore there is a general rule that a party cannot take on appeal a point which he did not take in the court below.[56]

To this rule there are two important exceptions. The first occurs where the point of law was expressly reserved in the court below. This might occur where the court below was not free to consider the point because it was bound by precedent on that point, whereas the Court of Appeal might be free to reconsider the precedent in question. Secondly, an appeal court will allow a point to be taken, and indeed will take the point itself, where not to do so would result in an abuse of the court's process. Thus the illegality of a contract may be raised on appeal even though the point was overlooked in the court below.[57]

2 APPEAL AGAINST A FINDING OF FACT

An appeal is not, generally, by way of rehearing, and thus an appeal court will be reluctant to interfere with findings of fact made by the judge. However, an appeal court can allow an appeal where the decision being appealed was 'wrong' and make draw such inference of fact which it considers justified on the evidence.[58] This has been held to mean that an appeal court must consider and make up its mind about findings of fact.[59] Whether a judge on appeal will overturn findings of fact, or inferences from fact, will depend on all the circumstances: did the trial judge reach the conclusion based on assessment or oral testimony, in which circumstance the trial judge will have had the advantage of hearing the evidence. By contrast inferences from primary facts may be more susceptible to the appeal court taking a different view.[60] Appeal is by way of rehearing, the Court of Appeal has power to substitute its own finding of fact, direct or inferential, for that of the trial judge or jury. However, the appeal court does not have the advantage, which the judge, or, occasionally judge and jury had, of seeing the trial witnesses and observing their demeanour. Consequently the jurisdiction exercised by the Court of Appeal in relation to findings of fact is confined to inferential findings of fact. The Court has the power to substitute its own

---

[56] See *Meco Pak AB* v *Electropaint Ltd* [2001] EWCA Civ 1537.
[57] See *Snell* v *Unity Finance Ltd* [1964] 2 QB 203; *Oscroft* v *Benabo* [1967] 2 All ER 548.
[58] CPR, 52.11.   [59] See *Todd* v *Adam* [2002] EWCA Civ 509.
[60] *Assicurazioni Generali Spa* v *Arab Insurance Group BSC* [2002] EWCA 1642.

inference from the facts as found for that of the trial judge or jury and will not hesitate to do so. In a pre-CPR case, involving a claim of medical negligence, where the crucial issue of fact was whether a hospital registrar had pulled 'too long and too hard' on the head of the infant plaintiff in the course of his birth, Lord Bridge explained his willingness to uphold an appeal from the trial judge's finding in the plaintiff's favour in the following words:[61]

My Lords, I recognise that this is a question of pure fact and that in the realm of fact, as the authorities repeatedly emphasise, the advantages which the judge derives from seeing and hearing the witnesses must always be respected by an appellate court. At the same time the importance of the part played by those advantages in assisting the judge to any particular conclusion of fact varies through a wide spectrum from, at one end, a straight conflict of primary fact between witnesses, where credibility is crucial and the appellate court can hardly ever interfere, to, at the other end, an inference from undisputed primary facts, where the appellate court is in just as good a position as the trial judge to make the decision.

Where a jury has returned a general verdict it is impossible to distinguish direct findings of fact from inferential findings and, indeed, the jury cannot be asked, after they have returned a general verdict, to state what their direct findings of fact were. An appeal court, therefore, can only upset the general verdict of a jury if it cannot be supported by the evidence or is a verdict which no reasonable men could have reached. In *Grobbellar* v *News Group Newspapers*[62] an attempt by the Court of Appeal to overturn a defamation finding because it flew in the face of the evidence as it was read by the Court of Appeal was overturned by the House of Lords. The jury's verdict could not be dismissed as irrational or perverse, though the House of Lords reduced the damages award from £88,000 to a derisory £1.

3 APPEAL AGAINST THE EXERCISE OF A DISCRETION

In many circumstances the judge has a discretion as to whether, and in what manner, to exercise his powers. Commonly encountered instances of judicial discretion are the discretion as to costs, the discretion whether to grant or refuse an injunction, and the discretion as to the mode of trial, in particular in relation to the question of whether or not to order jury trial. However, no discretion is absolute and there may be a successful appeal in relation to the exercise of a judicial discretion if the appellant can show that the judge exercised his discretion under a mistake of law, or under a misapprehension as to the facts, or that he took into account irrelevant matters or gave insufficient weight, or too much weight, to certain factors, or that he failed to exercise his discretion at all.[63] If the judge gives no reasons, or insufficient reasons for the exercise of his discretion, the court may infer that he has gone wrong in one respect or another, and, indeed, the conclusion may be that there is a breach of the fair

61 *Whitehouse* v *Jordan* [1981] 1 All ER 267 at 286.
62 [2002] 1 WLR 3024, HL, overturning [2001] 2 All ER 437.
63 For challenge on judicial review to the exercise of discretionary powers, see p 207, *ante*.

trial provisions of Article 6 of the Convention.[64] It is vital for proper reasons to be stated, not only because of the requirements of fairness to the parties but also that the appellate court can perform its function of review.

The burden of proof is on the party who alleges that the discretion was wrongly exercised and, in any event, the Court of Appeal will only allow the appeal if satisfied that the judge's conclusion is one which involves injustice or was clearly wrong. In *Hadmor Productions Ltd* v *Hamilton* Lord Diplock explained the extent of an appellate court's powers as follows:[65]

Before adverting to the evidence that was before the judge and the additional evidence that was before the Court of Appeal, it is I think appropriate to remind your Lordships of the limited function of an appellate court in an appeal of this kind. An interlocutory injunction is a discretionary relief and the discretion whether or not to grant it is vested in the High Court judge by whom the application for it is heard. On an appeal from the judge's grant or refusal of an interlocutory injunction the function of an appellate court, whether it be the Court of Appeal or your Lordships' House, is not to exercise an independent discretion of its own. It must defer to the judge's exercise of his discretion and must not interfere with it merely on the ground that the members of the appellate court would have exercised the discretion differently. The function of the appellate court is initially one of review only. It may set aside the judge's exercise of his discretion on the ground that it was based on a misunderstanding of the law or of the evidence before him or on an inference that particular facts existed or did not exist, which, although it was one that might legitimately have been drawn on the evidence that was before the judge, can be demonstrated to be wrong by further evidence that has become available by the time of the appeal, or on the ground that there has been a change of circumstances after the judge made his order that would have justified his acceding to an application to vary it. Since reasons given by judges for granting or refusing interlocutory injunctions may sometimes be sketchy, there may also be occasional cases where even though no erroneous assumption of law or fact can be identified the judge's decision to grant or refuse the injunction is so aberrant that it must be set aside on the ground that no reasonable judge regardful of his duty to act judicially could have reached it. It is only if and after the appellate court has reached the conclusion that the judge's exercise of his discretion must be set aside for one or other of these reasons that it becomes entitled to exercise an original discretion of its own.

4 APPEAL AGAINST AN AWARD OF DAMAGES

The approach adopted when determining an appeal against an award of damages differs according to whether the award was made by a jury or by a judge sitting alone. Where unliquidated damages are claimed, historically the Court has not interfered with the award of a jury unless the damages awarded were so large or, more rarely, so small that no jury could reasonably have given them.[66]

---

[64] See p 180, *ante*, and p 521, *post*.   [65] [1983] 1 AC 191 at 220.

[66] *Johnson* v *Great Western Railway Co* [1904] KB 250; *Cassell & Co Ltd* v *Broome* [1972] AC 1027, [1972] 1 All ER 801.

However a new trial may be ordered if it appears to the Court either that the jury took into account irrelevant factors or failed to consider matters which it ought to have considered and in consequence awarded damages which were excessive or inadequate. The case of *Lewis* v *Daily Telegraph Ltd*[67] provides a good example. In that case two national newspapers published on the same day paragraphs alleged to be defamatory of the plaintiffs. The jury in the first action awarded the plaintiffs a total of £100,000; in the second action two days later in which there were factors which a jury might be entitled to take into account as aggravating damages, a different jury awarded the plaintiffs a further £117,000. New trials of both actions were ordered on the ground (inter alia) that the damages in each case were excessive. The House of Lords, affirming the decision of the Court of Appeal, stated that in such a case, pursuant to section 12 of the Defamation Act 1952, each jury should be directed to consider how far the damage suffered can reasonably be attributed solely to the libel with which they are concerned, and how far it ought to be regarded as the joint result of the two libels, bearing in mind that the plaintiff ought not to be compensated twice for the same loss. In *Rantzen* v *Mirror Group Newspapers (1986) Ltd*[68] the plaintiff, a well-known television presenter, had been awarded £250,000 damages for defamation. The defendant appealed, on the basis that the award was excessive, and sought an order under section 8 of the Courts and Legal Services At 1990, which now provides that where the court has the power to order a new trial on the basis of excessive or inadequate damages, it may be given the power to substitute the proper sum instead of ordering that new trial. The Court of Appeal concluded that this power had to be exercised in the context of art. 10 of the European Convention on Human Rights, which permitted restrictions on freedom of expression only where they were necessary in a democratic society to meet a pressing social need. On this basis large awards of damages were to be subjected to very close scrutiny. The question now to be asked is whether a reasonable jury could have thought the award necessary to compensate the plaintiff. On the facts the award was excessive by any objective standard of reasonable compensation, and an award of £110,000 was substituted for that of the jury. Where the award of damages appealed against was made by a judge sitting alone the Court of Appeal will not hesitate to interfere with the assessment, not only on the ground that the judge applied a wrong principle of law in making the assessment, but also on the ground that the award is out of scale with awards in similar cases.

The matter was considered again by the Court of Appeal in *John* v *MGN Ltd*,[69] where the Court held that when assessing compensatory damages in a defamation case a jury could in future properly be referred by way of comparison to the conventional compensation scales in personal injury cases as well as to previous libel awards made or approved by the Court of Appeal, and there was no reason why the judge, in his directions, or counsel, should not indicate to the jury the level of award which they considered appropriate. Those changes of practice would not undermine but rather

---

[67] [1964] AC 234, [1963] 2 All ER 975. [68] [1994] 2 QB 670, [1993] 4 All ER 975.
[69] [1996] 2 All ER 35.

buttress the constitutional role of the libel jury by rendering their proceedings more rational and so more acceptable to public opinion. The same principle also applies in actions against the police for unlawful conduct.

There is, of course, no prescribed scale of damages in any type of action but, nevertheless, there is a certain degree of parity in awards in respect of similar types of damage particularly in actions for damages for personal injuries. In such cases the Court of Appeal will not make small adjustments to the sum awarded though it will make a substantial adjustment if that is found necessary. In practice the Court will rarely interfere unless an adjustment of at least 20 per cent or 25 per cent is envisaged. It is this diversity of approach to awards of damages made by judges and juries respectively that has led to the virtual disappearance of jury trial in personal injuries actions.

The Court of Appeal has power under section 17 of the Supreme Court Act 1981 to order a new trial. It may exercise this power on an appeal from a judge and jury or from a judge alone just as it can on a motion for a new trial following a trial with a jury. A new trial may be ordered on any one issue without disturbing the finding of the court below on any other issue. Thus the Court of Appeal may order a new trial on the issue of damages while affirming the decision on the question of liability. Indeed if the only ground of application is the amount of damages the court should limit the new trial to that issue and leave the findings as to liability undisturbed. If there is a new trial, that trial is completely independent of the first trial. The mode of trial need not be the same, no estoppel arises as a result of the first trial and the parties may raise new points and may contest issues left uncontested at the first trial. The costs of the first trial are sometimes ordered to await the outcome of the new trial though, as a rule, the successful applicant ought to be allowed the costs of his application.

PART IV

CRIMINAL PROCEEDINGS

18

CRIMINAL PROCEEDINGS AND THE CRIMINAL JUSTICE SYSTEM

A INTRODUCTION

1 THE 'SYSTEM'

The use of the word 'system' in the context of the English criminal justice system may be misleading. With a multitude of different Government Departments, agencies, and others making 'separate and sometimes conflicting'[1] contributions, and in excess of 400,000 staff,[2] the problem of consistent and coherent planning and action is obvious.

In the recent past, several Government Departments (principally the Home Office and Department of Constitutional Affairs),[3] some forty-two police forces, the Crown Prosecution Service, Magistrates' Courts Committees, the Prison Service, and Courts Service have each had major roles, quite apart from the roles that defence lawyers and defendants themselves play. The Auld Review observed that administrative complexities and muddle of responsibilities had a practical and visible effect on the efficient and effective working of the 'system'.[4] It considered that efficiency and effectiveness are as important as the formal procedural and substantive rules in ensuring that the aims of the criminal justice system are in fact achieved. This objective is not always easily achieved in the current 'system'.

More recently, emphasis has been placed on the achievement of a more 'joined-up', co-ordinated, approach. A new National Criminal Justice Committee was established following the Auld Review and the White Paper *Justice for All*.[5] It comprises leading civil servants from relevant Government Departments, comprising the Director of Public Prosecutions, the Chief Executives of relevant Criminal Justice agencies, a representative of the Association of Chief Police Officers, and a senior judge. The Committee reports to a Cabinet Committee and is responsible for overall criminal justice system delivery. For wider involvement of all those involved in the criminal justice system, a new National Criminal Justice Board comprises representatives not

---

[1] See Auld Review, *op cit*, Ch 8, para 1.
[2] See http://www.cjsonline.gov.uk/the_cjs/departments_of_the_cjs.
[3] Formerly the preserve of the Lord Chancellor's Department: see Ch 1, *ante*.
[4] Ibid, Ch 8, para 12.   [5] *Op cit*, Ch 9, para 5.

only of the Bar, magistracy, and judiciary, but also the representatives of of the Commission for Racial Equality, the Law Society, victim and witness organizations, and senior academics. It acts as a consultative and advisory body on the criminal justice system, and gives a voice to a wide range of interests within the criminal justice system, advising on criminal justice reform so that all who work within, or with, the 'system' can have their say and influence decision-making. Some forty-two local Criminal Justice Boards were established during 2002–2003.

A variety of other initiatives have, in recent years, been launched. The Youth Justice Board[6] was established in 1998,[7] with its objectives including monitoring the operation of the youth justice system, to publish information about that system, to advise on necessary changes, and to promote good practice. The Courts Act 2003 established a unified court service and management structure,[8] aiming to establish decentralized management and local accountability within a national framework.[9] A new national Courts Agency has functions which include setting performance indicators, monitoring performance standards, and managing projects for common systems (such as information technology). It is hoped that, soon, all criminal justice agencies will be able to exchange case information electronically, with victims being able to follow the progress of their case on-line. Through overall co-ordination and liaison, common IT systems, and better case management it is hoped that cases will be dealt with quicker, more efficiently, and in a more consistent way. Changes in police structures and organization,[10] the creation of the National Probation Service,[11] and now its merger with the Prison Agency into the National Offender Management Service are each a response to the need for co-ordinate efficient and consistent management of process and of punishments.[12]

So where, then, does actual responsibility lie in this complex structure? Within central government, there are three Government Departments who have responsibility for 'the system':

(a) Home Office

Oversees the Police and the National Offender Management Service, and sponsors the Youth Justice Board, Criminal Injuries Compensation Authority, and the Criminal Cases Review Commission.

(b) Department of Constitutional Affairs

Oversees the magistrates' courts, the Crown Court, the Appeal Courts and the Legal Service Commission.

---

[6] See p 642, *post.*   [7] Crime and Disorder Act 1998, s 41.   [8] See p 19, *ante.*
[9] *Justice for All, op cit,* 9.17.   [10] See ch 12, *ante.*
[11] Criminal Justice and Courts Services Act 2000, s 2, creates, inter alia, a National Probation Service. Section 2 states that the Home Secretary, local probation boards and probation officers must have regard to (1) the protection of the public; (2) the reduction of re-offending, and (3) the proper punishment of offenders.
[12] See Ch 22, *post.*

(c) Office of the Attorney-General

Oversees the Crown Prosecution Service, the Serious Fraud Office, and Customs and Excise prosecutors.

The work of these three Departments is co-ordinated by yet another government body, the Office for Criminal Justice Reform, a cross-departmental organization which reports to Ministers in each of the three Government Departments. Its task is to drive through improvements set out by the National Criminal Justice Board described above. One recent example is the publication by the OCJR of the Victims Code of Practice.[13]

2 THE AIMS OF THE CRIMINAL JUSTICE SYSTEM

The Auld Review identified two main aims that were set by government for the criminal justice system.[14] One was the reduction of crime and the fear of crime and its social and economic costs. The other was the dispensing of justice fairly and efficiently, to promote confidence in the law. This second aim had several more specific objectives: to secure just processes and just and effective outcomes; to deal with cases with appropriate speed; to meet the needs of victims, witnesses and jurors within the system; to respect the rights of defendants and treat them fairly; and to promote confidence in the criminal justice system.

These aims and objectives were accepted by that Review as an appropriate starting point, although it counselled against expecting too much of the criminal justice system, and in particular urged that the courts should not be seen as 'a medium for curing the ills of society'.[15] Nonetheless, as noted above, the trend of recent legislation has been to seek greater co-ordination between the different agencies who deal with the administration of the criminal justice system and those who have some responsibility for policies that may diminish criminal activity, or which might divert persons from the criminal justice system. We have already noted the co-ordinating role of the Youth Justice Board.[16] The Crime and Disorder Act 1998 created a new framework for the development and management of crime and disorder strategies, requiring police authorities and chief police officers to act in co-operation with each other, and formulate strategies for the reduction of crime and disorder.[17] It also placed an obligation on local authorities to consider the crime and disorder implications of what they do. Section 37 of the 1998 Act states a clear aim for the youth justice system, which deals with those under the age of eighteen: the principle aim of the youth justice system is to prevent offending by children and young persons. It is the duty of all persons and bodies carrying out functions in relation to the youth justice system to have regard to that aim.

More recent legislation has identified for the first time the purposes of sentencing.

---

[13] See p 517, *post.*   [14] *op cit*, Ch 1, para 7.   [15] Ibid, Ch 1, para 9.
[16] *Ante*, and see p 642, *post.*
[17] Crime and Disorder Act 1998, ss 5–6, based largely on the Report of the Morgan Cmtte *Safer Communities: the Local Delivery of Crime Prevention through the Partnership Approach*, Home Office, 1991.

Section 126 of the Criminal Justice Act 2003 states that these are:[18] (a) the punishment of offenders, (b) the reduction of crime (including its reduction by deterrence and its reduction by the reform and rehabilitation of offenders), (c) the protection of the public, and (d) the making of reparation by offenders to persons affected by their offences. Of course, the statement of aims and purposes tells us nothing about how different aims or purposes can be reconciled, or how the detailed processes, rules, and punishments should be used.

All these examples demonstrate that there are many interested parties affected by the criminal justice system, and who may view the purpose of what they are doing in different lights. Clearly, ensuring a fair trial for a defendant is fundamental, and a right enshrined in Article 6 of the European Convention.[19] There are, though, other legitimate interests: those of prosecutors, in ensuring that the guilty are in fact convicted; those of victims, in receiving 'justice'; those of government and other public authorities, in reducing the incidence of crime. These competing interests have to be balanced, and this is reflected in the trial and in pre-trial processes. Ensuring that some of these wider aims are achieved may, however, mean adopting approaches such as diverting offenders away from the criminal process to address offending behaviour, through cautioning or youth offender programmes, or using a combination of criminal and civil process to prevent repeat offending behaviour. The White Paper *Justice for All*[20] identified what were seen as weaknesses in critical areas throughout the criminal justice system: the police only detected 23 per cent of the 5.5 million offences recorded during 2000–2001; too many defendants offend whilst on bail;[21] the system brings defendants to trial too slowly; too many go unconvicted; and too many are not given the sentence they need. It recommended a more integrated strategy to reduce crime and deliver justice, through a 'virtuous circle'[22] of prevention, detection, prosecution, punishment, and rehabilitation. In this context, the trial process is fundamental, but forms only a part of a wider system designed to meet these diverse interests and objectives. The extent to which the failings identified above can be overcome depends crucially on the success or otherwise of the large number of provisions contained in the extremely complex Criminal Justice Act 2003,[23] to be brought into force between 2004 and 2007.

3 YOUTH JUSTICE[24]

Distinct issues arise in the context of juveniles (those aged under eighteen). Section 44 of the Children and Young Persons Act 1933 requires any court, in fulfilling its duties,

---

[18] See p 658, *post.*   [19] See p 180, *ante,* and p 521, *post.*

[20] 2002, Cm 5563, Home Office.

[21] Some 25 per cent, rising to 38 per cent of under-18's: ibid, para 1.6.   [22] Ibid, para 1.12.

[23] Containing some 339 sections and thirty-eight Schedules. Only some of the provisions had been brought into force as at the date of going to press: see Criminal Justice Act 2003 (Commencement No 1) and (Commencement No 2) Orders 2003 and 2004 respectively (SI 2003/3282, 2004/81).

[24] See, generally, Ward, *Young Offenders* (Jordans 2001).

to take account of the welfare of the child or young person before it. More recently, considerable debate has occurred as to the role and functions of the youth justice system. In a Consultation Paper,[25] the government stated its belief that action was needed to bring about greater consistency in the approach to working with young offenders in the community and to ensure that all the relevant local agencies play a full part. It also believed that the youth justice system should seek to prevent crime. For that reason, section 37 of the Crime and Disorder Act 1998 states that:

It shall be the principal aim of the youth justice system to prevent offending by children and young persons.

It is the duty of all persons and bodies carrying out functions in relation to the youth justice system to have regard to that aim. This is a broad statement of an overall duty that applies not only to local authorities, health authorities, probation services, voluntary agencies, and the police, but also to the courts in dealing with young offenders after conviction.

The role of local authorities in establishing youth offending teams and creating youth justice strategies should be noted. Each local authority is under a duty to secure that, to such extent as is appropriate for their area, all youth justice services are available,[26] performed in partnership with other agencies such as the police. Local Authorities operate within the overall guidance given by the Youth Justice Board.[27] This comprises ten, eleven, or twelve members, appointed by the Home Secretary, and includes persons with extensive recent experience of the youth justice system. Its functions are set out by section 42(5) of the Crime and Disorder Act 1998, and include:

(a) the monitoring of the operation of the youth justice and the provision of youth justice services;

(b) advising the Home Secretary on the operation of that system and the provision of such services; how the principal aim of that system might most effectively be pursued; the content of any national standards he may see fit to set with respect to the provision of such services, or the accommodation in which children and young persons are kept in custody; and the steps that might be taken to prevent offending by children and young persons;

(c) the monitoring and collection of information about the youth justice system and the provision of services by local authorities;

(d) the identification and promotion of good practice in the context of the operation of the youth justice system and the provision of youth justice services, the prevention of offending by children and young persons; and in respect of working with children and young persons who are or are at risk of becoming offenders.

---

[25] *No More Excuses—A New Approach to Tackling Youth Crime in England and Wales*, Cm 3809, 1997.
[26] 1998 Act, s 38.   [27] Ibid, s 41.

Central to the implementation of strategy in relation to young offenders are youth Offending teams (YOT). These teams are intended to 'pull together all the relevant local agencies in delivering community-based interventions with, and supervision of, young offenders.'[28] At least one team has been established in each local authority area, and include at least one probation officer, local authority social worker, police officer, and nominee of a health authority and of the local education authority. They are under a duty to co-ordinate the provision of youth justice services within the local authority area, and to carry out such functions as are assigned to the team in the local authority's youth justice plan made under section 41.[29] Not only should youth offending teams co-ordinate local provision relating to work with young offenders, but they also play a key role in the reprimand and caution system introduced by the 1998 Act,[30] and in respect of various of the orders that may be made by a court when dealing with young offenders. Their primary functions include report-writing for courts, the preparation of reparation or action plans, and the supervision of young offenders within the community, based upon an inter-agency partnership philosophy.[31]

4 VICTIMS OF CRIME

For the lawyer, the primary emphasis of the criminal justice has traditionally been on the detection of crime, and the prosecution of those accused of it. The objectives of that process have, of course, always been the prevention of crime, and the punishment of those who engage in it. Yet the victims of criminal conduct have not always been regarded as fundamental players within the criminal justice 'system'. Although the power to have regard to the injury or loss suffered by the victim is reflected in the power of the court to make a compensation order,[32] or to receive compensation through the Criminal Injuries Compensation Authority,[33] victims have generally had little role in the criminal justice process, beyond giving evidence. Even in that regard, the process has not always been 'victim friendly'. The White Paper *Justice for All*[34] observed:

Justice is not simply about punishment for its own sake. Many victims, when asked, say that they simply want to ensure that no one else has to go through the kind of experience by themselves have. And the best way of ensuring that is to catch, convict and rehabilitate offenders and prevent further crime. Victim's own evidence is crucial in bringing offenders to justice. They must be nurtured and not subject to a host of delays, postponements and barriers . . . The criminal justice agencies have a particular responsibility to support

---

[28] *No More Excuses: New National and Local Focus on Youth Crime*, Home Office, 1997, para 1.21. See also Morgan Report, *Safer Communities: the Local Delivery of Crime Prevention through the Partnership Approach*, Home Office 1991.

[29] *Ante.*　　　[30] See p 530, *post*. Note, in particular, the role of Youth Offender Panels.

[31] Consultation Paper, *op cit*; see also Morgan Report, *Safer Communities: The Local Delivery of Crime Prevention through the Partnership Approach (1991)*.

[32] See p 677, *post.*　　　[33] See p 677, *post.*

[34] Cm 5074, July 2002 (available at www.homeoffice.gov.uk) at paras 2.11–2.12.

victims and witnesses . . . This includes ensuring that they are protected, if vulnerable from intimidation or further crime, and taking into account the impact of the offence on victims when sentencing offenders. . . .

To address this, another White Paper, *A Better Deal for Victims and Witnesses*[35] reviewed what was working well, and what was not. Amongst the positive developments identified were the development of victim support, which, in 2004, helped in excess of one million victims, and the special measures provisions introduced by the Youth Justice and Criminal Evidence Act 1999 to help vulnerable witnesses.[36] Yet a range of problems remained: the need to abandon trials because witnesses and victims refuse to testify, the fact that many victims and witnesses felt badly treated by the criminal justice process, in particular by failure to keep them informed of the progress of cases, or informed of significant events such as the release of an offender from prison. Some of these problems have arisen because responsibility for victims and witnesses is distributed too widely across the criminal justice system, causing confusion, inefficiency and delay. Whatever, victim satisfaction with the police in particular fell from 67 per cent in 1984 to 58 per cent in 2000. The White Paper observed:[37]

Everyone has the right to justice including those accused of crime. But many victims feel that the rights of defendants take precedence over theirs. Public confidence in [the criminal justice system] is dependant on how people perceive that they, or their family or friends, will be treated as a victim or witness to a crime. Too often the perceptions that victims and witnesses are the ones on trial rather than the suspect.

A variety of measures—administrative and evidential—have been introduced to address some of the problems that lead to this perception. Greater powers for the police to impose conditions on police bail,[38] greater protection for witnesses,[39] the use of witness statements in some cases to avoid vulnerable witnesses having to go to court,[40] the greater regard for the victim in the sentencing process,[41] and a range of pilot projects and initiatives, often in liaison with the voluntary sector are examples of the types of measures put in place. This need to address issues relating to victims was recognized by the passage of the Domestic Violence, Crime and Victims Act 2004, which requires the Home Secretary to issue a Code of Practice as to the services to be provided to a victim of criminal conduct by a person who appears to have functions relating to the victims of criminal conduct, or in respect of any aspect of the criminal justice system.[42] These are likely to include the Courts Service, Magistrates' Courts Committees (and, from April 2005) the Courts Agency, the Criminal Cases Review Commission, the Criminal Injuries Compensation Authority, the Criminal Injuries Compensation Appeals Panel, Crown Prosecution Service, the police, the Parole Board, probation boards, the National Association of Victim Support Schemes, and Youth Offending teams.

---

[35] Home Office, 2003.   [36] By means of special measures directions: see p 613, *post.*
[37] *Op cit,* p 2.   [38] See p 411, *ante.*   [39] See p 613, *post.*   [40] See p 614, *post.*
[41] See p 656 et seq.   [42] 2004 Act, s 32(1). This provision will be implemented during 2005.

Those who have responsibilities under the code will be under an obligation to provide services and information to specified classes of victims of crime, particularly victims of offences against the person (including sexual offences) and victims of some offences against property. Special protections will be given to vulnerable victims: a victim falls within this class if he or she is under seventeen, mentally disordered, has experienced domestic violence, been the subject of harassment or religious or racially aggravated crime, or has been the subject of intimidation. The general nature of the duty was described as follows:[43]

Under the [Code] all the services that come into contact with victims . . . have new responsibilities to ensure that the needs of victim's are met . . . The police . . . will be responsible for providing information if a suspect is arrested, cautioned or charged; telling them whether the suspect is on bail; protecting them from intimidation; informing them promptly of the date of any court hearing and ensuring that the victim is put in such with Victim Support Services. The National Probation Service will be responsible for keeping victims informed about a prisoner's release and arrangements for their supervision and any licence conditions.

Particular responsibilities are placed on the Crown Prosecution Service.[44] Under a scheme funded by some £11 million by government the CPS already provides victims with an explanation when the prosecution decision is to discontinue the case or to alter the charges substantially. In certain sex offences or racially aggravated crime in serious cases such as those involving a death or child abuse the CPS offer to meet the victim or victim's family to explain the basis of the decision.

Amongst the rights conferred upon some (though not all) victims are the right to be informed of key stages and decisions, the right to make representations on certain matters relating to release of offenders on licence,[45] and the right to make complaint to the Parliamentary Commissioner for Administration.[46] Section 48 and Schedule 8 of the 2004 Act create the office of Commissioner for Victims and Witnesses. The functions of the Commissioner will be (under s 49) the promotion of the interests of victims and witnesses, the taking of necessary steps with a view to encouraging good practice in the treatment of victims and witnesses, and the keeping under review of then operation of the code of practice.

B THE CRIMINAL PROCESS

1 ADVERSARIAL NATURE

Despite the trend towards diverting offenders away from the criminal justice process, the trial remains at the heart of the criminal justice process. It is, essentially, adversarial

---

[43] *Justice for All* op cit, para 2.43.   [44] For the CPS, see p 356, *ante*.   [45] See p 669, *post*.
[46] 2004 Act, s 47, Schedule 7, amending Parliamentary Commissioner Act 1967.

in nature.[47] The process of investigation and evidence-gathering is conducted by the police or other investigating body, but with the Crown Prosecution Service (CPS)[48] playing an increasing role in supervising the investigation and determining what charges, if any, are to be brought.[49] Traditionally the court plays no significant part in the preparation of the case. The trial itself in not an investigation into events or allegations, but rather a hearing to decide, within complex rules of evidence,[50] whether the prosecution has proved, to the appropriate standard,[51] whether the defendant is guilty of the particular offences with which the prosecution have charged him.[52] By contrast, in many civil law jurisdictions the process is inquisitorial in nature. This term is used to describe systems where judges or magistrates supervise the pre-trial investigations and preparation of the case, to a greater or lesser extent, and play a significant part in the questioning of the witness at trial, and in the decisions as to what evidence should be considered by the court. Simply put, the trial is much more of an investigation than a contest, although some inquisitorial systems have adversarial characteristics, and over-rigid distinctions should be avoided.

This adversarial characteristic has often been viewed as one of the strengths of the English system. These strengths were identified by the Court of Appeal in *R v McIlkenny*:[53]

Another feature of our law, which goes hand in hand with trial by jury, is the adversarial nature of criminal proceedings. Clearly a jury cannot embark on a judicial investigation. So the material must be placed before the jury. It is sometimes said that the adversarial system leaves too much power in the hands of the police. But that criticism has been met, at least in part, by the creation of the Crown Prosecution Service. The great advantage of the adversarial system is that it enables the defendant to test the prosecution case in open court. Once there is sufficient evidence to commit a defendant for trial, the prosecution has to prove the case against him by calling witnesses to give oral testimony in the presence of the jury. We doubt whether there is a better example of exposing the weaknesses in the prosecution case, whether the witness be a policeman, a scientist or a bystander, than by cross examination.

Yet, despite these perceived advantages, in recent years focus has turned to whether

---

[47] For assessment generally of the adversarial process, see the various submissions of evidence to the Royal Commission on Criminal Justice, 1993, Cm 2263, HMSO, and the Royal Commission on Criminal Procedure, 1981, Cmn 8292, HMSO, at para 1.8.

[48] See p 356, *ante*.

[49] See p 534, *post*. When in force, Police and Criminal Evidence Act 1984 (PACE), s 37B, inserted by Criminal Justice Act 2003, Schedule 3, para 2, will give the decision as to whether to charge, and with what, to the CPS.

[50] Detailed consideration of the rules of evidence is beyond the scope of this book. See, generally, Dennis, *The Law of Evidence*, (2nd edn, 2003).

[51] The criminal standard is often described that the court must be satisfied of the defendant's guilt beyond any reasonable doubt. For difficulties in establishing the nature of the standard, see Ch 1, *ante*, and p 615, *post*.

[52] Whilst a judge has a discretion to call witnesses not called by the prosecution or defence, this power should be used sparingly, and only where necessary in the interests of justice: *R v Roberts* (1984) 80 Cr App R 89.

[53] [1992] 2 All ER 417, at 425–6.

the criminal trial in fact achieves its purpose, and, more fundamentally, whether the criminal justice system itself delivers what society expects of it. The adversarial approach of the trial, best exemplified by jury trial in the Crown Court,[54] has not seriously been challenged. The Royal Commission on Criminal Procedure,[55] Royal Commission on Criminal Justice,[56] and the Review of the Criminal Courts of England and Wales[57] (the Auld Review) each considered that:

> there is no persuasive case for a general move away from our adversarial process. Not only is it the norm throughout the common law world, it is beginning to find favour in a number of civil law jurisdictions which have become disenchanted with their inquisitorial tradition.[58]

Yet this general acceptance of a broadly adversarial approach should not disguise the fact that an increasing degree of case management by the court itself has developed. Examples of this are the process of pleas and directions hearings and preparatory hearings,[59] the increased duties of disclosure of evidence on both prosecution and defence,[60] the courts' role in protecting witnesses through special measures directions,[61] and in dealing with applications to withhold evidence.[62] These together constitute a significant inroad in the basic principle that the court does not get involved in what is put before it, and how that is done. In fact, the basic duty on a trial judge to ensure a fair trial, and, now, the wider right to a fair trial under art. 6 of the European Convention on Human Rights,[63] require a judge to perform a key role.[64] In R v Ward[65] the appeal court, in quashing a conviction wrongly obtained, stated that it was the responsibility of a trial judge to ensure a fair trial, to reduce the risk of wrongful conviction to a minimum.

In part, this debate about the nature of the criminal trial and trial process arose because of a series of *causes celebre*[66] where the trial, and indeed pre-trial, process failed to operate in a way to prevent injustice and miscarriage of justice. That was the situation in *Ward*. In R v McIlkenny itself, the appeal court identified some of the weaknesses of the adversarial process, such as the imbalance in resources between prosecution and defence, and the need for proper disclosure of prosecution evidence to the defence. Above all, the effectiveness of any system depends upon it not being abused by those who work within it. Many, though not all, of the miscarriages of justice that made headline news stemmed not from failures in the trial process itself,

---

[54] See ch 10, *ante*.   [55] *Op cit*, para 1.8.   [56] *Op cit*, paras 11–14.
[57] The Auld Review, 2001, HMSO.   [58] Ibid, Ch 1, para 28.   [59] See p 596, *post*.
[60] See p 574, *post*.   [61] See p 613, *post*.
[62] A court may allow relevant evidence to be withheld if a claim of public interest immunity is made out. For the procedure to be followed, see in particular, R v H, R v C, The Times 6 February 2004, following the decision of ECHR in *Edwards and Lewis v United Kingdom*, The Times 29 July 2003.
[63] See Ch 5, *ante*, and p 521, *post*.   [64] See p 522, post.   [65] [1993] 2 All ER 577.
[66] See, e.g., R v McIlkenny, *ante*; R v Maguire [1992] QB 936, [1992] 2 All ER 433; R v Silcott, Braithwaite and Raghip, The Times, 9 December 1991; R v Kisko (1992), unreported. See, generally, Walker and Starmer, *Justice in Error* (1994). For a host of examples see the various annual reports of the Criminal Cases Review Commission, at http://ccrc.gov.uk, and p 684, *post*.

but, rather from failures in the investigation process or from failures to apply properly the processes designed to protect the fairness of the trial itself.[67]

Concerns about the workings of the wider criminal justice process, and the balance between its competing aims, have been increasing in recent years. Back in 1993 the Royal Commission on Criminal Justice made some 352 separate recommendations.[68] As already noted, it did not recommend a fundamental change of approach, doubting whether a general move away from the adversarial approach would be desirable. It concluded that a system which keeps separate the roles of the police, prosecutor, and judge offers a basic protection against the risk of 'unnecessarily prolonged detention prior to trial'.[69] Instead, its recommendations were intended to make the pre-existing system 'more capable of serving the interests of justice and efficiency', and intended to deal with matters that seemed to the Commission to turn what ought to be a search for the truth into 'a contest played between opposing players according to a set of rules which the jury does not necessarily accept or even understand'.[70] It recognized that the criminal trial and the criminal justice process had a wider purpose other than simply to protect defendants, although that is a fundamental characteristic of a 'fair trial'. In achieving this balance, the Commission identified certain principles against which detailed rules, and any suggested changes to those rules, had to be judged: 'Are they fair'? 'Are they open?' 'Are they workable?'

Some, though not all, of the recommendations of the Royal Commission formed the basis of subsequent legislation, or informed the deliberations of other committees, commissions or working groups. The 1990's saw a plethora of government and parliamentary activity, with significant quantities of criminal justice legislation,[71] and culminating in the Auld Committee Report in 2000.[72] That Report, with its 328 recommendations, has itself informed the most recent legislation, the Criminal Justice Act 2003. This constant flow of legislation addressed not only changes to the adversarial pre-trial, trial, and sentencing powers and processes, but also wider and more fundamental questions about the structure and aims of the criminal justice system.

2 THE RIGHT TO A FAIR TRIAL

However we characterize the nature of the process, the right to a fair trial is fundamental, and enshrined in Article 6 of the European Convention on Human Rights.[73] Article 6 states:

---

[67] Many of the cases in question involved alleged police malpractice: see, e.g. *R v Maguire, ante.*

[68] The Commission did not consider police powers (which had been the subject of change in PACE following Royal Commission on Criminal Procedure, 1981, Cmnd 2263, HMSO), the rules relating to bail or sentencing. The various Research Studies published by the Royal Commission are a valuable source of data relating to, and analysis of, the trial system.

[69] Ibid, Ch 1, para 14.   [70] Ibid, Ch 1, para 11.

[71] See, e.g., Criminal Justice Act 1991; Criminal Justice Act 1993; Criminal Justice and Public Order Act 1994; Criminal Procedure and Investigations Act 1996; Crime (Sentences) Act 1997; Crime and Disorder Act 1998, Youth Justice and Criminal Evidence Act 1999.

[72] See n 57, *ante.*   [73] See also, p 180, *ante.*

(1) In the determination of his civil rights and obligations or of any criminal charge against him, everyone is entitled to a fair and public hearing within a reasonable time by an independent and impartial tribunal established by law. Judgment shall be pronounced publicly but the press and public may be excluded from all or part of the trial in the interest of morals, public order or national security in a democratic society, where the interests of juveniles or the protection of the private life of the parties so require, or to the extent strictly necessary in the opinion of the court in special circumstances where publicity would prejudice the interests of justice.

(2) Everyone charged with a criminal offence shall be presumed innocent until proved guilty according to law.

(3) Everyone charged with a criminal offence has the following minimum rights:

(a) to be informed properly, in a language which he understands and in detail, of the nature and cause of the accusation against him;

(b) to have adequate time and facilities for the preparation of his defence;

(c) to defend himself in person or through legal assistance of his own choosing or, if he has no sufficient means to pay for legal assistance, to be given it free when the interests of justice so require;

(d) to examine or have examined witnesses against him, and to obtain the attendance and examination of witnesses on his behalf under the same conditions as witnesses against him; to have the free assistance of an interpreter he cannot understand or speak the language used in court.

It confers protection on those who are subject to a determination of a criminal charge (Article 6(1)). Whether a matter involves a criminal charge will depend on the classification of the proceedings in domestic law, the nature of the offence; and the nature and degree of severity of the penalty that the person concerned risks incurring.[74] Amongst the instances of matters being classified as criminal are the investigation of an allegation of assault with no formal punishment,[75] penalties imposed for breach of military discipline,[76] a regulatory traffic offence,[77] administrative proceedings for customs regulations,[78] and fines imposed by tax authorities.[79] Recent English authorities serve to demonstrate the types of issue that arise. In *R v M; Kerr; H*,[80] it was held that Article 6 does not apply to proceedings under sections 4 and 4A of the Criminal Procedure (Insanity) Act 1964, which relate to the fitness to plead of a defendant. Such proceedings are not criminal, because they do not result in a conviction or a penalty, but merely determine whether the defendant can stand trial. Even if they were criminal, provided the disadvantages to a defendant under a disability are minimized, the trial could be fair and the defendant's disability would not usually, of itself, found an application for abuse of process.[81] Again, in *Han and another v Commissioners of Customs and Excise*[82] the issue arose as to whether the imposition of penalties on

---

[74] *Engel v Netherlands (No 1)* (1976) 1 EHRR 647; *AP v Switzerland* (1997) 26 EHRR 541.
[75] *Adolf v Austria* (1982) 4 EHRR 313.   [76] *Engel v Netherlands (No 1), ante.*
[77] *Ozturk v Germany* (1984) 6 EHRR 409.   [78] *Benedenoun v France* (1994) 18 EHRR 54.
[79] *AP v Switzerland, ante.*   [80] [2001] All ER (D) 67.
[81] See p 604, *post.*   [82] [2001] 4 All ER 687.

taxpayers for dishonest evasion of VAT (described as civil penalties) gave rise to criminal charges for the purpose of Article 6 of the Convention. It was held by the VAT and Duties Tribunal that they did, and that the taxpayers were entitled to the minimum rights contained in Article 6(3) On appeal, the Commissioners of Customs and Excise argued that the classification of the penalty was a civil penalty, that civil penalties had been introduced deliberately to decriminalize the VAT system, and there was an absence of any threat of imprisonment. In rejecting this argument, the Court noted in particular that alternative regimes existed under the legislation (one of them clearly criminal in nature) and with routes to move from one to another. A further example is the administration of a reprimand or warning under section 65 of the Crime and Disorder Act 1998,[83] which was held in *R (on the Application of U)* v *Metropolitan Police Commissioner*[84] to be the determination of a criminal charge. Because the offender had not been told that the effect of a reprimand would be registration as a sex offender,[85] there was a breach of Article 6.

Article 6 is not concerned with the fairness of provisions of substantive law. For that reason a challenge in *R* v *G*[86] to the test of recklessness in respect of the crime of arson failed. The question that Article 6 requires a court to answer is simply: 'is the trial fair'. Nor art. 6 does does prescribe rules for the admissibility of evidence:[87] In *Khan (Sultan)* v *United Kingdom*[88] the Court of Human Rights found there to be no breach of Article 6 in admitting evidence obtained by interception of conversations obtained by an interference with the property rights of the applicant, even though there might in some circumstances be a breach of the Article 8 rights of the applicant. There was no evidence of unreliability or unfairness. Article 6 does not directly address questions of errors of law or misuse of judicial discretion, unless a wider Convention right is infringed.[89]

The right to a fair trial cannot be limited.[90] A court must, though, be mindful that, although it should not accord a margin of appreciation[91] to the national authority, it should give weight to the decisions of a representative legislature and democratic government within the areas of discretionary judgment accorded to them. In deciding what the right to a fair trial involves, a court may ask whether a limit on a right is reasonable, directed by national authorities towards a clear and proper public objective and proportionate to that objective. Thus in *Brown* v *Stott (Procurator Fiscal: Dunfermline)*[92] the Privy Council, on an appeal from Scotland, held that provisions in section 172 of the Road Traffic Act 1988 requiring the registered owner of a motor vehicle to supply information as to the driver of a vehicle at any date and time did not infringe Article 6 rights protection against being required to self-incriminate. There was a clear public interest in dealing with driving that imperils the safety of others.

---

[83] See p 528, *post.*   [84] [2003] 1 All ER 419.   [85] Under Sexual Offences Act 2003.
[86] [2002] EWCA 1992.
[87] *Schenk* v *Switzerland* (1998) 13 EHRR 242; *Doorson* v *The Netherlands* (1996) 22 EHRR 330; *Trivedi* v *United Kingdom* [1997] EHRLR 520.
[88] [2000] Crim LR 683.   [89] *Ali* v *United Kingdom* (1997).
[90] See p 180, *ante.*   [91] See p 171, *ante.*   [92] [2001] 2 All ER 97.

The concept of applying legal rules to secure a fair trial is, of course, not one that is new, and which only arises under Article 6: English criminal procedure and evidential rules has long proceeded on this basis. Both at common law and under section 78 of Police and Criminal Evidence Act 1984 (PACE) a trial court must always act to secure a fair trial. It has been described as an 'elementary right of every defendant',[93] and as a 'constitutional right'.[94] One mechanism for achieving this has long been the basic common law discretion, which exists to permit the exclusion of evidence the probative value of which is low compared with its prejudicial effects.[95] However, Article 6 does raise certain key issues in the context of the criminal process. Amongst these are questions as to the presumption of innocence,[96] the principle against self-incrimination,[97] the right to legal advice and representation,[98] and the obligation to employ rules and procedures in a fair way. It also impacts significantly on issues relating to sentence.[99] The detailed issues that it raises are discussed as they arise.

Most fundamental of all, though, is the right to be tried by an independent and impartial tribunal. Justice must not only be done, but be seen to be done. If it can be shown that a court is the subject of actual bias, or, much more likely, gives the appearance of bias or lack of impartiality (judged objectively) then Article 6 rights will be infringed.[100] The question is whether there is a real danger of bias.[101] A court should ascertain the circumstances, and then '. . . ask itself whether, having regard to those circumstances, there was a real danger of bias on the part of the relevant member of the tribunal in question, in the sense that he might unfairly regard (or have unfairly regarded) with favour, or disfavour, the case of a party to an issue under consideration.' The matter must be viewed from the perspective of the 'informed observer'.[102] R v Gough is a good example. The brother of the appellant was the next-door neighbour of one member of the jury. The House of Lords concluded that there was not a real danger that the appellant had received a trial that was unfair, the juror having sworn a statement that she was unaware of the connection until after the jury had delivered its verdict.

In a criminal case, one aspect of the problem is whether a judge who has made pre-trial rulings or findings can, fairly, preside over the trial itself. The will usually be a legitimate doubt about impartiality if the judge has been involved in the case before trial in a way that involves the formulation of an opinion as to the guilt or innocence of the defendant.[103] There will also be a breach of Article 6 where the prosecuting authority appointed the judge.[104]

---

[93] per Lord Hope in R v Brown (Winston) [1998] AC 367.   [94] Ibid per Lord Steyn.

[95] R v Sang [1980] AC 402.   [96] See p 635, post.   [97] See p 635, post.

[98] See p 180, ante.   [99] See p 656, post.

[100] See Piersack v Belgium (1982) 5 EHRR 69; De Cubber v Belgium (1984) 7 EHRR 236; Hauschildt v Denmark (1989) 12 EHRR 416; Langborger v Sweden (1989) 12 EHRR 416.

[101] R v Gough [1993] AC 646.   [102] Locobail (UK) Ltd v Bayfield Properties [2000] 2 WLR 870.

[103] Brown v United Kingdom (1985) 8 EHRR 272.

[104] Findlay v United Kingdom (1997) 24 EHRR 221; De Cubber v Belgium (1984) 7 EHRR 236 (trial judge was previously the investigating judge).

C CASE MANAGEMENT

As noted above, a fair trial for the defendant must be the prime objective of the criminal trial. In a note written to the Lord Chancellor, Lord Woolf CJ wrote that '. . . the presumption of innocence and a robust adversarial process are essential features of English legal tradition and of the defendant's right to a fair trial . . .'. However, the efficient and effective management of cases is crucial if, on the one hand, a defendant is to be tried fairly and expeditiously, and, on the other, that the process is efficient, and effective in ensuring that those who *are* guilty are convicted and punished. To achieve this, one important pre-condition are procedural rules which are clear and concisely expressed, and which can be changed without complex legislative intervention.[105] To achieve this, new Criminal Procedure Rules which came into force on 4 April 2005, have been introduced, and aim to consolidate the rules and practices that govern the process from beginning to end. They are intended to create a culture change, making everybody involved in a case responsible for helping to make the case go ahead efficiently, under the supervision of the court,[106] and are the first step in the creation of a 'comprehensive criminal procedural code'. The Rules have been made by a new Criminal Procedure Rule Committee.[107] Reference is made in this book to these Rules during detailed consideration of the trial process, where it is necessary to do so. Rule 1.2 imposes a duty on every participant in the case to prepare and conduct the case in accordance with a new overriding objective. This is that 'criminal cases be dealt with justly'.[108] This is, by rule 1.2, to comprise seven elements:

(a) acquitting the innocent and convicting the guilty;

(b) dealing with the prosecution and the defence fairly;

(c) recognizing the rights of a defendant, particularly those arising under Article 6;

(d) respecting the interests of witnesses, victims, and jurors and keeping them informed of the progress of the case;

(e) dealing with the case efficiently and expeditiously;

(f) ensuring that appropriate information is available to the court when bail and sentence are being considered;

(g) dealing with a case in ways that take into account the gravity of the offence charged, the complexity of the matters in issue, the severity of the consequences for the defendant and others affected, and the needs of other cases.

---

[105] Auld Review, *op cit*, Ch 10.   [106] http://www.dca.gov.uk/criminal/crimpr.htm.
[107] For the relevant legislative framework, see Courts Act 2003, ss 69–74.   [108] CPR 2005, 1.1.

These may be thought not to be controversial, although (g) above gives to the possible danger of the downgrading of the procedural standards in cases perceived as less serious. The Rules place a duty on all those involved to ensure compliance with their provisions, and to report any 'significant failure', defined as being a failure which might hinder the court in furthering the overriding objective.

19

PRE-TRIAL PROCEDURE

A THE DECISION TO COMMENCE PROCEEDINGS

1 DISCRETION AND CAUTIONING

The fact that an offence is believed to have been committed does not mean that the commencement of a prosecution is inevitable. Discretion exists at various stages as to whether a prosecution should be commenced, or the suspect cautioned formally or informally. The police and the Crown Prosecution Service or other prosecution authority each has discretion at appropriate times. That discretion may be reviewable on normal judicial review principles.[1] It is also the duty of prosecuting authorities to keep under review the decision whether or not to prosecute.

At the policing level, an individual officer has discretion as to what action, if any, he should take. He can informally caution, make an arrest,[2] or formally report a suspect with a view to prosecution. These decisions will often be made in the light of the overall policies adopted by the police force of which the officer is a part. At a later stage a decision will have to be taken whether an individual should be charged, and, if so, with what offence, or whether a caution should be administered.

The practice of formally cautioning, rather than prosecuting, can be traced back to 1929, but until 2003 never had a statutory basis. It was first regulated in 1978.[3] but, despite these attempts to achieve greater consistency, cautioning practices varied widely between individual police forces, and were confined, in the main to elderly offenders, those suffering mental stress and young first offenders who had committed minor offences.[4] In 1991, some 279,000 offenders were dealt with by way of caution, some 179,000 of these relating to indictable or either-way offences. The Royal Commission on Criminal Justice[5] recommended an extension of cautioning to more petty

---

[1] See p 212, *ante*.

[2] Arrest for the purposes of cautioning is lawful only if the grounds for arrest in fact exist, and are being used. There is no power to detain for the purposes of cautioning: *Collins* v *Wilcock* [1984] 3 All ER 374, and p 405, *ante*.

[3] Home Office Circular 70/1978, replaced by Circular 14/1985.

[4] See Wilkinson and Evans, 'Police Cautioning of Juveniles: The Impact of Circular 14/1985' [1990] Crim LR 165; Westwood, 'The Effects of Home Office Guidelines on the Cautioning of Offenders' [1991] Crim LR 591; Evans, 'Police Cautioning and the Young Offender' [1991] Crim LR 598.

[5] *Op cit*, Ch 5, para 57.

offenders, but also recognized a need for national guidelines within which cautioning could occur, thus achieving greater consistency. It recommended that consideration should be given to combining cautions with other support, through social services or the probation service but recognized that a failure to prosecute an individual can itself damage confidence in the criminal justice system.

In 1994, Circular 18/1994 was issued. It encouraged the police to caution formally rather than prosecute in some circumstances. It required there to be evidence of the suspect's guilt sufficient to raise a reasonable prospect of conviction: the suspect must have admitted guilt. The caution amounts to a conviction for the purposes of registration under the provisions of the Sex Offender Notification Requirements.[6] The Circular deals with how the cautioning power was to be used. It stated:

(a) in deciding whether to charge or to summons an offender, no account will be taken of any previous conviction, or an earlier caution;

(b) the seriousness of the accused's action will determine whether a prosecution should take place. The police will take into account aggravating features, such as the age of the victim, and whether violence was used;

(c) the views of the victim may be important;

(d) there was a presumption in favour of cautioning for juveniles, and a high probability of a caution for young adults, aged between eighteen and twenty;

(e) If a caution is appropriate, regard will then be had to previous cautions or pending prosecutions of the offender.

The Auld Review observed that some 260,000 cautions were issued in 1999, amounting to some 25 per cent of 'solved' offences.[7] The offences were mainly, but not totally, in respect of less serious offences, with cautioning rates significantly high in respect of minor thefts, and drug offences, but, paradoxically, the cautioning-rate for summary-only offences was lower than for either-way offences. This may change under the 'caution-plus' provisions introduced by the Criminal Justice Act 2003 following the recommendations of the Auld Review. The incidence of cautioning was also higher in respect of juveniles. Juveniles are now dealt with under a separate scheme of reprimands and warnings introduced by the Crime and Disorder Act 1998.[8]

This extra-statutory scheme had its drawbacks. There was no sanction in respect of the original offence for an offender who re-offends. The power to caution did not have a power associated with it requiring an offender to engage in activities such as reparation to the victim, to pay compensation, or attend appropriate activities such as a drug or alcohol treatment programme, or sex offender programme. The Auld Review concluded that the cautioning system paid no regard to the feelings of the

---

[6] R (On the application of U) v MPC [2002] 4 All ER 593.
[7] Op cit, Ch 10, paras 41–47. The equivalent figures for 2000, excluding motoring offences, was 239,000 offenders: Cautions Court Proceedings and Sentencing 2000 Home Office Statistical Bulletin 20/01, Nov 2001.
[8] See p 530, post.

victim, lacked rigour, and posed a temptation to hard-pressed police forces to use cautions to effect a better clear-up rate. It therefore proposed, for adult offenders a new system of 'caution-plus', which forms the basis for the conditional caution provisions of the Criminal Justice Act 2003.

2 CONDITIONAL CAUTIONS FOR ADULT OFFENDERS

As noted above, until the passage of the 2003 Act,[9] no statutory power existed governing the cautioning of adult offenders at all, still less one which permitted the imposition of a requirement that the offender should make reparation for his offending behaviour, such as the payment of compensation for the damage done by vandalism, or apology to the victim, or a requirement of attendance at particular forms of activity which could address the offending behaviour. This was in stark contrast to the approach taken in respect of young offenders by the Crime and Disorder Act 1998.

Section 22 of the 2003 Act defines a conditional caution as one 'given in respect of an offence and which has conditions attached with which the offender must comply'. Conditions can be imposed only to the extent that they either ensure or facilitate the rehabilitation of the offender or to make sure that he makes some reparation. The caution (which amounts to a criminal conviction) is to be administered by the police, or by the CPS, or by any other designated person,[10] thus allowing cautioning in respect of minor offences investigated by non-police bodies, such as the Department of Social Security, or the RSPCA.

There are five pre-requisites prescribed by section 23, and which must each be satisfied:

(1) the cautioner must have evidence that the suspect committed the crime;

(2) the CPS must be satisfied that there is sufficient evidence to charge the suspect with the offence, and that a caution should be given. The CPS thus is the decisive decision-maker, and no doubt will be reluctant to caution in serious cases, or where the suspect has similar convictions, a poor record, or where the offence merits imprisonment.

(3) the suspect must admit the offence to the cautioner;

(4) the nature of the caution, and the consequences of the breach must be made clear to the suspect;[11]

(5) the suspect must sign a document recording the details of the offence and the admission of it by him. This in law amounts to a confession,[12] and will be evidence against the offender if he is subsequently prosecuted following non-compliance with the conditions attached to the caution.

---

[9] The conditional caution provisions are being piloted, and not universally in force.

[10] 2003 Act, s 22(4).

[11] See by analogy, *R v R and R* [2002] Crim LR 349, where there was a failure to explain that acceptance of a caution would result in registration under the sex offender legislation.

[12] Defined by PACE, s 82(3) as a statement wholly or partly adverse to its maker.

The Act does not prescribe any limits to the conditions that may be imposed. Guidance under a Code of Practice has been issued, but any conditions must be compliant with the Article 8 rights of the offender (right to respect for private and family life, etc).[13] Clearly, if the conditions impose any restrictions or requirements that affect the Article 8 rights of the offender, those conditions must be necessary and proportionate to ensure Convention-compliance, but, if justified, could include a requirement to clean up graffiti, make financial reparation, or attend treatment or behaviour programmes. If they are broken, the power exists to prosecute the offender for the original offence, a powerful sanction that may well make the conditional caution an effective way of dealing with the lower-level type of offence, whilst at the same time reducing the workload on the courts.

3 REPRIMANDS AND WARNINGS FOR JUVENILES

Circular 18/94 created a presumption in favour of cautioning of juveniles (i.e. those aged under eighteen)[14] Under the Circular, juveniles were more likely to cautioned than adults, but no support for the juvenile to address the offending behaviour was linked to the caution, at any rate in a formal sense. The Royal Commission on Criminal Justice[15] concluded that consideration should be given to combining cautions with other support, through social services or the probation service. It also recognized that failure to prosecute can damage confidence in the criminal justice system. Research showed that those children who display criminal behaviour at an early age are more likely to become serious or persistent offenders.[16] Cautions could best work for young offenders, diverting them from the criminal justice system if the response was clear and firm: cautions were shown to be of decreasing effectiveness as they are repeated.[17] It was to achieve a more effective and consistent scheme that the Crime and Disorder Act 1998 introduced reprimands and final warnings.

Under the 1998 Act, a constable may administer either a reprimand or a final warning where he has evidence that a child or young person[18] has committed an offence, and he considers that the evidence is such that, if the offender were prosecuted for the offence, there would be a realistic prospect of him being convicted.[19] The power only arises if the offender admits to the constable that he committed the offence, has not previously been convicted of an offence, and the constable is satisfied that it would not be in the public interest for the offender to be prosecuted.

The constable may reprimand the offender if the offender has not previously been reprimanded or warned. The offender must be warned rather than given a reprimand

---

[13] See p 184, *ante.*   [14] See p 514, *ante.*   [15] *Op cit,* at Ch 5, paras 57 *et seq.*

[16] *Young People and Crime* Home Office Research Study No 145, 1996.

[17] *No More Excuses—A New Approach to Tackling Youth Crime in England and Wales* Cm 3809, 1997, para 5.9.

[18] Probably to be determined as at the date of the offence, not court proceedings: see *Ghafour* [2002] Crim LR 739.

[19] 1998 Act, s 65(1).

if the constable considers the offence to be so serious to require a warning, but an offender may not be warned more than once. Guidance exists to indicate the circumstances in which a reprimand or a warning is appropriate, and form of the reprimand or warning. The scheme envisages that a first offence might be met with a reprimand, provided it is not too serious. Any further offence should be met with a warning: no offender should receive two reprimands, and any offence after a warning should result in prosecution, except where it is minor in nature and at least two years have elapsed since the administration of the warning.

The reprimand or warning is given at the police station by the constable in the presence of an appropriate adult, who will be a parent, guardian, representative of the local authority if the juvenile is in care, local authority social worker, or other responsible adult other than a police employee. The effect is the same as a conviction for that offence, although reprimands and final warnings do not become 'spent' under the Rehabilitation of Offenders Act 1974.[20] Where a warning is given the constable must refer the juvenile to a youth offending team,[21] which will assess the juvenile referred and, unless it is considered inappropriate to do so, that person shall arrange for that juvenile to participate in a rehabilitation programme. Thus might include, for example, meeting the victim, apologising for the crime and hearing about its effects, a programme of work, or payment of compensation. A failure to comply with the rehabilitation programme is not of itself punishment, but a 'failure to participate' in the programme may be cited in criminal proceedings just like a previous conviction.[22] That appears to relate only to total non participation, not inadequate participation.

4 JUDICIAL SCRUTINY OF THE DECISION TO PROSECUTE OR CAUTION

The decision to caution, or to prosecute instead of cautioning, is not beyond judicial scrutiny.[23] In R v *Chief Constable of Kent County Constabulary, ex parte L*[24] the Divisional Court considered that a decision to prosecute a twelve year-old girl, which was claimed to be in breach of the policy for cautioning of juveniles, was susceptible to judicial review, although on the facts it was found to be a proper exercise of discretion. Watkins LJ considered that the policy of cautioning, instead of prosecuting, was well settled and played a prominent part in the process of decision-making in an individual case. Care should be taken, however, to avoid 'the danger of opening too wide the door of review of the discretion to continue a prosecution', and the Court appeared to draw a distinction between decisions involving adults and those involving juveniles. Another Divisional Court in R v *Inland Revenue Commissioners, ex parte Mead*[25] has stressed that decisions relating to adults are not beyond judicial review,

---

[20] Which treats certain convictions as 'spent' after periods specified in the Act.

[21] 1998 Act, s 66(1). For youth offending teams, see p 516, *ante*.   [22] Ibid, s 66(5).

[23] There are distinct limits to judicial review of the decisions of a prosecution authority: see Watkin LJ in R v *General Council of the Bar, ex parte Percival* [1991] 1 QB 212, [1990] 3 All ER 137, and Ch 6 p 212, *ante*.

[24] [1993] 1 All ER 756.   [25] [1993] 1 All ER 772.

although the situations in which the courts would in fact intervene will be rare.[26] The criteria for the administration of reprimands and final warnings, and conditional cautions, are now set out in statutory form. An individual will have a legitimate expectation that Guidance issued will be adhered to.[27]

5 POLICE BAIL

Questions of bail arise at various stages of the criminal process. An arrested person need not, now,[28] always be taken to the police station. Where a suspect's identity and address are known and the offence is minor, there is often no need to go through the time-consuming process of the custody process at the police station. New provisions in PACE[29] permit a constable to release a suspect on 'street bail' before reaching the police station. The change is intended to simplify procedures, reduce administrative burden, save police resources, and speed up the process.[30] The bailed person must be given, or sent a notice telling him when and where he must answer to his bail, which may be at any time in the future, although it is anticipated that a period of two weeks should be the norm, and should not in any event exceed six weeks.[31] A constable should, in deciding whether to use this power, have regard to the nature of the offence, the ability to progress the case at the police station, the level of confidence in the suspect answering bail, and the level of understanding and awareness of the suspect. The likelihood of further offending, risk to the safety or welfare of the suspect, and the age of the suspect are also relevant.[32]

If an arrested person is in fact taken to the police station, a custody officer must order his release from police detention either on bail or without bail, in which case he goes to prison. The powers and duties of the police when dealing with the continued detention of those in custody have already been discussed.[33] The power to order bail is subject to limitations, which apply where the name and address of the arrested person is unknown, if detention is necessary for his protection or for the protection of other persons or property, if the defendant is not likely to answer to his bail, or is likely to interfere with the administration of justice, or, in the case of an imprisonable offence, detention is necessary to prevent his committing further offences.[34]

---

[26] The fact that there are alternative remedies, for example, to challenge for abuse of process, does not prevent the exercise of discretion itself from being challenged by way of judicial review.

[27] See p 214, *ante*.

[28] From 20 January 2004, when Criminal Justice Act 2003, s 4, came into force.

[29] PACE, ss 30A–30D. The Criminal Justice Act 2003, s 4, also amends PACE, ss 30, 34–36, 41, and 47.

[30] *Justice for All op cit*, para 3.10.

[31] Home Office Circular 61/2003, *Bail Elsewhere than at a Police Station*.

[32] Circular 61/2003, *ante*.   [33] See p 409, *ante*.   [34] PACE, s 38(1).

6 THE DECISION TO PROSECUTE

(a) Commencement—the pre-existing position

The decision to commence proceedings was generally in the hands of the police, although other organizations have law enforcement powers as well. In most cases the police have charged, taken a suspect into custody, or provided the information for the issue of a summons or warrant for arrest. It has been, though, the duty of the Director of Public Prosecutions to take over the conduct of all criminal proceedings instituted on behalf of a police force.[35] In reality, the DPP and Crown Prosecution Service have played a central role in the decision-making process, as has, in the case of serious or complex fraud, the Serious Fraud Office. The role of the CPS has now changed radically, with the implementation of new provisions contained in the Criminal Justice Act 2003.[36]

Other persons or bodies other than the police may institute proceedings. The Royal Commission on Criminal Procedure[37] in 1981 concluded that it would be both impracticable and undesirable to bring all prosecutions within the ambit of the CPS, although it suggested that a private prosecutor should first be under a duty to notify the Crown prosecutor, who should then decide whether to take over the prosecution. That latter suggestion was not implemented. The Auld Review[38] likewise considered that the right of private prosecution should remain, even though it is rarely used. Section 6 of the Prosecution of Offences Act 1985 states that nothing in the Act precludes any person from instituting any criminal proceedings to which the Director's duty under the Act does not apply. There are, though, safeguards. By section 42 of the Supreme Court Act 1981, if on an application by the Attorney-General the High Court is satisfied that any person has habitually and persistently and without any reasonable ground instituted vexatious prosecutions (whether against the same or different persons) the court may make a criminal proceedings order. This has the effect that no information shall be laid before a justice of the peace, and no application for leave to prefer a Bill of indictment shall be made by that person without the leave of the court. Leave is not to be granted unless the High Court is satisfied that the institution of proceedings does not amount to an abuse of process. In addition, in some cases the consent of the Attorney-General is needed.[39]

The Auld Review rejected any system of pre-charge check or approval. It did, though, endorse the recommendation of the Law Commission[40] that any court before

---

[35] Prosecution of Offences Act 1985, s 3(2)(a). In difficult, important or otherwise appropriate cases the DPP may institute proceedings: s 3(2)(b). For the office of the DPP, see p 23 and 356, *ante*.

[36] *Infra*.   [37] *Op cit*, paras 7.40–7.52.   [38] *Op cit*, Ch 12, paras 46–51.

[39] See, e.g., offences of incitement to racial hatred (Public Order Act 1986, s 27); offences under the Terrorism Act 2000. Some 150 statutes require the consent of either the Attorney-General or the DPP. See, p 000, *ante*. The Law Commission, and the Auld Review recommended general abolition of these requirements.

[40] Auld Review, *op cit*, Ch 12, para 50, citing Law Commission *Consents to Prosecution* Law Comm No 255, paras 7.4–7.8.

which a private prosecution is initiated should be under a duty forthwith to notify the DPP in writing. The DPP could decide whether to take over the proceedings, or take them over and then discontinue them. That recommendation has not been implemented, but since private prosecutions will in reality be known to Crown Prosecutors as some stage, there is nothing to prevent this practice from occurring routinely.

(b) The new procedure—the Criminal Justice Act 2003

The 2003 Act gives the CPS much greater involvement in the decision to prosecute and choice of charge. The Auld Review took the view that the CPS 'has still to fill its proper role which . . . should be closer to the more highly regarded Procurator Fiscal in Scotland or the Office of the Director of Public Prosecutions in Northern Ireland.'[41] It recommended that CPS should, generally, determine the initial charge. Following implementation of changes recommended by the Glidewell Report[42] and the Narey Report,[43] with CPS staff increasingly located in or close to police stations ('co-location'), or on call, greater CPS involvement is, for the first time, a practical proposition. Studies showed, however, that a voluntary approach did not inevitably create the closer involvement in the charging process.[44] Given the automatic sending for trial procedure now in place for trial on indictment,[45] the need for speed and efficiency, and the obligation in the Code for Crown Prosecutors not only to consider whether there is sufficient evidence (the 'sufficiency of evidence' test) but also whether it is in the public interest to prosecute (the 'public interest' test),[46] the Auld Review considered that change was essential.

That recommendation has to be viewed in the context of a continuing failure always to get the charge right in the first place. The Government White Paper *Justice for All*[47] stated that some 13 per cent of cases have to be discontinued by the CPS, either because there was not enough evidence to convict or because it is not in the public interest to proceed. Some 45 per cent of police files submitted to the CPS are not properly compiled, leading to the collapse of some cases, due to lack of evidence.[48] A failure to get the charge right early also makes the plea before venue procedure[49] less useful that it could be. *Justice for All* reported that pilot co-location projects saved, in cost, some 14 per cent of what would otherwise have been spent in monetary terms, and the number of cases disposed of at first hearing increased by some 20 per cent.

---

[41] *Op cit*, Ch 12, para 12. For the CPS generally, and recent reforms see p 356, *ante*.

[42] *A Review of The Review of the Crown Prosecution Service*, HMSO, 1998: see p 356, *ante*.

[43] *Review of Delay in the Criminal Justice System*, Home Office, 1997.

[44] *Reducing Delay in the Criminal Justice System: Evaluation of Pilot Schemes*, Ernst & Young, Home Office, 1999.

[45] See p 567, *post*.

[46] See p 635, *post*. The police in charging have regard, under Code C, only to the sufficiency of evidence.

[47] *Op cit*, Ch 3, p 52. The CPS Inspectorate in its Annual Report 1999–2000 found that some 22 per cent of police charges relating to assault, public order and road traffic were incorrect.

[48] See Ward and Davies, *Practitioners' Guide to the Criminal Justice Act 2003* (2004) para 3.2.

[49] See p 547, *post*, and Herbert, 'Mode of Trial and Magistrates' Sentencing Powers: Will increased powers inevitably lead to a reduction in the committal rate?' [2003] Crim LR 314.

A new section 37B of PACE[50] sets out the duties of the police. Except in minor and road traffic cases, the police must supply the CPS with information specified in Guidance. The CPS will then decide whether a charge should be laid, and, if so, what it should be using the sufficiency of evidence and public interest test. Alternatively, the CPS may decide that a conditional caution[51] is appropriate. The decision will be communicated in writing on the police and be binding on them. Co-location should make this process relatively speedy, but no time-limit is specified by section 37B, and section 37 of PACE has been amended to allow bail to be granted to a suspect whilst this decision-making process occurs.

(c) The criteria

By section 10 of the 1985, the Director of Public Prosecutions is under a duty to issue a Code for Crown Prosecutors, giving guidance on the general principles to be applied by them in determining, in any case, whether proceedings should be instituted, discontinued, or what charges should be made. The is to be found in works such as *Archbold* or *Blackstone's Criminal Practice*.

The first question to be decided is whether there is sufficient evidence. There must be admissible, substantial and reliable evidence that a criminal offence has been committed by an identified individual. In deciding this, a prima facie case is not enough: the test is whether there is a realistic prospect of conviction. This is an objective test. It means that a jury, or bench of magistrates (or district judge), properly directed in law is more likely than not to convict the defendant of the charge alleged.[52] In deciding that, a careful study of the available evidence will be undertaken. The possibility that evidence might be inadmissible in law, nor be excluded because of failure to comply with relevant rules, the possibility that a confession may be unreliable, the possibility that a witness may be hostile or likely to be unreliable, or not likely to tell the truth, the impression a witness will make in court, the availability of all necessary witnesses or the likelihood of the court accepting documentary evidence and competence of young children are all factors which are relevant. The prosecutor will look at the overall weight of the case, whether dangers of concoction of evidence exists, whether a case can be sustained against more than one defendant (if there is more than one), and whether the public might consider a prosecution to be oppressive. The prosecutor will also consider what the defence case may be.

Having decided whether there is a sufficiency of evidence, the prosecutor is then required to consider the wider public interest, although the interests of the victim also should be borne in mind. The graver the offence the less likelihood there will be that the public interest will permit the case to be dealt with by anything other than prosecution, although the Code does urge prosecutors to strive to ensure that the

---

[50] Created by Criminal Justice Act 2003, s 28 and Schedule 2. The provisions came into force on 29 January 2004.

[51] See p 529, *ante*.   [52] The so-called '51 per cent' rule.

spirit of cautioning guidelines is observed, where the seriousness of the offence allows. In particular the following factors may provide an indication that prosecution may not be required—

(a) where a court is likely to impose a small or nominal penalty only;

(b) where the offence was committed as a result of a genuine mistake or misunder-standing (balanced against the seriousness of the offence);

(c) where the loss or harm is minor, and results from a single incident (and particularly if it was caused by misjudgment)

(d) where the offences are stale. However, the staleness may have been caused by the offender himself, the offences may only just have come to light, there may have been the need for a long, complex investigation, or the offences may be serious;

(e) prosecution may have a very bad effect on the health of the victim, again bearing in mind the seriousness of the offence;

(f) old-age or infirmity;

(g) mental disorder at the time of the commission of the offence. Where the effect of proceedings on the health of the accused is not outweighed by a wider public interest in favour of prosecution, proceedings should not be com-menced, or may be discontinued. In this type of case other relevant factors will be the nature of the mental condition and the likelihood of further offending;

(h) changes in attitude by the complainant, including the making of reparation or putting right loss. However, prosecution cannot be avoided simply by an ability to pay compensation.

In addition to the Code of Practice, the CPS and police have developed charging standards for certain types of offence. These include certain assaults and other offences against the person, driving offences, and public order offences. The intention is to ensure fairness and consistency in the approach to certain types of offence. Certain principles are stated in all the charging standards. Charges should accurately reflect the extent of the defendant's involvement and responsibility, the choice of charges should accurately reflect the defendant's involvement and responsibility, the choice of charges should ensure the clear and simple presentation of the case; it is wrong to encourage a defendant to plead guilty to a few charges by selecting more charges than are necessary, and it is wrong to select a more serious charge not sup-ported by the evidence in order to encourage a plea of guilty to a lesser allegation.

(d) Discontinuance

Under section 23 of the Prosecution of Offences Act 1985 notice of discontinuance can be issued, provided this is done in summary cases before the hearing of the evidence, or, in cases to be tried on indictment, before sending for trial. This can be done by correspondence, and without the expense and inconvenience of a court hearing. It does not replace the power of a prosecutor to go before a court and offer no evidence or withdraw a charge, both of which remain options[53] although the leave of the court is needed.[54] Nor does it interfere with the power of the Attorney-General to prevent proceedings from continuing by the issue of a writ of *nolle prosequi*.

In deciding how to use these powers it is the duty of prosecutors to keep a case under review. In the case of juveniles it may become clear that a reprimand or final warning is a more appropriate way of dealing with the matter. In respect of those suffering illness the effect on health may make it appropriate for the case to be withdrawn.[55]

This power of review has been shown to be important. Since the creation of the Crown Prosecution Service in 1985 the incidence of discontinuance or withdrawal has risen from 7 per cent in 1985 to 13 per cent in 2001. In part this is due to the defects in the charging process, now addressed by the 2003 Act. The Narey Report considered[56] that the CPS, should not be permitted to discontinue cases on public interest grounds because they consider the offence is not serious. This recommendation, designed to resolve differences between police and CPS, is unlikely to be implemented given the key role in charging is now given to the CPS itself.

(e) Time-limits for prosecution and abuse of process

The right to trial within a reasonable time is part of the Article 6 rights of a defendant, that period being judged from the date on which the defendant is charged or officially notified that he is to be prosecuted,[57] and which continues all the way through the proceedings until a sentence is fixed.[58] Thus, it applies to decisions in respect of the enforcement of compensation orders or fines.[59] The reasonableness of the length of proceedings must be assessed in the light of all the circumstances of the case, having regard to the complexity of the case, the conduct of the applicant and of the prosecution authorities, and the importance of what is at stake. Where there is a breach of Article 6 there must be such remedy as is just, effective, and proportionate.[60]

Increasing concern has arisen about delays in the criminal justice system.[61] In general there is no time-limit on the prosecution of an indictable offence, although by contrast, summary proceedings must be brought within six months from the date of commission of the offence.[62] Even in some cases triable on indictment Parliament has,

---

[53] *R v Director of Public Prosecutions, ex parte Cooke* (1991) 95 Cr App R 233.

[54] The Royal Commission on Criminal Justice recommended that the CPS should have the power to discontinue a case without the leave of the court at any time prior to the start of the trial: *op cit*, Ch 5, para 37.

[55] This power to discontinue remains throughout the trial itself. In *R v Seelig* (1993) the defendant was discharged because he was medically unable to cope with the strains of a long trials in which he was defending himself: see *The Times*, 15 February 1993.

[56] Op cit, p 460.

[57] *Eckle* v *Germany* (1982) 5 EHRR 1; *Ewing* v *United Kingdom* (1986) 10 EHRR 141.

[58] *Findlay* v *United Kingdom* (1997) 24 EHRR 221; *Phillips* v *United Kingdom* (2001).

[59] *Crowther* v *United Kingdom* [2005] All ER (D) 06 (Feb); *Lloyd* v *Bow Street Magistrates' Court* [2003] EWHC 2294.

[60] *Attorney-General's Reference (No 2 of 2001)* [2004] 1 Cr App R 25.   [61] See p 514, *ante.*

[62] Or six months from when the matter of complaint arose: see Magistrates' Courts Act 1980, s 127.

for reasons of policy, imposed a time-limit: thus a prosecution for unlawful sexual intercourse with a girl under the age of sixteen may not be commenced more than twelve months after the commission of the offence.[63] However, even where no specific time-limit exists the court is not powerless, and can intervene to correct abuse of process caused by delay. The elapsing of time may also be a ground leading to a conviction being quashed. In R v B[64] it was held that a residual discretion existed to set aside a conviction considered to be unsafe because of the elapsing of time between offence and prosecution. That decision, though, was exceptional, and distinguished in R v E(T)[65] where there was a twelve-year gap between alleged sexual offences against children and their prosecution. The crucial in factor in E(T) was that there was supporting evidence independent of the allegations by the complainant, and unlike B, it was possible for the defendant to defend himself by cross-examination of the complainant.

A court can, as part of its inherent power, order a stay to prevent abuse of process.[66] Thus if the prosecution has manipulated or misused the process of the court:

so as to deprive the defendant of a protection provided by the law or if there has been such delay so that prejudice or unfairness to the defendant arises . . .[67]

then the court can order that the prosecution does not proceed. This is a power 'of great constitutional importance',[68] and arises in two classes, which may, of course, overlap. But, whichever class into which the case falls, the crucial factor is the public interest. In *Attorney-General's Refence (No 2 of 2001)*[69] the majority of the House of Lords held that it was not appropriate to stay proceedings unless (a) there could no longer be a fair hearing, or (b) it would be otherwise unfair to try the defendant. If the proposed trial would actually be unfair, then there would be an infringement of the fair trial provisions of Article 6. However, where matters of fairness can be dealt with at the trial they should be, rather than the proceedings being stayed for an abuse of process. In *Attorney-General's Reference (No 2 of 2001)* the court observed that a charge should not be stayed or dismissed if any lesser remedy would be just and proportionate. This was the case in R v *Hopkins*,[70] where an application to stay proceedings for abuse of process failed. Despite the fact that the prosecution was in respect of complaints of sexual abuse and violence which the police had originally investigated and decided not to proceed with the subsequent investigation and prosecution did not create unfairness that could not be dealt with at the trial.

The second class of case is where, although the fairness of the trial is not in question, nevertheless it would be unfair to the defendant because of the abuse that

---

[63] See Sexual Offences Act 2003, s 9.   [64] [2003] 2 Cr App R 197.
[65] [2004] 2 Cr App R 36.
[66] *Connolly* v *Director of Public Prosecutions* [1964] AC 1254, (1964) 48 Cr App R 183.
[67] R v *Derby Magistrates' Court, ex parte Brooks* (1984) 80 Cr App R 164.
[68] per Lord Salmon in *DPP* v *Humphrys* [1976] 2 All ER 479, at 527.   [69] [2004] 1 Cr App R 25.
[70] [2004] All ER (D) 356 (Feb).

has occurred. In *R v Croydon Justices, ex parte Dean*[71] this was applied and a conviction quashed, the accused having been assured that he would not be prosecuted. Again, in *R v Horseferry Road MC, ex parte Bennett*[72] the House of Lords held that the doctrine of abuse of process applied to prevent the trial of an accused who had been brought to the United Kingdom through the collusion of the UK and South African authorities, in breach of extradition procedures. Despite the fact that the fairness of the trial itself was not in issue, the court considered that the judiciary had a responsibility for the maintenance of the rule of law. A third example is where criminal proceedings are brought vexatiously by a private prosecutor.[73] Nonetheless, the ultimate objective of the discretionary power to stay proceedings is to ensure that there should be a fair trial. It is usually only in cases where there has been prosecution misconduct that the proceedings will be stayed under this second class, as *ex parte Dean* and *ex parte Bennett* illustrate.[74]

Dealing with a case involving delay, Viscount Dilhorne in *Director of Public Prosecutions v Humphrys*[75] warned that use of this power should only occur 'in the most exceptional circumstances'. This was an approach echoed by Lord Lane CJ in *A-G's Reference (No 1 of 1990)*[76] where he stated that even if delay was unjustifiable the imposition of a stay:

should be the exception rather than the rule. Still more rare should be cases where a stay can properly be imposed in the absence of any fault on the part of the complainant or prosecution.

This remains true despite the provisions of the Human Rights Act 1998, which incorporate the right to a fair trial within a reasonable time.[77] The defendant must show on the balance of probabilities that, owing to the delay, he will suffer serious prejudice to the extent that no fair trial can be held. In deciding this, the ability of the court through the rules of evidence to regulate what is placed before it, and the ability of the judge to warn and to give appropriate directions to the jury, should both be borne in mind. The reasons for delay may also be relevant. Prosecution inefficiency is one factor,[78] as is the nature of the case. A longer period of preparation for the prosecution is only to be expected in complex cases, particularly fraud cases.[79] Delay may also arise because of the nature of the offence alleged, and the reluctance of a victim to come forward.[80] Whatever the reason, long delay is not, inevitably, a

---

71 [1993] QB 769, [1993] 3 All ER 129; see also *R v Bow Street Stipendiary Magistrates' ex parte Director of Public Prosecutions* (1989) 91 Cr App R 283; *R v Crown Court at Norwich, ex parte Belsham* [1992] 1 All ER 394, [1992] 1 WLR 54.

72 [1994] 1 AC 42; see also *R v Beckford* [1996] 1 Cr App R 94.

73 See, e.g., *R v Belmarsh Magistrates' Court, ex parte Watts* [1999] 2 Cr App R 198.

74 See *R (On the application of Ebrahim) v Feltham MC; Muoat v DPP* [2001] 3 All ER 381.

75 [1977] AC 1, [1976] 2 All ER 497.

76 [1992] QB 630, [1992] 3 All ER 169; *R v H* [2003] All ER (D) 403 (Feb).

77 *R v H* [2003] All ER (D) 403. For Article 6, see p 180 and p 521, *ante*.

78 *R v West London Magistrates' Court, ex parte Anderson* (1984) 80 Cr App R 143.

79 See Narey Report, *op cit*, p 460.   80 *R v LPB* (1990) 91 Cr App R 359.

justification for a stay. In *R v Central Criminal Court, ex parte Randle and Pottle*[81] a delay of twenty years in a case of assisting the Soviet spy, George Blake, in escaping from lawful custody was held, on the facts, not to justify a stay. Again, in *R v V*[82] a twenty-year gap between alleged acts of sexual abuse and the prosecution was held to be no bar to prosecution, the court stressing that staying proceedings for delay should be exceptional. The delay could be explained by the fact that the complainant of the sexual offence was seven years younger than the defendant (his brother) and the defendant had threatened the complainant, had been violent in the past, and the complainant had been reluctant to tell because of the effect on her family.

Statute has created a framework within which prosecutors must work. By section 2 of the Prosecution of Offences Act 1985, and regulations made hereunder, there are time-limits regulating how long a defendant may be kept in custody pending the start of summary trial, between the first appearance at court and sending for trial, and between sending for trial and the start of the trial.[83] These are seventy days between first appearance and sending for trial,[84] eighty-six days from date of first appearance to the opening day of the trial and 112 days from, sending for trial until arraignment.[85] Application can be made for extension of those limits, and a right of appeal exists in respect of the decision of a magistrates' court to extend, or a refusal to extend, these time limits. By contrast, no power exists in respect of such an order made by the Crown Court, but since this is not a matter 'relating to trial on indictment' an aggrieved person could seek judicial review of the decision.

Of course, delay may arise not only in respect of the commencement of the proceedings but also in their conduct. The reduction of delays in the criminal justice system is regarded by the government as a matter of high priority. Despite a significant reduction in the number of cases coming before the courts, custody time limits are not always met.[86] This issue is discussed in due course.[87]

B BRINGING THE SUSPECT BEFORE THE COURT

1 THE OLD PROCEDURE

A suspect could of course have been charged, and thus brought before the court, or alternatively, bailed, and under a duty to surrender to bail. Otherwise proceedings could, prior to the implementation of provisions of the Criminal Justice Act 2003, be commenced by the defendant being brought before the court in one of three ways. Firstly, by a summons; secondly, by warrant for arrest; thirdly by arrest without

---

[81] (1992) 92 Cr App R 323.

[82] [2004] All ER (D) 207 (Feb); see also *R v V* [2004] All ER (D) 207 (Feb).

[83] See Prosecution of Offences (Custody Time Limits) Regulations 1987, SI 1987/698.

[84] See p 564, *post.*   [85] See p 598, *post.*   [86] See Narey Report, *op cit.*

[87] See p 572, *post.*

warrant. In respect of arrest without warrant, the available powers have already been discussed.[88]

A summons and a warrant for arrest were obtained by the laying of an information, a statement by which a magistrate is informed of the offence for which the summons or warrant is required.[89] The summons, if issued, would state shortly the matter of the information and then set out the time and place at which the defendant is required by the summons to appear. It can be issued by a single magistrate or justices' clerk.[90] Provided the magistrate or clerk acts judicially, he did not to have to make any further enquiries,[91] and normally the proposed defendant will have no right to be heard.[92] When issued it is served on the defendant. Rules exist governing how this should be effected, and how it should be proved.

A warrant is an order for the arrest of the defendant. It contains a statement of the offence charged, addressed to the officers of the police area in which the warrant is issued, and any other named persons, and directs the arrest of a named person: general warrants (not naming the person to be arrested) were declared illegal at common law in a series of constitutionally famous cases.[93] If the person arrested is to be released on bail, the warrant is described as 'backed for bail'.[94]

Before issuing 'process' (i.e. a summons or warrant) a magistrate, clerk, or authorized person must be satisfied on two matters:

(a) that jurisdiction to do so exists. It will do so if the person accused resides in that petty session area, or is believed to do so; if the alleged offence was committed in that area; or if it is necessary or expedient for the person to be tried in the same area as another person.[95] This may be because the offences should be tried together, perhaps because they are so closely connected that the same witnesses are involved.[96]

(b) The evidence is sufficient to do so.

The issue of process is discretionary, subject to challenge on normal judicial review principles.[97]

---

[88] See CL12, *ante.*

[89] Huddleston B in *R v Hughes* (1879) 4 QBD 614, cited with approval by the House of Lords in *R v Manchester Stipendiary Magistrate, ex parte Hill* [1983] 1 AC 328, *sub nom Hill v Anderton* [1982] 2 All ER 963.

[90] See Justices Clerks Rules 1999, SI 1999/2784, rr 2–3. 'Justices clerk' includes a member of staff with delegated authority.

[91] *R v Clerk to Bradford Justices, ex parte Sykes and another* [1999] Crim LR 748.

[92] *R v West London Stipendiary Magistrate, ex parte Klahn* [1979] 1 WLR 933. In an exceptional case a defendant may be permitted to make representations.

[93] *Money v Leach* (1765) 3 Burr 1742; *Entick v Carrington* (1765) 19 Sate Tr 1029.

[94] Magistrates' Courts Act 1980, s 117.   [95] 1980 Act, s 1(2).

[96] See, e.g., *R v Blandford, R v Freestone* [1955] 1 All ER 681, [1955] 1 WLR 331.

[97] See p 214, *ante.*

2 THE NEW PROCEDURE

The Auld Review pointed to the antiquated and inefficient nature of the system described above.[98] Many cases begun by summons were adjourned at the first hearing due to the non-appearance of the accused, which could be compelled only by the issue of a warrant, resulting in a further adjournment. Some cases could in fact be dealt with in absence of the defendant: they are, however, limited to cases where the charges are summary-only and carried a maximum punishment of no greater than three months imprisonment.[99]

Sections 28 to 31 of the Criminal Justice Act 2003 implement the recommendations of the Auld Review, and bring both greater simplicity and efficiency to the commencement of proceedings. A prosecutor will issue a *written charge* setting out the allegation, issue a *requisition* requiring the accused to appear before the magistrates' court at the specified date, and serve both on the court and defendant. It is hoped to cut-out wasted first and second appearances in motoring, local authority, and breach of community penalty cases.[100] Informations as a means of obtaining a summons are abolished, but remain as an option of obtaining a warrant, and for private prosecutors.

Section 308 of the 2003 Act removes some of the restrictions on dealing with a case in the absence of the defendant. However, this change is not as sweeping as may first appear, because a court must require those whom it is considering dealing with in a manner greater than an absolute discharge or fine to attend in person.

C CLASSIFICATION OF OFFENCES

Some 95 per cent of all criminal cases are tried summarily in the magistrates' or youth court. It is only a small minority of cases that are tried on indictment in the Crown Court.[101] The decision as to whether a charge is tried in the magistrates' court, with its advantages of speed, relative informality, and cost, or on indictment by judge and jury turns initially on the classification of the offence charged. Prior to the implementation of Part III of the Criminal Law Act 1977 the law relating to the classification of criminal offences and the determination of the appropriate Mode of Trial, summary or on indictment, was complex. Thus there were provisions for summary offences to be tried on indictment and for indictable offences to be tried summarily, while there was a third class of offences, colloquially (though not by statute) called 'hybrid' offences which might take on the character of either summary offences or indictable offences according to the election of the parties. These classifications were reviewed by

---

[98] *Op cit*, Ch 10, paras 416–422.   [99] Magistrates' Courts Act 1980, s 12.

[100] Ward and Davies, *op cit*, para 3.24.

[101] See the admonition by Darbyshire in 'An Essay on the Importance and Neglect of the Magistracy' [1997] Crim LR 639.

the James Committee in 1975,[102] which had as its twin aims a simplification of the procedure and possible reduction in the case loads of the Crown Court. Its recommendations were in part controversial, but the majority of them were adopted, and implemented by Part III of the Criminal Law Act 1977.

As regards Mode of Trial there are now three classes of offence namely:

(a) offences triable only on indictment;[103]

(b) offences triable only summarily;[104] and

(c) offences triable either way.[105]

1 OFFENCES TRIABLE ONLY ON INDICTMENT

Because offences can only fall within one of the other two categories if statute so provides, it follows that where there is no express statutory provision an offence is triable only on indictment. This involves a trial by judge and jury[106] in the Crown Court. The case will not now require committal proceedings and will be sent or transferred for trial.[107]

In practice only the gravest indictable offences are triable only on indictment; these include murder, genocide, manslaughter, infanticide, child destruction, abortion, rape, sexual intercourse with a girl under thirteen, sedition, mutiny, piracy, offences under section 1 of the Official Secrets Act 1911, robbery, wounding or causing grievous bodily harm 'with intent', blackmail, assault with intent to rob, aggravated burglary, and burglary comprising the commission of, or an intention to commit, an offence triable only on indictment. It will, however, be recalled that these are triable only on indictment if committed by an adult. As we shall see, in the case of children and young persons, all indictable offences (other than homicide) may, and in most cases must, be tried summarily.[108]

2 OFFENCES TRIABLE ONLY SUMMARILY

The expressions 'summary offence' and 'offence triable only summarily' may be taken as synonymous. A statute creating a summary offence will first define the offence and then state that it is punishable 'on summary conviction' with a particular penalty, thereby indicating that the offence is a summary one. In addition a number of

---

[102] *The Distribution of Criminal Business between the Crown Court and Magistrates' Courts* Cmnd 6323, HMSO.

[103] This should be distinguished from the phrase 'indictable offences', which means offences which, if committed by an adult, are triable on indictment, either exclusively or because they are 'either-way' offences: Interpretation Act 1978, s 5, Schedule 1.

[104] A 'summary offence' means an offence which, if committed by an adult, is triable only summarily.

[105] An offence 'triable either way' means an offence which, if committed by an adult, is triable either on indictment or summarily.

[106] For limited exceptions, see pp 552 and 643, *post*.   [107] See p 564, *post*.

[108] See p 552, *post*.

offences which, prior to the Criminal Law Act 1977, were not summary offences according to the statute creating them, became so.[109]

Special rules apply to some offences under the Criminal Damage Act 1971: offences under section 1 of this Act (excluding arson) are triable only summarily if the 'value involved' does not exceed £5,000. Section 22 of the Magistrates' Courts Act 1980 prescribes a procedure for determining whether such offences are to be regarded as summary or as triable either way (if the value involved exceeds £5,000). The court begins by hearing any representations made by the prosecutor or the accused as to the value involved; if it appears to the court clear that the value involved does not exceed the prescribed sum, it will proceed to summary trial. If it is clear that it does exceed that sum, then it will treat the offence as triable either way (which, of course, it then is).[110] If it is not clear whether or not the value involved does exceed the prescribed sum, then the defendant is given the choice and told that if he consents to summary trial, his liability to imprisonment or to a fine will be limited to the maximum that magistrates have power to impose; the nature of the offence will then be determined in accordance with the accused's decision. If a person is convicted, either by a magistrates' court or by the Crown Court, he cannot appeal on the ground that the magistrates were mistaken as to the value involved.[111]

3 OFFENCES TRIABLE EITHER WAY

The third class of offence is offences triable either way. In respect of these offences, the court has to determine whether the case is suitable for summary trial, or should be sent to the Crown Court. The defendant must, though, agree to summary trial if the court considers that summary trial is appropriate, and can himself elect jury trial, a right not generally open to a defendant until 1855.[112] The perceived inadequacy of prosecution disclosure, the potential for offence negotiation, the fact that mode of trial is often agreed informally between prosecutor and defendant and the perception, justified or not, the Crown Court process is superior have all been cited as factors which have encouraged defendants to elect for trial by jury.[113]

The offences which are either way are listed in Schedule 1 to the Magistrates' Courts Act 1980, which consists of thirty-five paragraphs incorporating some sixty-six separate offences; these include unlawful wounding or inflicting grievous bodily harm,

---

[109] See, now, Magistrates' Courts Act 1980, s 17 and Schedule 1.

[110] The court must hear 'representations', meaning submissions, assertions of fact and sometimes production of documents; however, the court is not bound to hear evidence of the value involved: *R v Canterbury and St Augustine Justices, ex parte Klisiak* [1982] QB 398, [1981] 2 All ER 129. Moreover, it is possible in cases of doubt for the prosecution to limit the charge to certain items clearly below the prescribed value, even though in fact other damaged items would take the value above the prescribed value (so as to ensure summary trial). In *R (DPP) v Prestatyn Magistrates' Court* [2002] Law Society Gazette, 1 July 2002, it was held, in the case of genetically modified maize that it was impossible to ascribe a value, and thus the offence was triable either-way.

[111] Magistrates' Courts Act 1980, s 22(8). [112] *Op cit*, Ch 5, para 123.

[113] See, e.g., Herbert, 'Mode of Trial and Magistrates' Sentencing Powers' [2003] Crim LR 315.

with or without a weapon, assault occasioning actual bodily harm, common assault, bigamy, certain forms of perjury and forgery, unlawful sexual intercourse with a girl under sixteen, all indictable offences under the Theft Act 1968 (except robbery, blackmail, assault with intent to rob and certain burglaries), arson, offences under section 1 of the Criminal Damage Act 1971 where the value exceeds £5,000 (*ante*), and indecent assault. In addition many other statutes expressly provide for an offence to be triable either summarily or on indictment (the former 'hybrid' offences) and these are now triable either way.[114]

4 POSSIBLE REFORM

This division of functions between Crown Court and magistrates' court has been the subject of continued discussion over many years. The James Committee[115] recommended the creation of the three-fold division outlined above,[116] though noted that the English system was 'unusual' in giving a defendant a right to choose his court of trial.[117] It also considered that it was appropriate to reclassify offences of low value theft as summary offences, thus restricting the right to jury trial. This proposal met considerable resistance, in the light of the impact any conviction for theft might have on a person's reputation and career. The Royal Commission on Criminal Justice[118] concluded that the distribution of work between magistrates' court and Crown Court was neither rational, nor always amounted to an efficient use of resources recommending that the decision should be by agreement, or, where there was a dispute as to mode of trial, the magistrates' court should determine the matter. This, it anticipated, would lead to fewer mode of trial hearings and fewer cases going to the Crown Court than the 37 per cent of cases the Commission found were electing jury trial. The Commission 'found that those electing trial had one of three or more main objectives: first a wish to put off trial with a view to securing in the meantime the advantages of a more liberal prison regime which would count towards a sentence if convicted and imprisoned; second, a well-founded belief that there was a better chance of acquittal in the Crown Court than before magistrates; and third, a mistaken belief that, if convicted the sentence would be lighter.'[119]

A government consultation paper in 1995[120] placed emphasis on the resource implications. It identified a large increase in the proportion of cases involving either way offences being committed to the Crown Court for trial.[121] In relation to defendants aged seventeen or over, the proportion of such cases rose from 15 per cent in 1980 to 23 per cent in 1987, before falling to 17 per cent in 1992. A significant proportion of these cases were committed to the Crown Court because the magistrates themselves declined jurisdiction. In 1987 the relevant percentage was 47 per cent,

---

114 Ibid, s 17(2).   115 *Op cit*, Cmnd 6323.
116 Implemented by the Criminal Law Act 1977.   117 *Op cit*, para 60.
118 *Op cit*, Ch 6, para 13–19.   119 *Op cit*, Ch 6, paras 6–8.
120 *Mode of Trial: A Consultation Paper* 1995, Cm 2908, HMSO.   121 Ibid, para 2.

rising to 64 per cent in 1991 and then falling to 63 per cent in 1992. This increase in committals had an affect not only on the workload of the court itself, but upon the size of the prison population, on the police, the Crown Prosecution Service and the Legal Aid Fund. The Consultation Paper considered one option to be a reclassification of the mode of trial of minor thefts and certain other offences. In doing so it mirrored the approach taken by the James Committee. Two other options related not so much to the classifications themselves, but rather to the decision-making process as to where 'either way' offences should be tried. The first option came from the Royal Commission on Criminal Justice. It recommended that a person accused of an either way offence should no longer be entitled to insist on trial in the Crown Court, but that the mode of trial should be a matter of agreement between the accused and the Crown Prosecution Service, and, in the absence of such agreement, be determined by magistrates. The other option considered was a change in the law relating to the mechanics of the decision-making process, so that magistrates could be aware, at the time of making the choice of mode of trial, of how the accused intends to plead at trial. The Consultation Paper estimated that a significant number of cases (38,000 in the year ending June 1993) were sent for trial in the Crown Court only for the accused to plead guilty on arraignment, and be given a sentence which the magistrates themselves could have imposed. It identified the fact that a 'significant proportion' of accused falling into that category would in fact be prepared to plead guilty in a magistrates' court to an either way charge and be dealt with by the magistrates. Such cases were often sent to the Crown Court because magistrates declined jurisdiction. It was this last option that found favour. Amended procedures (Plea before Venue) were introduced by the Criminal Procedure and Investigations Act 1996.[122]

The question of either-way offences was one of the major issues addressed by the Auld Review[123] whose consideration of this issue followed hard on the heels of two Mode of Trial Bills which had attempted, in effect, to give the decision-making power as to mode of trial of either-way offences to the magistrates' court, not the defendant.[124] Auld, like the Royal Commission on Criminal Justice and Narey Report[125] before him, took the view that it was for the court, not the defendant to determine mode of trial. The Review rejected the notion that there was some 'ancient, constitutional, fundamental or even broad right of the citizen to jury trial.'[126] The right to elect in fact began as a right to elect summary trial to avoid the rigour of trial on indictment in a limited number of cases, in the context of a harsh system which provided few protections for defendants. The Review considered that the public has 'a legitimate interest in the financial and human cost of the criminal justice system and how best to apply its finite resources and with justice to all.' It is for the court to

[122] See, generally, procedure for mode of trial.   [123] *Op cit*, Ch 5, paras 119–172.
[124] Both Bills (Mode of Trial and Mode of Trial (No 2)) were rejected by the House of Lords essentially on the grounds of it diminished the fundamental right to trial by jury for a serious offence, although considerable criticism of their detail was made.
[125] *Op cit*, Ch 1 p 2, and Ch 8, p 33.
[126] *Op cit*, Ch 5, para 166. All references in this discussion are to paras 66 *et seq*.

determine whether the circumstances of the case merit the more elaborate, costly, and time-consuming procedures of the Crown Court. It also concluded that the fact that some defendants perceive juries as more ready to acquit than magistrates is not a sound reason for leaving the power to elect with the defendant. There may many reasons why juries are more ready to acquit. If procedures in the magistrates' courts are unfair these should be addressed.[127] The Review's recommendations, that the court should decide with a limited right of appeal, that committal proceedings for either-way offences and committals for sentence should be abolished, have, however, only been partially implemented. The most recent interventions in this area, contained in the Criminal Justice Act 2003, do not proceed along the same lines as the ill-fated Modes of Trial Bills. Instead they sought to address the issue by modified Plea before Venue procedures and powers,[128] and by increased powers of sentencing for magistrates.[129]

D PROCEDURE FOR DETERMINING MODE OF TRIAL

The procedure for determining the Mode of Trial differs according to whether or not the accused is an adult. If he is, then, as has been noted, he will always be tried on indictment for an offence triable only on indictment and will always be tried summarily for a summary offence; only in the case of an 'either way' offence are there alternative possibilities. In the case of juveniles the position is quite different. Before considering these procedures it should be noted that if magistrates mistakenly adopt a procedure which is not permitted, for example by 'trying' a case which is triable only on indictment or by sending for trial in the case of an offence triable only summarily, then their 'trial' or 'committal' will be a complete nullity. Even if the defendant has been 'sentenced' he may later be committed for trial and properly tried, if the offence was triable only on indictment.[130]

The choice of charge is that of the prosecution. If the charge preferred is appropriate on the facts given their seriousness, then the defence cannot challenge that charge on the basis that the preferment of another, different charge would have permitted trial on indictment. Problems may also arise where fresh charges are leveled by the prosecutor, which, in reality, amount to attempts to deprive the justices of jurisdiction to try the case themselves. In R v Brooks (Christopher)[131] the appellant appeared before magistrates on a charge under section 20 of the Offences against the Person Act 1861. The appellant was content to be tried summarily, and the justices so ordered. The chief prosecuting solicitor then advised the bringing of a new charge under section 18

---

[127] Citing Ashworth *The Criminal Process: An Evaluation Study* (1998), p 262, and Derbyshire; 'For the new Lord Chancellor—some causes for concern about magistrates' [1997] Crim LR 869.

[128] See p 548, *post.*   [129] See p 637, *post.*

[130] See, e.g., *R v West* [1964] 1 QB 15; [1962] 2 All ER 624.   [131] [1985] Crim LR 385.

of the 1861 Act. In quashing the conviction obtained on such a charge O'Connor LJ observed that the prosecutor was seeking:

to act as an appellate tribunal from the justices. There is no other explanation for it, and he said as much.

However, in *R v Redbridge Justices, ex parte Whitehouse*[132] it was made clear that it was the abuse of power that led to the irregularity in *Brooks*. If the facts are capable of supporting a fresh charge, the justices must decide whether it is both proper and appropriate. If they have already decided on summary trial, any further charge which would have the effect of making summary trial impossible should be scrutinized with care, but is not totally prohibited. The operation of this principle was seen in *R v Sheffield Justices, ex parte Director of Public Prosecutions*[133] where the defendant elected trial on a charge of assault occasioning actual bodily harm. The Crown then substituted a charge of common assault. Upon the magistrates staying the proceedings, the prosecutor successfully applied for judicial review. The substitution was a proper one, despite the fact that it deprived the accused of his right to trial by jury. There was no evidence of manipulation, and the defence had been notified of the proposal at an earlier stage. It was an appropriate charge on the facts.

1 THE PLEA BEFORE VENUE PROCESS—ADULTS

As noted above, the plea before venue process is the means by which the decision is taken as to whether an either way offence is tried by the magistrates' court or sent to the Crown Court for trial by jury. Amended by the Criminal Procedure and Investigations Act 1996 to allow an indication of plea to be given, so that cases where a guilty plea is forthcoming are not sent unnecessarily to the Crown Court, but retained at magistrates' courts level, significant further amendments have been made by the Criminal Justice Act 2003. These amendments are part of a strategy to retain more either-way offences at magistrates' court level. The new provisions recognize the inextricable links between mode of trial and sentencing powers, and are designed to achieve fewer cases going to the Crown Court. The Royal Commission on Criminal Justice found[134] that Crown Courts were imposing sentences that were within the powers of the magistrates' court. The amended plea before venue system was not working as it should.[135] The early plea provisions introduced in 1996 were not overcoming some of the objections to, or reservations about, summary trial. In that context the 2003 Act will, when fully in force, allow a suspect to seek an indication of likely sentence, so that he can gauge what is his likely fate if he pleads guilty. At the

---

[132] (1991) 94 Cr App R 332.   [133] [1993] Crim LR 136.

[134] *Op cit*, para 6.12, relying on research conducted by Hedderman and Moxon, *Magistrates' Court or Crown Court? Mode of Trial Decisions and Sentencing*, Home Office Research Study No 125, HMSO, 1992.

[135] See also Herbert, 'Mode of Trial and Magistrates' Courts Powers' [2003] Crim LR 315.

same time the sentencing powers of magistrates are to be extended,[136] committals for sentence largely abolished,[137] and magistrates allowed to take into account previous convictions of the defendant.[138] By this combination of measures it is hope to achieve a greater number of guilty pleas and significantly reduce the number of cases going to the Crown Court, with a consequent cost saving.

Before any evidence is called, a magistrates' court before whom a person aged seventeen or over appears charged with an offence triable either way must adopt the following procedure:

(1) If the prosecution is being carried on by the Attorney-General, the Solicitor-General, or the Director of Public Prosecutions and he applies for the offence to be tried on indictment, then it must be tried in that way and send the case for trial. In any other case the following steps apply.

(2) The court must first cause the charge to be written down, if this has not already been done, and read to the accused.

(3) The court must explain to the defendant in ordinary language that he may indicate whether (if the offence were to proceed to trial) he would plead guilty or not guilty (1980 Act, s 17A).

(4) The defendant must also be warned that if he indicates that he intends to plead guilty the court will proceed to summary trial.

(5) If the defendant does indicate he would plead guilty then the court must proceed to summary trial with, of course, the power to commit for sentence which exists under section 3 of the Powers of Criminal Courts (Sentencing) Act 2000,[139] though if the court has given an indication of sentence (see below) this is a power which is unlikely to be used often. This indication of plea does not indicate the formal taking of a plea (1980 Act, s 17A(9)). Thus, if the accused indicates that he intends to plead not guilty, then, if the case is committed for trial, it is necessary for a formal plea to be taken in the Crown Court.

(6) If the accused indicates that his intention is to plead not guilty, then the magistrates' court proceeds to determine Mode of Trial, in accordance with the procedure set out below (s 18 of the 1980 Act, as amended).

(7) The prosecutor and then the accused are given an opportunity to make representations as to which Mode of Trial would be more suitable. The prosecutor

[136] Probably not to be brought into force until 2006: see p 638, *post*.

[137] See p 550, *post*.

[138] This is part of a wider theme of the 2003 Act in allowing a greater use of evidence of bad character at trial. See p 619, *post*.

[139] A new s 3 is substituted for the pre-existing provision, by Schedule 3, para 22 of Criminal Justice Act 2003. For changes to power to commit for sentence, see p 639, *post*.

will be invited to give details of the defendant's previous convictions (1980 Act, s 19(2))[140]

(8) The court then considers whether the offence appears more suitable for summary trial or for trial on indictment, having regard to the representations referred to in (7) above, to the nature of the case, whether the circumstances make the offence one of serious character, whether the punishment which a magistrates' court would have power to inflict for it would be adequate, and 'any other circumstances which appear to the court to make it more suitable for the offence to be tried in one way rather than the other.'[141] The Court must also have regard to allocation guidelines made by the new Sentencing Guidance Council[142] These new Allocation Guidelines, will replace the pre-existing Mode of Trial Guidelines, are intended to promote consistency in decisions made as to mode of trial.[143]

(9) If, following consideration as above, it appears to the court that the offence is more suitable for trial on indictment, then it must tell the defendant that it has so decided and will then proceed to send the case for trial, the defendant having no power to prevent this course even if neither he nor the prosecution has requested it.

(10) If, on the other hand, it appears to the court that the offence is 'more suitable for summary trial', then the court must explain to the defendant in ordinary language that he can either consent to summary trial or, if he wishes, be tried by a jury. Magistrates' courts have, increasingly limited, powers to commit to the Crown Court for sentence, if, having dealt with the case summarily, they consider their sentencing powers inadequate.[144] The magistrates' court must inform the defendant of that power. Those powers have mostly been abolished by the Criminal Justice Act 2003,[145] the power to commit to be (when the provision is brought into force) under a new section 3A of the Powers of Criminal Court (Sentencing) Act 2000, introduced by the 2003 Act. This will permit committal for sentence only if the defendant is found convicted of a 'specified offence'.[146] The effect of this is that once a magistrates' court accepts jurisdiction it must, in most cases, sentence the defendant, if convicted, within its own sentencing powers, reducing the number of cases that end up at the Crown Court.

---

[140] As substituted by Criminal Justice Act 2003, Schedule 3. This provision is not yet in force, but amounts to a change from the pre-existing position: see *R v Colchester Justices, ex parte North Essex Building Co Ltd* [1977] 3 All ER 567; *R v Doncaster Magistrates' Court, ex parte Goulding* [1993] 1 All ER 435; *R v South Hackney Juvenile Court, ex parte RB and C* (1983) 4 Cr App R 294.

[141] 1980 Act, s 19(4).

[142] See p 659, *post*. These replace the pre-existing Mode of Trial Guidelines.

[143] Criminal Justice Act 2003, s 170(5).

[144] Powers of Criminal Courts (Sentencing) Act 2000, s 3.

[145] Schedule 3. That provision is not yet in force.

[146] See, further, p 639, *post*. This provision is not yet in force.

(11) After explaining to the defendant his options, the court must ask him whether
      he consents to be tried summarily or wishes to be tried in the Crown Court.
      Before making his choice, the defendant may (when a new s 20 of the 1980
      Act is fully brought into force)[147] ask the court for an indication of likely
      sentence. The rationale for this new provision is that if the defendant receives
      an indication of likely sentence, particularly if it amounts to a statement that
      the defendant does not face a custodial sentence, he may be more willing to
      accept summary trial and not exercise his right to elect for jury trial. Again,
      this is part of the overall strategy of reducing jury trial.

      A court is not bound to give such an indication, and some courts may be
      unwilling in the early stages of operation of the new provisions to do so. An
      indication is not the taking of a plea,[148] and a defendant may elect trial by
      jury, or maintain his initial not guilty plea if the indication is one that is not
      favorable to him.

      The defendant may, after the indication of likely sentence, reconsider his
      initial indication of plea. If he does, he will again be invited to give such an
      indication (1980 Act, s 20(5),(6)). The court will then deal with the mode of
      trial issues in the way outlined above.

(12) If the defendant If he consents to summary trial, the magistrates proceed to
      try him; if he does not consent, they deal with matters such as bail and send
      him for trial (see below)

There are provisions in section 25 of the 1980 Act whereby the magistrates may
change from summary trial to proceed to decline jurisdiction. Where the court has
begun to try an either way offence summarily it may, at any time before the conclusion of the evidence for the prosecution, discontinue the summary trial and proceed
to send for trial. This will necessitate starting all over again and the court must
adjourn the hearing, and is not required to remand the defendant.

The defendant must usually be present in court in person during the proceedings
at which the Mode of Trial is determined.[149] However, the court may proceed in
the absence of the defendant if they consider that by reason of his disorderly conduct
before them it is not practicable for the proceedings to be conducted in his presence.
In addition, where the defendant is represented by counsel or a solicitor who in his
absence signifies to the court the defendant's consent to the proceedings for determining how he is to be tried for the offence being conducted in his absence, and the court
is satisfied that there is good reason for proceeding in the absence of the defendant,
then the court may proceed in the defendant's absence.[150] In either case the consents
required either to summary trial may be given by the defendant's counsel or
solicitor.[151]

---

[147] Introduced by Schedule 3, Criminal Justice Act 2003.
[148] 1980 Act, s 20A(4), not yet in force.   [149] 1980 Act, s 18(2).
[150] Ibid, s 18(3), 23(1).   [151] Ibid, ss 23(3), (4).

2 CHILDREN AND YOUNG PERSONS

The law has given significant protection to children and young persons. An attempt was made by the Children and Young Persons Act 1969 to prohibit the prosecution of children[152] for all crimes except murder, and severely limit the prosecution of young persons. However, these provisions were never brought into force, and were repealed in 1991,[153] leaving children and young persons open to prosecution, but with restrictions as to how proceedings shall be heard. Cases involving juveniles are nearly always tried in the Youth Court.[154]

A child under the age of ten is irrebuttably presumed to be *doli incapax*, that is, incapable in law of committing a criminal offence.[155] This minimum age of criminal responsibility has been criticized[156] and was unsuccessfully challenged in the Court of Human Rights in *T v United Kingdom, V v United Kingdom*.[157] The Court concluded that there was no clear common standard amongst the countries who were signatories to the Convention: even if the age of ten could be said to be low, it could not be regarded as so disproportionate to the stance taken by some other countries.

Whenever a child or young person appears before a youth court charged with any indictable offence except 'homicide' he must, subject to certain exceptions, be tried summarily.[158] This rule does not apply to an offence of homicide. Nor does it apply:

(a) in the case of a young person charged with an offence for which the penalty is in the case of an adult fourteen years' imprisonment or more, not being an offence for which the sentence is fixed by law, and the court considers that if he is found guilty it ought to be possible to sentence him to detention under section 53(2) of the Children and Young Persons Act 1933;[159] or

(b) in the case of a child or young person charged jointly with an adult (eighteen or over) if the court considers it necessary in the interests of justice to commit them both for trial.[160] In this case the court may also commit the child or young person for any other indictable offence with which he is charged at the same time (whether jointly with an adult or not) if that other offence arises out

---

[152] A child is a person aged ten–thirteen inclusive. A young person is a person aged fourteen–seventeen.

[153] Criminal Justice Act 1991, Schedule 13.   [154] See p 543, *ante*.

[155] The rebuttable presumption that a child under 14 was incapable of committing an offence unless it was proved that the child knew that what he had dome was seriously wrong was abolished by Crime and Disorder Act 1998, s 34.

[156] See, e.g. Family Studies Centre Briefing Paper No 3, 1998.

[157] [2000] 2 All ER 1024, (2000) 30 EHRR 121.

[158] Magistrates' Courts Act 1980, s 24(1): 'appears' means appears or is brought before the court when the court makes its decision as to mod of trial, so that a defendant who attains the age of eighteen before this occasion is treated as an adult despite the fact that he was a young person when he appeared at an earlier remand hearing: *R v Islington North Juvenile Court, ex parte Daley* [1983] 1 AC 347; *sub nom Re Daley* [1982] 2 All ER 974, approving *R v St Albans Juvenile Court, ex parte Goodman* [1981] 2 All ER 311 and disapproving *R v Amersham Juvenile Court, ex parte Wilson* [1981 2 All ER 315, which suggested otherwise. Under, Crime and Disorder Act 1998, s 47, where a person attains the age of eighteen before the start of the trial it may send the case to the Crown Court for trial.

[159] See p 646, *post*.   [160] Magistrates' Courts Act 1980, s 24.

of circumstances which are the same as or connected with those giving rise to the first offence.[161]

The power to try a juvenile in an adult court was criticized by the Court of Human Rights in *T v United Kingdom* and *V v United Kingdom*. In this notorious case, where two juveniles were tried and convicted of the murder of a young boy in circumstances that aroused public disgust and anger, the two defendants were tried in an adult Crown Court. The Court concluded that the nature of the proceedings against each of the defendants was a breach of Article 6, in that the defendants were, in the context of a public hearing in the Crown Court, unable to participate effectively in the criminal proceedings. Despite the special measures taken the formality and ritual of a Crown Court trial must have seemed incomprehensible to the defendants. As a result, a Practice Direction was issued[162] It is clear from that Practice Direction that separate trial, rather than joint trial in an adult court should be held where the interests of justice did not necessitate a joint trial.[163]

A child or young person not accused jointly with an adult will be tried in a youth court. However, if charged jointly with an adult he will be tried in an ordinary magistrates' court unless the adult pleads guilty or is not tried summarily (so that they are no longer jointly charged) in which event the court may before any evidence is called in the case of the child or young person remit him to a youth court for trial.[164]

The provisions set out above regarding plea before venue apply equally to juveniles in respect of the limited circumstances when a case can in fact be dealt with in an adult court.[165]

3 FACTORS THAT INFLUENCE MODE OF TRIAL

It has been noted that, in respect of 'either way' offences, the mode of trial is determined both by the magistrates' court and by the defendant. Magistrates were given specific guidance as to how these powers should be used by the National Mode of Trial Guidelines now set out in the *Practice Direction: Consolidated Criminal Practice*.[166] A revised version of the Guidelines was issued by the Criminal Justice Consultative Committee in early 1995, but not as a Practice Direction. The Practice Note, having identified the requirements of section 19 of the Magistrates' Courts Act 1980, states:

(a) the court should never make a decision on the ground of convenience or expedition;

---

[161] Ibid, *s* 24(2).

[162] *Practice Direction (Crown Court: trial of Children and Young Persons)* [2000] 2 All ER 285. See now *Practice Direction (Consolidated Criminal Practice)* [2002] 3 All ER 904.

[163] See, further, p 643, *post*.

[164] Ibid, s 29. This is a power to remit for trial, not for mode of trial to be determined: *R v Tottenham Youth Court, ex parte Fawzy* [1998] 1 All ER 365.

[165] Magistrates' Courts Act 1980, ss 24A–24D, inserted by Criminal Justice Act 2003, Schedule 3 (not yet in force).

[166] [2002] 3 All ER 904.

(b) the court should assume that the prosecution version of the facts is correct;

(c) the fact that the offences are specimen charges is relevant. By contrast, the fact that the defendant will be asking for other offences to be taken into consideration is not;

(d) where complex questions of fact, or difficult points of law, arise, the court should consider [sending for trial];[167]

(e) where two or more defendants are jointly charged with an offence, each has an individual right to elect his mode of trial;

(f) either way offences should be tried summarily unless the particular case has one of the specified features, and the court considers that its sentencing powers are insufficient;

(g) the court should consider its power to commit for sentence if evidence arises during the course of the hearing which leads the court to conclude that the offence is so serious, or the offender such a risk to the public, that its powers to sentence him are inadequate.[168]

The Note then goes into considerable detail, and in respect of each offence identifies relevant factors that may indicate that it ought to be tried on indictment. Thus, for example, burglary is made more serious if it is at night, or if during a daytime burglary persons are present on the property, if soiling or vandalism occurs, if the burglary displays professional hallmarks or is one of a series of similar offences.

As noted above, the Sentencing Guidelines Council promulgates Allocation Guidelines.[169] A magistrates' court will have to have regard to those Guidelines.

E COURT BAIL

1 NATURE OF BAIL

A person is 'granted bail' when he is released from the custody of the law subject to a duty to surrender to custody at some future time. The 'custody' is the custody of a court unless bail was granted by a police officer, in which event it is the custody of the officer. Considerable changes in the law were effected by the Bail Act 1976, which gave effect to many, though not all, of the recommendations of a Home Office Working Party Report[170] which identified the deficiencies of the old law. Previously, bail

---

[167] Committals for trial (the phrase used by the Practice Direction) are abolished by Criminal Justice Act 2003, Schedule 3 (not yet in force). Cases will now either be sent or transferred for trial.

[168] But note that the power to commit for sentence is heavily restricted by the provisions of Criminal Justice Act 2003 (not yet in force). See p 547, *ante* and p 639, *post*.

[169] Criminal Justice Act 2003, s 170. See p 553, *ante*.

[170] *Bail Procedures in Magistrates' Courts*, Home Office, 1974.

involved entering into a 'recognizance' which is an acknowledgement of a debt to the Queen payable on default of compliance with the conditions of the recognizance. The 1976 Act abolished personal recognizances from the defendant but preserved them for sureties (where these are required). If granted bail the defendant is under a duty to surrender to custody when required; if he fails without reasonable cause to do so he commits an offence under section 6(1) of the 1976 Act, punishable either on summary conviction or as a contempt of court.[171]

Bail may be granted either unconditionally or, in some circumstances, subject to conditions. Before any conditions can be imposed it must appear to the court that such conditions are necessary to prevent a failure to surrender to custody, to prevent the commission of an offence while on bail, to prevent interference with witnesses or an obstruction of the course of justice, or to allow inquiries or reports to be made to assist the court in dealing with him for the offence.[172] A court, in the future, may also impose a condition on a defendant for his own protection or welfare, irrespective of the age of the defendant.[173] These factors are, in fact, similar to those a court may rely upon in refusing bail where the court believes that 'substantial grounds' to believe that any of them apply exist,[174] and in R v Mansfield Justices, ex parte Sharkey[175] it was argued that 'substantial grounds' likewise had to exist before a court could impose conditions. This argument was rejected by the Court of Appeal. It was enough that a court considered that there was a real and not fanciful risk of an offence being committed whilst the defendant was on bail. In this case, the justices were entitled to impose conditions preventing the defendants from picketing or demonstrating at places other than their own places of work, during a major industrial dispute in the coal industry and where the court knew that disturbances at coal pits had occurred.

Where conditions can be imposed, they may cover a wide variety of matters. They may comprise the provision of a surety or sureties to secure the person's surrender to custody; the provision of security (if it appears that he is unlikely to remain in Great Britain until the time appointed for him to surrender to custody); requirements to secure that he surrenders to custody, does not commit any offence while on bail, does not interfere with witnesses or otherwise obstruct the course of justice or make himself available for the purpose of enabling inquiries or a report to be made to assist the court in dealing with him for the offence.[176] A court can also impose a condition requiring a defendant to attend an interview with a legal representative.[177] Failure to obtain legal advice or representation is one of the most common reasons for delay,

---

171 Bail Act 1976, s 3(2).   172 Ibid, s 3(6).

173 Bail Act 1976, s 3, as amended by Criminal Justice Act 2003, s 13.

174 Ibid, Schedule 1, para 1.   175 [1985] QB 613, [1985] 1 All ER 193.

176 Bail Act 1976. These conditions may now be imposed not only by a court but by a police officer. In murder cases, unless satisfactory reports on the defendant's mental condition have already been obtained, the court must impose as conditions of bail (a) a requirement that the defendant shall undergo examination by two medical practitioners for the purpose of enabling such reports to be prepared, and (b) a requirement that he shall for that purpose attend such an institution or place as the court directs (ibid, s 3(6A)).

177 Crime and Disorder Act 1998, s 54(2).

because the necessary steps to enable the case to proceed have not been taken. What is clear is that any condition must be necessary and proportionate, because the restriction of liberty invokes Convention rights under Article 5 and Article 8, and thus the restrictions must be justifiable.[178] Conditions commonly imposed include conditions of residence, as to surrender of passport, reporting to a police station at prescribed times, not visiting specified premises, and not approaching specified persons. Such conditions can be onerous in their effect. They can be varied by a court on the application of the person bailed, the prosecutor or a constable. In addition, section 16 of the Criminal Justice Act 2003 confers a right of appeal to the Crown Court against certain conditions. These are:

(a) that the person reside away from a particular place or area;

(b) that the person resides at a particular place other than a bail hostel;

(c) for the provision of a surety or the giving of a security;

(d) that the person concerned remains indoors between certain hours;

(e) requirements in respect of electronic monitoring; that the person makes no contact with another person.

The Crown Court may vary any such condition, a power that previously belonged to the High Court. Presumably, it is open to the Crown Court to vary conditions by deleting a condition entirely, or by adding new, alternative conditions.

2 OCCASIONS FOR THE GRANT OF BAIL

The question of when bail may be granted to a person may arise at various stages of his case, from the moment that he is arrested to the final determination of any appeal arising out of his conviction. Bail in cases of treason can only be granted by order of a High Court judge or the Home Secretary.[179] We have also noted the powers of the police regarding bail. In the context of the courts, bail may be granted as follows.

(a) By magistrates

Magistrates have power to grant bail at various stages of proceedings, subject to certain restrictions. When a defendant is first brought before a magistrates' court charged with an offence it quite often happens that the prosecution is not ready to proceed in which event the proceedings are adjourned and the accused is remanded, either in custody or on bail. This may arise in the course of summary proceedings or where the offence is triable only on indictment (in which event the magistrates will eventually send the case for trial) or where it is triable 'either way'.[180] If magistrates decide to send for trial a defendant to the Crown Court for trial, that sending for trial may be in custody or on bail.[181] Following summary conviction, the magistrates have

---

[178] See p 170, ante.   [179] Magistrates' Courts Act 1980, s 41.   [180] See p 544, ante.
[181] Bail Act 1976, s 6(3).

(now) limited power to commit the defendant to the Crown Court for sentence.[182] If they do they may commit in custody or on bail.[183] Finally, following conviction, if the magistrates adjourn for the purpose of considering sentence they may remand the defendant on bail or in custody[184] and, having imposed a custodial sentence, they may, if a person has given notice of appeal or applied to the magistrates to state a case,[185] grant bail.[186]

If bail is refused on a remand, the maximum period of remand is eight clear days[187] unless the accused is already serving a custodial sentence, in which event it is twenty-eight clear days.[188] There may, of course, be further remands thereafter.[189]

Where magistrates adjourn a summary trial, or the determination of the method of trial of any either way offence and remand the defendant in custody, they may, if the defendant is an adult, order that he be brought up for any subsequent remands before an alternative magistrates' court nearer to the prison where he is to be confined on remand. I the defendant's presence is required, this may be achievable through live TV link.[190] This is, again, designed to reduce delays, in this instance delays which arise where escorted prisoners arrive late at court.

Although successive applications for bail may be made to a magistrates' court (or to any court having power to grant bail), the Bail Act 1976 restricts the scope for continued applications. If bail has been refused a second application for bail can be supported with any argument that is desired, whether or not put before the court before. At any subsequent hearings the court need not hear arguments as to fact or law that it has heard previously.[191]

(b) By the Crown Court

The Crown Court may grant bail to any person:[192]

   (a) who has been committed in custody for appearance (trial or sentence) before the Crown Court; or

   (b) who is in custody pursuant to a sentence imposed by a magistrates' court and has appealed against conviction or sentence; or

   (c) who is in the custody of the Crown Court pending the disposal of his case by the Crown Court; or

---

[182] See p 547, *ante*, and p 639, *post*.

[183] See the terms of ss 3A and 4 of the Powers of Criminal Courts (Sentencing) Act 2000, as amended by Criminal Justice Act 2003.

[184] Magistrates' Courts Act 1980, s 128(1). If the remand is for medical examination and report it must not be for more than three weeks, if in custody, for four weeks, if on bail, and, if on bail, conditions as to undertaking medical examination must be imposed (ibid, s 30).

[185] See p 651, *post*.   [186] Magistrates' Courts Act 1980, s 113.

[187] Ibid, s 128(6): 'clear days' means omitting the day of the remand and the day fixed for the appearance. In certain circumstances this may be exceeded—see 1980 Act, s 128A. The key condition is that a previous remand must have been made.

[188] 1980 Act, s 131(1).   [189] Ibid, *s* 129(1).   [190] Crime and Disorder Act 1998, s 57.

[191] Even if refused bail on remand, a defendant is entitled to have his right to bail fully reviewed at the stage of sending for trial: R v *Reading Crown Court, ex parte Malik* [1981] QB 451, [1981] 1 All ER 249.

[192] Supreme Court Act 1981, s 81 (as amended).

(d) who, after the decision of the Crown Court in his case, has applied to the Crown Court to state a case for the High Court;[193] or

(e) who has applied to the High Court for an order of certiorari, or for leave to apply, in respect of proceedings in the Crown Court;[194] or

(f) to whom the Crown Court has granted a certificate under the Criminal Appeal Act 1968 (case fit for appeal); or

(g) who has been remanded in custody by a magistrates' court, where he has been refused bail by that court after hearing full argument.

The prosecution also has some rights of appeal against the grant of bail, first introduced in 1993.[195] in respect of an offence punishable by imprisonment for a term of five years or more. That has been changed to extend to any offence punishable with imprisonment,[196] a change designed to overcome the problem of mistaken grant of bail at a time when it can be rectified. For this right to exist the prosecution must have objected to bail at the hearing before the magistrates' court, and have to show that there is a risk to the public of serious harm if the defendant is bailed. The appeal is by way of rehearing.[197] The Crown Court may remand the defendant in custody or on bail subject to such conditions as it thinks fit.

(c) By the High Court

Hitherto, an appeal against a magistrates' court withholding bail, or the imposition of conditions, lay to the High Court. That jurisdiction has largely been abolished.[198]

(d) By the Court of Appeal

The Court of Appeal has power to grant bail pending appeal to that court or pending a retrial ordered by that court following such an appeal[199] or pending appeal from that court to the House of Lords.[200] It is rare for the Court of Appeal to grant bail, but it occasionally does so, for example where the sentence appealed against is a short one so that it might be served by the time the appeal comes on for hearing, or where there is a strong prima facie likelihood of success.[201]

---

[193] See p 651, *post*.

[194] This only applies to appellate proceedings in the Crown Court, because whilst it is sitting as a court of first instance it is not amenable to judicial review: see p 213, *ante*.

[195] Bail (Amendment) Act 1993.   [196] Criminal Justice Act 2003, s 16.

[197] For the relevant procedure, see Supreme Court Act 1981, s 18(2). Where notice of appeal is given orally, the magistrates' court must remand the defendant in custody pending hearing of the appeal.

[198] See Criminal Justice Act 2004, s 17. For the original jurisdiction, see Criminal Justice Act 1967, s 22, as amended by Bail Act 1976, Schedule 2.

[199] Criminal Appeal Act 1968, ss 8(2), 19; the power may be exercised by a single judge (ibid, ss 31, 45(2)).

[200] Ibid, s 36. By s 37, if the prosecutor is appealing to the House of Lords and, but for the decision of the Court of Appeal, the appellant would be liable to be detained, the Court of Appeal may make an order providing for his detention or directing that he shall not be released except on bail; there is similar provision on prosecution appeals from the Queens Bench Divisional Court (Administration of Justice Act 1960, s 5).

[201] R v *Wattam* (1978) 68 Cr App R 293.

3 THE RIGHT TO BAIL

The marginal note to section 4 of the Bail Act 1976 is 'General right to bail of accused persons and others' (the 'others' being persons who are brought up for breach of the requirements of certain community orders,[202] or persons who have been remanded following conviction for reports). The section created a statutory presumption in favour of granting bail and provides that, except as provided in Schedule 1 to the Act, bail shall be granted to a person who appears before a magistrates' court or the Crown Court in the course of or in connection with proceedings or who applies for bail in connection with proceedings. It does not apply (save in the case of remand for reports) after conviction.

The right to bail was restricted by section 25 of the Criminal Justice and Public Order Act 1994, which originally provided that a person charged with, or convicted of, murder, attempted murder, manslaughter, rape, or attempted rape must not be granted bail. This provision, intended to prevent repeat offences being committed by a person whilst on bail, was introduced despite the lack of clear empirical evidence that it was needed. It is now being modified, to restore an element of discretion in the hands of the court. Section 56 of the Crime and Disorder Act 1998 modified this to permit a grant of bail where 'exceptional circumstances' exist. The Act carefully avoided defining what might be regarded as exceptional circumstances.

Schedule 1 contains detailed provisions relating to circumstances in which bail may justifiably be withheld. The wider Human Rights Act context should not be overlooked. Article 5 of the Convention does indeed permit the deprivation of liberty, but the presumption is in favour of liberty and the state must show that there are 'relevant and sufficient' reasons to justify detention.[203] The period of pre-trial detention must be limited to a reasonable period of time, the public interest in detention must be balanced with the presumption of innocence, and the withholding of bail must be based on individual circumstances and not stereotypes.[204] There is a need to balance the competing interests in preventing interference with the administration of justice, preservation of public order, and the need to protect the defendant. It is in this context that the following grounds permitting refusal of bail, and in some cases the presumption against bail, must be judged. These vary according to whether the accused is charged with an 'imprisonable offence' or a 'non-imprisonable offence', that is to say whether or not the offence is punishable with imprisonment (even if the accused himself, for example by reason of his age, would not be liable to be imprisoned for it).

If the offence is non-imprisonable the only circumstances in which bail may be withheld are:

(1) if the defendant having previously been granted bail, has failed to comply with

---

[202] See s 4(3), as amended by Criminal Justice Act 1991. For these orders, see p 675, *post.*
[203] *Letellier* v *France* (1991) 14 EHRR 83.
[204] *Yagci and Sargan* v *Turkey* (1995) 20 EHRR 505; *A* v *France* (1999).

his obligation to surrender to custody and the court believes that he would so fail again;

(2) if the court is satisfied that the defendant should be kept in custody for his own protection or, if he is a child or young person, for his own welfare;

(3) if he is already in custody pursuant to a court sentence;[205]

(4) if, having been granted bail in the instant proceedings, he has been arrested for absconding or breaking the conditions of his bail.[206]

If the offence is imprisonable, there is a much wider range of circumstances in which bail may be justifiably withheld, in addition to those listed above.[207] These provisions were significantly amended by the Criminal Justice Act 2003 in the light of research conducted for the White Paper *Justice for All*, which showed that some 18 per cent of adults and 38 per cent of under eighteens, and 12 per cent of all those bailed subsequently fail to attend court or offend whilst on bail.[208] The Auld Review[209] reported police disenchantment at the lack of CPS vigour (as it was perceived) in respect of those who abscond, or re-offend, and are later granted bail. The amended Schedule 1 to the Bail Act 1976 addresses some of these issues. A court may refuse bail in the following circumstances:

(5) if the court is satisfied that there are substantial grounds for believing that the defendant, if released on bail (whether subject to conditions or not) would:
(a) fail to surrender to custody; or
(b) commit an offence while on bail; or
(c) interfere with witnesses or otherwise obstruct the course of justice;

(6) where it has not been practicable for want of time to obtain sufficient information to enable the court to make its decision;

(7) where a case is adjourned for inquiries or report and it appears that it would be impracticable to complete the inquiries or make the report without keeping the defendant in custody.

In considering the grounds referred to under (5) above the court must have regard to the nature and seriousness of the offence or default, the character, antecedents, associations, and community ties of the defendant, the defendant's record in relation to fulfilling his obligations under previous grants of bail in criminal proceedings, the strength of the evidence against him and any other considerations which appear to be relevant.[210] A further restriction was introduced into Schedule 1 in 1994[211] in an attempt to reduce the incidence of offending by persons on bail. In 1993, a study conducted by the Metropolitan Police showed that some 40 per cent of suspects

---

[205] Or a sentence of an authority acting under the Army, Air Force, or Naval Discipline Acts.
[206] Bail Act 1976, Schedule 1, Part II.	[207] Ibid, Schedule 1, Part I.
[208] *Justice for All*, Cm 5563, at Ch 3.	[209] *Op cit*, p 429, para 81.
[210] Schedule 1, para 9.	[211] Criminal Justice and Public Order Act 1994, s 26.

arrested in one week were already on bail.[212] Further amendments made by the 2003 Act mean that a court must 'give weight' to the fact that the defendant is already on bail when assessing whether there is a substantial risk that the defendant would commit a further offence if released on bail.[213] This applies in respect of a person accused of any imprisonable offence. It effectively amounts to a presumption against bail. A court should re-bail such a defendant only if it is satisfied that there is no significant risk of committing an offence whilst on bail. It is by no means certain that this presumption complies in all circumstances with Article 5 of the Convention. As the Parliamentary Joint Committee observed in 2003:[214]

... the court would be prevented from granting bail in at least some circumstances even though it is not satisfied that there is a sufficient public interest in detaining the defendant pending trial ... In some cases (for example, where a minor offence has been committed and the defendant poses no real risk to the community) the court would be prevented from granting bail where detaining the defendant in custody would be self-evidently disproportionate to any purpose, and in other cases it might be clear that the public interest in detaining the defendant is outweighed by other considerations ... [such as] the other Convention rights of the defendant, members of his or her family or other dependants. . . .

Further, section 15 of the 2003 Act requires a court to refuse to bail an adult defendant who fails without reasonable cause to answer bail in the same proceedings unless the court is satisfied that there is no significant risk that the defendant would fail to surrender if released on bail. In respect of juveniles there is no such presumption against bail, but the fact of absconding is a relevant fact for the court to consider in deciding whether there is a substantial risk that the juvenile would fail to surrender to bail.

A still further restriction on bail is contained in Schedule 1 to the Bail Act 1976[215] as part of a range of measures introduced to address the issue of drug-taking and drug-related crime. A court may deny bail, unless the court is satisfied that there is no significant risk of re-offending whilst on bail, or the defendant declines to take up the offer of a 'relevant assessment' in respect of his drug-taking, or, having agreed to one, fails to comply with it. In order for this power to exist:

(a) the defendant must be aged eighteen or over;

(b) the presence in his body of Class A drugs must have been detected,

(c) either he has been charged with an offence under section 5(2) or 5(3) of the Misuse of Drugs Act 1971, or the court is satisfied that his misuse of Class A drugs caused or contributed to his behaviour, or his offending was wholly or partly motivated by his intended misuse of a Class A drug.

---

[212] Debates in 1994 Act, Mr Robert McLennan MP, HC Cmtte.
[213] Bail Act 1976, Schedule 1, Part I, para 2A, inserted by Criminal Justice Act 2003, s 14.
[214] Cited by Ward and Davies, *Criminal Justice Act 2004—A Practitioners' Guide* (2004), at para 3.30.
[215] Inserted by Criminal Justice Act 2003, s 19.

The Act[216] contains detailed provisions for recording the decisions of both courts and police officers in relation to bail and entitling defendants to copies of records of such decisions. Where a court withholds bail or imposes or varies conditions of bail in the case of a person who has a 'right to bail' in criminal proceedings, it must give reasons and these are recorded with the record of the decision.[217]

4 SURETIES

As already noted, the 1976 Act abolished personal recognizances from defendants (although a person may be required to provide security[218]). Recognizances still exist, however, in relation to sureties; these are persons who are sometimes colloquially said to 'stand bail' for the accused. If a person is granted bail subject to the provision of sureties, the court must fix the amounts of the sureties and must also be satisfied that the proposed sureties are suitable having regard to their financial resources, character, and any previous convictions and proximity (whether in point of kinship, place of residence, or otherwise) to the defendant.[219] In practice courts are usually guided by the police in matters relating to the suitability of proposed sureties.

Before sureties are taken it is the practice to explain the nature of the obligations being undertaken so as to ensure that the proposed surety understands them and to warn of the consequences of the defendant failing to answer to his bail. These are, prima facie, forfeiture of the amount of the recognizance and possible imprisonment in default. The court has power to order the surety, in the event of default by the defendant, to forfeit the whole of the amount of the recognizance or part thereof.[220] Before exercising its discretion the court must, in some circumstances,[221] give the surety the opportunity to be heard and must take into account circumstances relating either to means or to the surety's culpability for the non-appearance of the defendant which might make it fair and just for the surety not to be ordered to forfeit the whole amount of the recognizance. Although not decisive, the conduct of the surety will be an important factor in the decision of the court as to whether or not to order forfeiture, either in whole or in part. In *R v Southampton Justices, ex parte Green*[222] Lord Denning MR stated that if the surety was guilty of no want of diligence and used every effort to secure the appearance of the accused it might be proper to remit the sum entirely. Imprisonment may be ordered in default of payment, of up to twelve months.

It is an offence, punishable on summary conviction or as a contempt of court, to

---

[216] Bail Act 1976, s 5.   [217] Ibid, s 5(3), (4).

[218] Hitherto limited to persons unlikely to remain in the United Kingdom, but, now, see Crime and Disorder Act 1998, s 54.

[219] Ibid, s 8(2).   [220] Magistrates' Courts Act 1980, s 120(3).

[221] See Crime and Disorder Act 1998: where recognizances not conditioned for the appearance of the defendant, the court is not bound.

[222] [1976] QB 11, [1975] 2 All ER 1073.

agree to indemnify a surety in criminal proceedings (or, in the case of the surety himself, to be indemnified).[223]

An order of the Crown Court entreating the recognizance of a surety for a defendant who has failed to surrender to his bail to stand trial is not a 'matter relating to trial on indictment' (within section 29(3) of the Supreme Court Act 1981) so that the order is subject to judicial review.[224]

---

[223] Bail Act 1976, s 9.
[224] *Re Smalley* [1985] AC 622, *sub nom Smalley* v *Crown Court at Warwick* [1985] 1 All ER 769.

20

TRIAL ON INDICTMENT

A SENDING AND TRANSFER FOR TRIAL

1 INTRODUCTION

The first stage of the trial of an indictable offence has, in recent legal history, been, been the committal for trial, or, as it is sometimes known, the preliminary inquiry before justices. Increasingly this has been only of a formal nature. Over the years the nature of committal for trial has significantly changed, with numerous legislative attempts to change its nature and purpose: indeed, the whole legislative history might be regarded as a case study into governmental and legislative indecision. That history is set out below. Currently, a hybrid (and confusing) system exists:

  (a) certain cases involving serious or complex fraud, or children, are transferred for trial;[1]

  (b) indictable-only offences are sent for trial;[2]

  (c) either-way cases to be tried in the Crown Court are committed for trial, without the consideration of the evidence.[3]

When the provisions of Schedule 3 to the Criminal Justice Act 2003 are fully brought into force, all cases, other than those transferred for trial, will be sent for trial. Committal proceedings will have been abolished.

2 THE BACKGROUND

Prior to 1967, committal proceedings were always held is to provide a mechanism for initial scrutiny by a court of the prosecution case against the defendant, so as to ensure that sufficient evidence exists to justify requiring the defendant to stand trial on indictment, with the expense and personal suffering that inevitably follows. Fundamental changes were made by the Criminal Justice Act 1967. Prior to that Act committal proceedings were always oral in nature: prosecution witnesses had to give

---

[1] See p 567, *post.*   [2] See p 571, *post.*   [3] See p 568, post.

evidence orally, their evidence was recorded in the form of a document known as a deposition, and the court had to decide whether or not sufficient evidence existed to justify sending the accused for trial on indictment. This procedure had to be followed even where the sufficiency of the prosecution evidence was not being questioned, even by the defendant. Furthermore, since the magistrates often sat in open court, the resulting publicity in notorious cases sometimes gave rise to the creation of a real risk of prejudice to the trial itself. The 1967 Act therefore introduced new procedures, permitting committal for trial without the consideration of the evidence, thus saving much time and expense. It also introduced changes limiting the publicity that can be given to the evidence or the details of the offence.

As long ago as 1981 the Royal Commission on Criminal Procedure[4] concluded that committal proceedings did not operate as an effective filter to prevent weak cases from reaching court. It proposed their abolition and replacement by a new procedure, to be known as an 'application for discharge'. This procedure would have given the defence the option of a hearing before magistrates at which to make a submission of no case to answer, after the prosecution had disclosed its case in writing. These proposals were not implemented at that time.

In 1986 the matter was considered further by the Fraud Trials Committee,[5] which identified a whole series of objections to committal proceedings. These included the length of time taken by full committals, with the consequent delays, the potential for abuse, whereby proceedings were undertaken in the hope of acquiring material to use as a defence, in the hope that advantage could be gained if witnesses die, go abroad, or suffer from fading memories. In addition, the difficulties magistrates had in dealing with serious fraud cases, the cost of such proceedings, and the small number of defendants discharged in fraud cases were all noted. The committee recommended an interim procedural reform, until action might be taken by government on the Royal Commission recommendations in respect of serious fraud cases. The resulting changes were introduced in the Criminal Justice Act 1987,[6] which introduced a notice of transfer procedure and which remains in being. Four years later, in 1991, a similar procedure was introduced in some cases involving children.[7] Where these provisions apply, a notice of transfer can be served which effectively deprives the magistrates of jurisdiction and leads to automatic transfer to the Crown Court. As already noted these cases involving transfer to the Crown Court remain in force.

This approach commended itself to the Royal Commission on Criminal Justice,[8] which, in its research, found that full committal proceedings involving a hearing occurred in only about eight per cent of cases tried on indictment. It also found evidence to support a conclusion that the committal process does not act as an effective filter to weed out weak cases: a significant number of cases fail at the Crown

---

[4] Cmnd 8092, HMSO, 1981.   [5] HMSO, 1986.
[6] Criminal Justice Act 1987, s 4.   [7] Criminal Justice Act 1991, s 53.
[8] Report, Ch 6, paras 26–32.

Court because of a direction by the judge to the jury to acquit. It recommended the abolition of the full committal procedure, but with the defence being able to make oral submissions of no case to answer, to be considered on the evidence contained in the case papers. In respect of either way offences, submissions would have been to a magistrates' court, and be dealt with by a stipendiary magistrate, but in respect of offences triable only on indictment such submissions would be to the Crown Court.[9]

The principle of limiting committal proceedings was accepted by the government, who, however, took a different view on the detail. The Criminal Justice and Public Order Act 1994 introduced a new scheme of transfers for trial,[10] subject to rights to make written representations to dismiss the case. These provisions were never implemented. The government found it difficult to create a scheme that would work effectively, and met strong criticism from professional bodies. It sought to remedy some of these difficulties by further provisions in the Criminal Procedure and Investigations Act 1996. The provisions initially contained in that Act had themselves to be abandoned, again because of practical difficulties and of representations by professional bodies. There followed the extraordinary spectacle of the government then abandoning the original proposals of the 1994 Act, and abandoning its proposals to amend the 1994 Act in the 1996 Act, and, instead, introducing revised provisions into the 1996 Act.[11] These revised provisions, ultimately enacted, kept committal proceedings in place, but modified the rules under which they are conducted.

The result was that committal proceedings remained, subject to the changes in the 1996 Act. These had the effect of limiting the evidence to be considered at such proceedings to documentary evidence and exhibits tendered by the prosecution. However, the right to a hearing remained, and magistrates continued to be able to consider any representations made by either the defence or the prosecution, to assist the court in reaching its decision as to whether the case should be committed for trial. This modified procedure did not, however, remain unchanged for long. The Crime and Disorder Act 1998 abolished committal proceedings in cases where an adult is charged with an indictable only offence.[12] Instead a scheme was introduced which basically requires service of the prosecution case in writing, followed by an opportunity for the defendant to make an application to the Crown Court for the case to be dismissed. Such an application may in some circumstances be an oral application. This new procedure governed cases of serious or complex fraud, or which involve children, in indictable-only cases, hitherto which had been within the notice of transfer procedures. The effect was to achieve a scheme not dissimilar from that recommended by the Royal Commission on Criminal Justice, with three distinct processes:

---

[9] The Royal Commission made consequential recommendations about the appropriate court for an application for bail, and in respect of the time-limits for making such applications of no case to answer: paras 29 and 31.

[10] 1994 Act, s 44 and Schedule 4.   [11] 1996 Act, ss 51–52, and Schedule 3.

[12] 1998 Act, s 51–52, and Schedule 3.

(a) the automatic transfer to the Crown Court of cases of an adult which include an indictable only offence, under the 1998 Act;

(b) committal proceedings in respect of most either way offences, subject to the limitations as to evidence introduced in the 1996 Act;

(c) the notice of transfer procedures contained in the 1987 and 1991 Acts, when they apply, in cases other than indictable-only offences.

As noted above, the Criminal Justice Act 2003 makes further changes.[13] The changes were intended to give effect to the recommendations of the Auld Review and the White Paper *Justice for All*, to create greater speed and efficiency in the handling of criminal cases. Their effect is to provide for common offences (i.e. those linked together) and linked offenders to sent to the Crown Court automatically. The court will not have to wait for committal papers to be prepared, although arraignment in the Crown Court will not occur until service of the prosecution's evidence, normally within forty-two days.[14]

3 PROCEDURE

(a) Indictable only offences

Under the provisions contained in the Crime and Disorder Act 1998, where an adult is charged with an indictable only offence (other than one to which the transfer for trial provisions apply) he must be sent forthwith to the Crown Court.[15] The person committed will be committed also in respect of any either way offences or summary offences with which he is also charged which:

(a) appear to the court to be related to the indictable only offence, and

(b) in the case of summary offences, are punishable with imprisonment or involve obligatory or discretionary disqualification from driving.[16] A summary offence is related to an indictable only offence if it arises out of circumstances which are the same as, or connected with, those giving rise to the indictable only offence.[17] In cases where an adult is jointly charged with an either way offence that appears to be related to the indictable only offence he also must be sent for trial. 'Related to' in this context means if the offence could be joined in the same indictment.[18] By contrast if a child or young person is jointly charged with that same indictable only offence the court may send for trial, but is not required to do so.

---

[13] 2003 Act, Schedule 3. These provisions are not yet in force.

[14] Crime and Disorder Act (Service of Prosecution Evidence) Regulations 2000, SI 2000/3305.

[15] 1998 Act, ss 51–52 and Schedule 3. When in force s 51 will be as substituted by Criminal Justice Act 2003, Schedule 3, para 18.

[16] Ibid, s 51(2), (4), (6), (11).

[17] Ibid, s 51(11). When the 2003 Act is in force the relevant provision is a new s 51E of the 1998 Act.

[18] See n 17, *ante*. For joinder of counts in an indictment, see p 587, *post*.

A person who has been sent for trial under the 1998 Act is entitled to receive copies of the documents containing the evidence on which the charge or charges are based.[19] When he has received that evidence, and before arraignment, he may apply either orally (provided he has given notice of intention to so) or in writing to the Crown Court sitting in the place specified, for the charge, or any of them, to be dismissed.[20] A defendant is only be entitled to adduce oral evidence at such a hearing if he is granted leave to do so, and that will only be granted if it appears to the judge, having regard to any matters stated in the application for leave, that the interests of justice require him to do so. The 1998 Act contains detailed provisions that govern the power of the Crown Court to deal with any summary offence.[21] A Crown Court has the power to take a plea of guilty, but not to try such an offence if a plea of not guilty is entered. It can dismiss such a charge if the CPS does not propose to offer evidence on that charge. A complex procedure applies where, for whatever reason, there ceases to be an indictable only offence before the court, but an either way offence remains. In such a case, following an inquiry as to the intended plea, the court has to decide whether trial on indictment or summary trial is more suitable.[22]

When a case is sent for trial the court must specify in a notice, the offence or offences which are being sent, and the place at which he is to be tried.[23]

(b) Either-way offences

The Criminal Procedure and Investigations Act 1996 introduced significant modifications to the relevant provisions of the Magistrates' Courts Act 1980. Under these provisions, as amended,[24] it has been open for a magistrates' court (which comprises for this purpose a single justice, or in some circumstances a justices' clerk or member of his staff)[25] to commit the accused for trial without consideration of the evidence, where the parties agree. Where, however, committal for trial is contested, the magistrates have had to consider the evidence, that evidence being confined to documentary evidence and exhibits tendered by the prosecution, provided these meet the conditions set out in the 1980 Act.[26]

These provisions are repealed by the Criminal Justice Act 2003, which substitutes new provisions into the Crime and Disorder Act 1998. The effect of a new section 50A of the 1998 Act[27] is that, in the case of an either-way offence not sent for trial because it is related to an indictable only offence, the court having followed the normal procedure for determining mode of trial, must send the defendant for trial on that charge unless it is transferred for trial (see below). The sending for trial procedure is the same as that for indictable only offences.

---

[19] Ibid, Schedule 3, para 1.   [20] Ibid, para 2.   [21] Ibid, paras 5–6.
[22] Ibid, para 6.   [23] See p 572, post.   [24] See Magistrates' Courts Act 1980, s 6.
[25] See p 631, post.
[26] Magistrates' Courts Act 1980, ss 5A–5F, introduced by 1996 Act, s 47 and Schedule 1. Those provisions are repealed by Criminal Justice Act 2003, Schedule 32 (not yet in force).
[27] Inserted by 2003 Act, Schedule 3, para 17 (not yet in force).

(c) Notices of transfer

In certain cases involving serious or complex fraud, the notice of transfer provisions that were contained in the Criminal Justice Act 1987 apply. When in force these provisions are superseded by new provisions in the Crime and Disorder Act 1998.

As already noted, committal proceedings in serious fraud cases were abolished in 1987, section 46 of the Criminal Justice Act 1987 providing for some such cases to be automatically transferred to the Crown Court. If in the opinion of an appropriate officer[28] there is sufficient evidence for the accused to be committed for trial and the evidence reveals a case of fraud of such seriousness or complexity[29] that it is appropriate that the management of the case should without delay be taken over by the Crown Court, then a notice of transfer could be served. This must be done before the magistrates' court begins any summary trial, or before the case is sent for trial under section 51 of the 1998 Act: when the notice is served, the magistrates' court loses all jurisdiction. The decision to serve the notice of transfer appears to be beyond judicial challenge or appeal.[30] These provisions are repealed and substantially re-enacted by the creation of a new section 51B of the Crime and Disorder Act 1998 in 2003.[31] There one difference of substance is the removal of the procedure introduced in 1987 which permitted a defendant to make an application for dismissal. Such a procedure would be anomalous following the general re-jigging of the sending for trial procedures, which contain no such right.

The Criminal Justice Act 1991 introduced similar provisions in cases where a child was the victim of, or witnessed, certain offences of violence or of a sexual nature, and where the case should be taken over and proceeded with by the Crown Court to avoid prejudice to the welfare of the child.[32] Again, these provisions are repealed and similarly re-enacted by the Criminal Justice Act 2003, which creates a new section 51A of the Crime and Disorder Act 1998. Where they apply,[33] the Director of Public Prosecutions can serve a notice of transfer. The evidence must be sufficient for the person charged to be committed for trial. Similar provisions did exist in respect of war crimes, but have now been repealed.[34]

---

[28] A term given a wide meaning by 1987 Act, s 4(2) to include the DPP, Director of the Serious Fraud Office, Commissioners of Inland Revenue, Commissioners of Customs and Excise, and the Secretary of State. The definition is re-enacted in identical terms by Crime and Disorder Act 1998, s 51B(9), as introduced by Criminal Justice Act 2003, Schedule 3, para 17.

[29] These terms reflect amendments made by Criminal Justice and Public Order Act 1994, Schedule 9, in response to recommendations made by Royal Commission on Criminal Justice.

[30] Criminal Justice Act 1987, s 6(2): see, now, 1998 Act, s 51B(8).

[31] See Criminal Justice Act 2003, Schedule 3, para 17 (not yet in force).

[32] Criminal Justice Act 2001, s 53.

[33] The provisions apply to cases involving specified violent or sexual offences, defined now by 1998 Act, s 51C(3), where a child under seventeen would be called as a witness and the DPP is of the opinion that for the purpose of avoiding any prejudice to the welfare of the child the case should be taken over and proceeded with without delay by the Crown Court.

[34] War Crimes Act 1991, Schedule 1, para 4, repealed by the Criminal Procedure and Investigations Act 1996, s 47 and Schedule 5.

(d) Voluntary bills of indictment

Historically there has been one way by which a case could reach the Crown Court without committal, sending or transfer for trial. By a procedure known as the voluntary Bill procedure, the prosecution can apply to a High Court judge[35] for leave to prefer a Bill of indictment against the accused. The judge in his discretion grants or refuses leave,[36] with the result that if leave is granted the Bill is preferred forthwith and there is no need for any proceedings. The defendant lost the advantage of knowing in advance the substance of the case against him. The applicant himself cannot attend unless permitted by the judge to do so, whilst the defendant is not entitled to attend at all. Even where there is a hearing it is not in open court.[37]

The use of this power has always been problematic[38] because it by-passed normal procedures and safeguards. To overcome this, the law now provides safeguards.[39] Except where there is good reason for doing otherwise, a defendant must receive notice of an application to seek a voluntary Bill, with supporting documentation, and must have an opportunity to make representations, in writing, and if desirable, orally. It is, though, exceptional, to be used only when the interests of justice rather than administrative convenience justify it. In one case,[40] the DPP had sought a voluntary Bill of indictment when he was concerned at the failure of a youth court to commit a young person to the Crown Court for sentence.[41] It was held that proceedings by way of judicial review[42] were more appropriate than seeking to obtaining a voluntary Bill of indictment.

(e) Publicity

Following a well-publicized murder trial where pre-trial publicity created a severe risk of prejudice to the trial itself,[43] restrictions on the reporting of committal proceedings were introduced in 1967,[44] and are now contained in the Magistrates' Courts Act 1980. Those provisions are now in turn replaced by those introduced into

---

[35] A circuit judge has no power to grant leave to prefer a Bill of indictment: R v *Thompson* [1975] 2 All ER 1028, [1975] 1 WLR 1425.

[36] See, e.g., Re *Roberts* [1967] 1 WLR n474. The issue of a voluntary Bill is not susceptible to judicial review: R v *Manchester Crown Court, ex parte Williams* (1990)154 JP 589.

[37] See, generally, R v *Raymond* [1981] QB 910, [1981] 2 All ER 246, where an attempt to challenge the validity of the voluntary Bill procedure (on the grounds that it infringed standards of procedural fairness) was rejected by the Court of Appeal. Such conclusions might, now, have to be reconsidered in the light of the terms of Article 6 but, for the reasons stated in the body of the text the issue is unlikely to arise.

[38] See, e.g. *Practice Direction* [1990] 1 WLR 633.

[39] *Consolidated Criminal Practice Direction* [2002] 1 WLR 2870, paras 35.5–35.6.

[40] R *(Director of Public Prosecutions)* v *Camberwell Youth Court* [2005] 1 Cr App R 6.

[41] As to which, see, p 643, *post.*   [42] See Ch 6, *ante.*

[43] The trial of Dr John Bodkin Adams in 1957. Devlin J stated that it would have been far better if the preliminary proceedings were held in private.

[44] Criminal Justice Act 1967, implementing the recommendations of the Tucker Report, Cmnd 479, HMSO, 1958.

the Crime and Disorder Act 1998,[45] designed to reflect the regime described above.

The effect of these provisions is that it is unlawful to publish anything other than the matters specified in section 52A(7) of the 1998 Act. These are:

(a) the identity of the court and the name of the justice or justices;

(b) the name, age, home address, and occupation of the defendant;

(c) in the case of a defendant charged with a case being transferred under section 51B (serious or complex fraud), and relevant business information;

(d) details of the offence or offences;

(e) the name of counsel or solicitors engaged in the proceedings;

(f) the date and place of any adjournment;

(g) the arrangements as to bail;

(h) whether a right to representation funded by the Legal Services Commission[46] has been granted.

This limitation can be lifted by the court, though, if the defendant objects, the court must consider such a course of action to be in the interests of justice.[47] In such cases any wider restrictions on reporting may come into effect.[48] Of course, the process of sending for trial (when fully in force) will render such provision unnecessary.

4 SENDING FOR TRIAL

When a case is sent for trial, it will be in respect of the offences with which the defendant is charged, in accordance with the principles already discussed. The notice of sending for trial will specify those offences, and the place at which the defendant is to be tried. In the selection of the place of trial the court must have regard to the convenience of the defence, the prosecution, and the witnesses, the desirability of expediting the trial, and any direction given by or on behalf of the Lord Chief Justice in respect of location for trial.[49]

The structure of the Crown Court has already been discussed.[50] It is not a single court but sits in a number of different locations. These are described as first-tier, second-tier, and third-tier centres. First-tier centres deal with both civil and criminal cases and are visited by High Court and circuit judges; second-tier centres deal with criminal cases only but are visited by both High Court and circuit judges, while third-tier centres deal with criminal cases only and are visited only by circuit judges. Each circuit contains a number of each type of centre. Offences in turn are divided into

---

[45] Crime and Disorder Act 1998, s 52A, introduced by Criminal Justice Act 2003, Schedule 3, para 17 (not yet in force).

[46] For details of funding in criminal cases, see p 000, *ante*.   [47] 1998 Act, s 52A(2).

[48] See Ch 8, *ante*.

[49] 1998 Act, s 51D(4), inserted by Criminal Justice Act 2003, Schedule 3, para 17.

[50] See p 256, *ante*.

four classes,[51] each containing a number of offences. Offences in Class 1 must normally be tried by a High Court judge although cases of murder may be released by the presiding judge, for trial by a circuit judge approved for that purpose by the Lord Chief Justice; examples are murder and the rare offences for which a person may be sentenced to death. Offences in Class 2 must be tried by a High Court judge unless a presiding judge of the circuit releases any particular case for trial by a circuit judge or recorder; examples are manslaughter, abortion, and rape. Offences in Class 3 may be tried by a High Court judge, or by a circuit judge or recorder; these are all offences triable only on indictment not falling within any other class.

Offences in Class 4 will normally be tried by a circuit judge or recorder, although they may also be tried by a High Court judge; examples are wounding or causing grievous bodily harm with intent, conspiracy, and all offences triable either way.

Therefore, when a magistrates' court sends for trial a person charged with any offence within Classes 1 or 2, it must specify, as the place of trial, the location of the Crown Court where a High Court judge regularly sits. In the case of an offence in Class 4 the magistrates' court must simply specify the most convenient location of the Crown Court. In selecting the most convenient location, the justices must have regard to the location of the Crown Court designated by the presiding judge as the location to which cases should normally be committed from their petty sessions area.[52] The magistrates will also need to have regard to whether live TV link facilities exist, if this is likely to be necessary because of a special measures direction or for any other reason.[53]

The magistrates must consider whether to release the defendant on bail, or to send in custody. Factors which must be considered, including the imposition of conditions, have already been explained.[54]

B DELAY AND TIME-LIMITS

It has already been seen that the Prosecution of Offences Act 1985 imposes time-limits upon the length of time an accused person may be held in custody.[55] The potential for delay to lead to application to stay the proceedings because of abuse of process also exists, although it will only be an exceptional case where delay is likely to lead to a successful application.[56]

Trial within a reasonable time is one important characteristic of the right to a fair trial under Article 6 Delay is a particular matter of concern in criminal proceedings, leading to the potential for an unfair trial, because of the time between the event in question and the determination of guilt. It also prolongs the effect of the alleged crime on the victim, witnesses and, indeed, the defendant. It was because of increasing, and

---

[51] By the directions set out in *The Consolidated Practice Direction*. See now Criminal Procedure Rules, *op cit*, p 525, *ante*.

[52] Ibid, para 3.　　　[53] See p 613, *post*.　　　[54] See p 554, *ante*.　　　[55] See p 540, *ante*.
[56] See p 539, *ante*.

unacceptable, delays that the government in 1996 established the Narey Committee to review delays within the criminal justice system. The Narey Report was published in February 1997,[57] and contained some thirty-three different recommendations. These recommendations, discussed at the appropriate parts of this book,[58] ranged over a wide area, including the operation and powers of the CPS, the role of justices' clerks, limitations on trial by jury, abolition of committal proceedings in respect of indict-able only offences, changes to the pleas-and-direction hearing, and major changes to the youth justice system. Many of them, although not all, have been accepted and are the subject of implementation through legislative and administrative changes.[59] Many of the procedural changes made by the Criminal Justice Act 2003, including the revised provisions relating to charging and sending for trial, are based on proposals made by the Auld Review and the White Paper *Justice for All*, intended to create efficiency and reduce delay.

One area of importance is the question of time-limits under the 1985 Act. The effect of the custody time-limits is that, if a defendant is in custody, proceedings need to be commenced within the prescribed limits. If, for whatever reason, delay occurs, the prosecution has to obtain an extension of time from the court under section 22(3) of the 1985 Act. The power to make regulations under section 22 of that Act permits time-limits generally to be set and to provide sanctions for non-compliance. Power exists to extend the regulations beyond custody time-limits. Section 40 of the Crime and Disorder Act 1998 confers a wider power to make regulations which govern different types of offence, of accused, or different areas of the country. Statutory time-limits will be set for all non-custodial cases, both in relation to adults and to juveniles, although with tougher time-limits in cases involving persistent young offenders, and young offenders on bail.[60] This latter proposal is part of the general reform of the youth justice system, with the objective of halving the time from arrest to sentence.[61] For adults, it is proposed that statutory time-limits be set for the pre-trial stage of all proceedings, both indictable and summary, broken down into three stages: the first listing of the case to start of summary trial; first appearance to committal or transfer; committal or transfer to start of Crown Court trial. It is not intended to set time-limits for the period between trial and conviction. To do so would, of course, place the fairness of proceedings in individual cases at risk.

Accompanying this extension of time-limit provision are changes in the rules governing enforcement, contained in the Crime and Disorder Act 1988. Section 22(3) of the 1985 Act now provides that an extension of the time-limit may be granted by a court, before the expiration of the time-limit, provided the court is satisfied that the need for the extension is due to:

(i)   the illness or absence of the accused, a necessary witness, a judge or magistrate; or

---

[57] *Review of Delay in the Criminal Justice System*, 27 February 1997, HMSO.
[58] See Chs 18, 19, 21.   [59] See, in particular, Crime and Disorder Act 1998, ss 43–47.
[60] Ibid, s 41.   [61] See p 641, *post*.

(ii) a postponement which is occasioned by the ordering by the court of separate trials in the case of two or more accused; or

(iii) what is some other good and sufficient cause. In addition the court will have to be satisfied that the prosecution has acted with all due diligence and expedition, which will be a question of fact for the court to consider in the context of the individual application and its effects. No extension of time-limits will be needed in respect of periods during which the accused is unlawfully at large.[62] If, because of prosecution delay, proceedings are stayed, fresh proceedings may in some circumstances be commenced, in cases where the stay is by a Crown Court, by the preferment of a voluntary Bill or indictment,[63] and in other cases by the laying of a new charge.[64]

C DISCLOSURE OF EVIDENCE

1 INTRODUCTION

The effective working of the adversarial system depends, in part, upon proper disclosure.[65] Unlike in civil proceedings where production of evidence (discovery) generally is available, the duties of pre-trial disclosure in criminal cases have in the past been limited. The prosecution has always been under a duty to disclose at the stage of committal, or to serve within a certain period in the case of sending for trial,[66] the evidence upon which it proposes to rely, subject only to the right to call additional evidence in some circumstances and subject to certain conditions.[67] Historically, a defendant has been under no general duty to disclose his defence. A defendant, or a suspect, in criminal proceedings, has a 'right of silence'. This 'right of silence'[68] has traditionally permitted the defence at any stage to adduce evidence without notice, and without adverse inferences being drawn in law from that non-disclosure. That rule was modified in 1967 in respect of evidence of alibi,[69] in respect of the adducing of expert evidence,[70] and, more recently, by the provisions that permit inferences from silence in respect of certain matters in particular circumstances.[71] The general right to

---

[62] Ibid, s 40(5).   [63] See p 570, *ante.*   [64] See s 40.

[65] See p 519, *ante,* and note, in particular, *R v McIlkenny* [1992] 2 All ER 417.

[66] See Crime and Disorder (Service of Prosecution Evidence) Regulations 2000, SI 2000/3305. The specified period thereunder is forty-two days, although authorities conflict as to whether this is mandatory: see *Gallagher, White Burke and Morris* (2002) Criminal Law Weekly (CLW) 20/05; *R v Haynes* (2002) CLW 25/6; *Re Fehily* (2002) CLW 26/9.

[67] Service of the witness statements.

[68] For the various meanings of this term, see Lord Mustill in *R v Director of Serious Fraud Office, ex parte Smith* [1993] AC 1, *sub nom Smith v Director of Serious Fraud Office* [1992] 3 All ER 456.

[69] Criminal Justice Act 1967, s 12.

[70] Crown Court (Advance Disclosure of Expert Evidence) Rules 1987.

[71] Criminal Justice and Public Order Act 1994, ss 34–38.

silence remains, although the practical effect of recent changes in the law may well be to limit or reduce reliance on the right.

A common law duty of disclosure on the prosecution in respect of unused material[72] reflected the fact that fairness to a defendant depends on material that might assist his case, or weaken that of the prosecution being made known, and produced, to him. The precise extent of that duty was, though, uncertain,[73] and Guidelines were issued by the Attorney-General[74] to rectify that. These formed the corner-stone of the rules relating to disclosure, and were regarded as 'to all intents and purposes' as having the force of law,[75] until the scope of the common law obligations was settled by the Court of Appeal.[76]

The effect of this change of approach was to meet some of the concerns of the Royal Commission on Criminal Justice, which, in 1993, stated[77] that:

the defence can require the police and prosecution to comb through large masses of material in the hope either of causing delay or chancing upon something which will induce the prosecution to drop the case rather than to have to disclose the material concerned. The defence may do this by successive requests for more material, far beyond the stage at which it could be reasonably claimed that the information was likely to cast a doubt upon the prosecution case. Although it may be time consuming and wasteful of the sources for the police to check all the materials requested they may have to do so if they are to be sure that it can properly be released.

Despite the development by the common law of a modified approach, in 1995 a government consultation paper[78] proposed the introduction of a statutory scheme of disclosure, governing both prosecution and defence. This scheme was implemented by Parts I and II of the Criminal Procedure and Investigations Act 1996. The 1996 Act introduced a new and complex scheme of disclosure, applicable to both prosecution and defence, supplemented by a Code of Practice made by the Home Secretary.[79] This now governs how material acquired during an investigation is recorded, preserved, and produced to the prosecutor by the investigator, and provides for the recording of material generally, and for the separate recording of what is known as 'sensitive material'. This Code is important, because, self-evidently, only if the prosecutor is in possession, or has access to, all the potentially relevant material can he make a judgment as to what, if anything, should be disclosed.

---

[72] See *R v Bryant and Dickson* (1946) 31 Cr App R 146.

[73] See Royal Commission On Criminal Procedure, Cmnd 8092, HMSO, 1981, which found the practices of police forces to be inconsistent and variable.

[74] (1981) 74 Cr App R 302.   [75] Royal Commission on Criminal Justice.

[76] *R v Melvin and Dingle* 20 September 1993, unreported; *R v Brown* [1995] 1 Cr App R 191; *R v Keane* (1994) 99 Cr App R 1. The test adopted was as follows—'I would judge to material in the realm of disclosure that which can be seen on a sensible appraisal by the prosecution: (1) to be relevant or possibly relevant to an issue in the case; (2) to raise or possibly raise a new issue whose existence is not apparent from the evidence the prosecution proposes to use; (3) to hold out a real (as opposed to fanciful) prospect of providing a lead on evidence which goes to (1) or (2)'.

[77] Op cit, Ch 6, para 42.   [78] Cm 2262, HMSO, 1993.

[79] Under Part II of the Criminal Procedure and Investigations Act 1996.

The 1996 Act creates a scheme of disclosure which is basically constructed in three stages. The first is primary prosecution disclosure. The second is the giving of a defence statement, to be followed by the third and final stage, secondary prosecution disclosure. This three-stage process was itself significantly modified by provisions contained in the Criminal Justice Act 2003 mostly brought into force on 4 April 2005. Despite the youth of the 1996 Act provisions, the Auld Review found them to be unsatisfactory in key respects, and not working as Parliament had intended. It also considered that the duties imposed on the defence did not go far enough. These issues are addressed as we deal with the detailed provisions below.

2 PROSECUTION DISCLOSURE

Section 3(1) originally provided that prosecutor must disclose to the accused any prosecution material which has not been previously disclosed to the accused, and which, *in the prosecutor's opinion*, might undermine the case for the prosecution against the accused. Alternatively, he must give to the accused a written statement that there is no such material. At the same time, the prosecutor gives to the accused a schedule of non-sensitive material which he has received from the disclosure officer. By these means, the accused should be provided with relevant unused material, together with a schedule of material which is relevant and which has been acquired by the prosecutor, and, through these documents, judge what further documents may, or should, be disclosable in the light of the needs of the defence. Thus, statements by witnesses who contradict the testimony of those who will be called to testify for the prosecution, inconsistent forensic evidence, the previous convictions of prosecution witnesses, matters relating to the credibility of prosecution witnesses, and inconsistent versions of the events in question are all examples of material that fall within the scope of section 3.

This first stage, known originally as *primary prosecution disclosure* but renamed *initial prosecution disclosure* by the Criminal Justice Act 2003, made the test at this stage essentially subjective. That, though, was open to criticism, putting the judgment of the prosecutor on this matter effectively beyond judicial scrutiny, and is changed by the 2003 Act.[80] The words in section 3 (highlighted above in italics) are repealed, and the duty extended to include evidence that might be considered capable of assisting the defence's case. The decision of the prosecutor is, henceforth, reviewable if any challenge is made by the defence.

3 SENSITIVE MATERIAL

A court has the power to refuse to disclose certain types of information in the public interest. The rule of evidence known as public interest immunity permits the withholding of otherwise relevant material from a party to proceedings on the grounds

---

[80] Criminal Justice Act 2003, s 32.

that its disclosure is not in the public interest.[81] For example, it may deal with matters relating to national security, or reveal the identity of a member of the security services thus rendering that person operationally ineffective. One general class of case where the courts have been prepared to uphold claims of public interest immunity is that relating to information concerning law enforcement. The right of the police to withhold information concerning police informers was recognized in *Marks v Beyfus*,[82] and has been extended to the location, and identity of occupants, of police observation posts.[83] Other successful claims of public interest immunity have related to records relating to the welfare of children.[84] The 1996 Act leaves the substantive rules governing disclosure of sensitive material unchanged, but changes the procedure to be followed. Provisions in the 1996 Act[85] permit such material to be withheld where disclosure would be contrary to the public interest.

The definition of sensitive material goes that protected by public interest immunity, and extends to material that is confidential in nature. What is, or is not sensitive material, will initially be determined by the disclosure officer, but subject to the ultimate decision of the court. Examples of such material given by the Code of Practice include the following:

(a) material relating to national security;

(b) material received from the intelligence and security agencies;

(c) material relating to intelligence from foreign sources which reveals intelligence gathering methods which are sensitive;

(d) material such as telephone subscriber cheques and itemized billing which is supplied to an investigator for intelligence purposes only;

(e) material given in confidence;

(f) material relating to the identity or activities of informants, or undercover police officers, or other persons supplying information to the police who may be in danger if their identities are revealed;

(g) material revealing the location of premises or other places used for police surveillance or the identity of any person allowing a police officer to use them for surveillance;

(h) material revealing, either directly or indirectly, techniques and methods relied on by a police officer in the course of a criminal investigation, for example covert surveillance techniques, or other methods of detecting crime;

---

[81] See, generally, *Conway v Rimmer* [1968] AC 910; *Air Canada v Secretary of State for Trade* [1983] 1 All ER 96; *Makanjuola v Commissioner of Police for the Metropolis* [1992] 3 All ER 617.

[82] (1890) 25 QBD 494.

[83] See *R v Hackett* [1986] Crim LR 462; *R v Hennessy* (1979) 68 Cr App R 419; *R v Agar* [1990] Crim LR 183; *R v Rankine* [1986] 2 All ER 566.

[84] *R v K (Trevor Douglas)* (1993) 97 Cr App R 342; *Re D (An Infant)* [1970] 1 All ER 1088.

[85] See ss 3(6), 7(5), 8(5), 9(8).

(i)   material whose disclosure might facilitate the commission of other offences or hinder the prevention and detection of crime;

(j)   internal police communications such as management minutes;

(k)   material on the strength of which search warrants were obtained;

(l)   material containing details of persons taking part in identification parades;

(m) material supplied to an investigator during a criminal investigation which has been generated by an official other body concerned with the regulation or supervision of bodies corporate or of persons engaged in financial activities;

(n)   material supplied to an investigator during a criminal investigation which relates to a child witness and which has been generated by a local authority social services department or other party contacted by the investigator during the investigation.

The disclosure officer in the first instance compiles a list of sensitive material, which is supplied to the prosecutor. It is for the prosecutor to decide whether or not a claim to withhold relevant material is to be made. Clearly, if a document is not relevant and material, it need not be disclosed, and issues of public interest immunity do not arise. Where a claim of immunity is made in respect of documents that are relevant, the court has to balance the respective public interest in maintaining the sensitivity of the document, on the one hand, and in ensuring a fair trial of an accused, on the other. This balancing function, in a criminal case, is not at all easy, and, although the case law[86] suggests that relevant material can be withheld in a criminal case, it is unlikely to be withheld where material may assist the defence. The Scott Report into the Arms for Iraq scandal observed that there was no reported case:

in which the judge has concluded that documents would be of assistance to the defendant that is none the less declined on public interest immunity grounds to order them to be disclosed. The firm conclusion is, in my opinion justified, that in criminal cases the only question should be whether the documents might be of assistance to the defendant.

This obviously raises fundamental issues, both in terms of the principle of withholding material and the decision-making process to determine the matter. At common law the law recognized that the prosecution might have to make an application without the defendant being present, or, exceptionally, without even knowing about the application (known as an *ex parte* application).[87] The 1996 Act sets out a similar procedure for dealing with applications to withhold sensitive material. The question as to how such cases are to be dealt with, consistent with the Article 6 rights of a defendant, was authoritively dealt with by the House of Lords in *R v H and C*,[88] in

---

[86] See *R v Chief Constable of the West Midlands Police, ex parte Wiley* [1995] 1 AC 274, [1994] 3 All ER 420. *R v Governor of Brixton Prison, ex parte Osman* [1992] 1 All ER 108, [1991] 1 WLR 281; *R v Clowes* [1992] 3 All ER 440.

[87] *R v Ward* [1993] 2 All ER 577.   [88] [2004] 2 Cr App R 10.

dealing with an appeal where the appellant contended that the trial judge was right to require the Attorney-General to appoint special counsel to represent the defendants in an *ex parte* hearing held in their absence and that of their own lawyers.[89] The court considered that derogation from the principle of full disclosure might be justified where there is a risk to an important public interest, but only to the minimum necessary to protect that public interest and never at the expense of the overall fairness of the trial itself. If material did not weaken the prosecution case, or strengthen that of the defence, there was no obligation to disclose it. If it were neutral, again no obligation to disclose existed, but it should be brought to the attention of the court. There would be very few cases where the prosecution could not make some measure of disclosure to the defence, even if that is confined to telling the defendant that an *ex parte* application is being made. If material is of serious help to a defendant, there was a serious question as to whether a defendant could receive a fair trial at all, even if special counsel were, wholly exceptionally, appointed by the Attorney-General to safeguard the interests of the defendant. Special counsel should only be appointed where the trial judge was satisfied that no other course would adequately meet the overriding requirement of fairness to the defendant. On the particular facts, in a drugs case turning on observation evidence and alleged police impropriety, the trial judge had not fully examined the nature of the prosecution evidence and the basis of the claim, and thus the decision to appoint special counsel was premature.

4 DEFENCE DISCLOSURE

The law has, since 1967, required an accused to give seven days' notice of his intention to adduce evidence in support of an alibi.[90] A failure to do so meant that the evidence could not be adduced without the leave of the court.[91] The purpose of the rule is to enable checks to be made by the prosecution as to the truth or otherwise of the claims of the accused that he was elsewhere at the time of the commission of the offence. Further, in cases of serious or complex fraud where a preparatory hearing is held,[92] the defence might have been required to disclose the general nature of its defence (though not the names of the witnesses it proposes to call), and the principal areas of disagreement.

Apart from these cases, and the obligation to disclose expert evidence, discussed above, there was no general duty on the defence to disclose in advance the nature and content of the defence upon which it is proposed to rely. This so-called 'right to silence' meant that it was not open to a court to invite a jury to draw adverse inferences from a failure to disclose pre-trial the facts relied upon by the defence.[93] Various calls for change were made. In 1972, the 11th Report of the Criminal Law Revision

---

[89] Relying on *Edwards and Lewis v United Kingdom*, App 396457/98 and 40451/98, unreported, 22 July 2003.

[90] An 'alibi' is an assertion that the accused person was elsewhere at the time of the commission of the offence.

[91] Criminal Justice Act 1967, s 11. [92] See p 596, *post*.

[93] *R v Gilbert* (1977) 66 Cr App R 237.

Committee recommended that a court should be permitted to draw inferences from silence in court, or from a failure to disclose facts subsequently relied upon by the defence.[94] The report was highly controversial,[95] and not acted upon. More recently, the Court of Appeal in *R v Alladice*[96] considered that it was 'high time' that some change in the law was made. This was indeed recommended in 1988 by the Working Group on the Right to Silence,[97] established by the Home Secretary. The question of defence disclosure was one of the most controversial issues considered by the Royal Commission on Criminal Justice. It took the view that no change should be made in respect of the 'right to silence', except in respect of disclosure of the defence proposed to be relied upon. The majority[98] believed that those who intended to contest the charges against them should be obliged to disclose the substance of their defence in advance of trial, or indicate that they would not be calling any evidence but simply argue that the prosecution has failed to prove its case.[99] A failure to do so, or an explanation at trial different from the one given in advance, or the advancing of mutually exclusive alternative defences, should be a matter from which the jury could draw adverse inferences, subject to the discretion of the court to prevent this where good reasons existed. A defendant who did not disclose would not generally be entitled to further disclosure of material from the prosecution.

The rationale for such proposals was a desire to reduce 'trial by ambush' involving springing a defence upon the prosecution without warning. The Royal Commission did not consider the proposals to infringe the right of defendants not to incriminate themselves, but accepted that a problem existed only in a minority of cases.[100] By contrast, the dissenting opinion in essence questioned whether the fundamental right of the defence not to respond until trial, and to require the prosecution to prove its case, should be changed where no real problem exists. It also pointed to the ineffectiveness of the advance disclosure powers in serious fraud cases.[101] These recommendations were, broadly, implemented by the 'right to silence' provisions contained in the Criminal Justice and Public Order Act 1994.

The scheme of disclosure introduced by the Criminal Procedure and Investigations Act 1996 contained provisions relating to defence disclosure. The Act made a significant change by requiring defence disclosure following primary prosecution disclosure. Under the original section 5, once the prosecutor has complied or purported to comply, with the duty of primary prosecution disclosure, the accused was under a duty to serve on the prosecutor a defence statement. A defence statement was defined as a written statement:

---

[94] Cmnd 4991 (HMSO, 1972).　　　　[95] See, e.g., MacKenna at [1972] Crim LR 605.

[96] (1988) 87 Cr App R 380.

[97] See Zuckerman, 'Trial By Unfair Means—The Report of the Working Group on the Right to Silence' [1989] Crim LR 855.

[98] With one dissentient: see RCCJ, pp 221–35.　　　　[99] Ibid, Ch 6, paras 56–73.

[100] Ch 4, para 19, relying on data from the Crown Court survey.

[101] Page 222, para 8, relying on Levi, *The Investigation, Prosecution and Trial of Serious Fraud* (Royal Commission on Criminal Justice Research Study No 14, HMSO, 1993).

(a) setting out in general terms the nature of the accused's defence;

(b) indicating the matters on which he takes issue with the prosecution;

(c) setting out, in the case of each such matter, the reason why he takes issue with the prosecution.

The purpose of this scheme was to avoid so called 'trial by ambush', with the accused coming up with a defence at a late stage[102] but also was intended to permit a prosecutor to re-assess what has been disclosed, and what further needs to be disclosed, in the light of positive knowledge as to what the defence actually is. Similar provisions applied specifically in the context of alibi evidence.[103] Yet even these provisions were considered inadequate by the Auld Review, which observed:[104]

I can understand why, as a matter of tactics, a defendant might wish to prefer to keep his cards close to his chest. But that is not a valid reason for preventing a full and fair hearing on the issues canvassed at the trial. A criminal trial is not a game under which a defendant should be presented with a sporting chance. It is a search for the truth.

It concluded that defence statements under pre-existing provisions disclosed very little. Further despite section 11(3) of the 1996 Act (which allows inferences to be drawn from a failure to make adequate defence disclosure, similar to those in the Criminal Justice Act 1987 concerning cases of serious or complex fraud,[105] and to the provisions in sections 34, 36, and 37 of the Criminal Justice and Public Order Act 1994 governing silence at or before trial)[106] there were few effective sanctions for failure to comply. The results were sometimes aborted trials, poorly prepared prosecution files, wasted witness or victim time through unnecessary attendance at court, and consequential knock-on financial costs to the courts, CPS, and Criminal Defence Service. Changes were thus introduced by the Criminal Justice Act 2003, the effect of which is to widen the requirement for defence disclosure.

A new section 6A of the 1996 Act[107] amends the definition of a defence statement. It must be in writing[108] and:

(a) set out the nature of the accused's defence including any particular defences on which he intends to rely;

(b) indicate the matters of fact on which he takes issue with the prosecution;

(c) set out, in the case of each matter, why he takes issue with the prosecution; and

(d) indicate any point of law (including any point as to the admissibility of evidence) which he wishes to take, and any authority on which he intends to rely for that purpose.

---

[102] See p 569, *ante.*   [103] Section 11 of the Criminal Justice Act 1967 is repealed.
[104] Auld Review Ch 10, para 154.
[105] See Criminal Justice Act 1987, s 10.   [106] See p 618, *ante.*
[107] See Criminal Justice Act 2003, s 33(3).
[108] Such a statement is deemed to be given with the authority of the defendant: see 1996 Act, s 6E, inserted by Criminal Justice Act 2003, s 38.

Further, a new section 6C[109] requires a defendant to indicate whether he intends to call any persons (other than himself) as witnessses, unless that detail has already been given as part of details of an alibi. The details to be given include names, addresses, and dates-of-birth (where known). A failure to give this detail does not prevent the witness being called, but, rather, allows comment to be made and inferences to be drawn from, a failure to do so. The purpose of this additional detail is so that investigators can run checks on proposed defence witnesses to look at any criminal record or antecedents, as well as to diminish the effects of 'surprise witnesses'. It facilitates the prosecution examining the veracity of any potential witnesses, although, on the other hand, may deter some potential witnesses from coming forward (not wishing to have details given, in advance, to the police). Because of concerns that witnesses may be, or feel, intimidated, new provisions impose obligations on the Home Secretary to issue a Code of Practice for police interviews of defence witnesses.[110]

Thus a greater measure or more specific information is required by the new law. The Royal Commission on Criminal Justice had envisaged only brief details as to the offence[111] and the Auld Review itself did not think that changes of this type to defence statement provisions were necessary.[112] The practical difficulties involved in providing this level of detail, within tight time limits, may be substantial. Which facts are in dispute and what points of law are to be taken often will not be clear because of the need to evaluate and investigate the prosecution case, and even changes to legal representation may complicate matters, without always being necessary. Relevant points of law may be obvious on the face of the documentation, or from pleas- and-directions hearings or preparatory hearings. The provisions as a whole perhaps mark an on-going trend towards the criminal trial becoming more inquisitorial in nature and less of a 'contest', perhaps a conclusion supported also by the additional provisions on expert evidence.[113]

5 FURTHER PROSECUTION DISCLOSURE

The third stage of the disclosure scheme is further prosecution disclosure. Once the defence has engaged in defence disclosure, it is the duty of the prosecutor to keep the issue of disclosure under review. This duty, formally marked by secondary prosecution disclosure under section 7 of the 1996 Act[114] requires the disclosure of prosecution material which might reasonably be considered capable of undermining the case for the prosecution or assisting the case for the defence (i.e. the same test as for initial prosecution disclosure). Material must be disclosed as soon as practicable. This test is objective in nature, i.e. it is open to a court to review the judgment made and its reasonableness, but judged by the state of affairs existing at the time.

---

[109] See Criminal Justice Act 2003, s 34.
[110] 1996 Act, s 21A, inserted by Criminal Justice Act 2003, s 40.
[111] Royal Commission, *op cit*, para 68, p 99.   [112] Op cit, Ch 10, para 180.
[113] See p 583, *post*.   [114] Repealed and replaced by a new s 7A by Criminal Justice Act 2003, s 33.

6 EXPERT EVIDENCE

Section 81 of the Police and Criminal Evidence Act 1984 authorizes the making of rules regarding the disclosure of expert evidence. The Crown Court (Advance Notice of Expert Evidence) Rules 1987 have been made under that power, and apply to trials on indictment.[115] Following committal or sending for trial the party who is seeking to rely on expert evidence, whether of fact or opinion, must furnish to the other party a statement in writing of any finding or opinion upon which he proposes to rely, and, on request in writing, provide a copy of (or access to, if that is more practicable) the records of any observation, test, calculation, or other procedure in respect of which the finding or opinion is based. A failure to disclose means that the evidence cannot be adduced without the leave of the court.

This obligation of disclosure is not the only obligation. In *R v Ward*[116] the Court of Appeal stressed that there is a common law obligation upon a government forensic scientist to act impartially, and to disclose any scientific evidence that might arguably assist the defence. Failure to comply with this obligation was one of the principal reasons for quashing the convictions of the defendant in that case. It was failure to disclose fully in this way that caused problems in *R v Ward* and other cases.[117] Such an obligation to disclose does not meet the criticism of those who argue that the trial process is unfairly tilted in favour of the prosecution because of its command of forensic science and other scientific facilities,[118] and generally the imbalance of resources. Some argue that the court itself should appoint its own expert witnesses, to report impartially to the court.[119] The whole question was examined extensively by the Royal Commission on Criminal Justice.[120]

The Commission considered, but rejected, a proposal to create an independent forensic science agency, as opposed to one being part of a government department or police authority. Instead, it proposed[121] the establishment of a Forensic Science Advisory Council to report to the Home Secretary on the performance, achievements, and efficiency of the forensic science laboratories, in both the private and public sectors. Subject to a rule that the same laboratory should not take on work for both prosecution and defence in the same case, public sector laboratories should look on themselves as equally available to defence and prosecution. This is important in the light of research findings[122] that defence solicitors sometimes encounter difficulty in finding suitable independent experts to interpret prosecution findings.[123] In respect of

---

[115] The power to make rules in respect of expert evidence in summary cases has been conferred by the Criminal Procedure and Investigations Act 1996, s 19. See the Criminal Procedure Rules 2005.

[116] [1993] 2 All ER 577, [1993] 1 WLR 619.

[117] See, e.g. *R v Maguire* [1992] QB 936, [1992] 2 All ER 433.

[118] For a description of the organisation of forensic science facilities, see the RCCJ, *op cit*, Ch 7, para 6–36.

[119] See Spencer [1992] Crim LR.   [120] Report, Ch 9.   [121] Ch 7, para 3.2.

[122] Roberts and Willmore, The Role of Forensic Science Evidence in Criminal Proceedings (Royal Commission on Criminal Justice Research Study No 11 (HMSO, 1992)); Steventon, The Ability to Challenge DNA Evidence (Royal Commission on Criminal Justice Research Study No 9 (HMSO, 1992)).

[123] See RCCJ, Ch 9, paras 50–53.

the general duty of disclosure, the Royal Commission welcomed the approach taken in R v Ward.[124] It also recommended streamlining legal aid provision to assist in this respect.

Of significance is the approach taken by the majority of the Commission towards a more inquisitorial system in respect of forensic science evidence. The Royal Commission found[125] that a sizeable minority of contested Crown Court cases involve scientific evidence. In approximately 25 per cent of such cases there was a defence challenge to such evidence, and in some 800 cases a year not only was such a challenge made but also expert evidence was called on behalf of the defence. In these cases the duty of disclosure applies equally to the defence as to the prosecution. Hitherto, however, the defence has been under no duty to disclose the evidence it has obtained from experts whom it does not intend to call, perhaps because it is unfavourable. Nor was there a duty to disclose expert evidence acquired by the defence for the purposes of discrediting prosecution evidence through cross-examination. The Royal Commission recommended changes which would have had the effect of requiring a greater measure of pre-trial discussion between experts, and imposed a duty to indicate the areas of prosecution expert evidence which are not agreed.[126] It also made recommendations as to the handling of expert evidence at the trial.[127] It emphatically rejected the appointment of a court expert, or an assessor, whose views would not be susceptible to examination or cross-examination.

Changes to the law were not made until the passage of the Criminal Justice Act 2003 following the recommendations of the Auld Review. Section 35 of the 2003 Act inserts in the Criminal Procedure and Investigations Act 1996 a new section 6D, which provides that if the accused instructs a person with a view to his providing an expert opinion for possible use as evidence at the trial of the accused, he must give to the court and the prosecutor a notice specifying that person's name and address unless that has already been specified in the defence statement. This duty is confined to the supply of details as to the name and address of the possible witness. It does not require disclosure of the expert's report, which is likely to be protected from disclosure by the doctrine of legal professional privilege.[128] Curiously, section 11 of the 1996 Act (inferences from failure to supply defence statement) does not apply to the new section 6D, and there is no sanction for non-compliance, which may lead to patchy compliance. Concerns also arise about how this requirement may affect the way defence lawyers interact with experts, in particular as to amount and type of privileged information given to the expert instructed.

---

[124] Ibid, para 47.

[125] Crown Court Survey: see RCCJ, para 57. The estimates ranged from 30 per cent–40 per cent of cases, in quantity some 10,000 cases per year.

[126] Royal Commission, op cit, paras 62–64.   [127] Ibid, Ch 9, para 4.

[128] As to which, see p 128, ante.

D THE INDICTMENT

1 INTRODUCTION

A Bill of indictment is a written or printed accusation of crime made at the suit of the Crown against one or more persons. A Bill of indictment may be preferred by any person[129] against any other person before the Crown Court, generally within twenty-eight days of sending for trial or notice of transfer, or within a period to be specified following a person being sent for trial under Schedule 3 of the 1998 Act.[130] However, a Bill of indictment is of no legal validity in itself. It only becomes a legal document when it is turned into an indictment proper by being signed by the appropriate officer of the court, who in turn can only sign the draft Bill if he is satisfied that the accused is validly before the court.[131] The judge of the court may direct the appropriate officer to sign the Bill, either on his own motion or on the application of the prosecution. After it has been signed, the proper officer must on request supply to the defendant a copy free of charge.[132]

Where the Bill is preferred following sending for trial it may charge any offence which appears on the statements, in addition to or in place of the offence or offences for which he was committed, subject to the normal rules as to joinder of offences.[133] It is immaterial that the 'added' offences involve a higher penalty than the original charge or charges. Although the accused will necessarily have knowledge of the facts alleged to constitute the offence, if not of the precise charge based on those facts, there are obvious possibilities of injustice, and the Court of Appeal has said[134] that whenever it is decided to bring such 'fresh' charges, the police ought to see the defendant and warn him of the charges under caution, so that he may make a statement in answer if he wishes.

The whole of the indictment may consist of such 'substitute' charge or charges. If the defendant considers that one or more of such charges does not fairly arise out of the facts in the depositions he may move to quash the indictment. It is then for the trial judge to rule on the sufficiency of the indictment. Where however the defendant was sent for trial in respect of two offences which had been repealed by statute, it was held that he was never lawfully committed at all, and it was immaterial that the third count of the indictment was in respect of an offence which both existed and was disclosed by the depositions.[135]

---

[129] Except in those cases where a private person has no right to institute proceedings: see p 533, *ante.*

[130] See p 571, *ante.*

[131] Through notice of transfer, voluntary Bill, or by direction of the Court of Appeal. An alternative procedure under the Perjury Act 1911, s 9, existed until abolished by the Prosecution of Offences Act 1985, s 28.

[132] Indictment Rules 1971, r 10(1).   [133] See p 587, *post.*

[134] In *R v Dickson* [1969] 1 All ER 729, [1969] 1 WLR 405, where the defendant's solicitors had six days' notice of 'fresh' charges.

[135] *R v Lamb* [1969] 1 All ER 45, [1968] 1 WLR 1946.

2 FORM AND CONTENTS

The rules as to the form of indictments are now contained in the Indictments Act 1915 and the Indictment Rules 1971. The drafting of the indictment is the responsibility of counsel for the prosecution,[136] whose duty it is to ensure that it is in proper form for the particular case. In most cases, other than those of complexity or difficulty, the actual drafting is undertaken by, or on behalf of, the Crown Prosecution Service.

An indictment is in three parts; introductory matters, statement of offence, and particulars of offence. The introductory matters are twofold, first the court of trial and secondly the name of the defendant, appearing in the form:

THE QUEEN v [Defendant] charged as follows:

As regards the statement of offence and particulars of offence, the rules provide[137] that every indictment must contain, and need not contain more than, a statement of the specific offence with which the defendant is charged, describing the offence shortly, together with such particulars as are necessary to give reasonable information as to the nature of the charge. Where, however, the offence is created by statute, there must be a reference to the statute and to the relevant section, and all the essential elements of the offence must be disclosed in the particulars, unless the defendant is not prejudiced or embarrassed by failure to describe any such element.[138] The fact that an indictment is defective does not render the trial a nullity. Whether a conviction obtained on an indictment that is deficient can stand will turn, ultimately, upon whether injustice or unfairness has been caused to the defendant. Whether these provisions are effective is open to doubt. The Royal Commission on Criminal Justice observed[139] that indictments were largely formal in nature, giving little information. It found widespread evidence of a failure to comply with the duty to give reasonable information as to the nature of the charge, and agreed with the Law Commission when that body observed:

There are strong reasons of justice and efficiency why the particulars in each count in an indictment should contain sufficiently clear factual allegations to inform the jury of the issues it will have to decide, and more generally, to enable the indictment to operate as a practical agenda for the trial.[140]

---

[136] *R v Newland* [1988] QB 402; [1988] 2 All ER 891.

[137] Indictment Rules 1971, r 5(1). Cf. the rules for the content of an information: see p 000, *post*. There may also be approved forms of indictment for individual offences: ibid.

[138] Ibid, r 6. It is not necessary for the indictment to specify or negative any exception, exemption, excuse, proviso, or qualification. There is, again, an analogy with the rules for the content of an information.

[139] Ch 8, para 5.   [140] Counts in an Indictment (Law Commission, 1992).

3 JOINDER; SEPARATE TRIALS

Hitherto we have considered an indictment charging one offence only. However, within certain limits, a single indictment may charge more than one offence, or be drawn in respect of more than one defendant, or both. This is known as joinder.

(a) Joinder of offenders

The basic rule is that where two or more persons join in the commission of an offence, all or any number of them may be jointly indicted for that offence, or each may be indicted separately. If they are in fact indicted separately there would be no power in any court to order 'consolidation' of the indictments, however desirable this might seem from the point of view of saving time and expense,[141] but, of course, the same result could be achieved through the use of the voluntary Bill procedure[142] to supersede existing indictments. However, joinder is now very common. The matter is one of judicial discretion, and what is in the interests of justice. Where the individual offences of the different accused are related to each other by virtue of time or some other link, then it may well be appropriate for them to be tried together.[143] The fact that evidence against one accused is inadmissible against another will be a relevant factor, though not necessarily decisive. Another consideration will be the length of the trial that will ensue should they be tried together. This is returned to later.[144]

(b) Joinder of offences

The basic rule is to be found in rule 9 of the 1971 Rules:

Charges for any offences may be joined in the same indictment if those charges are found on the same facts or form or are a part of a series of offences of the same or a similar character.

It should also be noted that in some limited circumstances summary offences may be tried with offences that are to be tried on indictment.[145]

It is a matter of fact and degree in each case as to whether this rule is satisfied, in accordance with principles set out in the cases. In *Ludlow* v *Metropolitan Police Commissioner*[146] the House of Lords indicated that in deciding whether offences were of a similar character, regard should be had both to their legal and factual characteristics. To show a 'series of offences' the prosecution must be able to show some nexus between them, a 'feature of similarity which in all the circumstances of the case enables the offences to be tried together'. It is not necessary that the evidence in respect of one charge should be admissible on another, a conclusion left ambiguous and unclear by the House of Lords in *Director of Public Prosecutions* v *P*,[147] where the tests for the use

---

141 *Crane* v *Director of Public Prosecutions* [1921] 2 AC 299   142 See p 570, *ante*.
143 *R* v *Assim* [1966] 2 QB 249, [1966] 2 All ER 881.   144 See p 589, *post*.
145 Criminal Justice Act 1988, s 40. The charge must be founded on the same facts or evidence, or be part of a series of offences.
146 [1971] AC 29, [1970] 1 All ER 567. The House was considering the appropriate provision of the 1915 Rules, which were materially the same as r 9. See also: *R* v *Kray* [1970] 1 QB 125, [1969] 3 All ER 941.
147 [1991] 2 AC 447; *sub nom R* v *P* [1991] 3 All ER 337. See *R* v *Tickner* [1992] Crim LR 44.

of evidence relevant to one count to prove another were reviewed and clarified, but appeared to conclude that the tests for admissibility and joinder in a sexual case were the same.[148]

The application of the principle was seen in a non-sexual case in *R v Cannan*[149] where the Court of Appeal held that a trial judge was entitled in his discretion to order the trial together of six offences involving three separate women. Three counts involved abduction, rape and buggery against one woman, another alleged attempted kidnapping against a second, and two more counts of alleged abduction and murder of a third. Sexual cases, by contrast, are particularly difficult because of the prejudice that may arise. In *Director of Public Prosecutions v Boardman*[150] Lord Cross seemed to equate the test for joinder of offences with their admissibility as evidence. He stated that if each count was inadmissible in respect of the other offences then they ought to be tried separately. It is, he said, asking too much of any jury to disregard the other charges when considering each individual charge.

This approach is contrary to the wording of rule 9 itself. Despite the House of Lords not putting the matter beyond doubt in *DPP v P*, the wording of rule 9 is clear. In *R v Christou*[151] the House of Lords held that where an accused person was charged with sexual offences against more than one person, where the evidence of one complainant was not admissible on charges concerning other complainants, the trial judge had a discretion to order that the charges be tried together. The judge is not obliged to exercise that discretion in favour of the accused simply because the evidence is not admissible on more than one count of the indictment. The key issue is simply: can the issues be resolved fairly? In that case the appellant was charged with sexual offences against his two young female cousins, C and M, with whom he had been living at the time of the alleged offences. The House of Lords concluded that the trial judge had acted properly in requiring that they be tried together, notwithstanding the fact that the evidence of C was not admissible on the counts that related solely to M. Further, in the case of *R v West*,[152] the court had to consider the same issue in the context of a non-sexual offence. The appellant had been tried and convicted of ten counts of murder. The evidence on many of these counts was admissible on other counts, under the so-called similar fact evidence rule. The Court of Appeal held, however, that the trial judge had acted properly in declining to sever the indictment and order separate trials in respect of three counts which were unaffected by similar fact evidence. This was a matter for the judge's discretion, which he had not exercised improperly.[153]

---

[148] Evidence can only be considered if it is both relevant and admissible. Admissibility in these circumstances depended on the operation of the so-called similar fact evidence rule. This rule, and others relating to bad character, were significantly altered by Criminal Justice Act 2003, ss 98–114 which came into effect in December 2004.

[149] (1990) 92 Cr App R 16.

[150] [1975] AC 421; *sub nom Boardman v Director of Public Prosecutions* [1974] 3 All ER 887.

[151] [1997] AC 117.   [152] [1996] 2 Cr App R 375.   [153] *R v Trew* (1996).

4 LONG TRIALS: THE NUMBER OF COUNTS AND ACCUSED

It has already been seen that the joinder of offenders, and of charges, is permissible. The danger exists that an indictment may become so overloaded that, as a result, the trial becomes too complex in terms of the issues the jury has to comprehend and decide, or unmanageable in terms of time. On many occasions the courts have complained of indictments which are overloaded.

In *R v Novac*[154] where a large number of counts of sexual offences were laid against four defendants, Bridge LJ observed:

whatever advantages were expected to accrue from one long trial they were heavily outweighed by the disadvantages. A trial of such dimensions puts an immense burden on both judge and jury. In the course of a four or five day summing up the most careful and conscientious judge may so easily overlook some essential matter. Even if the summing up is faultless, it is by no means cynical to doubt whether the average juror can be expected to take it all in and apply all the directions given. Some criminal prosecutions involve considerations of matters so plainly inextricable and indivisible that a long and complex trial is an ineluctable necessity. But we are convinced that nothing short of the criterion of absolute necessity can justify the imposition of the burden of a very long trial on the court.

The problem has arisen particularly in two different situations. The first concerns the use of conspiracy charges. There may be both evidential and tactical reasons why prosecutors may wish to lay a count of conspiracy in addition to counts alleging specific offences. This practice was disapproved in a Practice Note in 1977.[155] The onus is on the prosecution to justify a joinder of a conspiracy charge with other substantive offences. If it cannot, it must elect to proceed either upon the conspiracy charge or the substantive offences. Justification might exist where the substantive offences which the prosecution is in a position to prove do not adequately reflect the extent and persistence of the defendants' criminality. Thus, for example, there might be evidence to show that a person had been engaged for some time in the importation of drugs of various kinds, although the prosecution might only be able to prove one specific importation.

Secondly, a number of long complex fraud cases has placed great strain upon the jury trial system.[156] In *R v Cohen*[157] the trial was so long that the judge's summing-up (itself of considerable length) dealt only with one of the issues before the court. In passing sentence following convictions, later quashed on appeal, McKinnon J observed:

All involved in this case have been called upon to achieve what no-one in our courts should be asked to achieve. That applies to the defendants, to the jury and to me.

---

[154] (1976) 65 Cr App R 107.

[155] [1977] 2 All ER 540; *sub nom Practice Direction* [1977] 1 WLR 537.

[156] See, generally, the Roskill Committee, *op cit*, and Royal Commission on Criminal Justice Report, Ch 7, paras 59–67.

[157] [1992] NLJR 1267. The jury retired on the 184th day of the trial.

Even more startling, a recent fraud case collapsed after over two years, at a cost estimated at over £60m, having 'lurched from problem to problem, finally [folding] after sickness, jury problems, lengthy delays and disruptions'.[158] Following that fiasco, a Protocol was issued providing detailed guidance as to how such cases should be managed.[158A]

The Roskill Report on Fraud Trials[159] advocated the abolition of jury trial in complex fraud cases to be replaced by trial by judge and two specialist assessors. Such recommendations were a response to a recognition that such trials are inevitably long, causing unacceptable disruption to the lives of jurors, and unduly complex, the evidence often being beyond the comprehension of jurors. Such claims are, of course, difficult to gauge in the light of the prohibition on study of how in fact juries reach their verdicts, and upon what evidence.[160] By contrast, others have argued for the simplification of such cases. In its evidence to the Royal Commission, the Law Society[161] argued that such trials should be simplified by not including superfluous counts, and by keeping prosecution evidence within strict limits, principally by limiting the number of accused in the indictment. The Royal Commission itself considered the restriction of jury trial to be beyond its scope, but echoed the calls set out above for the number of counts or particulars on an indictment to be kept to a minimum.[162] In that regard, its recommendation for a review of the relationship between the criminal law and non-criminal action by financial regulators may be important in reducing the scope of criminal trials in such cases.[163] The Auld Review recommended trial on indictment without a jury.

5 NON JURY TRIAL ON INDICTMENT

(a) Long or complex cases

Section 43 of the Criminal Justice Act 2003, if and when it is brought into force,[164] will permit a prosecutor to apply for a judge-only trial where the subject matter is likely to be complex, the trial long or both long and complex. This change was supported by the Auld Review, which envisaged specialist fraud judge, trial by judge and experts, or trial by judge and lay assessors.[165] A White Paper[166] identified the great strain that long trials imposed on many jurors. Such trials may last for many months, with the juror away from work, perhaps with childcare problems, unable to talk with non jurors about the case in question, unable to make future plans, or to take time off without

---

[158] *The Times*, 23 March 2005.

[158A] See Ch 10, *ante*. Protocol for the control and management of heavy fraud and other complex cases [2005] 2 All ER 249.

[159] See p 339 *ante*.

[160] Contempt of Court Act 1981, s 8. For discussion of jury trial generally, see p 338, *ante*.

[161] Evidence of the Law Society to the Royal Commission on Criminal Justice (1992).

[162] Ch 8, para 79.   [163] Ch 7, para 64.

[164] The government gave an undertaking to review further the whole question of non-jury trial before s 43 is brought into effect but is now unlikely to be introduced during 2005/2006.

[165] Auld Review, *op cit*, Ch. 5, para 1097.   [166] *Justice for All*, Cm 5563, 2002.

adjournments granted by the court. The subject matter may be dry and technical, even tedious.

Examples of failure of high-profile fraud trials are well known. During the period 1988 to 1993, long trials following trials relating to the take-over of the company Guinness led to the conviction of only two of four defendants. In 1995 to 1996, trials of defendants arising out of the dealings of the publisher Robert Maxwell were unsuccessful, costs of up to £30m having been incurred. And of course the spectacular collapse of the Jubilee line case involving six defendants, after two years and at an estimated cost of £60m, seeming makes the case for reform irresistible. Yet, despite these problems, the success rate in cases of serious fraud has been good, in 2002 around 86 per cent.[167] It is a moot question as to whether the system should be judged by the conviction rate alone, but even on that basis the above statistics show that there are many aspects to this problem, particularly as one of the key questions that arises is whether a jury can ever understand a long and complex case. It was, though, the fact that non-jury trial in the Crown Court was seen a wrong in principle by opponents of the change being proposed by the legislation in 2003 that caused this change, and another in section 44, to be so fiercely resisted. Whether in fact it is brought into effect could have been a matter of some doubt in the light of new provisions in Domestic Violence, Crime and Victims Act 2004,[168] although the latest causes celebre have reignited the debate.

Section 43 will permit non-jury trial where because of length or complexity, the trial would be too burdensome for a jury. What that amounts to will be a matter for a judge to decide when an application is made for a non-jury trial at a preparatory hearing.[169] Many shorter cases can involve issues of complexity, and length alone does not signify complexity. They are, though, alternatives. When deciding an application, the judge must look at ways in which the trial could be simplified so that the length or complexity may be reduced. However, no step is to be regarded as reasonable if it would significantly disadvantage the prosecution.[170]

(b) Danger of jury interference

Section 44 of the Criminal Justice Act 2003 addresses the issue of jury 'nobbling', allowing the prosecution to apply for trial by judge alone in cases where there is, first, a real and present danger of interference with the jury, and, secondly, there is a risk that despite the fact that steps could be taken to protect from these malign influences, the prospect of jury tampering is so substantial that a non-jury trial is necessary in the interests of justice.

This change was prompted by a perceived increase[171] in the numbers of trials

---

[167] See HC Cmtte debate on Criminal Justice Bill, HC Cmtte, 4 January 2003, col 321.

[168] As to which, see p 592, post.

[169] As to which, see p 596, post, and Criminal Justice Act 2003, s 45. An order for non-jury trial will require the approval of the Lord Chief Justice.

[170] 2003 Act, s 43(6), (7).

[171] The White Paper, Justice for All, op cit, contained no statistical evidence on this point.

collapsing, particularly but not exclusively in London, with interference, or attempted interference, with the jury necessitating the discharge of the jury and the re-commencement of the trial. Section 43 requires there to be a danger of jury tampering. There must be a real and present danger of tampering, and the judge on an application must be satisfied that protection of then jury will not alleviate that risk. Section 44(6) gives examples of where may be a real and present danger of jury tampering:

(a) where the trial is a re-trial and the jury in the previous trial was discharged because of jury tampering;

(b) where tampering has taken place in previous criminal proceedings involving the defendant or any of the defendants;

(c) where there has been intimidation, or attempted intimidation of any person who is likely to be a witness at the trial.

This last example is extremely wide, with witness intimidation, regrettably, not being uncommon. Its breadth may perhaps be reduced by the fact that the prosecution must show that that risk exists even though steps could be taken to protect the witness. A court will also consider whether that danger can be reduced by adoption of special measures,[172] or by using as evidence the out-of-court statements given to the police by the witness.[173]

The jury tampering may occur during a trial. The effect of section 44 is that the judge will have the power to discharge the jury and continue the trial without a jury, subject to first allowing the parties to make representations. In such cases the judge will be the judge both or fact and law, and of course will be aware of evidence that the jury might not have been allowed to be aware of. This is likely to raise Article 6 issues in the future, following the decision of the Court of Human Rights in *Edwards and Lewis* v *United Kingdom*[174] that the trial judge might have been influenced, unconsciously, by material he was aware of because of an application for public interest immunity which he had dealt with and of which the defence were unaware.

(c) The non jury trial

Where a non-jury trial is ordered under either section 43 or section 44, the judge decides the case in exactly the same way as the jury would have done, and has all the powers, duties, and rights of the jury.[175] There is, though, one difference: unlike a jury, the judge must state reasons for his decision.

(d) Trial of multiple counts without a jury

The provisions in the Domestic Violence, Crime and Victims Act which permit trial in the Crown Court without a jury in certain circumstances were far less controversial

---

[172] See p 609, *post.*
[173] Under Criminal Justice Act 2003, s 116. See p 614, *post.*
[174] *The Times*, 29 July 2003.   [175] Criminal Justice Act 2003, s 48.

than those discussed above, for several reasons. First, they implement a Law Commission Report[176] designed to overcome practical problems caused by the Court of Appeal decision in *R v Kidd*.[177] Secondly, they do not dispense with the role of the jury totally in any one case.

The problem faced by a jury in trying a case with many, multiple, counts (particularly in fraud cases) has already been noted. To overcome those problems, prosecutors have been encouraged to indict on sample counts, counts which are indicative of the nature and type of offending. It was long the practice of courts to try a defendant on sample counts, and then to sentence for the totality of the offending identified by the court. However, in *R v Kidd* it was decided that it was improper for a court to have regard, when sentencing, to offences for which the defendant had not been tried and convicted, or had not admitted. That had the effect in some cases of limiting the power of a sentencing court to reflect in the total sentence the multiple nature of the offending. For example, in a case of multiple benefit fraud the totality of the offending may involve many individual procurement of benefit cheques of a total value far in excess of anything that could be adequately reflected by sample counts.[178]

To overcome this problem section 17 of the 2004 Act permits a prosecutor to apply, at a preparatory hearing,[179] that the trial of some, but not all, counts on an indictment be conducted without a jury. The judge must be satisfied that the number of counts on the indictment is likely to mean that trial by jury on all of them would be impracticable, that sample counts could be identified, and that it is in the interests of justice for an order to be made. The effect is that the sample counts will be tried by judge with a jury in the normal way, and then, at the conclusion of that trial the judge is able to order trial of the remaining counts (which are reflected by the sample counts) by a judge without a jury. The judge is not to be bound by the verdict of the jury, but clearly it is highly unlikely that trial by judge only would occur in respect of multiple counts where the defendant had been acquitted on the relevant sample counts. On the other hand, the normal rules of evidence will apply: evidence of the multiple offences may well be admissible at the trial before the jury,[180] and convictions in respect of the sample counts will certainly be admissible at the trial without a jury of the multiple examples. The nature of the judge only trial is the same as that identified above.

It remains to be seen what the effect of section 17 is. It may, paradoxically, have the effect of encouraging prosecutors to include more counts in indictments, not less as the courts have consistently urged. And it *could* render unnecessary the introduction of the more controversial powers contained in section 43 of the Criminal Justice Act 2003 unnecessary.

---

176 Law Com No 277, October 2002 *The Effective Prosecution of Multiple Offending*.
177 [1998] 1 WLR 604 (otherwise known as *R v Canavan*).
178 The facts of a pre-*Kidd* case, *R v Evans* [1992] NLJR 1267.   179 See p 596, *post*.
180 See Criminal Justice Act 2003, s 101.

6 DUPLICITY

Where two or more offences are joined in one indictment each one must be alleged in a separate count or paragraph of the indictment.[181] If an indictment in fact charges more than one offence in a single count then it is bad for duplicity. This must be distinguished from the analogous situation which, more accurately, may be described as uncertainty. This arises where a statutory provision contains one offence, which may be committed by a variety of means, or by virtue of different states of mind. Whether a count in an indictment may charge simply by reference to the statutory provision, or must allege the specific ingredients in each count, charging more than one count if necessary, is a question of construction of the relevant statute.[182]

A good example of the problem is contained in section 5 of the Domestic Violence, Crime and Victims Act 2004,[183] which creates an offence or allowing the death of a child or vulnerable adult. The offence can be committed is various ways, and s 5(2) provides that the prosecution do not have to prove which. The question arises as to whether one count in an indictment can allege all or any of the different variants. Of course, a prosecutor can avoid the whole problem in indicting in different counts.

In deciding whether a count is bad for duplicity, regard should be had to the question of whether different maximum punishments exist according to the presence or absence of specific factual ingredients.[184] Where that is so, it is likely that a court will consider the statute to create separate offences, which should therefore be indicated separately. In *Courtie*[185] Lord Diplock (with whom the other Law Lords concurred) held that where one provision involved the imposition of different penalties depending on whether the prosecution established particular factual ingredients then Parliament had created two different offences, which should be the subject of separate counts or informations.[186]

7 OBJECTING TO THE INDICTMENT: AMENDMENT

If the defendant desires to object to the validity of the indictment he should do so before he is arraigned. The grounds of objection have already been explained[187] though the power of the court to quash an indictment to prevent abuse of the process of the court should also be noted.

The Court of Appeal does not readily hear objections to the validity of an indictment where the objection was not taken at the trial, although failure to take it is not insuperable. When objection is taken the court may (unless it rules against the objection altogether) either quash the indictment or amend it. The Indictments Act 1915

---

[181] Indictment Rules 1971, r 4(2). Each count is equivalent to a separate indictment. Counts must be numbered consecutively: r 4(2).

[182] See p 627, *post*, for similar issues in respect of duplicity of charges of summary offences.

[183] Which came into force on 21 March 2005.

[184] *R v Courtie* [1984] AC 463, [1984] 1 All ER 740.   [185] See n 184, above.

[186] See p 586, *post*.   [187] See p 587, *ante*.

permits a court to make such order of amendment as it thinks necessary to meet the circumstances of the case, unless amendment cannot be made without injustice.[188]

A new count may be added before the defendant is arraigned, and even after arraignment a count can be added charging a completely new offence;[189] the question is one of degree depending on the facts of the particular case.[190]

Application for amendment may be made by either side and at any time or amendment made by the judge of his own motion. Since counsel for the prosecution has general responsibility for the correctness of the indictment he should not open his case without being satisfied on the point and should make any necessary application for amendment before the defendant is arraigned, having inspected the indictment for the purpose. Defending counsel should also inspect, in his own client's interests.

E PRE-TRIAL REVIEW

Except in cases of serious or complex fraud[191] no formal system for pre-trial review by the court of trial existed until 1996, although informal arrangements operated. Pre-trial reviews in fact operated in Crown Courts across the country, providing a basis for voluntary discussion of matters affecting a forthcoming trial, such as the plea to be entered, length of trial, points of law, or admissibility of evidence.[192] Such reviews appear to have occurred in approximately 25 per cent of cases.[193] The Royal Commission considered one trial project that had involved all cases being listed for a 'pleas and directions' hearing.[194] The majority of the Commission considered such a scheme to be both unnecessary and impracticable. Instead it proposed a scheme based on the automatic completion of forms with details of plea. The disclosure obligations recommended by the Commission[195] would then have been complied with, and both prosecution and defence would then indicate whether a preparatory hearing was needed and for what purpose.[196] Such hearings would occur in a minority of cases, usually those anticipated to last at least five days, although it would be open to the parties to require a hearing in shorter cases.[197] Such hearings would deal with plea, matters of evidence (including issues of admissibility), and expert opinion, matters

---

[188] Section 5(1).

[189] *R v Radley* (1973) 58 Cr App R 394, where the amendment was made at the conclusion of the prosecution opening; cf. *R v Tirado* (1974) 59 Cr App R 80.

[190] It seems that an amendment on immaterial matter may be made at or after verdict: *R v Dossi* (1918) 87 LJKB 1024.

[191] See Criminal Justice Act 1987, s 7(1).

[192] The Royal Commission on Criminal Justice (at Ch 7, para 10) identified also a scheme based on the exchange of forms, recommended by a Working Party chaired by Watkins LJ. The results obtained in a pilot scheme were disappointing.

[193] Ibid, para 11, relying on the Crown Court Survey.

[194] Working Group on Pre-trial Issues: Recommendation 92 (cited by RCCJ, Ch 7, para 12).

[195] See p 574, *ante*.   [196] RCCJ, para 20.   [197] Ibid, para 17.

generally relating to the trial. Such decisions would be binding on the trial judge and counsel. For this reason the Royal Commission was concerned that the practice of returned briefs be minimized as much as possible.[198]

Pleas and directions hearings ('PDH') in Crown Court cases have become in effect mandatory. The advantages of the hearing lie in the ability of the court to engage in effective case-management, to the benefit not only of the workload of the court in general but also to the effective handling of individual cases. However, the Narey Report[199] did accept that there may be some merit in the claim that PDH should not be mandatory in all cases since in straightforward ones they may involve an additional and unnecessary burden.

Following the recommendations of the Royal Commission, the government published in 1995 a consultation paper.[200] This paper recognized the desirability of achieving the objectives identified by the Royal Commission, namely the achievement of shorter and more efficient trials. However, it did not adopt the Royal Commission's proposals for pre-trial exchange of papers in less complex cases, and considered that the way forward was creation of a system based on a mixture of binding rulings at pleas and directions hearings, coupled with preparatory hearings to be held in complex or potentially lengthy cases. The government's approach was given statutory effect by Parts III and IV of the Criminal Procedure and Investigations Act of 1996.

By section 40 of the 1996 Act, a judge may, at a pre-trial hearing make a binding ruling as to:

(a) any question as to the admissibility of evidence;

(b) any other question of law relating to the case concerned.

A 'pre-trial hearing' can be held after sending for trial and before the commencement of the trial itself, and thus permits not simply questions of law to be determined, but also whether material should be disclosed, whether counts on an indictment should be quashed, and whether or not orders should be made, for example, under section 4 of the Contempt of Court Act 1981.

In addition, by section 29(1) of the 1996 Act, where it appears to a Crown Court judge that an indictment reveals a case of such complexity, or a case whose trial is likely to be of such length, that substantial benefits are likely to accrue from a preparatory hearing, such a hearing may be held. The purpose of the preparatory hearing is defined by section 29(2) as:

(a) identifying issues which are likely to be material to the verdict of the jury;

(b) assisting the comprehension of any such issues;

(c) expediting the proceedings before the jury;

---

[198] Ibid, para 36.   [199] See p 573, ante.
[200] Improving the effectiveness of pre-trial hearings in the Crown Court (HMSO, 1995, Cm 2924).

(d) assisting the judge's management of the trial.

(e) determining applications for non jury trial[201]

These provisions are not, in principle, new, and are similar to those found in section 7 of the Criminal Justice Act of 1987, dealing with cases of serious or complex fraud. The significance of a preparatory hearing is made clear by section 31(4). Under that sub-section, a judge at a preparatory hearing may order the prosecutor:

(1) to give to the court and the accused a written statement of certain matters which include the principal facts of the case for the prosecution, the witnesses who will speak to them, any exhibits relevant to those facts, any proposition of law on which the prosecutor proposes to rely, and the consequences that flow from any of those matters.

(2) to prepare the prosecution evidence and any explanatory material in such a form as required by the court;

(3) to give to the court and the accused written notice of documents the truth of contents of which ought in the prosecutor's view to be admitted, and of any such matters which in his view ought to be agreed;

(4) to make any amendments of any case statement given as appear to the judge to be appropriate.

F ARRAIGNMENT AND PLEAS

1 ATTENDANCE OF THE ACCUSED

On the day fixed the accused will, if he has been detained in custody, be brought from the prison or remand centre where he has been detained and lodged in the cells. If he has been on bail he must surrender to his bail and will then be placed in the cells to await his trial. It may be that the defendant has been on bail and does not appear, in which case the court of trial may issue a warrant, called a 'bench warrant' for the arrest of the defendant; this is a summary procedure and will not normally be used unless the arrest of the defendant is a matter of urgency.

Still further powers are provided by section 7(3) of the Bail Act 1976 by which a constable may arrest without a warrant any person who has been released on bail in criminal proceedings if, inter alia, he has reasonable grounds for believing that the person is unlikely to appear at the time and place required.

---

[201] See p 590, *ante.*

2 ARRAIGNMENT

Assuming that the defendant has appeared at, or has been brought to, the court, the first formal step in his trial will be the arraignment, which is the process of calling an accused forward to answer an indictment. The defendant will be brought from the cells into the dock[202] and the proper officer will first ask him his name. Assuming that he is the person named in the indictment he will then be asked to plead. The indictment will be read to him (omitting only the introductory matters) and he will be asked to plead to it; further, where the indictment contains more than one count, each should be put to the defendant separately and he should be asked to plead separately, for each count is equivalent to a separate indictment.[203]

On arraignment the defendant may, of course, simply say nothing. If this occurs, the first question is whether the defendant is mute of malice, that is to say, able to speak but refusing to do so, or whether he is mute by visitation of God, that is to say, temporarily or permanently unable to speak. If there is any doubt a jury must be sworn to try the issue. Witnesses may be called on either side and counsel may address the jury; the judge will then sum up the case to the jury, who will retire if necessary and then give a verdict.[204] If the finding is that the defendant is mute of malice the court may then order the proper officer of the court to enter a plea of not guilty on behalf of the defendant (assuming that he still declines to speak);[205] the trial will then proceed as if the defendant had himself pleaded not guilty. If, however, the finding is that the defendant is mute by visitation of God, the defendant may yet be perfectly well able to defend himself, and a plea of not guilty should be entered by the court and the trial should proceed in the ordinary way.

However there may well be some question of whether the defendant is fit to plead, the test for which is whether he is fit to challenge jurors, instruct counsel, understand the evidence, and give evidence himself.[206] The procedure to be followed is contained in the Criminal Procedure (Insanity) Act 1964, which was substantially amended in 2004.[207] Such matters used to be dealt with by a jury, but are now, generally to be dealt with by a judge, research showing that in the vast majority of cases the function of the jury was largely ritualistic, with the clear majority of questions of unfitness not being contested.[208] Evidence may be called by either side and speeches will be made; the judge will direct the jury, who will return a verdict. If the finding is that the defendant

---

[202] The Royal Commission did not recommend that docks be abolished. It considered that they should be situated as near as possible to the accused's legal representatives: Ch 8, para 109.

[203] *R v Boyle* [1954] 2 QB 292, [1954] 2 All ER 721.

[204] This may in some circumstances be by a majority: see p 620, *post*.

[205] Criminal Law Act 1967, s 6(1)(c).

[206] *R v Berry* (1977) 66 Cr App R 156; not whether he is able to defend himself properly or well: *R v Robertson* [1968] 3 All ER 557, [1968] 1 WLR 1767.

[207] As amended by the Criminal Procedure (Insanity and Unfitness to Plead) Act 1991. See ss 4, 4a, and 5 of the 1964 Act. The provisions were also substantially amended by Domestic Violence, Crime and Victims Act 2004, s 22.

[208] See Mackay and Kearns, 'The Trial of the Issue of Unfitness to Plead' [2000] Crim LR 536.

is unfit to plead, the trial does not proceed, but the defendant is not free to go; he is liable to be detained in hospital or made subject to various orders.[209] The court has power, in the interests of the accused, to postpone trial of the issue of fitness to plead until any time up to the opening of the case for the defence. If, before such time, the defendant is acquitted (on a submission of no case to answer) his fitness or otherwise will not be determined.[210] This is to ensure that the case against the person being detained is in fact tested, and to ensure that an innocent person is not subject to detention. If the finding is one of fitness to plead, the defendant will then be called upon to plead to the indictment; if he still declines to answer, a plea of not guilty will be entered on his behalf.

3 PLEAS

Assuming that all questions of fitness to plead have been disposed of adversely to the defendant, in the sense that the trial on the substantive issues must go on, various pleas are open to the defendant. In the vast majority of cases the alternatives are pleas of guilty or not guilty.

The decision to accept a plea to a lesser charge is that of the prosecutor, and does not require the consent of the court unless the decision arises after the prosecution has called its evidence and a case to answer has been found.[211] Such decisions may often assist in avoiding the time and expense of a trial, and are one explanation for the problem of 'cracked trials'. These are cases that are listed for trial but where on the day of trial the defendant pleads guilty.[212] By contrast, the holding of discussions informally with the trial judge to ascertain attitudes to likely sentence is a practice that has been heavily criticized by the Court of Appeal.[213] Out-of-court discussions with the trial judge should not occur unless absolutely essential, and then subject to various conditions. The Royal Commission proposed[214] a modification to this rule, so that judges may indicate the highest sentence that they would impose at that point on the basis of the facts put to them.[215] This might occur at pre-hearing, and encourage an accused to plead guilty. There is, of course, a danger that some defendants might plead guilty when they were, in fact, innocent.[216] The Crown Court Survey[217] found some evidence of this, but the significance of the data obtained is open to doubt.[218]

---

[209] Ibid, s 5.   [210] Ibid, s 4; see, for such a case, *R v Burles* [1970] 2 QB 191, [1970] 1 All ER 642.

[211] *R v Grafton* [1993] QB 101, [1992] 4 All ER 609. The position is different if counsel expressly asks for the approval of the judge: *R v Broad* (1978) 68 Cr App R 281. See, generally, Farquharson Committee Report (1986) LS Gaz 3599.

[212] RCCJ, Ch 7, para 13. The Crown Court Study showed that 'cracked' trials were 26 per cent of all cases, creating serious problems (para 45).

[213] *R v Turner* [1970] 2 QB 321, [1970] 2 All ER 281; *R v Coward* (1979) 70 Cr App R 70.

[214] Op cit.   [215] Report, Ch 7, para 50.

[216] It is for this reason that an accused must plead personally, not through counsel.

[217] See generally Ashworth, 'Plea, Venue and Discontinuance' [1993] Crim LR 830.

[218] RCCJ, Ch 7, para 45.

In fact the majority of accused persons at Crown Court plead guilty.[219] Therefore they obtain a 'discount' on the otherwise justified sentence.[220] The Royal Commission proposed a formalized system, of graduated discounts, to encourage early pleas of guilty.[221] In 1994, changes were made to allow credit to be given for an early plea of guilty, and are now to be found in section 144 of the Criminal Justice Act 2003. It does not formally enact that those offenders who falls within its terms must receive a discount on sentence, but that is the effect of sentencing policy and practice.[222] On the other hand, the research shows that approximately 50 per cent of those pleading not guilty are in fact acquitted,[223] with a significant number of 'non-jury' acquittals. These non-jury acquittals merit further mention: the statistical evidence suggests that discharge, usually where the prosecution offers no evidence, is far more common than judges directing a jury to enter a 'not guilty' verdict because of the inadequacy of the evidence before the court.[224]

(a) Plea of guilty

On the assumption that the plea covers the whole indictment, counsel briefed for the prosecution will give a brief outline of the facts and then call a police officer to give the antecedent history of the defendant, in the form of a sheet setting out the defendant's home and educational background, previous jobs, criminal record, and anything else thought to be relevant. He may be cross-examined by defending counsel. The court will then usually consider a pre-sentence report,[225] presented usually on behalf of a probation officer, and, sometimes, a victim impact statement. There is then a plea in mitigation made by counsel for the defence, sometimes supported by witnesses (very rarely the defendant). The defendant will then usually be given the opportunity of saying something himself to the court, after which sentence will be passed. If there are two defendants, one of whom is pleading guilty and the other not guilty, the one pleading guilty will not normally be sentenced until the trial of the other defendant is concluded.[226]

It is customary for the normal rules of evidence to be relaxed at proceedings following a plea of guilty. The rules of evidence do not apply to 'antecedent evidence', which is invariably given by a single police officer on the basis of files concerning the defendant which the officer has in court. Nevertheless the officer should not make allegations against the defendant which he has reason to think that the latter would

---

[219] *Op cit*, Ch 6.   [220] See, e.g., *R v Hollington and Emmens* (1985) 82 Cr App R 281.

[221] Ibid, para 47.

[222] See p 668, *post* and Reduction in Sentence for Guilty Plea (Sentencing Guidelines Council, 2005).

[223] Vennard, 'The Outcome of Contested Trials' in Moxon (ed) *Managing Criminal Justice* (1985).

[224] Ordered and Directed Acquittals in the Crown Court, RCCJ Research Study No 15 (HMSO, 1993).

[225] Criminal Justice Act 1991, s 3. These were formerly known as Social Inquiry Reports. See further, p 664, *post*.

[226] *R v Weekes* (1982) 74 Cr App R 161. The position may be different if the accused is going to give evidence for the prosecution against his co-accused.

deny and which he cannot properly prove.[227] Of course, if matters of importance are disputed, then the court may require them to be formally proved. In addition, where despite the plea of guilty there is a factual dispute that will affect the basis upon which the court will sentence the accused, the trial judge will hear evidence to determine that question, a so called 'Newton' hearing.[228]

If the defendant pleads guilty to some, but not all, counts or pleads guilty to a lesser offence, the prosecution must decide whether to proceed on the remaining counts or 'accept' the defendant's pleas, in which event the counts to which he has not pleaded guilty will be left 'on the file'. Although the defendant will never have been in peril of conviction on those counts, so that he could theoretically be tried on them, in practice this would not be permitted without leave of the court and, indeed, the counts on the file are sometimes ordered to be marked with words such as 'not to be proceeded with without the leave of this court or of the Court of Appeal'. However, even if the prosecution is content to adopt this course, the judge must, if asked, consent to it and, if he does not, he may order the trial to proceed.[229]

(b) Plea of not guilty

It should be noted that this is not necessarily a positive assertion that the defendant is innocent but merely a request or a challenge to the prosecution to prove the case against him. A defendant may plead guilty to one count in the indictment but not guilty to another, or even admit part of an offence contained in a single count but not the rest of the offence.[230] He may also plead not guilty to the offence charged but guilty to some other offence of which he may lawfully be convicted by way of alternative verdict; thus he may plead not guilty to murder but guilty to manslaughter. The whole question of alternative verdicts is now regulated by section 6(3) of the Criminal Law Act 1967. This enables the jury to acquit of the offence charged, but to convict of another offence which the court has jurisdiction to try and which is expressly or by implication alleged in the indictment.[231]

The point arises, often acutely, when the judge comes to sum up the case to the jury. Where nothing appears on the statements which can be said to reduce the crime charged to the lesser offence of which the defendant wishes to plead guilty, it is the duty of counsel for the Crown to present the offence charged in the indictment, leaving it to the jury 'in the exercise of their undoubted prerogative' to return a verdict of guilty of the lesser offence.[232] Even where there is material on the statements

---

227 Cf. *R v Robinson* (1969) 53 Cr App R 314, where the officer described the defendant as 'the principal drug pusher' in the Midlands, evidence the reception of which the Court of Appeal described as a 'clear and obvious injustice'. See also *R v Wilkins* (1977) 66 Cr App R 49.

228 *R v Newton* (1982) 77 Cr App R 13.　　　　　229 *R v Broad* (1978) 68 Cr App R 281.

230 *Machent v Quinn* [1970] 2 All ER 255.

231 What is included 'by implication' is often difficult to decide. The test is whether the allegations in the indictment are capable of including the elements of the alternative offence: *Metropolitan Police Commissioner v Wilson* [1984] AC 242; *sub nom R v Wilson* [1983] 3 All ER 448.

232 *R v Soanes* [1948] 1 All ER 289.

capable of sustaining a lesser charge, the prosecution is entitled to formulate its charges as it thinks fit. However, it is for the discretion of the trial judge whether to direct the jury as to the potential for an alternative verdict.

Secondly, the defendant may change his plea once the trial has started but in this case the appropriate verdict must be returned by the jury which will have been sworn to try the case;[233] it may seem a formality that if the defendant changes his plea, for example, from 'not guilty' to 'guilty', the foreman of the jury should be required to stand up and say that the defendant is guilty, but:

> once a prisoner is in charge of a jury he can only be either convicted or discharged by the verdict of the jury.[234]

(c) Autrefois acquit and autrefois convict

These are by far the most important of a number of so-called 'special pleas in bar' which can be raised by the defendant when the indictment is put to him.[235] The substance of the pleas in bar is that there is some reason why the court should not proceed to try the defendant, which should be made the subject of immediate inquiry, so that if the reason is found to be a valid one the defendant should be released and further proceedings stayed.[236] The general principle of the two pleas of *autrefois acquit* and *autrefois convict* is that the same person should not be put in jeopardy twice for the same offence founded on the same facts, not merely for the same facts. *Autrefois acquit* was well explained by a United States judge[237] as follows:

> The underlying idea ... is that the state with all its resources and power should not be allowed to make repeated attempts to convict an individual for an alleged offence, thereby subjecting him to embarrassment, expense and ordeal and compelling him to live in a continuing state of anxiety and insecurity, as well as enhancing the possibility that even though innocent he may be found guilty.

The two pleas were extensively considered by the House of Lords in *Connelly* v *Director of Public Prosecutions*.[238] The following principles emerge from that and subsequent cases:

> (1) A man cannot be tried for a crime in respect of which he has previously been convicted or acquitted. The reason for this is that an accused should not be put in peril twice. It is for this reason that the doctrine does not apply where the accused was never in fact in jeopardy. In *R* v *Dabhade*[239] a charge was

---

[233] *R* v *Heyes* [1951] 1 KB 29, [1950] 2 All ER 587.

[234] Ibid per Lord Goddard CJ [1951] 1 KB at 30, [1950] 2 All ER at 588.

[235] Others are demurrer (that the facts alleged do not constitute the offence charged); plea to the jurisdiction (that the court has no jurisdiction to try); pardon (that a pardon has been granted). These are extremely rare.

[236] See the remarks of Lord Goddard CJ in *R* v *County of London Quarter Sessions, ex parte Downes* [1954] 1 QB 1 at 5–6; [1953] 2 All ER at 750.

[237] Justice Black in *Green* v *United Kingdom* 355 US 184 (1957), 2 Led 2nd 199 at 201.

[238] [1964] AC 1254, [1964] 2 All ER 401.   [239] [1993] QB 329, [1992] 4 All ER 796.

formally dismissed, because in law it was defective. The accused was committed for trial on a substituted charge of theft. In dismissing an appeal against conviction, based upon the principle of *autrefois acquit*, the Court of Appeal indicated that where a charge was dismissed because it was defective, or because the evidence was insufficient to sustain a conviction, or because of a rationalization of the prosecution case, the appellant was never in fact in jeopardy.

(2) The same rule applies where a person could have been convicted of the alleged offence on a previous indictment. In this context the rule as to alternative verdict offences is of importance. As has already been seen,[240] a defendant on being charged with certain crimes may plead, or be found, guilty of certain other crimes and not guilty of the offence charged, without the need for a fresh indictment. Thus on a charge of murder the accused may be convicted of manslaughter. The doctrines of *autrefois acquit* and *autrefois convict* apply to any offence which was an alternative verdict offence to the original offence, and of which the accused was acquitted or convicted. Thus if the defendant is acquitted of murder, the defence of *autrefois acquit* will be open to him if charged with manslaughter or attempted murder arising out of the death of the same person.

(3) The rule applies if the crime in respect of which he is charged is in effect, or substantially the same as, the crime of which he was earlier acquitted or could have been (or was) convicted. This is in reality a matter for the common sense of the court.

(4) One test[241] of when the rule applies is to ask whether the evidence necessary to support the second indictment, or whether the facts which constitute the second offence, would have been sufficient to procure a legal conviction on the first indictment either as to the offence charged or of an offence of which the accused could have been found guilty.

(5) The matter is not decided simply by comparing indictments, but on the overall facts. The accused may adduce evidence as to the identity of the persons involved, and as to dates and other facts necessary to show that the doctrine applies.

(6) It is not within the doctrine that the facts under examination, or the witnesses being called in the later proceedings, are the same as those in the earlier proceedings.

---

[240] See p 601, *ante*.

[241] Lords Pearce and Devlin disagreed on this point, identifying this as abuse of process rather than *autrefois acquit*. See, in support, *R v Beedie* [1997] 2 Cr App R 167, adding that both the third and fourth principle amounts to an abuse of process, the difference being that *autrefois* is a complete answer to the prosecution case, whereas an abuse of process argument is launched to persuade the judge that it is unfair to try the defendant, the quashing of the indictment being a discretionary remedy not one available.

(7) Irrespective of the above, a person may be able to show that a matter has in fact been decided already by a court competent to decide it, in the sense of a finding or plea of guilty and a sentence passed pursuant to that finding or plea. The matter must, though, in fact have been decided. In *Richards* v *R*[242] the accused pleaded guilty to manslaughter, but had not been sentenced. At a resumed hearing the prosecution was halted, and the appellant subsequently tried and convicted and sentenced to death[243] for murder. In dismissing the appeal against conviction the Privy Council was of the view that the plea of *autrefois convict* did not assist the accused, because the adjudication was not in fact complete.

The Law Commission considered the rule in 1999,[244] and recommended change, which occurred in 2003. Section 75 of the Criminal Justice Act 2003 allows a prosecutor to apply to the Court of Appeal for an order that an individual be retried for a qualifying offence[245] of which he has been acquitted.[246] Clearly, if such an order is made, *autrefois acquit* is no bar, but the terms of section 84 of the 2003 Act apply. The re-trial must be on an indictment preferred by direction of the Court of Appeal, and on which the defendant is arraigned within two months of the order of the Court of Appeal

4 MOTION TO QUASH THE INDICTMENT

Instead of entering any plea, general or special, the defendant may move to quash the indictment. This may be done on several grounds. If any of the rules, already described,[247] as to the framing of the indictment have not been followed this may be made the ground for a motion to quash; however it has already been seen that the court possesses ample power to amend the indictment and it will only be rarely that a motion to quash on this ground will succeed. It could only do so on the ground of some grave defect of substance, such as the insufficiency of the particulars of offence, or duplicity. An indictment may also be quashed on the ground that the offence charged in it is not one known to the law. Yet another ground is that the appropriate officer did not have jurisdiction to sign it; as has already been seen he can sign it only if certain conditions are satisfied. An indictment can also be quashed if it amounts to an abuse of the process of the court.[248]

---

[242] [1993] AC 217, [1992] 4 All ER 807.

[243] It was a Privy Council appeal from Jamaica, where the death penalty still exists.

[244] Law Com No 156, 1999, *Double Jeopardy*.

[245] Defined by Criminal Justice Act 2003, Schedule 5, and include serious offences against the person, some sexual offences, serious drugs offences and some criminal damage offences.

[246] See p 620, *post*.   [247] See p 586, *ante*.   [248] See p 539, *ante*.

5 PRELIMINARY POINTS OF LAW

It sometimes happens that there is a point of law involved in a case the decision of which may effectively dispose of the whole case. Thus, for example, the basic facts alleged by the prosecution may be admitted by the defence, the sole issue being whether those admitted facts amount to the offence charged. In cases of this sort it is obviously a sterile exercise to go through the motions of trial by jury when the outcome of the case will depend entirely upon the judge's decision as to the law. The judge hears argument upon the law (before empanelling a jury); if a ruling is given which, in the view of the accused and his advisers, is fatal to the defence, the accused can then change his plea.[249] The point may, in fact, be dealt with at a preliminary hearing, or through a pre-trial ruling.[250] However it is necessary for a plea of not guilty to be taken before the point of law is argued.

If points of law are taken successfully at the commencement of the case in this way (or indeed, at any other time) the ruling may prevent the case from continuing. This is known as a terminating ruling. A terminating ruling is any ruling whether on law or evidence that is fatal to the prosecution case: a dismissal for abuse of process, a ruling of *autrefois acquit*, a successful submission of no case to answer, a ruling of public interest immunity adverse to the Crown, and a ruling that the conduct alleged does not form a known criminal offence are each examples. The Auld Review[251] and the Law Commission[252] each recommended changes in the law: as the latter put it:

If a case is to fall on a legal argument it is better for public confidence in the criminal justice system that it should be susceptible to the second opinion of a higher court, that it be appealable.

That is achieved by provisions in the Criminal Justice Act 2003 which confer rights of appeal against terminating rulings.[253]

6 EMPANELLING THE JURY: CHALLENGES

Assuming that there is a plea of not guilty to some part of the indictment the next stage of the trial will be the swearing of the jury. The Juries Act confers on the Lord Chancellor general responsibility for the summoning of jurors,[254] a function in reality performed locally. From all the jurors summoned, twelve will be chosen by ballot; a jury should be randomly selected[255] and a court has no power to interfere with the selection of a jury except in the rarest of cases, and for cause, for example relating to the physical or mental fitness of the proposed juror.[256] The selected jurors will take

---

[249] See, e.g., *Director of Public Prosecutions* v *Doot* [1973] AC 807, [1973] 1 All ER 940. An accused who has pleaded guilty in such circumstances can appeal against his conviction on the ground that the preliminary point of law was wrongly decided against him.

[250] See p 596, *ante*.   [251] *Op cit*, Ch 12, paras 47–65.

[252] Report on *Double Jeopardy and Prosecution Appeals, op cit.*

[253] 2003 Act, ss 57–66. See, further, p 000, *post*.   [254] Juries Act 1974, s 2.

[255] See RCCJ, Ch 8, paras 52–64.   [256] See p 332, *ante*.

their places in the jury box. Before the jury is sworn the defendant is given the opportunity to challenge members of the jury for cause, either to the whole panel summoned or to an individual juror. The burden is on the party making the challenge to show such a cause, the issue being tried by the trial judge. Prior to 1988 an accused had a right of peremptory challenge of up to three jurors, which meant that, unlike for cause, the defendant did not have to state any reason for challenge. This right was abolished by the Criminal Justice Act 1988. By contrast the right of the Crown to require jurors to 'stand by' still exists.[257] By this procedure, the juror is asked to stand down, but consideration of the cause of challenge (since a challenge by the Crown must be for cause) is postponed. It will usually then happen that there are enough 'spare' jurors for a whole jury to be assembled, however many more challenges are made, so that the trial can proceed and the cause of the Crown's challenge is never made the subject of enquiry. The Crown will usually act on the basis of knowledge of a potential juror's criminal record[258] or, in exceptional cases of other matters disclosed on an authorized check of police records.[259]

Each member of the jury having been sworn individually, the appropriate officer of the court then tells the jury of the terms of the offences to which the defendant has pleaded not guilty and informs them that it is their duty, having heard the evidence, to say whether he is guilty or not. The trial judge may also explain certain features about a criminal trial to the jury.[260]

G COURSE OF THE TRIAL

1 PUBLICITY

English law regards 'open justice' as a fundamental principle[261] which therefore means that the trial, including the process of arraignment described above, should be open to the public, and may be reported. Despite this, the principle is not unlimited, and may be departed from where necessary where openness or publicity would harm the interests of justice.[262] Powers exist to postpone the reporting of all or part of a trial,[263] to prevent reporting,[264] or in some situations to sit in camera. In addition, a variety of statutory powers exist that limit the principle.[265]

---

[257] See Attorney General's Guidelines [1988] 3 All ER 1086.

[258] These may disqualify a juror from service: see Ch 10, *ante*.

[259] *Attorney General's Guidelines on Jury Checks* [1988] 3 All ER 1086, and p 332, *ante*.

[260] Royal Commission on Criminal Procedure, Cmnd 8092 (HMSO, 1981), para 67.

[261] *Scott* v *Scott* [1913] AC 417, [1911–13] All ER Rep 1.   [262] See p 231, *ante*.

[263] Contempt of Court Act 1981, s 4(2). A right of appeal against such an order exists: criminal Justice Act 1988, s 159.

[264] Contempt of Court Act 1981, s 11.   [265] See p 231, *ante*.

2 PROCEDURE AT THE HEARING

Prosecuting counsel starts by making an opening speech. This will be an outline of the allegations against the defendant and of the evidence which it is proposed to call in support of the allegations. No reference should be made to any item of evidence if counsel has been informed that there is going to be an objection to the admissibility of that evidence. The fact that evidence is relevant[266] is not sufficient: for it to be considered at a trial it must also be admissible, and there are a number of rules of evidence which exclude evidence that might be thought to be relevant. Examples of these include evidence of the character of the accused unless it is directly relevant to the issue before the court and evidence of out-of-court statements.[267] A judge may also exclude from evidence relevant material where the fairness of the trial demands that that be done.[268] Therefore, in opening the case prosecuting counsel must take care not to refer to evidence that is not admissible, or which is likely to be excluded. Objections to the admissibility of evidence, or for the exclusion of evidence will be tried by the judge, usually (although not always) in the absence of the jury, at the time in the trial when the evidence would otherwise have been called. This procedure is known as a 'voir dire', taking its name from the name of the oath taken by witnesses during that hearing.

The institution of the opening speech has been criticized on the ground that counsel may make allegations which are not borne out by the evidence of his witnesses (even before they are the subject of cross-examination) yet the jury may recollect only the statements of counsel, since they came first. It is a strict rule that prosecuting counsel should limit his observations to what appears in the depositions, or witness statements. The only exception arises in the case of those witnesses in respect of whom a notice of additional evidence has been served. Even this practice is not strictly required by law, but the court has an inherent discretion to prevent oppressive conduct towards the defendant[269] and it is most unlikely that a judge would allow additional evidence to be called unless a notice of additional evidence, setting out a summary of that witness's evidence, had been served on the defendant.

---

266 'Relevance' was defined in *Stephen's Digest* as meaning that '. . . any two facts to which it is applied are so related to each other that according to the common course of events one either taken by itself or in connection with other facts proves or renders probable the past, present or future existence or non existence of the other.' For the difficulties in determining whether evidence is sufficiently relevant, see *R v Blastland* [1986] AC 41, [1985] 2 All ER 1095; *R v Kearley* [1992] 2 AC 228, [1992] 2 All ER 345.

267 The use of out-of-court statements as proof of their contents has traditionally been prohibited by the hearsay rule, subject to a number of statutory and common law exceptions. The law relating to hearsay has been significantly changed by Criminal Justice Act 2003, ss 114–131, and is beyond the scope of this book. The effect of the changes may be to allow out-of-court statements in lieu of oral testimony in a greater number of circumstances.

268 See, in particular PACE, s 78, discussed at p 391, *ante*.

269 See the remarks of Lord Devlin in *Connelly v Director of Public Prosecutions* [1964] AC 1254 at 1346 *et seq*.

Prosecution witnesses will then be called[270] and will be subject to examination in chief by prosecuting counsel, cross-examination by defending counsel, and re-examination by prosecuting counsel. Examination in chief is the first stage in the examination of a witness, and is carried out by the party calling the witness. The purpose of examination in chief is to elicit the testimony the witness has to give on the relevant matters. An advocate cannot ask the witness leading questions. A leading question is one which suggests to the witness the answer that is expected or which assumes a fact still to be proved. It is sometimes said that any question that can be answered with a simple 'Yes' or 'No' is a leading question. This is often, although not invariably, true. Leading questions are often permitted on formal matters, such as name, address, and occupation, and it is permissible for a party to lead a witness with the concurrence of the other parties and the court. Nor can an advocate cross-examine his own witness by putting previous inconsistent statements to the witness, unless the court rules that that witness is 'hostile'. A witness is hostile if that witness is 'not desirous of telling the truth at the instance of the party calling him'.[271] Some hostility or animosity is called for: it is not enough that the evidence is unfavorable to the party calling him. If the witness is hostile, then, at common law, he may be asked leading questions by the party calling him, and, under section 3 of the Criminal Procedure Act 1865, previous inconsistent statements may be put to him, which will affect the 'credit' of the witness in the eyes of the jury, and, now, may in some circumstances be evidence of the truth of their contents.[272] More usually, a witness will ask, or be invited, to refresh his memory from an out-of-court statement made when the events were still fresh in the mind.[273] The answers of a witness must be accepted by the advocate calling that witness, even if the witness has 'not come up to proof' (i.e. not testified as anticipated).

Following examination in chief, a witness will be cross-examined by the advocate for the party not calling that witness. The purpose of cross-examination is to weaken the testimony of the witness, either by casting doubt about his testimony, or by eliciting facts favourable to the cross-examiner, or by discrediting the credit of the

---

[270] It is the duty of the prosecution to take all reasonable steps to secure the attendance at the trial of all witnesses (other than those subject to a conditional witness order) named on the back of the indictment (*R v Cavanagh* [1972] 2 All ER 704, [1972] 1 WLR 676). However the prosecution has a discretion whether to call a particular witness and, having called him, whether to adduce his evidence-in-chief or merely to tender him for cross-examination. Where the witness's evidence is capable of belief the prosecution should call him even though his evidence is unfavourable to the prosecution case and if they do not do so, the judge may intervene and direct that he be called; on the other hand if the witness's evidence does not appear to be capable of belief the prosecution need not call him and it will then be for the defence to call him if they wish to do so; *R v Oliva* [1965] 3 All ER 116, [1965] 1 WLR 1028.

[271] *Ewer v Ambrose* (1825) 3 B & C 746.   [272] See Criminal Justice Act 2003, s 119.

[273] *R v Da Silva* [1990] 1 All ER 29, [1990] 1 WLR 31. If the witness wishes to refresh his memory, and have the document with him, actually whilst testifying, it must be contemporaneous, i.e. made whilst the events were still fresh in the mind of the maker of the statement: *R v Richardson* [1971] 2 QB 484. See also *A-G's Reference (No 3 of 1979)* (1979) 69 Cr App R 411 and cf. *R v Chisnell* [1992] Crim LR 507. (police officers allowed to refresh memory from notes transcribed many months earlier, but at a time when the events were still fresh in the mind).

witness in the eyes of the jury. An advocate may, for this purpose, ask leading questions and, indeed, there are few limits on what may be asked in cross-examination: normally, any question relevant to the issues in the case will be allowed.[274] Exceptions to this general rule exist in respect of questions relating to the interception of communications,[275] in respect of matters for which a claim of public interest immunity is successfully made.[276] By contrast, the law imposes limits on questions that may be asked and which affect the credit or credibility of the witness. The basic rule is that the question must, if asked, relate to the likely standing of the witness in the eyes of the court.[277] There are complex and special rules about the questions that may be asked about the bad character of both non-defendants and defendants alike,[278] and in sexual cases section 41 of the Youth Justice and Criminal Evidence Act 1999 imposes strict limits on what may or may not be asked in a sexual case. A complainant may not, subject to limited exceptions, be asked questions relating to his or her sexual experience. Such limitations are designed to give some protection for the witness, and to ensure that rape complainants in particular are not deterred from coming forward by the potential of unnecessary and intrusive questioning. One key authority, R v A, highlights the restrictive nature of section 41. In a preliminary ruling, the House of Lords ruled that, potentially, section 41 did not prevent questions about the sexual relationship that the appellant and complainant had had, if that was necessary to secure a fair trial. The 'reading down' of section 41 to ensure compliance with Article 6 has already been noted.[279]

Even where questions relating to credit are permitted, the law imposes strict limits as to how far the cross-examiner may adduce other evidence to contradict (i.e. rebut) the testimony of that witness. The reason for this is that there is a need to keep the trial to the issues at hand, and to prevent the trial from becoming an exploration of a multiplicity of other matters. This is known as the collateral evidence rule: the answers of a witness in cross-examination to matters that relate to credit are regarded as final, and can only be rebutted if one of the exceptions to the rule exists.[280] There are four such exceptions that potentially arise. The first is if the witness denies a previous conviction: the denial may be rebutted.[281] Secondly, if the witness denies making a previous inconsistent statement, that denial may be rebutted.[282] Thirdly, the cross-examiner may rebut a denial of bias.[283] Finally, if the witness denies having a general reputation for untruthfulness, that denial may be rebutted.[284]

Cross-examination is followed, sometimes, by re-examination by the advocate for the party calling the witness. The purpose of re-examination is limited to clarifying matters that have arisen out of the testimony the witness has given to the court, usually in the hope of bolstering testimony which has been shaken under cross-examination.

---

274 CT Hobbs v Tinling & Co [1929] 2 KB 1; R v Funderburk [1990] 2 All ER 482.
275 Regulation of Investigatory Powers Act 2000, s 17.   276 See p 578, ante.
277 See Hobbs v Tingling, ante, n 274.   278 See Criminal Justice Act 2003, s 98, s 100, s 101.
279 See p 56, ante.   280 Harris v Tippett (1810) 2 Camp 637.
281 Criminal Procedure Act 1865, s 6.   282 Ibid, s 4.
283 A-G v Hitchcock (1847) 1 Exch 91.   284 R v Richardson (1977) 66 Cr App R 6.

As in examination in chief, leading questions may not be asked. Furthermore, a party cannot use re-examination as an opportunity for raising matters which he omitted to raise in examination in chief unless the form of the cross-examination justifies this.

When all the witnesses for the prosecution have been examined, prosecuting counsel will close his case by saying 'that is the case for the prosecution' or words to that effect. There may then be a submission by defending counsel that there is no case to answer as regards the whole or some part of the indictment. This may be put in two ways; first that there is no evidence that the crime alleged against the accused was committed by him; secondly that the evidence, taken at its highest, is so tenuous that a jury could not properly convict on it.[285] This is a matter for the judge to determine and, although there is no set rule, it is usually regarded as desirable that the argument on the submission should take place in the absence of the jury. Prosecuting counsel has, of course, a right to reply to defending counsel's submission. If the submission is upheld the trial will end as regards that part of the indictment at least, though that will be a terminating ruling potentially giving right to a possible right of appeal.[286] The jury should in such a case be instructed to return a formal verdict of not guilty; this is analogous to the case where the defendant changes his plea to guilty in the course of the trial. Even if no formal verdict is taken, the case, once withdrawn from the jury, is completely 'dead' and cannot be revived by the defendant's own evidence or evidence given by a prosecution witness who is allowed to be recalled.[287] Similarly where two men are jointly charged, and a successful submission is made on behalf of one of them, he is to be regarded as no longer charged during what remains of the trial.[288]

The role of the judge at this stage is crucial. If the prosecution evidence is such that no properly directed jury could convict upon it then it is the duty of the judge to stop the case.[289] This is particularly so where the prosecution rely wholly on the confession of a person who suffers a significant degree of mental handicap, the confession itself being unconvincing. Such a case should be withdrawn from the jury.[290] By contrast, if the case is one where the strengths or weaknesses of the case depend upon the view to be taken as to the reliability of a witness or other matters properly within the remit of the jury, then the case should be left to the jury to decide. If the submission is simply rejected, the trial will proceed. Even if no submission is made the judge may at any time after the close of the prosecution's case ask the jury whether they think that the prosecution case has been proved and invite them to return a verdict of not guilty if they think that it has not;[291] the more desirable practice is for the judge to take the initiative and direct the jury to return a verdict of not guilty.

The defence case will then open, assuming that the trial is proceeding as to part or

---

[285] R v Galbraith [1981] 2 All ER 1060.   [286] Under the Criminal Justice Act 2003.

[287] R v Plain [1967] 1 All ER 614, [1967] 1 WLR 565. The corollary of this is that if the submission is wrongly rejected the accused is entitled to have his subsequent conviction quashed by the Court of Appeal, even though evidence subsequently given would support that conviction; R v Cockley [1984] Crim LR 429.

[288] R v Meek (1996) 110 Sol J 867.   [289] R v Galbraith n 285, ante.

[290] R v McKenzie [1993] 1 WLR 453.   [291] R v Young [1964] 2 All ER 480.

all of the indictment. Defence counsel has no right to make an opening speech to the jury unless he is calling witnesses as to fact other than the defendant (whether or not he is also calling the defendant); even then the matter is in his discretion.[292] Witnesses for the defence are then called. If the defendant is giving evidence it is the general rule that he must give evidence before other witnesses; he must be in court, and if he heard the evidence of other witnesses before him,[293] he might be tempted to 'trim' his own evidence. A witness about whose evidence there could be no controversy may of course be taken before the defendant. What evidence is called for the defence depends on the nature of the case. An accused person is not a compellable witness in his own defence.[294] However, if he fails to testify in his own defence without good cause, or refuses without good cause to answer any question, the court may draw such inference as it thinks proper.[295] An exception to this is where it appears to the court that the physical or mental condition of the accused makes it undesirable for him to give evidence.

Whether an inference is in fact drawn is a matter for the jury, based on their own perception of common-sense.[296] If good cause is argued by the accused, an evidential basis to establish it must exist: it is not enough for the accused simply to assert.[297] Age is not a barrier. Until 1998, no inference could be drawn in respect of an accused aged under fourteen. This was considered illogical by the government, in the light of the fact that an inference can be drawn from the silence of a suspect aged under fourteen at the investigatory stage, and the Crime and Disorder Act 1998 removed the age limitation.

All defence witnesses are subject to examination in chief, cross-examination, and re-examination in the normal way. Where there is more than one defendant, cross-examination of prosecution witnesses and speeches will normally be taken in the order in which the defendants' names appear on the indictment, although there is no fixed rule on the matter. Once the case for the defence has been closed the prosecution may be allowed to call rebutting evidence, in the discretion of the judge. The general rule is that rebutting evidence should be allowed only where evidence has been called on behalf of the defendant which could not fairly have been foreseen by the prosecution.[298] In determining this it should be borne in mind that in most cases the defence will have given a defence statement pursuant to section 5 of the Criminal Procedure and Investigations Act 1996.[299] Rebutting evidence may be called at any time up to the conclusion of the summing-up and retirement of the jury and defending counsel has a right to cross-examine the witnesses called in rebuttal. Further, if evidence is called after the conclusion of the speeches, counsel may deliver supplemental speeches dealing with the new evidence.

---

[292] The Royal Commission recommended that the right of the defence to make a speech at the commencement of the case should be extended to all cases, in substitution for the right here described.

[293] PACE, s 79.   [294] PACE, s 80.

[295] Criminal Justice and Public Order Act 1994, s 35.

[296] R v Cowan [1996] QB 373; Murray v DPP [1999] 1 WLR 1.

[297] See Practice Direction: Crown Court (Defendants Evidence) [1995] 2 Cr App R 192.

[298] R v Picher (1974) 60 Cr App R 1.   [299] See p 581, ante.

The judge has a right to recall witnesses himself or even call witnesses whom neither side has called; he may also question witnesses to clarify matters of doubt or to probe further into matters which he thinks have not been sufficiently investigated. However, a judge must be careful not to overstep the mark. In *R v Grafton* prosecuting counsel decided during his case to offer no further evidence. The trial judge disagreed with that decision, and called the one remaining prosecution witness. In quashing the resulting conviction, the Court of Appeal stressed that the judge's power to call witnesses should be used sparingly, and only to advance the ends of fairness and justice. Until the case for the Crown is complete it is the Crown's decision as to whether or not the prosecution should proceed.

Closing speeches and the summing-up then follow. These are dealt with later.[300]

3 WITNESSES

The procedure to be followed in the calling of evidence has been noted above. The general rule is that any person who is capable of giving intelligible testimony is a competent witness. A person who is incapable of such testimony because of mental capacity, whether of a permanent or temporary nature,[301] will not be competent and thus will not be heard. Until recently, it was thought that special rules applied to young children, but widespread criticism led to changes in the law. These have the effect of applying the same test of competence to a child as to an adult.[302] Special rules continue to apply to accused persons: an accused is not a competent witness for the prosecution, although he is competent in his own defence.

A witness who is competent is usually compellable. In other words, the witness can be required to attend court to testify, on pain of being punished for contempt of court. The attendance of a witness at the Crown Court is compelled by the issue of a witness order or witness summons, issued by the Crown Court.[303] A witness can resist the granting of a witness summons only if he has no relevant evidence to give, or if the witness is entitled to claim public interest immunity to resist the claim that he should testify or produce relevant documents.[304] To the general rule that a witness is compellable there are certain exceptions. An accused person is never compellable in his own defence. The spouse of the accused is only compellable in certain limited situations, contained in section 80(3) of the Police and Criminal Evidence Act 1984. These situations are as follows:

(1) where the offence charged involves an assault on, or injury or threat of injury to, the spouse or a person at the time of the offence under the age of sixteen years;

(2) a sexual offence alleged to have been committed against a person under the age of sixteen years;

---

[300] See p 619, *post.*   [301] *R v Bainews* [1987] Crim LR 508.
[302] *DPP v M* [1997] 2 All ER 749; *G v DPP* [1997] 2 All ER 755.
[303] Criminal Procedure (Attendance of Witnesess) Act 1965, s 2.   [304] See p 577, *ante.*

(3) an offence of attempting, conspiring, aiding or abetting, counseling, or inciting such an offence.

Where the spouse is competent but not compellable the trial judge is under a duty to inform the witness of that witness' right not to testify.[305] If the witness then decides to give evidence, that witness can then be treated in the normal way, for example, he or she may be declared hostile.

Various other persons are not compellable witnesses. This includes the sovereign, as well as foreign sovereigns, ambassadors, High Commissioners, and various grades of diplomatic staff. In any legal proceedings to which a bank is not a party, a bank or bank officer cannot be compelled to produce any banker's book the contents of which can be proved by secondary evidence, e.g. by the production of documentary evidence.[306]

Where a witness testifies he usually does so orally. The general rule is that all witnesses must give evidence on oath, but a child under the age of fourteen always gives unsworn evidence.[307] Any person having authority to hear evidence has the power to administer an oath,[308] but it is usually administered by the clerk to the court. The usual form of oath runs as follows:

I swear by Almighty God that the evidence I shall give shall be the truth, the whole truth and nothing but the truth.

The witness holds the New Testament, or in the case of Jews the Old Testament, in his uplifted hand.[309] This form of oath is only appropriate to members of the Christian and Jewish faiths. Any person who objects to taking the usual oath may take any other form of oath, according to his religious beliefs, which he declares to be binding on his conscience. As an alternative, a person who objects to being sworn is permitted to 'make his solemn affirmation' instead of taking the oath. This substitutes the words 'I (name) do solemnly sincerely and truly declare and affirm' for 'I swear by Almighty God . . .'. A witness is also permitted to affirm if it is not reasonably practicable without inconvenience or delay to administer the form of oath appropriate to the witness' beliefs (for example, because the book on which the witness wishes to swear is not available).[310] An affirmation is not unsworn testimony: it is equivalent to an oath and a false statement on affirmation amounts to perjury.[311]

Once sworn, or having affirmed, a witness gives evidence orally, usually in open court. Exceptions to this are permitted where it is essential for the administration of justice, or where statute specifically authorizes. In 1999, the Youth Justice and Criminal Evidence Act conferred the power to make special measures directions in respect of children or vulnerable witnesses in some circumstances. For example, a witness may give evidence from behind a screen, so that the witness does not have to face the alleged perpetrator of the offence, or through a live TV link. The use of video links is

[305] R v Thompson (1976) 64 Cr App R 96.   [306] Bankers Book Evidence Act 1879.
[307] Criminal Justice Act 1991, s 52.   [308] Evidence Act 1851, s 16.
[309] Oaths Act 1978, s 1.   [310] Oaths Act 1978, s 5(2).   [311] Ibid, s 5(4).

particularly important in cases involving children's evidence, especially where it is alleged that the child is the victim of abuse. In such cases the law is increasingly concerned to ensure that the child does not have the damage of the alleged offence compounded by the experience of having to face the alleged perpetrator in open court. This power to take evidence through a live TV link also extends to cases where an adult witness is outside the United Kingdom. In addition, a video recorded interview with a child may sometimes be admissible as the evidence in chief of that child. This is dealt with below.

(a) Out of court statements

Normally, the evidence given by a witness is oral in nature. Historically, a technical rule of evidence, the hearsay rule, prevents the out-of-court statements of a person being adduced to prove the truth of the assertions contained in those statements. The reasons for this general rule reflect the oral nature of the criminal trial: an out-of-court statement may, if it is made orally, be prone to distortion or inaccuracy. If the maker of the statement is available to testify, his out-of-court statement is self-serving and adds nothing to what he can tell the court. If, by contrast, the maker of the statement is unavailable to testify, the witness cannot be cross-examined on what is alleged to have been said in that statement.

Yet it can clearly be seen that the out-of-court statements of an individual may be both relevant and reliable, often made at a time when the events or matters in issue were fresh in the mind of that person. For that reason the hearsay rule has been severely criticized, and is subject to a wide range of exceptions. Changes have been made by the Criminal Justice Act 2003. Section 114 of that Act has recast the rule to preserve some of the common law and statutory exceptions that existed prior to the 2003 Act, and created a new 'safety valve' that can be used to admit evidence of out-of-court statements that infringes the rule but which it is in the interests of justice to receive. As a result of this recasting of the rules the following are the main forms of evidence now potentially admissible in evidence:

(1) Statements made by a witness who is unavailable for a variety of reasons. These include death, the fact that the person is physically or mentally unfit to be a witness, the fact that the witness is outside the UK and it is not reasonably practicable to secure his attendance, or cannot be found, or the witness does testify because of fear.[312]

(2) Where statements contained in documents are made or received in the course of a trade business or profession.[313]

(3) Statements in public documents.

---

[312] Criminal Justice Act 2003, s 115. This largely replicates the provisions of Criminal Justice Act 1968, s 23, but extends to both documentary and oral statements.

[313] Criminal Justice Act 2003, s 116. This largely replicates the provisions of Criminal Justice Act 1968, s 24.

(4) Spontaneous statements made by individuals where events dominate the mind of the individual (known as *res gestae statements*).[314]

(5) Confessions made by a defendant.[315]

(6) Statements used to refresh memory.[316]

(7) Some previous consistent or inconsistent statements.[317]

(8) Statements within the 'safety valve' described above. A good example may be a confession to the crime made by a person other than the defendant, which would technically be hearsay but nonetheless of strong evidential value.

One particular exception to the rule, mentioned above, is the power to consider a video recording of an interview with a child. In cases involving offences of violence, or sexual offences, the video recording of the interview with a child may, with leave of the court, be adduced. If such a video is shown, what the child says is evidence and can be used to prove the truth of the matters to which the child speaks. Leave will be granted unless:

(a) it appears to the court that the child will not be available for cross-examination;

(b) rules of court governing disclosure of the circumstances in which the recording was made have not been complied with;

(c) the court is of the opinion that, in the interests of justice, the recording ought not to be admitted. In considering whether or not leave should be granted, the court must consider whether any prejudice to the accused which might result is outweighed by the desirability of showing the whole, or substantially the whole, of the video. A *Memorandum of Good Practice* has been adopted intended to govern how such video recorded interviews should be conducted so as to ensure that the interview can safely be relied on.

4 THE BURDEN OF PROOF AND THE RIGHT OF SILENCE

The burden of proof in a criminal case is on the prosecution. The prosecution must prove each element of the crime charged. This includes, subject to certain limited exceptions,[318] disproving any defence that is raised. This fundamental principle was well demonstrated in *Woolmington v Director of Public Prosecutions*[319] where the accused, charged with murdering his wife, claimed that the killing was an accident. The trial judge in his summing up directed the jury that if the Crown proved that the accused killed the deceased the burden rested on the accused to prove provocation

---

[314] For the pre-existing common law see *R v Andrews* [1987] AC 281.

[315] Subject to the requirements of PACE s 76 being satisfied.

[316] Criminal Justice Act 2003, s 139.   [317] 2003 Act, ss 119–120.

[318] These include the burden of proving a plea in bar (e.g. *autrefois acquit*) insanity, diminished responsibility, unfitness to plead as well as under certain specific statutory exceptions.

[319] [1935] AC 462. Cf. *R v Bone* [1968] 2 All ER 644, [1968] 1 WLR 983 in which the defendant's conviction was quashed because of the trial judge's failure to direct that, in relation to the defence of duress, it was for the prosecution to disprove the defence rather than for the defendant to prove it.

or accident. The conviction was quashed in the House of Lords because of this misdirection. In the famous words of Lord Sankey LC:

... throughout the web of the English criminal law one golden thread is always to be seen, that is the duty of the prosecution to prove the prisoner's guilt, subject to. .... The defence of insanity and subject also to any statutory exception.[320]

The circumstances in which the law departs from the principle are limited. The burden of proving a special plea in bar is on the accused. Thus, if it is claimed that the accused has been previously acquitted on the same charge, then the doctrine of *autrefois acquit* will apply.[321] The burden of proof on this point will be on the accused. Another example is the defence of insanity: the burden of proving insanity is on the defence where this issue is raised by the defence, as is the burden of proving diminished responsibility or unfitness to plead.[322] Certain statutory exceptions also exist, which raises important issues in the context of Article 6, discussed below.[323] Whenever a burden of proof is placed on the accused, the standard of proof is not that normally imposed on the prosecution ('beyond reasonable doubt') but the lesser, civil, standard of the balance of probabilities.[324]

The fact that the burden of proof is on the prosecution is crucially connected with the basic principle that an accused person has the right not to self-incriminate. As already noted,[325] this is a right recognized both by English law and by the European Convention of Human Rights.[326] It is for this reason that an accused person cannot, generally, be required to self-incriminate or required to testify in his own defence. An accused is a competent, but not compellable, witness in his own defence. Further, if self incriminatory statements are obtained from an accused person unfairly, or by a trick, or in circumstances where they should not be relied on because safeguards created by the law have been evaded or ignored,[327] they will be excluded for evidence. Inroads into these principles have in recent years been made by Parliament. The fact that inferences may now be drawn from a failure to mention facts at the investigatory stage, or from a failure to disclose the nature of the defence later relied on, has already been seen, but, as already noted, section 35 of the Criminal Justice and Public Order Act 1994 permits a court to draw such inference as it thinks proper from a failure of an accused to give evidence or his refusal, without good cause, to answer any question.

---

[320] Ibid, at p 481.   [321] See p 521, *ante.*

[322] Homicide Act 1957, s 2(2); *R v Dunbar* [1958] 1 QB 1, [1957] 2 All ER 737.

[323] See, e.g. Road Traffic Act 1988, s 5(2).; Prevention of Crime Act 1953, s 1. For a general, and important statutory exception, see Magistrates' Courts Act 1980, s 101 which provides that, on summary trial, where an enactment makes the commission of a particular act an offence subject to a proviso, exception, excuse or qualification, the burden of proving that falls on the accused. For the application of s 101, see *R v Hunt* [1987] AC 352, [1987] 1 All ER 1.

[324] *R v Carr-Briant* [1943] KB 607, [1943] 2 All ER 156. Note though that the civil standard may not be absolute, and may vary according to the nature of what has to be proved.

[325] See p 180, *ante.*

[326] *Murray v United Kingdom* (1966) 22 EHRR 29; *Condron v United Kingdom* [2000] Crim LR 679.

[327] *R v Mason* [1987] 3 All ER 481, [1988] 1 WLR 139.

Whether an inference is in fact drawn will depend on all the circumstances and whether an evidential basis has been established to explain the failure to testify or to answer the relevant question.[328]

This right not to be required to self-incriminate is at the heart of the debate as to whether burdens of proof which raise a presumption of guilt, and place a burden of proof on a defendant are consistent with Article 6. In *Saliabaku v France*[329] the Court of Human Rights observed:

Presumptions of fact or of law operate in every legal system. Clearly the Convention does not prohibit such presumptions in principle. It does, however, require the Contracting States to remain within certain limits . . . *art 6(2)* does not regard presumptions of fact or of law provided for in the criminal law with indifference. It requires States to confine them within reasonable limits which take into account the importance of what is at stake an maintain the rights of the defence. . . .

The effect of this is to require the court in each case to take a view as to whether the legislative interference with the presumption of innocence is justified and proportionate.[330] The constituent rights Article 6 are not absolutes.[331] In respect of any statutory provision the first step is to determine whether it does in fact impose a burden of proof on the defendant.[332] If it does not, then clearly no issue arises. But if it does the court must be assessed in the context of Article 6(2). Whilst Article 6 does not inevitably prohibit a burden of proof being placed on a defendant, it will be open to challenge.

Although these principles appear straightforward, they have generated significant debate and disagreement as the courts have sought to implement them in a principled but pragmatic way.[333] In *Lambert* conflicting opinions were delivered by the House of Lords, when it concluded that section 28 of the Misuse of Drugs Act 1971 was to be read as imposing only an evidential burden on the defendant, leaving on the prosecution the legal burden (i.e. of satisfying the court so that it is sure of the guilt of the accused). A five-strong Court of Appeal in *Attorney-General's Reference (No 1 of 12004, R v Edwards and others*[334] examined and explained *Lambert,* but preferred statements made by Lord Nichols made in yet another case, *R v Johnstone.*[335] These differences of emphasis were described by Lord Bingham in *Sheldrake v DPP*[336] as explicable in the light of differences in the subject matter of the two cases. Section 5 of

---

[328] See *R v Cowan* [1996] QB373; [1995] 3WLR 818.   [329] (1988) 13 EHRR 379.

[330] See Lord Steyn in *R v Lambert* [2001] 3 All ER 577 at 590.

[331] See Lord Bingham in *Brown v Stott (Procurator Fiscal, Dunfermiline)* [2001] 2 All ER 97.

[332] See *R v Hunt* [1987] 1 All ER 1; Magistrates' Courts Act 1980, s 101.

[333] Amongst the authorities to which regard should be had are the following: *R v Lambert, ante* n 330; *R v DPP, ex parte kebiline* [1999] 4 All ER 801; *L v DPP* [2002] 1 Cr App R 420; *R v Drummond* [2002] All ER (D) 70; *R v Johnstone* [2003] 3 All ER 884; *R (On application of Grundy & Co Excavations Ltd) v Halton Division Magistrates' Court* (20030 167 JP; *Attorney-General's reference (No 1 of 2004), R v Edwards* [2004] All ER (D) 318.

[334] See n 333, *ante.*

[335] See n 333, *ante. Trade Marks Act 1994, s 91(5) held not to infringe Article 6.

[336] [2005] 1 All ER 337.

the 1971 Act (*Lambert*) and section 91 of the 1994 Act (*Johnstone*) were directed to serious social and economic problems, but the justifiability and fairness of the respective reverse-onus provisions had to be judged in the particular context of each case. In the latter case the offence was committed by dealers and traders of goods who might be expected to exercise some care about the provenance of goods in which they dealt. The correct approach, concluded the House of Lords in *Sheldrake*, is never to decide whether a reverse burden should be imposed on a defendant, but always to assess whether a burden imposed by Parliament unjustifiably infringes the presumption of innocence. It should not inevitably be assumed that 'Parliament would not have made an exception without good reason': that approach may lead the court to give too much weight to the enactment under review and too little to the presumption of innocence and the obligation imposed on it by section 3 of the Human Rights Act 1998.[337] Applying these principles, the court in *Shedrake* held that section 5 of the Road Traffic Act 1998[338] imposed a reverse onus, but was plainly directed to a legitimate objective, the prevention of death, injury and damage on the roads. By contrast, the reverse burden provision in section 12 of the Terrorism Act 2000 was not a proportionate and legitimate response to the problem being addressed. Although a defendant might reasonably be expected to show that an organization of which he was a member was not proscribed for the purpose of the offence under section 11 of the 2000 Act, it would be all but impossible for him to show that he had not taken part in activities of the organization at the time when it was proscribed. It thus was to be read as imposing only an evidential burden.

The clear effect of this mass of case law is to leave cases to be dealt with on their own particular facts, a conclusion that is likely to mean an on-going stream of case law.

5 PROTECTION OF THE DEFENDANT

An accused has always had special protections. The right not to be required to self-incriminate has already been noted. It extends not only to the trial itself but to the pre-trial process. In *Saunders v United Kingdom*[339] the Court of Human Rights concluded that the principle against self incrimination extended to the prosecution not being allowed to use evidence obtained through methods of coercion or oppression. That does not mean to say that the use of evidence obtained through self incrimination by an accused is prohibited. A confession obtained from an accused is admissible provided it has been obtained fairly and in compliance with the terms of section 76 of PACE. Again, a requirement for information, obtained on pain of penalty, as to the identity of the driver of a motor vehicle was held not to contravene Article 6 in *Brown v Stott (Procurator Fiscal, Dunfermiline)*[340] because it was a necessary and

---

[337] per Lord Bingham in *Sheldrake v DPP, ante*, disapproving dicta of the Court of Appeal in *A-G's Reference (No 1 of 2004)*. For the role of the court in applying Human Rights Act 1998, s 3, see p 157, *ante*.

[338] In respect of excess alcohol in blood:, defence to prove no likelihood of driving whilst over prescribed limit.

[339] (1997) 2 BHRC 358.   [340] [2001] 2 All ER 97.

proportionate limitation of the basic right not to be required to self incriminate. The provisions in sections 34, 37, and 38 of the Criminal Justice and Public Order Act 1994, which permit inferences to be drawn from a failure, in some circumstances, to supply information are, again, within Article 6 provided they do not provide the sole or main evidence against the accused.

At trial, the right of the accused not to testify has already been noted.[341] It used to be the case that, under section 1(3) of the Criminal Evidence Act 1898, an accused had a unique 'shield' about being asked questions about previous convictions or bad character. This has been significantly changed by the passage of sections 98 and 101 of the Criminal Justice Act 2003, which still give the accused some protections, but place him or her on a much more similar basis to other witnesses. Those rules are complex and outside the scope of this book.

6 CONCLUSION OF THE CASE

Each side may address the jury, except that where a defendant is unrepresented and either gives no evidence at all or only gives evidence himself the prosecution have no right to sum up their case.[342] In all cases the rule is that prosecuting counsel speaks first and is then followed by counsel for the defendant. The judge will then sum up.

The purpose of the summing-up is to instruct the jury as to the burden and standard of proof, the role of judge and jury, and to give directions on points of law where it is necessary to do so. The Judicial Studies Board has prepared model directions on common issues and points of law for the benefit of judges. The judge will also usually give a summary of the facts: indeed, in R v Gregory[343] the Court of Appeal suggested that there must be a reminder of the facts in all cases. However, in R v Wilson[344] the Court of Appeal upheld a conviction in a case where a judge considered the trial so short that a summary of the facts was unnecessary.

Criticism of this part of the judicial function has from time to time been made,[345] that summings-up can unwittingly, and occasionally deliberately, influence the jury's view of the facts. Some suggested to the Royal Commission that, as in the United States, no summing-up of the facts should be given. This was rejected, but the Commission did disagree with the approach taken in R v Gregory, and indicated that it is in each case a question of fairness and balance.[346]

---

[341] See p 583, ante.

[342] R v Harrison (1923) 17 Cr App R 156. Where the defendant is represented but calls no evidence, counsel for the prosecution has a right to make a closing speech but the Court of Appeal has stated that it is a right which it should rarely be necessary to exercise save in long and complex cases: R v Bryant [1979] QB 108; [1978] 2 All ER 689, an instructive case on the history of the procedure relating to speeches in criminal trials.

[343] [1993] Crim LR 623.   [344] [1991] Crim LR 838.

[345] See RCCJ, Ch 8, para 20.   [346] Ibid, para 22.

7 VERDICT

No pressure should be placed on a jury to reach a verdict.[347] The jury generally retire to the jury room to consider their verdict. They are put in charge of officers of the court called jury bailiffs who must take an oath not, without the leave of the court, to allow any person to speak to the jury or to speak to them themselves without such leave, except only to ask them if they are agreed upon their verdict. Once they have retired to consider their verdict, the jury can separate only with leave of the court, which in turn can be given only in cases of 'evident necessity' such as a juror being taken ill in the course of the jury's deliberations. They do not have to stay in the same jury room until they have reached a conclusion, but they must not separate, subject to the very limited exception noted above, and it is desirable if not essential for them always to be in the custody of one of the court bailiffs while, for example, staying at a hotel overnight.[348] The jury may, of course, ask for further guidance from the judge upon any point of law or evidence arising in the case, but both the request for information and the answer to it must be given in open court; if the jury have asked for guidance in the form of a note sent to the judge, this note should be read out verbatim and then the answer given.[349]

When the jury have concluded their deliberations they will return to court and one of their number, whom they have appointed foreman, will stand up and, subject to the possibility of a majority verdict, in answer to questions put by the appropriate officer of the court, deliver the verdict of the jury. The Criminal Justice Act 1967 introduced into English law the majority verdict. A verdict need not be unanimous if when there are not less than eleven jurors, ten agree on the verdict, and when there are ten, if nine agree. The law cannot accept any majority verdict unless the jury have had not less than two hours of deliberation, or such longer period as the court thinks reasonable having regard to the nature and complexity of the case,[350] nor can the court accept a majority verdict of guilty unless the foreman of the jury states in open court the number of jurors who agreed on, and dissented from, the verdict.[351] A Practice Direction

---

[347] R v McKenna [1960] 1 QB 411, [1960] 1 All ER 326: judge told jury that they would be kept overnight if they failed to agree a verdict within ten minutes. A guilty verdict was returned after six minutes. The resulting conviction was quashed on appeal. See also: Bushell's case (1670) Vaugh 135, 124 ER 1006.

[348] It may be necessary to restrict their reading or television viewing: see Re Central Independent Television [1991] 1 All ER 347, [1991] 1 WLR 4.

[349] R v Neal [1949] 2 KB 590, [1949] 2 All ER 438. Breach of this rule will almost invariably amount to a material irregularity resulting in a subsequent conviction being quashed; R v Goodson [1975] 1 All ER 760, [1975] 1 WLR 549 (where a juror, after retirement, was permitted by the jury bailiff to leave the jury room, following which he was seen making a telephone call); but compare R v Alexander [1974] 1 All ER 539, [1974] 1 WLR 422 in which the irregularity was a trifling one (juror returned to court simply to collect one or more of the exhibits and was observed throughout) and was held to be of insufficient gravity to justify quashing the conviction.

[350] Juries Act 1974, s 17(4).

[351] Ibid, s 17(3). The requirement of this subsection is mandatory so that if, for whatever reason, the foreman does not so state the conviction will inevitably be quashed: R v Barry [1975] 2 All ER 760, [1975] 1 WLR 1190.

contains procedure whereby it is hoped to conceal the fact that an acquittal was by a majority. In *R v Pigg*[352] the House of Lords held that the words 'ten agreed' (in answer to the question how many agreed and how many dissented) was sufficient compliance with the statute. If after such discussion as is practicable in the circumstances the jury still cannot reach the necessary measure of agreement the judge has no option but to discharge them. The defendant will then be remanded in custody or on bail to be tried afresh. Theoretically this could happen several times, but if successive juries disagree the practice is for the prosecution to offer no evidence at a third trial. On a re-trial, the fact that there has been a previous trial is usually irrelevant and inadmissible, but it may become necessary to refer to it, for example for the purpose of proving that the defendant or a witness made some particular statement or admission. Thus in *R v McGregor*.[353] the defendant was charged with receiving. At an earlier, abortive, trial he had admitted possession. A police officer was allowed to give evidence of this admission.

Other circumstances in which the jury may be discharged are:[354]

(1) illness. If during the course of a criminal trial a juror falls ill he may be discharged by the judge from further service, and depending on the facts, normally will be so discharged. The judge may then discharge the whole jury, but does not have to do so; neither is discharge of the single juror fatal to the continuance of the trial, since statute now provides that when, in the course of a trial, any member of the jury dies or is discharged the trial may nevertheless continue provided that the number of jurors does not fall below nine. If, however, the charge is murder or any offence punishable by death the prosecution and every accused must consent in writing to the trial continuing, even if only one juror is discharged or dies;

(2) misconduct of a juror, such as holding improper conversations with a member of the public about the case or absenting himself from his colleagues at the time when the jury were in the course of retiring to consider their verdict; and

(3) improper revelation to the jury of the defendant's past criminal record. In such a case the jury is frequently discharged.

8 POST VERDICT ORDERS AND SENTENCE

If the defendant pleads guilty, or is convicted by the jury, questions of sentence arise. That is dealt with in chapter 22. But even if the defendant is acquitted that may not,

---

[352] [1983] 1 All ER 56, [1983] 1 WLR 6.   [353] [1968] 1 QB 371, [1967] 2 All ER 267.

[354] Juries Act 1974, s 16. The judge may discharge a juror who 'being through illness incapable of continuing to act or for any other reason' (s 16(1)). This is a matter left to the discretion of the trial judge, although the Court of Appeal will interfere if injustice has resulted. In *R v Hambery* [1977] QB 924, [1977] 3 All ER 561 the trial judge discharged a lady juror in order to permit her to go away on holiday, a course which the Court of Appeal saw no reason to criticize.

now, quite be the end of it, because the Domestic Violence, Crime and Victims Act 2004 has given courts the right to impose restraining orders in some circumstances, despite the fact that the defendant has been acquitted. For convenience those are dealt with later.[355]

---

[355] See p 679, *post*.

21

SUMMARY PROCEDURE
AND APPEALS

The often forgotten,[1] central role of the magistrates' courts[2] in dealing with criminal cases has already been noted.[3] In excess of 95 per cent of criminal business is dealt with summarily,[4] including virtually all cases involving children and young persons which are dealt with in the youth court. This level of work is increasing in the light of recent legislation and practice changes.[5] The issues raised by this, in terms of the composition of the court and the choice of mode of trial have already been noted.[6] In this chapter, the main procedural differences between trial on indictment and summary trial are discussed. For this purpose, summary trial refers to trial irrespective of whether it is the trial of a summary-only offence or of an either-way offence in fact being tried summarily. It also refers to trial in the youth court.

At the outset of any discussion of summary procedure two basic points must be noted. First the overarching purpose of the Criminal Procedure Rules. These rules[7] provide a detailed framework for the operation of magistrates' court procedure and practice, as have in the past the various Magistrates' Courts Rules.[8] Secondly, note should be taken of the wide, and increasing, role of the justices' clerk, discussed below.[9]

A PROCESS

Summary procedure is commenced by process. The way an accused person may be brought before a court has already been discussed,[10] and is changing once the relevant parts of the Criminal Justice Act 2003 are in force.[11] Under current procedure, as the

---

[1] See the admonition of Darbyshire, 'An Essay on the Importance and Neglect of the Magistracy' [1997] Crim LR 639.

[2] For this purpose we can include the youth courts.   [3] See chapter 18, *ante.*

[4] Auld Review Ch 3, para 2. This may be an underestimate: see Auld Review *op cit*, and Derbyshire, *op cit*, n 1.

[5] See p 545, *ante.*   [6] See pp 545–6, *ante.*

[7] Made pursuant to Courts Act 2003, s 63. See SI 2005/384.

[8] See Magistrates' Courts Rules 1981, SI 1881/552 and related rules.   [9] See p 629, *post.*

[10] See p 540, ante.   [11] See p 541–2, *ante*, and p 629, *post.*

result of the laying of information,[12] either a summons to appear in court or a warrant to arrest the accused is obtained. Alternatively, the criminal proceedings can be commenced by bringing the offender to court following arrest,[13] assuming the power of arrest to be available. A warrant cannot be issued in any case where a summons has already been issued. In any event, as has already been noted, a warrant cannot be issued for the arrest of an adult in the case of a summary offence, unless the offence is punishable with imprisonment or the defendant's address is 'not sufficiently established' for a summons to be served on him. Even where a warrant may lawfully be issued, it is rarely thought necessary in the case of any summary offence. The position therefore is that a summons or a warrant may be issued if:

(a) the summary offence was committed or is suspected to have been committed within the area; or

(b) it appears to the magistrate issuing process necessary or expedient, with a view to the better administration of justice, that the person charged should be tried jointly with or in the same place as some other person who is charged with an offence and who is in custody or is to be proceeded against within the area; or

(c) the person charged resides, or is believed to reside or be within the area; or

(d) under any enactment the magistrates' court has jurisdiction to try the offence. In this context, there should be noted section 2(6) of the Magistrates' Courts Act 1980, permitting a magistrates' court to try a number of offences provided that it has jurisdiction to try any one of them; or

(e) the offence was committed outside England and Wales and, where it is an offence exclusively punishable on summary conviction, if a magistrates' court for the area would have jurisdiction to try the offence if the offender were before it.[14]

The Auld Review considered this procedure to be 'antiquated'.[15] A prosecutor could charge, summons, or lay an information, but only a charge brings with it an obligation to attend court, and many cases in fact begun by summons have to be adjourned due to the non-appearance of the defendant. This is because the issue of a summons does not place the defendant on bail, and thus create an obligation to surrender to bail. This analysis led the Auld Review to recommend change, which is effected by the Criminal Justice Act 2003. A new system of requisition and written charge will apply.[16] The power to issue an information is abolished,[17] though will remain an option for public prosecutors as a means of obtaining a warrant under section 1 of the Magistrates' Courts Act 1980 (issue of summons or warrant for arrest) to bring a charge

---

[12] For this see Criminal Procedure Rules 2005, r 7.1.   [13] As to which, see Ch 12, *ante*.

[14] Magistrates' Courts Act 1980, s 1(2).   [15] Auld Review, *op cit*, Ch 10 paras 416–422.

[16] See p 542, *ante*.   [17] Criminal Justice Act 2003, s 29(4).

against someone already in custody, or for someone other than a public prosecutor to obtain a summons or warrant.[18]

B JURISDICTION

A magistrates' court for an area[19] has jurisdiction to try summary offences committed within that area. It also has jurisdiction as a court of trial in the following circumstances:

(1) where a person is brought before the court on a summons or warrant issued under section 1(2) (b) of the Act (to be tried jointly with another person over whom the court has jurisdiction);[20]

(2) in relation to either way offences, in any case where it has jurisdiction to conduct preliminary hearings;[21]

(3) in relation to the trial of a young defendant for an indictable offence, in any case where it has jurisdiction to conduct preliminary hearings;

(4) where it has jurisdiction to try a defendant for a summary offence, it can also try him for any other summary offence.

C THE COURSE OF THE TRIAL

1 TIME-LIMIT

Unless expressly provided to the contrary a magistrates' court cannot try a summary offence unless the information was laid[22] or charge and requisition within six months from the time when the offence was committed.[23] However, it may try summarily an either-way offence outside that period, since this statutory time-limit is confined to summary offences.[24] Time runs from the time of commission of the offence, not from the time of its discovery; however, it is sufficient if the information is laid within the six months, even if the trial takes place outside that time. It is in each case a question of construction of the statute whether the offence in question is a continuing offence,

---

[18] For private prosecutions generally, see p 533, *ante*.

[19] County, a London commission area, or the City of London (Magistrates' Courts Act 1980, s 2(1)).

[20] See p 627, *ante*.   [21] See p 567 et seq, *ante*.

[22] See *R v Kennet JJ, ex parte Humphrey* [1993] Crim LR 787 (letter stating intention to charge sufficient); *R v Pontypridd Juvenile Court, ex parte B* [1988] Crim LR 842 (feeding of an information into a computer link to magistrates' court sufficient, irrespective of receipt).

[23] Magistrates' Courts Act 1980, s 127(1).

[24] Ibid, s 127(2); see also *Kemp v Liebherr (Great Britain) Ltd* [1987] 1 All ER 885, [1987] 1 WLR 607.

that is, committed each day that the act or state of affairs in question continues, or whether it is a 'once and for all' offence in that it is committed on one day and one day only. Thus in *R v Wimbledon Justices, ex parte Derwent*[25] a statute made it an offence to let or offer to let a house in excess of a certain rent. The Divisional Court held that a person lets a house once and for all when he demises it by means of a lease and that an information laid six months after the date of the demise was out of time. Proceedings could therefore be restrained by prohibition since:

If in a case brought before justices it can be seen on the face of the proceedings that the offence is alleged to have been committed more than six months before the information was laid, justices have no power to enter upon the case at all, because they have no jurisdiction to sit on a court of summary jurisdiction in the case of an offence alleged to have been committed more than six months before the proceedings were instituted.[26]

Even where the offence is continuing it seems that the time-limit runs from each day, so that the magistrates cannot hear any charge in respect of an offence as occurring more than six months before the date of the information;[27] in other words the matter is to be regarded as if the defendant committed the offence once every day. Where an information or charge and requisition is laid in time it may be amended to charge a different offence, after the expiry of six months from the commission of that offence, provided that this does not cause injustice.[28]

The general need to avoid delay in criminal proceedings has already been noted.[29] So, too, has the doctrine of abuse of process.[30] This doctrine applies to summary proceedings equally as to proceedings on indictment. In *R v Willesden Justices, ex parte Clemmings*,[31] Lord Bingham CJ indicated that magistrates had the power to stop a prosecution where there was an abuse of process, because:

(a) the prosecution have manipulated or misused the process of the court so as to deprive the accused of a protection provided by law or to take unfair advantage of a technicality; or

(b) the accused has been, or would be, prejudiced in the preparation or conduct of his defence by delay on the part of the prosecution, which was unjustifiable.

The principles on which these rules will be exercised are broadly those as apply more generally.[32] The court will consider whether the wrongdoing is deliberate, whether prejudice has been caused or the potential for it arises.[33] One example is *R v Brentford*

---

[25] [1953] 1 QB 380, [1953] 1 All ER 390.

[26] [1953] 1 QB 380, at 385, [1953] 1 All ER 390, at 391, per Lord Goddard CJ.

[27] *R v Chertsey Justices, ex parte Franks* [1961] 2 QB 152, [1961] 1 All ER 825.

[28] *R v Newcastle-upon-Tyne Justices, ex parte John Bryce (Contractors) Ltd* [1976] 2 All ER 611, [1976] 1 WLR 517.

[29] See p 537, *ante*.   [30] See p 538, *ante*.   [31] (1987) 87 Cr App R 280.

[32] See p 538, *ante*.

[33] See generally, *R v Oxford City Justices, ex parte Smith* (1987) 75 Cr App R 200, *R v Canterbury and St Augustine Justices, ex parte Turner* (1983) 147 JP 193; *R v Watford Justices, ex parte Outrim* [1983] RTR 26.

Justices, ex parte Wong[34] In that case an information for careless driving was laid two days before the expiration of the statutory six-months time-limit. At the time the information was laid the prosecution had not decided whether or not to prosecute and did not advise the defendant of the decision to do so until he was informed (by letter) some two months later. The summons consequent on the information was not served until some five months after the laying of the information, and the trial did not commence until some nine months after the laying of the information. On appeal for the refusal of the magistrates' court to stay the proceedings for abuse of process, the Divisional Court held that the police conduct amounted to 'a deliberate attempt to gain further time . . .', and stayed the proceedings.

2 NUMBER OF OFFENCES

A magistrates' court must not proceed to the trial of a charge which charges more than one offence.[35] This is a natural rule, since the charge fulfils the same function in summary trial as the indictment in the case of trial at the Crown Court; the same considerations of, inter alia, fairness to the defendant, which prohibit duplicity in an indictment, also prohibit the charging of more than one offence as one charge. Thus in *Ware v Fox*[36] an information charged the defendant with being concerned in the management of premises which were used for the purpose of smoking cannabis or cannabis resin or dealing in cannabis or cannabis resin. The Queen's Bench Divisional Court held that on the proper construction of the relevant statute[37] the information alleged two offences, namely managing premises used for smoking and managing premises used for dealing and was bad for duplicity. By contrast, section 5 of the Public Order Act 1936 created[38] the offence of using 'threatening, abusive or insulting words or behaviour with intent to provoke a breach of the peace or whereby a breach of the peace is likely to be occasioned'. It was held in *Vernon v Paddon*[39] that the section created one offence, the essential feature of which is conduct intended to provoke a breach of the peace or whereby such a breach was likely to be occasioned.

The issue as to whether an information is bad for duplicity is not always easy to decide. In *R v Courtie*[40] Lord Diplock suggested that where one provision involved the imposition of different penalties depending on whether the prosecution established particular factual ingredients then Parliament had created two separate offences, and these should be the subject of separate informations. Applying this principle a Divisional Court in *Director of Public Prosecutions v Corcoran*[41] held that an information

---

[34] [1981] 1 QB 445.

[35] Criminal Proceedings Rules, r 7.3. However, two or more informations may be set out in a single document (ibid, r 7.3(3))); see *Shah v Swallow* [1984] 2 All ER 528; *sub nom Director of Public Prosecutions v Shah* [1984] 1 WLR 886.

[36] [1967] 1 All ER 100, [1967] 1 WLR 379.   [37] Dangerous Drugs Act 1965, s 5.

[38] Now repealed and replaced by Public Order Act 1986, s 5.

[39] [1973] 3 All ER 302, [1973] 1 WLR 663.   [40] [1984] AC 463, [1984] 1 All ER 740.

[41] [1993] 1 All ER 912.

charging an offence of failure, without reasonable excuse, to provide a specimen of breath, blood, or urine, contrary to section 7(6) of the Road Traffic Act 1988, was bad for duplicity, because the maximum punishment for this offence depended on the purpose for which the specimen was being sought. However, a short time later a differently constituted Divisional Court, in dismissing appeals in several cases,[42] over-ruled the earlier ruling and distinguished *R v Courtie*. On a construction of the statutory provisions, this was one offence; the question of punishment was relevant to sentence only.

Where a charge amounts to more than one offence the prosecutor should be called on to elect before the trial begins on which offence to proceed; if he declines to make his election the charge should be dismissed.[43] It is important that the matter should be put right at the outset, since, as will be noted below, the magistrates must state the substance of it to the defendant and ask him to plead to it. However, even after a trial has started a charge bad for duplicity can be cured, by the court requiring the prosecutor to elect, just as it can prior to the trial itself.[44] The prosecutor will elect as to which offence he wishes to proceed on, the remainder will be struck out and the trial begun afresh. Again, if the prosecutor declines to elect, the charge as a whole will be struck out.

Details of the charge will be before the court.[45] It is however quite permissible, and indeed common, for two informations against the same defendant, or (where the cases are related) against different defendants, to be tried together. It was formerly thought that this could only be done by consent but the House of Lords in *Chief Constable of Norfolk v Clayton*[46] held that, although magistrates should first seek consent to such a course, they could nevertheless in the exercise of their discretion order a joint trial even without the consent of the parties, although they should not do so where it would not be fair and just to a defendant.[47]

Where the charges allege an offence and an attempt to commit that offence, these may be ordered to be tried together without the consent of the defendant[48] and this will usually be done.

---

[42] *Shaw* v *Director of Public Prosecutions (and other cases)* [1993] 1 All ER 918.

[43] *Edwards* v *Jones* [1947] KB 659, [1947] 1 All ER 830. See now Criminal Procedure Rules r 7.3(4).

[44] Criminal Procedure Rules, r 7.3(3).

[45] Per Lord Parker CJ and Salmon J (as he then was) in *Hargreaves* v *Alderson* [1964] 2 QB 159, [1962] 3 All ER 1019; see also *Garman* v *Plaice* [1969] 1 All ER 62, [1969] 1 WLR 19.

[46] [1983] 2 AC 473; *sub nom Clayton* v *Chief Constable of Norfolk* [1983] 1 All ER 984. This does not, however, enable a summons and cross-summons to be tried together; this cannot be done semble even by consent: *R v Epsom Justices, ex parte Gibbons* [1984] QB 574, [1983] 3 All ER 523.

[47] The wishes of the parties should not lightly be overruled: *R v Highbury Corner Magistrates' Court, ex parte McGinley* (1986) 150 JP 257.

[48] Criminal Attempts Act 1981, s 4(2).

3 PRE-TRIAL PROCEDURES

(a) Administrative hearings

The general approach now being pursued in respect of the criminal justice process is the need to ensure that delay is reduced and kept to a minimum. It was with this aim that the Narey Report[49] recommended a wide range of structural and procedural reforms, including reforms to summary process. In particular, it recommended the establishment of procedures that will permit administrative hearings, giving case-management powers to justices' clerks in much the same way as, on indictment, the court may engage in pleas and directions hearings and preparatory hearings. Clearly such hearings could deal with a variety of administrative matters, thus saving court time, and reducing its waste through unnecessary adjournments. Although experiments along these lines had from time to time occurred,[50] the basis on which they had been conducted was open to some doubt, and necessary changes were introduced by the Crime and Disorder Act 1998. It did this in two ways.

The first was by early administrative hearings. Section 47 of the 1998 Act provides that the first hearing before a magistrates' court following the charging of a person with an offence at a police station may be conducted by a single justice. Justices' clerks were also given some case management functions[51] At such a hearing the accused must be asked whether he wishes to receive legal aid, if he does his eligibility is to be determined and, if he is in fact eligible, the necessary arrangement must be put in hand for him to obtain it. The single justice may also exercise any other power exercisable by a single justice (see below). The second was the extension of the powers which may be exercised by a single justice. By section 49 of the Crime and Disorder Act 1998, a range of powers was conferred on a single justice, or, where rules provide,[52] on a justices' clerk. These powers comprise authority:

(a) to extend bail or to impose or vary conditions of bail;

(b) to mark an information as withdrawn;

(c) to dismiss an information or discharge an accused where no evidence is offered by the prosecution;

(d) to make an order for the payment of the accused's costs out of central funds;

(e) to request a pre-sentence report[53] following a guilty plea, and, for that purpose, to give an indication of the seriousness of the offence;

(f) to request a medical report and, for that purpose to remand the accused in custody or on bail;

(g) to remit an offender to another court for sentence;

---

[49] Review of Delay in the Criminal Justice System, 27 February 1997.
[50] Although with no clear basis in law.
[51] Powers to extend this jurisdiction to justices' clerks were conferred by s 48(2). See further, p 630, *post*.
[52] See *ante*, n 15C.
[53] Where required by Criminal Justice Act 1991, s 3.

(h) to determine mode of trial on an amended charge;

(i) to vary the time for appearance at court specified by police bail;

(j) to extend, with the consent of the accused, a custody or other time limit;

(k) to grant representation for the Crown Court under the Legal Aid Act 1988;

(l) to order production of a driving licence;

(m) to give a direction prohibiting the publication or disclosure of certain matters;

(n) to give, vary or revoke directions, which may include directions as to a timetable for the proceedings, the attendance of the parties, the service of documents, and the manner in which evidence is to be given.

Further changes to the range of powers exercisable by a single justice were made by the Criminal Justice Act 2003. A single justice will be able to deal with the revised process for determination of mode of trial for either-way offences.[54]

These changes individually focus on matters of considerable detail. Together, they provided a means whereby summary cases are not subject to continual or unnecessary adjournments or unnecessary hearings on what are important, but often administrative or preparatory, matters and are conducted efficiently and, so far as possible, speedily. The practice as to how they have in fact been used has varied, in particular as to the respective roles of the single justice and the justices' clerk or legal adviser. The Auld Review noted[55] that courts in two-thirds of magistrates' courts commission areas held at least some early administrative hearing presided over by a single magistrate nor clerk or adviser. It noted:

Some sit in the normal way with a bench of magistrates and a clerk, but the clerk deals with the directions and the magistrates deal with matters reserved to them. Some sit in split session, starting with the clerk alone and then bring in the magistrates to deal with anything outside the clerk's jurisdiction. And some sit, as they always have, as a full directions court, consisting of a bench of magistrates and the clerk, with the magistrates' dealing both with matters reserved to them and otherwise exercisable by the clerk.

The powers of justices' clerks are now to found specified by rules made in 1999 and re-enacted with amendments in 2005.[56] These powers now extend to dealing with informations, summonses, and (in some cases) the issue of warrants of arrest Adjournments by consent, the ascertaining of plea, the issue of directions, requests for pre-sentence reports, and varying or amendment of some community orders are amongst the long list of matters in respect of which power is conferred on a clerk, all designed to ensure effective case-management and disoposal. This is not crucial in the light of the provisions of the Criminal Procedure Rules. In pursuit of the overriding

---

[54] Criminal Justice Act 2003, Schedule 3. For mode of trial, see, p 544, *ante.*

[55] *Op cit*, Ch 4., para 56.

[56] See Justices' Clerks Rules 2005 SI 2005 No 545, replacing Justices Clerks Rules 1999.

objective that applies now to all criminal proceedings,[57] a magistrates' court must actively manage a case.[58] This includes:

(a) the early identification of the real issues;

(b) the early identification of the needs of witnesses;

(c) achieving certainty as to what must be done, by whom and when, in particular by the early setting of a timetable for the progress of the case;

(d) monitoring the progress of the case and compliance with directions;

(e) ensuring that evidence, whether disputed or not, is presented in the shortest and clearest way;

(f) discouraging delay, dealing with as many aspects of the case as possible on the same occasion, and avoiding unnecessary hearings;

(g) encouraging the participants to co-operate in the progression of the case; and

(h) making use of technology.

These are, of course, matters that apply equally to trial on indictment.[59] In their fulfillment each party must nominate a person responsible for the progression of the case (a 'case progression officer'), which may cause some organizational difficulties for smaller defence teams. He monitors compliance with directions, keeps the court informed, and must be available during normal working hours. A court may nominate a magistrate, or clerk to manage the case, and to make and deal with directions, including matters as to the date and length of a hearing. The rules provide for matters relating to case preparation and progression, readiness for trial, and identification of matters relevant to the trial itself, such as the witnesses to be called and points of law to be raised. In short, the framework for active case management is established, supplemented by a whole host of other relevant regulations and provisions.

(b) Disclosure

The regime for the disclosure of unused material by the prosecution and for defence disclosure, both contained in the Criminal Procedure and Investigations Act 1996, has already been discussed.[60] Until the passage of that Act the position regarding prosecution disclosure in summary proceedings had been unclear. In one case[61] a Divisional Court decided that the interests of justice required that decisions as to whether material should be disclosed should be restricted to the Crown Courts and were not matters for consideration by magistrates. However, that was a case concerned with committal proceedings, and did not address the more general question of disclosure on summary trial. Logically, there should be no fundamental difference between trial on indictment and summary trial in this respect, although various practical issues arise, and the position was clarified by another Divisional Court in *R v Bromley*

---

[57] See p 525, *ante.*   [58] Criminal Procedure Rules, 3.2.   [59] See p 525, *ante.*

[60] See pp 574–84, *ante.*

[61] *R v South Worcestershire Magistrates, ex parte Lilley* [1995] 4 All ER 186, (1995) 159 JP 598.

Magistrates' Court, ex parte Smithy and Wilkins,[62] where Simon Brown LJH observed that an accused in a summary case is as much entitled to the safeguards designed to secure a fair trial in a magistrates' court as in the Crown Court.

Section 1 of the 1996 Act applies the disclosure provisions of that Act (i.e. prosecution and defence disclosure) to cases where a person is charged with a summary offence in which a court proceeds to summary trial and the accused pleads not guilty, and to cases where a magistrates' court proceeds to summary trial on an either-way offence to which the accused pleads not guilty. It also applies to the trial in the youth court of an indictable offence in respect of a person under the age of eighteen. The effect of this is that the duty of prosecution initial disclosure and further prosecution disclosure arises.[63] A court will also have powers to determine questions as to whether material should be withheld in the public interest.[64] In respect of defence disclosure, the position is slightly different. There is no obligation on the defence to disclose the nature of the defence. However, section 6 of the 1996 Act creates a power for voluntary defence disclosure in summary cases, with the potential for an inference to be drawn[65] for inadequate or incomplete disclosure. The advantage for the accused in engaging in voluntary defence disclosure is that only if he does so will the prosecutor be under an obligation to engage in further prosecution disclosure.[66] If, of course, there is voluntary defence disclosure under section 6, then the extended obligations created by the Criminal Justice Act 2003[67] will apply.

One further change made by the 1996 Act should be noted. In cases of trial on indictment the law requires advance notice to be given of expert evidence which is to be called. No such obligation has existed hitherto in summary cases. There can be no real justification for this distinction, and the 1996 Act rectifies the omission by authorizing the making of rules which will extend to summary cases.[68] No such rules have yet been made. The new section 6D of the 1996 Act,[69] which requires details to be given as to experts who have been consulted is, read literally, wide enough to extend to summary proceedings but it is far from clear that it does so.

4 HEARING

If the defendant appears at the hearing, the court must state to him the substance of the information and ask him whether he pleads guilty or not guilty. In spite of these words, the same pleas as are open to a defendant charged with an indictable offence may be raised by a defendant charged with a summary offence. If the plea is one of not guilty the prosecutor may make an opening speech, and will then call his evidence. Where the prosecutor is unrepresented, it is open to the magistrates, in their discre-

---

[62] [1995] 4 All ER 146, (1994) 159 JP 251.   [63] See p 580, *ante.*

[64] Criminal Procedure and Investigations Act 1996, s 3(6) and s 14. See, further, p 576, *ante.*

[65] See 1996 Act, s 11. The inference will be of the same type as may be drawn under Criminal Justice and Public Order Act 1994, ss 34–38, as to which see p 616, *ante.*

[66] Under 1996 Act, s 7. See p 582, *ante.*   [67] See p 581, *ante.*   [68] 1996 Act, s 19(1).

[69] As to which see p 583, *ante.*

tion, to permit their clerk to examine prosecution witnesses.[70] Section 97 of the Magistrates' Courts Act 1980 will apply, and the witnesses will be subject to cross-examination and re-examination according to the circumstances of the case, and in accordance with the procedures and rules of evidence already noted.[71] If necessary, a witness can be summonsed to the court to give evidence by witness summons issued under section 97 of the 1980 Act. Alternatively, in some circumstances the written statement of the witness may be considered by the court.[72] Clearly, such out-of-court statements may infringe the rule of evidence relating to hearsay[73] and the relevant exceptions, whether statutory or common law, will need to be considered.

The procedure followed during the examination and cross-examination of witnesses mirrors that in trial on indictment, although rules of evidence may sometimes be applied less strictly here are, of course, important differences. Detailed matters of procedure are dealt with by Part 37 of the Criminal Procedure Rules 2005. Since there is no jury, the magistrates are both the tribunal of law and tribunal of fact: in other words, all decisions are for them irrespective of whether they are matters of fact or law. Thus the magistrates will decide questions of admissibility of evidence, although the procedures for doing so (which are quite clear in trial on indictment) are less clear on summary trial. It has been noted[74] that a Crown Court may hold a hearing (known as a *voir dire*, after the name of the oath taken by witnesses who testify at such a hearing) in order to decide questions of admissibility of evidence. Such a hearing is held in the absence of the jury, so that the jury does not hear evidence which may later be ruled inadmissible. The concept of a *voir dire* in magistrates' courts is wholly artificial, and the cases leave unclear the extent to which a magistrates' court, on summary trial, must conduct a 'trial within a trial' in order to decide whether evidence is admissible.[75]

It is also pertinent to consider the role of the justices' clerk. The functions of justices' clerks are considered elsewhere.[76] The clerk will generally advise on matters of law and procedure, and ensure that the trial is conducted properly, but must take great care to ensure that he plays no part in decisions on matters of fact, which are for the justices themselves.[77] The clerk may assist a party to present his case.[78] Care should be taken to avoid influencing the decisions of the justices on matters of fact or sentence, or to avoid giving the appearance of doing so.

At the conclusion of the evidence for the prosecution the defendant may address the court, whether or not he calls evidence; if he is calling evidence it will follow at

---

[70] *Simms v Moore* [1970] 2 QB 327, [1970] 3 All ER 1. [71] See p 608, *ante*.

[72] Under Criminal Justice Act 1988, ss 23–26; see also Magistrates' Courts Act 1980, s 102; Criminal Justice Act 1967, s 9.

[73] Prior to the implementation of the hearsay provisions of the Criminal Justice Act 2003 (not yet in force) the pre-existing principles apply.

[74] See p 607, *ante*.

[75] See, in particular, *R v Liverpool Juvenile Court, ex parte R* [1988] QB 1, which provides that a voir dire should be held in respect of confession evidence.

[76] See p 262, *ante*. [77] *R v Sussex Justices, ex parte MacCarthy* [1924] 1 KB 256.

[78] See *ante*.

once. The defendant may then address the court a second time but only if he himself has given evidence, another witness has been called on his behalf, and the court gives leave.[79] If the defendant addresses the court twice the prosecutor has a right to address the court a second time immediately before the defendant's second speech. The court will then retire if necessary and convict the defendant or dismiss the charge. If on the other hand the defendant pleads guilty the court may convict him without hearing evidence.[80] The wording of the subsection shows that it is often desirable to hear some evidence, particularly where it is part of the prosecution's case that the offence was committed in circumstances of aggravation, or perhaps if a committal for sentence to the Crown Court is contemplated or if the plea of guilty tendered may be 'equivocal'.[81] In any event the court retains full power over the case until sentence is passed and has discretion to allow a change of plea until that time if justice so requires.[82] Whether there is a plea of guilty or finding of guilt, there will normally be such an inquiry into the past record of the defendant as follows conviction of an indictable offence; the court may then adjourn, for not more than four weeks at a time, for inquiries to be made or for the purpose of determining the best way to deal with the case.[83] When the court resumes it need not be composed of the same magistrates; if, however, there are any newcomers the court which sentences or deals with the offender must make such inquiry into the facts and circumstances of the case as are necessary to acquaint the newcomers fully with those facts and circumstances.[84] This must be done even though the court will 'ex hypothesi' have held some such inquiry before; the use of the words 'the court' seems to prohibit the newcomers being given information privately before the court sits.[85]

Finally, note should be taken of the power which magistrates have under the Justices of the Peace Act 1361 to bind over a defendant to keep the peace or be of good behaviour even where he is acquitted.[86]

---

[79] Criminal Procedure Rules 2005, r 37.1.   [80] Magistrates' Courts Act 1980, s 9(3).

[81] See p 600, *ante*.

[82] *S (An Infant)* v *Manchester City Recorder* [1971] AC 481, [1969] 3 All ER 1230.

[83] Magistrates' Courts Act 1980, s 10(3); the period is three weeks if the defendant is in custody.

[84] Magistrates' Courts Act 1980, s 98(7). This is perhaps the nearest that English law comes to allowing special 'sentencing tribunals'.

[85] In the event of a question arising which might require reference to the European Court for a preliminary ruling the justices may, on application or otherwise, order the question to be referred and the hearing will then be adjourned pending receipt of the European Court's ruling; for a case in which this was done, and observations as to the approach which magistrates should adopt to this problem, see *R* v *Plymouth Justices, ex parte Rogers* [1982] QB 863, [1982] 2 All ER 175.

[86] See *Veater* v *G* [1981] 2 All ER 304, [1981] 1 WLR 567; *Hughes* v *Holley* (1986) 86 Cr App R 130.

D ABSENCES

1 GENERAL EFFECTS OF ABSENCE[87]

It sometimes happens that one or both of the parties fails to appear at the trial or adjourned trial of the information. If the defendant does not appear the court may hear the case in his absence provided that, where a summons was issued, either the court is satisfied that the summons was served on the defendant within what appears to be a reasonable time before the hearing, or the defendant appeared on a previous occasion to answer the information.[88] Alternatively the court may adjourn the hearing, with or without issuing a warrant for the arrest of the defendant; but a warrant can only be issued if the court is satisfied as to the matters stated above, and if the information is substantiated on oath. There is a further restriction on the issue of a warrant; if the court adjourns the trial after hearing evidence, or convicting the defendant without hearing evidence on a plea of guilty, the court must not issue a warrant unless it thinks it undesirable, by reason of the gravity of the offence, to continue the hearing in his absence. In any event, a warrant cannot be issued unless the offence is punishable by imprisonment or unless the court, having convicted the defendant, proposes to disqualify him.

The accused may be represented at the hearing by solicitor or counsel,[89] in such circumstances the accused being deemed to be present even if not physically in court. If the accused in fact is present he may be assisted by another person,[90] although the court may decline this if the level or nature of the assistance is unreasonable.

If the prosecutor fails to appear the court may dismiss the information or, if evidence has been received on a previous occasion, continue the hearing.[91] This is one example of the importance of the stage of the trial at which the justices begin to hear evidence. Alternatively the court may adjourn the trial, or may in an appropriate case dismiss the information for want of prosecution under section 15(1) of the Magistrates' Courts Act 1980. However, this power should not be used for this purpose save in exceptional cases. In *R v Hendon Justices, ex parte Director of Public Prosecutions*[92] a magistrates' court dismissed an information for want of prosecution when the defendants, their advocates, and the prosecution witnesses were all at court, but the prosecuting solicitor was not. This absence occurred because of an error in court administration, and the court was aware that a solicitor was on his way to rectify

---

[87] Magistrates' Courts Act 1980, ss 11–16. As to absence during the initial procedure on information for an offence triable either way, see p 000, *ante*. See now Magistrates' Courts (Procedure) Act 1998.

[88] The mode of service is prescribed by the Criminal Procedure Rules. If the court proceeds in the absence of the defendant in a case where he has not been duly served in accordance with this rule, the 'hearing' is a complete nullity: *R v Seisdon Justices, ex parte Dougan* [1983] 1 All ER 6, [1982] 1 WLR 1476.

[89] Magistrates' Courts Act 1980, s 12.

[90] *R v Leicester City Justices, ex parte Barow* [1991] 2 QB 60, [1991] 3 All ER 935.

[91] Magistrates' Courts Act 1980, s 15.　　　　[92] [1994] QB 167, [1993] 1 All ER 411.

the position. In quashing the order of the justices the Divisional Court stressed that the duty of the magistrates' court is to hear informations properly brought before it. The prosecution had a right to be heard; the proper course was to adjourn until the hearing could proceed.

If neither side appears, the court may again dismiss the information or, if evidence has been received on a previous occasion, continue the hearing;[93] alternatively the hearing may simply be adjourned.

2 PLEADING GUILTY BY POST

The Magistrates' Courts Act 1957 provided a new and convenient procedure whereby the defendant can plead guilty in cases where his appearance at court would be no more than a formality, if not a serious waste of time and money. It is now governed by section 12 of the 1980 Act. The procedure laid down by the Act is generally acknowledged to have worked well and is extensively used, particularly in motoring cases; however, it has no application at all to: (1) youth court proceedings in respect of persons under sixteen years; (2) offences triable either way; or (3) offences for which the accused is liable to be sentenced to imprisonment for a term exceeding three months. Where the Act does apply, the procedure is as follows. The prosecutor will serve with the summons a notice in prescribed terms as to the effect of section 12 of the Act and a concise statement of such facts as he will place before the court if the defendant does decide to plead guilty by post. Although the Act is silent on the point it seems that it is entirely within the discretion of the prosecutor as to whether he will make use of the Act and serve the above documents with the summons, even on the assumption that the Act applies to the offence charged. Where, however, the prosecutor does elect to use the procedure, he must serve the documents and then inform the clerk to the justices that he has done so. It is then for the defendant or his solicitor to inform the clerk that he desires to plead guilty without appearing, if that is so, by sending, appropriately completed, the part of the notice described above. He does not, of course, have to use the procedure, and even if he does at first give notification that he is not going to appear he may change his mind and appear.

If, however, he does not appear the court may proceed to hear the case in his absence (whether or not the prosecutor is also absent) provided that it is satisfied that the notice and statement of facts were served on the defendant with the summons. Before accepting the plea of guilty and convicting the defendant in his absence the court must cause to be read out aloud the defendant's notification that he is going to plead guilty, the statement of facts served on the defendant, and any statement by way of mitigation which the defendant himself may have submitted. The statement of facts read out must be precisely the same as that served upon the defendant. These rules must be meticulously observed, and breach of them may be a ground for quashing the conviction by means of certiorari:

---

[93] Magistrates' Courts Act 1980, s 16.

we all know that these matters have to be dealt with expeditiously.[94] It seems to me, however, to be quite clear that, before the magistrates can exercise jurisdiction in a case of this sort, they must strictly observe the conditions of the statute. Mere knowledge of the contents of the accused's submission, the mere reading of it themselves, is not sufficient; the submission must be read in open court.[95]

The rule that the precise statement of facts must be read out is also important, because after hearing it the magistrates may decide that the case is too grave to be dealt with in the way contemplated by the parties and may adjourn the case for the defendant to be present.

Assuming that, after hearing the notification of intention to plead guilty, the statement of facts and the submissions in mitigation, the magistrates accept the plea, they will record a conviction and (in the majority of cases to which the Act applies) impose a fine. Where they think it desirable to imprison the defendant or to impose any disqualification on him they must adjourn the hearing[96] without imposing any penalty whatever. There must then be sent to the defendant a notice stating the time and place of the adjourned hearing and the reason for the present adjournment (that is that the court is considering imprisonment or disqualification). If he chooses not to appear after receiving notice of what the court has in mind the court can proceed to disqualify him in his absence;[97] they cannot however sentence him to imprisonment or detention in his absence.[98] In such a case the proper course is to issue a warrant for the defendant's arrest.[99] Thus a person can never be sentenced to imprisonment in his absence and can only be disqualified in his absence following an adjournment for the purpose of giving him an opportunity to appear. However, a person may be committed to prison, for default in payment of a fine, in his absence.[100]

E SENTENCE

The types of sentence imposable by magistrates are basically similar to those available to the Crown Court, although the extent of magistrates' powers in relation to severity of sentence is more limited. They can, at the moment, normally only sentence to imprisonment for up to six months in respect of any one offence[101] (or twelve months

---

[94] Section 12, as amended by the Criminal Justice Act 1991, s 69.

[95] *R v Oldham Justices, ex parte Morrissey* [1958] 3 All ER 559n, at 560, [1959] 1 WLR 58, at 59, per Lord Parker CJ.

[96] Under the Magistrates' Courts Act 1980, s 10(3). This applies even if disqualification is mandatory under the 'totting-up' provisions; further there may even in this case be grounds for mitigating the normal consequences of conviction, which the defendant should have the chance to state: *R v Llandrindod Wells Justices, ex parte Gibson* [1968] 2 All ER 20, [1968] 1 WLR 598.

[97] Ibid, s 11(4). But, now, see Magistrates' Courts (Procedure) Act 1998.   [98] Ibid, s 11(3).

[99] Ibid, s 13(3).

[100] Ibid, s 82(5); *R v Dudley Magistrates' Court, ex parte Payne* [1979] 2 All ER 1089, [1979] 1 WLR 891.

[101] Magistrates' Courts Act 1980, s 31(1); they can, of course, commit to the Crown Court for sentence in the circumstances noted at pp 639–641, *post*.

in the case of consecutive sentences),[102] although that is to change when the provisions of Criminal Justice Act 2003 are brought into force.[103]

Their powers relating to the imposition of fines and the making of compensation orders are restricted. Since all summary jurisdiction derives from statute the amount of the maximum fine for any offence is prescribed by statute. However where a statute provides for imprisonment or other detention but makes no express provision for a fine, there is a general power to fine instead of imposing a custodial sentence.[104]

As a result of inflation statutory fines may quickly become too low and, to combat this phenomenon, the Criminal Justice Act 1982, section 37 introduced 'the standard scale' of fines for summary offences. This scale consists of five levels and the ensuing sections of the 1982 Act provided for the substitution of a level on the standard scale for the figures prescribed by existing statutory provisions. Thus, for example, a summary offence formerly punishable with a fine of £100 became punishable with a fine up to level 3. To keep pace with inflation these levels may be increased by order of the Secretary of State,[105] although it should be remembered that the fine that may be imposed in respect of an either way offence will be determined by the terms of the specific statutory provision. The maximum compensation that magistrates can order under a compensation order is similarly limited.[106]

The position regarding the appropriate level of fines for summary offences has proved somewhat controversial. In an attempt to create some equal impact of fines upon those of different incomes, the Criminal Justice Act 1991 introduced[107] a system of 'unit fines', whereby the actual amount of a fine depended upon a complex formula that sought to multiply an amount related to the seriousness of the offence with a multiple reflecting the level of disposable income of the defendant. After widespread public concern, the scheme was abandoned. The position is now governed by a revised section 18 of the Criminal Justice Act 1991,[108] which requires the sentencing court to take in to account both the seriousness of the offence and the ability of the defendant to pay.[109]

Finally, reference should be made to the provisions, now contained in section 39 of the 1980 Act, whereby a person aged seventeen or over who has been convicted before different magistrates' courts of two or more offences punishable with imprisonment or disqualification from driving, may be remitted to be dealt with by one of the courts concerned.

A wide range of special rules govern the sentencing and treatment of young offenders by the youth court. These are dealt with later.[110]

---

[102] Ibid, s 133.   [103] See p 666, *post.*   [104] Magistrates' Courts Act 1980, s 34(3).

[105] Magistrates' Courts Act 1980, s 143 (as amended by the Criminal Justice Act 1982, s 48). They were increased by the Criminal Justice Act 1991, s 17, under which the maximum fine for a level 5 offence is £5,000.

[106] Ibid, s 40(1); s 143 applies to s 40(1).   [107] Criminal Justice Act 1991, ss 18–19.

[108] As substituted by Criminal Justice Act 1993, s 65(1).

[109] Powers of Criminal Courts (Sentencing) Act 2000, s 128.

[110] See p 646–9, *post.*

F COMMITTALS FOR SENTENCE

In some instances a defendant who has been tried in the magistrates' court may be committed to the Crown Court to be sentenced or otherwise dealt with. The case then becomes:

a sort of composite case in which power is given to one court to convict and to another to give judgment; and until the judgment is given the hearing of the case is not complete[111]

The basic justification for the power to commit for sentence has been that a magistrates' court, having accepted jurisdiction in respect of an either-way offence, may consider, after conviction, that it sentencing powers are inadequate. Currently its powers of imprisonment are limited, in respect of a single offence, of six months, and in total twelve months in respect of multiple offences.[112] Section 3 of the Powers of Criminal Courts (Sentencing) Act 2000 (as amended currently) provides for committal to the Crown Court where the magistrates' court considers that the offence, or the combination of the offence and other offences associated with it,[113] is so serious that greater punishment should be inflicted than the magistrates' court has power to impose. A power to commit also arises in respect of an offence in respect of which the defendant has already indicated a guilty plea where the defendant is sent for trial on one or more related offences.[114]

As already noted,[115] the Royal Commission on Criminal Justice in 1993 observed[116] that the Crown Court was often passing sentences that were within the powers of the Crown Court. It was to address this issue that the Criminal Justice Act 2003 has altered mode of trial provisions,[117] and (when implemented) will increase magistrates' sentencing powers.[118] When these new provisions are fully in force, changes to the power to commit for sentence will be implemented. The 2003 Act inserts a new section 3 into the Powers of Criminal Courts (Sentencing) Act 2000.[119] Under this new section 3, the power to commit for sentence will only apply where the offender is convicted having indicated, when venue was determined, that he would plead guilty. There will be no power to commit for sentence where a defendant is convicted, the magistrates' court having accepted jurisdiction and convicted him after a non-guilty plea.

Committal will normally be to the most convenient location of the Crown Court. In selecting this the justices may have regard to directions given by the presiding judge

---

111 Lord Goddard CJ in R v Norfolk Justices, ex parte Director of Public Prosecutions [1950] 2 KB 558, at 568; sub nom R v Greenhoe Justices, ex parte Director of Public Prosecutions [1950] 2 All ER 42, at 46.

112 See p 666, post.   113 See p 667, post.

114 Powers of Criminal Courts (Sentencing) Act 2000, s 4.   115 See p 545, ante.

116 Royal Commission, op cit, para 6.12, relying on research conducted by Hedderman and Moxon, Magistrates' Court or Crown Court: Mode of Trial Decisions and Sentencing Home Office Research Study No 125, HMSO 1982. See now Herbert, 'Mode of Trial and Magistrates' Sentencing Powers' [2003] Crim LR 315.

117 See p 547, ante.   118 See p 666, post.   119 2003 Act, Schedule 3, para 22.

or judges of the circuit. Committal may be in custody or on bail, but the Court of Appeal has indicated that:

the cases must be rare when magistrates' courts can properly commit for [sentence] on bail because the whole purpose of the committal is to have the man sent to prison, and have him sent to prison for a longer period than the magistrates' court could impose.[120]

However, the defendant may give notice of appeal against conviction and may then, *qua* appellant, be released on bail, although, where a possibly severe sentence awaits him, bail will only be granted 'with extreme care, and only in really exceptional cases'.[121] There is no appeal against the order of committal as such;[122] if the defendant thinks that the committal was bad in law, for example because he was not warned that he might be committed, he should apply to a Divisional Court of the Queen's Bench Division for a quashing order or prohibition order; the Crown Court will not, of course, sentence him until the result of his application is known, since the order of committal may be held to be a nullity. On such an application the Divisional Court can only hear argument as to the legality of the committal and cannot entertain any suggestion that the committal was too harsh a step to take having regard to the facts; this is an argument to be addressed (although not in so many words) to the Crown Court when the defendant appears there for sentence.

On such appearance, procedure is as if the defendant had been committed for trial to the Crown Court and had pleaded guilty to the charge. No actual plea will be taken, since that stage of the trial is concluded, but otherwise the position is as if the defendant had pleaded guilty at the Crown Court itself. Thus notices required to be served 'three days before the trial' may be served three days before the hearing at the Crown Court,[123] and, if the defendant has been granted bail, but fails to surrender, the Crown Court may issue a bench warrant.[124] It might then be thought that the Crown Court could allow the defendant to withdraw his plea of guilty (if such was tendered) in the magistrates' court, before he was sentenced, and it is now clear from *R v Mutford and Lothingland Justices, ex parte Harber*[125] following the decision of the House of Lords in *S (An Infant) v Manchester City Recorder*[126] that this is permissible. The Crown Court certainly has such a power when trying a case on indictment.[127]

At the hearing there should be formal identification by the police of the defendant as the person who appeared at the magistrates' court and was committed; if there is no police officer present who can give this information, the defendant may, it seems, be asked whether he was the person who appeared and was committed. The Crown Court will inquire into the circumstances of the case as it would following a plea of

---

[120] *R v Coe* [1969] 1 All ER 65, at 68, [1968] 1 WLR 1950, at 1954.

[121] *Re Whitehouse* [1951] 1 KB 673, at 675, [1951] 1 All ER 353, at 354.

[122] *R v London Sessions Appeal Committee, ex parte Rogers* [1951] 2 KB 74, [1951] 1 All ER 343.

[123] *R v Grant* [1951] 1 KB 500, [1951] 1 All ER 28.   [124] Bail Act 1976, s 7.

[125] [1971] 2 QB 291, [1971] 1 All ER 81. The Crown Court can only take into consideration what took place in the magistrates' court: *R v Marylebone Justices, ex parte Westminster City Council* [1971] 1 All ER 1025, [1971] 1 WLR 567.

[126] [1971] AC 481, [1969] 3 All ER 1230.   [127] See p 600, ante.

guilty before itself; prosecuting counsel will give the court an outline of the facts. It should be noted that if there is a dispute as to the facts of the offence upon which the defendant has been committed for sentence, the Crown Court can either resolve that matter itself, if necessary by hearing evidence, or can remit the case to the magistrates' court for such dispute to be resolved.[128] The court will then consider the defendant's antecedents, and usually a pre-sentence report;[129] defending counsel (or solicitor) will then address the court in mitigation. The Crown Court can then pass any sentence up to the maximum which the particular indictable offence carries and can deal with the defendant in any manner in which it could deal with him if he had just been convicted of the offence on indictment before the court.[130] The position as to appeal itself against this sentence has already been considered.[131]

If the defendant appeals against conviction, as well as being committed for sentence, the Crown Court will of course hear his appeal first, since, if this succeeds, there will be no cause to sentence him.

G   YOUTH JUSTICE

Procedures in the youth court mirror those that apply on summary trial in the magistrates' court, although a clear division between the two courts exists,[132] those who sit in the youth court are members of a youth court panel,[133] and special restrictions apply on the reporting of proceedings.[134] The child or young person will be accompanied by parent, guardian, or social worker, and the proceedings will be very much more informal than those in the magistrates' court, clearly essential because of the age of the person before the court.

1   AIMS AND PROVISION OF YOUTH JUSTICE

Although no fundamental differences exist in terms of procedure, youth justice raises very distinct issues which are reflected in the powers, and objectives of the youth court (and of the Crown Court when dealing with children and young persons). Section 44 of the Children and Young Persons Act 1933 requires any court, in fulfilling its duties, to take account of the welfare of the child or young person before it. More recently considerable debate has occurred as to the role and functions of the youth justice system. In a Consultation Paper,[135] the government stated its belief that action was needed to bring about greater consistency in the approach to work with young offenders in the community and to ensure that all the relevant local agencies play a

---

128 *Munroe v Crown Prosecution Service* [1988] Crim LR 823.   129 See p 664, *post.*
130 Powers of Criminal Courts Act 1973, s 42.   131 See p 235, *ante.*
132 See generally Chapter 8.   133 Ibid.   134 See p 646, *post.*
135 *No More Excuses—A New Approach to Tackling Youth Crime in England and Wales,* Cm 3809 (1997).

full part. It also believed that the youth justice system should seek to prevent crime. For that reason, section 37 of the Crime and Disorder Act 1998 states that:

It shall be the principal aim of the youth justice system to prevent offending by children and young persons.

By section 37(2) it shall be the duty of all persons and bodies carrying out functions in relation to the youth justice system to have regard to that aim. This is a broad statement of an overall duty that will apply not only to local authorities, health authorities, probation services, voluntary agencies, and the police, but also to the courts in dealing with young offenders after conviction.

The role of local authorities in establishing youth offending teams and creating youth justice strategies should be noted. Each local authority is under a duty to secure that, to such extent as is appropriate for their area, all youth justice services are available there,[136] performed in partnership with other agencies such as the police. Local Authorities will operate within the overall guidance given by a new Youth Justice Board.[137] This will comprise ten, eleven, or twelve members, appointed by the Home Secretary, and who will include persons with extensive recent experience of the youth justice system. Its functions are set out by section 42(5) of the Crime and Disorder Act 1998, and include:

(a) the monitoring of the operation of the youth justice and the provision of youth justice services;

(b) advising the Home Secretary on the operation of that system and the provision of such services; how the principal aim of that system might most effectively be pursued; the content of any national standards he may see fit to set with respect to the provision of such services, or the accommodation in which children and young persons are kept in custody; and the steps that might be taken to prevent offending by children and young persons;

(c) the monitoring and collection of information about the youth justice system and the provision of services by local authorities;

(d) the identification and promotion of good practice in the context of the operation of the youth justice system and the provision of youth justice services, the prevention of offending by children and young persons; and in respect of working with children and young persons who are or are at risk of becoming offenders.

Youth justice teams are an important element in the strategy to deal with youth offending which was introduced by the Crime and Disorder Act 1998. At least one team exists in each local authority area, and includes at least one probation officer, local authority social worker, police officer, and nominee of a health authority and of the local education authority. These youth justice teams are under a duty to co-

---

[136] 1998 Act, s 38.   [137] Ibid, s 41.

ordinate the provision of youth justice services within the local authority area, and to carry out such functions as are assigned to the team in the local authority's youth justice plan made under section 41. Not only is it intended that youth offending teams should co-ordinate local provision relating to work with young offenders, but they also play a key role in the reprimand and caution system introduced by the 1998 Act, and in respect of several of the orders that may be made by a court when dealing with young offenders. Their primary functions include report-writing for courts, the preparation of reparation or action plans, and the supervision of young offenders within the community, based upon an inter-agency partnership philosophy.[138]

2 COURT OF TRIAL

(a) Committal to the Crown Court

Young defendants (i.e. those aged under eighteen when the mode of trial decision is made)[139] must generally be tried in the youth court. The exceptions to this are in respect of murder,[140] and those cases which fall within section 91 of the 2000 Act. These exceptions are:

(1) where the young defendant has attained the age of fourteen, and the offence is one to which section 91 of the Powers of Criminal Courts (Sentencing) Act 2000 applies. These are offences which, if committed by an adult, attract a maximum term of imprisonment of fourteen years or more, or indecent assault on a woman, and certain other specified offences.[141] The offence must not be one for which the sentence is fixed by law;

(2) where the young defendant is charged jointly with a person who has attained the age of eighteen and the court considers it necessary in the interests of justice to commit the young defendant for trial.

In addition where a young defendant is sent for trial under section 91, the court may also send for trial any other indictable offences with which he is charged at the same time, whether jointly with an adult or not, if that offence could be joined on the same indictment.[142]

These provisions have to be considered in the light of the fact that the maximum term of detention (under a detention and training order) that a youth court can impose is two years. If it considers longer detention is appropriate, the powers under

---

[138] Consultation Paper, *op cit*; see also Morgan Report, *Safer Communities: the Local Delivery of Crime Prevention through the Partnership Approach* (1991).

[139] *R v Islington North Juvenile Court, ex parte Daley* [1983] 1 AC 487, *sub nom Re Daley* [1982] 2 All ER 974.

[140] Which includes murder, manslaughter, causing death by reckless driving, killing in pursuance of a suicide pact, and infanticide: Magistrates' Courts Act 1980, s 24.

[141] Indecent assault on a woman, an offence of causing death by dangerous driving, an offence of causing death by careless driving whilst under the influence of drink or drugs.

[142] For joinder, see p 587, *ante*.

section 91 must be used. When deciding whether to commit the young defendant for trial in respect of a grave offence (as defined above) the court should not consider what sentence should be imposed if the young defendant is convicted, but, instead, should consider whether the court that sentences the defendant if convicted should have the option to impose a greater term of detention than generally available. In *R v Devizes Youth Court, ex parte M*[143] the charge was one of arson. The Divisional Court concluded that right course was to consider whether the Crown Court should have the power to order detention to impose a term of indefinite detention under what is now section 91.[144] That, though, has to be considered in the context of the basic principle inherent in *T v United and V v United Kingdom*[145] that the application of adult trial procedures to young defendants may potentially give rise to a breach of Article 6 (and possibly other provisions) of the European Convention. Magistrates should start with a presumption that the case will not be sent to the Crown Court, unless that is clearly required, either because their powers to order detention under a detention and training order[146] are inadequate or, alternatively, the likely sentence approaches the maximum of two years.[147] A committal under section 91 in respect of a defendant under fifteen years should only rarely occur.[148] Because detention is not available to a youth court in respect of a defendant under fifteen, the presumption is that is that a non-custodial sentence is the appropriate response unless a sentence of two years or more could be justified.

(b) Trial in an adult magistrates' court

The normal rule is that a young defendant will be tried in the youth court, unless committed to the Crown Court. To that rule, there is an exception where a young defendant is jointly charged with an adult. Such a case must be heard in the adult court,[149] but the case may be remitted to the youth court if the adult pleads guilty and the young defendant pleads not guilty, or where the adult is committed for trial or is discharged and the young defendant pleads not guilty.[150]

3 THE TRIAL

One of the key purposes of the youth court is to ensure process and procedure which is appropriate to the age of the defendant. Trying the young defendant in an adult court, especially the Crown Court, raises difficult issues. The European Convention on Human Rights, the United Nations Standard Minimum Rules for the Administration of Juvenile Justice (the Beijing Rules), the United Nation Convention on the

---

[143] 22 January 2000, unreported.

[144] The case was decided under the predecessor Children and Young Persons Act 1933, s 53.

[145] [2000] 2 All ER 1054.   [146] See p 647, *post*.

[147] *R v Southampton Crown Court, ex parte K* [2002] EWHC 1640 (Admin).

[148] *R (on the application of M) v Waltham Forest Youth Court and the DPP; R (on the application of W) v Thetford Youth Court and the DPP* (2002) 166 JP 453.

[149] Children and Young Persons Act 1933, s 46.   [150] Magistrates' Court Act 1980, s 29.

Rights of the Child, and Article 14 of the International Covenant on Civil and Political Rights of 1966 all focus on the essential principle that the age and welfare of the child or young person are key matters to which the courts must have regard.[151] That is also inherent in domestic law, section 44 of the Children and Young Persons Act 1933 requiring a court to have regard to the welfare of the child.

The trial process in the youth court reflects the needs of the child or young person. Limitations exist on publicity (including restrictions on publishing the name of the defendant) and limitations on those on those entitled to be present in court.[152] The limitation on reporting can be lifted if it is in the interests of justice to do so, but not simply for the purpose of adding to the punishment of the defendant by publishing his name.[153] The trial itself will follow normal procedures, and be conducted under the normal rules of evidence, but should reflect the age and maturity of the defendant. In some circumstances it may be possible to proceed in the absence of the child himself, provided that that attendance is not essential to the just hearing of the case, in the context of the rights to a fair trial.[154]

Particular problems arise in the Crown Court, as was vividly demonstrated by *T* v *United Kingdom; V* v *United Kingdom.*[155] T and V were tried, and convicted, for murder in the Crown Court. The Court of Human Rights concluded that whilst not all the complaints made by T and V were justified,[156] the nature of the proceedings amounted to a breach of Article 6, in that T and V were, in the context of a public hearing in the Crown Court, unable to participate effectively in the criminal proceedings. At the trial of T and V special measures were taken in the light of the age of the defendants (eleven years), and to promote understanding of the nature of the proceedings. The defendants had trial procedures explained to them, and shown the court room in advance of the trial itself. The hearing times were shortened in order not to tire the defendants excessively. Despite this the Court of Human Rights concluded that the formality and ritual of the Crown Court must have seemed incomprehensible and intimidating to a child aged eleven. There was evidence that certain of the modifications to the court room, particularly the raised dock (designed to allow the defendants to see what was going on, had the effect of increasing the defendant's sense of discomfort during the trial, leaving them exposed to the scrutiny of press and public. The trial generated high levels of press interest, given the notoriety of the alleged crime (the murder of B, a three year-old boy). There was also evidence that T suffered from post-traumatic stress disorder, which, combined with

---

[151] For recognition in domestic law of these international obligations, see *McKerry* v *Teesdale and Wear Valley Justices* [2000] Crim LR 594.

[152] Children and Young Persons Act 1933, ss 43, 47.

[153] *McKerry* v *Teesdale and Wear Valley Justices* [2000] Crim LR 594.

[154] 1933 Act, s 42. For the requirements of the 'fair trial' provisions of Article 6, see Ch 5, and p 521, *ante*.

[155] [2000] 2 All ER 1024.

[156] In particular, the Court rejected a submission that the procedure amounted to inhuman or degrading treatment under Article 3. The Court did also find that there *was* also a breach of Article 5, in that the procedure for determining and reviewing the tariff for the indeterminate sentence imposed was unfair and contravened Article 5. For this latter issue, see p 673, *post*.

the lack of therapeutic work since the date of the offence, had limited T's ability to consult his lawyers and adequately testify in his own defence. It was insufficient that T was represented by skilled and experienced lawyers. The Court considered it unlikely that T would have felt able to adequately consult with them whilst under public scrutiny in a tense courtroom, or in the light of his lack of maturity.

These findings highlighted the difficulties faced in attempting to try young defendants in adult courts. A Practice Direction was issued in response, addressing the needs of young defendants in the Crown Court.[157] It requires henceforth appropriate steps addressing these issues, in terms of the layout of the courtroom and the familiarization of the defendant with it; the hours the court sits, and the need to dispense with the formal court dress of wigs and gowns; and appropriate measures to control attendance by the public or press. Above all, a young defendant should, where at all possible, be tried separately from an adult. This, of course, then raises the issue as to whether the charge should be tried in the youth court or Crown Court. Clearly, in the case of T, only Crown Court trial was appropriate given the nature of the charge, but that will not always be the case.

4 YOUTH OFFENDER CONTRACTS

In 1999 a new method of dealing with young offenders was introduced, and now to be found in Part III of the Powers of Criminal Courts (Sentencing) Act 2000. Section 16 provides that a youth court or magistrates' court may, and in some cases must, refer a young offender to a youth offender panel, where the pre-conditions it creates are satisfied. Essentially, the power to make a referral arises when it is proposing to impose a non-custodial sentence. The duty to refer arises when an offender, who has never before been convicted of an offence, pleads guilty.[158] The objective of the procedure is to address the causes of the offending behaviour. A youth offender panel, created by section 21) will agree a contract with the young offender, which may involve reparation to the victim and measures to address the needs of the offender, in the hope of removing or reducing the causes of the offending behaviour. If a contract cannot be agreed, or is broken the offender is returned to the sentencing court to be sentenced for the original offence.

The power to make a referral is one vested in the youth court or magistrates' court. The Crown Court has no such power. The power to refer, as already noted, is the means for dealing with the offender without a custodial term, and cannot be combined with any community order.[159]

5 IMPRISONMENT AND COMMUNITY PUNISHMENT

The Crown Court, following trial on indictment, has various powers. Section 90 of the Powers of Criminal Courts (Sentencing) Act 2000 prescribes a mandatory detention

---

[157] See also Criminal Procedure Rules, op cit, p 525, *ante*.   [158] 2000 Act, s 17.
[159] For sentences generally, see p 656, *post*.

during Her Majesty's Pleasure for conviction for murder committed by an offender under eighteen at the time of the offence, and a term of detention for certain specified offences of seriousness, where the court is satisfied that no other method of dealing with the case is appropriate. However, the powers of the youth court have historically been limited. In respect of offenders aged under fifteen, no power of detention exists, other than to require detention in secure accommodation under a supervision order. In respect of those aged fifteen and under eighteen, section 100 of the 2000 Act provides for detention under a detention and training order. This allows a court to sentence a young offender to a detention and training order requiring the offender to be subject to a period of detention and training, followed by a period of supervision. Where a child or young person is convicted of an offence which is punishable with imprisonment in the case of a person aged twenty-one or over, and the court is satisfied that a custodial sentence is justified by the seriousness of the offence or the need to protect the public,[160] the sentence that the court can pass is a detention and training order. There are also pre-conditions on the imposition of the order on certain offenders: in the case of an offender under the age of fifteen at the time of the conviction, the court must be of the opinion that he is a persistent offender; in the case of an offender under the age of twelve at that time, the court must consider that only a custodial sentence would be adequate to protect the public from further offending by him; and the offence was committed on or after such date as the Home Secretary may appoint.

A detention and training order is an order that the offender in respect of whom it is made shall be subject, for the term specified in the order, to a period of detention and training followed by a period of supervision. The term of a detention and training order shall be four, six, eight, ten, twelve, eighteen, or twenty-four months. Thus the length of sentence that a youth court may impose has been increased. The order will be served in such secure accommodation as may be determined by the Secretary of State or by such other person as may be authorized by him for that purpose. The period of detention is half the length of the order.[161] The other half of the order is a period of supervision by a probation officer, local authority social worker, or member of a youth offending team.[162] Where a detention and training order is in force in respect of an offender and it appears on information to a justice of the peace acting for a relevant petty sessions area that the offender is in breach of the order, a summons may be issued, and the youth court may order the offender to be detained, in such secure accommodation as the Home Secretary may determine, for such period, not exceeding the shorter of three months or the remainder of the term of the detention and training order, as the court may specify; or impose on the offender a fine not exceeding level 3 on the standard scale.

A range of community or other orders exists[163] and is available in respect of young offenders. These include community rehabilitation orders (in respect of offenders

---

[160] See p 667, *post*.   [161] 2000 Act, s 100.   [162] As to which, see p 642, *ante*.
[163] See generally, p 675, *post*.

aged sixteen or over), community punishment orders (in respect of offenders aged sixteen or over), community punishment and rehabilitation orders, supervision orders and attendance sentence orders.[164] Other available orders include a reparation order, a sentence requiring a young offender to make reparation to the victim of the offence or a person otherwise affected by it, or to the community at large. The order is intended to help show young offenders the harm which they have done to the community and to their victims, and enable the courts to impose punishments which make some amends to the victim, or to the community generally. Another order is the action plan order.[165] This requires a young offender to comply with an action plan intended to address his offending behaviour. The intention is that the action plan order should provide the opportunity for a short but intensive programme of work with the young offender constructed by or on behalf of the youth offending team, in consultation with the offender's parents, to tackle the causes of offending at an early stage.

6 OTHER ORDERS

A youth court may fine a young offender an amount not exceeding £1,000, and may order the fine to be paid by a parent or guardian.[166] It may impose absolute or conditional discharges,[167] make compensation orders,[168] or impose disqualifications.[169]

H APPEALS FOLLOWING SUMMARY TRIAL

Wider issues relating to the appellate system are dealt with later.[170] Here we address specific procedures which apply in cases of summary trial.

A defendant convicted by a magistrates' court may appeal either:

(1) to the Crown Court, and thence by way of case stated to the Queen's Bench Division of the High Court; or

(2) by case stated to the Queen's Bench Division of the High Court;

(3) from the Queen's Bench Divisional Court to the House of Lords, in certain circumstances.

In addition to those rights of appeal there is the possibility of applying for judicial review. Each of these will be considered in turn.

---

[164] Powers of Criminal Courts (Sentencing) Act 2000, s 60.   [165] 2000 Act, s 12.
[166] 2000 Act, s 137.   [167] See p 677, *post.*   [168] See p 677, *post.*
[169] See p 678, *post.*   [170] See p 680, *post.*

1 APPEAL TO THE CROWN COURT

Where the defendant has been convicted in the magistrates' court of either a summary offence or an either way offence tried summarily he may appeal to the Crown Court, if he pleaded guilty against his sentence only, or if he pleaded not guilty against both conviction and sentence.[171] It will be seen that there is an express statutory prohibition against an appeal against conviction if the defendant pleaded guilty. This may be contrasted with the position following trial on indictment, where there is nothing in the Criminal Appeal Act to prevent an appeal against conviction to the Court of Appeal even if the defendant pleaded guilty.[172] It has been observed that the judges have laid down that appeals against conviction following a plea of guilty will only be entertained by the Court of Appeal in certain exceptional circumstances; so in the case of appeals to the Crown Court also, the judges have given a construction to the statute which evades the effect of the exact words used by Parliament, but on this occasion in favour of the defendant. It has been held that to make a plea of guilty binding and effective it must be unambiguous;[173] if therefore the defendant says the actual word 'guilty' but adds to it a statement which, if true, amounts to a defence to the charge, or if from the circumstances it is clear that he is denying the charge but has pleaded guilty through ignorance of the law, a plea of guilty accepted in these circumstances is a nullity.[174] The Crown Court can, therefore, hear an appeal against the 'conviction' which is equally a nullity, and under powers presently to be considered can remit the case to the magistrates with an expression of opinion that a plea of not guilty ought to be entered. Where on the other hand there has been a deliberate and unequivocal plea of guilty, no appeal against conviction can be entertained.[175]

The expression 'sentence' includes any order made on conviction by a magistrates' court, with an exception in respect of an order for absolute or conditional discharge, although if on a later date sentence is passed in respect of the offence for which the order for conditional discharge was made, that is following 'breach' of the order, there may be:

(1) an appeal against that later sentence;

(2) an order for the payment of costs;

(3) an order for the destruction of an animal, made under the Protection of Animals Act 1911; and

(4) any order, if the court has no discretion as to the making of the order or its terms, for example if the court is bound to order endorsement of a driving licence.[176] It has already been noted that there is no appeal against a committal for sentence, in the cases already discussed in which there may be such a

---

[171] Magistrates' Courts Act 1980, s 108(1).   [172] See p 683, *post.*

[173] *R v Durham Quarter Sessions, ex parte Virgo* [1952] 2 QB 1, [1952] 1 All ER 466.

[174] *R v Blandford Justices, ex parte G* [1967] 1 QB 82, [1966] 1 All ER 1021.

[175] *P Foster (Haulage) Ltd v Roberts* [1978] 2 All ER 751.

[176] Magistrates' Courts Act 1980, s 108(3).

committal, although there may be an appeal against the conviction on which the committal is based.

There is a right of appeal against an order to enter into recognizances to keep the peace or be of good behaviour,[177] and this right exists where such an order has been made following acquittal.[178]

With limited exceptions only the defendant may appeal. The procedure[179] is that an appeal must be commenced by giving notice of appeal, to the clerk of the magistrates' court, and to the other party, within twenty-one days after the day on which the decision of the magistrates' court was given (meaning the day on which sentence is passed if there is an adjournment of the case after conviction). The Crown Court may extend the time, either in relation to a notice not yet given or to a notice already given but out of time.

Proceedings before the Crown Court on an appeal against conviction take the form of a complete rehearing of the case;[180] the prosecution must open the case and call its witnesses afresh and either side may introduce fresh evidence without any leave. This is of course in sharp contrast to proceedings in the Court of Appeal. The Crown Court may confirm, reverse, or vary the decision of the magistrates' court,[181] or remit the case with an expression of their opinion;[182] as already seen this latter procedure will be appropriate where an 'equivocal' plea of guilty has been entered, which in all the circumstances the Crown Court considers should have been treated as a plea of not guilty. The Crown Court must give reasons for its decision except where they are obvious.[183] As regards appeals against sentence, the Crown Court may impose any sentence which the magistrates' court could have passed, whether more or less severe than that which they actually passed. The court may also do this if the appeal is against conviction only.[184] Again, there is a sharp contrast between appeals to the Crown Court and appeals to the Court of Appeal following trial on indictment, since the Court of Appeal never has had the power to interfere with the sentence in any way if the appeal is against conviction only and, in addition, cannot now increase sentence;[185] the Crown Court can do both. Finally, the Crown Court may:

---

[177] Magistrates' Courts (Appeals from Binding Over Orders) Act 1956.

[178] *Shaw* v *Hamilton* [1982] 2 All ER 718, [1982] 1 WLR 1308.

[179] See Criminal Procedure Rules, r 63.

[180] Supreme Court Act 1981, s 48. Although the prosecution cannot alter the case by amending the information (*Garfield* v *Maddocks* [1974] QB 7, [1973] 2 All ER 303).

[181] Supreme Court Act 1981, s 48(2)(a).   [182] Ibid, s 48(2)(b).

[183] *R* v *Snaresbrook Crown Court, ex parte Input Management Ltd* (1999) 163) JP 533; *R* v *Kingston Crown Court, ex parte Bell* (200) 164 JP 901.

[184] Ibid, s 9(4). However the Crown Court cannot impose a sentence which the magistrates could not have imposed. Thus an unrepresented defendant who has not previously been sentenced to imprisonment cannot (subject to minor exceptions) be sentenced to imprisonment (Powers of Criminal Courts Act 1973, s 21(1)). Accordingly, on appeal in such a case, the Crown Court cannot impose a sentence of imprisonment even though the accused is legally represented on his appeal: *R* v *Birmingham Justices, ex parte Wyatt* [1975] 3 All ER 897, [1976] 1 WLR 260. It can also vary a sentence passed at the same time and not appealed: *R* v *London Crown Court, ex parte Mentesh* [2001] 1 Cr App R (S) 323.

[185] See p 695, *post*.

make such other order in the matter as the court thinks just, and by such order exercise any power which the said authority might have exercised.[186]

The wording is liberal, but it was held[187] on an almost identical provision in the previous legislation, that quarter sessions had no power to vary the sentence by quashing the sentence passed at the magistrates' court and committing to itself for sentence. The reason lies in the point already noted[188] that committal for sentence is not itself a sentence; if therefore magistrates elect to sit as a sentencing court instead of as a committing court quarter sessions could not go behind that election. Their power was to interfere with a sentence, not a decision as to whether the defendant should be committed or sentenced. This is presumably still true for the Crown Court.

If the appeal is against sentence only it may proceed on the basis of the facts relevant to sentence produced before the magistrates, if counsel for the appellant agrees to that course; there will then be no need for any evidence whatever to be called before the Crown Court. The same strictness of proof is not demanded in matters relevant to sentence as in matters relevant to conviction. In fact proceedings on an appeal against sentence normally take the same course as if the defendant had just been convicted, or had pleaded guilty, before the court.[189]

From the Crown Court a further appeal lies by way of case stated to the Queen's Bench Division of the High Court; this will be considered below.

2 APPEAL BY CASE STATED TO THE QUEEN'S BENCH DIVISION FROM MAGISTRATES' COURTS AND THE CROWN COURT

(a) Magistrates' courts and youth courts

Any person who was a party to proceedings before a magistrates' court (or youth court) or (although not a party) is aggrieved by the conviction, order, determination, or other proceeding may appeal against the proceeding on the ground that it is wrong in law or in excess of jurisdiction by applying to the magistrates' court to state a case for the opinion of a Divisional Court of the Queen's Bench Division of the High Court.[190] The power to appeal by way of case stated is not normally a proper way of challenging a sentence that has been imposed, the proper procedure for which is appeal to the Crown Court.[191] Only where the sentence is, by any acceptable standard 'astonishing' will proceedings by way of case stated be entertained.[192]

Thus, either the defendant or the prosecutor in a criminal case may make application for a case to be stated. Application may also be made by a person aggrieved, but:

the words 'person aggrieved' do not really mean a man who is disappointed of a benefit

---

186 Supreme Court Act 1981, s 48(2)(c).
187 In *R* v *Bullock* [1964] 1 QB 481, [1963] 3 All ER 506.   188 See p 639, *ante*.
189 See p 600, *ante*.   190 Magistrates' Courts Act 1980, s 111(1).
191 *Tucker* v *Director of Public Prosecutions* [1992] 4 All ER 901.   192 Ibid, per Pill J.

which he might have received if some other order had been made (still less does it mean someone having a merely sympathetic interest in the proceedings). A 'person aggrieved' must be a man who has suffered a legal grievance, a man against whom a decision has been pronounced which has wrongfully deprived him of something, or wrongfully refused him something, or wrongfully affected his title to something.[193]

A party to proceedings who has succeeded in part only may appeal against the incompleteness of his success. Executors of a person who has died since the hearing of the case in the magistrates' court are 'interested', at any rate if a fine has been imposed, since the money to pay this would come out of the estate of the deceased; they may accordingly bring an appeal by way of case stated.[194] If the deceased had been sentenced to imprisonment the executors appear not to be 'interested'.[195]

Application must be made in writing, within twenty-one days after the day on which the decision of the magistrates' court was given;[196] again, if the magistrates adjourn after conviction, the day on which sentence is actually passed is the first day on which time begins to run.[197] The application should be delivered to the clerk of the magistrates' court whose decision is being questioned or sent to him by post; the names of the magistrates constituting the court do not have to be given and it is therefore immaterial that there is an error in their names.[198]

The application must identify the point of law on which the opinion of the High Court is sought.[199]

The magistrates may refuse to state a case only on the ground that the application is in their opinion frivolous, and may not refuse to state a case if the application is made by or under the direction of the Attorney-General, even in the unlikely event of such an application being considered frivolous.[200] On refusal the magistrates must give the applicant a certificate of refusal if he so requires; he may then apply to the High Court for an order directing the justices to state a case.[201] On the making of the application, whether granted or refused, the applicant loses his right to appeal to the Crown Court.[202]

A 'case' will normally contain a statement of the information as laid, the facts found, the contentions of the parties, the cases cited, the decision, and the question or questions for the decision of the High Court. If one or other of the parties is contending

---

[193] *Ex parte Sidebotham* (1880) 14 Ch D 458, at 465, per James LJ, described as 'the best definition of the expression "aggrieved" ' in *R v London Sessions, ex parte Westminster Corporation* [1951] 2 KB 508, at 511, [1951] 1 All ER 1032, at 1033, per Lord Goddard CJ.

[194] *Hodgson v Lakeman* [1943] 1 KB 15. The position is otherwise in an appeal following trial on indictment: *R v Jefferies* [1969] 1 QB 120, [1968] 3 All ER 238.

[195] *R v Rowe* [1955] 1 QB 573, [1955] 2 All ER 234.

[196] Magistrates' Courts Act 1980, s 111(2), (3).   [197] Ibid.

[198] *R v Oxford (Bullingdon) Justices, ex parte Bird* [1948] 1 KB 100.

[199] Magistrates' Courts Rules 1981, r 76(1).

[200] Magistrates' Courts Act 1980, s 111(5). See *R v Mildenhall Magistrates' Court, ex parte Forest Heath District Council* (1997) 161 JP 401.

[201] Magistrates' Courts Act 1980, s 111(6).

[202] Ibid, s 111(4). See *Sunworld Ltd v Hammersmith & Fulham LBC; R v Blackfriars Crown Court, ex parte Sunworld Ltd* [2000] 2 All ER 837.

that there was no evidence on which the magistrates could come to their decision, a statement of the evidence should be included. This form, originally settled by Lord Goddard CJ, should always be used. The case may be stated by all the justices whose decision is questioned or by any two of them[203] and may be stated in relation to a number of different prosecutions, even against different defendants on different days, provided that they raise precisely the same point. Under no circumstances should the case state that the decision was that of a majority, if that was the position.[204] The case should in any event be submitted to both parties for their consideration and in the event of any difficulty it should be left to the parties themselves to produce a draft and submit it to the magistrates for their consideration.[205] If, in spite of this, a party to an appeal considers that the facts have been improperly stated in the case he may apply to the Queen's Bench Division for the case to be remitted to the justices for restatement of the facts, the application being accompanied by an affidavit setting out the facts which it is alleged should go in the case.[206] Periods of twenty-one days are allowed for delivering the draft case to the parties, for the parties to make representations and for the justices to prepare the final case.[207] These time-limits are not inflexible and may be extended, but in such event a written statement of the reasons for the delay must accompany the final case.[208]

On the hearing the court will hear and determine the questions of law arising, after argument by counsel for the parties. The court may allow argument on a point not raised in the court below or even take such a point itself,[209] provided that in each case the point is one of pure law, not requiring any evidence. The magistrates themselves may file an affidavit, setting out the grounds of the decision and any facts which they may consider to have a bearing on the issues;[210] in view of the existence of the case this procedure will rarely be appropriate. Unless misconduct is alleged there is no need for the justices to be represented by counsel. The court may reverse, affirm, or amend the decision in respect of which the case has been stated, or may remit the matter to the magistrates with its opinion, or make such other order as it sees fit.[211]

(b) The Crown Court

The Crown Court may also state a case for the opinion of the High Court. Either party to any order, judgment, or other decision of the Crown Court, other than one relating

---

[203] Criminal Procedure Rules 2005, r 64.

[204] *More O'Ferrall Ltd* v *Harrow Urban District Council* [1947] KB 66, at 70, [1946] 2 All ER 489, at 491.

[205] *Cowlishaw* v *Chalkley* [1955] 1 All ER 367n, [1955] 119 JP 171.

[206] *Spicer* v *Warbey* [1953] 1 All ER 284, [1953] 1 WLR 334.

[207] Criminal Procedure Rules 2005, r 68.   [208] Ibid, r 68.

[209] *Whitehead* v *Haines* [1965] 1 QB 200, [1964] 2 All ER 530.

[210] Review of Justices Decisions Act 1872.

[211] Summary Jurisdiction Act 1857, s 6. If a question arises which is appropriate to be referred to the European Court for a preliminary ruling (as to which, see p 596, *ante*) the court may, of its own motion or on application, make an order whereupon proceedings will be stayed pending receipt of the ruling, unless the Divisional Court otherwise orders: RSC, Ord 114. A rehearing is only appropriate where a fair trial is still possible; cf. *Griffith* v *Jenkins* [1992] 2 AC 76, [1992] 1 All ER 65 in which case the House of Lords laid down guidelines as to the circumstances in which the power to order a rehearing should be exercised.

solely to trial on indictment, may apply for a case to be stated on the ground that the decision is wrong in law or in excess of jurisdiction.[212] Thus, either party to an appeal from the magistrates' court, against conviction or sentence may apply, as (apparently) may a person sentenced at the Crown Court after committal for sentence from a magistrates' court. These provisions are in several respects an extension of the old law; however, a person aggrieved by the Crown Court's decision, but not a party, still has no right of appeal. Application should be made in writing to the appropriate officer of the Crown Court within twenty-one days after the decision; again, the Crown Court may only refuse to state a case if the application is considered frivolous.[213] The powers of the Queen's Bench Division appear to be the same as those exercisable on an appeal from the magistrates.[214]

3 APPEAL TO THE HOUSE OF LORDS

Finally it should be noted that an appeal to the House of Lords may be made from the Divisional Court of the Queen's Bench Division, subject to the same conditions as those governing appeals from the Court of Appeal in the case of trial on indictment.[215] Thus there must be a certificate from the Divisional Court that a point of law of general public importance is involved in its decision and either the Divisional Court or the House of Lords must give leave to appeal on the ground that the point is one which ought to be considered by the House of Lords. In this way a summary offence may be considered by four courts; the magistrates' court, the Crown Court, the Divisional Court of the Queen's Bench Division and the House of Lords.[216]

I JUDICIAL REVIEW

Magistrates' courts and the Crown Court, in the exercise of their jurisdiction over summary offences, are inferior courts and therefore their proceedings are amenable to

---

[212] Supreme Court Act 1981, s 28. Certain decisions of the Crown Court are made final; see s 28(2)(b).

[213] Criminal Procedure Rules 2005, r 64.

[214] The case of *Harris, Simon & Co Ltd* v *Manchester City Council* [1975] 1 All ER 412, [1975] 1 WLR 100 demonstrated a little known legal oddity whereby under the Manchester General Improvement Act 1851 an objection to the Manchester City Council's resolution to stop up two streets was made by way of appeal to the Crown Court (as successor to the jurisdiction of quarter sessions) where the objection is heard as an appeal by judge and jury. Since juries do not make detailed findings of fact, the Divisional Court on an appeal by way of case stated approached the case on the basis that the appeal could succeed only if the judge had misdirected the jury or if their conclusion was perverse, in the sense of being a conclusion which no reasonable jury could have reached. This instance of an appeal by way of case stated of the verdict of a jury appears to be unique.

[215] Administration of Justice Act 1960, s 1.

[216] *Spicer* v *Holt* [1977] AC 987, [1976] 3 All ER 71 is a case in which this happened. It might, in addition, be considered by the European Court, to the extent that a question arising in the proceedings was referred to that court for a preliminary ruling; see p 596, *ante*.

judicial review by the High Court.[217] This procedure may be appropriate where there is no right of appeal. Thus, for example, it has been noted[218] that there is no right of appeal from an order for the payment of costs; nevertheless the High Court has on *Wednesbury* principles[219] been prepared to quash an order for costs which was so far outside the normal sum imposed as to involve an error of law.[220] Similarly, following an appeal against sentence from a magistrates' court to the Crown Court, there is no further appeal (except by way of case stated if a point of law is involved); nevertheless in *R v St Albans Crown Court, ex parte Cinnamond*[221] a disqualification of eighteen months for careless driving, although within the jurisdiction of the court, was quashed as being so far outside the normal sentence imposed by courts for this offence as to enable the Divisional Court to hold that it must have involved an error of law.

[217] See Chapter 6, *ante* for details of this jurisdiction and procedure.   [218] See p 650, *ante*.
[219] As to which see p 215, *ante*.
[220] *R v Tottenham Justices, ex parte Joshi* [1982] 2 All ER 507, [1982] 1 WLR 631.
[221] [1981] QB 480, [1981] 1 All ER 802.

22

SENTENCES

The law governing the sentencing of offenders has undergone frequent, and radical, changes in recent years. In part these changes have been a response to the stated desire of political parties to reduce the incidence of crime, and in part due to the often competing philosophies as to the purpose of custodial sentences. The result has been a plethora of statutes making new provision, or amending existing provision, or even substituting new changes for those that reached the statute book but which never were fully implemented.[1] The position in respect of sentencing legislation reached such a level of complexity that the Lord Bingham CJ in *R v Governor of Brockhill Prison, ex parte Evans*[2] was moved to observe (in the context of the date of release of prisoners) as follows:

The Law Commission has described it as an important feature of any criminal justice system that sentencing provisions should be accessible and comprehensible and has recommended the enactment of a comprehensive statutory consolidation of such provisions . . . We hope that this may be seen as a task commanding a high degree of priority. . . .

That consolidation occurred in 2000, with the passage of the Powers of Criminal Courts (Sentencing) Act 2000. Any belief that that would provide the desired clarity and ease of access to the statutory provisions was misplaced, with at least one amendment of the 2000 Act before it came into effect,[3] and significant further changes made by the Criminal Justice Act 2003.

A GENERAL PRINCIPLES

1 THE HALLIDAY REPORT

At the heart of current approaches to the sentencing process are the recommendations of the Halliday Report,[4] the latest in a long line of reports and studies examining

---

[1] See, e.g. Crime and Disorder Act 1998, ss 69–74, which introduced the new detention and training orders (as to which see p 674, *post*) for the never implemented secure training order provisions in Criminal Justice and Public Order Act 1994, ss 1–18.

[2] [1997] QB 443, [1997] 1 All ER 439.   [3] See Criminal Justice and Courts Services Act 2000.

[4] *Making Punishments Work: Report of a Review of the Sentencing Framework for England and Wales*, Home Office 2001, available at www.homeoffice.gov.uk/docs/halliday.html.

aspects of the sentencing framework. It was born out of a belief that the then existing sentencing structure suffered from serious deficiencies that reduced its effectiveness to contribute to crime reduction and public confidence. Amongst those deficiencies were the lack of any clear message about the effect repeat offending should have on sentence, the absence of reality as to what sentences in fact mean, and unexplored opportunities for non-custodial sentences, including reparation for victims.[5] The Criminal Justice Act 1991 had required sentencers to concentrate on the nature of the offences (the principle of 'just deserts'), and although that approach was diluted by various legislative inroads (such as the taking into account of previous convictions of offenders when sentencing, or requirements relating to mandatory or minimum sentences) the basic approach was proportionality of the sentence to the offence. That did not encourage sentencers to think wider, and address the needs of crime reduction or reparation. Community sentences were perceived as weak and ineffective.

Those were not the only perceived deficiencies. Despite the work done by the Sentencing Advisory Panel, in partnership with the Court of Appeal, sentencing law was confusing and obscure, and was not such as to inspire public confidence. There needed to be a more accessible framework, and decisions in individual cases needed to be understood. Community punishments[6] were not considered as sufficiently punitive or protective. Arrangements for the enforcement of community punishments were, again, uncertain and unclear. Yet, at the same time structural re-organization provided real opportunities. Management of offenders in custody was the responsibility of the Prison Service. Management of those offenders serving punishments within the community was the responsibility of the probation service. By means of a new National Offender Management Service, integrating the two,[7] and the development of sophisticated risk assessment techniques and of programmes of treatment accredited by the Home Office there were real opportunities to address offending behaviour. Research considered by Halliday confirmed the potential benefits of such programmes, but an appropriate sentencing framework was needed to maximize their chances of success.

A change in framework might also help achieve changes in sentencing behaviour,[8] by placing emphasis on the incapacitation of persistent and dangerous offenders, and on reparation and reform for others. Resources should be targeted on those most likely to re-offend and on those who commit offences serious enough to re-offend. This approach led Halliday to conclude that there should be clear principles of sentencing, clear sentencing guidelines, and a mass of important detailed changes in sentencing law. Many of the recent changes deal with hereafter owe their origin, in whole or in part, to the Halliday Report.

---

[5] Ibid, Introduction.   [6] See p 675, *post*.

[7] As to which see *Correctional Services Review* (the Carter Review), 11 December 2003, available at www.homeoffice.gov.uk.

[8] Halliday Report, *op cit*, para 1.25.

2 PRINCIPLES OF SENTENCING

The Crime and Disorder Act 1998 had, in the context of young offenders, set out the basic objective of the prevention of re-offending.[9] Surprisingly, no statutory statement existed of the principles to which a sentencer should have regard when dealing with an adult.[10] Section 142 of the Criminal Justice Act 2003 now requires a court when passing sentence[11] to have regard to the purposes of sentencing it identifies. These are:

(a) the punishment of offenders;

(b) the reduction of crime (including its reduction by deterrence);

(c) the reform and rehabilitation of offenders;

(d) the protection of the public;

(e) the making of reparation by offenders to persons affected by their offences. In this context reparation might be financial or non-financial, and those affected might by individuals such as a victim, or the public more generally.

It is not intended that the principles will be applied uniformly. Sentencing courts will retain the right to reflect local conditions, problems, and issues, but, paradoxically, that may limit the worth of general statements such as these, because section 142 does not (and cannot) specify what weight is to be given in an individual case by the sentencing court. Nor do the principles apply to offences which have mandatory sentences (e.g. murder) or minimum sentences.[12]

3 CONSISTENCY OF SENTENCING AND APPROPRIATE SENTENCE

A already noted, It is of considerable importance that different courts sentence consistently for the same type of offence, and impose a penalty appropriate to the level of seriousness of the offence of which the offender is convicted. On the other hand, the fact that a sentencing court has, or should have, a discretion to sentence in accordance with the circumstances of the particular offence is equally important and, to some, a basic constitutional principle. It was well explained as follows:

Attempts by the executive arm of government to influence sentencing are unconstitutional, attempts by the legislature to interfere with the discretion of the courts are, even if not strictly unconstitutional, bound to result in potential confusion and injustice to defendants,

---

[9] 1998 Act, s 37: see p 515, *ante*.

[10] i.e. a person aged eighteen or over.

[11] Which includes any order made by a court made when dealing with the offender. This is wide enough to include compensation orders, sex offender orders, and restraining orders, as to which see p 679, *post*.

[12] 2003 Act, s 142(2). For minimum sentences, see p 669, *post*.

the sentencing powers of the courts should therefore be left to the wisdom of the courts under the guidance of the Court of Appeal.[13]

It was this last concern that led to trenchant opposition to the introduction in the Crime (Sentences) Act 1997 of mandatory and minimum sentences.[14] Certain offences carry a mandatory sentence. Others carry a minimum sentence.[15] Consistency is also achieved through the Attorney-General's power to make a reference to the Court of Appeal in a case where the sentence imposed is considered to be unduly lenient,[16] and through the practice of the Court of Appeal of issuing guideline judgments setting out the appropriate approach to offences of similar types.[17] In respect of summary offences the Magistrates' Association has issued Guidelines in respect of a wide range of offences.[18]

Nonetheless existing mechanisms to ensure sentencing consistency proved inadequate. For that reason the Crime and Disorder Act 1998 created a Sentencing Advisory Panel.[19] It also imposed a duty on the Court of Appeal to issue guidance on appropriate sentences for specific types of offence.[20] The Sentencing Advisory Panel had the power to propose to the Court of Appeal (Criminal Division) that guidelines for sentencing in particular categories of indictable offence be framed or revised. It was required to do so if so directed to do so by the Home Secretary. The Panel was under a duty to consult, to formulate its own views, and communicate them to the Court of Appeal and to furnish information to the Court of Appeal about the sentences imposed by courts in England and Wales for offences of the relevant category, the cost of different sentences, and their relative effectiveness in preventing re-offending.[21] The recommendations of the Panel did not in any way bind the Court of Appeal but have a highly persuasive effect. Likewise the 1998 Act[22] imposed a duty on the Court of Appeal to consider whether to frame guidelines as to the sentencing of offences of particular categories.

This process worked seemingly well, with a series of guideline judgments following consideration by the Council.[23] However, section 167 of the Criminal Justice Act 2003

---

[13] Ashworth, *Sentencing and Penal Policy* (1983) at p 54. See also Ashworth, *Sentencing and Criminal Justice* (2nd edn, 1995) at pp 40–51; cf. Walker and Padfield, *Sentencing Theory, Law and Practice* (1996) at p 380, who see no constitutional principle which forbids or even discourages Parliament from limiting the discretion of sentences if that has advantages.

[14] See, e.g. Lord Woolf CJ, in the 2nd Reading, Debate of Crime (Sentences) Act 1997, *op cit*, col 997 where he complained of 'the legislature taking over what has been accepted to be the proper role of the judiciary'.

[15] See p 669, *post.*   [16] See p 660, *post.*

[17] See the following guideline cases for examples: see, e.g. *R v Billham; R v Bibi* (1980) 71 Cr App R 360; *R v Willis* (1974) 60 Cr App R 146; *R v Taylor, Roberts and Simons* (1977) 64 Cr App R 182.

[18] See p 660, *post.*

[19] Crime and Disorder Act 1998, s 81. Both s 80 and s 81 are repealed by the 2003 Act, but s 169 provides for the continuation of the Panel.

[20] Ibid, s 80.   [21] Ibid, s 81.   [22] Section 75.

[23] There include: *R v Millberry, Morgan and Lackenby* [2003] Crim LR 561 (rape); *R v Oliver, Hartley and Baldwin* [2003] Crim LR 127 (child pornography); *R v Celaire and Poulton* [2003] Crim LR 124 (possession of offensive weapons); *R v McInerney and Keating* [2003] Crim LR 209 (domestic burglary); *R v R* [2003] Crim

established a Sentencing Guidelines Council, whilst the Panel is preserved (by section 169). This Council has a mixed judicial and non judicial membership,[24] is chaired by the Lord Chief Justice, and with the non judicial element intended to reflect wider interests of society. It remains unclear as to why this non-judicial element was not equally reflected in the composition of the Panel.

The purpose of the Council is to develop the work done by the Court of Appeal through guideline judgments and the Magistrates' Association through its sentencing guidelines. Now, it is the Council which will issue sentencing and allocation guidelines. Nothing in the 2003 Act regulates the interaction of the Council and Panel, who will, presumably report to the Council. The task of the Council will be to formulate sentencing guidelines, having regard to the need to promote consistency in sentencing. It will also formulate allocation guidelines to provide consistency in decision making as to the allocation of mode of trial for either-way offences.[25] A sentencing court will be obliged to have regard to the sentencing guidelines.[26] The first such guidelines were published in December 2004, when it produced guidelines on discounts for early guilty pleas, offence seriousness, and the implementation of new sentences. The Lord Chief Justice was at pains to stress the improved quality of the guidelines following input of the non judicial members of the Council.

4 THE ROLE OF THE ATTORNEY-GENERAL

The prosecution has a limited role in the sentencing process. It is under a duty to bring to the attention of the sentencing court matters relating to the power of the court, and has the right to correct misstatements of fact that may be made by an accused during the sentencing process. However, the prosecution has no specific right of appeal in an individual case against a sentence perceived as being unduly lenient. It was to permit some higher court review of such sentences that the Criminal Justice Act 1988 introduced powers which entitle the Attorney-General to refer to the Court of Appeal cases in which he considers an over-lenient sentence to have been imposed. Where such a reference is made the Court of Appeal may quash any sentence imposed and, in its place, impose such sentence as it thinks appropriate, within the powers that were available to the sentencing court. The Court of Appeal will not intervene unless the sentencing judge's sentence was wrong in principle, so that public confidence would be damaged if the sentence were not altered.[27]

LR 898 (street robbery); *R v Cooksley* [2003] Crim LR 564 (causing death by dangerous driving. The Lord Chief Justices' *Practice Direction on Life Sentences for Murder* [2002] 4 All ER 1089 were issued after consultation with the Panel.

[24] Four non judicial members will reflect the experience of the police, criminal prosecution, criminal defence, and welfare services. The DPP will also be annex officio *member*.

[25] See p 544, *ante.*   [26] 2003 Act, s 172(1).

[27] *Attorney-General's Reference (No 5 of 1989) (R v Hill-Trevor)* (1989) 90 Cr App R 358.

5 VICTIMS

Traditionally, the victims of crime had not had a significant formal role within the process of the offender being convicted and dealt with. A government White Paper, *Justice for All*[28] observed:

Justice is not simply about punishment for its own sake. Many victims, when asked, say they simply want to ensure that non-one else has to go through the kind of experience they themselves have. And the best way of ensuring that is to catch, convict and rehabilitate offenders and prevent further crime. Victim's own evidence is crucial in bringing offenders to justice. They must be nurtured and not subject to a host of delays, postponement and barriers . . . the criminal justice agencies have a particular responsibility to support victims and witnesses . . . This includes . . . taking into account the impact of the offence on victims when sentencing offenders . . .

In recent years, a variety of measures have been taken to improve the position of victims and how they are treated. Victim Support has been developed, and assists in excess of one million victims each year; witnesses when giving evidence are now eligible for special measures to protect them;[29] the Witness Service assists those who have to testify; and the police and Crown Prosecution Service have received better training in respect of how better to deal with vulnerable witnesses. Yet various studies demonstrated that more could be done, in particular as to informing victims of the progress of their case, the verdict, or plea, the sentence, if any, imposed, and the disposition and release of those sent to prison.[30] To remedy this, the Domestic Violence, Crime and Victims Act 2004 contained major provisions aimed at supporting the victims of crime. The provisions are 'intended to give victims guaranteed[31] and consistent levels of advice support and information . . .'.

The 2004 Act requires the Home Secretary to issue a Code of Practice setting out the minimum standards expected of individuals and agencies who deal with victims of crime, particularly the police and Crown Prosecution Service. It will primarily concentrate on victims of violence and sexual offences, the victims of property crime, and vulnerable victims. The detailed provisions of the Code will set minimum standards for the transmission of information about charge, date of hearings, progress of the case, the result, and sentence. Victims of violent or sexual offences will have the right to receive information and make representations about the treatment of the offender after sentence and his potential release, including as to matters relating to conditions of licence,[32] and in respect of matters relating to hospital orders.[33]

Provisions also exist for financial support for victims of crime. The Criminal Injuries

---

[28] *Op cit*, paras 2.11b–2.12.   [29] See p 613, *ante*.

[30] See, in particular, *A Better Deal for Victims and Witnesses*, Home Office Consultation Paper, 2003; *Compensation and Support for the Victims of Crime*, Home Office Consultation Paper, 2004.

[31] Baroness Scotland, Minister of State, Home Office, HL 2nd Reading, 15 December 2003.

[32] 2004 Act, s 45(2), replacing and extending Criminal Justice and Courts Services Act 2000, s 69.

[33] Hospital orders may be made following a finding of disability under Criminal Procedure (Insanity) Act 1994.

Compensation Act 1995 placed on a statutory footing the arrangements for the compensation of some victims of crime, and which had been formally dealt with on a non statutory basis.[34] The 2004 Act envisages the creation of a victims' fund, which will be created from surcharges imposed on offenders following conviction,[35] and partly by money recovered from offenders in respect of compensation paid by the Criminal Injuries Compensation Scheme.[36] Statutory powers are being changed to permit a greater number of compensation orders.[37] But it is often not possible for such an order to be made or paid and the victim of a crime of violence may depend on compensation being paid from the Criminal Injuries Compensation scheme. To that end the 2004 Act creates powers that enable the recovery of compensation paid by the Criminal Injuries Compensation Scheme.

A variety of other statutory changes have been made to support victims, including access to the Parliamentary Commissioner for Administration in respect of complaints of maladministration, and the creation of the office of Commissioner for Victims and Witnesses to champion their cause.

B THE SENTENCING PROCESS AT THE CROWN COURT

A judge will sentence on the basis of the guilty plea or verdict of the jury. If there is a significant dispute about what factually occurred, then, following a plea of guilty, unless the prosecution accepts the defence version, a hearing is held to decide any dispute.[38] However, if there is a verdict (as opposed to a plea) of guilty, the judge sentences on the basis of the facts as they appear to him, provided that that view is consistent with the verdict of the jury.

1 PASSING SENTENCE

If the defendant has been found guilty on any part of the indictment the court will then proceed to sentence, in a similar manner to that following a plea of guilty. There is first an inquiry into the defendant's antecedents. A pre-sentence report[39] is then considered. The defendant, through his advocate, makes a speech in mitigation. In the course of this part of the trial it not infrequently happens that the defendant asks for other offences to be taken into consideration. This practice is based on convention and has no statutory foundation; yet at the same time it is extremely convenient both from the point of view of the police and of the defendant. If there are other offences which the defendant has committed but which are still untried (or unknown), then

---

[34] See R v Criminal Injuries Compensation Board, ex parte Lain [1967] 2 All ER 770.
[35] See p 678, post.   [36] See p 677, post.   [37] See Courts Act 2003.
[38] Known as a Newton hearing: R v Newton (1982) 77 Cr App R 13.   [39] See p 664, post.

the defendant may admit them to the court of trial and ask the judge to take them into consideration when sentencing him for the offence of which he has just been convicted. In practice he will probably tell the police well before the hearing that he wishes certain offences to be taken into consideration or the police may suggest the matter to him and he will then be supplied with an appropriate form of admission; however there seems to be nothing to prevent a court taking an offence into consideration even if the defendant does not either admit it or ask for it to be taken into consideration until the actual trial. However:

If justice is to be done it is essential that the practice should not be followed except with the express and unequivocal assent of the offender himself. Accordingly, he should be informed explicitly of each offence which the judge proposes to take into consideration; and should explicitly admit that he committed them and should state his desire that they should be taken into consideration in determining the sentence to be passed on him.[40]

Once the defendant has served his sentence he will not, by long established custom, be prosecuted in respect of any of the offences which have been taken into consideration, although if he were prosecuted the defence of *autrefois convict* would not be open to him, there having been no trial, let alone conviction, in respect of those offences.[41] If, however, his conviction were quashed, a prosecution might be brought. The mere fact that the defendant asks for the offence to be taken into consideration does not, of course, compel the court to do so. Certain limitations have been laid down in the cases. Broadly, the offence to be taken into consideration should be of the same character as the offence of which the defendant has been convicted; if the defendant has already been separately committed for trial in respect of the offence to be taken into consideration the judge should obtain the consent of the prosecution before doing so.[42] Even if the prosecution does consent, the judge ought to consider whether the public interest requires a separate inquiry. Neither ought the court to take into consideration an offence carrying disqualification from driving.[43] The reason is that in very many cases it will be desirable if not obligatory to disqualify the defendant, yet there can only be a disqualification on conviction, and taking other offences into consideration does not amount to a conviction in respect of them.

A sentence takes effect from the beginning of the day on which it is imposed, unless the court otherwise directs. The court should make clear whether any terms of imprisonment are concurrent or consecutive. Any sentence imposed, or other order made, by the Crown Court may, under section 47(2) of the Supreme Court Act 1981, be varied or rescinded by the Crown Court within the period of twenty-eight days from the date of such sentence or order.

---

[40] *Anderson* v *Director of Public Prosecutions* [1978] AC 964 at 977; *sub nom Director of Public Prosecutions* v *Anderson* [1978] 2 All ER 512, at 515–16, per Lord Diplock.

[41] *R* v *Nicholson* [1947] 2 All ER 535. [42] *R* v *McLean* [1911] 1 KB 332.

[43] *R* v *Williams* [1962] 3 All ER 639, [1962] 1 WLR 1268.

2 DEFERMENT OF SENTENCE

As an alternative to passing sentence immediately upon an offender, the judge has power to defer sentence for the purpose of enabling the court or any other court to which it falls to deal with him to have regard, in dealing with him to his conduct after conviction (including, where appropriate, the making by him of reparation for his offence) or to any change in his circumstances.[44] The deferment can only be made if the offender consents and the court is satisfied, having regard to the nature of the offence and the character and circumstances of the offender that it would be in the interests of justice to do so. The offender must also agree to comply with such requirements as to his conduct during the period of deferment that the court considers it appropriate to impose. There are no statutory limits as to what requirements may be imposed, although a court will need to ensure that any such requirements are necessary, proportionate, and reasonable in order to prevent arguments as to whether they infringe Article 8 of the European Convention.[45] A court will monitor the offender's progress against those requirements. Progress will continue to act as a mitigating factor in respect of the final sentence, and might, for example, persuade a court that a community sentence rather than a custodial term is appropriate.

The power to defer sentence is intended for cases such as those in which a persistent offender has at last shown an inclination to settle down and work or those in which persons have, under domestic or financial pressure, stolen from their employers sums which they say they propose to repay. Accordingly it will not be appropriate to defer sentence where the offence is so minor that it would not merit a sentence of imprisonment in any event. Nor is it appropriate to do so where the offence is so serious that it must inevitably result in a substantial custodial sentence. This is because it would not be appropriate to impose a custodial sentence if the information before the court about the offender's conduct during the period of deferment is favourable to him. The period of deferment may be anything up to six months and there must not be a further deferment on the specified date.[46] Furthermore, where sentence is deferred, all aspects of the sentence should be deferred; the sentence must not be 'split' by, for example, imposing an immediate disqualification from driving, but deferring the remainder of the sentence.

3 PRE-SENTENCE REPORTS AND OTHER REPORTS

A court must generally consider a pre-sentence report ('PSR')[47] before sentencing an offender to a custodial sentence. Such a report will also be a pre-condition to the

---

[44] See Powers of Criminal Courts (Sentencing) Act 2000, ss 1, 1A–1F, 2, as amended and substituted by Criminal Justice Act 2003, s 278 and Schedule 23.

[45] See p 184, *ante*.

[46] *R v Fairhead* [1975] 2 All ER 737. However, a restitution order may be made under the Theft Act 1968, even if the passing of the sentence is in other respects deferred: Theft Act 1968, s 28(1) (as amended by the Criminal Law Act 1977, Schedule 12).

[47] For the relevant statutory provisions, see Criminal Justice Act 2003, ss 156–159 re-enacting, with amendments, Powers of Criminal Courts (Sentencing) Act 2000, s 156.

imposition of certain community orders, or requirements in them.[48] A PSR is a written report usually prepared by the probation service, although it may well be prepared by a social worker or other member of the youth offending team[49] if the offender is under the age of eighteen. Failure to consider such a report does not invalidate a sentence passed, but in the event of an appeal the court must obtain one. The report, prepared in accordance with National Standards, will contain an assessment of the offence and its seriousness, of any factors that relate to the offender which may affect the assessment of seriousness, and especially of any risk that the offender poses. It should address the attitudes of the offender and other matters which may be relevant to the sentence ultimately imposed. It is not the practice of probation to prepare PSR in respect of those accused who indicate an intention to deny the offence. In such a case there will need to be an adjournment in order for a report to be prepared, causing delay. It was for this reason that the requirement to obtain a PSR was modified in 1994,[50] to permit a court to sentence without one where such a report is considered unnecessary. This exception does not apply in respect of offenders aged under eighteen, unless the offence for which the offender is being sentenced is triable only on indictment, and it is considered that sufficient information is available.

In addition to a PSR a court may wish, or be required, to consider other reports. Thus, a court may require a specialist report indicating the risk to the community that a sex offender poses. Other orders may require a report from a doctor or psychologist setting out details of a particular condition or addiction as a pre-requisite to the making of a particular order. Thus, for example, before a court can impose a community rehabilitation order with a requirement for medical treatment, it must first consider a report from a qualified medical practitioner. Where a PSR has been obtained a copy is given to the offender or his solicitor, the prosecutor, although statute limits the use to which the report may be put. The court has the power to require a financial circumstances statement,[51] which it will use where it is contemplating the imposition of a fine and wishes to find out the means of the offender.

4 PRE-SENTENCE DRUG TESTING

Drug misuse has long been recognised as one of the major causes of offending. On its back comes a range of acquisitive or violent offences.[52] Knowledge of the fact of addition or misuse may therefore be crucial if offending behaviour is to be addressed. Section 161 of the Criminal Justice Act 2003 confers a wide power to order a pre-sentence drug test. The court can make an order in respect of anyone aged fourteen or over, where the court is considering imposing a community sentence and, in the case of an adult, where it is considering a suspended sentence. The consent of the offender

---

[48] Where additional requirements are being considered: see s 156(2) of the 2003 Act.

[49] See p 674, *ante.*   [50] Criminal Justice and Public Order Act 1994, Schedule 9, paras 40–42.

[51] Criminal Justice Act 2003, s 162, re-enacting with amendments Powers of Criminal Courts (Sentencing) Act 2000, s 126.

[52] See Home Office Research Study 183, *Drugs and Crime,* 2002.

is not required: if the offender does not comply, and there is no reasonable excuse of that failure, a criminal offence is committed. In addition the court may draw its own conclusions, which may affect the nature and requirements of any order made on sentencing.

5 RESTRAINING ORDERS

Section 5 of the Protection from Harassment Act 1997 has, since 1997, permitted a court, when sentencing a defendant convicted of an offence under section 2 or section 4 of that Act,[53] to make a restraining order. That power has now been extended to any defendant, irrespective of the offence for which the defendant was convicted, and irrespective of whether the conviction is on indictment or on summary trial. The nature of the order is discussed later.[54] But, importantly, it also applies in some circumstances to cases even where the defendant was acquitted. A court will, in all relevant cases, irrespective of verdict, have to give consideration to the making of such an order.

C THE SENTENCING PROCESS IN THE MAGISTRATES' COURT

The sentencing process itself does not, in principle differ in cases tried summarily rather than on indictment, though the particular role of the Youth Court in dealing with young defendant should be borne in mind.[55] But the sentencing powers of the magistrates' courts are limited by statute. Those limitations, upon the maximum term of imprisonment or maximum fine, are important not only in respect of how the defendant is dealt with, but in wider issues about the proportion of cases that are sent for trial by the magistrates' courts.

Currently, magistrates' courts do not have the power to impose a term of imprisonment of more than six months in respect of any one offence and twelve

---

[53] A s 2 offence is committed by a person who pursues a course of conduct (a) which amounts to harassment of another, and (b) which he knows or ought to know amounts to harassment of another . . . A course of conduct does not fall within the above if the defendant shows—(a) that it was pursued for the purpose of preventing or detecting crime, (b) that it was pursued under any enactment or rule of law or to comply with any condition or requirement imposed by any person under any enactment; or (c) that in the particular circumstances the pursuit of the course of conduct was reasonable (see s 1 of the 1997 Act).

A s 4 offence is committed by a person whose course of conduct causes another to fear, on at least two occasions, that violence will be used against him, if the defendant knows or ought to know that his course of conduct will cause the other so to fear on each of those occasions. The exceptions stated in n 6 above (in the context of s 2) apply equally to s 4.

'Harassment' is further defined by 1997 Act, s 7 which states that references to 'harassment' include alarming the person or causing the person distress. A 'course of conduct' must involve conduct on at least two occasions.

[54] See p 679, *post*.   [55] See p 641, *ante*.

months in total for multiple offences. Powers of committal for sentence exist, where the sentencing powers of the magistrates' court are considered to be inadequate. Those limits are set to change when section 154 of the Criminal Justice Act 2003 is implemented. When that happens, magistrates' courts will have the power to impose a sentence of no more than fifty-one weeks[56] in respect of any one offence and a total, in the case of multiple offences, of sixty-five weeks. The rationale for this significant change is inextricably bound up with decisions relating to mode of trial.[57] The government wished to see fewer cases going for trial to the Crown Court. Whether inadequate sentencing powers is a primary reason for the numbers of cases being sent to trial at the Crown Court is arguable, with some evidence existing to show that significant cases which are committed attract sentences that the magistrates' court itself could in fact have imposed.[58]

As a consequential but necessary change, if the magistrates' court is to retain a greater number of cases for sentence, the powers of the magistrates' court to commit for sentence are restricted.

D OFFENCE SERIOUSNESS AND SENTENCING THRESHOLDS

The Criminal Justice Act 1991, which has provided the basis for approaches to sentencing in recent years, was primarily based on the concept of 'just deserts', a fact reflected in the basic principles stated in the Powers of Criminal Courts (Sentencing) Act 2000. Under that Act, a custodial sentence could not generally be imposed unless the offence, together with any associated offences,[59] were so serious that only a custodial sentence could be justified,[60] or that a custodial sentence (in the case of a violent or sexual offence) was necessary to protect the public. Further, a community sentence could only be imposed if the court was of the opinion that the offence, together with any associated offences, was serious enough to warrant such a sentence.

A hierarchy of seriousness was thus created. That hierarchy is maintained by new, replacement, provisions contained in the Criminal Justice Act 2003, but with amended wording.[61] The amended custody threshold is described to be where the offence and any associated with it '. . . was so serious that neither a fine alone or a community sentence can be justified . . .', the revised wording being intended to signify that

---

[56] For the significance of the period of fifty-one weeks, see p 670, *post*.   [57] See p 547, *ante*.

[58] See Herbert, 'Mode of Trial and Magistrates' Sentencing Powers' [2003] Crim LR 315; Royal Commission on Criminal Justice, *op cit*, para 6.12, citing research conducted by Hedderman and Moxon, *Magistrates' Court or Crown Court: Mode of Trial Decisions and Sentencing* Research Study No 125, HMSO, 1992.

[59] An 'associated offence' was an offence for which the offender is being dealt with on the same sentencing occasion, or which the offender is asking to be taken into consideration on that occasion.

[60] 2000 Act, s 79(2). For discussion of the custody threshold, see Ashworth and von Hirsch, 'Recognising Elephants The Problem of the Custody Threshold' [1997] Crim LR 187.

[61] 2003 Act, s 152.

custody really should be the sentence of last resort. Nothing, though, prevents the imposition of a custodial sentence where the defendant fails to signify his willingness to comply with a requirement proposed to be inserted into a community order.

By section 143 a court must, in considering the seriousness of any offence, consider the offender's culpability, and the harm or risk of harm that the offence was intended to cause. Culpability therefore does not depend solely on the consequences of the offence. The court must take into account the fact and nature of any previous convictions, and the fact (if that was the case) that the offence was committed whilst on bail.[62] The seriousness of an offence is aggravated by racial or religious motivation,[63] but mitigated by an early guilty plea.[64] The court must also have regard to sentencing guidelines issued by the Sentencing Guidelines Council[65] in determining levels of seriousness and how the offence is dealt with in terms of type and length of sentence.

E IMPRISONMENT

1 SUSPENDED SENTENCE

A sentence of imprisonment may be imposed but suspended, i.e. ordered not to take effect immediately.[66] The sentence must not be for more than two years and the period of suspension must be between one and two years. The effect of a suspended sentence is that so far as that sentence is concerned, the defendant is not liable to be imprisoned unless (1) during the period of suspension he commits another offence punishable with imprisonment, and thereafter (2) a court order that the sentence shall take effect. When suspended sentences were first introduced there was a tendency for courts to impose a suspended sentence upon persons who, but for the existence of the power to impose suspended sentences, would not have received a sentence of imprisonment at all. However, suspended sentences are custodial sentences, and therefore the criteria for the imposition of a custodial sentence (*ante*) must be satisfied before the decision whether it should be suspended is taken. In addition the Criminal Justice Act 1991[67] had made it harder for a court to impose a suspended sentence. Now, the power to suspend a sentence of imprisonment should only be used where the exceptional circumstances of the case justify it. The Act provides no guidance at to what might amount to exceptional circumstances for this purpose.

2 LENGTH OF CUSTODIAL SENTENCE

In cases of murder, a sentence of life imprisonment is mandatory. Life sentences are dealt with below.[68]

---

[62] 2003 Act, s 143. [63] 2003 Act, s 145. [64] 2003 Act, s 144.
[65] See p 660, *ante*. [66] 2000 Act, s 118. [67] See now 2000 Act, s 118.
[68] See p 673, *post*.

In any other case, the length of any custodial sentence imposed will be such as is commensurate with the seriousness of the offence, and in the light of sentencing guidelines. This does not prevent a sentence being imposed to deter future offences. In *R v Cunningham*[69] Lord Taylor CJ observed:

the sentence commensurate with the seriousness of the offence of this kind will be substantial to reflect the need both for punishment and deterrence. What [the Act] does prohibit is adding an extra length to the sentence by which those criteria is commensurate with the seriousness of the offence simply to make a special example of the defendant.

Special provisions apply to dangerous offenders, which replace pre-existing provisions introduced by the Criminal Justice Act 1991. It used to be the case that a longer than commensurate custodial sentence could be imposed if necessary, in the case of a violent or sexual offence, to protect the public from serious harm. Those provisions were repealed by the Criminal Justice Act 2003.

There are also special provisions relating to minimum sentences in some cases. The Crime (Sentences) Act 1997 introduced minimum sentences in respect of repeat drug trafficking and repeat burglary offences, although the provisions relating to burglary were never implemented. Where an offender aged eighteen or over commits a drug trafficking offence, having at that date already two separate and consecutive convictions for such offences, a court must impose a minimum term of seven years' imprisonment unless there are specific circumstances relating to the offence or the offender which justify it not so doing. Again, the rationale for the provision is open to doubt: the majority of such offences will in any event attract a long sentence.

The fact that an offender is sentenced to a particular term of imprisonment does not mean that that is the period actually served in prison or detention. Under provisions introduced in 1991,[70] a distinction was drawn between short-term prisoners (serving up to four years) and long-term prisoners. Short-term prisoners served half of their sentence, with release on licence then automatic, subject only to the possibility of earlier release under home detention curfew, which could contain curfew conditions and provide for electronic tagging if appropriate. Long-term prisoners (those serving four years or more) became eligible for release on licence by the Parole Board after having served half the term, and generally had the right to automatic release after two-thirds of the term. This regime lacked clarity, was not well understood by the public and did not engage with the need to continue to work with the offender in respect of his offending behaviour.[71] A new regime was introduced by the Criminal Justice Act 2003.[72] This abolished the distinction between short-term and long-term prisoners. Now, prisoners serve one half of their sentence in prison or detention, subject to eligibility for home detention curfew for those who are eligible up to 135 days early.[73] The remaining part of the sentence will be spent on licence, which may be

---

[69] (1993) 14 Cr App R (S) 444.   [70] Criminal Justice Act 1991.
[71] Halliday Report, *op cit*, paras 4.1–4.10.   [72] 2003 Act, ss 237–68.
[73] See 2003 Act, s 246.

subject to licence conditions. Special provisions apply in respect of 'custody plus', intermittent custody, extended sentences, and life prisoners.

3 CUSTODY PLUS

New provisions, known as 'custody plus' address issues relating to the usefulness of short sentences. The Halliday Report[74] highlighted the lack of utility as one of the significantly weaknesses of the sentencing framework. Only half of a term of imprisonment is ever served, because of automatic release at the halfway stage[75] and no power to impose conditions on the second six-month period existed. This is exacerbated by the fact that release under home detention curfew, permits release on licence at an even earlier stage. All this at a time when the number of short term sentences of less than twelve months was increasing—by 67 per cent in the period 1989 and 1999. In that same period there was an increase of 176 per cent in respect of the shortest sentences of three months or less. Halliday concluded that greater use could be made of community sentences, of intermittent custody,[76] but also of a scheme that combined custody with a period served, under supervision, in the community and subject to conditions.

Custody plus applies to offenders aged eighteen, and comprises[77] a custodial period of a minimum of two weeks and a maximum of thirteen in respect of any one offence.[78] This is to be followed by a licence period, of a period comprised by the remainder of the term once the custodial term has been served (i.e. the total sentence length less the custodial term). The total length of the sentence must not be less than twenty-eight weeks or more than fifty-one weeks in respect of any one offence,[79] a fact that explains the curious new maximum limit on magistrates' court sentencing powers.[80] Licence conditions can be imposed in respect of the licence period.

4 INTERMITTENT CUSTODY

Intermittent custody is an another innovation introduced by the Criminal Justice Act 2003, based on recommendations contained in the Halliday Report.[81] It is intended to deal with the negative and unhelpful consequences that can arise where a custodial sentence may mean loss of home or job, or damage to marriage or long-term relationships. These consequences may be the reduction of a custodial sentence in many instances, but intermittent custody may avoid some of these consequences if the offence seriousness and wider circumstances permit the imposition of such a sentence.

---

[74] Op cit, para 3.1 *et seq.*   [75] Criminal Justice Act 1991, s 33(1)(a).   [76] See below.
[77] Criminal Justice Act 2003, s 181. The provisions are not yet in force and not likely to be so for some time, probably 2007.
[78] Twenty-six weeks maximum for aggregate offences.
[79] Maximum sixty-five weeks for aggregate offences.   [80] See p 667, *ante*.
[81] It is currently being piloted.

It also potentially reduces the prison population, an additional benefit identified by Halliday.[82]

The scheme[83] is based on the same sentence length structure as is 'custody plus' (i.e. a maximum term for a single offence of fifty-one weeks. The offender must consent to an order, which is a custodial sentence. The intermittent custody order will then specify the number of days that must be served in custody before a licence period begins—not less than fourteen or less than ninety. The custodial term will be served during intermittent periods of custody. When the custodial term has finished a licence period will ensue for the residue of the term.

5 DANGEROUS OFFENDERS

We have already noted the repeal of the 'longer than commensurate sentence' provision that existed in respect of violent or sexual offence.[84] As part of the strategy, inherent in the Halliday Report and the Criminal Justice Act 2003, of concentrating on prioritizing resource and imprisonment on those who pose a danger to society, new indeterminate sentences (i.e. life imprisonment or detention for life) are introduced. The 1991 Act regime already discussed provided no protection once the normal release date for such offenders had passed. Different approaches were tried in the Crime (Sentences) Act 1997,[85] but never brought into force, and the Crime and Disorder Act 1998 modified but did not replace the 1991 Act scheme. This governmental indecision is ended by the 2003 Act.

The new powers apply to 'serious offences', defined by a long schedule of offences,[86] and which comprise more than sixty violent and more than forty sexual offences (known as 'specified offences') ranging (in the case of violent offences) from manslaughter, soliciting murder, and wounding with intent to causing grievous bodily harm to causing death by careless driving while under the influence of drink or drugs, carrying a firearm with criminal intent, racially aggravated assaults or racially aggravated public order offences. In respect of sexual offences the net is again cast widely, and includes rape, unlawful sexual intercourse, incest, indecent assault, the offence of causing prostitution of women, and possession of indecent photographs of children.

Four situations are identified and dealt with:

(a) Life sentence or imprisonment for public protection for serious offences by a person aged over eighteen[87]

If the court is of the opinion that there is significant risk to members of the public of serious harm[88] caused by the commission of further 'specified offences'[89] then the

---

82 Halliday Report op cit, para 5.4 See also Home Office *Alternatives to Custody* Cm 4174 (1998).

83 AS to which see Criminal Justice Act 2003, s 183.   84 See p 667, *ante*.

85 Which provided for an extended supervision regime.   86 2003 Act, Schedule 15.

87 2003 Act, s 225.

88 Defined as death or serious personal injury, whether physical or psychological: s 224(3).

89 The specified offence in respect of the risk in question does not have to be the same (or even the same type) as that which triggers the provision.

court must decide whether the offence is punishable by life or a fixed term of at least ten years. If a life sentence is available and appropriate on normal sentencing principles, that sentence must be imposed. If it is not, the court must determine whether the normal determinate sentence is adequate to protect the public. If it is not, it must pass a sentence for public protection, which is an indeterminate sentence, treated for release purposes in the same way as a life sentence.

(b) Detention for life or for public protection for serious offences committed by a person aged under eighteen[90]

This replicates, with necessary textual amendments to reflect that those under eighteen are subject to detention for life, the sentence discussed at (a) above in relation to adults

(c) Extended sentence for violent or sexual offences committed by a person aged eighteen or over[91]

This applies where the mandatory life sentence of imprisonment for public protection does not. Where there is a significant risk of serious harm to members of the public caused by the commission of further specified offences, and the term of imprisonment which it would pass would otherwise not be adequate for the purpose of protecting the public from serious harm from the commission of further specified offences, the court may impose an extended sentence. This is a term which equals the appropriate custodial term (defined by normal principles) and a further period (the 'extension period') for which the offender is to be subject to licence. The length of that licence will be of such length as the court considers necessary to prevent the commission of further specified offences, subject to the total period of the sentence not exceeding the maximum for the offence. The appropriate sentence on normal sentencing principles is six years, and if the maximum for the offence is ten years, the extended period must be no longer than four years. No automatic early release licence provisions apply to extended sentences: early release from the custodial term depends upon it being granted by the Parole Board.[92]

(d) Extended sentence for violent or sexual offences committed by a person aged under eighteen[93]

This replicates, with necessary textual amendments, the sentence discussed at (c) above in relation to adults.

These provisions are a significant addition to the armoury of the court, but care will be needed to be taken to ensure that the sentence imposed can be justified and is proportionate to the risk that the public face.

---

[90] 2003 Act, s 226.   [91] 2003 Act, s 227.   [92] 2003 Act, ss 247, 249.
[93] 2003 Act, s 228.

6 LIFE SENTENCES

We have seen that a life sentence in the case of a dangerous offender can be mandatory. That is always the situation in cases of murder, the death penalty having been
effectively abolished in 1965.[94]

Prior to December 2002, guidance as to the minimum period to be served by a
mandatory life sentence was given to the Home Secretary by the judiciary. Since 1983,
a tariff for mandatory life prisoners had been set by the Home Office, following
recommendations by the trial judge and Lord Chief Justice. The Home Secretary's
role was the subject of repeated challenge in domestic courts and under the Convention on Human Rights at Strasbourg.[95] Following a decision (in a case relating to a
discretionary life sentence) that the setting of the 'tariff' was a judicial not an executive function[96] the law was changed so that the trial judge set the tariff.[97] Following a
series of subsequent challenges,[98] the House of Lords ruled in R (Anderson) v Secretary
of State for the Home Department[99] that the Home Secretary should play no part in
fixing the tariff of a convicted murderer, even if he did no more than confirm what the
trial judge had recommended. The fixing of the tariff was a sentencing exercise involving a question of the quantum of punishment, Section 29 of the Crime (Sentences)
Act 1967 could not be read in a way compatible with Article 6 of the Convention,[100]
the court thus making a declaration of incompatibility. This was the catalyst for
change, first by judicial sentencing guidelines as to the minimum terms to be served
by life prisoners,[101] and then by the passage of section 269 of the Criminal Justice
Act 2003.

The effect of section 269 is that the sentencing court must, in most cases, specify a
minimum period of sentence. This must be done in open court, and set out the
reasons why the order is made. As soon as the prisoner has served the specified period,
he is eligible for release on licence, and must be released if the Parole Board (the body
responsible for determining early release questions) so directs.[102] The length of time
specified by the court is that which the court considers appropriate, taking into
account the nature of the offence and any associated offences.[103] This leaves the
question as to how the court is to determine the seriousness of the offence. Schedule
21 of the 2003 Act sets out the starting-points for different offences. For example, it

---

[94] It was not finally abolished for treason and piracy with violence until 1991.

[95] For the history, see Lord Bingham in R (Anderson) v Secretary of State for Home Affairs [2002] 4 All ER
1089 at 1097.

[96] Thynne v United Kingdom (1991) 13 EHRR 666.   [97] Crime (Sentences) Act 1997, s 28.

[98] V v United Kingdom [2002] All ER 1024: breach of Article 6 in setting tariff for young offender; R v
Secretary of State for the Home Department, ex parte Venables [1997] 3 All ER 97 unfair for Home Secretary to
set tariff in respect of individual detained during Her Majesty's Pleasure; Stafford v United Kingdom (2002) 13
BHRC 360.

[99] [200] 4 All ER 1089.

[100] See Easterbrook v United Kingdom, The Times 18 June 2003 which confirmed the correctness of that
conclusion in the context of ECHR.

[101] See Practice Statement (Crime: Life Sentences) [2002] 1 WLR 1789.

[102] Crime (Sentences) Act 1997, s 28.   [103] See p 667, ante.

identifies a starting point for murder of two or more persons as thirty years. It then identifies a range of aggravating and mitigating factors, such as pre-meditation, vulnerable victim, abuse of trust, concealment, destruction or dismemberment of the body (all aggravating), and an intention to cause serious harm rather than kill, the age of the offender, belief that the murder was an act of mercy (all mitigating). These principles are now being developed in detail by a series of guidelines and judicial decisions.[104]

7 YOUNG OFFENDERS

Generally, although not always, young offenders are dealt with in the youth court. However, for the most serious crimes they will be tried on indictment and, if found guilty, sentenced by that court. The general considerations that apply to young offenders have already been noted,[105] Irrespective of whether an offender is a young offender (i.e. under eighteen) there are restrictions on the power of a court to impose a custodial sentence on a person aged under twenty-one. Where an offender is not less than eighteen but under twenty-one, and a custodial sentence is justified, he may be sentenced to detention in a young offenders' institution. Where an offender is aged between twelve and eighteen, he may be sentenced to a detention and training order, which couples a period in custody in secure accommodation amounting to one-half of the length of the order, with an equivalent period of supervision. This order, introduced by the Crime and Disorder Act 1998,[106] is discussed in more detail in due course. That Act conferred the power to extend the operation of this order to ten- and eleven-year-olds, but such powers has never been brought into effect.

Two other provisions should be noted. Section 90 of the Powers of Criminal Courts (Sentencing) Act 2000[107] provides that a person convicted of an offence who appears to the court to have been under the age of eighteen years at the time the offence was committed shall not, if he is convicted of murder, be sentenced to imprisonment for life, but instead the court must sentence him to be detained during Her Majesty's Pleasure. If he is sentenced in that way, he is detained in such place and under such conditions as the Home Secretary directs. Section 90(2) provides that where:

(a) a young person is convicted on indictment of any offence punishable in the case of an adult with imprisonment for fourteen years or more, not being an offence the sentence for which is fixed by law; or

(b) a child is convicted of manslaughter, and the court is of opinion that none of the other methods in which the case may legally be dealt with is suitable, the court may sentence the offender to be detained for such period (not exceeding the maximum term of imprisonment with which the offence is punishable in

---

[104] See, in particular, *The Consolidated Criminal Practice Direction (Amendment No 8) (Mandatory Life Sentences [2005] 1 Cr App R 8.*

[105] See p 641, *ante.*   [106] See now Powers of Criminal Courts (Sentencing) Act 2000, ss 100–107.

[107] Re-enacting Children and Young Persons Act 1933, s 53.

the case of an adult) as may be specified in the sentence. Where such a sentence has been passed, the child or young person will be liable to be detained in such place and on such conditions as the Home Secretary directs.

The second special provision is that contained in section 93 of the 2000 Act. This provides that where a person aged eighteen or over but under the age of twenty-one years is convicted of any offence other than murder for which a person aged twenty-one years or over would be liable to imprisonment for life, the court shall, if it considers that a custodial sentence for life would be appropriate, sentence him to custody for life.

F COMMUNITY SENTENCES

If an offence is serious enough to warrant the passing of a community sentence, but not so serious so as to require a custodial sentence, the court may pass such a sentence.

A community sentence is, now[108] a single sentence which can comprise one or more community orders.[109] These are as follows:

(1) Community rehabilitation order (formerly known as Probation): where an offender, aged not less than sixteen years, is placed under the supervision of a probation officer for a period not exceeding three years. Such an order may contain requirements to keep in touch with a supervising officer, for the general purpose of securing the rehabilitation of the offender and for the protection of the public from him.

(2) Community punishment orders (formerly known as Community Service Orders): where an offender, aged not less than sixteen years, is required to perform work in the community for periods not less than forty hours or not more than 240 hours;

(3) Community punishment and rehabilitation order (formerly known as a combination order): these are a combination of community rehabilitation and community punishment orders, which may be imposed on a person aged at least sixteen years. It is an order which requires the offender:
(a) to be under the supervision of a probation officer for a period not less than twelve months or more than three years, and
(b) to perform unpaid work for a specified number of hours, not less than forty or more than 100.

(4) Curfew orders: where the power to make a curfew order exists a court may impose on an offender aged sixteen or over requirements to remain at a

---

[108] Since the implementation of Criminal Justice Act 2003, s 147.
[109] Defined by Criminal Justice Act 2003, s 177.

particular place specified in the order for specified periods. The period of restriction must not be less than two hours nor more than twelve hours in any one day, and an order cannot extend beyond a period of six months. An order can include provisions relating to electronic monitoring.

(5) Supervision orders: used for the supervision of offenders under eighteen years of age.

(6) Attendance centre orders: where an offender aged at least ten but under twenty-one years is required to attend an attendance centre for a specified number of hours. The number of hours that may be imposed varies according to the age of the offender.

(7) Drug treatment and testing orders: where a court considers that a person, aged not less than sixteen at the date of conviction for an offence, is dependent on or has a propensity to misuse drugs, and his dependency is such as requires and may be susceptible to treatment, the court may make a drug treatment and testing order. Such an order may include requirements that the offender submit to treatment, with a view to reduce or eliminate the dependency or propensity. The idea behind these orders is that offenders should be both punished and rehabilitated within the community. The particular order or orders forming part of the sentence must be commensurate with the seriousness of the offence and other offences associated with it, and be the most suitable for the offender, although the scope of such orders has been extended to include the use of community service and attendance centre orders for fine default, despite the fact that the normal threshold for the imposition of a community order has not been reached. Further, a community service order or a curfew order may be made in respect of persistent petty offenders. There are certain limits as to which community orders can be combined. Such orders have historically been viewed as being dependent on the offender being willing to consent to the making of such an order. The consent of the offender to the making of a probation order or community service or supervision order is no longer required.

Changes were made to the legislative regime governing community orders by the Criminal Justice Act 2003 to allow different requirements to be imposed as considered necessary by the court to reflect offence seriousness or the measures necessary to address the causes of the offending. Amongst the matters that can be included are unpaid work requirements, activity requirements, a requirement to attend specific programmes designed to tackle offending behaviour or the causes of offending, impose curfews and prohibit activities, provide for a residence requirement, or an exclusion requirement, or a drug rehabilitation requirement.

Failure to comply with the requirements of a community order can result in the offender being punished, or being re-sentenced for the original offence.[110]

---

[110] For the enforcement regime, see Criminal Justice Act 2003, Schedule 8.

G FINES

A court may impose a fine in lieu of, or in addition to, dealing with him in any other way. Unless a limit is fixed by the statute prescribing the offence (as it will usually be in the case of matters tried summarily, there is no limit to the amount of the fine. The court is obliged to fix a period of imprisonment or detention in default of payment.

H ABSOLUTE AND CONDITIONAL DISCHARGES

Where a court thinks it inappropriate to pass any sentence, or make a probation order, it may discharge the offender either absolutely, without any condition, or subject to the condition that he does not commit any further offence for a period fixed by the court, not exceeding three years. If he commits another offence in that period he is liable to be sentenced for his original offence.

I COMPENSATION AND RESTITUTION

A court by or before which a person is convicted of an offence may, instead of or in addition to dealing with him in any other way, make an order requiring him to pay compensation for any personal injury, loss, or damage resulting from that offence (or any other offence which is taken into consideration).[111] Some 14 per cent of those sentenced in the magistrates' court and 7 per cent of those sentenced at the Crown Court are ordered to pay compensation, most usually to those who receive a non custodial sentence. In 2001, the average amount ordered to be paid was £144 in the magistrates' court and £1,444 at the Crown Court.[112]

No compensation order may be made in favour of the dependants of a deceased person in consequence of his death, nor in respect of injury, loss, or damage due to a road accident. In determining whether to make an order and the amount of such order the court must have regard to the offender's means. In practice the power to make compensation orders has been exercised somewhat sparingly. In particular, the Court of Appeal has repeatedly stated that no order should be made where it might result in the accused committing further offences in order to discharge his obligations; for this reason a substantial compensation order will not usually be appropriate where the offender is imprisoned since the need to discharge the order may hinder his rehabilitation on his release.[113]

---

[111] Powers of Criminal Courts (Sentencing) Act 2000, s 130.
[112] *Consultation Paper, op cit*, p 11.
[113] See *R v Oddy* [1974] 2 All ER 666, and the cases therein cited.

If there are subsequent civil proceedings, the damages are assessed without reference to the order, but the order is taken into account when enforcing the judgment.[114] Compensation is of such amount as the court considers appropriate, having regard to any evidence and to any representations made by or on behalf of the accused or the prosecutor.

In future[115] an offender may be liable to pay a surcharge. These provisions are part of a strategy to ensure that funds are contributed by offenders to resource measures designed to support victims of crime.[116] Such surcharges are likely to vary from £5 to £30, and to be regarded as separate and distinct from any fine imposed. Surcharges are also liable to be paid in respect of on-the-spot penalties issued for disorderly behaviour,[117] and in respect of repeat road traffic offences.[118] 'Repeat' for this purpose means a second or subsequent offence.

J MISCELLANEOUS ORDERS[119]

The principal sentences and orders the court has power to make have been considered above. There are, in addition, various other forms of order which may be made, detailed consideration of which is beyond the scope of this work. However, it may be noted that the Crown Court has, in addition to the powers detailed above, power to make orders for costs[120] either out of central funds or inter partes, orders depriving offenders of property used, or intended for use, for the purpose of crime, orders disqualifying an offender from holding or obtaining a licence to drive a motor vehicle, orders authorizing the admission to and detention in specified hospitals of offenders suffering from mental illness, psychopathic disorder, subnormality, or severe subnormality,[121] and recommendations for deportation.[122] Significant powers of confiscation and forfeiture also exist under the Drug Trafficking Offences Act 1986. Where the Crown Court imposes a fine, forfeits a recognizance or makes an order for costs, it may order the person concerned to be searched and any money found on him to be applied towards payment of the fine or other sum.

---

[114] 2000 Act, s 134.

[115] When the provisions of Domestic Violence Crime and Victims Act 2004, ss 14–16 are brought into force.

[116] See Chapter 18, *ante.*

[117] See Domestic Violence Crime and Victims Act 2004, s 15; Criminal Justice and Police Act 2001.

[118] 2004 Act, s 16.

[119] See generally Powers of Criminal Courts (Sentencing) Act 2000.

[120] *Practice Direction on Costs in Criminal Proceedings* [2004] 2 Cr App R 26.

[121] Mental Health Act 1983, s 37.   [122] Immigration Act 1971, s 6.

K RESTRAINING ORDERS

The power to make a restraining order whether on sentencing or even after a defendant has been acquitted has already been noted.[123] Restraining orders are made under the terms of section 5 of the Protection from Harassment Act 1997. The effect of section 12 of the Domestic Violence and Crime Act 2004 is to permit such an order to be made when a person is convicted if *any* offence. The order must be 'for the purpose of protecting the victim of then offence'. Such an order may well be appropriate where future conduct might involve stalking, burglary, or criminal damage. Such an order may even be made following acquittal, for the same purpose. That raises important questions of proof. When an individual has been convicted, evidence can be heard as part of the sentencing process. By contrast the acquittal is, technically, the end of the case. Nonetheless, a court will be entitled to receive evidence about the level of risk or danger for the future. Such proceedings will be civil in nature. By contrast, breach of a restraining order is a criminal offence.

---

[123] See p 666, *ante.*

23

APPEALS AND
MISCARRIAGES OF JUSTICE

A INTRODUCTION

If a defendant is convicted on indictment at the Crown Court his appeal lies, if at all, to the Court of Appeal (Criminal Division). Appeals from the decisions of the magistrates' court acting summarily, and from the Crown Court acting in its appellate capacity, lie to the Divisional Court of the Queen's Bench Division.

The role and powers of the Court of Appeal (Criminal Division) have been the subject of a great deal of debate in recent years,[1] largely generated by a series of cases where convictions have had to be overturned, often some years after conviction and subsequent appeal.[2] In particular, the question of when the court should be able to overturn a conviction, how it should treat fresh evidence, and whether it should have greater powers to order re-trials following an appeal, and whether the Court of Appeal should have the right to order a retrial of a defendant who has, in fact, been acquitted, have each been raised, and the subject of consideration by the Royal Commission on Criminal Justice[3] and the Auld Review.[4] However, it is important to remember that controversy about the criminal appellate system is not new.

1 THE DEVELOPMENT OF THE COURT OF APPEAL (CRIMINAL DIVISION)

Until 1907 there was, in fact, no right of appeal at all. Where points of law arose on trial on indictment the trial judge could, but was not obliged to, refer such points for consideration by a court known as the Court for Crown Cases Reserved. Not until the passage of the Criminal Appeal Act 1907 was a formal appellate system introduced, and that Act was passed largely in response to a miscarriage of justice caused by the mistaken identification of an accused.[5] The 1907 Act created the Court of Criminal Appeal, which was given powers to allow appeals against conviction if that conviction was unreasonable or could not be supported having regard to the evidence, or if there

---

[1] See O'Connor, 'The Court of Appeal: Re-Trials & Tribulations' [1990] Crim LR 615; JUSTICE Report on Miscarriages of Justice (1989).

[2] See e.g. *R v Maguire* [1992] QB 936, [1992] 2 All ER 433; *R v McIlkenny* [1992] 2 All ER 417.

[3] Cm 2263 (1993, HMSO).   [4] Op cit, Ch 9.   [5] The Adolph Beck case.

was a wrong decision on a question of law. No power to order a re-trial existed at that time. The Criminal Appeal Act 1964 created a power to order a new trial, although only on the ground of 'fresh evidence',[6] a restriction that was not removed until the passing of the Criminal Justice Act 1988.[7] By the Criminal Appeal Act 1966, the jurisdiction of the Court of Criminal Appeal was transferred to the Court of Appeal (Criminal Division).[8]

The whole of the pre-existing legislation was consolidated in the Criminal Appeal Act 1968. However, the powers of, and the use of such powers by, the Court of Appeal attracted considerable attention, and concern, as miscarriages of justice came to light. The Royal Commission on Criminal Justice therefore considered the powers and functions of the Court of Appeal (Criminal Division). The result was a government consultation paper, followed by the passage of the Criminal Appeal Act 1995. That Act, based on the recommendations of the Royal Commission, significantly amends the existing legislation.

Before looking at the substance of the powers themselves, three general points need to be remembered:

(a) The right of appeal has traditionally been that of the defendant, except in cases referred to the court by the Home Secretary.[9] The prosecution has had no right of appeal against acquittal, or against unfavourable legal rulings although there is a limited power for points of law, and lenient sentences to be referred to the Court of Appeal by the Attorney-General.[10] Major changes in that context have now been introduced.[11]

(b) The court's powers derive solely from statute. The court has no inherent or residual power which entitles it to fill gaps in the statutory provisions. Criticism can fairly be made of the statutory provisions, not only in the obvious cases where the court's role has been limited, but also in other areas where gaps in the appellate system exist.

(c) The recent controversies about the actions of the court must be viewed in the light of the overall function and role of the court. This is dealt with below.

2 THE ROLE OF THE COURT OF APPEAL

The Court has been at pains to stress the limits of its powers. In R v McIlkenny[12] Lloyd, Mustill and Farquharson LJJ in a joint judgment observed:

Under jury trial juries not only find the facts; they also apply the law. Since they are not experts in the law, they are directed as to the relevant law by the judge. But the task of applying the law to the facts, and so reaching a verdict, belongs to the jury and the jury

---

[6] Section 1, re-enacted in Criminal Appeal Act 1968, s 7.   [7] See p 693, *post.*
[8] Being one of two divisions of the Court of Appeal: Supreme Court Act 1981, s 3(1).
[9] See p 684, *post.*   [10] See p 687, post.   [11] See p 688, *post.*
[12] [1992] 2 All ER 417.

alone. The primacy of the jury in the English criminal justice system explains why, historic-ally, the Court of Appeal had so limited a function Since justice is as much concerned with the conviction of the guilty as the acquittal of the innocent, and the task of convicting the guilty belongs constitutionally to the jury, not to us, the role [of the Court] is necessarily limited. Hence it is true to say that whereas the Civil Division of the Court of Appeal has appellate jurisdiction in the full sense, the Criminal Division is perhaps more accurately described as a court of review.

The point has also cogently been made that not only is the Court subordinate to the jury; also the jury's role is itself limited.[13] It is not the task of the jury within the adversarial system to pronounce innocence or guilt, but rather whether it has been proved, according to law, that the accused is guilty as charged. For these reasons the Court of Appeal has considered itself constrained in dealing with appeals, particularly those based upon new evidence. The extent to which these constraints are justifiable, or in the public interest, is a matter for debate. The Royal Commission on Criminal Justice concluded that such considerations as to the role of the jury have too heavily influenced the Court, and that the Court of Appeal should be 'readier to overturn jury verdicts than it has shown itself in the past'.[14] In particular it should be more prepared to consider arguments that a jury has made a mistake, and to admit evidence that might favour a defendant even if it was, or could have been, available at the trial. It is debatable as to how far the various legislative changes will, in fact, result in a greater willingness by the Court of Appeal to follow a more liberal approach.

B THE GROUNDS OF APPEAL

1 APPEAL AGAINST CONVICTION

By section 1 of the Criminal Appeal Act 1968, a person convicted on indictment may appeal to the Court of Appeal:

(a) against his conviction, on any ground which involves a question of law alone;

(b) with the leave of the Court of Appeal, against his conviction on any ground which involves a question of fact alone, or a question of mixed law and fact, or any other ground which appears to the court to be a sufficient ground of appeal.

Where leave to appeal is required, it may be granted in the first instance by a single judge of the Court; if he refuses, the applicant may have his case considered by the Court itself.[15] This process excludes a large proportion of cases. The Royal Commis-sion found that the chances of success are distinctly higher where the defendant is represented. In this regard the Commission found uneven and unsatisfactory provision

---

[13] See p 520, *ante*.   [14] Report, Ch 10.   [15] Criminal Appeal Act 1968, s 31(3).

for the giving of legal advice on appeal, which is part of the professional duty of solicitor and counsel. Initial advice after the case on appeal is within the scope of criminal legal aid (99 per cent of cases within the Crown Court). The research also found misunderstandings about the powers of the Court regarding length of sentence. The Commission concluded that interpreter facilities should be made available by the Prison Service to facilitate the giving of advice to those who do not understand English. The present requirement to obtain leave should be kept, and legal aid extended to cover advice as to whether an application should be renewed.

The trial judge may also grant a certificate that the case is fit for appeal, on a question of fact or mixed law and fact. This should only be done where the trial judge is satisfied that there is a substantial point, and one worthy of consideration by the Court of Appeal.[16]

Nothing in the Act prevents an appeal against conviction in a case where the accused in fact pleaded guilty at his trial. However, an appeal in such circumstances will only succeed if: (i) the defendant did not appreciate the nature of the charge; or (ii) he did not intend to admit that he was guilty of it; or (iii) on the admitted facts, he could not in law have been guilty of the offence to which he pleaded guilty. Such cases are rare, but not unknown.[17] In *R v Boal*[18] the Court was prepared to entertain an appeal where the defendant had pleaded guilty as a result of advice based upon a misunderstanding of the law by his barrister.

2 APPEAL AGAINST SENTENCE

The defendant may appeal against the sentence passed on him after conviction unless the sentence is one fixed by law. Such an appeal requires the leave of a single judge, or, if refused, of the full court.[19] The appeal can be not only against the sentence, but also against any order that forms part of the sentence, such as a compensation order,[20] disqualification from driving, a binding over order,[21] or recommendation for deportation.[22] There is no right of appeal against a recommendation that a defendant convicted of murder should serve a certain number of years, because this is not a recommendation binding on the Home Secretary.[23] By contrast, if a judge makes an order, in respect of a discretionary life sentence, specifying what part of the sentence must expire before the offender is able to have his case referred to the Parole Board, this has legal consequences and would appear to be a matter which can be subject to an appeal.[24]

---

[16] *R v Eyles* (1963) 47 Cr App R 260; cf. *R v Smith* [1974] QB 354, [1974] 1 All ER 6.32.

[17] *R v Forde* [1923] 2 KB 400, at 403; *R v Gould* [1968] 2 QB 65 [1968] 1 All ER 849; cf. *R v Vickers* [1975] 2 All ER 945, [1975] 1 WLR 811.

[18] [1992] QB 591; [1992] 3 All ER 177.   [19] Criminal Appeal Act 1968, s 1.

[20] Se p 677, ante.   [21] *R v Williams* [1982] 3 All ER 1092, [1982] 1 WLR 1398.

[22] See the Criminal Appeal Act 1968, s 50(1), defining sentence to include 'any order made by a court when dealing with an offender'.

[23] *R v Aitken* [1966] 2 All ER 453n, [1966] 1 WLR 1076.

[24] See the terms of Criminal Justice Act 1991, s 34(2).

The prosecution also has the right to have the sentence of a court reviewed.[25] If it appears to the Attorney-General that the sentencing of a person in a proceeding in the Crown Court has been unduly lenient, in respect of an offence triable only on indictment (or such other offence as the Secretary of State may order) then, with leave of the Court of Appeal, the case may be referred to them for the sentence to be reviewed. The application must be made within twenty-eight days of the sentence being passed.[26]

Concern was expressed at the time this power was introduced that a defendant is in jeopardy twice.[27] The power to review granted by the Act is in respect of a sentence perceived to be unduly lenient, not simply in respect of a sentence with which the court disagrees. The power is used where the judge has erred as a matter of sentencing principle, and thus is a means of achieving consistent application of sentencing policy.[28]

3 CRIMINAL CASES REVIEW COMMISSION

Once the avenues of appeal outlined above have been exhausted then, unless a final appeal to the House of Lords is permitted, the one remaining formal option open to an accused is the making of an application to the Criminal Cases Review Commission. The Commission was established by the 1995 Act following consistent, and justified, criticism of the pre-existing system under section 17 of the 1968 Act whereby a convicted person might apply to the Home Secretary for his case to be referred back to the Court of Appeal, or whereby the Home Secretary might of his own motion refer back a case, on a point arising in a case.[29] This is what occurred in *R v Berry (No 2)*[30] where a finding on a point of law by the Court of Appeal led to that court quashing a conviction, the court not determining another ground of appeal that was before the court. On appeal to the House of Lords by the prosecution, the decision of the Court of Appeal was reversed. The Court of Appeal now being without jurisdiction to deal with this further point, the only way in which it could now be dealt with by the Court was for the Home Secretary to make a reference under section 17, which is in fact what occurred. Yet the approach of the Home Office was on the whole slow and cautious, showing 'too great a constitutional deference' to the Court of Appeal.[31]

The operation of section 17, and, generally the role of the Home Office, was considered by the Royal Commission on Criminal Justice.[32] It noted that the Royal Prerogative of mercy in respect of trials on indictment was 'seldom exercised,'[33] and it noted also that section 17 references were made in only a small proportion of the cases

---

[25] Introduced by Criminal Justice Act 1988, s 36.   [26] Criminal Justice Act 1988, Schedule 3.
[27] See p 602, *post*.   [28] For wider issues in this context, see p 659, *ante*.
[29] 1968 Act, s 17(1)(a).
[30] [1991] 2 All ER 789, [1991] 1 WLR 125; for the resulting decision, see *R v Berry* (3 April 1992, unreported).
[31] See Nobles and Schiff, 'The Criminal Cases Review Commission: Establishing a Workable Relationship with the Court of Appeal' [2005] Crim LR 173
[32] *Op cit*, Ch 11.   [33] Ibid, para 3.

of those brought to the attention of the Home Office by the parties, or by campaign-ing groups such as JUSTICE.[34] The restrictive nature of the test[35] used by the Home Secretary to decide whether a reference should be made had been identified by the May Committee,[36] which also criticized the Home Office for not being pro-active in miscarriage cases. References back were only made in cases where fresh evidence had emerged since the trial and appeal. The view of the May Committee that there was a need for change was supported by the Royal Commission. It recommended that the Home Secretary's power to make references under section 17 should be abolished. Instead, the role now performed by the Home Office should be given to an indepen-dent body, a new Criminal Cases Review Authority. This authority, to comprise both lawyers and lay persons, would oversee any further investigations needed into cases referred to it by complainants, although it would not appear to have powers to instigate investigations on its own motion.

This recommendation was accepted in principle. The result was the creation, by the 1995 Act, of the Criminal Cases Review Commission. At least one-third of the mem-bers of the Commission must be lawyers,[37] and two-thirds persons who have know-ledge or expertise of any part of the criminal justice system.[38] Members are appointed by the Crown on the advice of the Prime Minister,[39] and hold office for an initial term of five years, renewable only once. The Commissioners are aided by caseworkers, and have a general power to undertake, or to arrange the undertaking by others, of inquir-ies.[40] The number, and type of cases, can be discovered by looking at the Annual Reports for the Commission. In evaluating that work, it is worth observing that legal aid is not available to lawyers pursuing miscarriage cases, a significant gap, convicted persons therefore being highly dependent on the public spiritedness of lawyers under-taking what amounts to *pro bono* work (i.e. without payment).

(a) The use of the powers

The Annual Report for 2003–2004 is illustrative. The Commission received 885 cases, making a cumulative intake of 6,647 since it was established. It referred twenty-three convictions and four sentences to the Court of Appeal. On the conviction referrals, eight were for murder, seven for dishonesty, four for sexual offences, two for non-fatal violence two for drugs offences, one for manslaughter, one for possession of a firearm, and one for membership of a proscribed organization. Of the cases decided by the Court of Appeal following reference, nine convictions were upheld. Referral of murder cases shows the greatest proportion of appeals which are dismissed.[41] Where convic-tions are overturned, the most common reason was fresh evidence casting doubt on

---

[34] A campaigning organisation with a primary aim of investigation of, and campaigning against, miscar-riages of justice. See, in particular, JUSTICE, *Miscarriages of Justice*, 1989.

[35] Royal Commission Report, *op cit*, Ch 1.

[36] Established to report on the miscarriage of justice in the Guildford and Woolwich pub bombings cases.

[37] Criminal Appeal Act, s 8(5).   [38] Ibid, s 8(6).   [39] Ibid, s 8(4).

[40] Ibid, s 21.   [41] CCRC Annual Report 2003–2004, p 14.

the reliability of prosecution witnesses.[42] Flawed or doubtful expert evidence is also an issue, as demonstrated vividly in a series of case relating to deaths of babies.[43] The Commission observed:[44]

The reasons for referral have been diverse but a strong underlying theme can be identified. In most cases there has been fresh evidence casting doubt on the reliability of prosecution witnesses. Concerns were identified about the way in which original exhibits had been handled in a rape case. Doubt was raised about the original medical evidence in a shaken baby case.

Psychological evidence suggests that a confession was unreliable . . . In other cases, referral resulted from the identification of defects in the investigative or trial process . . . In four cases the applicant had pleaded guilty and in three of those cases there had been no previous appeal but the Commission decided there were exceptional grounds to justify referral. This illustrates the fact that event though there may be no new evidence, careful analysis of the facts and circumstances at the time of trial can provide compelling reasons for referral on the basis of new argument.

Although the Commission has the power to undertake inquiries, this is likely to be exceptional. Rather, the intention is that inquiries be carried out by the police under the supervision and instruction of the Commission, a position regarded as inevitable by the Royal Commission on Criminal Justice. The Review Commission has the power to require the original investigatory body to appoint an investigating officer to report back to the Commission,[45] or to appoint an investigator from another police force.[46]

(b) The criteria

The Commission takes over the powers formerly exercised by the Home Secretary under section 17 of the 1968 Act. The powers to refer cases (which now include convictions on summary trial) are contained in section 13 of the 1995 Act. Firstly, there must be a real possibility that a conviction would not be upheld if a reference were made. Secondly, the reason for this must be that an argument or evidence was not raised at trial or on appeal. Finally, an appeal must have been heard or leave to appeal refused. The second and third criteria are not absolutes: the Commission can, despite them, refer a case where exceptional circumstances exist.[47]

The judgment therefore required of the Commission is a difficult one, and it is theirs alone.[48] It involves a prediction of the view the Court of Appeal may take, which may in turn require the Commission to assess what attitude the Court will take on a fresh evidence application.[49] The key words are therefore '*real possibility*', because it is at best a judgment. The Commission has to make this judgment even though the

---

[42] See *R v Mills and Poole* (1978) 68 Cr App R 154; *R v Cooper and McMahon* [1969] 1 QB 267.
[43] *R v Cannings*, [2004] 2 Cr App R 7, *R v Clark*.   [44] CCCRC, Annual Report, op cit, p 18.
[45] Ibid, s 19.   [46] Ibid, s 2.
[47] Ibid, s 13(2) Perhaps a good example is the referral of the case of *Mills* (1978) 68 Cr App R 154.
[48] See *R v Criminal Cases Review Commission, ex parte Pierson* (1999).
[49] For the powers of the Court of Appeal, see p 689, *post*.

criteria applied by the Court include a power to hear evidence when it is necessary or expedient in the interests of justice to do so.[50] One good example of the interrelationship between Commission and Court of Appeal is *R v Mills and Poole*.[51] In that case the Commission had decided not to refer a case following a libel case where a detective whose testimony was crucial was disbelieved. The Commission did so because it considered that the facts, which had been thoroughly examined at trial and on appeal, had not changed. On judicial review of the Commission's refusal the Divisional Court accepted the propriety of the Commission's decision but nonetheless invited a reference. That was duly made, and the Court of Appeal did not regard the situation as unfair, but quashed the conviction for a previously undiscovered legal error.

If the Commission decides to make a reference, then the case returns to the Court of Appeal to be dealt with in the normal way. The appeal may not be on any ground other than one related to reasons given by the Commission for making the reference.[52] There are no legal obstacles to old cases being referred. Cases have been referred that go back many years,[53] although the utility of referring old cases has been criticized, both judicially and extra-judicially.

The Court has the power itself to refer a case to the Commission for investigation and report.[54] Eleven such referrals have been made since the establishment of the Commission,[55] and the work of the Commission is likely to increase that allows Court referrals at the stage of application of leave to appeal, rather than simply at the appeal itself.[56] For that reason, the changes made by the 1995 Act to the powers of the Court are just as important as the creation of the Commission itself. If the Commission decides not to make a reference, it is required to state the reasons why it has so decided.[57]

4 REFERENCE FOLLOWING ACQUITTAL

The prosecution does not have any right to appeal against acquittal, unlike the position in cases of summary trial. However, the Criminal Justice Act 1972[58] gives to the prosecution a limited right to have points of law which arose during a trial resulting in an acquittal reconsidered by the Court of Appeal. The nature of the procedure is that of a reference of a point of law, rather than an appeal, for the outcome of the reference has no effect on the acquittal in the case.

---

[50] See, generally, powers of the Court.

[51] See [1998] 1 Cr App R 43, [2001] EWCA Crim 753, [2004] 1 Cr App R 7.

[52] Criminal Appeal Act 1965, s 14(4A) inserted by Criminal Justice Act 2003, s 315. This followed a case where the appeal went far beyond the reference: see *R v Day* [2003] EWCA Crim 1060.

[53] See, e.g., *R v Mattan Times*, 5 March 1998; *R v Hanratty* [2002] 2 Cr App R 30; *Ellis* [2003] EWCA Crim 3556; *Knighton* [2002] EWCA Crim 2227 (a seventy-five year-old conviction).

[54] Ibid, s 15.   [55] CCRC Annual Report, 2003–2004, p 46.

[56] See Criminal Justice Act 2003, s 315.

[57] Ibid, s 14(6). See, generally, *R v Secretary of State for the Home Department, ex parte Hickey (No 2)* [1995] 1 All ER 490, [1995] 1 WLR 734.

[58] 1972 Act, s 36(1).

The Act and the rules made hereunder go to great length to protect the acquitted person. Not only is his acquittal unaffected, he may appear to present argument in the Court of Appeal, is entitled to be represented by counsel, and have his costs paid out of central funds. His identity must not be disclosed during the proceedings in the Court of Appeal except by his consent.

The purpose of the power is to enable clarification of points of law which are important, and before wrong interpretations of law become entrenched at trial court level. The Court may, of its own motion or on application, refer the point to the House of Lords.

5 PROSECUTION RIGHTS OF APPEAL

Although defendants have many rights of appeal, the prosecutor has had only the extremely limited rights noted above. The position differed somewhat in the case of summary trial, where there has always been the power to apply to the High Court by way of case stated,[59] a right exercisable both by defence and the prosecution. That lack of a general means whereby the prosecution could seek recourse to appeal courts to correct legal error has been the subject of increasing concern. The Law Commission in 2001 observed:[60]

If a case falls on legal argument it is better for public confidence in the criminal justice system that it should be susceptible to the second opinion of a higher court, than it be unappealable.

The Auld Review likewise regarded the position as unsatisfactory.[61] It recommended that the prosecution should have three new rights: appeals from preparatory hearings against potentially terminating rulings; then a right to appeal against an acquittal resulting from a terminating ruling up to the end of the prosecution case; and a right of appeal against a finding of no case to answer. Those recommendations form for the basis of provisions in Part 9 of the Criminal Justice Act 2003. They apply to trials on indictment.

The general right of prosecution appeal in respect of rulings, subject to the leave of the trial judge or the Court of Appeal, are contained in section 58 of the 2003 Act. Section 58 does not use the expression 'terminating rulings', but it is such matters which section 58 is intended to address. The Solicitor-General in debate, put the matter graphically by observing:[62]

A terminating ruling is like an elephant. One can recognize it when it comes lumbering through the doors of the court. If it looks like a terminal ruling it is appealable.

The type of matters that are likely to 'lumber through the door' are matters which are so fatal to the prosecution case, and mean that it cannot, effectively, succeed. This

---

[59] Magistrates' Courts Act 1980, s 111. This is not technically an appeal but a review on certain grounds.
[60] *Double Jeopardy and Prosecution Appeals* Law Com No 267, 2001.
[61] Auld Review, *op cit*, Ch 12, paras 47–65.   [62] HC Cmtte, 25 February 2003.

might include stays for abuse of process,[63] a successful argument of *autrefois acquit* or *autrefois convict*;[64] a successful submission of no case to answer;[65] an adverse public interest immunity ruling;[66] or a ruling that the facts alleged disclose no offence known to English law. The effect of this power may be that a trial has to adjourn whilst the appeal is dealt with, presumably as a matter of some urgency.

A second prosecution right of appeal is in respect of evidentiary rulings, defined by section 62(2) as such rulings that significantly weaken the prosecution case. These need not be rulings that effectively are 'terminating' and thus fall within section 58.

C POWERS OF THE COURT

1 POWER TO QUASH A CONVICTION

The powers to quash a conviction are contained in section 2 of the 1968 Act. In its original form, section 2 set out three grounds, which were not mutually exclusive. These were as follows:

(a) under all the circumstances of the case the conviction[67] is unsafe and unsatisfactory;

(b) there was a wrong decision on a point of law;

(c) there was a material irregularity in the course of the trial.

In addition, section 2 contained a proviso. The Court of Appeal might, on an appeal against conviction, dismiss the appeal, even though of the opinion that the point raised might be decided in favour of the appellant, if it is considered that no miscarriage of justice has actually occurred. The test is whether a reasonable jury, after a proper summing-up, could have failed to convict the appellant:[68] in other words, the Court was putting itself in the place of the jury. It was often applied where there has been misdirection on a matter of law.

The relationship between the proviso and the powers contained in section 2(1) of

---

[63] See p 538, *ante*.   [64] See p 602, *ante*.

[65] In such a situation, the procedure to be adopted is dealt with by 2003 Act, s 58(7).

[66] See p 577, *ante*.

[67] 'Conviction' was substituted for 'verdict of the jury' by the Criminal Law Act 1977, s 44. The previous wording appeared to preclude an appeal if the accused pleaded guilty, unless the count to which the accused pleaded guilty disclosed no offence known to the law or (perhaps) on the admitted facts he could not in point of law have been guilty of the offence; this, presumably erroneous, drafting in the 1968 Act went judicially unnoticed until *Director of Public Prosecutions v Shannon* [1975] AC 717; *sub nom R v Shannon* [1974] 2 All ER 1009, in which case Lord Salmon drew attention to the need for some amendment to s 2(1) of the 1968 Act.

[68] *Stirland v Director of Public Prosecutions* [1944] AC 315, [1944] 2 All ER 13; see also (among many cases) *R v Haddy* [1944] KB 442, [1944] 1 All ER 319. For the proper attitude to application of the proviso in a murder case, see *Anderson v R* [1972] AC 100, [1971] 3 All ER 768.

the 1968 Act discussed was complex. If the conviction is found to be unsafe or unsatisfactory under section 2(1)(c) there was no room for the exercise of the proviso. In relation to the other grounds, the Court of Appeal in *R* v *Maguire*[69] equated the 'no miscarriage of justice' test in the proviso with whether the conviction could be regarded as safe or satisfactory:

If the court is unable to hold that 'no miscarriage of justice has actually occurred' in a case of irregularity then the conviction is not safe. If it does so hold then the court is effectively saying that the conviction is safe and satisfactory.

For this reason it has been argued that there was really only one test that the court should apply in deciding the use of section 2(1): has there been a miscarriage of justice?[70]

The majority of the Royal Commission took the view:[71]

(1) if a conviction was safe despite an error, then the appeal should be dismissed;

(2) if an error was made that rendered the conviction unsafe, then the conviction should be quashed;

(3) if an error may render a conviction unsafe, then the conviction should be quashed and a re-trial ordered. This would render the proviso redundant.

The majority also took the view that this should be the case even where appeals are based upon pre-trial malpractice or procedural irregularity. It is not the purpose of the appellate process to discipline the police or prosecution—the judge will have excluded tainted evidence anyway.

These arguments have not entirely disappeared as a result of the changes in the law made by the 1995 Act. That Act introduces a new section 2, containing a single test. The proviso is abolished. Henceforth, the test is this: the Court must allow an appeal against conviction if they think that the conviction is unsafe. This formulation should be compared with the recommendation of the Royal Commission that the single ground be 'the conviction is or may be unsafe'.[72] The difference in wording may in fact be of little consequence, in the light of the tests adopted by the courts to the question as to whether a conviction is unsafe, and in the light of parliamentary intent. The wording of the original section 2 ('unsafe or unsatisfactory') was considered by the House of Lords in *Stafford* v *Director of Public Prosecutions*,[73] where Viscount Dilhorne cited with approval a passage from the judgment of the court in *R* v *Cooper*.[74]

The court must in the end ask itself a subjective question, whether we are content to let the matter stand as it is, or whether there is not some lurking doubt in our minds which makes us wonder whether an injustice has been done. This is a reaction which may not be based

---

[69] [1992] QB 936, [1992] 2 All ER 433.   [70] See O'Connor, *op cit* at [1990] Crim LR 615.
[71] Report, *op cit*, Ch 10, para 38.   [72] Ibid, para 46.
[73] 1974] AC 878, [1973] 3 All ER 762.
[74] [1969] 1 QB 267, at 271, [1969] 1 All ER 32, at 34, per Widgery LJ (as he then was).

strictly on the evidence as such; it is a reaction that can be produced by the general feeling of the case as the court experiences it to be.

The Royal Commission received conflicting evidence about the application of this 'lurking doubt' approach. Research indicated that between 1968–89 only six cases applied the test, and in 1989 one out of 114 appeals. Yet the more recent research for the years 1991–92 showed a greater use of this power (fourteen out of 102).[75] However the language of lurking doubt was not always used by the Court. For the Court to conclude that a verdict was unsatisfactory because of an injustice in the case and in the verdict was no different from an application of the 'lurking doubt' test. Nevertheless, the Court in *R v Maguire*[76] stressed that it is the words of the Act that have to be applied, not some other reformulation of the question. Despite the fact that the word 'or' was used, the weight of authority suggests that 'unsafe' and 'unsatisfactory' in fact were regarded as bearing the same meaning.[77] This was a view supported by the Royal Commission. On this basis, the change in wording in section 2 does not change or limit the scope of the role of the Court.[78] Not only will the Court be able to interfere where the verdict of the jury is unsatisfactory on the evidence, but also on the various other grounds relating to errors of law, misdirections, and the like which underpinned the majority of successful appeals. Errors in summing up, misdirection on matters of law, a failure in appropriate cases to withdraw the case from the jury are all instances where section 2(1) (a) operate and will continue to do so. The unsafeness of the conviction may have arisen because of the way the case was conducted. In respect of appeals based upon error by lawyers, the test identified in *R v Ensor*[79] was whether injustice had been suffered as a result of flagrantly incompetent advocacy. This was, in the view of the Royal Commission,[80] too narrow:

It cannot possibly be right that there should be defendants serving prison sentences for no other reason than that their lawyers made a decision which later turns out to have been mistaken. What matters is not the degree to which the lawyers were at fault, but whether the particular decision, whether reasonable or unreasonable, caused a miscarriage of justice.

A wide variety of errors, usually of a procedural nature, may cause a conviction to be unsafe. These might include unfair conduct or undue interruption by the judge, improper disclosure to the jury of the defendant's character, tampering with a juror, misconduct on the part of a juror and failure to inform an undefended person of his right to call witnesses. In *R v Maguire*[81] it was held that a failure to comply with the requirements concerning disclosure of unused material amounted to a 'material irregularity'.

One area of uncertainty that remains are cases where a conviction for an offence, other than that for which the accused was tried, is upheld on appeal by virtue of the

---

75 Report, Ch 10 para 43.   76 *R v Maguire* [1992] QB 936, [1992] 2 All ER 433.

77 See O'Connor, op cit, n 1, p 546, *ante*; cf. Smith, 'The Criminal Appeal Act 1995' [1995] Crim LR 920.

78 See Smith, op cit, at p 924, as to parliamentary intent.

79 1989] 2 All ER 586, [1989] 1 WLR 497.   80 Report, para 59.

81 [1992] QB 936, [1992] 2 All ER 433.

proviso. One such case was R v *Pickford*[82] where the accused had pleaded guilty to an offence that, in law, he could not have committed as charged. The Court of Appeal upheld the conviction, applying the proviso, on the grounds that although the appellant had not in law committed the offence charged (incitement of a boy to commit incest with the boy's mother) he had in fact incited the mother to commit the incest (which was in law an offence). It is unclear as to whether this type of case is no longer good law on the grounds that the proviso has been abolished, or whether such a conviction would be regarded as 'safe'. The fact that the Court felt constrained to use the proviso provides clear evidence that such a conviction cannot be regarded as 'safe'.

It might also be noted that the conclusion that a conviction is 'unsafe' does not necessarily reflect on the trial process itself. In R v *B*[83] a conviction for sexual assault was overturned even though the trial had been conducted perfectly properly, because it had taken thirty years for the complainant to make the allegation.

2 POWER TO SUBSTITUTE AN ALTERNATIVE VERDICT

Where the defendant has been convicted of an offence and (1) the jury could on the same indictment have found him guilty of some other offence; and (2) it appears to the Court of Appeal that the jury must have been satisfied of the facts proving him guilty of that other offence, the Court may, instead of allowing or dismissing the appeal against conviction, substitute a verdict of guilty of that other offence and pass sentence on the defendant for it.[84] The sentence must not be greater than that passed on the defendant at the trial, and must not, of course, exceed the maximum permitted by law for the substituted offence.[85] The Court exercises this power with care, particularly in the light of (2) above, which involves some consideration of a verdict of a jury for which no reasons are given. Further, it is a material, though not decisive, point against exercising the power if the jury were not given any direction as to the alternative offence.[86] Where the indictment contains counts for two offences (such as theft and handling) which are in the circumstances alternative to each other, and the jury convict of one but acquit of the other, the court cannot substitute a verdict of guilty of the latter, even if that seems the correct verdict, since the jury expressly acquitted. The proper course, if there is a conviction on one, is for the jury to be discharged from giving a verdict on the other whereupon the Court of Appeal may substitute a verdict of guilty.[87] This may also be important from the point of view of a re-trial.

---

[82] [1995] 1 Cr App R 420. For other authorities in similar vein, see R v *Boal* [1992] QB 591; R v *Ayres* (1984) 78 Cr App R 232; R v *McHugh* (1976) 64 Cr App R 92.

[83] [2003] EWCA Crim 319.   [84] Criminal Appeal Act 1968, s 3(1).   [85] Ibid, s 3(2).

[86] See, generally, R v *Caslin* [1961] 1 All ER 246, [1961] 1 WLR 59. This case was decided under the corresponding provisions of the Criminal Appeal Act 1907, but appears still to be good law.

[87] R v *Melvin and Eden* [1953] 1 QB 481, [1953] 1 All ER 294.

3 POWER TO RECEIVE FRESH EVIDENCE AND TO ORDER A NEW TRIAL

The power to receive fresh evidence was contained in the 1907 Act, and is now to be found in section 23 of the 1968 Act, as now amended by the Criminal Appeal Act of 1995. This section contains both a duty and discretion. Originally worded in a restrictive way, which set too high a threshold,[88] section 23 was amended by the 1995 Act, Section 23(2) creates *a right* to admit fresh evidence (i.e. evidence not adduced at the trial) if they think it necessary or expedient in the interests of justice. It imposes a *duty* to do so if:

(a) the evidence is likely to be credible, and would have been admissible at the trial; and

(b) there is a reasonable explanation for the evidence not being adduced at trial.

Thus the intent of the change is that the Court now, when considering the exercise of the duty has to consider whether such evidence is capable of being believed without having to take a view as to whether, on the facts, it is likely to be so. The Court may decline to receive such evidence if it is satisfied that the evidence, if received, would not afford any ground for allowing the appeal.[89]

As noted, by section 23 (1) the Court has a discretion to admit the evidence of any witness or document if it thinks it necessary or expedient in the interests of justice to do so. It may be thought curious to have a discretion that in fact allows the Court to by-pass the more detailed criteria in section 23(2). That, though, simply reflects the basic role of the Court of Appeal in the criminal justice system, namely to ensure fairness and justice. It does, though, make the role of the Criminal Cases Review Commission more difficult in trying to predict how the Court of Appeal will deal with any particular case.[90] In this situation the evidence does not have to satisfy the criteria in section 23(2) of not being tendered at the trial. An example of the use of this discretion was seen in *R v Lattimore*,[91] where some of the evidence was in fact given at the trial, and all of it was in fact available. It was allowed to be heard because it cast doubt upon the confession evidence upon which the prosecution case largely depended. The Court will only exceptionally allow the discretion to be used as a means of different defences being put forward at the appellate stage. In *R v Ahluwalia*[92] the Court, exceptionally, allowed fresh medical evidence to be adduced to support a defence of diminished responsibility to the charge of murder of the appellant's husband, a defence which had not been raised at trial, an approach that did not reflect the balance of earlier authority[93] but which demonstrates the concern of the Court to ensure that any conviction is in fact safe. Although the Court warned against running

---

[88] And which required the evidence to be 'likely to be credible'.

[89] Criminal Appeal Act 1968, s 23(2).   [90] See p 686, *ante*.   [91] (1975) 62 Cr App R 53.

[92] [1992] 4 All ER 889.

[93] See *R v Dodd* (1971, Unreported); *R v Melville* [1976] 1 WLR 181; *R v Straw* [1995] 1 All ER 187 (decided in 1987, but not reported until 1995).

defences on appeal that had not been advanced at trial, the particular facts were such as to justify the course in fact taken.

Appeals on the grounds of fresh evidence used to be relatively rare, but of increasing importance given the role of the Criminal Cases Review Commission, and the nature of the cases it handles.[94] The case law has continued to demonstrate the real problems the courts fact in this area in deciding whether to admit the evidence, how to evaluate it, what judgments to make, whether to quash a conviction, and whether or not to order a retrial. The power to order a new trial was first introduced in 1964.[95] The Court may order a new trial if it considers that the interests of justice so require.[96] This power to order re-trial is not now confined to fresh evidence cases.[97] The power to order re-trials is at the heart of the debate as to how cases where fresh evidence comes to light should be dealt with. It was argued by Lord Devlin[98] that a conviction should always be quashed where fresh evidence has been received, since a conviction is bound to be unsafe or unsatisfactory if not based on all the evidence. That, though, is not the approach of the courts. In *Stafford* v *Director of Public Prosecutions*[99] the House of Lords considered that the verdict should be quashed if the Court itself considers the verdict to be unsafe or unsatisfactory, thus requiring the Court to take a view of the effect of the fresh evidence tendered. This approach was criticized as restricting the use of the re-trial powers,[100] but was considered in is affirmed as correct in the leading recent authority, the definitive re-statement of the law by the House of Lords in *R* v *Pendleton*.[101]

In *R* v *McIlkenny*[102] the Court of Appeal had described its approach as follows:

Nor is there any difficulty in fresh evidence cases, where the fresh evidence is discovered soon after the trial. If the evidence is incredible, or inadmissible, or would not afford a ground for allowing the appeal, we decline to receive it. If the fresh evidence surmounts that preliminary hurdle, we first quash the conviction, if we think it unsafe or unsatisfactory, and then order a retrial if the interests of justice so require. Where new evidence is conclusive, we quash the conviction without ordering a retrial. The difficulty becomes acute when there is no contest. For then we have to make up our minds whether the convictions are unsafe or unsatisfactory without having the benefit of having the evidence tested by cross-examination. Where a retrial is still possible, the quashing of the conviction is only the first half of a two stage process. Where a retrial is no longer possible, it is the end of the road.

Some ten years later the approach of the House of Lords in *Pendleton* was very much the same. If the Court is sure of innocence it should quash the conviction. If it is sure of guilt it should uphold the conviction. In less clear-cut cases it should ask itself the question: what might have been the effect of this evidence on the jury? The Court of Appeal should be aware that the primary decision maker is the jury, and that it may

---

[94] See p 684, *ante*.   [95] Criminal Appeal Act 1964, s 1.

[96] Criminal Appeal Act 1968 ss 7–8.

[97] See 1968 Act, s 7, amended by Criminal Justice Act 1988.

[98] See Royal Commission on Criminal Justice, Report, op cit, Ch 10, para 62.

[99] [1974] AC 898, [1973] 3 All ER 762.   [100] See Royal Commission, ibid, at para 66.

[101] [2002] 1 All ER 72.   [102] [1992] 2 All ER 417.

have an incomplete understanding of the full process that led the jury to convict. The Court of Appeal can make its own assessment, but it would usually be wise to test that assessment against the question: if the evidence had been tendered at trial, might reasonably it be thought that the conclusion would have been affected.

What is clear is that the courts, now, take the view that its discretion cannot be fettered by inflexible mechanistic rules.[103] The Court is also more likely to be generous in cases of expert medical evidence.[104]

4 *VENIRE DE NOVO*

The appeal court has always had the power to order a *venire de novo* where proceedings in the court of trial were so defective as to amount to a nullity. To the defendant this no doubt seems very like ordering a new trial, but strictly the Court is ordering not a new trial but a proper one. It has not, unfortunately, been established what degree of irregularity suffices to render proceedings a nullity; there are only particular examples in the cases of proceedings which have been held to be a nullity. This has been held to be so where the judge at the trial was not properly qualified,[105] where the defendant specifically asked for but was denied his right of peremptory challenges,[106] or where a plea of not guilty was misheard and dealt with as a plea of guilty.[107]

5 HOSPITAL ORDERS

The Court has certain powers to consider whether a hospital order was rightly made, and in some circumstances can substitute a verdict of guilty for an offence which was charged at the trial, of which the defendant could have been convicted, for the special verdict of not guilty by reason of insanity or against a finding of unfitness to plead reached at the trial.[108]

D APPEALS AGAINST SENTENCE

On an appeal against sentence the court may reduce the sentence, or may vary it, by substituting one form of detention for another. The Court will interfere with a sentence where it is 'wrong in principle', an approach that applies also to references made by the Attorney-General. Where the sentence is against conviction only there is no power to interfere with the sentence in any way. Nor, except on an Attorney-General's reference, has the Court the power to increase sentence, a power that once existed but was rarely used.

---

103 See *R* v *Mackerney and Pinfold* [2003] EWCA Crim 3643.
104 *R* v *O'Brian*, 2000, unreported.   105 *R* v *Cronin* [1940] 1 All ER 618.
106 But no such right now exists: see p 332, *ante*.   107 *R* v *Scothern* [1961] Crim LR 326.
108 See p 598, *ante*.

E PROCEDURE

Under section 9(d) and (e) of the Criminal Appeal Act 1907 the Court had the power to appoint a special commissioner to conduct an inquiry into documents and to appoint assessors where their special expert knowledge was likely to be required for the determination of a case. These powers were little, if ever used, and not re-enacted by the 1968 Act. The Royal Commission considered that the Court of Appeal is not well constituted to supervise or direct police or other investigations. Nor should the same body exercise judicial and investigatory functions.[109]

As noted above, some appeals to the Court may be brought without leave, but in most cases there must be an application to the Court itself for leave. The time limit for giving notice of appeal, or application for leave to appeal, is twenty-eight days from the date of conviction or sentence. This time may be extended by the Court. Such application is made in the first instance to a single judge of the Court, who considers it in private. A single judge has most of the powers of a Court of three judges (besides, of course, the power to grant leave); exceptionally he does not have any of the powers relating to fresh evidence. An application may of course be abandoned, and notice of abandonment cannot be withdrawn although it may be treated as a nullity if the abandonment was not the result of a deliberate and informed decision in the sense that 'the mind of the appellant did not go with his act of abandonment.'[110] For example, where an application for leave to appeal was granted but, because of a postal strike, was not communicated to the applicant before he gave notice of abandonment, he was permitted to withdraw his notice.[111] If the single judge refuses leave to appeal (or to exercise any other of his powers) the applicant may be considered by a Court of two judges. Both the single judge and the Court may grant legal aid and bail. Bail, for obvious reasons, is very rarely granted; indeed almost the only cases where it will be granted are where the defendant has obtained (or does not need) leave to appeal and has a very good chance of succeeding on appeal, or where the defendant has been given a comparatively short sentence after a long and complex trial. In the latter case he might otherwise have served much of his sentence before the appeal was heard.

F APPEAL TO THE HOUSE OF LORDS

A further appeal lies by either prosecution or defence from the Court of Appeal (Criminal Division) to the House of Lords if:

(1) the Court of Appeal certifies that a point of law of general public importance is involved in the decision; and

---

[109] Report, *op cit*, Ch 11, para 11.   [110] *R v Medway* [1976] QB 799.

[111] *R v Noble* [1971] 3 All ER 361.

(2) either the Court of Appeal or the House of Lords gives leave to appeal on the ground that the point is one which ought to be considered by the House.

The certificate was considered a necessary condition, to avoid the House of Lords being inundated with hopeless applications. This justification was not accepted by the Royal Commission, which recommended its abolition.[112] If the Court of Appeal is satisfied that there is a point of law of general public importance involved it will give the certificate, as it were, automatically. There will always, nevertheless, be an element of discretion as to whether an appeal is allowed to proceed, since even if the point were of general public importance it might still not be worthy of consideration by the House of Lords in the particular case; for example it might already be the subject of clear and satisfactory decisions of lower courts. This element of discretion is preserved by the requirement that there can be no further proceedings. On the other hand, the Court of Appeal may give a certificate and yet refuse leave, in which case a petition may be made to the House of Lords for leave to appeal, the petition being heard by the Appeals Committee of the House.

It is proper and convenient that the certificate should state what the point of law of general public importance is;[113] however, it seems likely that other points may be raised by either side once the case is before the House of Lords on the point certified.[114] However, the grant of a certificate on some point affecting the validity of the conviction does not enable the appellant to argue that the sentence is invalid. The House of Lords may exercise similar powers to those of the court below.

The procedure described above does not apply following the hearing of an Attorney-General's reference after acquittal. In these cases the Court of Appeal may of its own motion or in pursuance of an application refer the point of law in the case to the House of Lords 'if they appear to the court that the point ought to be considered by that House' and there is, accordingly, no need for a certificate that a point of law of general public importance is involved. Indeed the point of law need not be a point of general public importance, although no doubt the Court of Appeal would only refer such a point to the House as a matter of practice.

112 Report, *op cit*, Ch 10, para 79.
113 *Jones* v *Director of Public Prosecutions* [1962] AC 635, [1962] 1 All ER 569.
114 *A-G for Northern Ireland* v *Gallagher* [1963] AC 349, [1961] 3 All ER 299.

SELECTED READING

BOOks

ADLER and GULLAND, *Tribunal Users' Experiences, Perceptions and Expectations: A Literature Review* (Council on Tribunals: 2003)

ALLEN, *Law in the Making* (Oxford University Press: 7th edn, 1966)

ALSTON, HEENAN and BUSTELO, *The EU and Human Rights* (Oxford University Press: 1999)

ANDREWS, *English Civil Procedure* (Oxford University Press: 2003)

ASHWORTH, *Sentencing and Criminal Justice* (Butterworths: 3rd edn, 2000)

ASHWORTH, *Sentencing and Penal Policy* (Wiedenfeld and Nicholson: 1983)

ASHWORTH, *The Criminal Process: An Evaluation Study* (Oxford University Press: 2nd edn, 1998)

BAKER, *An Introduction to English Legal History* (Butterworths: 4th edn, 2002)

BALDWIN and McCONVILLE, *Jury Trials* (Clarendon Press: 1979)

BELL, *Anti-Discrimination Law and the European Union* (Oxford University Press: 2002)

BORRIE and LOWE, *The Law of Contempt* (Butterworths: 3rd edn, 1996)

BRIDGES, CHOONGH and McCONVILLE, *Ethnic-Minority Defendants and the Right to Elect Jury Trial* (Commission for Racial Equality: 2000)

CARD and WARD, *Criminal Procedure and Investigations Act 1996* (Jordans: 1996)

Citizens' Advice, *Geography of Advice* (Citizen's Advice: 2004)

CLAYTON and TOMLINSON, *The Law of Human Rights* (Oxford University Press: 2000)

CORNISH, *The Jury* (Penguin: 1970)

CRAIG and DE BÚRCA, *EU Law: Text, Cases and Materials* (Oxford University Press: 3rd edn, 2003)

DENNIS, *The Law of Evidence* (Sweet & Maxwell: 2nd edn, 2003)

DEVLIN, *Trial By Jury* (Stevens & Sons: 1956)

DICEY, *Introduction to the Study of the Law of the Constitution* (Macmillan: 10th edn, 1959)

ENGLISH and CARD, *Butterworth's Police Law* (Butterworths: 8th edn, 2003)

FAIRHURST and VINCENZI, *Law of the European Community* (Longman: 4th edn, 2003)

FENWICK, *Civil Liberties and Human Rights* (Cavendish: 3rd edn, 2002)

GARDNER, *Aspects of Incorporation of the European Convention on Human Rights* (British Institute of International and Comparative Law: 1993)

General Council of the Bar and the Law Society of the United Kingdom, *Civil Justice on Trial: The Case for Change Report* (General Council: 1993)

GENN and GENN, *The Effectiveness of Representation at Tribunals* (Lord Chancellor's Department: 1989)

GENN, *Paths to Justice* (Hart: 1997)

GOMIEN, HARRIS and ZWAAK, *Law and Practice of the European Convention on Human Rights and the European Social Charter* (Council of Europe: 1996)

GRIFFITH, *The Politics of the Judiciary* (Fontana: 5th edn, 1997)

HARRIS, O'BOYLE and WARBRICK, *Law of the European Convention on Human Rights* (Butterworths: 1995)

HART, *The Concept of Law* (Clarendon Press: 1961)

HARTLEY and CLAYTON, *The Foundations of European Community Law* (Oxford University Press: 5th edn, 2003)

HEWART, Lord Chief Justice, *The New Despotism* (Benn: 1929)

HOLLAND and SPENCER, *Without Prejudice? Sex Equality at the Bar and in the Judiciary* (TMS Management Consultants: 1992)

HUGHES, *The Circuit Bench: A Women's Place* (1991)

JACKSON, *The Machinery of Justice in England* (Cambridge University Press: 8th edn, 1989)

JACONELLI, *Open Justice: A Critique of the Public Trial* (Oxford University Press: 2002)

JANIS, KAY and BRADLEY, *European Human Rights Law: Text and Materials* (Oxford University Press: 2nd edn, 2000)

JASON-LLOYD, *Quasi Policing* (Cavendish: 2003)

JOWELL and COOPER (eds), *Understanding Human Rights Principles* (JUSTICE: 2001)

KENNEDY, *Eve Was Framed: Women and British Justice* (Vintage: 1992)

LEE, *Elements of Roman Law* (Sweet & Maxwell: 4th edn, 1986)

LEWIS, *Lord Hailsham: A Life* (Pimlico: 1997)

LOUGHLIN and GERLIS, *Civil Procedure* (Cavendish: 2nd edn, 2004)

LUSTGARTEN, *The Governance of the Police* (Sweet & Maxwell: 1986)

MAITLAND, *The Forms of Action at Common Law* (Cambridge University Press: 1948)

MALLESON, *The New Judiciary: The Effects of Expansion and Activism* (Aldershot: 1999)

McCABE and PURVES, *The Shadow Jury at Work* (Oxford University Penal Research Unit: 1974)

MILLER, *Contempt of Court* (Oxford University Press: 3rd edn, 2000)

MILSOM, *Historical Foundations of the Common Law* (Butterworths: 2nd edn, 1981)

MOORHEAD, SHERR and ROGERS, *Willing Blindness? OSS Complaints Handling Procedures* (Law Society: 2000)

MORGAN and RUSSELL, *The Judiciary in the Magistrates' Courts* (Home Office: 2000)

MOWBRAY, *Cases and Materials on the European Convention on Human Rights* (Oxford University Press: 2nd edn, 2004)

MOXON (ed), *Managing Criminal Justice* (HMSO: 1985)

NEWBURN (ed), *Handbook of Policing* (Willan: 2003)

OVEY and WHITE (eds), *Jacobs and White: European Convention on Human Rights* (Oxford University Press: 3rd edn, 2002)

PANNICK, *Judges* (Oxford University Press: 1987)

PLUCKNETT, *A Concise History of the Common Law* (Butterworths: 5th edn, 1965)

REINER, *The Politics of the Police* (Oxford University Press: 3rd edn, 2000)

ROBERTSON, *The Justice Game* (Chatto & Windus: 1998)

SCARMAN, *Why Britain Needs a Written Constitution* (Charter 88: 1992)

SIMPSON, *Human Rights and the End of Empire: Britain and the Genesis of the European Convention* (Oxford University Press: 2001)

SMART (ed), *Law, Crime and Sexuality: Essays in Feminism* (Sage: 1995)

STEINER and WOODS, *Textbook on EC law* (Oxford University Press: 8th edn, 2003)

STEVENS, *The English Judges: Their Role in the Changing Constitution* (Hart: 2002)

TEMKIN, *Rape and the Legal Process* (Oxford University Press: 1987)

VAN DIJK and VAN HOOF, *The Theory and Practice of the European Convention on Human Rights* (Kluwer: 3rd edn, 1998)

WADE, *Constitutional Fundamentals* (Stevens: 1980)

WADHAM and MOUNTFIELD, *Blackstone's Guide to the Human Rights Act 1998* (Blackstone Press: 2nd edn, 1999)

WALKER and PADFIELD, *Sentencing Theory, Law and Practice* (Butterworths: 1996)

WALKER and STARMER, *Justice in Error* (Blackstone Press: 1994)

WALKER and STARMER, *Miscarriages of Justice: A Review of Justice in Error* (Blackstone: 1999)

WALSH, *Working in the Family Justice System* (Bristol: 1997)

WARD and DAVIES, *Criminal Justice Act 2003: A Practitioners' Guide* (Jordans: 2004)

WARD, *Young Offenders: Law, Practice and Procedure* (Jordans: 2001)

WIKELEY, OGUS, and BARENDT, *The Law of Social Security* (Butterworths: 5th edn, 2002)

WILSON and GALPIN, *Maxwell on Interpretation of Statutes* (Sweet & Maxwell: 11th edn, 1962)

WYATT and DASHWOOD, *European Union Law* (Sweet & Maxwell: 4th edn, 2000)

YOURROW, *The Margin of Appreciation Doctrine in the Dynamics of European Human Rights Jurisprudence* (Martinus Nijhoff: 1996)

ZANDER, *A Bill of Rights* (Sweet & Maxwell: 4th edn, 1996)

ZUCKERMAN and CRANSTON (eds), *Reform of Civil Procedure: Essays on Access to Justice* (Clarendon Press: 1995)

ZUCKERMAN, *Civil Procedure* (LexisNexis: 2003)

ARTICLES AND OTHER PUBLICATIONS

AIRS and SHAW, 'Jury Excusal and Deferral' (Home Office Research Findings No 102: 1999)

ALLAN, 'The Conceptual Foundations of Judicial Review: Conceptual Conundrum or Interpretative Inquiry?' (2002) 61(1) CLJ 87

ALLAN, 'The Limits of Parliamentary Sovereignty' [1985] PL 614

AMOS, 'Can We Speak Freely Now? Freedom of Expression under the Human Rights Act' [2002] 6 EHRLR 750

AMOS, 'R v Secretary of State for the Home Department, ex parte Anderson: Ending the Home Secretary's Sentencing Role' (2004) 67(1) MLR 108

ANON, ' "Fat Cats" — the Facts behind "those Figures" ', Counsel, June 1998

ARNHEIM, 'The Rule of Law or the Rule of Lawyers?' (2004) 154 NLJ 776

ARNUL, 'The Direct Effect of Directives: Grasping the Nettle' (1986) 35 ICLQ 939

ARNULL, 'From Charter to Constitution and Beyond: Fundamental Rights in the New European Union' [2003] PL 774

ARNULL, 'The Use and Abuse of Article 177, EEC' (1989) 52(5) MLR 622

ASHWORTH and VON HIRSCH, 'Recognising Elephants: The Problem of the Custody Threshold' [1997] Crim LR 187

ASHWORTH, 'Plea, Venue and Discontinuance' [1993] Crim LR 830

BAKALIS, 'Anti-Social Behaviour Orders — Criminal Penalties or Civil Injunctions' [2003] 62(3) CLJ 583

BARENDT, 'Free Speech and Abortion' [2003] PL 580

BEERNAERT, 'Protocol 14 and New Strasbourg Procedures: Towards Greater Efficiency? And at What Price?' [2004] EHRLR 544

BELOFF and MOUNTFIELD, 'Unconventional Behaviour? Judicial uses of the European Convention in England and Wales' [1996] EHRLR 467

BENNION, 'The Law Commission's Criminal Law Bill: No Way to Draft a Code' (1994) 15 Stat LR 108

BENNION, 'What Interpretation is "Possible" Under s3(1) of the Human Rights Act 1998' [2000] PL 77

BEYLEVELD, 'The Concept of a Human Right and Incorporation of the ECHR' [1995] PL 577

BINGHAM, 'The European Convention on Human Rights: Time to Incorporate' [1993] LQR 390

BIRCH, 'A Better Deal for Vulnerable Witnesses?' [2000] Crim LR 22

BIRCH, 'The Pace Hots Up: Confessions And Confusions Under The 1984 Act' [1989] Crim LR 95

BLAKE, 'Importing Proportionality: Clarification or Confusion?' [2002] 1 EHRLR 19

BLOM-COOPER and MUNRO, 'The Hutton Inquiry' [2004] PL 472.

BLOM-COOPER, 'Witnesses and the Scott Inquiry' [1994] PL 1

BRADLEY, 'Judicial Independence Under Attack' [2003] PL 397

BROWN, 'The First Five Years of the Court of First Instance and Appeals to the Court of Justice' (1995) 32(3) CML Rev 743

BROWNE-WILKINSON, 'The Infiltration of a Bill of Rights' [1992] PL 397

BUCKE and BROWN, 'In Police Custody: Police Powers and Suspects' Rights under the Revised PACE Codes of Practice' (1997) HORS 174

BUXTON, 'Challenging and Discharging Jurors — Part 1' [1990] Crim LR 225

BUXTON, 'The Human Rights Act and Private Law' (2000) 116 LQR 48

CANOR, 'Primus Inter Pares: Who is the Ultimate Guardian of Fundamental Rights in Europe?' (2000) 25(1) EL Rev 3

CLAYTON, 'Judicial Deference and "Democratic Dialogue": the Legitimacy of Judicial Intervention under the Human Rights Act 1998' [2004] PL 33

CLAYTON, 'The Limits of What's "Possible": Statutory Construction Under the Human Rights Act' [2002] EHRLR 559

COOK, 'Environmental Rights as Human Rights' [2002] 2 EHRLR 196

CRAIG, 'Directives: Direct Effect, Indirect Effect and the Construction of National Legislation' (1997) 22 EL Rev 519

CRAIG, 'Public Law, Political Theory and Legal Theory' [2000] PL 211

CRAIG, 'The Fall and Renewal of the Commission: Accountability, Contract and Administrative Organisation' (2000) 6 ELJ 98

CRAIG, 'The Human Rights Act, Article 6 and Procedural Rights' [2003] PL 753

CRAM, 'Reporting Restrictions in Criminal Proceedings and Article 10 of the ECHR' [1998] EHRLR 742

CUMPER, 'The Protection of Religious Rights under s 13 of the Human Rights Act' [2000] PL 254

DARBYSHIRE, 'An Essay on the Importance and Neglect of the Magistracy' [1997] Crim LR 639

DARBYSHIRE, 'For the New Lord Chancellor: Some Causes for Concern about Magistrates' [1997] Crim LR 861

DARBYSHIRE, 'The Lamp that Shows that Freedom Lives: is it Worth the Candle?' [1991] Crim LR 740

DARBYSHIRE, Maughan and Stewart, What can the English Legal System Learn from Jury Research Published up to 2001? — Findings for the Criminal Courts Review (2001)

DREW, 'Human Trafficking: A Modern Form of Slavery?' [2002] 4 EHRLR 481

DREWERY, 'Judicial Inquiries and Public Reassurance' [1996] PL 368

DRZEMCZEWSKI, 'The Domestic Application of the European Human Rights Convention as European Community Law' (1981) 30 ICLQ 118

EDWARDS, 'Judicial Deference under the Human Rights Act' (2002) 65 MLR 859

ENRIGHT, 'Multi-racial Juries' (1991) 41 NLJ 992

EVANS, 'Police Cautioning and the Young Offender' [1991] Crim LR 598

FENWICK, 'The Right to Protest, the Human Rights Act and the Margin of Appreciation' (1999) 62 MLR 491

FORDHAM and de la MERE, 'Identifying the Principles of Proportionality', in Jowell and Cooper (eds), Understanding Human Rights Principles (JUSTICE: 2001)

FOSTER, 'The Effect of the European Communities Act 1972, s 2(4)' (1988) 51 MLR 775

FREEMAN, 'Law and Order in 1984' [1984] CLP 175

ZELLICK, 'Precedent in the Court of Appeal, Criminal Division' [1974] Crim LR 222

GLANVILLE WILLIAMS, 'The Definition of Crime' (1955) 8 CLP 107

GRIEF, 'The Domestic Impact of the European Convention on Human Rights as Mediated through Community Law' [1991] PL 555

GRIFFITHS, 'The Political Constitution' (1979) 42 MLR 1

HALE, 'Equality and the Judiciary: Why We Should Want More Women Judges' [2001] PL 489

HARMSEN, 'National Responsibility for EC Acts under the ECHR: Recasting the Accession Debate' (2001) 7 EPL 625

HARTSHORNE, 'The Human Rights Act 1998 and Damages for Non-Pecuniary Loss' [2004] EHRLR 660

HEDDERMAN and MOXON, 'Magistrates' Court or Crown Court: Mode of Trial Decisions and Sentencing' (Home Office Research Study No 125: 1982)

HERBERT, 'Mode of Trial and Magistrates' Sentencing Powers: Will increased powers inevitably lead to a reduction in the committal rate?' [2003] Crim LR 314

HILSON and DOWNES, 'Making Sense of Rights: Community Rights in EC Law' (1999) 24 EL Rev 121

Home Office, Statistics on Race and the Criminal Justice System, 2000, ch 3.

HOOD PHILLIPS, 'A Constitutional Myth: Separation of Powers' (1977) 93 LQR 11

HOWE, 'Procedure at the Scott Inquiry' [1996] PL 445

HUMPHRIES, 'Preparing for the New Order in Court', The Lawyer, 21 July 1998

HUNT, 'The 'Horizontal Effect' of the Human Rights Act' [1998] PL 424

IRVINE (Lord), 'Judges and Decision Makers: the Theory and Practice of Wednesbury Review' [1996] PL 59

IRVINE (Lord), 'The Development of Human Rights in Britain under an Incorporated Convention on Human Rights' [1998] PL 221

IRVINE (Lord), 'The Impact of the Human Rights Act: Parliament, the Courts and the Executive' [2003] PL 307

JACK STRAW MP and PAUL BOATENG MP, 'Bringing Rights Home: Labour's Plans to Incorporate the European Convention on Human Rights into UK Law' [1997] 1 EHRLR 71

JACOB, 'The Inherent Jurisdiction of the Court' (1970) CLP 23

JACOB, 'Administration of Justice: The Bowman Review of the Court of Appeal' (1998) 61(3) MLR 390

JASON-LLOYD, 'Police Reform — A Better Way?' (2003) 167 JP 805

JONES, 'The Devaluation of Human Rights Under the European Convention' [1995] PL 430

JOWELL, 'Heading for a Constitutional Crisis' (2004) 154 NLJ 401

JOWELL, 'Judicial Deference: Servility, Civility or Institutional Incapacity?' [2003] PL 592

KAVANAGH, 'Statutory Interpretation and Human Rights After Anderson: A More Contextual Approach' [2004] PL 537

KLUG and WADHAM, 'The "Democratic" Entrenchment of a Bill of Rights: Liberty's Proposals' [1993] PL 579

KLUG, 'Judicial Deference Under the Human Rights Act 1998' [2003] 2 EHRLR 125

LARDY, 'Prisoner Disenfranchisement: Constitutional Rights and Wrongs' [2002] PL 524

LAWS, 'Law and Democracy' [1995] PL 80

LAWS, 'The Constitution: Morals and Rights' [1996] PL 622

LE SUEUR, 'Three Strikes and it's out? The UK Government's Strategy to Oust Judicial Review from Immigration and Asylum Decision-Making' [2004] PL 22

LEIGH and LUSTGARTEN, 'Five Volumes in Search of Accountability: the Scott Report' (1996) 59(5) MLR 695

LESTER, 'Parliamentary Scrutiny Under the Human Rights Act 1998' [2002] 4 EHRLR 432

LESTER, 'The Art of the Possible — Interpreting Statutes Under the Human Rights Act' [1998] EHRLR 665

LESTER, 'The Mouse that Roared: The Human Rights Bill 1995' [1995] PL 198

LIGHTMAN, 'Civil litigation in the 21st Century' (1998) 17 CJQ 383

LIGHTMAN, 'The Civil Justice System and Legal Profession — the Challenges Ahead' (text of the 6th Edward Bramley Memorial Lecture) (2003) 22 CJQ 235

LOMAS, 'The Twenty-Fifth Annual Report of the Council on Tribunals — An Opportunity Sadly Missed' (1985) 48 MLR 694

LOVELAND, 'Does Homelessness Decision-Making Engage Article 6(1) of the ECHR?' [2003] 2 EHRLR 176

LUSTGARTEN, 'The Future of Stop and Search' [2002] Crim LR 603

LYELL, 'Whither Strasbourg? Why Britain Should Think Long and Hard Before Incorporating the European Convention on Human Rights' [1997] EHRLR 132

LYON, 'After Findlay — A Consideration of Some Aspects of the Military Justice System' [1998] Crim LR 109

MACDONALD, 'R (on the application of ProLife Alliance) v British Broadcasting Corporation' [2003] 6 EHRLR 651

MACKAY and KEARNS, 'The Trial of the Issue of Unfitness to Plead' [2000] Crim LR 536

MACMILLAN, 'Employment Tribunals: Philosophies and Practicalities' (1999) 28(1) ILJ 4

MALLESON and BANDA, 'Factors Affecting the Decision to Apply for Silk and Judicial Office' (2000) Lord Chancellor's Department Research Series 02/00

MALLESON, 'Creating a Judicial Appointments Commission: Which Model Works Best?' [2004] PL 102

MARRIOTT and NICOL, 'The Human Rights Act, Representative Standing and the Victim Culture' [1998] EHRLR 730

MARSHALL, 'The Lynchpin of Parliamentary Intention: Lost, Stolen or Strained?' [2003] PL 236

MATTHEWS, HANCOCK and BRIGGS, 'Jurors' Perceptions, Understanding, Confidence and Satisfaction in the Jury System: A Study in Six Courts' (Home Office Research Study No 227: 2004)

McCONVILLE and BRIDGES, 'Custodial Advice and the Right to Silence' (1993) RCCJ Research Study No 16

MEAD, 'Swallowing the Camel, Straining at the Gnat: The Implications of *Mendoza v Ghaidan*' [2003] 5 EHRLR 501

MEAD, 'The Likely Effect of the Human Rights Act on Everyday Policing Decisions in England and Wales' (2000) 5(1) J Civ Lib 5

MILLER, 'Getting the Focus Right for Civil Legal Aid' (2004) NLJ 1673

MILLER, BLAND and QUINTON, 'The Impact of Stops and Searches on Crime and the Community', Police Research Series Paper No 130 (2000)

MOORHEAD, 'Self-Regulation and the Market for Legal Services' — paper published by the Cardiff Centre for Ethics, Law and Society (Cardiff University: 2004)

MORRIS, 'Jury Trials in Personal Injury Claims — is there a Place for them?' [2002] 3 Journal of Personal Injury Law 310

MORRIS, 'Assisted Suicide Under the European Convention on Human Rights: a Critique' [2003] 1 EHRLR 65

MORRIS, 'Extending the Police Family: Issues and Anomalies' [1992] PL 670

NESIC, 'Mediation — On the Rise in the United Kingdom?' (2001) 13(2) Bond Law Review

NEWBURN and REINER, 'From PC Dixon to Dixon plc: Policing and Policing Powers since 1954' [2004] Crim LR 601

NÍ AOLÁIN, 'Truth Telling, Accountability and the Right to Life in Northern Ireland' [2002] 5 EHRLR 572

NICHOL, 'Available Dispute Resolution' Legal Action, Dec 1997, p 6

NICOL, 'Statutory Interpretation and Human Rights After Anderson' [2004] PL 274

NOBLES and SCHIFF, 'The Criminal Cases Review Commission: Establishing a Workable Relationship with the Court of Appeal' [2005] Crim LR 173

O'CONNOR, 'The Court of Appeal: Re-Trials & Tribulations' [1990] Crim LR 615

OLIVER, 'Functions of a Public Nature under the Human Rights Act' [2004] PL 329

ORMEROD and McKAY, 'Telephone Intercepts and their Admissibility' [2004] Crim LR 15

ORMEROD and ROBERTS, 'The Police Reform Act 2002 — Increasing Centralisation, Maintaining Confidence and Contracting out Crime' [2003] Crim LR 141

PARTINGTON, 'Alternative Dispute Resolution: Recent Developments, Future Challenges' (2004) 23 CJQ 99

PARTINGTON, 'Training the Judiciary in England and Wales' (1994) 13 CJQ 319

PHILLIPS and BROWN, 'Entry into the Criminal Justice System: A Survey of Police Arrests and their Outcomes' (1998) HORS 185

PHILLIPSON, 'The Human Rights Act: "Horizontal Effect" and the Common Law: A Bang or a Whimper?' (1999) 62(2) MLR 825

PRECHAL, 'Does Direct Effect Still Matter?' (2000) 37 CML Rev 1047

PRINCE, 'Court-based mediation: a preliminary analysis of the small claims mediation scheme at Exeter Crown Court', Research Report for the Civil Justice Council, March 2004

PRITCHARD, 'A Reform for Jury Trial?' (1998) 148 NLJ 45

REDMAYNE, 'The DNA Database: Civil Liberty and Evidentiary Issues' [1998] Crim LR 437

ROBERTS and WILLMORE, 'The Role of Forensic Science Evidence in Criminal Proceedings' (Royal Commission on Criminal Justice Research Study No 11: 1992)

RUFFERT, 'Rights and Remedies in European Community Law: A Comparative View' (1997) 34 CML Rev 307

SANDS, 'Human Rights, the Environment and the Lopez Ostra Case' [1996] 29 EHRLR 597

SCHOKKENBROEK, 'The Basis, Nature and Application of the Margin of Appreciation Doctrine in the Case-Law of the European Court of Human Rights' (1998) 19(1) HRLJ 30

SCOTT, 'Procedures at Inquiries: the Duty to be Fair' (1995) 111 LQR 596

SEDLEY, 'Human Rights: A Twenty-First Century Agenda' [1995] PL 386

SINGH and STRACHAN, 'Privacy Postponed' [2003] EHRLR Special Issue 12

SINGH, 'Is there a Role for the "Margin of Appreciation" in National Law after the Human Rights Act?' [1999] 1 EHRLR 15

SMITH, 'The Criminal Appeal Act 1995' [1995] Crim LR 920

SMITH, Paper for Legal Services Authority Conference on the Future of Community Legal Services: Law for those in Disadvantage (4th October 2002)

SMITH: 'The Law Commission's Criminal Law Bill — A Good Start for the Criminal Code' (1995) 16 Stat LR 105

STEVENS, 'Reform in Haste and Repent at Leisure: Iolanthe, the Lord High Executioner and Brave New World' (2004) 24 LS 1

STEYN, 'Democracy through Law' [2002] EHRLR 723

STEYN, 'Pepper v Hart: A Re-examination' (2001) 21 Oxford Journal of Legal Studies 59

STEYN: 'The Weakest and Least Dangerous Department of Government' [1997] PL 84

TAUSZ and ORMEROD 'Juries: Whether all white jury on case involving black defendant where victims all white contrary to European Convention on Human Rights' [2003] Crim LR 633

USHER: 'The Influence of National Concepts on Decisions of the European Court' [1976] 1 EL Rev 359

WADE, 'Horizons of Horizontality' (2000) 116 LQR 217

WADE, 'The Basis of Legal Sovereignty' [1955] CLJ 172

WALSON, 'Advocacy for the Unpopular' (1998) 162 JP 499

WESTWOOD, 'The Effects of Home Office Guidelines on the Cautioning of Offenders' [1991] Crim LR 591

WILKINSON and EVANS, 'Police Cautioning of Juveniles: The Impact of Circular 14/1985' [1990] Crim LR 165

WILLMOTT, 'A Presumption of Legal Representation at Judicial Inquiries' (2003) 12(2) Nott LJ 34

WINETROBE, 'Inquiries After Scott: the Return of the Tribunal of Inquiry' [1997] PL 18

WINTER, 'Direct Applicability and Direct Effects' (1972) 9 CML Rev 425

WOOLF (Lord), 'Public Law — Private Law: Why the Divide? A Personal View' [1986] 2 PL 220

WOOLF (Lord), 'The Rule of Law and a Change in the Constitution' (2004) 63(2) CLJ 317

WOOLF (Lord), 'Droit Public — English Style' [1995] PL 57

ZANDER, 'The Government's Plans on Civil Justice' (1998) 61 MLR 383

ZANDER, 'Forwards or Backwards for the New Lord Chancellor' (1997) 16 CJQ 208

ZANDER, 'The Complaining Juror' (2000) 150 NLJ 723

ZELLICK, 'Precedent in the Court of Appeal, Criminal Division' [1974] Crim LR 222

ZUCKERMAN, 'Trial by Unfair Means — The Report of the Working Group on the Right to Silence' [1989] Crim LR 85

INDEX

Absences,
  summary trials,
    general effects of 635
    pleading guilty by post
      636–637
Acte clair doctrine,
  references for a preliminary
    ruling 143
Acts of Parliament
  see Statutes
Administration of justice,
  see under individual headings,
  Civil process
  Courts
  Inquiries
  Judicial review
  Judiciary
  Juries
  Legal services
  Police
  Royal prerogative
  Tribunals
Administration of the civil
    justice system,
  see Civil process
Admiralty Court,
  Queen's Bench Division and
    252
Advocates-General,
  European Court of Justice
    139
All England Reports,
  present system of law
    reporting 106
Alternative dispute resolution
    (ADR),
  arbitration,
    generally 437–438
    intervention by the court
      440–441
    procedure 438–440
  introduction 436–437
  mediation,
    contractual disputes
      442–443
    court based schemes
      443–445
    court led ADR
      requirements 443–445
    family matters 441–442

    regulatory disputes
      442–443
  negotiation,
    contractual disputes
      442–443
    court based schemes
      443–445
    court led ADR
      requirements 443–445
    family matters 441–442
  regulatory disputes 442–443
Ambiguity,
  construction of statutes
    46–47
  interpretation of statutes
    46–47
Anton Piller orders,
  administration of the civil
    justice system 434
Appeals,
  civil,
    against a finding of fact
      504–505
    against an award of
      damages 506–508
    against exercise of
      discretion 505–506
    appeal on a point of law
      504
    introduction 498–499
    powers on appeal 502–503
    procedure on appeal
      502–503
    rights of appeal 499–501
  criminal,
    appeal against conviction
      682–683
    appeal against sentence
      683–684, 695
    appeal to House of Lords
      696–697
    Court of Appeal (Criminal
      Division) development
      680–681
    Criminal Cases Review
      Commission 684–687
    hospital orders 695
    introduction 680
    power to order a 'venire de
      novo' 695

power to order new trial
    693–695
power to quash conviction
    689–692
power to receive fresh
    evidence 693–695
power to substitute an
    alternative verdict 692
procedure 696
prosecution rights of
    appeal 688–689
references following
    acquittal 687–688
role of the Court of Appeal
    681–682
summary trials 648–654
summary trials and,
    case stated to Queen's
        Bench Division 651–654
    Crown Court 649–651
    House of Lords 654
    generally 648
Arbitration,
    generally 437–438
    intervention by the court
        440–441
    procedure 438–440
Arraignment,
    trial on indictment,
        attendance of the accused
            597
        generally 598–599
Arrest,
    consequences of arrest 409
    generally 405–406
    mechanics of 408–409
    powers of arrest 406–408
Assizes,
    history of 224
Attorney-General,
    administration of the English
        legal system 22–23
    criminal justice system 513
    sentences and the role of 660
Autonomic legislation,
    form of legislation 38–39
Autrefois acquit,
    plea of 602–604
Autrefois convict,
    plea of 602–604

Bail,
    court,
        Court of Appeal 558
        Crown Court 557–558

High Court 558
        magistrates 556–557
    nature of bail 554–556
    right to bail 559–562
    sureties 562–563
    police 532
Bar Council,
    regulation of legal services 361
Barristers,
    Bar Council 361
    complaints against 367
    education and training 359
    employed 355–356
    Inns of Court 353
    practice at the bar 353–354
    relationship between barrister
        and client 354–355
Bias,
    challenging the composition of
        the jury 335
Breaches of the peace,
    police powers and 398–400

Canon law,
    source of law 9
Case law,
    law reporting, present system
        of,
        All England Reports 106
        electronic sources 107
        European cases 107
        Law Reports 105–106
        newspapers 107
        neutral citation of
            judgments 107–108
        'Official' reports 106
        periodicals 107
        specialist reports 107
        weaknesses of 109
        Weekly Law Reports 106
        private reports 104–105
        year books 103–104
    non binding precedents,
        European Court of Human
            Rights decisions 86–87
        former rules of
            international law 89
        inferior courts decisions 85
        Judicial Committee of the
            Privy Council decisions
            85–86
        persuasive authorities
            85–87
        statements of law made per
            incuriam 87–89

precedents, operation of the
      doctrine of,
   binding element 81–85
   binding precedent 78–80
   distinguishing 92–93
   hierarchy of the Courts
      93–102
   impact of Human Rights
      Act 1998 on 80–81
   overruling 90–92
   reversing 90
   relationships between Law
      Reports and the doctrine
      of 77–78
   sources of community law
      and 122–126
Chancery Division,
   Court of Protection 252
   introduction 250–251
   jurisdiction 251
   patents court 251
Circuit judges,
   judiciary 301
Civil procedure,
   see under individual headings
   Appeals
   Civil process
   Civil trials
   Costs
   Pre-trial process
Civil procedure rules,
   civil trials,
      disclosure 477–479
      discontinuance and 468–
         469
      inspection of documents
         477–479
      offers to settle,
         effects of payment into
            Court 471–472
         principle of 470–471
      Part 36 payments,
         effects of payment into
            Court 471–472
         principle of 470–471
      settlement 469–470
      statements of case
         476–477
      striking out 468–469
      three track approach to
         464–467
   overriding objectives of
      434–435
   rules of court 433
   terminology of the 435

Civil process,
   administration of the civil
      justice system,
      civil procedure rules and
         overriding objective
         434–435
      generally 432–433
      Middleton Report 432
      rules of court 433–434
      terminology of civil
         procedure rules 435
   alternative dispute resolution,
      arbitration 436–441
      introduction 436–437
      mediation 441–445
      negotiation 441–445
   introduction 425–426
   settlement,
      arbitration 437–441
      introduction 436
      mediation 441–445
      negotiation 441–445
   Woolf analysis of the,
      adversarial nature 426–428
      complexity 430
      court of trial 430–431
      delay of civil litigation
         426–428
      expense 428–430
      recommendations 431–432
Civil trials,
   appeals,
      against a finding of fact
         504–505
      against an award of
         damages 506–508
      against exercise of
         discretion 505–506
      introduction 498–499
      on a point of law 504
      powers on appeal 502–503
      procedure on appeal
         502–503
      rights of appeal 499–501
   directions 481
   disclosure of documents,
      action for disclosure
         480–481
      background 477–479
      disclosure against other
         persons 480
      inspection against other
         persons 480
      relevant principles 477–479
   discontinuance 467–469

fast track 466
inspection of documents,
  action for disclosure
    480–481
  background 477–479
  disclosure against other
    persons 480
  inspection against other
    persons 480
  relevant principles 477–479
interim relief,
  interim payment of
    damages 474–475
  interlocutory injunction
    472–474
introductory matters 464
multi-track 466–467
offers to settle,
  effects of payment into
    Court 471–472
  principle of 470–471
Part 36 payments,
  effects of payment into
    Court 471–472
  principle of 470–471
preparation of evidence,
  documents 483
  evidence 482–483
  introduction 481–482
  notices under Civil
    Evidence Act 1995,
    483–484
  witnesses 482
pre-trial process,
  see also **Pre-trial process**
  choice of court 446–448
  commencing a civil action
    449–456
  pre-action protocols
    448–449
  pre-commencement order,
    disclosure of documents
    456–457
  freezing injunctions
    460–463
  inspection of
    documents 456–457
  Norwich Pharmacal
    principle 458
  search orders 458–460
procedure at the trial,
  case for the claimant
    484–485
  case for the defence 485
  introduction 484

  judgment 486–487
  right to begin 484
  verdict 486–487
  settlement 469–470
  small claims track 465
  statements of case,
    background 475–477
  striking out 467–469
  summary judgment 470
  three track approach
    464–465
Classification of offences,
  criminal process,
    indictment 543
    introduction 542–543
    reform possibilities
      545–547
    summarily 543–544
    triable either on indictment
      or summarily
      544–545
Clementi report,
  regulation of 362–364
Codes of Practice,
  form of legislation 39–40
  status of 40–41
Commercial court,
  Queen's Bench Division and
    252
Common law,
  evolution of equity and 4
  source of law 5–6
Community Legal Service,
  eligibility for assistance
    379–380
  generally 377–378
  not-for-profit organizations
    and partnerships with
    380
  work covered by Community
    Legal Service contracts
    378–379
Conditional fee agreements,
  costs and 495–496
  generally 372–373
contempt of court,
  civil 239–240
  criminal 236–239
  jurisdiction to punish
    240–241
Coroners' courts,
  jurisdiction 267–268
  office of coroner 266
  review of Coroners' services
    268–269

Costs,
  assessment of costs,
    amount 493–495
    indemnity costs 494–495
    process 492–493
    standard costs 49–495
  conditional fee agreements
    495–496
  multi party proceedings 497
  power to award,
    discretion 488–490
    introduction 488
    misconduct 491–492
    orders against non parties
     490–491
    wasted costs order 491–492
County Court rules,
  administration of the civil
    justice system 433
County Courts,
  constitution 255
  hierarchy of courts 102
  jurisdiction 255–256
Court of Appeal,
  constitution,
    ex officio judges 245–246
    Lords Justices of Appeal
     245–246
  hierarchy of courts 96–100
  introduction 245
  jurisdiction,
    civil division 246–248
    criminal division 248
Court of Chancery,
  history of 226
  history of the English legal
    system 1
Court of Common Pleas,
  history of 223
Court of Exchequer,
  history of 222
Court of First Instance,
  European Court of Justice 139
Court of King's Bench,
  history of 223
Court of Protection,
  Chancery Division and 252
Courts,
  see also **European Court of**
    Human Rights and
    European Court of
    Justice
  administration of 229–231
  classification of,
    appellate 227

    civil 227
    courts of record 228
    criminal 227
    inferior courts 228–229
    original jurisdiction 227
    superior courts 228–229
    tribunals 227–228
  contempt of court,
    civil 239–240
    criminal 236–239
    jurisdiction to punish
     240–241
Coroners' courts,
  jurisdiction 267–268
  office of coroner 266
  review of Coroners'
    services 268–269
County Courts,
  constitution 255
  hierarchy of courts 102
  jurisdiction 255–256
Court of Appeal,
  constitution 245–246
  hierarchy of 96–100
  introduction 245
  jurisdiction 246–248
Courts-martial,
  Appeal Court 273–274
  introduction 272–273
  issues of fairness 274–276
Crown Court,
  constitution 257–258
  creation of 256–257
  hierarchy of 102
  jurisdiction 258–259
  procedure 258–259
Ecclesiastical courts,
  introduction 276–277
hierarchy of the 93–102
High Court,
  constitution 249
  divisions 250–255
  hierarchy 101–102
  jurisdiction 249–250
history,
  Assizes 224
  Court of Chancery 226
  Court of Common Pleas
    223
  Court of Exchequer 222
  Court of King's Bench
    223
  courts of Exchequer
    Chamber 223
  Curia Regis 222

Justices of the Peace
    224–225
  Star Chamber 225–226
House of Lords,
  constitution 241–242
  hierarchy 93–96
  jurisdiction 242–243
  procedure 241–242
  reform 243–245
Judicial Committee of the
    Privy Council,
  constitution 269–270
  jurisdiction 270–272
Magistrates' courts,
  constitution 259–261
  hierarchy 102
  jurisdiction 264–266
  Justices of the Peace 261–
    262
  Justices' chief executive
    262–264
  Justices' clerks 262–264
  organization 259–261
open justice principle,
  hearing in open court
    232–233
  introduction 231–232
  reporting of proceedings in
    court 235–236
  withholding of particular
    information/ evidence
    from public 233–235
  organization of the 229–231
Courts-martial,
  Appeal Court 273–274
  introduction 272–273
  issues of fairness 274–276
Courts of Exchequer Chamber,
  history of 223–224
Criminal Cases Review
    Commission,
  criteria of 686–687
  introduction 684–685
  use of the powers 685–686
Criminal Defence Service,
  generally 380–381
  public defender service 381
Criminal Justice system,
  aims of 514
  Attorney-General,
    administration of the
      English legal system
      22–23
    criminal justice system
      513

Department of Constitutional
    Affairs,
    administration of the civil
      justice system and the
      433
    administration of the
      English legal system
      19–22
    criminal justice system and
      512
    Tribunals Service and
      284512
  Home Office 512
  introduction to 511–512
  victims of crime 516–518
  youth justice 514–516
Criminal proceedings,
  see under individual headings
  Appeals
  Criminal justice system
  Criminal process
  Indictment, trial on
  Miscarriages of justice
  Sentences
  Summary trials
Criminal process,
  adversarial nature 518–521
  bringing suspect before the
    court,
    new procedure 542
    old procedure 540–541
  case management 525–526
  classification of offences,
    indictment 543
    introduction 542–543
    reform possibilities
      545–547
    summarily 543–544
    triable either on indictment
      or summarily 544–545
  court bail,
    Court of Appeal 558
    Crown Court 557–558
    High Court 558
    magistrates 556–557
    nature of bail 554–556
    right to bail 559–562
    sureties 562–563
  pre-trial procedure,
    cautioning 527–529
    conditional cautions for
      adult offenders
      529–530
    decision to prosecute
      533–540

discretion as to whether
prosecution should be
commenced 527–529
judicial scrutiny of the
decision to prosecute or
caution 531–532
police bail 532
reprimands for juveniles
530–531
warnings for juveniles
530–531
procedure for determining
mode of trial,
children 552–553
factors that influence mode
of trial 553–554
introduction 547–548
plea before venue process:
adults 548–551
young persons 552–553
right to a fair trial 521–524
Crown Court,
constitution 257–258
creation of 256–257
hierarchy of 102
jurisdiction 258–259
procedure 258–259
sentences,
deferment of sentence
664
passing sentence 662–663
pre-sentence drug taking
665–666
pre-sentence reports and
other reports 664–665
restraining orders 666
Crown Prosecution Service,
administration of the English
legal system 19,
22–23
generally 356–357
Curia Regis,
history of 222
Custom,
source of law 7–9

Decisions,
relationship between
Community and
national law 134
Delegated legislation,
introduction 34–37
scrutiny of 37–38
Department for Constitutional
Affairs,

administration of the civil
justice system and the
433
administration of the English
legal system 19–22
criminal justice system and
512
Tribunals Service and 284
Derogation,
nature of Convention rights
protected 172–173
Detention,
powers of police 409–412
Director of Public Prosecutions,
administration of the English
legal system 22–23
generally 356–357
Directives,
relationship between
Community and
national law 129
District judges,
judiciary 301
Disclosure of documents,
civil trials,
action for disclosure
480–481
background 477–479
disclosure against other
persons 480
inspection against other
persons 480
relevant principles
477–479
pre-trial process 456–457

Ecclesiastical courts,
introduction 276–277
Equality of treatment,
Community law, principle of
122
Equity,
evolution of common law and
4
source of law 6
European Community law,
Charter of Fundamental
Rights 113
Constitution for Europe
113–114
European Court of Justice,
Advocates-General 139
composition 138–139
Court of First Instance 139
jurisdiction 139–141

preliminary rulings
141–146
procedure 138–139
impact upon English Courts,
interpretation 136–138
supremacy 134–136
institutions,
Commission 119
Council 117–119
Court of Justice 120–121
Parliament 119–120
introduction 110
relationship between
community and national
law,
direct applicability
127–128
direct effect 128
general approach of the
Court of Justice 126–127
scope of European law
114–117
Single European Act 111
sources of community law,
case law 122–126
legislation 121–122
Treaty of Amsterdam 111–112
Treaty on European Union
111
Treaty of Nice 113
**European Convention on
Human Rights,**
see also **Human Rights Act
1998**
incorporation into national
law 152
history 147–149
nature of rights protected,
derogation 172–173
introduction 170
margin of appreciation
171–172
proportionality 170–171
specific rights under,
discrimination against with
regard to other
Convention rights
194–197
fair trial 180–183
freedom of expression
190–193
freedom of thought,
conscience and religion
188–190
liberty 177–180

life 173–175
marry and found a family
194
peaceful assembly and
association with others
193–194
prohibition of slavery and
forced labour 176–177
prohibition of torture and
inhuman or degrading
treatment 175–176
respect for a person's
private and family life,
home and
correspondence
184–188
retrospective criminal
liability or penalties
183–184
security of the person
177–180
status before Human Rights
Act 1998,
impact of findings of the
European Court of
Human Rights 149
indirect influence on
domestic courts
150–151
influence through European
Community/European
Union 151
introduction 149
source of law 7
European Court of Justice,
Advocates-General 139
composition 138–139
Court of First Instance 139
hierarchy of the courts 93
jurisdiction 139–141
preliminary rulings,
discretion to refer
144–146
introduction 141–142
power to refer 142
reference mandatory
142–143
when decision on a point of
European law is
necessary 143–144
procedure 138–139
**European Court of Human
Rights,**
admissibility of complaints
200–201

composition of Court
198–200
introduction 197–198
procedure of Court 198–200
European Union,
Charter of Fundamental
Rights 113
Constitution for Europe
113–114
European Court of Justice,
Advocates-General 139
composition 138–139
Court of First Instance 139
jurisdiction 139–141
preliminary rulings
141–146
procedure 138–139
impact upon English Courts,
interpretation 136–138
supremacy 134–136
institutions,
Commission 119
Council 117–119
Court of Justice 120–121
Parliament 119–120
introduction 110
relationship between
community and national
law,
direct applicability
127–128
direct effect 128
general approach of the
Court of Justice 126–127
scope of European law
114–117
Single European Act 111
sources of community law,
case law 122–126
generally 6–7
legislation 121–122
Treaty of Amsterdam
111–112, 121
Treaty on European Union
111, 121
Treaty of Nice 113, 119–121
Evidence,
disclosure of,
defence disclosure 579–582
expert evidence 583–584
further prosecution
disclosure 582
introduction 574–576
prosecution disclosure 576
sensitive material 576–579

power to receive fresh
evidence 693–695
preparation of evidence,
documents 483
evidence 482–483
introduction 481–482
notices under Civil
Evidence Act 1995,
483–484
witnesses 482
withholding of particular
information/evidence
from public 233–235

Family Division,
High Court and 253–254
Fast track,
civil trials 466
Fines,
sentences 677
Fingerprints,
treatment of suspects 413–414
Force,
police powers 401
Freezing injunctions,
jurisdiction 460–461
Mareva injunctions 434,
461–462
position of third parties 463
principles on which the court
acts 462–463
procedure 461–462
Fundamental rights,
Community law, principle of
122

**Geographical operation of
statutes,**
introduction 41–42
Golden rule,
judicial approaches to
interpretation of statutes
49–50

Halliday report,
sentencing and 656
Hierarchy of the courts,
County courts 102
Court of Appeal,
Civil division 96–99
Criminal division 99–100
Crown courts 102
European Court of Justice 93
High Court,
Divisional courts 101

judges at first instance
101–102
House of Lords 93–96
Magistrates' courts 102
tribunals 102–103
High Court,
constitution 249
divisions,
Chancery 250–252
Family 253–254
Queen's Bench Division
252–253
hierarchy,
Divisional courts 101
judges at first instance
101–102
judicial review,
historical origin of the
powers of the High
Court 206–207
jurisdiction 249–250
High Court judges,
generally 300
**History of the English legal
system,**
administration of the English
legal system,
Department for
Constitutional Affairs
19–22
Home Office 22
introduction 19
law officers 22–23
Lord Chancellor 19–22
common law, evolution of 4
distinction between civil and
criminal matters,
decision whether matter
civil or criminal 15–18
importance of 13–15
equity, evolution of 4
introduction 3
monarch, role of 4
principal sources of law,
canon law 9
common law 5–6
custom 7–9
equity 6
European Convention on
Human Rights 7
European Union 6–7
legislation 5
other 7–13
roman law 9
textbooks 9–13

Home Office,
administration of the English
legal system,
Home Office 22
criminal justice system 512
Hospital order,
power of Court of Appeal
695
House of Lords,
appeal to,
from Court of Appeal
(Criminal Division)
696–697
from summary trials 654
constitution 241–242
hierarchy of the courts 93–96
jurisdiction 242–243
procedure 241–242
reform 243–245
Human Rights Act 1998,
see also **European Convention
on Human Rights**
breach of the peace police
power 399–400
direct enforcement of
Convention rights,
challenging public
authorities under the
Act 167–169
horizontal effect 166–167
judicial deference 165–166
proportionality 165–166
public authorities 163–165
remedies 169
freedom of expression
155–157, 190–193
freedom of religion 155–157,
188–190
impact on legislation,
declarations of
incompatibility 159–162
interpretative obligation
157–159
ministerial statements of
incompatibility 162–163
remedial orders 159–162
introduction 153–157
jurisprudence 153–157
rights protected 153
status of Convention rights
153–157
Strasbourg case law 153–155

Identification,
police powers 420–421

Imprisonment,
custody plus 670
dangerous offenders 671–672
intermittent custody 670–671
length of custodial sentence
668–670
life sentences 673–674
suspended sentence 668
young offenders 674–675
Indictment, trial on,
arraignment,
attendance of the accused
597
generally 598–599
course of the,
burden of proof 615–618
conclusion of the case 619
post verdict orders 621–622
procedure at the hearing
607–612
protection of the defendant
618–619
publicity 606
right of silence 615–618
sentence 621–622
verdict 620–621
witnesses 612–615
criminal appeals,
against conviction 682–683
against sentence 683–684,
695
appeal to House of Lords
696–697
Court of Appeal (Criminal
Division) development
680–681
Criminal Cases Review
Commission 684–687
hospital orders 695
introduction 680
power to order a 'venire de
novo' 695
power to order new trial
693–695
power to quash conviction
689–692
power to receive fresh
evidence 693–695
power to substitute an
alternative verdict 692
procedure 696
prosecution rights of
appeal 688–689
references following
acquittal 687–688

role of the Court of Appeal
681–682
summary trials 648–654
criminal process 543
delay 572–574
disclosure of evidence,
defence disclosure 579–582
expert evidence 583–584
further prosecution
disclosure 582
introduction 574–576
prosecution disclosure 576
sensitive material 576–579
empanelling the jury,
challenges 605–606
indictment,
amendment of 594–595
duplicity 594
form and contents 586
introduction 586
joinder of offences 587–588
joinder of offenders 587
long trials 589–590
non-jury trial on
indictment 590–593
objecting to the 594–595
motion to quash 604
pleas,
autrefois acquit 602–604
autrefois convict 602–604
generally 599–600
guilty 600–601
not guilty 601–602
preliminary points of law 605
pre-trial review 595–597
sending for trial 571–572
time-limits 572–574
transfer for,
background 564–567
either-way offences
procedure 568
indictable only offences
procedure 567–568
introduction 564
notices of transfer 569
publicity 570–571
voluntary bills of
indictment 570
Injunctions,
Freezing,
jurisdiction 460–461
position of third parties
463
principles on which the
court acts 462–463

procedure 461–462
Mareva,
    administration of the civil
        justice system 434
    generally 461–462
Inns of Court,
    functions of 353
Inquiries,
    see also **Tribunals**
    generally 296
    statutory inquiries 296–297
    tribunals of inquiry,
        inquiries under the
            Inquiries Act 2005
        Ministers acting under
            specific statutory
            provisions 297
        non-statutory inquiries
            298–299
Inspection of documents,
    civil trials,
        inspection of documents,
        action for disclosure
            480–481
        background 477–479
        disclosure against other
            persons 480
        inspection against other
            persons 480
        relevant principles 477–479
    pre-trial process 456–457
Interviews,
    police powers,
        cautions 418
        conduct of interviews
            418–419
        generally 417
        records of interviews 419
        right to silence 417–418
        vulnerable suspects
            419–420

**Judicial approaches to
    construction of statutes,**
    introduction 48
    literal 48–51
    purposive,
        introduction 51–53
        trend towards 53–54
    statutory interpretation under
        Human Rights Act 1998,
        55–58
**Judicial Committee of the Privy
    Council,**
    constitution 269–270

jurisdiction,
    admiralty jurisdiction 271
    appeals from courts outside
        United Kingdom
        270–271
    appeals from ecclesiastical
        courts 271
    devolution questions 271
    special references 272
Judicial review,
    Crown Court 654–655
    grounds for 214–217
    historical origin of the powers
        of the High Court
        206–207
    limits to jurisdiction 209–214
    magistrates' courts and
        654–655
    police accountability and
        396
    procedure 217–221
    scope of 207–209
Judiciary,
    appointments,
        diversity in the judiciary
            317–319
        present system 313–314
        reform 314–317
    constitutional position of
        judges,
        changing political climate
            304–311
        generally 303–304
        new balance of power
            312–313
    hierarchy,
        generally 300–301
        specific judicial offices
            301–303
    judicial function,
        administrative functions
            328
        common law 324–328
        introduction 323
        statutes 323–324
    judicial immunity 322–323
    security of tenure,
        fixed term appointments
            320–321
        removal and discipline
            319–320
        retirements 321
        salaries 321
        Starrs v Ruxton 320–321
    training 321–322

Juries,
 challenging the composition of
   the jury,
  challenging for cause
   334–337
  challenging the array 337
  judge's discretion to
   discharge 337–338
  jury vetting 333–334
  standing by for the Crown
   334
 empanelling,
  challenges 605–606
 historical growth of the jury
   system 329
 merits of jury trial 344–346
 qualifying for jury duty
   330–332
 selecting and summoning
   juries 332
 use of the jury trial,
  civil proceedings 340–341
  criminal cases 338–340
  generally 338
  jury secrecy 342–344
 vetting 333–334
Jury vetting,
 empanelling the jury: trial on
   indictment 605–606
 juries and 333–334
Justices' clerks,
 courts and 262–264
Justices of the Peace,
 courts and 261–262

Law Commission,
 law reform and the 25–26
Law enforcement,
 see Police
Law officers,
 Attorney-General 22, 358
 generally 358
 Solicitor-General 22, 358
Law reform,
 introduction 24–25
 Law Commission 25–26
Law reports,
 present system of,
  All England Reports 106
  electronic sources 107
  European cases 107
  Law Reports 105–106
  newspapers 107
  neutral citation of
    judgments 107–108

'Official' reports 106
  periodicals 107
  specialist reports 107
  weaknesses in 109
  Weekly Law Reports 106
 private reports 104–105
 year books 103–104
Law Society,
 complaints against solicitors
   364–366
 regulation of legal services
   359–361
Lawyers,
 see Legal services
Legal aid,
 generally 374–375
Legal profession,
 see Legal services
Legal services,
 barristers,
  Bar Council 361
  complaints against 367
  education and training 359
  employed 355–356
  Inns of Court 353
  liability to client 369–370
  liability to third parties
    370
  practice at the bar 353–354
  relationship between
    barrister and client
    354–355
 civil liability,
  barristers 369–370
  solicitors 368
 complaints against lawyers,
  barristers 367
  generally 364
  legal services ombudsman
    367–368
  solicitors 364–367
 Crown Prosecution Service
   356–357
 Director of Public
   Prosecutions 356–357
 funding of,
  see also Costs
  'access to justice': new
    funding regime 375–383
  conditional fee agreements
    372–373, 495–496
  cost of the law 373–374
  legal aid 374–375
  litigation funding
    agreements 373

remuneration of lawyers
371–373
law officers 358
legal profession,
Access to Justice Act
348–349
Court and Legal Services
Act 1990, 348
generally 347
regulation of,
Bar Council 361
Clementi report 362–364
Law Society 359–361
review by the courts
361–362
solicitors,
complaints against
364–367
conveyancing monopoly
350
education and training
358–359
Law Society 359–361
liability to client 368
liability to third party
368–369
probate monopoly 350
relationship between
solicitor and client
352–353
right to conduct litigation
349
rights of audience
350–352
Legal Services Commission,
administration of the English
legal system 19
Community Legal Service,
eligibility for assistance
379–380
generally 377–378
not-for-profit organizations
and partnerships with
380
work covered by
Community Legal
Service contracts
378–379
Criminal Defence Service,
generally 380–381
public defender service
381
funding of legal services,
contracts 377
generally 376–377

Legal Services Ombudsman,
administration of the English
legal system 19
generally 367–368
Legislation,
citation of statutes 32–34
codification 27–28
collection of revenue 28
consolidation of enactments
26–27
construction of statutes,
European Community
legislation 76
Interpretation Act 1978,
60–61
judicial approaches to
48–58
language 58–61
need for 45–48
presumptions of substance
61–66
material aids to
construction 66–76
rules of interpretation
58–61
delegated 34–38
disbursement of revenue 28
forms of,
Acts of Parliament 29–34
autonomic legislation
38–39
Codes of Practice 39–41
delegated legislation 34–38
private Acts 31
public Acts 31
interpretation of statutes,
European Community
legislation 76
Interpretation Act 1978,
60–61
judicial approaches to
48–58
language 58–61
need for 45–48
presumptions of substance
61–66
material aids to
construction 66–76
rules of 58–61
law reform and,
introduction 24–25
Law Commission 25–26
legislative process 31–32
operation of statutes,
geographical 41–42

temporal 42–45
social 28
treaties,
    implementation of 28
Lord Chancellor,
    administration of the civil
        justice system and 433
    administration of the English
        legal system 19–22
    generally 301–303
Lord Chief Justice,
    generally 303
Lord Justices of Appeal,
    judiciary 303

Magistrates' courts,
    constitution 259–261
    hierarchy 102
    jurisdiction,
        civil 265
        criminal 264–265
        family proceedings courts
            265
        youth courts 265
        youth justice 265
    Justices of the Peace 261–262
    Justices' chief executive
        262–264
    Justices' clerks 262–264
    organization 259–261
    reform under the Courts Act
        2003, 260
Mareva injunctions,
    administration of the civil
        justice system 434
Margin of appreciation,
    nature of Convention rights
        protected 171–172
Master of the Rolls,
    judiciary and 303
Mediation,
    contractual disputes 442–443
    court based schemes 443–445
    court led ADR requirements
        443–445
    family matters 441–442
    regulatory disputes 442–443
Middleton Report,
    civil process and the 432
Miscarriages of justice,
    appeals in criminal cases,
        appeal against conviction
            682–683
        appeal against sentence
            683–684, 695

appeal to House of Lords
    696–697
Court of Appeal (Criminal
    Division) development
    680–681
Criminal Cases Review
    Commission 684–687
hospital orders 695
introduction 680
power to order a 'venire de
    novo' 695
power to order new trial
    693–695
power to quash conviction
    689–692
power to receive fresh
    evidence 693–695
power to substitute an
    alternative verdict 692
procedure 696
prosecution rights of
    appeal 688–689
references following
    acquittal 687–688
role of the Court of Appeal
    681–682
'mischief rule'
    judicial approach to
        interpretation of statutes
        51–52
Monarch,
    role of the 4
Multi party proceedings,
    costs and 497
Multi track,
    civil trials 466–467

Natural justice,
    Community law, principle of
        122
Negotiation,
    contractual disputes 442–443
    court based schemes 443–445
    court led ADR requirements
        443–445
    family matters 441–442
    regulatory disputes 442–443
Neutral citation of judgments,
    present system of law
        reporting 107–108

Obiter dicta,
    binding element of precedents
        82–83
    non binding precedents 85

Offences,
    see Classification of offences
    joinder of 587–588
'Official' reports,
    present system of law
        reporting 106
Open justice principle,
    hearing in open court 232–
        233
    introduction 231–232
    reporting of proceedings in
        court 235–236
    withholding of particular
        information/ evidence
        from public 233–235

Parole Board,
    administration of the English
        legal system 19
Patents Court,
    Queen's Bench Division and
        251
Pleas,
    autrefois acquit 602–604
    autrefois convict 602–604
    generally 599–600
    guilty 600–601
    not guilty 601–602
Police,
    accountability,
        civil actions 395–396
        complaints against the
            police 396–397
        criminal proceedings
            394–395
        judicial review 396
        rules of evidence
            391–394
    bail 532
    law enforcement function,
        civilian officers 390–391
        generally 384
        organization of the police
            386–391
        role of the individual 385
    organization of the police,
        chief constables and
            individual officers
            389–390
        generally 386
        police authorities and
            central government
            387–388
        police authorities and Chief
            Constables 388–389

powers,
    access to legal advice
        415–417
    arrest 405–409
    breaches of the peace
        398–400
    Codes of Practice 401
    detention 409–412
    force 401
    generally 397–398
    identification 420–421
    interviews 417–420
    reasonable belief 400
    reasonable suspicion 400
    stop and search 401–404
    surveillance 404–405
    treatment of suspects
        412–415
Pre-trial process,
    choice of court 446–448
    commencing a civil action,
        contents of claim 450
        contributions 455–456
        counterclaims 455–456
        indemnities 455–456
        introduction 449–450
        issue of the claim 454–455
        multi-party actions
            452–454
        parties to proceedings 451
        public law involvement 455
        representative actions
            452–454
        service of the claim
            454–455
    pre-action protocols 448–449
    pre-commencement order,
        disclosure of documents
            456–457
        freezing injunctions
            460–463
        inspection of documents
            456–457
        Norwich Pharmacal
            principle 458
        search orders 458–460
Precedents,
    binding element of,
        ascertaining the ratio
            decidendi 83–85
        obiter dicta 82–83
        ratio decidendi 81–82
    distinguishing 92–93
    hierarchy of the Courts and,
        County courts 102

Court of Appeal 96–100
Crown courts 102
European Court of Justice
93
High Court 101–102
House of Lords 93–96
Magistrates' courts 102
tribunals 102–103
non binding precedents,
European Court of Human
Rights decisions 86–87
former rules of
international law 89
inferior courts decisions
85
Judicial Committee of the
Privy Council decisions
85–86
persuasive authorities
85–87
statements of law made per
incuriam 87–89
operation of the doctrine of,
binding element 81–85
binding precedent 78–80
impact of Human Rights
Act 1998 on 80–81
overruling 90–92
relationships between Law
Reports and the doctrine
of 77–78
reversing 90
Prison Service,
administration of the English
legal system 19
Private reports,
law reporting 104–105
Proportionality,
Community law, principle of
122
direct enforcement of
Convention rights
165–166
nature of Convention rights
protected 170
'Puisne judges'
see High Court judges

Queens Bench Division,
Admiralty court 252
civil jurisdiction 252
commercial court 252
criminal jurisdiction 253
introduction 252
supervisory jurisdiction 253

Technology and Construction
court 252–253

Race,
challenging the composition of
the jury 335
Ratio decidendi,
ascertaining the 83–85
binding element of precedents
81–82
Regulations,
relationship between
Community and
national law 129
Restitution,
sentences 677–678
Roman law,
source of law 9
Royal prerogative,
introduction 205–206

Sentences,
appropriate sentencing
658–660
community 675–676
compensation 677–678
consistency of sentencing
658–660
Crown Court,
deferment of sentence 664
passing sentence 662–663
pre-sentence drug taking
665–666
pre-sentence reports and
other reports 664–665
restraining orders 666
discharges,
absolute 677
conditional 677
fines 677
Halliday report 656
imprisonment,
custody plus 670
dangerous offenders
671–672
intermittent custody
670–671
length of custodial sentence
668–670
life sentences 673–674
suspended sentence 668
young offenders 674–675
introduction 656
Magistrates' court 666–667
miscellaneous orders 678

offence seriousness
  667–668
principles of sentencing 658
restitution 677–678
restraining orders 679
role of the Attorney-General
  660
sentencing thresholds
  667–668
victims 661–662
Serious Fraud Office,
administration of the English
  legal system 22–23
Small claims track,
civil trials 465
Solicitor-General,
administration of the English
  legal system 22–23
Solicitors,
complaints against,
  handling by Law Society
    364–366
  Solicitors Disciplinary
    Tribunal 366–367
conveyancing monopoly 350
education and training
  358–359
probate monopoly 350
relationship between solicitor
  and client 352–353
right to conduct litigation
  349
rights of audience 350–352
Solicitors Disciplinary Tribunal,
generally 366–367
Sources of English law
see under individual headings
Case law
European Community law
European Convention on
  Human Rights
History of the English legal
  system
Human Rights Act 1998
Law reports
Legislation
Precedents
Textbooks
Star Chamber,
history of 225–226
Statutes,
citation 32
codification 27–28
consolidation of enactments
  26–27

construction of,
  European Community
    legislation 76
  Interpretation Act 1978,
    60–61
  judicial approaches to
    48–58
  language 58–61
  need for 45–48
  presumptions of substance
    61–66
  material aids to
    construction 66–76
  rules of interpretation
    58–61
interpretation of,
  ambiguity 46–47
  European Community
    legislation 76
  Human Rights Act 1998, 55
  Interpretation Act 1978, 31,
    60–61
  judicial approaches to
    48–58
  language 58–61
  need for 45–48
  presumptions of substance
    61–66
  material aids to
    construction 66–76
  rules of 58–61
  uncertainty 47–48
operation of,
  geographical 41–42
  temporal 42–45
private Acts 31
public Acts 31
rules of interpretation,
  Interpretation Act 1978,
    60–61
  statute read as whole 58–60
statutory duties,
  enforcement of 33–34
words of 46
Stop and search,
police power of 401–404
Summary trials,
absences at,
  general effects of 635
  pleading guilty by post
    636–637
appeals following,
  case stated to Queen's
    Bench Division 651–654
  Crown Court 649–651

House of Lords 654
generally 648
course of the trial,
hearing 632–634
number of offences 627–628
time-limit 625–627
introduction 623
judicial review and 654–655
jurisdiction 625
pre-trial procedures,
administrative hearings 629–631
disclosure 631–632
hearing 632–634
process 623–625
sentence,
committals to Crown Court for 639–641
generally 637–638
youth justice,
aims 641
community punishment 646–648
court of trial 643
imprisonment 646–648
miscellaneous orders 648
provisions of 641–643
trial 644–646
youth offenders contracts 646

Supreme Court rules,
administration of the civil justice system 433

Technology and Construction Court,
Queen's Bench Division and 252–253
Temporal operation of statutes,
retrospective operation 43–44
statute begins to be operative 42–43
statute ceases to b operative 44–45
Textbooks,
books of authority 10–13
modern 11–13
source of law 9–13
Three track approach,
civil trials,
fast track 466
multi track 466–467
small claims track 465

Treasury Solicitors Office,
administration of the English legal system 22–23
Treaties,
relationship between Community and national law 129
Treatment of suspects,
access to legal aid 415–417
detention conditions 414
fingerprints 413–414
information about rights 413
police and 412–415
search 412–413
taking of samples 413–414
vulnerable suspects 414–415
Trial,
see under individual headings
Civil trials
Criminal process
Indictment, trial on
Summary trials
Tribunals,
see also **Inquiries**
administrative tribunals,
Appeals Service 286–287
Asylum and Immigration Tribunal 288–290
Criminal Injuries Compensation Appeals Panel 287–288
characteristics of 278–279
composition 279–281
control by the courts,
appeals from tribunals 294–295
challenging decisions of 'private' disciplinary bodies 295–296
supervisory control 295
hierarchy of the courts 102–103
introduction 278
organization and control,
Council on Tribunals 282–283
Franks Committee 282
introduction 281
Leggatt Review of Tribunals 283–284
transforming public services 284–285
party and party tribunals,
domestic tribunals 294

Employment Appeal
    Tribunal 292–294
employment tribunals
    290–292
generally 290

Verdict,
civil trials 486–487
Court of Appeal power to
    substitute alternative
    verdict 692
trial on indictment,
    post verdict orders
    621–622
Vice-Chancellor,
judiciary 303

Weekly Law Reports,
present system of law
    reporting 106
Witnesses,
generally 612–614
out of court statements
    614–615
Woolf analysis of civil process,
adversarial nature 426–428
complexity 430
court of trial 430–431

delay of civil litigation
    426–428
expense 428–430
recommendations 431–432

Year books,
law reporting 103
Young offenders,
sentencing and 674–675
Youth courts,
Magistrates' Courts and 265
Youth justice,
aims 641–643
community punishment
    646–648
court of trial,
    committal to Crown Court
    643–644
    adult magistrates' court
    644
imprisonment 646–648
miscellaneous orders 648
provisions of 641–643
trial 644–646
youth offenders contracts 646
Youth Justice Board,
administration of the English
    legal system 19